Handbook of Computational Economics, Volume 4

Handbook of Computational Economics, Volume 4

Heterogeneous Agent Modeling

Edited by

Cars Hommes
Blake LeBaron

North-Holland

An imprint of Elsevier

North-Holland is an imprint of Elsevier
Radarweg 29, PO Box 211, 1000 AE Amsterdam, Netherlands
The Boulevard, Langford Lane, Kidlington, Oxford OX5 1GB, United Kingdom

Notices

Knowledge and best practice in this field are constantly changing. As new research and experience broaden our understanding, changes in research methods, professional practices, or medical treatment may become necessary.

Practitioners and researchers must always rely on their own experience and knowledge in evaluating and using any information, methods, compounds, or experiments described herein. In using such information or methods they should be mindful of their own safety and the safety of others, including parties for whom they have a professional responsibility.

To the fullest extent of the law, neither the Publisher nor the authors, contributors, or editors, assume any liability for any injury and/or damage to persons or property as a matter of products liability, negligence or otherwise, or from any use or operation of any methods, products, instructions, or ideas contained in the material herein.

Library of Congress Cataloging-in-Publication Data
A catalog record for this book is available from the Library of Congress

British Library Cataloguing-in-Publication Data
A catalogue record for this book is available from the British Library

ISBN: 978-0-444-64131-1
ISSN: 1574-0021

For information on all North-Holland publications
visit our website at https://www.elsevier.com/books-and-journals

www.elsevier.com • www.bookaid.org

Publisher: Zoe Kruze
Acquisition Editor: Jason Mitchell
Editorial Project Manager: Alina Cleju
Production Project Manager: Vignesh Tamil
Designer: Greg Harris

Typeset by VTeX

Contents

PART 1 MACROECONOMICS

PART 2 FINANCE

PART 4 NETWORKS

PART 6 PERSPECTIVES ON HETEROGENEITY

Contributors

Jasmina Arifovic
Simon Fraser University, Burnaby, BC, Canada

Robert Axtell
Department of Computational and Data Sciences, Department of Economics, and Center for Social Complexity, Krasnow Institute for Advanced Study, George Mason University, Fairfax, VA, United States

Christoph Aymanns
Swiss Institute of Banking and Finance, University of St. Gallen, St. Gallen, Switzerland

Richard Bookstaber
Office of the Chief Investment Officer, University of California, Oakland, CA, United States

Jean-Philippe Bouchaud
Capital Fund Management, Paris, France

William A. Branch
University of California, Irvine, CA, United States

Herbert Dawid
Department of Business Administration and Economics and Center for Mathematical Economics, Bielefeld University, Bielefeld, Germany

Domenico Delli Gatti
Complexity Lab in Economics (CLE), Department of Economics and Finance, Università Cattolica del Sacro Cuore, Italy
CESifo Group Munich, Germany

Roberto Dieci
University of Bologna, Bologna, Italy

John Duffy
University of California, Irvine, CA, United States

J. Doyne Farmer
Institute for New Economic Thinking at the Oxford Martin School, University of Oxford, Oxford, United Kingdom
Mathematical Institute, University of Oxford, Oxford, United Kingdom
Department of Computer Science, University of Oxford, Oxford, United Kingdom
Santa-Fe Institute, Santa Fe, NM, United States

Sanjeev Goyal
Faculty of Economics and Christ's College, University of Cambridge, Cambridge, United Kingdom

Xue-Zhong He
University of Technology Sydney, Sydney, NSW, Australia

Giulia Iori
Department of Economics, City, University of London, London, United Kingdom

Alan Kirman
School for Advanced Studies in the Social Sciences (EHESS), Paris, France

Alissa M. Kleinnijenhuis
Institute for New Economic Thinking at the Oxford Martin School, University of Oxford, Oxford, United Kingdom
Mathematical Institute, University of Oxford, Oxford, United Kingdom
Oxford-Man Institute of Quantitative Finance, University of Oxford, Oxford, United Kingdom

Thomas Lux
Christian Albrechts Universität zu Kiel, Germany

Rosario N. Mantegna
Department of Physics and Chemistry, University of Palermo, Palermo, Italy
Department of Computer Science, University College London, London, United Kingdom
Complexity Science Hub Vienna, Vienna, Austria

Felix Mauersberger
Department of Economics and Business, Universitat Pompeu Fabra, Barcelona GSE, Barcelona, Spain

Bruce McGough
University of Oregon, Eugene, OR, United States

Rosemarie Nagel
Department of Economics and Business, Universitat Pompeu Fabra, Barcelona GSE, ICREA, Barcelona, Spain

Xavier Ragot

SciencesPo, CNRS, and OFCE, France

Leigh Tesfatsion

Economics Department, Iowa State University, Ames, IA, United States

Thom Wetzer

Institute for New Economic Thinking at the Oxford Martin School, University of Oxford, Oxford, United Kingdom

Oxford-Man Institute of Quantitative Finance, University of Oxford, Oxford, United Kingdom

Faculty of Law, University of Oxford, Oxford, United Kingdom

Remco C.J. Zwinkels

Vrije Universiteit Amsterdam and Tinbergen Institute, The Netherlands

Introduction to the Series

The aim of the Handbooks in Economics series is to produce Handbooks for various branches of economics, each of which is a definitive source, reference, and teaching supplement for use by professional researchers and advanced graduate students. Each Handbook provides self-contained surveys of the current state of a branch of economics in the form of chapters prepared by leading specialists on various aspects of this branch of economics. These surveys summarize not only received results but also newer developments, from recent journal articles and discussion papers. Some original material is also included, but the main goal is to provide comprehensive and accessible surveys. The Handbooks are intended to provide not only useful reference volumes for professional collections but also possible supplementary readings for advanced courses for graduate students in economics.

Kenneth J. Arrow[†]
Michael D. Intriligator[†]

[†]Deceased.

Introduction to the Handbook of Computational Economics, Volume 4, Heterogeneous Agent Modeling

1 INTRODUCTION

Over ten years ago, volume 2 of the *Handbook of Computational Economics* introduced Agent-Based Computational Economics (ACE).[1] Over the years the field has evolved considerably. With this new handbook we have tried to provide an update to much of the material from volume two, while also including and emphasizing new directions in the field.

The most obvious change is that the name of the field has drifted to the more general Agent-Based Modeling (ABM), or Heterogeneous Agent Modeling (HAM). The former name has taken hold across many different fields both in the social and biological sciences, so using it provides a natural bridge. The latter, HAM, is sometimes used to refer to a more narrow set of stylized agent-based models. Dropping the term "computational" from the title does allow acceptance of some models which do not require computational tools for analysis. However, it can generate questions and controversy, since many fields in economics make the case that they are "agent-based".

Beyond naming issues, this handbook acknowledges a wider scope of subject matter. The content is less about the difficulty to define the ABM world, and more about behavioral heterogeneity in general. A defining feature of agent-based models is that heterogeneity is fundamental, both through its emergence and dynamics. These are models where heterogeneity is not an exogenous nuisance, but a critical part of the modeling framework. Chapters in the handbook reflect this. They are all concerned with some aspect of heterogeneity both in modeling, and in empirical work. Heterogeneity has been declared a kind of key objective for economic modeling as we moved past the economic crisis of the early 21st century.[2] The Great Recession of 2007–2008 has revealed the weaknesses of models that ignore heterogeneity of both firms and consumers in macroeconomic decision making.

Comparing this issue of the handbook with volume 2 gives some interesting measures of how the field has progressed and some design decisions made by the editors. The first notable change is that the topics in macroeconomics and finance

---

[1] Tesfatsion and Judd (2006).

[2] Yellen (2016) stresses heterogeneity as a critical key to understanding macroeconomic dynamics.

see greater attention than in the previous handbook. The new volume has four chapters on macroeconomics and four chapters on finance, while volume 2 had only two chapters on finance and no chapter focusing on macroeconomics at all. A second key change is the concentration on data. Most chapters now have at least some empirical content, and some are completely dedicated to empirical topics. This acknowledges that the entire field of agent-based modeling has moved toward fitting and explaining data. There is also now much more emphasis on direct policy recommendations. A good fraction of the chapter by Aymanns et al. (2018) is dedicated to current and future macro-financial regulatory policies. In another chapter, Tesfatsion (2018) explores market design questions that are currently under consideration for residential electric power markets. The two chapters on networks represent the dramatic surge in research in this area since the previous volume, which contained only a single chapter on the topic. A similar doubling in chapters on experimental work also reflects major activity in this field. Finally, there are very few general overview/methodology chapters in this volume. In volume 2 these provided statements about what the field was, and where it was going. This is less necessary as the field has matured.

2 MACROECONOMICS

The new volume starts off with four chapters on macroeconomics. The detailed dynamics of learning and heterogeneity in agent-based economics is critical for understanding their empirical and policy implications. Branch and McGough (2018) survey a wide class of heterogeneous agent models and their dynamics under various forms of learning. They provide the micro-foundations of boundedly rational decision making and aggregation of individual decision rules in various macroeconomic models, such as the New Keynesian framework, with heterogeneous expectations. The authors refer to the wide range of research in macro and finance which shows how these models can generate excess volatility and bubbles in asset prices and trading inefficiencies in monetary economies. Also, they often call into question standard policy recommendations as derived from traditional New Keynesian macroeconomic models.

Agent-based macro economic models have become a key part of the ABM research agenda in the last decade. The need to envision the macro economy as a complex set of interacting behaviors from many different economic actors was realized many years ago. Dawid and Delli Gatti (2018) provide a survey of this literature which can be somewhat intimidating on first exposure. They provide a useful taxonomy of the many different model structures in use, and some of their key empirical features. They also outline the critical design questions faced by researchers as they attempt to build an entire working economy from the "bottom up". By comparing the structure and modeling assumptions of a set of macroeconomic ABMs they identify what could be considered an emerging common core of macroeconomic agent-based modeling. Finally, the models are examined along the dimensions of various policy recommendations including fiscal and monetary policy, financial stability, growth and convergence.

Axtell (2018) presents an agent-based model of the U.S. macro economy using a "micro scale" perspective with a large number of simple agents utilizing detailed census information on employment, productivity, and firm creation and destruction. He reminds us that under the relative stability of aggregate economic time series is an economy which is constantly in flux. In this system of continual change, a stable equilibrium is impossible, though aggregates can appear stable. The data is summarized with a relatively parsimonious agent-based model that describes firms' birth, growth, and death, along with endogenous labor flows supporting the firm dynamics. The model is calibrated to the U.S. economy with full scale agent-size – 120 million agents – and recreates many stylized features of firms in the cross-section including size and age distributions, growth rates, and labor productivity. Detailed labor market data also is replicated including wages, job tenure, and network properties of labor flows. These stylized facts are reproduced through the interactions of many agents, without any external stochastic shocks. The chapter stands as a useful summary of the U.S. economy at micro scale using a simple motivating agent-based model.

In early agent-based research, authors often suggested a stark contrast to the more traditional Dynamic Stochastic General Equilibrium (DSGE) approach. The latter was said to be restricted to many tractability assumptions that forced it into a representative agent space where agent heterogeneity had been assumed away. Since at least the late 1990s this characterization of DSGE models is false.[3] Ragot (2018) surveys the extensive literature that adds agent heterogeneity into traditional DSGE frameworks.[4] Much of this research was driven by a need to understand uninsurable idiosyncratic shocks that lead to money and other assets being used for self-insurance. The survey explores in detail some types of models where different subsets of optimizing agents are considered. They may differ in wealth levels, preferences, or access to asset markets. Imposing key constraints on heterogeneity can yield some tractable outcomes, and even models that fall into the modeling domain of DYNARE, which is the key software tool in the DSGE world. The chapter finishes by comparing the DSGE models with those coming out of the agent-based modeling area. The latter class of models often stress deviations from rational expectations, and heterogeneity in agent forecasting models. However, this often comes with a cost of imposing limited myopically optimizing behaviors. Ragot (2018) conjectures that there may be a middle ground where tools from the heterogeneous DSGE world can be used to model heterogeneity in beliefs, but still maintaining more traditional intertemporal optimization methods. It is possible that there may be a convergence of these two distinct research tracks in the future.

---

[3] Krusell and Smith Jr. (1998) was the pioneering paper in this area.
[4] Related surveys can be found in the previous *Handbook of Computational Economics* (Schmedders and Judd, 2014).

3 FINANCE

In finance a large body of research has been driven by work on Heterogeneous Agent Models (HAMs). This family of models usually consists of a small set of strategies with agents adaptively choosing to switch to better performing trading rules. Often these strategies consist of trend following, destabilizing behavior, along with mean reverting, stabilizing behavior. The tension between these two expectational beliefs drives the dynamics. Though this sounds like a simple and intuitive market structure, its dynamics have proved to be rich and revealing. In their chapter, Dieci and He (2018) begin with examples of some of the earliest versions of these models, and their empirical linkages to stylized facts in financial markets. They then document almost 30 years of progress that the models have made. This includes models in continuous time, multi-asset dynamics, and markets incorporating real estate price dynamics. Finally, they survey HAM approaches in markets with high frequency trading and limit order books.

Multi-agent models have been proposed as a useful test bed for various policies relating to macro-financial stability. The chapter by Aymanns et al. (2018) gives an agent-based perspective of models generating endogenous volatility fluctuations. It begins by presenting a few simple models where various leverage and dynamic risk policies can self-generate coordination and price volatility. They also overview some basic models of financial networks and how they can also allow financial instabilities to spread through an interlinked set of financial institutions. Finally, they provide an extensive overview of macro and microprudential policy making as currently practiced. These sections give detailed descriptions of various current implementations of stress tests along with some of their strengths and weaknesses. They finish with a detailed policy overview of what stress testing of the future may look like.

Market microstructure, the study of detailed mechanics of financial markets at high frequency, has been an area where agent-based models have been very successful. Bouchaud (2018) provides a useful reference to the key puzzles and results in this area along with some useful simplified models. It covers the basic stylized facts which have been generally observed in high frequency financial data. Several of these features present serious tensions for theoretical models trying to explain simple limit order book dynamics. Some of these are related to the coexistence of the extreme persistence of order flows along with the near random walk behavior of price series. The survey overviews some of the basic models that attempt to hit all these features. Most are extensions of a simple "zero intelligence" framework using the most basic agent behavior. The chapter ends by looking into the critical debate as to what really drives most of market volatility, endogenous order flow and liquidity dynamics, or the arrival of new exogenous information. This still remains and open question in market micro-structure, but agent-based models are becoming a useful tool for finally getting an answer to this question.

The fact that agent-based modeling has been moving steadily in the direction of empirical modeling is evident in several chapters. The chapter by Lux and Zwinkels (2018) is an extensive survey of empirical validation of ABMs, mainly to financial data. This rich area has produced many results, and lots of new techniques for model fitting and testing. This chapter broadly covers many new econometric tools and their uses in a wide range of fields including epidemiology, climate research, and ecology. They examine many different types of models and how they have been fit to data at both the macro and micro level. The use of micro level data is particularly useful for definitive validation of any agent-based model. The authors perform a very interesting small scale estimation experiment of the model of Gaunersdorfer and Hommes (2007). They also cover some related model fitting issues from macroeconomics as well. Interesting challenges remain, such as modeling fundamental values, and getting a precise estimate of the intensity of choice parameter. Finally, they comment on our current abilities for testing across different types of models, and incorporating fitted smaller models into a larger framework.

4 EXPERIMENTS

The connection between agent-based modeling and experimental economics has long and natural history. Both fields are relatively open to deviations from strict rationality, and consider learning and adaptation an important part of human behavior. Arifovic and Duffy (2018) survey the experimental literature in macro and finance from a perspective of heterogeneity, along with computational tools used to replicate various results. They repeat the key message of experimental economics that heterogeneity seems almost ever present in the laboratory. This is true in experimental setups including public goods, intertemporal optimization, expectations formation, and various models of monetary policy. The authors give many examples from all these fields. In most cases computational models are also available which can replicate initial heterogeneity along with convergent learning dynamics. The search for an optimal learning agent to use is still a work in progress, and some comparisons are given between tools such individual evolutionary learning (IEL), heuristic switching, and older basic reinforcement learning systems. In many instances these computational approaches provide an excellent fit to human laboratory subjects.

Beginning with the history of experimental economics, Mauersberger and Nagel (2018) summarize a large realm of experimental facts from a set of core experimental games which can be thought of as spanning most, if not all, critical economic situations. The authors make the case for the importance of coordination games as being foundational in economic behavior. They then take this line further by proposing the Keynesian Beauty Contest game as being a useful metaphor for many coordination situations both in microeconomic and macroeconomic environments. They show through a detailed taxonomy that by changing parameters, the beauty contest can be transformed into many of the core experimental games mentioned earlier. This taxonomy can also allow for classification of economic situations by their varying forms of strategic complementarity, or substitutability. Various forms of beauty contest games from the literature are summarized and explored with particular attention paid to how heterogeneity appears in the experimental subjects. They end the chapter by looking at some relatively complex experimental situations designed to closely mimic economic environments. In these experiments heterogeneity is very important to agent behavior, but these models still yield common behavioral regularities.

5 NETWORKS

The application of networks to financial markets has been one of the most active areas of network research. Much of this is driven by a rich supply of data, both public and confidential, and a large set of critical policy questions. Network models can explain how local instabilities can propagate through the financial system and cascade into a global financial crisis. Iori and Mantegna (2018) survey the empirical estimation of network structures in finance. They often connect modern financial references to much of the earlier work on networks coming from other social and physical sciences. As the authors comment, this area has contributions coming from researchers in economics, finance, physics, and computer science. They discuss the direct approach of using proprietary interbank network information both for gaining information on the overall banking system, but also to understand the propagation of shocks, and the development of better stress testing methods. They also discuss some of the tools used to reconstruct networks when only partial data is available. Network connections can both be formed with direct connections between financial institutions, and also more indirect linkages, often driven simply by similarities in portfolio holdings, or shock exposures. This is known as a proximity network structure, and the authors describe many of the tools used in this active area of statistical research.

Network structure can lead to extensive heterogeneity in observed behavior of economic actors. A growing literature documents how this may be the result of various theoretical concepts that may magnify heterogeneity. Goyal (2018) surveys this literature. This chapter both reviews some of the early literature on economic networks, and gives a useful perspective on the most recent work on how networks can be very influential in driving heterogeneity. The chapter covers both exogenous and endogenous network formation. It also ties to work on how underlying market structures may adapt to different connections in trading networks.

6 OTHER

Tesfatsion (2018) presents a very specific application for agent-based models, retail electric power markets. Given the diverse populations of consumers, and very dynamic nature of markets for electricity, these examples show agent-based models as an engineering test bed in an important market design situation. The computational nature of the markets Tesfatsion considers allows them to be tailored to exact power-grid characteristics. Also, in many situations the agents are not humans, but black box power negotiating algorithms installed in homes whose behavior can be easily implemented with computational modeling. Examples in the chapter show how simple markets can easily go into a cobweb price dynamic depending on supply and demand feedbacks, showing that highly active consumer behavior in retail electric power markets may lead to price instabilities. Tesfatsion shows some initial explorations into PowerMatcher, a market architecture that works to aggregate the behavior of individual agents. It has concentrator units which perform small scale demand and supply aggregation in the power grid. This concentration into a courser level of demand units works to smooth and stabilize the retail market. It is interesting that this result is somewhat similar to the role that banks play in economic stability in the agent-based banking model of Ashraf et al. (2017).

In the last chapter Bookstaber and Kirman (2018) give a perspective on the reality of modeling heterogeneous agent worlds. They examine how economic situations with a strong emphasis on heterogeneity often changes some key concepts of economic intuition. They focus on three separate characteristic examples motivated by data. In their most basic case, they look at properties of a fish market. Transaction level data shows that fish buyers can be classified into two groups. One group of loyalists, often stays with a given seller, but another group, shoppers, moves around. Loyalists pay a higher price, but often get faster and better fish delivery. The agent-based simulation begins with a completely homogeneous set of agents who eventually split into the different groups. In this case, heterogeneity is a completely emergent phenomenon for the model. This probably makes this example the most basic representation of key agent-based dynamics in the Handbook. The authors also look at two examples from finance. First, they outline the dynamics of volatility feedback in a world where several types of dynamic strategies designed both to control and profit from volatility changes are operating. Second, they give a brief outline of what a full multi-agent financial market might look like. This example is similar to the approach of Tesfatsion (2018) in that it tries to model many institutional details specific to current financial market players.

ACKNOWLEDGMENTS

The ideas for this handbook volume originated from early 2015. We are grateful to the handbook series editors Kenneth Arrow, Michael Woodford, and Julio Rotemberg for allowing us to put together a new volume of the Handbook of Computational Economics on heterogeneous agent modeling. As the 14 chapters of this volume reflect this has indeed become an important area of research in economics and finance. We are indebted to all authors for their efforts to write comprehensive survey chapters summarizing the state of the field. We thank all referees for their detailed and positive feedback on earlier chapter drafts. We would like to thank the Amsterdam School of Economics and the University of Amsterdam for financial support to run a handbook volume workshop in June 1–2, 2017, where earlier drafts of all chapters have been presented and discussed. Finally, we are grateful to Elsevier for their support, starting with Scott Bentley's early invitation in May 2015 and his encouragement, the help from Alina

Cleju with many practical issues in managing the volume process, and the assistance of Jason Mitchell and Vignesh Tamilselvvan with the final stage of the production process.

REFERENCES

Arifovic, J., Duffy, J., 2018. Heterogeneous agent modeling: experimental evidence. In: Hommes, C., LeBaron, B. (Eds.), Handbook of Computational Economics, vol. 4, Heterogeneous Agent Modeling. North-Holland, pp. 491–540.

Ashraf, Q., Gershman, B., Howitt, P., 2017. Banks, market organizations and macroeconomic performance: an agent-based computational analysis. Journal of Economic Behavior & Organization 135, 143–180.

Axtell, R., 2018. Endogenous firm dynamics and labor flows via heterogeneous agents. In: Hommes, C., LeBaron, B. (Eds.), Handbook of Computational Economics, vol. 4, Heterogeneous Agent Modeling. North-Holland, pp. 157–213.

Aymanns, C., Farmer, J.D., Kleinnijenhuis, A.M., Wetzer, T., 2018. Models of financial stability and their application in stress tests. In: Hommes, C., LeBaron, B. (Eds.), Handbook of Computational Economics, vol. 4, Heterogeneous Agent Modeling. North-Holland, pp. 329–391.

Bookstaber, R., Kirman, A., 2018. Modeling a heterogeneous world. In: Hommes, C., LeBaron, B. (Eds.), Handbook of Computational Economics, vol. 4, Heterogeneous Agent Modeling. North-Holland, pp. 769–795.

Bouchaud, J.-P., 2018. Agent-based models for market impact and volatility. In: Hommes, C., LeBaron, B. (Eds.), Handbook of Computational Economics, vol. 4, Heterogeneous Agent Modeling. North-Holland, pp. 393–436.

Branch, W.A., McGough, B., 2018. Heterogeneous expectations and micro-foundations in macroeconomics. In: Hommes, C., LeBaron, B. (Eds.), Handbook of Computational Economics, vol. 4, Heterogeneous Agent Modeling. North-Holland, pp. 3–62.

Dawid, H., Delli Gatti, D., 2018. Agent-based macroeconomics. In: Hommes, C., LeBaron, B. (Eds.), Handbook of Computational Economics, vol. 4, Heterogeneous Agent Modeling. North-Holland, pp. 63–156.

Dieci, R., He, X.-Z., 2018. Heterogeneous agent models in finance. In: Hommes, C., LeBaron, B. (Eds.), Handbook of Computational Economics, vol. 4, Heterogeneous Agent Modeling. North-Holland, pp. 257–328.

Gaunersdorfer, A., Hommes, C., 2007. A nonlinear structural model for volatility clustering. In: Kirman, A., Teyssiere, G. (Eds.), Micro Economic Models for Long Memory in Economics. Springer-Verlag, pp. 265–288.

Goyal, S., 2018. Heterogeneity and networks. In: Hommes, C., LeBaron, B. (Eds.), Handbook of Computational Economics, vol. 4, Heterogeneous Agent Modeling. North-Holland, pp. 687–712.

Iori, G., Mantegna, R.N., 2018. Empirical analysis of networks in finance. In: Hommes, C., LeBaron, B. (Eds.), Handbook of Computational Economics, vol. 4, Heterogeneous Agent Modeling. North-Holland, pp. 637–685.

Krusell, P., Smith Jr., A.A., 1998. Income and wealth heterogeneity in the macroeconomy. Journal of Political Economy 106 (5), 867–896.

Lux, T., Zwinkels, R.C.J., 2018. Empirical validation of agent-based models. In: Hommes, C., LeBaron, B. (Eds.), Handbook of Computational Economics, vol. 4, Heterogeneous Agent Modeling. North-Holland, pp. 437–488.

Mauersberger, F., Nagel, R., 2018. Levels of reasoning in Keynesian Beauty Contest: a generative framework. In: Hommes, C., LeBaron, B. (Eds.), Handbook of Computational Economics, vol. 4, Heterogeneous Agent Modeling. North-Holland, pp. 541–634.

Ragot, X., 2018. Heterogeneous agents in the macroeconomy: reduced-heterogeneity representations. In: Hommes, C., LeBaron, B. (Eds.), Handbook of Computational Economics, vol. 4, Heterogeneous Agent Modeling. North-Holland, pp. 215–253.

Schmedders, K., Judd, K.L. (Eds.), 2014. Handbook of Computational Economics, vol. 3. North-Holland.

Tesfatsion, L., 2018. Electric power markets in transition: agent-based modeling tools for transactive energy support. In: Hommes, C., LeBaron, B. (Eds.), Handbook of Computational Economics, vol. 4, Heterogeneous Agent Modeling. North-Holland, pp. 715–766.

Tesfatsion, L., Judd, K.L. (Eds.), 2006. Handbook of Computational Economics, vol. 2, Agent-Based Computational Economics. North-Holland.

Yellen, J.L., 2016. Macroeconomic Research After the Crisis. Technical report. Board of Governers of the Federal Reserve System.

Cars Hommes

University of Amsterdam and Tinbergen Institute, Amsterdam, The Netherlands

Blake LeBaron

Brandeis University, International Business School, Waltham, MA, United States

MACRO-
ECONOMICS

Heterogeneous Expectations and Micro-Foundations in Macroeconomics*

William A. Branch[*,1], **Bruce McGough**[†]
University of California, Irvine, CA, United States
[†]University of Oregon, Eugene, OR, United States
[1]Corresponding author: e-mail address: wbranch@uci.edu

CONTENTS

*We are grateful to the editors, Cars Hommes and Blake LeBaron, as well as Guillaume Rocheteau and three anonymous referees for many helpful comments.

Handbook of Computational Economics, Volume 4, ISSN 1574-0021, https://doi.org/10.1016/bs.hescom.2018.03.001

1 INTRODUCTION

Modern macroeconomic models are built on micro-foundations: households and firms are dynamic optimizers in uncertain environments who interact in markets that clear in general equilibrium. Because decision-making is intertemporal, and the future is uncertain, macroeconomic models impart an important role to households' and firms' expectations about future states of the economy. Despite the importance of expectations, the benchmark approach is to assume homogeneous rational expectations, where all agents in the economy hold similar and correct views about the dynamic evolution of economic variables. Even in models of adaptive learning, e.g. Evans and Honkapohja (2001), individuals and firms are typically assumed to forecast using the same econometric model.

Nevertheless, there is substantial empirical and experimental evidence that individuals and firms have *heterogeneous expectations*. For example, Fig. 1 plots the interquartile range from individual inflation probability forecasts published by the Survey of Professional Forecasters (SPF) over the period 1992.1–2010.4. The IQR gives a good measure of the range of views in the SPF. The left plot is the histogram of the IQR in the sample, while the right plot is the time-series of the median IQR in each quarterly survey. Evidently, there is substantial heterogeneity among professional forecasters and, importantly, the degree of heterogeneity evolves over time.

Fig. 2 plots an estimated time-series of likely forecasting methods used by respondents in the Michigan Survey of Consumers' inflation expectation series. This figure comes from Branch (2004) who estimates a model of expectation formation where households select from a set of standard statistical forecasting models, each differing in complexity and parsimony, in such a way that people favor predictors with lower forecast errors net of complexity costs. In this figure, and a substantial body of other research, there is strong evidence of time-varying expectational heterogeneity. Finally, in a series of learning-to-forecast experiments, Hommes (2013) shows

FIGURE 1

Heterogeneous expectations in the Survey of Professional Forecasters. All data are computed from the probability forecasts as detailed in Branch (2014). The left plot is the histogram of IQR for inflation forecasts, the right two panels are the time-series of the median IQR for inflation and output growth, respectively.

strong evidence of heterogeneous expectations even in simple, controlled laboratory environments.[1]

A burgeoning literature studies the implications of heterogeneous expectations for dynamic, stochastic, general equilibrium (DSGE) models. This literature, motivated by these empirical facts, introduce agents with different beliefs into micro-founded models. This step of bringing bounded rationality into models with micro-foundations brings certain challenges to modelers. In particular, we begin with a discussion of the following three key questions about how to model heterogeneous beliefs in DSGE models:

1. How to model individual behavior given the available forecasting models?
2. Given a distribution of individuals across forecasting models, how are endogenous variables determined?
3. How are individuals distributed across forecasting models?

To address these questions we adopt a stylized DSGE environment that nests benchmark models in monetary theory, asset-pricing, and New Keynesian business cycles. The framework, which is outlined in Section 2.2, is a simplified version of Rocheteau and Wright (2011) which combines the New Monetarist monetary model with search frictions by Lagos and Wright (2005) with a Lucas asset-pricing model. By turning the search frictions off, the model reduces to a standard asset-pricing model. If we set the dividend flow to zero, the model is isomorphic to a pure monetary economy. This simple framework is able to demonstrate many of the important implications of heterogeneous expectations for the macroeconomy and asset-pricing.

We then turn to address the first question, namely, how to model the decision making of boundedly rational agents. A substantial segment of the literature follows a reduced-form approach, where the conditional expectations in the equations derived under rational expectations are replaced with a convex combination of heterogeneous

---

[1] See Arifovic and Duffy (2018) and Mauersberger and Nagel (2018) in this volume for additional discussions and results on experiments involving expectations.

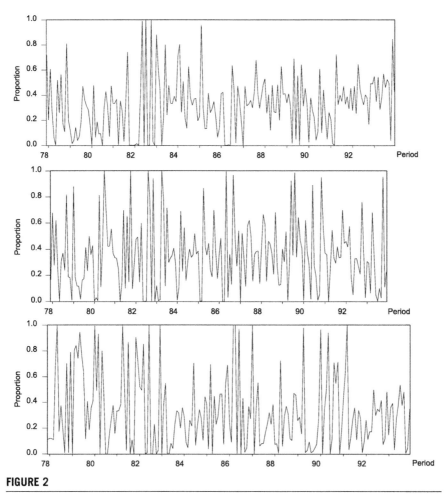

FIGURE 2

Rationally heterogeneous expectations in the Michigan Survey of Consumers (from Branch, 2004). Plots estimated proportions of consumers who form expectations from a VAR, an adaptive predictor, and a naive predictor.

expectations operators. More recently, the frontier of the adaptive learning literature adopts an "agent-level" approach that takes as given a set of behavioral primitives for individual decision-making. These behavioral primitives are based on two observations. First, agents who make boundedly rational forecasts may also make boundedly optimal decisions. Second, aggregation into equilibrium equations should follow a temporary equilibrium approach where aggregation occurs after imposing boundedly rational decision-making. The literature has proposed a variety of behavioral primitives, some based on anticipated utility maximization and others based on internal rationality. In Section 2.3 we review these approaches while discussing strengths and drawbacks of each alternative.

The link between individual decisions and aggregate outcomes is provided by temporary equilibrium: individual-level decision rules and the distribution of agents across forecasting rules are coordinated through market clearing. With properly specified forecasting rules, this leads to a temporary equilibrium law of motion that can be written entirely in terms of aggregate state variables. Section 2.4 briefly discusses this analysis in the context of our simple environment, and also discusses some potential impediments.

Our analysis is complete by specifying how the distribution of agents across forecasting models is determined as an equilibrium object. Most of the literature follows the seminal Brock and Hommes (1997) by modeling expectation formation as agents rationally choosing a predictor from a finite set of forecasting models. That is, expectation formation is a discrete choice in a random utility setting, where the distribution of agents across models is given by a multinomial logit (MNL) mapping. There have been two ways in which agents might not have rational expectations and select heterogeneous predictors. The first, called *rationally heterogeneous expectations*, is when rational expectations is available to agents, as well as other predictors such as adaptive and naive expectations, but they must pay a higher cost to do so. This cost is meant to proxy for computational and cognitive costs in forming rational expectations. If the utility associated with predictor choice is subject to an idiosyncratic preference shock, then heterogeneous beliefs can arise as an equilibrium object of the model. The second approach, based on Branch and Evans (2006), rules out that agents are able to form rational expectations and instead they must select from a set of parsimonious forecasting models. Branch and Evans (2006) define a *Misspecification Equilibrium* as occurring when individuals only select the best performing models from a restricted set.[2] Of course, which models are best performing is an equilibrium property and we demonstrate a variety of environments where *Intrinsic Heterogeneity* can arise.

Having laid out the key theoretical issues with incorporating, and deriving, heterogeneous expectations, the rest of the chapter focuses on applications. Section 4 focuses on asset-pricing applications. Here we show that asset-pricing models with heterogeneous expectations are able to explain key empirical regularities such as bubbles/crashes, regime-switching returns and volatilities, and excess volatility. We then, in Section 5, turn to a pure monetary economy and show how heterogeneous beliefs can alter the nature of trade in economies with over-the-counter frictions. An important result here is that trading between agents with heterogeneous beliefs must also specify higher-order beliefs and these may lead to a failure for buyers and sellers to successfully execute a trade. That is, there can be an extensive margin of trade that arises from heterogeneous expectations. However, these higher order beliefs also induce people to make more cautious offers, hoping to avoid times when their offers

---

[2] In a follow-up to their 1997 paper, Brock and Hommes (1998) also consider an environment in which agents select only from misspecified forecasting models, though, in contrast to Branch and Evans (2006), their work does not include adaptive learning.

are rejected, and so affect the intensive margin of trade as well. We show that heterogeneous expectations can have important welfare implications and can also explain puzzling experimental results.

We then extend the basic framework to the New Keynesian model. Here we show how a basic property of heterogeneous expectations models, "stability reversal," can have important implications for the design of monetary policy. A general principle of heterogeneous expectations is the tension between forward-looking rational expectations and backward-looking adaptive expectations and learning models. Homogeneous rational expectations models that are determinate (dynamically unstable) can be indeterminate (dynamically stable) with homogeneous adaptive expectations: adaptive beliefs can reverse the stability properties of rational expectations models. Thus, there is a tension between the repelling and attracting forces inherent to heterogeneous expectations. Brock and Hommes (1997) demonstrated, with masterful force, how these attracting/repelling forces can lead to periodic and complex dynamics. An important factor for the existence of complex belief dynamics is the self-referential property of the model, and, in New Keynesian models the policy rule followed by the central bank can alter the strength of expectational feedback. We demonstrate how a policy designed to adhere to the Taylor principle under rational expectations can destabilize an economy with even just a small amount of steady-state equilibrium fraction of adaptive agents. We also show that policy rules can affect that steady-state equilibrium fraction and potentially lead to hysteresis effects for plausibly strong inflation reaction coefficients in Taylor-type rules. Finally, we show how heterogeneous expectations can lead to multiple stable equilibria including the possibility of recurring collapses to a (stable under learning) liquidity trap.

This chapter proceeds as follows. Section 2 defines the notion of an expectations operator, introduces the model, and discusses the micro-foundations and aggregation of heterogeneous beliefs. Section 3 introduces the two types of equilibria considered in this chapter: rationally heterogeneous expectations and misspecification equilibria. The stability reversal principle is introduced in this section. Section 4 presents applications to asset-pricing models, while Section 5 focuses on pure monetary economies. Section 6 presents results for DSGE models.

2 EXPECTATIONS OPERATORS AND BOUNDED RATIONALITY

In macroeconomic models, economic agents make decisions in dynamic, uncertain environments and, thereby, confront two related, but conceptually distinct, issues: how to make forecasts given the available information; and, how to make decisions given the available forecasts. The rational expectations hypothesis joins these two aspects of agent-level behavior through the cross-equation restrictions imposed by the equilibrium, i.e. optimal forecasts depend on actions and optimal actions depend on forecasts. This chapter focuses on bounded rationality and heterogeneous expectations, an environment where the strict nature of the link is broken, and the agents' forecasting and decision-making problems may be treated separately. Before discussing the forecasting problem, the ways in which heterogeneous beliefs can arise in equilibrium, and the resulting applications, we begin with a review of boundedly rational decision-making.

In order to motivate an equilibrium with heterogeneous expectations, we follow the adaptive learning literature that has recently turned towards a more careful modeling of the decision-making process made by individuals given that forecasts are not fully rational. This "agent-level approach" is distinguished from reduced-form learning – where the conditional expectations in the equilibrium equations derived under rational expectations are replaced with a heterogeneous expectations operator – in two important ways: first, it is reasonable to assume that agents who make boundedly rational forecasts may also make boundedly optimal decisions; and second, aggregation into equilibrium equations should take place *after* boundedly-rational behavior has been imposed. The first point, the possibility of boundedly optimal decision-making, requires that we take a stand on – i.e. specify behavioral primitives governing – how agents make decisions given their forecasts; and the second point, concerning the aggregation of boundedly rational behavior, demands a temporary equilibrium approach. This section reviews several approaches pursued in the literature and shows how to aggregate the agent-level decision rules.

2.1 EXPECTATIONS OPERATORS

The literature on heterogeneous expectation formation is influenced, in part, by the adaptive learning literature (e.g. Evans and Honkapohja, 2001). In this class of models, fully rational expectations are replaced by linear forecasting rules with parameters that are updated by recursive least squares. In this chapter, we imagine different sets of agents who engage in economic forecasting while recognizing there may exist heterogeneity in forecasting rules. Some examples of heterogeneity consistent with our framework include the following: some agents may be rational while others adaptive, as has been examined in a cobweb model by Brock and Hommes (1997) and found empirically relevant in the data in Branch (2004); agents may have different information sets (e.g. Branch, 2007); or, they may use structurally different learning rules as in Honkapohja and Mitra (2006). Our goal is to extend this notion of agents as forecasters to the agents' primitive problem, and to characterize a set of admissible beliefs that facilitates aggregation.

Denote by $\hat{E}_t^\tau$ a (subjective) expectations operator; that is, $\hat{E}_t^\tau(x_{t+k})$ is the time t expectation of x_{t+k} formed by an agent of type τ. We require that

A1. Expectations operators fix observables.
A2. If x is a variable forecasted by agents and has steady state $\bar{x}$ then $\hat{E}^\tau \bar{x} = \bar{x}$.
A3. If x, y, $x + y$ and αx are variables forecasted by agents then $\hat{E}_t^\tau(x + y) = \hat{E}_t^\tau(x) + \hat{E}_t^\tau(y)$ and $\hat{E}_t^\tau(\alpha x) = \alpha \hat{E}_t^\tau(x)$.

A4. If for all $k \geq 0$, x_{t+k} and $\sum_k \beta^{t+k} x_{t+k}$ are forecasted by agents then

$$\hat{E}_t^\tau \left(\sum_{k \geq 0} \beta^{t+k} x_{t+k} \right) = \sum_{k \geq 0} \beta^{t+k} \hat{E}_t^\tau (x_{t+k}).$$

A5. $\hat{E}_t^\tau$ satisfies the law of iterated expectations (L.I.E.): If x is a variable forecasted by agents at time t and time $t + k$ then $\hat{E}_t^\tau \circ \hat{E}_{t+k}^\tau (x) = \hat{E}_t^\tau (x)$.

These assumptions impose regularity conditions consistent with the literature on bounded rationality and they facilitate aggregation in a linear, or linearized environment. Assumption A1 is consistent with reasonable specifications of agent behavior (the forecast of a known quantity should be the known quantity). Assumption A2 requires some continuity in beliefs in the sense that, in a steady state, agents' beliefs will coincide. Assumptions A3 and A4 require expectations to possess some linearity properties. Essentially, linear expectations require agents to incorporate some economic structure into their forecasting model rather than, say, mechanically applying a lag operator to every random variable.

Assumptions A5 restricts agents' expectations so that they satisfy the law of iterated expectations at an individual level. The L.I.E. at the individual level is a reasonable and intuitive assumption: agents should not expect to systematically alter their expectations. In deriving the New Keynesian IS curve, with heterogeneous expectations, Branch and McGough (2009) imposed an additional assumption of the L.I.E. at the aggregate level, essentially ruling out higher order beliefs. In other applications, such as the New Monetarist search model, we explicitly model higher-order beliefs by assuming that an expectation operator consists of two components, a point estimate given by E_t^τ and an uncertainty measure $F_t^\tau (\cdot, \Sigma)$.

2.2 THE ECONOMIC ENVIRONMENT

Before turning to a discussion of bounded optimality and aggregation of heterogeneous expectations, it is useful to describe a general economic environment that forms the basis for many of the applications in this chapter. The environment is based on a Lucas (1978) asset-pricing model with consumption risk in the form of a frictional goods market characterized by bilateral trading and a limited commitment problem. By opening and closing the frictional market we are able to nest a standard asset-pricing model or a search-based New Monetarist type model, depending on the desired application. We turn to a brief description of the environment, and then develop the analysis as the chapter progresses.

Time is discrete, and each time period is divided into two sub-periods. There are two types of non-storable goods: specialized goods, denoted q, that are produced and consumed in a market that opens during the first sub-period ("DM"); and general goods, denoted x, that are produced and consumed in a competitive market ("CM") during the second sub-period. There are two types of agents: "buyers" and "sellers".

All agents produce the general good using the same technology that is linear in labor. We assume that labor is traded in the competitive market at a real wage of w_t, which, in equilibrium, will equal the real wage in terms of the numeraire good. When we develop results for a standard Lucas asset-pricing model, we assume a perfectly inelastic labor supply so that the model reduces, essentially, to an endowment economy. Thus, the competitive market represents the part of the environment that is standard in macro DSGE models like the New Keynesian model or the Lucas asset-pricing model. In the specialized goods market, though, buyers can consume but not produce the specialized good while sellers can produce but cannot consume. Moreover, trade in these markets is characterized by a limited commitment friction where buyers are unable to commit to repay unsecured debt using their proceeds from producing in the competitive market. Thus, this part of the model captures environments with frictional goods markets where assets such as fiat money, stocks or bonds are used as payment instruments. Some of the most interesting, and recent, applications of heterogeneous expectations occur in such markets. We assume that with probability σ buyers will have preferences for the specialized goods. By setting $\sigma = 0$, the economic environment collapses into a standard environment without any real frictions.

There exists a single storable good, an asset a that yields a stochastic payoff y_t. This asset could be fiat money, with $y_t = 0$, a Lucas tree with a stochastic dividend, or a risk-free bond with a known payoff. Depending on the frictions in the specialized goods market, the asset can be used to smooth consumption or as a liquid asset used in *quid pro quo* trade in the specialized goods market. That is, the frictional goods market gives a precautionary savings motive to hold the asset to insure against random consumption opportunities for the specialized good. Assume that households have separable preferences over the general good, the specialized good, and leisure.

2.3 BOUNDED OPTIMALITY

We now turn to agent-level decision-making taking the expectations operators as given. To best illustrate the ideas reviewed here, we develop them within the context of a very simple asset-pricing model. We, therefore, take the economic environment described above and shut-down the frictional goods market.

2.3.1 Rational Expectations

Assume that there is a fixed quantity (unit mass) of the asset (Lucas trees) each of which yields per-period non-storable stochastic dividend $y_t = y + \varepsilon_t$, where ε_t is zero mean, i.i.d. and has small support (so that $y_t > 0$). Each agent is initially endowed with a unit of assets, discounts the future at rate β, and receives per-period utility from consuming the dividend, as measured by the function u. Note that agents are assumed identical, except possibly in the way they form forecasts and make decisions.

Under the rational expectations hypothesis (REH), it is sufficient to consider the behavior of a representative agent. This agent solves the following problem:

$$\max_{a_{t+1}\geq 0} E \sum_{t\geq 0} u(c_t)$$

$$p_t a_{t+1} = (p_t + y_t)a_t - c_t, \tag{1}$$

where a_t is the quantity of the asset held at the beginning of time t, c_t is consumption in time t, and p_t is the asset's (*ex* dividend) price in time t in terms of consumption goods.

Because in a rational expectations equilibrium agents are identical, $c_t = y_t$, the representative agent's Euler equation must be satisfied:

$$u'(y_t) = \beta E_t \left(\frac{p_{t+1} + y_{t+1}}{p_t} \right) u'(y_{t+1}).$$

Thus the non-stochastic steady state of this model (or the perfect-foresight REE in case income is non-stochastic) is given by

$$p = \left(\frac{\beta}{1 - \beta} \right) y, \tag{2}$$

which is the present value of the expected dividend flow.

The analysis of the model under the REH is quite straightforward from a modeler's perspective, but agents themselves are unrealistically sophisticated: they are assumed to know the endogenous distribution of p_t, fully solve their dynamic programming problem given this knowledge, and further, this knowledge must be *common* among agents.

In the following subsections we provide various models of decision-making that do not require these assumptions. Once departing from the rational expectations hypothesis, the modeler is confronted with whether to require that boundedly rational agents take the evolution of their beliefs as a constraint on their decision-making. Or, should they satisfy behavioral primitives that (mistakenly) take their beliefs as having come from a completed learning process? The latter approach – called the anticipated utility approach – is the benchmark in the literature and forms the basis for the discussion in the next several sections. Below, we discuss alternative implementations of the anticipated utility approach as well as some of the associated drawbacks.

2.3.2 The Shadow-Price Approach

The first approach to boundedly rational decision making that we consider is *shadow price learning*, developed by Evans et al. (2016) as a general approach to boundedly-optimal decision making. We now relax the representative agent assumption and consider agents who are identical except for expectations, indexed by type-j. Shadow-price learning is based on two simple assumptions: agents make linear forecasts and make decisions by contemplating trade-offs as measured by shadow prices.

Within the context of the current asset-pricing model, let λ_t^j be the perceived time-t value of an additional unit of the asset for an agent of expectations-type j. To make a time t consumption decision, the agent employs a variational thought experiment about the savings/consumption tradeoff: by reducing consumption by one unit today and increasing asset holdings tomorrow by $1/p_t$ an agent will equate

$$u'(c_t^j) = \frac{\beta}{p_t} \hat{E}_t^j \lambda_{t+1}^j.$$

(3)

To determine consumption, the modeler must take a stand on how $\hat{E}_t^j \lambda_{t+1}^j$ is formed, as well as a forecasting rule for p_t. Given a specification for the forecasting models, the modeler can solve for the consumption rule by combining the budget constraint (1) and Eq. (3). Plugging the consumption rule into the budget constraint determines the agent's asset demand as a function of price, dividend, asset holdings and beliefs:

$$a_{t+1}^j = a^{SP}(p_t, y_t, a_t^j, \hat{E}_t^j \lambda_{t+1}^j).$$

(4)

In the literature, and the examples presented below, boundedly rational beliefs are typically modeled as functions of past data. To update beliefs over time as new data become available some proxy data for λ_t must be computed, and for this the agent again employs another variational thought experiment: given the consumption choice, the benefit from an additional unit of the state today is

$$\lambda_t^j = (p_t + y_t)u'(c_t^j).$$

(5)

More generally, the envelope condition provides a way to compute the observed value for the shadow price. Thus, the shadow price approach provides a set of behavioral primitives consistent with optimization but does not require the full sophistication required of the agent in order to solve the complete dynamic programming problem.

2.3.3 The Shadow-Price Approach in the Linearized Model

A particularly nice feature of the shadow price approach is that it is easily employed in non-linear environments: no linearization was needed to determine demand (4). Further, note that this approach is amenable to any expectations operator satisfying the axioms (and based on linear forecasting models).[3] Most other implementations of boundedly-rational decision-making are developed in a linearized environment, and for comparison purposes, we consider a linearized version of shadow-price learning here.

---

[3]Evans et al. (2016) provide general conditions under which SP-learning as described here leads to asymptotic optimality; a more general expectations operator could potentially lead to very poorly behaved outcomes.

Log-linearizing (3) and (5) around the non-stochastic steady state (2) (and using $c = y$, which follows from the axioms) provides

$$c_t^j = v^{-1}(p_t - \hat{E}_t^j \lambda_{t+1}^j) \tag{6}$$
$$\lambda_t^j = -vc_t^j + \beta p_t + \beta y y_t,$$

where now all variables are written in proportional deviation from steady state form, and $v = -cu''(c)/u'(c)$. Eq. (6) is consistent with general expectations operators, but as above, it is standard to cast $E_t^j \lambda_{t+1}^j$ as a linear function of state variables. These equations can be coupled with the linearized budget constraint to compute the linearized asset demand equation

$$a_{t+1}^j = a_{lin}^{SP}(p_t, y_t, a_t^j, \hat{E}_t^j \lambda_{t+1}^j). \tag{7}$$

As long as beliefs are linear functions of prices and dividends, then asset-demand is a function only of state variables. Importantly, a_{lin}^{SP} is linear, which allows for tractable equilibrium analysis.

2.3.4 The Euler Equation Approach in the Linearized Model

Under shadow-price learning, the behavioral primitive is that agents make decisions based on tradeoffs measured by shadow prices. Here we take a different perspective, *Euler-equation learning* as advanced by Honkapohja et al. (2013): agents make decisions based on their perceived Euler equation. We continue to work within the linearized model.

The linearized Euler equation is given by

$$c_t^j = v^{-1} p_t + \hat{E}_t^j c_{t+1}^j - \beta v^{-1} \hat{E}_t^j p_{t+1} - \beta y v^{-1} \hat{E}_t^j y_{t+1}. \tag{8}$$

Note that (8) identifies the agent's decision in terms of a general expectations operator, but as in the shadow-price approach, it is common to assume agents use linear forecasting models to form expectations; however, rather than their shadow-value this time agents are required to forecast their own consumption plan. Coupled with the linearized budget constraint and perceived Euler equation, we can compute asset demand:

$$a_{t+1}^j = a_{lin}^{EL}(p_t, y_t, a_t^j, \hat{E}_t^j c_{t+1}^j, \hat{E}_t^j p_{t+1}), \tag{9}$$

which, as before, depends on beliefs, and is linear in prices. As before, provided that beliefs are linear functions of prices and dividends, the demand function can be written entirely in terms of state variables.

2.3.5 The Finite Horizon Approach in the Linearized Model

The shadow price and Euler equation approaches, as developed above, are based on one-step-ahead forecasts. When longer planning horizons are relevant, e.g. in case of anticipated structural change, a modification is in order. In this section we consider the implementation developed in Branch et al. (2012). The idea is simple: agents forecast their terminal asset position to solve their N-period consumption-savings problem. This finite-horizon learning approach places forecaster – who typically forecasts over a finite horizon – on equal footing with decision-makers.

While the model remains the same, it is convenient to change notation. First, go back to levels. Let $\hat{a}_t = p_{t-1}a_t$ be the goods-value of the asset held at time t and let $R_t = p_{t-1}^{-1}(p_t + y_t)$ be the return. The flow constraint may be written

$$c_t^j = R_t \hat{a}_t^j - \hat{a}_{t+1}^j.$$

Now let $D_{t+k} = \prod_{n=1}^{k} R_{t+n}^{-1}$, with $D_t = 1$, be the cumulative discount factor. The N-period budget constraint is then given by

$$\sum_{k=0}^{N} D_{t+k} c_{t+k} = R_t \hat{a}_t - D_{t+N} \hat{a}_{t+N+1}. \tag{10}$$

In differential form, we have

$$y \sum_{k=1}^{N} dD_{t+k} + \sum_{k=0}^{N} \beta^k dc_{t+k}^j = \hat{a} dR_t + \beta^{-1} da_t^j - \beta^N da_{t+N+1}^j - \hat{a} dD_{t+N},$$

where we have used that in steady state, $y = c$ and $R = \beta^{-1}$. Simplifying, using that $dD_{t+k} = -\beta^{k+1} \sum_{n=1}^{k} dR_{t+n}$ and returning to log-deviation form, we arrive at

$$y \sum_{k=0}^{N} \beta^k c_{t+k}^j = \hat{a}\beta^{-1} R_t + \beta^{-1} \hat{a} \hat{a}_t^j - \beta^N \hat{a} \hat{a}_{t+N+1}^j$$

$$+ \hat{a}\beta^N \sum_{n=1}^{k} R_{t+k} + y \sum_{k=1}^{N} \beta^k \sum_{n=1}^{k} R_{t+n}, \tag{11}$$

which is the agent's linearized budget constraint with planning horizon N.

The linearized Euler equation yields

$$\hat{E}_t^j c_{t+k}^j = c_t^j + \upsilon^{-1} \sum_{n=1}^{k} \hat{E}_t^j R_{t+n}. \tag{12}$$

Taking expectations of (11) (relying on the axioms), and using (12) to eliminate $\hat{E}_t^j c_{t+k}^j$, we may write current consumption as linear in $a_t^j, R_t, \hat{E}_t^j a_{t+N+1}^j$, and $\hat{E}_t^j R_{t+n}$, for $n = 1, \dots, N$. By providing the agent with linear forecasting models for asset holdings and returns, the current consumption and savings decisions may be determined in terms of beliefs and observable state variables.

2.3.6 The Infinite Horizon Approach in the Linearized Model

Letting the planning horizon N go to infinity and imposing the transversality condition provides the infinite horizon approach. Eq. (11) becomes the usual lifetime budget constraint, which is particularly simple in our case:

$$y \sum_{k=0}^{\infty} \beta^k E_t^\tau c_{t+k}^j = (1-\beta)^{-1} R_t + (1-\beta)^{-1} a_t^j + y(1-\beta)^{-1} \sum_{k=1}^{\infty} \beta^k R_{t+k}, \quad (13)$$

which, when coupled to the linearized Euler equation (12), yields

$$c_t^j = y^{-1} R_t + y^{-1} a_t^j + \frac{\upsilon - 1}{\upsilon} \sum_{k=1}^{\infty} \beta^k E_t^j R_{t+k}. \quad (14)$$

By providing the agent with linear forecasting models for returns, the current consumption and savings decisions may be determined in terms of beliefs and observables. Notice, unlike the previous approaches, with infinite-horizon learning they only need to forecast state variables beyond their own control.

The infinite horizon approach has advantages over the Euler equation in that the agents are behaving as optimizing anticipated utility maximizers. Thus, although the agents have non-rational and possibly heterogeneous expectations, they optimize given their subjective expectations. We show below that infinite horizon learning – by emphasizing decision rules that depend on expectations of state variables beyond an agent's control – can help aggregate decision rules across agents with heterogeneous expectations. From (14), the approach leads to a key result that long-run expectations play an important role in household consumption decisions. The infinite-horizon approach has been employed extensively by Preston (2005, 2006), Eusepi and Preston (2011), Woodford (2013), and recently surveyed in Eusepi and Preston (2018).

However, there are drawbacks as well. First, as a model of bounded rationality it seems unlikely that consumers hold such long-horizon expectations. Second, solving the infinite horizon problem can be technically challenging without log-linearizing the behavioral equations. While this may be appropriate in some environments such as the New Keynesian model which also is usually solved only after log-linearizing even when agents hold rational expectations, it is not a good approximation in other environments such as asset-pricing, pure monetary theory, and models with search and matching frictions. Finally, if the motivation for learning models is to place economist and economic agent on equal footing, it seems natural to model agents as finite-horizon learners who have a more limited horizon as most econometricians only forecast for so many periods into the future.

2.3.7 A Nod to Value Functions

As an alternative to the shadow-price approach, Evans et al. (2016) consider "value-function learning" within a linear-quadratic framework. Under this approach, agents estimate the value function based on a quadratic form specification and then make decisions conditional on the estimated value function. They show that asymptotic optimality obtains under the same conditions as for the shadow-price approach.

Value-function learning in the current environment is less natural: the analog to the linearized model would be to compute a second order approximation to the objective (after substituting in the non-linear budget constraint). On the other hand, the value-function approach is especially natural in discrete choice environments: Evans et al. (2016) develop a value-function learning analysis of the McCall (1970) search model where the agent must decide whether to accept an offer. They provide conditions under which a learning agent will behave optimally asymptotically.

The value function approach is also particularly convenient when special assumptions make it natural for the agent to know the value function's form. The LQ-environment considered by Evans et al. (2016) provides one framework, and the quasi-linear utility environment in many incarnations of the Lagos–Wright model provide another: Branch and McGough (2016) and Branch (2016) use precisely this approach, which is discussed below.

2.3.8 A Defense of Anticipated Utility

In models of learning and heterogeneous (non-rational) expectations, beliefs evolve over time. Households and firms solve intertemporal optimization problems that require expectations about future variables that are relevant to their decision making. Under rational expectations, an agent holds a well-specified probability distribution that, in equilibrium, is time invariant. Under learning, there is the issue of whether, and to what extent, agents explicitly account for the evolution of their beliefs when deciding on their optimal decision rules. That is, should an agent's beliefs be a state variable in their value functions?

The anticipated utility approach dictates that agents take their current beliefs as fixed when solving for their optimal plans. Given an expectation operator dated at time t, an agent is able to formulate expectations about variables relevant to their decision making over their particular planning horizon. They then solve for their optimal plan – consumption, labor hours, and asset holdings in the present environment – while assuming that their beliefs will not change in the future. As their beliefs change, they will discard their plan and formulate a new one. In a sense, an anticipated utility maximizing agent is dogmatic about their current beliefs. Conversely, a Bayesian agent would acknowledge that their beliefs evolve and treat those beliefs as a state variable with an associated law of motion. The literature on learning and heterogeneous expectations typically maintains the anticipated utility assumption for technical convenience: solving intertemporal optimization problems as a fully Bayesian agent is analytically and computationally challenging. Moreover, as we argue here the anticipated utility assumption is appealing from a bounded rationality perspective.

Cogley and Sargent (2008) directly address the inconsistency inherent to anticipated utility maximization. Each period the agent holds beliefs about all payoff-relevant variables over the planning horizon. Then when making decisions they act as if they will never change those beliefs again, that is, until the learning process has ended. In the next period they update beliefs and again pretend that they will not learn anymore. A fully Bayesian agent, however, would acknowledge their uncertainty, include their beliefs as a state variable, and assign posterior probabilities to all of the possible future paths, choosing the consumption plan that maximizes their expected utility, where expectations are taken with respect to their posterior distribution. Cogley and Sargent (2008) compare how anticipated utility consumption decisions compare to the fully Bayesian plan. They find that anticipated utility can be seen as a good approximation to fully Bayesian optimization.

This subsection briefly comments on their results, placing the discussion in the context of our present environment, and relating it to recent models of "Internal Rationality."[4] Cogley and Sargent's approach could be mapped into the present environment by assuming that the dividend growth process follows a two-state Markov chain and the agents know that the pricing function depends on the current realization of dividend growth. Cogley and Sargent's learning model imposes that the agents know that dividend growth, hence prices, follow the two-state process but they don't know the transition probabilities. Instead, they learn about these transition probabilities using past data and by updating their estimates using Bayes' rule. The Bayesian agents solve a dynamic programming problem including their beliefs about the transition probabilities in the state vector and, so, their learning rule becomes a part of the state transition equation. An anticipated utility maximizer, on the other hand, does not include the evolution of their beliefs in the state transition equation, and solves a standard dynamic programming problem assuming their beliefs are fixed.

Cogley and Sargent show that in this simple environment that the number of times that dividend growth is in a particular state is a sufficient statistic for agents' learning model. They focus on a model with finitely-lived agents. The agent considers each possible node which consists of a particular state at time t, and the number of times that it has been in a state, assigns probabilities to these nodes, and then chooses the consumption plan that maximizes expected utility. This can be done recursively using dynamic programming methods. As time advances, the number of nodes expands and the solution to the dynamic programming problem can run into the curse of dimensionality. If the agent has an infinite planning horizon, as is typical in macroeconomic and asset-pricing models, then the state space is unbounded and standard results for dynamic programming do not apply. Cogley and Sargent discuss an approximation, where since the agents are learning about an exogenous process, with no feedback from beliefs, the estimated probabilities eventually converge to their true values. So agents can take as given the value function that they will eventually converge to, and then recursively solve a finite horizon problem.

Adam et al. (2017) consider an asset-pricing model where agents are "internally rational." Like Cogley and Sargent they expand the state vector to include agents'

---

[4] See, for example, Adam and Marcet (2011).

beliefs. However, internally rational agents do not know the pricing function and so also forecast price-growth. With a continuous Markov process for dividend growth, and other restrictions on beliefs, they are able to numerically solve for the policy function. They find that such a model can explain key asset pricing and survey data empirical regularities.

This chapter focuses on bounded rationality and heterogeneous expectations. We do not present results on internal rationality because we do not find it a realistic model of individual behavior. The motivation for heterogeneous expectations and learning models is that forming rational expectations is complex and costly. The fully Bayesian model of decision making is, in essence, a hyper-rational model of agent decision-making. Besides considering what prices and other exogenous variables might be in the future, they also take into account how their beliefs might evolve along any history of shocks. Loosely speaking, an agent who is optimistic today has to forecast how they will behave in a few years if they become pessimistic and, continuing this internal thought experiment, will they switch to being optimistic in, say, another 10 years, and so on. Given the complexity for the modeler to solve such a dynamic programming problem, the potential for the curse of dimensionality, and the possibility that standard recursive tools are not available, it strikes us as not the most compelling way to describe real-life behavior.[5] The advantage of the internal rationality approach is to focus attention on the role of learning, without other assumptions about boundedly rational decision-making, and, as a benchmark like rational expectations, we agree that it is a useful theoretical approach. We are heartened that models with Euler equation learning and internal rationality produce similar asset-pricing implications.

However, the focus of this article is the extent to which bringing more realistic models of agent behavior can lead to distinct implications and provide explanations for real-world phenomena. Thus, we advocate for, and focus on, models of anticipated utility maximization.

2.4 AGGREGATING HOUSEHOLD DECISION RULES

Having derived the individual boundedly rational optimizing behavior of heterogeneous agents, equilibrium requires computing aggregate, or market-clearing consumption/output from which assets can then be priced. Many applications derive an aggregate asset-pricing equation that depends on the aggregate expectations operator. This section illustrates how to aggregate decision rules, while briefly discussing some challenges.

---

[5] Adam et al. (2017) make use of a recursive formulation. What is important is restrictions on beliefs so that the state-space expanded to include the belief transition equation is bounded, in contrast to Cogley–Sargent. It seems from their papers that it is sufficient to assume agents believe price growth follows a random-walk. Though, it remains an open question what other types of less-restrictive perceived laws of motion can be consistent with "internal rationality."

To illustrate, we adopt the Euler equation learning approach. Recall that the behavioral primitives, in the log-linearized economy, are

$$
\begin{aligned}
c_t^j &= \beta R \hat{E}_t^j c_{t+1}^j - \beta R \upsilon^{-1} \hat{E}_t^j R_{t+1} \\
c_t^j &= \hat{a} R(\hat{a}_t^j + R_t) - \hat{a} \hat{a}_{t+1}^j \equiv \Omega_t^j
\end{aligned}
$$

where Ω^j denotes (end of period) real-wealth. Iterating on the Euler equation, we have

$$
\Omega_t^j = \Omega_\infty^j - \beta R \upsilon^{-1} \hat{E}_t^j \sum_{k=1}^{\infty} (\beta R)^{k-1} R_{t+k}
$$

where $\Omega_\infty^j = \lim_{T\to\infty} (\beta R)^T \hat{E}_t^j c_T$. In the asset-pricing application, $\beta R = 1$ and so the Euler equation iterated forward depends on expected limiting wealth. In a model where there is a precautionary savings motivate, for instance in the version of the model with the specialized goods market and a limited commitment friction, it is possible that $R < \beta^{-1}$ and $\Omega_\infty^j = 0$. In this case, aggregation proceeds without any difficulty.

When $\beta R = 1$, then additional assumptions on higher-order beliefs are necessary for aggregation. To illustrate this, assume that there are two expectation-types, $j = 1, 2$. Then, $n\Omega_t^1 + (1-n)\Omega_t^2 = (1-\beta)^{-1} R_t$ in this linearized economy. Then

$$
\begin{aligned}
(1-\beta)^{-1} R_t &= n\Omega_t^1 + (1-n)\Omega_t^2 \\
&= n\Omega_\infty^1 + (1-n)\Omega_\infty^2 - \upsilon^{-1} \hat{E}_t \sum_{k\geq 1} R_{t+k} \\
&= \left[1 - \upsilon^{-1}(1-\beta) \right] \hat{E}_t R_{t+1} + n\Omega_\infty^1 + (1-n)\Omega_\infty^2 \\
&\quad - \hat{E} \left[n\Omega_\infty^1 + (1-n)\Omega_\infty^2 \right]
\end{aligned}
$$

where $\hat{E} = n\hat{E}^1 + (1-n)\hat{E}^2$. Thus, to have a (linearized) asset-pricing equation that depends on the aggregate expectations operator – i.e. a weighted average of heterogeneous expectations – requires that all agents agree on limiting wealth, an axiom needed for aggregation in the New Keynesian model as shown by Branch and McGough (2009). Alternatively, a model with $\beta R < 1$ also facilitates aggregation without difficulty.

3 EQUILIBRIA WITH HETEROGENEOUS EXPECTATIONS

Having developed both a general framework for non-rational expectations operators as well as a corresponding decision theory, we now turn to equilibrium considerations. There are two questions to address:

1. Given the distribution of agents across expectations operators, how are endogenous variables determined?
2. How are agents distributed across expectations operators?

The first question is straightforward to address: under the reduced form approach, a convex combination of expectations operators is imposed directly into the reduced-form expectational difference equations; while under a micro-founded approach, a temporary equilibrium is constructed by aggregating individual rules and imposing market clearing.

Three different broad mechanisms have been proposed to address the second question. Many, especially early, applications of heterogeneous expectations in macroeconomic models imposed the degree of heterogeneity exogenously, which we describe as *extrinsic heterogeneity*. Beginning with the seminal work by Brock and Hommes (1997), much of the literature has the distribution of agents across models as an equilibrium object. Here we review two ways in which heterogeneity can arise endogenously: first, where there is a cost to using certain types of predictors, i.e. *rationally heterogeneous expectations*; second, where forecasters miss-specify their models in different ways, but in equilibrium they only choose the best performing models, that is, *intrinsic heterogeneity*.

3.1 EXTRINSIC HETEROGENEITY

An equilibrium with extrinsic heterogeneity takes the distribution of agents across models as fixed and computes equilibrium prices and quantities. In particular, in the asset-pricing application developed in the previous section, each agent of type j, solves for their optimal consumption and asset holdings given their behavioral primitives (e.g. SP-learning, etc.), and then the temporary equilibrium pins down the price. For example, suppose J is a finite index set of types of SP-learning agents who differ only in their time-t beliefs. The asset demand of an agent of type $j \in J$ is then given by

$$a_{t+1}^j = a^{SP}(p_t, y_t, a_t^j, \hat{E}_t^j \lambda_{t+1}^j)$$

Let n_j be the measure of type j agents. Given y_t, beliefs $\{\hat{E}_t^j \lambda_{t+1}^j\}_{j \in J}$, and asset holdings $\{a_t^j\}_{j \in J}$, the equilibrium price is determined by

$$1 = \sum_{j \in J} n_j \cdot a^{SP}(p_t, y_t, a_t^j, \hat{E}_t^j \lambda_{t+1}^j)$$

Note that here we are using the non-linear version of SP-learning. The linearized market-clearing condition would set the sum to zero. Note also that, in this linearized case, an analytic expression for p_t in terms of beliefs, exogenous variables, and the distribution of asset holdings, is available.

3.2 RATIONALLY HETEROGENEOUS EXPECTATIONS

The theory of rationally heterogeneous expectations, as formulated by Brock and Hommes (1997), holds that expectation formation is a discrete choice from a finite set of predictors.

3.2.1 Predictor Selection

In order to illustrate how the approach works in the present environment, for ease of exposition, we assume the shadow value learning formulation, and risk-neutral preferences. In this case,

$$p_t = \beta y + \beta \hat{E}_t p_{t+1} \tag{15}$$

where $\hat{E}_t$ is a convex combination of expectations operators:

$$\hat{E}_t p_{t+1} = \sum_{j=1}^{N} n_j p_{t+1}^e(j)$$

where $p_{t+1}^e(j)$ is the forecast provided by predictor j, and n_j is the proportion of agents using that forecast.

Each individual i is assumed to select their predictor j by solving the following problem:

$$j_{t+1} = \arg \max_{j=1,\dots,J} \left\{ \Omega_i(j, p_t^e(j), p_t) \right\}$$

where

$$\Omega_i(j, p_t^e, p_t) = -\left(p_t - p_t^e(j)\right)^2 - C_{it}(j)$$

The objective function Ω_i can be thought of as consisting of two components: $-(p_t - p_t^e(j))^2$ captures the preference for predictors that forecast well; and, $C_{it}(j)$ is an idiosyncratic preference shock measuring individual i's relative ease of using predictor j, i.e. it is a "cost" to using the predictor.

The cross-sectional distribution of the preference shock determines the distribution of agents across the predictors. We follow the discrete choice approach of Brock and Hommes (1997) and assume that $C_{it}(j) = C(j) + \eta_{it}(j)$. Provided that the η_{it} are i.i.d. across time and individuals and, further, have the extreme value distribution, then the fraction of individuals using predictor j, denoted $n_t(j)$ is given by the multinomial logit (MNL) map:

$$n_t(j) = n_t \left(j, p_{t-1}, \{ p_{t-1}^e(\tau) \}_{\tau=1}^{J} \right) = \frac{\exp\left\{ \omega \times \Omega(j, p_{t-1}, p_{t-1}^e(j)) \right\}}{\sum_{\tau=1}^{N} \exp\left\{ \omega \times \Omega(\tau, p_{t-1}, p_{t-1}^e(\tau)) \right\}} \tag{16}$$

The MNL map has a long and venerable history in discrete choice decision making. It is a natural way of introducing randomness in forecasting and has a similar interpretation as mixed strategies in actions as a mechanism for remaining robust to forecast model uncertainty. The coefficient ω is referred to as the 'intensity of choice' and is inversely related to the variance of the idiosyncratic preference shock η_{it}. Finite values of ω, the intensity of choice, imply less than full utility maximization. The neoclassical case is when $\omega \to +\infty$.

One note about the formulation in (16). Here $n_t(j)$ is the fraction of agents holding predictor j at time t, i.e. it is the distribution at the time when markets clear and p_t is realized. We follow much of the adaptive learning literature in assuming a $(t-1)$-timing structure of information known to agents when they select predictors. Since these individuals are boundedly rational it is natural to assume that predictor choice and market outcomes are not determined simultaneously. Thus, when selecting the predictor to take into the market in time t the most recently observed data point is p_{t-1}.

3.2.2 Heterogeneous Beliefs and Economic Dynamics: Stability Reversal

Coupling predictor choice as in (16) with the pricing equation (15) can lead to interesting non-linear dynamics that exploit the mutual feedback between the pricing process – which is self-referential – and the choice of predictors. We illustrate these implications in this subsection.

Continue to assume that price is determined by (15). We will consider a simple example, as in Branch and McGough (2016), where individuals select from either a perfect foresight predictor, with a cost $C > 0$, or a simple adaptive predictor at no cost. That is, the predictors are

$$
\begin{aligned}
\hat{E}_t^1 p_{t+1} &= p_{t+1} \\
\hat{E}_t^2 p_{t+1} &= \bar{p} + \theta \left(p_{t-1} - \bar{p} \right)
\end{aligned}
$$

where $\bar{p} = \bar{y}/(1-\beta)$ is the steady-state price. Without loss of generality, set $\bar{y} = 0$. Then the actual law of motion is

$$
\begin{aligned}
p_t &= \left(\frac{1}{\beta n_{t-1}} \right) p_{t-1} - \left(\frac{1 - n_{t-1}}{n_{t-1}} \right) \theta p_{t-2} \\
n_t &= \frac{1}{2} \left\{ \tanh \left[\frac{\omega}{2} \left((p_{t-1} - \theta p_{t-2})^2 - C \right) \right] + 1 \right\}
\end{aligned}
$$

Predictor selection can lead to an endogenous attracting/repelling dynamic that can lead to periodic and complex fluctuations in price. The key intuition for complex dynamics is the *stability reversal* property of heterogeneous expectations:

Proposition 1. *Consider the case of rational versus adaptive expectations and (15) with extrinsic heterogeneity.*

a. *Let $n = 1$. The steady state is dynamically unstable and there exists a unique non-explosive perfect foresight equilibrium path.*

b. *Let $n = 0$. The steady state is dynamically stable provided that $\beta\theta < 1$.*

When $n = 1$, and all agents are rational, there is a unique rational expectations equilibrium that coincides with the steady-state. That is, the steady state is the only non-explosive solution to the forward expectational difference equation (15). The equilibrium is unique because the steady-state is dynamically unstable. Conversely, so long as θ is not too large – for example, $0 < \theta < 1$ would be sufficient – then the steady-state is dynamically stable and all paths from an initial condition on beliefs will converge to the steady-state.

The *stability reversal* property arises intuitively because perfect foresight requires forward-looking behavior and adaptive beliefs are backward-looking. This is most easily seen by noting that the expectational difference equation (15) reverses direction when, for instance, $\hat{E}_t p_{t+1} = p_{t-1}$. Therefore, forward stability implies backward stability, and vice versa. The possibility of stability reversal plays a prominent role in explaining the dynamic behavior of models with heterogeneous expectations. In subsequent sections, we present examples where stability reversal implies complex attracting/repelling dynamics.

3.3 INTRINSIC HETEROGENEITY

In the rationally heterogeneous expectations approach, heterogeneity arises because of a cost to using a particular predictor, and for finite intensities of choice, ω, i.e. because of the idiosyncratic preference shocks. In Branch and Evans (2006) an environment is presented where heterogeneity can arise even in the neoclassical case of $\omega \to +\infty$. The framework developed by Branch and Evans is an extension of Brock and Hommes to a stochastic environment where agents select among a set of misspecified forecasting models. In a Misspecification Equilibrium the parameters of the forecasting models, and the distribution of agents across models, are determined jointly as equilibrium objects. *Intrinsic Heterogeneity* arises if agents are distributed across more than one model even as $\omega \to \infty$. Branch and Evans (2006) developed their results within the context of a cobweb model, though Branch and Evans (2010) extend to an asset-pricing model, and Branch and Evans (2011) show existence of Intrinsic Heterogeneity in a New Keynesian model.

To illustrate the approach, we extend the basic modeling environment to include two different serially correlated shocks, a dividend shock and a share-supply shock. In Branch and Evans (2010) the share-supply shock arises in an OLG model through random variations in population growth, which affects the supply of trees per person. In Branch (2016) variations in the supply can arise in the search-based asset-pricing model outlined in the previous section. Here we will illustrate the approach in the context of the search-based asset-pricing model that, with large enough liquidity services role for the asset in facilitating specialized good consumption, can feature negative feedback as in the Cobweb and New Keynesian economies.

A log-linearization to the asset-pricing equation extended to include a liquidity premium can be written as

$$\hat{p}_t = \alpha_0 \hat{E}_t \hat{y}_{t+1} + \alpha_1 \hat{E}_t \hat{p}_{t+1} + \alpha_2 \hat{A}_t$$

for appropriately defined α_k, $k = 0, 1, 2$.[6] The stochastic process A_t is the supply of shares in the Lucas tree, which can be interpreted as asset float resulting from new share issuances, repurchases, and stock splits. Assume that the stochastic processes for dividends and share supply are stationary AR(1) processes, given by

$$\begin{align}
\hat{y}_t &= \rho \hat{y}_{t-1} + \varepsilon_t \\
\hat{A}_t &= \phi \hat{A}_{t-1} + \nu_t
\end{align}$$

where ε, ν are uncorrelated across time but are potentially correlated with each other. If there is sufficient curvature of the utility function over the specialized good then $\alpha_1 < 0$ and the model exhibits negative feedback. This arises when the liquidity premium is high: if the expected price of the asset is high then it will relax the liquidity constraint and individuals do not need to hold as much of the asset to facilitate specialized-goods consumption, demand for the asset goes down, and price decreases. Alternatively, for smaller liquidity premia then $\alpha_1 > 0$.

In a rational expectations equilibrium, agents would include in their forecasting model, or perceived law of motion (PLM), both dividends and share supply. In Branch and Evans (2006), agents were assumed to select from a set of underparameterized forecasting models. In the present application, the set of forecasting models are:

$$\begin{align}
\hat{p}_t = b^1 \hat{y}_t + \epsilon_t^1 &\quad \Rightarrow \quad \hat{E}_t^1 \hat{p}_{t+1} = b^1 \rho \hat{y}_t \\
\hat{p}_t = b^2 \hat{A}_t + \epsilon_t^2 &\quad \Rightarrow \quad \hat{E}_t^2 \hat{p}_{t+1} = b^2 \phi \hat{A}_t
\end{align}$$

Underparameterization is motivated by real life decisions encountered by professional forecasters. Often, degrees of freedom limitations lead forecasters to adopt parsimonious models.[7]

Denote by n the fraction of agents who adopt the dividend-only forecasting model, i.e. "model 1". Plugging in expectations, the actual law of motion can be written as

$$\hat{p}_t = \xi_0(b_1, n) \hat{y}_t + \xi_1(b_2, n) \hat{A}_t$$

In a *Misspecification Equilibrium*, agents only select the best-forming statistical models. Thus, in equilibrium we require that the coefficients of the forecasting models are determined by the least-squares projection of price onto the restricted set of regressors, i.e. b^1, b^2 satisfy the least-squares orthogonality conditions

$$E \hat{y}_t \left(p_t - b^1 \hat{y}_t \right) = 0 \tag{17}$$

$$E \hat{A}_t \left(p_t - b^2 \hat{A}_t \right) = 0 \tag{18}$$

---

[6]See Branch (2016) for details.

[7]There are various ways that forecasters underparameterize. For example, they could fit models with lower lag orders. The qualitative results are robust to these alternatives.

A *Restricted Perceptions Equilibrium* is a stochastic process for p_t, given n, such that b^1, b^2 satisfy (17)–(18). In a restricted perceptions equilibrium the agents forecasting models are misspecified but, within the context of their forecasting model, they do not recognize the misspecification. A restricted perceptions equilibrium can be justified in environments where data is slow to reveal the misspecification, a property shared by most time series data.

A Misspecification Equilibrium requires that the agents only select their best performing statistical model. Branch and Evans (2006) endogenize the distribution of agents across forecasting models, as in Brock–Hommes, by assuming they make a discrete choice and the distribution is determined by the MNL-map:

$$n = \frac{1}{2} \left\{ \tanh \left[\frac{\omega}{2} F(n) \right] + 1 \right\} \equiv T_\omega(n)$$

where $F(n)$ is the relative mean-squared error between predictor 1 and predictor 2 within a restricted perceptions equilibrium for a given n. Notice that the T-map: T_ω : $[0, 1] \rightarrow [0, 1]$ is continuous and so the set of equilibria is indexed by the intensity of choice ω and the properties of the function F.

Definition 2. A Misspecification Equilibrium is a fixed point, n^*, of T_ω.

The set of equilibria depend on the properties of F, and can be characterized in the following way.

Proposition 3. *The set of Misspecification Equilibria has one of the following properties.*

1. *If $F(0) > 0$ and $F(1) < 0$, then as $\omega \rightarrow \infty$, $n^* \rightarrow \tilde{n}$ where $F(\tilde{n}) = 0$. That is, the model exhibits Intrinsic Heterogeneity.*
2. *If $F(0) > 0$ and $F(1) > 0$, then as $\omega \rightarrow \infty$, $n^* \rightarrow 1$.*
3. *If $F(0) < 0$ and $F(1) < 0$, then as $\omega \rightarrow \infty$, $n^* \rightarrow 0$.*
4. *If $F(0) < 0$ and $F(1) > 0$, then as $\omega \rightarrow \infty$, the model has multiple Misspecification equilibrium with $n^* \rightarrow \in \{0, \tilde{n}, 1\}$ and $F(\tilde{n}) = 0$.*

Intrinsic Heterogeneity arises when agents do not want to mass on one or the other predictors, which occurs when $F(0) > 0$, $F(1) < 0$, i.e. there is always an incentive to deviate from expectations homogeneity. In the Branch–Evans papers it was shown that Intrinsic Heterogeneity requires negative feedback, $\alpha_1 < 0$, which can occur for large liquidity premia in the present environment. In the monetary policy application, negative feedback can arise when the central bank sets its policy rate according to an expectations-based Taylor-type rule with an aggressive response to expectations. Negative feedback implies that the asset pricing model features strategic substitution effects. There can also be multiple equilibria when there are sufficiently strong strategic complementarities, i.e. with $\alpha_1 > 0$. In this case, there are misspecification equilibria with all agents massed onto one model or the other, and a third misspecification equilibria that exhibits Intrinsic Heterogeneity.[8]

4 ASSET-PRICING APPLICATIONS

Heterogeneous expectations provide a promising avenue for generating more realistic movements in asset prices than what is capable with the representative agent counterpart. This section illustrates three mechanisms for generating empirical features of asset prices. First, we present a Misspecification Equilibrium, when combined with learning, that is able to generate regime-switching returns and volatilities consistent with the data. Second, we highlight two ways in which heterogeneous expectations can lead to the endogenous emergence of bubbles and crashes.

4.1 REGIME-SWITCHING RETURNS

Branch and Evans (2010) construct a mean-variance asset-pricing model where stock prices are driven by expected returns, which depend directly on dividends and asset share supply, and indirectly via the self-referential feature of the pricing Euler equation. As in the previous section, it was assumed that traders are distributed across underparameterized forecasting models that depend only on dividends or share supply. It was shown that multiple Misspecification Equilibria exist and a real-time adaptive learning version of the model generates regime-switching returns and volatilities.

The asset-pricing equation in Branch and Evans (2010) was derived from an overlapping generations model with mean-variance preferences. The dynamic structure of OLG models is quite similar to the sub-periods of the Lagos–Wright based model developed in Section 2. The CARA preferences underlying the mean-variance structure lead to a downward sloping demand curve, similar to what emerges in the search-based model where the limited demand is based on the liquidity properties of the asset. Thus, the results in Branch and Evans (2010) are robust to the version of the model with liquidity considerations provided that there are log preferences over the specialized good: see Branch (2016). For ease of exposition, this subsection deviates from the model derived in this chapter and presents the asset-pricing equation derived by Branch and Evans (2010).

The mean-variance asset-pricing model, with stochastic processes for dividends and share supply, has asset demand represented by equations of the form, for an agent

---

[8] It should be noted that in the applications with multiple Misspecification Equilibria considered by Branch and Evans, the Intrinsic Heterogeneity in the multiple equilibria case is unstable under real-time learning. It is an open question, whether there can exist stable Intrinsic Heterogeneity in models other than what was considered by Branch and Evans with positive feedback.

with expectations-type j,

$$a_{jt} = \frac{1}{\gamma \hat{\sigma}^2} \hat{E}_t^j (p_{t+1} + y_{t+1} - R p_t)$$

where γ is the coefficient of absolute risk aversion and $\hat{\sigma}^2$ is the (perceived) conditional variance of excess returns. The risk parameter $\hat{\sigma}$ is pinned down as an equilibrium object of the model. As in the previous section, assume that there are two-types of agents who differ based on whether they forecast with a dividends-based or share supply-based model. Then market equilibrium requires that

$$n a_{1t} + (1 - n) a_{2t} = A_t$$

where, again, A_t represents asset share supply (or, float). The equilibrium process for price is, then, given by

$$p_t = \beta \left[n \hat{E}_t^1 p_{t+1} + (1 - n) \hat{E}_t^2 p_{t+1} \right] + \beta \rho y_t - \beta a \hat{\sigma}^2 A_t \qquad (19)$$

where $\beta = 1/R$. As before, assume that dividends and share supply are represented as stationary AR(1) processes, written in deviation-from-mean form:

$$y_t = (1 - \rho) y_0 + \rho y_{t-1} + \varepsilon_t$$
$$A_t = (1 - \phi) A_0 + \phi A_{t-1} + v_t$$

Traders are assumed to form their forecasts by selecting from one of the following misspecified models:

$$\text{PLM}_1: \quad p_t = b_0^1 + b^1 y_t + \eta_t$$
$$\text{PLM}_1: \quad p_t = b_0^2 + b^2 A_t + \eta_t$$

where η_t is a perceived white noise error. As before, the distribution of agents, after selecting their predictor, is given by the MNL map:

$$T_\omega(n) = \frac{1}{2} \left\{ \tanh \left[\frac{\omega}{2} F(n) \right] + 1 \right\}$$

A *Misspecification Equilibrium* is a fixed point n^* to the T-map, i.e. $n^* = T_\omega(n^*)$.

Branch and Evans (2010) show theoretically that there can exist multiple misspecification equilibria. An example is given in Fig. 3, which is based on a calibrated version of the model with $\omega \to \infty$. Fig. 3 plots the T-map and $F(n)$ functions, where the T-map crosses the 45° line is a Misspecification Equilibrium. In the calibrated version of the model, there are multiple misspecification equilibria. When all agents use forecast model 1, then it is a best-response for an agent to use forecast model 1 as it delivers a lower mean-square forecast error. Similarly, for model 2. Notice that there is also an interior equilibrium exhibiting Intrinsic Heterogeneity. The right hand panels compute the volatility of returns for a given n. These figures reveal that there

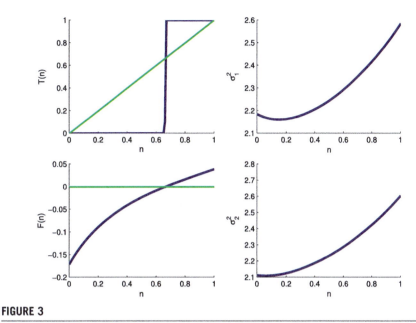

FIGURE 3

Misspecification Equilibria in an asset-pricing model (from Branch and Evans, 2010).

exist multiple misspecification equilibria, that differ in mean returns and volatilities. In particular, there exists a low return-low volatility and a high return-high volatility equilibrium.

The set of Misspecification Equilibria depends on the structural parameters of the model. In particular, the degree of risk-aversion – analogously, in the search-based model, the preferences for the differentiated good – plays an important role in determining whether multiple equilibria and whether Intrinsic Heterogeneity can exist. In Fig. 4, Branch and Evans (2010) compute the misspecification equilibria treating the degree of risk-aversion, a, as a bifurcation parameter. For low and high risk aversion there exist unique equilibria with homogeneous expectations. For moderate, and empirically realistic, degrees of risk-aversion there are multiple equilibria, including ones with Intrinsic Heterogeneity.

Branch and Evans (2010) exploited the existence of multiple misspecification equilibria to generate regime-switching returns and volatilities that match those estimated in the data by Guidolin and Timmermann (2007). To generate plausible dynamics, the Misspecification Equilibrium values for the belief parameters b^j, and the mean-square errors, were replaced by real-time recursive econometric estimators. Branch and Evans also specified a recursive estimator for the conditional variance $\hat{\sigma}^2$. The intensity of choice parameter was also calibrated to a finite value in order to match the Guidolin–Timmermann statistics. Fig. 5 illustrates a typical simulation that exhibits regime-switching returns and volatilities. As the distribution of heterogeneity n evolves in real-time, agents' beliefs fluctuate between neighborhoods of the

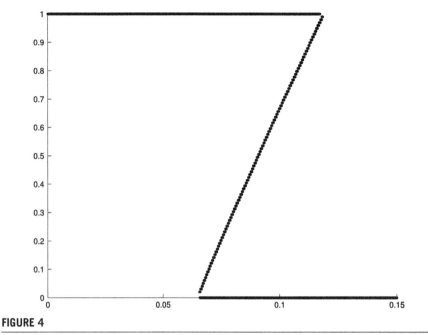

FIGURE 4

Bifurcating the set of Misspecification Equilibria in an asset-pricing model (from Branch and Evans, 2010).

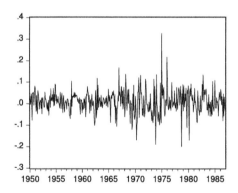

FIGURE 5

Real time learning dynamics of the Misspecification Equilibria in an asset-pricing model (from Branch and Evans, 2010).

low return/low volatility and high return/high volatility Misspecification Equilibria. Thus, misspecification and heterogeneity can lead to endogenous recurring regime switching asset returns.

4.2 BUBBLES WITH RATIONALLY HETEROGENEOUS EXPECTATIONS

Beginning with Brock and Hommes (1998), a large literature has developed studying paths from rationally heterogeneous expectations to excess volatility, bubbles, and crashes in otherwise standard asset-pricing models. Much of this literature is surveyed in Hommes (2013), with special attention to identifying simple forecasting heuristics that are consistent with learning-to-forecast experiments in asset pricing and other experimental economies. To illustrate the main mechanics, we turn now to a version of the model (19), but where agents choose between rational and adaptive expectations.

Consider a non-stochastic version of (19):

$$p_t = \mu + \beta \left[n_{t-1} \hat{E}_t^1 p_{t+1} + (1 - n_{t-1}) \hat{E}_t^2 p_{t+1} \right]$$

where $\mu = \beta \bar{y} - a\sigma^2 \bar{A}$, and we assume the following expectations operators:

$$
\begin{aligned}
\hat{E}_t^1 p_{t+1} &= p_{t+1} \\
\hat{E}_t^2 p_t &= \bar{p} + \theta (p_{t-1} - \bar{p}) \\
\hat{E}_t^2 p_{t+1} &= \bar{p} + \theta^2 (p_{t-1} - \bar{p})
\end{aligned}
$$

Predictor 1 is rational expectations (perfect foresight) and predictor 2 is an adaptive predictor that forecasts future prices as deviations from steady-state. Predictor 2 is an "anchor and adjustment" rule of the type that Hommes (2013) finds fits many experimental subjects' forecasts from the laboratory. In the example of this section, we assume that $\theta > 1$, so that agents who use this predictor are strongly extrapolative. Notice also that we have explicitly assumed a time-varying weight on n while preserving the typical $t - 1$-dating convention that forecasts made at time t are conditional on all information available through time t. This timing assumption breaks the simultaneity of expectations and equilibrium outcomes that are a defining feature of rational expectations equilibria but are not cognitively consistent in a model of bounded rationality. We also continue to assume that the distribution of predictor selection is given by the MNL map.

Given these assumptions, the actual law of motion for this economy is given by the following pair of non-linear difference equations:

$$
\begin{aligned}
p_t &= \hat{\mu} + \left(\frac{1}{\beta n_{t-1}} \right) p_{t-1} - \left(\frac{1 - n_{t-1}}{n_{t-1}} \right) \theta^2 p_{t-2} \\
n_t &= \frac{1}{2} \left\{ \tanh \left[\frac{\omega}{2} \left(U_t^1 - U_t^2 \right) \right] + 1 \right\}
\end{aligned}
$$

where $\hat{\mu} = -(\beta n)^{-1} \mu - (1 - n_{t-1})(1 - \theta^2) \bar{p}/n_{t-1}$ and $U_t^1 - U_t^2 = (p_t - \hat{E}_{t-1}^2 p_t)^2 - C$. For illustrative purposes, we measure predictor fitness as inversely related to the most recent squared forecast error net of the predictor cost, with the cost to using the adaptive predictor normalized to zero.

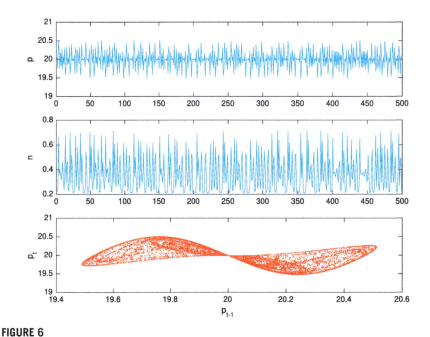

FIGURE 6

Rationally heterogeneous expectations and asset pricing dynamics.

Fig. 6 plots a typical simulation that exhibits complex price dynamics. This figure was generating assuming $\theta = 1.5, C = 1, \omega = 2.6, \beta = 0.95$, and $\mu = 1$. The first two panels plot the time paths for price and the fraction of rational agents along the stable attractor. The bottom panel plots the attractor in phase space. Price oscillates around the steady-state value with complex dynamics, featuring both excess volatility and bubbles/crashes. This simple example illustrates how rationally heterogeneous expectations can generate complex asset price dynamics. Other formulations of the predictors can lead to more realistic asset prices with larger bubbles and crashes, see, e.g. Hommes (2013) for examples.

The intuition for the complex dynamics arising from rationally heterogeneous expectations is based on attracting/repelling dynamics of predictor selection along with the stability reversal property discussed earlier. In this particular example, with forward- vs. backward-looking expectations, the steady-state is unstable when all agents adopt either rational or adaptive expectations. When the economy is close to steady-state the two predictors forecast equally well, so agents are unwilling to pay the cost for the rational predictor. This drives the economy away from the steady-state, i.e. the repelling dynamics. As price moves further from steady-state, the perfect foresight predictor's forecasting benefits begin to outweigh the cost, for some agents depending on their preference shocks, which balances the opposing repelling forces and tends to attract the system back towards the steady-state. These attracting/repelling forces combine to produce complex dynamics that can feature endogenous paths to bubbles and crashes.

4.3 RESTRICTED PERCEPTIONS AND ENDOGENOUS FLUCTUATIONS

A substantial body of research introduces volatility via fluctuations in expectations, for instance, through self-fulfilling sunspot shocks, news shocks, expectations shocks, sentiment shocks, forecasting add factors, exuberance shocks, etc. Broadly speaking, a drawback to these approaches to introducing expectations shocks, or animal spirits, is that it is difficult to construct instances where individuals and firms can coordinate their expectations. Branch and Zhu (2016), on the other hand, show how forecast model misspecification can expand the set of equilibria including restricted perceptions equilibria that depend on extrinsic noise. Interestingly, equilibria that depend on extrinsic noise do not necessarily exhibit more volatility than equilibria that only depend on fundamental economic variables. This is in contrast with much of the extant literature. Branch and Zhu (2016) show, however, that heterogeneity in forecast model misspecification can lead to more volatile equilibria that depend on extrinsic noise.

To illustrate the approach consider again the simplified asset-pricing model (19) with the share-supply shocks shut down:

$$p_t = \beta \left[n \hat{E}_t^1 p_{t+1} + (1-n) \hat{E}_t^2 p_{t+1} \right] + \gamma y_t$$

and $y_t = \rho y_{t-1} + \varepsilon_t, 0 < \rho < 1$ and ε is i.i.d. $N\left(0, \sigma_\varepsilon^2\right)$. Branch and Zhu (2016) follow the behavioral learning equilibria approach developed in Hommes and Zhu (2014), who assume that the exogenous shocks, y_t, are unobservable to all agents and so they instead fit autoregressive models to p_t, with the coefficients picked to ensure that the first autocorrelation of the data generating process and the approximating models coincide. In Branch and Zhu (2016) agents differ in a subset of their regressors, where the models can be thought of as ARMAX, so that agents may include more or less autoregressive terms, the fundamental exogenous variable y, or even moving average terms. The novelty in Branch and Zhu (2016) is that they also potentially include non-fundamental exogenous variables – loosely speaking, expectations shocks – in their forecasting model. To illustrate, we consider the simplest case in Branch and Zhu (2016):

$$\text{PLM}_1: \quad p_t = b p_{t-1} + d \eta_t$$
$$\text{PLM}_2: \quad p_t = c y_t + f \eta_t$$

where $\eta_t = \phi \eta_{t-1} + v_t$. The first predictor fits price to an AR(1) model plus a component common to the second predictor. The second predictor assumes these agents can observe the fundamental shocks, but also includes the common shock. The η_t can be thought of as all other information, exogenous to the fundamentals of the asset-pricing economy, i.e. a statistical sunspot variable. Whether agents coordinate on the η_t shock is determined as an equilibrium outcome. With these perceived laws of motion, the actual law of motion can be written as

$$p_t = \alpha_1 p_{t-1} + \alpha_2 y_t + \alpha_3 \eta_t \qquad (20)$$

for appropriately defined α_j, $j = 1, 2, 3$ that depend on the structural model parameters and, importantly, the belief coefficients b, c, d, f and the fraction of agents using model 1, n. Assume that n is an exogenous parameter in the model. Notice from (20) that the two predictors are misspecified: model 1 underparameterizes by excluding the fundamental shocks while model 2 omits lagged prices.

Because the two forecast models are misspecified, the appropriate equilibrium concept is *Restricted Perceptions Equilibrium* (RPE). Let $X_t^1 = (p_{t-1}, \eta_t)'$, $X_t^2 = (y_t, \eta_t)'$. Then, in an RPE the beliefs satisfy the least-squares orthogonality conditions:

$$EX_t^1 \left[p_t - (b, d)X_t^1 \right] = 0$$
$$EX_t^2 \left[p_t - (c, f)X_t^2 \right] = 0$$

If $n = 1$ and the RPE value $d = 0$ then the equilibrium value of b coincides with the behavioral learning equilibrium in Hommes and Zhu (2014). If $n = 0$ then there is a unique RPE value $f = 0$ and the value of c is the same as the rational expectations equilibrium coefficient. However, when $n = 1$ Branch and Zhu (2016) show that there can also exist non-fundamental RPE with $d \neq 0$. Thus, we focus on when $0 < n \leq 1$.

Branch and Zhu (2016) show that there always exists fundamental RPE where $d = 0$ and $f = 0$. In this case, the associated mappings from perceived parameters (b, c) to their least-squares projection values, computed using the implied actual law of motion, i.e. the "T-map" are

$$b \to \frac{b^2 n\beta + \rho}{1 + b^2 n\beta\rho}$$
$$c \to \frac{1 + c(1 - n)\beta\rho}{1 - b^2 n\beta\rho}$$

The fundamental RPE reveals an important insight for the existence of the non-fundamental RPE. In this simple example, the second perceived law of motion is only misspecified because of $n > 0$, i.e. the presence of the agents who do not observe or forecast with the dividend shocks as a regressor. The existence of these agents, though, alters the serial correlation properties of asset prices, which because of the cross-equation restrictions associated to the RPE least-squares orthogonality condition, impacts the regression coefficient c of the type-2 agents. Thus, the misspecification alters the equilibrium weight on the exogenous shocks.

Now consider the case where $d, f \neq 0$. Such equilibria can arise when the feedback effects in the model are strong, i.e. when β is close to one, a condition that will be satisfied in most asset-pricing models. In particular, the T-map components for the coefficients b, c now become

$$b \rightarrow \frac{1 - \beta\phi}{n\beta(1 - \phi^2)}$$

$$c \rightarrow \frac{1}{1 - (1 - n)\beta\rho - b^2 n\beta\rho}$$

and d is pinned down by a complicated quadratic expression in the structural parameters n, β, ρ, ϕ, and $f \rightarrow d/(1 - \beta\phi)$. The intuition for the existence of non-fundamental RPE is clear. The misspecification and heterogeneity introduce serial correlation in a temporary equilibrium sense. The agents optimally attribute some of that serial correlation to the endogenous variables – lagged prices for model 1 and serially correlated dividends for model 2 – and to the extrinsic variable η_t. The specific values of those regression coefficients depend on the distribution of agents across the two forecast models, as well as the stochastic properties of the shocks, i.e. ρ, ϕ. Importantly, the non-fundamental RPE are *self-fulfilling equilibria* that only arise when expectations play an important role in the pricing equation. There are, therefore, three important ingredients for the existence of these non-fundamental equilibria: misspecification, heterogeneity, and strong expectational feedback.

Fig. 7 illustrates the existence of the full set of RPE, including those depending on the statistical sunspots. This figure contains contour plots for the (b, c) components of the T-map.[9] The T_d component consists of a horizontal line at $d = 0$ and another vertical line at the non-fundamental value for b. The T_b mapping is the parabolic lines in the figure. The figure illustrates the fixed points to the T-map for two different values of n. The $n = 1$ T-maps provide the existence of RPE without heterogeneity, while the $n = 0.9$ consists of some degree of heterogeneous expectations. Notice that a fundamental RPE exists in both cases and that the RPE value of b are very close to each other for both values of n. For both values of n, there exist two non-fundamental RPE, symmetric around the $d = 0$ line. Increasing the degree of heterogeneity shifts the T_d line to the right, implying higher degrees of perceived autocorrelation. Similarly, the T_b shifts away from the $d = 0$ line, implying a relatively greater weight placed on the extrinsic noise d.

Branch and Zhu (2016) then ask the question of whether RPE that display dependence on extrinsic noise terms introduce more volatility into asset prices. It turns out that the effect is not obvious, as it depends on the equilibrium effect on all of the RPE belief coefficients. For example, bifurcating the equilibrium from a fundamental RPE to a non-fundamental RPE has a direct effect that increases asset-price volatility through the coordination of agents onto the extrinsic noise. However, there is a potentially competing effect on the equilibrium value for the AR(1) coefficient, b, in agents of type-one's forecasting model. These agents attribute, in part, some of

---

[9]Specifically, it computes the RPE in (b, c) space assuming that the remaining RPE coefficients (b, d) are set to their equilibrium values at each point in this space.

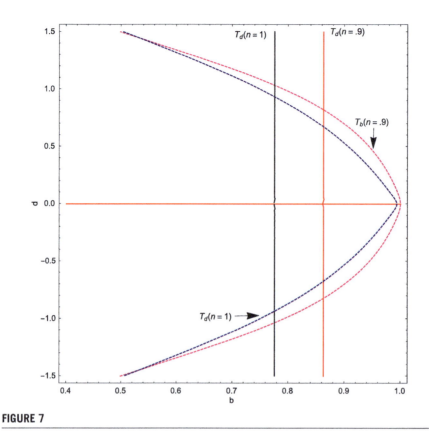

FIGURE 7

Restricted perceptions equilibria and endogenous fluctuations.

the serial correlation in prices to the extrinsic term, lowering their estimated value of b, which will tend to push down asset-price volatility. Thus, the effect on volatility is a balancing of these two effects. See, for example, a particular numerical case in Branch and Zhu (2016) that is plotted in Fig. 8. This figure plots the ratio of RPE price volatility to the volatility in the rational expectations equilibrium as a function of the degree of heterogeneity, n, for both the fundamental RPE (solid) and non-fundamental RPE (dashed). This particular example is for a very strongly serially correlated process η. Depending on the degree of heterogeneity, the RPE can introduce excess volatility, but it is not necessarily the case. Moreover, for relatively high values of n, that not too close to homogeneity, the excess volatility that arises from the non-fundamental RPE is greater than in the fundamental RPE. However, interestingly, when $n = 1$ the excess volatility is greater in the fundamental RPE, which coincides with the equilibrium identified by Hommes and Zhu (2014). The intuition for these findings can be seen in Fig. 7. The equilibrium with heterogeneous expectations is more volatile than the $n = 1$ equilibrium because the autoregressive coefficient b and the weight placed on the sunspot d is relatively higher. Thus, to have

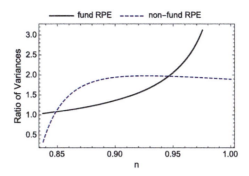

FIGURE 8

Endogenous volatility and asset prices.

statistical sunspots generate more volatility requires a self-reinforcing effect arising from heterogeneous expectations. However, if there is a sufficiently low n ($n < 0.85$ in the figure) then the non-fundamental RPE again produces less economic volatility. The reason is that as n decreases the T_d-map shifts to the right, and the forecasting models place less weight on both the sunspot (d, f) and the fundamental shock c.

4.4 RELATED LITERATURE

Much of the literature on asset-pricing in models with heterogeneous expectations was started by the seminal Brock and Hommes (1998), which applied the framework developed in Brock and Hommes (1997) to an asset pricing model where agents select between perfect foresight and a simple adaptive rule that nests extrapolative, contrarian, and trend-chasing expectations. These papers were inspired by LeBaron (1995) and other attempts at building artificial stock markets with heterogeneous, evolving technical trading strategies. Brock and Hommes (1998) demonstrated that rationally heterogeneous expectations could feature "a rational route to randomness" in asset prices for a wide specification of expectations-types. This launched an extensive literature with key contributions by Hommes and co-authors at the CENDEF at the University of Amsterdam. Important extensions include the "large-type limit" introduced by Brock et al. (2005), where agents select from a continuum of predictors, which has a natural Bayesian interpretation.

Importantly, this literature tackled the empirical foundations of heterogeneous expectations beyond their theoretical implications. A paper by Hommes et al. (2005) introduced "learning to forecast" experiments as a way to test for heterogeneous expectations in a simple laboratory environment. In this paper, a simple asset-pricing framework similar to Brock and Hommes (1998) was set in a laboratory where the only decision subjects were required to make was a forecast of the asset price in the next period, which automatically determines their portfolio allocation. Hommes et al. showed that the lab featured asset price dynamics that often converged to cycles around the fundamental price, i.e. bubbles and crashes. Moreover, they found that the best fit to the set of individual prediction strategies was a heterogeneous collection of simple autoregressive forecasting rules. Subsequent experiments across a range of model environments provide further evidence for heterogeneous beliefs and rationally evolving fractions of lab participants distributed across forecasting models. See, for instance, Hommes (2013) and Anufriev et al. (2015) for an extensive review.

There is also a literature that considers heterogeneity and adaptive learning. The seminal Marcet and Sargent (1989) featured a setting where agents had private information that creates for the other agents "hidden state variables," but differed in which sets of variables were unobservable. They focused on convergence to a limited information rational expectations equilibrium. Subsequent papers, such as Marcet and Sargent (1995), examine where agents fit heterogeneous ARMA models, similar to the class of forecasting models in Branch and Zhu (2016). Guse (2005) studies an environment with agents who have heterogeneous expectations derived from forecasting rules that fit the full set of rational expectations equilibria, i.e. one rule is based on the minimal state variable solution while the other is for an ARMA with sunspot, and derives conditions under which the MSV equilibrium is stable under learning in a general environment. Similarly, Berardi (2007) extends that framework to forward-looking models with a lag that nests the asset-pricing model considered here.

Besides Branch and Evans (2010), there have been other heterogeneous expectations models of adaptive learning and asset-pricing. LeBaron (2012) constructs a model with constant gain learning where agents differ in their gain size, i.e. their robustness to structural change of an unknown form. Markiewicz (2012) considers a form of misspecification equilibrium, where the distribution across predictors is determined by running statistical specification tests based on the Kullback–Leibler information criterion, and applies it to explaining exchange rate puzzles. Nakov and Nuno (2015) apply the learning-from-experience model of Malmendier and Nagel (2016) to an asset-pricing model. Finally, Parke and Waters (2007) construct an evolutionary model of learning that endogenously generates ARCH effects in asset-prices. Elias (2016) includes expectations shocks into an asset-pricing model with heterogeneous learning.

5 MONETARY APPLICATIONS

There is an extensive literature in monetary theory that studies the role of money as a medium of exchange. The modern workhorse monetary model is the Lagos–Wright New Monetarist framework which is equivalent to the model of Section 2 when the asset is reinterpreted as fiat money, i.e. the asset has zero payoff flows and is intrinsically worthless. Fiat money has value in the New Monetarist framework because the agents in the economy coordinate on a rational expectations equilibrium where fiat money is valued as a medium of exchange precisely because they expect that it will have value in the future. However, there is also an autarky equilibrium. Baranowski (2015) shows that when agents are homogeneous and adaptively learn about the value of money, the monetary equilibrium is locally stable. Branch and McGough

(2016) study the implications for monetary equilibria when agents have rationally heterogeneous expectations. They find that heterogeneous expectations have unique implications for trading efficiencies and the nature of trade in over-the-counter markets.

In particular, heterogeneous beliefs can account for some of the puzzling results in Duffy and Puzzello (2014), which are easily interpretable once the homogeneous expectations assumption is relaxed. From a theoretical perspective, this section shows how heterogeneous beliefs affect consumption and trade precisely because heterogeneity makes higher-order beliefs matter in a fundamental way, but only along dynamic paths. Therefore, the results surveyed here demonstrate that the type of dynamics highlighted in this survey can fundamentally alter economic mechanisms.

5.1 A MONETARY SEARCH MODEL WITH HETEROGENEOUS EXPECTATIONS

We begin by turning the preference shock, interpretable as a search friction, back on. With probability σ a buyer in the specialized good market will meet a seller. In this environment, the solution usually proceeds recursively, taking as given beliefs about the future. To set the stage, we turn to how a recursive solution can be found by starting with solving for equilibrium in the specialized goods sector. Following Branch and McGough (2016) we assume that the terms of trade are determined via take-it-or-leave-it offers made by buyers. If agents in this market are anonymous, buyers will be unable to commit to repaying any credit issued from sellers and all trade must be *quid pro quo*, i.e. the buyer must present a payment instrument, or equivalently, use an asset as collateral for a loan from the seller until the buyer receives proceeds from producing in the general goods market. We assume the existence of a single liquid asset, fiat money, which is a special case of the general framework where the asset has a zero payment flow, i.e. it is intrinsically worthless.

Buyers will decide on their asset holdings based on the discounted expected payoff of the asset, in terms of the general good, plus any expected liquidity services they provide. The literature has a number of ways of approaching how they decide on these asset holdings and consumption plans, depending on their beliefs about the future. To see this, denote by $V(a)$ the value function for a buyer at the beginning of the period before entering the specialized goods market. It is straightforward to see, using our earlier notation, that

$$V_t(a_t) = \max_{\phi_t q_t \le p_t a_t / w_t} \sigma \left[u(q_t) - p_t q_t \right] + \frac{p_t a_t}{w_t} + W_t(0)$$

and, the Bellman equation for the agent is

$$W(a_t) = \max_{x_t, h_t, a_{t+1}} v(x_t) - h_t + \beta \hat{E}_t V_{t+1}(a_{t+1})$$

subject to

$$x_t + p_t a_{t+1} = p_t a_t + w_t h_t$$

and $q_t = q(p_t a_t)$. The next section determines $q(\cdot)$ through bilateral bargaining in the specialized goods market. Now let $a_t = m_t$ denote holdings of real-money balances. Here we adopt the Bellman-equation learning approach, though with the quasi-linearity of the utility function, the asset-pricing equation is the same regardless of the assumed agent-level behavior. Because the value function is linear in wealth, the household chooses x so that $v'(x_t) = 1/w_t = 1$. The next section describes the implications of heterogeneous beliefs for bargaining and trade, and then optimal asset holdings.

5.2 HETEROGENEOUS BELIEFS AND BARGAINING

The departure point from Lagos and Wright (2005) in Branch and McGough (2016) is the common knowledge assumptions during trade between buyers and sellers. To illustrate the implications of heterogeneous beliefs for trading inefficiencies, we make two small changes to the benchmark model of Section 2: first, we assume the asset is fiat money, i.e. $y_t = 0$; second, we assume, like Lagos and Wright, that the differentiated good is traded in a decentralized market with search frictions. That is, we assume that in each decentralized market a buyer and seller are matched with probability σ. Trades in these markets are still subject to the limited commitment friction that precludes the use of unsecured credit. Once buyers and sellers are matched they bargain over the terms of trade, i.e. how much fiat money a buyer gives to a seller in exchange for a quantity of the specialized good. Branch and McGough (2016) focus on the set-up where buyers make take-it-or-leave-it offers as a natural way to relax common knowledge assumptions.

Assume as in Section 4.2 that buyers have rationally heterogeneous expectations: at the end of each period, after all markets clear, buyers choose their predictor for the following period. Then, in the subsequent period, given those beliefs, buyers and sellers are matched and buyers make a take-it-or-leave-it offer. Without loss of generality, Branch and McGough assume that sellers have perfect foresight. Thus, when a buyer is deciding on their money holdings they must forecast the value of money in the next period and the probability of actually trading in the decentralized market. The probability of trading depends on sellers' beliefs, which are assumed to not be common knowledge within a match. Thus, each buyer's predictor is assumed to have two components: point forecasts $p^e_{t+1}(j)$ and a bargaining uncertainty measure $F^j_{t+1}(\cdot, \Sigma)$, $j = 1, 2$. A buyer of type-j believes with certainty that the value of money will be $p^e_{t+1}(j)$, in the following CM, in order to make an offer to the seller they must hold beliefs about sellers' beliefs. This is where bargaining uncertainty is important.

With take-it-or-leave it offers there is not an extended period of bargaining, the buyer simply makes an offer and the seller chooses to accept or reject. Without an extended interaction, buyers will not learn any useful information from sellers. Thus, it is natural to assume that buyers and sellers' beliefs are not common knowledge within a match. Instead, we assume that buyers use their own forecasts as proxies for the seller's beliefs. However, buyers behave like a good Bayesian who acknowledges his uncertainty and places a prior on the seller's forecasts via the distribution function $F_t^j(\cdot, \Sigma)$, where the mean of the distribution is the buyer's own forecast $p^e(j)$ and the variance, or uncertainty, is parameterized by Σ. Branch and McGough (2016) consider cases where Σ is taken to be a parameter, and where it is endogenous. As the buyers learn over time they update their prior distribution.

A *Bayesian offer* balances the buyer maximizing his surplus against the subjective probability that the offer will be accepted. In particular, Branch and McGough (2016) show that Bayesian offers solve the following problem:

$$\max_{q,d \leq m} \left(u(q) - p^e(j)d\right)\left(1 - F_\Sigma\left(\frac{c(q)}{d}\right)\right)$$

A buyer makes an offer of d units of money in exchange for q units of the specialized good in order to maximize the expected surplus given that the offer cannot exceed their holdings of money m, and the expectation is taken with respect to their subjective prior over the seller's acceptance rule. The first term in the objective is the buyer's surplus, and the second term is the subjective probability that the offer will be accepted. The seller accepts an offer in time t if and only if

$$p_t d \geq c(q)$$

Branch and McGough (2016) show that Bayesian offers introduce caution into bargaining. Buyers, by acknowledging their uncertainty over the sellers' acceptance rule, demand fewer goods in exchange for their fiat money. While such offers sacrifice some surplus on the intensive margin, it raises the likelihood of trade on the *extensive margin*. Nevertheless, if buyers' beliefs are sufficiently different from sellers, the sellers may still reject the offer and heterogeneous beliefs can imply an extensive margin of trade that would not exist otherwise. Moreover, Branch and McGough derive the money-demand function for buyers and find that it depends on both the current price of money, expectations about future prices, and the uncertainty measure in their prior distribution. Thus, heterogeneity and uncertainty have important implications for the nature of trade, inflation and welfare.

5.3 EQUILIBRIUM WITH HETEROGENEOUS BELIEFS

Given the solution to the bargaining problem, and the definitions of the value functions, it follows that the optimal holdings of real-money balances solves:

$$\max_{m_{t+1}}\left\{-(p_t - \beta p_{t+1}^e(\tau_t))m_{t+1} + \beta\sigma\left(1 - F_\Sigma^{\tau_t}\left(\frac{c(q\left(m_{t+1}, p_{t+1}^e(\tau_t)\right))}{d\left(m_{t+1}, p_{t+1}^e(\tau_t)\right)}\right)\right)\right.$$
$$\left. \times \left(u(q\left(m_{t+1}, p_{t+1}^e(\tau_t)\right)) - p_{t+1}^e d\left(m_{t+1}, p_{t+1}^e(\tau_t)\right)\right)\right\}$$

The money-demand function depends on whether the buyers' Bayesian offer liquidity constraint $d \leq m$ binds. If the constraint binds, so that $p_{t+1}^e(\tau_t) < \beta^{-1}p_t$, then $d =$

m_{t+1} and m_{t+1} solves the interior F.O.C.

$$
\begin{aligned}
0 = {} & -p_t + \beta p_{t+1}^e(\tau_t) + \beta\sigma\left(1 - F_\Sigma^{\tau_t}\left(\frac{c\left(q\left(m_{t+1}, p_{t+1}^e(\tau_t)\right)\right)}{m_{t+1}}\right)\right) \\
& \times \left(u'\left(q\left(m_{t+1}, p_{t+1}^e(\tau_t)\right)\right) \times \frac{\partial}{\partial m_{t+1}}\left(q\left(m_{t+1}, p_{t+1}^e(\tau_t)\right)\right) - p_{t+1}^e(\tau_t)\right) \\
& - \beta\sigma dF_\Sigma^{\tau_t}\left(\frac{c\left(q\left(m_{t+1}, p_{t+1}^e(\tau_t)\right)\right)}{m_{t+1}}\right) \times \frac{\partial}{\partial m_{t+1}}\left(\frac{c\left(q\left(m_{t+1}, p_{t+1}^e(\tau_t)\right)\right)}{m_{t+1}}\right)
\end{aligned}
$$

(21)

This implies a money-demand function of the form $m\left(p_t, p_{t+1}^e(\tau)\right)$. Then an equilibrium price path is a sequence of prices p_t satisfying market clearing:

$$
\sum_{\tau=1}^N n_t\left(\tau, p_{t-1}, \{p_{t-1}^e(\omega)\}_{\omega=1}^N\right) m\left(p_t, p_{t+1}^e(\tau)\right) = M
$$

(22)

5.4 UNCERTAINTY AND WELFARE

Branch and McGough (2016) assume a form of rationally heterogeneous expectations that is the same as in Section 4.2, where agents select between a costly rational expectations predictor and an adaptive learning rule. Both predictors nest the steady-state, so the effects of heterogeneity and uncertainty only matter for out-of-steady-state dynamics. Branch and McGough (2016) show that the non-linear attracting/repelling dynamics that led to bubbles and crashes in Section 4.2 are at work in the monetary economy as well. For sufficient curvature in the utility function for specialized goods, i.e. a sufficiently large liquidity premium for money, there are periodic and aperiodic attractors that remain bounded around the monetary steady-state.

The extent to which buyers are cautious in their offers to sellers has important implications for welfare and economic dynamics. To illustrate this, we report on the experiments in Branch and McGough (2016). In that paper, they treat the uncertainty measure Σ as a bifurcation parameter and calculate welfare, offers, and acceptance rates along a stable attractor. Figs. 9 and 10 plot the results of a particular numerical example.

In Fig. 9 average welfare, relative to the rational expectations equilibrium, is calculated along a stable attractor, with the values of the specific variables plotted as a series of bifurcation plots in Fig. 10. In the center-left panel of Fig. 10 it is evident that for low values of Σ price is following a 2-cycle. As price fluctuates, the expectations of buyers with adaptive beliefs fluctuates as well, and they, in alternating periods, under-estimate the seller's willingness to accept the terms of their offer implying that the acceptance rate follows a 2-cycle (center-right). However, buyers introduce more caution into their offers as Σ increases (top-left) and so the average acceptance rate increases along the two-cycle. In Fig. 9 this shows up as an increase

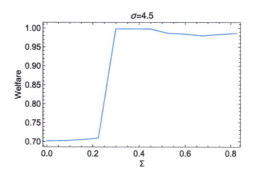

FIGURE 9

Heterogeneous beliefs and welfare in a monetary economy.

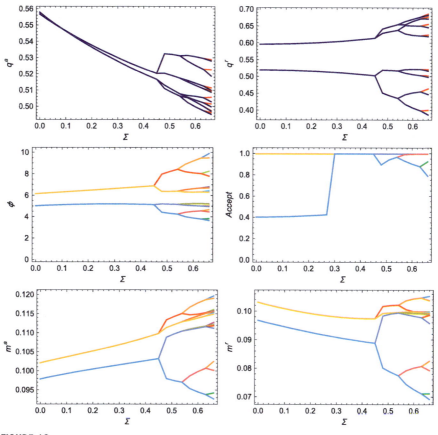

FIGURE 10

Heterogeneous beliefs and acceptance rates in a monetary economy.

in welfare, though welfare is always below what would arise under homogeneous beliefs. At $\Sigma \approx 0.30$, a threshold is crossed where offers are sufficiently cautious that the acceptance rate becomes one. In Fig. 9 this appears as a large increase in welfare accompanying the increase in the *extensive margin* of trade between heterogeneous agents. Then, conditional on the two-cycle, further increases in the uncertainty parameter only have a negative effect on the intensive margin and so welfare increases. Eventually, there is another bifurcation, with a 4-cycle appearing, an average acceptance rate below one, and a decrease in welfare.

These results illustrate how heterogeneous beliefs can lead to new dynamic phenomena. In many settings, differences in information can lead to more trading opportunities. In this setting, heterogeneous beliefs and uncertainty play subtle roles in determining trading inefficiencies and welfare. More uncertainty leads to more cautious offers, lowering welfare through the intensive margin, while increase the likelihood of trade and welfare. Branch and McGough (2016), though, show the importance that common knowledge assumptions play in trade between agents with heterogeneous expectations.

Branch and McGough also applied their model to help explain key puzzles in the experimental findings of Duffy and Puzzello (2014), who find laboratory support for the Lagos–Wright monetary theory. They also find, however, that

1. a large fraction of offers made by buyers are not accepted by sellers;
2. the accepted offers are different from the theoretical stationary equilibrium price and quantity;
3. there is a non-degenerate distribution of money holdings despite evidence of portfolio rebalancing in the centralized market;
4. higher-quantity (buyer) offers are more likely to be rejected.

These experimental results are consistent with the theoretical predictions of the monetary search model with heterogeneous expectations that is surveyed here. Furthermore, the model presented in this paper makes sharp predictions regarding the relationship between prices and the acceptance rate, as well as between prices and sellers' realized surpluses, which should be invariant to the price of money under rational expectations. These findings all present further empirical support for the role of heterogeneous expectations in macroeconomic models.

5.5 RELATED LITERATURE

While there is an active literature incorporating heterogeneous private information into monetary search environments, see Rocheteau and Nosal (2017), there have been few studies incorporating bounded rationality into the search environments. Baranowski (2015) was the first to introduce adaptive learning and showed how stability of a monetary equilibrium can arise when agents have homogeneous adaptive learning rules. Branch (2016) studied the asset-pricing implications of a form of extrinsic heterogeneity, where asset-holders form expectations about future asset prices with a real-time adaptive learning rule and firms have perfect foresight. Similarly, Branch et al. (2016) also features extrinsic heterogeneity in a two-sector model with labor and goods market search frictions, with workers and firms in different sectors having heterogeneous learning rules.

6 DSGE APPLICATIONS

A burgeoning literature, beginning with Branch and McGough (2009) and Branch and McGough (2010), examines the implications of heterogeneous expectations in New Keynesian and Real Business Cycle models. A takeaway from this literature is that heterogeneous expectations alters the propagation mechanism of exogenous shocks and the transmission of monetary policy. This section provides an overview by focusing on the implications for the design of monetary policy rules.

6.1 RATIONALLY HETEROGENEOUS EXPECTATIONS AND MONETARY POLICY RULES

The companion papers, Branch and McGough (2009) and Branch and McGough (2010), develop a theory of heterogeneous expectations in a New Keynesian model. In Branch and McGough (2009) conditions on the set of admissible heterogeneous expectations operators are derived that facilitates aggregation of heterogeneous individual agent behavior that leads to equilibrium conditions that have the same form as the familiar IS and AS relations in New Keynesian models. That paper shows that once the benchmark model is extended to include heterogeneity, the usual 'Taylor Principle' is not necessary or sufficient for monetary policy to guarantee determinacy of equilibrium. Branch and McGough (2010) extend the analysis to where there are rationally heterogeneous expectations and shows that even for monetary policy rules satisfying the Taylor principle it is possible for there to be inefficiently volatile periodic and complex dynamics.

Branch and McGough (2009) derive the following pair of equilibrium equations governing the evolution of the economy:

$$y_t = \hat{E}_t y_{t+1} - \upsilon^{-1}\left(i_t - \hat{E}_t \pi_{t+1}\right)$$
$$\pi_t = \beta \hat{E}_t \pi_{t+1} + \lambda y_t \tag{23}$$

where y_t is the output gap, π_t is the inflation rate, i_t is the nominal interest rate on one-period bonds and is the policy rate. All variables are in log-deviation from steady-state. The expectations operator $\hat{E}$ is a linear combination of the individual heterogeneous expectations operators. The parameters $\upsilon > 0$ is the intertemporal elasticity of substitution, $0 < \beta < 1$ is the discount rate, and λ is an expression of other structural parameters including the degree of price rigidity. The first line in (23) is the so-called IS equation, which relates aggregate demand in the current period to expected future demand and the *ex-ante* real interest rate. The second line in (23) is the New Keynesian Phillips curve which describes inflation as a function of discounted expected future inflation and the current output gap. Branch and Mc-Gough (2009) provide an axiomatic foundation to the expressions in (23). In addition, Branch and McGough also invoke two further axioms:

A6. If x is a variable forecasted by agents at time t and time $t + k$ then
$$E_t^\tau E_{t+k}^{\tau'}(x_{t+k}) = E_t^\tau x_{t+k}, \tau' \neq \tau.$$

A7. All agents have common expectations on expected differences in limiting wealth.

These additional restrictions on expectations are the law of iterated expectations at an individual and aggregate level (A6) and vanishing heterogeneity in the long-run (A7). Finally, Branch and McGough consider a set of Taylor-type policy rules with an expectations-based rule as the benchmark:

$$i_t = \chi_\pi E_t \pi_{t+1} + \chi_y E_t y_{t+1} \tag{24}$$

where here expectations are taken to be rational.

To illustrate the main results, we continue to maintain that expectations are the ones considered in Section 4.2, so that aggregate expectations are

$$\hat{E}_t y_{t+1} = n E_t y_{t+1} + (1 - n)\theta^2 y_{t-1}$$
$$\hat{E}_t \pi_{t+1} = n E_t \pi_{t+1} + (1 - n)\theta^2 \pi_{t-1}$$

Notice that the steady-state values for y, π are zero, and here we do impose type-1 expectations are rational but not necessarily perfect foresight.[10] While previous sections focused on adaptive expectations, i.e. $0 < \theta \leq 1$, Branch and McGough (2009) develop results also considering the case where $\theta > 1$, which is a case of extrapolative or trend-chasing expectations.

Assuming, for the moment, that n is exogenously given, plugging in expectations and the policy rule into (23) leads to the reduced-form dynamical system

$$F X_t = B E_t X_{t+1} + C X_{t-1}$$

where $X' = (y, \pi)$, and for appropriately conformable matrices F, B, C. This casts the heterogeneous expectations model into an associated rational expectations model. Since the associated rational model has the same form as a rational expectations model we can study the set of heterogeneous expectations equilibria by examining the determinacy properties of the associated model. In particular, the determinacy

---

[10]We consider policy rules that lead to indeterminacy, which under rational expectations can exhibit dependence on extrinsic noise – a sunspot – and so rational expectations do not necessarily align with perfect foresight.

properties can be determined from the eigenvalues of the matrix

$$M = \begin{pmatrix} B^{-1}F & -B^{-1}C \\ I_2 & 0 \end{pmatrix}$$

There are two pre-determined variables in the system and so the heterogeneous expectations model is determinate provided that there are two eigenvalues of M outside the unit circle. When there are fewer eigenvalues outside the unit circle then the model is indeterminate and can feature dependence on extrinsic noise or "sunspots." If there are three eigenvalues inside the unit circle then the model has order-1 indeterminacy and the equilibrium depends on a single sunspot variable. If all eigenvalues are inside the unit circle then the model has order-2 indeterminacy and there is dependence on two sunspot variables.

The main insight in Branch and McGough (2009) is that heterogeneous expectations can alter the determinacy properties of a model with homogeneous expectations. In particular,

Result 4.

1. *If $\theta \leq 1$ then policy rules that correspond to indeterminacy when $n = 1$ may yield determinacy when there is even a small proportion of adaptive agents in the economy. In this sense, heterogeneous expectations may be stabilizing.*
2. *If $\theta > 1$ then policy rules that correspond to determinacy when $n = 1$ may yield indeterminacy when there is even a small proportion of adaptive agents in the economy. In this case, heterogeneous expectations may be destabilizing.*

That the optimal design of monetary policy rules hinges on the nature of heterogeneity and the details of how precisely households and firms form expectations is an important takeaway. Policy rules that are thought to stabilize the economy may actually destabilize, and vice versa, depending on the nature of how agents form expectations. Importantly, these findings arise for even small fractions of adaptive agents with most other people holding rational expectations.

An example of how heterogeneity affects the number and nature of equilibria is presented in Fig. 11, from Branch and McGough (2009). This figure plots the determinacy properties in the policy-rule space (χ_y, χ_π). Each panel corresponds to a different proportion of rational agents n. The north-west plot is the determinacy properties under rational expectations which clearly demonstrates the Taylor principle: policy rules that are sufficiently active, i.e. $\chi_\pi > 1$ and χ_y not too large, lead to determinacy. However, as the degree of heterogeneity increases the diagonal line that determines the boundary between the determinate and indeterminate policy space, rotates clockwise. Policy rules that yield determinacy under rational expectations can lead to indeterminacy under heterogeneous expectations. Thus, the Taylor principle is not a necessary and sufficient condition for stability.

Fig. 11 also has important insights for the dynamics under rationally heterogeneous expectations, as shown in Branch and McGough (2010). The insight comes,

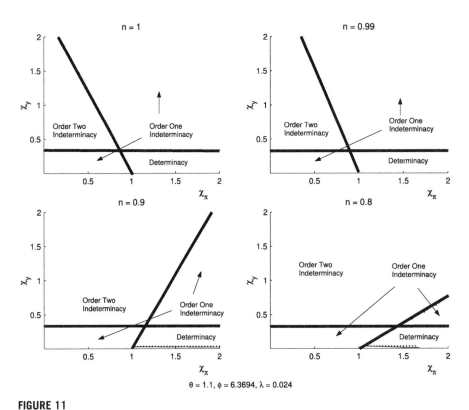

FIGURE 11

Heterogeneous beliefs and determinacy in a New Keynesian model.

again, from the stability reversal principle. Order-2 indeterminacy is equivalent to saying that the steady-state with rationally heterogeneous expectations, i.e. with the MNL map determining n_t in real-time, is locally stable. Order-1 indeterminacy, determinacy, and explosiveness when there are fewer contracting eigenvalues. Fig. 11 shows that as there are more adaptive agents in steady-state (for example by increasing the cost to using rational expectations C) that the steady-state can become stable. Branch and McGough (2010) show that if n becomes sufficiently small then the steady-state can become unstable with all eigenvalues outside the unit circle – this is the stability reversal property. Thus, as n fluctuates above and below the steady-state there can be the kind of attracting/repelling dynamics that lead to periodic and complicated dynamics. For example, suppose that the cost is sufficiently high so that there is a high proportion of adaptive agents and the steady-state is unstable. Then the dynamics will repel the system away from the steady-state. As the system moves away from the steady-state, the forecast errors for adopting rational expectations will be sufficiently lower than for the adaptive predictor that more and more agents will adopt the rational predictor. This moves the system into the "stable", or indeterminacy type-2, region and attracts the dynamics back toward the steady-state. Near the

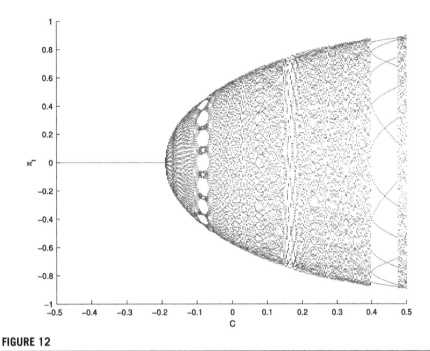

FIGURE 12

Rationally heterogeneous expectations and complex dynamics in a New Keynesian model.

steady-state, though, adaptive and rational expectations return very similar forecasts, the fraction of adaptive agents begins to increase, and the economy switches back into the unstable region. These attracting/repelling dynamics, depending on the steady-state value of adaptive agents, can lead to complex dynamics. For example, Fig. 12 plots a typical bifurcation diagram, where the cost of using rational expectations C is the bifurcation parameter.

6.2 INTRINSIC HETEROGENEITY AND MONETARY POLICY RULES

Monetary policy rules can also affect the number and nature of equilibria that agents coordinate on in stochastic environments. Branch and Evans (2011) embed the Misspecification Equilibrium framework in a New Keynesian model to see whether Intrinsic Heterogeneity and/or multiple misspecification equilibria can arise depending on the central bank's policy rule.

Branch and Evans (2011) consider a stochastic version of the New Keynesian model with heterogeneous expectations derived by Branch and McGough (2009):

$$
\begin{aligned}
y_t &= \hat{E}_t y_{t+1} - \sigma^{-1}\left(i_t - \hat{E}_t \pi_{t+1}\right) + g_t \\
\pi_t &= \beta \hat{E}_t \pi_{t+1} + \lambda y_t + u_t
\end{aligned}
\tag{25}
$$

where $g_t = \rho g_{t-1} + \varepsilon_t$ is a stationary stochastic process for "aggregate demand" shocks and $u_t = \phi u_{t-1} + v_t$ are "aggregate supply" shocks. The shocks g and u are (potentially) correlated, and $\hat{E}$ is an aggregate expectations operator to be specified below. Branch and Evans consider a variety of rules. Here we consider a rule that depends on contemporaneous private-sector expectations:

$$i_t = \chi_\pi \hat{E}_t \pi_t + \chi_y \hat{E}_t y_t$$

This rule is often advocated for as being close to the Taylor rule but depending on observable variables, in this case private-sector expectations. Branch and Evans show that the main qualitative results do not depend on the form of the policy rule.

As in Section 3.3, agents are assumed to underparameterize their forecasting models. In a determinate model, the rational expectations equilibrium depends linearly on the two shocks, g and u. The misspecification equilibrium approach assumes that agents prefer parsimony and instead select only the best-performing models from the set of underparameterized statistical models. Since there are only two stochastic driving variables, agents select from the following set of predictors, for variable x,

$$E_t^1 x_t = b^1 g_t, \quad E_t^1 x_{t+1} = b^1 \rho g_t$$
$$E_t^2 x_t = b^2 u_t, \quad E_t^2 x_{t+1} = b^2 \phi u_t$$

As usual, letting n denote the fraction that use forecast model 1, $\hat{E}x = nE^1x + (1-n)E^2x$.

Plugging in expectations leads to a reduced-form actual law of motion

$$x_t = \xi_1(n)g_t + \xi_2(n)u_t$$

The reduced-form expressions ξ_j, $j = 1, 2$ depend on the direct effect that g_t, u_t have on the economy, as well as the indirect effect that arises from the self-referential nature of the New Keynesian model. Thus, the distribution of agents across the two forecasting models depends on a balancing of the direct and indirect effects of the shocks. In a restricted perceptions equilibrium, the belief parameters b^j are pinned down to satisfy the least-squares orthogonality conditions

$$Eg_t \left(\xi_1(n)g_t + \xi_2(n)u_t - b^1 g_t \right) = 0$$
$$Eu_t \left(\xi_1(n)g_t + \xi_2(n)u_t - b^2 u_t \right) = 0$$

While the value of n is pinned down by the MNL map:

$$n = \frac{1}{2}\{\tanh[\omega F(n)] + 1\} \equiv T_\omega(n)$$

where $F(n) = EU1 - EU2$ and

$$EU^j = -E\left(x_{t+k} - E_t^j x_{t+k} \right)' W \left(x_{t+k} - E_t^j x_{t+k} \right)$$

where W is a weighting matrix, set to the identity matrix without loss of generality. A *Misspecification Equilibrium* is a fixed point of the T-map: $n^* = T_\omega(n^*)$. As before, the number and nature of equilibria depend on the function $F(n)$.

Branch and Evans (2011) prove the following result, which makes use of the notation for the correlation coefficients $r = Eg_t u_t / Eg_t^2, \tilde{r} = Eg_t u_t / Eu_t^2$.

Proposition 5. *Let $r, \tilde{r}$ be sufficiently small and assume that the intensity of choice ω is large.*

1. *For ξ_π, and/or ξ_y, sufficiently large, depending on $\frac{\sigma_\varepsilon^2}{\sigma_v^2}$, there either exists a Misspecification Equilibrium with Intrinsic Heterogeneity, or there exists a Misspecification Equilibrium with $n^* = 0$.*
2. *For $\frac{\sigma_\varepsilon^2}{\sigma_v^2}$ large, there exists a Misspecification Equilibrium with $n^* = 0$.*
3. *For $\frac{\sigma_\varepsilon^2}{\sigma_v^2}$ small, there exists a Misspecification Equilibrium with $n^* = 1$.*
4. *For intermediate values, there exists multiple Misspecification Equilibria.*

The restriction on the correlation coefficients ensures the existence of a unique RPE, given n. Then, the type of equilibria observed depends on the feedback of expectations through the policy rule, parameterized by the coefficients ξ_π, ξ_y. Similarly, the direct effect of the shocks, given by the ratio of the variances of their white noise shocks, affects whether there is an equilibrium with homogeneous expectations at either $n^* = 0$ or $n^* = 1$, or multiple equilibria.

Fig. 13 illustrates the possibilities in one particular numerical example from Branch and Evans (2011). The figure plots the bifurcation diagram where the central bank's reaction coefficient to inflation, χ_π is the bifurcating parameter. The figure considers values for χ_π that both satisfy and violate the Taylor principle. For weak central bank responses to inflation, there can exist multiple misspecification equilibria. Then for values just above the Taylor principle, there exists a unique misspecification equilibrium at $n = 1$, thus in accordance with case 3 in Proposition 5. Then as ξ_π becomes sufficiently large, as predicted by case 1 in Proposition 5, there exists a unique equilibrium exhibiting Intrinsic Heterogeneity. Thus, empirically realistic policy rule parameters can provide an explanation for heterogeneous expectations observed in survey data. The intuition is that they alter the feedback properties of the model so that a non-degenerate distribution of expectations-types will arise in equilibrium. For even larger values of χ_π multiple equilibria with Intrinsic Heterogeneity arises, and then eventually there is a unique equilibrium where all agents forecast with the supply shocks.

The bottom two panels plot the variances of the output gap and inflation within a Misspecification Equilibrium (as plotted in the top panel). The amount of economic volatility induced by a given policy rule choice depends on the particular equilibrium that agents coordinate on. Conditional on a particular type of equilibrium, more aggressive policy responses to inflation stabilizes both the output gap and inflation. However, a bifurcation can increase or reduce that volatility. Notice, in particular,

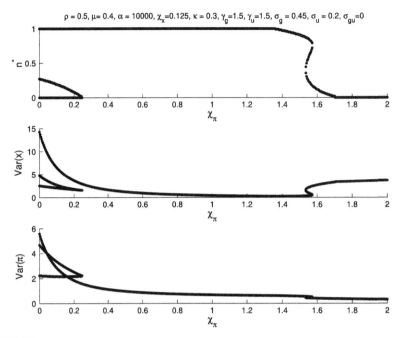

FIGURE 13

Intrinsic heterogeneity and Taylor rules.

that when the equilibrium bifurcates from the $n = 1$ equilibrium to the Intrinsic Heterogeneity equilibrium, there is a large jump in economic volatility, especially in the output gap. This happens because Intrinsic Heterogeneity has agents using both the lower volatility demand shocks and the higher volatility supply shocks.

Branch and Evans (2011) also draw other policy implications from the model. In some calibrations, there exists a unique misspecification equilibrium for lower values of χ_π and multiple equilibria for more aggressive policy stances. Thus, a policy-maker that becomes more aggressive in the policy rule can inadvertently bring the economy to coordinate on a more volatile equilibrium and there may be hysteresis effects if they, in turn, bring the reaction coefficient back down. A second implication is a bad luck shock that increases the variance and persistence of the supply shock – like the experience of the 1970's that preceded the Great Moderation, can lead to the existence of multiple equilibria and the possibility of an abrupt jump in volatility. Similar to a finding in Branch and Evans (2007) real-time learning can lead to endogenous regime-switching between high and low volatility regimes, as the result of policy hysteresis, similar to what was observed in US data with a switch into and out of the Great Moderation. A calibration exercise shows that this model does a good job matching statistics on volatility and persistence. Finally, it is shown that optimal discretionary policy leads to an expectations-based rule similar to Evans and

Honkapohja (2003). The optimal policy rule then features agents coordinating on the unique low volatility equilibrium.

6.3 HETEROGENEOUS EXPECTATIONS AND LIQUIDITY TRAPS

An insight of Branch and McGough (2009) is that heterogeneous expectations can alter the determinacy properties of a model. Branch and Kukacka (2016) use this insight in a New Keynesian model where there are multiple steady-states that arise from a zero lower bound constraint on the central bank's policy rule. While this framework has been studied in many papers, see for instance Evans and Honkapohja (2005), typically the so-called liquidity trap equilibrium is unstable under learning. Here we show how both the normal equilibrium and the liquidity trap equilibrium can be stable under learning by introducing heterogeneity of the type considered throughout this chapter.

Branch and Kukacka (2016) work with a version of the New Keynesian model with heterogeneous expectations extended to include a non-zero inflation target and a Taylor rule with a lower bound:

$$y_t = \hat{E}_t y_{t+1} - \upsilon^{-1} \left(i_t - \bar{i} - \hat{E}_t \pi_{t+1} + r_t^n \right)$$

$$\pi_t = \beta \hat{E}_t \pi_{t+1} + \kappa y_t + u_t$$

$$i_t = \max \left\{ \chi_\pi \left(\pi_t - \bar{\pi} \right) + \chi_y \left(y_t - \bar{y} \right) + \eta_t, 0 \right\}$$

For the purposes here, assume that the exogenous shocks r^n, u, η are mean-zero i.i.d. In Branch and Kukacka (2016) the central bank's target $\bar{\pi}$ follows a highly persistent serially correlated process that is unobservable to agents. There are two steady-states to the model. The first corresponding to the central bank's long-run inflation target $\tilde{\pi} = \bar{\pi}$ and the corresponding steady-state output gap $\tilde{x} = \bar{x} \equiv (1 - \beta)\bar{\pi}/\kappa$. There is also an unintended "liquidity trap" steady-state with $i = 0$ and $\tilde{\pi} = -\bar{r}$, $\tilde{x} = -(1 - \beta)\bar{r}/\kappa$. The paper studies the extent to which changes in that process and structural change in the supply shocks affects the basin of attraction of the liquidity trap equilibrium, i.e. the likelihood of escapes to the zero lower bound. Throughout, the model is parameterized so that around each equilibrium there is a locally unique rational expectations equilibrium.

As before, we assume that agents are distributed across two forecasting models. We assume that a fraction n of agents adopt a perceived law of motion that has the same form as the unique rational expectations equilibrium. The remaining fraction, $1 - n$, of agents adopt an anchoring-and-adjustment rule:

$$w_t = \tilde{w} + \theta \left(w_{t-1} - \tilde{w} \right)$$

for some state variable w. Without loss of generality, we assume that the anchoring-and-adjustment agents know the steady-state value of interest $\tilde{w}$. Branch and Kukacka (2016) assume a learning process for the anchor. Plugging in expectations from these agents leads to a stacked system of equations:

$$X_t = A + F\hat{E}_t^1 X_{t+1} + B X_{t-1} + C Z_t$$

where $X' = (y, \pi)$ and $Z' = (r^n, u, \eta)$, for appropriate matrices A, B, C, F.

The rational expectations equilibrium properties for a neighborhood of the targeted steady-state are well-known: the targeted steady-state is determinate provided that χ_π is sufficiently large and χ_y is not too big. Assuming $\hat{E}^1$ is a rational predictor, it is possible to follow Branch and McGough (2009) and also characterize the determinacy properties of the model near the liquidity trap steady-state:

- For $\theta < 1$, and n sufficiently small, there exists a unique rational expectations equilibrium in a neighborhood of the liquidity trap steady-state. For n sufficiently large, the liquidity trap steady-state exhibits order-one indeterminacy.
- For $\theta > 1$, and n sufficiently small, the liquidity trap steady-state exhibits order-two indeterminacy.

Thus, the case of a model where $\theta < 1$ and $n < 1$ is sufficiently small, then the liquidity trap is determinate. When $n = 1$, i.e. under rational expectations, the liquidity trap equilibrium is indeterminate and, as a result, it is typically unstable under learning. Thus, the interesting case is $\theta < 1$ and a sufficient number of adaptive agents so that the liquidity trap equilibrium is determinate.

In the neighborhood of a determinate steady-state, there exists a unique rational expectations equilibrium of the form

$$X_t = a + b X_{t-1} + \text{noise}$$

Rather than rational expectations, a fraction n adopt a predictor that has a VAR(1) form:

$$\hat{E}_t^1 X_{t+1} = a(1 + b) + b^2 X_{t-1}$$

Plugging in these beliefs, leads to an actual law of motion:

$$X_t = A + F(I + b)a + (Fb^2 + B)X_{t-1} + C Z_t$$

Notice that because of the heterogeneity, the actual law of motion depends on lags of the endogenous state variables. Thus, agents of type-1 beliefs have a properly specified statistical model of the economy. The T-map coefficients of the perceived law of motion into the actual law of motion are:

$$a \to A + F(I + b)a$$
$$b \to Fb^2 + b$$

A rational expectations equilibrium, i.e. a heterogeneous expectations equilibrium, arises when the coefficients (a, b) are fixed points of the T-map. Moreover, the T-map contains useful information about the stability of the REE under adaptive learning.

For reasonable learning algorithms, such as recursive least-squares, asymptotic stability is governed by the "E-stability" o.d.e.:

$$\frac{d(a,b)'}{d\tau} = T(a,b) - (a,b)'$$

An REE is a resting point of the E-stability o.d.e. Moreover, the E-stability principle holds that if an REE is a stable resting point of the E-stability o.d.e. then it will be stable under adaptive learning. Thus, it suffices to check whether the unique REE is E-stable. Branch and Kukacka (2016) provide a detailed analysis that shows under reasonable calibrations of the model, the liquidity trap equilibrium is stable under learning. For example, with the parameterization, $n = 0.7, \theta = 0.2, \beta = 0.99, \upsilon = 0.167, \kappa = 0.15$ the liquidity trap equilibrium is determinate and E-stable.

The stability of the liquidity trap arises because of the heterogeneity in expectations. The role that heterogeneity plays in altering the dynamic properties of otherwise standard models can help explain many features of the data. In Branch and Kukacka (2016) it can explain how an economy can endogenously collapse to a liquidity trap, and then remain in the liquidity trap for a long period of time. Most models of learning and heterogeneous expectations find that either the economy will eventually converge back to the targeted steady-state on its own, or else the time paths will feature deflationary spirals. Neither feature is observed in data for economies that have been at zero nominal interest rates for long stretches of time.

6.4 HETEROGENEITY AND BUSINESS CYCLES AMPLIFICATION

Branch and McGough (2011) study the implications for business cycle dynamics in a real business cycle (RBC) model with extrinsically heterogeneous expectations. It is well-known (see Cogley and Nason, 1995) that real business cycle models have very little internal propagation as output inherits most of its time series properties from the assumed exogenous process for technology. Branch and McGough (2011) show that a real business cycle model extended to include heterogeneous expectations can have output effects that significantly amplify technology shocks.[11]

In the model, households choose consumption, labor supply and savings. A competitive rental market for capital exists that channels savings into capital accumulation which is then rented to firms in a competitive market. All production takes place with a constant returns to scale production technology that combines consumption and labor. Branch and McGough (2011) assume that agents are identical except for their expectations operator.

Households are, further, assumed to be anticipated utility maximizers who choose their consumption, labor and savings plans in order to satisfy an N-step Euler equa-

---

[11] Eusepi and Preston (2011), in a homogeneous expectations environment with correctly specified learning rules and infinite-horizon decision-making, were the first to generate empirically plausible business cycle dynamics in a learning model.

tion, found by log-linearizing the Euler and iterating N periods ahead. Specifically, the household's first-order conditions for an agent of expectations-type τ are:

$$c_t^\tau = \hat{E}_t^\tau c_{t+N}^\tau - \beta r \sum_{i=1}^N \hat{E}_t^\tau r_{t+i}$$

$$c_t^\tau + \eta \frac{h}{l} h_t^\tau = w_t$$

(26)

and the household's flow budget constraint. The first equation in (26) is the N-step Euler equation. Thus, (26) is a form of finite-horizon learning, which was generalized and studied in Branch et al. (2012).

Branch and McGough (2011) specify expectations as a mixture of rational expectations and forecasts that are generated from a parsimonious forecasting rule that depends linearly on the lagged capital stock. The boundedly rational forecasts are underparameterized because in the RBC model the state variables are the capital stock and the real interest rate. Thus, Branch and McGough (2011) focus on a restricted perceptions equilibrium with the agents who adopt parsimonious forecasting models choosing the parameters of their model as optimal within the restricted class. Branch and McGough (2011) then study the effect that heterogeneity, and in particular the planning horizon N, has on the propagation of technology shocks to output.

Fig. 14 presents a key result from Branch and McGough (2011). In this figure an impulse response to a technology is plotted for various parameterizations of the degree to which there is extrinsic heterogeneity. The parameter n is the fraction of households with rational expectations implying that $1 - n$ is the fraction with restricted perceptions. The model was calibrated using standard parameters, and the impulse response was computed within a restricted perceptions equilibrium holding the planning horizon fixed at $N = 20$, i.e. households have a planning horizon of five years. The dashed line is the impulse response under homogeneous rational expectations. Then the solid lines correspond to the impulse response assuming heterogeneous expectations with each line corresponding to a fraction of rational agents, as indicated by the arrow in Fig. 14.

The rational expectations model features very little additional propagation and very little persistence from the shock. In contrast, the impulse response under heterogeneous expectations features a hump-shaped response to the technology shock, in line with results from structural VAR models. Notice also that as the fraction of rational agents decreases the output response to a technology shock becomes stronger and more persistent. In particular, with a value of $n = 0.1$ the peak effect on output from a one standard deviation technology shock exhibits a strong hump-shaped effect with a peak response of approximately 50%. Thus, heterogeneous expectations can bring a strong propagation mechanism into a business cycle model with very little internal propagation.

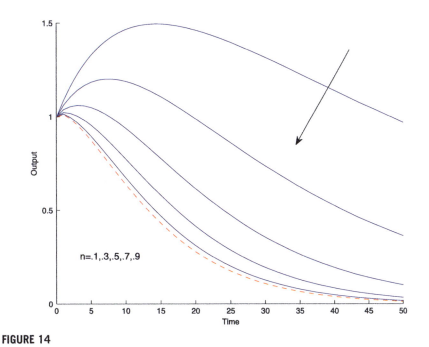

FIGURE 14

Impulse response to output from a 1% technology shock in a real business cycle model with heterogeneous expectations (from Branch and McGough, 2011).

6.5 RELATED LITERATURE

Following Branch and McGough (2009) an extensive literature studies the monetary policy implications of heterogeneous expectations in New Keynesian type models. Massaro (2013) considers rationally heterogeneous expectations – and the large type limit – in a New Keynesian model with long-horizon expectations. Massaro shows that the long-horizon approach generalizes the aggregation result in Branch and McGough (2009) without requiring some of the more restrictive axioms regarding higher-order beliefs. Harrison and Taylor (2012) apply the Massaro approach of long-horizon expectations to a stochastic model and show that it does a good job explaining business cycle facts. Anufriev et al. (2013) show that the Taylor principle is not sufficient to guarantee stability in a Fisherian type model with the large-type-limit beliefs. Lines and Westerhoff (2010) develop a rationally heterogeneous expectations model in a simple textbook model of the economy. Gasteiger (2014) studies the optimal monetary policy problem in the New Keynesian with heterogeneous expectations framework. Similarly, Gasteiger (2017) illustrates the implications of heterogeneity for monetary/fiscal policy interactions in a fiscal theory of the price level environment. Di Bartolomeo et al. (2016) study the fully optimal policy problem where the social welfare function is derived assuming the existence of heterogeneous expectations in a micro-founded NK model. Finally, Hommes and Lustenhouwer (2015) and Hommes and Lustenhouwer (2016) extend the New Keynesian environment of

Branch and McGough (2009) to include a zero lower bound on policy rates and where predictors are distributed around the central bank's long-run inflation target.

There is also an extensive literature that incorporates heterogeneous expectations using alternative approaches. For example, Kurz et al. (2013) develop a rational belief equilibrium in a New Keynesian model. De Grauwe (2011) uses a stylized New Keynesian model with biased heterogeneous beliefs, with the distribution evolving adaptively, to show existence of waves of optimism and pessimism. A similar framework set in an overlapping generations monetary model was developed by Brazier et al. (2008). Pfajfar (2013) develops an extension to the rationally heterogeneous expectations approach where agents decide both on their predictor and, in a second stage, whether to update their information sets. Applications of rationally heterogeneous expectations to survey data are made by Branch (2004), Branch (2007), and Pfajfar and Santoro (2010). Heterogeneity that arises from a genetic algorithm were applied to a New Keynesian model by Arifovic et al. (2013) who show that Taylor rules that would lead to indeterminacy under rational expectations can be stable with evolutionary learning. Gibbs (2017) uses forecast combination as a proxy for heterogeneous expectations in a pure currency economy. Nakagawa (2015) addresses the conditions under which monetary policy rules can ensure the expectational stability of misspecification equilibria.

Following the Great Recession and the 2007–2009 financial crisis, a number of papers have used expectations misspecification and heterogeneity to address relevant issues in the housing market and the macroeconomy. For example, Bofinger et al. (2013) incorporate heterogeneous expectations via simple heuristics in a New Keynesian model extended to include housing services and a collateral constraint. Similarly, Ascari et al. (2017) use heterogeneous expectations (chartists vs. fundamentalists) to explain the housing boom and bust in a DSGE model with a financing constraint. In a model with two sectors and labor market and goods market frictions, Branch et al. (2016) show that learning is essential to generate a housing boom and bust that leads to equilibrium unemployment rates consistent with those observed in the data over the period 1996–2010.

7 CONCLUSION

Heterogeneous expectations are increasingly being employed in macroeconomics. Heterogeneity in beliefs can alter the nature of trade in decentralized markets with important implications for welfare. An empirically realistic model of time-varying heterogeneous beliefs can lead to bubbles and crashes as the distribution of agents across forward- and backward-looking expectations evolves along with the state variables in DSGE and asset-pricing models that exhibit strong expectational feedback effects. Heterogeneity of beliefs also has implications for the set of equilibria and for the design of monetary policy rules that stabilize the economy near a central bank's objectives.

There are also substantive modeling issues associated with incorporating heterogeneous expectations into DSGE models. Section 2 of the chapter presented several frameworks for modeling bounded optimality. That is, we considered a variety of behavioral primitives that describe the decision-making of agents with boundedly rational expectations. We considered two alternatives based on a variational principle, shadow-price learning and Euler equation learning. We also considered a formulation where long horizon – both finitely and infinitely long – expectations matter for decision-making. We showed the implications of these behavioral rules for aggregating the decision rules of individual agents who hold heterogeneous expectations. Finally, we demonstrated two ways in which heterogeneous expectations can arise endogenously as an equilibrium object.

Despite considerable experimental and empirical evidence in favor of heterogeneous expectations, the DSGE literature incorporating heterogeneous beliefs is still in its infancy. This chapter provided an overview of many of the key contributions, but there is still much work to be done. Especially in models with market frictions, such as labor and money search models, the welfare and policy implications are starkly different from what arises under homogeneous, rational expectations. There is a need for more research on establishing the terms of trade in decentralized markets between buyers and sellers who hold different beliefs, a situation that describes most economic transactions.

REFERENCES

Adam, K., Marcet, A., 2011. Internal rationality, imperfect market knowledge and asset prices. Journal of Economic Theory 146, 1224–1252.

Adam, K., Marcet, A., Beutel, J., 2017. Stock price booms and expected capital gains. The American Economic Review 107 (8), 2352–2408.

Anufriev, M., Assenza, T., Hommes, C., Massaro, D., 2013. Interest rate rules and macroeconomic stability under heterogeneous expectations. Macroeconomic Dynamics 17 (8), 1574–1604.

Anufriev, M., Hommes, C.H., Makarewicz, T., 2015. Simple Forecasting Heuristics that Make Us Smart: Evidence from Different Market Experiments. Working paper.

Arifovic, J., Bullard, J., Kostyshyna, O., 2013. Social learning and monetary policy rules. The Economic Journal 123 (567), 38–76.

Arifovic, J., Duffy, J., 2018. Heterogeneous agent modeling: experimental evidence. In: Handbook of Computational Economics, vol. 4. Elsevier, pp. 491–540 (this Handbook).

Ascari, G., Pecora, N., Spelta, A., 2017. Booms and busts in a housing market with heterogeneous agents. Macroeconomic Dynamics, 1–17.

Baranowski, R., 2015. Adaptive learning and monetary exchange. Journal of Economic Dynamics and Control 58, 1–18.

Berardi, M., 2007. Heterogeneity and misspecifications in learning. Journal of Economic Dynamics and Control 31 (10), 3203–3227.

Bofinger, P., Debes, S., Gareis, J., Mayer, E., 2013. Monetary policy transmission in a model with animal spirits and house price booms and busts. Journal of Economic Dynamics and Control 37 (12), 2862–2881.

Branch, W.A., 2004. The theory of rationally heterogeneous expectations: evidence from survey data on inflation expectations. The Economic Journal 114, 592–621.

Branch, W.A., 2007. Sticky information and model uncertainty in survey data on inflation expectations. Journal of Economic Dynamics and Control 31 (1), 245–276.

Branch, W.A., 2014. Nowcasting and the Taylor rule. Journal of Money, Credit, and Banking 46 (5), 1035–1055.

Branch, W.A., 2016. Imperfect knowledge, liquidity and bubbles. Journal of Economic Dynamics and Control 62, 17–42.

Branch, W.A., Evans, G.W., 2006. Intrinsic heterogeneity in expectation formation. Journal of Economic Theory 127, 264–295.

Branch, W.A., Evans, G.W., 2007. Model uncertainty and endogenous volatility. Review of Economic Dynamics 10, 207–237.

Branch, W.A., Evans, G.W., 2010. Asset return dynamics and learning. The Review of Financial Studies 23 (4), 1651–1680.

Branch, W.A., Evans, G.W., 2011. Monetary policy and heterogeneous expectations. Economic Theory 27, 365–393.

Branch, W.A., Evans, G.W., McGough, B., 2012. Finite horizon learning. In: Vilmunen, J., Sargent, T. (Eds.), Macroeconomics at the Service of Public Policy. Cambridge University Press.

Branch, W.A., Kukacka, J., 2016. The Great Moderation and Liquidity Traps. Working paper.

Branch, W.A., McGough, B., 2009. A New Keynesian model with heterogeneous expectations. Journal of Economic Dynamics and Control 33, 1036–1051.

Branch, W.A., McGough, B., 2010. Dynamic predictor selection in a New Keynesian model with heterogeneous expectations. Journal of Economic Dynamics and Control 34 (8), 1492–1504.

Branch, W.A., McGough, B., 2011. Business cycle amplification with heterogeneous expectations. Economic Theory 47, 395–421.

Branch, W.A., McGough, B., 2016. Heterogeneous expectations and trading inefficiencies. Journal of Economic Theory 163, 786–818.

Branch, W.A., Petrosky-Nadeau, N., Rocheteau, G., 2016. Financial frictions, the housing market, and unemployment. Journal of Economic Theory 164, 101–135.

Branch, W.A., Zhu, M., 2016. Restricted Perceptions and Endogenous Volatility. Working paper.

Brazier, A., Harrison, R., King, M., Yates, T., 2008. The danger of inflation expectations of macroeconomic stability: heuristic switching in an overlapping-generations monetary model. International Journal of Central Banking.

Brock, W.A., Hommes, C.H., 1997. A rational route to randomness. Econometrica 65, 1059–1095.

Brock, W.A., Hommes, C.H., 1998. Heterogeneous beliefs and routes to chaos in a simple asset pricing model. Journal of Economic Dynamics and Control 22, 1235–1274.

Brock, W.A., Hommes, C.H., Wagener, F., 2005. Evolutionary dynamics in markets with many trader types. Journal of Mathematical Economics 41, 7–42.

Cogley, T., Nason, J., 1995. Output dynamics in real business cycle models. The American Economic Review 85, 492–511.

Cogley, T., Sargent, T.J., 2008. Anticipated utility and rational expectations as approximations of Bayesian decision making. International Economic Review 49.

De Grauwe, P., 2011. Animal spirits and monetary policy. Economic Theory 47, 423–457.

Di Bartolomeo, G., Di Pietro, M., Giannini, B., 2016. Optimal monetary policy in a New Keynesian model with heterogeneous expectations. Journal of Economic Dynamics and Control 73, 373–387.

Duffy, J., Puzzello, D., 2014. Gift exchange versus monetary exchange: theory and evidence. The American Economic Review 104 (6), 1735–1736.

Elias, C.J., 2016. Asset pricing with expectation shocks. Journal of Economic Dynamics and Control 65, 68–82.

Eusepi, S., Preston, B., 2011. Expectations, learning and business cycle fluctuations. The American Economic Review 101, 2844–2872.

Eusepi, S., Preston, B., 2018. The science of monetary policy: an imperfect knowledge perspective. Journal of Economic Literature 56 (1), 3–59.

Evans, D., Evans, G.W., McGough, B., 2016. Learning When to Say No. Working paper.

Evans, G.W., Honkapohja, S., 2001. Learning and Expectations in Macroeconomics. Princeton University Press, Princeton, NJ.

Evans, G.W., Honkapohja, S., 2003. Expectations and the stability problem for optimal monetary policies. The Review of Economic Studies 70, 807–824.

Evans, G.W., Honkapohja, S., 2005. Policy interaction, expectations and the liquidity trap. Review of Economic Dynamics 8, 303–323.

Gasteiger, E., 2014. Heterogeneous expectations, optimal monetary policy and the merit of policy inertia. Journal of Money, Credit, and Banking 46 (7), 1535–1554.

Gasteiger, E., 2017. Do heterogeneous expectations constitute a challenge for policy interaction? Macroeconomic Dynamics, 1–34. https://doi.org/10.1017/S1365100516001036.

Gibbs, C., 2017. Forecast combination, non-linear dynamics, and the macroeconomy. Economic Theory 63, 653–668.

Guidolin, M., Timmermann, A., 2007. Asset allocation under multivariate regime switching. Journal of Economic Dynamics and Control 31, 3503–3544.

Guse, E., 2005. Stability properties for learning with heterogeneous expectations and multiple equilibria. Journal of Economic Dynamics and Control 29 (10), 1623–1642.

Harrison, R., Taylor, T., 2012. Misperceptions, Heterogeneous Expectations and Macroeconomic Dynamics. Discussion paper, Bank of England Working Paper No. 449.

Hommes, C.H., 2013. Behavioral Rationality and Heterogeneous Expectations in Complex Economic Systems. Cambridge University Press.

Hommes, C.H., Lustenhouwer, J., 2015. Inflation Targeting and Liquidity Traps Under Endogenous Credibility. Discussion paper, CeNDEF Working Paper No. 15-03.

Hommes, C.H., Lustenhouwer, J., 2016. Managing Heterogeneous and Unanchored Expectations: A Monetary Policy Analysis. Discussion paper, CeNDEF Working Paper No. 16-01.

Hommes, C.H., Sonnemans, J., Tuinstra, J., van de Velden, H., 2005. Coordination of expectations in asset pricing experiments. The Review of Financial Studies 18 (3), 955–980.

Hommes, C.H., Zhu, M., 2014. Behavioral learning equilibria. Journal of Economic Theory 150, 778–814.

Honkapohja, S., Mitra, K., 2006. Learning stability in economies with heterogeneous agents. Review of Economic Dynamics 9, 284–309.

Honkapohja, S., Mitra, K., Evans, G.W., 2013. Notes on agents' behavioral rules under adaptive learning and recent studies of monetary policy. In: Sargent, T., Vilmunen, J. (Eds.), Macroeconomics at the Service of Public Policy. Oxford University Press.

Kurz, M., Piccillo, G., Wu, H., 2013. Modeling diverse expectations in an aggregated New Keynesian model. Journal of Economic Dynamics and Control 37 (8), 1403–1433.

Lagos, R., Wright, R., 2005. A unified framework for monetary theory and policy analysis. Journal of Political Economy 113, 463–484.

LeBaron, B.D., 1995. Experiments in evolutionary finance. In: Arthur, W., Lane, D., Durlauf, S. (Eds.), The Economy as an Evolving Complex System: II. Addison-Wesley.

LeBaron, B.D., 2012. Heterogeneous gain learning and the dynamics of asset prices. Journal of Economic Behavior & Organization 83 (3), 424–445.

Lines, M., Westerhoff, F., 2010. Inflation expectations and macroeconomic dynamics: the case of rational versus extrapolative expectations. Journal of Economic Dynamics and Control 34, 246–257.

Lucas Jr., R.E., 1978. Asset prices in an exchange economy. Econometrica 46, 1429–1445.

Malmendier, U., Nagel, S., 2016. Learning from inflation experiences. The Quarterly Journal of Economics 131 (1), 53–87.

Marcet, A., Sargent, T.J., 1989. Convergence of least-squares learning in environments with hidden state variables and private information. Journal of Political Economy 97, 1306–1322.

Marcet, A., Sargent, T.J., 1995. Speed of convergence of recursive least squares: learning with autoregressive moving-average perceptions. In: Kirman, A., Salmon, M. (Eds.), Learning and Rationality in Economics. Basil Blackwell, Oxford, pp. 179–215 (Chapter 6).

Markiewicz, A., 2012. Model uncertainty and exchange rate volatility. International Economic Review 53 (3), 815–844.

Massaro, D., 2013. Heterogeneous expectations in monetary DSGE models. Journal of Economic Dynamics and Control 37, 680–692.

Mauersberger, F.J., Nagel, R., 2018. Levels of reasoning in Keynesian Beauty Contests: a generative framework. In: Handbook of Computational Economics, vol. 4. Elsevier, pp. 541–634 (this Handbook).

McCall, J.J., 1970. Economics of information and job search. The Quarterly Journal of Economics 84 (1), 113–126.

Nakagawa, R., 2015. Learnability of an equilibrium with private information. Journal of Economic Dynamics and Control 59, 48–74.

Nakov, A., Nuno, G., 2015. Learning from experience in the stock market. Journal of Economic Dynamics and Control.

Parke, W., Waters, G., 2007. An evolutionary game theory explanation of arch effects. Journal of Economic Dynamics and Control 31 (7), 2234–2262.

Pfajfar, D., 2013. Formation of rationally heterogeneous expectations. Journal of Economic Dynamics and Control 37 (8), 1434–1452.

Pfajfar, D., Santoro, E., 2010. Heterogeneity, learning and information stickiness in inflation expectations. Journal of Economic Behavior & Organization 75, 426–444.

Preston, B., 2005. Learning about monetary policy rules when long-horizon expectations matter. International Journal of Central Banking 1, 81–126.

Preston, B., 2006. Adaptive learning, forecast-based instrument rules and monetary policy. Journal of Monetary Economics 53, 507–535.

Rocheteau, G., Nosal, E., 2017. Money, Payments, and Liquidity, second ed. MIT Press.

Rocheteau, G., Wright, R., 2011. Liquidity and asset market dynamics. Journal of Monetary Economics. Forthcoming.

Woodford, M., 2013. Macroeconomic analysis without the rational expectations hypothesis. Annual Review of Economics.

Agent-Based Macroeconomics*

Herbert Dawid[*,1], **Domenico Delli Gatti**[†,‡]

*Department of Business Administration and Economics and Center for Mathematical Economics,
Bielefeld University, Bielefeld, Germany
†Complexity Lab in Economics (CLE), Department of Economics and Finance,
Università Cattolica del Sacro Cuore, Italy
‡CESifo Group Munich, Germany
[1]Corresponding author: e-mail address: hdawid@wiwi.uni-bielefeld.de

CONTENTS

*The authors are grateful for helpful comments and suggestions from Tiziana Assenza, Jean-Philippe Bouchaud, Silvano Cincotti, Giovanni Dosi, Giorgio Fagiolo, Edoardo Gaffeo, Mauro Gallegati, Gavin Goy, Philipp Harting, Cars Hommes, Sander van der Hoog, Peter Howitt, Blake LeBaron, Marco Raberto, Andrea Roventini, Alberto Russo, and Isabelle Salle.

Handbook of Computational Economics, Volume 4, ISSN 1574-0021, https://doi.org/10.1016/bs.hescom.2018.02.006

63

1 INTRODUCTION

Starting from the early years of the availability of digital computers, the analysis of macroeconomic phenomena through the simulation of appropriate micro-founded models of the economy has been seen as a promising approach for Economic research. In an article in the *American Economic Review* in 1959 Herbert Simon argued that

> *"The very complexity that has made a theory of the decision-making process essential has made its construction exceedingly difficult. Most approaches have been piecemeal-now focused on the criteria of choice, now on conflict of interest, now on the formation of expectations. It seemed almost utopian to suppose that we could put together a model of adaptive man that would compare in completeness with the simple model of classical economic man. The sketchiness and incompleteness of the newer proposals has been urged as a compelling reason for clinging to the older theories, however inadequate they are admitted to be. The modern digital computer has changed the situation radically. It provides us with a tool of research—for formulating and testing theories—whose power is commensurate with the complexity of the phenomena we seek to understand. [...] As economics finds it more and more necessary to understand and explain disequilibrium as well as equilibrium, it will find an increasing use for this new tool and for communication with its sister sciences of psychology and sociology." (Simon, 1959, p. 280).*

This quote, which calls for an encompassing macroeconomic modeling approach building on the interaction of (heterogeneous) agents whose expectation formation and decision making processes are based on empirical and psychological insights, might be seen as the first formulation of a research agenda, which is now referred to as "Agent-Based Macroeconomics." Cohen (1960) provides a very insightful discussion of the potential and the challenges of the use of computer simulations for the development of a behavioral theory of the firm, as well as for the analysis of aggregate economic models. An early example of an actual simulation-based macroeconomic model is the evolutionary model of economic growth discussed in Nelson and Winter (1974) and Nelson et al. (1976). In the 1970s micro-founded simulation models of the Swedish economy (the MOSES model, see Eliason, 1977, 1984) and the US economy (the "Transactions Model", see Bergman, 1974; Bennett and Bergmann, 1986) have been developed as a tool for the analysis of certain economic policy measures. Although calibrated for specific countries, the structure of these models was rather general and as such they can be seen as very early agent-based macroeconomic models.

At the same time, starting in the 1970s the attention of the mainstream of macroeconomic research has shifted towards (dynamic) equilibrium models as a framework for macroeconomic studies and policy analyses. At least in their original form these models are built on assumptions of representative agents, rational expectations, and equilibrium based on inter-temporally optimal behavior of all agents. The clear conceptual basis, as well as the relatively parsimonious structure of these models, and the fact that they address the Lucas critique has strongly contributed to their appeal and has resulted in a large body of work dedicated to this approach. In particular, these models have become the workhorse for macroeconomic policy analysis.

Nevertheless, already early in this development different authors have pointed out numerous problematic aspects associated with using such models, in particular Dynamic Stochastic General Equilibrium (DSGE) models, for economic analysis and policy studies. Kirman (1992) nicely summarizes results, showing that in general aggregate behavior of a heterogeneous set of (optimizing) agents cannot be interpreted as the optimal decision of a representative agent and that, even in cases where it can, the sign of effects of policy changes on the utility of that representative agent might be different from the sign of the induced utility changes of all agents in the underlying population, which makes the interpretation of welfare analysis in representative agent models problematic. Furthermore, an extensive stream of literature has shown that under reasonable informational assumptions no adjustment processes ensuring general convergence to equilibrium can be constructed (see Kirman, 2016). Hence, the assumption of coordination of all agents in an equilibrium is very strong, even if a unique equilibrium exists, which in many classes of models is not guaranteed. As argued, e.g., in Howitt (2012) this assumption also avoids addressing coordination issues in the economy, which are essential for understanding the phenomena like the emergence of crises and also the impact of policies. Similarly, the assumption that all agents have rational expectations about the future dynamics of the economy has been criticized as being rather unrealistic, and indeed there is little experimental or empirical evidence suggesting that the evolution of expectations of agents is consistent with the rational expectations assumption (see, e.g., Carroll, 2003 or Hommes et al., 2005).

From a more technical perspective, studies in the DSGE literature typically rely on local approximations of the model dynamics around a steady state (e.g., log-linearization) and thereby do not capture the full global dynamics of the underlying model. This makes it problematic to properly capture global phenomena like regime changes or large fluctuations in such a framework. Business cycles and fluctuations are driven by shocks to fundamentals or expectations, whose structure is calibrated in a way to match empirical targets. Hence, the mechanisms actually generating these fluctuations are outside the scope of the model and therefore the model can only be used to study propagation of shocks, but is silent about which mechanisms generate such phenomena and which measures might reduce the risk of the emergence of cycles and downturns in the first place.

In the aftermath of the crises developing after 2007, policy makers, as well as economists, have acknowledged that several of the properties mentioned above substantially reduce the ability of standard DSGE models to inform policy makers about suitable responses to the unfolding economic downturn. New generations of DSGE-type models have been developed addressing several of these issues, in particular introducing more heterogeneity (see Ragot, 2018 in this handbook), heterogeneous non-rational expectations (see Branch and McGough, 2018 in this handbook) or the feedback between real and financial dynamics (e.g., Benes et al., 2014); however, also in each of these extensions several of the points discussed above, which seem intrinsic associated with this approach, still apply.[1]

Related to these new developments also a stream of literature has emerged, which, although relying on the backbone of a standard DSGE-type model, in certain parts of the model incorporates explicit micro-level representations of the (local) interaction of agents and relies on (agent-based) simulation of the emerging dynamics. Although these contributions (e.g., Anufriev et al., 2013; Arifovic et al., 2013; Assenza and Delli Gatti, 2013, 2017; Lengnick and Wohltmann, 2016) can be considered to be part of the agent-based macroeconomic literature, they are more hybrid in nature and this literature is treated in the chapter by Branch and McGough (2018) in this handbook, rather than in this chapter.[2]

The agent-based approach to macroeconomic modeling, which has started to attract increasing attention from the early 2000s onwards, is similar in spirit to Simon's quote above and hence differs in several ways from mainstream dynamic equilibrium models. In agent-based macroeconomic models, different types of heterogeneous agents endowed with behavioral and expectational rules interact through explicitly represented market protocols and meso- as well as macroeconomic variables are determined by actual aggregation of the output in this population of agents. They are mainly driven by the desire to provide empirically appealing representations of individual behavior and interaction patterns at the micro level and at the same time to validate the models by comparing the characteristics of their aggregate level output with empirical data. The global dynamics of the models are studied relying on (batches of) simulation runs and typically no ex-ante assumptions about the coordination of individual behavior are made.

Already early contributions to this stream of literature have shown that such models can endogenously generate fluctuations resembling actual business cycles without

---

[1] More extensive critical discussions of different aspects of the DSGE approach to macroeconomic modeling can be found in Colander et al. (2008), Fagiolo and Roventini (2012, 2017), or Romer (2016), where in particular Fagiolo and Roventini (2017) also consider different recent extensions to the DSGE literature.

[2] Early predecessors in a similar spirit are, e.g., Arifovic (1995, 1996), in which agent-based computational learning models have been incorporated into standard macroeconomic settings.

relying on external shocks (e.g., Dosi et al., 2006) and have highlighted, before the outbreak of the crises of 2007, mechanisms by which contagion (e.g., through credit networks) and feedback between the real and financial side of the economy can induce instability and sudden downturns (see Battiston et al., 2007). These properties, together with the ability to incorporate a wide range of behavioral assumptions and to represent institutional characteristics, which might be relevant for the analysis of actual policy proposals, have fostered interest of policy makers for agent-based macroeconomic modeling[3] and resulted in a vast increase in research in this area in general, and in agent-based policy analysis in particular. As has to be expected from a new emerging paradigm, the evolution of the field has progressed in several weakly coordinated streams, and in light of the large body of work that has been produced so far, a systematic review of the progress that has been made seems to be in order. This chapter is an attempt to provide such a review.

1.1 COMPLEXITY AND MACROECONOMICS

The notion of complexity is general enough to encompass a broad class of phenomena and models in nature and society. We interpret complexity as an attribute of a system. In particular, following the approach pioneered at the Santa Fe Institute by an interdisciplinary group of prominent scientists, *complex adaptive systems* (CAS) are systems consisting of a large number of "coupled elements the properties of which are modifiable as a result of environmental interactions. [...] In general complex adaptive systems are highly non-linear and are organized on many spatial and temporal scales" (cited from Cowan and Feldmann in Fontana, 2010, p. 173).

Macroeconomic dynamics are characterized by the interaction of a large number of heterogeneous individuals who take a plethora of decisions of different kinds to produce and exchange a large variety of goods, as well as information. These transactions are governed by institutional rules which might vary significantly between different regions, industries, time periods, and other contexts. Based on this, economic systems must certainly be seen as very complex adaptive systems. This makes it extremely challenging to develop appropriate models for studying economic systems and to derive any insights of general validity about the (future) dynamics of key economic variables or the effect of certain economic policy measures.

In order to study CAS, a natural tool is an *Agent Based Model (ABM)*, i.e., a model in which a *multitude of (heterogeneous) elements or objects interact* with each other and the environment. The single most important feature of an ABM is the *autonomy* of the elements, i.e., the absence of a centralized ("top down") coordinating or controlling mechanism. ABMs are, by construction, computationally intensive. The output of the model typically cannot be determined analytically but must be computed and consists of simulated time series. A key feature of CAS is that it often gives rise to emerging properties, i.e., stable, orderly aggregate structures resulting

---

[3]Clear indications of the potential that central banks see in agent-based macroeconomics can be found in Trichet (2010) or Haldane (2016).

from the interaction of the agents' behavior. A phenomenon is emergent whenever the whole achieves properties which its elements, if taken in isolation, do not have.

1.2 THE AGENT-BASED APPROACH TO MACROECONOMIC MODELING

Agent-based Computational Economics (ACE) is the application of AB modeling to economics or: "The computational study of economic processes modeled as dynamic systems of interacting agents." (Tesfatsion, 2006). Surveys of the ample literature on ACE work in different areas of Economics are provided in the second volume of the Handbook of Computational Economics (Tesfatsion and Judd, 2006). It is worthwhile noting that in this handbook no separate chapter on agent-based macroeconomics was included, which is a signal of the limited work in this area that has been completed before 2006.

A defining feature of *macroeconomic ABMs (MABMs)* is that although concerned with the dynamics of aggregate economic variables, such as GDP, consumption, etc., they explicitly capture the micro-level interaction of different types of heterogeneous economic agents and allow computing the aggregate variables "from the bottom up", i.e., summing individual quantities across agents. The bottom-up approach to macroeconomics consists therefore in deducing the macroscopic patterns and phenomena in terms of a multitude of elementary microscopic objects (microeconomic variables) interacting according to certain rules and protocols.

Developing and using an MABM typically requires a number of steps:

- *Model Design and Theory:*
  - determine the type of agents included to be in the model (households, firms, banks, etc.);
  - for each agent of each type define the set of decisions to be taken, the set of internal states (e.g., wealth, skills, savings, etc.), structure of each decision rule (inputs, how is decision made), the potential information exchange with other agents and the potential dynamic adjustment of internal states and decision rules; decide on the theoretical, empirical or experimental foundations on which these choices are based;
  - define interaction protocols for all potential interactions.
- *Codification*: translate the rules into computer code, do proper testing of the code (e.g., unit testing) to ensure proper implementation of the model.
- *Parameter Choice and Validation*: estimate and calibrate the parameters; run simulations; analyze the *emerging properties* of the simulated data, both at the cross-sectional level (e.g., firms' size distribution) and at the macroeconomic level (GDP growth and fluctuations, inflation/unemployment trade-off); compare these properties with real world "stylized facts."
- *Model Analysis*: study the effects of changes in key model parameters (e.g., policy parameters) based on proper statistical analysis of the output of batch runs across different parameter settings; use micro-level simulation data to highlight the mechanisms responsible for the observed findings and to foster economic intuition for the findings.

Several properties are common to MABMs and have been encountered in many agent-based models in Economics, among them several of the models reviewed in this chapter. First and foremost, in MABMs GDP tends to *self-organize* towards a growth path with endogenously generated fluctuations, such that business cycles are driven by the mechanics of the model rather than by properties of exogenous shocks. Furthermore, these models typically generate persistent heterogeneity of agents, giving rise to stable population distributions of firm size, productivity, profitability, growth rate or household income and thereby can reproduce also empirical patterns with respect to distributions of such variables. In particular, distributions with fat tails, which are observed for many real world variables (see, e.g., Axtell, 2018 in this handbook), have been reproduced in many instances by MABMs. Being able to jointly reproduce empirical stylized facts with respect to time series properties and distributional properties at different levels of aggregation is certainly a very appealing feature of MABMs, which is hard to obtain in the framework of alternative macroeconomic modeling approaches.

Many MABMs are characterized by *externalities* and *nonlinearities* (due to interaction), which generate dynamic processes with *positive feedbacks*. Due to the presence of such feedbacks path dependencies might arise such that initial conditions or random events in the transient phase can have decisive impact on the long run dynamics. These properties of MABMs are also the basis for endogenously generating extreme events, like crashes and economic crises, as well as fast transitions between different quasi-stable regimes. MABMs capture the actual dynamic mechanisms generating such potential fast economic transitions and therefore are natural tools to study how to prevent or mollify economic crises, e.g., through appropriate institutional designs or policy measures. Generally speaking, the fact that agent-based models allow for global analysis of macroeconomic dynamics in frameworks which endogenously generate dynamic and cross-sectoral patterns, which closely resemble empirical data, arguably is a main reason for the appeal of this approach.

1.3 BEHAVIOR, EXPECTATIONS, AND INTERACTION PROTOCOLS

In dynamic equilibrium models, individual behavior is typically determined by the optimal solution of some (dynamic) optimization problem an agent with rational expectations faces. Quite differently, in agent-based macroeconomic models it is not assumed that the economy is in equilibrium and that individuals have rational expectations. Hence, the agents in the model, similarly to real-world decision makers, are *"necessarily limited to locally constructive actions, that is, to actions constrained by their interaction networks, information, beliefs, and physical states."* (Sinitskaya and Tesfatsion, 2015, p. 152). The design of behavioral rules determining such locally constructive actions is a crucial aspect of developing an agent-based macroeconomic model. The lack of an accepted precise common conceptual or axiomatic basis for the modeling of bounded rational behavior has raised concerns about the *"wilderness of bounded rationality"* (Sims, 1980); however, agent-based modelers have become increasingly aware of this issue, providing different foundations for their approaches to model individual behavior.

Generally speaking, in many MABMs the design of the behavioral rules builds on the extensive psychological and empirical literature showing the prevalence of relatively simple heuristics and rules of thumb for making decisions, including economic decisions in complex environments (see, e.g., Gigerenzer and Gaissmaier, 2011; Artinger and Gigerenzer, 2016). Such rules might be derived from optimization within the framework of a simplified internal model of the surrounding environment, or might evolve over time based on adjustment dynamics that take into account which types of rules generate desirable results for the decision maker.[4] In a number of agent-based models the chosen behavioral rules are strongly motivated by experimental[5] or empirical observations of how actual decision makers behave in certain types of decision problems.[6] As will become clear in our survey below, the literature shows substantial heterogeneity with respect to the approach that underlies the design of the behavioral rules. Similar statements apply to the expectation formation of agents. The absence of the assumption of rational expectations typically gives rise to models with evolving heterogeneous expectations and also in this domain different approaches have been followed.

Given the heterogeneity in the way decision making and expectation formation are modeled, it would be desirable to have a clear understanding of how robust results obtained in the framework of a certain model are with respect to the use of alternative plausible behavioral rules. A step in this direction is taken by Sinitskaya and Tesfatsion (2015), who compare in a simple macroeconomic framework how key outcomes of the model compare across settings with different types of decision rules; however, in particular in large macroeconomic models such robustness tests are not feasible and the chosen design of the behavioral rules might therefore be an important determinant of the model output.

In most macroeconomic agent-based models the interaction of the different agents in markets or other interaction structures are governed by explicit protocols that represent the institutional design of the considered economic system. This allows capturing details of the institutional setting and also allows representing in a natural way potential rationing of both market sides, as well as the occurrence of frictions in a market. The degree of detail with which the interactions structures in different markets are described, of course, varies substantially across the agent-based macroeconomic models that have been developed and is strongly influenced by the main focus of the model.

---

[4] Seminal contributions to the development of theories capturing (bounded rational) firm behavior and the evolution of routines determining activities in firms are Cyert and March (1963) and Nelson and Winter (1982).

[5] See Hommes (2013) or Assenza et al. (2015b) for a discussion of the use of laboratory experiments as the foundation for the formulation of heuristic behavioral rules.

[6] With respect to firm decisions, the "Management Science Approach" (see Dawid and Harting, 2012) has been put forward as a way to incorporate decision rules into agent-based models that resemble heuristics developed in the literature on managerial decision making. The underlying rationale of this approach is that actual decision making of managers is likely to be guided by these heuristics which are put forward in textbooks and taught in business schools.

1.4 OUTLINE OF THE CHAPTER

In this chapter we discuss the main developments in Agent-Based Macroeconomics during the last decade. The treatment is essentially split into two parts. In the first part, consisting of Sections 2 and 3, we focus on the design of macroeconomic agent-based models. In particular, in Section 2 we address in some detail several main challenges of macroeconomic agent-based modeling, in particular the design of the behavioral rules of different types of agents for several of the most crucial decisions to be taken. We illustrate how these challenges were treated in eight macroeconomic agent-based models that have been well perceived in the literature. In Section 3, we provide more of a bird's-eye view on these model by summarizing the detailed discussion of Section 2 and providing a systematic comparison of these eight MABMs along a larger number of modeling dimensions. Section 3 also contains a discussion of the way these models have been linked to empirical data. The discussion in Section 3 is based on Tables A1 and A2, provided in Appendix A, in which a short summary of the main features of all eight models is given. Overall, we hope that Sections 2 and 3 of the chapter do not only provide a survey of the literature, but are also helpful in identifying what could be considered a common core of macroeconomic agent-based modeling. The second part of the chapter, essentially Section 4, provides an overview of macroeconomic policy analyses that have been carried out using agent-based models. Although the eight models discussed in Sections 2 and 3 are the basis for a considerable fraction of this policy oriented work, numerous studies reviewed in Section 4 do not fall into this category. This highlights the breadth of work in agent-based macroeconomics during the last years and the fact that a chapter like this, due to space constraints, cannot properly capture the full status of the literature. The chapter concludes with some remarks about challenges for the future development of this line of research and about areas in which, in our opinion, the potential for agent-based analysis is particularly high.

2 DESIGN OF AGENT-BASED MACROECONOMIC MODELS
2.1 FAMILIES OF MABMS

Macroeconomic Agent-Based Models (MABMs) can be classified according to different criteria. First of all, we can distinguish between large, medium sized, and small MABMs.

Medium sized and large MABMs feature at least three agent types – households, firms, and banks – interacting at least on five markets: consumption goods (C-goods hereafter), capital or investment goods (K-goods), labor, credit, deposits. Small MABMs generally feature just two types of agents – households and firms – interacting on two markets: C-goods and labor.

Some MABMs are able to replicate growth, i.e., a long-run exponential trend around which actual GDP irregularly fluctuates, some other focus only on the short run, i.e., they can replicate only business fluctuations.

In this section and the next, we will focus on medium-sized MABMs, grouping them into seven families:

1. The framework developed by Ashraf, Gershman, and Howitt (AGH hereafter)[7];
2. The family of models proposed by Delli Gatti, Gallegati, and coauthors in Ancona and Milan exploiting the notion of *Complex Adaptive Trivial Systems* (CATS)[8];
3. The framework developed by Dawid and coauthors in Bielefeld as an offspring of the EURACE project,[9] known as Eurace@Unibi (EUBI)[10];

---

[7]In the following we will refer mainly to Ashraf et al. (2016, 2017). For an extension and application to monetary and macroprudential policy, see Popoyan et al. (2017).

[8]The acronym CATS incorporates seemingly contradictory concepts: How can a *Complex* system be *Trivial* at the same time? The apparent paradox is easily explained: Complex aggregate behavior stems from the *interaction* of simple (almost Trivial) behavioral heuristics. A very early attempt at building a computational macroeconomic model is Albin (1989). Ideas on how to model complex adaptive trivial systems can be found in Leijonhufvud (1993). Delli Gatti et al. (2005) is the most significant early example of a CATS model, populated by myopic optimizing firms, which use only capital to produce goods. Russo et al. (2007) develop an early model along similar lines, with an application to fiscal policy. Some reflections on building macro ABMs stimulated by these early experiences can be found in Gaffeo et al. (2007). Gaffeo et al. (2015) put forward a model with learning and institutions. The single most important CATS framework, which is at the core of a wave of subsequent models, is described in Chapter 3 of the book "Macroeconomics from the Bottom Up" (Delli Gatti et al., 2011). We will refer to this framework as CATS/MBU. It features households, firms, and banks. Firms use only labor to produce consumption goods. The properties of this model in a stripped-down version (without banks) have been analyzed in depth in Gualdi et al. (2015). A CATS/MBU setup has been used by Delli Gatti and Desiderio (2015) to explore the effects of monetary policy (hereafter CATS/DD). Klimek et al. (2015) use a variant of CATS/MBU to analyze bank resolution policies. Assenza et al. (2015a) have extended the model introducing capital goods (hereafter CATS/ADG). Following the lead of Aoki (Aoki, 2001, 2008, 2011), Landini et al. (2017) provide an example of a computable MABM of the CATS type. There are quite a few networked MABMS of the CATS family. A first wave of network based financial accelerator models consists of Delli Gatti et al. (2006, 2009), further developed in Delli Gatti et al. (2010). A new wave of networked MABMS exploits the dynamic trade off theory: Riccetti et al. (2013), Bargigli et al. (2014), and Riccetti et al. (2016b). Using a similar setup, Catullo et al. (2015) develop early warning indicators of an incoming financial crisis. A medium-to-large model (so called "modellone") is an extension of the previous framework; see Riccetti et al. (2015). For applications of this model to different topics, see Riccetti et al. (2013, 2016a), Russo et al. (2016), Riccetti et al. (2018). Caiani et al. (2016a) develop a medium-to-large model with emphasis on stock-flow consistency (so called "modellaccio"). For an application of this model to inequality and growth, see Caiani et al. (2016b).

[9]The EURACE project was funded by the European Commission during 2006–2009 under the 6th Framework programme, and was carried out by a consortium of 7 universities (located in France, Germany, Italy, UK, and Turkey), coordinated by Silvano Cincotti (University of Genoa). The agenda of the project was to develop an agent-based simulation platform that is suitable for (macro)economic analysis and the evaluation of the effect of different types of economic policy measures. See Holcombe et al. (2013), Deissenberg et al. (2008), and Cincotti et al. (2012a) for descriptions of the agenda of the project and the version of the model as developed during the EURACE project.

[10]For an extensive presentation of the model, see Dawid et al. (2018d). A concise discussion can be found in Dawid et al. (2018a). For an application to firm dynamics, see Dawid and Harting (2012). Fiscal policies are analyzed in Harting (2015) and Dawid et al. (2018c). Two papers on financial and macroprudential issues are van der Hoog and Dawid (2018) and van der Hoog (2018). The nexus of skill dynamics, innovation, and growth in multiregional settings is explored in Dawid et al. (2008, 2014, 2018b). Labor market

4. The EURACE framework maintained by Cincotti and coauthors in Genoa (EUGE)[11];
5. The *Java Agent based MacroEconomic Laboratory* developed by Salle and Seppecher (JAMEL)[12];
6. The family of models developed by Dosi, Fagiolo, Roventini, and coauthors in Pisa, known as the "Keynes meeting Schumpeter" framework (KS)[13];
7. The LAGOM model developed by Jaeger and coauthors.[14]

We will also present the relatively simple small model developed by Lengnick (LEN) for comparison.[15] Key references for these models are given in Tables A1 and A2.

By selecting these eight families of models, on the one hand, we tried to pick those that seem to have had the strongest impact on the literature and have been used as the basis for interesting economic analyses and policy experiments, and, on the other hand, also present some variety to show the range of approaches that have been developed to deal with the challenges of agent-based macroeconomic modeling. Clearly, any such selection is highly subjective and, as will also become clear in the discussion of agent-based policy analyses in Section 4, the selection made here misses a substantial number of important contributions to this area. Nevertheless, we

---

integration policies are analyzed in Dawid et al. (2012). In Dawid and Gemkow (2014) social networks are integrated into the model and their role for the emergence of income inequality is studied.

[11] After the end of the EURACE project, the EURACE model has been maintained at the university of Genoa and adapted both in size and scope to different research questions. The group we will refer to as EUGE is currently running different specifications of the framework. For applications to the interaction between the banking system and the macroeconomy and the analysis of the effects of financial regulation, see Cincotti et al. (2010), Teglio et al. (2010, 2012), Cincotti et al. (2012b), Raberto et al. (2012, 2017). For the analysis of monetary policy, see Raberto et al. (2008). For the analysis of the effects of fiscal policy and sovereign debt, see Raberto et al. (2014), Teglio et al. (2018). For applications to the housing and mortgage markets, see Erlingsson et al. (2013, 2014), Teglio et al. (2014), Ozel et al. (2016). For an application to the issues pertaining to energy, see Ponta et al. (2018). Finally, a multicountry version is analyzed in Petrovic et al. (2017). In this section we will refer to the most general features of the model, which we retrieve mainly from Cincotti et al. (2012a).

[12] The building blocks of the JAMEL model are described in Seppecher (2012). Seppecher and Salle (2015) explore the emergent properties of the model, namely the alternating macroeconomic regimes of boom and bust. A model with emphasis on stock-flow consistency is presented in Seppecher et al. (2018). The role of expectations in macro ABMs is thoroughly analyzed in Salle et al. (2013) and Salle (2015).

[13] Early examples of ABMs which will eventually develop into the KS framework are Dosi et al. (2006, 2008). In the following we will discuss mainly the model in Dosi et al. (2010), which has been extended to introduce banks and macrofinancial interactions (and to be used for fiscal, monetary, and prudential policy exercises) in Dosi et al. (2013, 2015, 2017a). The model has been used to analyze labor market issues and the effects of structural reforms in Napoletano et al. (2012), Dosi et al. (2017b, 2017c, 2018). For an application to the analysis of the effects of climate change, see Lamperti et al. (2017). For a general overview of this KS literature, see Dosi et al. (2017a).

[14] LAGOM is not an acronym (as in the case of the other families of MABMs) but a Swedish word which means equilibrium and harmony "perhaps akin to the Chinese 'Tao'." (Haas and Jaeger, 2005, p. 2). In the following we will discuss mainly the model in Wolf et al. (2013), Mandel et al. (2010).

[15] In the following we will discuss mainly the model in Lengnick (2013). See also Lengnick and Wohltmann (2016, 2011).

believe that presenting such a survey is not only useful for newcomers to the field, but also helps to provide transparency about the status of the field of agent-based macroeconomics. Due to the rather complex structure of many models in this field, which often makes a full model description rather lengthy, such transparency is not easy to obtain.

The interested reader who ventures for the first time into this literature may feel the excitement of exploring a new world and, at the same time, the disorientation and discouragement of getting lost in the wilderness. At first sight, in fact, these models look very different from one another so that it's extremely difficult for the beginner to "see the forest" above and beyond a wide variety of trees. In our opinion, however, there are *common denominators*, both in the basic architecture of the models and in the underlying theory of the way in which agents form behavioral rules and interact on markets.

2.2 A MAP OF THIS SECTION

Let us set the stage by considering the *architecture* of an MABM. The economy is populated, at a minimum, by households and firms (as in LEN). Medium-sized MABMs are populated also by banks.

Households supply labor and demand C-goods. In most MABMs, households are "surplus units", i.e., net savers. Savings are used to accumulate financial wealth.

The corporate sector consists, at a minimum, of producers of C-goods (C-firms). Most MABMs, however, are now incorporating also producers of K-goods (K-firms). C-firms demand labor and K-goods in order to produce and sell C-goods to households. K-firms supply K-goods to C-firms.

In most MABMs firms are "deficit units", i.e., firms' internal funds may not be sufficient to finance costs. Therefore they resort to external finance to fill the financing gap. In most MABMs, external finance coincides with bank loans. Banks receive deposits from households and extend loans to firms.

In small MABMs, such as LEN, there are markets for C-goods and labor. In medium-sized MABMs, there are typically markets for C-goods, K-goods, labor, credit, and deposits.[16] Given this architecture, we can allocate agents in markets according to the grid shown in Table 1. Each column of the table represents a group of agents, each row a market. For instance, H/C/d represents **H**ouseholds acting on the market for **C**-goods on the side of **d**emand.

Instead of reviewing the models one after another, in each of the following subsections we will discuss the characterizations that the proponents of different MABMs adopt to describe the *behavioral rules* that each type of agent (on the columns) follows in each of the different markets the agent is active (on the rows). We will also

---

[16]It should be mentioned that for several of the MABMs there exist also variants including additional markets, e.g., for housing and electricity, see Lamperti et al. (2017), Ozel et al. (2016).

Table 1 *H* stands for households; *F* denotes firms; *B* stands for banks; *N* denotes the labor market; *L* denotes the market for loans; and *A* denotes the market for assets

	Households	**Firms**	**Banks**
C-goods	H/C/d	F/C/s	
K-goods		F/K/d,s	
Labor	H/N/s	F/N/d	
Credit		F/L/d	B/L/s
Assets	H/A/d	F/A/s	

devote some space to the description of the interaction of buyers and sellers on markets (*market protocols*) which Tesfatsion labels "procurement process."[17]

We aim at bringing to the fore the similarities among different MABMs. As mentioned above, assumptions and modeling choices come from a variety of sources, first and foremost from the empirical and experimental evidence. It is worth noting, moreover, that these assumptions have a varying degree of kinship with the current macroeconomic literature. MABMs are not developed in a vacuum, the shapes of their building blocks come also from the theoretical debate in macroeconomics. For this reason, at the beginning of each subsection, we will succinctly present the microeconomic backbone of a standard New Keynesian DSGE (NK-DSGE) model (the *standard model* hereafter) pertaining to that class of agents,[18] then present the behavioral rules and market protocols of MABMs concerning the same class. In this way we can discuss similarities and differences (i) between the standard model and the MABMs, and (ii) among MABMs. In order to make the comparison easier, we will adopt our own notation, which will be uniform across different MABMs. We will also slightly simplify the analytical apparatus of a specific MABM under review to make the modeling choices starker in the eyes of the reader. Notice finally that we will consider each MABM as the result of a collective effort (with the exception of LEN). Hence we will conjugate a verb describing the action of the group behind the label of each MABM in the third person plural. To foster readability, we provide in Appendix B a list of symbols with their meaning that are used in this section.

In our presentation of MABMs, due to space limitations, we will not discuss three relevant features.

The first concerns the *sequence of events*, which may differ from one model to another. By construction, MABMs are *recursive* sequential models. Agents decide

---

[17]For a discussion of this notion, see Tesfatsion (2006).

[18]The NK-DSGE literature is immense. The prototypical small standard model is the micro-founded NK-DSGE "three equation model", which is routinely taught in core macroeconomics courses at the graduate level. Among textbooks, the obvious reference is Gali (2008). This model features only two classes, households and firms (epitomized by a representative agent per class), and two markets, goods and labor. The introduction of the banking system is due to Bernanke et al. (1999) (BGG). Nowadays, BGG is the standard medium-sized NK-DSGE model with financial frictions.

on the desired level of their choice variables (planned level) following behavioral rules and then enter markets one after another in order to implement those decisions by suitable transactions. Search of trading opportunities and matching of supply and demand occur in fully decentralized markets, i.e., in the absence of a top-down mechanism to enforce equilibrium. Therefore, transactions typically occur at prices which do not clear the market. This may cause a disruption of plans, which must be revised accordingly.

Consider, for instance, a C-firm. Once the quantity to be produced has been established, the firm determines desired employment. If desired employment is greater than the current workforce, the firm tries to hire new workers by posting vacancies. It may not be able to fill the vacancies, however, because not enough workers will visit the firm or accept the position.[19] In this case, the firm has to downsize its production plans. Generally, due to unexploited trading opportunities, three constraints may limit the implementation of decisions, e.g., firms may be unable to (i) find enough external funds to fill the financing gap and/or (ii) hire enough workers and/or (iii) acquire enough capital to implement the desired level of production.

The second feature concerns *time discretization*. By construction, in MABMs time is discrete. MABMs can differ, however, as far as the minimal time unit is considered (a day, a week, a month, a quarter). Moreover, transactions can occur at different time scales. For instance, in LEN C-goods are traded every day but labor services are traded on a monthly basis. In the following, for simplicity we will not be specific on the time unit which will be referred to with the generic term "a period."

The third feature concerns the *characterization of interaction*. A few MABMs are networked, i.e., they have an explicit *network structure*: agents are linked by means of trading relationships which take the form of persistent partnerships. In LEN, for instance, each household trades with a finite set of firms.[20] Most of the MABMs we will consider below, however, do not assume a fixed network of trading relationships. Partners in a trade today may not trade again tomorrow. In a sense, trading relationships de facto connect people in a network which is systematically reshuffled every period.[21]

2.3 HOUSEHOLDS

In the following, we will consider a population of H households. Variables pertaining to the hth household will be denoted with the suffix h. Households may be active or inactive on the labor market. If active, they supply labor (in most MABMs, labor supply is exogenous). In some MABMs, households searching the labor market

---

[19] In most MABMs the labor market is riddled with frictions: each unemployed worker visits only a limited number of firms, and/or the posted vacancies are advertised only to a certain number of unemployed workers. Hence, after a round of transactions on the market, there will still be unfilled vacancies, as well as unemployed workers.

[20] This is also the case, for instance, of variants of the CATS framework, e.g., Delli Gatti et al. (2010).

[21] To be precise, also in the case of networked MABMs, the network can be rewired. Typically, with a certain probability and a certain periodicity, an agent switches from one partner to another.

have a reservation wage, which may be constant or decreasing with the length of the unemployment spell. If employed, the household earns a wage. In some MABMs, if unemployed, the household receives an unemployment subsidy, which amounts to a fraction of the wage of employed households.

Households are also firm owners. Firm ownership may be limited to a fraction of inactive households or spread somehow also to active households. As a firm owner, the household receives dividends. Current income is the sum of the wage bill and dividends. Households purchase C-goods. Generally, households are surplus units, i.e., they do not get into debt. Unspent income is saved and generates financial wealth. In most MABMs, financial wealth consists of bank deposits only.

In **LEN**, households are linked in a network of trading relationships to a finite set of firms from which they buy C-goods and firms for which they work. Since there are no banks, households hold wealth in liquid form (money holding).

In **AGH**, each household ("person") is denoted by the type (i, j) where i is the household's labor/product type and j are the types of goods the household wants to consume. By assumption the household consumes only two goods, different from the good it can produce.[22] A household of type i can be a worker if employed by a firm ("shop") of the same type. If a worker, she earns a wage. Otherwise, the household can be a firm owner.

In the **CATS** framework, households can be either workers or "capitalists." Workers supply labor, earn a wage (if employed), consume, and save. Capitalists are the owners of firms. For simplicity there is one capitalist per firm. Capitalists earn dividends (if the firm is profitable), consume, and save (therefore they behave as *rentiers*). Both workers and capitalists accumulate their savings in the form of deposits at banks. If the firm goes bankrupt, the owner of the bankrupt firm employs his personal wealth to provide equity to the entrant firm. In other words, the capitalist is *de facto* recapitalizing the defaulting firm to make it survive.

In **KS**, **EUBI**, **EUGE**, and **LAGOM**, each household supplies labor and owns firms at the same time. This alternative approach poses the problem of attributing ownership rights, dividends, and recapitalization commitments to heterogeneous households. For instance, in EUBI, the household holds financial wealth in the form of deposits at banks and an index of stocks which define property rights and the distribution of dividends.

In **JAMEL**, some of the households (chosen at random) are firm owners and remain firm owners for a certain time period (typically a run of a simulation).

2.3.1 The Demand for Consumption Goods

In this section we will first recall the basic tenets of the standard model of household's consumption/saving decisions, which we will refer to as the Life Cycle/Permanent Income (LCPI) benchmark. We will then present the *most general specification* of the

---

[22] In other words, technology is one-to-one. Each household is endowed with a unit of specific labor – say, labor of the ith type – so that it can produce one unit of the ith product.

consumption behavioral rule which we can extract from the MABM literature. The specific behavioral rules adopted by different MABMs can be conceived as *special cases* of this general specification.

The Life Cycle/Permanent Income Benchmark

The standard approach to households' behavior (incorporated in NK-DSGE models) is based on "two-stage budgeting." In the first stage, the representative infinitely lived household maximizes expected lifetime utility subject to the intertemporal budget constraint, determining the optimal *size* of consumption expenditure $C_{h,t}$, which we will sometimes refer to hereafter as the *consumption budget*.

In the second stage the household determines the *composition* of $C_{h,t}$, i.e., the fraction $C_{i,h,t}/C_{h,t}$ for each variety $i = 1, 2, \ldots, F_c$ where F_c is the cardinality of the set of C-goods (and of C-firms).[23]

As far as the first stage is concerned, optimal consumption turns out to be a function of expected future consumption $E_t C_{h,t+1}$ and the real interest rate r (*consumption Euler equation*).

Notice now that consumption expenditure is equal by definition to permanent income, $C_{h,t} = Y_{h,t}^p$. Hence, after some algebra, we get

$$C_{h,t} = \hat{r}(W_{h,t}^h + W_{h,t}^f) \tag{1}$$

where $\hat{r} = \hat{R} - 1$ is the (net, real) interest rate, $W_{h,t}^h$ is *human capital*, and $W_{h,t}^f$ is financial wealth. Eq. (1) can be interpreted as a benchmark *Life Cycle/Permanent Income (LCPI) consumption function*. In this framework, by construction, the consumption budget is equal to the annuity value of total (financial and human) wealth.

Human capital, in turn, is defined as the discounted sum of current income and expected future incomes accruing to the household:

$$W_{h,t}^h = \frac{1}{\hat{R}} \sum_{s=0}^{\infty} \left(\frac{1}{\hat{R}}\right)^s E_t Y_{h,t+s} = \frac{1}{\hat{R}} Y_{h,t} + \frac{1}{\hat{R}} \sum_{s=1}^{\infty} \left(\frac{1}{\hat{R}}\right)^s E_t Y_{h,t+s}. \tag{2}$$

Substituting (2) into (1), the LCPI consumption function becomes

$$C_{h,t} = \frac{\hat{r}}{\hat{R}} Y_{h,t} + \frac{\hat{r}}{\hat{R}} \sum_{s=1}^{\infty} \left(\frac{1}{\hat{R}}\right)^s E_t Y_{h,t+s} + r W_{h,t}^f. \tag{3}$$

In words, consumption is a linear function of current and expected future incomes and of financial wealth.

By definition, in the LCPI benchmark, $W_{h,t+1}^f = \hat{R} W_{h,t}^f + Y_{h,t} - C_{h,t}$. Therefore savings, i.e., the change in financial wealth $S_{h,t} = W_{h,t+1}^f - W_{h,t}^f$, turns out to be

---

[23]By construction, in a Dixit–Stiglitz setting $C_{h,t}$ is a CES aggregator of individual quantities.

equal to $S_{h,t} = \hat{r} W^f_{h,t} + Y_{h,t} - C_{h,t}$. Since consumption is equal to permanent income, savings can be specified as follows:

$$S_{h,t} = \hat{r} W^f_{h,t} + (Y_{h,t} - Y^p_{h,t}) \tag{4}$$

where the expression in parentheses is *transitory* income. All the income in excess of permanent income will be saved and added to financial wealth. If, on the other hand, current income falls short of permanent income, the household will stabilize consumption by decumulating financial wealth.

As far as the second stage is concerned, it is easy to show that in a Dixit–Stiglitz framework the (optimal) fraction of each good in the bundle is

$$\frac{C_{i,h,t}}{C_{h,t}} = \left(\frac{P_{i,t}}{P_t} \right)^{-\varepsilon} \tag{5}$$

where $P_{i,t}$ is the price of the ith variety, P_t is the general price level,[24] and ε is the absolute value of the price elasticity of demand. In words, the fraction of the consumption budget allocated to each variety is a decreasing function of the *relative price* $\frac{P_{i,t}}{P_t}$.

Generally, households are assumed to be identical. If household members are heterogeneous (for instance, because of the employment status, or the level and the source of income), in standard models *complete markets* are assumed so that idiosyncratic risk can always be insured. Within the household, "full consumption insurance" follows from the assumption that household members pool together their incomes (wages, unemployment subsidies, dividends) and consume the same amount in the same proportions. Thanks to this assumption, heterogeneity, albeit present, is irrelevant because the household may still be dealt with as a unique (representative) agent. If idiosyncratic income risk is uninsurable, then heterogeneity cannot be assumed away.[25]

The Agent Based Approach to Consumption/Saving Decisions

A two stage procedure is also generally adopted in MABMs. In the first stage household h determines the *consumption budget* $C_{h,t}$, i.e., the amount of resources (income, wealth) to be allocated to consumption expenditure. In the second stage the household determines the composition of the bundle of consumption goods, i.e., the quantities $C_{i,h,t}$, $i = 1, 2, \ldots, F_c$ of the goods which enter the consumption bundle. Notice, however, that in general agents do not follow explicit optimization procedures. Markets are generally incomplete and within-household consumption insurance is ruled out.

---

[24] By construction, the general price level is a CES aggregator of individual prices.

[25] Incomplete markets is the basic assumption of the literature on Standard Incomplete Market (SIM) models with heterogeneous agents, both of the new Classical and New Keynesian type. The New Keynesian variants are known as Heterogeneous Agents New Keynesian (HANK) models. For an exhaustive survey, see the chapter by Ragot (2018) in this handbook.

The Choice of the Consumption Budget

As far as the first stage is concerned, the most general behavioral rule adopted to set the consumption budget in the MABM literature can be specified as follows:

$$C_{h,t} = c_h W^h_{h,t} + c_f W^f_{h,t} \tag{6}$$

where $W^f_{h,t}$ is the household's financial wealth (deposited at the bank and/or invested in financial assets), $W^h_{h,t}$ is human capital, c_h and c_f are propensities to consume, both positive and smaller than one. In words, consumption is a linear function of human and financial wealth.

By definition, $W^f_{h,t} = \hat{R} W^f_{h,t-1} + Y_{h,t} - C_{h,t}$ and $S_{h,t} = W^f_{h,t} - W^f_{h,t-1}$. Consumption is defined as in (6). Hence, in a generic MABM savings turn out to be

$$S_{h,t} = Y_{h,t} + (\hat{r} - c_f) W^f_{h,t-1} - c_h W^h_{h,t}. \tag{7}$$

If positive, savings increase financial wealth. In some MABMs saving can be involuntary: it may happen that the household cannot find enough consumption goods at the limited number of firms it visits. Savings will turn negative, i.e., the household will decumulate financial wealth, if the consumer does not receive income, for instance, because a worker becomes unemployed and/or financial income (interest payments on financial wealth) is too low. In most MABMs, household do not get into debt so that consumption smoothing is limited or absent (in the jargon of NK-DSGE models, asset market participation is limited).

Specifications of the general rule (6) differ from one MABM to another.

AGH set $c_h = c_f = c$. Moreover, they define human capital as the capitalized value of permanent income $W^h_{h,t} = k^h Y^P_{h,t}$ where k^h is a capitalization factor.[26] Permanent income $Y^P_{h,t}$ is computed by means of an *adaptive* algorithm, $Y^P_{h,t} - Y^P_{h,t-1} = (1 - \xi)(Y_{h,t-1} - Y^P_{h,t-1})$ where $\xi \in (0, 1)$ is a memory parameter. By iterating, it is easy to see that permanent income (and therefore human capital) turns out to be a weighted sum of *past incomes* only, $Y^P_{h,t} = (1 - \xi) \sum_{s=0}^{-\infty} \xi^s Y_{h,t-s-1}$. Hence the AGH behavioral rule for consumption expenditure is

$$C_{h,t} = c k^h (1 - \xi) \sum_{s=0}^{-\infty} \xi^s Y_{h,t-s-1} + c W^f_{h,t}. \tag{8}$$

In words, consumption is a linear function of past incomes and financial wealth.

In the **CATS/ADG** framework, human capital is defined by the following *adaptive* algorithm: $W^h_{h,t} = \xi W^h_{h,t-1} + (1 - \xi) Y_{h,t}$. By iterating, one gets $W^h_{h,t} = (1 - \xi) Y_{h,t} + (1 - \xi) \sum_{s=1}^{-\infty} \xi^s Y_{h,t-s}$, i.e., human capital is a weighted average of *current and past*

---

[26] In AGH k^h is endogenous as it is a function of projections of inflation and the interest rate elaborated by the central bank and made available to the general public.

incomes.[27] Substituting this definition into (6), the behavioral rule specializes to

$$C_{h,t} = c_h(1 - \xi)Y_{h,t} + c_h(1 - \xi)\sum_{s=1}^{-\infty} \xi^s Y_{h,t-s} + c_f W_{h,t}^f. \qquad (9)$$

While human capital in the neoclassical approach is a linear combination of current and expected *future* incomes, and therefore is formed in a forward looking way, the proxy for human capital in AGH and CATS/ADG is a linear combination of current and *past* incomes, i.e., it is determined by a backward looking algorithm.[28]

Setting $\xi = 0$, i.e., assuming that there is no memory, human capital boils down to current income, so that (9) specializes to

$$C_{h,t} = c_y Y_{h,t} + c_f W_{h,t}^f \qquad (10)$$

where c_y is the propensity to consume out of income.[29]

Setting $c_f = 0$, from (10) we get a specification of the consumption function sometimes adopted in MABMs of a strictly Keynesian flavor

$$C_{h,t} = c_y Y_{h,t}. \qquad (11)$$

In many models of the **KS** family, the behavioral rule is (11) with $c_h = 1$:

$$C_{h,t} = Y_{h,t}. \qquad (12)$$

This specification describes the behavior of "hand-to-mouth" consumers.[30]

LAGOM adopts a rule such as (10) with $c_y = 0$. Moreover, since financial wealth coincides with money holding ($W_{h,t}^f = \frac{M_{h,t}}{P_t}$), the consumption budget turns out to be

---

[27] In ADG income accruing to the household is $Y_{h,t} = w$ if the consumer is a worker with an active labor contract, $Y_{f,t} = \tau \pi_{f,t-1}$ if the consumer is a capitalist receiving dividends; τ is the dividend-payout ratio and $\pi_{f,t-1}$ are profits of the firm realized in the previous period and accruing as income to the capitalist in the current period.

[28] This difference reflects the fact that forward looking expectation formation is marred with insurmountable difficulties in a complex heterogeneous agents context. In this context, the obvious candidate for expectation formation is an adaptive algorithm. Notice, however, that the empirical work on consumption has extensively used adaptive algorithms.

[29] c_y in (10) coincides with c_h in (9) because, in the absence of memory, human capital coincides with current income.

[30] This is the specification used in NK models with "rule of thumb" consumers, i.e., consumers who cannot smooth consumption over the life cycle due to "limited asset market participation" or "liquidity constraints."

an increasing linear function of real money balances[31]

$$C_{h,t} = c_f \frac{M_{h,t}}{P_t}. \tag{13}$$

In **CATS/DD**, consumption is a special case of (10) obtained by setting $c_y = c_f = c$. Therefore

$$C_{h,t} = c(Y_{h,t} + W_{h,t}^f). \tag{14}$$

The expression in parentheses is one of the possible specifications of "cash-on-hand", which can be defined in the most general way as *liquid assets* which can be used to carry on transactions. In small MABMs which do not feature banks such as LEN, cash-on-hand coincides with currency. In a setting with banks such as CATS/DD, cash-on-hand coincides with new deposits, which in turn amount to the sum of income and old deposits. This is in line with Deaton (1991), who defines cash-on-hand as the sum of income and financial assets.

In **EUBI** and **EUGE**, saving behavior aims at achieving a target for wealth, namely $S_{h,t} = v(\omega^f Y_{h,t} - W_{h,t}^f)$ where ω^f is the target wealth-to-income ratio and v is the velocity of adjustment of wealth to targeted wealth. Since by definition $S_{h,t} = Y_{h,t} - C_{h,t}$, simple algebra shows that under this assumption the consumption budget can be written as

$$C_{h,t} = (1 - v\omega^f)Y_{h,t} + vW_{h,t}^f \tag{15}$$

which is a special case of (10) with $c_y = 1 - v\omega^f$ and $c_f = v$.

Carroll has shown that in an uncertain world consumption is a *concave function* of cash-on-hand which he defines as the sum of human capital and beginning of period wealth.[32] In Carroll's framework, for low values of wealth, the propensity to consume (out of wealth) is high due to the precautionary motive: a reduction of wealth would in fact lead to a sizable reduction of consumption to rebuild wealth (*buffer stock rule*). In some MABMs the consumption function is adjusted to mimic Carroll's precautionary motive, i.e., to reproduce the *nonlinearity* of the relationship between consumption and wealth. This theoretical setting has been corroborated by a number of empirical studies (see Carroll and Summers, 1991; Carroll, 1997), such that using this approach in MABMs is consistent with the agenda to rely on behavioral rules which have strong empirical foundations.

---

[31] In LAGOM firms enter the market for C-goods to purchase raw materials and wholesale goods (circulating capital). The demand for C-goods of the ith firm is $K_{i,t}^c = (1/k^c)Y^T - K_{i,t-1}^c$ where Y^T is the production target of the firm, k^c is the marginal productivity of circulating capital and $K_{i,t-1}^c$ is the stock of circulating capital inherited from the past.

[32] See Carroll (1992, 1997, 2009).

For instance, in EUBI the specification of the consumption function discussed above gives rise to a piecewise linear heuristic based on the buffer-stock rule. Also EUGE adopt a specification of the consumption budget which adopts Carroll's rule.

In the **CATS/MBU** framework, consumption is specified as in (11) but c_y is a nonlinear function of wealth. This allows capturing the interaction between income and wealth in the determination of consumption.

LEN explicitly models the consumption budget as an increasing concave function of money holdings by

$$C_{h,t} = \left(\frac{M_{h,t}}{P_t} \right)^c \tag{16}$$

where $c \in (0, 1)$.[33]

JAMEL presents a variant of Carroll's framework. The household computes "average income" (which can be considered a proxy of permanent income) as the mean of incomes received over a certain time span occurred in the past, $Y^a_{h,t} = \frac{1}{n} \sum_{\tau=t-n}^{t} Y_{h,\tau}$.[34] Moreover, JAMEL define desired or targeted cash on hand as a fraction of average income, $m^T_{h,t} = s Y^a_{h,t}$, where $m^T_{h,t} = M^T_{h,t}/P_t$ are real money balances and $s \in (0, 1)$ is the desired propensity to save (out of average income). The consumption budget is defined as follows:

$$C_{h,t} = \begin{cases} c Y^a_{h,t} & \text{if } m_{h,t} < m^T_{h,t}, \\ Y^a_{h,t} + c_m (m_{h,t} - m^T_{h,t}) & \text{if } m_{h,t} > m^T_{h,t} \end{cases} \tag{17}$$

where $c = 1 - s$ and $c_m \in (0, 1)$ is the propensity to consume. In words, if liquid assets are (relatively) "low", the household spends a fraction c of average income. If liquidity is "high", the household consumes the entire average income and a fraction c_m of excess money balances, defined as the difference between the current and targeted money holding.

With the help of some algebra, the behavioral rule above can be written as follows:

$$C_{h,t} = \begin{cases} c Y^a_{h,t} & \text{if } Y^a_{h,t} > \bar{Y}^a_{h,t}, \\ c' Y^a_{h,t} + c_m M_{h,t} & \text{if } Y^a_{h,t} < \bar{Y}^a_{h,t} \end{cases} \tag{18}$$

where $\bar{Y}^a_{h,t} = \frac{1}{s} m_{h,t}$ is the cut-off value of average income and $c' = 1 - c_m(1 - c) = (1 - c_m)(1 - c) + c$. Notice that $c' > c$. The cut-off value of average income is a multiple of current money holdings. The specification above highlights the basic tenets of

---

[33] Of course, consumption cannot be greater than money holding. Hence $(M_{h,t}/P_t) > 1$.

[34] In JAMEL the minimal time unit is a month; $Y_{h,t}$ therefore is current income in month t. Average income in month t is the mean of monthly incomes in the last 12 months up to t, i.e., $Y^a_{h,t} = \frac{1}{12} \sum_{\tau=t-12}^{t} Y_{h,\tau}$. Since permanent income is a weighted average of all the past incomes over an infinite time span with exponentially decaying weights (see above), average income is defined on a shorter time span and with equal instead of decaying weights.

Carroll's buffer stock theory in a very simple piecewise linear setting. When average income is below the threshold, i.e., when the threshold is relatively high because the household is wealthy/liquid, the marginal propensity to consume is c', i.e., it is relatively high. When average income surpasses the threshold, the marginal propensity drops to c.

JAMEL also incorporates *consumer sentiment* and *opinion dynamics* in the consumption function. The propensity to save, s, can take on two values. When "optimistic", the household is characterized by s^L while if "pessimistic" it sets s to s^H, with $s^H > s^L$. Pessimism leads to a reduction of the propensity to consume: households save more for rainy days.

Each household switches from a low to a high propensity to save (and vice versa) depending on its *employment status*. The household turns pessimistic if unemployed. In each period, the household observes the consumer sentiment (proxied by the employment status) of a finite subset of other households (a neighborhood, for short). With probability π^m it adopts the *majority opinion*, i.e., the prevailing consumer sentiment, of the neighborhood; with probability $1 - \pi^m$ the household relies on its own situation: if it is unemployed (employed), it will be pessimistic (optimistic) and will choose s^H (s_L). The probability of adopting the sentiment of the majority can be interpreted as the strength of the households' "animal spirits."

The Choice of the Goods to Buy

As to the second stage, the choice of the goods to buy is generally influenced by the relative price. EUBI and EUGE introduce a multinomial logit model, CATS posit a search mechanism.

In **LEN** each household is linked to a fixed number of firms from which it can buy. The network can change over time. Each period, with a certain probability, the household chooses at random a firm in the neighborhood of current trading partners and a firm outside it, compares the prices, and switches to the new firm if the price of the price set by the current partner exceeds the price of the new firm by at least a certain margin. In the end, therefore, the household searches for better trading opportunities based on relative price.[35]

AGH posit that the household can buy only from two firms ("stores", i.e., shops where the household purchases its consumption goods). Hence it has to choose the quantity to be demanded from each firm. AGH derives behavioral rules by solving a simple optimization problem. The household maximizes $U_{h,t} = U(C_{1,h,t}, C_{2,h,t})$ subject to $p_{1,t}C_{1,h,t} + p_{2,t}C_{2,h,t} = C_{h,t}$ where $p_{i,t} = \frac{P_{i,t}}{P_t}$, $i = 1, 2$. Hence the quantity demanded for each variety turns out to be

$$C_{i,h,t} = f_i(p_{1,t}, p_{2,t}, C_{h,t}), \quad i = 1, 2, \tag{19}$$

---

[35] The household leaves the current partner and switches to a different one also when the household is demand constrained, i.e., when current trading partners are unable to satisfy demand.

which can be easily compared with (22). The household explores the goods market looking for stores supplying the goods it wants to consume. The household buys from store j only if the posted price $P_{j,t}$ is smaller than a reservation price equal to the price paid by the household in the past $P_{h,j,t-1}$ (appropriately indexed): $P_{h,i,t-1}(1 + \pi^T) > P_{j,t}$ where π^T is expected inflation, anchored to the inflation target of the central bank.[36]

In the **CATS** framework, households collect information and pick goods by visiting firms chosen at random. The hth household visits Z_c randomly selected firms, ranks them according to the price they charge and purchases C-goods starting from the firm charging the lowest price. If it does not spend the entire consumption budget at the first firm, it will move up to the second firm in the ranking, and so on. If it has not spent all the consumption budget after visiting Z_c firms, it will save involuntarily. This implies that the demand for the good produced by the ith C-firm is implicitly decreasing with the relative price $p_{i,t}$. Notice, however, that the implicit demand curve that the ith firm is facing is shifting over time. A given firm may be visited by different sets of consumers on subsequent days. The search and matching mechanism leads to the coexistence of queues of unsatisfied consumers (involuntary savers) at some firms and involuntary inventories of unsold goods at some other firms.

LAGOM adopts a similar market protocol as **CATS** for the market for C-goods. In the LAGOM model also firms enter the market for C-goods as they use circulating capital together with fixed capital for production.

EUBI and **EUGE** assume that the consumer receives information about the range of products, their prices, and their availability at (local) malls. The choice of the good to buy is random and the probability of buying a certain product is determined by a multinomial logit model:

$$P[\text{consumer } h \text{ selects good } i] = \frac{\exp(-\gamma \log P_{i,t})}{\sum_j \exp(-\gamma \log P_{j,t})} \tag{20}$$

where the sum in the denominator includes all products for which the consumer has received information.[37] As has been discussed in Dawid et al. (2018d), this formulation can also be interpreted as a representation of a situation in which the product offered by the different C-firms are horizontally differentiated along dimensions not explicitly captured in the model. The parameter γ governs the intensity of (price) competition between the C-firms and typically has strong influence on the emerging economic dynamics on the aggregate level. Dawid et al. (2018d) also point out that the use of logit-choice models for the representation of consumer choice has strong empirical foundations, e.g., in the Marketing literature.[38]

---

[36] Of course, this assumption is implicitly based on the credibility of the central bank's announced inflation target.

[37] In Dawid et al. (2018c) this setting is extended by assuming that consumers have a "home-bias" in consumption, such that the attractiveness of a product depends in addition to the price also on the fact whether it has been produced by a firm located in the same region as the consumer.

[38] An axiomatic behavioral foundation for multinomial logit models can be found in Breitmoser (2016).

2.3.2 Labor Supply

On the labor market, households are suppliers of labor. The hth worker supplies inelastically one unit of labor.

LEN assumes that each household has a reservation wage, denoted with w_h. It supplies its labor only to a finite subset of the population of firms, a neighborhood of potential employers. However, the network can be rewired. If the household is employed, say, at firm i, and its current wage is higher than the reservation wage ($w_i > w_h$), it will search for a better position infrequently, i.e., with probability less than one. When searching, it will visit only one new firm chosen at random. If at this new firm, say j, it finds $w_j > w_i$, so it will quit the current job and move to the jth firm. If, for any reasons, its current wage falls below the reservation wage ($w_i < w_h$),[39] it will intensify the quest for a better position by exploring a new firm every period (i.e., with certainty). If the household is unemployed, it will search for a job every period by visiting a fixed number Z_e of firms chosen at random. If the household switches to a new employer, the former employer drops out of the set of employers of the households and is replaced by the new one.

Also in **LAGOM** each household has a reservation wage. If the household is employed, say, at firm i, and its current wage is lower than the reservation wage ($w_i < w_h$), so it will quit the job and search for a better position at a finite set of firms chosen at random.

In **AGH**, as we saw above, a household type is defined by the production good it can produce with its labor type. If employed, the household is working in the same firm which produces its production good. If unemployed, the household engages in job search with a given probability π^s. It explores the labor market looking for a firm (with the same product type) posting a vacancy. The household accepts the job offer if the previous wage $w_{h,i,t-1}$ (appropriately indexed) is smaller than the posted wage $w_{i,t}$, i.e., if $w_{h,i,t-1}(1 + \pi^T) < w_{i,t}$.

In **CATS/MBU** and **CATS/ADG**, the hth household, if unemployed, looks for a job by visiting Z_e firms chosen at random and applying to those with open vacancies. In **CATS/MBU** the posted wage is firm-specific and cannot drop below a lower bound represented by a minimum wage, which is changing over time due to indexation. The unemployed worker will accept a job from the firm with open vacancies which pays the highest wage. For simplicity in **CATS/ADG** the posted wage is given and is uniform across firms so that the unemployed worker accepts the job at the first chance of finding an open vacancy. If it doesn't find an open vacancy, the household remains unemployed and funds consumption by dissaving, i.e., consuming out of accumulated wealth. For simplicity CATS assume that there are neither hiring nor firing costs. If a firm wants to scale down activity in a certain period, it can fire workers at no cost. Fired workers become unemployed and start searching for a job in the same period.

In **EUBI** the household is characterized by a specific skill and has a reservation wage. If unemployed, it explores the labor market with a given probability. Firms post

---

[39]This case may be due to the decision of the firm to cut the posted wage.

vacancies and wages. The unemployed household ranks the wage offers and applies only to firms that make a wage offer (for the worker's skill group) which is higher than its reservation wage. If the unemployed job searcher receives several acceptable job offers he/she accepts the offer with the highest wage. The reservation wage of the worker is adjusted downwards during periods of unemployment.

In **JAMEL** the household's reservation wage is stochastically reduced if the unemployment spell is greater than an exogenous upper bound. In symbols,

$$
w_{h,t} = \begin{cases} w_{h,t-1}(1 - \eta^h) & \text{if } d^u_{h,t} > \bar{d}^u, \\ w_{h,t-1} & \text{if } d^u_{h,t} < \bar{d}^u \end{cases} \tag{21}
$$

where $\eta^h \geq 0$ is a random draw from a uniform distribution, $d^u_{h,t}$ is the duration of the unemployment spell and $\bar{d}^u$ is the threshold value of this spell.

2.3.3 The Demand for Financial Assets

In a small MABM such as **LEN**, households can hold wealth only in the most liquid form (cash). Most medium-sized MABMs assume that there is at least one other financial asset such as deposits at banks. For **CATS**, **KS**, **JAMEL**, and **LAGOM**, households' wealth consists only of deposits. In **AGH**, households can hold cash, deposits, and government bonds. In **EUBI** and **EUGE** the household can hold wealth as liquidity (deposits at banks), as a portfolio of shares issued by firms and banks, and in EUGE also as government bonds. Households therefore receive dividends according to the composition of their portfolio of shares. For simplicity, in EUBI the allocation of households' savings to bank deposits and shares is random. Modeling the portfolio choice for each household, however, may be quite complex. For instance, the preference structure of "investors" in EUGE, i.e., households trading in financial markets, takes into account insights from behavioral finance, namely myopic loss aversion. Transactions on financial markets occur at higher frequency than on real markets (daily as against monthly). Prices are determined in equilibrium through a clearinghouse mechanism. In CATS households can be of two types, workers and capitalists. Assuming that there is one capitalist per firm, each firm distributes part of its profits to the firm owner as dividends. KS adopt the extreme assumption that all the profits are retained within the firm and used to accumulate net worth. In this case, by assumption there will be no dividends. In JAMEL some households (chosen at random) are firm owners and therefore receive dividends which will be distributed only if the firm's net worth is higher than a threshold (defined by a target level for leverage). Opinion dynamics play a role in dividend distribution. Firms switch from "optimistic" (characterized by high target leverage and high dividends) to "pessimistic" (low target leverage and low dividends). Also in LAGOM households are firm owners and receive both wages and dividends.

2.4 FIRMS

In this section we will consider a population of F firms, which produce either consumption goods (C-firms) or capital goods (K-firms). Variables pertaining to the ith C-firm will be denoted with the index $i = 1, 2, \ldots, F_c$. Variables pertaining to the kth K-firm will be denoted with the index $k = 1, 2, \ldots, F_k$. In most MABMs, C-firms demand labor and K-goods in order to produce and sell C-goods to households; K-firms demand labor in order to produce and sell K-goods to C-firms.[40]

Firms have market power, hence they set the quantity and the price of the goods they produce and sell. Generally, market power is rooted in transaction costs. Due to uncertainty and the costs of exploring market conditions, in fact, buyers do not have enough information on the prices and quantities set by all the sellers so that they purchase goods from a limited set of suppliers. Each supplier, therefore, operates in condition of monopolistic competition or oligopoly on the market for its own good.

The planned (or desired) scale of activity is the main determinant of the demand for inputs, namely the demand for capital and the demand for labor.

On the market for K-goods, demand comes from C-firms and supply comes from K-firms. The ith C-firm's demand for K-goods, i.e. investment, is driven mainly by production requirements. If production planned at period t for period $t + 1$ can be carried out with the capital stock inherited from the past (after depreciation), the firm simply adjusts capacity utilization. If capital inherited from the past is insufficient to undertake planned production, the ith firm should expand capacity by purchasing new K-goods (sometimes referred to as "machine tools"). In some MABMs, this is feasible. In other MABMs, investment at period t is driven by long-run production requirements and cannot be used to face short-run peaks of demand. Hence the firm will be constrained to produce at full capacity but less than desired.

On the market for labor, demand comes from all the firms and supply comes from households. Firms whose workforce is insufficient to undertake planned production will post vacancies and a wage offer (which may be firm-specific or uniform across firms, constant or time-varying because of indexation and/or because of labor market conditions.)

Firms may have a financing gap, i.e., a positive difference between operating costs and internally generated funds. They generally ask for a loan to fill this gap. The quantity and price of credit are set by banks.

Firms may be unable to achieve the desired scale of activity for lack of funds (if they are rationed on the credit market), of capital (if investment is disconnected from short-run production need and/or if they don't find enough machine tools to buy) or of labor (if they don't find enough workers to hire).

---

[40] In some MABMs, firms use also raw materials, energy, and wholesale/intermediate goods as inputs. We will be more specific below.

2.4.1 The Supply of Consumption Goods

The Dixit–Stiglitz Benchmark

As far as the corporate sector is concerned, NK DSGE models are based on monopolistic competition: each firm behaves as a monopolist on its own market. The firm's market power is due to product heterogeneity. Products may be different in the eyes of consumers for a number of reasons: spatial dispersion, product differentiation, or transaction costs which may generate captive markets.

In the Dixit–Stiglitz benchmark, the demand of the hth household for the ith good is represented by Eq. (5). Summing across H households and rearranging, one gets the demand function for the ith good:

$$C_{i,t} = \left(\frac{P_{i,t}}{P_t}\right)^{-\varepsilon} \frac{C_t}{F_c} \tag{22}$$

where $C_t = \sum_{h=1}^{H} C_{h,t}$ is total consumption (economywide).[41]

With a linear technology and only the labor input, the marginal cost will be w_t/α where w_t is the wage and α is the marginal productivity of labor. Optimal pricing yields

$$P_{i,t}^* = (1 + \mu)\frac{w_t}{\alpha} \tag{23}$$

where $\mu = (\varepsilon - 1)^{-1}$ is the mark-up.

Substituting (23) into (22), one gets the optimal scale of production

$$Y_{i,t}^* = C_{i,t}^* = \left(\frac{1 + \mu}{\alpha} \frac{w_t}{P_t}\right)^{-\varepsilon} \frac{C_t}{F_c}. \tag{24}$$

Since the manager of the firm knows the production function and input costs, and therefore can compute the marginal cost, if she knows also the demand curve she will choose an optimal mark-up (i.e., ratio of the individual price to marginal cost) and an optimal scale of activity. In other words, in the absence of uncertainty on market demand, the firm will choose a point on the demand curve in such a way as to maximize profits. In this case supply will always be equal to demand: the firm will neither accumulate involuntary inventories of unsold goods nor face queues of unsatisfied consumers; output will always be sold and no potential customer will leave the firm's premises empty handed.

Moreover, in the absence of frictions on the labor market, the firm will always be able to carry out planned production. In the end therefore, planned output will be equal to actual output and actual output will be equal to sales.

---

[41] For the sake of comparison with MABMs, Eq. (22) concerns the case of a "large" but finite number of firms. Eq. (5) is derived assuming a continuum of firms of unit mass.

From (23) and (24) we can predict the following: the firm will react to (i) an increase of elasticity of demand by reducing the mark up and therefore the individual price and increasing production; (ii) an increase of the real wage by increasing the price and reducing production; (iii) an increase in productivity by reducing the price and increasing production; (iv) an increase in total consumption by increasing production.

Since firms have the same technology, incur the same labor cost, and face the same demand function, a *symmetric equilibrium* in which all firms charge the same price, is considered: $P_{i,t} = P_t$, so that the real wage will be equal to $(w_t/P_t)^* = \alpha/(1+\mu)$. At that wage, employment is determined by labor supply, the labor market clears, and there is full employment.[42] Total output is equal to the full employment level of GDP.[43] In the absence of investment, output is equal to consumption. Each firm therefore will produce the same quantity, i.e., a fraction $1/F_c$ of total consumption, which is equal to total full employment output. In the presence of *nominal rigidities* (e.g., Calvo pricing), this level of output is unattainable, at least in the short run.

Price/Quantity Decisions when Demand Is Unknown

In order to understand the price/quantity strategies of firms in MABMs and compare them with firms' decisions in the standard model, in this "intermezzo" we will keep the basic structure of the Dixit–Stiglitz framework, but will relax the assumption of perfect information as far as market demand is concerned. We will assume instead that, at the moment decisions on price and quantity must be made, the firm *does not know the position of the demand curve* on the price/quantity space.

Uncertainty on market demand may be due to the fact that transactions do not occur at the same time on all markets. There is a *sequence of events* which take place at different times on different markets. For instance, we can envisage the following 4 steps: (1) At the beginning of period t (before the market for C-goods opens), the firm decides the price and the quantity. On the basis of the production plan, it decides whether to hire or fire workers. Suppose the workforce must be expanded to fulfill the production plan. (2) The firm enters the labor market by posting vacancies at a certain wage. These vacancies may or may not be filled depending on the number of matches between demand (job offers) and supply (unemployed workers) of labor. Suppose all the vacancies are filled. (3) The firm can therefore implement the desired production plan. (4) The quantity produced is then sold on the market of C-goods. Production must be decided in step (1) but actual demand will be revealed to the firm only in step (4).

---

[42]In the standard model, labor supply derives from expected lifetime utility maximization when leisure is an argument of the period utility function. It turns out that labor supply is increasing with the real wage. The real wage in the symmetric equilibrium with monopolistic competition is smaller than in perfect competition, because in the latter case the mark-up is zero. Hence full employment with monopolistic competition will be smaller than in the case of perfect competition.

[43]This is the characterization of total output in the equilibrium with *flexible prices* of the standard NK DSGE model.

The information set of the firm at the moment the scale of activity must be decided may contain precise information on the pricing behavior of competitors and the total number of firms but information may be incomplete and imperfect on the price elasticity of demand and/or total households' consumption. In order to maximize expected profits, the firm must estimate the elasticity of demand and total consumption planned by households. The market demand that the ith firm expects is

$$C_{i,t}^e = \left(\frac{P_{i,t}}{P_t}\right)^{-\varepsilon_t^i} \frac{C_t^i}{F_c} \tag{25}$$

where ε_t^i and C_t^i are price elasticity and total consumption expected or estimated by firm i. In order to maximize profits in this informational scenario, the firm could set the price as a mark up over marginal cost, the mark-up being a function of the estimated price elasticity:

$$P_{i,t} = \frac{1 + \mu_t^i}{\alpha} w_t \tag{26}$$

where $\mu_t^i = (\varepsilon_t^i - 1)^{-1}$. Plugging (26) into (25), one gets

$$C_{i,t}^e = \left(\frac{1 + \mu_t^i}{\alpha} \frac{w_t}{P_t}\right)^{-\varepsilon_t^i} \frac{C_t^i}{F_c}. \tag{27}$$

The firm uses expected demand to plan production, $Y_{i,t}^* = C_{i,t}^e$. For the sake of discussion, let's assume that actual production is equal to desired production, $Y_{i,t} = Y_{i,t}^*$. Hence[44]

$$Y_{i,t} = Y_{i,t}^* = C_{i,t}^e = \left(\frac{1 + \mu_t^i}{\alpha} \frac{w_t}{P_t}\right)^{-\varepsilon_t^i} \frac{C_t^i}{F_c}. \tag{28}$$

At the beginning of time t (step (1) in the sequence above) the *status quo* for the ith firm is the point $(P_{i,t}, Y_{i,t})$ on the price/quantity space. The coordinates are determined by (26) and (28). Once production has been carried out, transactions can take place. Once transactions are completed, the ith firm can observe the amount of goods actually sold $Q_{i,t} = \min(Y_{i,t}, C_{i,t})$ where $C_{i,t}$ is *actual* demand.

Since sales occur only after the firm has carried out production, actual demand can differ from current production. If $Q_{i,t} = C_{i,t} < Y_{i,t}$, there will be involuntary inventories whose size is $\Delta_{i,t} = Y_{i,t} - C_{i,t} > 0$. This is a signal of excess supply, i.e., of a positive *forecasting error* (demand has been overestimated).

---

[44]Notice that, in principle, desired production may not always be carried out because there may be constraints on the attainment of planned production. For instance, in step (2) of the sequence above, not all the vacancies may be filled. Therefore, in step (3) the firm cannot implement the desired scale of activity.

If $Q_{i,t} = Y_{i,t} < C_{i,t}$, all the output will be sold and therefore there will not be involuntary inventories, $\Delta_{i,t} = 0$. The difference $Y_{i,t} - C_{i,t} > 0$ measures the demand of unsatisfied consumers, who may turn to other producers (goods are substitutable, albeit only imperfectly) or save involuntarily. This is a signal of excess demand. The firm has made a negative forecasting error (demand has been underestimated).

It can also happen, of course, that demand equals production, $Y_{i,t} = C_{i,t}$. There will be no forecasting error (no inventories and no queues) in this case.

Inventories are defined as

$$\Delta_{i,t} = \min(Y_{i,t} - C_{i,t}, 0). \tag{29}$$

In the case of excess demand or excess supply the firm is underperforming,[45] and has an incentive to choose a different price/quantity in the future, say $(P_{i,t+1}, Y_{i,t+1})$.

One possible strategy consists in setting the *direction* of the change in price and quantity in line with the sign of the forecasting error. For instance, if $\Delta_{i,t} > 0$, the firm has an incentive to scale down production and cut the price. The *size* of the change may be linked to the magnitude of the error.

Notice that by making mistakes the firm collects new information on market conditions. As an alternative strategy, the firm can therefore make new estimates of demand and set the price and the quantity accordingly (see Eqs. (26) and (28)).

In the end, uncertainty and imperfect knowledge induce the firm to *adapt* period by period to evolving market conditions. This adaptation takes the form of price and quantity updating rules. There is no guarantee that this adaptation will lead to the type of equilibrium discussed above.

The Agent-Based Approach to Price/Quantity Decisions

The MABMs we are surveying generally conceive firms as production/trading units immersed in a market environment which is utterly uncertain. Uncertainty is due to the sequential nature of the market economy (which is easily replicated in an agent based framework) and to the ever changing conditions of demand and supply.

Different MABMs deal with price/quantity strategies in different ways. For most of the models we can detect a general pattern, however, in the description of the behavioral rules the firm adopts.[46] The firm starts with an initial pair of price and quantity, $(P_{i,t}, Y_{i,t})$, which we define the *status quo*. At the end of period t, once transactions have been carried out, the firm observes actual sales $Q_{i,t} = \min(Y_{i,t}, C_{i,t})$ and learns also the average price P_t, which is a proxy of the price charged on average by the firms' competitors.

If $Q_{i,t} = C_{i,t} < Y_{i,t}$, there will be an inventory equal to $\Delta_{i,t} = Y_{i,t} - C_{i,t} > 0$. Notice that the firm may want to hold a buffer stock of finished goods (desired or voluntary or target inventories). Desired inventories may be an interval, $\Delta_{i,t} \in [\Delta_{i,t}^m, \Delta_{i,t}^M]$,

---

[45] In other words, the level of profits is smaller than in the optimal position.
[46] As will become clear below, EUBI, EUGE, and KS follow approaches somehow different from this general pattern.

where the extremes are the minimum and maximum levels of desired inventories, or collapse to a single point, $\Delta_{i,t}^*$. In the first case there will be a shortage of inventories if $\Delta_{i,t} < \Delta_{i,t}^m$ and excess (or involuntary) inventories $\Delta_{i,t}^u = \Delta_{i,t} - \Delta_{i,t}^M$ if $\Delta_{i,t} > \Delta_{i,t}^M$. In the second case there will be a shortage of inventories (resp. involuntary inventories) if $\Delta_{i,t} < \Delta_{i,t}^*$ (resp. $\Delta_{i,t} > \Delta_{i,t}^*$). It is reasonable to assume that planned production for period t will take into account expected demand in the same period and desired inventories.

Of course, desired inventories may be zero, $\Delta_{i,t}^* = 0$. In this case, planned production is equal to expected demand, $Y_{i,t} = C_{i,t}^e$, the difference $e_{i,t} = C_{i,t} - Y_{i,t} = C_{i,t} - C_{i,t}^e$ therefore is the forecasting error. A positive inventory will always be involuntary and coincide with the absolute value of the (negative) forecasting error, $e_{i,t} < 0$ and $\Delta_{i,t} = |e_{i,t}| > 0$. If $Q_{i,t} = Y_{i,t} < C_{i,t}$, the forecasting error is positive ($e_{i,t} > 0$), there are no inventories ($\Delta_{i,t} = 0$) but a fringe of unsatisfied consumers.

Desired inventories are generally determined by applying a desired or target *inventory-to-sales ratio* δ^* to current production $\Delta_{i,t}^* = \delta^* Y_{i,t}$. This ratio represents the number of periods of production at the current rate necessary to build desired inventories. Hence the minimum and maximum levels of voluntary inventories are determined as follows: $\Delta_{i,t}^m = \delta_m Y_{i,t}$ and $\Delta_{i,t}^M = \delta_M Y_{i,t}$, $0 < \delta_m < \delta_M$. The parameters δ_m and δ_M are the minimum and the maximum inventory-to-sales ratios. If there are no desired inventories, then $\delta^* = 0$.

The firm receives two types of *signals* of market conditions: (i) an excess or shortage of inventories (with respect to the target, which may be an interval, a positive value or zero); (ii) the relative price, i.e., the ratio or difference between the individual price and average price. From signals of type (i) the firm infers that it has underestimated or overestimated the strength of demand: a shortage of inventories reveals stronger than expected demand; an involuntary inventory signals weaker than expected demand. From signals of type (ii) the firm infers its position relative to competitors: if the firm's price is lower than the average price, the firm is undercutting competitors (and its market share is bigger than the average market share); if the opposite holds true, the good produced by the firm is overpriced with respect to competitors (and its market share is smaller than the average market share).[47] The sign and size of signals determine the *direction* of the price and quantity change to be implemented. The *magnitude* of the price and quantity change is stochastic and/or governed by the signals. The change in price and quantity therefore will be governed by behavioral rules which take the form of updating algorithms.

The most general form of a *quantity updating* algorithm we can detect in the MABMs under scrutiny is

$$Y_{i,t+1}^* = \begin{cases} Y_{i,t}(1 + \eta^y) & \text{if } \Delta_{i,t} < \Delta_{i,t}^m \text{ and } P_{i,t} > P_t, \\ Y_{i,t}(1 - \eta^y) & \text{if } \Delta_{i,t} > \Delta_{i,t}^M \text{ and } P_{i,t} < P_t. \end{cases} \tag{30}$$

---

[47] The average market share is the share of total consumption that each firm would obtain in a situation of symmetry, i.e., $1/F_c$.

In words, the firm revises production plans up (resp. down) by η^y if there is a shortage (resp. excess) of inventories and the current price is greater (resp. smaller) than the competitors' price. The assumption of an upper and a lower bound on the level of desired inventories introduces inertia in quantity updating: if actual inventories fall in the desired interval, the firm does not change the scale of activity.

The most general form of a *price updating* algorithm is

$$
P^*_{i,t+1} = \begin{cases} P_{i,t}(1 + \eta^p) & \text{if } \Delta_{i,t} < \Delta^m_{i,t} \text{ and } P_{i,t} < P_t, \\ P_{i,t}(1 - \eta^p) & \text{if } \Delta_{i,t} > \Delta^M_{i,t} \text{ and } P_{i,t} > P_t. \end{cases} \tag{31}
$$

In words, the firm revises the price up (resp. down) by η^p if there is a shortage (excess) of inventories and the current price is smaller (greater) than the competitors' price.

We will now survey the specifications of these general rules adopted in some of the MABMs under scrutiny. Let's start with a small MABM. **LEN** posits the following quantity updating rule:

$$
Y^*_{i,t+1} = \begin{cases} Y^*_{i,t} + 1 & \text{if } \Delta_{i,t} < \Delta^m_{i,t}, \\ Y^*_{i,t} - 1 & \text{if } \Delta_{i,t} > \Delta^M_{i,t}. \end{cases} \tag{32}
$$

In words, the firm scales up production by one unit if inventories are "too low", i.e., smaller than the minimum. On the other hand, the firm scales down production if inventories are "too high", i.e., greater than the maximum. LEN assumes the firm has a one-to-one technology which uses only labor as input, $Y_{i,t} = N_{i,t}$. Therefore, in order to scale up production by one unit, the firm has to post a vacancy. The firm scales down production by one unit by firing a worker chosen at random in the employed workforce.[48]

The rule (32) is a special case of (30), in which the signal coming from the relative price is ignored. Moreover, the change in quantity is a discrete step of size one.

As to pricing, LEN assumes that the firm wants the actual mark-up $\mu_{i,t} = \frac{P_{i,t}}{MC_{i,t}} - 1$ to fall into a prespecified interval $\mu^m < \mu_{i,t} < \mu^M$ where $0 < \mu_m < \mu_M$. The introduction of an upper and a lower bound on mark-ups mitigates price volatility. In fact, the current price is deemed adequate if $P^m_{i,t} < P_{i,t} < P^M_{i,t}$ where $P^m_{i,t} = (1 + \mu_m)MC_{i,t}$ and $P^M_{i,t} = (1 + \mu_M)MC_{i,t}$ are the minimum and maximum prices. LEN posits the following price updating rule:

$$
P_{i,t+1} = \begin{cases} P_{i,t}(1 + \eta^p) & \text{if } \Delta_{i,t} < \Delta^m_{i,t} \text{ and } P_{i,t} < P^M_{i,t}, \\ P_{i,t}(1 - \eta^p) & \text{if } \Delta_{i,t} > \Delta^M_{i,t} \text{ and } P_{i,t} > P^m_{i,t} \end{cases} \tag{33}
$$

---

[48]LEN introduces an asymmetry in quantity updating by assuming that there are firing costs: the decision to fire is implemented one month after it has been taken. The output response of the firm to an excess of inventories is therefore slower than the response to a shortage of inventories.

where η^p is a random draw from a uniform distribution. In words, the firm raises the posted price if inventories are "too low" provided the current price is smaller than the maximum. On the other hand, the firm cuts the price if inventories are "too high" provided the current price is higher than the minimum. The size of the rate of change is stochastic.

LEN introduces inertia in price changes which may result in stickiness. In fact, there is an interval of values for inventories such that the firm does not change the price.[49]

Expression (33) is a special case of (31), in which the signal coming from the relative price has been replaced by an upper and lower bound on the range of the mark-up (with no reference to the prices charged by the competitors).

In **AGH**, before deciding to enter the market and produce, the firm conducts market research by sending out a message to people who are prospective buyers. This message contains the "normal" posted price $P_{i,t} = (1 + \mu)w_{i,t}$ where $w_{i,t}$ is the posted wage.[50] The mark-up μ is drawn from a uniform distribution.

As in LEN, AGH assume that the firm wants to keep a buffer stock of finished goods. Contrary to LEN, however, the desired size of inventories is unique, $\Delta_{i,t}^* = \delta^* Y_{i,t}$. AGH assume a fairly simple price updating rule:

$$P_{i,t+1} = \begin{cases} P_{i,t}(1 + \eta^p) & \text{if } \Delta_{i,t} < \Delta_{i,t}^*, \\ P_{i,t}(1 - \eta^p) & \text{if } \Delta_{i,t} > \Delta_{i,t}^* \end{cases} \tag{34}$$

where η^p is a random draw from a uniform distribution. Rule (34) is a special case of (31), in which $\delta_m = \delta_M = \delta^*$ and the relative price has no role to play.

The prospective customer (household h) decides to buy if the price posted by firm i is smaller than the price the household previously paid – by purchasing goods at firm j – updated by means of expected inflation, equal to the inflation target of the central bank. In symbols, $P_{j,t-1}(1 + \pi^T) > P_{i,t}$.

Transactions occur in the following way. The household visits two stores, 1 and 2. Consider one of the two, say, store 1, which has inventories $\Delta_{1,t}$. The household can place an order for $C_{1,h,t}$[51] if a cash-in-advance constraint is satisfied, $P_{1,t}C_{1,h,t} < M_{h,t}$ where $M_{h,t}$ are the household's money holdings. The store offers an amount $Y_{1,t} = \min(C_{1,h,t}, \Delta_{1,t})$. Suppose the household previously purchased goods at firm 2. The households decides to buy from firm 1 if $P_{1,t} < P_{2,t-1}(1 + \pi^T)$.

Upon entering the market, according to AGH, the firm sets a target for the labor input $N_{i,t}^*$, which must satisfy the requirement to produce desired output $Y_{i,t}^*$, given the fixed labor input (overhead costs) F and the need to move closer to desired

---

[49]Moreover, LEN assumes Calvo pricing, i.e., in each period a fraction of firms cannot change their price even if the rule (33) would suggest to do so.

[50]Since technology is linear and productivity is normalized to one, w_t is also the average cost.

[51]The amounts $C_{1,h,t}$ and $C_{2,h,t}$ are determined as shown above, in the section on "The Choice of the Goods to Buy."

inventories:

$$N_{i,t}^* = Y_{i,t}^* + F + \lambda_\Delta(\delta^* Y_{i,t}^* - \Delta_{i,t}) \tag{35}$$

where λ_Δ is the inventory adjustment speed.

In **CATS**, firms explore the price-quantity space around their status quo $(P_{i,t}, Y_{i,t})$ in order to maximize profits by adapting to the market environment. For simplicity, in this overview of firms' behavior in CATS, we will assume that planned production can be always carried out, $Y_{i,t}^* = Y_{i,t}$.[52] Notice that desired inventories are zero in this setting, i.e., $\delta^* = 0$.

Once transactions have been carried out, the information set of the firm $\Omega_{i,t} = (P_t, e_{i,t})$ consists of two signals: the average price P_t and the forecasting error $e_{i,t} = C_{i,t} - Y_{i,t}$. These signals capture – albeit imprecisely – the distance between the firm's actual position (the status quo) and the "benchmark", i.e., a situation in which all firms charge the same price and demand equals supply: $P_{i,t} = P_t$ and $Y_{i,t} = C_{i,t}$.[53] There are four cases: (a) $P_{i,t} > P_t, e_{i,t} > 0$; (b) $P_{i,t} < P_t, e_{i,t} > 0$; (c) $P_{i,t} > P_t$, $e_{i,t} < 0$; (d) $P_{i,t} < P_t, e_{i,t} < 0$. On the basis of this information, the firm decides (i) whether to change the price or the quantity in period $t+1$ (with respect to the status quo in period t), (ii) in which *direction*, and (iii) the *size* of such a change.

As to quantity, the firm sets in period t desired production $Y_{i,t+1}^*$ for period $t+1$ at the level of *expected future demand*, i.e., $Y_{i,t+1}^* = C_{i,t+1}^e$. Expectations of future demand are based on the forecasting error $e_{i,t}$. CATS/ADG assume that the firm decides to update the desired scale of activity as follows:

$$Y_{i,t+1}^* = C_{i,t+1}^e = Y_{i,t}(1 + \rho e_{i,t}) \quad \text{if} \quad \begin{cases} e_{i,t} > 0 \text{ and } P_{i,t} > P_t, \\ e_{i,t} < 0 \text{ and } P_{i,t} < P_t \end{cases} \tag{36}$$

where $\rho \in (0, 1)$. The firm revises expected demand (and desired production) up if there is a queue of unsatisfied consumers $(e_{i,t} > 0)$ and the price is higher than the average price (case (a)). The change in the scale of activity is proportional to the size of the error. If the firm's price is smaller than the average price, the firm does not adjust production even in the presence of a queue (case (b)). As we will see below, in case (b) the firm will revise the price up.

The firm revises expected demand and desired production down if $e_{i,t} = -\Delta_{i,t} < 0$ and the price is lower than the average price (case (d)). The decrease in activity in this case is proportional to the level of involuntary inventories, $Y_{i,t+1} - Y_{i,t} = -\rho\Delta_{i,t}$. If $e_{i,t} < 0$ but the price is higher than the average price, on the contrary, the firm will cut the price, keeping the quantity constant (case (c)).

---

[52] Both in CATS/MBU and in CATS/ADG there may be constraints, which prevent the attainment of desired production.

[53] The benchmark coincides with the symmetric equilibrium in a Dixit–Stiglitz setting, in which all firms charge the same price, and each firm produces a fraction $1/F_c$ of total output as shown in the section "The Dixit–Stiglitz Benchmark."

Expression (36) is a special case of (30) with $\eta^y = \rho(C_i - Y_i)$ in case of excess demand and $\eta^y = -\rho\Delta_{i,t}$ in case of excess supply.

This updating rule is based implicitly on an *adaptive scheme* to compute expected future demand, $C^e_{i,t+1} = C^e_{i,t} + \rho(C_{i,t} - C^e_{i,t})$. Recalling that $C^e_{i,t} = Y_{i,t}$, by iterating, it is easy to see that *expected future demand is a weighted average of current and past demand* with exponentially decaying weights:

$$Y_{i,t+1} = C^e_{i,t+1} = \rho \sum_{s=0}^{\infty} (1 - \rho)^s C_{i,t-s}. \tag{37}$$

As to the price, CATS/ADG assume the following updating rule:

$$P_{i,t+1} = \begin{cases} P_{i,t}(1 + \eta^p) & \text{if } e_{i,t} > 0 \text{ and } P_{i,t} < P_t, \\ P_{i,t}(1 - \eta^p) & \text{if } e_{i,t} < 0 \text{ and } P_{i,t} > P_t \end{cases} \tag{38}$$

where $\eta^p \geq 0$ is drawn from a uniform distribution. The firm revises the price up if there is a queue of unsatisfied consumers and the price is lower than the average price (case (b)): an increase of the price will mitigate excess demand for the good in question. If the firm's price is higher than the average price, in the presence of a queue the firm adjusts not the price but quantity (case (a)).

It is easy to see that (38) is a special case of (31) with $\delta^* = 0$.

The firm revises the price down if there is an involuntary inventory and the price is higher than the average price (case (c)): a reduction of the price will boost demand (and will allow increasing the market share). If the firm's price is lower than the average price, in the presence of inventories the firm adjusts not the price but quantity (case (d)).

The mark-up therefore is determined residually by the joint dynamics of the price – governed by the stochastic adjustment mechanism described in (38) – and the average cost, which is determined endogenously.

It is worth noting that once the *direction* of the price change has been decided on the basis of the signals, the *size* of the price change is determined by a random draw. Contrary to the updating rule for the quantity, in the updating rule for the price the size of the adjustment does not depend on the size of the error. In CATS/MBU, there is symmetry in the updating rules because the sizes of both the price and quantity adjustments are stochastic.

In this MABM an (unexpected) upward shift of the demand function (due, for instance, to an increase of total output, which will boost the consumption budget of each and every household) will create a queue and bring about an increase of production if the price is above the average price (case (a)); an increase of the price if the latter is below the average price (case (b)).

Financial factors seem to play no role in the price and quantity decisions of firms. This is not true. First, CATS assume there is a lower bound of the firm's price: the firm will never set the price below the average cost, which consists of operating costs (incurred to hire workers and purchase capital goods) and debt commitments. If interest payments increase, the average cost goes up and this may affect price and quantity decisions.

Second, once the scale of production has been decided, the firm goes to the bank asking for a loan to fill the financing gap (see below, Section 2.4.5). But the bank may refuse to extend a loan of the requested size. In this case the firm is rationed and has to scale down production. In other words, the firm is subject to an *ex post* borrowing constraint.

In a couple of CATS models characterized by a network based financial accelerator, planned production is financially constrained *ex ante*. For instance, Riccetti et al. (2013, 2016b) assume that the firm takes explicitly into account its balance sheet in deciding production. The production function is $Y_{i,t} = K_{i,t}^{\beta}$ where $K_{i,t}$ is the firm's capital stock and $\beta \in (0, 1)$. The firm sets a leverage target $\lambda_{i,t}^{T} t$ where leverage is defined as the ratio of debt (bank loans) to net worth.[54] Hence the target level of debt is $L_{i,t}^{T} = \lambda_{i,t}^{T} E_{i,t}$ where $E_{i,t}$ is net worth. Since $K_{i,t} = L_{i,t}^{T} + E_{i,t}$ by definition, it turns out that

$$Y_{i,t} = \left[(1 + \lambda_{i,t}^{T}) E_{i,t} \right]^{\beta}. \tag{39}$$

In a previous model, Delli Gatti et al. (2010) posit a *financially constrained* output function $Y_{i,t} = E_{i,t}^{\beta}$ which is a special case of Riccetti et al. (2013, 2016b).

In **EUBI**, following the "Management Science" approach, the procedure determining a firm's price and quantity is based on heuristics put forward in the literature on Operations Management and strategic pricing. A given firm (say firm i) in a given period t_0 knows the market size (total consumption expenditure) in the past n periods, i.e., $C_{t_0-\tau} = \sum_{h=1}^{H} C_{h,t_0-\tau}$ for $\tau = 1, 2, \ldots, n$. This means that the firm has a time series of aggregate consumption consisting of n data points. The firm estimates total consumption by simple linear regression, the regressor being time: $C_t^e = \hat{C} + \hat{g}t$ where $\hat{C}$ and $\hat{g}$ are the estimated intercept and slope of the regression line. Hence the estimated current market size will be $C_{t_0}^e = \hat{C} + \hat{g}t_0$ and the future market size at time $t_0 + T$ can be estimated as follows: $C_{t_0+T}^e = \hat{C} + \hat{g}(t_0 + T) = C_{t_0}^e + \hat{g}T$. From this simple statistical exercise, the firm derives a way of updating expectations of aggregate demand for C-goods.

Then the firm adopts a market research procedure to estimate the distribution of demand C_i for different own price levels given the price of competitors. The firm conducts a survey on a sample of consumers[55] asking whether they would buy product i at Z different prices P_z^i, $z = 1, 2, \ldots, Z$, given the prices of the F^i competitors, P_j, $j = 1, 2, \ldots, F_i$. This survey will determine a discrete distribution: each of the Z prices will be associated with the fraction of sampled households who would buy

---

[54]The target leverage is time varying as it is assumed to increase with expected profits.

[55]In the managerial literature this procedure has been labeled as simulated purchase interviews.

the product at that price, say, π_z^i. In this way, the firm determines a cross-section of Z data points, (P_z^i, π_z^i), $z = 1, 2, \ldots, Z$.[56]

Using the Z data points, the firm performs a regression of the fraction of buying households on the price according to the following specification: $\pi^i = \hat{b} \exp(-\hat{a} P^i)$ where $\hat{a}$ and $\hat{b}$ are estimated parameters.[57] Current expected demand is $C_{i,t_0}^e = \hat{b} \exp(-\hat{a} P^i) C_{t_0}^e$ where $C_{t_0}^e = \hat{C} + \hat{g} t_0$.

EUBI assume that the firm adopts an autoregressive model to estimate the future value of the fraction. Therefore the demand curve in period $t_0 + T$ estimated by the firm using data available up to t_0 will be $C_{i,t_0+T}^e = \pi_{t_0+T}^i C_{t_0+T}^e$ where $C_{t_0+T}^e = \hat{C} + \hat{g}(t_0 + T)$.

The firm then uses this estimates to determine its expected profit over a given planning horizon for each price and chooses the price which maximizes this profit.[58] The pricing procedure adopted in EUBI essentially leads to mark-ups determined by the estimated price elasticity of the firm's demand and therefore is well in accordance with standard results on optimal pricing discussed in the beginning of this subsection.

Since demand is uncertain and the firm may incur "stock-out costs" because consumers will switch to competitors if the firm's inventory at a mall is empty, the firm estimates the volatility of demand (standard deviation of the demand distribution denoted by σ_C) and uses this estimate to determine a desired buffer stock.[59] Production therefore must satisfy expected demand for the chosen price and generate a desired inventory:

$$Y_{i,t_0+T}^* = C_{i,t_0+T}^e + q_\chi \sigma_C \tag{40}$$

where q_χ is the χ quantile of the standard normal distribution and $\Delta^* = q_\chi \sigma_C$ are desired inventories.

In **EUGE** the firm estimates future demand using a linear regression on its own past sales. Given inventories, the firm sets the quantity to be produced as follows:

$$Y_{i,t+1} = \begin{cases} 0 & \text{if } C_{i,t+1}^e < \Delta_{i,t}, \\ C_{i,t+1}^e - \Delta_{i,t} & \text{if } C_{i,t+1}^e < \Delta_{i,t}. \end{cases} \tag{41}$$

As to pricing, EUGE assume a standard mark up pricing rule

$$P_{i,t} = (1 + \mu) AC_{i,t} \tag{42}$$

---

[56] The fraction can be determined also by means of the multinomial logit model.

[57] Hence the estimated market share of firm i when it charges the price $P_{z_0}^i$ is $\pi^i | P_{z_0}^i = \hat{b} \exp(-\hat{a} P_{z_0}^i)$.

[58] The level of detail reached in the model is much deeper as there are malls in different regions. Estimates should therefore be carried out at the local level.

[59] Problems of this kind (often referred to as "newsvendor problems") have been treated extensively in the Operations Management literature, which also provides simple decision heuristics to deal with such problems.

where μ is an exogenous mark up (uniform across firms) and $AC_{i,t}$ is a weighted average of the unit cost of current production and past production stocked in inventories. Costs consist of the wage bill, interest payments, and the cost of capital depreciation.

In **KS**, the firm plans production in period t in such a way as to satisfy expected demand $C^e_{i,t+1}$ in period $t+1$ and to generate the desired inventory:

$$Y^*_{i,t+1} = C^e_{i,t+1} + \Delta^*_{i,t+1}. \tag{43}$$

The expectation of future demand $C^e_{i,t+1}$ is generated by past demand on the basis of an adaptive rule such as (37).

As to pricing, KS assume the following mark up pricing rule:

$$P_{i,t} = \left(1 + \mu_{i,t}\right) AC_{i,t} \tag{44}$$

where $AC_{i,t} = \frac{w_t}{A^\tau_j}$ represents unit labor cost; A^τ_j is labor productivity due to use in production of the machine tool purchased at the jth K-firm (see Section 2.4.2).

Whereas in the MABMs reviewed so far the mark-up is either fixed or determined implicitly by the choice of the price, given the average cost, KS posit an *updating rule for the mark-up*:

$$\mu_{i,t} = \mu_{i,t-1} \left(1 + v \frac{f_{i,t-1} - f_{i,t-2}}{f_{i,t-2}}\right) \tag{45}$$

where v is a parameter and f_i is the firm's *market share*. In words, the rate of change of the mark-up between $t-1$ and t is assumed to be proportional to the rate of change of the market share between $t-2$ and $t-1$.

The change in market share, in turn, is governed by the change in *competitiveness* E_i according to a "quasi-replicator dynamics":

$$f_{i,t} = f_{i,t-1} \left(1 + \chi \frac{E_{i,t} - \bar{E}_t}{\bar{E}_t}\right) \tag{46}$$

where $\bar{E}_t = \sum_{n=1}^{F_c} E_{n,t} f_{n,t-1}$ is average competitiveness of C-firms. In words, the rate of change of the market share of firm i is proportional to *relative competitiveness* $\frac{E_{i,t} - \bar{E}_t}{\bar{E}_t}$. If relative competitiveness is positive, i.e., if the ith firm is more competitive than the average, its share increases (and vice versa). In the evolutionary environment of KS models, relative competitiveness is a *selection criterion* as it governs industry dynamics, i.e., expansion, contraction, and extinction of firms.

Finally, $E_{i,t}$ is defined as a decreasing function of the firm's price and of unfilled demand, $E_{i,t} = -\zeta_1 P_{i,t} - \zeta_2 U D_{i,t-1}$. In fact, customers dissatisfied with a firm, which is unable to provide the goods they want to purchase, will switch to competitors. Since $\bar{E}_t$ is a weighted average of the individual measures of competitiveness, it will be a linear function of the average price level P_t and average unfilled demand. In the end therefore, the relative competitiveness of the ith firm is determined by the *relative price* $P_{i,t}/P_t$ and the relative performance in fulfilling demand. It is worth noting, for comparison, that in the Dixit–Stiglitz benchmark, when prices are fully flexible, the mark-up is determined only by price elasticity. In the presence of nominal rigidities, the mark up is anticyclical: in a Calvo setting, when the firm is unable to change the price, a demand boost will make the mark-up shrink.

In **JAMEL** given the capital stock (see Section 2.4.2), $Y_{i,t}$ is proportional to the stock of workers $N_{i,t}$. Changes in production, therefore, require proportional changes in employment obtained by hiring/firing workers. JAMEL assume that there is a maximum level of inventories the firm can hold, which is proportional to the desired level of inventories. The desired level of inventories is $\delta Y_{i,t}$. The maximum level of inventories is $\delta Y_{i,t}(1 + \eta^d)$ where $\eta^d \geq 0$ is a random draw from a uniform distribution. Employment and output decisions are determined by the distance between actual inventories and the maximum level of inventories:

$$Y^*_{i,t+1} = \begin{cases} Y^*_{i,t}(1 + \eta^y) & \text{if } \Delta_{i,t} < \delta Y_{i,t}(1 + \eta^d), \\ Y^*_{i,t}(1 - \eta^y) & \text{if } \Delta_{i,t} > \delta Y_{i,t}(1 + \eta^d) \end{cases} \tag{47}$$

where $\eta^y \geq 0$ is a random draw from a uniform distribution. Pricing follows a similar updating rule, namely

$$P_{i,t+1} = \begin{cases} P_{i,t}(1 + \eta^p) & \text{if } \Delta_{i,t} < \delta Y_{i,t}(1 + \eta^d), \\ P_{i,t}(1 - \eta^p) & \text{if } \Delta_{i,t} > \delta Y_{i,t}(1 + \eta^d) \end{cases} \tag{48}$$

where $\eta^p \geq 0$ is a random draw from a uniform distribution.

In words, the firm scales up production (by posting vacancies) and increases the price if inventories are "too low"; it scales down production by firing workers and cuts the price if inventories are "too high".[60,61]

If desired production is equal to expected demand, $Y^*_{i,t+1} = C^e_{i,t+1}$, and involuntary inventories are a symptom of a forecasting error, the quantity updating rule above can be reinterpreted as follows. The firm revises expected demand up (stochastically) if (i) it has underestimated demand (there are no inventories) or (ii) it has overestimated demand but "not too much"; the firm revises expected demand down if it has overestimated demand by a "large" margin.

In **LAGOM** the firm is assumed to have a moving target for production:

$$Y^*_{i,t+1} = Y^*_{i,t} + f\left(\pi_{i,t}, \Delta_{i,t}, K_{i,t}, C_{i,t}\right) \tag{49}$$

where $f(\cdot)$ is increasing with all the arguments, except inventories. The price is updated using a similar algorithm.

---

[60] In JAMEL the stochastic parameters η^d and η are correlated.

[61] In JAMEL, as in LEN, there is inertia in pricing of the Calvo type. Each firm, in fact, is assumed to be able to set the price every d^p periods. The fraction of firms which are able to set the price per period, therefore is $1/d^p$.

2.4.2 Technology

In **LEN**, production is carried out by means of a one-to-one technology which uses only labor. In **AGH**, capital plays a role only as collateral. Each household supplies one unit of labor of a specific type which is transformed through production in one unit of goods of the same type. The technology in some of the CATS models does not use capital (e.g., CATS/MBU) or does not use labor (Delli Gatti et al., 2005).

In this section we will refer to **CATS/ADG** as a benchmark CATS model with capital. In CATS/ADG the ith firm produces output $Y_{i,t}$ by means of capital $K_{i,t}$ and labor $N_{i,t}$. For simplicity ADG assume a Leontief technology. *In a condition of full capacity utilization* the output will be

$$Y_{i,t} = \min(\alpha N_{i,t}, \kappa K_{i,t}) \tag{50}$$

where α and κ are the productivities of labor and capital, respectively, both exogenous, constant, and uniform across firms. Assuming that labor is always abundant, $Y_{i,t} = \kappa K_{i,t}$. Hence labor requirements at full capacity utilization is $N_{i,t} = \frac{\kappa}{\alpha} K_{i,t}$, where κ/α is the reciprocal of the (given and constant) capital/labor ratio. When capacity is not fully utilized, only a fraction $\omega_{i,t} \in (0, 1)$ of the capital stock will be used in production. Here $\omega_{i,t}$ represents the *rate of capacity utilization*. In this context, the marginal cost of production is constant and independent of the scale of production, $MC_{it} = \frac{w_t}{\alpha} + \frac{r_t}{\kappa}$.

JAMEL posits the same Leontief production function but assumes $\alpha = \kappa$ so that the capital/labor ratio is equal to one. Contrary to CATS/ADG, each firm has a given endowment of capital K (measured in numbers of identical machine tools) which does not depreciate and is not accumulated by means of investment. "Capital" therefore is a nonreproducible and durable input which is available in fixed supply, evenly spread across firms. Hence $Y_{i,t} = \kappa K$ and labor requirement is $N_{i,t} = K$: each machine is operated by a worker. Production takes time. Each machine needs n periods to produce κ units of output. Output is added to inventories of finished goods. As we saw above, there is a desired level of inventories (identical for all firms) $\delta \kappa K$ where δ is the desired inventories-to-output ratio.

LAGOM posit a variant of (50), namely $Y_{i,t} = \min(\alpha N_{i,t}, \kappa K_{i,t}, \kappa^c K_{i,t}^c)$ where $K_{i,t}^c$ is the firm's stock of circulating capital (e.g., raw materials) and κ^c is the productivity of circulating capital. In the production process which takes place in one period, circulating capital is depleted completely while fixed capital and inventories of finished goods depreciate at a constant rate.

In EUBI, as well as in KS, capital goods ("machine tools") are heterogeneous since different *vintages* of machine tools are characterized by different productivities. We will denote with A^v the productivity of a machine tool of vintage v, $v = 1, 2, \ldots, V$.

In **KS** K-firms develop new vintages over time by means of innovation and imitation. The probability for a K-firm to innovate or imitate $\pi_{k,t}^z$ with $z =$ innovate, imitate is assumed to be increasing with its R&D expenditure $RD_{k,t}$:

$$\pi_{k,t}^z = 1 - e^{-\zeta_z RD_{k,t}} \tag{51}$$

where $\pi^z_{k,t}$ is the parameter characterizing the Bernoulli distribution. Notice that R&D expenditure, in turn, is proportional to past sales. Hence the probability to innovate/imitate is driven by high demand coming from C-firms, which in turn is high when households' demand for C-goods is high. The innovating K-firm draws a new machine embodying a technology inducing productivity A^{v+1}_k given by

$$A^{v+1}_k = A^v_k(1 + x^A_{k,t}),\tag{52}$$

where $x^A_{k,t}$ is drawn from a Beta distribution characterized by parameters α_1. Changes in these parameters, and therefore in the shape of the distribution, capture technological opportunities for the economy under scrutiny.

In **EUBI** there is *complementarity* between the productivity of each vintage and the skill composition of the labor force. For each vintage v, the actual productivity of the machine of that vintage employed in production at firm i, denoted with A^v_i, is constrained by the average skill of the workforce, denoted with B_i.[62] In symbols, $A^v_{i,t} = \min(A^v, B_{i,t})$.[63] If $B_{i,t} < A^v$, then $A^v_i = B_{i,t} < A^v$. In words, a machine tool with a built-in "high" productivity will underperform if operated by relatively unskilled workforce.

Technology to produce output with a machine tool of the vth vintage $Y^v_{i,t}$ is represented by a Leontief production function, whose arguments are capital of the same vintage $K^v_{i,t}$ and labor employed with capital of that vintage, which we will denote with $N^v_{i,t}$, $Y^v_{i,t} = A^v_{i,t} \min(K^v_{i,t}, N^v_{i,t})$.[64] For simplicity the capital-to-labor ratio is 1. The complementarity between skill of the workforce and vintage of the machine tool allows anchoring the incentive of the firm to invest in new vintages to the skill of its workforce (see Piva and Vivarelli, 2009). Summing across vintages, one gets the production function

$$Y_{i,t} = \sum_{v=1}^{V} A^v_{i,t} \min(K^v_{i,t}, N^v_{i,t}).\tag{53}$$

We denote with $I^v_{i,t}$ the purchase of a machine tool of vintage v. The firm will choose the vintage on the basis of the ratio of the expected future productivity of each vintage for a firm relative to the price of the machine tool of that vintage P^v_t. When calculating the estimated future productivity of a vintage, $\hat{A}^v_{i,t}$, the firm takes into account that the skills of its workforce will evolve over time and that this evolution is influenced by the vintage the workers are matched with. The probability of selecting

---

[62] B_i is the average skill level at firm i, obtained by averaging across its workers, $B_i = \frac{1}{N_i} \sum_{h=1}^{N_i} B_{h,i}$.

[63] Notice that A_v is constant but B_i is time varying, hence also A^v_i is time varying.

[64] $N^v_{i,t} = N_{i,t} - \sum_{v'=v+1}^{V} K^{v'}_{i,t}$.

a given vintage is then determined by means of the multinomial logit model:

$$P[\text{firm } i \text{ selects vintage } v] = \frac{\exp\left(-\gamma^v \log \frac{\hat{A}_{i,t}^v}{P_t^v}\right)}{\sum_{v=1}^{V} \exp\left(-\gamma^v \log \frac{\hat{A}_{i,t}^v}{P_t^v}\right)} \tag{54}$$

where $\gamma^v > 0$. In EUBI the K-firm sets the price P_t^v using a weighted average between a cost- and value-based pricing component. To determine the value-based component, the firm estimates the expected future productivity of each vintage for a firm with a labor force whose skill profile matches the average profile in the economy.

MABMs considered so far rule out substitutability among inputs (they assume indeed perfect complementarity). An exception to this rule is **EUGE**. The setting is similar to EUBI: there is complementarity between the quality of the capital stock and the skill composition of the labor force. The actual productivity of firm i is determined by the average quality of its capital stock, $A_{i,t}$, and the average skill of the workforce, $B_{i,t}$. EUGE, however, assume that technology to produce output is represented by a Cobb–Douglas production function:

$$Y_{i,t} = \min[A_{i,t}, B_{i,t}] N_{i,t}^\alpha K_{i,t}^{1-\alpha}. \tag{55}$$

Hence inputs are substitutable. While technology in EUBI is characterized by complementarity (i) of skill and vintage and (ii) of labor and capital, in EUGE there is complementarity of skill and quality of capital, but substitutability of labor and capital.

2.4.3 Demand and Supply of Capital Goods

In the market for K-goods (K-market, for short), C-firms are buyers and K-firms are sellers.

Decisions of C-firms concerning capital accumulation have long term effects on the production possibilities of the firm. A few approaches have been proposed to describe and interpret investment decisions in a complex environment in which firms cannot perfectly anticipate future developments on goods and factor markets.

In **LAGOM** firms enter the market for K-goods with demand $K_{i,t}^* = (1/\kappa)Y_{i,t}^* - K_{i,t-1}$ where $Y_{i,t}^*$ is the production target of the firm.

In **CATS/ADG**, in each period the firm decides on capacity utilization and on investment. The two decisions are carried out independently. By assumption, the firm copes with short run oscillations of demand by adjusting capacity utilization (if feasible). Investment, on the contrary, is driven by long run production requirements, as we shall see momentarily.

Let's assume that, on the basis of expected demand, the firm plans in period t to produce $Y_{i,t+1}^*$ in period $t + 1$. In period $t + 1$, the capital stock will be $K_{i,t+1} =$

$K_{i,t}(1 - \delta^r \omega_{i,t}) + I_{i,t}$ where δ^r is the depreciation rate, $\omega_{i,t}$ is the utilization rate, and $I_{i,t}$ is investment decided in period t. There are two scenarios.

If the capital stock is "large", i.e., $Y_{i,t+1}^* < \kappa K_{i,t+1}$, the firm will reach the desired scale of activity by setting capacity utilization at the required level $\omega_{i,t+1}^* = Y_{i,t+1}^* / \kappa K_{i,t+1}$ with $\omega_{i,t+1}^* < 1$.

If, on the contrary, the capital stock is "insufficient", i.e., $Y_{i,t+1}^* > \kappa K_{i,t+1}$, the firm will use machinery and equipment at full capacity but will produce less than desired because its scale of activity is constrained by the available capital stock $K_{i,t+1}$.

Investment decisions in period t are based on the stock of capital the firm has used *on average* until period $t - 1$, computed by means of the following adaptive rule: $\hat{K}_{i,t-1} = \xi \hat{K}_{i,t-2} + (1 - \xi)\omega_{i,t-1} K_{i,t-1}$ where $\xi \in (0, 1)$. By iterating, it is easy to see that $\hat{K}_{i,t-1}$ is a weighted average of past utilized capital with exponentially decaying weights:

$$\hat{K}_{i,t} = (1 - \xi) \sum_{s=0}^{\infty} \xi^s \omega_{i,t-s-1} K_{i,t-s-1}. \tag{56}$$

The history of capacity utilization in the past, therefore, will influence the decision to purchase new capital goods in period t and this decision, in turn, will impact on capacity in the future.

The firm is assumed to have a target *long run capacity utilization* rate ω^T. Therefore the capital desired at the investing stage t for $t + 1$ is $K_{i,t+1}^* = \hat{K}_{i,t-1}/\omega^T$. Investment to replace worn out capital is $\delta^r \hat{K}_{i,t-1}$. Hence total investment will be $I_{i,t} = \left(\frac{1}{\omega^T} + \delta^r\right)\hat{K}_{i,t-1} - K_{i,t}$ where $K_{i,t} = (1 - \delta^r \omega_{i,t-1})K_{i,t-1} + I_{i,t-1}$.

CATS/ADG assume, moreover, that there are *adjustment costs* of the capital stock such that only a fraction of C-firms is capable to purchase new capital goods in each period. Hence the firm has to take into account the fact that investment can be carried out only infrequently. Durability and stickiness imply that the capital stock available for production at the beginning of period $t + 1$ keeps memory of the entire history of the capital stock in the past.

The demand side of the market for K-goods if populated by C-firms. The ith C-firm plans to purchase K-goods in the amount $I_{i,t}$.

Consider now the supply side, which is populated by F_k K-firms. Each K-firm has market power due to transaction costs (e.g., incompleteness of the information set) which force C-firms to visit only a subset of the population of K-firms. The ith C-firm, in fact, does not interact globally with all the producers of machine tools but randomly selects Z_k K-firms, sorts them by selling price and demand capital goods starting from the firm charging the lowest price. K-firms with lower prices, therefore, will get, in principle, higher demand.

At the beginning of time t the kth producer of capital goods ($k = 1, 2, \ldots, F_k$) sets the *status quo* $(P_{k,t}, Y_{k,t})$.

Once production has been carried out[65] and search and matching has taken place, the kth firm observes the amount of K-goods actually sold $Q_{k,t} = \min(Y_{k,t}, J_{k,t})$ where $J_{k,t}$ is actual demand, coming from C-firms which placed orders at firm k.

If production is greater than demand, the firm will pile up an involuntary inventory of unsold goods. Since K-goods are storable, inventories accumulated in period t can be used to satisfy demand in the future. If, on the contrary, demand is greater than production, the firm can satisfy excess demand by depleting inventories carried oven from the past.

K-firms receive two signals like C-firms: the price charged by competitors and the change of inventories or the presence of queues. On the basis of these signals, the firm changes the price or the quantity. Price and quantity updating rules for K-firms are similar to those adopted by C-firms, the major difference being the assumption that machine tools can be stored in warehouses in period t and sold to C-firms in the future.

In **EUBI** the ith C-firm purchases new machine tools if the current capital stock is not sufficient to produce planned output. EUBI define *potential output* as production the firm can carry out in period t using at full capacity the capital stock inherited from the past in the absence of investment, i.e., $\hat{Y}_{i,t} = \sum_{v \in V}(1 - \delta^r)A_{i,t}^v K_{i,t-1}^v$. The investment decision is the outcome of a comparison between potential output and desired output $Y_{i,t}^*$.

If the capital stock inherited from the past is "large", $\hat{Y}_{i,t} > Y_{i,t}^*$, the firm can produce desired output by adjusting capacity utilization and there is no investment. If desired production is greater than potential output, so that the capital stock inherited from the past is "insufficient", the firm expands the capital stock and investment is positive. The size of the investment depends on the vintage v chosen by the firm for the investment in that period (see (54)):

$$I_{i,t}^{v*} = \begin{cases} 0 & \text{if } Y_{i,t}^* \leq \hat{Y}_{i,t}, \\ (Y_{i,t}^* - \hat{Y}_{i,t})/A_{i,t}^v & \text{if } Y_{i,t}^* > \hat{Y}_{i,t}. \end{cases} \tag{57}$$

Due to the flexibility in production due to input substitutability, in **EUGE** the capital-to-labor ratio is a function of the relative costs of the inputs:

$$\frac{K_{i,t}}{N_{i,t}} = \frac{(1-\alpha)\hat{w}_{i,t}}{\alpha c_{i,t}^k} \tag{58}$$

where $\hat{w}_{i,t}$ is the real wage and $c_{i,t}^k$ is the user cost of capital, a function of the real interest rate, the depreciation rate, and the price of K-goods.

Plugging (58) into (55) and rearranging, we get the demand for capital as

$$K_{i,t}^* = \left(\frac{(1-\alpha)\hat{w}_{i,t}}{\alpha c_{i,t}^k}\right)^\alpha \frac{Y_{i,t}^*}{A_{i,t}}. \tag{59}$$

---

[65]For simplicity, K-firms produce machine tools using only labor.

If the current capital stock in the absence of investment is smaller than desired capital, the firm adjusts capacity utilization. If the opposite holds true, the firm purchases new capital goods to bring capital up to the desired size.

K-firms produce and sell tailor-made machine tools to each purchasing C-firm, using only energy and raw materials, imported from abroad. The price of machine tools is a mark-up on energy prices. Since they follow a job production process, K-firms don't have inventories. By construction, moreover, they don't have financing needs.

In **KS**, as in CATS/ADG, for simplicity, K-firms produce machine tools of different vintages using only labor. K-firms send "brochures" to selected C-firms advertising the price and the *quality* of the machine tools they produce. C-firms compare brochures and then choose the machines with the lowest price and unit cost of production and send their orders to the corresponding machine manufacturer. Gross investment of each C-firm is the sum of expansion and replacement investment, where, as above, expansion happens if the desired level of production is higher than what can be produced with the current capital stock.

2.4.4 The Demand for Labor

In LEN, AGH, and JAMEL, quantity decisions translate immediately into hiring/firing decisions. In **LEN**, thanks to the one-to-one technology, vacancies are derived straightforwardly from the quantity adjusting rule. If inventories are "too low", the firm will post a new vacancy to increase production. In symbols, $V^*_{i,t+1} = +1$ if $\Delta_{i,t} < \delta_m Y_{i,t}$. If, on the contrary, inventories are "too high", the firm will fire a worker in order to reduce production, $N_{i,t+1} = N_{i,t} - 1$ if $\Delta_{i,t} > \delta_M Y_{i,t}$.

The firm adjusts the posted wage according to the following rule:

$$w_{i,t+1} = \begin{cases} w_{i,t}(1 + \eta^w) & \text{if } \Delta_{i,t} \leq \delta_0 Y_{i,t}, \\ w_{i,t}(1 - \eta^w) & \text{if } \Delta_{i,t} > \delta_1 Y_{i,t} \end{cases} \tag{60}$$

where $\eta^w \geq 0$ is drawn from a uniform distribution.

In **JAMEL** maximum employment per firm coincides with the capital stock. Hence we can define capacity utilization $\omega_{i,t} = N_{i,t}/K$. JAMEL assume also that there is a target or desired utilization rate ω^T. The firm adjusts the posted wage according to the following rule:

$$w_{i,t+1} = \begin{cases} w_{i,t}(1 + \eta^w) & \text{if } \omega_{i,t} - \omega^T > \tilde{\omega}, \\ w_{i,t}(1 - \eta^w) & \text{if } \omega_{i,t} - \omega^T < \tilde{\omega} \end{cases} \tag{61}$$

where $\eta^w \geq 0$ is drawn from a uniform distribution and $\tilde{\omega}$ is a stochastic cut-off value.

In **AGH** the firm conducts market research before deciding to enter the market and produce by sending out messages to people who are prospective employees. This message contains the posted wage. AGH assume that the wage is set by the firm as

$$w_{i,t} = v_{i,t} w_{i,t-1}(1 + \pi^T) \tag{62}$$

where $v_{i,t}$ is a function of the ratio of desired employment to the workforce, $v_{i,t} = f(N^*_{i,t}/N_{i,t-1})$, and π^T is expected inflation, which is equal to the (time invariant) inflation target of the central bank. AGH assume that the central bank's target for inflation is the anchor agents used in expectation formation.

In most MABMs with capital, the demand for labor is determined by planned production and the size of the capital stock, with limited substitutability between labor and capital. Consider, for instance, **CATS/ADG**. Let's assume that, on the basis of expected demand, the C-firm plans to produce $Y^*_{i,t+1}$ in period $t+1$. Suppose that technology is represented by a Leontief production function (see above). If the capital stock is "large", then $\omega^*_{i,t+1} < 1$. Hence the firm could reach the desired scale of activity by setting capacity utilization at the required level and adjust desired employment accordingly. In symbols, $N^*_{i,t+1} = (1/\alpha)Y^*_{i,t+1} = \omega_{i,t+1}(\kappa/\alpha)K_{i,t+1}$.

If, on the contrary, the capital stock is "insufficient", the firm will use the stock of capital at full capacity ($\omega_{i,t+1} = 1$) and $Y_{i,t+1} = \kappa K_{i,t+1}$ so that desired employment in this case will be $N^*_{i,t+1} = (\kappa/\alpha)K_{i,t+1}$. Hence planned employment will be

$$N^*_{i,t+1} = \omega_{i,t+1}\frac{\kappa}{\alpha}K_{i,t+1} \tag{63}$$

where $0 < \omega_{i,t+1} \leq 1$ and $K_{i,t+1} = (1 - \delta^r\omega_{i,t})K_{i,t} + I_{i,t}$.

In **EUBI** and **EUGE**, if the capital stock is "too low" in a given period, say, $t+1$, investment can be carried out in the same period to overcome bottlenecks in production, also in the short run (see previous section) so that $K_{i,t+1} = (1-\delta^r)K_{i,t} + I_{i,t+1}$.

In **EUBI**, with a Leontief technology, the demand for labor is

$$N^*_{i,t+1} = \frac{\kappa}{\alpha}K_{i,t+1}. \tag{64}$$

The same equation defines the demand for labor in **LAGOM**.

In EUGE, with a Cobb–Douglas technology, the demand for labor is

$$N^*_{i,t+1} = \frac{\alpha c^k_{i,t}}{(1-\alpha)\hat{w}_{i,t}}K_{i,t+1}. \tag{65}$$

Given planned employment $\hat{N}_{i,t+1}$ and actual employment, $N_{i,t}$, at the beginning of period $t+1$ the firm posts vacancies as follows:

$$V^*_{i,t+1} = \max(N^*_{i,t+1} - N_{i,t}, 0). \tag{66}$$

Suppose $N^*_{i,t+1} > N_{i,t}$. In CATS/ADG, a vacancy is filled only if the firm is visited by an unemployed worker. The probability of filling the vacancy depends on the posted wage and on the number of unemployed workers visiting the firm. Thus actual employment $N_{i,t+1}$ may be smaller than desired employment $N^*_{i,t+1}$, the difference between the two being unfilled vacancies. In this case the planned scale of activity will not be reached.

Suppose now $N^*_{i,t+1} < N_{i,t}$, i.e., the number of actual workers exceeds the level of desired employment. In this scenario the firm fires $n_{i,t+1} = N_{i,t} - N^*_{i,t+1}$ workers selected at random. Similarly, in EUBI the actual workforce can differ from planned employment due to search frictions and differences in wages offered by different firms If employment is too high, there is random firing.

Summing up, the firm enjoys full flexibility in adjusting production when production must be scaled down (first scenario) and when output should be increased but "not too much" (i.e., when capacity utilization can be adjusted adequately). When the desired increase in output is sizable the firm hits a capacity constraint.

Actual production may be smaller than desired if the firm does not succeed in achieving the "appropriate" level of capital but also if the firm does not succeed in achieving the "appropriate" level of employment (for instance because of unfilled vacancies) and/or she does not get enough credit.

Consider now K-firms. In CATS/ADG, the kth firm produces output $Y_{k,t}$ by means of a linear technology which uses only labor, $Y_{k,t} = \alpha N_{k,t}$ where α is the productivity of labor, exogenous, constant, and uniform across firms. Desired employment will be $N^*_{i,t+1} = Y^*_{i,t+1}/\alpha$. The firm posts vacancies $V_{k,t+1} = \max(N^*_{k,t+1} - N_{k,t}, 0)$. These vacancies add to those posted by C-firms.

On the labor market C-firms and K-firms are competing for labor services: labor is a homogeneous input. Unemployed workers search for a job visiting Z_e firms (out of a population of F firms) irrespective of the type of goods they produce. In other words, the unemployed worker is indifferent between finding a job at a C-firm or a K-firm.

2.4.5 The Demand for Credit

In most MABMs, the demand for credit comes from the corporate sector only and is determined by the firms' financing needs. Consider a generic firm, say, f (where $f = i, k$), with operating costs $X_{f,t}$ and internal funds $M_{f,t-1}$. If the latter is greater than the former, the firm can finance costs by means of internal funds only. If, on the contrary, costs are greater than internal funds, the firm has a financing gap

$$F_{f,t} = \max(X_{f,t} - M_{f,t-1}, 0), \tag{67}$$

which must be filled by means of a bank loan. The demand for credit, therefore, coincides with the financing gap.[66]

Consider a C-firm. If technology requires only labor, operating costs coincide with the wage bill. Hence the financing gap is $F_{i,t} = \max(w_{i,t}N_{i,t} - M_{i,t-1}, 0)$. This is essentially the demand for credit in **AGH**, **LEN**, and **JAMEL**.[67]

---

[66] In EUGE firms can obtain external finance also in other ways.

[67] In AGH the firm has a financing need already at entry because there are *setup costs* that should be financed.

If the firm employs labor and capital, the firm has to finance also the purchase of new K-goods. For example, in **CATS/ADG** the expenditure on capital goods is $P^K_{t-1}I_{i,t}$ where P^K represents the price index of K-goods.[68]

Consider now a K-firm. If technology requires only labor, the financing gap is $F_{k,t} = \max(w_{k,t}N_{k,t} - M_{k,t-1}, 0)$.

We can posit, therefore, the following general specification of the demand for credit:

$$F_{f,t} = \max(w_{f,t}N_{f,t} + \mathbf{1_k}P^K_{t-1}I_{f,t} - M_{f,t-1}, 0) \tag{68}$$

where $\mathbf{1_k}$ is an indicator function which assumes value 1 if the firm employs capital and labor and 0 if it employs only labor.

2.5 THE BANK

In most MABMs, C-firms demand labor and K-goods in order to produce and sell C-goods to households.

2.5.1 Credit Risk and the Interest Rate

The Benchmark: Financial Frictions

In the most recent literature, a special and crucial role for financial factors in macroeconomic performance stems from the assumption of "financial frictions", i.e., imperfections in the transmission of funds from surplus units (lenders) to deficit units (borrowers).[69] There are essentially three types of financial friction.

Costly State Verification

Building on Bernanke and Gertler (1989, 1990), Bernanke et al. (1999) (BGG hereafter) develop an NK-DSGE model, in which a financial friction arises from *ex post asymmetric information* between borrowers ("entrepreneurs"[70]) and lenders (banks) in the presence of *costly state verification* á la Townsend. Information on the return of investment becomes asymmetric ex post, i.e., after the investment has been carried out. While the entrepreneur can observe the return on investment at zero cost, the bank can ascertain the "true return" only incurring a monitoring cost.

To be more specific, consider the balance sheet of the representative entrepreneur

$$q_t K_t = L_t + E_t \tag{69}$$

---

[68]In CATS/ADG, at the moment of deciding investment in period t the C-firm does not have sufficient information about the prices charged by K-firms (a decision also taken in period t). Therefore, in order to evaluate the financing gap, the firm uses the mean of the prices determined in period $t-1$.

[69]Lenders are generally banks, borrowers are generally firms. These frictions generate a "financial accelerator." Hence financial instability is interpreted as the *amplification* of the macroeconomic effects of a shock in a linear impulse-propagation framework.

[70]In Bernanke et al. (1999), entrepreneurs are firms which purchase K-goods to produce wholesale, homogeneous goods. These goods are sold to "retailers" who differentiate them and sell final goods to households and K-firms.

where K is physical capital (a durable asset), q is the market value of the firm's assets, L is debt towards banks, and E is net worth. Hence $\lambda_t := q_t K_t / E_t$ is leverage.[71] The optimal financial contract between the entrepreneur and the bank in such a setting yields a risk premium, i.e., a wedge between the interest rate on loans and the risk free interest rate, which BGG label the "External Finance Premium" (EFP), $EFP_t = R_L / R$.[72] They show that the EFP is increasing with the borrower's leverage, $EFP_t = \phi(\lambda_t)$ with $\phi' > 0$. In the end, therefore

$$R_t^L = R_t \phi(\lambda_t). \tag{70}$$

In BGG the bank sets (optimally) the interest rate on loans (i.e., the price of credit) as a mark-up over the risk free interest rate, the mark-up being increasing with leverage. At that price all the credit demanded is extended. The quantity of credit is demand-driven.

Costly Enforcement

Kiyotaki and Moore (1997) (KM hereafter) assume that the *human capital* of the producer/borrower is critical to production and "inalienable" á la Hart and Moore. In this setting there is financial friction due to *costly enforcement* of the debt contract: if the borrower "takes the money and runs", the lender cannot replace him with a new producer as producers are not substitutable. In a default scenario the lender is bound to experience a loss. Therefore she will design the debt contract in such a way as to minimize this loss.

The debt contract specifies the interest rate (R^L), the size of the loan (L), maturity (one period), and the provision of collateral (K) on the part of the borrower. Due to costly enforcement, the borrower is subject to a *financing constraint*

$$L_t = \frac{q_{t+1} K_t}{R^L} \tag{71}$$

where L_t is the loan the lender is willing to extend, K_t is a durable asset pledged by the borrower as collateral, which we will identify with "capital",[73] q_{t+1} is the price of capital at maturity, R^L is the interest rate on loans, uniform across agents, given and constant. The financing constraint states that the lender extends a loan in period t of a size such that debt commitments (interest and principal) $R^L L_t$ at maturity, i.e., at time $t + 1$, is equal to the market value of collateral $q_{t+1} K_t$. Thanks to the

---

[71] A more encompassing balance sheet is $M_t + q_t K_t = L_t + E_t$ where M is the firm's liquidity. If the firm produces using only labor, durable assets do not show up in the balance sheet. Liquidity, therefore, of both internal and external origin, is used to finance the wage bill only: $M = wN$ and $L = M - E = wN - E$.

[72] To be precise, the EFP is $EFP = R^K / R$ and the interest rate on loans, R_L, is somehow proportional to the rate of return on capital.

[73] Kiyotaki and Moore (1997) interpret K as land, which is nonreproducible and available in fixed supply. Capital is durable (as land) but also reproducible and in variable supply. However, both capital and land can be used as collateralizable wealth.

financing constraint, if the borrower defaults, at maturity the lender can repossess capital and sell it, earning sales proceeds $q_{t+1} K_t$ exactly equal to the borrower's debt commitments. The lender's loss in case of default therefore is reduced to zero.

Plugging (71) into (69) and rearranging, we get $K_t = \lambda_t E_t$ where $\lambda_t = \left(q_t - \frac{q_{t+1}}{R^L}\right)^{-1}$ is leverage.[74] Hence, leverage is increasing with q_{t+1} but decreasing with q_t and R^L.

In KM the quantity of credit is set by the lender as a proportion of the market value of collateral. The price of credit is exogenous.

If the production function is $Y_t = Y(K_t)$, then the scale of activity of the producer will be constrained by his wealth (net worth):

$$Y_t = Y(\lambda_t E_t). \tag{72}$$

Costly Bankruptcy

Greenwald and Stiglitz (1993) (GS hereafter) shift the burden of *bankruptcy costs* from the lender to the borrower. For GS it is the borrower who incurs the (pecuniary and reputational) costs due to default. These costs are the source of financial friction, which shows up as a wedge between the interest rate on loans as perceived by the borrower and the cost of credit set by the lender.

Consider a generic firm which gets a loan L_t from a bank at the rate R. Debt commitments therefore are RL_t. The firm incurs bankruptcy costs CB_t with probability π_t^d. GS assume that the costs of bankruptcy are increasing with size: $CB_t = c^d Y_t$ where c^d is the (given) cost of default per unit produced. Moreover, they show that when revenues are uncertain, the probability of default is increasing with leverage, $\pi_t^d = \pi(\lambda_t)$, $\pi' > 0$. Hence total costs (the sum of debt commitments and expected bankruptcy costs) are $[R + c^d y^d \pi_t^d]L_t$ where y^d is output per unit of credit. The actual cost of credit (i.e., the interest rate on loans for the borrower) therefore is

$$R_t^L = R + c^d y^d \pi(\lambda_t). \tag{73}$$

The actual cost of credit is the interest rate set by the bank augmented by a risk premium $c^d y^d \pi(\lambda_t)$ borne by the borrower. It is the borrower who perceives the risk of default. In Bernanke et al. (1999), the risk of default is borne by the lender.[75]

---

[74]Leverage is the reciprocal of the "down-payment" in Kiyotaki and Moore (1997). The down-payment is the ratio of equity (internal funds) to the market value of the durable asset the agent wants to hold. For each unit of a durable asset the agent wants to hold (land, capital), the down-payment defines the amount of internal funds the agent has to provide. The size of the loan per unit of asset is provided by the lender as a loan. Hence, the complement to unity of the down-payment is the loan-to-value ratio.

[75]If operating costs are X_t and credit fills the financing gap, then total costs are $[R + c^d y^d \pi(\lambda_t)](X_t - E_t)$. Suppose that, with DRS, $X_t = \frac{x}{2} Y_t^2$. Then the profits are $\Pi_t = Y_t - [R + c^d y^d \pi(\lambda_t)](\frac{x}{2} Y_t^2 - E_t)$. The optimum is $Y_t = ([R + c^d y^d \pi(\lambda_t)]x)^{-1}$. Here output is decreasing with leverage, because otherwise an increase of leverage increases marginal cost. In KM, an increase of leverage boosts output because this makes more credit available per unit of equity and therefore more capital.

The Agent-Based Approach to Interest Rate Setting

In **AGH**, there is a bank in each sector of the economy, loosely defined as a subset of the number of goods. The bank accepts deposits from people in its sector and extend loans to firm owners. Loans are collateralized by inventories and fixed capital (which plays only the role of collateral, it is not an input). If a firm is unable to reimburse debt the bank can repossess all the collateral and the wealth of the firm owner (money and deposits) ("full recourse"). The interest rate on deposits is equal to the interest rate set by the central bank. In many ABMs the interest rate set by the central bank is either fixed or follows a Taylor rule. For instance, in AGH, LAGOM, KS, and EUGE, the interest rate is assumed to follow a standard Taylor rule in the flexible inflation targeting regime

$$r = \max[r^T + \gamma_\pi (\pi - \pi^T) + \gamma_y (y - y^T), 0] \tag{74}$$

where r^T is the target for the "long run" interest rate[76] and π^T, y^T are the targets for inflation and output, respectively. While π^T is fixed, in AGH the target for potential output and the target for the long run interest rate are updated. The interest rate on loans is a fixed markup on this rate, uniform across firms.

In **CATS/ADG** firms demand credit according to their production plans and the resulting financing gaps (as shown above). For simplicity, there is only one bank, which has to decide both the price (interest rate) and the quantity of loans to extend to each firm on the basis of the assessment of the firm's financial fragility proxied by *leverage*.

For each borrowing firm f in each period the bank can compute the *leverage ratio* $\lambda_{f,t}$.[77]

The bank will estimate the relationship between the individual bankruptcy probability $\pi_{f,t}^d$ and the individual leverage $\lambda_{f,t}$ as $\pi_{f,t}^d = \pi(\lambda_{f,t})$. The estimated default probability is an increasing function of leverage.

For simplicity, the bank is assumed to be risk neutral: it will lend to a risky firm inasmuch as the return on lending to that firm is not smaller than the return on investing in an alternative risk free asset which measures the opportunity cost of lending.[78]

Once all the arbitrage opportunities have been exploited, the following equality will hold true: $R_{f,t}(1 - \pi_{f,t}^d) = R$. Hence

$$R_{f,t} = \frac{R}{1 - \pi(\lambda_{f,t})}. \tag{75}$$

From (75) it follows that the interest rate charged by the bank to the fth firm is increasing with the risk free rate and with the firm's leverage. This is a reduced for a BGG type of friction. If the firm goes bankrupt, the equity of the bank will decrease.

---

[76] Natural rate.

[77] To be precise, CATS/ADG use a definition of leverage $\lambda' = \frac{L}{E}$, which is a linear transformation of the one used in this paper and elsewhere in the literature, $\lambda = \frac{L+E}{E}$. In fact, $\lambda = 1 + \lambda'$.

[78] This is the definition of the *participation constraint* for the lender.

Also in **JAMEL** there is only one bank, which accommodates the demand for credit at a fixed interest rate r and maturity d_L (uniform across borrowing firms). If a firm, say, firm i, enters a period of financial distress and becomes unable to validate debt commitments as scheduled, the loan becomes "doubtful" so that the bank raises the interest rate to $r_i > r$ and extends maturity to $d_i > d_L$.

In **EUBI** and **EUGE**, the bank assesses the probability of default as follows:

$$\pi^d_{f,t} = 1 - e^{-\lambda_{f,t}}. \tag{76}$$

The interest rate charged by the bank to the firm therefore is given by

$$R_{f,t} = R + k\pi^d_{f,t} \tag{77}$$

where k is a parameter.

2.5.2 Supply of Loans

In most MABMs, the bank is subject to a regulatory prudential constraint consisting of a minimum "capital requirement" of the Basel type: the bank must have "capital" (net worth) $E_{b,t}$ at least equal to a given fraction of risky assets $RA_{b,t}$. Defining the bank's leverage as $\lambda_{b,t} = RA_{b,t}/E_{b,t}$, the regulatory constraint can be recast in terms of maximum leverage: the bank can hold illiquid (risky) assets up to a maximum equal to a multiple λ^M_b of net worth. In symbols, $RA_{b,t} \leq \lambda^M_b E_{b,t}$ where λ^M_b is the bank's upper bound on bank's leverage set by the regulator.

In AGH, risky assets are $RA_{b,t} = L_{b,t} + K_{b,t}$ where $K_{b,t}$ is the level of seized collateral. The probability for the bank to approve new loan applications is

$$\pi^L_{b,t} = \min\left[k_b \left(\frac{\lambda^M_b E_{b,t}}{L_{b,t} + K_{b,t}} - 1 \right), 1 \right]. \tag{78}$$

The bank will extend loans for sure if $L_{b,t} + K_{b,t} \leq \frac{k_b}{1+k_b}\lambda^M_b E_{b,t}$, i.e., if $\lambda_{b,t} < \lambda^M_b \frac{k_b}{1+k_b}$. When this threshold is achieved, the probability of approving a new loan becomes less than one. It becomes zero when the maximum regulatory requirement is reached, i.e., $\lambda_{b,t} = \lambda^M_b$.

In **CATS/ADG** and **KS**, risky assets coincide with loans. Hence the regulatory constraint boils down to $L_{b,t} \leq \lambda^M_b E_{b,t}$. Suppose the constraint is binding. Hence the maximum amount of credit the bank can extend to all firms/borrowers is constrained by the availability of internal finance:

$$L_{b,t} = \lambda^M_b E_{b,t}. \tag{79}$$

At this point the bank has to allocate credit to each firm. CATS/ADG assume that bank b opens a credit line $\Lambda_{f,t}$ to firm f up to a maximum represented by a fraction $\psi_{f,t}$ of total credit $L_{b,t}$. This fraction is decreasing with the firm's leverage: $\psi_{f,t} = \psi(\lambda_{f,t})$ with $\psi' < 0$. In symbols, $\Lambda_{f,t} = \psi(\lambda_{f,t})L_{b,t}$. KS posit a similar procedure: borrowing firms are ordered in terms of financial fragility, captured by the ratio of net worth to past sales.

If the loan demanded by the firm (i.e., the financing gap $F_{f,t}$) is smaller than the maximum loan the bank is willing to extend (i.e., $\Lambda_{f,t}$), then the bank will accommodate the demand for credit, $L_{f,t} = F_{f,t}$; if, on the contrary, the financing gap is greater than the credit line the bank is willing to extend, the bank will limit credit to the borrower, $L_{f,t} = \Lambda_{f,t}$. In the end therefore,

$$L_{f,t} = \min(F_{f,t}, \Lambda_{f,t}). \tag{80}$$

From the inequality above, given the definition of a financing gap, it follows that an increase of the net worth of the bank and/or of the borrowing firm – so that the firm's leverage and the estimated probability of bankruptcy go down – relaxes the constraint represented by the maximum admissible loan supply and makes credit rationing less likely.

In **EUBI** and **EUGE**, the bank computes the budget available to fund firms as follows:

$$L_{b,t} = \lambda_b^M E_{b,t} - A_{b,t} \tag{81}$$

where $A_{b,t}$ is the sum of risk weighted assets in the bank's portfolio. The bank has to decide now how much credit to extend to each firm. In EUBI, the firm's financing gap is funded completely if the credit risk exposure remains below the budget, while the firm is fully rationed if the loan exceeds this limit.

3 COMPARISON OF EXISTING AGENT-BASED MACROECONOMIC MODELS

Whereas in the previous section we have discussed in some detail several key issues in designing MABMs, the purpose of this section is to provide a more general survey and comparison over several agent-based macroeconomic models, which have been developed during these years. We discuss the variance of the model structure and the behavioral assumptions across the different approaches and examine in how far an established "core" of modeling assumptions has emerged for agent-based macroeconomics. The basis for this discussion are Tables A1 and A2 in Appendix A, which provide a systematic overview of main properties of the eight agent-based macroeconomic models that have already been the basis for the discussion in Section 2.

The different models covered here have been designed and implemented for various research purposes in macroeconomics and with different agendas in mind.

- MABMs, in which *"financial factors"* play a major role in business fluctuations: AGH, CATS, EUGE;
- MABMs, in which *capital accumulation, embodied technical progress*, and *skill dynamics* generate growth, fluctuations, and inequality dynamics: KS, EUBI;

- MABMs with focus on policy analyses, in particular on certain measures in fiscal, monetary or climate policy: KS, EUBI, EUGE, LAGOM;
- MABMs, which capture the effects of learning of agents, social influence, and opinion dynamics: JAMEL;
- MABMs with minimal complexity that are able to reproduce key stylized facts like endogenous business cycles, Phillips and Beveridge curves: LEN.

The presentation of the models in Tables A1 and A2, as well as our discussion of the similarities and differences between the different models, is structured along eight broad categories covering different aspects of the setup of the models and their main output. As observed in Section 2, in terms of the general model structures, we observe that almost all share the same set of types of agents (households, C-firms, K-firms, banks, policy makers) and considered markets (consumption goods, capital, labor, credit, stocks) except for LEN, which does not include physical capital, credit, and banks in the model, and AGH, which also abstracts from physical capital accumulation. Recent literature on agent-based macroeconomics has stressed the importance of the concept of stock-flow consistency for models of this type (e.g., Caiani et al., 2016a). Stock-flow consistency entails that the model is closed in a sense that for any transaction the (real and financial) flows of all involved agents sum up to zero, such that there are no (hidden) inflows or outflows. This can be most easily ensured if the model encompasses explicit balance sheets for all agents, but only a fraction of the MABMs have these properties, and therefore it is not straightforward to verify this property if it is not directly reported by the authors.

In terms of other general properties, it becomes clear that in most MABMs expectations are mainly considered with respect to the future development of firm demand, whereas expectation formation of households about future income or economic developments is often not considered. The employed expectation rules are in most MABMs naive or linear forecasts. An exception in this respect is JAMEL, which models the dynamics of household expectations driven by evolving sentiments in the population. In term of agent demographics, the considered MABMs do not incorporate an evolving age structure of individuals and keep the number of agents of different types constant over time. Firm entry occurs in most models only after a firm has exited the market and thereby is essentially a replacement of the exiting firm (with different firm characteristics and equity). Only the AGH model captures, in a rather sophisticated way, the market entry of firms and the associated decisions of potential entrants as well as financial transactions. A simple endogenous firm entry process, in which the (stochastic) number of entrants in a sector depends positively on the number of incumbents in the industry, as well as on the sectoral ratio between firms' liquid assets and debt, has also been incorporated in a recent version of the KS model (see Dosi et al., 2017b). Although the possibility to consider spatial structures and (emerging) heterogeneities of distributions of agents characteristics across regions arguably is a merit of the agent-based modeling approach most of the models so far have not considered multiregional settings. Exceptions in this respect are EUBI and LAGOM, which have been used for numerous analyses of economies with multiple regions or countries. Recently, also multicountry versions of the KS (Dosi et al., 2017d) and the EUGE model (Petrovic et al., 2017) have been put forward and Caiani et al. (2017) have developed a stock-flow consistent multicountry model to analyze different fiscal regimes in a currency union.

Considering the consumption goods market, the focus of the different models, in particular whether they aim to explain endogenously economic growth and technological change, shows clearly in the way the production process is covered. Whereas KS and EUBI incorporate vintage structured capital goods and endogenous vintage choices of firms, the other MABMs consider capital with homogeneous productivity,[79] which is typically combined in fixed proportion with labor to produce the consumption good. As discussed in the previous section, assuming mark-up pricing is most common, where the mark-up is typically adjusted over time based on the firms' market share or its inventory level (relative to expected demand). Only EUBI features a different approach in which firms explicitly estimate the form of the demand function they are facing. Quantity choices in most models are determined by the expected demand (typically adjusted by a security buffer and the current stock of inventory), in JAMEL and LEN the output quantity is determined by the size of the labor force, which, however, is adjusted over time based on the relationship between expected demand and inventory.

The size of the physical investment of consumption good firms is in most models simply derived from the potential need of expansion due to the current production plan. In these investment rules long run planning has no effect on the investment patterns, which is arguable rather myopic, since the acquired physical capital will be available for the firm for an extended period of time. An exception in this respect is CATS, where investment is based on a target level of capital, which is calculated from past capital requirement over an extended time interval. Whereas this rule seems less myopic, it still does not involve any explicitly forward looking planning of the firm. Harting (2015) has developed an extension of the EUBI model, in which investment is determined in a forward looking way using a real-option approach. Also, in most MABMs the firm's demand for inputs (capital and labor) are dictated by the decision on the scale of activity, which is typically driven by observed past demand for the goods produced by the firm. Potential changes in the price of the different inputs do not play any allocative role. For instance, the demand for capital (labor) by a C-firm is determined by the expected sales of the firm, which in turn is determined by the (past) consumer's demand. Changes in the price of capital (labor) hence do not enter the considerations determining the current demand for these inputs. Exceptions in this respect are EUBI, where the estimated unit costs of production, which are determined by input prices, influence price, and quantity decisions, and EUGE, where, although input prices do not influence the planned production level, they determine the desired capital-to-labor ratio.

With respect to the determination of the households' consumption budget, (piecewise) linear rules based on the wealth and income have emerged as the dominant

---

[79] In the version of EUGE in Raberto et al. (2018), capital is differentiated with respect to its energy efficiency.

choice in the design of MABMs. In particular, a large fraction of model relies on buffer stock rules put forward in Carroll and Summers (1991), which also have strong empirical and theoretical foundations. Also the matching between households and consumption good producers is modeled in similar ways across the considered models, in which explicit protocols for this matching procedure are given. Consumers observe the prices of a randomly selected subset of consumption good producers and then select (with high probability) the cheapest ones. If they cannot purchase the full amount they demand, households move to the next best option, and so on. A different approach in this respect is chosen in AGH, where customers have evolving networks of stores to which they have relations and then buy from these firms in a way to maximize their utility.

The capital good markets in the considered MABMs typically have a much simpler structure than the consumption goods markets, since it is usually assumed that there is no explicit quantity choice of producers who simply produce based on orders they have received. Also, apart from the KS and the CATS model, no competition between capital good producers is considered. With respect to pricing there is a large heterogeneity of the considered pricing rules including fixed mark-up rules, prices based on anticipated value of the capital good for consumption good producers and pricing rules based on expected demand and inventory similar to approaches used for the consumption good market. In the EUBI and the KS model, endogenously evolving sets of multiple vintages of capital goods are considered. Whereas in the EUBI model new vintages emerge randomly, the KS model incorporates an explicit representation of the innovation activities in the capital goods sector such that the probability of a firm to innovate depends on its R&D investments.

Also with respect to the interactions on the labor market there is considerable uniformity across the MABMs. Labor demand is derived from the planned output, and with the exception of Dosi et al. (2017b, 2017c) none of the considered models explicitly captures inertia in the adjustment of the stock of workers that might, for example, be driven by labor market regulations or labor contract durations.[80] The majority of MABMs relies on random search of job-seekers in combination with posted wages of firms having vacancies, where posted wages are adjusted if the searching firms are unable to fill their vacancies. In several MABMs (EUBI, EUGE, KS, LAGOM) wages are also adjusted according to the evolution of labor productivity. In EUBI and EUGE the productivity of a worker is strongly influenced by her skills, which evolve endogenously over time. No such skill differentiation is present in the other (standard) models although a recent version of the KS model also exhibits heterogeneous and endogenously evolving skills of workers (Dosi et al., 2017b). Furthermore, dynamically adjusting reservation wages, which rely mainly on the worker's current (wage or unemployment) income, determine in several of the models, whether workers accept the jobs with the posted wages.

---

[80]Frictions of such type have been considered; however, in Goudet et al. (2015) in the framework of an agent-based labor market model.

External financing of firms is in all considered models, with the exception of EUGE, restricted to bank loans. With respect to the interest rate the banks charge to firms, the majority of MABMs follows an approach where a mark-up, whose size depends on the borrowers leverage and riskiness, is applied to the Central Bank interest rate. On the other hand, there is substantial heterogeneity across the models with respect to possible rationing of firms on the credit market. Whereas in some MABMs all credit demands are satisfied (JAMEL, LAGOM), others introduce probabilities of loan approvals (AGH, CATS) or assume (regulatory) upper bounds on the volume of credit a bank can grant (EUBI, EUGE, KS). A common feature of the credit market in combination with the investment rules in the considered models is that firms do not take into account the induced interest payments when deciding on their output and investment targets, although the amount of credit they need influences their financial standing and thereby their interest rate and size of interest payments. Hence, the impact of the central bank base rate and of the shape of the interest rule the banks use typically is weak in these models. With exception of the Eurace models, none of the MABMs includes a stock market. Also in EUBI only a minimalistic stock market is considered in which an index share, containing all firms in the economy, is traded. EUGE incorporates a more complex stock market in which different shares are traded.

Only a subset of the considered models assigns an active role to the government, and also in these models government activity essentially reduces to collecting income and profit taxes in order to be able to pay out unemployment benefits and potentially implement additional fiscal policy measures, like paying out firm subsidies. In all these models, tax rates are dynamically adjusted over time to fulfill a balanced budget or a target debt to GDP ratio. Different variations of the Taylor rule are the dominant choice to determine the central bank interest rate; however, in several of the MABMs the interest rule is also treated as fixed model parameter.

This brief discussion highlights that in spite of the heterogeneity with respect to the agenda and objective of the different MABMs a consensus has emerged in the MABM community about a number of key features of behavioral rules and interaction protocols. A similar statement can certainly be made about empirical validation of the models. The reproduction of stylized facts has become a standard way to show that the developed MABMs are able to capture important economic mechanisms that are responsible for business cycle properties and distributional characteristics in real economies. As Tables A1 and A2 clearly show, many of the MABMs have been very successful in qualitatively matching stylized facts on different levels of aggregation, combining the reproduction of average levels of key variables with time series properties and distributional patterns. Clearly, this point is one of the perceived main strengths of the agent-based approach in (macro)economics, although it has to be observed that clear quantifiable standards for what is exactly meant by the "reproduction" of a stylized fact is so far missing. The last few years have seen a significant increase in the work trying to quantify the quality of the match between simulation output generated by agent-based models and empirical data (e.g., Guerini and Moneta, 2017; Barde, 2017), as well as approaches for systematic estimation of agent-based models in Economics (e.g., Grazzini et al., 2017). This work is discussed in more detail in the chapter by Lux and Zwinkels (2018) in this handbook, and we refrain from a detailed treatment here.

4 POLICY ANALYSIS

Early work in agent-based macroeconomics, as well as in agent-based studies of individual markets, was mainly concerned with showing that agent-based models are able to capture important empirical features of real world economic dynamics and with exploring implications of different assumptions about individual behavior and interaction schemes. The last ten years, however, have seen a considerable increase in agent-based work with a policy focus. Several reasons might have contributed to this development. First, the financial and economic crisis unfolding after 2008 highlighted the need of building policy analyses on models capable of capturing mechanisms, which are potentially responsible for the outbreak of crises, as well as describing economic dynamics far away from an equilibrium state. In particular, the interplay between real and financial markets, contagion effects, dynamic expectation formation, and similar issues came to the forefront of attention for policy makers, and clearly agent-based models are well suited to deal with these issues. Second, the work in agent-based macroeconomics has seen some consolidation in the sense that a number of models (many of them have been discussed in the previous sections) have been systematically developed and improved over a considerable time span. Improved confidence in the ability of these models to capture key economic mechanisms, e.g., by building on their ability to reproduce a wide range of stylized facts, has also made them a more reliable basis for policy analysis. Some of these models have been developed into something like "workhorse" models for policy analysis and have been used for the exploration of the effects of policies in a diverse range of domains. Third, the accumulating evidence in Experimental and Behavioral Economics that individual behavior is often not determined by (intertemporal) optimization and rational expectations has generated increasing attention in macroeconomics for studying learning and adaptive expectation formation and for investigating policy effects in models capturing these phenomena. Several of the agent-based contribution to the policy literature are addressing this point.

Apart from these developments, several other well-known properties of the agent-based approach models seem particularly useful in the context of policy analyses. This includes the ability to distinguish explicitly between short-, medium-, and long-run effects of policies, as well as to capture potential path dependencies and hysteresis effects triggered by policies. Furthermore, the fact that agent-based models are designed to represent the evolution and emergence of heterogeneities of different kinds makes them well suited to generate insights about the implications of different policies for the distribution of key economic indicators and therefore also for studying inequality in the economy.

In the following subsections we briefly review agent-based policy analysis in different key policy domains. We have decided to organize the discussion of existing policy studies in this way although several of the covered papers combine the analysis of different types of policy measures, as well as their interaction, in a unified framework. Hence, several papers will appear in more than one of the following subsections. Having discussed several contributions in different policy areas, we will conclude this section with some general comments about how agent-based policy analyses have developed over the last decade.

It should be stressed that we restrict our coverage to contributions which analyze policy effects in the framework of macroeconomic models. For several of the policy domains covered there is also a very active agent-based literature relying on partial models, e.g., addressing issues of systemic risk. Furthermore, also in some areas outside the domains, which are covered in the following sections, policy related work using an agent-based approach has been done. This includes in particular the area of environmental and climate policy, where some recent contributions develop integrated assessment models linking the approaches developed in agent-based macroeconomics with some climate module capturing dynamics and effects of climate change. These models seem to have high potential for the analysis of different types of climate-relevant policies. A survey over this emerging literature can be found in Balint et al. (2017).

4.1 FISCAL POLICY

An early analysis of fiscal policy effects in the framework of an agent-based macromodel is carried out in Russo et al. (2007). The main agenda of this paper is to compare the effect of demand oriented versus technology oriented fiscal measures in the presence of endogenous technological change. A simple macroeconomic model containing only goods and labor markets is considered with random matching protocols on both markets (incorporating loyalty effects on the labor market) and simple adaptive behavioral rules governing price and wage adjustment. Production technology is linear with labor as the single input and the firm-specific labor productivity stochastically evolves over time where the expected increase depends on the firm's R&D investment. Since it is assumed that firms invest a fixed fraction of their profits in R&D, the model exhibits a positive relationship between firm sales and the speed of technological change.

After the discussion of emergent properties of the model and of several empirical stylized facts it is able to reproduce, Russo et al. (2007) focus on a computational experiment aimed at exploring the qualitative consequences of alternative fiscal policies. In particular, they consider two scenarios in which a public agency introduces a (flat) tax rate on firms' profits. In the first scenario these tax revenues are paid out as unemployment benefits, whereas in the second scenario they are redistributed to firms on a per-capita basis increasing their R&D expenditures. The simulations show a strongly diverging effect of the tax on the average growth rate in these two scenarios. In the first scenario, in which the tax is used to boost demand, the effect on growth is clearly negative and becoming stronger the higher the tax rate. In the technology oriented scenario, a positive effect on growth is detected, which grows with the tax rate as long as the rate stays below an upper threshold. These results show that in the considered setting the multiplier generated by higher demand is not sufficiently large to outweigh the direct negative effects of the tax on R&D spending, which hinges on after-tax profits. The main driver of the positive effect of a technology oriented redistributive tax policy seems to be the intensification of R&D activities per se rather than the redistribution between firms. This is demonstrated by comparing the effect of an increase in tax rate with a scenario without the tax in which firms increase their R&D rates by the same amount. It is shown that the growth rate in the second scenario, referred to as private R&D scenario, is always above that in a corresponding public R&D scenario, in which R&D is entirely financed through the tax. This suggests that the tax per se has a negative effect on economic performance. The question whether it is needed to induce the desirable level of R&D expenditures cannot be addressed in the considered setting since the R&D rate is a given exogenous parameter rather than an endogenous result of firms' decision making.

Whereas in Russo et al. (2007) the positive effects of fiscal policy measures are rather limited, most of the following agent-based fiscal policy analyses come to much more positive conclusions about the effectiveness of fiscal measures, both with respect to fostering growth and to reducing business cycle fluctuations. Haber (2008) uses the agent-based macroeconomic model "AS1", incorporating geographical structure, evolving product ranges, a rather sophisticated banking sector, and explicit expectation formation processes, to analyze the effect of an expansionary fiscal policy on key economic indicators. In particular, the implications of a reduction of the tax rate on income and firm profits is studied. It is shown that such a reduction leads to an increase in economic growth, as well as a reduction in unemployment and increase in inflation. Using the fact that the model can capture a variety of different expectation formation rules, Haber (2008) also demonstrates that the positive effect of the fiscal expansion is reduced if the agents employ more sophisticated foresight mechanisms. In any case, the reduction of the tax rate induces a higher level of public debt, which in the framework of the model is covered through bank credit.

The potential growth enhancing effect of an expansionary fiscal policy has also been an important theme in the analysis of fiscal measures in the framework of the "Keynes meeting Schumpeter" (KS) model. In Dosi et al. (2010) the effects of a rise in the level of unemployment benefits financed by an increase of the tax rate on firm profits is studied. It is shown that increasing the rate of unemployment subsidies relative to wages (and therefore also the tax rate) from zero to a positive level has a significant positive effect on the growth rate of productivity and output, where the actual size of the positive rate has only little influence. The authors explain this observation in a way that in the absence of unemployment subsidies the low demand negatively affects firms' R&D investment and thereby also negatively affects productivity growth leading to a vicious cycle associated with low growth and strong fluctuations. A minimal level of fiscal stimulation is needed to avoid such a low growth scenario and to allow the economy to fully exploit the technological opportunities for productivity growth arising in the considered framework. Whereas the level of a positive unemployment and tax rate hardly affects the speed of growth, increasing these rates leads to reduced output volatility and reduced unemployment. This analysis is extended in Dosi et al. (2013), where it is shown that the positive effects of such a fiscal policy, which redistributes firm profits to households, is larger the more market power the firms have. More precisely, the authors establish that the reduction in volatility and unemployment induced by higher unemployment subsidies and tax rates is more pronounced if firms charge a high price mark-up on consumption goods. If mark-ups are so low that the economy is persistently in (almost) full employment an increase in the unemployment subsidy/tax rate yields an increase of growth rate volatility. These observations reinforce that in the framework of this model the main role of the considered fiscal measures is to channel funds from firm savings to households, where it stimulates demand. The authors stress that their results highlight the importance of the interactions between income distribution regimes and redistributive fiscal policies.

The observation in Dosi et al. (2010, 2013) that fiscal measures can reduce economic fluctuations illustrates a theme that has been an important motivation of numerous agent-based studies of fiscal policy, namely that this type of policy models are well suited to examine the mechanisms by which fiscal policies might trigger or avoid crises and to explore potential fiscal policy responses to crises once they have emerged. In Dosi et al. (2015) the dynamics of the KS model in the benchmark case with constant unemployment subsidy/tax rate is compared to scenarios in which these rates are adjusted according to rules resembling the European Stability and Growth Pact (SGP) and the European Fiscal Compact (FC). In particular, under these rules the level of unemployment subsidies is reduced if the deficit is above 3% of GDP, in case of SGP, or, in case of FC, public expenditures have to be cut also if public debt exceeds the target of 60% of GDP. For both types of rule also an adjusted version with escape clause is considered, in which these constraints do not apply in periods in which the growth rate is negative. The simulation results clearly indicate that compared to the benchmark both rules without escape clauses have significant and large negative effects on growth and employment. Furthermore, they strongly increase output volatility and the likelihood of economic crises. Due to these negative implications for the level of economic activity in the framework of this model, the considered rules even induce exploding dynamics of public debt to GDP ratios. In the presence of escape clauses the negative implications of these fiscal rules are much weaker, however, with the exception of the effects on the growth rate, still significant. The authors conclude from these observations that an unconstrained fiscal policy allowing automatic stabilizers is needed to dampen economic fluctuations and to reduce the likelihood of crises. They also discuss the interplay of such a policy with different variants of monetary policies (see Section 4.2).

The results of Dosi et al. (2015) that fiscal contraction in bad times yields negative implications for recovery and growth is consistent with evidence presented in the framework of other agent-based macroeconomic models. A study closely related to that of Dosi et al. (2015) is carried out by Teglio et al. (2018) in the framework of the Eurace simulator (EUGE). They also consider the effects of fiscal rules, corresponding in a stylized way to the European Stability and Growth Pact (SGP) and the European Fiscal Compact (FC), and combine them with an escape clause and a "fiscal accommodation" (reduction of tax rates during crises), as well as with quantitative easing by the central bank. Similar to Dosi et al. (2015) they find that applying escape clauses and fiscal accommodation both to the SGP and the FC reduces the probability of depressions and increases average growth rates. Napoletano et al. (2015) study in the framework of a simple endowment economy with a credit market the effectiveness of different fiscal policies in the aftermath of a (household) bankruptcy shock. They show that a deficit-spending rule is able to reduce the negative impact of the bankruptcy shock on the economy and to favor a fast recovery from the recession more effectively than balanced-budget policies. Furthermore, the size of the fiscal multiplier is time-varying and is largest in the downturn several periods after the shock. Neveu (2013) uses a model, which in structure is similar to that of Russo et al. (2007), however, with a slightly different fiscal setup. Fiscal revenues are generated by a combination of a corporate profit tax and a progressive income tax and are spent partly on unemployment benefits and partly on R&D subsidies for firms, which are distributed across firms proportionally to last period profits. Three fiscal rules are considered, in which special measures are activated once the economy contracts for four successive periods: (i) fiscal spending is increased while the tax rate is kept constant; (ii) spending and taxes are cut such that a balanced budget is maintained; (iii) the tax rate is reduced while spending is kept constant. Under the first and the third rule, public debt is accumulated during downturns, and during growth periods taxes are adjusted to repay this debt. It turns out that all three rules have no significant effect on average growth or unemployment, however, differently from rules (i) and (ii) the third rule reduces the number of long downturns significantly and substantially. Hence, a debt financed stimulation of demand and R&D during bad times helps to avoid long and deep recessions without negatively affecting growth perspectives even if the debt accumulated during downturns is repaid during growth periods.

Similarly to Neveu (2013), also Harting (2015) studies the implications of different fiscal responses to downturns on the growth rate and volatility of the economy. In the framework of an extended version of the Eurace@Unibi model (EUBI), the following three scenarios are compared, where in each a special fiscal policy is activated once the growth rate of output drops below a given threshold. In the first scenario households receive a direct fiscal transfer, thereby increasing their consumption budget, in the second scenario all firms receive subsidies on any investment they make, whereas in the third scenario subsidies are paid out only to firms investing in the best available vintage of the capital good. Since in the Eurace@Unibi model the vintage choice of firms is determined by the comparison of the ratio of expected future return to price of each vintage, the third rule influences the technology choice of firms and fosters the acquisition of frontier vintages. Main insights from the analysis in Harting (2015) are that all three policies are able to reduce the volatility in the economic dynamics. However, in order to achieve the same reduction of volatility, the demand oriented first measure requires substantially larger fiscal expenditures during the downturns than the other two technology oriented rules. Furthermore, the three rules differ substantially with respect to their growth effects. No such effects are induced by the second measure, i.e., the payout of subsidies to all investing firms. The other two rules have positive growth effects and these effects are much stronger if the third rule is used, in which only firm investment in frontier technology is subsidized. These results imply that the facilitation of diffusion of new technologies in the economy is the main driver of the positive effects of these policies.

While the papers reviewed in the previous paragraphs have focused on the role of fiscal policy measure as automatic stabilizers and as instruments to prevent crises and economic fluctuations, Dawid et al. (2018c) examine which types of fiscal measures are most effective in fostering recovery and growth in a region which is in an economic crisis. The agenda of the paper is motivated by the developments associated with the public debt crises in southern European countries unfolding after 2010. This paper uses a two-region version of the Eurace@Unibi (EUBI) model and considers a scenario where the two regions are in an economic union with integrated consumption and capital goods markets but differ substantially with respect to size as well as the technological level of firms and the (specific) skill endowment of workers. In particular, a scenario is considered in which the smaller and technologically lagging region has accumulated so much public debt that it no longer has access to the credit market. Without any fiscal transfers from the larger and faster growing region this situation would lead to a rigorous decline in output and consumption in the small region. The paper compares the effects of different union-wide financed fiscal transfer schemes to the crisis region and shows that technology oriented subsidy policies, which are able to positively influence the technology choice of firms in the lagging region is the only option to foster long-run catch-up of the that region. The effect of this policy becomes significant only after a considerable delay, whereas measures strengthening demand in the lagging region have a positive short-run effect on consumption in that region, however, with little positive impact on production and productivity. A policy in which only the debt burden of the lagging region is taken over by the union has no significant positive effect on the economic dynamics in that region. The paper shows that under none of the considered policy measures the larger and stronger region in the union, which covers the majority of the fiscal expenditures, experiences significant negative effects on consumption or production.

4.2 MONETARY POLICY

A strong focus of agent-based work with a policy orientation has also been on monetary policy issues and the optimal design of regulatory schemes for banks and the financial market. We will survey contributions concentrating on regulatory issues in the next subsection and concentrate here on studies of classical monetary policy instruments, in particular interest rate rules.

Dosi et al. (2013) study the implications of a variation of the (constant) central bank interest rate in the framework of the KS model. In their setting a variation of the interest rate in the range between 0% and 10% essentially has no impact on the level or on the fluctuations of growth rates. Only as the rate is increased beyond this level to some value, which depends on the firms' market power, a strong negative impact on the growth rate associated with increasing fluctuations emerges. For sufficiently high levels of firm mark-up such negative impact of interest rate increases is, however, avoided. The intuition underlying these results is that the interest rate negatively affects growth performance mainly by increasing the danger of firm bankruptcies, which destabilize the economy, and by reducing the frequency of full employment states. Under sufficiently high mark-ups the risk of bankruptcies is negligible and hardly affected by the interest rate. Hence the effect of interest rate hikes are very minor.

While Dosi et al. (2013) assume a fixed central bank interest rate, the majority of contributions rely on variations of the Taylor rule to model the central bank's interest rate policy. Raberto et al. (2008) demonstrate that a simple output gap oriented interest rule, at least if it is sufficiently strong, leads to better economic performance in terms of output and worker utility compared to a random interest rule. In a related work, Delli Gatti and Desiderio (2015) compare the performance of an economy under a fixed central bank rate and an output and inflation oriented Taylor rule in the aftermath of a negative productivity shock. They show that with a Taylor rule the decrease in output is much weaker and the price level stays lower compared to the fixed interest scenario. The main positive effect of the Taylor rule in this setting is that it helps to keep the firms' credit demand and liquidity higher than under a fixed central bank rate. Ashraf et al. (2016) consider in the framework of the AGH model a Taylor rule based on inflation and output gap and study the implications of a variation of the central bank's (fixed) inflation target on output, inflation, and volatility. Quite in accordance with the insights in Dosi et al. (2013), they find that increasing the inflation target above a certain threshold leads to a deterioration of output and an increase in volatility. The interpretation of Ashraf et al. (2016) for these results is that a large inflation target induces a large dispersion of relative prices increasing the frictions on the goods market and thereby the bankruptcy risk of sellers.

Several agent-based studies have explored how changes in the set of target variables as well as in the values of the reaction coefficients in the Taylor rule affect the emerging economic dynamics and also how these effects depend on various properties of the considered economy. Dosi et al. (2015) compare the economic dynamics emerging in the KS model if the central bank targets only inflation with that under a Taylor rule with dual mandate reacting to inflation and unemployment. They find that the dual mandate rule significantly increases the growth rate in the economy and that the positive growth effect is particularly strong if a restrictive fiscal policy is in place. This growth effect also is associated with a reduction in unemployment. Furthermore, the dual mandate leads to less GDP volatility compared to a purely inflation oriented monetary policy. The authors explain the positive effect of the dual mandate rule by a better performance of the banking sector, reducing the rate of bank failures and increases the number of investment projects that are financed and implemented.

Contributions by Krug (2015) and Chiarella and Di Guilmi (2017) use different agent-based macroeconomic models to examine in how far a Taylor rule, which takes into account some indicator of economic instability, can improve economic performance and stability. Krug (2015) develops an agent-based macromodel, which combines a simple real sector with exogenous growth with a quite detailed representation of the money market and the financial sector. He examines the implications of an extension of a dual mandate Taylor rule (inflation and output gap), which either reacts also to the deviation of a financial stability indicator from its target value or reacts also to the deviation of the credit to GDP ratio from its long term trend. A main finding of the paper is that also with such an extension of the policy rule, monetary policy alone cannot achieve significant improvements with respect to financial stability if the goal of macroeconomic stability remains the main focus. Combining a dual mandate Taylor rule with macroprudential policy in form of a more rigid regulation of the financial sector seems much more efficient in this respect. The paper highlights also that implementing a "leaning against the wind" monetary policy (i.e., a Taylor rule reacting with a central bank rate increase to an increase of the financial instability indicator) in a restrictive regulatory environment is counterproductive and actually leads to higher financial fragility. Chiarella and Di Guilmi (2017) also study the effects of a policy oriented towards financial stability by considering a Taylor rule which includes the deviation of the current fraction of Ponzi firms from its past moving average as a financial instability indicator. Motivated by the seminal work of Minsky (1963), firms are classified as Ponzi if they have positive debt and negative profit. Quite in accordance to the main insights from Krug (2015), they also find that increasing the (positive) reaction coefficient of the central bank rate to the fraction of Ponzi firms leads to a larger rather than a smaller fraction of Ponzi firms in the economy and does not reduce the bankruptcy rate. Furthermore, such a change in the monetary policy has a negative impact on aggregate output.

While the work discussed in the previous paragraph has highlighted the suitability of an agent-based approach to study the interplay of monetary policy and regulation, works by Salle et al. (2013) and Salle (2015) exploit the ability of this approach to capture heterogeneous expectation formation processes and learning in a macroeconomic framework. They consider a macroeconomic model with social learning among households and individual learning of firms in which the central bank uses a nonlinear Taylor rule responding to inflation and unemployment. Salle et al. (2013) examine the impact of an increase of the reaction coefficients of inflation and unemployment under different credibility scenarios for the central bank. They find that monetary policy is much more effective if the central bank's target rate can be communicated with full credibility and is perceived without noise. In Salle et al. (2013) the inflation expectations of households are formed in a very simple way as a weighted average between the perceived inflation target and the past inflation. In Salle (2015) a much more sophisticated and flexible expectation formation process is inserted into this macroeconomic model. This process is modeled using artificial neural network with different sets of input variables which vary according to the considered transparency scenario. These input variables might also include the central banks internal inflation forecasts, based on VAR models, or the trend of these forecasts. The analysis of extensive simulation exercises under the different scenarios shows that transparency of the central bank reduces the trade-off between the goals of inflation targeting and minimization of the output gap. In particular, it turns out that a central bank which communicates not only its objectives but also its forecasts reduces the inflation-output gap trade-off and should use smaller reaction coefficients to these two objectives than a central bank restricting communication to its objectives.

In addition to the extensive work studying the impact of different interest rate rules of the central bank on economic performance, agent-based models have also been used to explore the macroeconomic effect of quantitative easing. Cincotti et al. (2010) use the Eurace simulator (EUGE) to compare quantitative easing scenarios, in which the central bank purchases government bonds, thereby financing public deficits, with fiscal tightening. Under fiscal tightening the deficit of the government is funded by issuing new bonds in the market and by an increase of tax rates. The effects of the two policies are compared under different assumptions about the dividend payout ratio of firms, where higher dividend ratios imply a larger demand of firms for external credit and therefore a higher amount of credit in the economy. The authors show that quantitative easing leads to higher growth rates in the economy and to higher inflation compared to the fiscal tightening scenario. The effect is much stronger in scenarios with a relatively small dividend payout rate. Also Chiarella and Di Guilmi (2017) combine their analysis of variations of the Taylor rule, which was discussed above, with policy experiments based on a central bank rule determining the supply of money. In particular, the supply of central bank money is assumed to depend negatively on inflation and on the number of Ponzi firms in the economy. In the exogenous money scenario, in which only the central bank, but not the financial sector, can generate money, an increase of each parameter capturing the effect of inflation and Ponzi firms on money supply reduces the number of Ponzi firms. In the endogenous money scenario, in which the financial sector endogenously generates all credit demanded by firms and liquidity demanded by investors, increasing the sensitivity parameter with respect to inflation also reduces the variance of output fluctuations.

4.3 FINANCIAL REGULATION AND CRISIS RESOLUTION MECHANISMS

On of the main policy lessons learned from the financial and economic crisis of 2007 is that systemic risk matters and should be taken into account when designing regulatory policies. This has not only led to the development of the Basel III framework for the regulation of the financial sector, but also to an explosion of academic work studying the implications of different regulatory schemes from a systemic perspective, which acknowledges the interconnectedness of the players in the financial sector, as well as the feedbacks between the real and the financial sector. An agent-based approach seems a natural choice to transform such a perspective into concrete models and indeed a number of contributions based on such an approach have improved our understanding of the macroeconomic effects of different regulatory instruments discussed in the aftermath of the crisis.

Teglio et al. (2012) use the Eurace simulator (EUGE) to analyze the effect of making the regulatory capital requirement, defined in terms of the ratio of equity to risk-weighted assets, more restrictive. They find that a very strong requirement, which implies some credit rationing of firms from the start of the simulation, has negative implications for short-term GDP in the economy, however, induces higher output and lower unemployment in the long-run compared to a looser regulatory scheme. They argue that under a more restrictive scheme the buildup of financial fragility of firms is avoided, which leads to more significant credit rationing of firms in the long-run under loose regulatory schemes. In Cincotti et al. (2012b) this analysis is extended by considering capital requirements which are adapted over time in a countercyclical way, i.e., they become more tight in good times compared to bad times. Two versions of such rules are considered, where the level of unemployment and the amount of total credit are used as indicators of the state of the economy. Simulations indicate that in the long run output is higher and unemployment is lower under such adaptive policies compared to fixed capital requirements. This effect is particularly strong if the countercyclical policy is based on total credit in the economy. Raberto et al. (2018) explore in the framework of the Eurace simulator (EUGE) how a capital adequacy requirement for banks, which requires lower reserves for firm loans compared to household mortgages, might foster firms investment in new technologies and the transition to green energy production. They find that such regulatory schemes in the short-run indeed speed up firm investment in new technologies, but at the same time reduce overall growth due to stronger constraints on household expenditures. In the long-run this negative effect outweighs the positive one even with respect to firm investment.

van der Hoog and Dawid (2018) pose the question which type of banking regulation is best suited to avoid large downturns in an economy. Within the framework of the Eurace@Unibi model (EUBI) they use indicators developed in the empirical literature to identify amplitude and duration of recessions and expansions in the simulation data and analyze how the distribution of these indicators depends on the regulatory environment. In particular, they compare the effects of strengthening the capital requirement with those of making the reserve requirement, which focuses on a bank's liquidity, more stringent. They find that if the capital requirement becomes more restrictive, the distribution of recession amplitudes shifts in a way that the amplitudes of the most severe recession become larger and overall strong recessions become more likely. If the reserve requirement becomes more restrictive, an opposite effect is observed and the distribution of amplitudes becomes more concentrated around smaller values. Based on their examination of the mechanisms underlying these observations, which involves the categorization of firms according to their financial status, the authors argue that a liquidity constraint is able to prevent banks from fueling a debt bubble that is mainly caused by the financially unsound firms requiring new debt to roll-over old debt. Hence, strict liquidity requirements reduce the risk of large downturns. In a related work van der Hoog (2018) shows, again in the framework of the Eurace@Unibi (EUBI) model, that a stringent reserve requirement reduces the output fluctuations without negatively affecting the (average) dynamics of total output.

An extensive agent-based analysis of the effect of different types of regulatory schemes for banks is also carried out in Popoyan et al. (2017). They build their analysis on an extension of the AGH model, in which the banks' rule for granting loans to shops is based on a frequently used approach for determining creditworthiness, the "6C" approach. The main objectives of the study are to compare the economic dynamics under a Basel II type regulation of banks with that under a Basel III approach, and to analyze which aspects of the Basel III regulation are most crucial for the effectiveness of that scheme. In particular, the paper distinguishes between the following four regulatory instruments, which are all part of the Basel III scheme: (i) a static capital requirement; (ii) a countercyclical buffer, as an add-on to the capital requirement, which is determined based on the aggregate private sector credit-to-GDP ratio; (iii) a leverage requirement; (iv) a liquidity requirement. Considering the level and the volatility of output gap and unemployment, as well as the likelihood of crises, the authors find that the Basel III scheme performs significantly better than Basel II. More specifically, the combination of the static capital requirement with the countercyclical buffer seems to be the crucial aspect of the Basel III approach. Implementing just these two instruments already yields results that are only slightly worse than those under the full Basel III package. However, applying only the leverage requirement or only the liquidity requirement produces significantly larger output gaps and unemployment values, as well as more volatility. The authors show that in their setting these instruments alone perform worse than the Basel II rule. These claims are verified across different Taylor rules that are inserted into the model. Comparing these findings with those of van der Hoog and Dawid (2018) and van der Hoog (2018) discussed above, one has to acknowledge that, whereas the importance of the countercyclical buffer seems consistent with the intuition of the importance of bubble prevention in these papers, the negative role of the liquidity constraint is at odds with the main findings in van der Hoog and Dawid (2018) and van der Hoog (2018). This observation highlights the importance of taking into account the details of the underlying macroeconomic setup when interpreting the qualitative insights from policy analyses. Riccetti et al. (2018) employ still another agent-based macroeconomic framework and show that, similar to the finding reported above, also in their setting a too loose capital-based banking regulation increases financial fragility with potential negative implications for the real economy. However, they also point out that an overly tight regulation, which restricts the availability of credit too strongly, is detrimental for the performance of the economy.

The papers we have discussed in this section so far have focused on the regulation of regular commercial banks. Krug and Wohltmann (2016) point out that in recent years actors other than commercial banks, which are not subject to the corresponding regulation, have taken over a more important role of financial intermediaries in the economy. They analyze the impact of such shadow banks on the dynamics and stability of the economy in a stock-flow-consistent agent-based macroeconomic model, in which banks are subject to Basel III type regulation. Inserting unregulated shadow banks into a benchmark scenario, in which only commercial banks offer financial services, the authors find a destabilizing effect of the informal financial sector on the economy. At the same time they find a small positive impact of the informal financial sector on the growth rate. If the shadow banks are also subject to regulation and share the traditional banks' access to central bank liquidity, then the variance of output, as well as that of inflation, is, however, substantially lower than in the benchmark. Based on this, the authors argue that including the shadow banks in the regulation and giving them access to the central bank as lender of last resort is helpful for reaching the central bank's dual mandate of price and output stabilization. At the same time the average growth rate of output is substantially smaller in such a scenario with regulated shadow banks compared to the benchmark.

The regulatory environment of the financial sector is not only determined by the constraints banks face while solvent, but also by the mechanisms that apply in case a bank is defaulting. Klimek et al. (2015) compare the macroeconomic effect of three different types of such crisis resolution mechanisms in the framework of a simple agent-based macroeconomic model. These mechanisms are: (i) a purchase and assumption (P&A) operation under which assets and liabilities of the defaulting bank are taken by the other banks; (ii) a bail-out under which households and firms provide equity for the bank; (iii) a bail-in under which unsecured claims of creditors are written off or transformed to equity. In all cases the mechanism is activated if the equity of a bank falls below a certain (negative) threshold. The effect of these different mechanisms on output, unemployment, and credit volume is compared for different levels of the banks refinancing interest rate (which drives the size of the interest rate the bank is charging the firms). For low interest rates, the choice of the crisis resolution mechanism has little effect, but for higher interest rates bail-in and bail-out lead to better results than P&A. In particular, in the highest interest rate regime, which is characterized by high unemployment and low household savings the bail-in mechanism leads to highest output and lowest unemployment because in such a setting the financial burden for firms and households, implied by the bail-out of banks, significantly affects their level of economic activity reducing the overall output in the economy.

4.4 LABOR MARKET POLICY

The discussion in the previous subsection highlights that, in particular after the crisis of 2008, the focus of the (agent-based) literature dealing with market regulation has been on the financial and credit market. However, in the framework of agent-based macroeconomic models also the effects of regulatory schemes on other markets, in particular the labor market has been studied. An example in this respect is Seppecher (2012), who in the framework of the JAMEL model, shows that higher flexibility of (reservation) wages decreases unemployment duration, but through the demand channel reduces consumption and real wages and increases unemployment.[81] The

---

[81] It should be pointed out that we cover here only papers using macroeconomic agent-based models. There are also several studies of the implications of changes in the labor market design using partial agent-based

introduction of a minimum wage in such a scenario can help to eliminate such negative effects of increased wage flexibility.

The findings of Seppecher (2012) are consistent with results obtained in the framework of other agent-based studies, like Napoletano et al. (2012) and Dosi et al. (2017c). In the latter paper the authors compare the effects of different labor market regimes in the framework of a version of the KS model with a decentralized labor market. A "Fordist" regime, in which wages are indexed to productivity, firms do not dismiss workers as long as profits are positive and workers do not search on the job, is compared to different variations of a "Competitive" regime, in which wage changes respond to unemployment, firms immediately adjust the size of their work force to their current production plan and workers search for a job. The main insight from their analysis is that in scenarios, where growth is mainly driven by demand, the Competitive regime's no full indexation of minimum wages and no unemployment benefits are associated with higher unemployment, slower growth, and a higher risk of economic crises compared to the Fordist regime. The main mechanism underlying this observation is that, under the Competitive regime without wage indexation, wages and thereby demand are strongly diminished during downturns, which reduces firm investment in R&D and new vintages, which reduces the rate of productivity growth. In a similar setting and following a similar logic, Dosi et al. (2018) show that the Fordist regime also induces lower unemployment and lower income inequality than alternative regimes under which firms have higher flexibility in dismissing workers. In Dosi et al. (2017b) the Fordist and Competitive labor market regimes are compared with respect to the question how much hysteresis an economy exhibits under these regimes. The model of Dosi et al. (2017c) is extended by incorporating endogenous skill dynamics of workers into the model and also introducing endogenous firm entry and the main focus of the analysis is on the question how strong and how long lasting the negative impact of a crisis on future growth is. Quite consistent with the results of the two papers just discussed, the authors find that under a Fordist regime the negative impact of a crisis is substantially less severe and also shorter-lived than under a competitive regime.

In Dawid et al. (2018b) the effect of increasing the flexibility of the labor market is studied in a two-region version of the EUBI model in which the two regions differ with respect to (initial) firm productivity and worker skills (see also Section 4.5). In particular, it is studied how the growth and inequality in the weaker region is affected if the wage replacement rates in that region are decreased and the pressure to find work are increased such that the workers' reservation wages adjust downwards much faster if they are unemployed. Whereas such measures induce a decrease of the growth rate of output in that region, they also reduce the income inequality in the region. Both effects arise because under a more flexible labor market technologically less advanced firms in the region have better chances to hire workers who have been earning higher wages at firms with higher productivity before. This reduces the wage

---

model of the labor market, see, e.g., Haruvy et al. (2006), Goudet et al. (2015), or the survey by Neugart and Richiardi (2018).

dispersion in the population and at the same time increases competition for the high productivity firms reducing their investment and thereby reducing overall productivity growth.

4.5 REGIONAL GROWTH, CONVERGENCE, AND COHESION POLICY

In a stream of papers different versions of the Eurace@Unibi model (EUBI) have been used to study how different types of (region-specific) policies influence the regional dynamics of growth and technological change in an economy consisting of several heterogeneous regions. In Dawid et al. (2008) a two-region version of the model is considered and it is assumed that a certain budget is available to improve the general skills, i.e., the speed by which workers can acquire specific skills that increase their productivity. The main question posed is how the effects of an equal distribution of the skill upgrading measures across the two regions compare to an approach where all effort is concentrated in one region ("lighthouse policy"). It is shown that the equal distribution leads to higher average productivity and output in the economy in the long-run, whereas a concentration of effort induces faster growth in the short-run. A crucial assumption for this finding is that labor is immobile across regions. This implies that firms in the lighthouse region, which due to their productivity advantages in the short-run also have cost and price advantages relative to firms from the other region, face problems filling their vacancies with local workers once the demand for their products becomes too large. These rationing problems on the labor market inhibit output expansion and growth and also induce upwards pressure on wages in the lighthouse region. If the upgrading of skills is equally distributed across the regions such effects do not occur, which explains why such an equal distribution yields better outcomes in terms of economy-wide output and productivity growth.

The importance of spatial labor market frictions for the results in Dawid et al. (2008) is highlighted in Dawid et al. (2009), where the same policy experiment is carried out under a completely integrated labor market of the two regions (no commuting costs for workers working in the other region from where they live) and a market with positive, but small commuting costs. Not surprisingly, in the case of a completely integrated labor market the allocation of the skill upgrading measures between regions is irrelevant, however, for small positive commuting costs the opposite result to Dawid et al. (2008) is obtained. Concentrating all skill upgrading measures in one region here leads to higher economy-wide output in the long-run. The impact of different degrees of labor market integration on regional economic dynamics and economy wide output is studied in more detail in Dawid et al. (2012). Again, a two-region version of the Eurace@Unibi (EUBI) is studied, in which the first region (the "high-tech" region) is characterized by a larger fraction of workers with high general skills and an initial advantage of the local firms with respect to the quality of their physical capital stock compared to the second region ("low-tech"). Inspired by discussions about the integration of labor markets between EU member countries after the EU enlargement in 2004, the authors compare the economic dynamics emerging under four different policies: (i) full separation of labor markets; (ii) full integration (no commuting costs); (iii) integration with small commuting costs between regions; (iv) integration with small commuting costs with some delay (after the integration of the product markets). A main finding of this paper is that, whereas in terms of economy-wide long-run output open labor markets clearly outperform closed ones, the ranking of the different policies differs crucially depending on which region and which time horizon is considered. For the high-tech region closed labor markets are preferable in terms of the level of produced output if the planning horizon is short, while under a long-run consideration open labor market with small frictions perform best. For the low-tech region the opposite holds true. Closed labor markets are harmful in the short-run but have positive long run implications for this region. The underlying mechanisms are again closely related to the induced labor flows across regions, the resulting pressure on wages, and the associated investment incentives of firms.

A demonstration how multiregion agent-based macromodels can be used to provide insights into the effects and the effectiveness of cohesion policies aiming at the fostering of convergence between regions is given in Dawid et al. (2014, 2018b). In particular, these papers incorporate policy measures resembling instruments the European Union applies as part of its cohesion policy in a two-region setting of the Eurace@Unibi (EUBI) model, in which, similar to Dawid et al. (2012), one region has an initial advantage with respect to physical and human capital endowment. In Dawid et al. (2014) the effects of two types of cohesion policies are analyzed, namely a human capital oriented policy, under which the distribution of general skills in the low-tech region is improved, and a technology oriented policy, under which firms in the low-tech region receive subsidies if they invest in new physical capital at the technological frontier. It is shown that in a scenario with integrated labor markets between the two regions the human capital policy fails to achieve its objective of fostering convergence between the two regions, but, quite on the contrary, affects only the output in the high-tech region positively. The output in the low tech region, which is the target of the policy, is, however, negatively influenced. The reason for this observation is that the human capital policy induces a flow of highly skilled workers from the low tech region to firms in the high tech region, which due to their higher productivity offer higher wages. This has second order effects on firms' investment incentives, which give rise to this result. If labor markets are separated, then the human capital policy indeed facilitates growth in the low-tech region and therefore fosters convergence. Considering the effect of the technology policy, it is shown that it always fosters convergence, and that the effect is stronger if labor markets are integrated. Dawid et al. (2018b) focuses entirely on the effects of technology policies and shows that the positive convergence effect identified in Dawid et al. (2014) disappears if the policy becomes "undirected" in a sense that investing firms in the low-tech region receive subsidies even if they invest off the technological frontier. In this paper the effect of cohesion policies is not only studied with respect to the income differences between the two regions but also with respect to income inequality within each region.

4.6 TAKING STOCK: WHAT IS THE POTENTIAL OF AGENT-BASED MACROECONOMICS FOR POLICY ANALYSIS?

Several general observations about the use of agent-based models for policy analysis can be made based on the literature review in this section. There seems to be a clear development both with respect to content and to methodological standards. Whereas the earlier contributions reviewed above, let's say most of the papers from 2008 to 2013, have mostly focused on rather generic and traditional policy issues, like interest rate policies or demand versus supply oriented fiscal polices, many of the more recent publications explore the implications of rather detailed aspects of actual policy proposals. These contributions exploit the ability of the agent-based approach to capture institutional details of environments and policies to disentangle the implications of different aspects of programs like the Basel III regulations or the EU cohesion policies. Clearly, such insights about the expected effects of details in the policy design should be highly relevant for policy makers. Similarly, the consideration of the interplay of different types of policy measures, as well as the feedback between policies, expectations, and credibility of policy makers, which has been the focus of several of the reviewed contributions, seems to be an important aspect of the agent-based work in the policy domain.

From a methodological perspective, a trend towards statistical rigor in the analysis of policy effects can be observed over the last decade. The (often graphical) comparison of the means across Monte Carlo runs of certain considered variables between different policy scenarios, which has been quite common in earlier contributions, has more or less disappeared in more recent publications. Providing meaningful statistical tests for the significance of certain policy effects, or at least confidence bands around for the considered variables under the different policy variants has become a standard in the literature. Also, more sophisticated methods have been applied, like the use penalized spline methods for the estimation (also providing confidence bands) of the dynamics of the isolated effects of certain policies in simulation models (Dawid et al., 2014, 2018b, 2018c; Harting, 2015) or regression analyses of the impact of policy parameters across certain relevant parameter spaces. For the latter it is essential to rely on appropriate methods for sampling the parameter space and in this respect nearly-orthogonal Latin hypercubes (Cioppa and Lucas, 2007) have been used (e.g., Salle et al., 2013).

Important challenges certainly remain to increase the potential impact of this work for actual policy design. First, the appeal of a policy recommendation certainly increases if it is backed up not only by careful analysis within the considered model framework, but also by a clear intuition for the causal mechanisms driving the policy effects. Given the rich structure many of the agent-based models have, developing such a narrative is typically difficult, even more so if the intention is to demonstrate that the mechanisms highlighted in that narrative can actually be identified in the simulation data. Second, in many areas of application, it is common to carry out a calibration of the model based on some empirical data before entering the policy analysis. As discussed in the previous section, at this point the agent-based macroeconomic models employed in policy analyses are typically not calibrated in the traditional way, but are linked to empirical data through a mix of parameter estimation and matching of stylized facts. Developing more clear standards of linking these models to data could be useful to improve clarity and also credibility of the derived policy recommendations.

5 CONCLUSIONS AND OUTLOOK

In this chapter we have attempted to provide a systematic overview of the state-of-the-art in agent-based macroeconomic modeling, as well as of the main areas of economic policy analysis in which these models have been applied. Our survey highlights that, in spite of a substantial number of different models that have been developed in the literature, a quite significant common core has emerged with respect to the design of agents' behavioral rules and interaction protocols, as well as to the approaches for testing empirical validity of the models and to carrying out rigorous and meaningful analyses of the simulation outcomes. Also, a rich stream of policy related literature relying on MABMs has evolved, addressing issues in more or less all main areas of economic policy.

Nevertheless, it is evident that agent-based macroeconomic analysis is still a very young area of economic research facing numerous challenges and also the need for consolidation. A stronger standardization towards some "canonical" MABMs (at least for certain parts of the model) would certainly increase the comparability across obtained results and the transparency about the main mechanisms responsible for them. However, also in light of the ongoing debate in the agent-based community about the appropriate size and granularity of agent-based macroeconomic models (see, e.g., Richiardi, 2017), a certain diversity of approaches is certainly desirable and should pertain. A main challenge from a methodological perspective is certainly the development of empirical calibration methods for MABMs, which are computationally feasible even for large size models. As indicated in this chapter, promising conceptual work has been done during the last few years and in light of the ever increasing computational speed it can be expected that we will see the emergence of suitable standard methods and algorithms for this purpose very soon.

From an economic perspective, several areas can be identified for which the potential payoff of using MABMs seems particularly high. As discussed above, one important area of work in this respect is the analysis of economic crises, taking into account the interplay of the real and the financial sector and the mechanisms generating systemic risk. Another topical area, for which the ability of MABMs to model the dynamic evolution of populations of heterogeneous individuals, who differ in different relevant aspects, is crucial, is the study of inequality dynamics and the mechanisms fostering and reducing inequality (see, e.g., Dawid and Gemkow, 2014; Dosi et al., 2013; Russo et al., 2016 for MABM analyses with such focus). Also, MABMs seem to be the natural tool to examine in a systematic way how the implications and effectiveness of certain policy measures depend on the level of inequality and the population distribution with respect to key economic characteristics.

APPENDIX A SUMMARY OF SELECTED AGENT-BASED MACROECONOMIC MODELS

Table A1 Overview over agent-based macroeconomic models (Part 1)

Model Name/Acronym	AGH	CATS	Eurace@Unibi (EUBI)	Eurace Simulator (EUGE)
Key references	Ashraf et al. (2016, 2017)	Delli Gatti et al. (2011), Assenza et al. (2015a)	Dawid et al. (2014, 2018a, 2018b, 2018d)	Cincotti et al. (2012a), Teglio et al. (2018), Ponta et al. (2018)
1. General Properties				
Stock-flow consistent?	Yes	Yes	Yes	Yes
Expectations	CoG firms: inflation, sales; entrants: profits and opportunity costs of opening shop	CoG firms: future demand	CoG firms: demand, evolution of productivity of capital goods	CoG firms: demand and inflation; HH: stock and bond returns
Type of expectation rules	(inflation adjusted) naive expectations for wage, price, income; expected inflation given by CB target rate or by CB predictions	adaptive (in some cases: naive)	simple linear extrapolation models	adaptive based on linear regression on past values
Entry of agents?	entry of shops: financial viability and profitability tests, positive signals not to be rationed on consumption and labor market	one-to-one replacement of exiting (bankrupt) firms	reentry of firms after bankruptcy	reentry of firms after bankruptcy
Spatial structure?	No	No	multiple regions	multiple countries in Petrovic et al. (2017)
2. Consumption Goods Market				
Consumption Goods Producers				
Single/multiple goods?	n products	differentiated goods	single CoG sector, horizontal differentiation	single CoG sector
Production technology	fixed capital needed for production; output linear in labor input	linear technology with labor input/ Leontief technology with capital and labor input	vintage capital plus skill differentiated labor with fixed capital–labor ratio	Cobb–Douglas with labor and capital input, fixed ratio with energy input
Pricing rule	fixed mark-up with upwards (downwards) adjustment if inventory/expected sales ratio is too low (high)	price adjustment based on involuntary inventories/queue of unsatisfied consumers and changes in competitors' prices	profit maximization based on estimated demand	fixed mark-up

(continued on next page)

Table A1 (continued)

Model Name/Acronym	AGH	CATS	Eurace@Unibi (EUBI)	Eurace Simulator (EUGE)
Quantity choice	expected sales plus inventory adjustment	based on expected demand	newsboy heuristics based on estimated demand distribution	newsboy heuristics based on estimated demand distribution
Physical investment	fixed investment (in terms of consumption goods) upon market entry	based on long run (adaptive) estimate of capital requirements	derived from quantity choice, vintage choice based on maximum of expected future profit	derived from quantity choice and based on net present value of future expected cash flows
Households				
Consumption budget	fixed fraction of total wealth	fixed fraction of total wealth	fixed fraction of total wealth	piecewise linear heuristic based on buffer-stock rule
Purchasing decision	utility maximization subject to budget constraint	search for the best bargain by visiting CoG producers and ranking their prices	piecewise linear heuristic based on buffer-stock rule	stochastic choice of firms by HHs based on posted prices (logit choice)
Interaction Protocol	evolving customer relationship with two stores due to (random) search for lower prices	Households search by visiting a subset of CoG producers and chose the best bargain	stochastic choice of firms by HHs based on posted prices (logit choice)	market platforms (malls), posted prices, inventory stocks
			region-specific market platforms (malls), inventory stocks of goods, posted prices	
3. Capital Goods Market				
Capital Goods Producers				
Differentiated physical capital?	no capital goods in the model	Yes	multiple vintages	differentiated w.r.t. energy efficiency
Technological change	not applicable	none	new better vintages added to vintage range over time due to exogenous stochastic process	exogenously-given energy efficiency growth path
Pricing rule	not applicable	price adjustment based on involuntary inventories/queue of unsatisfied CoG (investing) producers	combination of cost based and value based pricing using expected returns of vintage for average firm	fixed mark-up
Interaction Protocol	not applicable	CoG producers search by visiting a subset of CaG producers, matching of CoG to CaG producers without capacity constraints, instantaneous delivery	posted prices, production based on received orders without capacity constraints, instantaneous delivery	posted prices, production based on received orders, instantaneous delivery

(continued on next page)

Table A1 (continued)

Model Name/Acronym	AGH	CATS	Eurace@Unibi (EUBI)	Eurace Simulator (EUGE)
4. Labor Market				
Firms				
Labor demand	derived from sales target	derived from sales target (expected demand)	CoG: derived from quantity choice; CaG firms: no labor input	CoG: derived from cost minimization given the planned output; CaG firms: no labor input
Wage offers	adjusted after fixed time interval based on ratio of target employment and people with employment relationship	posted wage, may be fixed or indexed to inflation	take it or leave it offer based on expected productivity of the worker, adjustment of offer if firm is rationed	wage offer adjusted upwards if firm is rationed
Workers				
Differentiated workers?	different types of workers; employment relationships only between workers and firms with matching types	no differentiation between workers	heterogeneous general skills and specific skills	heterogeneous general skills and specific skills
Labor supply	supply of one unit	exogenous	supply of one unit if wage offer above reservation wage	supply of one unit if wage offer above reservation wage
Reservation wage	no reservation wage	No	current wage if employed; dynamically adjusting toward unemployment benefit if unemployed	current wage if employed; dynamically adjusting toward unemployment benefit if unemployed
Interaction Protocol	labor relationships evolving due to wage oriented search of workers and lay-off of workers by firms	unemployed workers search by visiting a subset of firms, matching of workers to firms once a vacancy is found	applications to random set of firms based on posted vacancies; skill-based sorting of candidates and wage offers leading to matches	applications to random set of firms based on posted vacancies; skill-based sorting of candidates and wage offers leading to matches
5. Credit Market				
Firms				
Demand for external financing	liquidity needs that cannot be financed internally from the own stock of liquid assets	liquidity needs that cannot be financed internally	only CoG: liquidity needs that cannot be financed internally from the payment account	only CoG: liquidity needs that cannot be financed internally from liquid resources
External financing options	only bank loans	only bank loans	only bank loans	CoG: bank loans, if rationed then new shares can be issued

(continued on next page)

Table A1 (continued)

Model Name/Acronym	AGH	CATS	Eurace@Unibi (EUBI)	Eurace Simulator (EUGE)
Bankruptcy rule	negative financial wealth exceeds credit limit	negative net worth	illiquidity bankruptcy or insolvency bankruptcy (negative net worth)	illiquidity bankruptcy or insolvency bankruptcy (negative net worth)
Banks				
Credit supply	probability of loan approval increasing with ratio of equity/required capital	decreasing with borrower's leverage	full service of demand up to regulatory constraints	full service of demand up to regulatory constraints
Interest rate	CB rate plus fixed spread (uniform across banks)	increasing with borrower's leverage	risk-adjusted mark-up on CB rate	risk-adjusted mark-up on CB rate
Regulatory constraints	lower bound on equity/asset ratio	minimal capital requirement	capital adequacy requirement; reserve requirement ratio	capital requirement
Bank exit	bank failure if equity is negative; full recapitalization by the government	if the bank has negative net worth, there will be full recapitalization by the government	no bank exit; banks become inactive if net worth is negative or capital and reserve requirements are violated	no bank exit; infinite access to CB standing facility; if net worth is negative lending activity is stopped
Interaction Protocol	one bank per sector; agent can approach only bank in her/his sector	one bank which extend loans at different interest rates to producers	firms contact randomly chosen set of banks; select the bank with lowest interest rate offer	firms contact randomly chosen set of banks; select the bank with lowest interest rate offer
6. Stock Market/Financial Management				
Firms				
Dividend payout	single firm owner accrues all profits	firm owner gets a fraction of profits	fixed proportion of (positive) profits as long as firms payment account below a threshold, above threshold full distribution of profits	CoG: variable fraction of previous month net earning; Banks: dividend paid only if credit supply restriction is not binding
Households				
Financial investment	cash holdings to carry out expected transactions, the remainder goes to bank deposits	none	random allocation of savings between bank deposit and index bond of all firms	allocation between bank deposits and stocks/bonds according to decision rationale inspired by prospect theory
Interaction Protocol	no stock market	no stock market	only index bond, adjustment of index bond price based on excess demand/supply	clearinghouse with daily determination of market clearing prices

(continued on next page)

Table A1 (*continued*)

Model Name/Acronym	AGH	CATS	Eurace@Unibi (EUBI)	Eurace Simulator (EUGE)
7. Policy Makers				
Government				
Fiscal measures	sales tax; bank recapitalization	none	unemployment benefits; firm subsidies; taxes on income and profits	unemployment benefits; household transfers; taxes on income (labor and capital), corporate earnings, and consumption (VAT)
Balanced budget?	adjustment of tax rate based on target debt/GDP ratio	no public expenditures and taxes	yes, dynamic adjustment of tax rates	dynamic adjustment of tax rates based on different fiscal policies
Central Bank				
CB interest rate	Taylor rule based on inflation and output gap; dynamic adjustment of target rate	risk free rate as model parameter	constant CB rate	Taylor rule based on inflation and output gap (proxied by the employment rate)
8. Reproduced Stylized Facts	Matching of median outcomes with US data: inflation; real interest rate; unemployment rate; unemployment duration; volatility of output gap; volatility of inflation; autocorrelation of gap; autocorrelation of inflation; average mark-up; firm exit rate; job-loss rate; price-change frequency; bank failure rate	Business cycle: persistent irregular fluctuations of GDP around a stationary long run mean (quasi-equilibrium) punctuated by sudden recessions of sizable magnitude followed by slow recoveries	Business cycle: persistent growth and persistent endogenous fluctuations; investment, output, employment, firm debt procyclical; wages, unemployment, mark-up countercyclical; investment more volatile, consumption less volatile than output; Beveridge curve; persistence in firm market-shares. Micro-level distributions: fat-tailed firm size distribution; persistent heterogeneity of productivity and prices; cross regional negative relationship between average income level and income Gini	Levels of debt/GDP, deficit/GDP, bond yields; Business cycle: endogenous fluctuations; investment, consumption; mortgages, firm loans procyclical; unemployment, prices countercyclical; firm liquidity lead business cycle; bond yield positively correlated with government debt and with CB rate; negative correlation between stock and bond price; investment more volatile than consumption; Phillips curve, Okun law

Table A2 Overview over agent-based macroeconomic models (Part 2)

Model Name/Acronym	JAMEL	Keynes meeting Schumpeter (KS)	LAGOM	LEN
Key References	Seppecher (2012), Seppecher and Salle (2015), Seppecher et al. (2018)	Dosi et al. (2010, 2013, 2015, 2017c)	Wolf et al. (2013), Mandel et al. (2010)	Lengnick (2013)
1. General Properties				
Stock-flow consistent?	Yes	not reported	Yes	Yes
Expectations	demand (all firms); leverage target (CoG) and consumption budget (HH)	CoG firms: demand	CoG firms: demand; HHs: income	CoG firms: demand
Type of expectation rules	naive expectations; Seppecher and Salle (2015): evolving sentiments	naive expectations	simple linear extrapolation models	naive expectations
Entry of agents?	firm entry only as replacement for exited firms	firm entry only as replacement for exited firms	entry/exit of firms in a sector if average profit rate is above/below average interest rate plus a risk premium	No
Spatial structure?	No	No	No	Yes (regional version)
2. Consumption Goods Market				
Consumption Goods Producers				
Single/multiple goods?	single CoGood	single CoGood	multiple goods (identified with sectors of production)	single CoGood
Production technology	homogeneous capital and labor with fixed capital/labor ratio	vintage capital plus labor with fixed capital–labor ratio	Production functions. Different types available: CES, Cobb–Douglas, Leontieff	linear, labor as single input
Pricing rule	price adjustment if inventory is below/above target level and last period production has/has not been fully sold; Seppecher et al. (2018): evolving mark-up adjustment	mark-ups evolving based on firms' market share	mark-up over costs with mark-up rate following evolution dynamics	dynamic adjustment based on ratio of inventory and expected demand
Quantity choice	implied by size of labor force	proportional to expected demand taking into account current inventory	expected demand	implied by size of labor force

(continued on next page)

Table A2 (continued)

Model Name/Acronym	JAMEL	Keynes meeting Schumpeter (KS)	LAGOM	LEN
Physical investment	only Seppecher et al. (2018); derived from past sales based on NPV calculations and leverage target	derived from quantity choice plus replacement inventory (technical obsolescence); vintage choice based on price and induced prod. costs	derived from quantity choice: investment at a fixed rate whenever capacity utilization rate passes a threshold	no physical capital in the model
Households				
Consumption budget	buffer-stock rule	HHs every period consume their entire income	Deaton rule: save/unsave if income is greater/smaller than expected	concave function of wealth
Purchasing decision	cheapest observed price	not applicable (only single CoG)	allocation across sectors based on (evolving) expenditure weights; for each good cheapest available price is selected	HHs purchase from randomly selected firm in their network
Interaction Protocol	firms post prices; HHs observe randomly selected group of offers	no explicit interaction protocol; market shares of firms determined by prices and unfilled demand in the previous period	HHs order firms according to price and visit them till demand is fulfilled	evolving network of connections between HHs and CoG firms based on price and unfilled demand
3. Capital Goods Market				
Capital Goods Producers				
Differentiated physical capital?	homogeneous capital (in each sector)	multiple vintages	differentiated capital	no capital goods in the model
Technological change	no endogenous technological change; only in Seppecher et al. (2018): exogenous technological shocks	competing CaG firms update their offered vintage through innovation and imitation, process modeled in the spirit of Nelson and Winter (1982)	endogenous (at the sectoral level)	not applicable
Pricing rule	only in Seppecher et al. (2018): evolutionary adjustment of mark-ups	fixed mark-up	mark-up over costs with mark-up rate following evolutionary dynamics	not applicable
Interaction Protocol	only in Seppecher et al. (2018): capital goods firms post prices, investing firms observe randomly selected group of offers	production based on received orders, potential friction due to labor market rationing, delivery after one period	delivered upon orders based on expected demand; no frictions	not applicable

(continued on next page)

Table A2 (continued)

Model Name/Acronym	JAMEL	Keynes meeting Schumpeter (KS)	LAGOM	LEN
4. Labor Market				
Firms				
Labor demand	adjustment relative to current labor force with a probability depending on the gap between inventory and inventory target level	CoG + CaG: derived from quantity choice	based on expected demand and minimum ratio between labor and capital	dynamic adjustment based on ratio of inventory and expected demand
Wage offers	adjustment of wage offer based on difference between vacancies and target vacancy rate	homogeneous wage in the economy, adjusted over time based on average productivity, inflation, unemployment	reference wage at the sectoral level evolves according to productivity; firm wage adjusted according to share of vacancies filled	adjusted upwards if firm is rationed; adjusted downwards if all positions have been filled for several periods
Workers				
Differentiated workers?	no differentiation between workers	no differentiation between workers	no differentiation between workers	no differentiation between workers
Labor supply	supply of one unit if wage offer above reservation wage	aggregate labor supply is exogenous and inelastic	supply of one unit if wage offer above reservation wage constant, randomly chosen	supply of one unit
Reservation wage	current wage if employed; if unemployed downward adjustment with a probability that increases with duration of unemployment	not applicable		if employed equal to maximum of current wage and previous reservation wage; decreased if unemployed
Interaction Protocol	firms post wage offers; unemployed worker chooses highest wage offer within randomly selected group of observed offers, if above reservation wage	no explicit interaction protocol; rationing of firms/unemployment if labor supply differs from demand; in Dosi et al. (2017c): decentralized labor market with random matching, where firms make offers first to applicants with lowest requested wage	firms access the labor market in a random order and workers with lowest reservation wages are employed first	workers approach randomly chosen firm, if firm has vacancy worker accepts if offered wage above reservation wage
5. Credit Market				
Firms				
Demand for external financing	liquidity needs that cannot be internally financed; in Seppecher et al. (2018); also long term loans as a fraction of investment costs	liquidity needs that cannot be financed internally from the own stock of liquid assets	liquidity needs that cannot be financed internally from the own stock of liquid assets (deficit computed at the end of the period)	no credit market

(continued on next page)

Table A2 (*continued*)

Model Name/Acronym	JAMEL	Keynes meeting Schumpeter (KS)	LAGOM	LEN
External financing options	only bank credit	only bank credit	only bank credit	not applicable
Bankruptcy/exit rule	inability to pay off a loan; in Seppecher et al. (2018): liabilities exceed assets	CoG and CaG: firms with near-zero market shares and/or negative net liquid assets	firm exit if profit rate below average interest rate	no bankruptcies; automatic wage cuts to keep liquidity nonnegative
Banks				
Credit supply	all credit demands are satisfied	supply to firms based on ranking w.r.t. liquidity/sales ratio up to (bank specific) upper bound on credit	all credit demands are satisfied	not applicable
Interest rate	fixed interest rate, increased if extension of due date is needed by firm	Dosi et al. (2013): fixed mark-up on CB rate; Dosi et al. (2015): risk-adjusted mark-up on CB rate	Taylor rule (one interest rate for the financial sector)	not applicable
Regulatory constraints	none	Dosi et al. (2013): global upper bound on credit proportional to previous period total deposits; Dosi et al. (2015): bank specific upper bound based on deposits and bad debt	none	not applicable
Bank exit	single bank; exit if insolvent	bank failure if net worth becomes negative; automatic bailout by the government (only Dosi et al., 2015)	only financial sector as a whole considered	not applicable
Interaction Protocol	single bank accommodates all requests	Dosi et al. (2013): single bank; Dosi et al. (2015): fixed firm–bank network	financial sector accommodates all requests	not applicable
6. Stock Market/Financial Management				
Firms				
Dividend payout	difference between target level of net wealth (derived from leverage target) and actual net wealth (if positive) constrained by available cash-at-hand	no firm dividends	fixed dividend rate; distributed only if no debt	profits net of liqidity buffer distributed to HHs proportional to HHs liquidity
Households				
Financial investment	all savings kept in cash	no HH savings	only savings accounts receiving interests	all savings kept in cash
Interaction Protocol	no stock market	not applicable	no stock market	no stock market

(continued on next page)

Table A2 (continued)

Model Name/Acronym	JAMEL	Keynes meeting Schumpeter (KS)	LAGOM	LEN
7. Policy Makers				
Government				
Fiscal measures	no fiscal measures	unemployment benefits, taxes on income, and profits	unemployment benefits, taxes on income	no fiscal measures
Balanced budget?	not applicable	fixed rates for taxes, subsidies, and unemployment benefits and endogenously evolving government deficit	yes, dynamic adjustment of tax rates	not applicable
Central Bank				
CB interest rate	Seppecher et al. (2018): Taylor rule (implemented by unique bank representing the whole banking sector)	Dosi et al. (2013): fixed CB rate; Dosi et al. (2015): Taylor rule based on inflation and unemployment	Taylor rule based on inflation and unemployment gaps	no CB
8. Reproduced Stylized Facts	Business cycle: endogenous persistent fluctuations; positive correlation between consumption & output; higher volatility of output; procyclical consumption, employment, inventory change, inflation, vacancy, velocity of money; countercyclical unemployment rate and duration; Beveridge curve; Phillips curve; output autocorrelation; persistence of inflation & GDP; Micro-level distributions: firms size distribution right skewed and not normal; upper part of income distribution Pareto; average level of Gini	Business cycle: endogenous persistent fluctuations; procyclical consumption, investment, change in inventory, employment, productivity, inflation, firm debt (partially with lags); countercyclical unemployment, prices, mark-ups, bank deposits; investment more volatile than GDP; consumption less volatile than GDP; distribution of aggregate growth rates with fat tails; micro-level distributions: firm size distribution skewed and not log-normal; firm growth rate distribution tent-shaped; persistent heterogeneity of labor productivity; Laplace distribution of productivity growth rates; power-law type distribution of bad debt at time of bankruptcy; lumpiness of investment; clustering of bankruptcies in time; fat tails of distribution of banking crises costs (relative to GDP)	endogenous growth; Business cycle: endogenous persistent fluctuations; investment more volatile than consumption	Business cycles: endogenous persistent fluctuations; correlation between output & lagged prices for different lags; Beveridge curve; Phillips curve; micro-level distributions: firms size distribution right skewed; right skewed distribution of frequency of price change

APPENDIX B **LIST OF SYMBOLS**

Symbol	Meaning
C_h	total consumption of household h
Y_h	income of household h
S_h	saving of household h
$C_{i,h}$	consumption of variety i by household h
C	total households' consumption
C_i	households' demand for variety i
$C_{i,t}^e$	expected demand for variety i
Y_i	output of the ith C-firm
Y_k	output of the kth K-firm
J_k	demand for the kth K-good
K_i	physical capital of firm i
I_i	investment of firm i
E_i	net worth or equity of firm i
π_i	profit of firm i
ω_i	capacity utilization of firm i
N_i	employment at firm i
L_i	bank loans received by firm i
Y_i^*	desired or optimal output of firm i
Y	total output/income (GDP)
MC_i	marginal cost of firm i
AC_i	average cost of firm i
Q_i	sales of firm i
Δ_i	inventories of firm i
α	marginal productivity of labor
F_c	number of C-goods and of C-firms
F_k	number of K-goods and of K-firms
F	total number of firms
H	total number of households
Y_h^p	permanent income of household h
Y_h^a	average income of household h
$\bar{Y}_h^a$	cut-off value of the average income of household h
$R = 1 + r$	gross nominal interest rate
W_h^h	human capital of household h
W_h^f	financial wealth of household h
M_h	money balances of household h
w_h	reservation wage of household h
w_i	wage posted by firm i

(continued on next page)

Symbol	Meaning
w	wage
P_i	price of the ith C-good
P_k	price of the kth K-good
P	general price level
p_i	relative price of the ith variety
y_i	output-to-loan ratio of firm i
π	inflation rate
k^h	capitalization factor (in AGH)
ξ	memory parameter in permanent income algorithm (AGH)
δ	desired inventory-to-sale ratio
β	exponent of capital in the production function
ω^f	desired wealth-to-income ratio
χ	parameter of quasi-replication dynamics of market share (KS)
υ	parameter of mark-up dynamics (KS)
ζ_1, ζ_2	parameters of competitiveness equation (KS)
Ω_i	information set of firm i
e_i	forecasting error of firm i
π_z^i	fraction of sampled household that would good i at the price P_z^i
λ_i	leverage of firm i
λ_i^T	target leverage of firm i
μ_i	mark-up of firm i
ν	velocity of adjustment of wealth to targeted wealth (EUBI)
ε	price elasticity of demand
ε^i	price elasticity of demand expected/estimated by firm i
C_h^i	total consumption expenditure estimated/expected by firm i
η	stochastic rate of change of the price set by each firm
η^w	stochastic rate of change of the wage posted by each firm
η^h	stochastic rate of change of the reservation wage
d_h^u	duration of the unemployment spell (JAMEL)
$\bar{d}^u$	cut-off value of the unemployment spell (JAMEL)

(continued on next page)

Symbol	Meaning
γ	intensity of (price) competition among C-firms (EUBI)
ρ	intensity of adjustment of output to changes in inventories (ADG)
c_h	propensity to consume out of human capital
c_f	propensity to consume out of financial wealth
c_y	propensity to consume out of income
f_i	market share of firm i (KS)
E_i	competitiveness of firm i (KS)
$\bar{E}$	average competitiveness of C-firms (KS)
s^H	propensity to save when optimist (JAMEL)
s^L	propensity to save when pessimist (JAMEL)
π^m	probability of adopting the consumer sentiment of the majority (JAMEL)
π^s	probability of searching for a job if unemployed (AGH)
π^T	inflation target of the central bank (AGH)
v	vintage of a machine tool
V	total number of vintages of a machine tool
Z_c	number of C-firms visited by a household to buy C-goods
Z_k	number of K-firms visited by a C-firm to buy a machine tool
Z_e	number of firms visited by a household searching for a job

REFERENCES

Albin, P., 1989. Qualitative effects of monetary policy in "rich" dynamic systems. In: Semmler, W. (Ed.), Financial Dynamics and Business Cycles. M.E. Sharpe.

Anufriev, M., Assenza, T., Hommes, C., Massaro, D., 2013. Interest rules and macroeconomic stability under heterogeneous expectations. Macroeconomic Dynamics 17, 1574–1604.

Aoki, M., 2001. Modeling Aggregate Behavior and Fluctuations in Economics, Stochastic Views of Interacting Agents. Cambridge University Press.

Aoki, M., 2008. Modeling New Approaches to Macroeconomic Modeling: Evolutionary Stochastic Dynamics, Multiple Equilibria and Externalities as Field Effects. Cambridge University Press.

Aoki, M., 2011. Reconstructing Macroeconomics: A Perspective from Statistical Physics and Combinatorial Stochastic Processes. Cambridge University Press.

Arifovic, J., 1995. Genetic algorithms and inflationary economies. Journal of Monetary Economics 36, 219–243.

Arifovic, J., 1996. The behavior of the exchange rate in the genetic algorithm and experimental economies. Journal of Political Economy 104, 510–541.

Arifovic, J., Bullard, J., Kostyshyna, O., 2013. Social learning and monetary policy rules. The Economic Journal 123, 38–76.

Artinger, F., Gigerenzer, G., 2016. Heuristic Pricing in an Uncertain Market: Ecological and Constructivist Rationality. Working paper.

Ashraf, Q., Gershman, B., Howitt, P., 2016. How inflation affects macroeconomic performance: an agent-based computational investigation. Macroeconomic Dynamics 20, 558–581.

Ashraf, Q., Gershman, B., Howitt, P., 2017. Banks, market organization, and macroeconomic performance: an agent-based computational analysis. Journal of Economic Behavior & Organization 135, 143–180.

Assenza, T., Delli Gatti, D., 2013. E pluribus unum: macroeconomic modelling for multi-agent economies. Journal of Economic Dynamics and Control 37, 1659–1682.

Assenza, T., Delli Gatti, D., 2017. The financial transmission of shocks in a simple hybrid macroeconomic agent based model. Journal of Evolutionary Economics. https://doi.org/10.1007/s00191-018-0559-3. Forthcoming.

Assenza, T., Delli Gatti, D., Grazzini, J., 2015a. Emergent dynamics of a macroeconomic agent based model with capital and credit. Journal of Economic Dynamics and Control 50, 5–28.

Assenza, T., Grazzini, J., Hommes, C., Massaro, D., 2015b. PQ strategies in monopolistic competition: some insights from the lab. Journal of Economic Dynamics and Control 50, 62–77.

Axtell, R., 2018. Endogenous firm dynamics and labor flows via heterogeneous agents. In: Handbook of Computational Economics, vol. 4. Elsevier, pp. 157–213 (this Handbook).

Balint, T., Lamperti, F., Mandel, A., Napoletano, M., Roventini, A., Sapio, A., 2017. Complexity and the economics of climate change: a survey and a look forward. Ecological Economics 158, 252–265.

Barde, S., 2017. A practical, accurate, information criterion for nth order Markov processes. Computational Economics 50, 281–324.

Bargigli, L., Riccetti, L., Russo, A., Gallegati, M., 2014. Network analysis and calibration of the "leveraged network-based financial accelerator". Journal of Economic Behavior & Organization 99 (C), 109–125.

Battiston, S., Delli Gatti, D., Gallegati, M., Greenwald, B., Stiglitz, J., 2007. Credit chains and bankruptcy propagation in production networks. Journal of Economic Dynamics and Control 31, 2061–2084.

Benes, J., Kumhof, M., Laxton, D., 2014. Financial Crises in DSGE Models: A Prototype Model. IMF Working Paper 14/57. International Monetary Fund.

Bennett, R., Bergmann, B., 1986. A Microsimulated Model of the United States Economy. The John Hopkins University Press, Baltimore.

Bergman, B., 1974. A microsimulation of the macroeconomy with explicitly represented money flows. Annals of Economic and Social Measurement 3, 475–489.

Bernanke, B., Gertler, M., 1989. Agency costs, net worth, and business fluctuations. The American Economic Review 79, 14–31.

Bernanke, B., Gertler, M., 1990. Financial fragility and economic performance. The Quarterly Journal of Economics 105, 87–114.

Bernanke, B., Gertler, M., Gilchrist, S., 1999. The financial accelerator in a quantitative business cycle framework. In: Taylor, J., Woodford, M. (Eds.), Handbook of Macroeconomics, vol. 1. North-Holland, Amsterdam, pp. 1341–1393.

Branch, W., McGough, B., 2018. Heterogeneous expectations and micro-foundations in macroeconomics. In: Handbook of Computational Economics, vol. 4. Elsevier, pp. 3–62 (this Handbook).

Breitmoser, Y., 2016. The Axiomatic Foundation of Logit. MPRA Paper No. 74334.

Caiani, A., Catullo, E., Gallegati, M., 2017. The Effects of Fiscal Targets in a Currency Union: A Multi-Country Agent Based-Stock Flow Consistent Model. Working paper. Università Politecnica delle Marche.

Caiani, A., Godin, A., Caverzasi, E., Gallegati, M., Kinsella, S., Stiglitz, J.E., 2016a. Agent based-stock flow consistent macroeconomics: towards a benchmark model. Journal of Economic Dynamics and Control 69, 375–408.

Caiani, A., Russo, A., Gallegati, M., 2016b. Does Inequality Hamper Innovation and Growth? An AB-SFC Analysis. Working paper. Available at SSRN: http://papers.ssrn.com/sol3/papers.cfm?abstract_id=2790911.

Carroll, C., 1992. How Does Future Income Affect Current Consumption? Working Paper 126. Board of Governors of the Federal Reserve System.

Carroll, C., 1997. Buffer-stock saving and the life cycle/permanent income hypothesis. The Quarterly Journal of Economics 112 (1), 1–55.

Carroll, C., 2003. Macroeconomic expectations of households and professional forecasters. The Quarterly Journal of Economics 118, 269–298.

Carroll, C., 2009. Precautionary saving and the marginal propensity to consume out of permanent income. Journal of Monetary Economics 56 (6), 780–790.

Carroll, C., Summers, L., 1991. Consumption growth parallels income growth: some new evidence. In: Bernheim, B., Shoven, J. (Eds.), National Saving and Economic Performance. University of Chicago Press, Chicago, pp. 305–348.

Catullo, E., Gallegati, M., Palestrini, A., 2015. Towards a credit network based early warning indicator for crises. Journal of Economic Dynamics and Control 50, 78–97.

Chiarella, C., Di Guilmi, C., 2017. Monetary policy and debt deflation: some computational experiments. Macroeconomic Dynamics 21, 214–242.

Cincotti, S., Raberto, M., Teglio, A., 2010. Credit money and macroeconomic instability in the agent-based model and simulator Eurace. Economics: The Open-Access, Open-Assessment E-Journal 4, 1–32.

Cincotti, S., Raberto, M., Teglio, A., 2012a. The Eurace macroeconomic model and simulator. In: Aoki, M., Binmore, K., Deakin, S., Gintis, H. (Eds.), Complexity and Institutions: Markets, Norms and Corporations. Palgrave Macmillan, New York, pp. 81–106.

Cincotti, S., Raberto, M., Teglio, A., 2012b. Macroprudential policies in an agent-based artificial economy. Revue de l'OFCE 124, 205–234.

Cioppa, T., Lucas, T., 2007. Efficient nearly orthogonal and space-filling Latin hypercubes. Technometrics, 45–55.

Cohen, K.J., 1960. Simulation of the firm. The American Economic Review: Papers and Proceedings 50, 534–540.

Colander, D., Howitt, P., Kirman, A., Leijonhufvud, A., Mehrling, P., 2008. Beyond DSGE models: toward an empirically based macroeconomics. The American Economic Review: Papers and Proceedings 98, 236–240.

Cyert, R., March, J., 1963. A Behavioral Theory of the Firm. Blackwell.

Dawid, H., Gemkow, S., 2014. How do social networks contribute to wage inequality? Insights from an agent-based analysis. Industrial and Corporate Change 23, 1171–1200.

Dawid, H., Gemkow, S., Harting, P., Neugart, M., 2009. On the effects of skill upgrading in the presence of spatial labor market frictions: an agent-based analysis of spatial policy design. Journal of Artificial Societies and Social Simulation 12, 4.

Dawid, H., Gemkow, S., Harting, P., Neugart, M., 2012. Labor market integration policies and the convergence of regions: the role of skills and technology diffusion. Journal of Evolutionary Economics 22, 543–562.

Dawid, H., Gemkow, S., Harting, P., Neugart, M., Kabus, K., Wersching, K., 2008. Skills, innovation and growth: an agent-based policy analysis. Journal of Economics and Statistics 228, 251–275.

Dawid, H., Gemkow, S., Harting, P., van der Hoog, S., Neugart, M., 2018a. Agent-based macroeconomic modeling and policy analysis: the Eurace@Unibi model. In: Chen, S.-H., Kaboudan, M., Du, Y.-R. (Eds.), The Oxford Handbook on Computational Economics and Finance. Oxford University Press.

Dawid, H., Harting, P., 2012. Capturing firm behavior in agent-based models of industry evolution and macroeconomic dynamics. In: Bünsdorf, G. (Ed.), Evolution, Organization and Economic Behavior. Edward Elgar. Chapter 6.

Dawid, H., Harting, P., Neugart, M., 2018b. Cohesion Policy and Inequality Dynamics: Insights from a Heterogeneous Agents Macroeconomic Model. Journal of Economic Behavior & Organization. Forthcoming.

Dawid, H., Harting, P., Neugart, M., 2014. Economic convergence: policy implications from a heterogeneous agent model. Journal of Economic Dynamics and Control 44, 54–80.

Dawid, H., Harting, P., Neugart, M., 2018c. Fiscal transfers and regional economic growth. Review of International Economics. https://doi.org/10.1111/roie.12317. Forthcoming.

Dawid, H., Harting, P., van der Hoog, S., Neugart, M., 2018d. A heterogeneous agent macroeconomic model for policy evaluation: improving transparency and reproducibility. Journal of Evolutionary Economics. Forthcoming.

Deaton, A., 1991. Saving and liquidity constraints. Econometrica 59, 1221–1248.

Deissenberg, C., van der Hoog, S., Dawid, H., 2008. Eurace: a massively parallel agent-based model of the European economy. Applied Mathematics and Computation 204, 541–552.

Delli Gatti, D., Desiderio, S., 2015. Monetary policy experiments in an agent-based model with financial frictions. Journal of Economic Interaction and Coordination 10, 265–286.

Delli Gatti, D., Di Guilmi, C., Gaffeo, E., Giulioni, G., Gallegati, M., Palestrini, A., 2005. A new approach to business fluctuations: heterogeneous interacting agents, scaling laws and financial fragility. Journal of Economic Behavior & Organization 56, 489–512.

Delli Gatti, D., Gallegati, M., Cirillo, P., Desiderio, S., Gaffeo, E., 2011. Macroeconomics from the Bottom-Up. Springer-Verlag, Berlin.

Delli Gatti, D., Gallegati, M., Greenwald, B., Russo, A., Stiglitz, J., 2010. The financial accelerator in an evolving credit network. Journal of Economic Dynamics and Control 34, 1627–1650.

Delli Gatti, D., Gallegati, M., Greenwald, B., Russo, A., Stiglitz, J.E., 2006. Business fluctuations in a credit-network economy. Physica A: Statistical Mechanics and Its Applications 370 (1), 68–74.

Delli Gatti, D., Gallegati, M., Greenwald, B., Russo, A., Stiglitz, J.E., 2009. Business fluctuations and bankruptcy avalanches in an evolving network economy. Journal of Economic Interaction and Coordination 4 (2), 195–212.

Dosi, G., Fagiolo, G., Napoletano, M., Roventini, A., 2013. Income distribution, credit and fiscal policies in an agent-based Keynesian model. Journal of Economic Dynamics and Control 37, 1598–1625.

Dosi, G., Fagiolo, G., Napoletano, M., Roventini, A., Treibich, T., 2015. Fiscal and monetary policies in complex evolving economies. Journal of Economic Dynamics and Control 52, 166–189.

Dosi, G., Fagiolo, G., Roventini, A., 2006. An evolutionary model of endogenous business cycles. Computational Economics 27, 3–34.

Dosi, G., Fagiolo, G., Roventini, A., 2008. The microfoundations of business cycles: an evolutionary multi-agent model. Journal of Evolutionary Economics 18, 413–432.

Dosi, G., Fagiolo, G., Roventini, A., 2010. Schumpeter meeting Keynes: a policy-friendly model of endogenous growth and business cycles. Journal of Economic Dynamics and Control 34, 1748–1767.

Dosi, G., Napoletano, M., Roventini, A., Treibich, T., 2017a. Micro and macro policies in the Keynes plus Schumpeter evolutionary models. Journal of Evolutionary Economics 27, 63–90.

Dosi, G., Pereira, M., Roventini, A., Virgillito, M., 2017b. Causes and Consequences of Hysteresis: Aggregate Demand, Productivity and Employment. LEM Working Paper No. 2017/07.

Dosi, G., Pereira, M., Roventini, A., Virgillito, M., 2017c. When more flexibility yields more fragility: the microfoundations of Keynesian aggregate unemployment. Journal of Economic Dynamics and Control 81, 162–186.

Dosi, G., Roventini, A., Russo, E., 2017d. Endogenous Growth and Global Divergence in a Multi-Country Agent-Based Model. LEM Working Paper No. 2017/32.

Dosi, G., Pereira, M., Roventini, A., Virgillito, M., 2018. The effects of labour market reforms upon unemployment and income inequalities: an agent based model approach. Socio-Economic Review. Forthcoming.

Eliason, G., 1977. Competition and market processes in a simulation model of the Swedish economy. The American Economic Review 67, 277–281.

Eliason, G., 1984. Micro-heterogeneity of firms and the stability of industrial growth. Journal of Economic Behavior & Organization 5, 249–274.

Erlingsson, E.J., Raberto, M., Stefánsson, H., Sturluson, J.T., 2013. Integrating the housing market into an agent-based economic model. In: Teglio, A., Alfarano, S., Camacho-Cuena, E., Ginés-Vilar, M. (Eds.), Managing Market Complexity. In: Lecture Notes in Economics and Mathematical Systems. Springer.

Erlingsson, E., Teglio, A., Cincotti, S., Stefansson, H., Sturluson, J.T., Raberto, M., 2014. Housing market bubbles and business cycles in an agent-based credit economy. Economics: The Open-Access, Open Assessment E-Journal 8.

Fagiolo, G., Roventini, A., 2012. On the scientific status of economic policy: a tale of alternative paradigms. Knowledge Engineering Review 27, 163–185.

Fagiolo, G., Roventini, A., 2017. Macroeconomic policy in DSGE and agent-based models Redux: new developments and challenges ahead. Journal of Artificial Societies and Social Simulation 20, 1.

Fontana, M., 2010. The Santa Fe perspective on economics: emerging patterns in the science of complexity. History of Economic Ideas 18, 167–196.

Gaffeo, E., Catalano, M., Clementi, F., Delli Gatti, D., Gallegati, M., Russo, A., 2007. Reflections on modern macroeconomics: can we travel along a safer road? Physica A: Statistical Mechanics and Its Applications 382 (1), 68–74.

Gaffeo, E., Gallegati, M., Gostoli, U., 2015. An agent-based "proof of principle" for Walrasian macroeconomic theory. Computational and Mathematical Organization Theory 21, 150–183.

Gali, J., 2008. Monetary Policy, Inflation and the Business Cycle. Princeton University Press, Princeton, New Jersey.

Gigerenzer, G., Gaissmaier, W., 2011. Heuristic decision making. Annual Review of Psychology 62, 451–482.

Goudet, O., Kant, J.-D., Ballot, G., 2015. Forbidding fixed duration contracts: unfolding the opposing effects with a multiagent model of the French labour market. In: Amblard, F., Miguel, F., Blanchet, A., Gaudou, B. (Eds.), Advances in Artificial Economics. In: Lecture Notes in Economics and Mathematical Systems, vol. 676. Springer, Berlin, pp. 151–167.

Grazzini, J., Richiardi, M.G., Tsionas, M., 2017. Bayesian estimation of agent-based models. Journal of Economic Dynamics and Control 77, 26–47.

Greenwald, B., Stiglitz, J., 1993. Financial markets imperfections and business cycles. The Quarterly Journal of Economics 108, 77–113.

Gualdi, S., Tarzia, M., Zamponi, F., Bouchaud, J., 2015. Tipping points in macroeconomic agent-based models. Journal of Economic Dynamics and Control 50 (1), 29–61.

Guerini, M., Moneta, A., 2017. A method for agent-based models validation. Journal of Economic Dynamics and Control 82, 125–141.

Haas, A., Jaeger, C., 2005. Agents, Bayes, and climate risks – a modular modelling approach. Advances in Geosciences 4, 3–7.

Haber, G., 2008. Monetary and fiscal policy analysis with an agent-based macroeconomic model. Journal of Economics and Statistics 228, 276–295.

Haldane, A., 2016. The dappled world. http://www.bankofengland.co.uk/publications/pages/speeches/2016/937.aspx.

Harting, P., 2015. Stabilization Policies and Long Term Growth: Policy Implications from an Agent-Based Macroeconomic Model. Bielefeld Working Paper in Economics and Management No. 06-2015.

Haruvy, E., Roth, A., Unver, U., 2006. The dynamics of law clerk matching: an experimental and computational investigation of proposals for reform of the market. Journal of Economic Dynamics and Control 30, 457–486.

Holcombe, M., Coakley, S., Kiran, M., Chin, S., Greenough, C., Worth, D., Cincotti, S., Raberto, M., Teglio, A., Deissenberg, C., van der Hoog, S., Dawid, H., Gemkow, S., Harting, P., Neugart, M., 2013. Large-scale modeling of economic systems. Complex Systems 22, 175–191.

Hommes, C., 2013. Behavioral Rationality and Heterogeneous Expectations in Complex Economic Systems. Cambridge University Press.

Hommes, C., Sonnemans, J., Tuinstra, J., van de Velden, H., 2005. Coordination of expectations in asset pricing experiments. The Review of Financial Studies 18, 955–980.

Howitt, P., 2012. What have central bankers learned from modern macroeconomic theory? Journal of Macroeconomics 34, 11–22.

Kirman, A., 1992. Whom or what does the representative individual represent? The Journal of Economic Perspectives 6, 117–136.

Kirman, A., 2016. Ants and nonoptimal self-organization: lessons for macroeconomics. Macroeconomic Dynamics 20, 601–621.

Kiyotaki, N., Moore, J., 1997. Credit cycles. Journal of Political Economy 105, 211–248.

Klimek, P., Poledna, S., Farmer, J., Thurner, S., 2015. To bail-out or to bail-in? Answers from an agent-based model. Journal of Economic Dynamics and Control 50, 144–154.

Krug, S., 2015. The Interaction Between Monetary and Macroprudential Policy: Should Central Banks "Lean Against the Wind" to Foster Macrofinancial Stability? Economics Working Paper No. 2015-08. Christian-Albrechts-Universität Kiel, Department of Economics.

Krug, S., Wohltmann, H.-W., 2016. Shadow Banking, Financial Regulation and Animal Spirits: An Ace Approach. Economics Working Paper No. 2016-08. Christian-Albrechts-Universität Kiel, Department of Economics.

Lamperti, F., Dosi, G., Napoletano, M., Roventini, A., Sapio, A., 2017. Faraway, So Close: Coupled Climate and Economic Dynamics in an Agent-Based Integrated Assessment Model. LEM Working Paper 2017/12.

Landini, S., Di Guilmi, C., Gallegati, M., 2017. Interactive Macroeconomics: Stochastic Aggregate Dynamics with Heterogeneous and Interacting Agents. Cambridge University Press.

Leijonhufvud, A., 1993. Towards a not-too-rational macroeconomics. Southern Economic Journal 1, 1–13.

Lengnick, M., 2013. Agent-based macroeconomics: a baseline model. Journal of Economic Behavior & Organization 86, 102–120.

Lengnick, M., Wohltmann, H.-W., 2011. Agent-Based Financial Markets and New Keynesian Macroeconomics: A Synthesis. Economics Working Paper No. 2011-09. Christian-Albrechts-Universität Kiel, Department of Economics.

Lengnick, M., Wohltmann, H.-W., 2016. Optimal monetary policy in a new Keynesian model with animal spirits and financial markets. Journal of Economic Dynamics and Control 64, 148–165.

Lux, T., Zwinkels, C., 2018. Empirical validation of agent-based models. In: Handbook of Computational Economics, vol. 4. Elsevier, pp. 437–488 (this Handbook).

Mandel, A., Jaeger, C., Fuerst, S., Lass, W., Lincke, D., Meissner, F., Pablo-Marti, F., Wolf, S., 2010. Agent-Based Dynamics in Disaggregated Growth Models. Centre d'Economie de la Sorbonne Working Paper 10077.

Minsky, H., 1963. Can "it" happen again. In: Carson, D. (Ed.), Banking and Monetary Studies. Richard D. Irwin, Homewood.

Napoletano, M., Dosi, G., Fagiolo, G., Roventini, A., 2012. Wage formation, investment behavior and growth regimes: an agent-based analysis. Revue de l'OFCE 124, 235–261.

Napoletano, M., Roventini, A., Gaffard, J.-L., 2015. Time-Varying Fiscal Multipliers in an Agent-Based Model with Credit Rationing. GREDEG Working Paper No. 2015-30.

Nelson, R., Winter, S., 1974. Neoclassical vs. evolutionary theories of economic growth: critique and prospectus. The Economic Journal 84, 886–905.

Nelson, R., Winter, S., 1982. An Evolutionary Theory of Economic Change. Belknap, Cambridge, MA.

Nelson, R., Winter, S., Schuette, H., 1976. Technical change in an evolutionary model. The Quarterly Journal of Economics 90, 90–118.

Neugart, M., Richiardi, M., 2018. Agent-based models of the labor market. In: Chen, S.-H., Kaboudan, M., Du, Y.-R. (Eds.), The Oxford Handbook of Computational Economics and Finance. Oxford University Press.

Neveu, A., 2013. Fiscal policy and business cycle characteristics in a heterogeneous agent macro model. Journal of Economic Behavior & Organization 90, 224–240.

Ozel, B., Nathanael, R., Raberto, M., Teglio, A., Cincotti, S., 2016. Macroeconomic Implications of Mortgage Loans Requirements: An Agent Based Approach. Working Paper 2016/05. Economics Department, Universitat Jaume I, Castellón.

Petrovic, M., Ozel, B., Teglio, A., Raberto, M., Cincotti, S., 2017. Eurace Open: An Agent-Based Multi-Country Model. Working Paper No. 2017/09. Economics Department, Universitat Jaume I.

Piva, M., Vivarelli, M., 2009. Corporate skills as an ex-ante incentive to R&D investment. International Journal of Manpower 30, 835–852.

Ponta, L., Raberto, M., Cincotti, S., 2018. An agent-based stock-flow consistent model of the sustainable transition in the energy sector. Ecological Economics 145, 274–300.

Popoyan, L., Napoletano, M., Roventini, A., 2017. Taming macroeconomic instability: monetary and macroprudential policy interactions in an agent-based model. Journal of Economic Behavior & Organization 134, 117–140.

Raberto, M., Cincotti, S., Teglio, A., 2014. Fiscal consolidation and sovereign debt risk in balance-sheet recessions: an agent-based approach. In: Manica, P.T.L. (Ed.), Economic Policy and the Financial Crisis. Routledge.

Raberto, M., Nathanael, R., Ozel, B., Teglio, A., Cincotti, S., 2017. Credit-driven business cycles in an agent-base macro model. In: Scholz-Wäckerle, M., Hanappi, H., Katsikides, S. (Eds.), Theory and Method of Evolutionary Political Economy. Routledge.

Raberto, M., Ozel, B., Ponta, L., Teglio, A., Cincotti, S., 2018. From financial instability to green finance: the role of banking and monetary policies in the Eurace model. Journal of Evolutionary Economics. https://doi.org/10.1007/s00191-018-0568-2. Forthcoming.

Raberto, M., Teglio, A., Cincotti, S., 2008. Integrating real and financial markets in an agent-based economic model: an application to monetary policy design. Computational Economics 32, 147–162.

Raberto, M., Teglio, A., Cincotti, S., 2012. Debt, deleveraging and business cycles: an agent-based perspective. Economics: The Open-Access, Open-Assessment E-Journal 6, 2012-27.

Ragot, X., 2018. Heterogeneous agents in the macroeconomy: reduced-heterogeneity representations. In: Handbook of Computational Economics, vol. 4. Elsevier, pp. 215–253 (this Handbook).

Riccetti, L., Russo, A., Gallegati, M., 2013. Leveraged network-based financial accelerator. Journal of Economic Dynamics and Control 37 (8), 1626–1640.

Riccetti, L., Russo, A., Gallegati, M., 2015. An agent based decentralized matching macroeconomic model. Journal of Economic Interaction and Coordination 10 (2), 305–332.

Riccetti, L., Russo, A., Gallegati, M., 2016a. Financialisation and crisis in an agent based macroeconomic model. Economic Modelling 52 (PA), 162–172.

Riccetti, L., Russo, A., Gallegati, M., 2016b. Stock market dynamics, leveraged network-based financial accelerator and monetary policy. International Review of Economics & Finance 43 (C), 509–524.

Riccetti, L., Russo, A., Gallegati, M., 2018. Financial regulation and endogenous macroeconomic crises. Macroeconomic Dynamics. https://doi.org/10.1017/S1365100516000444. Forthcoming.

Richiardi, M., 2017. The future of agent-based modeling. Eastern Economic Journal 43, 271–287.

Romer, P., 2016. The trouble with macroeconomics. Working Paper. New York University.

Russo, A., Catalano, M., Gaffeo, E., Gallegati, M., Napoletano, M., 2007. Industrial dynamics, fiscal policy and R&D: evidence from a computational experiment. Journal of Economic Behavior & Organization 64, 426–447.

Russo, A., Riccetti, L., Gallegati, 2016. Increasing inequality, consumer credit and financial fragility in an agent based macroeconomic model. Journal of Evolutionary Economics 26, 25–47.

Salle, I., 2015. Modeling expectations in agent-based models—an application to central bank's communication and monetary policy. Economic Modelling 46, 130–141.

Salle, I., Yıldızoglu, M., Senegas, M.-A., 2013. Inflation targeting in a learning economy: an ABM perspective. Economic Modelling 34, 114–128.

Seppecher, P., 2012. Flexibility of wages and macroeconomic instability in an agent-based computational model with endogenous money. Macroeconomic Dynamics 16, 284–297.

Seppecher, P., Salle, I., 2015. Deleveraging crises and deep recessions: a behavioural approach. Applied Economics 47, 3771–3790.

Seppecher, P., Salle, I., Lavoie, M., 2018. What drives markups? Evolutionary pricing in an agent-based stock-flow consistent macroeconomic model. Industrial and Corporate Change. Forthcoming.

Simon, H., 1959. Theories of decision-making in economics and behavioral science. The American Economic Review 49, 253–283.

Sims, C., 1980. Macroeconomics and reality. Econometrica 48, 1–48.

Sinitskaya, E., Tesfatsion, L., 2015. Macroeconomies as constructively rational games. Journal of Economic Dynamics and Control 61, 152–182.

Teglio, A., Cincotti, S., Erlingsson, E., Raberto, M., Stefansson, H., Sturluson, J., 2014. Subprime lending and financial inequality in an agent-based model. In: Leitner, S., Wall, F. (Eds.), Artificial Economics and Self Organization. In: Lecture Notes in Economics and Mathematical Systems. Springer.

Teglio, A., Mazzocchetti, A., Ponta, L., Raberto, M., Cincotti, S., 2018. Budgetary rigour with stimulus in lean times: policy advices from an agent-based model. Journal of Economic Behavior & Organization. https://doi.org/10.1016/j.jebo.2017.09.016. Forthcoming.

Teglio, A., Raberto, M., Cincotti, S., 2010. Endogenous credit dynamics as source of business cycles in the Eurace model. In: Calzi, M.L., Milone, L., Pellizzari, P. (Eds.), Progress in Artificial Economics. Computational and Agent-Based Models. In: Lecture Notes in Economics and Mathematical Systems. Springer.

Teglio, A., Raberto, M., Cincotti, S., 2012. The impact of banks' capital adequacy regulation on the economic system: an agent-based approach. Advances in Complex Systems 15.

Tesfatsion, L., 2006. Agent-based computational economics: a constructive approach to economic theory. In: Tesfatsion, L., Judd, K. (Eds.), Handbook of Computational Economics, vol. II. North-Holland, pp. 831–880.

Tesfatsion, L., Judd, K.E., 2006. Handbook of Computational Economics II: Agent-Based Computational Economics. North-Holland.

Trichet, J., 2010. Reflections on the nature of monetary policy non-standard measures and finance theory. http://www.ecb.europa.eu/press/key/date/2010/html/sp101118.en.html.

van der Hoog, S., 2018. The limits to credit growth: mitigation policies and macroprudential regulations to foster macrofinancial stability and sustainable debt. Computational Economics. https://doi.org/10.1007/s10614-017-9714-4. Forthcoming.

van der Hoog, S., Dawid, H., 2018. Bubbles, crashes and the financial cycle: the impact of banking regulation on deep recessions. Macroeconomic Dynamics. https://doi.org/10.1017/S1365100517000219 . Forthcoming.

Wolf, S., Fürst, S., Mandel, A., Lass, W., Lincke, D., Pablo-Martí, F., Jaeger, C., 2013. A multi-agent model of several economic regions. Environmental Modelling & Software 44, 25–43.

Endogenous Firm Dynamics and Labor Flows via Heterogeneous Agents*

3

Robert Axtell

Department of Computational and Data Sciences, Department of Economics, and Center for Social Complexity, Krasnow Institute for Advanced Study, George Mason University, Fairfax, VA, United States
e-mail address: rax222@gmu.edu

CONTENTS

Support from the John D. and Catherine T. MacArthur Foundation, the National Science Foundation (0738606), the Small Business Administration (SBAHQ-05-Q-0018), and the Mercatus Center at George Mason is gratefully acknowledged. I have no relevant or material financial interests that relate to the research described in this paper or the associated model. Earlier versions of this work were presented at research institutions (Aix-en-Provence, Arizona State, Brookings, Carnegie Mellon, Emory, Esalen, Essex, George Mason, Georgia, Georgia Tech, James Madison, Leicester, Leiden, Limerick, Nanyang Technological University, New School for Social Research, Office of Financial Research, Oxford, Queen Mary and Westfield, Sant' Anna (Pisa), Santa Fe Institute, Turino) and conferences (Eastern Economic Association, INFORMS, Society for Computational Economics, Southern Economic Association) where comments from attendees yielded significant improvements. For helpful feedback on the manuscript I am grateful to Zoltan Acs, Luis Amaral, Brian Arthur, David Audretsch, Bob Axelrod, Bob Ayres, Eric Beinhocker, Margaret Blair, Pete Boettke, David Canning, Kathleen Carley, John Chisholm, Alex Coad, Herbert Dawid, Art DeVany, Bill Dickens, Kathy Eisenhardt, Joshua Epstein, Doyne Farmer, Rich Florida, Duncan Foley, Xavier Gabaix, Chris Georges, Herb Gintis, Joe Harrington, John Holland, Stu Kauffman, Steve Kimbrough, Paul Kleindorfer, Blake LeBaron, Axel Leijonhufvud, Bob Litan, Francesco Luna, Jim March, Michael Maouboussin, Greg McRae, Benoit Morel, Scott Moss, Paul Omerod, J. Barkley Rosser Jr., Martin Shubik, Gene Stanley, Dan Teitelbaum, Leigh Tesfatsion, Sid Winter and several people who are no longer with us: Per Bak, Michael Cohen, Ben Harrison, Steve Klepper, Sam Kotz, and Benoit Mandelbrot. The late Herb Simon inspired and encouraged the work. Anna Nelson and Omar Guerrero each advanced the work through their Ph.D. dissertations. Thanks are due Miles Parker and Gabriel Balan for implementing the model in Java, first in Ascape and then in Mason. Errors are my own.

> *Human beings, viewed as behaving systems, are quite simple. The apparent com-*
> *plexity of our behavior over time is largely a reflection of the complexity of the*
> *environment in which we find ourselves.*
>
> **Herbert Simon (1996, p. 53)**

1 INTRODUCTION

While it is conventional, in a wide variety of economic models, to assume that the
economy is in general equilibrium, there is, in fact, substantial dynamism in real

economies. Consider the U.S. private sector: over the last decade the workforce has ranged from 115 to 120 million employees annually, with nearly 3 million workers changing employers *each month* on average (Davis et al., 2006). Over this same period there were, each year, 5.7–6.0 million firms with employees of which, on average, nearly 100 thousand went out of business *monthly* while a comparable number started up (Fairlie, 2012). Such high levels of turnover in the American economy—1 in 40 workers changing employers monthly, 1 in 60 firms terminating its operations—portrays a kind of *perpetual economic flux* in the U.S. How are we to interpret such persistent adjustments and reorganizations of productive activities? Conventionally, they are believed to represent the reallocation of human resources to more productive uses (Caves, 1998). But do they generate actual productivity gains at the firm level? Do such fluxes partially result from previous changes, e.g., filling jobs previously opened? Do they cause new fluxes in the next period? Are they produced by *exogenous* shocks, whether aggregate or firm-specific (e.g., technological or productivity-related), or are they due to *endogenous* agent interactions and decisions? If we stipulate that the economy is in general equilibrium then there is no way to realize micro-dynamics except by the imposition of external shocks. Can microeconomic models *endogenously* produce the kinds of dynamics observed empirically when the incentives agents have to change jobs are fully represented?

The main result of the research described here is a microeconomic model capable of producing, *without* exogenous shocks, firm and labor dynamics of the size and type experienced by the U.S. economy prior to the recent financial crisis. In addition to the nearly 3 million people who change jobs in the U.S. each month, about half as many, some 1.5 million workers, separate from their employers monthly without new jobs, becoming unemployed, while a comparable number move off unemployment into new jobs; another 1.5 million people either leave the workforce for a spell or else begin a job after being out of the workforce. These flows sum to approximately 9 million labor market events per month at steady-state (Fallick and Fleischman, 2004). Further, many of the vacancies created by such *inter-firm* flows are filled by *intra-firm* job changes, about which there are few data. All told, perhaps 12 million distinct job change events occur each *month* in the U.S., primarily among the 120 million people in the private sector. Clearly, over the course of a year there is enormous turnover in the matching of people to jobs in the U.S. While conventional explanations for these large labor flows exist (e.g., Krusell et al., 2011, 2017), here I provide a microeconomic explanation *without the need for aggregate shocks*.

This model also reproduces a variety of cross-sectional properties of U.S. businesses. Over the past decade there have appeared increasing amounts of micro-data on U.S. firms, including administratively *comprehensive* (tax record-based) data on firm sizes, ages, growth rates, labor productivity, job tenure, and wages. Extant theories place few restrictions on these data.[1] Lucas (1978) derives Pareto-distributed firm sizes from a postulated Pareto distribution of managerial talent. Luttmer (2007, 2010)

---

[1] A generation ago Simon noted the inability of the neoclassical theory of the firm to explain the empirical size distribution (Ijiri and Simon, 1977, pp. 7–11, 138–140; Simon, 1997). Transaction cost (e.g.,

obtains Zipf-distributed firm sizes and exponential firm ages (2011) in a variety of general equilibrium settings, driven by exogenous shocks. Rossi-Hansberg and Wright (2007) study establishment growth and exit rates arising in general equilibrium due to industry-specific productivity shocks. Elsby and Michaels (2013) and Arkolakis (2013) simulate heterogeneous firm growth rates due to productivity shocks. However, there are *many* more data on firms and labor to be explained. The model described below reproduces more than three dozen features of the empirical data *without* recourse to exogenous shocks—such shocks are not necessary in a model with worker-level dynamics.

The model draws together threads from various theoretical literatures. It is written at the level of individual agents and incentive problems of the type studied in the principal-agent literature manifest themselves. The agents work in perpetually novel environments, so contracts are incomplete and transaction costs are implicit. Each firm is a coalition of agents making the theory of coalition formation relevant (Ray, 2007). Agent decisions generate firm growth and decline in the spirit of evolutionary economics (Nelson and Winter, 1982).

Specifically, the model consists of a heterogeneous population of agents with preferences for income and leisure. Production takes place under increasing returns to scale, so agents who work together can produce more output per unit effort than by working alone. However, agents act non-cooperatively[2]: they select effort levels that improve their own welfare, and may migrate between firms or start-up new firms when it is advantageous to do so. Analytically, Nash equilibria within a firm can be unstable. Large firms are ultimately unstable because each agent's compensation is imperfectly related to its effort level, making free-riding possible. Highly productive agents eventually leave large firms and such firms eventually decline. All firms have finite lives. The dynamics of firms perpetually forming, growing and perishing are studied. It will be shown that *this non-equilibrium regime provides greater welfare than equilibrium.*

These dynamics mean it is analytically difficult to relate agent level behavior to aggregate outcomes. Therefore, features that emerge at the firm population level are studied using agent-based computing (Holland and Miller, 1991; Vriend, 1995; Axtell, 2000; Tesfatsion, 2002). In agent computing individual software objects represent people and have behavioral rules governing their interactions. Agent models are 'spun' forward in time and regularities emerge from the interactions (e.g., Grimm et al., 2005). The shorthand for this is that macro-structure "grows" from the bottom-up.[3] No equations governing the aggregate level are specified. Nor do agents have either complete information or correct models for how

---

Williamson, 1985) and game theoretic explanations of the firm (e.g., Hart, 1995; Zame, 2007) make few empirical claims. Sutton (1998) bounds the extent of intra-industry concentration, constraining the shape of size distributions.

[2]For a cooperative game theoretic view of firms see Ichiishi (1993).

[3]'Growing' social phenomena in this way automatically entails sufficient explanation, since a demonstration is provided that the phenomenon to be explained (the explanandum) directly results from agents following certain behavioral rules (explanans); to wit: a social phenomenon has been explained if it has

the economy will unfold. Instead, they glean data inductively from the environment and from their social networks, through direct interactions, and make imperfect forecasts of economic opportunities (Arthur, 1994b). The macroscopic properties of the model *emerge* from the agent interactions. This methodology facilitates modeling agent heterogeneity (Kirman, 1992), non-equilibrium dynamics (Arthur, 2006), local interactions (Kirman, 1997), and bounded rationality (Arthur, 1991; Kirman, 1993).

2 DYNAMICS OF TEAM PRODUCTION

Consider a group of agents A, $|A| = n$, engaged in team production, each agent contributing some amount of effort, generating team output.[4] Specifically, agent i has endowment $\omega_i > 0$ and contributes effort level $e_{i \in A} \in [0, \omega_i]$, to the group. The total effort of the group is then $E \equiv \sum_{i \in A} e_i$. The group produces output, O, as a function of E, according to $O(E) = aE + bE^\beta$, $\beta > 1$, without capital as in Hopenhayn (1992).[5] For $b > 0$ there are increasing returns to effort.[6] Increasing returns in production means that agents working together can produce more than they can as individuals.[7] To see this, consider two agents having effort levels e_1 and e_2, with $\beta = 2$. As individuals they produce total output $O_1 + O_2 = a(e_1 + e_2) + b(e_1^2 + e_2^2)$, while working together they make $a(e_1 + e_2) + b(e_1 + e_2)^2$. Clearly this latter quantity is at least as large as the former since $(e_1 + e_2)^2 \geq e_1^2 + e_2^2$. Agents earn according to a compensation rule. For now consider agents sharing total output equally: at the end of each period all output is sold for unit price and each agent receives an O/N

---

been 'grown' in this sense. By contrast, Epstein (2006) has asserted that if a phenomenon has not been 'grown' then it has not been explained, a much stronger claim. Insofar as Newton, Darwin, and Maxwell did not 'grow' gravity, evolution, or electromagnetism, respectively, from the bottom up, i.e., in terms of lower level principles, yet each provided scientific explanations for the natural phenomena they investigated, Epstein's position is not tenable as philosophy, although perhaps useful as a motto, a kind of rallying cry for the science of emergence (Laughlin and Pines, 2000). Rather, the converse of Epstein's claim— if a phenomenon has not been explained then it has not been grown—is defensible as the contrapositive version of the original claim, that if one has 'grown' a phenomenon then it has been explained.

[4] The model derives from Canning (1995), Huberman and Glance (1998), and Glance et al. (1997).

[5] While $O(E)$ relates inputs to outputs, like a standard production function, E is not the choice of a single decision-maker, since it results from the actions of autonomous agents. Thus, $O(E)$ cannot be made the subject of a math program, as in conventional production theory, yet does describe production possibilities.

[6] Increasing returns at the firm level goes back at least to Marshall (1920) and was the basis of theoretical controversies in the 1920s (Sraffa, 1926; Young, 1928). Recent work on increasing returns is reprinted in Arthur (1994a) and Buchanan and Yoon (1994). Colander and Landreth (1999) give a history of the idea.

[7] There are many ways to motivate increasing returns, including 'four hands problems': two people working together are able to perform a task that neither could do alone, like carrying a piano up a flight of stairs.

share of the total output.[8] Agents have Cobb–Douglas preferences for income and leisure, parameterized by θ.[9] All time not spent working is spent in leisure, so agent i's utility can be written as a function of its effort, e_i, and the effort of other agents, $E_{\sim i} \equiv E - e_i$ as

$$U_i(e_i) = \left(\frac{a(e_i + E_{\sim i}) + b(e_i + E_{\sim i})^\beta}{n} \right)^{\theta_i} (\omega_i - e_i)^{1-\theta_i}. \tag{1}$$

2.1 EQUILIBRIUM OF THE TEAM PRODUCTION GAME

Consider the individual efforts of agents as unobservable. From team output, O, each agent i determines E and, from its contribution to production, e_i, can figure out $E_{\sim i}$. Agent i then selects the effort level that maximizes its utility, i.e.,

$$e_i^* (\theta_i, \omega_i, E_{\sim i}, a, b) = \arg \max_{e_i} U_i (e_i; \theta_i, \omega_i, E_{\sim i}, n, a, b, \beta).$$

For $\beta = 2$, in symbols,

$$e_i^* = \max \left\{ 0, \frac{2b(\theta_i \omega_i - E_{\sim i}) - a + \sqrt{4b\theta_i^2 (\omega_i + E_{\sim i})[a + b(\omega_i + E_{\sim i})] + a^2}}{2b(1 + \theta_i)} \right\}. \tag{2}$$

Note that e_i^* does not depend on n but does depend on $E_{\sim i}$—the effort put in by the other agents. To develop intuition for the general dependence of e_i^* on its parameters, Fig. 1 plots it for $a = b = 1$ and $\omega_i = 10$, as functions of $E_{\sim i}$ and θ_i. Optimal effort decreases monotonically as 'other agent effort,' $E_{\sim i}$, increases. For each θ_i there exists some $E_{\sim i}$ beyond which it is rational for agent i to put in no effort. For constant returns, i.e. $b = 0$, e_i^* falls linearly with $E_{\sim i}$ with slope $\theta_i - 1$.

Singleton Firms

The $E_{\sim i} = 0$ solution of (2) corresponds to agents working alone in single agent firms. For this case the expression for the optimal effort level is

$$e^* = \frac{2b\theta\omega - a + \sqrt{4b\theta^2\omega[a + b\omega] + a^2}}{2b(1 + \theta)}. \tag{3}$$

For $\theta = 0$, $e^* = 0$ while for $\theta = 1$, $e^* = \omega$.

---

[8] The model yields roughly constant total output, so in a competitive market the price of output would be nearly constant. Since there are no fixed costs, agent shares sum to total cost, which equals total revenue. The shares can be thought of as either uniform wages in pure competition or profit shares in a partnership.
[9] Appendix A gives a more general model of preferences, yielding qualitatively identical results.

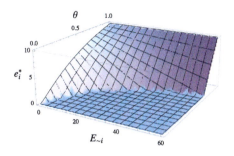

FIGURE 1

Dependence of e_i^* on $E_{\sim i}$ and θ for $a = 1$, $b = 1$, $\omega_i = 10$.

Nash Equilibrium

Equilibrium in a team corresponds to each agent working with effort e_i^* from (2), using $E_{\sim i}^*$ in place of $E_{\sim i}$ such that $E_{\sim i}^* = \sum_{j \neq i} e_j^*$. This leads to:

Proposition 1. *Nash equilibrium exists and is unique (Rosen, 1965; Watts, 2002).*

Proof. From the continuity of the *RHS* of (2) and the convexity and compactness of the space of effort levels, a fixed point exists by the Brouwer theorem. Each fixed point is a Nash equilibrium, since once it is established no agent can make itself better off by working at some other effort level. $\square$

Proposition 2. *There exists a set of efforts that Pareto dominate Nash equilibrium (Hölmstrom, 1982), a subset of which are Pareto optimal. These (a) involve larger effort levels than the Nash equilibrium, and (b) are not individually rational.*

Proof. To see (a) note that

$$dU_i(e_i^*) = \frac{\partial U_i}{\partial e_i} de_i + \frac{\partial U_i}{\partial E_{\sim i}} dE_{\sim i} > 0,$$

since the first term on the *RHS* vanishes at the Nash equilibrium and

$$\frac{\partial U_i}{\partial E_{\sim i}} = \frac{\theta_i \, (a + 2b \, (e_i + E_{\sim i})) \, (\omega_i - e_i)^{1-\theta_i}}{n^{\theta_i} \, [(e_i + E_{\sim i}) \, (a + b \, (e_i + E_{\sim i}))]^{1-\theta_i}} > 0.$$

For (b), each agent's utility is monotone increasing on the interval $[0, e_i^*)$, and monotone decreasing on $(e_i^*, \omega_i]$. Therefore, $\partial U_i / \partial e_i < 0 \; \forall e_i > e_i^*$, $E_{\sim i} > E_{\sim i}^*$. $\square$

The effort region that Pareto-dominates Nash equilibrium is the space where individuals who are part of the firm can achieve higher welfare than they do either working alone or at Nash equilibrium within the team.

Example 1 (*Nash equilibrium in a team with free agent entry and exit*). Four agents having θs of $\{0.6, 0.7, 0.8, 0.9\}$ work together in a team in which $a =$

$b = 1$ and the agents have equal endowments, $\omega_i = 1$. Equilibrium, from (2), has agents working with efforts $\{0.15, 0.45, 0.68, 0.86\}$, respectively, producing 6.74 units of output. The corresponding utilities are $\{1.28, 1.20, 1.21, 1.32\}$. If these agents worked alone they would, by (3), put in efforts $\{0.68, 0.77, 0.85, 0.93\}$, generating outputs of $\{1.14, 1.36, 1.58, 1.80\}$ and total output of 6.07. Their utilities would be $\{0.69, 0.80, 0.98, 1.30\}$. Working together they put in less effort and receive greater reward. This is the essence of team production. Now say a $\theta = 0.75$ agent joins the team. The four original members adjust their effort to $\{0.05, 0.39, 0.64, 0.84\}$—i.e., all workless—while total output rises to 8.41. Their utilities increase to $\{1.34, 1.24, 1.23, 1.33\}$. The new agent works with effort 0.52, receiving utility of 1.23, above its singleton utility of 0.80. If another agent having $\theta = 0.75$ joins the team the new equilibrium efforts of the original group members are $\{0.00, 0.33, 0.61, 0.83\}$, while the two newest agents contribute 0.48. The total output rises to 10.09 with utilities $\{1.37, 1.28, 1.26, 1.34\}$ for the original agents and 1.26 for each of the twins. Overall, even though the new agent induces one co-worker to free ride, the net effect is a Pareto improvement. Next, an agent with $\theta = 0.55$ (or less) joins. Such an agent will free ride and not affect the effort or output levels, so efforts of the extant group members will not change. However, since output must be shared with one additional agent, all utilities fall. For the 4 originals these become $\{1.25, 1.15, 1.11, 1.17\}$. For the twins their utility falls to 1.12 and that of the $\theta = 0.9$ agent is now below what it can get working alone (1.17 vs. 1.30). Since agents may exit the group freely, it is rational for this agent to do so, causing further adjustment: the three original agents work with efforts $\{0.10, 0.42, 0.66\}$, while the twins add 0.55 and the newest agent free rides. Output is 7.52, yielding utility of $\{1.10, 0.99, 0.96\}$ for the original three, 0.97 for the twins, and 1.13 for the free rider. Unfortunately for the group, the $\theta = 0.8$ agent now can do better by working alone—utility of 0.98 versus 0.96, inducing further adjustments: the original two work with efforts 0.21 and 0.49, respectively, the twins put in effort of 0.61, and the $\theta = 0.55$ agent rises out of free-riding to work at the 0.04 level; output drops to 5.80. The utilities of the originals are now 0.99 and 0.90, 0.88 for the twins, and 1.07 for the newest agent. Now the $\theta = 0.75$ agents are indifferent between staying or starting new singleton teams.

Homogeneous Teams

Consider a team composed of agents of the same type (identical θ and ω). In a homogeneous group each agent works with the same effort in equilibrium, determined from (2) by substituting $(n - 1) e_i^*$ for $E_{\sim i}$, and solving for e^*, yielding:

$$e^* = \frac{2bn\theta\omega - a\left(\theta + n\left(1 - \theta\right)\right) + \sqrt{4bn\theta^2\omega\left(a + bn\omega\right) + a^2\left(\theta + n\left(1 - \theta\right)\right)^2}}{2bn\left(2\theta + n\left(1 - \theta\right)\right)}.$$

(4)

It is easy to see that (4) specializes to (3) in the case of $n = 1$. These efforts are shown in Fig. 2 as a function of θ with $a = b = 1$ and various n, for two values of ω. Clearly, effort in monotonically increasing in preference for income, θ. Note that agents with

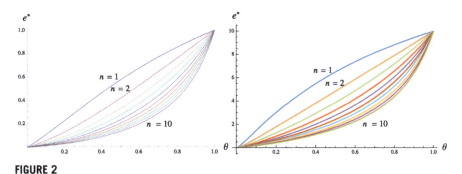

FIGURE 2

Optimal agent effort in homogeneous teams as a function of n for various θ, with $a = b = 1$ and $\omega = 1$ (left) and $\omega = 10$ (right).

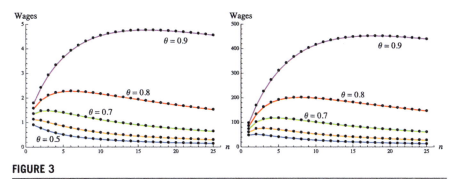

FIGURE 3

Agent wages in homogeneous teams as a function of n for various θ, with $a = b = 1$ and $\omega = 1$ (left) and $\omega = 10$ (right).

$\theta = 0$ do work not at all, i.e., $e^*(0, \omega, n) = 0$, while those with $\theta = 1$ contribute everything to production, $e^*(1, \omega, n) = \omega$, and nothing to leisure, independent of the size of the team, n. Also note that $e^*(\theta, \omega, i) > e^*(\theta, \omega, i + 1)$, that is, effort levels decrease as team size increases, other things being equal.

From (4) wages as a function of agent preference, θ, endowment, ω, and team size, n, can be determined explicitly for homogeneous teams. There results a long expression that is not terribly revealing so it is omitted here. Instead, wages as a function of n for $a = b = 1$ are plotted in Fig. 3, for $\theta \in \{0.5, 0.6, 0.7, 0.8, 0.9\}$, and for two values of endowments, ω. Note that teams with high endowments earn *much* more than low endowment teams. For agents with relatively low preference for income and low endowment, wages are monotonically decreasing as team size increases. For sufficiently large preference for income or endowment there is a team size that maximizes wages. For instance, in the left plot of Fig. 4, for $\theta = 0.9$ the team size that maximizes wages is 16.

But wages are only part of what motivates our agents. They also care about leisure, i.e., the non-contributions to production: $\omega - e^*$. Fig. 4 plots utilities as a function of

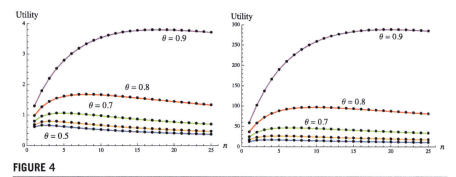

FIGURE 4

Agent utility in homogeneous teams as a function of n for various θ, with $a = b = 1$ and $\omega = 1$ (left) and $\omega = 10$ (right).

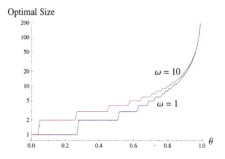

FIGURE 5

Optimal sizes of homogeneous teams as a function of θ, with $a = b = 1$ and $\omega = 1, 10$.

n for $a = b = 1$ and $\theta \in \{0.5, 0.6, 0.7, 0.8, 0.9\}$. Now note that each curve in Fig. 5 is single-peaked, so there is an optimal team size for every θ. Since utility involves both wages and leisure, the team size that maximizes utility will not generally be the same as team size that maximizes wages. For example, in the left plot of Fig. 5, for $\theta = 0.9$ the team size that maximizes utility is 18, versus 16 for maximizing wages. In a team of size 18 each agent has almost the same income as in a 16 person team and somewhat more leisure time. Utility maximizing team sizes are shown in Fig. 5 as a function of θ for two values of ω. For high θ agents the curves are approximately coincident. When homogeneous agents are arranged into optimal teams, how much utility do they receive? Once again, an analytical expression can be written down but it is long and its overall shape not obvious. Se we plot it numerically in Fig. 6, as a function of θ, and compare it to singleton utility, for two values of endowments, ω. Optimal team sizes rise quickly with θ (note log scale in the higher endowment case). Gains from being in a team are greater for high θ agents.[10]

---

[10]For analytical characterization of an equal share (partnership) model with perfect exclusionary power see Farrell and Scotchmer (1988); an extension to heterogeneous skills is given by Sherstyuk (1998).

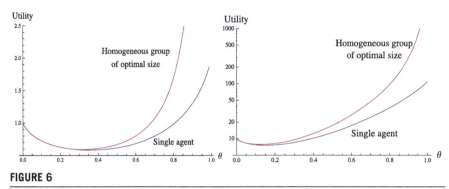

FIGURE 6

Agent utility in optimally-sized homogeneous teams as a function of θ, with $a = b = 1$ and $\omega = 1$ (left) and $\omega = 10$ (right).

For homogeneous teams it is instructive to study the effort that would be contributed at the (symmetric) Pareto solution. This can be explicitly determined by substituting $(n-1)e_i$ for $E_{\sim i}$ in (1) then differentiating with respect to e_i, setting the resulting expression equal to 0 and solving for e^*. Doing this yields

$$e^*_{Pareto} = \frac{2bn\theta\omega - a + \sqrt{4bn\theta^2\omega(a + bn\omega) + a^2}}{2bn(1+\theta)}. \tag{5}$$

Conceptually, it must be the case that the Pareto effort level exceeds the Nash level, i.e., (5) always greater than (4). To demonstrate this involves lengthy algebra so instead, to build up some intuition for what the difference between the two terms looks like, we simply plot it in Fig. 7 for a specific parameterization. Clearly this surface is everywhere greater than 0, numerically confirming the general result that agents under-supply effort in Nash equilibrium.

Example 2 (*Graphical depiction of the solution space 2 two identical agents*). Consider two agents with $\theta = 0.5$ and $\omega = 1$. Solving (2) for e^* with $E_{\sim i} = e^*$ and $a = b = 1$ yields $e^* = 0.4215$, corresponding to utility level 0.6704. Effort deviations by either agent alone are Pareto dominated by the Nash equilibrium, e.g., decreasing the first agent's effort to $e_1 = 0.4000$, with e_2 at the Nash level yields utility levels of 0.6700 and 0.6579, respectively. An effort increase to $e_1 = 0.4400$ with e_2 unchanged produces utility levels of 0.6701 and 0.6811, respectively, a loss for the first agent while the second gains. If both agents decrease their effort from the Nash level their utilities fall, while joint increases in effort are welfare-improving. There exist symmetric Pareto optimal efforts of 0.6080 and utility of 0.7267. However, efforts exceeding Nash levels are not individually rational—each agent gains by putting in less effort. Fig. 8 plots iso-utility contours for these agents as a function of effort. The U-shaped lines are for the first agent, utility increasing upwards. The C-shaped curves refer to the second agent, utility larger to the right. Point 'N' is the Nash equilibrium.

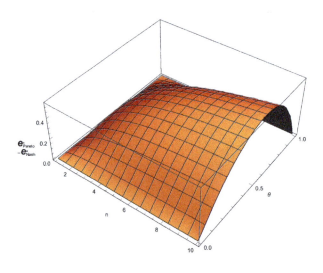

FIGURE 7

Difference in effort levels between Pareto and Nash solutions in team production as a function of n and θ, with $a = b = 1$ and $\omega = 1$.

The 'core' shaped region extending above and to the right of 'N' is the set of efforts that Pareto-dominate Nash. The set of efforts from 'P' to 'P' are Pareto optimal, with the subset from 'D' to 'D' being Nash dominant.

For two agents with different θs the qualitative structure of the effort space shown in Fig. 8 is preserved, but the symmetry is lost. Increasing returns insures the existence of effort levels that Pareto-dominate the Nash equilibrium.

2.2 STABILITY OF NASH EQUILIBRIUM, DEPENDENCE ON TEAM SIZE

A unique Nash equilibrium always exists but for sufficiently large group size it is unstable. To see this, consider a team operating away from equilibrium, each agent adjusting its effort. As long as the adjustment functions are decreasing in $E_{\sim i}$ then one expects the Nash levels to obtain. Because aggregate effort is a linear combination of individual efforts, the adjustment dynamics can be conceived of in aggregate terms. In particular, the total effort level at time $t + 1$, $E(t + 1)$, is a decreasing function of $E(t)$, as depicted notionally in Fig. 9 for a five agent firm, with the dependence of $E(t + 1)$ on $E(t)$ shown as piecewise linear. The intersection of this function with the 45° line is the equilibrium total effort. However, if the slope at the intersection is less than -1, the equilibrium will be unstable. Thus, every team has a maximum stable size, dependent on agent θs.

Consider the n agent group in some state other than equilibrium at time t, with effort levels, $e(t) = (e_1(t), e_2(t), \ldots, e_n(t))$. At $t + 1$ let each agent adjust its effort

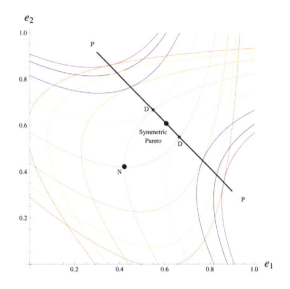

FIGURE 8

Effort level space for two agents with $\theta = 0.5$ and $a = b = \omega = 1$; colored lines are iso-utility contours, 'N' designates the Nash equilibrium, the heavy line from P–P are the Pareto optima, and the segment D–D represents the Pareto optima that dominate the Nash equilibrium.

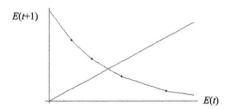

FIGURE 9

Phase space of effort level adjustment, $n = 5$.

using (2), a 'best reply' to the previous period's value of $E_{\sim i}$,[11]

$$e_i(t+1) = \max \left\{ 0, \frac{2b[\theta_i \omega_i - E_{\sim i}(t)] - a + \sqrt{4b\theta_i^2(\omega_i + E_{\sim i}(t))[a + b(\omega_i + E_{\sim i}(t))] + a^2}}{2b(1+\theta_i)} \right\}.$$
(6)

---

[11] Effort adjustment functions that are decreasing in $E_{\sim i}$ and increasing in θ_i yield qualitatively similar results; see Appendix A. While this is a dynamic strategic environment, agents make no attempt to deduce optimal multi-period strategies. Rather, at each period they myopically 'best respond'. This simple behavior is sufficient to produce very complex dynamics, suggesting sub-game perfection is implausible.

This results in an n-dimensional dynamical system, for which it can be shown:

Proposition 3. *All teams are unstable for sufficiently large group size.*

Proof. Start by assessing the eigenvalues of the Jacobian matrix[12]:

$$J_{ij} \equiv \frac{\partial e_i}{\partial e_j} = \frac{1}{1+\theta_i} \left\{ \theta_i^2 \frac{a + 2b(\omega_i + E_{\sim i}^*)}{\sqrt{a^2 + 4b\theta_i^2(\omega_i + E_{\sim i}^*)[a + 2b(\omega_i + E_{\sim i}^*)]}} - 1 \right\} \quad (7)$$

with $J_{ii} = 0$. Since each $\theta_i \in [0, 1]$ it can be shown that $J_{ij} \in [-1, 0]$, and J_{ij} is monotone increasing with θ_i. The *RHS* of (7) is independent of j, so each row of the Jacobian has the same value off the diagonal, i.e., $J_{ij} \equiv k_i$ for all $j \neq i$. Overall,

$$J = \begin{bmatrix} 0 & k_1 & \cdots & k_1 \\ k_2 & 0 & \cdots & k_2 \\ \vdots & & \ddots & \vdots \\ k_n & \cdots & k_n & 0 \end{bmatrix},$$

with each of the $k_i \leq 0$. Stability of equilibrium requires that this matrix's dominant eigenvalue, λ_0, have modulus strictly inside the unit circle. It will now be shown that this condition holds only for sufficiently small group sizes. Call ρ_i the row sum of the ith row of J. It is well-known (Luenberger, 1979, pp. 194–195) that $\min_i \rho_i \leq \lambda_0 \leq \max_i \rho_i$. Since the rows of J are comprised of identical entries

$$(n - 1) \min_i k_i \leq \lambda_0 \leq (n - 1) \max_i k_i. \quad (8)$$

Consider the upper bound: since the largest $k_i < 0$ there is some value of n beyond which $\lambda_0 < -1$ and the solution is unstable. Furthermore, since large k_i corresponds to agents with high θ_i, it is these agents who determine group stability. From (8), compute the maximum stable group size, $N^{\max}$, by setting $\lambda_0 = -1$ and rearranging:

$$n^{\max} \leq \left\lfloor \frac{\max_i k_i - 1}{\max_i k_i} \right\rfloor, \quad (9)$$

where $\lfloor z \rfloor$ refers to the largest integer less than or equal to z. Groups larger than $n^{\max}$ will never be stable, that is, (9) is an upper bound on group size. $\qquad \square$

For any of b, $E_{\sim i}$ or $\omega_i \gg a$, such as when $a \sim 0$, $k_i \approx (\theta_i - 1)/(\theta_i + 1)$. Using this together with (9) we obtain an expression for $n^{\max}$ in terms of preferences

$$n^{\max} \leq \left\lfloor \frac{2}{1 - \max_i \theta_i} \right\rfloor. \quad (10)$$

---

[12] Technically, agents who put in no effort do not contribute to the dynamics, so the effective dimension of the system will be strictly less than n when such agents are present.

Table 1 Onset of instability in a group having $\theta = 0.7$; Nash equilibrium in groups larger than 6 are unstable

n	e^*	$U(e^*)$	k	$\lambda_0 = (n-1)k$
1	0.770	0.799	not applicable	not applicable
2	0.646	0.964	−0.188	−0.188
3	0.558	1.036	−0.184	−0.368
4	0.492	1.065	−0.182	−0.547
5	0.441	1.069	−0.181	−0.726
6	0.399	1.061	−0.181	−0.904
7	0.364	1.045	−0.180	−1.082

The agent with *highest* income preference thus determines the maximum stable group size. Other bounds on λ_0 can be obtained via column sums of J. Noting the ith column sum by γ_i, we have $\min_i \gamma_i \leq \lambda_0 \leq \max_i \gamma_i$, which means that

$$\sum_{i=1}^{n} k_i - \min_i k_i \leq \lambda_0 \leq \sum_{i=1}^{n} k_i - \max_i k_i. \tag{11}$$

These bounds on λ_0 can be written in terms of the group size by substituting $n\bar{k}$ for the sums. Then an expression for $n^{\max}$ can be obtained by substituting $\lambda_0 = -1$ in the upper bound of (11) and solving for the maximum group size, yielding

$$n^{\max} \leq \left\lfloor \frac{\max_i k_i - 1}{\bar{k}} \right\rfloor. \tag{12}$$

The bounds given by (9) and (12) are the same (tight) for homogeneous groups, since the denominators are identical in this case.

Example 3 (*Onset of instability with increasing team size*). Consider a homogeneous group of agents having $\theta = 0.7$, with $a = b = \omega = 1$. From (8) the maximum stable group size is 6. Here we investigate how instability arises as the group grows. For an agent working alone the optimal effort, from (3), is 0.770, utility is 0.799. Now imagine two agents working together. From (4) the Nash efforts are 0.646 and utility increases to 0.964. Each element of the Jacobian (6) is identical; call this k. For $n = 2$, $k = -0.188 = \lambda_0$. For $n = 3$ the utility is higher and $\lambda_0 = -0.368$. The same qualitative results hold for group sizes 4 and 5, with λ_0 approaching -1. At $n = 6$ efforts again decline and now each agent's utility is lower. Adding one more agent to the group ($n = 7$) causes λ_0 to fall to -1.082: the group is *unstable*—any perturbation of the Nash equilibrium creates dynamics that do not settle down. All of this is summarized in Table 1. Groups of greater size are also unstable in this sense. For lesser θ instability occurs at smaller sizes, while groups having higher θ can support larger numbers. Fig. 10 shows the maximum stable firm size (in green) for all θ with $a = b = 1$ and $\omega = 1$, with the smallest size at which instability occurs (red). The

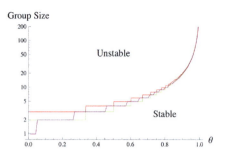

FIGURE 10

Unstable Nash equilibria in homogeneous teams as a function of income preference θ.

lower (magenta) line is the optimal firm size (Fig. 5), which is very near the stability boundary, sometimes in the unstable region. This is reminiscent of the 'edge of chaos' literature, for systems poised at the boundary between order and disorder (Levitan et al., 2002).

Unstable Equilibria and Pattern Formation Far from Agent Level Equilibria

Unstable equilibria may be viewed as problematical if one assumes agent level equilibria are *necessary* for social regularity. Games in which optimal strategies are cycles have long been known (e.g., Shapley, 1964; Shubik, 1997). Solution concepts can be defined to include such possibilities (Gilboa and Matsui, 1991). While agent level equilibria are *sufficient* for macro-regularity, they are not *necessary*. When agents are learning or in combinatorially rich environments, as they are here, fixed points are unlikely to be realized. Non-equilibrium models in economics include Papageorgiou and Smith (1983) and Krugman (1996).[13]

Real firms are inherently dynamic: workers leave, new ones arrive, everyone adjusts.[14] Indeed, there is vast turnover of jobs and firms, as already indicated. Of the largest 5000 U.S. firms in 1982, in excess of 65% of them no longer existed as independent entities by 1996 (Blair et al., 2000)! 'Turbulence' well describes such volatility (Beesley and Hamilton, 1984; Ericson and Pakes, 1995).

3 FROM ONE TEAM TO SIX MILLION FIRMS, COMPUTATIONALLY

The U.S. private sector consists of some 120 million employees who work in 6 million firms. How can we relate the abstract team production model described in the

---

[13] Non-equilibrium models are better known and well-established in other sciences, e.g., in mathematical biology the instabilities of certain PDE systems are the basis for pattern formation (Murray, 1993).

[14] Arguments against firm equilibrium include Kaldor (1972, 1985), Moss (1981), and Lazonick (1991).

previous section to a real economy? Analytically, there would appear to be little hope of linking the model to data without thinking in terms of to some kind of 'representative firm,' unless heroic assumptions were made about employee agents being substantially homogeneous, for otherwise how could large numbers of equations be solved? Alternatively, since there are millions of workers and firms, perhaps probabilistic or statistical reasoning could be brought to bear on the analytical model to connect it to the data, just as statistical mechanics relates the microscopic behavior of atoms or molecules to aggregate properties of a gas or liquid. While it might be possible to make progress using these approaches, we have employed, instead, an emerging computational technique known as agent-based modeling (*ABM*). In this approach, agents are created in software as objects, each having internal data and purposive behavioral rules. The agents interact and over time patterns and regularities emerge at the population level. With sufficient computational resources it is possible to instantiate very large populations of agents—indeed, below we report results for an *ABM* at full-scale with the U.S. economy, some 120 million worker agents. The question then becomes what specific rules of agent behavior are sufficient to produce teams that quantitatively resemble U.S. business firms, in terms sizes, ages, productivities, growth rates, entry and exit rates, and so on? Perhaps surprisingly, it turns out that basing agent behavior on the analytical model of the previous section is one way to accomplish this, when supplemented with rules for changing jobs and starting up new firms. Specifically, consider agents arranged in teams, with each agent perpetually adjusting its effort level according to (6), based on the adjustments of others, with new people being hired and co-workers leaving for new employment elsewhere. If a specific agent's team becomes unstable or populated by other agents who are not working very hard we permit it to look for employment in other teams and to consider forming a new team as well. What happens overall? Do lots of little teams form or a few big ones? Is a static equilibrium of specific agents in particular teams reached if we wait long enough? Are patterns produced in the population of teams that are recognizable vis-á-vis real firms? Parameterizing the firm formation model of the previous section appropriately, adding rules for how individuals seek new employment, yields an *ABM* that is capable of producing patterns and regularities that can be made to closely resemble the data on U.S. firms.

3.1 SET-UP OF THE COMPUTATIONAL MODEL USING AGENTS

To study the formation of teams within a population using software agents the *ABM* follows the analytical model. Total output of a firm consists of both constant and increasing returns, requiring specification of three parameters for each firm, a, b, and β; probability distributions for each will be used so the realized firms will be heterogeneous. Preferences and endowments, θ and ω respectively, are also specified probabilistically, so agents are heterogeneous. When agent i acts it searches over $[0, \omega_i]$ for the effort maximizing its next period utility. It makes no explicit forecast about future utility, knowing that the composition of its team will likely change—in essence, it knows it will adapt to changing circumstances so its 'default forecast'

Table 2 'Base case' configuration of the computational model

Model attribute	Value
number of agents	120,000,000
constant returns coefficient, a	uniform on [0, 1/2]
increasing returns coefficient, b	uniform on [3/4, 5/4]
increasing returns exponent, β	uniform on [3/2, 2]
distribution of preferences, θ	uniform on (0, 1)
endowments, ω	1
compensation rule	equal shares
number of neighbors, v	uniform on [2, 6]
activation regime	uniform (all agents active each period)
probability of agent activation/period	4% of total agents (4,800,000)
time calibration: one model period	one month of calendar time
initial condition	all agents in singleton firms

is that thing will remain about the same and when things begin to go downhill it will move on. Many firms arise in the *ABM* and each agent, when activated, always evaluates the utility it could receive from working elsewhere. Thus it is necessary to specify how agents search other firms for employment opportunities. Here each agent is given an exogenous social network consisting of v_i other agents, connected at random with uniform probability, effectively an Erdös–Renyi random graph. When activated, each agent considers (a) staying in its current firm, (b) joining v_i other firms—in essence an on-the-job search over its social network (Granovetter, 1973; Montgomery, 1991)—and (c) starting up a new firm. It chooses the option that yields greatest utility. Since agents evaluate only a small number of firms their information is very limited. We utilize 120 million agents, roughly the size of the U.S. private sector.[15] Specifically, about 5 million agents are activated each period, corresponding to one calendar month, in rough accord with job search frequency (Fallick and Fleischman, 2001). The 'base case' parameterization of the model is shown in Table 2. This was developed by heuristically seeking good fits to the many empirical data described in the next several subsections.[16]

---

[15] For many years we labored under the constraint of not having enough computing power to work at full-scale, instead using 10 million agents, or 1 million, or even 10,000 in our earliest efforts (Axtell, 1999). So the pros and cons of small and large models are well-known to us. While it may appear to not be parsimonious to work with full-scale models involving hundreds of millions of agents, the one great advantage of doing so is that the many model outputs do *not* have to be re-scaled in order to be compared to data emanating from the actual economy. In practice, each output measure from a sub-scale model has to be at least be interpreted in order to be compared to reality, such as in explaining a cut-off in the upper tail of a distribution, as when a 1 million agent model fails to produce a firm bigger than 10,000. But more problematically, many outputs have to be quantitatively adjusted for the different variability, skewness, and so on produced by the smaller model. The bottom line is that a 1 million agent economy is not simply a (1/100)th scale replica of a 100 million agent economy.

[16] For model attributes with random values, each agent or firm is given a single value when it is instantiated.

- • **INSTANTIATE and INITIALIZE time, agent, firm, and data objects;**
- • **REPEAT:**
  - ○ **FOR each agent, activate it probabilistically; if active:**
    - ■ **Compute e^* and $U(e^*)$ in current firm;**
    - ■ **Compute e^* and $U(e^*)$ for starting up a new firm;**
    - ■ **FOR each firm in the agent's social network:**
      - • **Compute e^* and $U(e^*)$;**
    - ■ **IF current firm is not best choice THEN leave:**
      - • **IF start-up firm is best THEN form start-up;**
      - • **IF another firm is best THEN join other firm;**
  - ○ **FOR each firm:**
    - ■ **Sum agent inputs and then do production;**
    - ■ **Distribute output according to compensation rule;**
  - ○ **COLLECT monthly and annual statistics;**
  - ○ **INCREMENT time and reset data objects;**

ALGORITHM 1

High-level representation of the ABM code.

Execution of the model is summarized in Algorithm 1, presented as pseudo-code, with the parameters of Table 2 calibrated such that each pass through the main RE-PEAT loop represents one month of calendar time in the real world. Each worker is represented as an agent in this model, and both agents and firms are software objects. It is important to emphasize that this is *not* a numerical model: there are no (explicit) equations governing the aggregate level; each agent does some calculations to figure out *how hard* to work in its own firm and in other firms it evaluates, and then compares the various alternatives in order to come to a decision about *where* to work. "Solving" an *ABM* means marching it forward in time to see what patterns emerge (cf. Axtell, 2000).

The ways individual worker agents form firms are described in Section 3.2. The aggregate steady-state that eventually emerges in the model is the subject of Section 3.3. Then in Section 3.4 the population of *firms* in the steady-state is studied—distributions of firm sizes, ages, growth rates, and so on. In Section 3.5 the population of *employees* in the steady-state is characterized, including distributions of income, job tenure, etc. Section 3.6 looks at the movement of workers between firms. The final Section 3.7 investigates the welfare advantages of an economy organized into firms, from the perspective of individual workers as well as from an aggregate/social planner point of view.

3.2 A TYPICAL REALIZATION OF THE MODEL: AGENTS FORM FIRMS

As specified in Table 2, we start the model with all agents working for themselves, in one person firms.[17] However, this configuration of the economy immediately breaks

---

[17]This is not strictly necessary, and the code base supports starting agents in teams, but beginning as singletons serves two purposes. First, running from the most extreme 'atomized' initial condition and

down as each agent, when activated, discovers it can do better working with another agent to jointly produce output, taking advantage of increasing returns to effort. Over time some teams expand as certain agents find it welfare-improving to join those teams, while other teams contract as their employee agents discover better opportunities elsewhere. New firms are started-up by agents who do not find better opportunities.[18] Overall, once an initial transient passes,[19] an approximately stationary macrostate emerges.[20] In this macro steady-state agents continue to adjust their efforts and change jobs, causing firms to evolve, and so there is no static equilibrium at the agent level, at least not in the entire population—there can be 'pockets' of agents who are in temporary equilibrium but this never lasts. Nor can the agent-level behavior be characterized by some form of mixed strategy Nash equilibria, since in even modestly-sized populations the specific social situation each agent finds itself in at any time is idiosyncratic and essentially never repeats. In the next subsection we shall attempt to characterize this steady-state, but first we investigate the formation, evolution, and eventual death of a 'typical' firm.

During a realization of the model, when a firm starts operating it adds agents who contribute effort to production. Generally this is good for the firm since through the increasing returns mechanism current employees of the firm will either receive more income when new employees add effort or, by reducing their effort levels, current employees gain utility. However, there is no guarantee that the new employee will work as hard as the current employees. That is, at the margin it is always hard to find people who will contribute as much effort, on average, as current workers, and it particularly difficult to find people who will *raise* firm productivity. So after a period of growth, in which the firm attracts some number of productive new employees, it inevitably enters a phase in which agents continue to adjust their effort levels downward and it soon becomes preferable—typically for those having the largest preference for income including those who founded the firm—to leave, either to take a job elsewhere or to start-up a new firm. By withdrawing their efforts from the firm the exiting agents impact the rest of the firm in two ways, first by reducing

---

targeting empirically-credible results is a high-bar which, if accomplished, is strong evidence that the behavioral rules employed are reasonably correct, that they are doing all the work. By contrast, if agents were initially arranged in groups that closely resembled the real world then it would be unclear whether the final result was due to the model or the initial condition. Second, it turns out to be quite hard to initialize agents into teams that are even temporarily stable, where the agents are willing to stay, even briefly. That is, for most group initial conditions large numbers of agents change jobs right away, leading to unrealistically high job turnover initially, which may take a long time to settle down.

[18] To give some intuition for how this works, movies of this process in a small population of agents are available at css.gmu.edu/~axtell/Rob/Research/Pages/Firms.html#6.

[19] The duration of the transient depends on model parameters.

[20] As is typical of all *ABMs*, while each run of the model is deterministic—distinct runs made with the same stream of pseudo-random numbers always produce the same output—there can be substantial run-to-run variation in the evolution of the economy at the agent level due to the underlying stochasticity of both the agent population (set by the parameters of Table 2) and the behavioral rules. However, for a given parameterization of the model the aggregate steady-state eventually produced is statistically the same across individual runs.

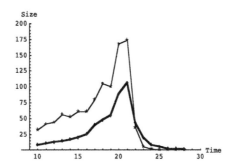

FIGURE 11

Evolution of the number of workers (heavy line) and output (thin line) over the lifetime of a firm.

the superlinear gains produced by increasing returns, and second because their effort contributions are typically above average, often considerably so. Taken together these effects may subsequently induce other employees to work harder (shirk less), partially stabilizing the firm, as was illustrated in Example 1. Then, if the loss of hard-working agents can be partially compensated for by the addition of new employees the demise of the firm may be at least delayed for some time, if not stopped altogether. Alternatively, the loss of highly productive agents may lead to rapid decline. Ultimately, every firm declines in this model, as in the real world—no firm lives forever—despite the fact that the individual agents do live forever, unlike the real world. That is, each firm has a *lifecycle*.

To illustrate the basic firm lifecycle it is instructive to look at the history of a particular firm. In Fig. 11 the evolution of the number of employees and the output of a specific firm are displayed over the course of its life from its birth at time 9 through its demise at time 28. This firm grew nearly exponentially to the point of having some 100 workers around time 21, at which time its production peaked at approximately 175 units, but soon after it went into decline with both its production and its workforce declining monotonically. To see the type of agents who joined this firm and to understand their behavior over time we plot in Fig. 12 the preferences for income, θ, and effort levels among the employees, averages represented by dark lines with ranges in each period also shown. The firm begins life with agents having high θ but over time agents having lower preference for income progressively populate the firm (left figure), although some high θ individuals stay through to the late stages. From the start there is almost monotone decreasing effort contributed (right figure), on average, over time, although right from the start there is a wide range of effort levels, with some agents contributing little and others working hard. As the workers leave this firm they migrate to other firms where they can earn more or have more leisure, gaining utility in the process.

In summary, a typical firm is founded by high θ agents who work hard. Subsequent hires work less hard but the firm prospers due to increasing returns. Eventually the most productive agents leave and the firm goes into decline.

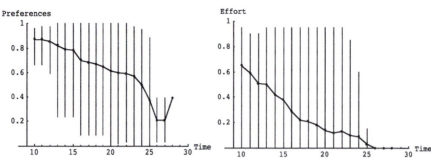

FIGURE 12

Evolution of average preference for income (left figure) and average effort levels (right figure) over the lifetime of a firm, showing minimum and maximum values as well.

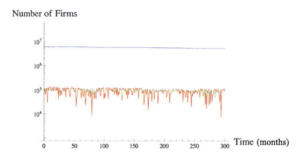

FIGURE 13

Typical time series for the total number of firms (blue), new firms (green), and exiting firms (red) over 25 years (300 months); note higher volatility in exits.

3.3 AN AGGREGATE STEADY-STATE EMERGES: PROPERTIES

While agents perpetually adjust their efforts and change jobs in this model, causing individual firms to evolve, a steady-state emerges at the aggregate level.

Number of Firms, Entrance and Exit, and Average Firm Size

The number of firms varies over time, due both to entry—agents leaving extant firms for start-ups—and the demise of failing firms. In the U.S. about 6 million firms have employees. Fig. 13 shows the number of firms (blue) once a steady-state has been achieved, nearly unchanging over 300 months (25 years) and in good agreement with the data. Before the Financial Crisis of 2008–2009 there were nearly 100K startups with employees in the U.S. monthly (Fairlie, 2012), quite close to the number produced by the model as shown in Fig. 14 (green). Counts of firm exits shown in Fig. 14 (red) are comparable but more volatile. Note that this plot has a logarithmic ordinate, so despite the volatility of entrants and exits the total number of firms is relatively constant.

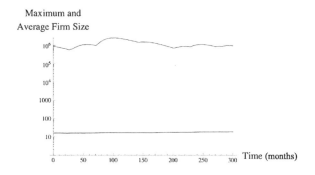

FIGURE 14

Typical time series for average firm size (blue) and maximum firm size (magenta).

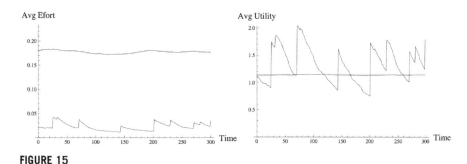

FIGURE 15

Typical time series for average effort level (left) in the population (blue) and in the largest firm (magenta), and (right) average utility (blue) and in the largest firm (magenta).

Mean firm size in the U.S. is about 20 workers/firm (Axtell, 2001). Since there are 120 million agents in the model and the number of firms that emerges is approximately 6 million, mean firm size, as shown in Fig. 14 (blue), is very close to 20. Also shown in Fig. 14 is the size of largest firm (red), which fluctuates around a million. The largest firm in the U.S. (Wal-Mart) employs some 1.4 million Americans today. The several abrupt changes in the size of the largest firm in the figure represent distinct firms, each temporarily having the largest size in the artificial economy.

Typical Effort and Utility Levels

Agents who work together improve upon their singleton utility levels through reduced effort, as shown in Fig. 15. This is the *raison d'être* of firms. While efforts in large firms fluctuate, average effort overall is quite stable (Fig. 15, left). Much of the dynamism in the 'large firm' time series is due to the identity of the largest firm changing. Fig. 15 (right) shows the average agent utility (blue) is usually less than that in the largest firm (red). Occasionally utility in large firms falls below average, signaling that the large firm is in decline.

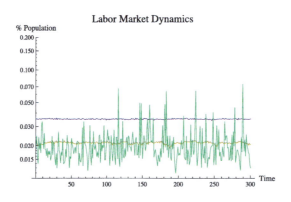

FIGURE 16

Typical monthly job-to-job changes (blue), job creation (yellow), and destruction (green).

Labor Flows

In the U.S. economy people change jobs with, what is to some, "astonishingly high" frequency (Hall, 1999, p. 1151). Job-to-job switching (also known as employer-to-employer flow) represents 30–40% of labor turnover, and is larger than un-employment flows (Fallick and Fleischman, 2001; Faberman and Nagypál, 2008; Nagypál, 2008; Davis et al., 2012). Moving between jobs is intrinsic to the agent-based model. In Fig. 16 the level of monthly job changing at steady-state is shown (blue)—just over 3 million/month—along with measures of jobs created (red) and jobs destroyed (green). Job creation occurs in firms with net monthly hiring, while job destruction means firms lose workers (net). Job destruction is more volatile than job creation, as is the case in the U.S. data (Davis et al., 1996).

Overall, Figs. 13–16 develop intuition about typical dynamics of firm formation, growth and dissolution. They are a 'longitudinal' picture of typical micro-dynamics of agents and firms. We now turn to cross-sectional properties.

3.4 THE STEADY-STATE POPULATION OF FIRMS: SIZES, PRODUCTIVITIES, AGES, SURVIVAL RATES, LIFETIMES, AND GROWTH RATES

Watching firms form, grow, and die in the model movies (see footnote 18), one readily sees the coexistence of big firms, medium-sized ones, and small ones.

Firm Sizes (by Employees and Output)

At any instant there exists a distribution of firm sizes in the model. In the steady-state firm sizes are skew, with a few big firms and larger numbers of progressively smaller ones. Typical model output is shown in Fig. 17 for firm size measured by employees (left) and output (right; arbitrary units). The modal firm size is 1 employee with the median between 3 and 4, in agreement with the data on U.S. firms. Firm sizes, S, are

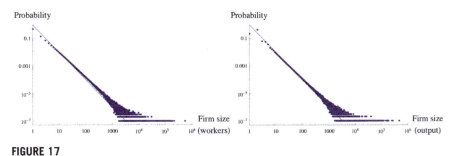

FIGURE 17

Stationary firm size distributions (PMFs) by employees (left) and output (right).

approximately Pareto distributed, the complementary *CDF* of which, $\overline{F}_S(s)$, is

$$Pr[S \geq s] \equiv \overline{F}_S(s; \alpha, s_0) = \left(\frac{s_0}{s}\right)^\alpha, \quad s \geq s_0, \; \alpha \geq 0$$

where s_0 is the minimum size, unity for size measured by employees. The U.S. data are well fit by $\alpha \approx -1.06$ (Axtell, 2001), the line in Fig. 17 (left), a *PMF*. The Pareto distribution is a power law and for $\alpha = 1$ is known as Zipf's law. Note that the power law fits almost the *entire distribution* of firm sizes. A variety of explanations for power laws have been proposed.[21] Common to these is the idea that such systems are far from (static) equilibrium at the microscopic (agent) level. Our model is clearly non-equilibrium with agents regularly changing jobs.

Labor Productivity

Firm output per employee is labor productivity. Fig. 18 plots average firm output as a function of firm size. Fitting a line by several methods indicates that $\ln(O)$ scales linearly with $\ln(S)$ with slope close to 1. This represents nearly constant returns to scale, also a feature of U.S. output data; see Basu and Fernald (1997). That nearly *constant returns* occur at the *aggregate* level despite *increasing returns* at the *micro*-level suggests the difficulties of making inferences across levels, i.e., the dual fallacies of division and composition. An explanation of why this occurs is apparent. High productivity firms grow by adding agents who work less hard than incumbents, thus such firms are driven toward the average productivity. That is, firms whose position in the (output, worker) space of Fig. 18 put them above the 45 degree line find that, over time, they evolve toward that line. In essence, when agents change jobs they push their new firm toward the average labor productivity.[22]

It is well known that there is large heterogeneity in labor productivity across firms (e.g., Dosi, 2007). Shown in Fig. 19 (left) are data on gross output per worker for

---

[21] Bak (1996, pp. 62–64), Marsili and Zhang (1998), Gabaix (1999), Reed (2001), and Saichev et al. (2010); for a review see Mitzenmacher (2004).

[22] As output per worker represents wages in our model, there is only a small wage–size effect (Brown and Medoff, 1989; Even and Macpherson, 2012).

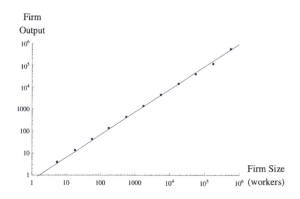

FIGURE 18

Constant returns at the aggregate level despite increasing returns at the micro-level.

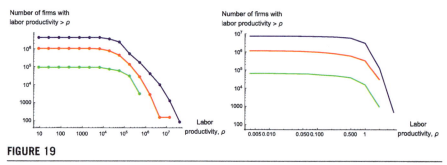

FIGURE 19

Complementary distribution functions of gross labor productivity in the U.S. (left) and in model output (right), by firm size.

all U.S. companies for three size classes: from 1 to 99 employees (blue), between 100 and 9999 (red) and 10,000 and larger (green). Note that log–log coordinates are being used in Fig. 19, meaning the right tail is very nearly a power law. Souma et al. (2009) have studied the productivity of Japanese firms and find similar results. Fig. 19 (right) is model output for the same sizes with productivity measured in arbitrary units. Note its qualitative similarity to the U.S. data, although fewer medium-sized firms having high productivity arise in our model, and the slope of the distribution for small firms appears to be significantly steeper in the model than in the data.

Firm Ages, Survival Rates, and Lifetimes

Using data from the BLS Business Employment Dynamics program, Fig. 20 gives the age distribution (*PMF*) of U.S. firms, in semi-log coordinates, with each colored line representing the distribution reported in a recent year. Model output is overlaid on the raw data as points and agrees reasonably well. Average firm lifetime is about 14 years

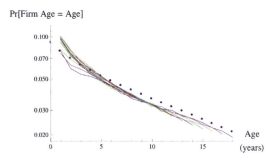

FIGURE 20

Firm age distributions (PMFs), U.S. data 2000–2011 (12 lines) and model (points).

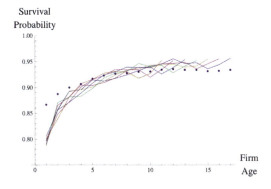

FIGURE 21

Firm survival probability increases with firm age, U.S. data 1994–2000 (7 lines) and model (points).

here, ranging from 12 to 15 over the several years shown. The curvature in the data implies that firm ages are better fit by the Weibull distribution than the exponential, the latter more commonly employed in the literature on firm ages (Coad, 2010; West, 2017).

If firm ages were exactly exponentially distributed then the survival probability would be constant, independent of age (Barlow and Proschan, 1965; Kalbfleisch and Prentice, 1980; Klein and Moeschberger, 1997). The curvature in Fig. 18 indicates that survival probability depends on age. Empirically, survival probability *increases* with age (Evans, 1987a; Hall, 1987; Haltiwanger et al., 2011). This is shown in Fig. 21 for U.S. companies in recent years (lines) along with model output (points). The model over-predicts the survival probabilities of the youngest firms.

Data on U.S. firm ages is right censored in age, thus little systematic information is known about long-lived firms, except that they are rare (de Geus, 1997).

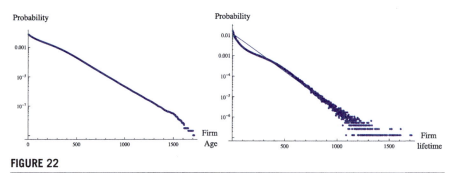

FIGURE 22

Firm age distributions and lifetime distributions (PMFs) in the long run (months).

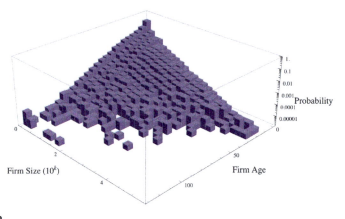

FIGURE 23

Histogram of the steady-state distribution of firms by log (size) and age in the model.

Further, the role of mergers and acquisitions (M&A) makes the lifetime of very long-lived firms ambiguous, as when a younger firm buys an older one. When this model has run for a sufficiently long time in the steady-state approximately stationary firm age and lifetime distributions emerges, as shown in Fig. 22. The durations (ages, lifetimes) shown here approach 150 years. As such, they represent predictions, since we lack appropriate data at present, for how firm lives play out over the long run.

Joint Distribution of Firms by Size and Age

The joint distribution of size and age is shown in Fig. 23, a normalized histogram in log probabilities. Note that log probabilities decline approximately linearly as a function of age and log(S). Many of the largest firms in the model are relatively young ones that grow rapidly, much like in the U.S. economy (e.g., Luttmer, 2011, Fig. 1).

Firm Growth Rates

Call S_t a firm's size at time t. Its one period growth rate is $G \equiv S_{t+1}/S_t \in \boldsymbol{R}_+$.[23] In a population of firms consider G to be a stationary random variable. Gibrat's (1931) law of proportional growth implies that if all firms have the same G then $S_{t+1} = GS_t$ is lognormally distributed for large t while the mean and variance of S grows with time (Sutton, 1997, p. 40), i.e., S is not stationary. Adding firm birth and death processes can lead to stationary firm size distributions (e.g., Simon, 1955; Ijiri and Simon, 1977; Ijiri, 1987; Mitzenmacher, 2004; or de Wit, 2005).

Historically, determination of the overall structure of G was limited by relatively small samples of firm data (e.g., Hart and Prais, 1956). Beginning with Stanley et al. (1996), who analyzed data on publicly-traded U.S. manufacturing firms (Compustat), there has emerged a consensus that $g \equiv \ln(G) \in \boldsymbol{R}$ is well-fit by the Subbotin or exponential power distribution.[24] This distribution embeds the Gaussian and Laplace distributions and has *PDF*

$$\frac{\eta}{2\sigma_g \Gamma\left(1/\eta\right)} \exp\left[-\left(\frac{|g - \overline{g}|}{\sigma_g}\right)^{\eta}\right],$$

where $\overline{g}$ is the average log growth rate, σ_g is proportional to the standard deviation, Γ is the gamma function, and η is a parameter; $\eta = 2$ corresponds to the normal distribution, $\eta = 1$ the Laplace or double exponential.[25]

Data on g for all U.S. establishments[26] has been analyzed by Perline et al. (2006), shown as a histogram in Fig. 24 for 1998–1999, decomposed into seven logarithmic size classes. Note the vertical axis is ln (frequency). In comparison to later years, e.g., 1999–2000, 2000–2001, these data are very nearly stationary. Perline et al. (2006) find that $\eta \sim 0.60$ for the size 32–63 size class, lesser for smaller firms, larger for bigger ones. The gross statistical features of g are:

i. Growth rates *depend* on firm size—small and large firms have different g. This means that *Gibrat's law is false*: all firms do *not* have the same G.

ii. The mode of $g \sim 0$, so mode(G) ~ 1, i.e., many firms do not grow.

iii. There is more variance for firm decline ($g < 0$) than for growth ($g > 0$), i.e., there is more variability in job destruction than job creation (Davis et al., 1996), requiring an asymmetric Subbotin distribution (Perline et al., 2006).

---

[23] An alternative definition of G is $2(S_{t+1} - S_t)/(S_t + S_{t+1})$, making $G \in [-2, 2]$ (Davis et al., 1996). Although advantageous because it keeps exiting and entering firms in datasets for one additional period, it obscures differences in growth rate tails by artificially truncating them. Because part of our focus will be tail behavior (high and low growth-rate firms), we will not use this alternative definition here.

[24] Subsequent work includes European pharmaceuticals (Bottazzi et al., 2001) and Italian and French manufacturers (Bottazzi et al., 2007, 2011). Bottazzi and Secchi (2006) give theoretical reasons why g should have $\eta \sim 1$, having to do with the central limit theorem for the number of summands geometrically distributed (Kotz et al., 2001). Schwarzkopf (2010, 2011) argues that g is Levy-stable.

[25] For g Laplace-distributed, G follows the log-Laplace distribution, a kind of double-sided Pareto distribution (Reed, 2001), a combination of the power function distribution on $(0, 1)$ and the Pareto on $(1, \infty)$.

[26] Due to details of tracking firms (enterprises) longitudinally, only establishment data are available.

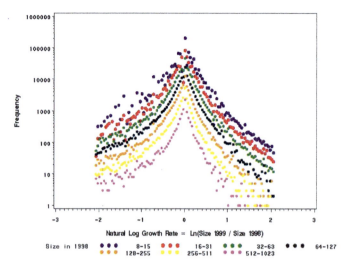

FIGURE 24

Histogram of annual g for all U.S. establishments, by size class. Source: Census.

iv. Growth rate variance declines with firm size (Hymer and Pashigian, 1962; Mansfield, 1962; Evans, 1987a, 1987b; Hall, 1987; Stanley et al., 1996).

There are at least five other well-known regularities concerning firm growth rates that are *not* illustrated by the previous figure:

v. Mean growth is positive, slightly above 0;
vi. Mean grow rate declines with firm size, and is positive for small firms, negative for large firms (Mansfield, 1962; Birch, 1981; Evans, 1987a, 1987b; Hall, 1987; Davis et al., 1996; Neumark et al., 2011);
vii. Mean growth *declines* with age (Evans, 1987a, 1987b; Haltiwanger et al., 2008);
viii. Mean growth *rises* with size, controlling for age (Haltiwanger et al., 2011);
ix. Growth rate variance *declines* with firm age (Evans, 1987a, 1987b).

With these empirical features of firm growth rates as background, Fig. 25 shows distributions of g produced by the model for seven classes of firm sizes, from small (blue) to large (purple) ones. In this plot we can see at least half of the empirical properties of firm growth: g clearly depends on firm size (i), with mode$(g) = 0$ (ii) and $\bar{g} \sim 0.0$ (v). It is harder to see that there is more variance in firm decline than growth (iii) but it is the case numerically. Clearly, variance declines with firm size (iv). Fig. 26 shows mean growth rates as a function of firm (left) size and (right) age. It is clear from these figures that $\bar{g}$ declines with size (vi) and similarly for age (vii). For more than 30 years, since the work of Birch (1981, 1987), economists have debated the meaning of figures like Fig. 26 (left). Specifically, it is not clear whether

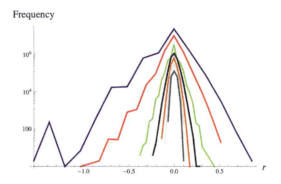

FIGURE 25

Distribution of annual g by firm size: 8–15 (blue), 16–31 (red), 32–63 (green), 64–127 (black), 128–255 (orange), 256–511 (yellow), and 512–1023 (purple).

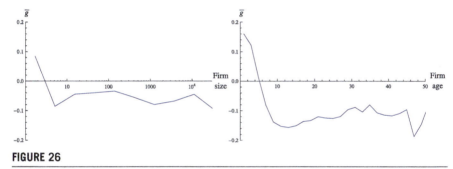

FIGURE 26

Dependence of $\bar{g}$ on (left) firm size and (right) firm age, model output.

size or age plays the larger role in determining positive growth rates. Haltiwanger and co-workers (2008, 2009, 2011) control for age and argue that it is not small firms that create jobs but rather young ones. The problem with such 'controls' for non-monotonic relationships is that they mix effects across distinct (size, age) classes. A different way to understand the distinct effects of size and age is to show how they each effect $\bar{g}$. This is done in Fig. 27, where each firm is placed into a (size, age) bin and the average g computed locally. To see precisely whether size or age matters most, a no growth ($\bar{g} = 0$) plane is superimposed on the model's $\bar{g}$ (size, age). From this we can see that *young* and *small* firms grow the most in our model.

Firm growth rate variability falls with size (iv) and age (ix). Fig. 28 shows these unconditionally for the model. Specifically, the standard deviation of g falls with size in the left plot of Fig. 28. Based on central limit arguments one expects this to be proportional to $S^{-\kappa}$, $\kappa = 1/2$ meaning the fluctuations are independent while $\kappa < 1/2$ implies they are correlated. Stanley et al. (1996) find $\kappa \sim 0.16 \pm 0.03$ for publicly-traded firms (Compustat data) while Perline et al. (2006) estimate $\kappa \sim 0.06$ for all U.S. establishments. From the model output $\kappa = 0.054 \pm 0.010$. A variety of

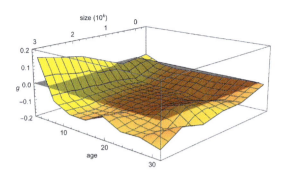

FIGURE 27

Dependence of $\bar{g}$ on firm size and age.

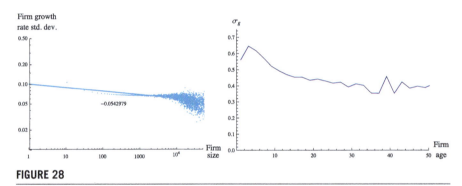

FIGURE 28

Dependence of the standard deviation of g on firm size (left) and firm age (right).

explanations for $0 \le \kappa \le 1/2$ have been proposed (Buldyrev et al., 1997; Amaral et al., 1998; Sutton, 2002; Wyart and Bouchaud, 2002; Fu et al., 2005; Riccaboni et al., 2008), all involving firms having internal structure. Note that no internal structure exists for the firms in our model, since they are simply collections of agents, yet dependence of the standard deviation of g on size is present nonetheless. In our model the weak correlation that develops between firm fluctuations has to do with the flow of workers between firms.

Over any epoch of time some firms grow and others decline. Expanding firms may shed some workers while shrinking firms may do some hiring. Fig. 29 shows that growing firms in our model experiences some separations while declining firms continue to hire, even when separations are the norm. These results are quite similar to U.S. data (Davis et al., 2006). The 'hiring' line from the model is quite comparable to the empirical result, but the 'separations' line is somewhat different for declining firms—there are too few separations in the model. Having explored firms cross-sectionally we now turn to the properties of the population of agents in the steady-state configuration of the model.

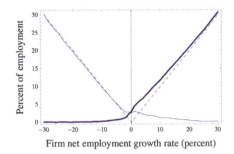

FIGURE 29

Labor transitions as a function of firm growth rate, model output.

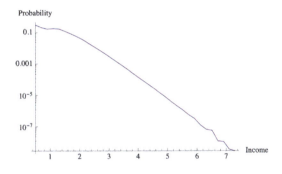

FIGURE 30

Wage distribution (arbitrary units).

3.5 THE STEADY-STATE POPULATION OF AGENTS: WAGES EARNED, JOB TENURE, AND EMPLOYMENT AS A FUNCTION OF FIRM SIZE AND AGE

Worker behavior in firms is characterized here across the agent population. While each agent's situation adjusts uniquely and idiosyncratically, at the population level there emerge robust statistical features.

Wage Distribution

While income and wealth are famously heavy-tailed (Pareto, 1971; Wolff, 1994), *wages* are less so. A recent empirical examination of U.S. adjusted gross incomes argues that an exponential distribution fits the data below about $125K, while a power law better fits the upper tail (Yakovenko and Rosser, 2009). Fig. 30 gives the income distribution from the model. Since incomes are nearly linear in this semi-log coordinate system, they are approximately exponentially-distributed.

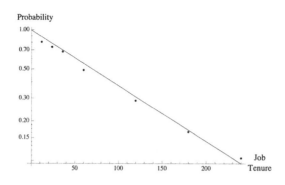

FIGURE 31

Job tenure (months) is exponentially-distributed in the U.S. (dots, binned) and in the model (line). Source: BLS and author calculations.

Job Tenure Distribution

Job tenure in the U.S. has a median near 4 years and a mean of about 8.5 years (BLS Job Tenure, 2010). The complementary-cumulative distribution for 2010 is Fig. 31 (points) with the straight line being the model output. As with income, these data are well-approximated by an exponential distribution. The base case of the model is calibrated to make these distributions nearly coincide. That is, the number of agent activations per period is specified in order to make the line go through the points, thus defining the meaning of one unit of time in the model, here a month. The many other dimensions of the model having to do with time—e.g., firm growth rates, ages— derive from this basic calibration.

Employment as a Function of Firm Size and Age

Calling $f(s)$ the firm size distribution function (*PDF or PMF*), the worker-weighted firm size distribution, $w(s) = sf(s)$. Whereas each firm is one data 'point' in $f(s)$, each worker is a 'point' in $w(s)$, so large firms 'count' more, in proportion to their size. Because $f(s)$ is a power law, so is $w(s)$, which can usefully be thought of as the fraction of total employment as a function of firm size. It turns out that the worker-weighted firm size distribution has some interesting properties. For example, the so-called *Florence median* (Pryor, 2001) is the firm size for which half of the labor force works in larger firms and half in smaller—it is the number you would get if you asked all 120 million private sector employees how big their firm was and then averaged the result. This quantity is about 500 for the U.S., roughly invariant over time—half of the American workforce is employed in firms having more than 500 employees and half in firms having 500 or fewer. It turns out that since the firm size distribution produced by the model is very close to the empirical data (Fig. 17, left), the weighted firm size distribution is also quite similar.

A related notion is the dependence of employment on firm *age*. In Fig. 32 the fraction of total employment as a function of firm age is shown. About half of Amer-

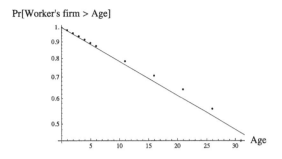

Pr[Worker's firm > Age]

FIGURE 32

Counter cumulative distribution of employment by firm age in years in the U.S. (line) and in the model (dots). Source: BLS (BDM), available online.

ican workers are in firms younger than 25 years of age, half in older. The U.S. data are shown as a counter-cumulative distribution while the model output is shown as points. Again there is good agreement between the model and the data. Employment changes by age (Haltiwanger et al., 2008) have also been studied with our model.

3.6 STEADY-STATE JOB-TO-JOB FLOWS: THE LABOR FLOW NETWORK

In the model, as in the real world, workers regularly move between jobs, as shown in Fig. 16. Here the *structure* of such flows is studied, using a graph theoretic representation of inter-firm labor flows. Let each firm be a node (vertex) in such a graph, and an edge (link) exists between two firms if a worker has migrated between them. Elsewhere this has been called the *labor flow network* (Guerrero and Axtell, 2013). In Fig. 33 four properties of this network for the base case of the model are shown. The upper left panel gives the degree distribution, while the upper right is the distribution of edge weights. The lower plots are the clustering coefficient (left) and the assortativity (average neighbor degree), each as a function of the degree. These closely reproduce data from Finland and Mexico (Guerrero and Axtell, 2013), shown as insets.[27] Three of these plots are in log–log coordinates. The heavy-tailed character of the relationships reflects the underlying Pareto distribution of firm sizes.

3.7 STEADY-STATE AGENT WELFARE

Each time an agent is activated it seeks higher utility, which is bounded from below by the singleton utility. Therefore, it must be the case that all agents prefer the non-equilibrium state to one in which each is working alone—the state of all firms being size one is Pareto-dominated by the dynamical configurations above.

---

[27]Comparable data for the U.S. are not available at this time.

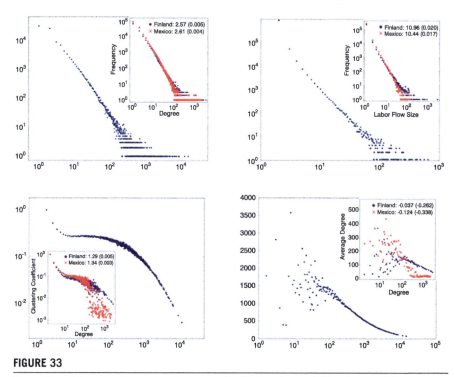

FIGURE 33

Properties of the labor flow network: degree distribution (upper left), edge weight distribution (upper right), clustering as a function of degree (lower left), and average neighbor degree (assortativity) vs. degree (lower right).

To analyze welfare of agents, consider homogeneous groups of maximum stable size, having utility levels shown in Fig. 6, replotted in Fig. 34. Overlaid on these smooth curves is the cross-section of utilities in realized groups. The main result here is that most agents prefer the non-equilibrium world to the equilibrium outcome with homogeneous groups.

4 MODEL VARIATIONS: SENSITIVITY AND ROBUSTNESS

In this section the base model of Table 2 is varied in certain ways and the effects described. The main lesson is that some aspects of the model can be modified while preserving the empirical character of the results, relaxation of certain core model specifications, individually, is sufficient to break its connection to the data. Another way to say this is that the combination of the models' main components—increasing returns, agent heterogeneity, imperfect compensation, limited information—is a minimal set of specifications that is sufficient to produce a close connection to the empirical data.

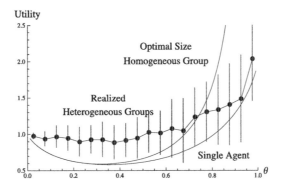

FIGURE 34

Utility in single agent firms, optimal homogeneous firms, and realized firms (averages and standard deviations), by θ.

First we investigate the importance of purposive behavior. Since certain stochastic growth processes are known to yield power law distributions, perhaps the model described above is simply a complicated way to generate random behavior. That is, although the agents are behaving purposively, this may be just noise at the macro level. If agent behavior were simply random, would this yield realistic firms too? We have investigated this in two ways. First, consider that agents randomly select whether to stay in their current firm, leave for another firm, or start-up a new firm, while still picking an optimal effort where they end up. It turns out that this specification yields only small firms, under size 10. Second, if agents select the best firm to work in but then choose an effort level at random, again nothing like skew size distributions arise. These results suggest that any systematic departure from (locally) purposive behavior is unrealistic.

One specification found to have no effect on the model in the long run is the initial condition. Starting the agents in groups seems to modify only the duration of the initial transient.

Next how does the number of agents matter? While the base case of the model has been realized for 120 million agents, Fig. 35 gives the dependence of the largest firm realized as the population size is varied. The maximum firm size rises sub-linearly with the size of the population for the parameters of Table 2. This means that a less than full-scale model would produce somewhat different statistics than the base model of Table 2, e.g., a 1000 agent model can yield a 100 person largest firm, too large proportionally.

Next, consider alternative agent activation schemes. While it is well-known that *synchronous* activation can produce anomalous output (Huberman and Glance, 1993), *asynchronous* activation can also lead to subtle effects based on whether agents are activated randomly or uniformly (Axtell et al., 1996). Moving from uniform to ran-

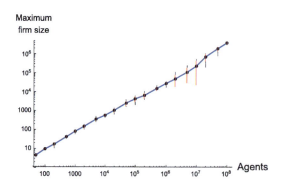

FIGURE 35

Largest firm size realized as a function of the number of agents.

dom activation produces *quantitative* changes in output but only small *qualitative* changes.

How does the specification of production matter? Of the three parameters that specify the production function, a, b, and β, as increasing returns are made stronger, larger firms are realized and average firm size increases. For $\beta > 2$, very large firms arise; these are 'too big' empirically.[28]

Are the results presented above robust to different kinds of agent heterogeneity? With preferences distributed uniformly on $(0, 1)$ in the base case a certain number of extreme agents exist: those with $\theta \approx 0$ are leisure lovers and those with $\theta \approx 1$ love income. Other distributions (e.g., beta, triangular) were investigated and found to change the results *quantitatively* but not *qualitatively*. Removing agents with extreme preferences from the population may result in too few large firms forming, but this can be repaired by increasing β. If agent preferences are *too homogeneous* the model output is qualitatively different from the empirical data. Finally, CES preferences do not alter the general character of the results. Overall, the results are robust to alternative specifications of heterogeneous preferences, as long as there is sufficient heterogeneity.

Social networks play an important role in the model. In the base case each agent has 2 to 6 friends. This number is a measure of the size of an agent's search or information space, since the agent queries these other agents when active to assess the feasibility of joining their firms. The main qualitative impact of increasing the number of friends is to slow model execution. However, when agents query *firms* for jobs something different happens. Asking an agent about a job may lead to working at a big firm. But asking a firm at random usually leads to small firms and empirically-irrelevant model output because most firms are small.

---

[28] If β is sufficiently large the model can occasionally 'run away' to a single firm employing all the agents!

How does compensation matter to the results? Pay proportional to effort[29]:

$$U_i^p(e_i; \theta_i, E_{\sim i}) = \left(\frac{e_i}{E} O(E)\right)^{\theta_i} (\omega_i - e_i)^{1-\theta_i}$$

leads to a breakdown in the basic model results, possibly with one giant firm forming. The reason for this is that there are great advantages from the increasing returns to being in a large firm and if everyone is compensated in proportion to their effort level no one can do better away from the one large firm. Thus, while there is a certain 'perfection' in the microeconomics of this pay scheme, it completely destroys all connections of the model to empirical data. Consider instead a mixture of compensation schemes, with workers paid partially in proportion to how hard they work and partially based on total output. Calling the U of Eq. (1) U_i^e, a convex combination of utility functions is

$$U_i(e_i) = f U_i^e(e_i) + (1 - f) U_i^p(e_i)$$
$$= \left(\frac{f}{n^{\theta_i}} + \frac{(1-f)e_i^{\theta_i}}{(E_{\sim i} + e_i)^{\theta_i}}\right) \left[O(e_i, E_{\sim i})\right]^{\theta_i} (\omega_i - e_i)^{1-\theta_i}.$$

Parameter f moves compensation between 'equal' and 'proportional'. This expression can be maximized analytically for $\beta = 2$, but produces a messy result. Experiments varying f show the *qualitative* character of the model is insensitive to the value of f except in the limit of f approaching 0. Additional sensitivity tests and model extensions are described in the appendix, including variants in which one agent in each firm acts as a residual claimant and hires and fires workers, relaxing the free entry and exit character of the base model.

5 SUMMARY AND CONCLUSIONS

A model in which individual agents form firms has been analyzed mathematically, realized computationally, and tested empirically. Stable equilibrium configurations of firms *do not exist* in this model. Rather, agents constantly adapt to their economic circumstances, changing jobs when it is in their self-interest to do so. Firms are born and enter the economy, they live and age, and then they exit. No firm lives forever. This multi-level model, consisting of a large number of simple agents in an environment of increasing returns, is sufficient to generate macro-statistics on firm sizes, ages, growth rates, job tenure, wages, networks, etc., that closely resemble some three dozen data, summarized in Table 3.

---

[29]Encinosa et al. (1997) studied compensation systems empirically for team production environments in medical practices. They find that "group norms" are important in determining pay practices. Garen (1998) empirically links pay systems to monitoring costs. More recent work is Shaw and Lazear (2008).

Table 3 Empirical data to which the model output is compared; similar data similarly colored

	Datum or data compared	Source	In text
1	Size of the U.S. workforce: 120 million	Census	Table 2
2	Number of firms with employees: ~6 million	Census	Fig. 13
3	Number of new firms monthly: ~100 thousand	Fairlie 2012	Fig. 13
4	Number of exiting firms monthly: ~100 thousand	Fairlie 2012	Fig. 13
5	Variance higher for exiting firms than new firms	various	Fig. 13
6	Average firm size: 20 employees/firm	Census	Fig. 14
7	Maximum firm size: ~1 million employees	Fortune	Fig. 14
8	Number of job-to-job changes monthly: ~3+ million	Fallick and Fleischman (2004)	Fig. 16
9	Number of jobs created monthly: ~2 million	Fallick/Fed spreadsheet	Fig. 16
10	Number of jobs destroyed monthly: ~2 million	Fallick/Fed spreadsheet	Fig. 16
11	Variance higher for jobs destroyed than jobs created	Davis et al. (1996)	Fig. 16
12	Firm size distribution (employees): ~Zipf	Axtell (2001)	Fig. 17 (left)
13	Firm size distribution (output): ~Zipf	Axtell (2001)	Fig. 17 (right)
14	Aggregate returns to scale: constant	Basu and Fernald (1997)	Fig. 18
15	Productivity distribution: Pareto tail	Souma et al. (2009)	Fig. 19
16	Firm age distribution: Weibull; mean ~14 years	Bureau of Labor Statistics	Fig. 20
17	Firm survival probability: increasing with age	Bureau of Labor Statistics	Fig. 21
18	Joint dist. of firms, size and age: linear in age, log size	Haltiwanger et al. (2011)	Fig. 23

(continued on next page)

Table 3 (continued)

	Datum or data compared	Source	In text
19	Firm growth rates depend on firm size	various, see text	Figs. 24, 25
20	Log firm growth rates (g) are Subbotin-distributed	Stanley et al. (1996)	Figs. 24, 25
21	Mode(g) = 0.0, many firms do not grow	various, see text	Figs. 24, 25
22	More variance for firm decline than firm growth	Davis et al. (1996)	Fig. 24, 25
23	Mean of $\bar{g}$ near 0.0, + for small firms, − for large	Birch (1981), others	Fig. 26 (left)
24	Variance of g declines with firm size	Stanley et al. (1996)	Fig. 28 (left)
25	Mean of g declines with firm age	Haltiwanger et al. (2011)	Fig. 26 (right)
26	Variance of g declines with firm age	Evans (1987a, 1987b)	Fig. 28 (right)
27	Mean of g as function of size, age: young firms grow	Haltiwanger et al. (2011)	Fig. 27
28	Simultaneous hiring and separation	Davis et al. (2006)	Fig. 29
29	Wage distribution: exponential	Yakovenko and Rosser (2009)	Fig. 30
30	Job tenure dist.: exponential with mean 90 months	Bureau of Labor Statistics	Fig. 31
31	Employment vs. age: exp. with mean 25 years	Bureau of Labor Statistics	Fig. 32
32	Florence (firm size weighted) median: 500 employees	Census	Around Fig. 32
33	Degree distribution of the labor flow network (LFN)	Guerrero and Axtell 2013	Fig. 33
34	Edge weight distribution of the LFN	Guerrero and Axtell 2013	Fig. 33
35	Clustering coefficient vs. firm size in the LFN	Guerrero and Axtell 2013	Fig. 33
36	Assortativity (degree of neighbors) vs. firm size, LFN	Guerrero and Axtell 2013	Fig. 33

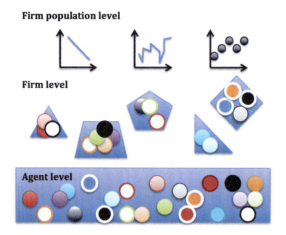

FIGURE 36

Multi-level schematic of firm formation from agents.

Overall, firms are vehicles through which agents realize greater utility than they would by working alone. The general character of these results is robust to many model variations. However, it is possible to sever connections to empirical data with agents who are too homogeneous, too random, or too rational.

5.1 EMERGENCE OF FIRMS, OUT OF MICROECONOMIC EQUILIBRIUM

The main result of this research is to connect an explicit microeconomic model of team formation to emerging micro-data on the population of U.S. business firms. Agent behavior is specified at the micro-level with firms emerging at a meso-level, and the population of firms studied at the aggregate level (Fig. 36). This micro–meso–macro picture has been created with agent computing, realized at full-scale with the U.S. private sector.[30] However, despite the vast scale of the model, its specification is actually very *minimal*, so spare as to seem rather unrealistic[31]—no product markets are modeled, no prices computed, no consumption represented, no industries appear, and agent behavior is relatively simple. Furthermore, there is no technological change and thus no economic growth—all the dynamics are produced simply through rear-rangements of firm personnel to achieve local improvements in the *social* technology of production (Beinhocker, 2006). How is it that such a stripped-down model could ever resemble empirical data?

This model works because its *dynamics* capture elements of the real world more closely than conventional models involving static equilibria, either with or without external shocks. This is so despite the agents being unequipped to figure out optimal

---

[30] It is folk wisdom that agent models are 'macroscopes,' illuminating macro patterns from the micro rules.
[31] In this it is reminiscent of Gode and Sunder and their zero-intelligence traders (Gode and Sunder, 1993).

multi-period strategies. In defense of such *simple* agents, the environments in which they find themselves are *too complex* for them to compute rational behaviors—each agent's team contains difficult-to-forecast contingencies concerning co-worker effort levels, the tenure of current colleagues, the arrival of new personnel, and fluctuating outside opportunities.[32] A major finding of this research is that we are able to *neglect* strategic behavior at the firm level—price and quantity-setting, for instance—yet explain many empirical properties of firms. Strategic decisions certainly matter for the fortunes of individual firms, but seem to not be needed to explain the gross properties of the *population* of firms.

More generally, the belief that social (aggregate) equilibria require agent-level equilibria is problematical (Foley, 1994; Axtell, 2015), a classical fallacy of division. The goal of social science is to explain *social* regularities realized at some level 'above' the agent behavioral level. While agent-level equilibria are commonly treated as *necessary*, such equilibria are, in fact, only *sufficient*—macroscopic regularities that have the character of statistical steady-states (e.g., stationary distributions) may result when there do not exist stable agent-level equilibria, as we have seen above. The assumption of similarity across levels, whether explicitly made or implicitly followed as a social norm, can be fallacious. Important regularities and patterns may arise at the macro-level without the agent level being in Nash or Walrasian equilibrium. Furthermore, when stable equilibria exist but require huge amounts of time to be realized, one may be better off looking for regularities in long-lived transients. This is particularly relevant to coalition formation games in large populations, where the number of coalitions is given by the unimaginably vast Bell numbers, meaning that anything like optimal coalitions could never be realized during agent lifetimes. Perpetual flux in the composition of groups leads naturally to the conclusion that microeconomic equilibria have little explanatory power.

5.2 FROM THEORIES OF THE FIRM TO A THEORY OF FIRMS

Unfortunately, most extant theories of the firm are steeped in this kind of micro-to-macro homogeneity. They begin innocuously enough, with firms conceived of as being composed of a few actors. They then go on to derive firm performance in response to rivals, strategic uncertainty, information processing constraints, and so on. But these derivations interpret the overall performance of multi-agent groups and organizations in terms of a few agents in equilibrium,[33] and have little connection to the empirical regularities documented above.[34]

---

[32] Anderlini and Felli (1994) assert the impossibility of complete contracts due to the complexity of nature. Anderlini (1998) describes the kinds of forecasting errors that are intrinsic in such environments.

[33] Least guilty of this charge is the evolutionary paradigm.

[34] For example, the industrial organization textbooks of both Shy (1995) and Cabral (2000) fail to make any mention whatsoever of firm size, age, or growth rate distributions, nor do they note either the number of firms or the average firm size, either in the U.S. or in other countries!

There are two senses in which the model described above is a theory of firms. First, from a purely descriptive point of view, the model reproduces the gross features of U.S. firms, while extant theories of the firm do not.[35] Nor are most theories sufficiently explicit to be operationalized, mathematically or computationally, their focus on equilibrium leaving behavior away from equilibrium unspecified.[36] In the language of Simon (1976), these theories are substantively rational, not procedurally so. Or, if micro-mechanisms are given, the model is only notionally related to data (e.g., Hopenhayn, 1992; Kremer, 1993; Rajan and Zingales, 2001), or else the model generates the wrong patterns (e.g., Cooley and Quadrini, 2001 get *exponential* firm sizes; Klette and Kortum, 2004 get *logarithmic* sizes and incorrect dependence of firm growth rate variance on size).

The second sense in which my model is a theory of firms is that agent models are *explanations* of the phenomena they reproduce.[37] In the philosophy of science an explanation is defined with respect to a theory,[38] which has to be general enough to provide explanations of whole classes of phenomena, while not being so vague that it can rationalize all phenomena. Each parameterization of an agent-based model is an instance of a more general agent 'theory'. Executing an instance yields patterns that can be compared to data, thus making it falsifiable.[39]

My 'explanation' for firms is simple: purposive agents in increasing returns environments form quasi-stable coalitions. The ability of agents to move between such transient teams 'arbitrages' away superlinear returns. In effect, firms compete for high effort individuals. Successful firms in this environment are ones that can attract and keep productive workers. This model, suitably parameterized, can be compared directly to emerging micro-data on firms. Today we do not have a *mathematical derivation* of the aggregate (firm population) properties of our model from the micro (agent behavioral) specifications, so for now we must content ourselves with the *computational discovery* that such firms result from purposive agents in economic environments having increasing returns.

This model is a first step toward a more realistic, dynamical theory of the firm, one with explicit micro-foundations. Clearly this approach produces empirically-rich results. We have produced these results computationally. Today computation is used by economists in many ways, to numerically *solve* equations (e.g., Judd, 1998), to *execute* mathematical programs (Scarf, 1973; Scarf and Shoven, 1984; Scarf, 1990), to *run* regressions (e.g., Sala-i-Martin, 1997), to *simulate* stochastic processes (e.g., Bratley et al., 1987), or to *perform* micro-simulations (e.g., Bergmann,

---

[35] A variety of models aim for one of these targets, often the firm size distribution (e.g., Lucas, 1978; Kwasnicki, 1998) and only a handful attempt to get more (Luttmer, 2007, 2011; Arkolakis, 2013).

[36] I began this work with the expectation of drawing heavily on extant theory. While I did not expect to be able to turn Coase's elegant prose into software line-for-line, I did expect to find significant guidance on the micro-mechanisms of firm formation. These hopes were soon dashed.

[37] According to Simon (Ijiri and Simon, 1977, p. 118): "To 'explain' an empirical regularity is to discover a set of simple mechanisms that would produce the former in any system governed by the latter."

[38] This is the so-called deductive-nomological (D-N) view of explanation; see Hempel (1966).

[39] In models that are intrinsically stochastic, multiple realizations must be made to find robust regularities.

1990)—all complementary to conventional theorizing. Agent computing enriches these approaches. Like microsimulation, it facilitates heterogeneity, so representative agents (Kirman, 1992) are not needed. Unlike microsimulation, it features direct (local) interactions, so networks (Kirman, 1997; Vega-Redondo, 2007) are natural to consider. Agents possess limited information and are of necessity boundedly rational, since full rationality is computationally intractable (Papadimitriou and Yannakakis, 1994). This encourages experimentally-grounded behavioral specifications. Aggregation happens, as in the real world, by summing over agents and firms. Macro-relationships *emerge* and are not limited *a priori* to what the 'armchair economist' (Simon, 1986) can first imagine and then solve for analytically. There is no need to postulate the attainment of equilibrium since one merely interrogates a model's output for patterns, which may or may not include stable equilibria. Indeed, agent computing is a natural technique for studying economic processes that are far from (agent-level) equilibrium (Arthur, 2006, 2015).

5.3 ECONOMICS OF COMPUTATION AND COMPUTATIONAL ECONOMICS

We have entered the age of *computational synthesis*. Across the sciences, driven by massive reduction in the cost of computing, researchers have begun to reproduce fundamental structures and phenomena in their fields using large-scale computation. In chemistry, complex molecules have their structure and properties investigated digitally before they are manufactured in the lab (Lewars, 2011). In biology, whole cell simulation, involving thousands of genes and millions of molecules, has recently been demonstrated (Karr et al., 2012). In fluid mechanics, turbulence has resisted analytical solution despite the governing equations being known since the 19th century. Today turbulent flows are studied computationally using methods that permit transient internal structures (e.g., eddies, vortices) to arise spontaneously (Hoffman and Johnson, 2007). In climate science whole Earth models couple atmospheric and ocean circulation dynamics to study global warming at ever-finer spatio-temporal resolution (Lau and Ploshay, 2013). In planetary science the way the moon formed after a large Earth impact event has been simulated in great detail (Canup, 2012; Cuk and Stewart, 2012). In neuroscience high frequency modeling of billions of neurons is now possible, leading to the drive for whole brain models (Markram, 2006, 2012).

Surely economics cannot be far behind. Across the social sciences people are utilizing 'big data' in a variety of ways (Lazer et al., 2009; Watts, 2013; Alvarez, 2016). The time has come for a computational research program focused on creating economies in software at full scale with real economies. Perhaps such a new endeavor needs a name—*synthetic economics* might work. More than a generation ago an empirically-rich computational model of a specific firm was created and described by Cyert and March (1963) in their book entitled *A Behavioral Theory of the Firm*. I hope the present work can begin for the *population* of U.S. firms what Cyert and March accomplished for an *individual* organization. At this point we have merely scratched the surface of the rich intersection between large-scale agent computing and economics. Let the computing begin!

APPENDIX A GENERALIZED PREFERENCE SPECIFICATIONS

The functional forms of Section 2 can be relaxed without altering the main conclusions. Consider each agent having preferences for income, I, and leisure, Λ, with more of each being preferred to less. Agent i's income is monotone nondecreasing in its effort level e_i as well as that of the other agents in the group, $E_{\sim i}$. Its leisure is a non-decreasing function of $\omega_i - e_i$. The agent's utility is thus $U_i(e_i; E_i) = U_i(I(e_i; E_{\sim i}), \Lambda(\omega_i - e_i))$, with $\partial U_i/\partial I > 0$, $\partial U_i/\partial \Lambda > 0$, and $\partial I(e_i; E_{\sim i})/\partial e_i > 0$, $\partial \Lambda(e_i)/\partial e_i < 0$. Furthermore, assuming $U_i(I = 0, \cdot) = U_i(\cdot, \Lambda = 0) = 0$, U is single-peaked. Each agent selects the effort that maximizes its utility. The first-order condition is straightforward. From the inverse function theorem there exists a solution to this equation of the form $e_i^* = \max[0, \zeta(E_{\sim i})]$. From the implicit function theorem both ζ and e_i^* are continuous, non-increasing functions of $E_{\sim i}$.

Team effort equilibrium corresponds to each agent contributing its e_i^*, and that the other agents are doing so as well, i.e., substituting $E_{\sim i}^*$ for $E_{\sim i}$. Since each e_i^* is a continuous function of $E_{\sim i}$ so is the vector of optimal efforts, $e^* \in [0, \omega]^n$, a compact, convex set. By the Leray–Schauder–Tychonoff theorem an effort fixed point exists. Such a solution constitutes a Nash equilibrium, which is Pareto-dominated by effort vectors having larger amounts of effort for all agents.

For any effort adjustment function $e_i(t + 1) = h_i(E_{\sim i}(t))$, such that

$$\frac{dh_i(E_{\sim i})}{dE_{\sim i}} = \frac{\partial h_i(E_{\sim i})}{\partial e_j} \leq 0,$$

for all $j \neq i$, there may exist an upper bound on firm size. Under these circumstances the Jacobian matrix retains the structure described in Section 2.2, where each row contains $N - 1$ identical entries and a 0 on the diagonal. The bounds on the dominant eigenvalue derived in Section 2.2 guarantee that there exists an upper bound on the stable group size, as long as the previous inequality is strict, thus establishing the onset of instability above some critical size.

APPENDIX B GENERALIZED COMPENSATION AND NASH STABILITY

It was asserted in Section 4 that proportional or piecemeal compensation breaks our basic results. What it does is dramatically reduce the incentive problems of team production. To see this we redo Fig. 1 for this compensation function, as shown in

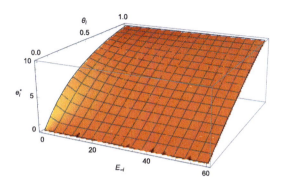

FIGURE 37

Dependence of e_i^* on $E_{\sim i}$ and θ_i for $a = 1$, $b = 1$, $\omega_i = 10$.

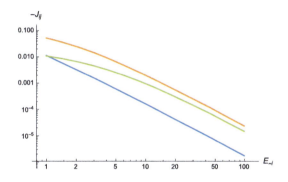

FIGURE 38

Dependence of the elements of the Jacobian matrix on $E_{\sim i}$ for $a = 1$, $b = 1$, and $\omega_i = 1$, for three values of θ_i (0.1, 0.5, and 0.9).

Fig. 37. Note that there is no longer a region of zero effort. We next compute the Jacobian matrix and evaluate its elements as the size of the group increases. This is shown in Fig. 38. The values decline sufficiently rapidly (note the log–log coordinates) that no instability will be induced by the dynamical effort level adjustments of the agents to one another, no matter how large the group.

For mixtures of compensation we recover the general properties of equal compensation. The way that effort, e_i^*, depends on $E_{\sim i}$ and θ_i for $f = 1/2$ is shown in Fig. 39. Note the region of zero effort for agents with low preference for income. For this mixture of compensation policies the eigenvalues of the Jacobian matrix can be computed numerically for various values of n (Fig. 40). While these values still decline as an approximate power law, they do so sufficiently slowly that it becomes possible to produce eigenvalues outside the unit circle, particularly for large n, since the matrix entries begin plateauing then.

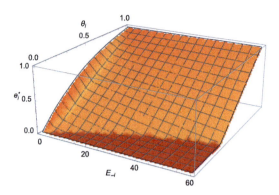

FIGURE 39

Dependence of e_i^* on $E_{\sim i}$ and θ_i for $a = 1$, $b = 1$, $\omega_i = 10$, and $f = 1/2$.

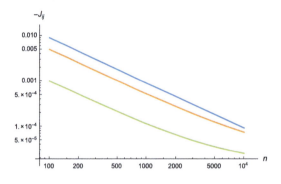

FIGURE 40

Dependence of the elements of the Jacobian matrix on n for $a = 1$, $b = 1$, $\omega_i = 1$, $f = 1/2$, and $E_{\sim i} = 100$, for three values of θ_i (0.1 (blue), 0.5 (orange), and 0.9 (green)).

APPENDIX C SENSITIVITY TO 'STICKY' EFFORT ADJUSTMENT

In the base model agents adjust their effort levels to anywhere within the feasible range $[0, \omega]$. A different behavioral model involves agents making only small changes from their current effort level each time they are activated. Think of this as a kind of prevailing *work ethic* within the group or *individual habit* that constrains the agents to keep doing what they have been, with small changes.

Experiments have been conducted for each agent searching over a range of 0.10 around its current effort level: an agent working with effort e_i picks its new effort from the range $[e_L, e_H]$, where $e_L = \max(0, e_i - 0.05)$ and $e_H = \min(e_i + 0.05, 1)$. This slows down the dynamics somewhat, yielding larger firms. This is because as large firms tend toward non-cooperation, this kind of sticky effort adjustment dampens the downhill spiral to free riding. I have also experimented with agents who 'grope' for welfare gains by randomly perturbing current effort levels, yielding similar results.

APPENDIX D EXTENSION: STABILIZING EFFECT OF AGENT LOYALTY

In the basic model an agent moves immediately to a new firm when its subjective evaluation is that it will be better off by doing so. Behaviorally, this seems implausible for certain kinds of workers, especially those who feel some *loyalty* to their firm. The formulation of agent loyalty used here involves agents not changing jobs right away, as soon as they figure out that they can do better elsewhere. Rather, they let χ better job opportunities arrive before separating from their current firm. Think of an agent's χ as a kind of counter. It starts off with some value and each time the agent determines there are higher payoffs elsewhere but does not leave its firm the value of χ declines by 1. When $\chi = 0$ the next preferable position it can find it takes and χ is reset. The base case of the model corresponds to no loyalty, that is, $\chi = 0$.

I have experimented with homogeneous and heterogeneous χs, in the range from $[0, 10]$. Even a modest amount of loyalty reduces worker turnover and firm volatility, especially in large firms, and increases job tenure, firm age, and firm lifetime, holding other parameters constant. Increasing loyalty makes large firms bigger while reducing labor flows. In order to maintain the close connection of the model output to empirical data in the presence of agent loyalty it would be necessary to recalibrate the model, something reserved for future work.

APPENDIX E EXTENSION: HIRING

One aspect of the base model is very unrealistic: that agents can join whatever firms they want, as if there is no barrier to getting hired by any firm. The model can be made more realistic by instituting local hiring policies.

Let us say that one agent in each firm does all hiring, perhaps the agent who founded the firm or the one with the most seniority. We will call this agent the 'boss'. A simple hiring policy has the boss compare current productivity to what would be generated by the addition of a new worker, *assuming that no agents adjust their effort levels*. The boss computes the minimum effort, $\phi E/n$, for a new hire to raise productivity as a function of a, b, β, E, and n, where ϕ is a fraction:

$$\frac{aE + bE^{\beta}}{n} < \frac{a\left(E + \phi \frac{E}{n}\right) + b\left(E + \phi \frac{E}{n}\right)^{\beta}}{n+1} = \frac{aE\left(1 + \frac{\phi}{n}\right) + bE^{\beta}\left(1 + \frac{\phi}{n}\right)^{\beta}}{n+1}. \quad \text{(A.8)}$$

For $\beta = 2$ this can be solved explicitly for the minimum ϕ necessary

$$\phi_* = \frac{-n(a + 2bE) + \sqrt{n^2(a + 2bE)^2 + 4bEn(a + bE)}}{2bE}.$$

Table 4 Dependence of the minimum fraction of average effort on firm size, n, and increasing returns parameter, β

n	β			
	1.0	**1.5**	**2.0**	**2.5**
1	1.0	0.59	0.41	0.32
2	1.0	0.62	0.45	0.35
5	1.0	0.65	0.48	0.38
10	1.0	0.66	0.49	0.39
100	1.0	0.67	0.50	0.40

For all values of ϕ_* exceeding this level the prospective worker is hired. For the case of $a = 0$, (A.8) can be solved for any value of β:

$$\phi_* = n\left(\frac{n+1}{n}\right)^{1/\beta} - n;$$

this is independent of b and E. The dependence of ϕ_* on β and n is show in Table 4.

As n increases for a given β, ϕ_* increases. In the limit of large n, ϕ_* equals $1/\beta$. So with sufficient increasing returns the boss will hire just about any agent who wants a job! These results can be generalized to hiring multiple workers.

Adding this functionality to the computational model changes the behavior of individual firms and the life trajectories of individual agents but does not substantially alter the overall macrostatistics of the artificial economy.

APPENDIX F EXTENSION: EFFORT MONITORING AND WORKER TERMINATION

In the base model, shirking goes completely undetected and unpunished. Effort level monitoring is important in real firms, and a large literature has grown up studying it; see Olson (1965), the models of mutual monitoring of Varian (1990), Bowles and Gintis (1998), and Dong and Dow (1993b), the effect of free exit (Dong and Dow, 1993a), and endowment effects (Legros and Newman, 1996); Ostrom (1990) describes mutual monitoring in institutions of self-governance.

It is possible to *perfectly* monitor workers and fire the shirkers, but this breaks the model by pushing it toward static equilibrium. All real firms suffer from imperfect monitoring. Indeed, many real-world compensation systems can be interpreted as ways to manage incentive problems by substituting reward for supervision, from efficiency wages to profit-sharing (Bowles and Gintis, 1996). Indeed, if incentive problems in team production were perfectly handled by monitoring there would be no need for corporate law (Blair and Stout, 1999).

To introduce involuntary separations, say the residual claimant knows the effort of each agent and can thus determine if the firm would be better off if the least hard working one were let go. Analogous to hiring we have:

$$\frac{aE + bE^\beta}{n} < \frac{a\left(E - \phi\frac{E}{n}\right) + b\left(E - \phi\frac{E}{n}\right)^\beta}{n-1} = \frac{aE\left(1 - \frac{\phi}{n}\right) + bE^\beta\left(1 - \frac{\phi}{n}\right)^\beta}{n-1}.$$

Introducing this logic into the code there results unemployment: agents are terminated and do not immediately find another firm to join. Experiments with terminations and unemployment have been undertaken and many new issues are raised, so we leave full investigation of this for future work.

REFERENCES

Alvarez, R.M. (Ed.), 2016. Computational Social Science: Discovery and Prediction. Analytical Methods for Social Research. Cambridge University Press, New York, N.Y.

Amaral, L.A.N., Buldyrev, S.V., Havlin, S., Leschhorn, H., Maass, P., Salinger, M.A., Stanley, H.E., 1998. Power law scaling for a system of interacting units with complex internal structure. Physical Review Letters 80, 1385–1388.

Anderlini, L., 1998. Forecasting errors and bounded rationality: an example. Mathematical Social Sciences 36, 71–90.

Anderlini, L., Felli, L., 1994. Incomplete written contracts: indescribable states of nature. Quarterly Journal of Economics 109, 1085–1124.

Arkolakis, C., 2013. A Unified Theory of Firm Selection and Growth. NBER working paper.

Arthur, W.B., 1991. Designing economic agents that act like human agents: a behavioral approach to bounded rationality. American Economic Review 81 (2), 353–359.

Arthur, W.B., 1994a. Increasing Returns and Economic Theory. University of Michigan Press, Ann Arbor, M.I.

Arthur, W.B., 1994b. Inductive reasoning and bounded rationality. American Economic Review 84 (2), 406–411.

Arthur, W.B., 2006. Out-of-equilibrium economics and agent-based modeling. In: Judd, K., Tesfatsion, L. (Eds.), Handbook of Computational Economics, vol. 2: Agent-Based Computational Economics. North-Holland, New York, N.Y.

Arthur, W.B., 2015. Complexity and the Economy. Oxford University Press, New York, N.Y.

Axtell, R.L., 1999. The Emergence of Firms in a Population of Agents: Local Increasing Returns, Unstable Nash Equilibria, and Power Law Size Distributions. Working paper. Santa Fe Institute, Santa Fe, N.M.

Axtell, R.L., 2000. Why agents? On the varied motivations for agent computing in the social sciences. In: Macal, C.M., Sallach, D. (Eds.), Proceedings of the Workshop on Agent Simulation: Applications, Models, and Tools. Argonne National Laboratory, Chicago, I.L, pp. 3–24.

Axtell, R.L., 2001. Zipf distribution of U.S. firm sizes. Science 293 (5536), 1818–1820.

Axtell, R.L., 2015. Beyond the Nash Program: Aggregate Steady-States Without Agent-Level Equilibria. Working paper.

Axtell, R.L., Axelrod, R., Epstein, J.M., Cohen, M.D., 1996. Aligning simulation models: a case study and results. Computational and Mathematical Organization Theory 1 (2), 123–141.

Bak, P., 1996. How Nature Works: The Science of Self-Organized Criticality. Copernicus, New York, N.Y.

Barlow, R.E., Proschan, F., 1965. Mathematical Theory of Reliability. John Wiley & Sons, New York, N.Y.

Basu, S., Fernald, J.G., 1997. Returns to scale in U.S. manufacturing: estimates and implications. Journal of Political Economy 105 (2), 249–283.

Beesley, M.E., Hamilton, R.T., 1984. Small firms' seedbed role and the concept of turbulence. Journal of Industrial Economics 33 (2), 217–231.

Beinhocker, E., 2006. The Origin of Wealth: How Evolution Creates Novelty, Knowledge, and Growth in the Economy. Harvard Business School Press, Cambridge, M.A.

Bergmann, B.R., 1990. Micro-to-macro simulation: a primer with a labor market example. Journal of Economic Perspectives 4 (1), 99–116.

Birch, D.L., 1981. Who creates jobs? The Public Interest 65, 3–14.

Birch, D.L., 1987. Job Creation in America: How Our Smallest Companies Put the Most People to Work. Free Press, New York, N.Y.

Blair, M.M., Kruse, D.L., Blasi, J.R., 2000. Is employee ownership an unstable form? Or a stabilizing force? In: Blair, M.M., Kochan, T.A. (Eds.), The New Relationship: Human Capital in the American Corporation. Brookings Institution Press, Washington, D.C.

Bottazzi, G., Cefis, E., Dosi, G., Secchi, A., 2007. Invariances and diversities in the patterns of industrial evolution: some evidence from Italian manufacturing industries. Small Business Economics 29 (1–2), 137–159.

Bottazzi, G., Coad, A., Jacoby, N., Secchi, A., 2011. Corporate growth and industrial dynamics: evidence from French manufacturing. Applied Economics 43 (1), 103–116.

Bottazzi, G., Dosi, G., Lippi, M., Pammolli, F., Riccaboni, M., 2001. Innovation and corporate growth in the evolution of the drug industry. International Journal of Industrial Organization 19, 1161–1187.

Bottazzi, G., Secchi, A., 2006. Explaining the distribution of firm growth rates. Rand Journal of Economics 37 (2), 235–256.

Bratley, P., Fox, B.L., Schrage, L.E., 1987. A Guide to Simulation. Springer-Verlag, New York, N.Y.

Brown, C., Medoff, J., 1989. The employer size–wage effect. Journal of Political Economy 97, 1027–1059.

Buchanan, J.M., Yoon, Y.J., 1994. The Return to Increasing Returns. University of Michigan Press, Ann Arbor, M.I.

Buldyrev, S.V., Amaral, L.A.N., Havlin, S., Leschhorn, H., Maass, P., Salinger, M.A., Stanley, H.E., Stanley, M.H.R., 1997. Scaling behavior in economics: II. Modeling company growth. Journal de Physique I 7, 635–650.

Cabral, L.M.B., 2000. Introduction to Industrial Organization. MIT Press, Cambridge, M.A.

Canning, D., 1995. Evolution of Group Cooperation through Inter-Group Conflict. Queens University of Belfast, Belfast, Northern Ireland.

Canup, R.M., 2012. Forming a Moon with an Earth-like composition via a giant impact. Science 338 (6110), 1052–1055.

Caves, R.E., 1998. Industrial organization and new findings on the turnover and mobility of firms. Journal of Economic Literature XXXVI, 1947–1982.

Coad, A., 2010. The exponential age distribution and the Pareto firm size distribution. Journal of Industrial Competition and Trade 10, 389–395.

Colander, D.C., Landreth, H., 1999. Increasing returns: who, if anyone, deserves credit for reintroducing it into economics? Paper presented at the American Economic Association Annual Meetings. New York, N.Y.

Cooley, T.F., Quadrini, V., 2001. Financial markets and firm dynamics. American Economic Review 91 (5), 1286–1310.

Cuk, M., Stewart, S.T., 2012. Making the Moon from a fast-spinning Earth: a giant impact followed by resonant despinning. Science 338 (6110), 1047–1052.

Cyert, R.M., March, J.G., 1963. A Behavioral Theory of the Firm. Prentice-Hall, Englewood Cliffs, N.J.

Davis, S.J., Faberman, R.J., Haltiwanger, J.C., 2006. The flow approach to labor markets: new data sources and micro–macro links. Journal of Economic Perspectives 20 (3), 3–26.

Davis, S.J., Faberman, R.J., Haltiwanger, J.C., 2012. Labor market flows in the cross section and over time. Journal of Monetary Economics 59, 1–18.

Davis, S.J., Haltiwanger, J.C., Schuh, S., 1996. Job Creation and Job Destruction. MIT Press, Cambridge, M.A.

de Geus, A., 1997. The Living Company: Growth, Learning and Longevity in Business. Nicholas Brealey Publishing.

de Wit, G., 2005. Firm size distributions: an overview of steady-state distributions resulting from firm dynamics models. International Journal of Industrial Organization 23, 423–450.

Dosi, G., 2007. Statistical regularities in the evolution of industries. A guide through some evidence and challenges for the theory. In: Malerba, F., Brusoni, S. (Eds.), Perspectives on Innovation. Cambridge University Press, Cambridge, UK.

Elsby, M.W.L., Michaels, R., 2013. Marginal jobs, heterogeneous firms, and unemployment flows. American Economic Journal: Macroeconomics 5 (1), 1–48.

Encinosa III, W.E., Gaynor, M., Rebitzer, J.B., 1997. The Sociology of Groups and the Economics of Incentives: Theory and Evidence on Compensation Systems. Graduate School of Industrial Administration working paper. Carnegie Mellon University, Pittsburgh, P.A.

Epstein, J.M., 2006. Generative Social Science: Studies in Agent-Based Computational Modeling. Princeton University, Princeton, N.J.

Ericson, R., Pakes, A., 1995. Markov-perfect industry dynamics: a framework for empirical work. Review of Economic Studies 62 (1), 53–82.

Evans, D.S., 1987a. The relationship between firm growth, size, and age: estimates for 100 manufacturing industries. Journal of Industrial Economics 35, 567–581.

Evans, D.S., 1987b. Tests of alternative theories of firm growth. Journal of Political Economy 95 (4), 657–674.

Even, W.E., Macpherson, D.A., 2012. Is bigger still better? The decline of the wage premium at large firms. Southern Economic Journal 78 (4), 1181–1201.

Faberman, R.J., Nagypál, É., 2008. Quits, Worker Recruitment, and Firm Growth: Theory and Evidence. Federal Reserve Bank of Philadelphia, Philadelphia, P.A, p. 50.

Fairlie, R.W., 2012. Kauffman Index of Entrepreneurial Activity: 1996–2012. Ewing and Marion Kauffman Foundation, Kansas City, K.S.

Fallick, B.C., Fleischman, C.A., 2001. The Importance of Employer-to-Employer Flows in the U.S. Labor Market. Washington, D.C., p. 44.

Fallick, B.C., Fleischman, C.A., 2004. Employer-to-Employer Flows in the U.S. Labor Market: The Complete Picture of Gross Worker Flows. Washington, D.C., p. 48.

Farrell, J., Scotchmer, S., 1988. Partnerships. Quarterly Journal of Economics 103 (2), 279–297.

Foley, D.K., 1994. A statistical equilibrium theory of markets. Journal of Economic Theory 62, 321–345.

Fu, D., Pammolli, F., Buldyrev, S.V., Riccaboni, M., Matia, K., Yamasaki, K., Stanley, H.E., 2005. The growth of business firms: theoretical framework and empirical evidence. Proceedings of the National Academy of Sciences of the United States of America 102 (52), 18801–18806.

Gabaix, X., 1999. Zipf's law for cities: an explanation. Quarterly Journal of Economics 114 (3), 739–767.

Garen, J., 1998. Self-employment, pay systems, and the theory of the firm: an empirical analysis. Journal of Economic Behavior & Organization 36, 257–274.

Gibrat, R., 1931. Les Inegalities Economiques; Applications: Aux Ineqalities des Richesses, a la Concentartion des Entreprises, Aux Populations des Villes, Aux Statistiques des Families, etc., d'une Loi Nouvelle, La Loi de l'Effet Proportionnel. Librarie du Recueil Sirey, Paris.

Gilboa, I., Matsui, A., 1991. Social stability and equilibrium. Econometrica 59 (3), 859–867.

Glance, N.S., Hogg, T., Huberman, B.A., 1997. Training and turnover in the evolution of organizations. Organization Science 8, 84–96.

Gode, D.K., Sunder, S., 1993. Allocative efficiency of markets with zero-intelligence traders: market as a partial substitute for individual rationality. Journal of Political Economy CI, 119–137.

Granovetter, M., 1973. The strength of weak ties. American Journal of Sociology 78, 1360–1380.

Grimm, V., Revilla, E., Berger, U., Jeltsch, F., Mooij, W.M., Reilsback, S.F., Thulke, H.-H., Weiner, J., Wiegand, T., DeAngelis, D.L., 2005. Pattern-oriented modeling of agent-based complex systems: lessons from ecology. Science 310, 987–991.

Guerrero, O.A., Axtell, R.L., 2013. Employment growth through labor flow networks. PLoS ONE 8 (5), e60808.

Hall, B.W., 1987. The relationship between firm size and firm growth in the U.S. manufacturing sector. Journal of Industrial Economics 35, 583–606.

Hall, R.E., 1999. Labor-market frictions and employment fluctuations. In: Taylor, J.B., Woodford, M. (Eds.), Handbook of Macroeconomics, vol. 1. Elsevier Science, New York, N.Y., pp. 1137–1170.

Haltiwanger, J.C., Jarmin, R., Miranda, J., 2009. High growth and failure of young firms. In: Business Dynamics Statistics Briefing, vol. 4. Ewing Marion Kauffman Foundation, Kansas City, M.O., p. 4.

Haltiwanger, J.C., Jarmin, R.S., Miranda, J., 2008. Business Formation and Dynamics by Business Age: Results from the New Business Dynamics Statistics. University of Maryland, College Park, M.D.

Haltiwanger, J.C., Jarmin, R.S., Miranda, J., 2011. Who Creates Jobs? Small vs. Large vs. Young. NBER, Cambridge, M.A.

Hart, O., 1995. Firms, Contracts and Financial Structure. Oxford University Press, New York, N.Y.

Hart, P.E., Prais, S.J., 1956. The analysis of business concentration: a statistical approach. Journal of the Royal Statistical Society, Series A 119, 150–191.

Hempel, C.G., 1966. Philosophy of Natural Science. Prentice-Hall, Englewood Cliffs, N.J.

Hoffman, J., Johnson, C., 2007. Computational Turbulent Incompressible Flow. Springer, New York, N.Y.

Holland, J.H., Miller, J., 1991. Artificial adaptive agents in economic theory. American Economic Review 81 (2), 363–370.

Hölmstrom, B., 1982. Moral hazard in teams. Bell Journal of Economics 13, 324–340.

Hopenhayn, H., 1992. Entry, exit and firm dynamics in long run equilibrium. Econometrica 60 (5), 1127–1150.

Huberman, B.A., Glance, N.S., 1993. Evolutionary games and computer simulations. Proceedings of the National Academy of Sciences of the United States of America 90, 7716–7718.

Huberman, B.A., Glance, N.S., 1998. Fluctuating efforts and sustainable cooperation. In: Prietula, M.J., Carley, K.M., Gasser, L. (Eds.), Simulating Organizations: Computational Models of Institutions and Groups. MIT Press, Cambridge, M.A.

Hymer, S., Pashigian, P., 1962. Firm size and the rate of growth. Journal of Political Economy 70 (4), 556–569.

Ichiishi, T., 1993. The Cooperative Nature of the Firm. Academic Press, New York, N.Y.

Ijiri, Y., 1987. Birth-and-death processes. In: Eatwell, J., Milgate, M., Newman, P. (Eds.), The New Palgrave: A Dictionary of Economics, vol. 1. Macmillan Press, London, pp. 249–250.

Ijiri, Y., Simon, H.A., 1977. Skew Distributions and the Sizes of Business Firms. North-Holland, New York, N.Y.

Judd, K., 1998. Numerical Methods in Economics. MIT Press, Cambridge, M.A.

Kalbfleisch, J.D., Prentice, R.L., 1980. The Statistical Analysis of Failure Time Data. Wiley, New York, N.Y.

Kaldor, N., 1972. The irrelevance of equilibrium economics. Economic Journal 82 (328), 1237–1255.

Kaldor, N., 1985. Economics without Equilibrium. University College Cardiff Press, Cardiff, UK.

Karr, J.R., Sanghvi, J.C., Macklin, D.N., Gutschow, M.V., Jacobs, J.M., Bolival, B.J., Assad-Garcia, N., Glass, J.I., Covert, M.W., 2012. A whole-cell computational model predicts phenotype from genotype. Cell 150, 389–401.

Kirman, A.P., 1992. Whom or what does the representative individual represent? Journal of Economic Perspectives 6 (2), 117–136.

Kirman, A.P., 1993. Ants, rationality and recruitment. Quarterly Journal of Economics 108, 137–156.

Kirman, A.P., 1997. The economy as an interactive system. In: Arthur, W.B., Durlauf, S.N., Lane, D.A. (Eds.), The Economy as an Evolving Complex System II. Addison-Wesley, Reading, M.A.

Klein, J.P., Moeschberger, M.L., 1997. Survival Analysis: Techniques for Censored and Truncated Data. Springer-Verlag, New York, N.Y.

Klette, T.J., Kortum, S., 2004. Innovating firms and aggregate innovation. Journal of Political Economy CXII, 986–1018.

Kotz, S., Kozubowski, T.J., Podgorski, K., 2001. The Laplace Distribution and Generalizations: A Revisit with Applications to Communications, Economics, Engineering, and Finance. Birkhäuser.

Kremer, M., 1993. The O-ring theory of economic development. Quarterly Journal of Economics CVIII, 551–575.

Krugman, P., 1996. The Self-Organizing Economy. Blackwell, New York, N.Y.

Krusell, P., Mukoyama, T., Rogerson, R., Sahin, A., 2011. A three state model of worker flows in general equilibrium. Journal of Economic Theory 146, 1107–1133.

Krusell, P., Mukoyama, T., Rogerson, R., Sahin, A., 2017. Gross worker flows over the business cycle. American Economic Review 107 (11), 3447–3476.

Kwasnicki, W., 1998. Skewed distribution of firm sizes—an evolutionary perspective. Structural Change and Economic Dynamics 9, 135–158.

Lau, N.-C., Ploshay, J.J., 2013. Model projections of the changes in atmospheric circulation and surface climate over North American, the North Atlantic, and Europe in the 21st century. Journal of Climate. https://doi.org/10.1175/JCLI-D-13-00151.1.

Laughlin, R.B., Pines, D., 2000. The theory of everything. Proceedings of the National Academy of Sciences of the United States of America 97 (1), 28–31.

Lazer, D., Pentland, A., Adamic, L., Aral, S., Barabasi, A.-L., Brewer, D., Christakis, N., Contractor, N., Fowler, J., Gutmann, M., Jebara, T., King, G., Macy, M.W., Roy, D., van Alstyne, M., 2009. Computational social science. Science 323 (5915), 721–723.

Lazonick, W., 1991. Business Organization and the Myth of the Market Economy. Cambridge University Press, New York, N.Y.

Levitan, B., Lobo, J., Schuler, R., Kauffman, S., 2002. Evolution of organization performance and stability in a stochastic environment. Computational and Mathematical Organization Theory 8 (4), 281–313.

Lewars, E.G., 2011. Computational Chemistry: Introduction to the Theory and Applications of Molecular and Quantum Mechanics. Springer, New York, N.Y.

Lucas Jr., R.E., 1978. On the size distribution of business firms. Bell Journal of Economics 9, 508–523.

Luenberger, D.G., 1979. An Introduction to Dynamical Systems: Theory, Models and Applications. John Wiley & Sons, New York, N.Y.

Luttmer, E.G.J., 2007. Selection, growth, and the size distribution of firms. Quarterly Journal of Economics 122 (3), 1103–1144.

Luttmer, E.G.J., 2010. Models of growth and firm heterogeneity. Annual Review of Economics 2, 547–576.

Luttmer, E.G.J., 2011. On the mechanics of firm growth. Review of Economic Studies 78 (3), 1042–1068.

Mansfield, E., 1962. Entry, Gibrat's law, innovation, and the growth of firms. American Economic Review 52 (5), 1023–1051.

Markram, H., 2006. The blue brain project. Nature Reviews. Neuroscience 7, 153–160.

Markram, H., 2012. A countdown to a digital simulation of every last neuron in the human brain. Scientific American (June).

Marshall, A., 1920. Principles of Economics. Macmillan, London.

Marsili, M., Zhang, Y.-C., 1998. Interacting individuals leading to Zipf's law. Physical Review Letters LXXX (12), 2741–2744.

Mitzenmacher, M., 2004. A brief history of generative models for power law and lognormal distributions. Internet Mathematics 1 (2), 226–251.

Montgomery, J.D., 1991. Social networks and labor-market outcomes: toward an economic analysis. American Economic Review 81 (5), 1408–1418.

Moss, S.J., 1981. An Economic Theory of Business Strategy: An Essay in Dynamics Without Equilibrium. Halsted Press, New York, N.Y.

Murray, J.D., 1993. Mathematical Biology. Springer-Verlag, New York, N.Y.

Nagypál, É., 2008. Worker Reallocation over the Business Cycle: The Importance of Employer-to-Employer Transitions. Northwestern University, Evanston, I.L, p. 55.

Nelson, R., Winter, S.G., 1982. An Evolutionary Theory of Economic Change. Harvard University Press, Cambridge, M.A.

Neumark, D., Wall, B., Zhang, J., 2011. Do small businesses create more jobs? New evidence for the United States from the national establishment time series. Review of Economics and Statistics 93 (1), 16–29.

Papadimitriou, C., Yannakakis, M., 1994. On complexity as bounded rationality. In: Proceedings of the Twenty-Sixth Annual ACM Symposium on the Theory of Computing. ACM Press, New York, N.Y, pp. 726–733.

Papageorgiou, Y.Y., Smith, T.R., 1983. Agglomeration as a local instability of spatially uniform steady-states. Econometrica 51 (4), 1109–1119.

Pareto, V., 1971. Manual of Political Economy. Augustus M. Kelley, New York, N.Y. Originally published in 1927.

Perline, R., Axtell, R., Teitelbaum, D., 2006. Volatility and Asymmetry of Small Firm Growth Rates over Increasing Time Frames. SBA Research Report. Washington, D.C.

Pryor, F.L., 2001. Will most of us be working for giant enterprises by 2028. Journal of Economic Behavior & Organization 44 (4), 363–382.

Rajan, R.G., Zingales, L., 2001. The firm as a dedicated hierarchy: a theory of the origins and growth of firms. Quarterly Journal of Economics 116 (3), 805–851.

Ray, D., 2007. A Game Theoretic Perspective on Coalition Formation. Oxford University Press, New York, N.Y.

Reed, W.J., 2001. The Pareto, Zipf and other power laws. Economics Letters 74, 15–19.

Riccaboni, M., Pammolli, F., Buldyrev, S.V., Ponta, L., Stanley, H.E., 2008. The size variance relationship of business firm growth rates. Proceedings of the National Academy of Sciences of the United States of America 105 (50), 19595–19600.

Rosen, J.B., 1965. Existence and uniqueness of equilibrium points for concave n-person games. Econometrica 33, 520–534.

Rossi-Hansberg, E., Wright, M.L.J., 2007. Establishment size dynamics in the aggregate economy. American Economic Review 97 (5), 1639–1666.

Saichev, A., Malevergne, Y., Sornette, D., 2010. Theory of Zipf's Law and Beyond. Springer-Verlag, New York, N.Y.

Sala-i-Martin, X., 1997. I just ran two million regressions. American Economic Review 87 (2), 178–183.

Scarf, H., 1973. The Computation of Economic Equilibria. Yale University Press, New Haven, C.T.

Scarf, H.E., 1990. Mathematical programming and economic theory. Operations Research 38 (3), 377–385.

Scarf, H.E., Shoven, J.B. (Eds.), 1984. Applied General Equilibrium Analysis. Cambridge University Press, New York, N.Y.

Schwarzkopf, Y., 2010. Complex Phenomena in Social and Financial Systems: From Bird Population Growth to the Dynamics of the Mutual Fund Industry. Ph.D. California Institute of Technology.

Schwarzkopf, Y., Axtell, R.L., Farmer, J.D., 2011. An Explanation of Universality in Growth Fluctuations. Working paper, p. 12.

Shapley, L.S., 1964. Some topics in two-person games. In: Dresher, M., Shapley, L.S., Tucker, A.W. (Eds.), Advances in Game Theory. Princeton University Press, Princeton, N.J.

Shaw, K., Lazear, E.P., 2008. Tenure and output. Labour Economics 15, 705–724.

Sherstyuk, K., 1998. Efficiency in partnership structures. Journal of Economic Behavior & Organization 36, 331–346.

Shubik, M., 1997. Why equilibrium? A note on the noncooperative equilibria of some matrix games. Journal of Economic Behavior & Organization 29, 537–539.

Shy, O., 1995. Industrial Organization: Theory and Applications. MIT Press, Cambridge, M.A.

Simon, H.A., 1955. On a class of skew distribution functions. Biometrika 42, 425–440.

Simon, H.A., 1976. From substantive to procedural rationality. In: Latsis, S. (Ed.), Method and Appraisal in Economics. Cambridge University Press, New York, N.Y.

Simon, H.A., 1986. The failure of armchair economics. Challenge 29 (5), 18–25.

Simon, H.A., 1996. The Sciences of the Artificial. MIT Press, Cambridge, M.A. First edition 1969.

Simon, H.A., 1997. An Empirically-Based Microeconomics. Cambridge University Press, Cambridge, UK.

Souma, W., Ikeda, Y., Iyetomi, H., Fujiwara, Y., 2009. Distribution of labour productivity in Japan over the period 1996–2006. Economics E-Journal 3, 2009-14.

Sraffa, P., 1926. The laws of returns under competitive conditions. Economic Journal XXXVI (144), 535–550.

Stanley, M.H.R., Amaral, L.A.N., Buldyrev, S.V., Havlin, S., Leschhorn, H., Maass, P., Salinger, M.A., Stanley, H.E., 1996. Scaling behaviour in the growth of companies. Nature 379 (29), 804–806.

Sutton, J., 1997. Gibrat's legacy. Journal of Economic Literature XXXV (1), 40–59.

Sutton, J., 1998. Technology and Market Structure. MIT Press, Cambridge, M.A.

Sutton, J., 2002. The variance of firm growth rates: the scaling puzzle. Physica A 312.

Tesfatsion, L., 2002. Agent-based computational economics: growing economies from the bottom up. Artificial Life 8 (1), 55–82.

Vega-Redondo, F., 2007. Complex Social Networks. Cambridge University Press, New York, N.Y.

Vriend, N.J., 1995. Self-organization of markets: an example of a computational approach. Computational Economics 8 (3), 205–231.

Watts, A., 2002. Uniqueness of equilibrium in cost sharing games. Journal of Mathematical Economics 37, 47–70.

Watts, D.J., 2013. Computational social science: exciting progress and future directions. The Bridge 43 (4), 5–10.

West, G., 2017. Scale: The Universal Laws of Growth, Innovation, Sustainability, and the Pace of Life, in Organisms, Cities, Economies, and Companies. Penguin Press, New York, N.Y.

Williamson, O.E., 1985. The Economic Institutions of Capitalism: Firms, Markets, Relational Contracting. Free Press, New York, N.Y.

Wolff, E.N., 1994. Top Heavy: A Study of the Increasing Inequality of Wealth in America. Twentieth Century Foundation, New York, N.Y.

Wyart, M., Bouchaud, J.-P., 2002. Statistical models for company growth. arXiv.

Yakovenko, V.M., Rosser, J.B., 2009. Statistical mechanics of money, wealth, and income. Reviews of Modern Physics 81 (4), 1703–1725.

Young, A., 1928. Increasing returns and economic progress. Economic Journal 38, 527–542.

Zame, W.R., 2007. Incentives, contracts, and markets: a general equilibrium theory of firms. Econometrica 75 (5), 1453–1500.

References for Appendices

Blair, M.M., Stout, L.A., 1999. A team production theory of corporation law. Virginia Law Review 85 (2), 247–328.

Bowles, S., Gintis, H., 1996. Efficient redistribution: new rules for markets, states and communities. Politics & Society 24, 307–342.

Bowles, S., Gintis, H., 1998. Mutual Monitoring in Teams: The Effects of Residual Claimancy and Reciprocity. Santa Fe Institute, Santa Fe, N.M.

Dong, X.-Y., Dow, G., 1993a. Does free exit reduce shirking in production teams? Journal of Comparative Economics 17, 472–484.

Dong, X.-Y., Dow, G., 1993b. Monitoring costs in Chinese agricultural teams. Journal of Political Economy 101 (3), 539–553.

Legros, P., Newman, A.F., 1996. Wealth effects, distribution, and the theory of organization. Journal of Economic Theory 70, 312–341.

Olson Jr., M., 1965. The Logic of Collective Action: Public Goods and the Theory of Groups. Harvard University Press, Cambridge, M.A.

Ostrom, E., 1990. Governing the Commons: The Evolution of Institutions for Collective Action. Cambridge University Press, New York, N.Y.

Varian, H., 1990. Monitoring agents with other agents. Journal of Institutional and Theoretical Economics 46 (1), 153–174.

Heterogeneous Agents in the Macroeconomy: Reduced-Heterogeneity Representations

4

Xavier Ragot

SciencesPo, CNRS, and OFCE, France
e-mail address: xavier.ragot@sciencespo.fr

CONTENTS

Handbook of Computational Economics, Volume 4, ISSN 1574-0021, https://doi.org/10.1016/bs.hescom.2018.02.001

215

1 INTRODUCTION

Heterogeneity is now everywhere in the macroeconomy. Both on the normative and on the positive side, considering redistribution across agents with different wealth levels or economic behaviors is obviously key for economic analysis. Economists mostly use the term "heterogeneity" to refer to the multiple dimensions according to which economic agents could differ. The public debate is mostly concerned by "inequalities", which refer to differences in income, wealth or consumption. Inequality should thus be understood as a subset of the broadest concept of heterogeneity for which a simple cardinal ranking of agents is possible (along the wealth dimension for instance). This being said, two lines of research dealing with agents heterogeneity have coexisted since many years.

A first line of research assumes that agents are rational, such that their differences come either from characteristics they have before starting economic activities or from different histories of "shocks" they face in their life. The notion of shocks should be broadly understood, including income shocks, but also health shocks, "family" shocks (see Heathcote et al., 2009 for a discussion of sources of risk). The key tool to model agent heterogeneity is the class of models with uninsurable idiosyncratic risks, which have different names in the literature: They are called either the Bewley–Huggett–Imohoroglu–Aiyagari models, or the Standard Incomplete Market model (SIM), or even simply Heterogeneous Agent models. This source of heterogeneity can be mixed with the introduction of the age dimension, in overlapping generation models, to obtain a very rich representation of heterogeneity across households (see Rios-Rull, 1995, 1997 for an early survey). After the contribution of Krusell and Smith (1998) these models are solved with aggregate shocks (see Algan et al., 2014 for a comparison of numerical methods).

Recent research now introduces many relevant frictions in this class of model, which were originally developed in the Dynamic Stochastic General Equilibrium (DSGE) literature with a representative agent. These frictions are sticky-prices, search-and-matching frictions on the labor market, and habit-formation or limited-participation in financial markets (see Krusell et al., 2010; Gornemann et al., 2012; Ravn and Sterk, 2013; Kaplan et al., 2016; Challe et al., 2017 among others). These recent contributions have shown that heterogeneity is important for macroeconomists for positive and not only normative analysis. The effect of technology shocks, of fiscal or monetary policy shocks are different between representative-agent world, and models where agents face uninsurable risks. To give a concrete example, Challe et al. (2017) show that agents facing an expected increase in unemployment save to self-insure, as they are afraid to fall into unemployment. This contributes to a fall in aggregate demand, which reduces the incentives to post vacancies and increases unemployment. This negative feedback loop is a form of a "paradox of thrift", which is absent in representative agent models. This may explain a third of the fall in the consumption of non-durable goods with respect to trends after 2008. Krueger et al. (2015) present other evidence of the importance of heterogeneity/inequality among households in the subprime crisis.

The goal of this chapter is to review recent methods to solve these models, which allow for an easy introduction of these frictions in general equilibrium. These methods are based on a simplification of the structure of heterogeneity (motivating the title of this chapter) and on simple perturbation methods. The models generate a finite number of equations to describe agent heterogeneity. The gain of this reduction in heterogeneity is threefold. First, it allows deriving clear analytical insights in this class of model. Second, the model can be solve very rapidly. It allows the use of econometric techniques, such as estimation of the model with Bayesian tools. Third, one can derive normative implications from optimal policies in these environments. This class of model also has some drawbacks, resulting from the simplifying assumptions that are necessary to obtain a finite number of agent types in equilibrium. The use of perturbation methods for the aggregate risk (as in the DSGE literature) generates well-known problems about the determinacy of equilibrium portfolios with multiple assets. Recent papers emphasize non-convex portfolio adjustment costs, which could help in this dimension (see Kaplan et al., 2016 and Ragot, 2014). Finally, on the quantitative side, the models using truncated idiosyncratic histories may be more promising in matching relevant wealth distribution, as the wealth distribution can be made close to the full-fledge model when one increases the number of equations (see Section 7 below).

The balance of the costs of benefits of using this class of model obviously depends on the problem under consideration, as will be clear in this chapter. For some problems, the simulation of the full-heterogeneity model with aggregate shocks may be necessary. The limitations and possible developments in the reduced-heterogeneity literature are further discussed at the end of this survey, in Section 7.

The tools used in this chapter are designed to solve models with rational expectations (in a broad sense). These models differ from a second line of research on heterogeneous agents that depart from rational expectations. The models are labeled Agent-Based Models (ABM) and are developed in a vast literature that assume some specific behavioral rules. Section 8 is dedicated to the discussion of the these two lines of research.

This chapter is mostly methodological. It details benchmark models generating reduced heterogeneity and it sketches algorithms to solve them. Other approaches to solve heterogeneous-agent models with perturbation methods are used in the literature. The discussion and comparison with these alternative approaches is left for Section 7.

The presentation of this chapter follows the order of the complexity of the models. First, the basic problem is presented in Section 2 to lay down notations. Then, some economic problems can be quantitatively investigated in environments where agents don't trade in equilibrium. These no-trade equilibria are presented in Section 3. No-trade is too strong an assumption for models where the endogeneity of the amount of insurance (or self-insurance) is key for the economic problems under investigation. Section 4 presents an alternative class of models with small-heterogeneity where heterogeneity is preserved only for a subgroup of agents. Section 5 presents a general approach to reducing heterogeneity in incomplete insurance market models. In a nutshell, this theory is based on truncations of idiosyncratic histories, which endogenously delivers a finite (but arbitrarily large) number of different agents. Section 6 discusses the derivation of optimal policies in these environments. Section 7 discusses the relationship between the reduced-heterogeneity approach of this chapter and other methods using perturbation methods. Section 8 discusses the possible use of reduced-heterogeneity approaches for models not using rational expectations, such as Agent-Based Models. Section 9 concludes. Empirical strategies to discipline and discriminate among the general class of heterogeneous-agent models are discussed.

2 THE ECONOMIC PROBLEM AND NOTATIONS
2.1 THE MODEL

Time is discrete, indexed by $t \geq 0$. The aggregate risk is represented[1] by state variables $h_t \in \mathbb{R}^N$ in each period t. Typically, h_t can be the level of technology, the amount of public spending, and so on. It is assumed to be N-dimensional for the sake of generality. Key to the methods described below is the fact that h_t is continuous to allow for perturbation methods. We will indeed solve for small variations in h_t or, in other words, for small changes in the aggregate state of the world. The idea is the same as linearizing a model around a well-defined steady-state for a representative agent model. It will always be possible to take higher-order approximation, but usually a first-order approximation (linearizing the model) is enough to obtain key insights. The history of aggregate shocks up to period t is denoted $h^t = \{h_0, ..., h_t\}$.

---

[1]More formally, the aggregate risk is represented by a probability space $(\mathcal{S}^\infty, \mathcal{F}, \mathbb{P})$. See Heathcote (2005) or Miao (2006) for a more formal presentation.

Agents' problem. The specificity of heterogeneous agent models is that, on top of aggregate risk, each agent faces uninsurable idiosyncratic risk, such that they will differ as time goes by, according to the realization of their idiosyncratic risk. More formally, assume that there is a continuum of length 1 of agents indexed by i.

Agents face time-varying idiosyncratic risk. At the beginning of each period, agents face an idiosyncratic labor productivity shock $e_t \in \mathcal{E} \equiv \{e_1, ..., e_E\}$ that follows a discrete first-order Markov process with transition matrix $M(h_t)$, which is an $E \times E$ Markov matrix. The probability $M_{e,e'}(h_t)$, $e, e' \in \mathcal{E}$ is the probability for an agent to switch from individual state $e_t = e$ at date t to state $e_{t+1} = e'$ at date $t + 1$, when the aggregate state is h_t in period t. At period t, $e^t = \{e_0, ..., e_t\} \in \mathcal{E}^{(t+1)}$ denotes a history of the realization of idiosyncratic shocks, up to time t. The fact that the idiosyncratic state space is discrete is crucial for the methods presented below, but it is not restrictive for the application found in the literature. The idiosyncratic states considered are often employment–unemployment or a 2-state endowment economy (as in Huggett, 1993), or different idiosyncratic productivity levels to match the empirical process of labor income (Heathcote, 2005 uses a 3-state process; Aiyagari, 1994 uses a 7-state process). More generally, any continuous first-order process can be approximated by a discrete process, using the Tauchen (1986) procedure.

In what follows, and without loss of generality, I will consider a two-state process where agents can be either employed, when $e_t = 1$, or unemployed, when $e_t = 0$. In this latter case, the agent must supply a quantity of labor δ for home production to obtain a quantity of goods δ: the labor choice is constrained. The probability to stay employed is denoted $\alpha_t \equiv M_{1,1}(h_t)$, thus $1 - \alpha_t$ is the job-separation rate. The probability to stay unemployed is denoted as $\rho_t \equiv M_{0,0}(h_t)$, such that $1 - \rho_t$ is the job finding rate in period t.

Agents have a discount factor β and a period utility function $U(c, l)$, which is increasing in consumption c and decreasing in labor supply l. In addition U is twice-differentiable and has standard concavity properties for consumption.

Market structure. Agents can't buy assets contingent on their next-period employment status (otherwise, they could buy some insurance), but can only save in an "aggregate" asset, whose return depends only on the history of the aggregate states h^t.

The typical problem of an agent facing incomplete insurance markets is the following

$$\max_{\left(a_{t+1}^i, c_t^i\right)_{t \geq 0}} \mathbb{E}_0 \sum_{t=0}^{\infty} \beta^t \ U\left(c_t^i, l_t^i\right) \tag{1}$$

$$a_{t+1}^i + c_t^i \ = \ e_t^i w_t l_t^i + (1 - e_t^i)\delta + (1 + r_t)a_t^i, \text{ for all } e^N \in \mathcal{E}^N \tag{2}$$

$$c_t^i, l_t^i \geq 0, \qquad a_t^i \geq -\bar{a}, \text{ for all } e^N \in \mathcal{E}^N \tag{3}$$

$$a_0^i \quad \text{are given} \tag{4}$$

where w_t is the wage rate in period t and r_t is the return on saving between period $t - 1$ and period t. a_{t+1}^i is the saving of agent i in period t, and c_t^i, l_t^i are respectively the consumption and labor supply of agent i in period t. More rigorously, aggregate variables should be understood as a function of the history of aggregate shock h^t, thus as $r(h^t)$ and $w(h^t)$, whereas idiosyncratic variables should be understood as functions of both aggregate and idiosyncratic histories, as $a_{t+1}^i(e^{i,t}, h^t)$ for instance. The decisions in each period are subject to the non-negativity constraints (3). Importantly, agents can't borrow more than the amount $\bar{a}$ in each period.

Production. Markets are competitive and a representative firm produces with capital and labor. The production function is $Y_t = A_t K_t^\lambda L_t^{1-\lambda} + (1 - \mu) K_t$, where μ is the capital depreciation rate, and A_t is the technology level, which is affected by technology shocks. The first-order conditions of the firm imply that factor prices are

$$r_t + \mu = \lambda A_t K_t^{\lambda-1} L_t^{1-\lambda}$$

and

$$w_t = (1 - \lambda) A_t K_t^\lambda L_t^{-\lambda}$$

where K_t is the aggregate capital stock and L_t is the aggregate labor supply.

The technology shock is defined as the standard AR(1) process $A_t \equiv e^{a_t}$, with

$$a_t = \rho^a a_{t-1} + \epsilon_t^a$$

with $\epsilon_t^a \sim \mathcal{N}\left(0, (\sigma^a)^2\right)$.

2.2 EQUILIBRIUM DEFINITION AND INTUITION TO REDUCE THE STATE SPACE

We can provide the equilibrium definition and the main idea to reduce the state space. First, in the general case, as time goes by, there is an increasing number of different agents, due to the heterogeneity in idiosyncratic histories. Instead of thinking in sequential terms (i.e. following the history of each agent from period 0 to any period t), Huggett (1993) and Aiyagari (1994) have shown that the problem can be stated in recursive form, if ones introduces an infinite-support distribution as a state variable, when there are no aggregate shocks.[2]

Indeed, define as $F_t : [-\bar{a}; +\infty) \times \{0, 1\} \to \mathbb{R}^+$ the cross-sectional cumulative distribution over capital holdings and idiosyncratic states in period t. For instance, $F(d, 1)$ is the mass of employed workers having a wealth level less than d at the beginning of period t. In the general case, an equilibrium of this economy is 1) a policy rule for each agent solving its individual maximization problem, 2) factor prices that are consistent with the firm first-order conditions, 3) financial and labor markets clear

---

[2]The structure of the recursive equilibrium with aggregate shocks is still an open theoretical question. See Miao (2006) for a discussion. This difficulty will not exist for the class of equilibria presented in this chapter, so I don't discuss this issue.

for each period $t \geq 0$:

$$\int a_{t+1}(a, e) dF_t(a, e) = K_{t+1} \tag{5}$$

where $a_{t+1}(a, e)$ is the saving in period t of a household having initial wealth a and being in state $e \in \{0, 1\}$, and

$$\int l_t(a, e) dF_t(a, e) = L_t \tag{6}$$

and finally 4) a law of motion for the cross-sectional distribution F_t that is consistent with the agents' decision rule at each date. This law of motion can be written as (following the notation of Algan et al., 2014)

$$F_{t+1} = \Upsilon(h_{t+1}, h_t, F_t)$$

The literature on heterogeneous-agent models has tried to find solution techniques to approximate the very complex object Υ, which maps distribution and shocks into distributions (Den Haan, 2010 for a presentation and discussion of differences in methods).

The basic idea. The basic idea for reducing the state space is first to go back to the sequential representation. If at any period t, only the last N periods are necessary to know the wealth of any agent, then only the truncated history $e^{N,t} = \{e_{t+1-N}, ..., e_t\} \in \mathcal{E}^N$ is necessary to "follow" the whole distribution of agents, in a sense made clear below. In this economy, there are only 2^N different agents at each period, instead of a continuous distribution. This number can be large, but it is finite and all standard perturbation techniques can be applied.

The next section presents different types of equilibria in the literature. The first one is the no-trade equilibrium where $N = 1$, the second one is the reduced-heterogeneity equilibrium, and the last one is the general case for arbitrary N.

3 NO-TRADE EQUILIBRIA

3.1 NO-TRADE EQUILIBRIA WITH TRANSITORY SHOCKS

A first simple way to generate a tractable model is to consider environments that endogenously generate no-trade equilibria with transitory shocks. This class of equilibrium was introduced by Krusell et al. (2011) to study asset prices with time-varying idiosyncratic risk. Recent developments show that they can be useful for macroeconomic analysis. Indeed, this equilibrium structure can be applied to a subgroup of agents.

3.1.1 Assumptions

These equilibria are based on two assumptions. First, assets are in zero net supply and production only necessitates labor ($\lambda = 0$ in the production function). The first consequence is that the total amount of saving must be equal to the total amount of borrowing *among* households. The second consequence is that the real wage is only the technology level in each period $w_t = A_t$. Second, it is assumed that the borrowing limit is 0, $\bar{a} = 0$. As agents can't borrow, there are no assets in which agents can save: $a_t^i = 0$ for all agents i in any period t. These equilibria are not interesting for generating a realistic cross-section of wealth, but they can be interesting to investigate the behavior of the economy facing time-varying uninsurable risk. Indeed, the price of any asset is determined by the highest price than any agent is willing to pay.

Denoting $\{1\}$ the employed agents and $\{0\}$ the unemployed agents, one can now state the problem recursively. The value functions for employed and unemployed agents are (I write these functions with the time index to facilitate the reading, although it is not necessary in this recursive formulation).

$$V(a_t, h_t, \{1\}) = \max_{c_t, l_t, a_{t+1}} U(c_t, l_t) + \beta \mathbb{E}\big(\alpha_{t+1} V(a_{t+1}, h_{t+1}, \{1\})$$
$$+ (1 - \alpha_{t+1}) V(a_{t+1}, h_{t+1}, \{0\})\big)$$
$$a_{t+1} + c_t = A_t l_t + a_t(1 + r_t)$$
$$a_{t+1} \geq 0$$

and

$$V(a_t, h_t, \{0\}) = \max_{c_t, a_{t+1}} U(c_t, \delta) + \beta \mathbb{E}\big(\rho_{t+1} V(a_{t+1}, h_{t+1}, \{0\})$$
$$+ (1 - \rho_{t+1}) V(a_{t+1}, h_{t+1}, \{1\})\big)$$
$$a_{t+1} + c_t = \delta + a_t(1 + r_t)$$
$$a_{t+1} \geq 0$$

where the expectation operator $\mathbb{E}$ is taken for the aggregate shock h only.

As no agent can save, we have $a_{t+1} = 0$ for all agents, and one can thus see that all employed agents consume $c_{1,t} = A_t l_{1,t}$ and supply the same quantity of labor $l_{1,t}$, whereas unemployed agents simply consume $c_{0,t} = \delta$ and the labor supply is obviously given by $l_{0,t} = \delta$.

The equilibrium can be derived using a guess-and-verify structure. Indeed, for general values of the parameters derived below, unemployed agents are credit-constrained: they would like to borrow, and employed agents would like to save. As a consequence, they are the marginal buyer of the asset (although in zero-net supply) and make the price.

Deriving the first-order conditions of the previous program and *then* using these values, one finds

$$A_t U_c(c_{1,t}, l_{1,t}) = \qquad\qquad - U_l(c_{1,t}, l_{1,t})$$
$$U_c(c_{1,t}, l_{1,t}) = \beta \mathbb{E}(1 + r_{t+1}) \big(\alpha_{t+1} U_c(c_{1,t+1}, l_{1,t+1}) + (1 - \alpha_{t+1}) U_c(c_{0,t+1}, \delta)\big)$$

and the conditions for unemployed agents to be credit-constrained at the current interest rate is

$$U_c(c_{0,t}, \delta) > \beta \mathbb{E}(1 + r_{t+1}) \big(\rho_{t+1} U_c(c_{0,t+1}, \delta) + (1 - \rho_{t+1}) U_c(c_{1,t+1}, l_{1,t+1})\big)$$

Specification of the functional forms. Assume that

$$
\begin{cases}
U(c,l) = \frac{c^{1-\sigma}-1}{1-\sigma} - \chi \frac{l^{1+\frac{1}{\phi}}}{1+\frac{1}{\phi}} & \text{if } \sigma \neq 1 \\[2ex]
U(c,l) = \log(c) - \chi \frac{l^{1+\frac{1}{\phi}}}{1+\frac{1}{\phi}} & \text{if } \sigma = 1
\end{cases}
$$

σ is the curvature of the utility function (not directly equal to risk aversion to the endogenous labor supply), and ϕ is the Frisch elasticity of labor supply, ranging from 0.3 to 2 in applied work (see Chetty et al., 2011 for a discussion). χ is a parameter scaling the supply of labor in steady state. With this specification one finds

$$
\begin{aligned}
A_t c_{1,t}^{-\sigma} &= \chi l_{1,t}^{\frac{1}{\phi}} \\
c_{1,t}^{-\sigma} &= \beta \mathbb{E}\left(1+r_{t+1}\right)\left(\alpha_{t+1} c_{1,t+1}^{-\sigma} + (1-\alpha_{t+1})\delta^{-\sigma}\right)
\end{aligned} \tag{7}
$$

and the conditions for unemployed agents to be credit-constrained at the current interest rate is

$$
\delta^{-\sigma} > \beta \mathbb{E}\left(1+r_{t+1}\right)\left(\rho_{t+1}\delta^{-\sigma} + (1-\rho_{t+1})c_{1,t+1}^{-\sigma}\right)
$$

From the budget constraint of employed agents $c_{1,t} = A_t l_{1,t}$ and the labor choice in (7), we obtain

$$
c_{1,t}^{1+\phi\sigma} = A_t^{1+\phi}/\chi^\phi
$$

The technology process is the following

$$
A_t = e^{a_t}
$$

where a_t is an AR(1) process specified above.

Assume that three shocks hit the economy: A shock to the technology level, a_t, a shock to the probability to stay employed α_t and a shock to the probability to stay unemployed ρ_t, which are AR(1) processes. More formally,

$$
\begin{bmatrix} a_t \\ \alpha_t - \bar{\alpha} \\ \rho_t - \bar{\rho} \end{bmatrix} = \begin{bmatrix} \rho^a & 0 & 0 \\ 0 & \rho^\alpha & 0 \\ 0 & 0 & \rho^\rho \end{bmatrix} \begin{bmatrix} a_{t-1} \\ \alpha_{t-1} - \bar{\alpha} \\ \rho_{t-1} - \bar{\rho} \end{bmatrix} + \begin{bmatrix} \epsilon_t^a \\ \epsilon_t^\alpha \\ \epsilon_t^\rho \end{bmatrix}
$$

where the innovations ϵ_t^a, ϵ_t^α, and ϵ_t^ρ are white noise with standard deviation equal to σ^a, σ^α, and σ^ρ respectively, $\mathcal{N}\left(0,(\sigma^a)^2\right)$, $\mathcal{N}\left(0,(\sigma^\alpha)^2\right)$, $\mathcal{N}\left(0,(\sigma^\rho)^2\right)$. In the previous processes, the covariation between the exogenous shocks are 0, but alternative specifications are easy to introduce. The steady-state value of α_t is $\bar{\alpha}$ and the steady-sate level of ρ_t is $\bar{\rho}$.

Steady state. To use perturbation methods, we first solve for the steady sate and then consider first-order deviation from the steady state. In steady state $A = 1$, and we get from the two equations in (7),

$$c_1 = \chi^{-\frac{\phi}{1+\sigma\phi}} \tag{8}$$

and

$$1 + r = \frac{1}{\beta} \left(\bar{\alpha} + (1 - \bar{\alpha}) \left(\frac{\delta}{c_1} \right)^{-\sigma} \right)^{-1}$$

Putting in some numbers allows estimating the order of magnitude. Consider the period to be a quarter. The previous equality shows that the effect of uninsurable risk on the interest rate is the consumption inequality between employed and unemployed agents (irrespective of labor-supply elasticity for instance). Chodorow-Reich and Karabarbounis (2014) estimate a decrease in consumption of non-durable goods of households falling into unemployment between 10% and 20%. As a consequence, one can take the conservative value $\frac{\delta}{c_1} = 0.9$. The quarterly job loss probability is roughly 5% and $\alpha = 0.95$ (see Challe and Ragot, 2016 for a discussion), and the discount factor is $\beta = 0.99$. One finds a real interest rate $r = 0.45\%$ for $\sigma = 1$, and $r = -0.002$ when $\sigma = 2$. In the complete market case, we have $\alpha = 1$ and $1 + r = 1/\beta$. We find $r = 1\%$. As is well known, market incompleteness contributes to a smaller steady-state interest rate compared to the complete market case (see Aiyagari, 1994 for a discussion).

3.2 PRESERVING TIME-VARYING PRECAUTIONARY SAVING IN THE LINEAR MODEL

The effect of time-varying precautionary saving is preserved in the linear model for all the environments studied in this chapter. This is best understood in this simple framework. I denote by $\hat{x}$ the proportional deviation of the variable x and by $\tilde{y}$ the level deviation of variables y (applied typically to interest rate and transition probabilities). For instance, $c_{1,t} = c_1 \left(1 + \hat{c}_{1,t} \right)$ and $\alpha_t = \alpha + \tilde{\alpha}_t$. Linearizing the Euler equation in (7), one finds that

$$\hat{c}_{1,t} = \mu_1 \mathbb{E}\hat{c}_{1,t+1} + \mu_2 \mathbb{E}\tilde{\alpha}_{t+1} - \frac{1}{\sigma}\mathbb{E}\tilde{r}_{t+1} \tag{9}$$

where

$$\mu_1 = \alpha\beta(1+r) \text{ and } \mu_2 = \frac{\beta(1+r)}{\sigma} \left(\frac{\delta^{-\sigma} - c_1^{-\sigma}}{c_1^{-\sigma}} \right)$$

With the values given above, one finds $\mu_1 = 0.94$ and $\mu_2 = 0.1$, when $\sigma = 1$. To give an order of magnitude, an increase in 10% in the expected job-separation rate (a decrease in α) has the same effect as an increase of 1% in the real interest rate.

A second key implication is the value of $\mu_1 < 1$ in front of $\mathbb{E}\hat{c}_{1,t+1}$. This has dramatic implications for monetary policy compared to the complete market case, where we have $\mu_1 = 1$. These implications are studied by McKay et al. (2016) in this type of environment, to study forward guidance.

One can see that the probability to stay employed α_t has a first-order effect on the consumption decision in (9) when markets are incomplete. The reason for this result is that we are not linearizing around a riskless steady state. We are linearizing around a steady state where idiosyncratic risk is preserved. As a consequence, there are two different marginal utilities that agents can experience in the steady state: either $c_1^{-\sigma}$ if employed, or $\delta^{-\sigma}$ if unemployed. As a consequence, the term $\frac{\delta^{-\sigma} - c_1^{-\sigma}}{c_1^{-\sigma}}$ in μ_2 represents the lack of insurance in steady state. This term scales the reaction of consumption to changes in the idiosyncratic probability to switch employment status. In the complete market case, we obviously have $\mu_2 = 0$.

Linearizing the labor-supply equation, one finds $\hat{c}_{1,t} = \frac{1+\phi}{1+\phi\sigma} a_t$. Plugging this expression into (9), one finds that the value of the interest rate is pinned down by the shocks (using $\mathbb{E}\tilde{\alpha}_{t+1} = \rho^\alpha \tilde{\alpha}_t$ and $\mathbb{E}a_{t+1} = \rho^a a_t$):

$$\mathbb{E}\tilde{r}_{t+1} = \sigma \mu_2 \rho^\alpha \tilde{\alpha}_t - \sigma \frac{1+\phi}{1+\phi\sigma} \left(1 - \mu_1 \rho^a\right) a_t$$

One observes that an increase in the uncertainty (decrease in $\tilde{\alpha}_t$) generates a fall in the expected real interest rate. Indeed, employed agents want to self-insure more in this case, and they accept a lower remuneration of their savings. An increase in productivity (a_t) also decreases the expected real interest rate, as agents also want to self-insure more to transfer income from today to the next-period state of the world where they are unemployed.

These no-trade equilibria are extreme representations of market incompleteness, as the consumption levels are exogenous. They can nevertheless be useful in DSGE models. For instance, Ravn and Sterk (2013) use the same trick to study an incomplete-insurance market model where households can be either employed or unemployed. The simplification on the households side allows to enrich the production side and to consider sticky prices, introducing quadratic costs of price adjustment à la Rotemberg, search-and-matching frictions on the labor market and downward nominal wage rigidities. In this environment, Ravn and Sterk consider two types of unemployed workers who differ in their search efficiency and therefore in their job-finding probabilities. They use this model to account for changes in the US labor market after the great recession. They focus in particular on the distinction of shifts in the Beveridge curve and of movements along the Beveridge curve. Werning (2015) uses this model to derive theoretical results about the effect of market incompleteness. Challe (2017) uses a no-trade equilibrium to analyze optimal monetary policy with sticky prices on the goods market and search-and-matching frictions on the labor market. He shows that optimal monetary policy reaction is more expansionary after a cost-push shock when markets are incomplete (compared to the complete market environment), because there are additional gains to reduce unemployment when markets are incomplete. McKay and Reis (2016a) analyze optimal time-varying unemployment insurance using this setup.

3.3 NO-TRADE EQUILIBRIUM WITH PERMANENT SHOCKS

A second line of literature to generate tractable no-trade equilibria is based on the Constantinides and Duffie (1996) environment. These authors consider permanent idiosyncratic risk (instead of transitory risk as in the previous framework) and show that one can study market allocations and asset prices with no-trade. Recently, Heathcote et al. (2014) generalized this framework to quantify risk-sharing and to decompose inequality into life-cycle shocks versus initial heterogeneity in preferences and productivity. Closed-form solutions are obtained for equilibrium allocations and for moments of the joint distribution of consumption, hours, and wages.

These no-trade equilibria are useful to provide a first quantification of new mechanisms generated by incomplete insurance markets. Nevertheless, they can't consider the macroeconomic effect of changes in savings after aggregate shocks. Small-heterogeneity models have been developed to consider this important additional channel in tractable environments.

4 SMALL-HETEROGENEITY MODELS

Small-heterogeneity models are classes of equilibria where agents do save but where the equilibrium distribution of wealth endogenously features a finite state space. Three classes of equilibria can be found in the literature. Each type of equilibrium has its own merit according to the question under scrutiny. I present the first one in detail, and the two others more rapidly, as the algorithms to solve for the equilibrium are very similar. The last class of equilibrium may be more suited for quantitative analysis, as the conditions for the equilibrium to exist are easier to check.

4.1 MODELS BASED ON ASSUMPTIONS ABOUT LABOR SUPPLY

4.1.1 Assumptions

The first class of equilibria is based on two assumptions.

First, it is assumed that agents choose their labor supply when employed and that the disutility of labor supply is linear. If c is consumption and l is labor supply, the period utility function is

$$U(c,l) = u(c) - l$$

The implication of this assumption is that the first-order condition for labor supply pins down the marginal utility of consumption of employed agents. This assumption is used in Scheinkman and Weiss (1986) and in Lagos and Wright (2005) to simplify heterogeneity in various environments.

The second assumption is that the credit constraint is tighter than the natural borrowing limit

$$\bar{a} > -\delta/r \tag{10}$$

where r is the steady-state interest rate. This concept is introduced by Aiyagari (1994), and it is the loosest credit constraint, which ensures that consumption is always positive. The implication of this assumption is that unemployed agents will hit the credit constraint after a finite number of periods of unemployment. This property is key to reduce the state space, and we discuss it below.

4.1.2 Equilibrium Structure

To simplify the exposition, the equilibrium is presented using a guess-and-verify strategy. For the sake of clarity, the time index is kept to variables (although not necessary in the recursive exposition). Assume that all employed agents consume and save the same amount in each period t, $c_{0,t}$ and $a_{0,t+1}$ respectively. In addition, assume that all agents unemployed for k periods consume and save the same amount, denoted $c_{k,t}$ and $a_{k,t+1}$, for $k \geq 1$ respectively. In addition, assume that agents unemployed for L periods are credit-constrained, and that this number is not time-varying (L is an equilibrium object). This last assumption is important and will be justified below.

Denote as $V_k(a_t, X_t)$ the value function of agents in state $k = 0, 1, \dots$ (0 is employed agents, here), where X_t is the set of variables specified below that are necessary to form rational expectations.[3]

We have for employed people

$$V_0(a_t, X_t) = \max_{c_{0,t}, a_{0,t+1}, l_t} u(c_{0,t}) - l_t + \beta \mathbb{E} \left(\alpha_{t+1} V_0(a_{0,t+1}, X_{t+1}) \right.$$
$$\left. + (1 - \alpha_{t+1}) V_1(a_{0,t+1}, X_{t+1}) \right)$$
$$a_{0,t+1} + c_{0,t} = w_t l_t + a_t(1 + r_t)$$
$$a_{0,t+1} \geq -\bar{a}$$

and for all unemployed people, $k \geq 1$

$$V_k(a_t, X_t) = \max u(c_t) - \delta + \beta \mathbb{E} \left(\rho_{t+1} V_0(a_{k,t+1}, X_{t+1}) \right.$$
$$\left. + (1 - \rho_{t+1}) V_{k+1}(a_{k,t+1}, X_{t+1}) \right)$$
$$a_{k,t+1} + c_{k,t} = \delta + a_t(1 + r_t)$$
$$a_{k,t+1} \geq -\bar{a}$$

As credit constraints bind for agents unemployed for $k \geq L$ periods, we have for these agents $a_{k,t+1} = -\bar{a}$.

---

[3] We introduce the time subscript in the recursive formulation to ease the understanding of the timing of the model.

We can derive the set of first-order conditions. For employed agents

$$u'(c_{0,t}) = 1/w_t$$
$$u'(c_{0,t}) = \beta\mathbb{E}(1+r_{t+1})\left(\alpha_{t+1}u'(c_{0,t+1})+(1-\alpha_{t+1})u'(c_{1,t+1})\right)$$

For unemployed agents, for $k = 1...L-1$.

$$u'(c_{k,t}) = \beta\mathbb{E}(1+r_{t+1})\left(\rho_{t+1}u'(c_{k+1,t+1})+(1-\rho_{t+1})u'(c_{0,t+1})\right)$$

Note that when $L = 1$, such that the credit constraints bind after one period of unemployment, then the previous equations don't exist. This case is studied more precisely below.

The conditions define a system of $2(L+1)$ equations.

$$1/w_t = \beta\mathbb{E}(1+r_{t+1})\left(\alpha_{t+1}/w_{t+1}+(1-\alpha_{t+1})u'(c_{1,t+1})\right)$$
$$u'(c_{k,t}) = \beta\mathbb{E}(1+r_{t+1})\left(\rho_{t+1}u'(c_{k+1,t+1})+(1-\rho_{t+1})/w_{t+1}\right),$$
$$\text{for } k = 1...L-1$$
$$a_{k,t+1}+c_{k,t} = \delta+a_{k-1,t}(1+r_t), \quad \text{for } k = 1...L$$
$$u'(c_{0,t}) = 1/w_t$$
$$a_{L,t} = -\bar{a}$$

These equations form a system in the $2(L+1)$ variables $(c_{k,t}, a_{k,t})_{k=0...L}$. These equations confirm the intuition that all employed agents consume and save the same amount.

How is this possible? This comes from the labor choice, which provides some insurance. Indeed, as soon as an unemployed agent for k period in period $t-1$ becomes employed in period t, then they work the necessary amount, denoted as $l_{k0,t}$ to consume $c_{0,t}$. This amount is given by the budget constraint of employed households

$$l_{k0,t} = \left(a_{0,t+1}+c_{0,t}-a_{k,t}(1+r_t)\right)/w_t, \quad k = 0, ..., L-1$$
$$l_{k0,t} = \left(a_{0,t+1}+c_{0,t}+\bar{a}(1+r_t)\right)/w_t, \quad k = L, ..., \infty \tag{11}$$

(The previous equation is indeed valid for $k = 0$.) Finally, note that for agents $k \geq L+1$, we simply have, from the budget constraint

$$c_{k,t} = \delta - r_t\bar{a}$$

Thanks to the assumption about the credit constraint given by (3) and the assumption of small aggregate shocks (to use perturbation methods), this amount will be positive.

This almost concludes the description of the agent's decision. The last step is to follow the number of employed and of each type of unemployed agent. Denote as

$n_{k,t}$ the number of agents in state $k = 0, ..., L$ in each period t. We have the law of motion of each type of agent

$$
\begin{aligned}
n_{0,t} &= \alpha_t n_{0,t-1} + (1 - \rho_t)(1 - n_{0,t-1}) \\
n_{k,t} &= \rho_t n_{k-1,t-1}, \qquad \text{for } k = 1, ..., \infty
\end{aligned}
$$

The first equation states that the number of employed agents is equal to the number of employed agents who keep their job (first) term, plus the number of unemployed agents, which is $1 - n_{0,t-1}$, who find a job. The second equation states that the number of agents unemployed for k periods at date t, are the number of agents unemployed for $k - 1$ periods at the previous date who stay unemployed.

The number of $k0$ agents (i.e. employed agents at date t, who were unemployed for k periods at date $t - 1$) is

$$
n_{k0,t} = (1 - \rho_t)n_{k,t-1}
$$

The number of credit-constrained agents is denoted as n_t^c and is simply

$$
n_t^c = 1 - \sum_{k=0}^{L-1} n_{k,t}
$$

In this equilibrium, the capital market equilibrium is simply

$$
K_t = \sum_{k=0}^{L-1} n_{k,t} a_{k,t} - n_t^c \bar{a}
$$

and

$$
L_t = \sum_{k=0}^{L-1} n_{k0,t} l_{k0,t} + (1 - \rho_t) n_{t-1}^c l_{L0,t}
$$

Here we used the fact that all constrained agents work the same amount when they find a job, due to condition (11).

Due to this assumption, the marginal utility of all employed agents is $u'(c_t) = 1/w_t$ in all periods. As a consequence, this marginal utility does not depend on the history of agents on the labor market, what considerably simplifies the equilibrium structure.

4.1.3 The System
We can now present the whole system of equations:

$$
\begin{aligned}
1/w_t &= \beta \mathbb{E}(1 + r_{t+1}) \left(\alpha_{t+1}/w_{t+1} + (1 - \alpha_{t+1}) u'(c_{1,t+1}) \right) \\
u'(c_{k,t}) &= \beta \mathbb{E}(1 + r_{t+1}) \left(\rho_{t+1} u'(c_{k+1,t+1}) + (1 - \rho_{t+1})/w_{t+1} \right), \\
&\qquad\qquad\qquad\qquad\qquad \text{for } k = 1, ..., L - 1
\end{aligned}
$$

$$a_{k,t+1} + c_{k,t} = \delta + a_{k-1,t}(1 + r_t), \qquad \text{for } k = 1, ..., L$$
$$u'(c_{0,t}) = 1/w_t$$
$$a_{L,t} = -\bar{a}$$
$$l_{k0,t} = \left(a_{0,t+1} + c_{0,t} - a_{k,t}(1 + r_t)\right)/w_t, \qquad \text{for } k = 0, ..., L-1$$
$$l_{L0,t} = \left(a_{0,t+1} + c_{0,t} + \bar{a}(1 + r_t)\right)/w_t$$
$$n_{0,t} = \alpha_t n_{0,t-1} + (1 - \rho_t)(1 - n_{0,t-1})$$
$$n_{1,t} = (1 - \alpha_t)n_{0,t}$$
$$n_{k,t} = \rho_t n_{k-1,t-1}, \qquad \text{for } k = 2, ..., L-1$$
$$n_{00,t} = \alpha_t n_{0,t}$$
$$n_{k0,t} = (1 - \rho_t)n_{k,t-1}, \qquad \text{for } k = 1, ..., L-1$$
$$n_t^c = 1 - \sum_{k=0}^{L-1} n_{k,t}$$
$$K_t = \sum_{k=0}^{L-1} n_{k,t} a_{k,t} - n_t^c \bar{a}$$
$$L_t = \sum_{k=0}^{L-1} n_{k0,t} l_{k0,t} + (1 - \rho_t) n_{t-1}^c l_{L0,t}$$
$$r_t = \lambda A_t K_t^{\lambda-1} L_t^{1-\lambda} - \mu$$
$$w_t = (1 - \lambda) A_t K_t^{\lambda} L_t^{-\lambda}$$

This system is large but finite. There are $5L + 8$ equations for $5L + 8$ variables $\left((c_{k,t}, a_{k,t+1}, l_{k0,t})_{k=0,...,L}, (n_{k,t}, n_{k0,t})_{k=0,...,L-1}, n_t^c, K_t, L_t, r_t, w_t\right)_{t=0...\infty}$. For any process for the exogenous shocks (α_t, ρ_t, A_t) one may think that it is possible to simulate this model. This is not the case because one key variable is not determined: L.

4.1.4 Algorithm: Finding the Value of L

The value of L can be found using steady-state solutions of the previous system. The idea is to find the steady-state for any L and iterate over L to find the value for which L agents are credit constrained, whereas $L - 1$ agents are not. The algorithm to find L and the steady state is the following (finding the steady state is not difficult because the problem is block-separable). I simply drop the time subscript to denote steady-state values.

Algorithm.

1. Take $L \geq 1$ as given.
   a. Take r as given.
      i. From r deduce w using the FOCs of the firms.
      ii. Solve for the consumption of agents $c_{k=0...L}$ using the Euler equations of the agents, from $k = 1$ to $k = L$.

    iii. Solve for the saving of the agents from a_L down to a_0 using the budget constraint of all agents, and the values $c_{k=0...L}$.

    iv. Solve for the labor supply of employed agents l_{k0} $k = 0, ..., L$.

    v. Solve for the share of agents n_k, n_{k0} for $k = 0, ..., L - 1$ and n^c.

    vi. Find the aggregate capital stock K.

  b. Iterate over r, until the financial market clears, i.e. until $r = \lambda K^{\lambda-1} L^{1-\lambda} - \mu$.

2. Iterate over L, until

$$
\begin{aligned}
a_{L-1} &> -\bar{a} \\
u'(c_L) &> \beta(1+r)\left((1-\bar{\rho})u'(c_0) + \rho u'(c_{L+1})\right)
\end{aligned}
\tag{12}
$$

where $c_{L+1} = \delta - r\bar{a}$.

4.1.5 Simulations

Once the steady-state value of L and the steady-state value of the variables are determined, one can simulate the model using standard perturbation methods. One can use DYNARE to simulate first and second approximations of the model, compute second moments, and so on. The distribution of wealth is summarized by the vector $(n_{k,t}, a_{k,t})_{k=0,...,L-1}$ and belongs to the state space of agents X_t to form rational expectations. In these simulations, one has to check that the aggregate shock is small enough such that L is indeed constant over time. One must thus check that the condition (12) is satisfied not only in the steady state but also during the simulations.

4.1.6 References and Limits

In the Bewley–Huggett–Aiyagari environment, Algan et al. (2011) use this framework to investigate the impact of money injections in a model where agents use money to self-insure against idiosyncratic shocks. Challe et al. (2013) use this assumption to study the effect of an increase in public debt on the yields curve in an environment where agents use safe assets of various maturities to self-insure against idiosyncratic risk. They show that an increase in idiosyncratic risk decreases both the level and the slope of the yield curve. In addition, an increase in public debt increases both the level and the slope of the yield curve. LeGrand and Ragot (2016a) use this assumption to consider insurance for aggregate risk in these environments. Introducing derivative assets, such as options, in an environment where agents use a risky asset to self-insure against idiosyncratic risk, they show that the time-variations in the volume of traded derivative assets are consistent with empirical findings.

    This framework is interesting to investigate the properties of time-varying precautionary saving in finance (for instance to study asset prices) but it is not well suited for the macroeconomy. Indeed, the elasticity of labor supply is much too high compared to empirical findings (the Frisch elasticity is here infinite, whereas it is between 0.3 and 1 in the data, see Chetty et al., 2011 for a discussion). In addition, all employed agents consume the same amount, which is pinned down by the real wage, which is obviously a counterfactual. For this reason, other frameworks with positive trade have been developed.

4.2 MODELS BASED ON LINEARITY IN THE PERIOD UTILITY FUNCTION

Challe and Ragot (2016) present an alternative environment, consistent with any value of the elasticity of the labor supply. This framework can thus be used in macroeconomic environments to model time-varying movements in inequality. We describe the empirical relevance and the modeling strategy in Section 4.2.3 after the presentation of the model.

4.2.1 Assumptions

The model relies on three assumptions.

First, instead of introducing linearity in the labor supply, the linearity is in the utility of consumption. More precisely, it is assumed that there exists a threshold c^* such that the period utility function is strictly concave for $c < c^*$ and linear for $c \geq c^*$. The linear-after-a-threshold utility function was introduced by Fishburn (1977) in decision theory to model behavior in front of gains and losses differently.

The period utility function is thus

$$
\tilde{u}'(c) = \begin{cases} u'(c) & \text{if } c < c^*, \\ \eta & \text{if } c^* \leq c, \end{cases} \tag{13}
$$

where the function $u(.)$ is increasing and concave. The slope of the utility function must be low enough to obtain global concavity, that is $u'(c^*) > \eta$.

Second, the borrowing limit is assumed to be strictly higher than the natural borrowing limit, as before.

Third, it is assumed that the discount factor of agents is such that all employed agents consume an amount $c_t > c^*$ and all unemployed agents consume an amount $c_t < c^*$.

4.2.2 Equilibrium Structure

To save some space, we now focus on the households' program. Assume that labor is inelastic as a useful benchmark (introducing elastic labor is very simple in this environment). All employed agents supply one unit of labor.

We have for employed people

$$
V_0(a_t, X_t) = \max_{c_{0,t}, a_{0,t+1} l_t} \tilde{u}(c_{0,t}) - 1 + \beta \mathbb{E} \left(\alpha_{t+1} V_0(a_{0,t+1}, X_{t+1}) \right.
$$
$$
\left. + (1 - \alpha_{t+1}) V_1(a_{0,t+1}, X_{t+1}) \right)
$$
$$
a_{0,t+1} + c_{0,t} = w_t + a_t(1 + r_t)
$$
$$
a_{0,t+1} \geq -\bar{a}
$$

and for all unemployed people, $k \geq 1$

$$V_k(a_t, X_t) = \max \tilde{u}(c_t) - \delta + \beta \mathbb{E}\left(\rho_{t+1} V_0(a_{k,t+1}, X_{t+1})\right.$$
$$\left. + (1 - \rho_{t+1}) V_{k+1}(a_{k,t+1}, X_{t+1})\right)$$
$$a_{k,t+1} + c_{k,t} = \delta + a_t(1 + r_t)$$
$$a_{k,t+1} \geq -\bar{a}$$

One can solve for the order conditions following the same steps as before. Using the same notations as in the previous section, denote as k agents the agents unemployed for k periods. Assuming that credit constraints are binding after L periods of unemployment, one can find consumption and saving choices.

The key difference between this environment and the one presented in the previous section is that employed agents will not differ according to their labor supply (which is inelastic), but by their consumption level. Denote as $c_{k0,t}$ the consumption at date t of employed agents who were unemployed for k periods at date $t - 1$, and denote (as before) as $c_{k,t}$ (for $k = 1, ..., L$) the consumption of unemployed agents who are unemployed for k periods at date t. The households are now described by the vector $(a_{k,t}, c_{k0,t})_{k=0,...,L}$ and $(c_{k,t})_{k=1,...,L}$ solving

$$\eta = \beta \mathbb{E}(1 + r_{t+1})\left(\alpha_{t+1}\eta + (1 - \alpha_{t+1})u'(c_{1,t+1})\right)$$
$$u'(c_{k,t}) = \beta \mathbb{E}(1 + r_{t+1})\left(\rho_{t+1}u'(c_{k+1,t+1}) + (1 - \rho_{t+1})\eta\right),$$
$$\text{for } k = 1, ..., L - 1$$
$$a_{k,t+1} + c_{k,t} = \delta + a_{k-1,t}(1 + r_t), \qquad \text{for } k = 1, ..., L$$
$$a_{0,t+1} + c_{k0,t} = w_t + a_{k,t}(1 + r_t), \qquad \text{for } k = 0, ..., L$$
$$a_{L,t} = -\bar{a}$$

One can check that this is a system of $3L + 2$ equations for $3L + 2$ variables. The number of each type of agent can be followed as in the previous section.

One may find this environment more appealing than the one in the previous section, as it does not rely on an unrealistic elasticity of labor supply. The problem is nevertheless that there are additional conditions for the equilibrium existence that limit the use of such a framework. Indeed, one has first to solve for steady-state consumption and savings for each type of agent, and for the steady-state value of L using the algorithm described in Section 4.1.4, and then one has to check the following ranking condition:

$$c_1 < c_{L0}$$

The previous condition is that the highest steady-state consumption of unemployed agents is lower than the lowest steady-state consumption of employed agents. Indeed, the consumption of households just becoming unemployed (and thus being employed in the previous period) c_1 is the highest consumption of unemployed agents, because consumption is falling with the length of the unemployment spell.

Moreover, the consumption of employed agents who were at the credit constraint in the previous period, c_{L0}, is the lowest consumption level of employed agents, because these agents have the lowest beginning-of-period wealth $-\bar{a}$. If the condition is fulfilled, one can always find a threshold c^* such that the period utility function is well behaved.

This framework can nevertheless be used in realistic dynamic models when applied to a subgroup of the population.

4.2.3 Using Reduced Heterogeneity to Model Wealth Inequality over the Business Cycle

Challe and Ragot (2016) apply the previous framework to model the bottom 60% of US households, based on the following observation. The wealth share of the poorest 60% of households in terms of liquid wealth is as low as 0.3%. Indeed, as the model is used to model precautionary saving in the business cycle, one should indeed focus on the net worth, which can readily be used for the short-run change in income. Define the period to be a quarter.

The modeling strategy is the following. Challe and Ragot (2016) model the top 40% of the households by a family, that can fully insure its members against unemployment risk. This family has a discount factor β^P for patient and it has thus a standard Euler equation (without the employment risk, which is insured).

$$u'(c_t^P) = \beta^P \mathbb{E}(1 + r_{t+1})u'(c_{t+1}^P)$$

As a consequence, the bottom 60% is modeled by agents having a quasi-linear utility function and having a lower discount factor, denoted as $\beta^I < \beta^P$ (I for impatient, P for patient). With such a low wealth shares of 0.3% (a few hundred dollars of savings), it is easy to show that the households spend all their saving after a quarter of unemployment. This implies that one can construct an equilibrium for the bottom, where $L = 1$. In other words, these households face the credit constraint after one period (one quarter) of unemployment.

The inter-temporal choice of employed agents can be simply written as

$$\eta = \beta^I \mathbb{E}(1 + r_{t+1})\left(\alpha_{t+1}\eta + (1 - \alpha_{t+1})u'(\delta + a_{0,t+1}(1 + r_{t+1}) + \bar{a})\right)$$

where we used the fact that $c_{1,t+1} = \delta + a_{0,t+1}(1 + r_{t+1}) + \bar{a}$.

One can linearize the previous equation to obtain a simple saving rule. Level-deviations from the steady state are denoted with a tilde, as before. Linearization gives

$$\tilde{a}_{0,t+1} = \Gamma_s \mathbb{E}\tilde{\alpha}_{t+1} + \Gamma_r \mathbb{E}\tilde{r}_{t+1}$$

where Γ_s, Γ_r are coefficients that depend on parameter values. One can show that $\Gamma_s < 0$, because agents facing a higher probability to stay employed decrease their precautionary savings. The coefficient Γ_r can be either positive or negative depending on parameter values, and on income and substitution effects.

Due to the saving rule, the model differs from hand-to-mouth DSGE models in the tradition of Kiyotaki and Moore (1997). In the previous model, the number of credit-constrained agents is very low, as households at the constraint are the fraction of impatient agents who are unemployed and not the full population of impatient agents. Finally, the conclusion of this model that poor households (the bottom 60% of the wealth distribution) react more to the unemployment risk than rich households is confirmed by household data (see Krueger et al., 2015). As a consequence, this framework is empirically more relevant than the no-trade equilibria presented above, or hand-to-mouth models following the seminal paper of Kiyotaki and Moore (1997).

Finally, Challe and Ragot (2016) show that this model does a relatively good job in reproducing time-varying precautionary saving (compared to Krusell and Smith, 1998), and that the model is not more complicated than a standard DSGE model. In particular, it can be solved easily using DYNARE.

4.2.4 Other References and Remarks

LeGrand and Ragot (2016c) extend this environment to introduce various segments in the period utility function to consider various types of agents. They apply this framework to show that such a model can reproduce a rich set of empirical moments when limited participation in financial markets is introduced. In particular, the model can reproduce the low risk free rate, the equity premium the volatility of the consumption growth rate of the top 50% together with the aggregate volatility of consumption.

The use of a quasi-linear utility function provides (with the relevant set of assumptions) a simple representation of household heterogeneity focusing on the poor households who indeed face a higher unemployment risk. The cost of this representation is that the existence conditions can be violated for big aggregate shocks or for an alternative calibration of the share of households facing the unemployment risk. As a consequence, this representation is not well-suited for Bayesian estimation, as it is not sure that existence conditions are fulfilled for any samples. To overcome this difficulty, other assumptions can be introduced.

4.3 MODELS BASED ON A "FAMILY" ASSUMPTION

The modeling strategy of previous models is based on the reduction of the state space by 1) reducing heterogeneity among high-income agents and 2) setting the credit constraints at a level higher than the natural borrowing limit (to be sure that low-income households reach the credit limit in a finite number of periods). The two previous modeling strategies played with utility functions to reach this goal. The last modeling strategy follows another route and considers directly different market arrangements for any utility function. It will be assumed that there is risk-sharing among employed agents. The presentation follows Challe et al. (2017), but it is much simpler because we do not introduce habit formation.

4.3.1 Assumptions

The model is based on limited insurance ("or the family assumption") often used in macro, but applied to a subgroup of agents. Assume that all agents belong to a family. The family head cares for all agents, but has a limited ability to transfer resources across agents. Indeed, the planner can transfer resources across agents on the same islands, but it cannot transfer resources across islands. More specifically:

1. All employed agents are on the same islands, where there is full risk-sharing.
2. All unemployed agents for k periods live on the same island, where there is full risk-sharing.
3. A representative of the family head implements the consumption-saving choice in all islands, maximizing total welfare.
4. The representative of the family head choose allocate wealth to households before knowing their next-period employment status.

The structure can be seen as a deviation from Lucas (1990) to reduce heterogeneity among employed agents. It will generate the same structure as the previous models: no heterogeneity among employed agents and heterogeneous unemployed agents according to the length of their unemployment spell.

4.3.2 Equilibrium Structure

As before, we use a guess-and-verify strategy to present the model. Assume that the unemployed agents reach the credit constraint after L consecutive periods of unemployment.

As before, denote as $n_{0,t}$ the number of employed agents at date t, and as $n_{k,t}$ the number of agents unemployed for $k \geq 1$ consecutive periods at date t. Denote as V^f the value function of the family head, and V^k as the value function of households unemployed for k periods. First, the value function of agents in the employed island is

$$
V^f \left(A_t^f, n_{0,t}, X_t \right) = \max_{S_{t+1}^f, c_{0,t}, l_t} n_{0,t} U(c_{0,t}, l_t)
$$

$$
+ \beta \mathbb{E} \left[V^f \left(A_{t+1}^f, n_{0,t+1}, X_{t+1} \right) + V^1 \left(a_{0,t+1}, X_{t+1} \right) \right]
$$

$$
c_{0,t} + a_{0,t+1} = w_t l_t + \frac{A_t^f}{n_{0,t}} (1 + r_t)
$$

$$
A_{t+1}^f = \alpha_{t+1} n_{0,t} a_{0,t+1}
$$

$$
+ (1 - \rho_{t+1}) \sum_{k=1}^{L-1} n_{k,t} a_{k,t+1} - (1 - \rho_{t+1}) n_t^c \bar{a}
$$

Let's explain this problem. The family head maximizes the utility of all agents in the employed island (imposing the same consumption and labor choice on all agents to maximize welfare). The head takes into consideration the fact that some employed agents will fall into unemployment next period (and will have the value function V^1 which is the inter-temporal welfare of agents unemployed for one period). The budget constraint is written in per capita terms: Per capita income is equal to per capita consumption and per capita savings, denoted as $a_{0,t+1}$. At the end of the period, all agents in the employed island have the same wealth, which is $a_{0,t+1}$. As the family head cannot discriminate between agents before they leave the island, this will be the next-period beginning-of-period wealth of agents leaving the island, i.e. just falling into unemployment.

Finally, the next-period wealth of employed agents is the next-period pooling of the wealth of agents staying or becoming employed. First, it sums the wealth of agents staying employed $\alpha_{t+1} n_{0,t} a_{0,t+1}$, and the wealth of unemployed agents not at the credit constraint in period t and finding a job in period $t+1$, $(1 - \rho_{t+1}) \sum_{k=1}^{L} n_{k,t} a_{k,t+1}$, and the wealth of agents constrained in period t and finding a job in period $t+1$. These agents have a wealth $-\bar{a}$ (recall that n_t^c is the number of agents at the credit constraint in period t).

The value function of unemployed agents for k periods is simpler

$$V^k\left(a_{k-1,t}, X_t\right) = \max_{a_{k,t+1}, c_{k,t}} n_{k,t} U(c_{k,t}, \delta)$$
$$+ \beta \mathbb{E}\left[V^f\left(A_{t+1}^f, n_{0,t+1}, X_{t+1}\right) + V^{k+1}\left(a_{k,t+1}, X_{t+1}\right)\right]$$
$$c_{k,t} + a_{k,t+1} = \delta + a_{k-1,t}(1 + r_t)$$
$$a_{k,t+1} \geq -\bar{a}$$

In this maximization, the representative of the family head in the island where agents are unemployed for k periods takes into account the fact that they will affect the next-period wealth of employed agents, because all agents belong to a whole family, and the wealth of agents unemployed for $k+1$ periods, in the next period. First-order and envelope conditions for employed agents are

$$w_t U_1(c_{0,t}, l_t) = -U_2(c_{0,t}, l_t)$$
$$U_1(c_{0,t}, l_t) = \beta \mathbb{E}\left[\alpha_{t+1} V_1^f\left(A_{t+1}^f, n_{0,t+1}, X_{t+1}\right)\right.$$
$$\left. + \frac{1}{n_{0,t}} V_1^1\left(a_{0,t+1}, X_{t+1}\right)\right]$$
$$V_1^f\left(A_t^f, n_{0,t}, X_t\right) = (1 + r_t) U_1(c_{0,t}, l_t)$$

First-order and envelope conditions for unemployed agents are

$$n_{k,t} U_1(c_{k,t}, \delta) = \beta \mathbb{E}\left[(1 - \rho_{t+1}) n_{k,t} V_1\left(A_{t+1}^f, n_{0,t+1}, X_{t+1}\right)\right.$$
$$\left. + V_1^{k+1}\left(a_{k,t+1}, X_{t+1}\right)\right]$$
$$V_1^k\left(a_{k-1,t}, X_t\right) = (1 + r_t) n_{k,t} U_1(c_{k,t}, \delta)$$

Combining these equations (and using the fact that $n_{1,t+1} = (1 - \alpha_{t+1})n_{0,t}$ and $n_{k+1,t+1} = \rho_{t+1}n_{k,t}$), one finds the set of equations defining the agents' choice.

$$U_1(c_{0,t}, l_t) = \beta\mathbb{E}(1 + r_{t+1})\left[\alpha_{t+1}U_1(c_{0,t+1}, l_{t+1}) + (1 - \alpha_{t+1})U_1(c_{1,t+1}, \delta)\right]$$

(14)

$$U_1(c_{k,t}, \delta) = \beta\mathbb{E}(1 + r_{t+1})\left[(1 - \rho_{t+1})U_1(c_{0,t+1}, l_{t+1}) + \rho_{t+1}U_1(c_{k+1,t+1}, \delta)\right],$$
$$\text{for } k = 1, ..., L - 1$$

$$w_t U_1(c_{0,t}, l_t) = -U_2(c_{0,t}, l_t)$$

(15)

$$A_{t+1}^f = \alpha_{t+1}n_{0,t}a_{0,t+1} + (1 - \rho_{t+1})\sum_{k=1}^{L-1}n_{k,t}a_{k,t+1} - (1 - \rho_{t+1})n_t^c\bar{a}$$

$$c_{0,t} + a_{0,t+1} = w_t l_t + \frac{A_t^f}{n_{0,t}}(1 + r_t)$$

(16)

$$c_{k,t} + a_{k,t+1} = \delta + a_{k-1,t}(1 + r_t), \text{ for } k = 1, ..., L$$

Given the prices r_t and w_t, this is a system of $2L + 3$ equations for the $2L + 3$ variables $((c_{k,t})_{k=0...L}, (a_{k,t})_{k=0...L-1}A_t^f, l_t)$. The key result of this construction is that the Euler equations of employed and unemployed agents are the same as those obtained in a model with uninsurable idiosyncratic risk. Indeed, using the law of large numbers (which is assumed to be valid in a continuum), the "island" metaphor transforms idiosyncratic probabilities into shares of agents switching between islands. The gain is that the state space is finite and the amount of heterogeneity is finite, as there are only $L + 1$ different wealth levels.

Note that the consumption of $c_{k,t}$ for $k \geq L + 1$ is $c_{k,t} = \delta + \bar{a}r_t$ because $a_{k,t+1} = \bar{a}$ for $k \geq L$.

The capital stock and total labor supply are simply

$$K_t = \sum_{k=0}^{L-1}n_{k,t}a_{k,t} - n_t^c\bar{a}$$

$$L_t = n_{0,t}l_t$$

Compared to the environments in Section 4.1 and in Section 4.2, the current equilibrium exhibits less heterogeneity, as all employed agents consume and work the same amount. The gain is that the period utility function can be very general.

4.3.3 Algorithm and Simulations

The algorithm to find the steady state is the following.

1. Guess a value for $L \geq 1$.
2. Guess a value for r; from r deduce w using the FOCs of the firms.
3. Guess a value for c_0; deduce the labor supply using (15).

a. Solve for the consumption of agents $c_{k=0...L}$ using the Euler equations of the agents, from c_1 to c_L.

b. Solve for the saving of the agents from a_0 to a_L using the budget constraint of all agents, and the values $c_{k=0...L}$.

c. Solve for the share of agents n_k for $k = 0, ..., L - 1$ and n^c.

d. Find the aggregate capital stock K and aggregate labor L.

4. Iterate on r, until the financial market clears, i.e. until $r = \lambda K^{\lambda-1} L^{1-\lambda} - \mu$.

5. Iterate on L, until

$$
\begin{aligned}
a_{L-1} &> & -\bar{a} \\
u'(c_L) &> & \beta(1+r)\left((1-\bar{\rho})u'(c_0) + \rho u'(c_{L+1})\right)
\end{aligned}
\tag{17}
$$

where $c_{L+1} = \delta - r\bar{a}$.

The model is again a finite set of equations, which can be simulated using DYNARE. The DYNARE solver could be used to double-check the values of the steady state.

4.3.4 Example of Quantitative Work

Challe et al. (2017) use this representation of heterogeneity to construct a full DSGE model with heterogeneous agents. Indeed, the authors assume that only the bottom 60% in the wealth distribution form precautionary saving, and that the top 40% can be modeled by a representative agent.

They then introduce many other features to build a quantitative model, such as 1) sticky prices, 2) habit formation (which complexifies significantly the exposition of the equilibrium), 3) capital adjustment costs, 4) search-and-matching frictions on the labor market, and 5) stochastic growth.

The general model is then brought to the data using Bayesian estimations. The information used in the estimation procedure includes thus the information set used to estimate DSGE models. In addition, information about time-varying consumption inequalities across agents can be used in the estimation process. The model is used to assess the role of precautionary saving during the great recession in the US. The authors show that a third of the fall in aggregate consumption can be attributed to time-varying precautionary saving due to the increase in unemployment during this period.

The possibility to use Bayesian estimation is a clear strength of this class of model. Indeed, as time-varying precautionary saving is preserved after linearization, the same techniques as in the representative-agent DSGE literature can be used, but lots of new data about time-varying moments of the distribution of income, wealth or consumption can be used to disciplined the model. This open the route for richer quantitative works.

4.4 ASSESSMENT OF SMALL-HETEROGENEITY MODELS

The three classes of small-heterogeneity model presented in this section have the merit to keep the effects of time-varying precautionary savings using perturbation methods. Compared to no-trade equilibria, the actual quantity of assets used to self-insure, i.e. the optimal quantity of liquidity in the sense of Woodford (1990), is endogenous. In addition, this can easily be applied to a relevant subset of households in a DSGE model.

An additional gain of these representations is that the state space is small. For an equilibrium where agents hit the borrowing constraint after L periods of unemployment, there are only $L + 1$ different wealth levels.

There are nevertheless two main drawbacks. First, when L grows, the state space doesn't converge toward a Bewley economy, because there is no heterogeneity across employed households. As a consequence, one cannot consider the full-fledged Bewley economy as the limit of these equilibria when there are no aggregate shocks. As a further consequence, one cannot use all the information about the cross-section of household inequality (for instance all employed agents are similar). Hence, the models capture only a part of time-varying precautionary saving. Admittedly, this a key part as the unemployment risk is the biggest uninsurable risk faced by households (Carroll et al., 2003).

The second drawback is that the number of periods of consecutive unemployment before the credit constraint binds (denoted as L) is part of the equilibrium definition: it has to be computed as a function of the model parameters. If aggregate shocks are small enough, this number is not time-varying, but this has to be checked during the simulations.

New developments provide environments without these drawbacks, at the cost of a bigger state space.

5 TRUNCATED-HISTORY MODELS

LeGrand and Ragot (2016b) present a general model to generate limited heterogeneity with an arbitrarily large but finite state space and which can be made close to the Bewley model. In this environment, the heterogeneity across agents depends only on a finite but possibly arbitrarily large number, denoted N, of consecutive past realizations of the idiosyncratic risk (as a theoretical outcome). As a consequence, the history of idiosyncratic risk is truncated after N periods. Agents sharing the same idiosyncratic risk realizations for the previous N periods choose the same consumption and wealth. As a consequence, instead of having a continuous distribution of heterogeneous agents in each period, the economy is characterized by a finite number of heterogeneous consumption and wealth levels. The model can be simulated with DYNARE and optimal policy can be derived solving a Ramsey problem in this environment. The presentation follows the exposition of the decentralized equilibrium of LeGrand and Ragot (2016b).[4]

---

[4]In the paper, LeGrand and Ragot show that this allocation can be represented as the allocation of a constrained planner. This insures existence and uniqueness for a given price dynamics.

5.1 ASSUMPTIONS

Truncated histories. Consider the following notations. First, the program is written in recursive forms to simplify the exposition, such that x' is the next-period value of the variable x. $\tilde{e}_0$ is the current beginning-of-period idiosyncratic state of the agent under consideration, $\tilde{e}_1$ is the beginning-of-period idiosyncratic state one period ago, and $\tilde{e}_k$ is the beginning-of-period idiosyncratic state k periods ago. As a consequence and for any N, each agent enters any period with an N-period history $\tilde{e}^N \in \mathcal{E}^N$, $\tilde{e}^N = \{\tilde{e}_{N-1}, ..., \tilde{e}_0\}$. This N-period history is a truncation of the whole history of each agent: It is the history of the agent for the last N periods, *before* the agent learns its current idiosyncratic shock $e \in \mathcal{E}$ for the current period.

After the idiosyncratic shock is realized, the agent has the $(N+1)$-period history denoted $e^{N+1} \equiv (\tilde{e}^N, e)$. Histories without a tilde are thus histories after the idiosyncratic shock is realized. We can also write $e^{N+1} = (\tilde{e}_{N-1}, e^N) = (\tilde{e}^N, e) = (\tilde{e}_{N-1}, \tilde{e}_{N-2}, ..., \tilde{e}_0, e)$. Indeed, e^{N+1} can be seen as the history $\tilde{e}^N$ with the successor state e, or as the state $\tilde{e}_{N-1}$ followed by the N-period history e^N.

The probability $\Pi_{\hat{e}^N, e^N}(X)$ that a household with end-of-period history (i.e. after the idiosyncratic shock is realized) $\hat{e}^N = (\hat{e}_{N-1}, ..., \hat{e}_0)$ in the current period experiences a next-period end-of-period history $e^N = (e_{N-1}, ..., e_0)$ is the probability to switch from state $\hat{e}_0$ in the current period to state e_0 in the next period, provided that histories $\hat{e}^N$ and e^N are compatible. More formally:

$$\Pi_{t, \hat{e}^N, e^N}(X) = 1_{e^N \succeq \hat{e}^N} M_{\hat{e}_0, e_0}(X) \tag{18}$$

where $1_{e^N \succeq \hat{e}^N} = 1$ if e^N is a possible continuation of history $\hat{e}^N$, and 0 otherwise.

From the expression (18) of the probability $\Pi_{\hat{e}^N, e^N}$, we can deduce the dynamics of the number of agents having history e^N in each period, denoted S_{e^N}:

$$S'_{e^N} = \sum_{\hat{e}^N \in \mathcal{E}^N} S_{\hat{e}^N} \Pi_{\hat{e}^N, e^N}(X) \tag{19}$$

The previous expression is the application of the law of large numbers in a continuum.

Preferences. For quantitative reasons that will appear clear below, we assume that the utility of each agent may be affected by its idiosyncratic history. More formally, it depends on the history of idiosyncratic risk e^N, recalling that $e^{N+1} = (\tilde{e}_{N-1}, e^N)$. As a consequence, preference depends on the current and the last $N-1$ idiosyncratic shocks. The period utility is thus $\xi_{e^N} U(c, l)$, where $\xi_{e^N} > 0$. The equilibrium can be derived for $\xi_{e^N} = 1$, as in LeGrand and Ragot (2016b). Adding the terms $\xi_{e^N} > 0$ is a trick to make the model more quantitatively relevant. It has the same role as the stochastic discount factor in Krusell and Smith (1998).

To simplify the algebra, it is assumed that the period utility function exhibits no wealth effect on the labor supply (which is consistent with empirical estimates). The period utility function is of the Greenwood–Hercowitz–Huffman (GHH) type

$$U(c, l) = u\left(c - \frac{l^{1 + \frac{1}{\varphi}}}{1 + \frac{1}{\varphi}}\right)$$

State vector. Denote by X the state vector in each period, which is necessary to form rational expectations. This state vector will be specified below. For now it is sufficient to assume that it is finite dimensional.

Transfer. The trick to reduce heterogeneity is to assume that each agent receives a lump-sum transfer, which depends on her $(N+1)$-history. This lump-sum transfer is denoted $\Gamma_{N+1}(e^{N+1}, X)$ and it will be balanced in each period.

Program of the agents. The agent maximizes her inter-temporal welfare by choosing the current consumption c, labor effort l, and asset holding a'. She will have to pay an after-tax interest rate and wage rate denoted as r and w, as before. The value function can be written as

$$V(a, e^{N+1}, X) = \max_{a',c,l} \xi_{e^N} u\left(c - \frac{l^{1+\frac{1}{\varphi}}}{1+\frac{1}{\varphi}}\right) + \beta \mathbb{E}\left[\sum_{e' \in \mathcal{E}} M_{e,e'}(X) V(a', (e^N, e'), X')\right]$$

(20)

$$a' + c = w(X) n_e l + \delta 1_{e=0} + (1 + r(X))a + \Gamma_{N+1}(e^{N+1}, X)$$ (21)

$$c, l \geq 0, \ a' \geq -\bar{a}$$ (22)

Denote by $\tilde{\eta}(a, e^{N+1}, X)$ the Lagrange multiplier of the credit constraint $a' \geq -\bar{a}$. The solution to the maximization program (20)–(22) is the policy rules denoted $c = g_c(a, e^{N+1}, X)$, $a' = g_{a'}(a, e^{N+1}, X)$, $l = g_l(a, e^{N+1}, X)$ and the multiplier $\tilde{\eta}$ satisfying the following first-order conditions, written in a compact form (I omit the dependence in X to lighten notations):

$$\xi_{e^N} u'\left(c - \frac{l^{1+\frac{1}{\varphi}}}{1+\frac{1}{\varphi}}\right) + \tilde{\eta} = \beta \mathbb{E}\left[\sum_{e' \in \mathcal{E}} M_{e,e'} \xi_{e'^N} u'\left(c' - \frac{l'^{1+\frac{1}{\varphi}}}{1+\frac{1}{\varphi}}\right)(1+r')\right]$$ (23)

$$l = (w n_e)^\varphi, \text{ if } e > 0$$ (24)

$$l = \delta, \text{ if } e = 0$$ (25)

$$\tilde{\eta}(a' + \bar{a}) = 0 \text{ and } \tilde{\eta} \geq 0$$ (26)

5.2 EQUILIBRIUM STRUCTURE

We can show that all agents with the same current history e^N have the same consumption, saving, and labor choices. To do so, we follow a guess-and-verify strategy. Assume that agents entering the period with a beginning-of-period history $\tilde{e}^N$ have the same beginning-of-period saving $a_{\tilde{e}^N}$. These agents have a current productivity shock e, and have thus a history $e^{N+1} = (\tilde{e}^N, e)$. There are $S_{\tilde{e}^N, -1}$ agents with a beginning-of-period history $\tilde{e}^N$ and S_{e^N} agents with a current (i.e. after the current shock) history e^N.

Under the assumption that for any $\tilde{e}^N \in \mathcal{E}^N$, agents having the history $\tilde{e}^N$ have the same beginning-of-period wealth $a_{\tilde{e}^N}$, the average welfare (before transfer) of agents having a current N-period history is

$$\tilde{a}_{e^N} = \sum_{\tilde{e}^N \in \mathcal{E}^N} \frac{S_{\tilde{e}^N}}{S'_{e^N}} \Pi_{\tilde{e}^N, e^N} a_{\tilde{e}^N}, \text{ for all } e^N \tag{27}$$

The term $\sum_{\tilde{e}^N \in \mathcal{E}^N} S_{\tilde{e}^N} \Pi_{\tilde{e}^N, e^N} a_{\tilde{e}^N}$ is the total wealth of agents having current history e^N. Dividing by the number of those agents, we find the per capita value $\tilde{a}_{e^N}$. The transfer is now easy to define:

$$\Gamma_{N+1}(e^{N+1}, X) \equiv (1+r)\left(\tilde{a}_{e^N} - a_{\tilde{e}^N}\right) \tag{28}$$

The transfer Γ_{N+1} swaps the remuneration of the beginning-of-period wealth $a_{\tilde{e}^N}$ of agents having history $\tilde{e}^N$ by the remuneration of the average wealth $\tilde{a}_{e^N}$ of agents having the current N-period history $e^N = (\tilde{e}_{N-2}, \dots, \tilde{e}_0, e)$. It is easy to see that this transfer is balanced, as it only reshuffles wealth across a sub-group of agents.

The impact of the transfer on agents' wealth. It is easy to see that all agents consider the lump-sum transfer Γ_{N+1} as given and thus do not internalize the effect of their choice on this transfer (because there is a continuum of agents for any truncated history). We consider the impact of transfer $\Gamma_{N+1}(e^{N+1}, X)$ for an agent with history $e^{N+1} = (\tilde{e}^N, e) \in \mathcal{E}^{N+1}$ and beginning-of-period wealth $a_{\tilde{e}^N}$. Her budget constraint (21) can be expressed using transfer expression (28) as follows:

$$a' + c = wn_e l + \delta 1_{e=0} + (1+r)\tilde{a}_{e^N} \tag{29}$$

The beginning-of-period and after-transfer wealth of agents with a beginning-of-period history e^{N+1} depends only on the current N-period history e^N. Moreover, as can be seen from (20), agents with the same N-period history e^N are endowed with the same expected continuation utility as long as they save the same amount a'. Therefore, agents with the same current N-period history e^N behave similarly: they consume the same level, they supply the same labor quantity, and they hold the same wealth.

State vector. The aggregate state of the economy X is the collection of: (i) the beginning-of-period wealth distribution depending on the N-period history $(S_{e^N}, a_{e^N})_{e^N \in \mathcal{E}^N}$ (i.e., the size of the agent population with history e^N, together with their respective wealth), and (ii) the aggregate state h, which affects transition probabilities.

5.3 EQUATIONS OF THE MODEL

We can now write the equations of the models with a truncation for N periods of idiosyncratic histories. We introduce the time subscript to simplify the reading and the numerical implementation. Define as $\mathcal{C}_t$ the set of N-period idiosyncratic histories for which agents face credit constraints (we show how to find $\mathcal{C}_t$ below). The histories $\mathcal{E}^N - \mathcal{C}_t$ are thus not credit-constrained.

$$a_{t,e^N} + c_{t,e^N} = w_t l_{t,e^N} + \delta 1_{e_t^N=0} + (1+r_t)\tilde{a}_{t,e^N}, \text{ for all } e^N \tag{30}$$

$$\xi_{e^N} u' \left(c_{t,e^N} - \frac{l_{t,e^N}^{1+\frac{1}{\varphi}}}{1+\frac{1}{\varphi}} \right) = \beta \mathbb{E}_t \left[\sum_{\hat{e}^N \in \mathcal{E}^N} \Pi_{t,e^N,\hat{e}^N} \xi_{\hat{e}^N} u' \left(c_{t+1,\hat{e}^N} - \frac{l_{t+1,\hat{e}^N}^{1+\frac{1}{\varphi}}}{1+\frac{1}{\varphi}} \right) \right.$$

$$\left. \times (1+r_{t+1}) \right], \quad \text{for } e^N \in \mathcal{E}^N - \mathcal{C}_t \tag{31}$$

$$l_{t,e^N} = w_t^{\varphi} 1_{e_t > 0} + \delta 1_{e_t = 0}, \text{ for all } e^N \tag{32}$$

$$a_{t,e^N} = -\bar{a}, \text{ for } e^N \in \mathcal{C}_t \tag{33}$$

$$\tilde{a}_{t,e^N} = \sum_{\tilde{e}^N \in \mathcal{E}^N} \frac{S_{t-1,\tilde{e}^N}}{S_{t,e^N}} \Pi_{t-1,\tilde{e}^N,e^N} a_{t-1,\tilde{e}^N}, \text{ for all } e^N \tag{34}$$

$$S_{t,e^N} = \sum_{\tilde{e}^N \in \mathcal{E}^N} S_{t-1,\tilde{e}^N} \Pi_{t-1,\tilde{e}^N,e^N}, \text{ for all } e^N \tag{35}$$

$$K_{t+1} = \sum_{e \in \mathcal{E}^N} S_{t,e^N} a_{t,e^N} \tag{36}$$

$$L_t = \sum_{e \in \mathcal{E}^N} S_{t,e^N} l_{t,e^N} \tag{37}$$

$$r_t = \lambda A_t K_t^{\lambda-1} L_t^{1-\lambda} - \mu \tag{38}$$

$$w_t = (1-\lambda) A_t K_t^{\lambda} L_t^{-\lambda} \tag{39}$$

For a given technology process A_t, this system has $5 \times E^N + 4$ equations for $5 \times E^N + 4$ variables $((a_{t,e^N}, c_{t,e^N}, l_{t,e^N}, \tilde{a}_{t,e^N}, S_{t,e^N})_{e^N \in \mathcal{E}^N}, K_{t+1}, r_{t+1}, w_t, L_t)_{t=0\ldots\infty}$. Before simulating the model, one has to find the set of histories facing credit constraint $\mathcal{C}_t$. To do so, we first solve the model under steady state to find $\mathcal{C}$, and then we assume that shocks are small enough to check that credit constraints are indeed binding.

5.4 ALGORITHM FOR THE STEADY STATE

For a given N, rank first the agents according to their idiosyncratic history. For instance, for the history $e^{N,t} = \{e_{N-1}, \ldots, e_0\} \in \mathcal{E}^N$, one can consider $k = 1 + \sum_{i=0}^{N-1} e_i E^{N-1-i}$. With this ordering, $k = 1$ for the agents who are unemployed for N periods $e^t = \{0, \ldots, 0\}$ and $k = E^N = 2^N$ for $e^t = \{1, \ldots, 1\}$. In other words, agents with a low k have been unemployed recently for a long period of time. All the steady-state variables will be indexed by k instead of e^N. We thus look for $((a_k, c_k, l_k, \tilde{a}_k, S_k)_{k=1\ldots E^N}, K, r, w, L)$.

The algorithm for the steady state is the following.

1. Assume that the set of histories $\mathcal{C}$ is credit constrained. For all $k \in \mathcal{C}$, we have
$a_k = -\bar{a}$.

a. Consider an interest rate r such that $\beta(1 + r) < 1$. Deduce the real wage w, using Eqs. (38) and (39).

b. Deduce l_k using (32).

    i. Assume values for the vector of consumption levels of constrained agents $c_k, k \in C$.

    ii. Using the Euler equations (31) and labor supply l_k find the consumption levels of unconstrained agents $c_k, k \notin C$.

    iii. Using the budget constraints (30) of unconstrained agents C and the risk-sharing equation (34) find the savings of unconstrained agents $a_k, k \notin C$.

    iv. Deduce from the budget constraint of constrained agents, $k \in S^c$, the implied consumption levels $\tilde{c}_k, k \in C$.

    v. Iterate over $c_k, k \in C$ until $c_k = \tilde{c}_k, k \in C$.

c. Compute the implied interest rate $\tilde{r}$ using Eqs. (36), (37), and (38).

d. Iterate on r until $r = \tilde{r}$.

2. Check that histories $k \in C$ are credit-constrained and histories $k \notin C$ are not, iterate on C otherwise.

5.5 DYNAMICS

The model can be easily simulated for small aggregate shocks at the first order, assuming that those shocks are small enough such that the set of constrained histories remains always the same. This can be checked during each simulation, checking that Euler equations hold with inequality for assumed constrained households. The simple way to simulate the model is 1) to write a code that writes the set of equations (30)–(39) as a DYNARE code, 2) specify the steady state found in the previous section as initial values to double-check that the steady state is correct, using the "resid" function of DYNARE, and 3) simulate the model using the "stoch_simul" function.

5.6 CHOOSING THE PREFERENCE SHIFTERS ξ_{e^N}

The simulations of the model can be done for any ξ_{e^N}. How can we choose these parameters? What are they useful for? The simplest choice is to set $\xi_{e^N} = 1$, $e^N \in \mathcal{E}^N$. But the choice of these ξ_{e^N} can be made to improve the fit of the equilibrium distribution to a given target. Indeed, if one has empirical average estimates of wealth levels of agents for an observed history on the labor market e^N, namely $\hat{a}_{e^N}$ for $e^N \in \mathcal{E}^N$, then one can iterate over ξ_{e^N}, until the steady savings values of the model are close enough to their empirical counterpart $a_{e^N} \simeq \hat{a}_{e^N}$ for $e^N \in \mathcal{E}^N$. For instance, one can simulate a Bewley–Aiyagari–Huggett model to get the model-generated averages $\hat{a}_{e^N}$ for $e^N \in \mathcal{E}^N$, and then iterate over ξ_{e^N} in the truncated economy for the steady-state outcome of the truncated model to be close to the "true" values $\hat{a}_{e^N}$ for $e^N \in \mathcal{E}^N$. The general ability of the truncated model to reproduce any given wealth distribution is still an open question.

Table 1 Parameter values

N	β	φ	σ	μ	λ	ρ^a	σ^a	$\bar{a}$
6	0.96	1	2	0.1	0.36	0.8	0.01	0

5.7 NUMERICAL EXAMPLE

As an example, one can now provide numerical simulations of the truncated model. The goal of this simulation is not to provide a quantitatively relevant model, but to show how the truncated economy can be simulated. First, assume that the period GHH-utility function is

$$U(c,l) = \frac{1}{\sigma - 1}\left(c - \frac{l^{1+\frac{1}{\varphi}}}{1 + \frac{1}{\varphi}}\right)^{\sigma-1}$$

where φ is the inter-temporal Frisch elasticity of labor supply. The period is a year. The discount factor is set equal to $\beta = 0.96$. The curvature of the utility function is $\sigma = 2$. The Frisch elasticity of the labor supply is also set to $\varphi = 0.1$. The quantity λ is the capital share, which is set to 0.36, while μ is the annual depreciation rate, set to 10%. The replacement ratio is set to $\delta/w = 0.3$, which is in the lower range of empirical estimates. The credit constraint is set to $\bar{a} = 0$. As a benchmark the model is solved with $\xi_{e^N} = 1$, $e^N \in \mathcal{E}^N$.

The autocorrelation of the technology shock ρ^a is 0.8, and the standard deviation $\sigma^a = 0.01$. Table 1 summarizes the parameter values.

Concerning the labor process, the following transition matrix is considered:

$$M = \begin{bmatrix} 0.2 & 0.8 \\ 0.05 & 0.95 \end{bmatrix}$$

When unemployed, agents have a yearly probability 0.2 to stay unemployed. This matrix corresponds more to a European labor market than the US labor market where the persistence of states is lower. This implies that the steady-state unemployment rate is roughly 6%.

The model is solved for $N = 6$. This implies that agents differ according to their idiosyncratic histories for the last 6 periods and that there are $2^6 = 64$ different agents in this economy. As a software like DYNARE can handle a few thousand equations, it implies that a maximum length of $N = 12$ (such that $2^{12} = 4096$) seems a number consistent with current standard computers.

In the steady state without aggregate shocks, one finds that only agents unemployed for $N = 6$ periods are credit constrained. All other agents have a positive saving. The simulation of the model with aggregate shocks take 3 seconds in DYNARE.

Table 2 provides first- and second-order moments for this economy. The gain of using perturbation methods and DYNARE is that the impulse response function can

Table 2 First- and second-order moments of key variables

	K	L	GDP	C^{tot}	r	w
Mean	4.07	0.95	1.60	1.21	0.0417	1.08
St. dev.	0.12	0.002	0.04	0.02	0.003	0.025

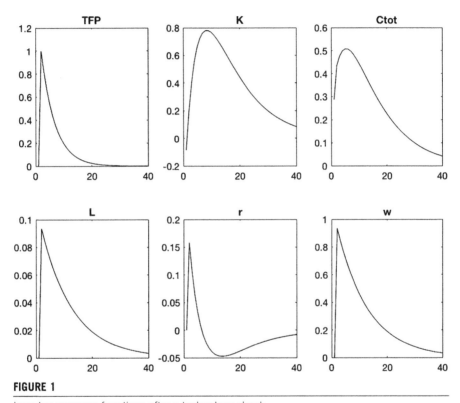

FIGURE 1

Impulse response functions after a technology shock.

be easily simulated for continuous exogenous shocks, as the state space for the aggregate variable is continuous. As an example, Fig. 1 plots IRFs after a TFP shock (first panel) for relevant variables. The variables are provided in percentage proportional deviation from steady state values, except the real interest rate which is in percentage level deviation from its steady state values.

Computing the amount of extra insurance provided by the truncation. The structure of the truncation provides an additional transfer to any agents, summarized by the amount $\Gamma_{N+1}(e^{N+1}, X)$ in Eq. (21). This transfer can be seen as an extra-insurance term, as it cancels the effect of past shocks to reduce heterogeneity. As the transfer is balanced, the average value of the transfer in any period is 0. In a full-fledge Bewley model, this transfer is exactly 0 for all agents, and the whole history of idiosyncratic shock matters for each individual agent. A measure of the contribution of the transfer to any agent's income is provided by the measure

$$\Delta_{e^{N+1}} = \frac{\Gamma_{N+1}(e^{N+1}, X)}{w(X)n_e l + \delta 1_{e=0} + (1 + r(X))a}$$

This ratio $\Delta_{e^{N+1}}$ is the relative contribution of the transfer to the income of an agent having a history e^{N+1}. For the case $N = 6$ used in the current calibration, one finds that $\text{sd}(\Delta_{e^N}) = 5.48\%$, which is a relatively small amount. LeGrand and Ragot (2016b) show that this standard deviation tends toward 0 as N increases. As a consequence, an increase in N reduces the amount of extra insurance provided by the truncation.

6 OPTIMAL POLICIES

A common outcome of the previous models is that one has a finite number of types of agents to follow, as an equilibrium outcome. This allows deriving optimal policies using Ramsey techniques developed in the representative agents environments (see Sargent and Ljungqvist, 2012 for a textbook presentation), which is an interesting methodology to investigate the distortions generated by market frictions. Ragot (2016) investigates optimal monetary policy in a model with capital accumulation and flexible prices. Bilbiie and Ragot (2017) study optimal monetary policy in a monetary model with sticky-prices. Challe (2017) analyzes optimal monetary policy in a no-trade model with unemployment risk.

Recently, LeGrand and Ragot (2016b) developed a general technique to solve for optimal policies in truncated economies. They study optimal fiscal policies in a model with heterogeneous agents and aggregate shocks, with four instruments: a positive transfer, two distorting taxes on capital and labor, and public debt. This may be a promising route, as the distortions generated by incomplete insurance markets are hard to identify (see Aiyagari, 1995 and Davila et al., 2012 for a contribution about the optimality of the level of the capital stock). Nuno and Thomas (2017) solve for optimal monetary policy in a model with heterogeneous agents in continuous time, and without aggregate shocks (see also references in LeGrand and Ragot, 2016b for many relevant papers deriving optimal policies with heterogeneous agents). As far as I know, deriving optimal policies (monetary, fiscal or unemployment benefits) with incomplete markets and aggregate shocks is only easily done in a reduced-heterogeneity equilibrium, whereas it is impossible at this stage in full-fledged incomplete-market models.

7 COMPARISON WITH OTHER APPROACH USING PERTURBATION METHODS

It maybe useful to compare the methods presented in this chapter with other methods using perturbation techniques. The key similarity of methods of this chapter is indeed to use perturbation methods around a steady state with idiosyncratic risk but with a finite state-space support as an equilibrium outcome. In addition, the state space for the aggregate risk has a continuous support, as in the DSGE literature. The model can be simulated with a finite number of equations using perturbations and software as DYNARE can be used.

Other strategies have been used to make possible the use perturbation methods.[5] First, Reiter (2009) uses perturbation methods to solve for aggregate dynamics around a steady-state equilibrium of a Bewley model, with idiosyncratic shock but no aggregate shock. These techniques, used for instance in McKay and Reis (2016b), linearize policy rules around an equilibrium distribution, which has an infinite support (but the aggregate state has a finite support).

Mertens and Judd (2012) use perturbation methods around a steady-state with neither aggregate nor idiosyncratic shock. They use a penalty function to pin down steady-state portfolios (which are not determined without risks). Other papers using perturbation method but restricting exogenously the state-space are Preston and Roca (2007) and Kim et al. (2010). For instance, one can solve the model using an exogenous finite grid for the saving decisions.

The techniques presented in this chapter implied that the reduction in heterogeneity appears has an equilibrium outcome. To summarize the previous remarks, the gain is threefold.

First, this allows to consider many assets. For instance, Challe et al. (2013) price arbitrarily large number of maturities of the yield curve. LeGrand and Ragot (2016a) price both assets and derivative assets in the same model. This last two papers consider a finite state space for the aggregate risk. Considering different assets, some recent contributions in households finance show that non-convex portfolio adjustment costs (such as fixed costs) are necessary to rationalize households reaction to fiscal stimulus. This is the outcome of the recent literature on wealthy hand-to-mouth agents (Kaplan et al., 2016 and Ragot, 2014). The ability of reduced heterogeneity models to reproduce the data with such costs is an open question. Indeed, participation decision would depends on idiosyncratic histories, but they would have not to change with aggregate shocks.

Second, having a finite number of equations (in a possibly large model) allows using econometric techniques, such as Bayesian estimation, which are then relatively easy to implement. This is done in Challe et al. (2017) to quantify the contribution of precautionary saving to the business cycle in the US.

---

[5]Global methods are also used to solve these models. See Algan et al. (2014) for a survey of methods and Krueger et al. (2015) for a recent application to the subprime crisis in the US. Den Haan (2014) discusses (global) solution methods for models with and without rational expectations.

Third, the finite number of equations permits the derivation of optimal policies in these environments. This last properties allow considering rich and relevant tradeoffs for both fiscal and monetary policies, about redistribution, insurance, and incentives.

The cost of using the models presented in this chapter is that the representation of inequality is simplified in all cases compared to full-fledged Bewley models. As a consequence, these models are less useful when one wants to describe in details inequalities generated by self-insurance for uninsurable risks. Nevertheless, models with truncation in the space of idiosyncratic histories can generate an arbitrarily high number of agents to match any targeted wealth distribution. As a consequence, this type of model is more suited for quantitative work focusing cross-sectional heterogeneity.

8 HETEROGENEOUS EXPECTATIONS

The previous models have been presented under the assumption that agents share the same information set and form rational expectations. The gain of this assumption is that expectations are consistent with the model, what is an appealing property, and that they are the same for all agents. This last outcome is not totally consistent with data surveys, which shows heterogeneity in expectation about aggregate variables (see Carroll, 2003; Branch, 2004; and Massaro, 2013) and heterogeneity in expectation formation for the same information set (see Hommes, 2011 and Coibion and Gorodnichenko, 2015). A second line of research, called Agent-Based Modeling (ABM) departs from rational expectations in assuming that agents follow simple rules, and change rules according to interactions, or that they use expectations formation rules that differ from rational expectations. Hommes (2006) and LeBaron (2006) provide early surveys of this literature; Branch and McGough (2018) and Dieci and He (2018) give up to date state of the art surveys of heterogeneous expectations models in macroeconomics and finance respectively. The frontier between these two lines of research (rational and non-rational expectations) is still visible in the reference lists of various papers, but it can be expected to disappear progressively, as a growing literature investigates relevant models of expectation formation.

The tools developed in this chapter could be useful to model heterogeneous expectations in a tractable way, and thus contribute to close the gap between these two literatures. First, in some models agents choose in each periods the rules to form expectations (Branch and McGough, 2009; Massaro, 2013) or how much effort to invest to form expectation, as in the *rational inattention* literature (see Andrade and Le Bihan, 2013; or Vellekoop and Wiederholt, 2017 and the references in this paper). As the various equilibrium structures presented in the previous sections don't depend on rational expectations to reduce heterogeneity, they could be useful to construct models with a finite number of different expectations. Models where expectations are a state variable, as in *learning models*, may also be consistent with previous models. For instance, if agents experiencing the same history of shocks for a long period of time converge to the same expectations, then a truncation in histories of idiosyncratic shocks could also be a satisfactory assumption. Finally, as noted by Den Haan (2014) the case where some agents form rational expectations whereas others are boundedly rational are difficult to solve. The models presented here could allow to reduce heterogeneity among rational agents and could help to solve some of those models.

9 CONCLUDING REMARKS

This chapter surveys a class of heterogeneous-agent models, where heterogeneity is finite as an equilibrium outcome. Agents differ according to "shocks" defined in a broad sense that occur in their life. We focused more precisely on representations of reduced heterogeneity with rational expectations which can be solved with perturbation methods for the aggregate shocks. This allows introducing many other "frictions" studied in the literature, such as search-and-matching in the labor market, sticky prices, heterogeneity in skills, habit formation, and son on. These models can be estimated, using a vast information set, including times-series and cross-sectional information. Integrated models with both uninsurable shocks, a role for forward-looking behavior together with relevant heterogeneous expectations would be a good laboratory to quantify the relative importance of these various ingredients.

Finally, the models of this chapter has focused on households heterogeneity, leaving aside other forms of heterogeneity among firms or financial intermediaries. This opens a deeper question about the relevant level of aggregation to think about heterogeneity, and which type of heterogeneity matters for economic analysis. If a recent consensus seems to emerge about the importance of households heterogeneity, the interactions of various types of heterogeneity seem an interesting line of research.

REFERENCES

Aiyagari, R.S., 1994. Uninsured idiosyncratic risk and aggregate saving. The Quarterly Journal of Economics 109 (3), 659–684.

Aiyagari, S.R., 1995. Optimal capital income taxation with incomplete markets, borrowing constraints, and constant discounting. Journal of Political Economy 103 (6), 1158–1175.

Algan, Y., Allais, O., DenHaan, W., Rendahl, P., 2014. Solving and simulating models with heterogeneous agents and aggregate uncertainty. In: Handbook of Computational Economics, vol. 3. Elsevier, pp. 277–324 (Chap. 6).

Algan, Y., Challe, E., Ragot, X., 2011. Incomplete markets and the output-inflation tradeoff. Economic Theory 46 (1), 55–84.

Andrade, P., Le Bihan, H., 2013. Inattentive professional forecasters. Journal of Monetary Economics 8 (60), 967–982.

Bilbiie, F., Ragot, X., 2017. Monetary Policy and Inequality when Aggregate Demand Depends on Liquidity. CEPR working paper. Centre for Economic Policy Research.

Branch, W., 2004. The theory of rationally heterogeneous expectations: evidence from survey data on inflation expectations. The Economic Journal 114 (497), 592–621.

Branch, W., McGough, B., 2009. Monetary policy in a new Keynesian model with heterogeneous expectations. Journal of Economic Dynamics and Control 33 (8), 1036–1051.

Branch, W., McGough, B., 2018. Heterogeneous expectations and micro-foundations in macroeconomics. In: Handbook of Computational Economics, vol. 4. Elsevier, pp. 3–62 (this Handbook).

Carroll, C., 2003. Macroeconomic expectations of households and professional forecasters. The Quarterly Journal of Economics 118, 269–298.

Carroll, C.D., Dynan, K.E., Krane, S.D., 2003. Unemployment risk and precautionary wealth: evidence from households' balance sheets. Review of Economics and Statistics 85 (3), 586–604.

Challe, E., 2017. Uninsured Unemployment Risk and Optimal Monetary Policy. Working paper.

Challe, E., LeGrand, F., Ragot, X., 2013. Incomplete markets, liquidation risk and the term structure of interest rates. Journal of Economic Theory 148 (6), 2483–2519.

Challe, E., Matheron, J., Ragot, X., Rubio-Ramirez, J., 2017. Precautionary saving and aggregate demand. Quantitative Economics 8 (3), 435–478.

Challe, E., Ragot, X., 2016. Precautionary saving over the business cycle. The Economic Journal 126 (590), 135–164.

Chetty, R., Guren, A., Manoli, D., Weber, A., 2011. Are micro and macro labor supply elasticities consistent? A review of evidence on the intensive and extensive margins. The American Economic Review, 1–6.

Chodorow-Reich, G., Karabarbounis, L., 2014. The Cyclicality of the Opportunity Cost of Employment. Working paper. Harvard University.

Coibion, O., Gorodnichenko, Y., 2015. Information rigidity and the expectations formation process: a simple framework and new facts. The American Economic Review 105 (8), 2644–2678.

Constantinides, G.M., Duffie, D., 1996. Asset pricing with heterogeneous consumers. Journal of Political Economy 104 (2), 219–240.

Davila, J., Hong, J., Krusell, P., Rios-Rull, J.-V., 2012. Constrained efficiency in the neoclassical growth model with uninsurable idiosyncratic shocks. Econometrica 80 (6), 2431–2467.

Den Haan, W., 2010. Comparison of solutions to the incomplete markets model with aggregate uncertainty. Journal of Economic Dynamics and Control 1 (34), 4–27.

Den Haan, W., 2014. Solving models with heterogeneous expectations. Presentation slides.

Dieci, R., He, X.X., 2018. Heterogeneous agent models in finance. In: Handbook of Computational Economics, vol. 4. Elsevier, pp. 257–328 (this Handbook).

Fishburn, P., 1977. Mean-risk analysis with risk associated with below-target returns. The American Economic Review 67 (2), 116–126.

Gornemann, N., Kuester, K., Nakajima, M., 2012. Monetary Policy with Heterogeneous Agents. Working Paper 12-21. Federal Reserve Bank of Philadelphia.

Heathcote, J., 2005. Fiscal policy with heterogeneous agents and incomplete markets. The Review of Economic Studies 72 (1), 161–188.

Heathcote, J., Storesletten, K., Violante, G., 2009. Quantitative macroeconomics with heterogeneous households. Annual Review of Economics 1, 319–354.

Heathcote, J., Storesletten, K., Violante, G., 2014. Optimal Tax Progressivity: An Analytical Framework. NBER Working Paper 19899. National Bureau of Economic Research.

Hommes, C., 2006. Heterogeneous agent models in economics and finance. In: Handbook of Computational Economics, vol. 2. Elsevier, pp. 1109–1186.

Hommes, C., 2011. The heterogeneous expectations hypothesis: some evidence from the lab. Journal of Economic Dynamics and Control 35, 1–24.

Huggett, M., 1993. The risk free rate in heterogeneous-agent incomplete-insurance economies. Journal of Economic Dynamics and Control 17 (5–6), 953–969.

Kaplan, G., Moll, B., Violante, G., 2016. The world according to HANK. Mimeo.

Kim, S.H., Kollmann, R., Kim, J., 2010. Solving the incomplete market model with aggregate uncertainty using a perturbation method. Journal of Economic Dynamics and Control 34 (1), 50–58.

Kiyotaki, N., Moore, J., 1997. Credit cycles. Journal of Political Economy 105 (2), 211–248.

Krueger, D., Mitman, K., Perri, F., 2015. Macroeconomics and heterogeneity, including inequality. Mimeo. University of Pennsylvania.

Krusell, P., Mukoyama, T., Sahin, A., 2010. Labour-market matching with precautionary savings and aggregate fluctuations. The Review of Economic Studies 77 (4), 1477–1507.

Krusell, P., Mukoyama, T., Smith, A.A.J., 2011. Asset prices in a Huggett economy. Journal of Economic Theory 146 (3), 812–844.

Krusell, P., Smith, A.A., 1998. Income and wealth heterogeneity in the macroeconomy. Journal of Political Economy 106 (5), 867–896.

Lagos, R., Wright, R., 2005. A unified framework for monetary theory and policy analysis. Journal of Political Economy 113 (3), 463–484.

LeBaron, B., 2006. Agent based computational finance. In: Tesfatsion, L., Judd, K. (Eds.), Handbook of Computational Economics, vol. 2: Agent-Based Computational Economics. Elsevier, pp. 1187–1233.

LeGrand, F., Ragot, X., 2016a. Incomplete markets and derivative assets. Economic Theory 62 (3), 517–545.

LeGrand, F., Ragot, X., 2016b. Optimal Policy with Heterogeneous Agents and Aggregate Shocks: An Application to Optimal Public Debt Dynamics. Working paper.

LeGrand, F., Ragot, X., 2016c. Asset Returns, Idiosyncratic and Aggregate Risk Exposure. Working paper.

Lucas, R.J., 1990. Liquidity and interest rates. Journal of Economic Theory 50 (2), 237–264.

Massaro, D., 2013. Heterogeneous expectations in monetary DSGE models. Journal of Economic Dynamics and Control 37, 680–692.

McKay, A., Nakamura, E., Steinsson, J., 2016. The Discounted Euler Equation: A Note. NBER Working Paper 22129. National Bureau of Economic Research.

McKay, A., Reis, R., 2016a. Optimal Automatic Stabilizers. Working paper.

McKay, A., Reis, R., 2016b. The Role of Automatic Stabilizers in the U.S. Business Cycle. Discussion Paper 84.

Mertens, T.M., Judd, K.L., 2012. Equilibrium Existence and Approximation for Incomplete Market Models with Substantial Heterogeneity. NYU Working Paper 2451/31656. New York University.

Miao, J., 2006. Competitive equilibria of economies with a continuum of consumers and aggregate shocks. Journal of Economic Theory 128 (1), 274–298.

Nuno, G., Thomas, C., 2017. Optimal Monetary Policy with Heterogeneous Agents. Banca de Espana working paper.

Preston, B., Roca, M., 2007. Incomplete Markets, Heterogeneity and Macroeconomic Dynamics. NBER Working Paper 13260. National Bureau of Economic Research.

Ragot, X., 2014. The case for a financial approach to money demand. Journal of Monetary Economics 62, 94–107.

Ragot, X., 2016. Money and Capital Accumulation over the Business Cycle. Working paper. SciencesPo.

Ravn, M., Sterk, V., 2013. Job uncertainty and deep recessions. Mimeo. University College London.

Reiter, M., 2009. Solving heterogeneous-agent models by projection and perturbation. Journal of Economic Dynamics and Control 33 (3), 649–665.

Rios-Rull, J.-V., 1995. Models with heterogeneous agents. In: Cooley, T. (Ed.), Frontiers of Business Cycle Research. Princeton University Press, Princeton, NJ, p. 16.

Rios-Rull, J.-V., 1997. Computation of Equilibria in Heterogeneous Agent Models. FRB of Minneapolis Research Department Staff Report 231.

Sargent, T.J., Ljungqvist, L., 2012. Recursive Macroeconomic Theory, third edn. MIT Press.

Scheinkman, J., Weiss, L., 1986. Borrowing constraints and aggregate economic activity. Econometrica 54 (1), 23–45.

Tauchen, G., 1986. Finite state Markov chain approximations to univariate and vector autoregressions. Economics Letters, 177–181.

Vellekoop, N., Wiederholt, M., 2017. Inflation Expectations and Choices of Households. Working Paper 2.

Werning, I., 2015. Incomplete Markets and Aggregate Demand. Working paper.

Woodford, M., 1990. Public debt as private liquidity. The American Economic Review 80 (2), 382–388.

PART

FINANCE

2

Heterogeneous Agent Models in Finance*

Roberto Dieci*, Xue-Zhong He[†],[1]
*University of Bologna, Bologna, Italy
†University of Technology Sydney, Sydney, NSW, Australia
1Corresponding author: e-mail address: tony.he1@uts.edu.au

CONTENTS

*Acknowledgments: We are grateful to the editors, Cars Hommes and Blake LeBaron, and three reviewers for their very helpful comments. We also thank the participants to the Workshop "Handbook of Computational Economics, Volume 4, Heterogeneous Agent Models", hosted by the Amsterdam School of Economics, University of Amsterdam, for insightful discussions and suggestions. We would like to dedicate this survey to the memory of Carl Chiarella who inspired and collaborated with us on a large body of research covered partially in this chapter. Financial support from the Australian Research Council (ARC) under Discovery Grant (DP130103210) is gratefully acknowledged.

1 INTRODUCTION

Economic and finance theory is witnessing a paradigm shift from a representative agent with rational expectations to boundedly rational agents with heterogeneous expectations. This shift reflects a growing evidence on the theoretical limitations and empirical challenges in the traditional view of homogeneity and perfect rationality in finance and economics.

The existence of *limitations to fully rational behavior* and the roles of psychological phenomena and behavioral factors in individuals' decision making have been emphasized and discussed from a variety of different standpoints in the economics and finance literature (see, e.g. Simon, 1982, Sargent, 1993, Arthur, 1994, Conlisk, 1996, Rubinstein, 1998, and Shefrin, 2005). Due to endogenous uncertainty about the state of the world and limits to information and computational ability, agents are prevented from forming rational forecasts and solving life-time optimization problems. Rather, agents favor simple reasoning and 'rules of thumb', such as the well documented technical analysis and active trading from financial market professionals.[1] In addition, *empirical investigations* of financial time series show a number of market phenomena (including bubbles, crashes, short-run momentum and long-run mean reverting in asset prices) and some common features, the so-called *stylized facts*,[2] which are difficult to accommodate and explain within the standard paradigm based on homogeneous agents and rational expectations.

Moreover, agents are *heterogeneous* in their beliefs and behavioral rules, which may change over time due to social interaction and evolutionary selection (see Lux, 1995, Arthur et al., 1997b, and Brock and Hommes, 1998). Such heterogeneity and diversity in individual behavior in economics, along with social interaction among individuals, can hardly be captured by a 'representative' agent at the aggregate level (see Kirman, 1992, 2010 for extensive discussions). For instance, as Heckman (2001), the 2000 Nobel Laureate in Economics, points out (concerning the contribution of

---

[1] See Allen and Taylor (1990) for foreign exchange rate markets and Menkhoff (2010) for fund managers.
[2] They include excess volatility, excess skewness, fat tails, volatility clustering, long range dependence in volatility, and various power-law behavior, as detailed in Pagan (1996) and Lux (2009b).

microeconometrics to economic theory), *"the most important discovery was the evidence on pervasiveness of heterogeneity and diversity in economic life. When a full analysis was made of heterogeneity in response, a variety of candidate averages emerged to describe the average person, and the longstanding edifice of the representative consumer was shown to lack empirical support."* Regarding agents' behavior during crisis periods and the role of policy makers, the former ECB president Jean-Claude Trichet writes *"We need to deal better with heterogeneity across agents and the interaction among those heterogeneous agents"*, highlighting the potential of alternative approaches such as behavioral economics and agent-based modeling.

Over the last three decades, empirical evidence, unconvincing justification of the assumption of unbounded rationality, and role of investor psychology have led to an incorporation of heterogeneity in beliefs and bounded rationality of agents into financial market modeling and asset pricing theory. This has changed the landscape of finance theory dramatically and led to fruitful development in financial economics, empirical finance, and market practice. In this chapter, we focus on the state-of-the-art of this expanding research field, denoted as Heterogeneous Agent Models (HAMs) in finance.

HAMs start from the contributions of Day and Huang (1990), Chiarella (1992), de Grauwe et al. (1993), Lux (1995), Brock and Hommes (1998), inspired by the pioneering work of Zeeman (1974) and Beja and Goldman (1980). This modeling framework views financial market dynamics as a result of the interaction of heterogeneous investors with different behavioral rules, such as fundamental and technical trading rules. One of the key aspects of these models is the expectation feedback mechanism. Namely, agents' decisions are based upon the predictions of endogenous variables whose actual values are determined by the expectations of agents. This results in the co-evolution of beliefs and asset prices over time. Earlier HAMs develop various nonlinear models to characterize various endogenous mechanisms of market fluctuations and financial crisis resulting from the interaction of heterogeneous agents rather than exogenous shocks or news. Overall, such models demonstrate that asset price fluctuations can be caused endogenously. We refer to Hommes (2006), LeBaron (2006), Chiarella et al. (2009a), Hommes and Wagener (2009), Westerhoff (2009), Chen et al. (2012), Hommes (2013), and He (2014) for surveys of these developments in the literature.

HAMs have strong connections with a broader area of Agent-Based Models (ABMs) and Agent-based Computational Economics (ACE). In fact, HAMs can be regarded as particular types of ABMs. However, generally speaking, ABMs are by nature very computationally oriented and allow for a large number of interacting agents, network structures, many parameters, and thorough descriptions of the underlying market microstructures. As such, they turn out to be extremely flexible and powerful, suitable for simulation, scenario analysis and regulation of real-world dynamic systems (see, e.g. Tesfatsion and Judd, 2006, LeBaron and Tesfatsion, 2008). By contrast, HAMs are typically characterized by substantial simplifications at the modeling level (few belief-types or behavioral rules, simplified interaction structures and reduced number of parameters). This makes HAMs analytically tractable to some extent, mostly within the theoretical framework of nonlinear dynamical systems. However, unlike computationally oriented ABMs, HAMs allow a deeper understanding of the basic dynamic mechanisms and driving forces at work, making it possible to identify different and clear-cut 'types' of macro outcomes in connection to specific agents' behavior.

Among the large number of HAMs in finance, this chapter is mostly concerned with analytically tractable models based on the interplay of two broad types of beliefs: *extrapolative* vs. *regressive* (or *technical* vs. *fundamental* rules, or *chartists* vs. *fundamentalists*). Since chartists rely on extrapolative rules to forecast future prices and to take their position in the market, they tend to sustain and reinforce current price trends or to amplify the deviations from the 'fundamental price'. By contrast, fundamentalists place their orders in view of a mean reversion of asset price to its fundamental in long-run. The interplay between such forces is able to capture, albeit in a simplified manner, a basic mechanism of price fluctuations in financial markets. Support to this kind of behavioral heterogeneity comes from survey evidence (Menkhoff and Taylor, 2007, Menkhoff, 2010), experimental evidence (Hommes et al., 2005, Heemeijer et al., 2009), and empirically grounded discussion on the profitability of momentum and mean reversion strategies in financial markets (e.g. Lakonishok et al., 1994, Jegadeesh and Titman, 2001, Moskowitz et al., 2012).

In this chapter, we focus on the state-of-the-art of HAMs in finance from five main strands of the literature developed approximately over the last ten years since the appearance of the previous contributions in Volume II of this Handbook series. This development can have profound consequences for the interpretation of empirical evidence and the formulation of economic policy.

The first strand of research (Section 2) emphasizes the lasting potential of stylized HAMs in discrete time (in particular, chartist-fundamentalist models) to address key issues in finance. Such models have been largely investigated in the past in a wide range of versions incorporating heterogeneity, adaptation, evolution, and even learning (Hommes, 2001, Chiarella and He, 2002, 2003, and Chiarella et al., 2002, 2006b). They have successfully explained various market behavior, such as the long-term swing of market prices from fundamental price, asset bubbles, and market crashes, showing a potential to characterize and explain the stylized facts (Alfarano et al., 2005, Gaunersdorfer and Hommes, 2007) and various power law behavior (He and Li, 2008 and Lux and Alfarano, 2016) observed in financial markets. In addition, the chartist-fundamentalist framework can still provide insight into various stylized facts and market anomalies, and relate them to the economic mechanisms, parameters and scenarios of the underlying nonlinear deterministic systems. Such promising perspectives have motivated further empirical studies, leading to a growing literature on the calibration and estimation of the HAMs. In particular, in Sections 2.1 and 2.2, we focus on a simple HAM of Dieci et al. (2006) to illustrate its explanatory power to volatility clustering through calibration and empirical estimation, and relate the results to the underlying mechanisms and bifurcations of the nonlinear deterministic 'skeleton'. Moreover, by considering an integrated approach of HAMs and incomplete information about the fundamental value, we provide a micro-foundation to the endogenous trading heterogeneity and switching behavior wildly characterized in HAMs (Section 2.3). We also survey fund flow effect among competing and evolving investment strategies (Section 2.4).

The second strand (Section 3) is on the development of a general framework in continuous time HAMs to incorporate historical price information in the HAMs. It provides a plausible way to deal with a variety of expectation rules formed from historical prices via moving averages over different time horizons, through a parsimonious system of stochastic delay differential equations. We introduce a time delay parameter to measure the effect of historical price information. Besides being consistent with continuous-time finance, this framework appears promising to understand the impact on market stability of lagged information (incorporated in different moving average rules and in realized profits recorded over different time horizons) and to explain a number of phenomena, particularly the long-range dependence in financial markets. We illustrate this approach and the main results in Section 3.1 by surveying the model in He and Li (2012). We emphasize the similarities to and differences from discrete-time HAMs. Moreover, Sections 3.2 and 3.3 demonstrate how useful the continuous-time HAMs can be in addressing the profitability of momentum and contrarian strategies and the optimal allocation with time series momentum and reversal, two of the most dominating financial market anomalies.

The third strand (Section 4) is on the impact of heterogeneous beliefs, expectations feedback and portfolio diversification on the joint dynamics of prices and returns of multiple risky assets. A related issue concerns the joint dynamics of international asset markets, driven by heterogeneous speculators who switch across markets depending on relative profit opportunities. In such models, often described by dynamical systems of large dimension, the typical nonlinear features of baseline HAMs interact with additional nonlinearities that arise naturally within a multi-asset setting, such as the beliefs about second moments and correlations. Section 4 surveys such models, starting from the basic setup developed by Westerhoff (2004), in which investors can switch not only across strategies but across markets (Section 4.1). Such models are not only able to reproduce various stylized facts, but also to offer some explanations to price comovements and cross-correlations of volatilities reported empirically (Schmitt and Westerhoff, 2014), as well as to address some key regulatory issues (Westerhoff and Dieci, 2006). Further research deals with asset comovements and changes in correlations from a different perspective. Based on models of evolving beliefs and (mean-variance) portfolios of heterogeneous investors, Section 4.2 is devoted to the multi-asset HAM of Chiarella et al. (2013b). This approach appears quite promising to address the issue of 'time-varying betas' within an evolutionary CAPM framework. It establishes a link between investors' behavior and changes in risk-return relationships at the aggregate level. Finally, Section 4.3 applies HAMs to illustrate the potentially destabilizing impact of the interlinkages between stock and foreign exchange markets (Dieci and Westerhoff, 2010, 2013b).

The fourth strand (Section 5) investigates the dynamics of house prices from the perspective of HAMs. Similar to financial markets, housing markets have long been characterized by boom-bust cycles and other phenomena apparently unrelated to changes in economic fundamentals, such as short-term positive autocorrelation and long-term mean-reversion, which are at odds with the predictions of the rational representative agent framework. Moreover, peculiar features of the housing market (such as the 'twofold' nature of housing, illiquidity, and supply-side elasticity) may interact with investors' demand influenced by behavioral factors. Section 5.1 surveys two recent HAMs of the housing market (Bolt et al., 2014 and Dieci and Westerhoff, 2016) which are based on mean-variance preferences and standard equilibrium conditions, with the fundamental price being regarded as the present value of future expected rental payments. However, within this framework, investors form heterogeneous expectations about future house prices, according to (evolving) regressive and extrapolative beliefs. Estimation of similar models supports the assumption of behavioral heterogeneity changing over time, based on the relative performance of the competing prediction rules. It highlights how such heterogeneity can produce endogenous house price bubbles and crashes (disconnected from the dynamics of the fundamental price). Moreover, the nonlinear dynamic analysis of such models can provide a simple behavioral explanation for the observed role of supply elasticity in 'shaping' housing bubbles and crashes, as widely reported and discussed in empirical and theoretical literature (see, e.g. Glaeser et al., 2008). Further 'disequilibrium' models, illustrated in Section 5.2, confirm the main findings about the impact of behavioral heterogeneity on housing price dynamics.

The fifth strand (Section 6) is on an integrated approach combining HAMs with traditional market microstructure literature to examine the joint impact of information asymmetry, heterogeneous expectations, and adaptive learning in limit order markets. As shown in Section 6.1, these HAMs are very helpful in examining complexity in market microstructure, providing insight into the impact of heterogeneous trading rules on limit order book and order flows (Chiarella and Iori, 2002, Chiarella et al., 2009b, 2012b, Kovaleva and Iori, 2014), and replicating the stylized facts in limit order markets (Chiarella et al., 2017). Earlier HAMs mainly examine the endogenous mechanism of interaction of heterogeneous agents, less so about information asymmetry, which is the focus of traditional market microstructure literature under rational expectations. Moreover, while the current microstructure literature focuses on informed traders by simplifying the behavior of uninformed traders substantially, a thorough modeling of the learning behavior of uninformed traders appears crucial for trading and market liquidity (O'Hara, 2001). Section 6.2 surveys a contribution in this direction by Chiarella et al. (2015a). By integrating HAMs with asymmetric information and Genetic Algorithm (GA) learning into microstructure literature, they examine the impact of learning on order submission, market liquidity, and price discovery. Finally, very recent contributions (in Sections 6.3 and 6.4) further examine the impact of high frequency trading (Arifovic et al., 2016) and different regulations (Lensberg et al., 2015) on market in a GA learning environment.

Most of the development surveyed in this chapter is based on a jointly theoretical and empirical analysis, combined with numerical simulations and Monte Carlo analysis from the latest development in computational finance. It provides very rich approaches to deal with various issues in equity market, housing market, and market microstructure. The results provide some insights into our understanding of the complexity and efficiency of financial market and policy implications.

2 HAMS OF SINGLE ASSET MARKET IN DISCRETE-TIME

Empirical evidence of various stylized facts and anomalies in financial markets, such as fat tails in return distribution, long-range dependence in volatility, and time series momentum and reversal, has stimulated increasing research interest in financial market modeling. By focusing on endogenous heterogeneity of investor behavior, HAMs play a very important role in providing insights into the importance of investor heterogeneity and explaining stylized facts and marker anomalies observed in financial time series. Early HAMs consider two types of traders, typically fundamentalists and chartists. Beja and Goldman (1980), Day and Huang (1990), Chiarella (1992), Lux (1995), and Brock and Hommes (1997, 1998) are amongst the first to have shown that interaction of agents with heterogeneous expectations can lead to market instability. These HAMs have successfully explained market booms, crashes, and the deviations of market price from fundamental price and replicated some of the stylized facts, which are nicely surveyed in Hommes (2006), LeBaron (2006), and Chiarella et al. (2009a). The promising perspectives of HAMs have stimulated further studies on empirical testing in different markets, including commodity markets (Baak, 1999, Chavas, 2000), stock markets (Boswijk et al., 2007; Franke, 2009; Franke and Westerhoff, 2011, 2012; Chiarella et al., 2012a, 2014; He and Li, 2015a, 2015b), foreign exchange markets (Westerhoff and Reitz, 2003; de Jong et al., 2010; ter Ellen et al., 2013), mutual funds (Gomes and Michaelides, 2008), option markets (Frijns et al., 2010), oil markets (ter Ellen and Zwinkels, 2010), and CDS markets (Chiarella et al., 2015b). HAMs have also been estimated with contagious interpersonal communication by Gilli and Winker (2003), Alfarano et al. (2005), Lux (2009a, 2012), and other works reviewed in Chen et al. (2012).

This development has spurred recent attempts at theoretical explanations and the underlying economic mechanism analysis, which is nicely summarized in a recent survey of Lux and Alfarano (2016). Several behavioral mechanisms on volatility clustering have been proposed based on the underlying deterministic dynamics (He and Li, 2007, 2015b, 2017, Gaunersdorfer et al., 2008, He et al., 2016b), stochastic herding (Alfarano et al., 2005), and stochastic demand (Franke and Westerhoff, 2011, 2012).

In this section, we use the simple HAM of Dieci et al. (2006) to illustrate the explanatory power of the model to investor behavior and provide some of the underlying mathematical and economic mechanisms to volatility clustering and long-range dependence in volatility. We first introduce the model of boundedly rational and adaptive switching behavior of investors in financial markets in Section 2.1. We then provide two particular mechanisms to explain volatility clustering and long memory in return volatility based on the underlying deterministic dynamics in Section 2.2.

Mathematically, the first is based on the local stability and Hopf bifurcation, explored in He and Li (2007), while the second is characterized by the coexistence of two locally stable attractors with different size, proposed initially in Gaunersdorfer et al. (2008) and further developed theoretically in He et al. (2016b). Economically, it demonstrates that the dominance of trend chasing behavior when investors cannot change their strategies or the intensive switching behavior of investors to switch to more profitable strategy can explain volatility clustering and long memory in return volatility, while the noise traders also play a very important role.

In Section 2.3, we briefly discuss He and Zheng (2016) about the emergence of trading heterogeneity due to information uncertainty and strategic trading of agents. Through an integrated approach of HAMs and incomplete information about the fundamental value, He and Zheng (2016) provide an endogenous *self-correction* mechanism of the market. This mechanism is very different from the HAMs with complete information, in which mean-reverting is channeled through some kind of nonlinear assumptions on the demand or order flow of risky asset and market stability depends exogenously on balanced activities from fundamental and momentum trading. The approach provides a micro-foundation to endogenous trading heterogeneity and switching behavior wildly characterized in HAMs. We complete the section with a discussion about an evolutionary finance framework in Section 2.4 to examine the effect of the flows of funds among competing and evolving investment styles on investment performance.

2.1 MARKET MOOD AND ADAPTIVE BEHAVIOR

Empirical evidence in foreign exchange markets (Allen and Taylor, 1990, Taylor and Allen, 1992, Menkhoff, 1998, and Cheung et al., 2004) and managing fund industrial (Menkhoff, 2010) suggests that agents have different information and/or beliefs about market processes. They use not only fundamental but also technical analyses, which are consistent with short-run momentum and long-run reversal behavior in financial markets. In addition, although some agents do not change their particular trading strategies, there are agents who may switch to more profitable strategies over time. Recent laboratory experiments in Hommes et al. (2005), Anufriev and Hommes (2012), and Hommes and in't Veld (2015) also show that agents using simple "rule of thumb" trading strategies are able to coordinate on a common prediction rule. Therefore heterogeneity in expectations and adaptive behavior are crucial to describe individual forecasting and aggregate price behavior.

Motivated by the empirical and experiment evidence, Dieci et al. (2006) introduce a simple financial market of fundamentalists and trend followers. Some agents switch between different strategies over time according to their performance, characterizing the *adaptively rational behavior* of agents. Others are confident and stay with their strategies over time, representing *market mood*. It turns out that this simple model is rich enough to illustrating the complicated price dynamics and to exploring different mechanisms in generating volatility clustering and long memory in volatility. In the following, we first outline the model, discuss calibration and empirical estimation of the model, and then provide an analysis on the two underlying mechanisms (see Dieci et al., 2006 and He and Li, 2008, 2017 for the detail).

Consider a financial market with one risky asset and one risk free asset. Let r be the constant risk free rate, p_t the price, and d_t the dividend of the risky asset at time t. Assume that there are four types of investors, fundamental traders (or fundamentalists), trend followers (or chartists) and noise traders, and one market maker. Let n_3 be the population fraction of the noise traders. Among $1 - n_3$, the fractions of the fundamentalists and trend followers have fixed, n_1 and n_2, and switching, $n_{1,t}$ and $n_{2,t} = 1 - n_{1,t}$, components respectively. Denote $n_0 = n_1 + n_2, m_0 = (n_1 - n_2)/n_0$ and $m_t = n_{1,t} - n_{2,t}$. Then the market fractions $Q_{h,t}$ $(h = 1, 2, 3)$ of the fundamentalists, trend followers, and noise traders at time t can be rewritten as, respectively,

$$\begin{cases} Q_{1,t} = \frac{1}{2}(1 - n_3)\left[n_0 (1 + m_0) + (1 - n_0)(1 + m_t)\right], \\ Q_{2,t} = \frac{1}{2}(1 - n_3)\left[n_0 (1 - m_0) + (1 - n_0)(1 - m_t)\right], \\ Q_{3,t} = n_3. \end{cases} \tag{1}$$

Let $R_{t+1} = p_{t+1} + d_{t+1} - Rp_t$ be the excess return and $R = 1 + r$. We model the order flow[3] $z_{h,t}$ of type-h investors from t to $t + 1$ by $z_{h,t} = E_{h,t}(R_{t+1})/(a_h V_{h,t}(R_{t+1}))$, where $E_{h,t}$ and $V_{h,t}$ are the conditional expectation and variance at time t and a_h is the risk aversion coefficient of type h traders. The order flow of the noise traders $\xi_t \sim N(0, \sigma_\xi^2)$ is an i.i.d. random variable. Then the population weighted average order flow is given by $Z_{e,t} = Q_{1,t} z_{1,t} + Q_{2,t} z_{2,t} + n_3 \xi_t$. To determine the market price, we follow Chiarella and He (2003) and assume that the market price is determined by the market maker as follows,

$$p_{t+1} = p_t + \lambda Z_{e,t} = p_t + \mu z_{e,t} + \delta_t, \tag{2}$$

where $z_{e,t} = q_{1,t} z_{1,t} + q_{2,t} z_{2,t}, q_{h,t} = Q_{h,t}/(1 - n_3)$ for $h = 1, 2$, λ denotes the speed of price adjustment of the market maker, $\mu = (1 - n_3)\lambda$ and $\delta_t \sim N(0, \sigma_\delta^2)$ with $\sigma_\delta = \lambda n_3 \sigma_\xi$.

We now describe briefly the heterogeneous beliefs of the fundamentalists and trend followers and the adaptive switching mechanism. The conditional mean and variance for the fundamental traders are assumed to follow

$$E_{1,t}(p_{t+1}) = p_t + (1 - \alpha)[E_t(p_{t+1}^*) - p_t], \qquad V_{1,t}(p_{t+1}) = \sigma_1^2, \tag{3}$$

---

[3]This order flow can be motivated by assuming that investors maximize their expected CARA utility under their beliefs. This is particular the case when prices or payoffs of the risky asset are assumed to be normally distributed, agents make a myopic mean-variance decision, and linear price adjustment rule is used by market maker. When prices are assumed to be log-normal, the order flow and price adjustment in log-linear price would be more appropriate (see Franke and Westerhoff, 2011, 2012 for the related discussion), though their micro-economic foundation becomes less clear with heterogeneous expectations.

where p_t^* is the fundamental value of the risky asset following a random walk,

$$p_{t+1}^* = p_t^* \exp(-\frac{\sigma_\varepsilon^2}{2} + \sigma_\varepsilon \varepsilon_{t+1}), \quad \varepsilon_t \sim \mathcal{N}(0,1), \quad \sigma_\varepsilon \geq 0, \quad p_0^* = p^* > 0, \quad (4)$$

ε_t is independent of the noise process δ_t, σ_1^2 is constant, and hence $E_t(p_{t+1}^*) = p_t^*$. Here $(1 - \alpha)$ measures the speed of price adjustment towards the fundamental price with $0 < \alpha < 1$. A high α indicates less confidence on the convergence to the fundamental price, leading to a slower adjustment of the market price to the fundamental. For the trend followers, we assume

$$E_{2,t}(p_{t+1}) = p_t + \gamma(p_t - u_t), \qquad V_{2,t}(p_{t+1}) = \sigma_1^2 + b_2 v_t, \qquad (5)$$

where $\gamma \geq 0$ measures the extrapolation of the trend, u_t and v_t are sample mean and variance, respectively. We assume that $u_t = \delta u_{t-1} + (1 - \delta) p_t$ and $v_t = \delta v_{t-1} + \delta(1 - \delta)(p_t - u_{t-1})^2$, representing limiting mean and variance of the geometric decay processes when the memory lag tends to infinity. Here $\delta \in (0, 1)$ measures the geometric decay rate and $b_2 \geq 0$ measures the sensitivity to the sample variance. For simplicity we assume that investors share a homogeneous belief about the dividend process d_t, which is i.i.d. and normally distributed with mean $\bar{d}$ and variance σ_d^2. Denote by $p^* = p_o^* = \bar{d}/r$ the long-run fundamental price.

Let $\pi_{h,t+1}$ be the realized profit between t and $t+1$ of type-h investors, $\pi_{h,t+1} = z_{h,t}(p_{t+1} + d_{t+1} - Rp_t)$ for $h = 1, 2$. Following Brock and Hommes (1997, 1998), the market fraction of investors choosing strategy h at time $t + 1$ is determined by

$$n_{h,t+1} = \frac{\exp[\beta(\pi_{h,t+1} - C_h)]}{\sum_i \exp[\beta(\pi_{i,t+1} - C_i)]}, \qquad h = 1, 2,$$

where β measures the *intensity of the choice* and $C_h \geq 0$ the cost. Together with (1) the market fractions and asset price dynamics are determined by the following random dynamic system in discrete-time,

$$\begin{cases} p_{t+1} = p_t + \mu(q_{1,t} z_{1,t} + q_{2,t} z_{2,t}) + \delta_t, & \delta_t \sim \mathcal{N}(0, \sigma_\delta^2), \\ u_t = \delta u_{t-1} + (1 - \delta) p_t, \\ v_t = \delta v_{t-1} + \delta(1 - \delta)(p_t - u_{t-1})^2, \\ m_t = \tanh\left[\frac{\beta}{2}(z_{1,t-1} - z_{2,t-1} - (C_1 - C_2))(p_t + d_t - Rp_{t-1})\right]. \end{cases} \quad (6)$$

2.2 VOLATILITY CLUSTERING: CALIBRATION AND MECHANISMS

By conducting econometric analysis via Monte Carlo simulations, He and Li (2015b, 2017) show that the autocorrelations of returns, absolute returns and squared returns of the model developed above share the same pattern as those of the DAX 30. They further characterize the power-law behavior of the DAX 30 and find that the estimates of the power-law decay indices, the (FI)GARCH parameters, and the tail index of

Table 1 Calibrated parameters of the no-switching (N), pure-switching (S), and full (F) models

	α	γ	a_1	a_2	μ	n_0	m_0	δ	b	σ	σ_δ	β	**Wald**
N	0.858	8.464	6.024	0.383	0.946	1	−0.200	0.292	6.763	0.24	3.473	0	112
S	0.513	0.764	7.972	0.231	2.004	0	–	0.983	3.692	0.231	3.268	0.745	108
F	0.488	1.978	7.298	0.320	1.866	0.313	−0.024	0.983	3.537	0.231	3.205	0.954	106

the model closely match those of the DAX 30. In the following we first report the calibrated results of the model developed in the previous subsection and then provide some insights into investor behavior and two underlying mechanisms of the volatility clustering.

When there is no switching between the two strategies, the above model reduces to the no-switching model in He and Li (2007), showing that the no-switching model is able to replicate the power-law behavior in return volatility. Based on the daily price index data of the DAX 30 from 11 August, 1975 to 29 June, 2007, He and Li (2015b, 2017) calibrate three scenarios of the above model: the no-switching (N) model with $\beta = 0$, pure-switching (S) model with $n_0 = 0$, and full (F) model of (6). The results are collected in Table 1 (with fixed $r = 5\% \, p.a.$ and $C_1 = C_2 = 0$). By conducting econometric analysis via Monte Carlo simulations based on the calibrated models, He and Li (2015b, 2017) find that, for all three scenarios, the estimates of the power-law decay indices d, the (FI)GARCH parameters, and the tail index of the calibrated model closely match those of the DAX 30. By conducting a Wald test $H_o : d_{DAX} = d$ at 5% and 1% significant levels (with the critical values of 3.842 and 6.635, respectively), He and Li (2017) show that switching model fits the data better than the no-switching and pure-switching models.

Comparing the estimates of the three scenarios leads to different investor behavior. The estimated annual return volatility σ is close to the annual return volatility of the DAX 30. Higher a_1 than a_2 implies that the fundamentalists are more risk averse compared to the trend followers. For the no-switching scenario, a higher value of α indicates a slow price adjustment of the fundamentalists toward the fundamental value, while a higher value of γ indicates that the trend followers extrapolate the price trend actively. Without switching, $m_o = -0.2$ indicates that both the fundamentalists and trend followers are active in the market, which is however dominated by the trend followers (about 60%). On the full model, the market is dominated by investors (about 70%) who constantly switch between the fundamental and trend following strategies, although some investors (about 30%) never change their strategies over the time. This is consistent with the empirical findings discussed at the beginning of this section.

We now provide two mechanisms based on the underlying deterministic dynamics. The first one is on the local stability and periodic oscillation due to Hopf bifurcation, explored in He and Li (2007). Essentially, on the parameter space of the deterministic model, near the Hopf bifurcation boundary, the fundamental steady state can be locally stable but globally unstable. Due to the nature of Hopf bifurcation, such global instability leads to switching between the locally stable fundamental price and the periodic oscillations around the fundamental price. Then triggered by the fundamental and market noises, He and Li (2007) show that the interaction of the fundamental, risk-adjusted trend chasing from the trend followers, and the interplay of the noises and the underlying deterministic dynamics can be the source of power-law behavior in return volatility. Mathematically, the calibrated no-switching and switching models share the same underlying deterministic mechanism. Economically, however, they provide different behavioral mechanisms. With no-switching, it is the dominance of the trend followers (about 60%) that drives the power-law behavior. However, with both switching and no-switching investors, dominated by these traders (about 70%) who constantly switch between the two strategies. It is therefore the adaptive behavior of investors that generates the power-law behavior. This is also in line with Franke and Westerhoff (2012, 2016) who estimate various HAMs and show that herding behavior plays a key role in matching the stylized facts. More importantly, the noise traders play an important role in generating insignificant ACs on the returns, while the significantly decayed AC patterns of the absolute returns and squared returns are more influenced by the fundamental noise. As pointed out in Lux and Alfarano (2016), noise traders is probably a central ingredient of these models.

The second mechanism proposed initially in Gaunersdorfer et al. (2008) is characterized by the coexistence of two locally stable attractors with different size, while such coexistence is not required in the previous mechanism. Dieci et al. (2006) show that the above model can display such co-existence of locally stable fundamental steady state and periodic cycle. The interaction of the coexistence of the deterministic dynamics and the noise processes then triggers the switching among the two attractors and endogenously generates volatility clustering. More recently, by applying normal form analysis and center manifold theory, He et al. (2016b) provide the following theoretical result on the coexistence of the locally stable steady state and invariant circle of the underlying deterministic model (we refer to He et al., 2016b for the details).

Proposition 2.1. *The underlying deterministic system of* (6) *has a unique fundamental steady state* $(p, u, v, m) = (\bar{p}, \bar{p}, 0, \bar{m})$ *with* $\bar{m} = \tanh \frac{\beta(C_2 - C_1)}{2}$. *The fundamental steady state is locally asymptotically stable for* $\gamma \in (0, \gamma^{**})$, *and it undergoes a Neimark–Sacker bifurcation at* $\gamma = \gamma^{**}$, *that is, there is an invariant curve near the fundamental steady state. Moreover, the bifurcated closed invariant curve is forward and stable when* $a(0) < 0$ *and backward and unstable when* $a(0) > 0$, *and a Chenciner (generalized Neimark–Sacker) bifurcation takes place when* $a(0) = 0$. *Here* $a(0)$ *is the first Lyapunov coefficient.*

Note that the market fractions of the fundamentalists and trend followers at the fundamental steady state are given by $q_1 = (1 + m_q)/2$ and $q_2 = (1 - m_q)/2$ with $m_q = n_0 m_0 + (1 - n_0)\bar{m}$, respectively. When the cost of the fundamental strategy C_1 is higher than the cost of the trend following strategy C_2, an increase in the switching intensity β leads to a decrease in γ^{**}, meaning that the fundamental price becomes less stable when traders switch their strategies more often. This is essentially the rational routes to randomness of Brock and Hommes (1997, 1998).

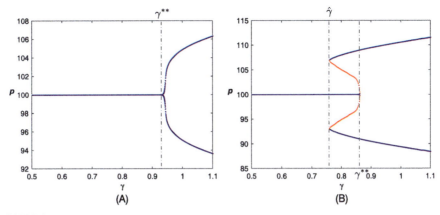

FIGURE 1

Bifurcation diagrams of the market price with respect to γ. Here $a = a_1 = a_2 = 0.5$, $\mu = 1$, $\alpha = 0.3$, $\delta = 0.85$, $b_2 = 0.05$, $C = C_1 - C_2 = 0.5$, $\beta = 0.5$, and $m_0 = 0$. (A) $n_0 = 0.8$; (B) $n_0 = 0.5$.

Fig. 1 illustrates two different types of Neimark–Sacker bifurcation. It is the sign of the first Lyapunov coefficient $a(0)$ that determines the bifurcation direction, either forward or backward, and the stability of the bifurcated invariant circles, leading to different bifurcation dynamics. When $a(0) < 0$, the bifurcation is forward and stable, meaning that the bifurcated invariant circle occurring for $\gamma > \gamma^{**}$ is locally stable. In this case, as γ increases and passes γ^{**}, the fundamental steady state becomes unstable and the trajectory converges to an invariant circle bifurcating from the fundamental steady state. As γ increases further, the trajectory converges to invariant circles with different sizes. This is illustrated in Fig. 1A with $\gamma^{**} \approx 0.93$ where the two bifurcating curves for $\gamma > \gamma^{**}$ indicate the minimum and maximum value boundaries of the bifurcating invariant circles as γ increases.

However, when $a(0) > 0$, the bifurcation is backward and unstable, meaning that the bifurcated invariant circle occurring at $\gamma = \gamma^{**}$ is unstable, illustrated in Fig. 1B (with $\gamma^{**} \approx 0.88$). There is a continuation of the unstable bifurcated circles as γ decreases initially until it reaches a critical value $\hat{\gamma}$, which is indicated by the two (red) dotted curves of the bifurcating circles for $\hat{\gamma} < \gamma < \gamma^{**}$. Then as γ increases from the critical value $\hat{\gamma}$, the bifurcated circles become forward and stable. This is illustrated by the two (blue) solid curves, which are the boundaries of the bifurcating circles, for $\gamma > \hat{\gamma}$ in Fig. 1B. Therefore, the locally stable steady state coexists with the locally stable 'forward extended' circles for $\hat{\gamma} < \gamma < \gamma^{**}$, in between there are backward extended unstable circles. For $\hat{\gamma} < \gamma < \gamma^{**}$, even when the fundamental steady state is locally stable, prices need not converge to the fundamental value, while may settle down to a stable limit circle. We call $\hat{\gamma} < \gamma < \gamma^{**}$ the 'volatility clustering region'. In addition, a Chenciner (generalized Neimark–Sacker) bifurcation takes place when $a(0) = 0$. Based on the above analysis, a necessary condition on the coexistence is

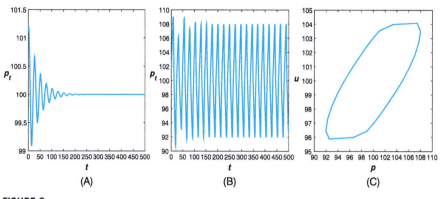

FIGURE 2

The deterministic trajectories of time series of price for $(p_0, u_0, v_0, m_0) = (\bar{p} + 1, \bar{p}, 0, \bar{m})$ in (A) and $(p_0, u_0, v_0, m_0) = (\bar{p} + 1, \bar{p} - 1, 0, \bar{m})$ in (B) and the phase plot of (p, u) in (C). Here the parameter values are the same as in Fig. 1 and $n_0 = 0.5$. (A) Price time series; (B) price time series; (C) phase plot.

that $a(0) > 0$. The coexistence of the locally stable steady state and invariant circle illustrated in Fig. 2 shows that the price dynamics depends on the initial values.

When buffeted with noises, the stochastic model can endogenously generate volatility clustering and long range dependence in volatility, illustrated in Fig. 3. Economically, with strong trading activities of either the fundamental investors or the trend followers, market price fluctuates around either the fundamental value with low volatility or a cyclical price movement with high volatility, depending on market conditions. When the activities of the fundamentalists and trend followers are balanced (to be in the volatility clustering region), the interaction of the fundamental noise and noise traders and the underlying co-existence dynamics then triggers an irregular switching between the two volatility regimes, leading to volatility clustering. In particular, volatility clustering becomes more significant when neither the fundamental nor the trend following traders dominate the market and traders switch their strategies more often. The results verify the endogenous mechanism on volatility clustering proposed by Gaunersdorfer et al. (2008) and provide a behavioral explanation on the volatility clustering.

2.3 INFORMATION UNCERTAINTY AND TRADING HETEROGENEITY

Traditional finance literature mainly explore the role of asymmetric information and information uncertainty. Most HAMs however mainly focus on endogenous market mechanism through the interaction among heterogeneous agents by assuming a complete information about the fundamental value of risky assets. An integration of HAMs and asymmetric and/or uncertain information would provide a micro-foundation on behavioral heterogeneity and a more broad framework to better explaining various puzzles and anomalies in financial markets. Instead of heuristi-

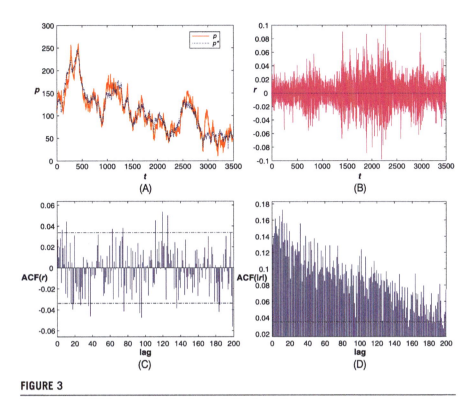

FIGURE 3

Time series of (A) the market price (red solid line) and the fundamental price (blue dotted line), (B) the market returns (r); the ACs of (C) the returns and (D) the absolute returns. Here the parameter values are the same as in Fig. 2 and $\sigma_\delta = 2$, $\sigma_\varepsilon = 0.025$.

cal heterogeneity assumption of agents' behavior, He and Zheng (2016) model the trading heterogeneity by introducing information uncertainty about the fundamental value to a HAM. Agents are homogeneous ex ante. Conditional on their private information about the fundamental value, agents choose optimally among different trading strategies when optimizing their expected utilities. This approach provides a micro-foundation to trading and behavioral heterogeneity among agents. It also offers a different switching behavior of agents from the current HAMs. In the following, we brief this approach.

Consider a continuum $[0, 1]$ of agents trading one risky asset and one risk-free asset in discrete-time. For simplicity, the risk-free rate is normalized to be zero. The fundamental value of the risky asset $\mu \sim \mathcal{N}(\bar{\mu}, \sigma_\mu^2)$ is not known publicly. Denote $\alpha_\mu = 1/\sigma_\mu^2$ the precision of the fundamental value μ. In each time period, agent i receives a private signal about the fundamental value μ, given by $x_{i,t} = \mu + \varepsilon_{i,t}$, where $\varepsilon_{i,t} \sim \mathcal{N}(0, \sigma_x^2)$ is i.i.d. normal across agents and over time. Let $\alpha_x = 1/\sigma_x^2$ be the precision of the signal. Agents maximize CARA utility function $U\left(W_{i,t}\right) = -\exp\left(-a\,W_{i,t}\right)$, with the same risk aversion coefficient

a, in which $W_{i,t}$ is the wealth of agent i at time t. Let p_t be the (cum-)market price of the risky asset and denote $I_t = \{p_t, p_{t-1}, \cdots\}$ the public information of historical price. Conditional on the public information I_{t-1} and her private signal $x_{i,t}$, agent i seeks to maximize her expected utility, leading to the optimal demand $q_{i,t} = [E(p_t|x_{i,t}, I_{t-1}) - p_{t-1}]/[a\,Var(p_t|x_{i,t}, I_{t-1})]$, conditional on the public information I_{t-1} and her signal $x_{i,t}$.

Facing the information uncertainty on the fundamental value, the agent considers both fundamental and momentum trading strategies based on the public information of the history price and her private signal about the fundamental value. More explicitly, the fundamental trading strategy is based on

$$E^f(p_t|x_{i,t}, I_{t-1}) = (1-\gamma)p_{t-1} + \gamma\frac{\alpha_\mu\bar{\mu} + \alpha_x x_{i,t}}{\alpha_\mu + \alpha_x}, \tag{7}$$

$$Var^f(p_t|x_{i,t}, I_{t-1}) = \gamma^2 Var\left(\mu|x_{i,t}, I_{t-1}\right) = \frac{\gamma^2}{\alpha_\mu + \alpha_x}, \tag{8}$$

where $\gamma \in (0, 1]$ is a constant, measuring the convergence speed of the market price to the expected fundamental value. Note that $\frac{\alpha_\mu\bar{\mu} + \alpha_x x_{i,t}}{\alpha_\mu + \alpha_x}$ and $\frac{1}{\alpha_\mu + \alpha_x}$ are agent i's posterior updating of the mean and variance, respectively, of the fundamental value of the risky asset conditional on her signal $x_{i,t}$. Condition (7) means that the predicted price is a weighted average of the latest market price and the posterior updating of the fundamental value conditional on her private signal $x_{i,t}$; while (8) means that the conditional variance is proportional to the posterior variance conditional on the private signal $x_{i,t}$. In particular, when $\gamma = 1$, the conditional mean and variance (7)–(8) are reduced to the posterior mean and variance, respectively. Therefore the fundamental trading strategy reflects agent's belief that the future price is expected to converge to the expected fundamental value. Though the private signals $x_{i,t}$ are i.i.d. across agents and over time, they are partially incorporated through the current market price p_t and hence reflected in the prediction of the future prices. Consequently, the optimal demand based on the fundamental analysis becomes $q_{i,t}^f = [\alpha_\mu\bar{\mu} + \alpha_x x_{i,t} - (\alpha_\mu + \alpha_x)p_{t-1}]/(a\gamma)$, which is called the fundamental trading strategy f.

The momentum trading is however independent of the private signal $x_{i,t}$, but depends on a price trend,

$$E^c(p_t|x_{i,t}, I_{t-1}) = p_{t-1} + \beta(p_{t-1} - v_t), \qquad Var^c(p_t|x_{i,t}, I_{t-1}) = \sigma_{t-1}^2, \tag{9}$$

where v_t is a reference price or price trend (can be a moving average, a supporting/resistance price level, or any index derived from technical analysis), β measures the extrapolation of the price deviation from the trend, and σ_{t-1}^2 is a heuristic prediction on the variance of the asset price. Then the optimal demand becomes $q_{i,t}^c = \beta(p_{t-1} - v_t)/(a\sigma_{t-1}^2)$, which is called momentum strategy c. In particular, when v_t is a moving average of the historical prices and $\beta > (<)0$, strategy c is essentially a time-series momentum (contrarian) strategy (Moskowitz et al., 2012).

Given the information uncertainty, the agent compares the expected value functions based on the two optimal trading strategies and chooses the one with relative higher value. More explicitly, the agent firstly calculates the respective value functions based on strategy f and c,

$$E_{i,t}^{f}(U) = -\exp\left\{-A\left[W_{i,t-1} + \frac{\left[\alpha_{\mu}\bar{\mu} + \alpha_{x}x_{i,t} - (\alpha_{\mu} + \alpha_{x})p_{t-1}\right]^{2}}{2a(\alpha_{\mu} + \alpha_{x})}\right]\right\},$$

$$E_{i,t}^{c}(U) = -\exp\left\{-A\left[W_{i,t-1} + \frac{\beta^{2}(p_{t-1} - v_{t})^{2}}{2a\sigma_{t-1}^{2}}\right]\right\}.$$

The agent then compares the value functions and selects the one that yields a higher value. Note that $E_{i,t}^{f}$ is an increasing function of the absolute value of the signal $|x_{i,t}|$, while E_{i}^{c} is independent of $x_{i,t}$. Therefore there exists threshold signal values $\bar{x}_{t}$ for the private signal such that $E_{i,t}^{f} = E_{i,t}^{c}$, that is,

$$\frac{E_{i,t}^{f}(U)}{E_{i,t}^{c}(U)} = \exp\left\{-\left[\frac{\left[\alpha_{\mu}\bar{\mu} + \alpha_{x}\bar{x}_{t} - (\alpha_{\mu} + \alpha_{x})p_{t-1}\right]^{2}}{2(\alpha_{\mu} + \alpha_{x})} - \frac{\beta^{2}(p_{t-1} - v_{t})^{2}}{2\sigma_{t-1}^{2}}\right]\right\} = 1.$$

Solving for $\bar{x}_{t}$ yields

$$x_{t}^{\pm} = \frac{1}{\alpha_{x}}\left[(\alpha_{\mu} + \alpha_{x})p_{t-1} - \alpha_{\mu}\bar{\mu} \pm \frac{\beta\sqrt{\alpha_{\mu} + \alpha_{x}}}{\sigma_{t-1}}(p_{t-1} - v_{t})\right]. \tag{10}$$

Therefore, when $v_{t} = p_{t-1}$, the agent chooses strategy f. When $v_{t} \neq p_{t-1}$, the agent chooses strategy c if her signal is less informative, falling into the interval (x_{t}^{m}, x_{t}^{M}), and strategy f otherwise, where $x_{t}^{m} = \min(x_{t}^{\pm})$ and $x_{t}^{M} = \max(x_{t}^{\pm})$. Therefore, the optimal demand of agent i is given by $q_{i,t} = q_{i,t}^{f}$ for $x_{i,t} \leq x_{t}^{m}$ or $x_{i,t} \geq x_{t}^{M}$; otherwise $q_{i,t} = q_{i,t}^{c}$ when $x_{i,t} \in (x_{t}^{m}, x_{t}^{M})$. Intuitively, when agent's private signal is near the mean fundamental value, the private information becomes less valuable. However, when agent's private signal is far away from the mean fundamental value, the private information becomes more valuable and hence the agent favors the fundamental trading strategy.

The choice between the two strategies due to the informativeness of the private information about the fundamental value leads to endogenous heterogeneity and switching behavior of agents' choices. More explicitly, by aggregating the demand D_{t} in a closed form and considering noisy supply S_{t}, the market price is determined through a market maker scenario via $p_{t} = p_{t-1} + \lambda(D_{t} + S_{t})$ with $\lambda > 0$. He and Zheng (2016) first conduct an analysis on the underlying deterministic model when $\sigma_{t-1}^{2} = \sigma^{2}$ is a constant and $v_{t} = p_{t-2}$ (corresponding to a simple momentum trading based on the change in the last price). They show that the fundamental price is locally stable with small precisions of the fundamental information noise. That is, the fundamental price becomes unstable when the level of the fundamental information noise is small, leading to high price volatility. Intuitively, in this case, the fundamental information become more accurate and hence less valuable. Therefore the fundamental strategy becomes less profitable, while the momentum trading strategy becomes more popular. This is consistent with the literature on coordination game with imperfect information (see Angeletos and Werning, 2006).

When the fundamental price becomes unstable, the price dynamics can become very complicated. On the stochastic model, they have shown that the market fraction of the agents choosing the momentum (fundamental) strategy decreases (increases) as the mis-pricing increases. This underlies mean-reverting of market price to its fundamental price when mis-pricing becomes significant, burst of a bubble, and recover of a recession. This mechanism, together with the destabilizing role of the momentum trading and the stabilizing role of the fundamental trading, provides an endogenous *self-correction* mechanism of the market. This mechanism is very different from the HAMs with complete information, in which the mean-reverting is channeled through some nonlinear assumptions on the demand or order flow of risky asset. The market stability depends exogenously on balanced activities from fundamental and momentum trading. This integrated approach of HAMs and incomplete information about the fundamental value therefore provides a micro-foundation to endogenous trading heterogeneity and switching behavior wildly characterized in HAMs. Furthermore, He and Zheng (2016) conduct a time series analysis on the stylized facts and demonstrate that the model is able to match the S&P 500 in terms of power-law distribution in returns, volatility clustering, long memory in volatility, and leverage effect.

2.4 SWITCHING OF AGENTS, FUND FLOWS, AND LEVERAGE

Similar to Dieci et al. (2006), most HAMs employ the discrete-choice framework[4] to capture the way investors switch across different competing strategies/behavioral rules. However, since this approach models the changes of investors' proportions, not directly the flows of funds, it is not very suitable to capture the long-run performance of investment strategies (or 'styles') in terms of accumulated wealth, nor the impact of fund flows on the price dynamics. For this reason, LeBaron (2011) defines such forms of switching between strategies as *active learning*, capturing investors' tendency to adopt the best-performing rule, in contrast to *passive learning*, by which investors' wealth naturally accumulates on strategies that have been relatively successful. This second form of learning is closely related to the issue of survival and long-run dominance of strategies and to the evolutionary finance approach (see Blume and Easley, 1992, 2006, Sandroni, 2000, Hens and Schenk-Hoppé, 2005, as well as Evstigneev

---

[4]A further example of switching based on the discrete-choice approach is contained in the multi-asset model discussed in Section 4.2, whereas in the models described in Sections 5.1.2 and 5.2 investors' shares evolve through a simplified mechanism based on current market conditions.

et al., 2009 for a comprehensive survey of early results and recent research in this field).[5]

LeBaron (2011) argues that the dynamics of real-world markets are likely to be affected by some combinations of active and passive learning, and that exploring their interaction may improve our understanding of the dynamics of asset prices. Moreover, LeBaron (2012) proposes a simple framework that can simultaneously account for wealth dynamics and active search for new strategies, based on performance comparison. Besides reproducing the basic stylized facts of asset returns and trading volume, the model yields some insight into the dynamics of agents' strategies and their impact on market stability.

A further recent contribution on the interplay of active and passive learning is provided by Palczewski et al. (2016). They build an evolutionary finance framework in discrete time with fundamental, trend-following and noise trading strategies. Such strategies are interpreted as portfolio managers with different investment 'styles'. Individual investors can move (part of) their funds between portfolio managers. The total amount of freely flowing capital is a model parameter, capturing the clients' degree of impatience (similar to the proportion of *switching* investors in Dieci et al., 2006). Funds are reallocated based on the relative performance of competing fund managers, according to the discrete choice principle. Therefore, portfolio managers may experience an *exogenous* growth of their wealth, in addition to the *endogenous* growth due to returns on the employed capital. The model framework appears promising to investigate the market impact of the *fund flows* and to incorporate different types of 'behavioral biases' into HAMs. In particular, Palczewski et al. (2016) show that even a small amount of freely flowing capital can have a large impact on price movements if investors exhibit 'recency bias' in evaluating fund performance.

In a somewhat related framework with heterogeneous investment funds using 'value investing', Thurner et al. (2012) explore the joint impact of wealth dynamics and the flows of capital among competing investment funds. Evolutionary pressure generated by short-run competition forces fund managers to make leveraged asset purchases with margin calls. Simulation results highlight a new mechanism to fat tails and clustered volatility, which is linked to wealth dynamics and leverage-induced crashes. Moreover, this framework appears promising to test different credit regulation policies (Poledna et al., 2014) and to investigate the impact of bank leverage management on the stability properties of the financial system (Aymanns and Farmer, 2015).

---

[5]Note that, while most HAMs with strategy switching are based on CARA utility maximization, the evolutionary finance approach is consistent with CRRA utility. Other models where endogenous dynamics emerge due to the evolution of the wealth shares of heterogeneous investors are Levy et al. (1994), Chiarella and He (2001), Chiarella et al. (2006a), Anufriev and Dindo (2010), Bottazzi and Dindo (2014).

3 HAMS OF SINGLE ASSET MARKET IN CONTINUOUS-TIME

Historical information plays a very important role in testing efficient market hypothesis in financial markets. In particular, it is crucial to understand how quickly market prices reflect fundamental shocks and how much information is contained in the historical prices. Empirical evidence shows that stock markets react with a delay to information on fundamentals and that information diffuses gradually across markets (Hou and Moskowitz, 2005, Hong et al., 2007). Based on market underreaction and overreaction hypotheses, momentum and contrarian strategies are widely used by financial market practitioners and their profitability has been extensively investigated by academics. De Bondt and Thaler (1985) and Lakonishok et al. (1994) find supporting evidence on the profitability of contrarian strategies for a holding period of 3–5 years based on the past 3–5 years' returns. In contrast, Jegadeesh and Titman (1993, 2001) among many others, find supporting evidence on the profitability of momentum strategies for holding periods of 3–12 months based on the returns over the past 3–12 months. Time series momentum investigated recently in Moskowitz et al. (2012) characterizes a strong positive predictability of a security's own past returns. It becomes clear that the time horizons of historical prices play crucial roles in the performance of contrarian and momentum strategies. Many theoretical studies have tried to explain the momentum,[6] however, as argued in Griffin et al. (2003), "*the comparison is in some sense unfair since no time horizon is specified in most behavioral models*".

In the literature of HAMs, the heterogeneous expectations of agents, in particular of chartists, are formed based on price trends such as moving average of historical prices. In discrete-time models, with different time horizon, the dimension of the model is different. To examine the effect of time horizon analytically, we need to study the model with different dimension separately. Also, as the time horizon increases, it becomes more difficult analytically in dealing with high dimensional nonlinear dynamic system. This challenge is illustrated in Chiarella et al. (2006b) when examining the effect of different moving averages on market stability. Therefore, how different time horizons of historical prices affect price dynamics becomes a challenging issue in the current HAMs.

This section introduces some of the recent developments of HAMs of a single risky asset (and a riskless asset) in continuous time to deal with the price delay problems in behavioral finance and HAMs literature. In continuous-time HAMs, the time horizon of historical price information is simply captured by a time delay parameter. Such models are characterized mathematically by a system of stochastic delay differential equations, which provide a more broad framework to investigate the joint effect of adaptive behavior of heterogeneous agents and the impact of historical prices.

---

[6]See, for example, Fama and French (1996), Daniel et al. (1998), and Hong and Stein (1999).

Development of deterministic delay differential equation models to characterize fluctuation of commodity prices and cyclic economic behavior has a long history,[7] however the application to asset pricing and financial markets is relatively new. This section bridges HAMs with traditional approaches in continuous-time finance to investigate the impact of moving average rules over different time horizon (He and Li, 2012) in Section 3.1, the profitability of fundamental and momentum strategies (He and Li, 2015a) in Section 3.2, and optimal asset allocation with time series momentum and reversal (He et al., 2018) in Section 3.3.

3.1 A CONTINUOUS-TIME HAM WITH TIME DELAY

We now introduce the continuous-time model of He and Li (2012) and demonstrate first that the result of Brock and Hommes on rational routes to market instability in discrete-time also holds in continuous time. That is, adaptive switching behavior of agents can lead to market instability as the switching intensity increases. We then show a double edged effect of an increase in the time horizon of historical price information on market stability. An initial increase in time delay can destabilize the market, leading to price fluctuations. However, as the time delay increases further, the market is stabilized. This double edged effect is a very different feature of continuous-time HAMs from discrete-time HAMs. With noisy fundamental value and liquidity traders, the continuous-time model is able to generate long deviations of market price from the fundamental price, bubbles, crashes, and volatility clustering.

Consider a financial market with a risky asset and let $P(t)$ denote the (cum) price per share of the risky asset at time t. The market consists of fundamentalists, chartists, liquidity traders, and a market maker. The fundamentalists believe that the market price $P(t)$ is mean-reverting to the fundamental price $F(t)$, and their demand is given by $Z_f(t) = \beta_f[F(t) - P(t)]$, with $\beta_f > 0$ measuring the mean-reverting speed of the market price to the fundamental price. The chartists are modeled as trend followers, believing that the future market price follows a price trend $u(t)$, and their demand is given by[8] $Z_c(t) = \tanh\left(\beta_c[P(t) - u(t)]\right)$ with $\beta_c > 0$ measuring the extrapolation of the trend followers to the price trend. Among various price trends used in practice, we consider $u(t)$ as a normalized exponentially decaying weighted average of historical prices over a time interval $[t - \tau, t]$,

$$u(t) = \frac{k}{1 - e^{-k\tau}} \int_{t-\tau}^{t} e^{-k(t-s)} P(s)ds, \tag{11}$$

where time delay $\tau \in (0, \infty)$ represents time horizon of historical prices, $k > 0$ measures the decay rate of the weights on the historical prices. In particular, when

---

[7]See, for example, Kalecki (1935), Goodwin (1951), Larson (1964), Mackey (1989), Phillips (1957), Yoshida and Asada (2007), and Matsumoto and Szidarovszky (2011).

[8]The fact that the S-shaped demand function captures the trend following behavior is well documented in the HAM literature (see, for example, Chiarella et al., 2009a).

$k \to 0$, the weights are equal and the price trend $u(t)$ in (11) is simply given by the standard moving average (MA) with equal weights, $u(t) = \frac{1}{\tau} \int_{t-\tau}^{t} P(s)ds$. When $k \to \infty$, all the weights go to the current price so that $u(t) \to P(t)$. For the time delay, when $\tau \to 0$, the trend followers regard the current price as the price trend. When $\tau \to \infty$, the trend followers use all the historical prices to form the price trend, $u(t) = k \int_{-\infty}^{t} e^{-k(t-s)} P(s)ds$. In general, for $0 < k < \infty$, Eq. (11) can be expressed as a delay differential equation with time delay τ

$$du(t) = \frac{k}{1 - e^{-k\tau}} \left[P(t) - e^{-k\tau} P(t - \tau) - (1 - e^{-k\tau}) u(t) \right] dt.$$

The demand of liquidity traders is i.i.d. normally distributed with mean of zero and standard deviation of $\sigma_M (> 0)$.

Let $n_f(t)$ and $n_c(t)$ represent the market fractions of agents who use the fundamental and trend following strategies, respectively. Their net profits over a short time interval $[t, t + dt]$ can be measured, respectively, by $\pi_f(t)dt = Z_f(t)dP(t) - C_f dt$ and $\pi_c(t)dt = Z_c(t)dP(t) - C_c dt$, where C_f, $C_c \geq 0$ are constant costs of the strategies. To measure strategy performance, we introduce a cumulated profit over the time interval $[t - \tau, t]$ by $U_i(t) = \frac{\eta}{1 - e^{-\eta\tau}} \int_{t-\tau}^{t} e^{-\eta(t-s)} \pi_i(s)ds$, $i = f, c$, where $\eta > 0$ measures the decay of the historical profits. Consequently, $dU_i(t) = \eta \left[\frac{\pi_i(t) - e^{-\eta\tau} \pi_i(t-\tau)}{1 - e^{-\eta\tau}} - U_i(t) \right] dt$ for $i = f, c$. Following Hofbauer and Sigmund (1998, Chapter 7), the evolution dynamics of the market populations are governed by

$$dn_i(t) = \beta n_i(t)[dU_i(t) - d\bar{U}(t)], \qquad \text{for } i = f, c,$$

where $d\bar{U}(t) = n_f(t)dU_f(t) + n_c(t)dU_c(t)$ is the average performance of the two strategies and $\beta > 0$ measures the intensity of choice. The switching mechanism in the continuous-time setup is consistent with the one used in discrete-time HAMs. In fact, it can be verified that the dynamics of the market fraction $n_f(t)$ satisfy $dn_f(t) = \beta n_f(t)(1 - n_f(t))[dU_f(t) - dU_c(t)]$, leading to $n_f(t) = e^{\beta U_f(t)} / (e^{\beta U_f(t)} + e^{\beta U_c(t)})$, which is the discrete choice model used in Brock and Hommes (1998).

Finally, the price $P(t)$ is adjusted by the market maker according to $dP(t) = \mu \left[n_f(t)Z_f(t) + n_c(t)Z_c(t) \right] dt + \sigma_M dW_M(t)$, where $\mu > 0$ represents the speed of the price adjustment of the market maker, $W_M(t)$ is a standard Wiener process capturing the random excess demand process either driven by unexpected market news or liquidity traders, and $\sigma_M > 0$ is a constant. To sum up, the market price of the risky asset is determined according to the stochastic delay differential system

$$\begin{cases} dP(t) = \mu \left[n_f(t)Z_f(t) + (1 - n_f(t)) Z_c(t) \right] dt + \sigma_M dW_M(t), \\[2mm] du(t) = \dfrac{k}{1 - e^{-k\tau}} \left[P(t) - e^{-k\tau} P(t - \tau) - (1 - e^{-k\tau}) u(t) \right] dt, \\[2mm] dU(t) = \dfrac{\eta}{1 - e^{-\eta\tau}} \left[\pi(t) - e^{-\eta\tau} \pi(t - \tau) - (1 - e^{-\eta\tau}) U(t) \right] dt, \end{cases} \qquad (12)$$

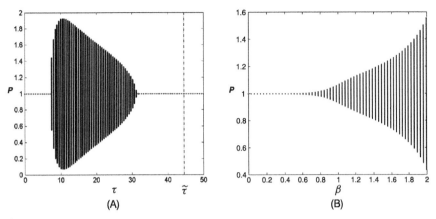

FIGURE 4

Bifurcation diagram of the market price with respect to τ in (A) and β in (B).

where $U(t) = U_f(t) - U_c(t)$, $n_f(t) = 1/(1 + e^{-\beta U(t)})$, $Z_f(t) = \beta_f(F(t) - P(t))$, $Z_c(t) = \tanh[\beta_c(P(t) - u(t))]$, $C = C_f - C_c$, and

$$\pi(t) = \pi_f(t) - \pi_c(t) = \mu[n_f(t)Z_f(t) + (1 - n_f(t))Z_c(t)][Z_f(t) - Z_c(t)] - C.$$

By assuming that the fundamental price is a constant $F(t) \equiv \bar{F}$ and there is no market noise $\sigma_M = 0$, system (12) becomes a deterministic delay differential system with $(P, u, U) = (\bar{F}, \bar{F}, -C)$ as the unique *fundamental steady state*. He and Li (2012) show that the steady state is locally stable for either small or large time delay τ when the market is dominated by the fundamentalists. Otherwise, the steady state becomes unstable through Hopf bifurcations as the time delay increases. This result is in line with the results obtained in discrete-time HAMs. However, different from discrete-time HAMs, the continuous-time model shows that the fundamental steady state becomes locally stable again when the time delay is large enough. This is illustrated by the bifurcation diagram of the market price with respect to τ in Fig. 4A.[9] It shows that there are two Hopf bifurcation values $0 < \tau_o < \tau_1$ occurring at $\tau = \tau_0 (\approx 8)$ and $\tau = \tau_1 (\approx 28)$. The fundamental steady state is locally stable when the time delay is small, $\tau \in [0, \tau_0)$, then becomes unstable for $\tau \in (\tau_o, \tau_1)$, and then regains the local stability for $\tau > \tau_1$. Due to the problem of high dimensionality, such analysis on the effect of historical price on market price in discrete-time HAMs can become very complicated, see Chiarella et al. (2006b) that examining the effect of different moving averages on market stability. It is the continuous-time model that facilitates such analysis on the stability effect of time horizon of historical prices and stability switching. The bifurcation diagram of the market price with respect to the

[9]Unless specified otherwise, the parameter values for Figs. 4 and 5 are: $k = 0.05$, $\mu = 1$, $\beta_f = 1.4$, $\beta_c = 1.4$, $\eta = 0.5$, $\beta = 0.5$, $C = 0.02$, $\bar{F} = 1$, $\sigma_F = 0.12$, and $\sigma_M = 0.05$.

switching intensity β is given in Fig. 4B. It shows that the fundamental steady state is locally stable when the switching intensity β is low, becoming unstable as the switching intensity increases, bifurcating to periodic price with increasing fluctuations. This is consistent with the discrete-time HAMs.

For the deterministic model, when the steady state becomes unstable, it bifurcates to stable periodic solutions through a Hopf bifurcation. The periodic fluctuations of the market prices are associated with periodic fluctuations of the market fractions, illustrated in Fig. 5A. Based on the bifurcation diagram in Fig. 4A, the steady state is unstable for $\tau = 16$. Fig. 5A shows that both price and market fraction fluctuate periodically. It shows that, when the fundamental steady state becomes unstable, the market fractions tend to stay away from the steady state market fraction level most of the time and a mean of n_f below 0.5 clearly indicates the dominance of the trend following strategy. To examine the effect of population evolution, we compare the case without switching $\beta = 0$ to the case with switching $\beta \neq 0$. Fig. 5A clearly shows that the evolution of population increases the fluctuations in both price and market fraction.

For the stochastic model with a random walk fundamental price process, Fig. 5B demonstrates that the market price follows the fundamental price closely when $\tau = 3$, while Fig. 5C illustrates that the market price fluctuates around the fundamental price in cyclical fashion for $\tau = 16$. To examine the effect of population evolution, we compare the case without switching $\beta = 0$ to the case with switching $\beta \neq 0$. Fig. 5B shows that the evolution of population has insignificant impact on the price dynamics when the fundamental steady state of the underlying deterministic model is locally stable for $\tau = 3$. However, when the fundamental steady state becomes unstable for $\tau = 16$, the fluctuations in both price and market fraction become more significant. Therefore the stochastic price behavior is underlined by the dynamics of the corresponding deterministic model. He and Li (2012) further explore the potential of the stochastic model in generating volatility clustering and long range dependence in volatility. The underlying mechanism and the interplay between the nonlinear deterministic dynamics and noises are very similar to the discrete-time HAM by He and Li (2007). The framework can be used to study the joint impact of many heterogeneous strategies based on different time horizons of historical prices on market stability.

3.2 PROFITABILITY OF MOMENTUM AND CONTRARIAN STRATEGIES

Momentum and contrarian strategies are widely used by market practitioners to profit from momentum in the short-run and mean-reversion in the long-run in financial markets. Empirical profitability of these strategies based on moving averages with different time horizon of historical prices and different holding period has been extensively investigated in the literature (Lakonishok et al., 1994, Jegadeesh and Titman, 1993, 2001, and Moskowitz et al., 2012).

To explain the profitability and the underlying mechanism of time series momentum and contrarian strategies, He and Li (2015a) propose a continuous-time HAM consisting of fundamental, momentum, and contrarian traders. They develop an intuitive and parsimonious financial market model of heterogeneous agents to study

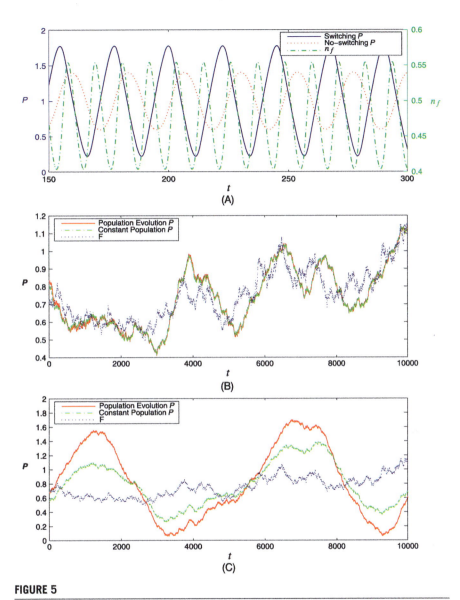

FIGURE 5

Time series of (A) deterministic market price P (solid line) and market fraction $n_f(t)$ of fundamentalists (dotted line) for $\tau = 16$ and stochastic fundamental price (the dotted line) and market price (the solid line) for two delays (B) $\tau = 3$ and (C) $\tau = 16$ with and without switching.

the impact of different time horizons on market price and profitability of fundamental, momentum and contrarian trading strategies. They show that the performance of momentum strategy is determined by the historical time horizon, investment holding period, and market dominance of momentum trading. More specifically, due to price continuity, the price trend based on the moving average of historical prices becomes very significant (apart from over very short time horizon). Therefore, when momentum traders are more active in the market, the price trend becomes very sensitive to the shocks, which is characterized by the destabilizing role of the momentum trading to the market. This provides a profit opportunity for momentum trading with short, not long, holding time horizons. When momentum traders are less active in the market, they always loose. The results provide some insights into the profitability of time series momentum over short, not long, holding periods. We now brief the main results of He and Li (2015a).

Consider a continuous-time model with fundamentalists who trade according to fundamental analysis and momentum and contrarian traders who trade differently based on price trend calculated from moving averages of historical prices over different time horizons. Let $P(t)$ and $F(t)$ denote the log (cum dividend) price and (log) fundamental value[10] of a risky asset at time t, respectively. The fundamental traders buy (sell) the stock when the current price $P(t)$ is below (above) the fundamental value $F(t)$. For simplicity, we assume that the fundamental return follows a pure white noise process $dF(t) = \sigma_F dW_F(t)$ with $F(0) = \bar{F}$, $\sigma_F > 0$, and $W_F(t)$ is a standard Wiener process.

Regarding the momentum and contrarian trading, as in the previous section, we assume that both momentum and contrarian traders trade based on their estimated market price trends, although they behave differently. Momentum traders believe that future market price follows a price trend $u_m(t)$, while contrarians believe that future market price goes opposite to a price trend $u_c(t)$. The price trend used for the momentum traders and contrarians can be different in general. Among various price trends used in practice, the standard moving average (MA) rules with different time horizons are the most popular ones, $u_i(t) = \frac{1}{\tau_i} \int_{t-\tau_i}^{t} P(s)ds$ for $i = m, c$, where the time delay $\tau_i \geq 0$ represents the time horizon of the MA. Assume the excess demand of the momentum traders and contrarians are given, respectively, by $Z_m(t) = g_m(P(t) - u_m(t))$ and $D_c(t) = g_c(u_c(t) - P(t))$, where $g_i(x)$ satisfies $g_i(0) = 0, g_i'(x) > 0, g_i'(0) = \beta_i > 0, x g_i''(x) < 0$ for $x \neq 0$ and $i = m, c$, and parameter β_i represents the extrapolation rate when the market price deviation from the trend is small.

Assume a zero net supply in the risky asset and let α_f, α_m, and α_c be the fixed market population fractions of the fundamental, momentum, and contrarian traders,[11] respectively, with $\alpha_f + \alpha_m + \alpha_c = 1$. Following Beja and Goldman (1980) and Farmer and Joshi (2002), the price $P(t)$ at time t is determined by

$$dP(t) = \mu[\alpha_f Z_f(t) + \alpha_m Z_m(t) + \alpha_c Z_c(t)]dt + \sigma_M dW_M(t), \qquad (13)$$

---

[10]For convenience of return calculations, we use log-price instead of price.

[11]To track the profitability of the trading strategies easily, we do not consider the adaptive evolution of the market fractions.

where $\mu > 0$ represents the speed of the price adjustment of the market maker, $W_M(t)$ is a standard Wiener process, independent of $W_F(t)$, capturing the random demand of either noise or liquidity traders, and $\sigma_M \geq 0$ is constant.

By assuming a constant fundamental price $F(t) \equiv \bar{F}$ and no market noise $\sigma_M = 0$, system (13) becomes a deterministic delay integro-differential equation,

$$\frac{dP(t)}{dt} = \mu\Big[\alpha_f \beta_f\big(\bar{F} - P(t)\big) + \alpha_m \tanh\Big(\beta_m\Big(P(t) - \frac{1}{\tau_m}\int_{t-\tau_m}^t P(s)ds\Big)\Big)$$

$$+ \alpha_c \tanh\Big(-\beta_c\Big(P(t) - \frac{1}{\tau_c}\int_{t-\tau_c}^t P(s)ds\Big)\Big)\Big]. \tag{14}$$

It is easy to see that $P(t) = \bar{F}$, the *fundamental steady state*, is the unique steady state price of system (14). He and Li (2015a) examine different role of the time horizon used in the MA by either the contrarians or momentum traders. When both strategies are employed in the market, the market stability of system (14) can be characterized by the following proposition.

Proposition 3.1. *If $\tau_m = \tau_c = \tau$, then the fundamental steady state price $P = \bar{F}$ of system (14) is*

1. *locally stable for all $\tau \geq 0$ when $\gamma_m < \gamma_c + \gamma_f/(1+a)$;*
2. *locally stable for either $0 \leq \tau < \tau_l^*$ or $\tau > \tau_h^*$ and unstable for $\tau_l^* < \tau < \tau_h^*$ when $\gamma_c + \gamma_f/(1+a) \leq \gamma_m \leq \gamma_c + \gamma_f$; and*
3. *locally stable for $\tau < \tau_l^*$ and unstable for $\tau > \tau_l^*$ when $\gamma_m > \gamma_c + \gamma_f$.*

Here $\tau_1^* = 2(\gamma_m - \gamma_c)/(\gamma_f - \gamma_m + \gamma_c)^2$, and $\tau_l^*(< \tau_1^*)$ and $\tau_h^*(\in (\tau_l^*, \tau_1^*))$ are the minimum and maximum positive roots, respectively, of the equation

$$\frac{\tau}{\gamma_m - \gamma_c}(\gamma_f - \gamma_m + \gamma_c)^2 - \cos\Big[\sqrt{2(\gamma_m - \gamma_c)\tau - (\gamma_f - \gamma_m + \gamma_c)^2\tau^2}\Big] - 1 = 0.$$

The three conditions (1) $\gamma_m < \gamma_c + \frac{\gamma_f}{1+a}$, (2) $\gamma_c + \frac{\gamma_f}{1+a} \leq \gamma_m \leq \gamma_c + \gamma_f$, and (3) $\gamma_m > \gamma_c + \gamma_f$ in Proposition 3.1 characterize three different states of market stability, having different implications to the profitability of momentum trading. For convenience, market state k is referred to condition (k) for $k = 1, 2, 3$ in the following discussion. Numerical analysis shows that for market state 1, the fundamental price is locally stable, independent of the time horizon; for market state 2, the fundamental price is locally stable when $\tau \in [0, \tau_l^*) \cup (\tau_h^*, \infty)$ and becomes unstable when $\tau \in (\tau_l^*, \tau_h^*)$ (the stability switches twice); while for market state 3, the first (Hopf bifurcation) value $\tau_l^*(\approx 0.22)$ leads to stable limit cycles for $\tau > \tau_l^*$ (the stability switches only once at τ_l^*).

The profitability of different strategies based on the stochastic model is closely related to the market states and holding period. In market state 1, the market is dominated jointly by the fundamental and contrarian traders (so that $\gamma_m < \gamma_c + \gamma_f/(1+a)$). In this case, the stability of the fundamental price of the underlying deterministic model is independent of the time horizon. Monte Carlo simulations show

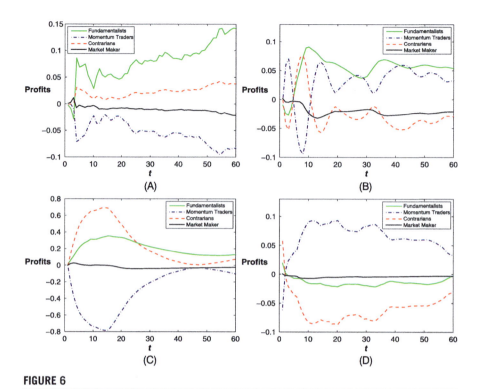

FIGURE 6

The average accumulated profits based on a typical simulation with different time horizon τ and holding period h in different market state: (A) $\tau = h = 0.5$ in market state 2; (B) $\tau = h = 0.5$ in market state 3; (C) $\tau = h = 3$ in market state 3; and (D) $\tau = 3$, $h = 0.5$ in market state 3. Here $\gamma_f = 20$, $\gamma_m = 22.6$, and $\gamma_c = 5$ in (A) and $\gamma_f = 2$, $\gamma_m = 20$, and $\gamma_c = 10$ in (B)–(D).

that the contrarian and fundamental strategies are profitable, but not the momentum strategy and the market maker, underlined by significant and negative ACs for small lags and insignificant ACs for large lags. This corresponds to market overreaction in short-run and hence the fundamental and contrarian trading can generate significant profits. Without under-reaction in this case, the momentum trading is not profitable.

In market state 2, the momentum traders are active, but their activities are balanced by the fundamental and contrarian traders. In this case, the fundamental and contrarian trading strategies are still profitable, but not the momentum traders and the market maker. This is illustrated by the average accumulated profits based on a typical simulation with time horizon $\tau = 0.5$ and holding period $h = 2$ in Fig. 6A. The return ACs based on Monte Carlo simulation show some significantly negative ACs over short lags, indicating the profitability of the fundamental and contrarian trading due to market overreaction, but not for the momentum trading.

In market state 3, the market is dominated by the momentum traders and their destabilizing role. Over short time horizon, the market price fluctuates due to the unstable fundamental price of the underlying deterministic system. When the market price increases, the price trend follows the market price closely and increases too. The momentum trading with short holding period hence becomes profitable by taking long positions. Similarly, when the market price declines, the price trend follows and hence the momentum trading with short holding period is profitable by taking short positions. Therefore, the momentum trading strategies are profitable, but not the contrarians, illustrated by Fig. 6B for $\tau = h = 0.5$ and Fig. 6C for $\tau = h = 3$ respectively. Over long time horizon, the market price fluctuates widely due to the unstable fundamental value of the underlying deterministic system. A longer time horizon makes the price trend less sensitive to the changes in price and the shocks. The dominance of the momentum trading and market price continuation make the momentum trading with short holding period more profitable, illustrated by Fig. 6D for $\tau = 3$ and $h = 0.5$. With long holding period, the momentum trading mis-matches the profitability opportunity and hence becomes less profitable. With long time horizon and long holding period, Fig. 6C also illustrates that the fundamental and contrarian strategies are profitable, but not the momentum strategy. For time horizon and holding period from 1 to 60 months, the model is able to replicate the time series momentum profit explored for the S&P 500. The results are consistent with Moskowitz et al. (2012) who find that the time series momentum strategy with 12 months horizon and one month holding is the most profitable among others.

In summary, the stochastic delay integro-differential system of the model provides a unified approach to deal with different time horizons of momentum and contrarian strategies. The profitability is closely related to the market states defined by the stability of the underlying deterministic model. In particular, in market state 3 where the momentum traders dominate the market, the momentum strategy is profitable with short, but not long, holding periods. Some explanations to the mechanism of the profitability through autocorrelation patterns and the under-reaction and overreaction hypotheses are also provided in He and Li (2015a).

3.3 OPTIMAL TRADING WITH TIME SERIES MOMENTUM AND REVERSAL

Short-run momentum and long-run reversal are two of the most prominent financial market anomalies. Though market timing opportunities under mean reversion in equity return are well documented (Campbell and Viceira, 1999 and Wachter, 2002), time series momentum (TSM) has been explored recently in Moskowitz et al. (2012). Intuitively, if we incorporate both return momentum and reversal into a trading strategy optimally, we would expect to outperform the strategies based only on return momentum or reversal, and even the market index. To capture this intuition, He et al. (2018) develop a continuous-time asset price model, derive an optimal investment strategy theoretically, and test the strategy empirically. They show that, by combining market fundamentals and timing opportunity with respect to market trend and volatility, the optimal strategy based on the time series momentum and reversal significantly outperforms, both in-sample and out-of-sample, the S&P 500 and pure strategies based on either time series momentum or reversal only. We now outline the main results and refer the details to He et al. (2018).

Consider a financial market with two tradable securities. A riskless asset B satisfies $dB_t/B_t = rdt$ with a constant risk-free rate r. The risky asset S_t satisfies

$$dS_t/S_t = [\phi m_t + (1-\phi)\mu_t]dt + \sigma_S'dZ_t, \qquad d\mu_t = \alpha(\bar{\mu} - \mu_t)dt + \sigma_\mu'dZ_t,$$

where $\alpha > 0$, $\bar{\mu} > 0$, and $m_t = (1/\tau)\int_{t-\tau}^t \frac{dS_u}{S_u}$. Here ϕ is a constant, $\bar{\mu}$ is the constant long-run expected return, α measures the speed of the convergence of μ_t to $\bar{\mu}$, σ_S and σ_μ' are two-dimensional volatility vectors, and Z_t is a two-dimensional vector of independent Brownian motions. Therefore, the expected return is given by a combination of a momentum component m_t based on a moving average of the past returns and a long-run mean-reversion component μ_t based on market fundamentals such as dividend yield.

Consider a typical long-term investor who maximizes the expected log utility of terminal wealth at time $T(>t)$. Let W_t be the wealth of the investor at time t and π_t be the fraction of the wealth invested in the stock. Then

$$\frac{dW_t}{W_t} = (\pi_t[\phi m_t + (1-\phi)\mu_t - r] + r)dt + \pi_t\sigma_S'dZ_t. \qquad (15)$$

By applying the maximum principle for optimal control of stochastic delay differential equations, He et al. (2018) derive the optimal investment strategy

$$\pi_t^* = \frac{\phi m_t + (1-\phi)\mu_t - r}{\sigma_S'\sigma_S}. \qquad (16)$$

That is, by taking into account the short-run momentum and long-run reversal, as well as the timing opportunity with respect to market trend and volatility, a weighted average of the momentum and mean-reverting strategies is optimal.

This result has a number of implications. (i) When the asset price follows a geometric Brownian motion process with mean-reversion drift μ_t, namely $\phi = 0$, the optimal investment strategy (16) becomes $\pi_t^* = \frac{\mu_t - r}{\sigma_S'\sigma_S}$. This is the optimal investment strategy with mean-reverting returns obtained in the literature (Campbell and Viceira, 1999 and Wachter, 2002). In particular, when $\mu_t = \bar{\mu}$ is a constant, the optimal portfolio collapses to the optimal portfolio of Merton (1971). (ii) When the asset return depends only on the momentum, namely $\phi = 1$, the optimal portfolio (16) reduces to $\pi_t^* = \frac{m_t - r}{\sigma_S'\sigma_S}$. If we consider a trading strategy based on the trading signal indicated by the excess moving average return $m_t - r$ only, with $\tau = 12$ months, the strategy of long/short when the trading signal is positive/negative is consistent with the TSM strategy used in Moskowitz et al. (2012). Therefore, if we only take fixed long/short positions and construct simple buy-and-hold momentum strategies over a large range of look-back and holding periods, the TSM strategy of Moskowitz et al. (2012) can be optimal when the mean reversion is not significant in financial markets.

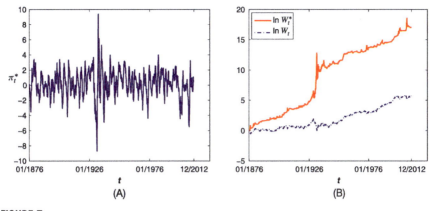

FIGURE 7

Time series of the optimal portfolio (A) and the utility (B) of the optimal portfolio wealth ($\ln W_t^*$) from January 1876 until December 2012 for $\tau = 12$.

He et al. (2018) then examine the performance of the optimal portfolio in terms of the utility of the portfolio wealth empirically. As a benchmark, the log utility of $1 investment in the S&P 500 index from January 1876 grows to 5.765 at December 2012. With a time horizon of $\tau = 12$ and one month holding period, the optimal portfolio wealth fractions and the evolution of the utility of the optimal portfolio wealth ($\ln W_t^*$) based on the estimated model from January 1876 to December 2012 are plotted in Fig. 7A and B, showing that the optimal portfolios outperform the market index measured by the utility of wealth ($\ln W_t$).

4 HAMS OF MULTI-ASSET MARKETS AND FINANCIAL MARKET INTERLINKAGES

A recent literature has been developed to understand the joint dynamics of multiple asset markets from the viewpoint of HAMs. In particular, research in this area investigates how investors' heterogeneity and changing behavior (including dynamic strategy and market selection) affect the comovement of prices, returns and volatilities in a multiple-asset framework. Modeling such interlinkages naturally introduces additional nonlinearities into HAMs and has the potential to address key issues in financial markets.

4.1 STOCK MARKET COMOVEMENT AND POLICY IMPLICATIONS

A number of models extend the single-risky asset frameworks of Brock and Hommes (1998), Chiarella and He (2002), and Westerhoff (2003) to allow agents to switch not only across strategies but also across different asset markets. Westerhoff (2004) provides one of the first HAMs of interconnected financial markets in which both fundamentalists and chartists are simultaneously active. In each market, chartist demand is positively related to the observed price trends but negatively related to the risk of being caught in a bursting bubble. Asset prices react to the excess demand according to a log-linear price impact function. Chartists may switch between markets depending on short-run profit opportunities. The basic model of interacting agents and markets can naturally produce complex dynamics. A simple stochastic extension of the model can mimic the behavior of actual asset markets closely, offering an explanation for the high degree of stock price comovements observed empirically.

Westerhoff and Dieci (2006) extend the basic framework of Westerhoff (2004) to investigate the effect of transaction taxes when speculators can trade in two markets, and the related issue of regulatory coordination. The market fractions of fundamentalists and chartists active in each market evolve depending on the realized profitability of each 'rule-market' combination, which is affected by the adoption of transaction taxes. Log-price adjustments depend on excess demand and are subject to i.i.d. random noise (uncorrelated across markets). The joint dynamics of the two markets is investigated with and without transaction taxes. Moreover, the effectiveness[12] of transaction taxes is assessed when tax is imposed in one market only and when uniform transaction taxes are imposed in both markets. It turns out that, while the market subject to a transaction tax becomes less distorted and less volatile, the other market may be destabilized. On the contrary, a uniform transaction tax tends to stabilize, by forcing agents to focus more strongly on fundamentals.

Building on the above frameworks, Schmitt and Westerhoff (2014) focus on co-evolving stock prices in international stock markets. In their model, the demand of heterogeneous speculators is subject to different types of exogenous shocks (global shocks and shocks specific to markets or to trading rules). Investors switch between strategies and between markets depending on a number of behavioral factors and market circumstances. Besides reproducing a large number of statistical properties of stock markets ('stylized facts'), the model shows how traders' behavior can amplify financial market interlinkages and generate stock price comovements and cross-correlations of volatilities.

Other recent papers are closely related to the above topics. For instance, Huang and Chen (2014) develop a nonlinear model with chartists and fundamentalists that generalizes the framework of Day and Huang (1990) to the case of two regional stock markets with a common currency, in order to investigate the global effects of financial market integration and of possible stabilization policies. In an agent-based model where portfolio managers allocate their funds between two asset markets, Feldman (2010) shows how fund managers' aggregate behavior can undermine global financial stability, whenever they enter the markets in large numbers, their leverage increases and their investment strategies are affected by behavioral factors (such as loss aversion). Overall, such models demonstrate the potential of HAMs for understanding the global effects of financial market interlinkages.

---

[12]Effectiveness refers to the ability of transaction taxes to reduce volatility, distortion (i.e. misalignment from the fundamental price), and weight of chartism.

4.2 HETEROGENEOUS BELIEFS AND EVOLUTIONARY CAPM

A further strand of research investigates the impact of behavioral heterogeneity in an evolutionary CAPM framework. More precisely, this literature adopts standard mean-variance portfolio selection across multiple assets (or asset classes/markets) and develops a dynamic CAPM framework with fundamental and technical traders. Investors update their beliefs about the means, variances and covariances of the prices or returns of the risky assets, based on fundamental information and historical prices. They may either use fixed rules (Chiarella et al., 2007, 2013a) or switch between different strategies based on their performance (Chiarella et al., 2013b). This framework is helpful to understand how investors' behavior can produce changes of the market portfolio and spillovers of volatility and correlation across markets. In particular, through the construction of a *consensus belief*, Chiarella et al. (2013b) develop a dynamic CAPM relationship between the market-average expected returns of the risky assets and their ex-ante betas in temporary equilibrium. Results show that systematic changes in the market portfolio and risk-return relationships may occur due to changes of investor sentiment (such as chartists acting more strongly as momentum traders). Besides providing behavioral explanations for the debated on *time-varying betas*, such models allow to compare theoretical ex-ante betas to commonly used ex-post beta estimates based on rolling-windows. The remainder of this section presents the model setup and key findings of Chiarella et al. (2013b).

4.2.1 A Dynamic Multi-Asset Model

Consider an economy with H agent-types, indexed by $h = 1, \cdots, H$, where the agents within the same group are homogeneous in their beliefs and risk aversion. Agents invest in portfolios of a riskless asset (with a risk-free gross return $R_f = 1 + r_f$) and N risky assets, indexed by $j = 1, \cdots, N$ (with $N \geq 1$). Vectors $\mathbf{p}_t = (p_{1,t}, \cdots, p_{N,t})^\top$, $\mathbf{d}_t = (d_{1,t}, \cdots, d_{N,t})^\top$, and $\mathbf{x}_t := \mathbf{p}_t + \mathbf{d}_t$ denote prices, dividends, and payoffs of the risky assets at time t. Assume that an agent of type h maximizes expected CARA utility, $u_h(w) = -e^{-\theta_h w}$, of one-period-ahead wealth, where θ_h is the agent's absolute risk aversion coefficient. Then the optimal demand for the risky assets (in terms of number of shares) is determined as the N-dimensional vector $\mathbf{z}_{h,t} = \theta_h^{-1} \mathbf{\Omega}_{h,t}^{-1} [E_{h,t}(\mathbf{x}_{t+1}) - R_f \mathbf{p}_t]$, where $E_{h,t}(\mathbf{x}_{t+1})$ and $\mathbf{\Omega}_{h,t} = [Cov_{h,t}(x_{j,t+1}, x_{k,t+1})]_{N \times N}$ are the subjective conditional expectation and variance-covariance matrix of the risky payoffs. Moreover, denote by $n_{h,t}$ the market fraction of agents of type h at time t. Market clearing requires:

$$\sum_{h=1}^{H} n_{h,t} \mathbf{z}_{h,t} = \sum_{h=1}^{H} n_{h,t} \theta_h^{-1} \mathbf{\Omega}_{h,t}^{-1} [E_{h,t}(\mathbf{x}_{t+1}) - R_f \mathbf{p}_t] = \mathbf{z}_t^s, \qquad (17)$$

where $\mathbf{z}_t^s = \mathbf{s} + \boldsymbol{\xi}_t$ is a N-dimensional supply vector of the risky assets, subject to random supply shocks satisfying $\boldsymbol{\xi}_t = \boldsymbol{\xi}_{t-1} + \sigma_\kappa \boldsymbol{\kappa}_t$, where $\boldsymbol{\kappa}_t$ is standard normal i.i.d. with $E(\boldsymbol{\kappa}_t) = \mathbf{0}$, $Cov(\boldsymbol{\kappa}_t) = \mathbf{I}$. Likewise, dividends $\mathbf{d}_t$ are assumed to follow a N-dimensional martingale process, $\mathbf{d}_t = \mathbf{d}_{t-1} + \sigma_\zeta \boldsymbol{\zeta}_t$, where $\boldsymbol{\zeta}_t$ is standard normal i.i.d. with $E(\zeta_t) = \mathbf{0}$, $Cov(\zeta_t) = \mathbf{I}$, independent of κ_t.[13] In spite of heterogeneous beliefs about asset prices, conditional beliefs about dividends are assumed to be homogeneous across agents and correct.

4.2.2 Price Dynamics Under Consensus Belief

Solving Eq. (17) one obtains the temporary equilibrium asset prices, $\mathbf{p}_t$, as functions of the beliefs, risk attitudes, and current market proportions of the H agent-types. The solution can be rewritten as if prices were determined by a homogeneous agent endowed with average risk aversion $\theta_{a,t} := (\sum_{h=1}^{H} n_{h,t}\theta_h^{-1})^{-1}$ and a 'consensus' belief about the conditional first and second moments of the payoff process, $\{E_{a,t}, \Omega_{a,t}\}$, where

$$\Omega_{a,t} = \theta_{a,t}^{-1}\left(\sum_{h=1}^{H} n_{h,t}\theta_h^{-1}\Omega_{h,t}^{-1}\right)^{-1},$$

$$E_{a,t}(\mathbf{x}_{t+1}) = \theta_{a,t}\Omega_{a,t}\sum_{h=1}^{H} n_{h,t}\theta_h^{-1}\Omega_{h,t}^{-1}E_{h,t}(\mathbf{x}_{t+1}).$$

From (17) and the assumption of homogeneous and correct beliefs *about dividends*, one obtains

$$\mathbf{p}_t = \frac{1}{R_f}\left[E_{a,t}(\mathbf{p}_{t+1}) + \mathbf{d}_t - \theta_{a,t}\Omega_{a,t}\mathbf{z}_t^s\right]. \tag{18}$$

Eq. (18) represents $\mathbf{p}_t$ in a standard way as the discounted value of the expected end-of-period payoffs. The adjustment for the risk takes place through a negative correction to the dividends. The equilibrium prices decrease with the discount rate and increase with the expectations of future prices and dividends (other things being equal), whereas they tend to be negatively affected by risk aversion, risk perceptions, and the supply of assets.

4.2.3 Fitness and Strategy Switching

Based on the discrete choice model adopted in HAMs, the fraction $n_{h,t}$ of agents of type h depends on their strategy's fitness $v_{h,t-1}$, namely, $n_{h,t} = e^{\eta v_{h,t-1}}/Z_t$, where $Z_t = \sum_h e^{\eta v_{h,t-1}}$ and $\eta > 0$ is the intensity of choice. The fitness is specified as $v_{h,t} = \pi_{h,t} - \pi_{h,t}^B - C_h$, where $C_h \geq 0$ measures the cost of the strategy, and

$$\pi_{h,t} := \mathbf{z}_{h,t-1}^{\top}(\mathbf{p}_t + \mathbf{d}_t - R_f\mathbf{p}_{t-1}) - \frac{\theta_h}{2}\mathbf{z}_{h,t-1}^{\top}\Omega_{h,t-1}\mathbf{z}_{h,t-1}, \tag{19}$$

$$\pi_{h,t}^B := \left(\frac{\theta_{a,t-1}}{\theta_h}\mathbf{s}\right)^{\top}(\mathbf{p}_t + \mathbf{d}_t - R_f\mathbf{p}_{t-1}) - \frac{\theta_h}{2}\left(\frac{\theta_{a,t-1}}{\theta_h}\mathbf{s}\right)^{\top}\Omega_{h,t-1}\left(\frac{\theta_{a,t-1}}{\theta_h}\mathbf{s}\right). \tag{20}$$

---

[13] Matrix σ_ζ is not necessarily diagonal; that is, the exogenous dividend processes may be correlated across assets. The same holds for matrix σ_κ, characterizing the supply process.

This performance measure generalizes the risk-adjusted profit introduced by Hommes (2001) represented by (19).[14] It views strategy h as a successful strategy only to the extent that portfolio $\mathbf{z}_{h,t-1}$ outperforms (in terms of risk-adjusted profitability) portfolio $\mathbf{z}_{h,t-1}^B := \frac{\theta_{a,t-1}}{\theta_h}\mathbf{s}$. The latter can be naturally interpreted as a 'benchmark' portfolio for type-h agents, based on their risk aversion θ_h.[15] Moreover, as shown in Chiarella et al. (2013b), the fitness measure $v_{h,t}$ is not affected by the differences in risk aversion across agents.

4.2.4 Fundamentalists and Trend Followers

In particular, the model focuses on the interplay of fundamentalists and trend followers, indexed by $h \in \{f, c\}$, respectively. Based on their beliefs in mean reversion, the price expectations of the fundamentalists are specified as $E_{f,t}(\mathbf{p}_{t+1}) = \mathbf{p}_{t-1} + \boldsymbol{\alpha}(E_{f,t}(\mathbf{p}_{t+1}^*) - \mathbf{p}_{t-1})$, where $\mathbf{p}_t^* = (p_{1,t}^*, \cdots, p_{N,t}^*)$ is the vector of fundamental values at time t, $\boldsymbol{\alpha} := diag[\alpha_1, \cdots, \alpha_N]$, and $\alpha_j \in [0, 1]$ reflects their confidence in the fundamental price for asset j. The beliefs of the fundamentalists about the covariance matrix of the payoffs are assumed constant, $\boldsymbol{\Omega}_{f,t} = \boldsymbol{\Omega}_0 := (\sigma_{jk})_{N \times N}$. Fundamental prices $\mathbf{p}_t^*$ are assumed to evolve exogenously as a martingale process, consistent with the assumed dividend and supply processes. Moreover, $\mathbf{p}_t^*$ is also consistent with Eq. (18) under the special case of homogeneous and correct first-moment beliefs, constant risk aversion $\bar{\theta}$, and constant second moment beliefs $\boldsymbol{\Omega}_0$. This results in

$$\mathbf{p}_t^* = \frac{1}{r_f}(\mathbf{d}_t - \bar{\theta}\boldsymbol{\Omega}_0(\mathbf{s} + \boldsymbol{\xi}_t)), \tag{21}$$

which implies $\mathbf{p}_{t+1}^* = \mathbf{p}_t^* + \boldsymbol{\epsilon}_{t+1}$, where $\boldsymbol{\epsilon}_{t+1} := \frac{1}{r_f}(\sigma_\zeta \boldsymbol{\zeta}_{t+1} - \bar{\theta}\boldsymbol{\Omega}_0 \sigma_\kappa \boldsymbol{\kappa}_{t+1}) \sim$ i.i.d. normal. The fundamental price process can be treated as 'steady state' of the dynamic heterogeneous-belief model.

Unlike the fundamentalists, trend followers form their beliefs about price trends based on the observed prices and (exponential) moving averages. Their conditional mean and covariance matrices are assumed to satisfy $E_{c,t}(\mathbf{p}_{t+1}) = \mathbf{p}_{t-1} + \boldsymbol{\gamma}(\mathbf{p}_{t-1} - \mathbf{u}_{t-1})$, $\boldsymbol{\Omega}_{c,t} = \boldsymbol{\Omega}_0 + \lambda \mathbf{V}_{t-1}$, where $\mathbf{u}_{t-1}$ and $\mathbf{V}_{t-1}$ are sample means and covariance matrices of historical prices $\mathbf{p}_{t-1}, \mathbf{p}_{t-2}, \cdots$. Moreover, $\boldsymbol{\gamma} = diag[\gamma_1, \cdots, \gamma_N] > 0$, γ_j measures the 'strength' of extrapolation for asset j, and λ measures the sensitivity of the second-moment estimate to the sample variance. Quantities $\mathbf{u}_t$ and $\mathbf{V}_t$ are updated recursively according to $\mathbf{u}_t = \delta\mathbf{u}_{t-1} + (1 - \delta)\mathbf{p}_t$ and $\mathbf{V}_t = \delta\mathbf{V}_{t-1} + \delta(1 - \delta)(\mathbf{p}_t - \mathbf{u}_{t-1})(\mathbf{p}_t - \mathbf{u}_{t-1})^\top$, where parameter $\delta \in [0, 1]$ is related to the weight of past information.

---

[14]Hommes (2001) considers a simplified case where the stock of the risky asset is endogenous ($\mathbf{z}_t^s \equiv \mathbf{0}$), in which case market clearing leads to $E_{a,t}(\mathbf{x}_{t+1}) = R_f \mathbf{p}_t$ and the performance measure reduces to the risk-adjusted profit (corrected for the strategy cost), $\pi_{h,t} - C_h$.

[15]Benchmark portfolio $\mathbf{z}_{h,t-1}^B$, proportional to the 'market portfolio' $\mathbf{s}$, is more (less) aggressive than the market portfolio iff θ_h is smaller (larger) than the average risk aversion $\theta_{a,t-1}$.

The optimal portfolios of fundamentalists and chartists are then given by, respectively,

$$\mathbf{z}_{f,t} = \theta_f^{-1}\boldsymbol{\Omega}_0^{-1}[\mathbf{p}_{t-1} + \mathbf{d}_t + \alpha(\mathbf{p}_t^* - \mathbf{p}_{t-1}) - R_f\mathbf{p}_t], \tag{22}$$

$$\mathbf{z}_{c,t} = \theta_c^{-1}[\boldsymbol{\Omega}_0 + \lambda\mathbf{V}_{t-1}]^{-1}[\mathbf{p}_{t-1} + \mathbf{d}_t + \gamma(\mathbf{p}_{t-1} - \mathbf{u}_{t-1}) - R_f\mathbf{p}_t]. \tag{23}$$

4.2.5 Dynamic Model and Stability Properties

The stochastic nonlinear multi-asset HAM with two belief-types results in the following recursive equation for asset prices

$$\begin{aligned}
\mathbf{p}_t = \frac{\theta_{a,t}}{R_f}\boldsymbol{\Omega}_{a,t}&\left[\frac{n_{f,t}}{\theta_f}\boldsymbol{\Omega}_0^{-1}\left(\mathbf{p}_{t-1} + \alpha(\mathbf{p}_t^* - \mathbf{p}_{t-1})\right)\right.\\
&\left. + \frac{n_{c,t}}{\theta_c}(\boldsymbol{\Omega}_0 + \lambda\mathbf{V}_{t-1})^{-1}\left(\mathbf{p}_{t-1} + \gamma(\mathbf{p}_{t-1} - \mathbf{u}_{t-1})\right) - \mathbf{s} - \boldsymbol{\xi}_t\right] + \frac{1}{R_f}\mathbf{d}_t, \tag{24}
\end{aligned}$$

where the average risk aversion and second-moment beliefs satisfy $\theta_{a,t} = \left(\frac{n_{f,t}}{\theta_f} + \frac{n_{c,t}}{\theta_c}\right)^{-1}$ and $\boldsymbol{\Omega}_{a,t} = \frac{1}{\theta_{a,t}}\left(\frac{n_{f,t}}{\theta_f}\boldsymbol{\Omega}_0^{-1} + \frac{n_{c,t}}{\theta_c}(\boldsymbol{\Omega}_0 + \lambda\mathbf{V}_{t-1})^{-1}\right)^{-1}$. In (24), market fractions evolve based on performances $v_{f,t-1}$ and $v_{c,t-1}$, as follows:

$$n_{f,t} = \frac{1}{1 + e^{-\eta(v_{f,t-1} - v_{c,t-1})}}, \quad n_{c,t} = 1 - n_{f,t},$$

where

$$\begin{aligned}
v_{f,t} = &\left(\mathbf{z}_{f,t-1} - \frac{\theta_{a,t-1}\mathbf{s}}{\theta_f}\right)^{\top}\left[\mathbf{p}_t + \mathbf{d}_t - R_f\mathbf{p}_{t-1} - \frac{\theta_f}{2}\boldsymbol{\Omega}_0\left(\mathbf{z}_{f,t-1} + \frac{\theta_{a,t-1}\mathbf{s}}{\theta_f}\right)\right]\\
&- C_f,
\end{aligned}$$

$$\begin{aligned}
v_{c,t} = &\left(\mathbf{z}_{c,t-1} - \frac{\theta_{a,t-1}\mathbf{s}}{\theta_c}\right)^{\top}\\
&\times\left[\mathbf{p}_t + \mathbf{d}_t - R_f\mathbf{p}_{t-1} - \frac{\theta_c}{2}(\boldsymbol{\Omega}_0 + \lambda\mathbf{V}_{t-2})\left(\mathbf{z}_{c,t-1} + \frac{\theta_{a,t-1}\mathbf{s}}{\theta_c}\right)\right] - C_c,
\end{aligned}$$

and $C_f \geq C_c \geq 0$.

Despite the large dimension of the dynamical system, insightful analytical results about the steady state and its stability properties are possible for the 'deterministic skeleton', obtained by setting the supply and dividends at their unconditional mean levels $\boldsymbol{\xi}_t = 0$, $\mathbf{d}_t = \bar{\mathbf{d}}$. The model admits a unique steady state[16] $(\mathbf{p}_t, \mathbf{u}_t, \mathbf{V}_t, n_{f,t}) = (\mathbf{p}^*, \mathbf{p}^*, \mathbf{0}, n_f^*) := \mathbf{F}^*$, where $\mathbf{p}^* = \frac{1}{r_f}(\bar{\mathbf{d}} - \theta_a^*\boldsymbol{\Omega}_0\mathbf{s})$ is the fundamental price vector of

---

[16]For consistency between the model's unique steady state and the fundamental price, we set $\bar{\theta} = \theta_a^*$ in Eq. (21).

the deterministic system, $\theta_a^* = 1/(n_f^*/\theta_f + n_c^*/\theta_c)$ is the average risk aversion and $n_f^* = 1/(1 + e^{\eta(C_f - C_c)})$, $n_c^* = 1 - n_f^*$ are the market fractions of the fundamentalist and chartist, respectively, at the steady state. It turns out that the local stability of $\mathbf{F}^*$ is based on clear-cut and intuitive analytical relationships between chartist extrapolation and memory, fundamentalist confidence, and switching intensity. We set $\theta_0 := \theta_f/\theta_c$, $C_\Delta := C_f - C_c$, and denote by $J_o \subseteq \{1, \cdots, N\}$ the subset of assets characterized by 'sufficiently' strong extrapolation from the chartists, namely, by $\gamma_j > R_f/\delta - 1$. In the typical case $C_\Delta > 0$, the local stability results can be summarized as follows:

(i) If the chartist extrapolation is not very strong in general (namely, $\gamma_j \leq R_f/\delta - 1$ for all $j \in \{1, \cdots, N\}$), the steady state $\mathbf{F}^*$ is locally stable for any level of the switching intensity η;

(ii) If chartist extrapolation is sufficiently strong for some (possibly for all) assets ($J_o \neq \emptyset$), then $\mathbf{F}^*$ is locally stable when the switching intensity is not too strong, namely $\eta < \widehat{\eta}_m := \min_{j \in J_o} \widehat{\eta}_j$, where $\widehat{\eta}_j$ for asset j is defined by

$$\widehat{\eta}_j := \frac{1}{C_\Delta} \ln \frac{R_f - \delta(1 - \alpha_j)}{\theta_0[\delta(1 + \gamma_j) - R_f]}. \tag{25}$$

Moreover, for increasing switching intensity $\mathbf{F}^*$ undergoes a Neimark–Sacker bifurcation at $\eta = \widehat{\eta}_m$.

Roughly speaking, investors' switching intensity η is not sufficient, *per se*, to destabilize the steady state $\mathbf{F}^*$ (case (i)), but the possibility that investors' behavior destabilizes the system depends on the joint effect of the switching intensity η and the chartists' strengths of extrapolation γ_j, $j = 1, 2, \ldots, N$. In case (ii), the threshold $\widehat{\eta}_j$ is determined for each asset according to (25), depending, amongst others, negatively on γ_j and positively on α_j. Hence, even when chartist extrapolation is strong enough for some asset j (so that $\gamma_j > R_f/\delta - 1$), the system can still be stable when the fundamentalists dominate the market at the steady state and the switching intensity is not too large. Conversely, since the stability depends on the lowest threshold amongst assets ($\widehat{\eta}_m$), a large extrapolation on one or few assets is sufficient for the whole system to be eventually destabilized for large enough η. Numerical investigations confirm that, by increasing η in case (ii), fluctuations are initially 'confined' to the asset with the lowest $\widehat{\eta}_j$ and then spill over to the whole system of interconnected assets. As for the 'non asset-specific' parameters, the above results show that increases in δ, C_f, and θ_f (respectively R_f, C_c, and θ_c) tend to reduce (respectively to increase) all thresholds $\widehat{\eta}_j$, $j = 1, 2, \ldots, N$. In particular, larger values of the ratio $\theta_0 = \theta_f/\theta_c$ of the fundamentalist and chartist risk aversion and of the strategy cost differential $C_\Delta = C_f - C_c$ reduce the stability domain, whereas a larger risk-free return R_f or a faster decay in chartist moving averages (i.e. a smaller δ) widens the stability domain.

4.2.6 Nonlinear Risk-Return Patterns

Further results concern the impact of the dynamic correlation structure on the global properties of the stochastic model. Although the *levels* of the fundamental prices do depend on the 'exogenous' subjective beliefs about variances and covariances, Ω_0, such beliefs have no influence on the *local stability* properties.[17] However, second-moment beliefs and their evolution turn out to be very important for the dynamics of the nonlinear system buffeted by exogenous noise. The nonlinear stochastic model is characterized by emerging patterns and systematic changes in risk-return relationships that can by no means be explained by the linearized model. One important example concerns the nonlinear stochastic nature of the time-varying *ex-ante* beta coefficients implied by the model (based on the consensus beliefs), and of the realized betas, estimated using rolling windows.[18] The value at time t and the payoff at time $t+1$ of the market portfolio are given by $W_{m,t} = \mathbf{p}_t^\top \mathbf{s}$ and $W_{m,t+1} = \mathbf{x}_{t+1}^\top \mathbf{s}$, respectively, while $r_{j,t+1} = x_{j,t+1}/p_{j,t} - 1$, $r_{m,t+1} = W_{m,t+1}/W_{m,t} - 1$ represent the returns of risky asset j and of the market portfolio, respectively. Hence, under the consensus belief, $E_{a,t}(W_{m,t+1}) = E_{a,t}(\mathbf{x}_{t+1})^\top \mathbf{s}$, $Var_{a,t}(W_{m,t+1}) = \mathbf{s}^\top \Omega_{a,t} \mathbf{s}$, $E_{a,t}(r_{j,t+1}) = \frac{E_{a,t}(x_{j,t+1})}{p_{j,t}} - 1$, $E_{a,t}(r_{m,t+1}) = \frac{E_{a,t}(W_{m,t+1})}{W_{m,t}} - 1$. Following Chiarella et al. (2011), one obtains the CAPM-like return relation[19]

$$E_{a,t}(\mathbf{r}_{t+1}) - r_f \mathbf{1} = \boldsymbol{\beta}_{a,t}[E_{a,t}(r_{m,t+1}) - r_f], \qquad (26)$$

where $\mathbf{r}_{t+1}$ is the vector collecting the risky returns and $\boldsymbol{\beta}_{a,t} = (\beta_{1,t}, \cdots, \beta_{N,t})^\top$, $\beta_{j,t} = \frac{Cov_{a,t}(r_{m,t+1}, r_{j,t+1})}{Var_{a,t}(r_{m,t+1})}$ are the *ex-ante* beta coefficients, in the sense that they reflect the temporary market equilibrium condition under the consensus beliefs $E_{a,t}$ and $\Omega_{a,t}$. In the case of two risky assets, Fig. 8 (from the top-left to bottom-right) shows the time series of asset prices ($\mathbf{p}_t$), asset returns ($\mathbf{r}_t$), the aggregate wealth shares invested in the risky assets (i.e. the market portfolio weights, denoted as $\boldsymbol{\omega}_t := (\omega_{1,t}, \omega_{2,t})^\top$), the ex-ante betas of the risky assets under the consensus belief ($\boldsymbol{\beta}_{a,t}$), and the estimates of the betas using rolling windows of 100 and of 300 periods.[20] In particular, the variation of the ex-ante beta coefficients is significant and

---

[17] Note that the threshold (25) for asset j is independent of the parameters specific to any other asset, since the fitness measure and the variance-covariance matrices are in higher order terms. They can affect the nonlinear dynamics, but not the dynamics of the linearized system.

[18] A large literature on time-varying betas has been developed within the conditional CAPM, which proves successful in explaining the cross-section of returns and a number of empirical 'anomalies' (see, e.g. Jagannathan and Wang, 1996). However, most models of the time-varying betas are motivated by econometric estimation and generally lack economic intuition.

[19] The CAPM relation (26) is *evolutionary*, since asset and market returns, as well as the corresponding consensus beliefs, co-evolve endogenously, based on the dynamic HAM with expectations feedback.

[20] The parameter used in Fig. 8 are $\theta_f = \theta_c = 1$, $C_f = 4$, $C_c = 1$, $\gamma = diag[0.3, 0.3]$, $\alpha = diag[0.4, 0.5]$, $\lambda = 1.5$, $\delta = 0.98$, $\eta = 1.5$, $\mathbf{s} = (0.1, 0.1)^\top$, $r_f := R_f - 1 = 0.025$, $\bar{d} = (0.08, 0.05)^\top$, $\Omega_0 = [\sigma_1^2, \rho\sigma_1\sigma_2; \rho\sigma_1\sigma_2, \sigma_2^2]$, where $\sigma_1 = 0.6$, $\sigma_2 = 0.4$, $\rho = 0.5$. Parameters r_f, Ω_0, α, γ, δ, $\bar{d}$, C_f, and C_c are expressed in annual terms and converted to monthly via the factor $1/12$ (δ is converted to a monthly

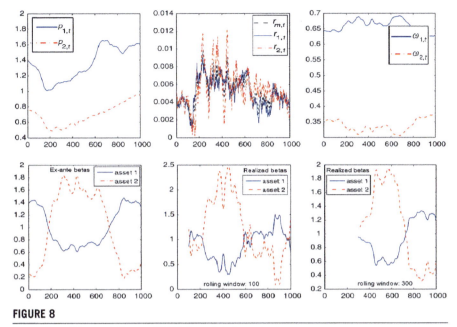

FIGURE 8

Dynamics of the evolutionary CAPM (monthly time step).

seems to indicate substantially different levels over different subperiods. Although the rolling estimates of the betas do not necessarily reflect the nature of the ex-ante betas implied by the CAPM (see also Chiarella et al., 2013a), the 100-period and the (smoother) 300-period rolling betas also reveal systematic changes in risk-return relationships, with patterns similar to the ex-ante betas.

Finally, further numerical results on the relationship between trading volume and volatility indicate that the ACs for both volatility and trading volume are highly significant and decaying over long lags, which is close to what we have observed in financial markets. Moreover, the correlation between price volatility and trading volume of the risky assets is remarkably influenced by the assets' correlation structure.

From a broader perspective, the results described in this section are part of a growing stream of research. They show that asset diversification in a dynamic setting where investors rebalance their portfolios based on heterogeneous strategies and behavioral rules may produce aggregate effects that different substantially from risk reduction and equilibrium risk-return relationships predicted by standard mean-variance analysis and finance theory. Amongst recent work in this area, Brock et al.

---

value of 0.9983, in such a way to preserve the average memory length). Supply and dividend noise parameters are $\sigma_\kappa = diag[0.001, 0.001]$ and $\sigma_\zeta = diag[0.002, 0.002]$. The parameter setting is one where the underlying deterministic model has a stable fundamental steady state, namely, $\eta < \widehat{\eta}_m := \min_{j \in J_o} \widehat{\eta}_j$. When the system is no longer stable due to larger switching intensity η, even stronger effects can be observed.

(2009) show that the introduction of additional hedging instruments in the baseline asset pricing setup of Brock and Hommes (1998) may have destabilizing effects in the presence of heterogeneity and adaptive behavior according to performance-based reinforcement learning. In an evolutionary finance setting that allows for the coexistence of different trading strategies, the stochastic multi-asset model of Anufriev et al. (2012) shows the existence of strong trading-induced excess covariance in equilibrium, which is a key ingredient of systemic risk. Corsi et al. (2016) investigate the dynamic effect of financial innovation and increasing diversification in a model of heterogeneous financial institutions subject to Value-at-Risk constraints. They show that this may lead to systemic instabilities, through increased leverage and overlapping portfolios. Similar channels of contagion and systemic risk in financial networks are investigated by Caccioli et al. (2015).

4.3 INTERACTING STOCK MARKET AND FOREIGN EXCHANGE MARKET

The recent work of Dieci and Westerhoff (2010) and Dieci and Westerhoff (2013b) investigates how the trading activity of foreign-based stock market speculators – who care both about stock returns and exchange rate movements – can affect otherwise independent stock markets denominated in different currencies and the related foreign exchange market. We brief the main findings in the following.

Let us abstract from the impact of international trade on exchange rates, and focus on the sole effect of financial market speculators. For simplicity, let us define *cross-market traders* the investors from one country who are active in the stock market of the other country, in contrast to *home-market traders*.[21] Quantities P_t, Q_t, and S_t denote the price of the domestic asset (in domestic currency), the price of the foreign asset (in foreign currency) and the exchange rate,[22] while P^*, Q^*, and S^* denote their fundamental values, respectively. We use lowercase letters for log-prices p_t, q_t, s_t, p^*, q^*, s^*, respectively.

Exchange rate movements are driven by the excess demand for domestic currency. As such, they are directly affected by foreign exchange speculators, but they also depend, indirectly, on stock transactions of cross-market traders. This is captured by:

$$s_{t+1} - s_t = \alpha_S(U_t + X_t + Y_t), \quad \alpha_S > 0, \tag{27}$$

where (positive or negative) quantities U_t, X_t, and Y_t are different components of the excess demand for *domestic* currency, expressed in currency units. More precisely, U_t is the excess demand for domestic currency due to direct speculation in the foreign exchange market (to be specified later), $X_t := P_t \widetilde{D}_t = \widetilde{D}_t \exp(p_t)$ is the currency

---

[21] In general, we use a 'tilde' to denote demand components and behavioral parameters characterizing cross-market traders, whereas analogous quantities without the tilde be related to home-market traders.

[22] For convenience, we define the exchange rate S as the price of one unit of domestic currency in terms of the foreign currency.

excess demand from foreign traders active in the domestic stock market (and demand-ing/supplying $\widetilde{D}_t$ units of domestic asset), and $Y_t := -Q_t \widetilde{Z}_t / S_t = -\widetilde{Z}_t \exp(q_t - s_t)$ is the excess demand generated by domestic traders active in the foreign stock mar-ket (since $\widetilde{Z}_t$ units of foreign stock correspond to $Q_t \widetilde{Z}_t$ units of foreign currency and thus result in a counter transaction of $-Q_t \widetilde{Z}_t / S_t$ units of domestic currency).

Similar price adjustment mechanisms are assumed for the two stock markets:

$$p_{t+1} - p_t = \alpha_P D_t^E, \quad q_{t+1} - q_t = \alpha_Q Z_t^E, \quad \alpha_P, \alpha_Q > 0 \tag{28}$$

where D_t^E and Z_t^E denote the excess demand for the domestic and foreign stock, respectively, including the components $\widetilde{D}_t$ and $\widetilde{Z}_t$ from cross-market traders, as explained below. In a framework with two agent-types, both D_t^E and Z_t^E can be modeled as the sum of four components, representing the demand of domestic and foreign chartists and fundamentalists. At time t, the excess demand D_t^E for the *do-mestic asset* is given by:

$$D_t^E = \beta(p_t - p_{t-1}) + \theta(p^* - p_t) + \widetilde{D}_t, \tag{29}$$

where $\widetilde{D}_t = \widetilde{\beta}(s_t + p_t - s_{t-1} - p_{t-1}) + \widetilde{\theta}(s^* - s_t + p^* - p_t)$ and $\beta, \theta, \widetilde{\beta}, \widetilde{\theta} \geq 0$. Both $\beta(p_t - p_{t-1})$ and $\theta(p^* - p_t)$ represent the demand from domestic chartists and fundamentalists, based on the observed price trend and the observed mispric-ing, respectively. Similar comments hold for demands $\widetilde{\beta}(s_t + p_t - s_{t-1} - p_{t-1})$ and $\widetilde{\theta}(s^* - s_t + p^* - p_t)$ from foreign chartists and fundamentalists, respectively, which depend also on the observed trend and misalignment of the exchange rate. Symmet-rically, demand Z_t^E for the *foreign asset* is given by:

$$Z_t^E = \gamma(q_t - q_{t-1}) + \psi(q^* - q_t) + \widetilde{Z}_t, \tag{30}$$

where $\widetilde{Z}_t = \widetilde{\gamma}(-s_t + q_t + s_{t-1} - q_{t-1}) + \widetilde{\psi}(-s^* + s_t + q^* - q_t)$ and $\gamma, \psi, \widetilde{\gamma}, \widetilde{\psi} \geq 0$. The four terms $\gamma(q_t - q_{t-1})$, $\psi(q^* - q_t)$, $\widetilde{\gamma}(-s_t + q_t + s_{t-1} - q_{t-1})$ and $\widetilde{\psi}(-s^* + s_t + q^* - q_t)$ represent the demands from foreign chartists, foreign fundamentalists, domestic chartists and domestic fundamentalists, respectively.

Dieci and Westerhoff (2013b) investigate the case without foreign exchange spec-ulators ($U_t \equiv 0$ in Eq. (27)). Even if demand in the stock markets is linear in (log-)prices, the joint dynamics (27)–(30) of the three markets results in a *nonlin-ear* dynamical system, by construction, due to the products, 'price×quantity', which govern the exchange rate dynamics (27).[23] Moreover, although system (27)–(30) is 6-dimensional, analytical stability conditions of the unique 'fundamental' steady state (FSS henceforth)[24] can be derived in the case of *symmetric* markets, namely, $\beta = \gamma$, $\widetilde{\beta} = \widetilde{\gamma}$, $\theta = \psi$, $\widetilde{\theta} = \widetilde{\psi}$, $q^* = p^* + s^*$, thanks to a factorization of the char-acteristic polynomial of the Jacobian matrix at the FSS. This allows an exhaustive

---

[23] Further nonlinearities may result from speculative demand U_t, as shown below.
[24] At the FSS, stock prices and the exchange rate are at their fundamental values.

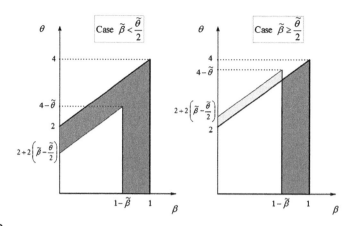

FIGURE 9

Destabilization of two symmetric markets, due to the entry of new cross-market speculators. For parameters (β, θ) in the dark grey region, the markets are stable when considered in isolation, but the system of interacting market has an unstable FSS. Left panel: case $\widetilde{\beta} < \widetilde{\theta}/2$. Right panel: case $\widetilde{\beta} \geq \widetilde{\theta}/2$.

comparison of the stability condition for the integrated system with that of otherwise independent stock markets.

Fig. 9 illustrates the impact of parameters $\widetilde{\beta}$ and $\widetilde{\theta}$ of the cross-market traders on the stability of the steady state of otherwise independent symmetric stock markets. The stability region is represented in the plane of parameters β and θ of home-market traders. In both panels, the area bounded by the axes and by the two (thick) lines of equations $\theta = 2(1 + \beta)$ and $\beta = 1$ is the stability region for isolated symmetric markets, which we denote by S. Therefore, the markets in isolation may become unstable in the presence of sufficiently large chartist extrapolation (β) or fundamentalist reaction (θ) from the home-market traders. If the two markets interact ($\widetilde{\beta}, \widetilde{\theta} \neq 0$), the FSS of the resulting integrated system is unstable for *at least* all the parameter combinations (β, θ) originally in area S and now falling within the dark grey region, say area $\mathcal{R} \subset S$. The shape and extension of area $\mathcal{R}$ depend on the behavioral parameters of the cross-market chartists and fundamentalists, $\widetilde{\beta}$ and $\widetilde{\theta}$. In particular, a larger chartist impact $\widetilde{\beta}$ tends to enlarge area $\mathcal{R}$. The left panel depicts the case $\widetilde{\beta} < \widetilde{\theta}/2$, in which the integration is *always* destabilizing (the new stability area is strictly a subset of the original one). A destabilizing effect prevails also in the opposite case, as shown in the right panel, for $\widetilde{\beta} \geq \widetilde{\theta}/2$. However, in this case there exists a parameter region (light grey area) in which the otherwise unstable isolated markets (due to overreaction of fundamentalists) may be stabilized by strong extrapolation of the cross-market traders.

We may interpret parameters β and θ as proportional to the total number of chartists and fundamentalists trading in their home markets, while $\widetilde{\beta}$ and $\widetilde{\theta}$ represent the number of additional cross-market traders of the two types. From this standpoint, the above results indicate a destabilizing effect of the *market entry* of additional cross-market speculators, once the two stock markets become interconnected. In addition, an even stronger result holds in the case of simple *relocation* of the existing mass of speculators across the markets, namely, the case when the total population of chartists $(\beta + \tilde{\beta})$ and fundamentalists $(\theta + \tilde{\theta})$ remains unchanged, while parameters $\tilde{\beta}$, $\tilde{\theta}$ are increased (and β, θ are decreased accordingly). In this case the stability conditions for the integrated system are definitely more restrictive than for the markets in isolation, as proven in Dieci and Westerhoff (2013b). Further numerical investigations show the robustness of such results to the introduction of asymmetries between the two stock markets.

In a related paper, Dieci and Westerhoff (2010) investigate the case in which instability originates in the foreign exchange market due to speculative currency trading, and then it propagates to the stock markets. Different from Dieci and Westerhoff (2013b), only the fundamental traders are active in the two stock markets, while the foreign exchange market is populated by the speculators who switch between two behavioral rules, based on extrapolative and regressive beliefs, depending on the exchange rate misalignment. Therefore, the general setup (27)–(30) is reduced to a special case where $\beta = \tilde{\beta} = \gamma = \tilde{\gamma} = 0$, whereas currency excess demand U_t is specified as:

$$U_t = n_{c,t} D_{c,t}^{FX} + (1 - n_{c,t}) D_{f,t}^{FX}, \tag{31}$$

$$D_{c,t}^{FX} = \kappa(s_t - s^*), \quad D_{f,t}^{FX} = \varphi(s^* - s_t), \quad n_{c,t} = \left[1 + \nu(s^* - s_t)^2\right]^{-1}, \tag{32}$$

where $\kappa, \varphi, \nu > 0$ and $n_{c,t}$ is the weight of extrapolative beliefs in period t. By Eqs. (31) and (32), chartist and fundamentalist demand are then proportional to the current exchange rate deviation. That is, the chartists believe that the observed misalignment will increase further, whereas the fundamentalists believe that the exchange rate will revert to the fundamental. However, the more the exchange rate deviates from its fundamental value, the more regressive beliefs gain in popularity at the expense of extrapolative beliefs, as speculators perceive the risk that the bull or bear market might collapse. Moreover, the higher parameter ν is in (32), the more sensitive the mass of speculators becomes with regard to a given misalignment.[25] Intuitively, when considered in isolation ($\tilde{\theta} = \tilde{\psi} = 0$), the foreign exchange market is unstable (since the extrapolative beliefs prevail and tend to increase the misalignment if s_t is sufficiently close to s^*), whereas the two stock markets converge to their fundamental prices, thanks to the stabilizing activity of fundamental traders.

Dieci and Westerhoff (2010) investigate the dynamics under market integration, which results in a 3-dimensional nonlinear dynamical system, having two additional non-fundamental steady states (NFSS), beside the FSS. Analytical conditions for the FSS to be locally stable can be derived in terms of the model parameters and compared with the stability conditions of each market, considered in isolation. Bifurcation

---

[25] Similar weighting mechanisms have also been used in de Grauwe et al. (1993), Bauer et al. (2009), and Gaunersdorfer and Hommes (2007).

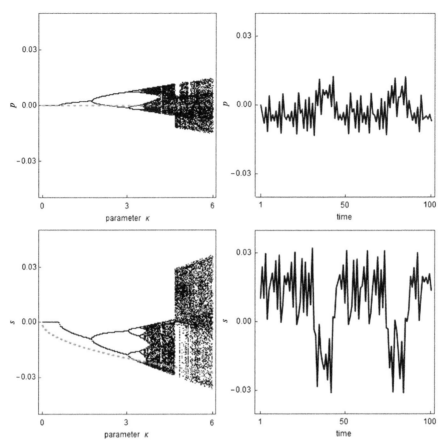

FIGURE 10

Bifurcation diagrams of log-price p and log-exchange rate s against extrapolation parameter κ (left panels) and their time paths under strong extrapolation (right panels). The superimposed dashed lines in the left panels depict the case of isolated markets. Parameters are: $p^* = q^* = s^* = 0$, $\alpha_P = 1$, $\alpha_Q = 0.8$, $\alpha_S = 1$, $\theta = 1$, $\psi = 1.5$, $\widetilde{\theta} = \widetilde{\psi} = 0.4$, $\varphi = 0.8$, $\nu = 10000$ and (in the right panels) $\kappa = 5.3$.

diagrams are particularly useful to understand how the 'strength' of the interaction between the stock markets (captured by parameters $\widetilde{\theta}$ and $\widetilde{\psi}$) and chartist extrapolation in the foreign exchange market (parameter κ) jointly affect the stability properties. In the left panels of Fig. 10, the asymptotic behavior of the domestic (log-)stock price p (top) and (log-)exchange rate s (bottom) is plotted against extrapolation parameter κ. In the no-interaction case (illustrated by the superimposed dashed lines), the fundamental (log-)exchange rate s^* is unstable and the exchange rate misalignment in the NFSS increases with κ, whereas the fundamental (log-)prices in the stock markets, p^* and q^*, are stable. The plots show that the connection with stable stock markets can be beneficial, to some extent, by bringing the exchange rate back to its fundamental value (for $\kappa < \hat{\kappa} \approx 0.6015$), or by reducing such misalignments. However, if κ is large enough, the integration can destabilize the stock markets, too, and introduce cyclical and chaotic behavior in the whole system of the interacting markets, with fluctuations of increasing amplitude. In particular, for $\kappa > \kappa^* \approx 4.856$, the fluctuations range across a much wider area than for $\kappa < \kappa^*$. While for $\kappa < \kappa^*$, two different attractors coexist, implying that the asymptotic dynamics of prices and exchange rate are confined to different regions depending on the initial condition ('bull' or 'bear' markets), at $\kappa = \kappa^*$ they merge into a unique attractor (through a *homoclinic* bifurcation).[26] The right panels of Fig. 10 represent the fluctuations of p (top) and s (bottom) for very large κ, characterized by sudden switching between bull and bear markets. The dynamic analysis thus reveals a double-edged effect of market interlinkages, where behavioral factors appear to play a substantial role.

The interaction of foreign and domestic investors using heterogeneous trading rules, and its effect on the dynamics of the foreign exchange market, has been the subject of further research in recent years. Amongst others, Kirman et al. (2007) show that the mere interplay of speculative traders with wealth measured in two different currencies and buying or selling assets of both countries can produce bubbles in foreign exchange market and realistic features of the exchange rate series. Corona et al. (2008) develop and investigate a computationally oriented agent-based model of two stock markets and a related foreign exchange market. They focus, in particular, on the resulting volatility, covariance and correlation of the stock markets, both during quiet periods and during a monetary crisis. Overall, such models highlight a number of dynamic features that are intrinsic to a system of asset markets linked *via* and *with* foreign exchange market and that simply arise from the structural properties of such interlinkages combined with the behavior of heterogeneous traders.

5 HAMS AND HOUSE PRICE DYNAMICS

This section surveys recent research on the impact of investors' behavioral heterogeneity on the dynamics of house prices and markets. Similarly to financial market dynamics, the main body of literature on house price dynamics relies on the theoretical framework of fully rational and forward looking investors (see, e.g. Poterba, 1984, Poterba et al., 1991, Clayton, 1996, Glaeser and Gyourko, 2007, Brunnermeier and Julliard, 2008). Broadly speaking, in this framework house price movements are due to sequences of *exogenous* shocks affecting the fundamentals of the housing market (rents, population growth, the user cost of capital, etc.), and to the resulting 'well-behaved' adjustments to new long-run equilibrium levels. Real estate market efficiency is an implication of such rationality assumptions.

---

[26] Tramontana et al. (2009, 2010) investigate how bull and bear market phases may arise in a HAM of stock and foreign exchange markets similar to Dieci and Westerhoff (2010), using techniques from nonlinear dynamics and the theory of global bifurcations.

Despite the remarkable achievements in this literature, a number of housing market phenomena are far from being fully understood. This includes the existence of boom-bust housing cycles unrelated to changes in underlying fundamentals (Wheaton, 1999, Shiller, 2007) – as the house price bubble and crash of the 2000s. Further empirical evidence challenges real estate market efficiency, in particular the short-term positive autocorrelation and long-term mean-reversion of house price returns (Capozza and Israelsen, 2007, Case and Shiller, 1989, 1990). For this reason, research on housing market dynamics has gradually accepted the view that investors' bounded rationality (optimism and pessimism, herd behavior, adaptive expectations, etc.) may play a role in house price fluctuations, for instance Cutler et al. (1991), Wheaton (1999), Malpezzi and Wachter (2005), Shiller (2005, 2008), Glaeser et al. (2008), Piazzesi and Schneider (2009), Sommervoll et al. (2010), and Burnside et al. (2012).

Recently, a number of HAMs of housing markets have been developed and estimated, inspired by the well-established heterogeneous-agent approach to financial markets. A stylized two-belief (chartist-fundamentalist) framework has been developed to incorporate in a tractable way the behavioral heterogeneity of agents. It proves to be a useful tool to understand housing bubbles and crashes and the way they interact with the 'real side' of housing markets, as well as other phenomena that are at odds with the standard approach. The framework of housing models is very close to HAMs of financial markets. It is based on housing demand consistent with mean-variance optimization and on a benchmark 'fundamental' price linked to the expected rental earnings (Bolt et al., 2014). However, unlike other asset markets, housing markets have specific features that need to be taken into account (such as the dual nature of housing, endogenous housing supply). Such features generate important interactions between the real and financial side of housing markets, which may be amplified by the interplay of heterogeneous speculators (Dieci and Westerhoff, 2012, 2016).

5.1 AN EQUILIBRIUM FRAMEWORK WITH HETEROGENEOUS INVESTORS

The housing market models developed by Bolt et al. (2014) and Dieci and Westerhoff (2016) are based on a common temporary equilibrium framework for house prices. This framework generalizes standard asset pricing relationships to the case of heterogeneous expectations. Denote by P_t the price of a housing unit at the beginning of the time interval $(t, t+1)$, P_{t+1} the end-of-period price, and Q_{t+1} the (real or imputed) rent in that period. The sum $P_{t+1} + Q_{t+1}$ represents the one-period payoff on the investment in one housing unit. Despite the time subscript, quantity Q_{t+1} is assumed to be known with certainty at time t (since rental prices are typically agreed in advance). At time t, housing market investors form expectations about price P_{t+1} by choosing among a number of available rules. Denote by $\mathbb{E}_{h,t}(\cdot)$ and $n_{h,t}$ the subjective expectation and the market proportion of investors of type h, respectively, and $P^e_{t,t+1} := \sum_h n_{h,t} \mathbb{E}_{h,t}(P_{t+1})$ the average market expectation. Note that price P_t is not known yet to investors when they form expectations about P_{t+1}. In a single-period setting, the current price is determined by the expectation as follows:

$$P_t = \frac{P_{t,t+1}^e + Q_{t+1}}{1 + k_t + \xi_t}, \tag{33}$$

where k_t represents the so-called *user cost* of housing and ξ_t can be interpreted as the risk premium for buying over renting a house. In particular, the user cost k_t includes the risk-free interest rate (or mortgage rate), denoted as r_t, as well as other costs, such as depreciation and maintenance costs, property tax, etc. (see, e.g. Himmelberg et al., 2005). As shown in Bolt et al. (2014) and Dieci and Westerhoff (2016), Eq. (33) is consistent with the assumptions of mean-variance demand and market clearing in the housing market.

5.1.1 Heterogeneous Expectations, Fundamentals, and Temporary Bubbles

In this section we discuss the model of Bolt et al. (2014). They address the issue of house price bubbles and crashes, disconnected from the dynamics of the rent and fundamental price, in a model of the housing market with behavioral heterogeneity and evolutionary selection of beliefs. Following Boswijk et al. (2007), the rent Q_t in (33) follows an *exogenous* process, namely, a geometric Brownian motion with drift, $Q_{t+1} = (1+g)\epsilon_t Q_t$, where $\{\epsilon_t\}$ are i.i.d. log-normal, with unit conditional mean. The user cost k_t (here reduced to the interest rate for simplicity) and the risk premium ξ_t in (33) are assumed constant $k_t = r_t = r$, $\xi_t = \xi$, with $r + \xi > g$.[27] In the reference case of homogeneous and correct expectations, a benchmark 'fundamental' solution P_t^* can be obtained from Eq. (33), namely, $P_t^* = \mathbb{E}_t \left[\sum_{s=1}^{\infty} Q_{t+s}(1+r+\xi)^{-s} \right] = Q_{t+1} \left[\sum_{s=1}^{\infty} (1+g)^{s-1}(1+r+\xi)^{-s} \right] = Q_{t+1}/(r+\xi-g)$.

Heterogeneity in expectations is captured by the interplay of regressive (fundamentalist) and extrapolative (chartist) beliefs (indexed by $h \in \{f, c\}$, respectively), with time-varying proportions $n_{c,t}$ and $n_{f,t} = 1 - n_{c,t}$. More precisely, investors form their beliefs about the relative deviation between the price and the fundamental in the next period, $X_{t+1} := (P_{t+1} - P_{t+1}^*)/P_{t+1}^*$, according to the linear rules $\mathbb{E}_{h,t}(X_{t+1}) = \phi_h X_{t-1}$, $h \in \{f, c\}$, where $\phi_f < 1$ and $\phi_c > 1$ characterize regressive and extrapolative beliefs, respectively. As a consequence,[28] asset pricing Eq. (33) takes the following recursive form in relative deviations from the fundamental price, given proportions $n_{c,t}$ and $n_{f,t}$:

$$X_t = \frac{(1+g)}{1+r+\xi}(n_{f,t}\phi_f + n_{c,t}\phi_c)X_{t-1}, \tag{34}$$

---

[27]Quantity ξ_t is positively related to investors' second-moment beliefs and risk aversion, and to the stock of housing at time t. This quantity is kept constant both for analytical tractability and for estimation purposes.
[28]Under the assumed belief types, Eq. (33) simplifies to (34) provided that X_{t+1} and Q_{t+2} are regarded as conditionally and mutually independent in agents' beliefs at time t.

where $(n_{f,t}\phi_f + n_{c,t}\phi_c)X_{t-1}$ is the average market expectation of X_{t+1}. It is also clear from (34) that the direction of the price change is remarkably affected by the current belief distribution. Strategies' proportions are determined by a logistic switching model with a-synchronous updating (see, e.g. Diks and van der Weide, 2005), according to $n_{c,t} = \delta n_{c,t-1} + (1 - \delta)\{1 + \exp[-\beta(U_{c,t-1} - U_{f,t-1})]\}^{-1}$, where $U_{c,t-1}$ and $U_{f,t-1}$ are fitness measures for chartists and fundamentalists, based on the realized excess profits in the previous period.[29] The model is described by a high-dimensional nonlinear dynamical system.

Based on earlier literature and on quarterly data on house price and rent indices from OECD databases, Bolt et al. (2014) calibrate the fundamental model parameters and obtain the price-fundamental deviations X_t for each of eight different countries (US, UK, NL, JP, CH, ES, SE, and BE).[30] In a second step, the behavioral parameters of the agent-based model are estimated based on the time series X_t (with the fundamental parameters fixed during the estimation). Since the model is governed by a nonlinear time-varying AR(1) process, once white noise is added to Eq. (34), it can be estimated by nonlinear least squares. In particular, among the estimated behavioral parameters, ϕ_c is significantly larger than 1 (chartists expect that the bubble will continue in the near future) and the difference $\Delta\phi := \phi_f - \phi_c$ is significant for all countries. This confirms the destabilizing impact of extrapolators and the presence of time-varying heterogeneity in the way agents form expectations. For all countries, long-lasting temporary house price bubbles are identified, driven or amplified by extrapolation (in particular, US, UK, NL SE, and ES display strong housing bubbles over the period 2004–2007). When these bubbles burst, the correction of housing prices is reinforced by investors' switching to a mean-reverting fundamental strategy. Remarkably, for all countries, the estimated parameters are close to regimes of multiple equilibria and/or global instability of the underlying nonlinear switching model. This fact has important policy implications, as the control of certain parameters may prevent the system from getting too close to bifurcation. For instance, the (mortgage) interest rate turns out to be one of the parameters that may shift the nonlinear system closer to multiple equilibria and global instability, whenever it becomes too low. The paper also shows that the qualitative in-sample and out-of-sample predictions of the non-linear switching model differ considerably from those of standard linear benchmark models with a rational representative agent, which is also important from a policy viewpoint.

---

[29] Performance measures $U_{c,t-1}$ and $U_{f,t-1}$ are related to investors' demand and realized returns in the previous period. Under simplifying assumptions, they can be rewritten as nonlinear functions of past *relative* deviations X_{t-i} ($i = 1, 2, 3$), as well.

[30] Calibration of the fundamental model parameters $\bar{R} := (1 + r)/(1 + g)$ and $\bar{\xi} := \xi/(1 + g)$ is based on estimates of average housing risk premia from earlier literature (in particular Himmelberg et al., 2005) and on average quarterly rental yields (average of Q_t/P_t) obtained from OECD housing datasets. Based on the datasets of prices and rents and the calibrated fundamental parameters, the time series $X_t = \ln P_t - \ln P_t^*$ is obtained. See Section 3 in Bolt et al. (2014) for detailed data description and parameter calibration.

5.1.2 Heterogeneous Beliefs, Boom-Bust Cycles, and Supply Conditions

In a similar two-beliefs asset pricing framework for housing markets, Dieci and West-erhoff, 2016 investigate how expectations-driven house price fluctuations interact with supply conditions (namely, housing supply elasticity and the existing stock of housing). For this purpose, an evolving mix of extrapolative and regressive beliefs is nested into a traditional *stock-flow* housing market framework (DiPasquale and Wheaton, 1992, Poterba, 1984) that connects the house price to the rent level and housing stock. Although the house price is still determined by a temporary equilibrium condition formally similar to (33), the model has a number of peculiar features. *First*, the (constant) user cost $k_t = k$ now includes also the depreciation rate d, namely, $k = r + d$. *Second*, the rent paid in period $(t, t+1)$, Q_{t+1}, is determined *endogenously* and, *ceteris paribus*, negatively related to the current stock of housing H_t, namely, $Q_{t+1} = q(H_t)$, with $q' < 0$. This is due to market clearing for rental housing, where supply of housing services is assumed to be proportional to the stock of housing while demand is a downward-sloping function of the rent. *Third*, the stock of housing evolves due to depreciation and new constructions, where the latter depends positively on the observed price level:

$$H_{t+1} = (1-d)H_t + h(P_t) \qquad h' > 0. \tag{35}$$

In each period, investment demand for housing based on standard mean-variance optimization (see, e.g. Brock and Hommes, 1998) results in the following market clearing condition[31]:

$$\frac{1}{\alpha}\left[P^e_{t,t+1} + q(H_t) - dP_t - (1+r)P_t\right] = H_t, \tag{36}$$

where $P^e_{t,t+1}$ is the average market expectation (across investors) and parameter $\alpha > 0$ is directly related to investors' risk aversion and second moment beliefs, assumed to be constant and identical across investors. The left-hand side of (36) represents the average individual demand (desired holdings of housing stock) and is proportional to the expected excess profit on one housing unit, taking both rental earnings and depreciation into account. Note that a larger stock H_t and/or a larger risk perception α require a larger expected excess profit in order for the market to clear, which results in a lower market clearing price, *ceteris paribus*. By defining the 'risk-adjusted' rent $\tilde{q}(H_t) := q(H_t) - \alpha H_t$, one obtains the following house pricing equation[32]:

$$P_t = \frac{P^e_{t,t+1} + \tilde{q}(H_t)}{1 + r + d}. \tag{37}$$

---

[31] Note that H_t is interpreted as the current housing stock *per* investor.

[32] In Eq. (37), the adjustment for risk affects the expected payoff instead of the discount rate in the denominator (similar to Eq. (18) in Section 4.2.2). This equation can be reduced to the standard form (33) by simple algebraic manipulations.

Dynamical system (37) and (35) admits a unique steady state, implicitly defined by $P^* = \frac{\tilde{q}(H^*)}{r+d}$ and $H^* = \frac{h(P^*)}{d}$, which can be regarded as the *fundamental steady state* (FSS), where the *fundamental price* P^* obeys to a standard 'discounted dividend' representation. Consistently, the price-rent ratio at the FSS can be expressed as the reciprocal of the user cost (including the required housing risk premium):

$$\pi^* = \frac{P^*}{Q^*} = \frac{1}{r+d+\xi}, \qquad \xi := \alpha H^*/P^*. \tag{38}$$

Although the model admits the same FSS under a wide spectrum of expectations schemes, investors' beliefs may remarkably affect the nature of the dynamical system, the way it reacts to shocks, and how it behaves sufficiently far from the FSS. In the reference case of *perfect foresight*, with homogeneous price expectation satisfying $P^e_{t,t+1} = P_{t+1}$, the FSS is saddle-path stable. In the presence of a 'fundamental' shock (e.g., an unanticipated and permanent interest rate reduction) shifting the FSS in the plane (P, H), the adjustment process towards the new FSS implies an initial price overshooting followed by a monotonic decline toward the new equilibrium price $P^{*'}$, whereas the stock adjusts to level $H^{*'}$ gradually, without overbuilding, as shown in Fig. 11. This dynamic pattern is due to the assumed full rationality of housing market investors, by which the system can jump to the new saddle path immediately after the shock. Remarkably, the *qualitative* pattern illustrated Fig. 11 is extremely robust to changes of the parameters (in particular, it is unaffected by the response of housing supply).

In contrast, by assuming *backward-looking* and heterogeneous expectations, the stability properties of the FSS and the nature of price and stock fluctuations depend on the way investors' beliefs coevolve with the housing market itself. The average price expectation is specified as

$$P^e_{t,t+1} = \varphi(P_{t-1}) = n_{c,t}\varphi_c(P_{t-1}) + n_{f,t}\varphi_f(P_{t-1}), \quad n_{f,t} = 1 - n_{c,t}, \tag{39}$$

where $\varphi_c(P) = P + \gamma(P - P^*)$ and $\phi_f(P) = P + \theta(P^* - P)$, $\gamma, \theta > 0$, represent the extrapolative and regressive components, respectively. Similar to (32), the market weight of extrapolative and regressive beliefs evolves endogenously, depending on market circumstances. The market proportion of extrapolators is specified as $n_{c,t} = w(P_{t-1})$, where $w(P) = [1 + v(P - P^*)^2]^{-1}$, is a 'bell-shaped' function of the observed mispricing, governed by a (possibly state-dependent) sensitivity coefficient $v > 0$.[33]

The rent and the supply of new constructions are modeled as isoelastic functions, namely, $q(H) = \lambda_0 H^{-\lambda}$, $h(P) = \mu_0 P^\mu$, $\lambda_0, \mu_0, \lambda, \mu > 0$. Dynamical system (37)

---

[33] See Section 4.3 for a behavioral interpretation of this endogenous rule. In Figs. 12 and 13, $v = v(P)$ is specified in such a way that the bell-shaped function $w(P)$ is asymmetric, featuring stronger reaction to negative mispricing.

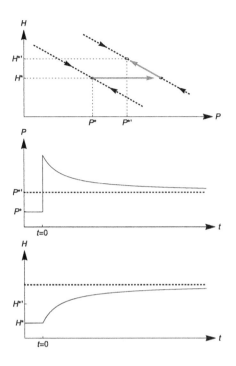

FIGURE 11

The case of *perfect foresight*: 'well-behaved' price and stock adjustments in response to an unanticipated shock.

and (35) has a locally stable FSS[34] only for sufficiently weak extrapolation (low parameter γ). For large enough γ, the model predicts that an initial positive deviation from the fundamental price tends to be amplified by investors' behavior. However, the stability loss generated by strong extrapolation may result in different scenarios, depending on the elasticity of housing supply, μ. Under a relatively inelastic housing supply, the extrapolation generates two additional (locally stable) non-fundamental steady states (NFSS), via a so-called *pitchfork bifurcation*. Such 'bubble equilibria' are characterized by higher (respectively lower) levels of the price-rent ratio than the fundamental price-rent ratio π^* in Eq. (38). Therefore, under a weak supply response, a positive mispricing at time $t = 0$ results in a long-lasting price bubble and overbuilding, in the absence of exogenous shocks (the top left panel of Fig. 12). Things are quite different under a more elastic housing supply. Although the initial price path is very similar, a prompt supply response results in a larger growth of the housing stock, which causes a price decline and, ultimately, the endogenous bursting of the bubble (the top right panel). This second scenario is associated with a stable

---

[34] Note, however, that the *local stability* of the FSS in this model is conceptually different from the saddle-path stability in the model with perfect foresight.

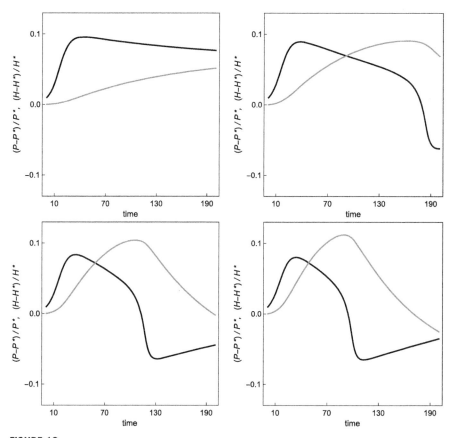

FIGURE 12

Impact of different degrees of supply elasticity (from top-left to bottom right: $\mu = 1$, $\mu = 2.5$, $\mu = 4$, $\mu = 5$), in the presence of strong extrapolative behavior. House price (black) and stock (grey) are expressed in relative deviations from their fundamental levels. Other parameters are: $P^* = H^* = 100$, $r = d = \xi = 0.5\%$, $\gamma = 0.15$, $\theta = 0.125$, $\alpha = 0.005$, $\lambda = 4$. State-dependent switching coefficient is modeled as $v = 1/100$ for $P \geq 100$, whereas $v = v(P) = (101 - P)/100$ for $P < 100$.

closed orbit, generated via a *Neimark–Sacker bifurcation*. The larger the supply response, the larger and faster the growth of the stock, the shorter the bubble period (the bottom panels of Fig. 12).

Fig. 13 illustrates a further scenario in which supply elasticity may affect bubbles in a similar manner. The top-left panel is a phase-space representation in the plane of house price and stock (in relative deviations from P^* and H^*, respectively) of the dynamics depicted in the top-left panel in Fig. 12. The underlying regime has three equilibria, two of which are visible in Fig. 13, namely, the FSS and the 'upper' NFSS. The light and dark gray regions represent the basins of attraction of the coexisting NFSS, whereas the (saddle) FSS lies on the boundary of the basins. The top panels

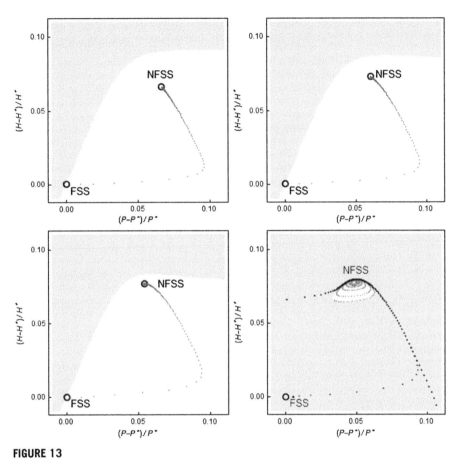

FIGURE 13

Changes of the basin (boundary) of the bubble steady state, for increasing supply elasticity (from top-left to bottom right: $\mu = 1$, $\mu = 1.2$, $\mu = 1.4$, $\mu = 1.57$). Other parameters are as in Fig. 12.

and the bottom-left panel indicate that, the larger the supply elasticity, the closer the NFSS gets to the boundary of its basin. The bubble equilibrium thus becomes less and less robust to exogenous noise, although it continues to be *locally* stable. In particular, its basin of attraction may become very small (white area in the bottom-right panel of Fig. 13).[35] From the viewpoint of nonlinear dynamics, the phenomena illustrated in Fig. 13 are *global*, in the sense that they are independent of the *local* stability properties of the coexisting steady states.

The qualitative results produced by this model are in agreement with recent research on housing market bubbles and urban economics, reporting that a more elastic

---

[35] In the bottom-right panel of Fig. 13, the dark gray region represents the basin of a coexisting attracting closed orbit.

housing supply is associated to shorter bubbles, smaller price increases and larger stock adjustments (see, e.g. Glaeser et al., 2008).[36] This model thus provides a 'non-linear economic dynamics' interpretation on the observed role of supply elasticity in shaping housing bubbles and crashes, based on bifurcation analysis and on a simple HAM framework.

5.2 DISEQUILIBRIUM PRICE ADJUSTMENTS

Further HAMs of the housing market depart from equilibrium asset pricing equation (33) and rest on the view that prices adjust to excess demand in each period in disequilibrium. This may lead to different dynamics from that observed under market clearing. However, the phenomena reported in the previous section appear to be quite robust to such alternative specifications. In particular, Dieci and Westerhoff (2012) consider the following linear price adjustment equation

$$P_{t+1} - P_t = \psi(D_t^R + D_t^S - H_t). \tag{40}$$

Housing stock H_t evolves similarly to (35), namely, $H_t = (1-d)H_{t-1} + m P_t$, $m > 0$. The housing demand $D_t^R + D_t^S := D_t$ (interpreted as the desired stock of housing) is made up of 'real demand' D_t^R (from consumers of housing services) and speculative demand D_t^S (from investors motivated by short-term capital gains). The two demand components are modeled, respectively, as follows:

$$D_t^R = a - b P_t, \quad a, b > 0, \tag{41}$$

$$D_t^S = n_{c,t} D_{c,t} + n_{f,t} D_{f,t} = n_{c,t}\hat{\gamma}(P_t - P^*) + n_{f,t}\hat{\theta}(P^* - P_t), \quad \hat{\gamma}, \hat{\theta} > 0, \tag{42}$$

where $D_{c,t}$ and $D_{f,t}$ are chartist and fundamentalist demand, respectively. Again, the proportion of extrapolators $n_{c,t} = w(P_t)$ evolves according to weighting function $w(P)$ introduced in Section 5.1.2. In particular, while real demand D_t^R depends linearly and negatively on the current price level, speculative demand D_t^S results in a nonlinear, cubic-like function of P_t.[37] In (42), P^* is the FSS, corresponding to the unique steady state of the baseline case without speculative demand, namely, $P^* := \frac{ad}{m+bd}$, $H^* = \frac{m}{d} P^* = \frac{am}{m+bd}$. Using the change of variables $\pi_t := P_t - P^*$, $\zeta_t := H_{t-1} - H^*$, one obtains the following two-dimensional nonlinear system in deviations from the FSS:

$$\pi_{t+1} = \pi_t - \psi\left[(b+m)\pi_t - \frac{\hat{\gamma}\pi_t - \hat{\theta}v\pi_t^3}{1 + v\pi_t^2} + (1-d)\zeta_t\right],$$

$$\zeta_{t+1} = m\pi_t + (1-d)\zeta_t.$$

---

[36] Further experimental evidence on the negative feedback and the stabilizing role of elastic housing supply is provided by Bao and Hommes (2015) in a related heterogeneous-agent setting.

[37] In an interesting recent paper, Diks and Wang (2016) find a similar cubic-type nonlinearity, by applying stochastic catastrophe theory to housing market dynamics.

The analytical and numerical study of the dynamical system delivers clear-cut results about the emergence of housing bubbles and crashes and the joint role played by chartist demand parameter, $\hat{\gamma}$, and the slopes of 'real' demand and supply schedules, b and m. In particular, similar to Dieci and Westerhoff (2016), parameter $\hat{\gamma}$ may destabilize the steady state via a pitchfork bifurcation, if the housing supply curve is sufficiently flat (low m), or via a Neimark–Sacker bifurcation, if the supply schedule is sufficiently sloped (large m). Moreover, in both scenarios, large $\hat{\gamma}$ results in a 'route' to complexity and endogenous irregular bubbles and crashes. In particular, in the pitchfork scenario, two locally attracting NFSS may evolve into more complex (disjoint) attractors and, ultimately, merge into a unique attractor (through a so-called *homoclinic* bifurcation). The motion of the system on this attractor is characterized by irregular dynamics in the bull or bear market regions, and by sudden, seemingly unpredictable switching between the bull and bear markets (the top-left panel of Fig. 14) and slow change of the stock level (the top-right panel).[38] In the Neimark–Sacker scenario, irregular bubbles of different size and duration, followed by sudden crashes, can be observed (the bottom-left panel), with larger and more frequent stock fluctuations (the bottom-right panel). This kind of motion is also due to a complex attractor, originally born as a regular closed curve via a Neimark–Sacker bifurcation.

Kouwenberg and Zwinkels (2015) develop and estimate a housing market model with a structure similar to Dieci and Westerhoff (2012). For estimation purposes, their model is expressed in log price, $p_t := \ln P_t$, and the log-fundamental $p_t^* := \ln P_t^*$ is modeled as a time-varying reference value. The demand functions from consumers and investors are interpreted as flows (desired transactions) and so is supply (identified with the flow of new constructions). While fundamentalist demand is based on current mispricing, chartist demand is based on the extrapolation of a time average of past returns. The proportions of chartists and fundamentalists evolve endogenously based on past performances (related to past observed forecast errors), according to a standard logit switching model. The model is expressed as:

$$\rho_{t+1} := p_{t+1} - p_t = \psi(d_t - h_t) + \epsilon_{t+1}, \tag{43}$$

where ρ_{t+1} is the log-return on housing investment, ϵ_{t+1} is a random noise term. The demand and supply are defined as follows:

$$d_t = (a - bp_t) + n_{c,t}\hat{\gamma}\sum_{l=1}^{L} \rho_{t-l+1} + n_{f,t}\hat{\theta}(p_t^* - p_t), \quad h_t = c + mp_t. \tag{44}$$

Chartist proportion is given by $n_{c,t} = \left[1 + \exp\left(-\beta A_t\right)\right]^{-1}$, where $A_t = (\Pi_{f,t} - \Pi_{c,t})/(\Pi_{f,t} + \Pi_{c,t})$, and $\Pi_{h,t} = \sum_{j=1}^{J} \left|\mathbb{E}_{h,t-j}(\rho_{t-j+1}) - \rho_{t-j+1}\right|$ is a sum of past

---

[38] See also Dieci and Westerhoff (2013a) for similar dynamics in a housing market model with different specifications of housing supply and demand.

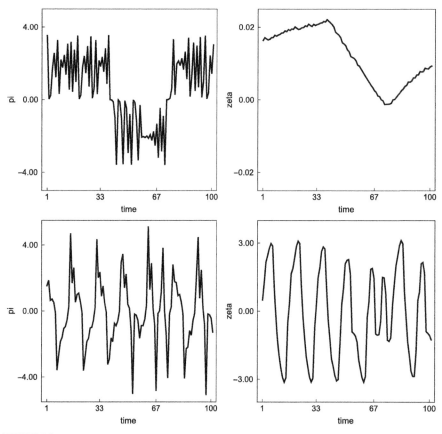

FIGURE 14

Irregular bubbles and crashes in the presence of strong extrapolation. Top panels: house price and stock (in deviations from the steady state) in the 'pitchfork scenario' ($b = 0.6$, $m = 0.0003$, $\hat{\gamma} = 7.28$). Bottom panels: house price and stock in the 'Neimark–Sacker' scenario ($b = 0.05$, $m = 0.5$, $\hat{\gamma} = 6$). Other parameters are $d = 0.02$, $\hat{\theta} = 1$, $v = 1$ for all panels.

absolute forecast errors of agents of type h, $h \in \{f, c\}$. Similar to Eqs. (41) and (42), the housing demand d_t in (44) includes the consumer demand component and the speculative demand terms due to chartists and fundamentalists, respectively.[39]

The model can be estimated by rewriting it as single non-linear equation and applying maximum likelihood estimation. Estimation results (based on U.S. quarterly time-series data on prices and rents)[40] reveal that the coefficients for the fundamen-

---

[39]Chartist and fundamentalist speculative demand is assumed to be proportional to their expected log-returns.

[40]Eichholtz et al. (2015) develop and estimate a similar HAM based on a long-term time series of house prices in Amsterdam.

talist and chartist rules are significant and have the expected signs. The positive and significant sign of the estimated intensity of choice parameter (β) implies that agents tend to switch following recent prediction performance. Interestingly, simulation of the deterministic skeleton of the model (with the parameters set equal to the estimated values) shows that the price does not converge to a stable steady state value, but to a stable limit cycle. Hence, an endogenous nonlinear motion appears to be an important part of U.S. housing market dynamics.

A widely reported empirical fact about real estate returns is the presence of short-term positive autocorrelation and long-term mean-reversion (see, e.g. Capozza and Israelsen, 2007, Case and Shiller, 1989, 1990). This fact is, more or less explicitly, part of the motivation for the chartist-fundamentalist framework adopted in the models reviewed in this section. Kouwenberg and Zwinkels (2014) build an econometric model that includes explicitly these two competing components of housing returns. The model is based on a VECM equation, modified to allow for smoothly changing weights of the autoregressive and error correction components, conditional on the value of a transition variable that depends on past relative forecast errors (a so-called *smooth transition* model). In fact, the econometric model is a particular case of the behavioral model described above (Kouwenberg and Zwinkels, 2015). The analysis shows that house prices are cointegrated with a rent-based estimate of the fundamental value. Estimation results (using quasi-maximum likelihood estimation, based on quarterly US national house price index data) indicate that the strength of the autocorrelation and the long-term mean reversion in housing returns vary significantly over time, depending on recent forecasting performances. The time variation captured by the smooth transition model can produce better out-of-sample forecasts of house price index returns than alternative models.

6 HAMS AND MARKET MICROSTRUCTURE

Limit order markets (LOM) are the most active and dominating financial markets (O'Hara, 2001; Easley et al., 2013; O'Hara, 2015). A core and challenging issue in dynamical LOM models is the endogenous order choice of investors to submit either market or limit orders. It is important to understand how investors trade based on their asymmetric information and what they can learn from order book information. The current literature of limit order market models faces two main challenges. First, they mainly focus on perfectly rational information-based trade and order choice of informed traders. However, within rational expectation equilibrium framework, "*a model that incorporates the relevant frictions of limit-order markets (such as discrete prices, staggered trader arrivals, and asymmetric information) does not readily admit a closed-form solution* (Goettler et al., 2009)". This limits the explanatory power of this framework. Second, rational expectation framework simplifies the order choice behavior of uninformed traders by introducing either private value or time preferences exogenously. However, as pointed out by O'Hara (2001), "*It is the uninformed traders who provide the liquidity to the informed, and so understanding their behavior can provide substantial insight and intuition into the trading process*". Therefore what uninformed traders can learn from order book information and how learning affects their order choice and the behavior of informed traders are not clear.

Recent development of HAMs and computationally oriented agent-based simulations provide a framework to deal with these challenges in LOM models. With great flexibility in modeling complexity and learning, this framework offers a very promising and integrated approach to the research in market microstructure. Within this framework, many features including asymmetric information, learning, and order choice can be articulated. It can provide an insight into the impact of heterogeneous trading rules on limit order book and order flows (Chiarella and Iori, 2002, Chiarella et al., 2009b, 2012b, Kovaleva and Iori, 2014), interplay of different market architectures and different types of regulatory measures, such as price limits (Yeh and Yang, 2010), transaction taxes (Pellizzari and Westerhoff, 2009), short-sales constraints (Anufriev and Tuinstra, 2013). It also sheds light on the costs and benefits of financial regulations (Lensberg et al., 2015).

This section discusses briefly the recent developments along this line, in particular the contributions of Chiarella et al. (2015a, 2017) and Arifovic et al. (2016). We first focus on how computationally oriented HAMs can be used to replicate the stylized facts in LOM and provide possible mechanism explanation to these stylized facts in Section 6.1. We then discuss how genetic algorithm (GA) learning with a classifier system can help to understand the joint impact of market information, market microstructure mechanisms, and behavioral factors on the dynamics of LOM characterized by information asymmetry and complexity in order flows and trading in Section 6.2. We also examine the impact of high frequency trading (HFT) and learning on information aggregation, market liquidity, and price discovery in Section 6.3, demonstrating that the incentive for high frequency traders not to trade too fast can be consistent with price information efficiency. We also discuss some implications on market design and regulation in Section 6.4.

6.1 STYLIZED FACTS IN LIMIT ORDER MARKETS

Agent-based computational finance has made a significant contribution to characterize the stylized facts in financial markets, as discussed in Section 2. As pointed out in Chen et al. (2012) and Gould et al. (2013), after several prototypes have successfully replicated a number of financial stylized facts of the low frequency data, the next milestone is to see whether HAMs can also be used to replicate the features in high frequency domain.

Various stylized facts in limit order markets have been documented in market microstructure literature. According to surveys by Chen et al. (2012) and Gould et al. (2013), apart from the stylized facts in the time series of returns, including fat tails, the absence of autocorrelation in returns, volatility clustering, and long memory in the absolute returns, the limit order market has its own stylized facts. They include long memory in the bid-ask spread and trading volume, hump shapes in order depth profiles of order books, non-linear relationship between trade imbalance and mid-price return, and diagonal effect or event clustering in order submission types, among the most common and important statistical regularities in LOM. They have become the most important criteria to justify the explanatory power of agent-based LOM.

A number of HAMs of market microstructure have been able to replicate some of the stylized facts. They include zero-intelligence models and HAMs (see Chen et al., 2012 and Gould et al., 2013 for surveys). The zero-intelligence models show that some of the stylized facts, such as fat tail and possible volatility and event clusterings, are generated by trading mechanism, instead of agents' strategic behavior. Different from the zero-intelligence models, HAMs consider agents' strategic behaviors as potential explanations to the stylized facts. Chiarella and Iori (2002) argue that substantial heterogeneity must exist between market participants in order for the highly non-trivial properties of volatility to emerge in real limit order markets. By assuming that agents use strategies that blend three components (fundamentalist, chartist, and noisy), Chiarella et al. (2009b) provide a computational HAM of an order-driven market to study order book and flow dynamics. Inspired by the theoretically oriented dynamic analysis of moving average rules in Chiarella et al. (2006b), Chiarella et al. (2012b) conduct a dynamic analysis of a more realistic microstructure model of continuous double auctions. When agents switch between either fundamentalists or chartists based on their relative performance, they show that the model is able to characterize volatility clustering, insignificant autocorrelations (ACs) of returns and significantly slow-decaying ACs of the absolute returns. The result suggests that both *behavioral* traits and *realistic microstructure* have a role in explaining several statistical properties of returns.

In a modified version of Chiarella et al. (2009b), Kovaleva and Iori (2014) investigate the interrelation between pre-trade quote transparency and stylized properties of order-driven markets populated by traders with heterogeneous beliefs. The model is able to capture negative skewness of stock returns and volatility clustering once book depth is visible to traders. Their simulation analysis reveals that full quote transparency contributes to convergence in traders' actions, while exogenously partial transparency restriction may exacerbate long-range dependencies. However, replicating most of these stylized facts in LOM simultaneously remains very challenging.

When modeling agents' expectation, *behavioral sentiment* plays an important role. Barberis et al. (1998) and Daniel et al. (1998) point out that certain well-known psychological biases, including conservatism, representativeness heuristic, overconfidence and biased self-attribution, not only characterize how people actually behave, but can also explain a range of empirical findings, such as underreaction and overreaction of stock prices to news, excess volatility and post-earnings announcement drift. By incorporating behavioral sentiment to a LOM model, Chiarella et al. (2017) show that the behavioral sentiment not only helps to replicate most of the stylized facts simultaneously in LOM, but also plays a unique role in explaining these stylized facts that cannot be explained by noise trading. They include fat tails in the return distribution, long memory in the trading volume, an increasing and non-linear relationship between trading imbalance and mid-price returns, as well as the diagonal effect or event clustering in order submission types.

6.2 INFORMATION AND LEARNING IN LIMIT ORDER MARKET

Because of information asymmetry and growing complexity in order flows and trading in LOM, the endogenous order choice based on the order book conditions is a core and challenging issue, as highlighted by Rosu (2012). How traders' learning, in particular uninformed traders, from order book information affect their order choice and limit order market becomes important. Recently, Chiarella et al. (2015a) provide a LOM model with adaptive learning through genetic algorithm (GA) with classifier system, trying to explore the joint impact of adaptive learning and information asymmetric on trading behavior, market liquidity, and price discovery.

Since introduced firstly by Holland (1975), GA and classifier system have been used in agent-based models to examine learning and evolution in Santa Fe Institute artificial stock market (SFI-ASM) (Arthur et al., 1997a, LeBaron et al., 1999) and economic models (Marimon et al., 1990, Lettau and Uhlig, 1999, Allen and Carroll, 2001). In LOM, LeBaron and Yamamoto (2008) employ GA to capture the imitation behavior among heterogeneous beliefs. Darley and Outkin (2007) use adaptive learning to evolve trading rules of market makers and apply their simulations to the Nasdaq market in 1998. The adaptive learning has been widely used in financial markets. However most HAMs with adaptive learning and trading are largely driven by the market price instead of asymmetric information, which is the focus of microstructure literature in LOM. This brings a significant difference in the dynamics of LOM.

Unlike informed traders, uninformed traders do not have the information about the current, but lagged fundamental value. By combining information processing of market conditions and order choice into GA with a classifier system, Chiarella et al. (2015a) show that behavior heterogeneity of traders is endogenously emerged from their learning and trading. This approach fills the gap between agent-based computational finance and the mainstream market microstructure since Kyle (1985). They show that, measured by the average usage of different market information, trading rules under the GA learning become stationary and hence effective in the long-run. In particular, the learning of uninformed traders improves market information efficiency, which is not necessarily the case when informed traders learn. The learning also makes uninformed traders submit less aggressive limit orders but more market orders, while it makes informed traders submit less market orders and more aggressive limit orders. In general, both informed and uninformed traders provide liquidity to market at approximately the same rate. The results provide some insight into the effect of learning on order submission behavior, market liquidity and efficiency.

6.3 HIGH FREQUENCY TRADING

With technology advance, high frequency trading (HFT) becomes very popular. It also brings a hot debate on the benefit of and market regulation on HFT (O'Hara, 2015). In particular, do financial market participants benefit from HFT and how does HFT affect market efficiency? To examine the effect of HFT and learning in limit order markets, Arifovic et al. (2016) extend the LOM model of Chiarella et al. (2015a) and introduce fast and slow traders with GA learning. Consistent with Grossman and Stiglitz (1980), they show a trade-off between information advantage and profit opportunity for informed HFT. This trade-off leads to a hump-shaped relation between HFT profit, market efficiency, and trading speed. When informed investors trade fast, their information advantage makes HFT more profitable. However, the learning, in particular from uninformed traders, improves information aggregation and efficiency. This then reduces the information advantage of HFT and hence the profit opportunity. HFT in general improves market information efficiency and hence price discovery. However, the trade-off between the information advantage and trading speed of HFT also leads to a hump-shape relation between liquidity consumption and trading speed. HFT improves liquidity consumption and price discovery in general due to information aggregation through the learning. When HFT trade too fast, they submit more market order, which enlarges the spread and reduces market liquidity. This implies that there is an incentive for not trading too fast, which in turn improves price efficiency. The results provide an insight into the profitability of HFT and the current debates and puzzles about the impact of HFT on market liquidity and efficiency.

6.4 HAMS AND MICROSTRUCTURE REGULATION

Lensberg et al. (2015) build an agent-based framework with market microstructure and delegated portfolio management in order to forecast and compare the equilibrium effects of different regulatory measures: financial transaction tax, short-selling ban and leverage ban. The financial market is characterized by fund managers who trade stocks and bonds in an order-driven market. The process of competition and innovation among different investment styles is modeled through a genetic programming algorithm with tournament selection. However, the heterogeneous trading strategies that emerge from the evolutionary process can be classified by a relatively small number of 'styles' (interpreted as value trading, news trading/arbitrage and market making/liquidity supply). The model contributes to understand the pros and cons of different regulations, by providing detailed information on the equilibrium properties of portfolio holdings, order flow, liquidity, cost of capital, price discovery, short-term volatility and long-term price dynamics. By including an exogenous business cycle process, the model also allows to quantify the effects of different regulations during periods of market distress. In particular, it turns out that a financial transaction tax may have a negative impact on liquidity and price discovery, and limited effect on long swings in asset prices.

7 CONCLUSION AND FUTURE RESEARCH

This chapter has discussed the latest development of heterogeneous agent models (HAMs) in finance over the last ten years since the publications of the *Handbook of Computational Economics* in 2006 and, in particular, the *Handbook of Financial Markets: Dynamics and Evolution* in 2009. It demonstrates a significant contribution of HAMs to finance theory and practice from five broad aspects of financial markets. First of all, inspired by the rich and promising perspectives of the earlier HAMs, we have witnessed a growing supporting evidence on the explanatory power of HAMs to various market anomalies and, in particular, the stylized facts through calibrations and estimations of HAMs to real data in various financial markets over the last decade. More importantly, different from traditional empirical finance and financial econometrics, HAMs provide some insights into economic mechanisms and driving forces of these stylized facts. They therefore lead to some helpful implications in policy and market design. Moreover, the basic framework of earlier HAMs has been naturally developed and extended in two different directions. The first extension to a continuous-time setup provides a unified framework to deal with the effect of historical price information. The framework can be used to examine profitability of fundamental and non-fundamental, such as momentum and contrarian, trading strategies that have been widely used and discussed in financial market practice and finance theory. It also enables to develop optimal asset allocation to incorporate time series momentum and reversal, two of the most important anomalies in financial markets. The second extension to a multiple-risky-asset framework helps to examine the impact of heterogeneous expectations on asset comovements within a financial market, as well as the spill-over effects across markets, and to characterize risk-return relations through an evolutionary CAPM. Moreover, inspired by HAMs of financial markets, a new heterogeneous-agent framework for housing market dynamics has been developed recently. It can well explain house bubbles and crashes, by combining behavioral facts and the real side of housing markets. Finally, the advantage of HAMs in dealing with market complexity plays a unique role in the development of market microstructure modeling. This provides a very promising approach to understand the impact of information, learning, and trading on trading behavior, market liquidity, and price discovery.

The research streams reviewed in this chapter can be developed further in several directions. First, instead of heuristic assumptions on agents' behavioral heterogeneity currently assumed in HAMs, there is a need to provide micro-foundation to endogenize such heuristic heterogeneity among agents. Most of the HAMs investigate the endogenous market mechanism by focusing on the interaction of heterogeneous agents with different expectations (typically fundamentalists and trend followers). Their explanatory power is mainly demonstrated by combining the insights from the nonlinear dynamics of the underlying deterministic model with various noise processes, such as fundamental shocks and noise trading. To a large extent, the HAM literature has not explored the impact of asymmetric information or information uncertainty on agents' behavioral heterogeneity. By considering asymmetric information, which is the focus of traditional finance literature and plays a very important role in financial markets, agents' heterogeneity can be endogenized and micro-founded. This has been illustrated in Section 2.3, based on He and Zheng (2016), by showing how trading heterogeneity can arise endogenously among traders due to uncertainty about the fundamental value information of the risky asset. The development along this line would help to provide economic foundation to the assumed behavioral heterogeneity of agent-based models, which is often critiqued by traditional finance.

Second, as a different aspect of information uncertainty, ambiguity has been introduced in the literature to address various market anomalies and asset pricing (Epstein and Schneider, 2006). More recently, Aliyev and He (2016) discuss the possibilities of capturing efficient market hypothesis and behavioral finance under a general framework based on a broad definition of rationality. They argue that the root of behavioral anomalies comes from the imprecision and reliability of information. A natural combination of heterogeneity and ambiguity would provide a broader framework to financial market modeling and to rationalize market anomalies.

Third, when asset prices are affected by historical price information, we need to develop a portfolio and asset pricing theory in continuous-time to characterize cross-section returns driven by time series momentum in short-run and reversal in long-run. The continuous-time HAMs discussed in Section 3 illustrate the challenging but promising perspectives of this development. Recently, Li and Liu (2016) study the optimal momentum trading strategy when asset prices are affected by historical price information. They provide an optimal way to hedge the momentum crash risk, a newly-found empirical feature, and to significantly improve momentum profits. The techniques developed can potentially be applied to a range of problems in economics and finance, such as momentum, long memory in volatility, post-earnings announcement drift, indexation lags in the inflation-linked bonds.

Fourth, incorporating social interactions and social networks to the current HAMs would be helpful for examining their impact on financial markets and asset pricing. Social interactions are well documented in financial markets, in particular when facing information uncertainty. He et al. (2016a) recently develop a simple evolutionary model of asset pricing and population dynamics to incorporate social interactions among investors with heterogeneous beliefs on information uncertainty. They show that social interactions can lead to mis-pricing and existence of multiple steady state equilibria, generating two different volatility regimes, bi-modal distribution in population dynamics, and stochastic volatility. As pointed out by Hirshleifer (2015), *[T]he time has come to move beyond behavioral finance to 'social finance'*. This would provide a fruitful area of research in the near future.

Fifth, HAMS of multiasset markets and financial market interlinkages could be developed further. An interesting research issue is understanding the effect of an increase in the number of risky assets in a setup similar to Chiarella et al. (2013b) and the extent to which standard results on the role of diversification continue to hold in the presence of momentum trading. A related issue concerns the profitability of different trading strategies in a multi-asset framework, their ability to exploit the emerging correlation patterns, and their joint impact on financial market stability. Furthermore, the ability of the evolutionary, heterogeneous-agent CAPM discussed in Section 4.2 to produce a time variation of ex-ante betas has been illustrated through simulation results only. There is a need to have formal statistical tests on the observations based on the numerical simulations. Finally, it would be interesting to see if the time variation of either beta coefficients or risk premia plays a role in explaining the cross section of asset returns.

Sixth, housing market dynamics has only very recently been investigated from the perspective of HAMs. The existing models are mainly aimed at qualitative or quantitative investigations of the role of price extrapolation in generating house price fluctuations. Among the possible interesting developments of this baseline setup is the joint impact of interest rate changes, credit conditions, and investor sentiment on house price fluctuations. In particular, the role of interest rates and credit in triggering house price booms and busts is crucial for policy makers and highly debated in academic literature (see, e.g. Himmelberg et al., 2005 and Jordà et al., 2015). A related issue concerns the dynamic interplay among housing, stock and bond markets, driven by both fundamental shocks, such as interest rate movements, and behavioral factors, such as investors switching to better investment opportunities. Dieci et al. (2017) provide a first attempt in this direction.

Finally, an integrated approach of agent-based models and market microstructure literature would provide a very promising approach, if not the only one, to understand information aggregation, learning, trading, market liquidity and efficiency when facing information asymmetry and growing complexity in market microstructure. This has been illustrated by the discussion in Section 6, but remains largely unexplored.

REFERENCES

Alfarano, S., Lux, T., Wagner, F., 2005. Estimation of agent-based models: the case of an asymmetric herding model. Computational Economics 26, 19–49.

Aliyev, N., He, X., 2016. Toward a General Model of Financial Markets. Technical report. Quantitative Finance Research Centre, University of Technology, Sydney.

Allen, H., Taylor, M., 1990. Charts, noise and fundamentals in the London foreign exchange market. Economic Journal 100, 49–59.

Allen, T., Carroll, C., 2001. Individual learning about consumption. Macroeconomic Dynamics 5, 255–271.

Angeletos, G.-M., Werning, I., 2006. Crises and prices: information aggregation, multiplicity, and volatility. The American Economic Review 96, 1720–1736.

Anufriev, M., Bottazzi, G., Marsili, M., Pin, P., 2012. Excess covariance and dynamic instability in a multi-asset model. Journal of Economic Dynamics and Control 36, 1142–1161.

Anufriev, M., Dindo, P., 2010. Wealth-driven selection in a financial market with heterogeneous agents. Journal of Economic Behavior and Organization 73, 327–358.

Anufriev, M., Hommes, C., 2012. Evolutionary selection of individual expectations and aggregate outcomes. American Economic Journal: Microeconomics 4, 35–64.

Anufriev, M., Tuinstra, J., 2013. The impact of short-selling constraints on financial market stability in heterogeneous agents model. Journal of Economic Dynamics and Control 37 (8), 1523–1543.

Arifovic, J., Chiarella, C., He, X., Wei, L., 2016. High Frequency Trading and Learning in a Dynamic Limit Order Market. Working Paper. University of Technology, Sydney.

Arthur, W., 1994. Inductive reasoning and bounded rationality. American Economic Review 84 (2), 406–411.

Arthur, W., Holland, J., LeBaron, B., Palmer, R., Tayler, P., 1997a. Asset pricing under endogenous expectations in an artificial stock market. Economic Notes 26 (2), 297–330.

Arthur, W., Holland, J., LeBaron, B., Palmer, R., Tayler, P., 1997b. Asset pricing under endogenous expectations in an artificial stock market. In: Arthur, W.B., Durlauf, S.N., Lane, D.A. (Eds.), The Economy as an Evolving Complex System II. Addison–Wesley, Reading, MA, pp. 15–44.

Aymanns, C., Farmer, J., 2015. The dynamics of the leverage cycle. Journal of Economic Dynamics and Control 50, 155–179.

Baak, S., 1999. Test for bounded rationality with a linear dynamics model distorted by heterogeneous expectations. Journal of Economic Dynamics and Control 23, 1517–1543.

Bao, T., Hommes, C., 2015. When Speculators Meet Constructors: Positive and Negative Feedback in Experimental Housing Markets. Working Paper 15-10. CeNDEF, University of Amsterdam.

Barberis, N., Shleifer, A., Vishny, R., 1998. A model of investor sentiment. Journal of Financial Economics 49, 307–343.

Bauer, C., de Grauwe, P., Reitz, S., 2009. Exchange rate dynamics in a target zone—a heterogeneous expectations approach. Journal of Economic Dynamics and Control 33 (2), 329–344.

Beja, A., Goldman, M., 1980. On the dynamic behavior of prices in disequilibrium. Journal of Finance 35, 235–247.

Blume, L., Easley, D., 1992. Evolution and market behavior. Journal of Economic Theory 58, 9–40.

Blume, L., Easley, D., 2006. If you're so smart, why aren't you rich? Belief selection in complete and incomplete markets. Econometrica 74, 929–966.

Bolt, W., Demertzis, M., Diks, C., Hommes, C., van der Leij, M., 2014. Identifying Booms and Busts in House Prices Under Heterogeneous Expectations. Technical Report 14-13, CeNDEF Working Paper. University of Amsterdam.

Boswijk, H., Hommes, C., Manzan, S., 2007. Behavioral heterogeneity in stock prices. Journal of Economic Dynamics and Control 31, 1938–1970.

Bottazzi, G., Dindo, P., 2014. Evolution and market behavior with endogenous investment rules. Journal of Economic Dynamics and Control 48, 121–146.

Brock, W., Hommes, C., 1997. A rational route to randomness. Econometrica 65, 1059–1095.

Brock, W., Hommes, C., 1998. Heterogeneous beliefs and routes to chaos in a simple asset pricing model. Journal of Economic Dynamics and Control 22, 1235–1274.

Brock, W., Hommes, C., Wagener, F., 2009. More hedging instruments may destabilize markets. Journal of Economic Dynamics and Control 33, 1912–1928.

Brunnermeier, M., Julliard, C., 2008. Money illusion and housing frenzies. Review of Financial Studies 21 (1), 135–180.

Burnside, C., Eichenbaum, M., Rebelo, S., 2012. Understanding Booms and Busts in Housing Markets. CQER Working Paper 12-02. Federal Reserve Bank of Atlanta.

Caccioli, F., Farmer, J., Foti, N., Rockmore, D., 2015. Overlapping portfolios, contagion, and financial stability. Journal of Economic Dynamics and Control 51, 50–63.

Campbell, J., Viceira, L., 1999. Consumption and portfolio decisions when expected returns are time varying. The Quarterly Journal of Economics 114, 433–495.

Capozza, D., Israelsen, R., 2007. Predictability in equilibrium: the price dynamics of real estate investment trusts. Real Estate Economics 35 (4), 541–567.

Case, K., Shiller, R., 1989. The efficiency of the market for single-family homes. The American Economic Review 79 (1), 125–137.

Case, K., Shiller, R., 1990. Forecasting prices and excess returns in the housing market. Real Estate Economics 18 (3), 253–273.

Chavas, J., 2000. On the information and market dynamics: the case of the U.S. beef market. Journal of Economic Dynamics and Control 24, 833–853.

Chen, S.-H., Chang, C., Du, Y.R., 2012. Agent-based economic models and econometrics. Knowledge Engineering Review 27 (2), 187–219.

Cheung, Y.-W., Chinn, M., Marsh, I., 2004. How do UK-based foreign exchange dealers think their market operates? International Journal of Finance and Economics 9, 289–306.

Chiarella, C., 1992. The dynamics of speculative behaviour. Annals of Operations Research 37, 101–123.

Chiarella, C., Dieci, R., Gardini, L., 2002. Speculative behaviour and complex asset price dynamics. Journal of Economic Behavior and Organization 49, 173–197.

Chiarella, C., Dieci, R., Gardini, L., 2006a. Asset price and wealth dynamics in a financial market with Heterogeneous agents. Journal of Economic Dynamics and Control 30, 1775–1786.

Chiarella, C., Dieci, R., He, X., 2007. Heterogeneous expectations and speculative behaviour in a dynamic multi-asset framework. Journal of Economic Behavior and Organization 62, 402–427.

Chiarella, C., Dieci, R., He, X., 2009a. Heterogeneity, market mechanisms and asset price dynamics. In: Hens, T., Schenk-Hoppe, K.R. (Eds.), Handbook of Financial Markets: Dynamics and Evolution. Elsevier, pp. 277–344.

Chiarella, C., Dieci, R., He, X., 2011. Do heterogeneous beliefs diversify market risk? European Journal of Finance 17 (3), 241–258.

Chiarella, C., Dieci, R., He, X., 2013a. Time-varying beta: a boundedly rational equilibrium approach. Journal of Evolutionary Economics, 609–639.

Chiarella, C., Dieci, R., He, X., Li, K., 2013b. An evolutionary CAPM under heterogeneous beliefs. Annals of Finance 9, 189–215.

Chiarella, C., He, X., 2001. Asset price and wealth dynamics under heterogeneous expectations. Quantitative Finance 1, 509–526.

Chiarella, C., He, X., 2002. Heterogeneous beliefs, risk and learning in a simple asset pricing model. Computational Economics 19, 95–132.

Chiarella, C., He, X., 2003. Heterogeneous beliefs, risk and learning in a simple asset pricing model with a market maker. Macroeconomic Dynamics 7, 503–536.

Chiarella, C., He, X., Hommes, C., 2006b. A dynamic analysis of moving average rules. Journal of Economic Dynamics and Control 30, 1729–1753.

Chiarella, C., He, X., Huang, W., Zheng, H., 2012a. Estimating behavioural heterogeneity under regime switching. Journal of Economic Behavior and Organization 83 (3), 446–460. https://doi.org/10.1016/j.jebo.2012.02.014.

Chiarella, C., He, X., Pellizzari, P., 2012b. A dynamic analysis of the microstructure of moving average rules in a double auction market. Macroeconomic Dynamics 16, 556–575.

Chiarella, C., He, X., Shi, L., Wei, L., 2017. A behavioral model of investor sentiment in limit order markets. Quantitative Finance 17, 71–86.

Chiarella, C., He, X., Wei, L., 2015a. Learning, information processing and order submission in limit order markets. Journal of Economic Dynamics and Control 61, 245–268.

Chiarella, C., He, X., Zwinkels, R., 2014. Heterogeneous expectations in asset pricing: empirical evidence from the s&p500. Journal of Economic Behavior and Organization 105, 1–16.

Chiarella, C., Iori, G., 2002. A simulation analysis of the microstructure of double auction markets. Quantitative Finance 2 (5), 346–353.

Chiarella, C., Iori, G., Perello, J., 2009b. The impact of heterogeneous trading rules on the limit order book and order flows. Journal of Economic Dynamics and Control 33 (3), 525–537.

Chiarella, C., ter Ellen, S., He, X., Wu, E., 2015b. Fear or fundamentals? Heterogeneous beliefs in the European sovereign CDS market. Journal of Empirical Finance 32, 19–34.

Clayton, J., 1996. Rational expectations, market fundamentals and housing price volatility. Real Estate Economics 24 (4), 441–470.

Conlisk, J., 1996. Why bounded rationality? Journal of Economic Literature 34, 669–700.

Corona, E., Ecca, S., Marchesi, M., Setzu, A., 2008. The interplay between two stock markets and a related foreign exchange market: a simulation approach. Computational Economics 32, 99–119.

Corsi, F., Marmi, S., Lillo, F., 2016. When micro prudence increases macro risk: the destabilizing effects of financial innovation, leverage, and diversification. Operations Research 64 (5), 1073–1088.

Cutler, D., Poterba, J., Summers, L., 1991. Speculative dynamics. Review of Economic Studies 58, 529–546.

Daniel, K., Hirshleifer, D., Subrahmanyam, A., 1998. A theory of overconfidence, self-attribution, and security market under- and over-reactions. Journal of Finance 53, 1839–1885.

Darley, V., Outkin, A.V., 2007. A NASDAQ Market Simulation, Vol. 1 of Complex Systems and Interdisciplinary Science. World Scientific.

Day, R., Huang, W., 1990. Bulls, bears and market sheep. Journal of Economic Behavior and Organization 14, 299–329.

de Grauwe, P., Dewachter, H., Embrechts, M., 1993. Exchange Rate Theory: Chaotic Models of Foreign Exchange Markets. Blackwell.

de Jong, E., Verschoor, W., Zwinkels, R., 2010. Heterogeneity of agents and exchange rate dynamics: evidence from the EMS. Journal of International Money and Finance 29 (8), 1652–1669.

DeBondt, W., Thaler, R., 1985. Does the stock market overreact? Journal of Finance 40, 793–808.

Dieci, R., Foroni, I., Gardini, L., He, X., 2006. Market mood, adaptive beliefs and asset price dynamics. Chaos, Solitons and Fractals 29, 520–534.

Dieci, R., Schmitt, N., Westerhoff, F., 2017. Interactions Between Stock, Bond and Housing Markets. Working Paper. University of Bamberg.

Dieci, R., Westerhoff, F., 2010. Heterogeneous speculators, endogenous fluctuations and interacting markets: a model of stock prices and exchange rates. Journal of Economic Dynamics and Control 34, 743–764.

Dieci, R., Westerhoff, F., 2012. A simple model of a speculative housing market. Journal of Evolutionary Economics 22 (2), 303–329.

Dieci, R., Westerhoff, F., 2013a. Modeling house price dynamics with heterogeneous speculators. In: Bischi, G.I., Chiarella, C., Sushko, I. (Eds.), Global Analysis of Dynamic Models in Economics and Finance. Springer, Berlin/Heidelberg, pp. 35–61.

Dieci, R., Westerhoff, F., 2013b. On the inherent instability of international financial markets: natural nonlinear interactions between stock and foreign exchange markets. Applied Mathematics and Computation 221, 306–328.

Dieci, R., Westerhoff, F., 2016. Heterogeneous expectations, boom-bust housing cycles, and supply conditions: a nonlinear economic dynamics approach. Journal of Economic Dynamics and Control 71, 21–44.

Diks, C., van der Weide, R., 2005. Herding, a-synchronous updating and heterogeneity in memory in a CBS. Journal of Economic Dynamics and Control 29, 741–763.

Diks, C., Wang, J., 2016. Can a stochastic cusp catastrophe model explain housing market crashes? Journal of Economic Dynamics and Control 69, 68–88.

DiPasquale, D., Wheaton, W., 1992. The markets for real estate assets and space: a conceptual framework. Real Estate Economics 20 (2), 181–198.

Easley, D., de Prado, M.L., O'Hara, M., 2013. High Frequency Trading—New Realities for Traders, Markets and Regulators. Risk Books. Chapter The Volume Clock: Insights into the High-Frequency Paradigm.

Eichholtz, P., Huisman, R., Zwinkels, R., 2015. Fundamentals or trends? A long-term perspective on house prices. Applied Economics 47 (10), 1050–1059.

Epstein, L., Schneider, M., 2006. Ambiguity, information quality, and asset pricing. Journal of Finance 63, 197–228.

Evstigneev, I., Hens, T., Schenk-Hoppé, K., 2009. Evolutionary finance. In: Hens, T., Schenk-Hoppé, K.R. (Eds.), Handbook of Financial Markets: Dynamics and Evolution. Elsevier, pp. 509–564.

Fama, E., French, K., 1996. Multifactor explanations of asset pricing anomalies. Journal of Finance 51, 55–84.

Farmer, J., Joshi, S., 2002. The price dynamics of common trading strategies. Journal of Economic Behavior and Organization 49, 149–171.

Feldman, T., 2010. Portfolio manager behavior and global financial crises. Journal of Economic Behavior and Organization 75, 192–202.

Franke, R., 2009. Applying the method of simulated moments to estimate a small agent-based asset pricing model. Journal of Empirical Finance 16, 804–815.

Franke, R., Westerhoff, F., 2011. Estimation of a structural stochastic volatility model of asset pricing. Computational Economics 38, 53–83.

Franke, R., Westerhoff, F., 2012. Structural stochastic volatility in asset pricing dynamics: estimation and model contest. Journal of Economic Dynamics and Control 36, 1193–1211.

Franke, R., Westerhoff, F., 2016. Why a simple herding model may generate the stylized facts of daily returns: explanation and estimation. Journal of Economic Interaction and Coordination 11, 1–34.

Frijns, B., Lehnert, T., Zwinkels, R., 2010. Behavioral heterogeneity in the option market. Journal of Economic Dynamics and Control 34, 2273–2287.

Gaunersdorfer, A., Hommes, C., 2007. A nonlinear structural model for volatility clustering. In: Teyssiere, G., Kirman, A. (Eds.), Long Memory in Economics. Springer, Berlin/Heidelberg, pp. 265–288.

Gaunersdorfer, A., Hommes, C., Wagener, F., 2008. Bifurcation routes to volatility clustering under evolutionary learning. Journal of Economic Behavior and Organization 67, 27–47.

Gilli, M., Winker, P., 2003. A global optimization heuristic for estimating agent-based model. Computational Statistics and Data Analysis 42, 299–312.

Glaeser, E., Gyourko, J., 2007. Housing Dynamics. Discussion Paper 2137. HIER.

Glaeser, E., Gyourko, J., Saiz, A., 2008. Housing supply and housing bubbles. Journal of Urban Economics 64 (2), 198–217.

Goettler, R.L., Parlour, C.A., Rajan, U., 2009. Informed traders and limit order markets. Journal of Financial Economics 93, 67–87.

Gomes, F., Michaelides, A., 2008. Asset pricing with limited risk sharing and heterogeneous agents. Review of Financial Economics 21, 415–448.

Goodwin, R., 1951. The nonlinear accelerator and the persistence of business cycles. Econometrica 19, 1–17.

Gould, M., Porter, M., Williams, S., McDonald, M., Fenn, D., Howison, S., 2013. Limit order books. Quantitative Finance 13, 1709–1742.

Griffin, J., Ji, X., Martin, J., 2003. Momentum investing and business cycle risk: evidence from pole to pole. Journal of Finance 58, 2515–2547.

Grossman, S., Stiglitz, J., 1980. On the impossibility of informationally efficient markets. American Economic Review 70, 393–408.

He, X., 2014. Recent developments in asset pricing with heterogeneous beliefs and adaptive behavior of financial markets. In: Bischi, G.I., Chiarella, C., Sushko, I. (Eds.), Global Analysis of Dynamical Models in Economics and Finance. Springer, pp. 3–34.

He, X., Li, K., 2012. Heterogeneous beliefs and adaptive behaviour in a continuous-time asset price model. Journal of Economic Dynamics and Control 36, 973–987.

He, X., Li, K., 2015a. Profitability of time series momentum. Journal of Banking and Finance 53, 140–157.

He, X., Li, K., Li, Y., 2018. Asset allocation with time series momentum and reversal. Journal of Economic Dynamics & Control. Forthcoming.

He, X., Li, K., Shi, L., 2016a. Social Interaction, Stochastic Volatility, and Momentum. Technical Report. Quantitative Finance Research Centre, University of Technology, Sydney.

He, X., Li, K., Wang, C., 2016b. Volatility clustering: a nonlinear theoretical approach. Journal of Economic Behavior and Organization 130, 274–297.

He, X., Li, Y., 2007. Power law behaviour, heterogeneity, and trend chasing. Journal of Economic Dynamics and Control 31, 3396–3426.

He, X., Li, Y., 2008. Heterogeneity, convergence and autocorrelations. Quantitative Finance 8, 58–79.

He, X., Li, Y., 2015b. Testing of a market fraction model and power-law behaviour in the DAX 30. Journal of Empirical Finance 30, 1–17.

He, X., Li, Y., 2017. The adaptiveness in stock markets: testing the stylized facts in the DAX 30. Journal of Evolutionary Economics 27 (5), 1071–1094.

He, X., Zheng, H., 2016. Trading heterogeneity under information uncertainty. Journal of Economic Behavior and Organization 130, 64–80.

Heckman, J., 2001. Micro data, heterogeneity, and evaluation of public policy: Nobel lecture. Journal of Political Economy 109 (4), 673–748.

Heemeijer, P., Hommes, C., Sonnemans, J., Tuinstra, J., 2009. Price stability and volatility in markets with positive and negative expectations feedback: an experimental investigation. Journal of Economic Dynamics and Control 33, 1052–1072.

Hens, T., Schenk-Hoppé, K., 2005. Evolutionary stability of portfolio rules. Journal of Mathematical Economics 41, 43–66.

Himmelberg, C., Mayer, C., Sinai, T., 2005. Assessing high house prices: bubbles, fundamentals and misperceptions. Journal of Economic Perspectives 19 (4), 67–92.

Hirshleifer, D., 2015. Behavioral finance. Annual Review of Financial Economics 7, 133–159.

Hofbauer, J., Sigmund, K., 1998. Evolutionary Games and Population Dynamics. Cambridge University Press.

Holland, J., 1975. Adaptation in Natural and Artificial Systems: An Introductory Analysis with Applications to Biology, Control, and Artificial Intelligence. University of Michigan Press.

Hommes, C., 2001. Financial markets as nonlinear adaptive evolutionary systems. Quantitative Finance 1, 149–167.

Hommes, C., 2006. Heterogeneous agent models in economics and finance. In: Tesfatsion, L., Judd, K.L. (Eds.), Handbook of Computational Economics, Vol. 2, Agent-based Computational Economics. North-Holland, pp. 1109–1186.

Hommes, C., 2013. Behavioral Rationality and Heterogeneous Expectations in Complex Economic Systems. Cambridge University Press, New York.

Hommes, C., in't Veld, D., 2015. Booms, Busts and Behavioural Heterogeneity in Stock Prices. Technical Report 15-088/II. Tinbergen Institute Discussion Paper, Amsterdam, The Netherlands.

Hommes, C., Sonnemans, J., Tuinstra, J., Velden, H.V.D., 2005. Coordination of expectations in asset pricing experiments. Review of Financial Studies 18, 955–980.

Hommes, C., Wagener, F., 2009. Complex evolutionary systems in behavioral finance (Chapter 4). In: Hens, T., In: Schenk-Hoppe, K. (Eds.), Handbook of Financial Markets: Dynamics and Evolution. In: Handbooks in Finance. North-Holland, pp. 217–276.

Hong, H., Stein, J., 1999. A unified theory of underreaction, momentum trading, and overreaction in asset markets. Journal of Finance 54, 2143–2184.

Hong, H., Torous, W., Valkanov, R., 2007. Do industries lead stock markets? Journal of Financial Economics 83, 367–396.

Hou, K., Moskowitz, T., 2005. Market frictions, price delay, and the cross-section of expected returns. Review of Financial Studies 18, 981–1020.

Huang, W., Chen, Z., 2014. Modeling regional linkage of financial markets. Journal of Economic Behavior and Organization 99, 18–31.

Jagannathan, R., Wang, Z., 1996. The conditional CAPM and cross-section of expected returns. Journal of Finance 51, 3–53.

Jegadeesh, N., Titman, S., 1993. Returns to buying winners and selling losers: implications for stock market efficiency. Journal of Finance 48, 65–91.

Jegadeesh, N., Titman, S., 2001. Profitability of momentum strategies: an evaluation of alternative explanations. Journal of Finance 56, 699–720.

Jordà, O., Schularick, M., Taylor, A., 2015. Betting the house. Journal of International Economics 96, S2–S18.

Kalecki, M., 1935. A macroeconomic theory of the business cycle. Econometrica 3, 327–344.

Kirman, A., 1992. Whom or what does the representative agent represent? Journal of Economic Perspectives 6, 117–136.

Kirman, A., 2010. The economic crisis is a crisis for economic theory. CESifo Economic Studies 56 (4), 498–535.

Kirman, A., Ricciotti, R., Topol, R., 2007. Bubbles in foreign exchange markets: it takes two to tango. Macroeconomic Dynamics 11, 102–123.

Kouwenberg, R., Zwinkels, R., 2014. Forecasting the US housing market. International Journal of Forecasting 30, 415–425.

Kouwenberg, R., Zwinkels, R., 2015. Endogenous price bubbles in a multi-agent system of the housing market. PLoS ONE 10 (6).

Kovaleva, P., Iori, G., 2014. Heterogenous beliefs and quote transparency in an order-driven market. In: Dieci, R., He, X., Hommes, C. (Eds.), Nonlinear Economic Dynamics and Financial Modelling: Essays in Honour of Carl Chiarella. Springer, pp. 163–181.

Kyle, A., 1985. Continuous auctions and insider trading. Econometrica 53, 1315–1335.

Lakonishok, J., Shleifer, A., Vishny, R., 1994. Contrarian investment, extrapolation and risk. Journal of Finance 49, 1541–1578.

Larson, A., 1964. The hog cycle as harmonic motion. Journal of Farm Economics 46, 375–386.

LeBaron, B., 2006. Agent-based computational finance. In: Tesfatsion, L., Judd, K.L. (Eds.), Handbook of Computational Economics, Vol. 2, Agent-based Computational Economics. North-Holland, pp. 1187–1233.

LeBaron, B., 2011. Active and passive learning in agent-based financial markets. Eastern Economic Journal 37, 35–43.

LeBaron, B., 2012. Heterogeneous gain learning and the dynamics of asset prices. Journal of Economic Behavior & Organization 83, 424–445.

LeBaron, B., Arthur, W., Palmer, R., 1999. Time series properties of an artificial stock market. Journal of Economic Dynamics and Control 23, 1487–1516.

LeBaron, B., Tesfatsion, L., 2008. Modeling macroeconomies as open-ended dynamic systems of interacting agents. American Economic Review 98 (2), 246–250.

LeBaron, B., Yamamoto, R., 2008. The impact of imitation on long-memory in an order-driven market. Eastern Economic Journal 34, 504–517.

Lensberg, T., Schenk-Hoppé, K., Ladley, D., 2015. Costs and benefits of financial regulation: short-selling bans and transaction taxes. Journal of Banking and Finance 51, 103–118.

Lettau, M., Uhlig, H., 1999. Rules of thumb versus dynamic programming. American Economic Review 89, 148–174.

Levy, M., Levy, H., Solomon, S., 1994. A microscopic model of the stock market. Economics Letters 45, 103–111.

Li, K., Liu, J., 2016. Optimal Dynamic Momentum Strategies. SSRN Working Paper. http://ssrn.com/abstract=2746561.

Lux, T., 1995. Herd behaviour, bubbles and crashes. Economic Journal 105, 881–896.

Lux, T., 2009a. Rational forecasts or social opinion dynamics? Identification of interaction effects in a business climate survey. Journal of Economic Behavior and Organization 32, 638–655.

Lux, T., 2009b. Stochastic behavioural asset pricing and stylized facts. In: Hens, T., Schenk-Hoppe, K.R. (Eds.), Handbook of Financial Markets: Dynamics and Evolution. Elsevier, pp. 161–215.

Lux, T., 2012. Estimation of an agent-based model of investor sentiment formation in financial markets. Journal of Economic Behavior and Organization 36, 1284–1302.

Lux, T., Alfarano, S., 2016. Financial power laws: empirical evidence, models, and mechanisms. Chaos, Solitons and Fractals 88, 3–18.

Mackey, M., 1989. Commodity price fluctuations: price dependent delays and nonlinearities as explanatory factors. Journal of Economic Theory 48, 495–509.

Malpezzi, S., Wachter, S., 2005. The role of speculation in real estate cycles. Journal of Real Estate Literature 13 (2), 141–164.

Marimon, R., McGrattan, E., Sargent, T., 1990. Money as a medium of exchange in an economy with artificially intelligent agents. Journal of Economic Dynamics and Control 14, 329–373.

Matsumoto, A., Szidarovszky, F., 2011. Delay differential neoclassical growth model. Journal of Economic Behavior and Organization 78, 272–289.

Menkhoff, L., 1998. The noise trading approach – questionnaire evidence from foreign exchange. Journal of International Money and Finance 17, 547–564.

Menkhoff, L., 2010. The use of technical analysis by fund managers: international evidence. Journal of Banking and Finance 34, 2573–2586.

Menkhoff, L., Taylor, P., 2007. The obstinate passion of foreign exchange professionals: technical analysis. Journal of Economic Literature 45, 936–972.

Merton, R., 1971. Optimum consumption and portfolio rules in a continuous time model. Journal of Economic Theory 3, 373–413.

Moskowitz, T., Ooi, Y.H., Pedersen, L.H., 2012. Time series momentum. Journal of Financial Economics 104, 228–250.

O'Hara, M., 2001. Overview: market structure issues in market liquidity. In: Market Liquidity: Proceedings of a Workshop Held at the BIS. Bank for International Settlements (BIS) Papers.

O'Hara, M., 2015. High frequency market microstructure. Journal of Financial Economics 116, 257–270.

Pagan, A., 1996. The econometrics of financial markets. Journal of Empirical Finance 3, 15–102.

Palczewski, J., Schenk-Hoppé, K., Wang, T., 2016. Itchy feet vs cool heads: flow of funds in an agent-based financial market. Journal of Economic Dynamics and Control 63, 53–68.

Pellizzari, P., Westerhoff, F., 2009. Some effects of transaction taxes under different microstructures. Journal of Economic Behavior and Organization 72 (3), 850–863.

Phillips, A., 1957. Stabilization policy and time forms of lagged responses in a closed economy. Economic Journal 67, 265–277.

Piazzesi, M., Schneider, M., 2009. Momentum traders in the housing market: survey evidence and a search model. American Economic Review 99 (2), 406–411.

Poledna, S., Thurner, S., Farmer, J., Geanakoplos, J., 2014. Leverage-induced systemic risk under Basle II and other credit risk policies. Journal of Banking and Finance 42, 199–212.

Poterba, J., 1984. Tax subsidies to owner-occupied housing: an asset-market approach. The Quarterly Journal of Economics 99 (4), 729–752.

Poterba, J., Weil, D., Shiller, R., 1991. House price dynamics: the role of tax policy and demography. Brookings Papers on Economic Activity 1991 (2), 143–203.

Rosu, I., 2012. Order choice and information in limit order markets. In: Market Microstructure: Confronting Many Viewpoints. Wiley, pp. 41–60.

Rubinstein, A., 1998. Modeling Bounded Rationality. MIT Press, Cambridge, MA.

Sandroni, A., 2000. Do markets favor agents able to make accurate predictions? Econometrica 68, 1303–1342.

Sargent, T., 1993. Bounded Rationality in Macroeconomics. Clarendon Press, Oxford.

Schmitt, N., Westerhoff, F., 2014. Speculative behavior and the dynamics of interacting stock markets. Journal of Economic Dynamics and Control 45, 262–288.

Shefrin, H., 2005. A Behavioral Approach to Asset Pricing. Academic Press Inc., London.

Shiller, R., 2005. Irrational Exuberance, 2nd edn. Princeton University Press, Princeton.

Shiller, R., 2007. Understanding Recent Trends in House Prices and Home Ownership. Technical Report. National Bureau of Economic Research.

Shiller, R., 2008. Historic turning points in real estate. Eastern Economic Journal 34 (1), 1–13.

Simon, H., 1982. Models of Bounded Rationality. MIT Press, Cambridge, MA.

Sommervoll, D., Borgersen, T., Wennemo, T., 2010. Endogenous housing market cycles. Journal of Banking and Finance 34 (3), 557–567.

Taylor, M., Allen, H., 1992. The use of technical analysis in the foreign exchange market. Journal of International Money and Finance 11, 304–314.

ter Ellen, S., Verschoor, W., Zwinkels, R., 2013. Dynamic expectation formation in the foreign exchange market. Journal of International Money and Finance 37, 75–97.

ter Ellen, S., Zwinkels, R., 2010. Oil price dynamics: a behavioral finance approach with heterogeneous agents. Energy Economics 32, 1427–1434.

Tesfatsion, L., Judd, K., 2006. Agent-Based Computational Economics. Handbook of Computational Economics, vol. 2. Elsevier.

Thurner, S., Farmer, J., Geanakoplos, J., 2012. Leverage causes fat tails and clustered volatility. Quantitative Finance 12 (5), 695–707.

Tramontana, F., Gardini, L., Dieci, R., Westerhoff, F., 2009. The emergence of bull and bear dynamics in a nonlinear model of interacting markets. Discrete Dynamics in Nature and Society 2009, 1–30.

Tramontana, F., Gardini, L., Dieci, R., Westerhoff, F., 2010. Global bifurcations in a three-dimensional financial model of bull and bear interactions. In: Bischi, G.-I., Chiarella, C., Gardini, L. (Eds.), Nonlinear Dynamics in Economics, Finance and Social Sciences: Essays in Honour of John Barkley Rosser Jr. Springer, pp. 333–352.

Wachter, J., 2002. Portfolio and consumption decisions under mean-reverting returns: an exact solution for complete markets. Journal of Financial and Quantitative Analysis 37, 63–91.

Westerhoff, F., 2003. Speculative markets and the effectiveness of price limits. Journal of Economic Dynamics and Control 28, 439–508.

Westerhoff, F., 2004. Multiasset market dynamics. Macroeconomic Dynamics 8, 591–616.

Westerhoff, F., 2009. Exchange rate dynamics: a nonlinear survey. In: Handbook of Research on Complexity. Edward Elgar, Cheltenham, pp. 287–325.

Westerhoff, F., Dieci, R., 2006. The effectiveness of Keynes–Tobin transaction taxes when heterogeneous agents can trade in different markets: a behavioral finance approach. Journal of Economic Dynamics and Control 30, 293–322.

Westerhoff, F., Reitz, S., 2003. Nonlinearities and cyclical behavior: the role of chartists and fundamentalists. Studies in Nonlinear Dynamics and Econometrics 7 (4). Article no. 3.

Wheaton, W., 1999. Real estate "cycles": some fundamentals. Real Estate Economics 27 (2), 209–230.

Yeh, C., Yang, C., 2010. Examining the effectiveness of price limits in an artificial stock market. Journal of Economic Dynamics and Control 34, 2089–2108.

Yoshida, H., Asada, T., 2007. Dynamic analysis of policy lag in a Keynes–Goodwin model: stability, instability, cycles and chaos. Journal of Economic Behavior and Organization 62, 441–469.

Zeeman, E., 1974. The unstable behavior of stock exchange. Journal of Mathematical Economics 1, 39–49.

Models of Financial Stability and Their Application in Stress Tests[*]

Christoph Aymanns[*], J. Doyne Farmer[†,‡,§,¶,1], Alissa M. Kleinnijenhuis[†,‡,‖],
Thom Wetzer[†,‖,**]

[*]*Swiss Institute of Banking and Finance, University of St. Gallen, St. Gallen, Switzerland*
[†]*Institute for New Economic Thinking at the Oxford Martin School, University of Oxford, Oxford, United Kingdom*
[‡]*Mathematical Institute, University of Oxford, Oxford, United Kingdom*
[§]*Department of Computer Science, University of Oxford, Oxford, United Kingdom*
[¶]*Santa-Fe Institute, Santa Fe, NM, United States*
[‖]*Oxford-Man Institute of Quantitative Finance, University of Oxford, Oxford, United Kingdom*
[**]*Faculty of Law, University of Oxford, Oxford, United Kingdom*
[1]*Corresponding author: e-mail address: doyne.farmer@inet.ox.ac.uk*

CONTENTS

[*]The authors thank Tobias Adrian, Fabio Caccioli, Agostino Capponi, Darrell Duffie, Luca Enriques, Cars Hommes, Sujit Kapadia, Blake LeBaron, Alan D. Morrison, Paul Nahai-Williamson, James Paulin, Peyton Young, Garbrand Wiersema, an anonymous reviewer, and the participants of the Workshop for the Handbook of Computational Economics for their valuable comments and suggestions. The usual disclaimers apply.

1 INTRODUCTION

The financial system is a classic example of a complex system. It consists of many diverse actors, including banks, mutual funds, hedge funds, insurance companies, pension funds and shadow banks. All of them interact with each other, as well as interacting directly with the real economy (which is undeniably a complex system in and of itself). The financial crisis of 2008 provided a perfect example of an emergent phenomenon, which is the hallmark of a complex system.

While the causes of the crisis remain controversial, a standard view goes like this: A financial market innovation called mortgage-backed securities made lenders feel more secure, causing them to extend more credit to households and purchase large quantities of securities on credit. Liberalized lending fueled a housing bubble; when it crashed, the fact that the portfolios of most major financial institutions had significant holdings of mortgage backed securities caused large losses. This in turn caused a credit freeze, cutting off funding for important activities in the real economy. This generated a global recession that cost the world an amount that has been estimated to be as high as fifty trillion dollars, the order of half a year of global GDP. Here we will present an alternative hypothesis, suggesting the possibility that the housing bubble was only the spark that lit the fire, and a deeper underlying cause might have been the build up of systemic risk over time. As we will discuss below, a substantial part of this systemic risk may have been due to backward looking, procyclical risk management of leveraged financial institutions.[1] In either case, the crisis provides a clear example of an emergent phenomenon.

The crisis has made everyone aware of the complex nature of the interactions and feedback loops in the economy, and has driven an explosive amount of research attempting to better understand the financial system from a systemic point of view. It has also underlined the policy relevance of the complex systems approach. Systemic risk occurs when the decisions of individuals, which might be prudent if considered in isolation, combine to create risks at the level of the whole system that may be qualitatively different from the simple combination of their individual risks. By its very nature systemic risk is an emergent phenomenon that comes about due to the nonlinear interaction of individual agents. To understand systemic risk we need to understand the collective dynamics of the system that gives rise to it.

The financial system is sufficiently complicated that it is not yet possible to model it realistically. Existing models only attempt a stylized view, trying to elucidate the underlying mechanisms driving financial stability. There are currently two basic approaches. The mainstream approach has been to focus on situations where it is possible to compute an equilibrium. This generally requires making very strong simplifications, e.g. studying only a few actors and interactions at a time. The equilibrium approach has been useful to clarify some of the key mechanisms driving financial instabilities and financial contagion, but it comes at the expense of simplifications that limit the realism of the conclusions. There is also a concern that, particularly during a crisis, the assumptions of rationality and equilibrium are too strong.

The alternative approach abandons equilibrium and rationality and replaces them with behavioral assumptions.[2] This approach often relies on simulation, which has the advantage that it is easier to study more complicated situations, e.g. with more actors and more realistic institutional constraints. It also makes it possible to study multiple channels of interaction; even though research in this direction is still in its early stages, it is clear that this plays an important role.

The use of behavioral assumptions as an alternative to utility maximization is controversial. Unlike utility, behavioral assumptions have the advantage of being directly observable, and in many cases the degree to which they are followed can be

---

[1] One example of procyclical risk management practices based on backward looking risk estimates are Value-at-Risk constraints. Such constraints were imposed on the trading book of banks under Basel II. However, many other leveraged institutions, not subject to Basel II, also used Value-at-Risk constraints in their internal risk management.

[2] Rationality vs. behavioral assumptions can be regarded as two poles in a continuum. A useful intermediate alternative is to place more emphasis on agents that learn. The computational approach is often forced to abandon rationality because in more realistic settings perfect rationality may be computationally intractable, but numerical approximations with optimizing behavior may be feasible.

confirmed empirically. The disadvantage of this approach is that behavior may be context dependent, and as a result, such models typically fail the Lucas critique. We will show examples here where models based on behavioral assumptions are nonetheless very useful because they make it possible to directly investigate the consequences of a given set of behaviors. We will show examples where it leads to simple models that make clear predictions, at the same time that it can potentially be extended to complex real world situations.

This review will focus primarily on the simulation approach, though we will attempt to discuss key influences and interactions with the more traditional equilibrium approach. Our view is that the two approaches are complements rather than substitutes. The most appropriate approach depends on the context and the goals of the modeling exercise. We predict that the simulation approach will become increasingly important with time, for several reasons. One is that this approach can be easier to bring to the data, and data is becoming more readily available. Many central banks are beginning to collect comprehensive data sets that make it possible to monitor the key parts of the financial system. This makes it easier to test the realism of behavioral assumptions, making such models less ad hoc. With such models it is potentially feasible to match the models to the data in a literal, one-to-one manner. This has not yet been done, but it is on the horizon, and if successful such models may become valuable tools for assessing and monitoring financial stability, and for policy testing. In addition, computational power is always improving. This is a new area of pursuit and the computational techniques and software are rapidly improving.

The actors in the financial system are highly interconnected, and as a consequence network dynamics plays a key role in determining financial stability. The distress of one institution can propagate to other institutions, a process that is often called *contagion*, based on the analogy to disease. There are multiple channels of contagion, including counterparty risk, funding risk, and common assets holdings. *Counterparty risk* is caused by the web of bilateral contracts, which make one institution's assets another's liabilities. When a borrower is unable to pay, the lender's balance sheet is affected, and the resulting financial distress may in turn be transmitted to other parties, causing them to come under stress or default. *Funding risk* occurs when a lender comes under stress, which may create problems for parties that routinely borrow from this lender because loans that they would normally expect to receive fail to be extended. Institutions are also connected in many indirect ways, e.g. by common asset holdings, also called *overlapping portfolios*. If an institution comes under stress and sells assets, this depresses prices, which can cause further selling, etc. There are of course other channels of contagion, such as common information, that can affect expectations and interact with the more mechanical channels described above.

These channels of contagion cause nonlinear interactions that can create positive feedback loops that amplify external shocks or even generate purely endogenous dynamics, such as booms and busts. Nonlinear feedback loops can also be amplified by behavioral and institutional constraints and by bounded rationality (often in the context of incomplete information and learning).

Behavioral and institutional constraints force agents to take actions that they would prefer to avoid in the absence of the constraint. Such behavioral constraints can be imposed by a regulator but they can also result from bilateral contracts between private institutions. In principle, regulatory constraints, such as capital or liquidity coverage ratios, are designed to increase financial stability. In many cases however, these constraints are designed to increase the resilience of an individual financial institution to idiosyncratic shocks rather than the resilience of the system as a whole. Take the example of a leverage constraint. If a financial institution has high leverage, a small shock may be enough to push it into insolvency. Hence, from a regulatory perspective, a cap on leverage seems like a good idea. However, as we will discuss below, a leverage constraint may have the adverse side effect that it forces distressed institutions to sell into falling asset markets, causing prices to fall further and amplifying a crisis. Of course, leverage constraints are needed, but the point is that their effects can go far beyond the failure of individual institutions, and the way in which they are enforced can make a big difference. Similar positive feedback can result from other behavioral constraints as well.

This brings up the distinction between *microprudential regulation*, which is designed to benefit individual institutions without considering the effect on the system as a whole, vs. *macroprudential regulation*, which is designed to take systemic effects into account. These can come into dramatic conflict. For example, we will discuss the base of Basel II, which provided perfectly sensible rules for risk management from a microprudential point of view, but which likely caused substantial systemic risk from a macroprudential point of view, and indeed may have been a major driver of the crisis of 2008. It is ironic that prudent behavior of an individual can cause such significant problems for society as a whole.

Rational agents with complete information might be able to navigate the risks inherent to the financial system. Indeed, optimal behavior might well mitigate the positive feedback resulting from interconnectedness and behavioral constraints. However, we believe that optimal behavior in the financial system is rare. Instead, agents are restricted by bounded rationality. Their limited understanding of the system in which they operate forces agents to rely on simple rules as well as biased methods to learn about the state of the system and form expectations about its future states (Farmer, 2002; Lo, 2005). Suboptimal decisions and biased expectations can exacerbate the destabilizing effects of interconnectedness and behavioral constraints but can also lead to financial instability on their own.

The remainder of this paper is organized as follows: In Section 2 we briefly contrast and compare traditional equilibrium models with agent-based models. In Section 3 we introduce the dynamical systems perspective on the financial system that will underlie many of the models of financial stability that we discuss in subsequent sections. In Sections 4 and 5 we discuss models of systemic risk resulting from leverage constraints and models of financial contagion due to interconnectedness, respectively. Sections 6 to 9 consider various different stress tests. In particular, Section 6 gives a brief conceptual overview of stress tests; Section 7 introduces and critically evaluates standard, micro-prudential stress tests; Section 8 discusses examples of macroprudential stress tests and how to bring them to data; finally Section 9 outlines a vision for the next generation of system-wide stress tests.

2 TWO APPROACHES TO MODELING SYSTEMIC RISK

As mentioned in the introduction, traditionally finance has focused on modeling systemic risk in highly stylized models that are analytically tractable. These efforts have improved our understanding of a wide range of phenomena related to systemic risk ranging from bank runs (Diamond and Dybvig, 1983; Morris and Shin, 2001), credit cycles (Kiyotaki and Moore, 1997; Brunnermeier and Sannikov, 2014), balance sheet (Allen and Gale, 2000), and information contagion (Acharya and Yorulmazer, 2008) over fire sales (Shleifer and Vishny, 1992), to the feedback between market and funding liquidity (Brunnermeier and Pedersen, 2009). A comprehensive review that does justice to this literature is beyond the scope of this paper. However, we would like to make a few observations in regard to the traditional modeling approach and contrast it with the agent-based approach.

Traditional models place great emphasis on the incentives and information structure of agents in a financial market. Given those, agents behave strategically, taking into account their beliefs about the state of the world, and other agents' strategies. The objects of interest are then the game theoretic equilibria of this interaction. This allows for studying the effects of properties such as asymmetric information, uncertainty or moral hazard on the stability of the financial system. While these models provide valuable qualitative insights, they are typically only tractable in very stylized settings. Models are usually restricted to a small number or a continuum of agents, a few time periods and a drastically simplified institutional and market set up. This can make it difficult to draw quantitative conclusions from such models.

Agent-based models typically place less emphasis on incentives and information, and instead focus on how the dynamic interactions of behaviorally simple agents can lead to complex aggregate phenomena, such as financial crises, and how outcomes are shaped by the structure of this interaction and the heterogeneity of agents. From this perspective, the key drivers of systemic risk are the amplification of dynamic instabilities and contagion processes in financial markets. Complicated strategic interactions and incentives are often ignored in favor of simple, empirically motivated behavioral rules and a more realistic institutional and market set up. Since these models can easily be simulated numerically, they can in principle be scaled to a large number of agents and, if appropriately calibrated, can yield quantitative insights.

Two common criticisms leveled against heterogeneous agent-based models are the lack of strategic interactions and the reliance on computer simulations. The first criticism is fair and, in many cases, highlights an important shortcoming of this approach. Hard wired behavioral rules need to be carefully calibrated against real data, and even when they are, they can fail in new situations where the behavior of agents may change. For computer simulations to be credible, their parameters need to be calibrated and the sensitivity of outcomes to those parameters needs to be understood.

The latter in particular is more challenging in computational models than in tractable analytical models.

In our view, what is not fair is to regard computer simulations as inherently inferior to analytic results. Analytic models have the benefit of the relative ease with which they can be used to understand the concepts driving structural cause-and-effect relationships. But many aspects of the economic world are not simple, and in most realistic situations computer simulations are the only possibility. Good practice is to make code freely available and well documented, so that results are easily reproducible.

Traditional and heterogeneous agent-based models are complements rather than substitutes. Some heterogeneous agent-based models already use myopic optimization, and in the future the line between the two may become increasingly blurred.[3] As methods such as computational game theory or multi-agent reinforcement learning mature, it may become possible to increasingly introduce strategic interactions into computational heterogeneous agent-based models. Furthermore, as computational resources and large volumes of data on the financial system become more accessible, parameter exploration and calibration should become increasingly feasible. Therefore, we are optimistic that, provided technology progresses as expected,[4] in the future heterogeneous agent-based models will be able to overcome some of the shortcomings discussed above. And as we demonstrate here, they have already led to important new results in this field, that were not obtainable via analytic methods.

3 A VIEW OF THE FINANCIAL SYSTEM

At a high level, it is useful to think of the financial system as a dynamical system that consists of a collection of institutions that interact via centralized and bilateral markets. An institution can be represented by its balance sheet, i.e. its assets and liabilities, together with a set of decision rules that it deploys to control the state of its balance sheet in order to achieve a certain goal. Within this framework, a market can be thought of as a mechanism that takes actions from institutions as inputs and changes the state of their balance sheets based on its internal dynamics. Anyone wishing to construct an agent model of the financial system therefore has to answer three fundamental questions: (i) what comprises the institutions' balance sheets, (ii) what determines their actions conditional on the state of the world, and (iii) how do markets respond to these actions? In the following, we will sketch the balance sheet of a generic leveraged investor, which will serve as the fundamental building block of the models of financial stability that we will discuss in this review. We will also

---

[3] In fact, this is already the case in the literature on financial and economic networks, see for example Goyal (2018).

[4] It seems unlikely that scientists' ability to analytically solve models will improve as quickly as numerical techniques and heterogeneous agent-based simulations, which benefit from rapid improvements in hardware and software.

briefly touch on (ii) and (iii) when discussing the important channels through which leveraged investors interact. In the subsequent sections we will then discuss concrete models of financial stability that fall within this general framework.

3.1 BALANCE SHEET COMPOSITION

When developing a model of a financial system, it is useful to distinguish between two types of agents which we refer to as "active" and "passive" agents. Active agents are the objects of interest and their internal state and interactions are carefully modeled. Passive agents represent parts of the financial system that interact with active agents but are not the focus of the model, and are therefore typically represented by simple stochastic processes. For the remainder of this review, consider a financial system that consists of a set $\mathcal{B}$ of active leveraged investors and a set of passive agents which will remain unspecified for now. We are particularly interested in systemic risk that is driven by borrowing, and thus we focus on agents that use leverage (defined as purchasing assets with borrowed funds). However, the setup below is sufficiently general to accommodate unleveraged investors as a special case with leverage equal to one.

Leveraged investors need not be homogeneous and may differ, among other aspects, in their balance sheet composition, strategies or counterparties. In practice, a leveraged investor might be a bank or a leveraged hedge fund and other active investors might include unleveraged mutual funds. Passive agents could be depositors, noise traders, fund investors that generate investment flows or banks that lend to hedge funds. The choice of active vs. passive investors of course varies from model to model.

The balance sheet of an investor $i \in \mathcal{B}$ is composed of assets A_i, liabilities L_i, and equity E_i, such that $A_i = L_i + E_i$. The investor's leverage is simply the ratio of assets to equity $\lambda_i = A_i/E_i$. It is useful to decompose the investor's assets into three classes: bilateral contracts A_i^B between investors, such as loans or derivative exposures; traded securities A_i^S, such as stocks; and external assets A_i^R, whose value is assumed exogenous. Throughout this review, we assume that the value A_i^S of traded securities is marked to market.[5] That is, the value of a traded security on the investor's balance sheet will be determined by its current market price. Of course we must have that $A_i = A_i^B + A_i^S + A_i^R$. Each asset class can be further decomposed into individual loan contracts, stock holdings and so on.

The investor's liabilities can be decomposed in a similar fashion. For now, let us decompose the investor's liabilities simply into bilateral contracts L_i^B between investors, such as loans or derivative exposures, and external liabilities L_i^R which can be assumed exogenous. In the case of a bank, these external liabilities might be deposits. Again we must have that $L_i = L_i^B + L_i^R$, and bilateral liabilities can be

---

[5] The term *marked to market* means that the value of assets is recomputed in every period based on current market prices. This is in contrast to valuing assets based on an estimate of their fundamental value.

further decomposed into individual bilateral contracts. Bilateral assets and liabilities might be secured, such as repurchase agreements, or unsecured such as interbank loans. Naturally, bilateral liabilities are just the flip side of bilateral assets such that summing over all investors we must have $\sum_i A_i^B = \sum_i L_i^B$.

3.2 BALANCE SHEET DYNAMICS

Of all the factors that affect the dynamics of the investors' balance sheets, three are of particular importance for financial stability: leverage, liquidity, and interconnectedness. Below, we discuss each factor in turn.

Leverage: Leverage amplifies returns, both positive and negative. Therefore, investors typically face a leverage constraint to limit the investors' risk.[6] However, at the level of the financial system, binding leverage constraints can lead to substantial instabilities. On short time scales, a leveraged investor may be forced to sell into falling markets when she exceeds her leverage constraint. Her sales will in turn depress prices further as we explain in the next paragraph on market liquidity. Leverage constraints can thus lead to an unstable feedback loop between falling prices and forced sales. On longer time scales dynamic leverage constraints that depend on backward looking risk estimates can lead to entirely endogenous volatility – so called leverage cycles.[7]

Liquidity: Broadly speaking, one can distinguish between two types of liquidity: market liquidity and funding liquidity.

Market liquidity can be understood as the inverse to price impact. When market liquidity is high, the market can absorb large sell orders without large changes in the price. If markets were perfectly liquid it would always be possible to sell assets without affecting prices and most forms of systemic risk would not exist.[8] Leverage is dangerous both because it directly increases risk, amplifying gains and losses proportionally, but also because the market impact of liquidating a portfolio to achieve a certain leverage increases with leverage. This point was stressed by Caccioli et al. (2012a), who showed how, due to her own market impact, an investor with a large leveraged position can easily drive herself bankrupt by liquidating her position. They showed that this can be a serious problem even under normal market conditions, and recommended taking market impact into account when valuing portfolios in order to reduce this problem. The problem can become even worse if investors are forced to

---

[6]This constraint may be imposed by a regulator, a counterparty or internal risk management.

[7]Beyond leverage, investors may also face other constraints. Regulators have imposed restrictions on the liquidity of assets that some investors may hold (with a preference for more liquid assets) and the stability of their funding (with a preference for more long term funding). The effect of these constraints on systemic risk is much less studied than the effect of leverage constraints. A priori however, one would expect these constraints to improve stability. This is because of the absence of feedback loops similar to the leverage-price feedback loop that drives forced sales.

[8]Prices would of course still change to reflect the arrival of new information.

sell too quickly, inducing *fire sales* in which a market is overloaded with sell orders, causing a dramatic decrease in liquidity for sellers.[9] Fire sales can be induced when investors hit leverage constraints, forcing them to sell, which in turn causes leverage constraints to be more strongly broken, inducing more selling.

Funding liquidity refers to the ease with which investors can borrow to fund their balance sheets. When funding liquidity is high, investors can easily roll over their existing liabilities by borrowing again, or even expand their balance sheets. In times of crises, funding liquidity can drop dramatically. If investors rely on short term liabilities they may be forced to liquidate a large part of their assets to pay back their liabilities. This forced sale can trigger fire sales by other investors.

Interconnectedness: Investors are connected via their balance sheets and so are not isolated agents. Connections can result from direct exposures due to bilateral loan contracts, or from indirect exposures due to investments into the same assets. Interconnectedness together with feedback loops resulting from binding leverage constraints and endogenous liquidity can lead to financial contagion. In analogy to epidemiology, financial contagion refers to the process by which "distress" may spread from one investor to another, where distress can be broadly understood as an investor becoming uncomfortably close to insolvency or illiquidity. Typically financial contagion arises when, via some mechanism or channel, a distressed investor's actions negatively affect some subset of other investors. This subset of investors is said to be connected to the distressed investor. A simple example of such connections are the bilateral liabilities between investors. Taken together, the set of all such connections form a network over which financial contagion can spread. For an in-depth review of financial networks see Iori and Mantegna (2018).

The aim of the subsequent sections is to introduce the reader to a number of models that tackle the effect of leverage, liquidity and interconnectedness on financial stability in isolation. These models then form the building blocks of more comprehensive models discussed in Section 6. Below, in Section 4, we first focus on the potentially destabilizing effects of leverage as they form the basis of fire sale models discussed later, and because they are thought to have contributed to the build up of risk prior to the great financial crisis. In Section 5 we then proceed to models of financial contagion as they form the scientific bedrock of the stress testing models that will be discussed in Section 6 and beyond. While liquidity is of great importance, we will only discuss it implicitly in Sections 4 and 5, rather than dedicating a separate section to it. This is because, unfortunately, there are currently only few dedicated models on this topic, see Bookstaber and Paddrik (2015) for an example. We will not be able to provide a complete overview of the agent-based modeling literature devoted to various aspects of financial stability. Important topics that we will not be able to discuss include the role of heterogeneous expectations or time scales in the

---

[9]There is always market impact from buying or selling. The term "fire sales" technically means selling under stress, but often means simply a case where the sale of assets is forced (even when markets remain orderly). See the discussion in Section 5.3.

dynamics of financial markets, see for example Hommes (2006), LeBaron (2006) for early surveys, and Dieci and He (2018) for a recent overview.

4 LEVERAGE AND ENDOGENOUS DYNAMICS IN A FINANCIAL SYSTEM

4.1 LEVERAGE AND BALANCE SHEET MECHANICS

Many financial institutions borrow and invest the borrowed funds into risky assets. Three simple properties of leverage are worth noting at this point. First, ceteris paribus, leverage determines the size of the investor's balance sheet. Second, leverage boosts asset returns. Third, leverage increases when the investor incurs losses, again ceteris paribus. In the following, we discuss each property in turn. For a fixed amount of equity, an investor can only increase the size of its balance sheet by increasing its leverage. Further, it is easy to show that, if r_t is the asset return, the equity return is $u_t = \lambda r_t$, where, as above, λ is the investor's leverage. In good times, leverage thus allows an investor to boost its return. In bad times however, even small negative asset returns can drive the investor into bankruptcy provided leverage is sufficiently high. Given the potential risks associated with high leverage, an investor typically faces a leverage limit which may be imposed by a regulator, as is the case for banks, or by creditors via a haircut[10] on collateralized debt. Finally, why does leverage increase when the investor incurs losses? Suppose the investor holds S units of a risky asset at price p such that $A = Sp$. Holding the investor's liabilities fixed, it is easy to see that $\lambda > 1$ implies $\partial \lambda / \partial p < 0$. In other words, whenever an investor is leveraged ($\lambda > 1$), a decrease (increase) in asset prices leads to an increase (decrease) in its leverage.

In what follows, we discuss how these three properties of leverage, in combination with reasonable assumptions about investor behavior, can lead to financial instability. We begin by discussing how leverage constraints can force investors to sell into falling markets even if they would prefer to buy in the absence of leverage constraints. We then show how a leverage constraint based on a backward looking estimator of market risk can lead to endogenous volatility and leverage cycles.

4.2 LEVERAGE CONSTRAINTS AND MARGIN CALLS

Consider again the simple investor discussed above. Suppose the investor faces a leverage constraint $\bar{\lambda}$ and has leverage $\lambda_{t-1} < \bar{\lambda}$.[11] The investor has to decide on an action at time $t - 1$ to ensure that it does not violate its leverage constraint at

---

[10]A *haircut* is the difference between the face value of a loan and the market value of the assets used as loan collateral. Typically, the haircut is such that the dollar amount of collateral is higher than the face value of the loan. This ensures that the lender can recover his investment in case of default of the borrower even if the collateral has lost some of its value.

[11]As mentioned above, a leverage constraint can be the result of regulation or contractual obligations.

time t. Suppose the investor expects the price of the risky asset to drop sufficiently from one period to the next, such that its leverage is pushed beyond its limit, i.e. $\lambda_t > \overline{\lambda}$. In this situation the investor has two options to decrease its leverage: raise equity or reduce its assets (or some combination of the two). Raising equity can be time consuming or even impossible during a financial crisis. Therefore, if the leverage constraint has to be satisfied quickly or if new equity is not available and no assets are maturing in the next period, the investor has to sell at least $\Delta A_{t-1} = \max\{0, (\mathbb{E}_{t-1}[\lambda_t] - \overline{\lambda})\mathbb{E}_{t-1}[E_t]\}$ of its assets to satisfy its leverage constraint, where $\mathbb{E}_t[\cdot]$ is the conditional expectation at time t. In the following we will set $\mathbb{E}_t[\lambda_{t+1}] = \lambda_t$ and $\mathbb{E}_t[E_{t+1}] = E_t$. This can be done for simplicity or because a contract forces the investor to make adjustments based on current rather than expected values. In this case we have simply $\Delta A_t = \max\{0, (\lambda_t - \overline{\lambda})E_t\}$. If λ_t exceeds the leverage limit due to a drop in prices, the investor will sell into falling markets which may lead to a feedback loop between leverage and falling prices as outlined in the previous section.

This simple mechanism has been discussed by a number of authors, see for example Gennotte and Leland (1990), Geanakoplos (2010), Thurner et al. (2012), Shleifer and Vishny (1997), Gromb and Vayanos (2002), Fostel and Geanakoplos (2008). Gorton and Metrick (2012) study the effect of haircuts on repo markets during the financial crisis empirically. Thurner et al. (2012) incorporate this mechanism in a heterogeneous agent model of leverage-constrained value investors. In the remainder of this section we will introduce their model and discuss some of the quantitative results they obtain for the effect of leverage constraints on asset returns.

Consider our set $\mathcal{B}$ of leveraged investors introduced in Section 3. Suppose that investors have no bilateral assets or liabilities and only invest into a single traded security, i.e. $A_i = A_i^S$. Furthermore, assume that the investor has access to a credit line from an unmodeled bank such that $L_i = L_i^R$. For brevity and to guide intuition, we will refer to these leveraged investors as funds for the remainder of this section. In addition to the funds, there is a representative noise trader and a representative "fund investor" that allocates capital to the funds. There is an asset of supply N with fundamental value V that is traded by the funds and the noise trader at discrete points in time $t \in \mathbb{N}$. Every period a fund i takes a long position $A_{it} = \lambda_{it} E_{it}$ provided its equity satisfies $E_{it} \geq 0$. The fund's leverage is given by the heuristic

$$\lambda_{it} = \min\{\beta_i m_t, \overline{\lambda}\},$$

where $m_t = \max\{0, V - p_t\}$ is the mispricing signal and β_i is the fund's aggressiveness. In other words, the fund goes long in the asset if the asset is underpriced relative to its fundamental value V. The noise trader's long position follows a transformed AR(1) process with normally distributed innovations. The price of the asset is determined by market clearing. Every period, the fund investor adjusts its capital allocation to the funds, withdrawing capital from poorly performing funds and investing into successful funds relative to an exogenous benchmark return.

Before considering the dynamics of the full model, let us briefly discuss the limit where the funds are small, i.e. $E_{it} \to 0$. In this case, in the absence of any significant effect of the funds, log price returns will be approximately iid normal due to the action of the noise trader. This serves as a benchmark. The authors then calibrate the parameters of the model such that funds are significant in size and prices may deviate substantially from fundamentals. This corresponds to a regime where arbitrage is limited as in Shleifer and Vishny (1997). The authors also assume that funds differ substantially in their aggressiveness β_i but share the same leverage constraint $\bar{\lambda}$ and initial equity E_{i0}.

In this setting the funds' leverage and wealth dynamics can lead to a number of interesting phenomena. When the noise trader's demand drives the price below the asset's fundamental value, funds will enter the market in proportion to their aggressiveness β_i. Due to the built-in tendency of the price to revert to its fundamental value due to the action of the noise traders, these trades will be profitable for the funds on average and even more profitable for more aggressive funds. Hence, the equity of aggressive funds grows quicker due to a combination of profits and capital reallocation of the fund investor. Importantly, as the equity of funds grows, their influence on prices increases and the volatility of the price decreases, due to the fact that they buy into falling markets and sell into rising markets.

Aggressive funds are also more likely to leverage to their maximum. Consider an aggressive fund i that has chosen $\lambda_{it-1} = \bar{\lambda}$. Now suppose the price drops such that $\lambda_{it} > \bar{\lambda}$. In response the fund sells parts of its assets as outlined above. Thurner et al. (2012) refer to this forced selling as a margin call, as they interpret the leverage constraint as arising from a haircut on a collateralized loan. Recall that the amount the fund will sell is $\Delta A_{it} = \max\{0, (\lambda_{it} - \bar{\lambda})E_{it}\}$, i.e. it is proportional to the fund's equity. As the aggressive fund is likely also the most wealthy fund, its selling can be expected to lead to a significant drop in prices. This drop may push other, less aggressive funds past their leverage limits. A margin spiral ensues in which more and more funds are forced to sell into falling markets. In an extreme outcome, most funds will exit or will have lost most of their equity in the price crash. As a result, their impact on prices is limited and the price is dominated by the noise trader. Thus following a margin spiral, price volatility increases due to two forces. First, it spikes due to the immediate impact of the price collapse. But then, it remains at an elevated level due to lack of value investors that push the price toward its fundamental value. These dynamics, which are illustrated in Fig. 1, reproduce some important features of financial time series in a reasonably quantitative way, in particular fat tails in the distribution of returns and clustered volatility (cf. Cont, 2001), as well as a realistic volatility dynamics profile before and after shocks (Poledna et al., 2014). These are difficult to reproduce in standard models.

One would expect these dynamics to be less drastic if funds took precautions against margin calls and stayed some $\epsilon > 0$ below their maximum leverage allowing them to more smoothly adjust to price shocks. However, it is important to note that a single "renegade" fund that pushes its leverage limit while all other funds remain well below it can be sufficient to cause a margin spiral.

It should be noted that the deleveraging schedule ΔA_{it} that a fund follows can depend on how the leverage constraint is implemented. In Thurner et al. (2012), the

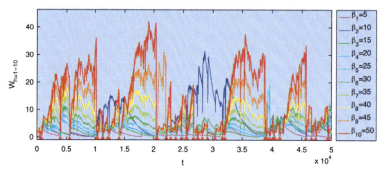

FIGURE 1

Time series of fund wealth dynamics from Thurner et al. (2012). Each time series corresponds to the wealth dynamics of a fund with different aggressiveness ranging from $\beta = 5$ to $\beta = 50$. Aggressive funds grow in size, become highly leveraged and susceptible to margin spirals and subsequent rapid collapse. The resulting asset return time series displays several realistic features including fat tails and clustered volatility.

leverage constraint results from a haircut applied to a collateralized loan, i.e. the fund obtains a short term loan from a bank, purchases the asset with the loan and its equity and then posts the asset as collateral for the loan. The haircut is equivalent to leverage and determines how much of its assets the fund can finance via borrowing. When the value of the asset drops, the bank will make a margin call as outlined above and the fund will have to sell assets immediately. However, a leverage constraint can, for example, also be imposed by a regulator. In this case, the fund may be allowed to violate the leverage constraint for a few time steps while smoothly adjusting to satisfy the constraint in later periods. Such an implementation will increase the stability of the system. Finally, the schedule $\Delta A_{it} = \max\{0, (\lambda_{it} - \bar{\lambda})E_{it}\}$ assumes the price remains unchanged from the current to the next period. A more sophisticated fund might take its own price impact into account when determining the deleveraging schedule.

4.3 PROCYCLICAL LEVERAGE AND LEVERAGE CYCLES

In the model presented in the previous section, funds actively increase their leverage when the price falls until they reach a leverage limit. Of course, a variety of other leverage management policies are possible. In an effort to study leverage management policies, Adrian and Shin (2010) analyze how changes in leverage $\Delta \lambda_t$ relate to changes in total assets ΔA_t (at mark-to-market prices) during the period 1963–2006 for three types of investors: households, commercial banks and security broker dealers (such as Goldman Sachs). Below we focus on households on one extreme and broker dealers on the other.

For households and broker-dealers the authors find a distinct correlation between leverage and asset changes, see Fig. 2. For households, changes in leverage are negatively correlated to changes in assets: $\text{Corr}(\Delta \lambda_t, \Delta A_t) < 0$. For broker dealers they find a positive correlation $\text{Corr}(\Delta \lambda_t, \Delta A_t) > 0$. This points toward at least two distinct leverage management policies.

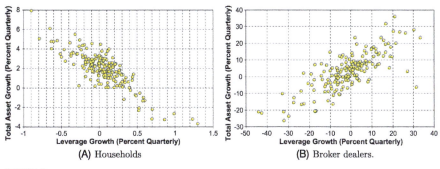

(A) Households   **(B)** Broker dealers.

FIGURE 2

Change in total assets vs change in leverage from Adrian and Shin (2010).

Households appear to be passive investors since leverage decreases when assets appreciate, ceteris paribus. Broker-dealers however, appear to follow a state-contingent target leverage which they try to reach through balance sheet adjustments. To see this, suppose an investor has a leverage target which is high in good times and low in bad times. Let us say that good times are identified by increasing asset prices while bad times are identified by falling asset prices (there are other ways of identifying the state of the world as we will discuss below). In this case, in response to an increase (decrease) in the price of the asset, the investor will increase (decrease) its target leverage and adjust its balance sheet accordingly. Importantly, the leverage adjustment often occurs via debt and asset adjustment rather than equity adjustment. Adrian and Shin (2010) call this a *procyclical* leverage policy. With such a leverage policy we expect $\text{Corr}(\Delta\lambda_t, \Delta A_t) > 0$. Hence, it appears that broker-dealers follow a procyclical leverage policy.

A procyclical leverage policy could arise if the broker-dealers face a time varying leverage constraint and choose to leverage maximally. In fact, Adrian and Shin (2010), Danielsson et al. (2004), and others show that a time varying leverage constraint arises when the investor faces a Value-at-Risk (VaR) constraint as was required under the Basel II regulatory framework. As we will show below, the effect of a VaR constraint is that the investor faces a leverage constraint that is inversely proportional to market risk. Thus, when market risk is high (low), the leverage constraint is low (high). In this setting the level of risk identifies the state of the world: in good times risk is low, while in bad times risk is high.

In summary, two leverage management policies are borne out by the data: passive leverage and procyclical target leverage. The type of leverage management policy used by the investor can have significant implications for financial stability. Indeed, at least anecdotally, the time series of broker-dealer leverage,[12] perceived risk (as

---

[12] Broker-dealer leverage is defined as the ratio of the series "Total Assets" (Fed time series identifier Z1/OTHER/FL664090663.Q) to "Equity capital" (Fed time series Z1/OTHER/FL665080003.Q), available at https://www.federalreserve.gov/datadownload/.

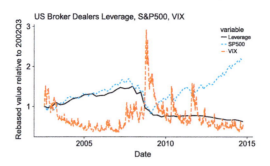

FIGURE 3

Time series of broker-dealer leverage, perceived risk (as measured by the VIX) and asset prices (as measured by the S&P500).

measured by the VIX) and asset prices (as measured by the S&P500) in Fig. 3 suggests a relationship between these three variables that is potentially induced by the dealers' procyclical leverage policy. In the following, we will introduce a model developed by Aymanns and Farmer (2015) that links leverage, perceived risk and asset prices in order to illustrate the effect of procyclical leverage and VaR constraints on the dynamics of asset prices.

Consider again our set $\mathcal{B}$ of leveraged investors (banks for short) and a representative noise trader. As above, we assume that there are no bilateral assets or liabilities. There is a risk free asset (cash) and a set $\mathcal{A}$ of risky assets that are traded by banks and the noise trader at discrete points in time $t \in \mathbb{N}$. At the beginning of every period, the banks and the noise trader determine their demand for the assets. For this, each bank i picks a vector $\mathbf{w}_{it}$ of portfolio weights and is assigned a target leverage $\overline{\lambda}_{it}$. The noise trader is not leveraged and therefore only picks a vector $\mathbf{v}_t$ of portfolio weights. Once the agent's demand functions have been fixed, the markets for the risky assets clear which fixes prices. Given the new prices, banks choose their next period's balance sheet adjustment (buying or selling of assets) in order to hit their target leverage. We refer the reader to Aymanns and Farmer (2015) for a detailed description of the model.

As mentioned above, banks are subject to a Value-at-Risk constraint.[13] Here, a bank's VaR is the loss in market value of its portfolio over one period that is exceeded with probability $1 - a$, where a is the associated confidence level. The VaR constraint then requires that bank holds equity to cover these losses, i.e. $E_{it} \geq \text{VaR}_{it}(a)$. We approximate the Value-at-Risk by $\text{VaR}_{it} = \sigma_{it} A_{it} / \alpha$, where σ_{it} is the estimated portfolio variance of bank i and α is a parameter. This relation becomes exact for normal asset returns and an appropriately chosen α. Rearranging the VaR constraint yields the bank's leverage constraint $\overline{\lambda}_{it} = \alpha / \sigma_{it}$. We assume that the bank chooses to be maximally leveraged, e.g. for profit motives. The leverage

---

[13] Within the context of this model the Value-at-Risk constraint should be understood as a placeholder for a procyclical leverage policy. We choose Value-at-Risk here for modeling convenience.

constraint is therefore equivalent to the target leverage we discussed above. To evaluate their VaR, banks compute their portfolio variance as an exponentially weighted moving average of past log returns.

Let us briefly discuss the implications of this set up. As mentioned at the outset of this section, banks follow a procyclical leverage policy. In particular, the banks' VaR constraint, together with its choice to be maximally leveraged at all times, imply a target leverage that is inversely proportional to the banks' *perceived risk* as measured by an exponentially weighted moving average of past squared returns. Why is such a leverage policy procyclical? Suppose a random drop in an asset's price causes an increase in the level of perceived risk of bank i. As a result the bank's target leverage will decrease (while its actual leverage simultaneously increases) and it will have to sell some of its assets, similar to the funds in the previous section.[14] The banks selling may lead to a further drop in prices and a further increase in perceived risk. In other words, the bank's leverage policy together with its perception of risk can lead to an unstable feedback loop. It is in this sense that the leverage policy is procyclical.

Banks in this model have a very simple, yet realistic, method of computing perceived (or expected) risk. Similar backward looking methods are well established in practice, see for example Andersen et al. (2006). It is important to note that perceived risk σ_{it} and realized volatility over the next time step can be very different. Since banks have only bounded rationality and follow a simple backward looking rule in this model, their expectations about volatility are not necessarily correct on average and tend to lag behind realizations.

Let us now consider the dynamics of the model in more detail. In Fig. 4 we show two simulation paths (with the same random seed) of the price of a single risky asset for two leverage policy rules. In the top panel, banks behave like the households in Adrian and Shin (2010) – they are passive and do not adjust their leverage to changes in asset prices or perceived risk. In the bottom panel, banks follow the procyclical leverage policy outlined above. The difference between the two price paths is striking. In the case of passive banks, the price follows what appears to be a simple mean reverting random walk. However, when banks follow the procyclical leverage policy, the price trajectory shows stochastic, irregular cycles with a period of roughly 100 time steps. These complex, endogenous dynamics are the result of the unstable feedback loop outlined above.

Aymanns and Farmer (2015) refer to these cycles as *leverage cycles*. Leverage cycles are an example of *endogenous* volatility – volatility that arises not because of the arrival of exogenous information but due to the endogenous dynamics of the agents in the financial system. To better understand these dynamics, consider the state of the system just after a crash has occurred, e.g. at time $t \approx 80$. Following the crash, banks' perceived risk is high, their leverage is low and prices are stable. Over time, perceived risk declines and banks increase their leverage. As they increase their leverage, they buy more of the risky assets and push up their prices. At some point

---

[14]Note that this selling will be spread across all assets according to the bank's portfolio weight matrix.

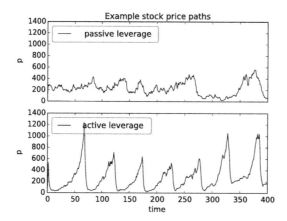

FIGURE 4

Example paths for the price of the risky asset from Aymanns and Farmer (2015). In the top panel, banks behave like households in Adrian and Shin (2010), i.e. they do not adjust their balance sheets following a change in leverage. Prices roughly follow a random walk – volatility is driven by the exogenous noise fed into the system. In the bottom panel, banks actively manage their leverage attempting to achieve a risk dependent target leverage, similar to broker-dealers in Adrian and Shin (2010). Prices now show endogenous, stochastic, irregular cycles.

leverage is sufficiently high and perceived risk sufficiently low, so that a relatively small drop of the price of an asset leads to large downward correction in leverage. A crash follows and prices fall until the noise trader's action stops the crash and the cycle begins anew. Naturally, these dynamics depend on the choice of parameters. In particular, when the banks are small relative to the noise trader, banks' trading has no significant impact on asset prices and leverage cycles do not occur. For a detailed discussion of the sensitivity of the results to parameters see Aymanns and Farmer (2015), and for a more realistic model that is better calibrated to the data, see Aymanns et al. (2016).

These results show that simple behavioral rules, grounded in empirical evidence of bank behavior (Adrian and Shin, 2010; Andersen et al., 2006), can lead to remarkable and unexpected dynamics which bear some resemblance to the run up to and crash following the 2008 financial crises. The results originate from the agents' bounded rationality and their reliance on past returns to estimate their Value-at-Risk. These features would be absent in a traditional economic models in which agents are fully rational. Indeed, rational models rarely display the dynamic instabilities that Aymanns and Farmer (2015) observe. If we believe that real economic actors are rarely fully rational, we should take note of this result. Of course, the agents in this model are really quite dumb. For example, they do not adjust to the strong cyclical pattern in the time series. However, they also live in an economy that is significantly simpler than the real world. Thus, their level of rationality in relation to the complexity of the world they inhabit might not be too far off from real economic agents' level of rationality.

The model discussed above can also yield insights for policy makers on how bank risk management might be modified in order to mitigate the effects of the leverage cycle. Aymanns et al. (2016) present a reduced form version of the model outlined above in order to investigate the implications of alternative leverage policies on financial stability. They show that, depending on the size of the banking sector and the properties of the exogenous volatility process, either a constant leverage policy or a Value-at-Risk based leverage policy is optimal from the perspective of a social planner. This finding lends support to the use of macroprudential leverage ratios as discussed in ESRB (2015). The authors also show that the timescale for the bubbles and crashes observed in the model is around 10–15 years, roughly corresponding to the run-up to the 2008 crash. Another important insight from Aymanns et al. (2016) is that the time scale on which investors need to achieve their leverage constraint plays a crucial role in the stability of the financial system: slower adjustment toward the constraint (corresponding to more slackness) increases stability.

The effect of leverage targeting on asset price dynamics has also been studied by other others in the multi-asset case. For example, Capponi and Larsson (2015) show that the deleveraging of banks may amplify asset return shocks and lead to large fluctuations in realized returns which in turn can cause spillover effects between different assets.

5 CONTAGION IN FINANCIAL NETWORKS
5.1 FINANCIAL LINKAGES AND CHANNELS OF CONTAGION

A channel of contagion is a mechanism by which distress can spread from one financial institution to another.[15] Often the channel of contagion is such that distress can only spread from one institution to a subset of all institutions in the system. These susceptible institutions are said to be linked to the stressed institution. The set of all links then forms a financial network associated with the channel of contagion.[16] Depending on the channel, links in this network may arise directly from bilateral contracts between banks, such as loans, or indirectly via the markets in which the banks operate. In the literature, one typically distinguishes between three key channels of contagion: counterparty loss, overlapping portfolios, and funding liquidity contagion.[17] Counterparty loss and overlapping portfolio contagion affect the value of the assets on the investors' balance sheet while funding liquidity contagion affects the availability of funding for the investors' balance sheets. In the following we will first introduce the investor's balance sheet relevant for this section. We will then

---

[15]For the first micro-level evidence of the transmission of shocks through the financial network, see Morrison et al. (2016).

[16]See Iori and Mantegna (2018) for a review of financial networks. For a review of models of financial contagion see Young and Glasserman (2016).

[17]Information contagion (cf. Acharya and Yorulmazer, 2008) is another channel of contagion but won't be discussed in this section.

give a brief overview of the channels of contagion before discussing each in more detail.

Balance sheet: Throughout this chapter we will consider a set $\mathcal{B}$ of leveraged investors (banks for short) whose assets can be decomposed into three classes: bilateral interbank contracts A_i^B, traded securities A_i^S that are marked to market and external, unmodeled assets A_i^R. Furthermore bank liabilities can be decomposed into bilateral interbank contracts L_i^B, and external, unmodeled liabilities L_i^R such that $L_i = L_i^B + L_i^R$. Note that bilateral interbank contracts need not be loans, they can also be derivative contracts for example. For simplicity however, we will think of bilateral interbank contracts as loans for the remainder of this section.

Counterparty loss: Suppose bank i has lent an amount C to bank j such that $A_i^B = L_j^B = C$. Now suppose the value of bank j's external assets A_j^R drops due to an exogenous shock. As a result the probability of default of bank j is likely to increase, which will affect the value of the claim A_i^B that bank i holds on bank j. If bank i's interbank assets are marked to market, a change in bank j's probability of default will affect the market value of A_i^B. In the worst case, if bank j defaults, bank i will only recover some fraction $r \leq 1$ of its initial claim A_i^B. If the loss of bank i exceeds its equity, i.e. $(1 - r)A_i^B > E_i$, bank i will default as well.[18] Now, how can this lead to financial contagion? To elaborate on the above stylized example, suppose that bank i in turn borrowed an amount C from another bank k such that $A_k^B = L_i^B = C$.[19] In this scenario, it can be plausibly argued that an increase in the probability of default of j increases the probability of default of i which in turn increases the probability of default of k. If all banks mark their books to market, an initial shock to j can therefore end up affecting the value of the claim that bank k holds on bank i. Again, in the extreme scenario, the default of bank j may cause bank i to default which may cause bank k to default. This is the essence of counterparty loss contagion. Naturally, in a real financial system the structure of interbank liabilities will be much more complex than in the stylized example outlined above. However, the conceptual insights carry over: the financial network associated with the counterparty loss contagion channel is the network induced by the set of interbank liabilities.

Overlapping portfolios: The overlapping portfolio channel is slightly more subtle. Suppose bank i and bank j have both invested an amount C in the same security l such that $A_{il}^S = A_{jl}^S = C$, where we have introduced the additional index to reference the security.[20] Now, suppose the value of bank j's external assets A_j^R drops due to some exogenous shock. How will bank j respond to this loss? In the extreme

---

[18] In reality, this scenario is excluded due to regulatory large exposure limits which require that $A_i^B < E_i$.
[19] We assume that the contract between i and j as well as i and k has the same notional purely for expositional simplicity and all conceptual insights carry over for heterogeneous notionals.
[20] Again, we assume that both banks invest the same amount purely of expositional simplicity.

case, when the exogenous shock causes bank j's bankruptcy ($E_i < 0$), the bank will liquidate its entire investment in the security in a fire sale. However, even if the bank does not go bankrupt, it may wish to liquidate some of its investment. This can occur for example when the bank faces a leverage constraint as discussed in Section 4. Bank j's selling is likely to have price impact. As a result, the market value of A_{il}^S will fall. If bank i also faces a leverage constraint, or even goes bankrupt following the fall in prices, it will liquidate part of its securities portfolio in response. How will this lead to contagion? Suppose that bank i also has invested an amount C into another security m and that another bank k has also invested into the same security, such that $A_{im}^S = A_{km}^S = C$. If bank i liquidates across its entire portfolio, it will sell some of security m following a fall in the price of security l. The resulting price impact will then affect the balance sheet of bank k which was not connected to bank j via an interbank contract or a shared security. This is the essence of overlapping portfolio contagion. Banks are linked by the securities that they co-own and the fact that they liquidate with market impact across their entire portfolios. Empirical evidence from the 2007 Quant meltdown for this contagion channel has been provided in Khandani and Lo (2011).

Funding liquidity contagion often occurs when a lender is stressed, and so often occurs in conjunction with overlapping portfolio contagion and counterparty loss contagion. To see this, let us reconsider the scenario we discussed for counterparty loss contagion. Suppose bank i has lent an amount C to bank j such that $A_i^B = L_j^B = C$. As before, suppose the value of bank j's external assets A_j^R drops due to some exogenous shock and as a result, the probability of default of bank j increases. Now, suppose that every T periods bank i can decide whether to roll over its loan to bank j. Further assume that bank i is bank j's only source of interbank funding and L_j^R is fixed. Given bank j's increased default probability, bank i may choose not to roll over the loan at the next opportunity. Ignoring interest payments, if bank i does not roll over the loan, bank j will have to deliver an amount C to bank i. In the simplest case, bank j may choose not to roll over its own loans to other banks which in turn may decide against rolling over their loans. This is the essence of funding liquidity contagion. As for counterparty loss contagion, the associated financial network is induced by the set of interbank loans. Empirical evidence on the fragility of funding markets during the past financial crisis has been provided for example by Afonso et al. (2011) and Iyer and Peydro (2011). In a further complication, bank j may also choose to liquidate part of its securities portfolio in order to pay back its loan. Funding liquidity contagion can therefore lead to fire sales and overlapping portfolio contagion and vice versa. This interdependence of contagion channels makes the funding liquidity and overlapping portfolio contagion processes the most challenging from a modeling perspective.

In the remainder of this section, we will discuss models for counterparty loss, overlapping portfolio and funding liquidity contagion, as well as models for the interaction of all three contagion channels.

5.2 COUNTERPARTY LOSS CONTAGION

Let P denote the matrix of nominal interbank liabilities such that banks hold interbank assets $A_i^B = \sum_j P_{ij}^T$, where T denotes the matrix transpose. In addition, banks hold external assets A_i^R which can be liquidated at no cost. Banks have interbank liabilities $L_i^B = \sum_j P_{ij}$ only. Assume all interbank liabilities mature at the same time and have the same seniority. We further assume that all banks are solvent initially. There is only one time period. At the end of that period all liabilities mature, external assets are liquidated and banks pay back their loans if possible. Now suppose banks are subject to a shock $s_i \geq 0$ to the value of their external assets such that $\hat{A}_i^R = A_i^R - s_i$. Given an exogenous shock, we can ask a number of questions. First, which loan payments are feasible given the exogenous shock? Second, which banks will default on their liabilities? And finally, how do the answers to the first two questions depend on the structure of the interbank liabilities P? There is a large literature that studies counterparty loss contagion in a set up similar to the above, including Eisenberg and Noe (2001), Gai and Kapadia (2010), May and Arinaminpathy (2010), Elliott et al. (2014), Acemoglu et al. (2015), Battiston et al. (2012), Amini et al. (2016), and Capponi et al. (2015). In the following, we will briefly introduce the seminal contribution by Eisenberg and Noe (2001), who provide a solution to the first two questions. We will then consider a number of extensions of Eisenberg and Noe (2001) and alternative approaches to addressing the above questions.

Define the relative nominal interbank liabilities matrix as $\Pi_{ij} = P_{ij}/L_i^B$ for $L_i^B > 0$ and $\Pi_{ij} = 0$ otherwise. The relative liabilities matrix corresponds to the adjacency matrix of the weighted, directed network $\mathcal{G}$ of interbank liabilities. Let $\mathbf{p} = (p_1, \ldots, p_N)$ denote the vector of total payments made by the banks when their liabilities mature, where $N = |\mathcal{B}|$. Naturally, a bank pays at most what it owes in total, i.e. $p_i \leq L_i^B$. However, it may default and pay less if the value of its external assets plus the payments it receives from its debtors is less than what it owes. The individual payments that bank i makes are given by $\Pi_{ij} p_i$ since by assumption all liabilities have equal seniority. The vector of payments, also known as the clearing vector, that satisfies these constraints is the solution to the following fixed point equation

$$p_i = \min\{L_i^B, \hat{A}_i^R + \sum_j \Pi_{ij}^T p_j\}. \tag{1}$$

Eisenberg and Noe (2001) show that such a fixed point always exists. In addition, if within each strongly connected component of $\mathcal{G}$ there exists at least one bank with $\hat{A}_i^R > 0$, Eisenberg and Noe (2001) show that the fixed point is unique.[21] In other words, there exists a unique way in which losses incurred due to the adverse shock $\{s_i\}$ are distributed in the financial system via the interbank liabilities matrix. The

---

[21] In a strongly connected component of a directed graph there exists a directed path from each node in the component to each other node in the component. The strongly connected component is the maximal set of nodes for which this condition holds.

clearing vector and the set of defaulting banks can be found easily numerically by iterating the fixed point map in Eq. (1). As the map is iterated, more and more banks may default, resulting in a default cascade propagating through the financial network.

It is important to note that in this setup losses are only redistributed and the system is conservative – contagion acts as a distribution mechanism but does not, in the aggregate, lead to any further losses to bank shareholders beyond the initial shock. To see this, define the equity of bank i prior to the exogenous shock as $E_i = A_i^B + A_i^R - L_i^B$ and after the exogenous shock as $\hat{E}_i = \hat{A}_i^B(\mathbf{p}) + A_i^R - s_i - \hat{L}_i^B(\mathbf{p})$. Note that post-shock both bank i's assets and liabilities depend on the clearing vector $\mathbf{p}$. Taking the difference and summing over all banks we obtain $\sum_i E_i - \hat{E}_i = \sum_i A_i^R - (A_i^R - s_i) = \sum_i s_i$ since $\sum_i A_i^B = \sum_i L_i^B$ and $\sum_i \hat{A}_i^B(\mathbf{p}) = \sum_i \hat{L}_i^B(\mathbf{p})$. Also note that, while bank shareholder losses are not amplified, losses to the total value of bank assets are amplified due to indirect losses, i.e. losses not stemming from the initial exogenous shock but due to revaluation of interbank loans. This can be seen by taking the difference between pre- and post-shock total assets in the system. The total pre-shock assets of bank i are $A_i = A_i^B + A_i^R$ and its total post-shock assets are $\hat{A}_i = \hat{A}_i^B(\mathbf{p}) + A_i^R - s_i$, then $\sum_i A_i - \hat{A}_i = \sum_i A_i^B - \hat{A}_i^B(\mathbf{p}) + s_i \geq \sum_i s_i$. Some authors argue that this total asset loss can be useful measure of systemic impact of the exogenous shock, see Glasserman and Young (2015). Finally, note that the mechanism of finding a clearing vector ignores any potential frictions in the financial system and ensures that the maximal payment is made given the exogenous shocks. Several authors have argued that this is too optimistic and assume instead that once a default has occurred, some additional bankruptcy costs are incurred, see for example Rogers and Veraart (2013) and Cont et al. (2010).[22,23] In this case, aggregate bank shareholder losses may be larger than the aggregate exogenous shock. Further shortcomings of the Eisenberg and Noe model include the lack of heterogeneous seniorities or maturities and the lack of the possibility of strategic default.

The extent of the default cascade triggered by an exogenous shock depends on the structure of the financial network induced by the matrix of interbank liabilities P. One key property of the financial network is the average degree of a bank, i.e. the number of other banks it lends to. A well-known result is that, as banks' interbank lending A_i^B becomes more diversified over $\mathcal{B}$, i.e. the average degree increases, the expected number of defaulting banks first increases and then decreases, see Fig. 5. If banks lend only to a very small number of other banks, the network is not fully connected. Instead, it consists of several small and disjoint components. A default in a particular component cannot spread to other components, hence limiting the size of the default cascade. As banks become more diversified, the network will become fully connected and default cascades can spread across the entire network. As banks

---

[22]Such bankruptcy cost might for example capture the cost of forced liquidation of the banks' external assets.

[23]Papers that do not assume bankruptcy costs are essentially treating the system as it were conservative in equity: losses to one party are gains to the other, but there is no deadweight loss that ravages welfare. Hence, they fail to capture the negative externalities imposed by the banking system on society.

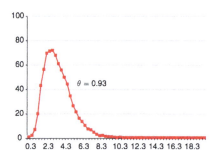

FIGURE 5

Expected number of defaults as a function of diversification in Elliott et al. (2014).

diversify further, the size of the individual loans between banks declines to the point that the default of any one counterparty becomes negligible for a given bank. Thus default cascades become unlikely. However, if they do occur, they will be very large. This is often referred to as the "robust-yet fragile" property of financial networks and has been observed for specifications of the financial network and the default cascade mechanism, see for example Elliott et al. (2014), Gai and Kapadia (2010), Battiston et al. (2012), or Amini et al. (2016). However, not only the average of the network's degree distribution is important for the system's stability. Caccioli et al. (2012b) show that if the degree distribution is very heterogeneous, i.e. there are a few banks that lend to many banks while most only lend to a few, the system is more resilient to contagion triggered by the failure of a random bank, but more fragile with respect to contagion triggered by the failure of highly connected nodes. In addition, Capponi et al. (2015) show that the level of concentration of the liability matrix, as defined by a majorization order, can qualitatively change the system's loss profile.

The models and solution methods discussed above tend to be simple to remain tractable and usually reduce to finding a fixed point.[24] However, these equilibrium models often form useful starting points for heterogeneous agent models that try to incorporate additional dynamic effects and more realism into the counterparty loss contagion process. See for example Georg (2013) where the effect of a central bank on the extent of default cascades is studied.

Finally, note that it is widely believed that large default cascades are quite unlikely for reasonable assumptions about the distribution of the exogenous shock and nominal interbank liabilities matrix, see for example Glasserman and Young (2015). For larger cascades to occur, default costs or additional contagion channels are necessary. Nevertheless, the existence of a counterparty loss contagion channel is important in practice as it affects the decisions of agents, for example in the way they form lending

---

[24]Gai and Kapadia (2010) for example make similarly restrictive assumptions on the structure of bank balance sheets as Eisenberg and Noe (2001). In addition several technical assumptions on the structure of the matrix of liabilities are necessary to solve for the fixed point of non-defaulted banks via a branching process approximation.

relationships. In other words, while default cascades are unlikely to occur in reality, they form an "off-equilibrium" path that shapes reality, see Elliott et al. (2014).

5.3 OVERLAPPING PORTFOLIO CONTAGION

In the following we will formally discuss the mechanics of overlapping portfolio contagion. To this end, consider again our set of banks $\mathcal{B}$. There is an illiquid asset whose value is exogenous and a set of securities $\mathcal{S}$, with $M = |\mathcal{S}|$, traded by banks at discrete points in time $t \in \mathbb{N}$. Let $\mathbf{p}_t = (p_{1t}, \ldots, p_{Mt})$ denote the vector of prices of the securities and let the matrix $\mathbf{S}_t \in \mathbb{R}^{N \times M}$ denote the securities ownership of all banks at time t. Thus S_{ijt} is the position that bank i holds in security j at time t. The assets of bank i are then given by $A_{it} = \mathbf{S}_{it} \cdot \mathbf{p}_t + A_i^R$, where A_i^R is the bank's illiquid asset holding. Let E_{it} and $\lambda_{it} = A_{it}/E_{it}$ denote bank i's equity and leverage, respectively. There are no interbank assets or liabilities.

As mentioned above, overlapping portfolio contagion occurs when one bank is forced to sell and the resulting price impact forces other banks with similar asset holdings to sell. What might force banks to sell? In an extreme scenario, a bank might have to liquidate its portfolio if it becomes insolvent, i.e. $E_{it} < 0$. But even before becoming insolvent, a bank might be forced to liquidate part of its portfolio if it violates a leverage constraint $\bar{\lambda}$ as we have shown in Section 4.[25] Both of these were considered by Caccioli et al. (2014) and by Cont and Schaanning (2017). In fact Caccioli et al. (2014) showed that such pre-emptive liquidations only make the problem worse due to increasing the pressure on assets that are already stressed. (This is closely related to the problem that liquidation can in and of itself cause default as studied by Caccioli et al. (2012a).) Other papers that discuss the effects of overlapping portfolios include Duarte and Eisenbach (2015), Greenwood et al. (2015), Cont and Wagalath (2016, 2013). An important early contribution to this topic is Cifuentes et al. (2005).

Let us first discuss the simpler case where liquidation occurs only upon default. Suppose bank i is subject to an exogenous shock $s_i > 0$ that reduces the value of its illiquid assets to $\hat{A}_{it}^R = A_{it}^R - s_i$. If $s_i > E_{it}$, the bank becomes insolvent and liquidates its entire portfolio. Let $Q_{jt} = \sum_{i \in \mathcal{I}_t} S_{ijt}$ denote the total amount of security j that is liquidated by banks in the set $\mathcal{I}_t$ of banks that became insolvent at time t. The sale of the securities is assumed to have market impact such that $p_{jt+1} = p_{jt}(1 + f_j(Q_{jt}))$, where $f_j(\cdot)$ is the market impact function of security j. Caccioli et al. (2014) assume an exponential form $f_j(x) = \exp(-\alpha_j x) - 1$, where x is volume liquidated and $\alpha_j > 0$ is chosen to be inversely proportional to the total shares outstanding of security j. In the next period, banks reevaluate their equity at the new securities prices. The change in equity is equal to $\Delta E_{it+1} = \sum_j S_{ijt} p_{jt} f_j(Q_{jt}) - s_i$. Note that

---

[25]Other "constraints" might also lead to forced sales and overlapping portfolio contagion. For example, investor redemptions that depend on past performance, as in Thurner and Poledna (2013), can force a fund to liquidate, which may result in an overlapping portfolio contagion similar to the one induced by leverage constraints.

in this setting we hold S_{ijt} fixed unless a bank liquidates its entire portfolio. Thus, banks who share securities with the banks that were liquidating in the previous period will suffer losses due to market impact. These losses may be sufficiently large for additional banks to become insolvent. If this occurs, contagion will spread and more banks will liquidate their portfolios, leading to further losses. Over the course of this default cascade, banks may suffer losses that did not share any common securities with the initially insolvent banks.

The evolution of the default cascade can be easily computed numerically by following the procedure outlined above until no further banks default. Caccioli et al. (2014) also show that the default cascade can be approximated by a branching process, provided suitable assumptions are made about the network structure. For their computations, Caccioli et al. (2014) assume that a given bank i invests into each security with a fixed probability μ_B/M, where μ_B is the expected number of securities that a bank holds. The bank distributes a fixed investment over all securities it holds. When μ_B/M is high, the portfolios of banks will be highly overlapping, i.e. banks will share many securities in their portfolios. Similar to the results for counterparty loss contagion, the authors find that as banks become more diversified, that is μ_B increases while M is held fixed, the probability of default (blue circles) first increases and then decreases, see Fig. 6. The intuition for this result is again similar to the counterparty loss contagion case. If banks are not diversified, their portfolios are not overlapping and price impact from portfolio liquidation of one bank affects only a few banks. As banks become more diversified, their portfolios become more overlapping and price impact spreads throughout the set of banks leading to large default cascades. Eventually, when banks become sufficiently diversified, the losses resulting from a price change in an individual security become negligible and large default cascades become unlikely. However, when they do occur, they encompass the entire set of banks. Thus, here again the financial network displays the robust-yet fragile property. Interestingly, the authors also show that for a fixed level of diversification, there exists a critical bank leverage λ_{it} at which default cascades emerge. The intuition for this result is that, when leverage is low, banks are stable and large shocks are required for default to occur, as leverage grows banks become more susceptible to shocks and defaults occur more easily.

As mentioned above, banks are likely to liquidate a part of their portfolio even before bankruptcy, if an exogenous shock pushes them above their leverage constraint. This is the setting studied in Cont and Schaanning (2017) and Caccioli et al. (2014). In this case, the shocks for which banks start to liquidate as well as the amount liquidated are both smaller than in the setting discussed above. If banks breach their leverage constraint due to an exogenous shock s_i to the value of their illiquid assets, Cont and Schaanning (2017) require that banks liquidate a fraction Γ_i of their entire portfolio such that $((1 - \Gamma_i)\mathbf{S}_{it} \cdot \mathbf{p}_t + \hat{A}_{it}^R)/E_{it} = \overline{\lambda}$. The corresponding liquidated monetary amount for a security j is then $Q_{jt} = \sum_{i \in \mathcal{B}} \Gamma_i S_{ijt} p_{jt}$. Again, the sale of the securities is assumed to have market impact such that $p_{jt+1} = p_{jt}(1 + f_j(Q_{jt}))$. In contrast to Caccioli et al. (2014), the authors assume that the market impact function $f_j(x)$ is linear in x, where x is the total monetary amount sold rather than the

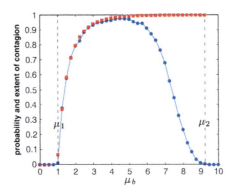

FIGURE 6

Blue circles: probability of contagion. Red squares: conditional on a contagion, the fraction of banks that fail (i.e. the extent of contagion). Taken from Caccioli et al. (2014).

number of shares. Similar market impact functions are used by Greenwood et al. (2015) and Duarte and Eisenbach (2015).

The shape and parameterization of the market impact function is crucial for the practical usage of models of overlapping portfolio contagion. There is a large body of market microstructure literature addressing this question. This literature begins with Kyle (1985), who derived a linear impact function under strong assumptions. More recent theoretical and empirical work indicates that under normal circumstances market impact is better approximated by a square root function (Bouchaud et al., 2008).[26]

The use of the term "fire sales" in this literature is confusing. Overlapping portfolio contagion can occur even if markets are functioning normally. A good example was the quant meltdown in August 2007. There are also likely to be circumstances in which normal market functioning breaks down due to overload of sellers, generating genuine fire sales; in this circumstance one expects market impact to behave anomalously and the square root approximation to be violated. There is little empirical evidence for this – genuine fire sales most likely occur only for extreme situations such as the crash of 1987 or the flash crash. In common usage the term "fire sale" often refers to any situation where selling of an asset depresses prices, even when the market is orderly.

Cont and Schaanning (2017) calibrate their model to realistic portfolio holdings and market impact parameters and obtain quantitative estimates of the extent of losses due to overlapping portfolio contagion. This provides a good starting point for more sophisticated financial system stress tests that will be discussed in the following sections. The models outlined above can be improved in many ways. Cont and Wagalath

[26]The market impact function takes the form $k\sigma\sqrt{\Delta V/V}$, where σ is volatility, ΔV is the size of the trade, V is market trading volume, and k is a constant of order one, whose value depends on the market.

(2016) study the effect of overlapping portfolios and fire sales on the correlations of securities in a continuous time setting, where securities prices follow a stochastic process rather than being assumed fixed up to the price impact from fire sales.

5.4 FUNDING LIQUIDITY CONTAGION

Funding liquidity contagion has been much less studied than overlapping portfolio or counterparty loss contagion. In the following we will briefly outline some of the considerations that should enter a model of funding liquidity contagion.

In modeling funding liquidity contagion, it is useful to partition an investor's funding into long term funding as well as short term secured and unsecured funding. Only short term funding should be susceptible to funding liquidity contagion as long term funding cannot be withdrawn on the relevant time scales. The availability of secured and unsecured short term funding may be restricted via two channels: a deleveraging channel and a default anticipation channel. The deleveraging channel applies equally to secured and unsecured funding: when a lender needs to deleverage, she can refuse to roll over short term loans, which may in turn force the borrower to deleverage, resulting in a cascade. This channel can be modeled using the same tools applied to overlapping portfolio and counterparty loss contagion. A paper that studies this channel is Gai et al. (2011). The default anticipation channel is different for secured and unsecured funding. In the case of secured funding, a lender might withdraw funding if the quality of the collateral decreases so that the original loan amount is no longer adequately collateralized. In the case of unsecured funding, a lender that questions the credit quality of one its borrowers might anticipate the withdrawal of funding of other lenders to that borrower and therefore withdraw her funding. This mechanism is similar to a bank run and therefore should be modeled as a coordination game, see Diamond and Dybvig (1983) and Morris and Shin (2001). This poses a challenge for heterogeneous agent models and might explain the relative scarcity of the literature on this topic. One notable exception that tries to combine both mechanisms is Anand et al. (2015).

5.5 INTERACTION OF CONTAGION CHANNELS

So far we have focused on counterparty loss and overlapping portfolio contagion in isolation. Of course, focusing on one channel in isolation only provides a partial view of the system and thus ignores important interaction effects. Indeed, it has been shown by a number of authors that the interaction of contagion channels can substantially amplify the effect of each individual channel (e.g. Poledna et al., 2015; Caccioli et al., 2015; Kok and Montagna, 2013; Arinaminpathy et al., 2012). Although constructing models with multiple contagion channels is difficult, some progress has been made.

Cifuentes et al. (2005) and Caccioli et al. (2015) study the interaction of counterparty loss and overlapping portfolio contagion by combining variants of the contagion processes outlined above into a comprehensive simulation model. In particular, using data from the Austrian interbank system, Caccioli et al. (2015) show that the expected size of a default cascade, conditional on a cascade occurring, can increase by orders of magnitude if overlapping portfolio contagion occurs alongside counterparty loss contagion, rather than in isolation.

In an equilibrium model Brunnermeier and Pedersen (2009) show that market liquidity and funding liquidity can be tightly linked. In particular, consider a market in which intermediaries trade a risky asset and use it as collateral for their secured short term funding. A decline in the price of the risky asset can lead to an increase in the haircut applied on the collateral. An increase in the haircut can be interpreted as a decrease in funding liquidity and can force intermediaries to sell some of their assets. This in turn can lead to a decrease in market liquidity of the asset. Aymanns et al. (2017) show that a similar link between market and funding liquidity can also result from the local structure of liquidity in over-the-counter markets (OTC). The authors show that, when the markets for secured debt and the associated collateral are both OTC, the withdrawal of an intermediary from the OTC markets can cause a liquidity contagion through the networks formed by the two OTC markets. Similar to Caccioli et al. (2015), the authors show that under certain conditions the interaction of two contagion channels – funding and collateral – can drastically amplify the resulting cascade.

Finally, Kok and Montagna (2013) construct a model that attempts to combine counterparty loss, overlapping portfolio and funding liquidity contagion. Such comprehensive stress testing models are the subject of the remainder of this chapter and will be discussed in detail in the following sections.

6 FROM MODELS TO POLICY: STRESS TESTS
6.1 WHAT ARE STRESS TESTS?

The insights from the models discussed so far are increasingly used in the tools designed to assess and monitor financial stability. After the crisis of 2008, maintaining financial stability has become a core objective of most central banks.[27] One example of such a tool, which has become increasingly prominent over the past years, has been the stress test.[28] Stress tests assess the resilience of (parts of) the financial system to crises (Siddique and Hasan, 2012; Scheule and Roesh, 2008; Quagliariello, 2009; Moretti et al., 2008). The central bank designs a hypothetical but plausible adverse scenario, such as a general economic shock (e.g. a negative shock to house prices or GDP) or a financial shock (e.g. a reduction in market liquidity, increased market volatility, or the collapse of a financial institution). Using simulations, the central bank then evaluates how this shock – in the event this scenario were to take

---

[27] For example, the mission statement of the US Federal Reserve (FED): 'The Federal Reserve promotes the stability of the financial system and seeks to minimize and contain systemic risks through active monitoring and engagement in the U.S. and abroad'; https://www.bankofengland.co.uk.

[28] Timothy Geither, who played a key role in fighting that crisis as President of the New York Fed and U.S. Secretary of the Treasury, has named his memories after the tool he helped introduce, see Geithner (2014).

place – would affect the resilience of the institution or financial system it tests. Say, for example, that the central bank submits a bank to a stress test. In this case, it would provide the bankers with a hypothetical adverse scenario, and ask them to determine the effect this scenario would have on the bank's balance sheet. If a bank's capital drops below a given threshold, it must raise additional capital. Stress tests evaluate resilience to shocks and link that evaluation to a specific policy consequence intended to enhance that resilience (e.g. raising capital). The process also provides valuable information to regulators and market participants, and helps both to better identify and evaluate risks in the financial system.

6.2 A BRIEF HISTORY OF STRESS TESTS

Stress tests are a relatively novel part of the regulatory toolkit. The potential utility of stress tests had been extensively discussed in the years preceding the financial crisis, and were already used by the International Monetary Fund to evaluate the robustness of countries' financial systems. Banks already designed and conducted stress tests for internal risk management under the Market Risk Amendment of the Basel I Capital Accord, but it was only during the financial crisis that regulators introduced them on a large scale and took a more proactive role in their design and conduct (Armour et al., 2016).

In February 2009 the U.S. Treasury Department introduced the Supervisory Capital Assessment Program (SCAP). This effort was led by Timothy Geither, at a time when uncertainty about the capitalization of banks was still paramount (Schuermann, 2014; Geithner, 2014). Under the auspices of this program the Federal Reserve Board introduced a stress test and required the 19 largest banks in the U.S. to apply it. The immediate motivation was to determine how much capital a bank would need to ensure its viability even under adverse scenarios, and relatedly, whether capital injections from the U.S. tax payer were needed. A secondary motivation was to reduce uncertainty about the financial health of these banks to calm markets and restore confidence in U.S. financial markets (Anderson, 2016; Tarullo, 2016).

In later years, SCAP was replaced by the Comprehensive Capital Analysis and Review (CCAR) and the Dodd–Frank Act Stress Test (DFAST), which have been run on an annual basis since 2011 and 2013, respectively (FED, 2017b, 2017a). These early stress tests gave investors, regulators and the public at large insight into previously opaque balance sheets of banks. They have been credited with restoring trust in the financial sector and thereby contributing to the return of normalcy in the financial markets (Bernanke, 2013).

Across the Atlantic European authorities followed suit and introduced a stress test of their own (EBA, 2017a). This resulted in the first EU stress tests in 2009, overseen by the Committee of European Banking Supervisors (CEBS) (Acharya et al., 2014). Due to concerns about their credibility, the CEBS stress test was replaced in 2011 by stress tests conducted by the European Banking Authority (EBA) (see Ong and Pazarbasioglu, 2014). These have been maintained ever since (EBA, 2017b).

In 2014 the Bank of England also introduced stress tests in line with the American example (BoE, 2014). Around that time, stress tests became a widely used regulatory

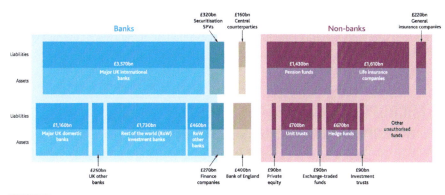

FIGURE 7

Map of the UK financial system. Source: Burrows et al. (2015).

tool in other countries too (Boss et al., 2007). Now stress tests are regarded as a cornerstone of the post-crisis regulatory and supervisory regime. Daniel Tarullo, who served on the board of the U.S. Federal Reserve from 2009 to 2017 and was responsible for the implementation of stress tests in the U.S., has hailed stress tests as 'the single most important advance in prudential regulation since the crisis' (Tarullo, 2014).

Stress tests are not a uniform tool. They can take a variety of forms, which can be helpfully classified along two dimensions. The first dimension concerns their *object*, or the types of agent that the stress test covers; does the stress test only cover banks, or non-banks as well? In the early days of stress testing, only banks were considered, but now there is an increasing trend toward including non-banks. Given the composition of the financial system in most advanced economies, and the importance of non-banks in these financial systems, it is increasingly acknowledged that excluding non-banks from stress tests would leave regulators with a partial picture of financial stability risks in their jurisdiction. In the United Kingdom, for example, almost half of the assets in the financial system are held by non-banks (Burrows et al., 2015), as is illustrated by a stylized map of the UK financial system depicted in Fig. 7.

The second dimension concerns the *scope* of the stress test. Generally speaking, stress tests can be used to evaluate the resilience of individual institutions (*microprudential* stress tests), but could also assess the resilience of a larger group of financial institutions or even of the financial system as a whole (*macroprudential* stress tests) (Cetina et al., 2015; Bookstaber et al., 2014a). Methodologically speaking, the key difference is that *macroprudential* stress tests take the feedback loops and interactions between (heterogeneous) financial institutions – as described in Section 4 and Section 5 of this chapter – into account, whereas the *microprudential* stress tests do not.

Perhaps more than any other financial stability tool, stress tests rely explicitly on the models introduced so far. The following sections will cover micro- and macroprudential stress tests in depth. In each instance, we will first review some representative stress tests and subsequently conclude with an evaluation of their strengths and weaknesses.

7 MICROPRUDENTIAL STRESS TESTS
7.1 MICROPRUDENTIAL STRESS TESTS OF BANKS

As noted, microprudential stress tests evaluate the resilience of an individual institution, in this case a bank. Regulators subject the bank to an adverse scenario and evaluate whether a bank has sufficiently high capital buffers[29] (and, in some cases, liquid assets[30]) to withstand it.[31] If this is not the case, regulators can require the bank to raise additional capital (or liquidity) to enhance its buffers. The idea is that this will make the bank more resilient, and by implication increase the resilience of the financial system as a whole.

Given this general approach, microprudential stress tests for banks tend to follow three steps. First, the regulator designs the adverse scenario the bank is subjected to. As noted, this scenario usually involves an economic and/or financial shock. In some cases, the scenario consists of multiple (exogenous) shocks operating at the same time, sometimes with specified ripple effects affecting other variables, which together create a 'crisis narrative' for the bank. The hypothetical scenario a bank is subjected to must be adverse, plausible and coherent. That is, it cannot consist of a set of shocks that, taken together, violate the relationships among variables historically observed or deemed conceivable. Typically, the exogenous shocks affect a set of macro-variables (such as equity prices, house prices, unemployment rate or GDP) as well as financial variables (such as interest rates and credit spreads).

Second, the effect of this scenario on the bank's balance sheet is determined. This determination primarily relates to the effect of the scenario on the bank's capital (and liquidity) buffer, usually expressed as a ratio of capital (liquidity) buffers to assets,[32]

---

[29] The simplest measure of a capital buffer is that of a bank's net assets – the value of its assets minus its liabilities. This represents a buffer that protects the bank against bankruptcy when its assets decline in value. In most models described earlier in this chapter, this buffer corresponds to a bank's equity. When describing whether a bank has a sufficiently high buffer, the term 'capital adequacy' is commonly used. For a more comprehensive overview, see Armour et al. (2016), Chapter 14.

[30] A liquidity buffer is intended to ensure that, when liquidity risks of the type discussed in Section 3.2 materialize, a bank has sufficient liquid assets to meet demands for cash withdrawals. Although microprudential liquidity stress tests for banks have been developed, they are currently not yet widely used for regulatory purposes. Hence, we will focus on microprudential capital stress tests here.

[31] Note that this capital buffer is an example of a regulatory leverage constraint as introduced in Section 3.2.

[32] When capital ratios are computed as capital over total (unweighted) assets, this amounts to the inverse of the leverage ratio, as defined in Section 4. Regulators typically use a more complex measure for the capital buffer to account for the fact that some assets are riskier than others. Suppose a bank holds two assets with the same value, but one (asset Y) is riskier than the other (asset X). When regulators take the riskiness of these assets into account, to meet regulatory requirements the bank would have to hold a higher capital

and profits. This calculation is based on an evaluation of how the shocks change the values of the assets and liabilities on the bank's balance sheet, as well as on the bank's expected income. Value changes on the balance sheet materialize either through a re-evaluation of the market value (if the asset or liability is marked-to-market), or through a credit shock re-evaluation. These effects are captured by market risk models and credit risk models (such as those described in Siddique and Hasan, 2012; Scheule and Roesh, 2008; Quagliariello, 2009; Moretti et al., 2008). Credit losses for specific assets or asset classes are commonly computed by multiplying the probability of default (PD), the exposure at default (EaD), and the loss given default (LGD). Estimating these variables is therefore key to the credit risk component of stress testing (Foglia, 2009). Value changes to the expected income stream result largely from shocks that affect income on particular assets or asset classes, such as interest rate shocks. This determination matters in the context of the stress test because such income can, in the form of retained earnings, feedback into capital buffers.[33] Usually, these microprudential stress test models therefore equate the post-stress regulatory capital buffer to the sum of post-stress retained earning plus regulatory capital[34] over the post-stress (risk-weighted[35]) assets.

Third, once the bank's post-stress capital buffer has been determined, regulators compare it to a hurdle rate. This hurdle rate is usually set at such a level that, when passing it, the bank would withstand the hypothetical scenario without being at risk of bankruptcy. Consequently, if the bank does not meet this hurdle rate, it fails the stress test and is said to be 'undercapitalized' (that is, its capital buffer is insufficient). When that happens, the regulator commonly has the authority to require the bank to raise extra capital to increase its buffer, so as to leave it better prepared for adverse scenarios. Microprudential stress tests are thus used as a tool to recapitalize undercapitalized banks, thereby reducing their leverage and increasing their resilience.

7.2 MICROPRUDENTIAL STRESS TEST OF NON-BANKS

Given the importance of non-bank financial institutions to the financial system,[36] it was only a matter of time before the scope of microprudential stress tests would be extended beyond banks. The rationale for doing so is similar to the one that applies to

---

buffer for asset Y than for asset X, corresponding to their relative riskiness. This process is referred to as 'risk-weighting', and the resulting capital buffer is commonly expressed relative to 'risk-weighted assets' (RWAs).

[33] This is true unless part of this income is being paid to shareholders as dividends, which stress tests commonly assume not to be the case.

[34] If the scenario results in a loss to the bank's equity and lowers its income, the capital buffer drops (ceteris paribus).

[35] In most cases the model also updates the assets' risk-weights to reflect that the adverse scenario has altered the riskiness of the asset (class). For an overview of the methodologies commonly used by banks, see Capgemini (2014). The 'standard' approach as proposed by regulators is set out in BIS (2015).

[36] See e.g. FSB (2015), ECB (2015), Burrows et al. (2015), Pozsar et al. (2010), Pozsar and Singh (2011), Mehrling et al. (2013), Pozsar (2013).

banks: regulators want to understand the resilience of non-bank financial institutions, and where they find fragility they want to be able to amend it. So far, at least three types of non-bank financial institutions are subjected to stress tests: insurers, pension funds and central clearing parties (CCPs).

Like the microprudential stress tests for banks, those for non-bank financial institutions are primarily used to assess capital adequacy in times of distress. However, the methodology used in that assessment differs between the various institutional types, because each type faces a different set (and type) of risks. For example, the balance sheet composition differs for each institution, which in turn means each institution is exposed to different tail risks which should be reflected in the scenario design used in the stress test. Moreover, because of the differences in balance sheet composition, losses materialize in different ways and should be determined using methodologies suitable to each institutional type. Finally, the benchmark each type of institution has to meet in order to 'pass' the stress test differs too, because the regulatory requirements vary among different institutional types.[37]

In sum, the heterogeneity of non-bank financial institutions requires bespoke microprudential stress tests. They all, however, follow the same pattern: they start by setting a hypothetical adverse scenario, evaluate the effect of that scenario on the institution's balance sheet, and compare the post-stress balance sheet to regulatory requirements (hurdles). Table 1 sets out some of the most salient differences between microprudential stress tests for various types of institutions. In what follows, we provide a high-level overview of regulatory stress tests for insurers, pension funds, and central clearing parties.

Insurers and Pension Funds: Insurance stress tests are becoming increasingly common, and have been conducted by the Bank of England (BoE, 2015), the IMF (under its FSAP Program) (Jobst and Andreas, 2014), the U.S. Federal Reserve (Accenture, 2015; Robb, 2015), and the European Insurance and Occupational Pensions Authority (EIOPA) (EIOPA, 2016). Similarly, pension fund stress tests have been conducted by the International Organisation of Pension Fund Supervisors (IOPFS) (Ionescu and Yermon, 2014) and, in the EU, by EIOPA (EIOPA, 2017).

EIOPA's 2016 stress test of life insurers tested each insurer's capital and liquidity adequacy[38] (EIOPA, 2016). When evaluating capital adequacy, the benchmark was that an insurer's assets should exceed its liabilities.[39] Liquidity adequacy was assessed by performing a cash-flow analysis to investigate whether the timing of insurer's incoming cash-flow (from its assets) matched the insurer's expected cash outflow (resulting from its insurance liabilities).

---

[37]This reflects the different loss absorption mechanisms that have been designed for each type of non-bank financial institution.

[38]For insurance companies, this refers to the ability to meet insurance obligations.

[39]In other words, its Assets-over-Liability ratio (AoL) should exceed a hundred percent.

Table 1 Key distinguishing characteristics of microprudential stress tests for banks, insurers, pension funds, and central clearing parties

	Banks	**Insurers**	**Pension Funds**	**CCPs**
Primary Objective	Capital Adequacy	Capital and Liquidity Adequacy		Capital Adequacy
Measure of Capital Adequacy	Capital Ratio	Assets over Liability Ratio (AoL)	Coverage Ratio	Default Waterfall
Loss Assessment	How asset losses affect capital buffers	How asset and liability re-evaluations affect capital, and whether[*] liabilities can be met		If, and how, clearing member default losses are absorbed by the default waterfall

[*] *Other than in the case of banks, insurance and pension fund liabilities re-evaluate significantly with certain types of adverse shocks, such as interest rate shocks. In such scenarios, the discounted future value of promised insurance schemes and pension fund schemes adjusts. Pension funds must also assess whether there is no significant maturity mismatch between promised pension fund payments (liabilities) and income from assets to meet them.*

EIOPA's 2015 stress test of occupational pension funds assessed whether pension payment promises[40] could be met in the face of adverse market conditions. The hypothetical adverse scenario was tailored to risks specific to a pension fund. For example, the effect of increased life expectancy (which lengthens the time a pension fund must pay out a pension, and thus increases the cumulative amount of pension payments a pension fund must make) on the pension fund's ability to meet its pension obligations was tested.

Central Clearing Parties: Central clearing parties (CCPs) have been created to mitigate counterparty risk, for example in (simple, or 'over-the-counter' (OTC)) derivatives transactions. By doing so, they also reduce the likelihood that counterparty risk causes a cascade of losses, and generates contagion (as has been discussed in Section 5). In this way, well-functioning CCPs can mitigate systemic risk in financial systems.

CCPs operate by stepping in between two contractual counterparties, and becoming, as is commonly noted, 'the buyer to every seller, and the seller to every buyer'.[41] Once a contract is 'cleared' through a CCP, its counterparties are referred to as 'clearing members'. As long as no clearing member defaults, the assets and liabilities of the CCP balance out, so that the CCP faces no market risk. That changes when clearing members default, in which case the CCP is exposed to losses. To absorb such

---

[40] Specifically, those related to defined benefit and hybrid pension schemes.

[41] Because many counterparties that are also exposed to each other engage in contractual relationships via the CCP, the CCP can also net out exposures, thereby reducing the complexity of exposures that counterparties must manage and reducing bilateral exposures (Cont and Kokholm, 2014).

losses, the CCP has an elaborate process in place that distributes these losses among all its clearing members as well as its own equity, which is referred to as a 'default waterfall' (see Murphy, 2013; Capponi et al., 2017). This default waterfall consists of various contributions of the clearing members (e.g. initial and variation margin, default fund contributions) and some of the CCPs own capital buffer (equity). When losses materialize, these are absorbed by each of the layers in turn, until the CCP's own capital buffer is exhausted and it defaults.[42]

CCPs have become increasingly important after the financial crisis, as regulators require counterparties to frequently-used contracts to clear these contracts through CCPs (ESMA, 2017; Ey, 2013). Individual CCPs have also grown substantially and process very high volumes of trades, leading some to argue that their failure would be catastrophic for the financial system in which they operate (and perhaps beyond) (ESMA, 2015; Murphy, 2013). That is why regulators around the world increasingly carry out microprudential stress tests for CCPs, including the Commodity Futures and Trading Commission (CFTC) in the U.S. (CFTC, 2016), the British and German regulatory authorities (Erbenova, 2015) (this will include a U.S. regulator in 2017) (Robb, 2015), and the European Securities and Markets Authority (ESMA) (ESMA, 2015).

Microprudential stress tests for CCPs focus on whether a CCP's capital buffer (its default waterfall) can absorb losses in a crisis event, to avoid that the CCP defaults. ESMA's CCP stress tests illustrates how such a stress test can be designed (ESMA, 2015).

In ESMA's microprudential CCP stress test from 2015, the adverse scenario included the default of the CCP's two largest clearing members (that is, those two clearing members with the largest contribution to the CCP's default fund),[43] while the CCP was simultaneously hit by a severe adverse market shift.[44] Because clearing members often trade in multiple CCPs, the two defaulted clearing members for each CCP were assumed to default in all CCPs where they cleared – which is referred to as cross default contagion.

To assess the extent to which the CCP's capital buffer has been depleted as a consequence of this adverse scenario, the test calculates the losses to each step of the CCP's default waterfall. Losses beyond the absorption capacity of the default

---

[42] A comprehensive overview of the operation of CCPs and the risks they create is beyond the scope of this chapter. Examples of excellent overviews include: Cont (2015), Murphy (2013), Duffie et al. (2015), Duffie and Zhu (2011).

[43] This scenario tests whether CCPs meet the minimum requirement set under the EU's EMIR regulation (see Art. 42(2)).

[44] It is important that both the default of two counterparties and a severe adverse market shift hit simultaneously. If two clearing members default, but there is no market shift, the total margin posted should be sufficient to absorb all losses of the defaulted clearing members. If only the market conditions change, the CCP is not at risk of default because its variation margin ensures it is not exposed to changes in market conditions.

waterfall are calculated as well. Taken together, these two criteria are used to judge whether a CCP is sufficiently capitalized.[45]

7.3 STRENGTHS AND WEAKNESSES OF CURRENT MICROPRUDENTIAL STRESS TESTS

Microprudential stress tests are valuable from at least three perspectives. First, they give market participants more insight into the opaque balance sheets of the financial institutions being evaluated (Bookstaber et al., 2014a). Opacity coupled with asymmetric information can, especially in times of financial distress, lead to a loss of confidence (Diamond and Dybvig, 1983; Brunnermeier, 2008). If the type and quality of a financial institution's assets and liabilities are unclear, outsiders may conceivably fear the worst and, for example, pull back their funding.[46] Such responses feed speculative runs which can turn into self-fulfilling prophecies and, ultimately, (further) destabilize the financial system at the worst possible time (He and Xiong, 2012; Diamond and Dybvig, 1983; Martin et al., 2014; Copeland et al., 2014). Credibly executed microprudential stress tests provide insight into an institution's balance sheet, can signal confidence about the institution's ability to withstand severe stress, and create a separating equilibrium that allows solid banks to avoid runs (Ong and Pazarbasioglu, 2014; Bernanke, 2013).[47]

Second, microprudential stress tests help financial institutions to improve their own risk-management. By forcing them to assess their resilience to a variety of novel scenarios, stress tests require banks to take a holistic look at their own risk-management practices (Bookstaber et al., 2014a). As a consequence, more banks are now also engaged in serious internal stress tests (Wackerbeck et al., 2016).

Third, microprudential stress tests have proven to be an effective mechanism to recapitalize banks (Armour et al., 2016). In the EU, the stress tests have forced banks to raise their capital by 260 billion euros from 2011 to 2016 (Arnold and Jenkins, 2016), and in the US the risk-weighted regulatory ratio of the banks that took part in the stress test went up from 5.6 percent at the end of 2008 to 11.3 at the end of 2012 (Bernanke, 2013). Against a backdrop of frequent questions about the adequacy of banks' capital buffers,[48] in part due to the gaming of risk weights (Behn et al., 2016;

---

[45] Although the 2015 ESMA CCP stress test was microprudential in nature, an attempt was made to make it somewhat macroprudential by capturing a (first-order) contagion effect. In case the adverse scenario affected the default fund contributions of the non-defaulting clearing members, the resulting hit to the equity of these clearing members was included. If that hit, in turn, caused a loss to the non-defaulting clearing member that exceeded a threshold percentage of its equity, that clearing member was said to be vulnerable. If that hit wiped out all of the previously non-defaulting clearing member's equity, it was said to default as well.

[46] The general economic principle at play is that of asymmetric information causing market failures, see Akerlof (1970).

[47] Weaker banks, however, may be exposed by the stress test. But regulators would learn this information first, giving them an opportunity to intervene before the information reaches the market.

[48] See, for example, Admati and Hellwig (2014).

Fender and Lewrick, 2015; Groendahl, 2015), many regulators have welcomed the role that stress tests have played to enhance the resilience of banks. Even if microprudential stress tests are not, strictly speaking, designed to assess and evaluate systemic risk, their role in raising capital adequacy standards can have the effect of enhancing resilience (Greenwood et al., 2015).

Despite their strengths in specific areas, the current microprudential stress tests have been criticized on at least four grounds. First, and most importantly from the perspective of this chapter, microprudential stress tests ignore the fact that economies are complex systems (as noted in Section 1) and therefore are ill-suited to capture systemic risk. As discussed in Sections 4 and 5 of this chapter, systemic risk materializes due to interconnections between heterogeneous agents (for example due to overlapping portfolios and funding liquidity contagion). By considering institutions in isolation, microprudential stress tests (largely[49]) ignore the interconnections and interaction between financial institutions that serve to propagate and amplify distress caused by the initial shock resulting from the adverse scenario. Empirical research suggests that this approach substantially underestimates the losses from adverse scenarios (Bookstaber et al., 2014b, also see Section 3). Bernanke (2015), for example, notes that the majority of the losses in the last financial crisis can be traced back to such interactions as opposed to the initial shock emerging from credit losses in subprime mortgage loans.

Second, microprudential stress tests tend to impose an unrealistically large initial shock. Because regulators are aware of the fact that a microprudential modeling strategy does not capture the higher order losses on the balance sheets of individual financial institutions, they use a more severe initial scenario that causes direct losses to compensate for that. To generate a sufficiently large initial shock, the scenario tends to depart quite strongly from reality. Often, the initial scenario posits a substantial increase in the unemployment rate as well as a sharp drop in GDP.[50] In reality, however, it is uncommon for these conditions to *precede* a financial crisis, so the stress test might be testing for the wrong type of scenario.[51] Imposing an unrealistic shock – and excluding higher-order effects – can also affect the outcome of the stress test in unexpected ways. In particular, while stress tests with large initial shocks might get the overall losses right, they might fail to accurately capture the distribution of losses across institutions, which ultimately determines which banks survive and which do not. For an investigation of this issue, see for example Cont and Schaanning (2017).

Third, the value of the information produced by microprudential stress tests is increasingly being questioned. The outcomes of stress tests have converged (Glasserman et al., 2015), perhaps because banks seem increasingly able to 'train to the test'. This has left some to wonder what the information produced by the stress tests is

---

[49] In some cases a proxy for such contagious effects is included in the microprudential stress test.

[50] See, for example, FED (2016), BoE (2016), ESRB (2016).

[51] Instead, exogenous shocks such as declining house prices or stock markets precede financial crises. These are commonly also part of the initial scenario.

actually worth (Hirtle et al., 2016), and others to conclude that the value of such information has declined over time (Candelon and Sy, 2015). Such concerns have been further fueled by the apparent willingness of some regulators to allow banks to pass the test on the basis of dubious assumptions.[52]

Finally, the stress tests are commonly calibrated to the losses incurred during the last financial crisis, raising questions about their relevance in relation to current, let alone future, scenarios – not least because the financial system constantly changes.

8 MACROPRUDENTIAL STRESS TESTS

Because the financial system is a complex system (see Section 1), the whole is different from the sum of its parts (Anderson et al., 1972; Farmer, 2012; Battiston et al., 2016). In other words, measures focused on the health of individual institutions (as microprudential stress tests would prescribe) will not necessarily guarantee the health of the financial system as a whole. In fact, such measures might destabilize the system. To understand the system as a whole – and, by implication, systemic risk – stress tests have to account for feedback loops and non-linearities.

The inability of microprudential stress tests to appropriately account for systemic risk has prompted the development of a specific type of stress tests focused on this goal; the macroprudential stress test. Macroprudential stress tests aim to assess the resilience of a whole sector, or even the whole financial system, rather than that of one particular institution. To do so, they extend the microprudential stress test by including contagion effects between interconnected financial institutions that can arise following the initial adverse scenario. This means that the regulators must not only assess the effect of the initial shocks on the individual balance sheets, but must capture how the balance sheets are interlinked (see Section 5). They should also address what consequences such interlinkages have for the potential of financial distress to propagate throughout the system. The contagion models discussed in Sections 4 and 5 can help inform regulators on how to model these higher order spill-over effects.

This section discusses two macroprudential models for banks, and one that combines banks and non-banks. The first two models, the Bank of England's 'Risk Assessment Model of Systemic Institutions' (RAMSI) and the Bank of Canada's 'MacroFinancial Risk Assessment Framework' (MFRAF), have been used in stress tests. The last model, U.S. Office of Financial Research's (OFR's) 'Agent-Based Model for Financial Vulnerabilities' (ABMFV), has not.[53]

---

[52]Deutsche Bank, which has seen its share price fall significantly in 2016 on fears that it could face a US fine of up to USD 14bn, was given special treatment by the European Central Bank in the 2016 EBA stress tests, so that it could use the result of the stress test as evidence of its healthy finances (Noonan et al., 2016).

[53]We focus on comparing these three models. However, other relevant macroprudential stress tests have recently been developed. Baranova et al. (2017), for example, study market liquidity in a corporate bond

The ABMFV and the RAMSI are examples of cases where heterogeneous agent models have been applied to macroprudential stress tests.[54] The MFRAF is an example of another, somewhat more traditional approach.

After introducing these three models, their differences and similarities are outlined. The section ends with a discussion of the strengths and weaknesses of these macroprudential stress tests.

8.1 THREE MACROPRUDENTIAL STRESS TESTS

8.1.1 RAMSI Stress Test of the Bank of England

The Bank of England has pioneered the development and use of a macroprudential banking stress test, called the RAMSI model.[55] The model evaluates how adverse shocks transmit through the balance sheets of banks and can cause further contagion effects (Burrows et al., 2012). It is based on earlier research that has been conducted by Bank of England researchers and others (Aikman et al., 2009; Kapadia et al., 2013; Alessandri et al., 2009).

The RAMSI stress test begins as a microprudential stress test. Subsequently, possible feedback effects within the banking system are considered. If the initial shocks have caused a bank to fall below its regulatory capital ratio, or have caused the bank to be shut off of all unsecured funding[56] markets, the bank respectively suffers an insolvency or illiquidity default. Subsequently, the default causes two interbank contagion effects: common asset holding contagion and interbank contagion. The combined effect of the marked-to-market losses and the credit losses can cause other banks to default through insolvency or illiquidity by being shut out of the funding market. If this happens, the loop is repeated. If this does not happen, each bank's net operating expenses are invested in assets such that the bank targets its regulatory risk-weighted target ratio. The credit losses persist, but the marked-to-market losses are assumed

---

market by modeling broker-dealers, hedge funds and (unlevered) asset managers. They capture common asset holding contagion. Like Baranova et al. (2017), Feroli et al. (2014) highlight that subdued leverage of financial intermediaries is no sufficient ground to rule out stability concerns. Instead, unlevered investors (such as unlevered funds) may be the locus of potential financial instability. Dees and Henry (2017) offer a host of macroprudential (stress testing) tools. The multi-layered network model (and ABM) of Kok and Montagna (2013) (discussed in Section 5.5) can also be considered to be macroprudential stress testing model, as it is a data-driven stress simulation of the European Union (EU) banking system. The model of Kok and Montagna (2013) is similar in style to the ABMFV discussed here.

[54] Indeed, these models combine the contagion models discussed in Section 5.

[55] The model is currently being phased-out. We discuss this model to showcase its strengths and weaknesses. These are further treated in Section 8.3.

[56] This causes funding liquidity contagion. The bank is shut off of all unsecured funding based on a rating system. Based on the shocked balance sheets and profit and losses (PL), the credit score for the bank is computed, which the authors assume affects the funding cost of the bank and its ability to access the long-term and short-term funding market. This credit score takes into account liquidity and solvency characteristics of the bank's balance sheet, but also system-wide market distress. If its credit score is above a certain threshold, the bank is shut out of the unsecured funding markets altogether (both long-term and short-term) and is assumed to default.

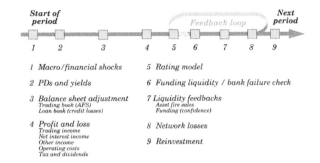

FIGURE 8

Description of the RAMSI stress test of the Bank of England. Source: Aikman et al. (2009).

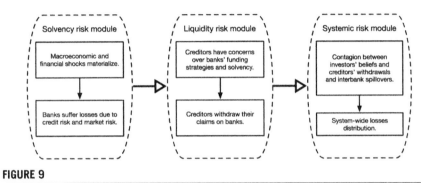

FIGURE 9

Description of the MFRAF stress test of the Canada. Source: Anand et al. (2014).

to disappear as each asset price returns to its fundamental value. Then, the next time step starts, and the process can be repeated, starting with a balance sheet that includes the credit losses incurred in the previous time step.

Thus, the RAMSI stress test turns a microprudential foundation into a macroprudential model by including interbank contagion effects via common asset holdings, interbank losses and funding liquidity contagion. Fig. 8 summarizes what happens at each step of the RAMSI model.

8.1.2 MFRAF Stress Test of the Bank of Canada

Contrary to the RAMSI model, the Bank of Canada's MacroFinancial Risk Assessment Framework (MFRAF) is at its core not a heterogeneous agent model, but a global games model, such as those described in Morris and Shin (2001). In the way it sets up funding runs (i.e. as a global coordination game) it is similar to the seminal model of Diamond and Dybvig (1983) (discussed in Section 5). It captures three sources of risk that banks face (Anand et al., 2014; BoC, 2014, 2012): solvency, liquidity, and spill-over risk (see Fig. 9).

The MFRAF stress test has been applied to the Financial Sector Stability Assessment (FSAP) of the Canadian financial sector conducted by the International

$t = 0$	$t = 1$ (round 1)	$t = 1$ (round 2)	$t = 2$
1. Debt issuance	1. Interim shock	1. Belief updated	1. Investment matures
2. Investments	2. Private signals	2. New pooling price	2. Final shock
	3. Debt withdrawals	3. New private signals	3. Debts honored
		4. Debt withdrawals	

FIGURE 10

Time steps in theoretical model of MFRAF stress test of the Bank of Canada. Source: Anand et al. (2015).

Monetary Fund (IMF) in 2014 (IMF, 2014). The 2014 FSAP stress test, which considers the direct effects of adverse shocks on the solvency of banks, is microprudential. When extending it to capture system-wide effects (i.e. liquidity effects and spill-over effects) using MFRAF, overall losses to the capital of the Canadian banks rose with 20 percent. This again shows that microprudential stress tests significantly underestimate system-wide losses. We will now discuss the theoretical underpinnings of the MFRAF stress tests, which builds on research at the Bank of Canada and elsewhere (Anand et al., 2015; Gauthier et al., 2012, 2014).

The theoretical model that underpins the MFRAF stress test is described in Anand et al. (2015) and will be discussed here.[57] The model captures how solvency risks, funding liquidity risks, and market risks of banks are intertwined. In essence, this works as follows: a coordination failure between a bank's creditors and adverse selection in the secondary market for the bank's assets interact, leading to a vicious cycle that can drive otherwise solvent banks to illiquidity. Investors' pessimism over the quality of a bank's assets reduces the bank's access to liquidity, which exacerbates the incidence of runs by creditors. This, in turn, makes investors more pessimistic, driving down other banks' access to liquidity. The model does not capture interbank contagion upon default, although this is captured in MFRAF (IMF, 2014).

The key components of the model according to the evolution of the model over time is summarized in Fig. 10.

8.1.3 ABM for Financial Vulnerabilities

The final system-wide stress testing model that will be discussed, the Agent-Based Model (ABM) for Financial Vulnerabilities (Bookstaber et al., 2014b),[58] captures similar contagion mechanisms as MFRAF, but it does so using a different methodology. The model is designed to investigate the vulnerability of the financial system to asset- and funding-based firesales that can lead to common asset holding contagion.

---

[57] The degree to which the theoretical model of Anand et al. (2015) is in unaltered form translated into the MFRAF stress tests is not made explicit in the IMF (2014) documentation of the MFRAF stress test.

[58] A further discussion of some agent-based models of the financial crisis and stress testing can be found in Bookstaber and Kirman (2018).

FIGURE 11

Map of the financial system and its flows, as considered in the ABM for Financial Vulnerabilities. Source: OFR (2014).

The financial system is modeled as a combination of banks that act as intermediaries between the cash provider (a representative agent for various types of funds) and the ultimate investors (i.e. the hedge funds). Hedge funds can receive funding from banks for long positions in return for collateral. Banks, in turn, receive funding from the cash provider in return for collateral. Funding and collateral therefore flow in opposite directions, as is illustrated in Fig. 11.

The role of the cash provider c in the model is to provide secured funding to banks.[59] Although the cash provider is not actively modeled, it can take two actions. First, it can set the haircut (this can force the hedge fund to engage in fire sales), and second it can pull funding from the banks (this may lead the bank to contribute to pre-default contagion or default).

Hedge funds have a balance sheet that consists of cash and tradable assets on the asset side, and secured loans and equity (and possibly short positions) on the liability side. A hedge fund funds its long positions in assets using funding from banks in the form of repurchase contracts (often referred to as repos).[60] When funding themselves this way, hedge funds receive cash in return for collateral they pledge to the bank. Although the hedge fund does not face a regulatory leverage constraint, it

---

[59]The cash provider is a representative agent that represents financial institutions that typically provide funding to banks, such as asset managers, pension funds, insurance companies, and security lenders, but most importantly, money market funds.

[60]In a repo, one party sells an asset to another party at one price at the start of the transaction and commits to repurchase the fungible assets from the second party at a different price at a future date. If the seller defaults during the life of the repo, the buyer (as the new owner) can sell the asset to a third party to offset his losses. The asset therefore acts as collateral and mitigates the credit risk that the buyer has on the seller. Although assets are sold outright at the start of a repo, the commitment of the seller to buy back the fungible assets in the future means that the buyer has only temporary use of those assets, while the seller has only temporary use of the cash proceeds of the sale. Thus, although repo is structured legally as a sale and repurchase of securities, it behaves economically like a collateralized loan or secured deposit. For an overview, see https://www.icmagroup.org/Regulatory-Policy-and-Market-Practice/repo-and-collateral-markets/icma-ercc-publications/frequently-asked-questions-on-repo/1-what-is-a-repo/.

faces an implicit leverage constraint based on the haircut it receives on its collateral. The haircut determines how much equity a hedge fund needs for a given amount of repo funding. If the haircuts on all types of collateral (i.e. on all types of assets that can be pledged as collateral) is the same, and assuming that the bank passes on the haircut it receives from the cash provider, the maximum leverage $\bar{\lambda}_{jt}$ of the hedge fund j at time t is given by $\bar{\lambda}_{jt} = \frac{1}{h_{cjt}}$. If the leverage of the hedge fund exceeds the maximum leverage,[61] the hedge fund is forced to de-lever. It will do so by fire selling assets. This can cause marked-to-market losses for other banks or hedge funds who hold the same assets.

The banks act as an intermediary between buyers and sellers of securities and between lenders and borrowers of funding.[62] On the whole, the bank can contribute to financial distress pre-default and post-default in various ways. Pre-default, the bank may have to fire sell assets or to pull funding from the hedge fund (which consequently may also have to engage in firesales) in order to raise cash, de-lever, or pay back funding to the cash provider (if the cash provider pulled its funding). In addition, by passing on an increased haircut to the hedge fund, it can trigger a hedge fund to engage in firesales. Post-default, the bank contributes to exposure losses and further firesale losses.

8.2 COMPARING AND EVALUATING MACROPRUDENTIAL STRESS TESTS: FIVE BUILDING BLOCKS

To comprehensively design, study and evaluate macroprudential stress tests, we introduce a general framework consisting of five building blocks that allow us to break down each stress test in discrete components: (1) types of financial institutions (agents), (2) financial contracts, (3) markets, (4) constraints, and (5) behavior.[63] This framework also offers an analytically coherent way to combine the various heterogeneous agent models discussed in Section 4 and Section 5 in order to capture their interactions (see Section 5.5). With such a framework one can capture *critical features* necessary to be able to capture systemic risk. This section covers these five building blocks and compares the three macroprudential stress tests discussed

---

[61] A hedge fund's leverage can exceed the maximum leverage due to asset price depreciations (as a consequence of firesales, for example) or increases in the haircut (due to the cash provider's downward assessment of the bank's solvency and/or liquidity). If the hedge fund is forced to de-lever, it will attempt to go back to a 'buffer leverage' level, which is below the maximum leverage value.

[62] In its role, it facilitates maturity, liquidity, and risk transformations. The banks have various desks that play a role in these processes: the prime broker, the finance desk, the trading desk, the derivatives desk, and the treasury. The various equations associated with the functioning of the bank dealer and its various subdesks can be found in Bookstaber et al. (2014b).

[63] With these five building blocks, many relevant features of a financial system can be captured by initializing bespoke implementations for each building block. Once financial institutions and financial contracts are defined, a multi-layered network can be initialized. When, subsequently, markets, constraints, and behavior are chosen, the dynamics of the system can be studied.

Table 2 Comparison between the three macroprudential stress tests (RAMSI, MFRAF, ABMFV) regarding the (system-wide stress test) building blocks: (1) financial institutions; (2) financial contracts; (3) markets; (4) constraints; and (5) behavior. Note that rc, cc, mc stand for regulatory, contractual and market-based constraints respectively. Remark that MFRAF captures unsecured inter-bank loans, counterparty loss contagion and a leverage constraint, the theoretical model of Anand et al. (2015) does not. We list the behavior that impacts the state of the system

		RAMSI	MFRAV	ABMFV
(1)	Financial institutions:			
	Banks	✓	✓	✓
	Creditors (exogenous)	✓	✓	✓
	Hedge funds	–	–	✓
(2a)	Financial contracts:			
	Traded securities	✓	✓	✓
	Unsecured interbank loans	✓	✓	–
	Unsecured term deposits	–	✓	–
	Secured interbank loans (repos)	–	–	✓
(2b)	Channels of contagion:			
	Overlapping portfolios	✓	✓	✓
	Counterparty loss	✓	✓	–
	Funding liquidity	✓	✓	✓
	Margin spirals	–	–	✓
(3)	Modeled markets:			
	Traded securities	✓	✓	✓
(4)	Constraints:			
	Leverage constraints (rc)	✓	✓	✓
	Liability payment obligations (cc)	✓	✓	✓
	Margin call obligations (cc)	–	–	✓
	Funding run (mc)	✓	✓	✓
(5)	Behavior:			
	Pre-default			
	– no action (banks)	✓	✓	–
	– action (banks, hedge funds)	–	–	• control leverage • meet contractual obligations • maximize profits
	– exogenous action (creditor run)	✓	✓	✓
	Post-default			
	– Default procedure	• fire sales • exposure losses	• fire sales (of collateral)	• fire sales (implicit)

above[64] as we go along (these findings are summarized in Table 2). We will see that these stress tests implement each building block with varying degrees of fidelity to the real world.

8.2.1 Financial Institutions

Financial institutions are at the heart of any financial stability analysis and form a key component of macroprudential stress tests. In most models they are represented by balance sheets filled out with a collection of financial contracts that are unique to that institution. Moreover, each institution comes with its own set of constraints and behavioral rules. By endowing an institution with its unique collection of financial contracts, combination of constraints, and behavioral rules, various types of heterogeneous financial institutions (e.g. banks, insurance companies, hedge funds, unlevered funds, central clearing parties) can be characterized. This allows for the inclusion of the many types of financial institutions that need to be studied to capture the dynamics of a financial system under stress.

None of the macroprudential models discussed in this chapter capture all relevant financial institutions, which limits their claim to be a truly 'system-wide' macroprudential stress test. Specifically, the RAMSI and MFRAF model only capture the banking system, and though the ABMFV also considers non-banks it only covers a subset (hedge funds and cash providers).[65]

8.2.2 Financial Contracts: Interlinkages and Associated Contagion Channels

Contracts sit on the balance sheet of each institution, but because contracts are between institutions, they also stipulate the interconnections between institutions. Taking institutions as the nodes in the network the contracts define the edges of the network. (Common asset holdings also define connections, though a more accurate approach is to treat these as bipartite networks.) Contagion dynamics, such as those described in Section 5, operate over these financial contracts to jump from institution to institution. It is therefore important to ensure that the models representing these contracts capture the features that create the interconnections between institutions (e.g. contractual counterparties) and enable contagion (e.g. valuation method, contractual obligations).

The three macroprudential stress tests capture these three contractual characteristics for a subset of contracts (leaving out some relevant contractual types), but do study how the contagion dynamics operating over them can interact. Specifically, models capture the interaction between contagion channels discussed in Section 5:

---

[64]See Section 8.1.1, Section 8.1.2, and Section 8.1.3.

[65]Each model also considers exogenous creditors. The balance sheets of exogenous agents are not explicitly modeled. As such exogenous agents cannot default. When exogenous creditors withdraw a loan, the cash exists the system.

common asset holding contagion, counterparty loss contagion, and funding liquidity contagion. The ABMFV also captures 'collateral contagion'.[66]

8.2.3 Markets

In most models (as in reality), markets are the places where asset prices are determined, as well as the place where new contracts are agreed upon and existing ones modified or terminated. It is their role in the price formation process and the provision of liquidity that makes the modeling of markets particularly relevant to macroprudential stress tests. Markets are diverse in their institutional characteristics; they can be bilateral (such as the interbank loan market), exchange-based (like the stock market), intermediated (like a dealer-based market for, say, corporate bonds), or centrally cleared (i.e. by a CCP). Typically, there is a specific market for each financial contract on the balance sheet of an institution.

However, although each of our three macroprudential models consider multiple types of contractual linkages, they only model one market: the market for common asset holdings.[67] Moreover, although all three models consider bilateral funding, they do not include a market for these contracts. Therefore, when an (un)secured loan is not rolled over, institutions have no opportunity to seek funding elsewhere. That potentially causes these models to overestimate financial distress.

Because financial stability critically depends on price formation and the ability of institutions to forge contractual links (or break them), it is important to model the markets that exist for each type of contract (and do so with sufficient realism).[68] An understudied challenge is thus to determine whether and how the dynamics in a given market contribute to financial (in)stability, and to reflect that in stress testing models. This is complicated, because ideally it would require an understanding of the supply and demand functions for each market.[69]

8.2.4 Constraints

Financial institutions typically face four types of constraints: regulatory constraints, contractual constraints, market-based constraints, and internal risk limits. Regulatory

---

[66]'Collateral contagion' refers to the contagious spill-overs that can arise from margin calls associated to repo contracts (e.g. secured funding contracts). Institutions receive a margin call when the asset collateral value drops (or haircuts increase) so that it is not enough to cover the loan amount. If institutions are not able to meet the margin call they may be forced to engage in fire sales. Collateral contagion is especially relevant as it interacts with common asset holding contagion. Indeed, price falls due to fire sales can trigger collateral contagion.

[67]The modeling of price formation is approached differently in the three models. In the case of the RAMSI and MFRAF model a price impact function is used. The MFRAF model updates prices based on the investors' beliefs about the quality of the assets.

[68]For example, Baranova et al. (2017) show for the case of corporate bond markets that market liquidity (and common asset holding contagion) critically depends on the ability of intermediaries to make markets.

[69]To capture price formation (or counterparties for a bilateral contract), the model must produce well-balanced supply and demand as observed in normal times and allow for imbalances in times of distress.

constraints are constraints set by the regulator. Most regulatory constraints are specific to a type of institution; banks face different regulatory constraints than insurers, for example. The models capture a subset of the regulatory constraints that banks face[70] and do not capture the regulatory constraints that non-banks confront.[71]

Contractual constraints arise out of contractual obligations. Because, as noted before, each financial institution holds a unique collection of contracts, the contractual constraints of each institution are unique too. Each model covers repayment obligations, because they capture (un)secured funding contracts. The ABMFV also considers margin call obligations as part of the secured funding contracts. Because each of the macroprudential stress tests discussed above only captures a subset of the relevant contracts, the contractual constraints they capture are incomplete as well. Banks, for example, typically hold derivatives contracts (e.g. credit default swaps) that can give liquidity shocks that may foster pre- or post-default contagion.

Market-based constraints (commonly referred to as 'market discipline') are those that are enforced by market participants. Sometimes, market participants set higher standards than regulators do; a bank might, for example, be cut off from funding markets because its leverage is judged to be too high, even though it still meets the regulatory leverage requirements. In this case, the market constraint could be formalized as a leverage constraint that is stricter than the regulatory leverage constraint. The most relevant market-based constraint, which entails that creditors run if the liquidity and/or solvency characteristics of a bank are sufficiently negative, is captured by all three models.[72]

Finally, internal risk limits are set by the financial institutions themselves, as part of their risk-management practices. An example could be a value-at-risk (VaR) constraint on a portfolio.[73]

Taken together, these constraints (and their various interactions) can drive an institution's behavior, especially under stress. First, institutions may act in a precautionary manner to avoid breaching constraints in order to avoid defaults. These actions, which are often prudent for each institution separately, may contribute to pre-default contagion (e.g. firesales in order to meet payment obligations). Second, institutions may fail to avoid breaching a constraint and default, which then leads to post-default con-

---

[70]The RAMSI model and the ABMFV consider one regulatory constraint for banks, an (unweighted) leverage ratio and a risk-weighted leverage ratio respectively. The theoretical model of Anand et al. (2015) that underpins the MFRAF stress test does not consider a regulatory leverage constraint. (But the MFRAF (IMF, 2014) stress test presumably does.) Banks default when they no longer meet their minimum (risk-weighted) leverage constraint. The models do not capture other regulatory constraints of banks that may affect financial stability, such as liquidity constraints (e.g. the liquidity coverage ratio) for banks.

[71]A few important (solvency) constraints that non-banks face have been covered in Section 7.2. As has been discussed in that section, insurers face a Solvency II constraint, pension funds face a coverage ratio, and CCPs must fulfill default fund requirements.

[72]The models consider the creditors to be exogenous to the system. A more realistic approach would be to make these creditors endogenous to the system. That way, cash does not leave the system but ends up in an institution's pockets.

[73]None of the macroprudential models discussed here consider internal risk limits.

tagion (e.g. due to exposure losses). Given their vital role in driving interactions under stressed conditions, it is important to consider whether the constraints included in a given stress test model represent those most relevant to the description of the system or sector that is being studied. More specifically, for any given institution the nature of its contribution to contagion will be critically determined by the set of constraints it faces. In sum, a failure to consider the relevant constraints makes it unlikely that the stress test model will correctly identify which channels of contagion operate and which institution are affected (Cetina et al., 2015).

8.2.5 Behavior

Behavior drives the dynamics of the financial system and the evolution of the multi-layered network representation thereof. It therefore critically affects the inherent stability of the financial system and can be an important driver of contagion. Behavior of institutions is typically not known and must thus be reasonably estimated.

Institutions can *affect the state of the system* when they default (*i.e. post-default*) or when they are still alive (*i.e. pre-default*). When institutions are alive they act for two reasons: *to fulfill objectives* (e.g. seek profits) and *to avoid default*.[74] When institutions default either through insolvency (i.e. breaching *regulatory constraints*) or illiquidity (i.e. when an institution does not meet its *contractual obligations*) they also affect the system. Through these pre- and post-default actions institutions can contribute to contagion.[75]

The three macroprudential stress testing models capture the critical drivers of financial stability dynamics to various degrees. The ABMFV most realistically simulates a financial market and its (contagious) dynamics. It captures that institutions can contribute to 'pre-default contagion' when they aim to avoid default,[76] but can also contribute to 'post-default contagion' once they have defaulted.[77] In addition, the ABMFV captures normal-time behavior, presumably to ensure that contagion is not overestimated (e.g. some may be willing to buy when others are forced to sell). The MFRAF and the Aikman et al. (2009), Alessandri et al. (2009) versions of the RAMSI model[78] assume that institutions are largely *passive*: they do not act until they default (only when they do default, institutions affect the system). Barring any

---

[74]Note that many financial stability models (see Section 5) abstract away from profit-seeking behavior. This may be a reasonable abstraction because in times of distress behavior is typically mostly driven by the objective to avoid default. However, by doing so, these models might overestimate contagion. As in crisis times, the institutions that are not under pressure (e.g. do not experience binding constraints) can stabilize the market.

[75]Or act as stabilizers.

[76]For example, institutions, which must meet the contractual obligation to repay a loan, may engage in fire sales to do so.

[77]To capture the contagion consequences that may ensue following a default, the relevant aspects of a default procedure must be modeled. For example, models must not only capture one contagion effect (e.g. exposure loss contagion), but various relevant contagion effects (e.g. including common asset holding contagion, etc.).

[78]The Kapadia et al. (2013) version of the RAMSI model does capture pre-default contagion.

defaults, these models thus only capture dynamics to a limited extent. By not capturing pre-default contagion, these may significantly underestimate losses (see e.g. Bardoscia et al., 2017). Table 2 summarizes the implementation of behavior in the three macroprudential stress testing models.

8.3 THE CALIBRATION CHALLENGE

Calibration is a process to ensure that the estimated parameters of a model match existing data (Turrell, 2016). The design of stress tests can make calibration easier or harder. Calibration is made easier when models are designed so as to either avoid free parameters entirely (by initializing all components to data), or to set up the model so that its parameters can be measured independently on input data rather than based on target data (the data that one wants to fit).[79] In general, it is therefore useful to design the stress test model so as to closely fit the market infrastructure, because this allows regulators to collect data on each component and then put it together – for example by using the five building blocks used above. A stress test that relies heavily on latent parameters[80] will require more assumptions will therefore introduce more uncertainty.

When using the five building blocks (institutions, contracts, markets, constraints and behavior) it becomes clear that the first four can (to a large extent) be data-driven.[81] Balance sheet data is already collected by regulators, although not always on a contractual level.[82] This latter step is important, given the importance of contractual constraints in driving specific contagion dynamics (as discussed in Section 8.2). Regulators increasingly recognize this, and have started collecting contract-level data for contractual types considered especially important to financial stability (e.g. Abad et al., 2016).[83] Because data gaps still persist, the (multi-layered) networks that make up system-wide financial models cannot be completely calibrated to data. In such cases, network reconstruction techniques can generate 'realistic' networks based on the known information (e.g. Anand et al., 2018).

Markets are complicated, because the market mechanism has to be modeled correctly. So far, most stress tests abstract away from market infrastructure and instead rely on price impact functions to move prices. The problem is that these functions are

---

[79] In other words, (loosely speaking) the more a model can be a one-to-one fit with the available data, the better.

[80] Latent parameters are unobservable and can – at best – only be calibrated by fitting model outputs to data.

[81] Provided, of course, that such data is indeed collected. On this front, more progress is desirable (see Section 9).

[82] Examples of data sources that capture contract level data are: the securities holding database and the trade reporting of derivatives (under EMIR). See https://sdw.ecb.europa.eu/browseExplanation.do?node=9691594 and https://www.esma.europa.eu/policy-rules/post-trading/trade-reporting, respectively.

[83] Regulators should collect data on three dimensions of contracts: counterparties, valuation methods (and inputs), and contractual obligations (and inputs). The first is needed stipulate interconnections, the second is needed to understand contagion dynamics arising through valuation and liquidity shocks.

driven by 'market depth', which is a latent variable and can only be approximated with data about the daily volume of trades and the volatility in the asset class (e.g. Cont and Schaanning, 2017).

The most relevant constraints that drive dynamics, regulatory and contractual constraints could in principle be calibrated to data,[84] but market constraints have to be inferred and can easily change over time. Internal risk limits can change too and are often proprietary.[85]

The building block for which calibration is most complicated is the last one, behavior. Although behavioral assumptions can be informed by supervisory data and surveys (Bookstaber, 2017), and perhaps even inferred using machine learning techniques, it is bound to change when a new type of crisis hits.[86] That is why it is important that even if the first four building blocks are (relatively closely) calibrated, the resulting stress tests are explicitly conditional on the behavioral assumption chosen.[87] It is then possible to change that assumption and run parameter sweeps to get a sense of the effect size of that behavioral assumption. In other words, stress tests might not predict exactly what will happen in a given scenario, but can explore directionally what might happen under a set of what-if scenarios.[88] This can be useful to (1) assess the level of systemic risk; (2) identify potential vulnerabilities in the system; and (3) evaluate the effectiveness of policies designed to mitigate systemic risk.

Calibrating the three macroprudential stress tests discussed above is challenging. The ABMFV may be the easiest to calibrate,[89] as it captures a realistic market infrastructure (consisting of the first four building blocks). Only behavioral parameters (related to block five) are uncertain, as is the usual case in a social system. It models realistic behavior, but it does not investigate how different behavioral parameters give different dynamics. The RAMSI model relies heavily on a careful calibration of the initial shock and the effect this has on the balance sheet.[90] That emphasis on calibrating the initial shock may distract from the most relevant function of any macroprudential model; its evaluation of a financial system's capacity for

---

[84]Regulatory constraints are typically publicly known. Most relevant contractual constraints can be known by a regulator that collects contract-level data, and includes the third dimension of contracts: contractual obligations.

[85]It is unclear whether, and how, these constraints will be enforced in times of crisis. It may be, for example, that a financial institution loosens its internal risk limits to avoid fire sales, or that contractual counterparties agree to suspend their obligations because strict enforcement would be costly for both.

[86]Based on a range of observations, representative behavior for certain types of institutions, and for various circumstances, can be inferred. Many models in the ABM literature capture somewhat realistic behavior (e.g. Kok and Montagna, 2013 discussed in Section 5.5).

[87]This is not a problem particular to macroprudential stress tests. Anyone who models a social system – rather than a physical system (where the dynamics are governed by physical laws) faces this problem.

[88]As far as we are aware, none of the financial stability models and macroprudential stress tests focus on prediction.

[89]Although, in practice, this model has not yet been calibrated.

[90]As noted, this is the microprudential component of the model.

shock amplification and endogenous dynamics.[91] Finally, Anand et al. (2015) is a more traditional model that seems much harder to calibrate to data. Its structure is more rigid, and therefore harder to map onto a given market structure. For example, the model's dynamics revolve around a two-period funding contract (and an abstract asset market), but it is not clear how the model can accommodate the variety of contracts that exist in the financial system. On the other hand, Anand et al. (2015) has been used in a data-driven MFRAF stress test.

8.4 STRENGTHS AND WEAKNESSES OF THE CURRENT MACROPRUDENTIAL STRESS TESTS

Macroprudential stress tests are strongly complementary to microprudential stress tests, because they allow regulators to assess the resilience of the financial system as a whole (or a larger subset of it) rather than that of individual financial institutions. The current macroprudential stress tests have three related strengths.

First, they provide insights into the interlinkages between financial institutions, mapping out how financial shocks transmit through individual balance sheets and affect other institutions. The data-driven methodology to establish the model setup (as well as the subsequent calibration) provide a promising avenue for future stress tests, but also for further data-driven research into the structure of the financial system (Aikman et al., 2009).

Second, they capture the interactions between various financial institutions and contagion channels that can drive distress, and therefore capture (some of) the feedback effects that characterize the complex nature of the financial system (see Section 4.1 and Section 5). Especially the ABM for Financial Vulnerabilities makes an important contribution by including heterogeneous financial institutions, which is key to allow for emergent phenomena (Bookstaber, 2017).

Third, in addition to capturing solvency risk, or separately investigating solvency and liquidity risk, the current macroprudential stress tests capture funding liquidity risk and the interactions between solvency and liquidity (the interaction between contagion channels has been discussed in Section 5.5). The RAMSI model, for example, not only considers defaults through insolvency, but also through illiquidity, and takes their interaction into account. In case of the MFRAF, a particular strength is that market risk and funding liquidity are endogenously determined. Market risk is based on the degree of adverse selection. Because of asymmetric information, investors offer banks a pooling price for their assets. The pooling price (and hence the market liquidity) lowers if investors become more pessimistic and the quality of the assets is

---

[91] In addition, the RAMSI model is a one-size fits all model. The aim seemed to be to flexibly use this model for multiple analyses and macroprudential policy purposes. But this was inhibited by rigid outfit of inflexible code and entangled parts in which it was dressed. In such a model it is harder to disentangle the effects of various components of the model, and such a model is easily prone to becoming a 'black box'. That is why we propose that, as a matter of model design, it is preferable to create a *modular* and *transparent* plug-and-play model, where (building block) components can be *flexibly* added and removed.

lower. Funding liquidity risk is determined as a function of the bank's credit and market losses (based on general market confidence, and thus as a function of information contagion), its funding composition and maturity profile, and concerns that creditors may have over its future solvency.

Despite these strengths, there is substantial scope for improvement. First, most macroprudential stress tests only cover banks and their creditors, and therefore fail to capture interactions with non-banks that make up a substantial part of the financial system. Non-banks have played an important role in amplifying distress to the banking sector during the 2007–2009 financial crisis (Bernanke, 2015). Therefore, failing to capture non-banks does not just exclude many institutions from the analysis, but also leaves regulators less well-equipped to understand the resilience of the subset of financial institutions they do study. The ABM for Financial Vulnerabilities is an exception, since it does include multiple types of financial institutions, but contrary to the RAMSI and the MFRAF models it is not used as a regulatory stress test.

Second, and relatedly, most macroprudential stress tests capture only a few types of interconnections, even though it is clear that the multiplicity of channels and interconnections between financial institutions plays a critical role in spreading distress (Brunnermeier, 2008) (see also Section 5.5). Notable examples of such contractual linkages include securitized products and credit default swaps.

Third, most current macroprudential stress tests only capture post-default contagion. However, in financial crises pre-default contagion is rampant, often resulting from actions that are prudent from a firm-specific risk-management perspective, but destabilizing from a system-wide perspective. A bank, for example, might engage in precautionary de-leveraging to avoid insolvency (i.e. breaking a leverage constraint), which can add to further negative price spirals. Not capturing such dynamics implies that the total size of contagion, as well as the timing of contagion, is misunderstood.

These three areas of improvement essentially come down to the same point: the current macroprudential stress tests insufficiently capture the diversity of agents and interactions that make up the financial system, and therefore do not do justice to the complex nature of the financial system (or, for that matter, to the insights of the heterogeneous agent model literature, see Sections 4 and 5). One of the important challenges is to devise a modeling strategy that can capture these various effects, and the ABM for Financial Vulnerabilities offers a promising start; the model could easily be extended to capture more types of financial institutions (e.g. central clearing parties, pension funds), financial contracts (e.g. derivative contracts, securitized products), and constraints that drive behavior under stressed circumstances (Cetina et al., 2015; Farmer et al., 2018).

Finally, macroprudential stress tests must be more data-driven[92] and more carefully calibrated to be credible. Thus, suitably designed system-wide stress tests are enabled to become more credible as regulators collect better (contract-level) data.

---

[92]This depends on data availability.

9 THE FUTURE OF SYSTEM-WIDE STRESS TESTS

So far, we have spoken largely about *what* is. When thinking about what *should be*, we start by setting an overarching objective: to study systemic risk in the financial system. Such risk would not exist if firms operated in isolation, so adopting a system-wide perspective that takes account of the heterogeneity of the agents that inhabit it, as well as their interconnectedness and interactions (see Section 4 and Section 5), is critical. This view is gaining popularity among central bankers. Alex Brazier, head of financial stability at the Bank of England, recently made a statement that aligns with our observation (made in Section 1) that the economy is a complex system.[93] Brazier warned that a salient principle for macroprudential policy is to realize that 'the system is not the sum of its parts'. Instead, he emphasized, 'feedback loops within the system mean that the entities in the system can be individually resilient, but still collectively overwhelmed by the stress scenario'. Brazier related this statement explicitly to the stress tests, suggesting that these tools should be developed so that they can take that system-wide view. We agree (Farmer et al., 2018), but also observe that current macroprudential stress tests are not yet 'system-wide'. What should a genuine system-wide stress test be able to do?

System-wide stress tests[94] serve at least three important goals: to monitor financial stability, identify vulnerabilities in the financial system, and evaluate policies designed to mitigate systemic risk. The first, monitoring financial stability, involves developing metrics that would allow regulators to track whether systemic risks are building up over time, and to have early-warning indicators to ensure that they can intervene in a timely manner.

The second, identifying vulnerabilities in the financial system, implies that stress tests should enable regulators to become aware of structural deficiencies in the financial system that render it vulnerable to systemic risk. Another way of phrasing the same point would be to say that it should identify sources of systemic risk, the factors that contribute to such risk, and the relative importance of those factors. For example, regulators should be able to analyze the network structure of the financial system (Cont et al., 2010; e Santos et al., 2010; Battiston et al., 2012; Caccioli et al., 2014; Acemoglu et al., 2015), evaluate asset-holding patterns and concentration risk, identify systemically important nodes (Battiston et al., 2012), and examine the maturity structure and leverage of a financial institution's balance sheet (Puhr et al., 2003; Hirtle and Lehnert, 2014).

The third objective of a system-wide stress test would be that it can evaluate policies designed to mitigate systemic risk. In part, this objective touches on the concerns related to *microprudential* policies.[95] Such policies, meant to enhance the

---

[93] A substantial body of research using network theory to study financial systems finds emergent properties at the system-level which arise out of interactions between agents, see e.g. Battiston et al. (2007).

[94] Note that our conception of a 'stress test' is broader than the one commonly used; when we describe a 'system-wide stress test', we are not merely referring to the regulatory tool, but also to the underlying models that enable it.

[95] In other words, risk regulation itself can cause systemic risk.

resilience of individual institutions, can increase the fragility of the system in times of crisis when these requirements have procyclical effects (Danıelsson et al., 2004; Aymanns and Farmer, 2015).[96] At the same time, the objective to be able to evaluate the system-wide effects of proposed policies recognizes the significant design challenges associated with the development of *macroprudential* policies. To evaluate their efficacy *ex ante* is a significant challenge, and one that by definition requires a system-wide evaluation of their impact (see Armour et al., 2016). The interaction of multiple risk management policies, each of which would be beneficial on its own, may combine to produce effects that are undesirable. A system-wide stress testing model should be able to evaluate this, even if not in point-estimate terms.[97]

An example that highlights the potential for policies to pro-actively dramatically reduce systemic risk is provided by the work of Poledna and Thurner (2016). They use the debt-rank methodology of Battiston et al. (2012) to quantify the marginal systemic risk contribution of a given transaction, in this case a potential new loan. They then tax individual transactions according to that transaction's marginal contribution to systemic risk. In an agent-based simulation of the economy they find that this tax causes the agents to alter their transactions to re-organize the network and drastically decrease systemic risk at little cost. They demonstrate that this is far more effective than a Tobin (transaction) tax, which is both ineffectual and has substantial and potentially detrimental side effects. More generally, agent-based models have the advantage for policy evaluation that it is easy to change policies and explore their effects, though of course here one must work to properly take into account the Lucas critique[98] (Turrell, 2016; Farmer et al., 2018).

Before system-wide stress tests can credibly serve these important goals, the frontiers of financial stability models have to be pushed. One of the frontiers of financial stability modeling is to better understand the effect of interacting channels of contagion, and more generally, of multi-layered networks (like the ones used in Kok and Montagna, 2013). Setting up a system-wide stress test using multi-layered networks is useful because it allows for the representation of different types of relationships between various agents. That in turn allows for the interaction between different contractual types, corresponding to different layers of the model, enabling a richer set of contagion and amplification mechanisms (see Poledna et al., 2015, discussed in Section 5.5). Using a fine grained and comprehensive dataset Poledna et al. (2015) quantify the daily contribution to systemic risk from four layers of the Mexican banking system from 2007 to 2013. They find that focusing on a single layer underestimates the total systemic risk by up to 90%. A lingering question is how the

---

[96] As Andrew Crockett of the BIS observed as early as in 2000: 'actions that may seem desirable from the perspective of individual institutions may result in unwelcome system outcomes' (Crockett, 2000).

[97] Instead, the model may produce stylized facts, which help policymakers evaluate whether the policy is directionally efficacious (Haldane and Turrell, 2018). That way, it could serve as a laboratory for policy experiments.

[98] For example, conditional on a particular calibration for a proposed macroprudential policy.

interaction between the layers is modeled. Often, systemic risk or contagion estimates in each layer are simply added up (albeit jointly considered), so that richness of the interaction effects between contractual types is ignored[99] – despite their importance to the overall contagion dynamics.

Another frontier is more realistic modeling of agent behavior. In most macroprudential stress tests agents are naive and often are simply static, so that they do not take precautionary action and often take no action at all, even when catastrophic events occur. There are good reasons why agents could be modeled using fixed heuristics (Bookstaber, 2017), whether geared toward leverage targeting or to avoiding default (Kok and Montagna, 2013; Bookstaber et al., 2014b). But operating on fixed heuristics is also a limiting factor. Lo (2017), for example, has noted that some of the most interesting and salient behavioral phenomena – which translate into the dynamics of financial markets – result from the updating of behaviors by agents in response to changing circumstances. Simple learning protocols such as reinforcement learning and switching between heterogeneous expectations (e.g. Brock and Hommes, 1997; Brock and Hommes, 1998; Hommes et al., 2017), that allow agents to display goal-seeking, optimizing behavior while learning from their past interactions, have been shown to be effective in explaining behavioral experiments.

Calibration and validation remain key challenges for heterogeneous agent modeling. Methodological advances are required to provide better solutions to this problem and to convince policymakers that system-wide stress testing models are reliable. A key aspect of this is creating fine grained data sets.[100] Heterogeneous ABMs typically model the behavior of agents at a detailed level, and with appropriate microdata, they can also be calibrated and validated at this level.[101] This potentially offers a huge advantage over aggregated models that can only be calibrated and validated at an aggregate level. It is also essential that fine-grained data in anonymized form be made available to academics. Such models need to be designed to be more modular and flexible, so that it is easy to test alternative hypotheses and understand the key factors that drive observed behavior, and so that they can be easily adapted to new situations.

---

[99]For example, common asset holding interacts with repo contracts – when collateral price falls this can lead to margin calls.

[100]An encouraging development in this respect is that central banks and other regulators have started to collect high-quality and fine-grained data. Perhaps the best example is the 'trade repository data set'. Art. 9 of the European Markets Infrastructure Regulation (EMIR) requires counterparties resident in the EU (including central clearing counterparties) to report the details of new and outstanding derivatives transactions to trade repositories on a daily basis. Sufficient information for each contract is gathered to determine the counterparties, the valuation and contractual obligations of a contract. To do so, around 85 variables are reported for each transaction. Such comprehensive reporting under EMIR implies huge data volumes. For a description of this data set, see Abad et al. (2016). On the basis of this data, it is possible to initialize derivatives networks and study contagion dynamics operating on that network.

[101]A good example is the housing ABM developed by Baptista et al. (2016).

10 CONCLUSION

Computational agent-based models provide a useful complement to more traditional equilibrium based methods. They have already been shown to be essential for understanding the dynamics of systemic risk and for investigating the network properties of the financial system. Their role is likely to become even more important in the future, as increasingly comprehensive fine-grained data becomes available, making it possible to carefully calibrate such models so that they can yield more quantitative conclusions. Due to the inherent complexity of the financial system, and in particular its nonlinear feedback loops, analytic methods are unlikely to be sufficient.

We expect that computational and simulation methods will soon begin to go beyond hard wired behavioral rules and move increasingly toward myopic optimization. Models of boundedly rational heterogeneous agents, who learn and adapt their behavior in response to observed market realizations and newly adopted policies, withstand the Lucas critique. Behavioral economists have documented more and more situations in which people are not fully rational, emphasizing the obvious point that realistic behavior lies somewhere between full rationality and zero intelligence. Computational models offer the possibility of implementing realistic levels of strategic behavior, while allowing one to model the complex institutional structure of the financial system. We think that computational models will play an expanding role for understanding financial stability and systemic risk.

REFERENCES

Abad, J., Aldasoro, I., Aymanns, C., D'Errico, M., Rousová, L.F., Hoffmann, P., Langfield, S., Neychev, M., Roukny, T., 2016. Shedding light on dark markets: first insights from the new EU-wide OTC derivatives dataset. ESRB Occasional Paper Series 10, 1–32.

Accenture, 2015. Federal Reserve Involvement in Insurance Industry Capital Standards. Technical report. Accenture.

Acemoglu, D., Ozdaglar, A., Tahbaz-Salehi, A., 2015. Systemic risk and stability in financial networks. The American Economic Review 105 (2), 564–608.

Acharya, V., Engle, R., Pierret, D., 2014. Testing macroprudential stress tests: the risk of regulatory risk weights. Journal of Monetary Economics 65, 36–53.

Acharya, V.V., Yorulmazer, T., 2008. Information contagion and bank herding. Journal of Money, Credit, and Banking 40 (1), 215–231.

Admati, A., Hellwig, M., 2014. The Bankers' New Clothes: What's Wrong with Banking and What to Do About It. Princeton University Press.

Adrian, T., Shin, H.S., 2010. Liquidity and leverage. Journal of Financial Intermediation 19 (3), 418–437.

Afonso, G., Kovner, A., Schoar, A., 2011. Stressed, not frozen: the federal funds market in the financial crisis. The Journal of Finance 66 (4), 1109–1139.

Aikman, D., Alessandri, P., Eklund, B., Gai, P., Kapadia, S., Martin, E., Mora, N., Sterne, G., Willison, M., 2009. Funding Liquidity Risk in a Quantitative Model of Systemic Stability. Bank of England Working Paper No. 372.

Akerlof, G.A., 1970. The market for "lemons": quality uncertainty and the market mechanism. The Quarterly Journal of Economics, 488–500.

Alessandri, P., Gai, P., Kapadia, S., Mora, N., Puhr, C., et al., 2009. Towards a framework for quantifying systemic stability. International Journal of Central Banking 5 (3), 47–81.

Allen, F., Gale, D., 2000. Financial contagion. Journal of Political Economy 108 (1), 1–33.

Amini, H., Cont, R., Minca, A., 2016. Resilience to contagion in financial networks. Mathematical Finance 26, 329–365.

Anand, K., Bédard-Pagé, G., Traclet, V., 2014. Stress testing the Canadian banking system: a system-wide approach. Financial System Review 61.

Anand, K., Gauthier, C., Souissi, M., 2015. Quantifying Contagion Risk in Funding Markets: A Model-Based Stress-Testing Approach. Technical report.

Anand, K., van Lelyveld, I., Banai, Á., Friedrich, S., Garratt, R., Hałaj, G., Fique, J., Hansen, I., Jaramillo, S.M., Lee, H., et al., 2018. The missing links: a global study on uncovering financial network structures from partial data. Journal of Financial Stability 35, 107–119.

Andersen, T.G., Bollerslev, T., Christoffersen, P.F., Diebold, F.X., 2006. Volatility and correlation forecasting. In: Handbook of Economic Forecasting, vol. 1, pp. 777–878.

Anderson, P.W., et al., 1972. More is different. Science 177 (4047), 393–396.

Anderson, R.W., 2016. Stress testing and macroprudential regulation: a transatlantic assessment. In: Stress Testing and Macroprudential Regulation, p. 1.

Arinaminpathy, N., Kapadia, S., May, R.M., 2012. Size and complexity in model financial systems. Proceedings of the National Academy of Sciences 109 (45), 18338–18343.

Armour, J., Awrey, D., Davies, P., Enriques, L., Gordon, J.N., Mayer, C., Payne, J., 2016. Principles of Financial Regulation. Oxford University Press.

Arnold, M., Jenkins, P., 2016. EBA boss says recapitalization of banks has been 'successful'. https://www.ft.com/content/5496cc86-5417-11e6-befd-2fc0c26b3c60.

Aymanns, C., Caccioli, F., Farmer, J.D., Tan, V.W., 2016. Taming the Basel leverage cycle. Journal of Financial Stability 27, 263–277.

Aymanns, C., Farmer, J.D., 2015. The dynamics of the leverage cycle. Journal of Economic Dynamics and Control 50, 155–179.

Aymanns, C., Georg, C.-P., Bundesbank, D., Golub, B., 2017. Illiquidity spirals in coupled over-the-counter markets. Posted on SSRN: https://papers.ssrn.com/sol3/papers.cfm?abstract_id=2881814.

Baptista, R., Farmer, J.D., Hinterschweiger, M., Low, K., Tang, D., Uluc, A., 2016. Macroprudential Policy in an Agent-Based Model of the UK Housing Market. Bank of England Working Paper No. 619.

Baranova, Y., Coen, J., Lowe, P., Noss, J., Silvestri, L., 2017. Simulating Stress Across the Financial System: The Resilience of Corporate Bond Markets and the Role of Investment Funds. Bank of England Financial Stability Paper 42.

Bardoscia, M., Barucca, P., Brinley, A., Hill, J., 2017. The Decline of Solvency Contagion Risk. Bank of England Staff Working Paper No. 662.

Battiston, S., Farmer, J.D., Flache, A., Garlaschelli, D., Haldane, A.G., Heesterbeek, H., Hommes, C., Jaeger, C., May, R., Scheffer, M., 2016. Complexity theory and financial regulation. Science 351 (6275), 818–819.

Battiston, S., Gatti, D.D., Gallegati, M., Greenwald, B., Stiglitz, J.E., 2007. Credit chains and bankruptcy propagation in production networks. Journal of Economic Dynamics and Control 31 (6), 2061–2084.

Battiston, S., Puliga, M., Kaushik, R., Tasca, P., Caldarelli, G., 2012. Debtrank: too central to fail? Financial networks, the Fed and systemic risk. Scientific Reports 2.

Behn, M., Haselmann, R.F., Vig, V., 2016. The Limits of Model-Based Regulation. ECB Working Paper No. 1928.

Bernanke, B., 2013. Stress testing banks: what have we learned? https://www.federalreserve.gov/newsevents/speech/bernanke20130408a.htm.

Bernanke, B., 2015. The Courage to Act: A Memoir of the Crisis and Its Aftermath. W.W. Norton and Company.

BIS, 2015. Revisions to the Standardised Approach for Credit Risk. Technical report. Bank for International Settlements, Basel Committee on Banking Supervision.

BoC, 2012. Understanding Systemic Risk in the Banking Sector: A Macrofinancial Risk Assessment Framework. Technical report. Bank of Canada.

BoC, 2014. Financial System Review. Technical report. Bank of Canada.

BoE, 2014. Stress Testing the UK Banking System: 2014 Results. Technical report. Bank of England.

BoE, 2015. General Insurance Stress Test 2015 – Scenario Specification, Guidelines and Instructions. Technical report. BoE.

BoE, 2016. Stress Testing the UK Banking System: Key Elements of the 2016 Stress Test. Technical report. Bank of England.

Bookstaber, R., 2017. The End of Theory: Financial Crises, the Failure of Economics, and the Sweep of Human Interaction. Princeton University Press.

Bookstaber, R., Cetina, J., Feldberg, G., Flood, M., Glasserman, P., 2014a. Stress tests to promote financial stability: assessing progress and looking to the future. Journal of Risk Management in Financial Institutions 7 (1), 16–25.

Bookstaber, R., Kirman, A., 2018. Modeling a heterogeneous world. In: Handbook of Computational Economics, vol. 4. Elsevier, pp. 769–795 (this Handbook).

Bookstaber, R., Paddrik, M., Tivnan, B., 2014b. An agent-based model for financial vulnerability. Office of Financial Research Working Paper Series 14 (05).

Bookstaber, R.M., Paddrik, M.E., 2015. An Agent-Based Model for Crisis Liquidity Dynamics. Office of Financial Research (OFR) Working Paper 15-18.

Boss, M., Krenn, G., Puhr, C., Schwaiger, M.S., et al., 2007. Stress Testing the Exposure of Austrian Banks in Central and Eastern Europe. Oesterreichische Nationalbank (ONB) Financial Stability Report 13.

Bouchaud, J.-P., Farmer, J.D., Lillo, F., 2008. How markets slowly digest changes in supply and demand. arXiv:0809.0822.

Brock, W.A., Hommes, C.H., 1997. A rational route to randomness. Econometrica, 1059–1095.

Brock, W.A., Hommes, C.H., 1998. Heterogeneous beliefs and routes to chaos in a simple asset pricing model. Journal of Economic Dynamics & Control 22 (8), 1235–1274.

Brunnermeier, M.K., 2008. Deciphering the Liquidity and Credit Crunch 2007–08. Technical report. National Bureau of Economic Research.

Brunnermeier, M.K., Pedersen, L.H., 2009. Market liquidity and funding liquidity. The Review of Financial Studies 22 (6), 2201–2238.

Brunnermeier, M.K., Sannikov, Y., 2014. A macroeconomic model with a financial sector. The American Economic Review 104 (2), 379–421.

Burrows, O., Learmonth, D., McKeown, J., Williams, R., 2012. RAMSI: a top-down stress-testing model developed at the Bank of England. Bank of England Quarterly Bulletin 52 (3), 204–212.

Burrows, O., Low, K., Cumming, F., 2015. Mapping the UK financial system. Bank of England Quarterly Bulletin 55 (2), 114–129.

Caccioli, F., Bouchaud, J.-P., Farmer, J.D., 2012a. Impact-adjusted valuation and the criticality of leverage. Risk, 74–77.

Caccioli, F., Catanach, T.A., Farmer, J.D., 2012b. Heterogeneity, correlations and financial contagion. Advances in Complex Systems 15 (Suppl. 02), 1250058.

Caccioli, F., Farmer, J.D., Foti, N., Rockmore, D., 2015. Overlapping portfolios, contagion, and financial stability. Journal of Economic Dynamics and Control 51, 50–63.

Caccioli, F., Shrestha, M., Moore, C., Farmer, J.D., 2014. Stability analysis of financial contagion due to overlapping portfolios. Journal of Banking & Finance 46, 233–245.

Candelon, B., Sy, A.N., 2015. How Did Markets React to Stress Tests? International Monetary Fund.

Capgemini, 2014. Basel III: Comparison of Standardized and Advanced Approaches. Technical report. Capgemini.

Capponi, A., Chen, P.-C., Yao, D.D., 2015. Liability concentration and systemic losses in financial networks. Operations Research 64 (5), 1121–1134.

Capponi, A., Cheng, W., Sethuraman, J., 2017. Clearinghouse default waterfalls: risk-sharing, incentives, and systemic risk. Available at SSRN: https://ssrn.com/abstract=2930099 or http://dx.doi.org/10.2139/ssrn.2930099.

Capponi, A., Larsson, M., 2015. Price contagion through balance sheet linkages. The Review of Asset Pricing Studies 5 (2), 227–253.

Cetina, J., Lelyveld, I., Anand, K., 2015. Making Supervisory Stress Tests More Macroprudential: Considering Liquidity and Solvency Interactions and Systemic Risk. BCBS Working Paper.

CFTC, 2016. Supervisory Stress Test of Clearinghouses. Technical report. Commodity Futures and Trading Commission.

Cifuentes, R., Ferrucci, G., Shin, H.S., 2005. Liquidity risk and contagion. Journal of the European Economic Association 3 (2–3), 556–566.

Cont, R., 2001. Empirical properties of asset returns: stylized facts and statistical issues. Quantitative Finance 1 (2), 223–236.

Cont, R., 2015. The end of the waterfall: default resources of central counterparties. Journal of Risk Management in Financial Institutions 8 (4), 365–389.

Cont, R., Kokholm, T., 2014. Central clearing of OTC derivatives: bilateral vs multilateral netting. Statistics & Risk Modeling 31 (1), 3–22.

Cont, R., Moussa, A., Santos, E.B., 2010. Network structure and systemic risk in banking systems. Available at SSRN: https://ssrn.com/abstract=1733528 or http://dx.doi.org/10.2139/ssrn.1733528.

Cont, R., Schaanning, E.F., 2017. Fire sales, indirect contagion and systemic stress-testing. Available at SSRN: https://ssrn.com/abstract=2541114 or http://dx.doi.org/10.2139/ssrn.2541114.

Cont, R., Wagalath, L., 2013. Running for the exit: distressed selling and endogenous correlation in financial markets. Mathematical Finance 23 (4), 718–741.

Cont, R., Wagalath, L., 2016. Fire sales forensics: measuring endogenous risk. Mathematical Finance 26 (4), 835–866. https://doi.org/10.1111/mafi.12071.

Copeland, A., Martin, A., Walker, M., 2014. Repo runs: evidence from the tri-party repo market. The Journal of Finance 69, 2343–2380.

Crockett, A.D., 2000. Marrying the Micro- and Macro-Prudential Dimensions of Financial Stability. Technical report. Bank of International Settlements.

Danıelsson, J., Shin, H.S., Zigrand, J.-P., 2004. The impact of risk regulation on price dynamics. Journal of Banking & Finance 28 (5), 1069–1087.

Dees, S., Henry, J., 2017. Stress-test analytics for macroprudential purposes: introducing stamp. In: Satellite Models, p. 13.

Diamond, D.W., Dybvig, P.H., 1983. Bank runs, deposit insurance, and liquidity. Journal of Political Economy 91 (3), 401–419.

Dieci, R., He, T., 2018. Heterogeneous agent models in finance. In: Hommes, C., LeBaron, B. (Eds.), Handbook of Computational Economics, vol. 4. Elsevier, pp. 257–328 (this Handbook).

Duarte, F., Eisenbach, T.M., et al., 2015. Fire-Sale Spillovers and Systemic Risk. Federal Reserve Bank of New York Staff Report No. 645. October 2013, revised February 2015.

Duffie, D., Scheicher, M., Vuillemey, G., 2015. Central clearing and collateral demand. Journal of Financial Economics 116 (2), 237–256.

Duffie, D., Zhu, H., 2011. Does a central clearing counterparty reduce counterparty risk? The Review of Asset Pricing Studies 1 (1), 74–95.

e Santos, E.B., Cont, R., et al., 2010. The Brazilian Interbank Network Structure and Systemic Risk. Technical report.

EBA, 2017a. CEBS stress testing results. http://www.eba.europa.eu/risk-analysis-and-data/eu-wide-stress-testing/2009.

EBA, 2017b. EU-wide stress testing. http://www.eba.europa.eu/risk-analysis-and-data/eu-wide-stress-testing.

ECB, 2015. Report on Financial Structures. Technical report. European Central Bank.

EIOPA, 2016. Insurance Stress Test 2016 Technical Specifications. Technical report. European Insurance and Occupational Pensions Authority.

EIOPA, 2017. Occupational pensions stress test. https://eiopa.europa.eu/financial-stability-crisis-prevention/financial-stability/occupational-pensions-stress-test.

Eisenberg, L., Noe, T.H., 2001. Systemic risk in financial systems. Management Science 47 (2), 236–249.

Elliott, M., Golub, B., Jackson, M.O., 2014. Financial networks and contagion. The American Economic Review 104 (10), 3115–3153.

Erbenova, M., 2015. Germany Financial Sector Assessment Program. Technical report. International Monetary Fund.

ESMA, 2015. EU-Wide CCP Stress Test 2015. Technical report. European Securities and Markets Authority.

ESMA, 2017. OTC derivatives and clearing obligation. https://www.esma.europa.eu/regulation/post-trading/otc-derivatives-and-clearing-obligation.

ESRB, 2015. The ESRB handbook on operationalising macroprudential policy in the banking sector, macroprudential leverage ratios. https://www.esrb.europa.eu/pub/pdf/other/140303_esrb_handbook_mp.en.pdf.

ESRB, 2016. Adverse Macro-Financial Scenario for the EBA 2016 EU-Wide Bank Stress Testing Exercise. Technical report. European Systemic Risk Board.

EY, 2013. Dodd–Frank's Title VII – OTC derivatives reform. http://www.ey.com/Publication/vwLUAssets/Key_questions_board_members_should_ask_about_Title_VII/$FILE/Americas_FAAS_Dodd_Frank_derivatives_reform.pdf.

Farmer, D., Kleinnijenhuis, A., Nahai-Williamson, P., Tanin, R., Wetzer, T., 2018. A Nesting Model for System-Wide Stress Tests. Working paper.

Farmer, J.D., 2002. Market force, ecology and evolution. Journal of Industrial and Corporate Change 11 (5), 895–953.

Farmer, J.D., 2012. Economics needs to treat the economy as a complex system. In: Papers for the INET Conference. Rethinking Economics and Politics, vol. 14.

FED, 2016. Dodd–Frank Act Stress Test 2016: Supervisory Stress Test Methodology and Results. Technical report. Board of Governors of the Federal Reserve.

FED, 2017a. Stress tests and capital planning: comprehensive capital analysis and review. https://www.federalreserve.gov/supervisionreg/ccar.htm.

FED, 2017b. Stress tests and capital planning: Dodd–Frank act stress tests. https://www.federalreserve.gov/supervisionreg/ccar.htm.

Fender, I., Lewrick, U., 2015. Calibrating the leverage ratio. BIS Quarterly Review. https://EconPapers.repec.org/RePEc:bis:bisqtr:1512f.

Feroli, M., Kashyap, A.K., Schoenholtz, K.L., Shin, H.S., 2014. Market tantrums and monetary policy. Chicago Booth Research Paper No. 14-09. Available at SSRN: https://ssrn.com/abstract=2409092 or http://dx.doi.org/10.2139/ssrn.2409092.

Foglia, A., 2009. Stress testing credit risk: a survey of authorities' approaches. International Journal of Central Banking 5 (3), 9–45.

Fostel, A., Geanakoplos, J., 2008. Leverage cycles and the anxious economy. The American Economic Review 98 (4), 1211–1244.

FSB, 2015. Global Shadow Banking Monitoring Report. Technical report.

Gai, P., Haldane, A., Kapadia, S., 2011. Complexity, concentration and contagion. Journal of Monetary Economics 58 (5), 453–470.

Gai, P., Kapadia, S., 2010. Contagion in financial networks. Proceedings of the Royal Society of London A: Mathematical, Physical and Engineering Sciences, rspa20090410.

Gauthier, C., Lehar, A., Souissi, M., 2012. Macroprudential capital requirements and systemic risk. Journal of Financial Intermediation 21 (4), 594–618.

Gauthier, C., Souissi, M., Liu, X., et al., 2014. Introducing funding liquidity risk in a macro stress-testing framework. International Journal of Central Banking 10 (4), 105–141.

Geanakoplos, J., 2010. The leverage cycle. NBER Macroeconomics Annual 24 (1), 1–66.

Geithner, T.F., 2014. Stress test: reflections on the financial crisis. Business Economics 49 (3), 201–203.

Gennotte, G., Leland, H., 1990. Market liquidity, hedging, and crashes. The American Economic Review, 999–1021.

Georg, C.-P., 2013. The effect of the interbank network structure on contagion and common shocks. Journal of Banking & Finance 37 (7), 2216–2228.

Glasserman, P., Tangirala, G., et al., 2015. Are the Federal Reserve's Stress Test Results Predictable? Technical report.

Glasserman, P., Young, H.P., 2015. How likely is contagion in financial networks? Journal of Banking & Finance 50, 383–399.

Gorton, G., Metrick, A., 2012. Securitized banking and the run on repo. Journal of Financial Economics 104 (3), 425–451.

Goyal, S., 2018. Heterogeneity and networks. In: Hommes, C., LeBaron, B. (Eds.), Handbook of Computational Economics, vol. 4. Elsevier, pp. 687–712 (this Handbook).

Greenwood, R., Landier, A., Thesmar, D., 2015. Vulnerable banks. Journal of Financial Economics 115 (3), 471–485.

Groendahl, B., 2015. Leverage ratio for banks can rise as high as 5%, BIS says. https://www.bloomberg.com/news/articles/2015-12-06/leverage-ratio-for-banks-can-be-raised-as-high-as-5-bis-says.

Gromb, D., Vayanos, D., 2002. Equilibrium and welfare in markets with financially constrained arbitrageurs. Journal of Financial Economics 66 (2), 361–407.

Haldane, A.G., Turrell, A.E., 2018. An interdisciplinary model for macroeconomics. Oxford Review of Economic Policy 34 (1–2), 219–251.

He, Z., Xiong, W., 2012. Dynamic debt runs. The Review of Financial Studies 25 (6), 1799–1843.

Hirtle, B., Kovner, A., Zeller, S., 2016. Are stress tests still informative. http://libertystreeteconomics.newyorkfed.org/2016/04/are-stress-tests-still-informative.html.

Hirtle, B., Lehnert, A., 2014. Supervisory Stress Tests. FRB of New York Staff Report 696.

Hommes, C.H., Jump, R., Levine, P., 2017. Internal rationality, heterogeneity, and complexity in the new Keynesian model. Available at SSRN: https://ssrn.com/abstract=3086851 or http://dx.doi.org/10.2139/ssrn.3086851.

Hommes, C.H., 2006. Heterogeneous agent models in economics and finance. In: Handbook of Computational Economics, vol. 2, pp. 1109–1186.

IMF, 2014. Canada Financial Sector Stability Assessment. Technical report. International Monetary Fund.

Ionescu, L., Yermon, J., 2014. Stress Testing and Scenario Analysis of Pension Plans. Technical report. International Organisation of Pension Fund Supervisors.

Iori, G., Mantegna, R., 2018. Empirical analyses of networks in finance. In: Hommes, C., LeBaron, B. (Eds.), Handbook of Computational Economics, vol. 4. Elsevier, pp. 637–685 (this Handbook).

Iyer, R., Peydro, J.-L., 2011. Interbank contagion at work: evidence from a natural experiment. The Review of Financial Studies 24 (4), 1337–1377.

Jobst, A., Andreas, S.N.B.T., 2014. Macroprudential Solvency Stress Testing of the Insurance Sector. Technical report. IMF.

Kapadia, S., Drehmann, M., Elliott, J., Sterne, G., 2013. Liquidity risk, cash flow constraints, and systemic feedbacks. In: Quantifying Systemic Risk. University of Chicago Press, pp. 29–61.

Khandani, A.E., Lo, A.W., 2011. What happened to the quants in August 2007? Evidence from factors and transactions data. Journal of Financial Markets 14 (1), 1–46.

Kiyotaki, N., Moore, J., 1997. Credit cycles. Journal of Political Economy 105 (2), 211–248.

Kok, C., Montagna, M., 2013. Multi-Layered Interbank Model for Assessing Systemic Risk. Technical report. European Central Bank.

Kyle, A.S., 1985. Continuous auctions and insider trading. Econometrica, 1315–1335.

LeBaron, B., 2006. Agent-based computational finance. In: Handbook of Computational Economics, vol. 2, pp. 1187–1233.

Lo, A.W., 2005. Reconciling efficient markets with behavioral finance: the adaptive markets hypothesis. Journal of Investment Consulting, 21–44.

Lo, A.W., 2017. Adaptive Markets: Financial Evolution at the Speed of Thought. Princeton University Press.

Martin, A., Skeie, D., Von Thadden, E.-L., 2014. Repo runs. The Review of Financial Studies 27, 957–989.

May, R.M., Arinaminpathy, N., 2010. Systemic risk: the dynamics of model banking systems. Journal of the Royal Society Interface 7 (46), 823–838.

Mehrling, P., Pozsar, Z., Sweeney, J., Neilson, D.H., 2013. Bagehot was a shadow banker: shadow banking, central banking, and the future of global finance. Available at SSRN: https://ssrn.com/abstract=2232016 or http://dx.doi.org/10.2139/ssrn.2232016.

Moretti, M., Stolz, S.M., Swinburne, M., 2008. Stress Testing at the IMF. Citeseer.

Morris, S., Shin, H.S., 2001. Global games: theory and applications.

Morrison, A.D., Vasios, M., Wilson, M.I., Zikes, F., 2016. Identifying Contagion in a Banking Network. Saïd Business School WP 2016-37. Available at SSRN: https://ssrn.com/abstract=2987848 or https://doi.org/10.2139/ssrn.2987848.

Murphy, D., 2013. OTC Derivatives: Bilateral Trading and Central Clearing: An Introduction to Regulatory Policy, Market Impact and Systemic Risk. Springer.

Noonan, L., Binham, C., Shotter, J., 2016. Deutsche Bank received special treatment in EU stress tests. https://www.ft.com/content/44768ea8-8c71-11e6-8aa5-f79f5696c731.

OFR, 2014. Office of Financial Research: 2014 Annual Report. Technical report. Office of Financial Research.

Ong, L.L., Pazarbasioglu, C., 2014. Credibility and crisis stress testing. International Journal of Financial Studies 2 (1), 15–81.

Poledna, S., Molina-Borboa, J.L., Martínez-Jaramillo, S., Van Der Leij, M., Thurner, S., 2015. The multilayer network nature of systemic risk and its implications for the costs of financial crises. Journal of Financial Stability 20, 70–81.

Poledna, S., Thurner, S., 2016. Elimination of systemic risk in financial networks by means of a systemic risk transaction tax. Quantitative Finance 16 (10), 1599–1613.

Poledna, S., Thurner, S., Farmer, J.D., Geanakoplos, J., 2014. Leverage-induced systemic risk under Basel II and other credit risk policies. Journal of Banking & Finance 42, 199–212.

Pozsar, Z., 2013. Shadow banking and the global financial ecosystem. VoxEU 6.

Pozsar, Z., Adrian, T., Ashcraft, A., Boesky, H., 2010. Shadow banking. New York 458, 3–9.

Pozsar, Z., Singh, M., 2011. The Nonbank–Bank Nexus and the Shadow Banking System. IMF Working Paper WP/11/289.

Puhr, M.C., Santos, M.A., Schmieder, M.C., Neftci, S.N., Neudorfer, M.B., Schmitz, M.S.W., Hesse, H., 2003. Next Generation System-Wide Liquidity Stress Testing. No. 12–13. International Monetary Fund.

Quagliariello, M., 2009. Stress-Testing the Banking System: Methodologies and Applications. Cambridge University Press.

Robb, G., 2015. Fed adopting stress test for insurance companies: Fisher. http://www.marketwatch.com/story/fed-adopting-stress-test-for-insurance-companies-fischer-2015-06-24.

Rogers, L.C., Veraart, L.A., 2013. Failure and rescue in an interbank network. Management Science 59 (4), 882–898.

Scheule, H., Roesh, D., 2008. Stress Testing for Financial Institutions. Risk Publications.

Schuermann, T., 2014. Stress testing banks. International Journal of Forecasting 30 (3), 717–728.

Shleifer, A., Vishny, R.W., 1992. Liquidation values and debt capacity: a market equilibrium approach. The Journal of Finance 47 (4), 1343–1366.

Shleifer, A., Vishny, R.W., 1997. The limits of arbitrage. The Journal of Finance 52 (1), 35–55.

Siddique, A., Hasan, I., 2012. Stress Testing: Approaches, Methods and Applications. Risk Books.

Tarullo, D.K., 2014. Stress Testing After Five Years: A Speech at the Federal Reserve Third Annual Stress Test Modeling Symposium, Boston, Massachusetts. Technical report. Board of Governors of the Federal Reserve System.

Tarullo, D.K., 2016. Next steps in the evolution of stress testing. In: Remarks at the Yale University School of Management Leaders Forum (September 26, 2016).

Thurner, S., Farmer, J.D., Geanakoplos, J., 2012. Leverage causes fat tails and clustered volatility. Quantitative Finance 12 (5), 695–707.

Thurner, S., Poledna, S., 2013. Debtrank-transparency: controlling systemic risk in financial networks. arXiv:1301.6115.

Turrell, A., 2016. Agent-based models: understanding the economy from the bottom up.

Wackerbeck, P., Saxena, A., Crijns, J., Karsten, C., 2016. Stress testing: from regulatory burden to strategic capability. https://www.strategyand.pwc.com/reports/stress-testing.

Young, P., Glasserman, P., 2016. Contagion in financial networks. Journal of Economic Literature 54 (3), 779–831.

Agent-Based Models for Market Impact and Volatility

Jean-Philippe Bouchaud

Capital Fund Management, Paris, France
e-mail address: Jean-Philippe.Bouchaud@cfm.fr

CONTENTS

1 INTRODUCTION

Understanding why and how prices move is arguably one of the most important problems in financial economics. The "why" question is intimately related to the information content of prices and the efficiency of markets, and the "how" question is related to the issue of price impact, that has become one of the main theme of research in the recent years, both in academic circles and in trading houses. From a theoretical standpoint, price impact is the transmission belt that allows private information to be reflected by prices. But by the same token, it is also the very mechanism by which prices can be distorted, or even crash, under the influence of uninformed trades and/or fire-sale deleveraging. Price impact is also a cost for trading firms – in fact the dominant one when assets under management become substantial.

Now, the simplest guess is that price impact should be linear, i.e. proportional to the (signed) volume of a transaction. This is in fact the central result of the seminal microstructure model proposed by Kyle in 1985 (Kyle, 1985). This paper has had a profound influence on the field, with over 9500 citations as of November 2017. A linear impact model is at the core of many different studies, concerning for example optimal execution strategies, liquidity estimators, agent-based models, volatility models, etc.

Quite surprisingly, however, the last 20 years have witnessed mounting empirical evidence invalidating classical assumptions. For example, the order flow is found to have long-range autocorrelations, in apparent contradiction with the (nearly) unpredictable nature of price changes. How can this be if order flow impact prices? More strikingly still, empirical results suggest a square-root like growth of impact with traded volume Q, often dubbed the "square-root impact law", see Section 3.2 below for precise statements and references. This finding is in our opinion truly remarkable, on several counts. First, it is to a large extent *universal*, across time, markets (including the options markets or the Bitcoin), and execution strategies, suggesting to call it a "law" akin to physical laws. Second, a square-root dependence entails that the last $Q/2$ trades have an impact that is only $\sim$40% of the first $Q/2$. The only possibility for such a strange behavior to hold is that there must exist some memory in the market that extends over a time scale longer than the typical time needed to complete an order (see below for more on this). The second ingredient needed to explain the concavity of the square-root impact is that the last $Q/2$ must experience more resistance than the first $Q/2$. In other words, after having executed the first half of the order, the liquidity opposing further moves must somehow increase. Still, it is quite a quandary to understand how such non-linear effects can appear, even when the bias in the order flow is very small.

In several recent publications, simple Agent-Based Models (ABM) have been proposed to rationalize the universal square-root dependence of the impact. The argument relies on the existence of slow "latent" order book, i.e. orders to buy/sell that are not necessarily placed in the visible order book but that only reveal themselves as the transaction price moves closer to their limit price. Using both analytical arguments and numerical simulations of an artificial market, one finds that the liquidity profile is V-shaped, with a minimum around the current price and a linear growth of the latent volume as one moves away from that price. This explains why the resistance to further moves increases with the executed volume, and provides a simple explanation – borne out by numerical simulations – for the square-root impact. By the same token, a vanishing expected volume available around the mid-price leads to very small trades having anomalously large impact, as indeed reflected by the singular behavior of the square-root function near the origin.

The aim of the present chapter is to review the recent progress in Agent-Based Microstructure models that attempt to account for the various emergent "stylized facts" of financial markets, in particular the square-root impact just described. We show in particular that zero-intelligence models of order flow fail in general at reproducing the most basic property of prices, namely a random walk like behavior. Interestingly, models must be poised at a "critical point" separating a super-diffusive (trending) market and a sub-diffusive (mean-reverting) market, in such a way that the long range correlation of order flow is precisely balanced by the inertia of the (latent) order book. While all the necessary ingredients seem to be present to understand how fat-tailed distributions and clustered activity effects may emerge within such artificial markets, the final steps needed to complete this program are still not convincingly established, and is an important research objective for the future.

While the literature on ABM for financial markets is extremely abundant (see LeBaron, 2000; Chiarella et al., 2009b; Cristelli et al., 2011 for recent reviews), such models often start from the "mesoscale" (say minutes to days). Agent-Based Models at "microscale" (trades and quotes) have however been considered as well, see Sections 4, 5 and, among others, Bak et al. (1997), Chiarella and Iori (2002), Challet and Stinchcombe (2003), Chiarella et al. (2009a), Preis et al. (2006).

2 THE STATISTICS OF PRICE CHANGES: A SHORT OVERVIEW

2.1 BACHELIER'S FIRST LAW

The simplest property of financial prices, dating back to Bachelier's thesis (Bachelier, 1900), states that typical price variations grow like the square root of time. More formally, under the assumption that price changes have zero mean (which is a good approximation on short time scales), then the *price variogram*

$$\mathcal{V}(\tau) := \mathbb{E}[(p_{t+\tau} - p_t)^2] \tag{1}$$

grows linearly with time lag τ, such that $\mathcal{V}(\tau) = D\tau$.

Subsequent to Bachelier's time, many empirical studies noted that the typical size of a given stock's price change tends to be proportional to the stock's price itself. This suggests that price changes should be regarded as multiplicative rather than additive, which, in turn, suggests the use of *geometric Brownian motion* for price-series modeling. However, over short time horizons – say intraday – there is empirical evidence that price changes are closer to being additive than multiplicative, so we will assume throughout this chapter an additive model of price changes. Still, given the prevalence of multiplicative models for price changes on longer time scales, it has become customary to define the volatility σ in relative terms (even for short timescales), according to the equation

$$D = \sigma^2 p_0^2, \tag{2}$$

where p_0 is either the current price or some medium-term average.

2.2 SIGNATURE PLOTS

Assume now that a price series is described by

$$p_t = p_0 \left[1 + \sum_{t'=1}^{t} r_{t'} \right], \tag{3}$$

where the return series r_t is covariance-stationary with zero mean and covariance

$$\text{Cov}(r_{t'}, r_{t''}) = \sigma_0^2 C_r(|t' - t''|). \tag{4}$$

The case of a random walk with uncorrelated price returns corresponds to $C_r(u) = \delta_{u,0}$, where $\delta_{u,0}$ is the Kronecker delta function. A trending random walk has $C_r(u) > 0$ and a mean-reverting random walk has $C_r(u) < 0$. How does this affect Bachelier's first law?

One important implication is that the volatility observed by sampling price series on a given time scale τ is itself dependent on that time scale. More precisely, the volatility at scale τ is given by

$$\sigma^2(\tau) := \frac{\mathcal{V}(\tau)}{p_0^2 \tau} = \sigma_0^2 \left[1 + 2 \sum_{u=1}^{\tau} \left(1 - \frac{u}{\tau} \right) C_r(u) \right]. \tag{5}$$

A plot of $\sigma(\tau)$ versus τ is called a *volatility signature plot*. The case of an un-correlated random walk leads to a flat signature plot. Positive correlations (which correspond to trends) lead to an increase in $\sigma(\tau)$ with increasing τ. Negative correlations (which correspond to mean reversion) lead to a decrease in $\sigma(\tau)$ with increasing τ.

2.3 HIGH-FREQUENCY NOISE

Another interesting case occurs when the price p_t is soiled by some high-frequency noise, coming e.g. from price discretization effects or from pricing errors. Consider the case where rather than being given by Eq. (3), p_t is instead assumed to be governed by

$$p_t = p_0 \left[1 + \sum_{t'=1}^{t} r_{t'} \right] + \eta_t, \tag{6}$$

where η_t is a mean zero, variance σ_η^2 noise, uncorrelated with r_t, but is autocorrelated as

$$C_\eta(\tau) = e^{-\tau/\tau_\eta}, \tag{7}$$

where τ_η is a short time scale time over which the high-frequency noise is correlated. Eq. (6) is standard in the microstructure (Hasbrouck, 2007), where the observed price is decomposed into a "fundamental" price plus microstructural noise.

How does this noise affect the observed volatility? By replacing $C_r(\tau)$ in Eq. (5) with $C_\eta(\tau)$, we see that compared to the volatility observed in a price series without noise, the addition of the η_t term in Eq. (6) serves to increase the lag-τ volatility by $2\sigma_\eta^2 \left(1 - e^{-\tau/\tau_\eta}\right)/\tau$. This additional noise term decays from $2\sigma_\eta^2/\tau_\eta$ for $\tau \to 0$, to 0 for $\tau \to \infty$. The effect of this high-frequency noise on a volatility signature plot is thus akin to mean-reversion, in the sense that it creates a higher short-term volatility than long-term volatility. Note that small pricing errors of $\sigma_\eta = 0.01\%$ with a one minute life-time would contribute to a very significant excess short-term volatility of 0.3% (daily), to be compared with a typical volatility of 1% for stock indexes.

2.4 VOLATILITY SIGNATURE PLOTS FOR REAL PRICE SERIES

Quite remarkably, the volatility signature plots of most liquid assets (stocks, futures, FX, ...) are nowadays almost flat for values of τ ranging from a few seconds to a few months (beyond which it becomes dubious whether the statistical assumption of stationarity still holds). For example, for the S&P500 E-mini futures contract, which is one of the most liquid contracts in the world, $\sigma(\tau)$ only decreases by about 20% from short time scales (seconds) to long time scales (weeks) – see Fig. 1. The exact form of a volatility signature plot depends on the microstructural details of the underlying asset, but most liquid contracts in this market have a similar volatility signature plot.

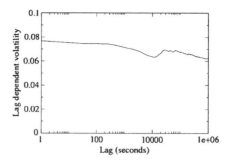

FIGURE 1

Volatility signature plot for the S&P500 E-mini futures contract for time lags between 1 second and 10^6 seconds corresponding to approximately 22 trading days. Note the semi-log scale.

The important conclusion from this empirical result is that long-term volatility is almost entirely determined by the short-term price formation process. Depending on how one views this result, it is either trivial (a simple random walk has this property) or extremely non-intuitive. In fact, one should expect a rather large fundamental uncertainty about the price of an asset, which would translate into substantially larger high-frequency volatility. Although empirical data shows that high-frequency volatility is larger than low-frequency volatility, the size of this effect is small (~20%). In a nutshell, long-term volatility seems is closely related to short-term volatility, itself determined by the high-frequency mechanisms of price formation.

2.5 HEAVY TAILS

An overwhelming body of empirical evidence from a vast array of financial instruments (including stocks, currencies, interest rates, commodities, and even implied volatility) show that unconditional distribution of returns has *fat tails*, which decay as a power law for large arguments and are much heavier than the corresponding tails of the Gaussian distribution, see e.g. Plerou et al. (1999), Gopikrishnan et al. (1999), Gabaix et al. (2006), Cont (2001), Bouchaud and Potters (2003).

On short time scales (between about a minute and a few hours), the empirical density function of returns r can be fit reasonably well by a Student's t distribution, with a distribution $f(r)$ decaying for large r as $|r|^{-1-\mu}$, is the *tail exponent*. Empirically, the tail parameter μ is consistently found to be around 3 for a wide variety of different markets, which suggests some kind of universality in the mechanism leading to extreme returns. This universality hints at the fact that fundamental factors are probably unimportant in determining the amplitude of most large price jumps. Interestingly, many studies indeed suggest that large price moves are often not associated to an identifiable piece of news that would rationally explain wild valuation swings (Cutler et al., 1989; Fair, 2002; Joulin et al., 2008).

2.6 VOLATILITY CLUSTERING

Although considering the unconditional distribution of returns is informative, it is also somewhat misleading. Returns are in fact very far from being IID random variables – although they are indeed nearly uncorrelated, as their flat signature plots demonstrate. Therefore, returns are not simply independent random variables drawn from the Student's t distribution. Such an IID model would predict that upon time aggregation, the distribution of returns would quickly converge to a Gaussian distribution on longer time scales. Empirical data indicates that this is not the case, and that returns remain substantially non-Gaussian on time scales up to weeks or even months (Bouchaud and Potters, 2003).

The dynamics of financial markets is in fact highly intermittent, with periods of intense activity intertwined with periods of relative calm. In intuitive terms, the volatility of financial returns is itself a dynamic variable that changes over time with a broad distribution of characteristic frequencies. In more formal terms, returns can be represented by the product of a time-dependent volatility component σ_t and a directional component ξ_t,

$$r_t := \sigma_t \xi_t. \tag{8}$$

In this representation, ξ_t are IID (but not necessarily Gaussian) random variables of unit variance and σ_t are positive random variables with long memory (Cont, 2001; Bollerslev et al., 1994; Muzy et al., 2000; Calvet and Fisher, 2002; Lux, 2008; Chicheportiche and Bouchaud, 2014).

It is worth pointing out that volatilities σ and scaled returns ξ are not independent random variables. It is well-documented that positive past returns tend to decrease future volatilities and that negative past returns tend to increase future volatilities (i.e., $\langle \xi_t \sigma_{t+\tau} \rangle < 0$ for $\tau > 0$). This is called the *leverage effect* (Bouchaud et al., 2001). Importantly, however, past volatilities do not give much information on the sign of future returns (i.e., $\langle \xi_t \sigma_{t+\tau} \rangle \approx 0$ for $\tau < 0$).

2.7 ACTIVITY CLUSTERING

In view of the long-range correlations of the volatility discussed in the last section, it is interesting to study the temporal fluctuations of market activity itself. Even a cursory look at the time series of mid-point changes suggests a strong degree of clustering in the activity as well.

A more precise way of characterizing this clustering property is to choose a time t and a small dt, and count the number dN_t of price changes that occur during the time interval $[t, t + dt]$ (i.e., count $dN_t = 1$ if the mid-point changed or $dN_t = 0$ if it did not). The empirical average of dN_t provides a way to define the average market activity $\bar{\lambda}$, while the covariance $\text{Cov}[dN_t, dN_{t+\tau}]$ characterizes the temporal structure of the fluctuations in market activity.

An increased activity at time t appears to trigger more activity at time $t + \tau$, much like earthquakes are followed by aftershocks. For example, a large jump is usually followed by an increased frequency of smaller price moves. More generally, some kind of "self-excitation" seem to be present in financial markets. This contagion takes place either in the time direction (some events trigger more events in the future) or across different assets (the activity of one stock spills over to other correlated stocks, or even from one market to another). Hawkes processes are mathematical models that capture (part) of these contagion effects, see Bacry et al. (2015) for a review, and Blanc et al. (2016) for some recent extensions.

2.8 LONG MEMORY IN THE ORDER FLOW

Another striking stylized fact of financial markets is the persistence in the sign of the order flow. More formally, let ε_t denote the sign of the tth market order, with $\varepsilon_t = +1$ for a buy market order and $\varepsilon_t = -1$ for a sell market order, where t is discrete and counts the number of market orders. In this event-time framework, one can introduce the sign autocorrelation function

$$C(\ell) := \operatorname{Cov}[\varepsilon_t, \varepsilon_{t+\ell}], \tag{9}$$

The surprising empirical result – that holds for many different asset classes (stocks, FX, futures, ...) – is that $C(\ell)$ decays extremely slowly with ℓ (see Bouchaud et al., 2004, 2006; Lillo and Farmer, 2004; Bouchaud et al., 2009 for a review). Its long time behavior is well-approximated by a power-law $\ell^{-\gamma}$ with $\gamma < 1$, corresponding to a so-called long-memory process (Beran, 1994). Typically, $\gamma \approx 0.5$ for stock markets and $\gamma \approx 0.8$ for futures markets (see for example Bouchaud et al., 2004, 2006, 2009; Lillo and Farmer, 2004; and, for futures markets, Mastromatteo et al., 2014a). The origin of this long-memory has been argued to be chiefly due to order splitting (LeBaron and Yamamoto, 2010; Tóth et al., 2015) rather than direct herding. Importantly, the long memory of order signs and long-memory in activity fluctuations are distinct phenomena, with no logical relation to one another (it is easy to build models that have one type of long memory, but not the other).

The persistence in the sign of the order flow leads to an apparent "efficiency paradox", which asks the question of how prices can remain unpredictable when order flow (which impacts the price directly) is so predictable. We will come back on this issue in Section 5.

2.9 SUMMARY

The above short review of the statistical properties of prices has left aside a host of other interesting regularities, in particular concerning inter-asset correlations, long-term behavioral anomalies, trend following effects and other "factor" dynamics, etc. The main message of this section is that price changes are remarkably uncorrelated over a large range of frequencies, with little signs of price adjustments or *tâtonnement* at high frequencies. The long-term volatility appears to be determined by the short-term, high frequency movements of the price.

In fact, the frequency of news that would affect the fundamental value of financial assets is much lower than the frequency of price changes themselves. As Cutler,

Poterba, and Summers state it: *The evidence that large market moves often occur on days without any identifiable major news releases, casts doubt on the view that stock price movements are fully explicable by news.* It is as if price changes *themselves* are the main source of news, and feedback as to create self-induced excess volatility and, most probably, price jumps that occur without any news at all. Interestingly, all quantitative volatility/activity feedback models (such as ARCH/GARCH models and the like, or Hawkes processes; see Bollerslev et al., 1994; Chicheportiche and Bouchaud, 2014; Bacry et al., 2015; Hardiman et al., 2013) suggest that at least 80% of the price variance is induced by self-referential effects. This adds credence to the idea that a lion's share of the short to medium term activity of financial markets is unrelated to any fundamental information or economic effects.

From a scientific point of view, this is extremely interesting, since it opens the path to building a theory of price moves that is mostly based on modeling the endogenous, self-exciting dynamics of markets, and not on long-term fundamental effects. One particularly important question is to understand the origin and the mechanisms leading to price jumps, which seem to have a similar structure on all traded, liquid markets (again indicating that fundamental factors are probably unimportant at short time scales).

3 THE SQUARE-ROOT IMPACT LAW

3.1 INTRODUCTION

Assume that following a decision to trade (whatever the underlying reason might be) one has to buy (or sell) some quantity Q on the market. Ideally, one would like to execute it immediately, "at the market price". However, unless the quantity Q is smaller than the available volume at the best quote, this is simply not possible. There is no such thing as a "market price". The market price is not only different for buy trades and sell trades, it really only makes sense for infinitesimal volumes, when the trade can be executed in one shot, such that impact on later trades can be neglected. For volumes typical of large financial institutions – say 1% of the market capitalization of a given stock – there is just not enough liquidity in the whole Limit Order Book (LOB) to match the required quantity Q.

Large trades should thus be split in small chunks. This incremental execution aims at allowing the latent liquidity to reveal itself and refill the LOB with previously undisclosed orders (what we call later the "latent" order book). This should, in principle, considerably improve the price obtained compared to an immediate execution with market orders that would otherwise penetrate deep into the book and possibly even destabilize the market.

The sequence of trades that comes from a single investment decision is known as a *metaorder*. How does a metaorder of size Q impact the price? From the point of view of investors: what is the true cost of trading? How does it depend on market conditions, execution strategies, and time horizon, etc.? From the point of view of regulators: can large metaorders destabilize markets? Is marked-to-market accounting wise when, as emphasized above, the market price is at best meaningful for infinitesimal volumes, but not for large investment portfolios that would substantially impact the price upon unwinding?

3.2 EMPIRICAL EVIDENCE

Naively, one expects the impact of a metaorder to be linear in its volume Q. It is also what standard theoretical models of impact predict, such as the famous Kyle model (Kyle, 1985). However, there is now overwhelming empirical evidence ruling out the simple linear impact law, and suggesting instead a concave, square-root-like growth of impact with volume, often dubbed the "square-root impact law". The impact of a metaorder is surprisingly universal: the square-root law has been reported in many different studies, both academic and professional, since the early eighties (Loeb, 1983). It appears to hold for completely different markets (equities, futures, FX, options (Tóth et al., 2016), or even the Bitcoin; Donier and Bonart, 2015), epochs (pre-2005, when liquidity was mostly provided by market makers, and post-2005, with electronic markets dominated by HFT), types of microstructure (small ticks versus large ticks), market participants and underlying trading strategies (fundamental, technical, etc.), and styles of execution (using limit or market orders). In all these cases, the impact of a meta-order of volume Q is well described by (Torre and Ferrari, 1997; Grinold and Kahn, 1999; Almgren et al., 2005; Moro et al., 2009; Tóth et al., 2011; Mastromatteo et al., 2014a; Gomes and Waelbroeck, 2014; Bershova and Rakhlin, 2013; Brokmann et al., 2015)[1]

$$\mathcal{I}(Q, T) \approx Y\sigma_T \left(\frac{Q}{V_T}\right)^{\delta} \qquad (Q \ll V_T) \qquad (10)$$

where δ is an exponent in the range 0.4–0.7, Y is a numerical coefficient of order unity ($Y \approx 0.5$ for US stocks), and σ_T and V_T are, respectively, the average contemporaneous volatility on the time horizon T and the average contemporaneous traded volume over time T. Note that Eq. (10) is dimensionally correct (in the sense that the dimension of Q and V_T cancel out, while impact and volatility are indeed expressed as price percentage). Kyle's model instead leads to $\delta = 1$, with a Kyle "lambda" parameter equal to $Y\sigma_T/V_T$.

3.3 A VERY SURPRISING LAW

This square-root impact law is extremely well established empirically but extremely surprising theoretically. As mentioned in the introduction, one finds that the second half of a metaorder of size impacts the price much less than the first half, in fact, a square-root impact gives $\sqrt{2} - 1 = 0.4142...$ times less. How can this be? Surely if

---

[1] For slightly conflicting results, see however Zarinelli et al. (2015).

one traded the second half a very long time after the first half, impact should be additive again, as the memory of the first trade would evaporate. This clearly shows that there must be some kind of "memory time" T_m in financial markets, such that impact is square root for $T \ll T_m$ but additivity is recovered for $T \gg T_m$, when all memory of past trades is lost. We will hypothesize in Sections 5, 6 that this memory is in fact imprinted in the "latent" order book alluded to above, that stores the outstanding liquidity that cannot be executed immediately.

Note that the relevant ratio here is the volume of the metaorder Q to the market volume V_T over the execution time, and not, as could have been naively anticipated, the ratio of Q over total the market capitalization $\mathcal{M}$ of the asset. That one should trade 1% of the market capitalization $\mathcal{M}$ of a stock to move its price by 1% would look reasonable at first sight. It was in fact common lore in the 80's, when impact was deemed totally irrelevant for quantities representing a few basis points of $\mathcal{M}$. But $\mathcal{M}$ is (for stocks) 200 times larger than V_T itself, so that $Q/\mathcal{M} \ll Q/V_T$. Therefore a $Q/\mathcal{M}$ scaling would have meant a much smaller impact than the one observed in practice. The non-linear square-root behavior for $Q \ll V_T$ furthermore substantially amplifies the impact of small metaorders: executing 1% of the daily volume moves the price (on average) by $\sqrt{1\%} = 10\%$ of its daily volatility. The main conclusion here is that impact, even of relatively small metaorders, is a surprisingly large effect.

Let us highlight another remarkable property of the strict square-root impact, which that $\mathcal{I}(Q, T)$ is approximately *independent* of the execution time horizon T, and only determined by the total exchanged volume Q. This follows from the fact that $\sigma_T \propto \sqrt{T}$ whereas $V_T \propto T$, so that the T dependence cancels out in Eq. (10). In economics term, this makes sense: the market price has to adapt to a certain change of global supply/demand εQ, quite independently on how this volume is actually executed. A more detailed, "Walrasian" view of this highly non-trivial statement is provided in Section 6.

Let us note however that the square-root impact law (10) is only approximately valid in a certain domain of parameters, as with any empirical law. For example, as we have mentioned already, the execution time T should not be longer than a certain "memory time" T_m of the market. The second obvious limitation is that the ratio Q/V_T should be small, such that the metaorder remains a small fraction of the total volume V_T and that the impact itself is small compared to the volatility. In the case where Q/V_T becomes substantial, one must enter a different regime as the metaorder becomes a large perturbation to the normal course of the market.

Finally, let us discuss some recurrent misconceptions or confusions that exist in the literature concerning the impact of metaorders:

- First, we emphasize that the impact of a metaorder of volume Q is *not* equal to the aggregate impact of order imbalance $\Delta V = Q$, which is in fact linear for small ΔV, and not square-root like (Bouchaud et al., 2009; Patzelt and Bouchaud, 2018). One cannot measure the impact of metaorders without being able to identify the origin of the trades, and correctly ascribe them to a given investor executing an order.

- The square-root impact law applies to slow metaorders composed of several individual trades, but *not* to these individual trades themselves. Universality, if it holds, can only result from some "mesoscopic" properties of the supply and demand in financial markets, that are insensitive to the way markets are organized at the microscale. This would explain, for example, why the square-root law holds equally well in the pre-HFT era (say before 2005) and since the explosion of electronic, high frequency market making (after 2005).
- Conversely, at the single trade level, one expects that microstructure effects (tick size, continuous markets vs. batch auctions, etc.) play a strong role. In particular, the impact of a single market order of size q does not behave like a square-root, although it behaves as a concave function of q (Bouchaud et al., 2009). But this concavity has no immediate relation with the concavity of the impact of metaorders.

3.4 THEORETICAL IDEAS

The square-root law was not anticipated by financial economists: classical models, such as the Kyle model, all suggested or posited a linear behavior. It is an interesting case where empirical data compelled the finance community to accept that reality was fundamentally different from theory. Several stories have been proposed since the mid-nineties to account for the square-root impact law.

The first attempt, due to the Barra group (Torre and Ferrari, 1997) and Grinold and Kahn (1999), argues that the square-root behavior is a consequence of market-markers getting compensated for their *inventory risk*. Assume that the metaorder of volume Q is absorbed by market-makers who will need to slowly offload their position later on. The amplitude of an adverse move of the price during this unwinding phase is given by $\sim \sigma \sqrt{T_{\text{off.}}}$, where $T_{\text{off.}}$ is the time needed to offload an inventory of size Q. It is reasonable to assume that $T_{\text{off.}}$ is proportional to Q and inversely proportional to the trading rate of the market V. If market-makers respond to the metaorder by moving the price in such a way that their profit is of the same order as the risk they take, then indeed $\mathcal{I} \propto \sigma \sqrt{Q/V}$, as found empirically. However, this story assumes no competition between market-makers. Indeed, inventory risk is diversifiable over time and on the long run averages to zero. Charging an impact cost compensating for the inventory risk of each metaorder would lead to formidable profits and necessarily attract competing liquidity providers.

Another story, proposed by Gabaix et al. (2003, 2006), ascribes the square-root impact law to the fact that the optimal execution horizon T^* for "informed" metaorders of size Q grows like $T^* \sim \sqrt{Q}$. Since during that time the price is expected to move linearly in the direction of the trade as information gets slowly revealed, the apparent peak impact behaves as $\sqrt{Q}$. However, this scenario would imply that the impact *during the metaorder* is linear in the executed quantity q, at variance with empirical data: the impact path itself behaves as a square-root of q, at least when the execution schedule is flat.

Recently, Farmer et al. (2013) have proposed yet another theory which is very reminiscent of the Glosten–Milgrom model (Glosten and Milgrom, 1985) that competitively sets the size of the bid–ask spread. One assumes metaorders with a power-law distributed volume Q come one after the other. Market-makers attempt to guess whether the metaorder will continue or stop at the next time step, and set the price such that (a) it is a martingale and (b) the average execution price compensates for the information contained in the metaorder ("fair pricing"). Provided the distribution of metaorder sizes behaves as $Q^{-5/2}$, these two conditions lead to a square-root impact law. Although enticing, this theory has difficulty explaining why the square-root law holds even when the average impact is smaller than, or of the same order as the bid–ask spread and/or the trading fees – which should in principle strongly affect the market-makers' fair pricing condition. Furthermore, the square-root impact law appears to be much more universal than the distribution of the size of metaorders. In the case of Bitcoin, for example, the square-root law holds very precisely while the distribution of metaorders behaves as Q^{-2} rather than $Q^{-5/2}$ (Donier and Bonart, 2015).

The universality of the square-root law suggests that its explanation should rely on minimal, robust ingredients that would account for its validity is different markets (from stocks to Bitcoin) and different epochs (from pit markets to electronic platforms). We will present in Sections 5 and 6 a minimal agent-based model of the dynamics of supply and demand. This framework, originally put forth by Tóth et al. (2011) and much developed since, provides a natural interpretation of the square-root law and its apparent universality.

4 THE SANTA-FE "ZERO-INTELLIGENCE" MODEL

In this section, we introduce a (over-)simplified framework for describing the co-evolution of liquidity and prices, at the level of the Limit Order Book.[2] This model was initially proposed and developed by a group of scientists then working at the Santa Fe Institute, see Daniels et al. (2003), Smith et al. (2003), Farmer et al. (2005).[3] After describing the Santa-Fe model and the price dynamics it generates, we will discuss some of its limitations. (Note that what we call here the Santa-Fe model is *not* the stock market agent-based model (Palmer et al., 1994) but rather the more recent particle-based limit order book model.)

4.1 MODEL DEFINITION

Consider the continuous-time temporal evolution of a set of particles on a one-dimensional lattice of mesh size equal to one tick ϑ. Each location on the lattice corresponds to a specified price level in the LOB. Each particle is either of type A,

---

[2]For an introduction to Limit Order Books, their empirical properties and models, see Gould et al. (2013).
[3]Similar zero-intelligence Poisson model have also been introduced to describe the queue dynamics of the best quotes in large tick assets, see e.g. Cont and De Larrard (2013).

which corresponds to a sell order, or of type B, which corresponds to a buy order. Each particle corresponds to an order of a fixed size v_0 which we can arbitrarily set to unity. Whenever two particles of opposite type occupy the same point on the pricing grid, an annihilation $A + B \to \emptyset$ occurs, to represent the matching of a buy order and a sell order. Particles can also "evaporate", to represent the cancellation of an order by its owner. The position of the leftmost A particle defines the ask price $a(t)$, and he position of the rightmost B particle defines the bid price $b(t)$. The mid-price is $m(t) = (b(t) + a(t))/2$, and the bid–ask spread $s(t)$ is $a(t) - b(t)$.

In the Santa-Fe "Zero-Intelligence" model, order flows are completely random and assumed to be governed by the following stochastic processes,[4] where all orders have size $v_0 = 1$:

- At each price level $p \le m(t)$ (resp. $p \ge m(t)$), buy (resp. sell) limit orders arrive as a Poisson process with rate λ, independently of p.
- Buy/Sell market orders arrive as Poisson processes, each with rate μ.
- Each outstanding buy (resp. sell) limit order is canceled according to a Poisson process with rate v.
- All event types are mutually independent.

The first two rules mean that the mid-price $m(t)$ is the reference price around which the order flow organizes. Whenever a buy (respectively, sell) market order x arrives at time t_x, it annihilates a sell limit order at the price $a(t_x)$ (respectively, buy limit order at the price $b(t_x)$), and thereby causes a transaction. Therefore, the interacting flows of market order arrivals, limit order arrivals, and limit order cancellations together fully specify the temporal evolution of the LOB, and in particular the mid-price $m(t)$.

4.2 BASIC INTUITION

Before investigating the model in detail, we first appeal to intuition to discuss some of its more straightforward properties. First, each of the parameters λ, μ, and v are rate parameters, with units of inverse time. Therefore, any observable related to the equilibrium distribution of volumes, spreads, or gaps between filled prices can only depend on ratios of λ, μ, and v, to cause the units to cancel out.

Second, the approximate distributions of queue sizes can be derived by considering the interactions of the different types of order flows at different prices. Because market order arrivals only influence activity at the best quotes, it follows that very deep into the LOB, the distribution of queue sizes V reaches a stationary state that is

---

[4]We will only consider the symmetric case where buy and sell orders have the same rates. The model can be extended by allowing different rate parameters on the buy and sell sides of the LOB. Note also that our specification slightly differs from the original model, in that we prevent limit orders to fall beyond the mid-point. This is a minor modification, that is more realistic. On this point see Mike and Farmer (2008).

independent of the distance from $m(t)$, given by

$$P_{\text{st.}}(V) = e^{-V^*} \frac{V^{*V}}{V!}, \qquad V^* = \frac{\lambda}{\nu}. \tag{11}$$

Two extreme cases are possible:

- A sparse LOB, corresponding to $V^* \ll \upsilon_0 = 1$, where most price levels are empty while some are only weakly populated. This case corresponds to very small-tick assets.
- A dense LOB, corresponding to $V^* \gg \upsilon_0 = 1$, where all price levels are populated with a large number of orders. This corresponds to large-tick assets, at least close enough to the mid-point so that the assumption that λ is constant is reasonable.

In reality, one observes that λ decreases with increasing distance from $m(t)$. Therefore, even in the case of large-tick stocks, we expect a cross-over between a densely populated LOB close to the best quotes and a sparse LOB far away from them. This does not, however, imply that there are no buyers or sellers who wish to trade at prices far away from the current mid-point. As we will argue in Sections 5, 6, the potential number of buyers (respectively, sellers) is expected to grow with increasing distance from $m(t)$, but most of the corresponding liquidity is latent, and only becomes revealed as $m(t)$ decreases (respectively, increases).

The above distribution of queue sizes is not accurate for prices close to $m(t)$. If d denotes the distance between a given price and $m(t)$, then for smaller values of d, it becomes increasingly likely that a given price was actually the best price in the recent past. Correspondingly, limit orders are depleted not only because of cancellations but also because of market orders that may have hit that queue. Heuristically, one expects that the average size of the queues is given by

$$V^* \approx \frac{\lambda - \mu \phi_{\text{eff}}(d)}{\nu},$$

where $\phi_{\text{eff}}(d)$ is the fraction of time during which the corresponding price level was the best quote in the recent past (of duration ν^{-1}, beyond which all memory is lost). This formula says that queues tend to be smaller on average close to the mid-point, simply because the market order flow plays a greater role in removing outstanding limit orders. One therefore expects that the average depth profile is an increasing function of d, at least close to $d = 0$ where λ can be considered as a constant. This is indeed what is observed in empirical data of LOB volume profiles, see Bouchaud et al. (2002, 2009), where a simple theory describing the shape of an LOB's volume profile is also given.

Next, we consider the size of the spread $s(t)$. For large-tick stocks, the bid and ask queues will both typically be long and $s(t)$ will spend most of the time equal to its smallest possible value of one tick, $s(t) = \vartheta$. For small-tick stocks, however, the spread may become larger. In this case, the probability per unit time that a new limit order arrives inside the spread is given by $(\widehat{s} - 1)\lambda$ (because both buy and sell limit orders can fall on the $\widehat{s} - 1$ available intervals inside the spread $s = \widehat{s}\vartheta$), and the probability per unit time that an order at the best quotes is removed by cancellation or by an incoming market order is given by $2(\mu + \nu)$. The equilibrium spread size is such that these two effects compensate,

$$s_{\text{eq.}} \approx \vartheta \left[1 + 2 \frac{\mu + \nu}{\lambda} \right].$$

Although hand-waving, this argument gives a good first approximation of the average spread. In particular, the result that a large flux of market orders μ opens up the spread sounds reasonable.

4.3 SIMULATION RESULTS

Deriving analytical results about the behavior of the Santa Fe model is deceptively difficult (Smith et al., 2003). By contrast, simulating the model is relatively straightforward. The Santa Fe model is extremely rich, so many output observables can be studied in this way. We restrict here to three particularly relevant topics:

1. The ratio between the mean first gap behind the best quote (i.e., the price difference between the best and second-best quotes) and the mean spread s;
2. The volatility and signature plot of the mid-price;
3. The mean impact of a market order and the mean profit of market-making.

Numerical results show that the model does a good job of capturing some of these properties, but a less good job at capturing others, due to the many simplifying assumptions that it makes. For example, when λ, μ, ν are calibrated on real data, the model makes good predictions of the mean bid–ask spread, as first emphasized by Farmer et al. (2005). However, the price series that it generates show significant mean-reverting behavior, except when the memory time $T_m = \nu^{-1}$ is very short (Daniels et al., 2003; Smith et al., 2003). As noticed in Section 2.4, such mean-reversion is usually not observed in real markets. Moreover, the model predicts volatility to be too small for large-tick stocks and too large for small-tick stocks, and furthermore creates strong arbitrage opportunities for market-making strategies that do not exist in real markets. These weaknesses of the model provide insight into how it might be improved, by including additional effects such as the long-range correlations of order flow or some simple strategic behaviors from market participants (see Section 5).

4.3.1 The Gap-to-Spread Ratio

Let us consider the mean gap between the second-best quote and the best quote, compared to the mean spread itself. We call this ratio the *gap-to-spread ratio*. The gap-to-spread ratio is interesting since it is to a large extent insensitive to the problem of calibrating the parameters correctly (and of reproducing the mean bid–ask spread exactly).

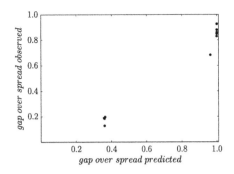

FIGURE 2

Empirical ratio of the gap between the best and second best quote to the spread versus its prediction from the Santa Fe model.

Fig. 2 shows the empirical gap-to-spread ratio versus the gap-to-spread ratio generated by simulating the Santa Fe model, for a selection of 13 US stocks with different tick sizes (Bouchaud et al., 2018). For large-tick stocks, the model predicts that both the spread and the gap between the second-best and best quotes are nearly always locked to 1 tick, so the ratio is itself simply equal to 1. In reality, however, the dynamics is more subtle. The bid–ask spread actually widens more frequently than the Santa Fe model predicts, such that the empirical gap-to-spread ratio is in fact in the range 0.8–0.95. This discrepancy becomes even more pronounced for small-tick stocks, for which the empirical gap-to-spread ratio typically takes values around 0.15–0.2, but for which the Santa Fe model predicts a gap-to-spread ratio as high as 0.4. In other words, when the spread is large, the second best price tends to be much closer to the best quote in reality than it is in the model. As we will see in below this turns out to have an important consequence for the impact of market orders in the model.

This analysis of the gap-to-spread ratio reveals that an important ingredient is missing from the Santa Fe model. When the spread is large, real liquidity providers tend to place new limit orders inside the spread, but still close to the best quotes, and thereby typically only improve the quote price by one tick at a time. This leads to gaps between the best and second-best quotes that are much smaller than those predicted by the assumption of uniform arrivals of limit orders at all prices beyond the mid-price. One could indeed modify the Santa Fe specification to account for this empirically observed phenomenon of smaller gaps for limit orders that arrive inside the spread, but doing so comes at the expense of adding extra parameters, see Mike and Farmer (2008).

4.3.2 The Signature Plot

When simulating the Santa Fe model, the lag-dependent volatility $\sigma(\tau)$ of the mid-price, and the corresponding signature plot (see Section 2.4), both reveal that the model exhibits some excess volatility at small values of τ, particularly when the cancellation rate ν is small. Put another way, the slow temporal evolution of the LOB

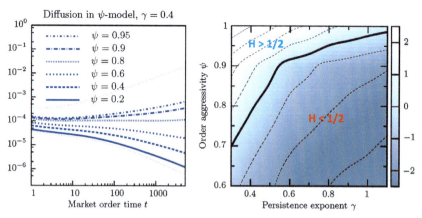

FIGURE 3

Left: Signature plots for the extended Santa-Fe model with power law selective liquidity taking, for various values of the ψ exponent. The parameters set is $\mu = 0.1$, $\lambda\vartheta = 5 \times 10^{-3}$, $\nu = 10^{-7}$, and $\gamma = 0.4$. The lower light gray line corresponds to the limiting cases $\psi = 0$ (corresponding to the Santa-Fe model), while the upper gray line corresponds to $\psi = 1$. Note that the long time behavior is sub-diffusive when $\psi < \psi_c$, super-diffusive for $\psi > \psi_c$, and exactly diffusive for $\psi = \psi_c \approx 0.8$. Right: "Phase diagram" of the model in terms of the value of the Hurst exponent H, in the plane ψ, γ, with a "critical line" $\psi_c(\gamma)$ where the dynamics is exactly diffusive ($H = 1/2$).

leads to a substantial mean-reversion in the mid price. This was already noted in the papers published by the Santa-Fe group (Daniels et al., 2003; Smith et al., 2003), and can be observed in the left graph of Fig. 3 in the case $\psi = 0$ that corresponds to the Santa-Fe limit. Intuitively, this strong mean-reverting behavior is explained by the following argument: imagine that the price has been drifting upwards for a while. The buy side of the book, below the current price, has had little time to refill yet, whereas the sell side of the book is full and creates a barrier resisting further increases. Subsequent sell market orders will therefore have a larger impact than buy orders, pushing the price back down.

Empirically, one observes some mean reversion for large-tick stocks, but very little – or even weak trending effects – for small-tick stocks (see e.g. Eisler et al., 2012; Taranto et al., 2016). Strong short term mean-reversion, and the consequent failure to reproduce realistic signature plots, is one of the main drawbacks of the Santa-Fe model. The problem manifests in many different ways. For example, the model predicts long-term volatility to be much too small for large-tick stocks and somewhat too large for small-tick stocks, and incorrectly predicts a negative correlation between the ratio of long-term volatility and short-term volatility and tick size.

For the parameter value estimates for large-tick stocks, the model in fact predicts that the queues almost never empty, and the mid-price almost never moves. In real markets, these extremely long emptying times are tempered, in part through the dynamical coupling between the bid queue and the ask queue, and in part because of the existence of large market orders that consume a substantial fraction the queue at once. Both of these important empirical effects are absent from the Santa Fe model.

For small-tick stocks, the model predicts values of volatility higher than those observed empirically. The main reason for this weakness is because of the absence of a mechanism that accurately describes how order flows adapt when prices change. In the model, once the best quote has disappeared, the order flow immediately adapts around the new mid-price, irrespective of whether the price change was caused by a cancellation, a market order arrival, or a limit order arrival inside the spread. In other words, the permanent impact of all of these events are identical, whereas in reality the permanent impact of a market order arrival is much larger than that of cancellations, as shown in Eisler et al. (2012).

4.3.3 Impact of Market Orders and Market-Making

Let us now analyze in more detail the lag-dependent impact of market orders in the Santa-Fe model. We define this impact as

$$\mathcal{R}(\tau) := \langle \varepsilon_t \cdot (m_{t+\tau} - m_t) \rangle_t, \tag{12}$$

where ε_t denotes the sign of the market order at event-time t, where t increases by one unit for each market order arrival, and the brackets mean an empirical average over t. In real markets the impact function $\mathcal{R}(\tau)$ is positive and grows with τ before saturating for large τs, see e.g. Bouchaud et al. (2004, 2006) and Wyart et al. (2008). In the Santa Fe model, however, $\mathcal{R}(\tau)$ is strictly constant, independent of τ, and is well approximated by

$$\mathcal{R}(\tau) \approx \mathbb{P}(V_{\text{best}} = 1) \times \frac{1}{2} \langle \text{first gap} \rangle, \tag{13}$$

where $\mathbb{P}(V_{\text{best}} = 1)$ is the probability that the best queue is of length 1. This approximation holds because a market order of size unity impacts the price if and only if it completely consumes the volume at the opposite-side best quote, and if it does so, it moves that quote by the size of the first gap, and thus moves the mid-price by half this amount. Since order flow in the Santa Fe model is uncorrelated and is always centered around the current mid-price, the impact of a market order is instantaneous and permanent. Therefore, the model predicts that $\mathcal{R}(\tau)$ is constant in τ. In real markets, by contrast, the signs of market orders show strong positive autocorrelation, which causes $\mathcal{R}(\tau)$ to increase with τ (Bouchaud et al., 2004, 2006; Wyart et al., 2008).

This simple observation has an important immediate consequence: The Santa Fe model specification leads to profitable market-making strategies. It is plain to see that market-making is profitable if the mean bid–ask spread is larger than twice the long-term impact $\mathcal{R}_\infty$ (Wyart et al., 2008). In the Santa Fe model, the mean first gap is found to be smaller than the bid–ask spread (see Fig. 2). Therefore, from Eq. (13), one necessarily has $\mathcal{R}_\infty < \langle s \rangle / 2$, so market-making is "easy" within this framework. If we want to avoid the existence of such opportunities, which are absent in real markets, we need to find a way to extend the Santa Fe model. One possible route for doing so is incorporating some strategic behavior into the model, such as introducing agents that specifically seek out and capitalize on any simple market-making opportunities that arise. Another route is to modify the model's assumptions regarding order flow to better reflect the empirical properties observed in real markets. For example, introducing the empirically observed autocorrelation in market order signs would increase the long-term impact $\mathcal{R}_\infty$ and thereby reduce the profitability of market-making. This is the direction taken in the next section.

5 AN IMPROVED MODEL FOR THE DYNAMICS OF LIQUIDITY

5.1 INTRODUCTION

The Santa-Fe model was originally proposed as a model of the *visible* LOB. However, most of the liquidity in financial markets remains *latent*, and only gets revealed when execution is highly probable. This latent order book is where the "true" liquidity of the market lies, at variance with the real order book where only a very small fraction of this liquidity is revealed, and that evolves on very fast time scales (i.e. large values of ν). In particular, market making/high frequency trading contributes heavily to the latter but only very thinly to the former, which corresponds to much smaller values of ν.[5] The vast majority of the daily traded volume in fact progressively reveals itself as trading proceeds: liquidity is a dynamical process – see Bouchaud et al. (2004, 2006, 2009), Weber and Rosenow (2005), and for an early study carrying a similar message, Sandas (2001). When one wants understand the impact of long metaorders – and in particular the square-root law, see Section 3.2 – it is clearly more important to model this latent liquidity, not seen in the LOB, than the LOB itself. We therefore need a modeling strategy that is able to describe the dynamics of the latent liquidity, and how it is perturbed by a metaorder. This is what we will pursue in the following sections.

In order to describe prices movements on medium to long time scales, one should therefore understand the dynamics of the "latent liquidity" (LL). The simplest model for the LL is again the Santa-Fe model, now interpreted in terms of latent intentions – rather than visible limit orders. We imagine that the volume in the latent order book materializes in the real order book with a probability that increases sharply when the distance between the traded price and the limit price decreases.

As we have seen in the previous section, one of the main drawback of the Santa-Fe model is the strong mean-reversion effects on time scales small compared to the renewal time of the LL $T_m = \nu^{-1}$, assumed to be large (hours or days – see below). Some additional features must be introduced to allow the price to be diffusive, with a "flat" signature plot (Tóth et al., 2011; Mastromatteo et al., 2014a). In the present

---

[5]It is actually worth noticing that the "square-root" impact law has not been much affected by the development of high-frequency trading; this is yet another strong argument in favor of the latent liquidity models.

extension of the Santa-Fe model, we still assume the deposition rate λ of limit orders and the cancellation rate ν to be constants, independent of the price level. The sign of market orders, on the other hand, is determined by a non-trivial process, such as to generate long-range correlations, in agreement with empirical findings (Bouchaud et al., 2009). More precisely, the sign ε_t of market order at (event) time t has zero mean, $\langle \varepsilon_t \rangle = 0$, but is characterized by a power-law decaying autocorrelation function $C(\ell) \propto \ell^{-\gamma}$ with $\gamma < 1$, see Section 2.8. A way to do this in practice is to use the Lillo–Mike–Farmer model (Lillo et al., 2005), or the so-called DAR(p) model (see e.g. Taranto et al., 2016).

Another ingredient of the model is the statistics of the volume consumed by each single market order. In the Santa-Fe model, each market order is of unit volume υ_0. However, this is unrealistic, since more volume at the best is a clear incentive to send larger market orders, in order to accelerate trading without immediately impacting the price. It is more reasonable to assume *selective liquidity taking*, i.e. that the size of market order V_{MO} is an increasing function of the prevailing volume at the best V_{best}. A simple specification is the following (Mastromatteo et al., 2014a):

$$V_{MO} = \upsilon_0^{1-\psi} V_{best}^{\psi} \tag{14}$$

with $\psi \in [0, 1]$, so that $\upsilon_0 \leq V_{MO} \leq V_{best}$. Clearly, larger values of ψ correspond to more aggressive orders, so that $\psi = 1$ corresponds to eating the all the available liquidity at the best price and $\psi = 0$ corresponds to unit size execution. In fact, the model with $\psi = 0$ and $\gamma \to \infty$ (no correlation of the order flow) precisely recovers the Santa-Fe specification of the previous section.

As already emphasized, the cancellation rate defines a time scale $T_m = \nu^{-1}$ which is of crucial importance for the model, since this is the memory time of the market. For times much larger than T_m, all limit orders have been canceled and replaced elsewhere, so that no memory of the initial (latent) order book can remain. Now, as we emphasized in Section 3.3, a concave (non-additive) impact law can only appear if some kind of memory is present. Therefore, we will study the dynamics of the system in a regime where times are small compared to T_m. From a mathematical point of view, rigorous statements about the diffusive nature of the price, and the non-additive nature of the impact, can only be achieved in the limit where $\nu/\mu \to 0$, i.e. in markets where the latent liquidity profile changes on a time scale very much longer than the inverse trading frequency. Although T_m is very hard to estimate directly using market data,[6] it is reasonable to think that trading decisions only change when the transaction price changes by a few percent, which leads to $T_m \sim$ a few days in stocks and futures markets. Hence, we expect the ratio ν/μ to be indeed very small, on the order of 10^{-5}, in these markets. (In other words, 10,000 to 100,000 trades take place before the memory of the latent liquidity is lost.)

---

[6]Remember again that ν is *not* the cancel rate in the real (visible) order book, which is extremely high, 10 s^{-1} or so, but the cancel rate of trading *intentions* in the latent order book, which are much slower.

5.2 SUPER-DIFFUSION VS. SUB-DIFFUSION

We first investigate the statistics of price changes in this extended Santa-Fe model, where market order signs are autocorrelated and where market orders adapt to the size of the opposite quote. We again focus on the price variogram $\mathcal{V}(\tau)$, defined by Eq. (1). Note that the averaging time window must be very large compared to T_m in order to be in the stationary state of the model.

As recalled above, $\sigma^2(\tau) = \mathcal{V}(\tau)/\tau$ is strictly independent of τ for a purely diffusive process (e.g. the Brownian motion). A "sub-diffusive" process is such that $\sigma^2(\tau)$ is a decreasing function of τ, signaling mean-reversion, whereas a "super-diffusive" process is such that $\sigma^2(\tau)$ is an increasing function of τ, signaling trends. A simple example is provided by the fractional Brownian motion, which is such that $\mathcal{V}(\tau) \propto \tau^{2H}$, where H is the so-called Hurst exponent of the process. The usual Brownian case corresponds to $H = 1/2$; $H > 1/2$ (resp. $H < 1/2$) is tantamount to super- (resp. sub-) diffusion. From a financial point of view, both super-diffusion and sub-diffusion lead to arbitrage opportunities, i.e. strategies that try to profit from the trends or mean-reversion patterns that exist when $H \neq 1/2$. The trading rules that emerge must be such that simple strategies are not profitable, i.e. prices are close to random walks with $H \approx 1/2$, a property often called "statistical efficiency".[7]

The above dynamical liquidity model contains an ingredient that favors super-diffusion (the long range correlated nature of the order flow), and an ingredient that favors sub-diffusion (the long memory time of the latent order book itself). Which of the two effects is dominant, and can one find a regime where they cancel out, so that prices are *exactly* diffusive?

When the memory time of the order book T_m is very short, the autocorrelation of the price changes is dominated by the autocorrelation of the order flow. It is easy to show that for a power-law autocorrelation with exponent γ, as defined above, the Hurst exponent of the price change is given by

$$H = \frac{1}{2}, \quad \text{when} \quad \gamma > 1; \qquad H = 1 - \frac{\gamma}{2} > \frac{1}{2}, \quad \text{when} \quad \gamma < 1. \quad (15)$$

For an *uncorrelated order flow* (i.e. $\gamma \to \infty$) in a quickly evolving environment the price process is obviously diffusive.

However, the same totally uncorrelated order flow $\gamma \to \infty$ but now with a very slowly evolving order book, turns out to be far from trivial, and leads to a strongly sub-diffusive short time dynamics. When $\psi = 1$, then $H = 1/2$ trivially since each market order removes the best quote completely, killing the mean-reversion effect. When $\psi = 0$, one recovers exactly the Santa-Fe model, and in the limit $\tau \ll T_m$,

---

[7]Whether or not this random walk behavior is indicating the markets are "efficient" in the sense that prices reflect fundamental values is another matter. We believe that while the former property is indeed obeyed, the mechanisms that lead to statistical efficiency have little to do with the activity of fundamental arbitrageurs. See Section 7 for an extended discussion of this point.

simulations show that the price motion is actually *confined*, i.e.

$$\sigma^2(\tau) \approx \sigma_\infty^2 - \frac{c}{\sqrt{\tau}}, \qquad 1 \ll \tau \ll T_m, \tag{16}$$

where c is a constant depending upon the values of μ and λ. This result can be intuitively understood after realizing that σ_∞ is proportional to the stationary value of the spread: in this regime the price bounces back and forth indefinitely in the region of the bid–ask spread, whereas the volumes of price levels outside that zone grow linearly in time, leading to a trapping effect.

When $0 < \psi < 1$ and $\gamma < 1$, a very interesting scenario appears. First note that since γ is empirically found to be smaller than unity, real markets must clearly in the regime $T_m \gg \mu^{-1}$ (where μ is the frequency of market orders) otherwise a super-diffusive behavior with $H = 1 - \gamma/2$ would necessarily ensue, for the reason explained above. Fig. 3 shows that the Hurst exponent H is a *continuously varying function* of γ and ψ, monotonically increasing from $H(\gamma, \psi = 0) = 0$ (confinement) to $H(\gamma < 1, \psi = 1) = 1 - \gamma/2$ (super-diffusion). For all $\gamma < 1$, there is therefore a critical value $\psi_c(\gamma)$ such that statistical efficiency is strictly recovered for $\mu^{-1} \ll \tau \ll T_m$ (Mastromatteo et al., 2014a). For $\tau \gg T_m$ and $\gamma < 1$ we expect, as explained above, super-diffusion to take over in all cases, so our artificial market tuned to be efficient on intermediate time scales would still show long term trends. The model is however, obviously, an approximate description of reality, which neglects many effects that play an important role on longer time scales. One is that the long memory in sign trades is probably cut-off beyond some time scale, although this is very difficult to establish empirically.

As Fig. 3 indicates, it is possible to find a line of parameters such that the price variogram is perfectly flat. This removes obvious arbitrage opportunities but does not yet make the artificial market completely consistent, since market making opportunities may still be present. As alluded to in the previous section, the average half bid–ask spread $\langle s \rangle / 2$ must be larger than the asymptotic response function $\mathcal{R}_\infty$ for such opportunities to exist. Although a detailed study of this point was not made in Mastromatteo et al. (2014a), we believe that the modeling framework is flexible enough to allow a choice of parameters such that $\mathcal{R}_\infty = \langle s \rangle / 2$.

5.3 THE CONCAVE IMPACT OF META-ORDERS

We now investigate the impact of metaorders in the efficient agent-based market that sits on the critical line $\psi_c(\gamma)$ where trending effects are counter-balanced by liquidity. We first define more precisely how meta-orders are introduced in the model, on top of the previously defined "background" order flow. An extra agent (the trader) is introduced, who buys (without loss of generality) Q shares within the time interval $[0, T]$, by executing *market orders* at a fixed time rate $\mu\phi$ (limit order execution can also be considered, with very similar results; Mastromatteo et al., 2014a). After time T, the meta-order ends, and the market order flow immediately reverts to its unperturbed state. The trading "style" is parameterized by an exponent ψ' possibly

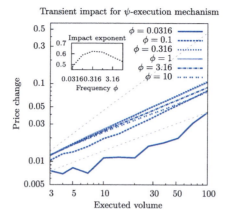

FIGURE 4

Metaorder impact $\mathcal{I}(Q, T)$ as a function of Q, for different frequencies ϕ, in a log–log representation. We consider here the case $\psi' = \psi = 0.75$ and $\gamma = 0.4$ for which the model is approximately diffusive. The other parameters are as in Fig. 3. The inset shows the fitted impact exponent δ as a function of the frequency ϕ.

different from the ψ of the background market. A larger ψ' corresponds to a more aggressive trader.

Because of the bias in the order flow, the average price change $\langle p_T - p_0 \rangle$ between the start and the end of the meta-order is no longer zero. The questions we want to ask are:

1. Is the dependence of the *peak impact* $\mathcal{I}(Q, T) = \langle p_T - p_0 \rangle$ on Q concave and how does it depend on the frequency ϕ?
2. Does the impact depend on the trading style?
3. What happens to the price at large times after the meta-order is over (i.e., what is the *permanent* part of the impact $\langle p_\infty - p_0 \rangle$)?

In all possible specifications, the impact $\mathcal{I}(Q, T)$ was numerically found to be a concave function of the volume Q, provided $T \ll T_m$:

$$\mathcal{I}(Q, T) \propto Q^\delta, \qquad \delta \approx 0.5\text{–}0.6, \tag{17}$$

as first reported in Tóth et al. (2011), and well compatible with the square-root impact law (see Section 3). For example, we plot in Fig. 4 the results obtained for the case $\gamma = 0.5$ and for $\psi' = \psi = 0.75$. The dependence of the impact exponent δ on ϕ is shown in the inset of Fig. 4.

The relaxation of impact after the end of a meta-order is a particularly important topic, which has attracted considerable attention recently. Farmer et al. (2013) argue that a 'fair price' mechanism should by at play, such that the impact of a meta-order reverts at long times to a value precisely equal to the average price at which the meta-order was executed. This seems to be confirmed by the empirical data analyzed in Bershova and Rakhlin (2013), Gomes and Waelbroeck (2014); however, such an analysis is quite tricky, as it involves some degree of arbitrariness in the choice of the timescale for the relaxation of price after the end of the meta-order and in the treatment of the correlations between successive metaorders, see Brokmann et al. (2015). Even within the above synthetic market framework, the long time behavior of the impact is quite noisy. Numerical results suggests that the impact decays to a finite value, which seems to be higher than the 'fair price' benchmark, although we cannot exclude a slow decay to a smaller value, with some dependence on the parameters of the model. More specifically, one finds that permanent and transient component of the impact obey two different scalings: while the transient component of the impact is described by a concave law, its permanent component is linear, and hence dominates the total impact for long enough trades. (On this point, see Almgren et al., 2005; Donier et al., 2015; and Benzaquen and Bouchaud, 2017.)

Alternative specifications of the model have also been studied in Mastromatteo et al. (2014a), for example a situation where price efficiency is maintained through a "stimulated liquidity refill" mechanism, whereby market orders attract a liquidity counter-flow – instead of adapting to the prevailing volume at best, as above. One can again fine-tune the parameters of the model such that prices are exactly diffusive. The execution of meta-orders again leads to a strongly concave shape of the impact as a function of the size of the meta-order, with an exponent $\delta \approx 0.4$–0.5 that only depends weakly on the participation rate – see Mastromatteo et al. (2014a).

6 WALRASIAN AUCTIONS AND THE SQUARE-ROOT LAW

The agent-based models introduced in the previous sections is easily studied using numerical simulations. However, a better insight on the mechanism leading to the square-root impact law is desirable. Here, we introduce (closely following Donier and Bouchaud, 2016) a mathematical model for the dynamics of the latent order book that lends itself to reasonably straightforward analytical calculations. The idea is to (temporarily) revert to the old scheme of Walrasian auctions to clear markets, and describe how the marginal supply and demand curve generically evolves between two such auctions. For a finite inter-auction time τ, one finds that impact is linear, as in the Kyle model, at least for small enough volumes Q. When $\tau \to 0$, as for modern continuous electronic market, the supply and demand vanish around the traded price, leading to an anomalous response of the market – the square-root law.

6.1 A DYNAMIC THEORY FOR SUPPLY AND DEMAND

6.1.1 Definitions

At any given time, some agents consider buying some quantity of an asset, while others consider selling. Each agent has a certain reservation price p, i.e. the maximum (minimum) price at which they are willing to buy (sell), and a corresponding volume.

The classical supply and demand curves $\mathcal{S}(p, t)$ and $\mathcal{D}(p, t)$ represent respectively the aggregate quantity agents are willing to sell (buy) above (below) price p.

In classical Walrasian framework, the transaction (or clearing) price p_{trade} is then set to the value that matches both quantities so that

$$\mathcal{D}(p_{\text{trade}}, t) = \mathcal{S}(p_{\text{trade}}, t). \tag{18}$$

This price is unique provided the curves are strictly monotonous, which is a very reasonable assumption.

As discussed in the previous section, however, only a minute quantity of the total supply and demand is revealed in the LOB. Most of it remain unexpressed intentions, which is what we define henceforth as the "latent" liquidity. In order to define its dynamics, we also introduce the *marginal supply and demand curves* (MSD), on which we will focus in the rest of this chapter. They are defined as

$$\rho^-(p, t) = \partial_p \mathcal{S}(p, t) \geq 0;$$
$$\rho^+(p, t) = -\partial_p \mathcal{D}(p, t) \geq 0,$$

In the Walrasian theory, supply and demand pre-exist and the Walrasian auctioneer gropes (*tâtonne*) to find the price p_{trade} that maximizes the amount of possible transactions. The auction then takes place at time t and removes instantly all matched orders. Assuming that all the supply and demand intentions close to the transaction price were revealed before the auction and were matched, the state of the MSD just after the auction is simple to describe, see Fig. 5:

$$\begin{cases} \rho^-(p, t^+) = \rho^-(p, t^-) & (p > p_{\text{trade}}) \\ \qquad\quad = 0 & (p \leq p_{\text{trade}}) \\ \rho^+(p, t^+) = \rho^+(p, t^-) & (p < p_{\text{trade}}) \\ \qquad\quad = 0 & (p \geq p_{\text{trade}}). \end{cases} \tag{19}$$

Now what happens next, once the auction has been settled? The aim of this section is to set up a plausible framework for the dynamics of the supply and demand curves. This will allow us to describe, among other questions, how the supply and demand curves evolve from the truncated shape given by Eq. (19) up to the next auction at time $t + \tau$.

6.1.2 General Hypotheses About the Behavior of Agents

The theoretical framework presented here relies on general assumptions on the behavior of market agents, that generalize in one crucial way the Santa-Fe model and its extension presented above: agents can update continuously their valuation and correspondingly change their position in the latent limit order book. The resulting equations lead, in certain limits, to a universal evolution of the MSD curves with only two relevant parameters: the price volatility, and the market activity (traded volume per unit time).

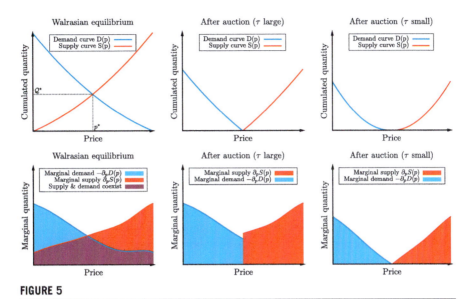

FIGURE 5

Top: Supply and demand curves in (left) Walrasian auctions, (center) immediately after infrequent auctions, and (right) immediately after frequent auctions. Bottom: Corresponding MSD curves. When transactions occur, supply and demand cannot cross (center and right). When the market is cleared frequently, supply and demand are depleted close to the price and exhibit a characteristic V-shape (right).

We will assume that market participants only have a partial knowledge of the "fundamental" price process, which they try to estimate each in their own way, i.e. with some idiosyncratic error around a certain reference price $p^F(t)$. In the absence of transactions, the MSD curves evolve according to three distinct mechanisms, that we model as follows:

1. **New intentions:** Intentions to buy/sell, not present in the MSD before time t, can appear. The probability for new buy/sell intentions to appear between t and $t + dt$ and between prices p and $p + dp$ is given by $\lambda_\pm(p - p^F(t))dpdt$, where $\lambda_+(x)$ is a decreasing function of x and $\lambda_-(x)$ is an increasing function of x. This is similar to the deposition rate in the Santa Fe model, except that the λ's are centered around the reference price $p^F(t)$ and not the current mid-price.
2. **Cancellations:** Already existing intentions to buy/sell at price p can simply be canceled and disappear from the supply and demand curves. The probability for an existing buy/sell intention around price p to disappear between t and $t + dt$ is chosen to be $\nu_\pm(p - p^F(t))dt$.
3. **Price revisions:** Already existing intentions to buy/sell at price p can be revised, because of e.g. new information, or because of idiosyncratic factors. We assume that between t and $t + dt$, each agent i revises his/her reservation price p_t^i as

$$p_t^i \longrightarrow p_t^i + \beta_t^i d\xi_t + dW_t^i, \tag{20}$$

where $d\xi_t$ is common to all i, representing some public information, while β_t^i is the sensitivity of agent i to the news, which we imagine to be a random variable with a mean normalized such that $\mathbb{E}_i[\beta_t^i] = 1$. Some agents may over-react ($\beta_t^i > 1$), others under-react ($\beta_t^i < 1$). The idiosyncratic contribution dW_t^i is an independent Wiener noise both across different agents and in time, with distribution of mean zero and variance $\Sigma^2 dt$ which we take for simplicity independent of i (but some agents could be more "noisy" than others). Both the variation of β_t^i across agents, and the noise contribution dW_t^i reflect the heterogeneity of agents' beliefs.

For simplicity, the "news" term $d\xi_t$ is chosen to a Wiener noise of variance $\sigma^2 dt$. Normalizing the mean of the β_t^i's to unity thus corresponds to the assumption that agents are on average unbiased in their interpretation of the news – i.e. their intentions remain centered around the fundamental price $p^F(t) = \int^t d\xi_{t'}$.

One final assumption is that the idiosyncratic behavior does "average out" in the limit of a very large number of agents, i.e., that no single market participant accounts for a finite fraction of the total supply or demand. This assumption leads to a deterministic aggregate behavior and allows one to gloss over some rather involved mathematics.

Note the similarities and differences with the Santa Fe model for the LOB, see Section 4. In the Santa Fe model, orders appear and get canceled with Poisson rates, much as postulated above for the latent supply and demand curves. However, the price revision process – with the common news driver $d\xi_t$ – is absent from the Santa Fe model. In other words, while the dynamics of the price is fully explained by the order flow in the Santa Fe model, the present specification allows one to include some exogenous factors as well.

6.1.3 The "Free Evolution" Equation for MSD Curves

Endowed with the above hypothesis, one can obtain stochastic partial differential equations for the evolution of the average marginal supply ($\rho^-(p, t) = \partial_p S(p, t)$) and the average marginal demand ($\rho^+(p, t) = -\partial_p \mathcal{D}(p, t)$) in the absence of transactions. The derivation of these equations in beyond the scope of this chapter; their final form is however quite intuitive and easy to interpret – see Mastromatteo et al. (2014b), Donier et al. (2015).[8] It turns out that these equations take a simple form in the moving frame of the reference price $p^F(t)$. Introducing the shifted price $x = p - p^F(t)$, one finds:

$$
\begin{cases}
\partial_t \rho^+(x, t) &= \underbrace{D\,\partial_{xx}^2 \rho^+(x, t)}_{\text{Revisions}} - \underbrace{v_+(x)\rho^+(x, t)}_{\text{Cancellations}} + \underbrace{\lambda_+(x)}_{\text{New orders}}; \\
\partial_t \rho^-(x, t) &= D\,\partial_{yy}^2 \rho^-(x, t) - v_-(x)\rho^-(x, t) + \lambda_-(x) ,
\end{cases}
\tag{21}
$$

---

[8] See also Lasry and Lions (2007), Lehalle et al. (2010) for similar ideas in the context of mean-field games.

where the three terms have a rather transparent origin. The diffusion coefficient D is given by $(\Sigma^2 + \sigma^2 \mathbb{V}[\beta_t^i])/2$, i.e. part of the diffusion comes from the purely idiosyncratic "noisy" updates of agents (Σ^2), and another part comes from the in-homogeneity of their reaction to news $(\sigma^2 \mathbb{V}[\beta_t^i])$, which indeed vanishes if all β_t^i's are equal to unity. One could argue that extra drift terms should be added to these equations, describing e.g. the propensity of agents to revise their price estimation towards the reference price $(x = 0)$. However, these drift terms play a relatively minor role in the following discussion.

Eqs. (21) describe the structural evolution of supply and demand around the reference price $p^F(t)$, which in fact does not appear explicitly in these equations. Interestingly, the dynamics of the MSD curves can be treated independently of the dynamics of the reference price itself, provided one describes the MSD in a moving frame centered around $p^F(t)$.

Eqs. (21) for $\rho^+(x, t)$ and $\rho^-(x, t)$ are linear and can be formally solved in the general case, starting from an arbitrary initial condition such as Eq. (19). This general solution is however not very illuminating, and we rather focus here in the special case where the cancellation rate $\nu_\pm(x) \equiv \nu$ does not depend on x nor on the side of the latent order book. The evolution of the MSD can then be written in a transparent way, as

$$
\begin{aligned}
\rho^\pm(x, t) &= \int_{-\infty}^{+\infty} \frac{dx'}{\sqrt{4\pi Dt}} \rho^\pm(x', t = 0^+) e^{-\frac{(x'-x)^2}{4Dt} - \nu t} \\
&+ \int_0^t dt' \int_{-\infty}^{+\infty} \frac{dx'}{\sqrt{4\pi D(t-t')}} \lambda_\pm(x') e^{-\frac{(x'-x)^2}{4D(t-t')} - \nu(t-t')}, \quad (22)
\end{aligned}
$$

where $\rho^\pm(x, t = 0^+)$ is the initial condition, i.e. just after the last auction. The first term describes the free evolution of this initial condition, whereas the second term describes new intentions, that appear between time 0 and t.

We will now explore the properties of the above solution at time $t = \tau^-$, i.e., just before the next auction, in the two asymptotic limits $\tau \to \infty$, corresponding to very infrequent auctions, and $\tau \to 0$, i.e. continuous time auctions as in modern financial markets. The upshot will be that while the liquidity around the auction price is in general finite and leads to a linear impact, this liquidity *vanishes* as $\sqrt{\tau}$ when the inter-auction time $\tau \to 0$. This signals the breakdown of linear impact and its replacement by the square-root law detailed in Section 3.2.

6.2 INFREQUENT AUCTIONS

The aim of this section is to show that the shape of the marginal supply and demand curves can be characterized in the limit of very infrequent auctions (corresponding to Walras' auctions), allowing one to characterize the famous Kyle impact parameter lambda (Kyle, 1985) in this framework.

Letting $t = \tau \to \infty$ in Eq. (22), one can see that the first term disappears exponentially fast, with rate ν. This means that after time $T_m = \nu^{-1}$, one reaches an *equilibrium solution* $\rho_{\text{st.}}^{\pm}(x)$, independently of the initial condition. After integrating over t', the second term can be simplified further to give the following general solution:

$$\rho_{\text{st.}}^{\pm}(x) = \frac{1}{2\sqrt{\nu D}} \int_{-\infty}^{+\infty} dx' \lambda_{\pm}(x') e^{-\sqrt{\frac{\nu}{D}}|x'-x|}. \tag{23}$$

A particularly simple case is when $\lambda_{\pm}(x) = \Omega_{\pm} e^{\mp x/\Delta}$, meaning that buyers(/sellers) have an exponentially small probability to be interested in a transaction at high/low prices; Δ is the price range within which typically pricing disagreements lie. In this toy-example, one finds that a stationary state only exists when the cancellation rate is strong enough to prevent accumulation of orders far away from $x = 0$. When $\nu \Delta^2 > D$, one finds:

$$\rho_{\text{st.}}^{\pm}(x) = \frac{\Omega_{\pm} \Delta^2}{\nu \Delta^2 - D} e^{\mp x/\Delta}.$$

The shape of $\rho_{\text{st.}}(x)$ is generically the one shown in Fig. 5 with an overlapping region where buy/sell orders coexist. The auction price $p_{\text{trade}} = p^F + x_{\text{trade}}$ is determined by the condition (18), or else

$$\int_{x_{\text{trade}}}^{\infty} dx \rho_{\text{st.}}^{+}(x) = \int_{-\infty}^{x_{\text{trade}}} dx \rho_{\text{st.}}^{-}(x) := V_{\text{trade}},$$

where V_{trade} is, by definition, the volume exchanged during the auction. For the simple exponential case above, this equation can be readily solved as

$$x_{\text{trade}} = \frac{\Delta}{2} \ln \frac{\Omega_{+}}{\Omega_{-}},$$

with a clear interpretation: if the new buy order intentions accumulated since the last auction happen to outsize the new sell intentions during the same period, the auction price will exceed the reference price, and vice versa. Would this be the case, one expects the imbalance to invert in the next period (by definition of the reference price), leading to short time mean reversion around p_t^F. When $\Omega_{+} \approx \Omega_{-} \approx \Omega_0$, one finds:

$$x_{\text{trade}} \approx \frac{\Omega_{+} - \Omega_{-}}{2\Omega_0} \Delta, \tag{24}$$

and

$$V_{\text{trade}} = \frac{\Omega_0 \Delta^3}{\nu \Delta^2 - D}. \tag{25}$$

Just after the auction, the MSD curves start again from $\rho_{\text{st.}}^{\mp}(x)$, truncated below (resp. above) x_{trade}, as in Eq. (19).

Let us now turn to price impact in this model, by imagining that a buy metaorder of volume Q is introduced in an otherwise balanced market (i.e. $\Omega_{+} = \Omega_{-}$), with a very high reservation price. For small enough Q's, the clearing price p_Q can be computed writing that $S(p_Q) = D(p_Q) + Q$ and Taylor expanding $S(p)$ and $D(p)$ around p^F to first order in Q. One readily gets a *linear impact* law:

$$S(p^F) + (p_Q - p^F)\partial_p S(p^F) = D(p^F) + (p_Q - p^F)\partial_p D(p^F) + Q$$
$$\Rightarrow \quad p_Q - p^F \approx \Lambda Q \tag{26}$$

where Kyle's lambda (noted here Λ) is given by

$$\Lambda^{-1} = \partial_p S(p^F) - \partial_p D(p^F) = 2\rho_{st.}(0). \tag{27}$$

Whenever the MSD do not simultaneously vanish at $y = 0$, the price response to a perturbation must be linear, as in the Kyle model. For the exponential case, one finds:

$$\Lambda = \frac{\Delta}{2V_{trade}},$$

which has an immediate interpretation: the price impact of a metaorder of volume Q is proportional to the typical mis-pricing Δ times the ratio of Q over the typical transacted volume at each auction V_{trade}. Note that for the exponential model, the impact law can be computed beyond the linear regime and reads:

$$\mathcal{I}(Q) = p_Q - p^F = \Delta \sinh^{-1}\left(\frac{Q}{2V_{trade}}\right), \tag{28}$$

which is linear for small Qs and logarithmic at large Qs.

The main point of the present section is that when the inter-auction time is large enough, each auction clears an equilibrium supply with an equilibrium demand, given by Eq. (23). This corresponds to the standard representation of market dynamics in the Walrasian context, since in this case only the long-term properties of supply and demand matter and the whole transients are discarded. The next section will depart from this limiting case, by introducing a finite inter-auction time such that the transient dynamics of supply and demand becomes a central feature.

6.3 HIGH FREQUENCY AUCTIONS

Let us now investigate the case where the inter-auction time τ tends to zero. Since all the supply (resp. demand) curve left (resp. right) of the auction price is wiped out by the auction process, one expects intuitively that after a very small time τ, the density of buy/sell orders in the immediate vicinity of the transaction price will remain small. We will show that this is indeed the case, and specify exactly the shape of the stationary MSD after many auctions have taken place. Consider again Eq. (22) just before the $(n+1)$th auction at time $(n+1)\tau^-$, in the case where the flow of new orders is symmetric, i.e. $\lambda_+(x) = \lambda_-(-x)$, such that the transaction price is always at the reference price ($x_{trade} = 0$). One can focus on the supply side and postulate that

$\rho^-(x, t = n\tau^-)$ can be written, in the vicinity of $x = 0$, as

$$\rho^-(x, t = n\tau^-) = \sqrt{\tau}\,\phi_n\left(\frac{x}{\sqrt{D\tau}}\right) + O(\tau) \tag{29}$$

when $\tau \to 0$. In that limit, one can show that the following iteration equation is exact up to order $\sqrt{\tau}$:

$$\phi_{n+1}(u) = \int_0^{+\infty} \frac{dw}{\sqrt{4\pi}}\phi_n(w)e^{-(u-w)^2/4} + O(\sqrt{\tau}). \tag{30}$$

Note that v has entirely disappeared from the equation (but will appear in the boundary condition, see below), and only the value of $\lambda(x)$ close to the transaction price is relevant at this order.

After a very large number of auctions, one therefore finds that the stationary shape of the demand curve close to the price and in the limit $\tau \to 0$ is given by the non-trivial solution of the following fixed point equation:

$$\phi_\infty(u) = \int_0^{+\infty} \frac{dw}{\sqrt{4\pi}}\phi_\infty(w)e^{-(u-w)^2/4}, \tag{31}$$

supplemented by the boundary condition $\phi_\infty(u \gg 1) \approx \mathcal{L}\sqrt{D}u$, where $\mathcal{L}$ can be fully determined by matching with the explicit solution for $\tau = 0$, leading to

$$\mathcal{L} = \frac{1}{D}\int_0^\infty dx'\left[\lambda(-x') - \lambda(x')\right]e^{-\sqrt{v/D}\,x'}. \tag{32}$$

In the exponential model, one finds explicitly:

$$\mathcal{L} = \frac{2\Omega_0\Delta}{\Delta v - D}, \tag{33}$$

which is a measure of liquidity (see below) that increases with the flux of incoming intentions (Ω_0) and decreases with the cancellation rate v. Note that $\mathcal{L}$ has dimensions of $1/[\text{price}]^2$.

Eq. (31) is of the so-called Wiener–Hopf type and its analytical solution can be found in e.g. Atkinson (1974). Its numerical solution is found to be very close to an affine function for $u > 0$: $\phi_\infty(u) \approx \mathcal{L}\sqrt{D}(u + u_0)$ with $u_0 \approx 0.824$.

In summary, the stationary shape $\rho^{\text{st.}}(x)$ of the MSD curve in the frequent auction limit $\tau \to 0$ and close to the reference price ($x = O(\sqrt{D\tau})$), has a *universal shape*, for a wide class of model specifications (i.e., the functions $v_\pm(x)$ and $\lambda_\pm(x)$). This MSD curve is given by $\sqrt{\tau}\phi_\infty(x/\sqrt{D\tau})$, where ϕ_∞ can itself be approximated by a simple affine function. In particular, one finds that the liquidity at the traded price goes to zero as $\sqrt{\tau}$:

$$\rho_{\text{st.}}(x = 0) \approx 0.824\mathcal{L}\sqrt{D\tau}. \tag{34}$$

We now turn to the interpretation of this result in terms of market liquidity and price impact. First, one can show that in the $\tau \to 0$ limit, the volume V_{trade} cleared at each auction is simply given by

$$V_{\text{trade}} = \mathcal{L}D\tau. \tag{35}$$

The total transacted volume V_T within a finite time interval of length T is given by $V_T = V_{\text{trade}}T/\tau$. Interestingly, this volume remains finite when $\tau \to 0$, and given by

$$V_T = \mathcal{L}DT. \tag{36}$$

This observation should be put in perspective with the recent evolution of financial markets, where the time between transactions τ has indeed become very small, while the volume of each transaction has simultaneously decreased, in such a way that the daily volume has remained roughly constant.

Now, looking back at Eq. (27), one notes that Kyle's Λ behaves as $\Lambda^{-1} \equiv 2\rho_{\text{st.}}(x=0) \propto \mathcal{L}\sqrt{\tau}$, which is the pivotal result of this present section. It means that the marginal supply and demand becomes very small around the transaction price as the auction frequency increases. Intuitively, this is due to the fact that close to the transaction price, liquidity has no time to rebuild between two auctions. From the point of view of price impact, the divergence of Kyle's Λ as $1/\sqrt{\tau}$ means that the auction price becomes more and more susceptible to any imbalance between supply and demand – as noted in Tóth et al. (2011), the market becomes *fragile* in the high-frequency limit.

6.4 FROM LINEAR TO SQUARE-ROOT IMPACT

From the shape of the MSD close to transaction price given by Eq. (29), one can compute the supply and demand curves just before an auction, when the inter-auction time τ tends to 0. From these curves one infers the impact of an extra buy order of size Q from the equation

$$\mathcal{D}(p_Q) + Q = \mathcal{S}(p_Q). \tag{37}$$

Using the results of the previous subsection, one can work out the corresponding impact $\mathcal{I}(Q) = p_Q - p^F$, with the following result, valid for $\tau \to 0$:

$$\mathcal{I}(Q) = \sqrt{D\tau} \times \mathcal{Y}\left(\frac{Q}{V_{\text{trade}}}\right); \qquad V_{\text{trade}} = \mathcal{L}D\tau, \tag{38}$$

where $\mathcal{Y}(u)$ is a certain function with the following asymptotic behavior:

$$\mathcal{Y}(u) \approx_{u \ll 1} 0.555u; \qquad Y(u) \approx_{u \gg 1} \sqrt{2u}. \tag{39}$$

The fact that $\mathcal{Y}(1)$ is a number of order unity means that trading the typical auction volume typically moves the price by $\sqrt{D\tau}$, i.e. its own volatility on time τ.

Eq. (38) means that the impact $\mathcal{I}(Q)$ is linear in a region where the volume Q is much smaller than $V_{\text{trade}} \sim \mathcal{L}D\tau$, i.e. when the extra volume is small compared to the typical volume exchanged during auctions. In the other limit, however, *one recovers the square-root impact law* analytically:

$$\mathcal{I}(Q \gg V_{\text{trade}}) \approx \sqrt{\frac{2Q}{\mathcal{L}}}.$$

The impact is universal when Q is small enough for the linear approximation of the MSD to hold. For very large Q's, this linear approximation breaks down, and one enters a presumably non-universal regime that is beyond the scope of the present discussion. Impact is Kyle-like for $Q < V_{\text{trade}}$ and crosses over to a square root regime when Q becomes greater that V_{trade}. Clearly, for $\tau \to 0$, the auction volume $V_{\text{trade}} = \mathcal{L}D\tau$ also tends to zero, so that the region where impact is linear in volume shrinks to zero. In other words, when the market clearing time becomes infinitely small, the impact of small trades is *never* linear.

6.5 SUMMARY AND CONCLUSIONS

The punchline of the above section is quite simple, and well summarized by the graphs plotted in Fig. 5, where we show (a) the standard Walrasian supply and demand curves just before the auction, from which the clearing price p_{trade} can be deduced; (b) the supply and demand curves just after an auction, when the inter-auction time τ is large enough – in which case the marginal supply and demand are both finite at p_{trade}; and (c) the supply and demand curves in the continuous time limit $\tau \to 0$, for which the marginal supply and demand curves vanish linearly around the current price, giving rise to a characteristic V-shaped latent liquidity curve.

Remarkably, one can check directly the above prediction on the shape of the MSD curves using Bitcoin data, where traders are much less strategic than in more mature financial markets and display their orders in the visible order book even quite far from the current price. Quite strikingly, the MSD curves are indeed found to be *linear* in the vicinity of the price that corresponds to about 5% range, in perfect agreement with our dynamical theory of supply and demand in the limit of frequent auctions, see Donier and Bouchaud (2016). Correspondingly, one expects that the impact of meta-orders is well accounted by a square-root law in this region, which is indeed also found empirically (see Donier and Bonart, 2015 for the special case of Bitcoin case).

7 THE INFORMATION CONTENT OF PRICES

After the above journey into agent-based, microstructural foundations of price dynamics where fundamental information is completely absent, it is important to discuss one of the most contentious questions in financial economics: what is the real information contained in prices and why do prices move?

7.1 **THE EFFICIENT MARKET VIEW**

The traditional point of view is that market prices reflect the fundamental value (of a stock, currency, commodity, etc.), up to small and short lived mispricings. Markets are *measurement apparatuses* that aggregate all private information about the "true" (but hidden) value of assets and provide prices, at the end of a quick and efficient digestion process. Prices are martingales because by definition any new piece of information that changes the value of the asset cannot be anticipated or predicted. In this view, microstructure effects, and trading itself, cannot affect prices except possibly on short time scales. The long term volatility of prices cannot be influenced by short term, microstructural effects.

7.1.1 *Three Major Puzzles*

This Platonian view of markets is however fraught with several difficulties, that have been the subject of thousands of academic papers in the last 30 years, with renewed insights from microstructure studies. Some of the well-known puzzles are (see Black, 1986 and Shleifer and Summers, 1990 for remarkably clear and lucid early discussions):

- *The excess trading puzzle*: If prices really reflect value and are unpredictable, why are there (still) so many people trading? While some amount of excess trading might be justified by risk management or cash management, it is difficult to explain the sheer orders of magnitude of the trading activity in, e.g. stock markets or currency markets.
- *The excess volatility puzzle*: Prices move around far too much to be explained by fluctuations of fundamentals (Shiller, 1981). In particular many large price jumps seem to occur without substantial news at all (Cutler et al., 1989; Fair, 2002; Joulin et al., 2008) and, conversely, move much less when markets are closed than when they are open, while the same amount of news continues to be released (French and Roll, 1986).
- *The trend-following puzzle*: Price returns tend to be positively autocorrelated on long times scales, such as weeks to months. In other words, some information about future price moves seems to be contained in the past price changes themselves. Trend following appears to be present in all asset classes (including stock indices, commodities, FX, bonds, and so on) and has persisted for at least two centuries, see e.g. Lempérière et al. (2014). This is in stark contradiction with the efficient market story, under which such autocorrelations should not be present. Given that the CTA/trend-following industry managed an estimated 325 billion dollars at the end of 2013, it is hard to argue that these strategies are economically insignificant.

7.1.2 *Noise Traders*

Faced with the excess volatility/trading puzzles, research in the 80's proposed to break away from the strict orthodoxy of rational market participants and introduce a new category of "noise traders", or uninformed agents. This, on the one hand, allows one get rid of the "no-trade theorem" and to account for excess trading. As illustrated by the Kyle model or the Glosten–Milgrom model (Kyle, 1985; Glosten and Milgrom, 1985), the existence of noise traders is actually crucial for the viability of market making – and thus of the very existence of markets. However, these models refrain from heresy, in the sense that the long term impact of noise trading on prices is assumed to be zero. Prices still follow fundamental values. This is quite clear in the Kyle model: if the volatility of the fundamental value was zero, the impact of trades would be zero as well. Price impact in this context merely means that trades *forecast* fundamental prices (Hasbrouck, 2007); but the volatility puzzle is still there since random trades cannot increase volatility.

7.2 ORDER-FLOW DRIVEN PRICES

7.2.1 Trades Impact Prices

After accepting the presence of non-rational agents, the next conceptual step is to open the Pandora Box and accept that all trades – informed or random, large or small – do impact prices. This, at least naively, offers a solution to the excess volatility puzzle: if trades by themselves move prices, excess trading should mean excess volatility. We return to this in the next subsection, but note that this view of markets is enticing for several reasons:

- As we have argued in Section 3, impact is indeed surprisingly large (a metaorder representing 1% of the average daily volume moves the price by ∼10% of its average volatility) and long-lived (the impact of an order only decays as a slow, power-law of the lag). Even small, random trades do significantly impact prices.
- Because *order flow* becomes by itself a dominant cause for price changes, market participants should attempt to predict future order flows rather than fundamentals (that may only play a role on much longer time scales). This ties up neatly with Keynes' famous beauty contest:

> *Investment based on genuine long-term expectation is so difficult [...] as to be scarcely practicable. He who attempts it must surely [...] run greater risks than he who tries to guess better than the crowd how the crowd will behave;*

which is much closer to the way market participants really operate. As reformulated by Shleifer and Summers (1990):

> *On that view, the key to investment success is not just predicting future fundamentals, but also predicting the movement of other active investors. Market professionals spend considerable resources tracking price trends, volume, short interest, odd lot volume, investor sentiment indexes, and other numerous gauges of demand for equities. Tracking these possible indicators of demand makes no sense if prices responded only to fundamental news and not to investor demand.*

In fact, artificial market experiments show that even when the fundamental value is known to all subjects, they are tempted to forecast the behavior of their fellow subjects and end up creating trends, bubbles, and crashes; see Smith et al. (1988) and Hommes (2013).

- This scenario allows one to understand why self-exciting, feedback effects are so prevalent in financial markets. As we have seen above, volatility and activity are clustered in time, strongly suggesting that the activity of the market itself leads to more trading which in turn, impact prices and generates more volatility – see Section 2. In fact, calibrating any of these self-exciting models on data lead to the conclusion that the lion's share of the activity/volatility is self-generated, rather than exogenous. In view of Shiller's excess volatility puzzle, this is quite satisfying.

7.2.2 The Statistically Efficient View

There are however at least two potential conundrums with the order-flow dominated theory of price changes.

One is the long-range correlation in order flows (see Section 2.8) that is a clear proof of the presence of long-lived imbalances between supply and demand which markets just cannot quickly digest. These imbalances should create trends and long-lived mispricings. However, we have seen that liquidity providing acts (in normal market conditions) to buffer these imbalances and remove any exploitable price pattern. In other words, competition at the *high-frequency end* of the spectrum is enough to whiten the time series of returns. Competition enforces a price-setting mechanism whereby liquidity providers/market makers must offer their best guess of future prices based on past order flow. This is essentially the content of the "propagator model" (Bouchaud et al., 2004, 2006) where impact decay, induced by liquidity providers, is fine-tuned to compensate the long-memory of order flow and allow the price to be close to a martingale. In this picture, the volatility of the resulting whitened process is however entirely dominated by high-frequency activity, and has therefore no reason whatsoever to be related to the volatility of the fundamental value. But in fact this is precisely the ingredient we need to account for the excess-volatility puzzle: high-frequency mechanisms set a volatility level that then trickles down unchanged to lower frequencies, generating a trading-induced volatility different from the fundamental volatility.

This is precisely the second conundrum on which many economists immediately pounce. In the words of French and Roll (1986):

> *Under the trading noise hypothesis, stock returns should be serially correlated [...]: unless market prices are unrelated to the objective economic value of the stock, pricing errors must be corrected in the long run. These corrections would generate negative autocorrelations.*

In other words, the (circular) argument is as follows: since in the long-run prices cannot err away from the economic value of the asset, the near-absence of negative autocorrelations is a proof that prices are *always* close to their fundamental values! The alternative is Black's famous "factor 2" inefficiency (Black, 1986; Bouchaud et al., 2017): prices do err away from their fundamental values by large amounts, and for long times. Back-of-envelope order of magnitude calculations suggest that mean reversion can be as long as a few years, as confirmed by data (Poterba and Summers, 1988; Bouchaud et al., 2017). As pointed out by Summers (1986), this long-term mean reversion hardly leaves any trace that econometricians or traders can exploit.

How can mis-pricing remain for so long, that is, why does the aggregation process that financial markets are supposed to realize fail so badly? One reason often evoked is that the fundamental value is so vaguely determined that the usual arbitrage mechanism – pushing the price back to its fundamental value – is not strong enough (Shleifer and Summers, 1990). Another interesting reason is that self-referential effects can prevent the market as a whole to converge to an unbiased best guess of the fundamental value (Bouchaud, 2013; Bouchaud et al., 2018). Note that in contrast to Kyle's world where the fundamental price is revealed at some time in the future, there is not any terminal time where the "true" level of – say – the S&P500 is announced. While this anchoring does happen at maturity for bond prices or option prices, this idea is not relevant for stock prices or currency levels.

7.2.3 Permanent Impact and Information

If order flow is the dominant cause of price changes, information is chiefly about correctly anticipating the behavior of others and not about fundamental value, as Keynes envisioned. The notion of *information* should then be replaced by the notion of *correlation* with future flows. For example, when all market participants interpret a piece of news as negative and trade accordingly, the correct anticipation for an arbitrageur would be to also interpret the news as negative, even if it did not rationally make sense. Of course if all market participants are rational and make trading decision based on their best guess of the fundamental value, order flow will just reflect deviation from fundamentals and the efficient market picture is recovered.

In an order-flow dominated market, the difference between a noise trader and an informed trader is merely the amount of correlation of their trades with the future order flow. Informed traders are positively correlated with it, allowing them to forecast future price changes, whereas noise traders are simply uncorrelated with the rest of the crowd. While the short-term, mechanical impact is similar in both cases (Tóth et al., 2017), on the long run the price reverts to its initial value for noise trades whereas a permanent component remains for "informed" trades. (See Gomes and Waelbroeck, 2014; Donier and Bonart, 2015; Brokmann et al., 2015 for empirical studies on how informed and noise trades impact the price differently on the long run.)

Now, it might well be that even random trades have a non-zero permanent impact – perhaps very small. This is what happens in the Santa-Fe model (see Section 4), while *all* trades are random, but the rest of the market acts as if they contained some information. This is also the case in Kyle's model when market-makers think there is information when there is none. In the absence of strong anchoring to a fundamental value, the price ends up wandering around because of the order-flow itself, with volatility generated by the price formation mechanism at the microscale.

8 CONCLUSIONS AND OPEN PROBLEMS

Financial markets display a host of universal "stylized facts" begging for a scientific explanation. The most striking ones, in our eyes, fall into two distinct categories:

- Excess volatility, fat tails, and clustered activity: these ubiquitous observations strongly suggest that strong self-exciting effects or positive feedback loops are at play. Although mathematical models such as GARCH or Hawkes processes explicitly describe such feedback effects, it is fair to say that there is at this stage no deep understanding of their "microscopic" origin.
- Order flow regularities, such as the long memory of the sign of market orders or the square-root impact of metaorders.

Agent-based models are attempts to account for these stylized facts in a unified manner. Devising faithful microstructural ABMs would allow one to answer crucial questions, such as those related to market stability. Can large metaorders destabilize markets? Is HFT activity detrimental? Can crashes be endogenously generated and can destabilizing feedback loops be mitigated by adequate regulation?

We have reviewed above some of the recent work in that direction. We have seen in Section 4 that the Santa-Fe zero-intelligence model offers a very interesting benchmark, but suffers from important drawbacks as well, in particular when one wants to use it to account for the square-root impact of metaorders, that requires long memory times for the underlying (latent) liquidity. In its original version, the Santa-Fe model with a long memory time leads to strong mean-reversion effects for the price, which are not observed. A way out of this conundrum is to enrich the Santa-Fe model by allowing market order signs to be autocorrelated – as empirically observed – and to adapt their volume to the available volume on the opposite side. This model is able to reproduce both a diffusive price, and the square-root dependence of the impact on the volume of metaorders (see Section 5). The underlying mechanism can be well understood in terms of a generic "reaction–diffusion" model for the dynamics of the liquidity (see Section 6), that allows one to *derive* the square-root law analytically in the limit of continuous time auctions (Mastromatteo et al., 2014b; Donier et al., 2015; Donier and Bouchaud, 2016). In a nutshell, a diffusive price leads to a vanishing liquidity in the vicinity of the current price. This naturally accounts for the fact that large metaorders have to be fragmented in order to be digested by the liquidity funnel, which leads to a long memory in the sign of the order flow. Second, the anomalously small local liquidity induces a breakdown of the linear impact model and its replacement by a square-root law.

Although the square-root impact is well reproduced, many open problems remain. One is the relevance of an "information-less" description of financial markets, where prices move around merely as a result of random trades, without any of the usual assumptions about the rationality of agents, the anchoring to fundamental prices through arbitrage, etc. We have argued in Section 7 that the role of information is probably overstated in classical theories, while a picture based on a self-reflexive price-impacting order flow has many merits. Although still hotly debated, this point of view has a strong tradition, going back to Keynes, followed by Shiller, Black, Summers, and others (see Black, 1986; Shleifer and Summers, 1990; Farmer and Geanakoplos, 2009 for inspiring pieces; and Bouchaud et al., 2017 for a recent discussion). The recent accumulation of microstructural stylized facts, allowing one to focus on the price formation mechanism, all but confirm that fundamental information plays a relatively minor role in the dynamics of financial markets, at least on short to medium time scales.

Related to this discussion, a particularly important question is to understand the mechanisms leading to price jumps, which seem to be mostly of endogenous origin and not to news affecting fundamental factors (Cutler et al., 1989; Fair, 2002; Joulin et al., 2008). The order flow driven picture may offer a way to understand why the structure of price jumps is so similar across all traded, liquid markets and all epochs. How might this idea be implemented within the ABM's considered in this chapter, which do *not* generate fat-tail distributions?[9]

Here, we offer a conjecture, that obviously requires further scrutiny. In Section 5, we have assumed that latent orders instantaneously materialize in the real order book as the distance to the price gets small. However, any finite conversion time or increased cancellation rates might induce liquidity droughts. These are usually and self-heal rapidly, but they can amplify when price changes accelerate and lead to an unstable feedback loop (Bouchaud, 2011; Fosset et al., 2018). The anomalously low liquidity in the vicinity of the traded price, suggested by the arguments in Section 6, surely contributes to the appearance of these micro-crises, that can eventually become macro-crashes. This simple mechanism could explain the universal power-law distribution of returns that appear to be unrelated to exogenous news but rather to unavoidable, self-induced liquidity crises. Whether this scenario is realized in real markets remains to be vindicated.

ACKNOWLEDGMENTS

I want to thank all my collaborators for sharing their precious insights on these issues: M. Benzaquen, G. Bormetti, F. Caccioli, J. De Lataillade, Z. Eisler, J.D. Farmer, A. Fosset, S. Gualdi, J. Kockelkoren, Y. Lempérière, F. Lillo, I. Mastromatteo, F. Patzelt, M. Potters, D. Taranto, B. Tóth. Special thanks to J. Bonart, J. Donier, and M. Gould, with whom a substantial part of the present material was elaborated (see Bouchaud et al., 2018). I also want to thank C. Hommes and B. LeBaron for giving me the opportunity to write this review piece.

REFERENCES

Almgren, R., Thum, C., Hauptmann, E., Li, H., 2005. Direct estimation of equity market impact. Risk 18 (7), 5762.

---

[9]Some ABM of limit order books do however lead to fat-tailed returns, see e.g. Preis et al. (2006) and Chiarella et al. (2009a), with mechanisms somewhat related to the one discussed here.

Atkinson, C., 1974. A Wiener–Hopf integral equation arising in some inference and queueing problems. Biometrika, 277–283.

Bachelier, L., 1900. Théorie de la spéculation. Annales scientifiques de l'École normale supérieure, 3e série 17, 21–86.

Bacry, E., Mastromatteo, I., Muzy, J.-F., 2015. Hawkes processes in finance. Market Microstructure and Liquidity 1 (01), 1550005.

Bak, P., Paczuski, M., Shubik, M., 1997. Price variations in a stock market with many agents. Physica A: Statistical Mechanics and Its Applications 246 (3–4), 430–453.

Benzaquen, M., Bouchaud, J.-P., 2017. Market impact with multi-timescale liquidity. Available at SSRN: https://ssrn.com/abstract=3050724.

Beran, J., 1994. Statistics for Long-Memory Processes. Chapman & Hall, New York.

Bershova, N., Rakhlin, D., 2013. The non-linear market impact of large trades: evidence from buy-side order flow. Quantitative Finance 13, 1759–1778.

Black, F., 1986. Noise. The Journal of Finance 41 (3), 528–543.

Blanc, P., Donier, J., Bouchaud, J.-P., 2016. Quadratic Hawkes processes for financial prices. Quantitative Finance, 1–18.

Bollerslev, T., Engle, R.F., Nelson, D.B., 1994. ARCH models. In: Engle, R.F., McFadden, D.L. (Eds.), Handbook of Econometrics, vol. 4. Elsevier/North-Holland, Amsterdam, pp. 2959–3038.

Bouchaud, J.-P., Matacz, A., Potters, M., 2001. Leverage effect in financial markets: the retarded volatility model. Physical Review Letters 87 (22), 228701, and references therein.

Bouchaud, J.-P., Mézard, M., Potters, M., 2002. Statistical properties of stock order books: empirical results and models. Quantitative Finance 2 (4), 251–256.

Bouchaud, J.-P., Potters, M., 2003. Theory of Financial Risk and Derivative Pricing: From Statistical Physics to Risk Management. Cambridge University Press.

Bouchaud, J.-P., Gefen, Y., Potters, M., Wyart, M., 2004. Fluctuations and response in financial markets: the subtle nature of 'random' price changes. Quantitative Finance 4, 176.

Bouchaud, J.-P., Kockelkoren, J., Potters, M., 2006. Random walks, liquidity molasses and critical response in financial markets. Quantitative Finance 6, 115.

Bouchaud, J.-P., Farmer, J.D., Lillo, F., 2009. How markets slowly digest changes in supply and demand. In: Handbook of Financial Markets: Dynamics and Evolution. Elsevier/North-Holland.

Bouchaud, J.-P., 2011. The endogenous dynamics of markets: price impact, feedback loops and instabilities. In: Lessons from the Credit Crisis. Risk Publications.

Bouchaud, J.-P., 2013. Crises and collective socio-economic phenomena: simple models and challenges. Journal of Statistical Physics 151 (3–4), 567–606.

Bouchaud, J.-P., Ciliberti, S., Lempérière, Y., Majewski, A., Seager, P., Ronia, K.S., 2017. Black was right: price is within a factor 2 of value. arXiv preprint arXiv:1711.04717.

Bouchaud, J.-P., Bonart, J., Donier, J., Gould, M., 2018. Trades, Quotes and Prices. Cambridge University Press.

Brokmann, X., Serie, E., Kockelkoren, J., Bouchaud, J.-P., 2015. Slow decay of impact in equity markets. Market Microstructure and Liquidity 1 (02), 1550007.

Calvet, L., Fisher, A., 2002. Multifractality in asset returns: theory and evidence. Review of Economics and Statistics 84, 381–406.

Challet, D., Stinchcombe, R., 2003. Non-constant rates and over-diffusive prices in a simple model of limit order markets. Quantitative Finance 3 (3), 155–162.

Chiarella, C., Iori, G., 2002. A simulation analysis of the microstructure of double auction markets. Quantitative Finance 2 (5), 346–353.

Chiarella, C., Iori, G., Perelló, J., 2009a. The impact of heterogeneous trading rules on the limit order book and order flows. Journal of Economic Dynamics and Control 33 (3), 525–537.

Chiarella, C., Dieci, R., He, X., 2009b. Heterogeneity, market mechanisms and asset price dynamics. In: Hens, T., Schenk-Hoppe, K.R. (Eds.), Handbook of Financial Markets: Dynamics and Evolution. Elsevier, pp. 277–344.

Chicheportiche, R., Bouchaud, J.-P., 2014. The fine-structure of volatility feedback I: multi-scale self-reflexivity. Physica A: Statistical Mechanics and Its Applications 410, 174–195.

Cont, R., 2001. Empirical properties of asset returns: stylized facts and statistical issues. Quantitative Finance, 223–236.

Cont, R., De Larrard, A., 2013. Price dynamics in a Markovian limit order market. SIAM Journal on Financial Mathematics 4 (1), 1–25.

Cristelli, M., Pietronero, L., Zaccaria, A., 2011. Critical overview of agent-based models for economics. arXiv preprint arXiv:1101.1847.

Cutler, D.M., Poterba, J.M., Summers, L.H., 1989. What moves stock prices? The Journal of Portfolio Management 15, 412.

Daniels, M.G., Farmer, J.D., Gillemot, L., Iori, G., Smith, E., 2003. Quantitative model of price diffusion and market friction based on trading as a mechanistic random process. Physical Review Letters 90 (10), 108102.

Donier, J., Bonart, J., 2015. A million metaorder analysis of market impact on the Bitcoin. Market Microstructure and Liquidity 1 (02), 1550008.

Donier, J., Bonart, J., Mastromatteo, I., Bouchaud, J.-P., 2015. A fully consistent, minimal model for non-linear market impact. Quantitative Finance 15 (7), 1109–1121.

Donier, J., Bouchaud, J.-P., 2016. From Walras' auctioneer to continuous time double auctions: a general dynamic theory of supply and demand. Journal of Statistical Mechanics: Theory and Experiment 2016 (12), 123406.

Eisler, Z., Bouchaud, J.-P., Kockelkoren, J., 2012. The price impact of order book events: market orders, limit orders and cancellations. Quantitative Finance 12 (9), 1395–1419.

Fair, R.C., 2002. Events that shook the market. The Journal of Business 75 (4).

Farmer, J.D., Patelli, P., Zovko, I.I., 2005. Proceedings of the National Academy of Sciences of the United States of America 102, 2254.

Farmer, J.D., Geanakoplos, J., 2009. The virtues and vices of equilibrium and the future of financial economics. Complexity 14 (3), 11–38.

Farmer, J.D., Gerig, A., Lillo, F., Waelbroeck, H., 2013. How efficiency shapes market impact. Quantitative Finance 13, 1743–1758.

Fosset, A., Benzaquen, M., Bouchaud, J.-P., 2018. Destabilizing feedback loops in order books. In preparation.

French, K.R., Roll, R., 1986. Stock return variances: the arrival of information and the reaction of traders. Journal of Financial Economics 17, 5–26.

Gabaix, X., Gopikrishnan, P., Plerou, V., Stanley, H.E., 2003. A theory of power law distributions in financial market fluctuations. Nature CDXXIII, 267–270.

Gabaix, X., Gopikrishnan, P., Plerou, V., Stanley, H., 2006. Institutional investors and stock market volatility. The Quarterly Journal of Economics 121, 461.

Glosten, L.R., Milgrom, P.R., 1985. Bid, ask and transaction prices in a specialist market with heterogeneously informed traders. Journal of Financial Economics 14 (1), 71–100.

Gomes, C., Waelbroeck, H., 2014. Is market impact a measure of the information value of trades? Market response to liquidity vs informed trades. Quantitative Finance. https://doi.org/10.1080/14697688.2014.963140.

Gopikrishnan, P., Plerou, V., Amaral, L.A., Meyer, M., Stanley, H.E., 1999. Scaling of the distribution of fluctuations of financial market indices. Physical Review E 60, 5305.

Gould, M.D., Porter, M.A., Williams, S., McDonald, M., Fenn, D.J., Howison, S.D., 2013. Limit order books. Quantitative Finance 13 (11), 1709–1742.

Grinold, R.C., Kahn, R.N., 1999. Active Portfolio Management. The McGraw-Hill Co., Inc., New York.

Hardiman, S.J., Bercot, N., Bouchaud, J.-P., 2013. Critical reflexivity in financial markets: a Hawkes process analysis. The European Physical Journal B 86 (10), 1–9.

Hasbrouck, J., 2007. Empirical Market Microstructure: The Institutions, Economics, and Econometrics of Securities Trading. Oxford University Press.

Hommes, C., 2013. Behavioral Rationality and Heterogeneous Expectations in Complex Economic Systems. Cambridge University Press.

Joulin, A., Lefevre, A., Grunberg, D., Bouchaud, J.-P., 2008. Stock price jumps: news and volume play a minor role. Wilmott Magazine (Sept./Oct.).

Kyle, A.S., 1985. Continuous auctions and insider trading. Econometrica, 1315–1335.

Lasry, J.M., Lions, P.L., 2007. Mean field games. Japanese Journal of Mathematics 2 (1), 229–260.

LeBaron, B., 2000. Agent-based computational finance: suggested readings and early research. Journal of Economic Dynamics and Control 24 (5), 679–702.

LeBaron, B., Yamamoto, R., 2010. Order-splitting and long-memory in an order-driven market. The European Physical Journal B 73 (1), 51–57.

Lehalle, C.-A., Guéant, O., Razafinimanana, J., 2010. High frequency simulations of an order book: a two-scales approach. In: Abergel, F., Chakrabarti, B.K., Chakraborti, A., Mitra, M. (Eds.), Econophysics of Order-Driven Markets, New Economic Windows. Springer.

Lempérière, Y., Deremble, C., Seager, P., Potters, M., Bouchaud, J.-P., 2014. Two centuries of trend following. Journal of Investment Strategies 3 (3), 41–61.

Lillo, F., Farmer, J.D., 2004. The long memory of the efficient market. Studies in Nonlinear Dynamics and Econometrics 8, 1.

Lillo, F., Mike, S., Farmer, J.D., 2005. Theory for long memory in supply and demand. Physical Review E 71 (6), 066122.

Loeb, T., 1983. Trading cost: the critical link between investment information and results. Financial Analysts Journal XXXIX, 39–44.

Lux, T., 2008. The multi-fractal model of asset returns: its estimation via GMM and its use for volatility forecasting. Journal of Business and Economic Statistics 26, 194.

Mastromatteo, I., Tóth, B., Bouchaud, J.-P., 2014a. Agent-based models for latent liquidity and concave price impact. Physical Review E 89, 042805.

Mastromatteo, I., Tóth, B., Bouchaud, J.-P., 2014b. Anomalous impact in reaction–diffusion financial models. Physical Review Letters 113, 268701.

Mike, S., Farmer, J.D., 2008. An empirical behavioral model of liquidity and volatility. Journal of Economic Dynamics and Control 32, 200–234.

Moro, E., Vicente, J., Moyano, L.G., Gerig, A., Farmer, J.D., Vaglica, G., Lillo, F., Mantegna, R.N., 2009. Market impact and trading profile of hidden orders in stock markets. Physical Review E 80 (6), 066102.

Muzy, J.-F., Delour, J., Bacry, E., 2000. Modelling fluctuations of financial time series: from cascade process to stochastic volatility model. The European Physical Journal B 17, 537–548.

Palmer, R.G., Arthur, W.B., Holland, J.H., LeBaron, B., Tayler, P., 1994. Artificial economic life: a simple model of a stockmarket. Physica D: Nonlinear Phenomena 75 (1–3), 264–274.

Patzelt, F., Bouchaud, J.-P., 2018. Universal scaling and nonlinearity of aggregate price impact in financial markets. Physical Review E 97 (1), 012304.

Plerou, V., Gopikrishnan, P., Amaral, L.A., Meyer, M., Stanley, H.E., 1999. Scaling of the distribution of price fluctuations of individual companies. Physical Review E 60, 6519.

Poterba, J.M., Summers, L.H., 1988. Mean reversion in stock prices: evidence and implications. Journal of Financial Economics 22 (1), 27–59.

Preis, T., Golke, S., Paul, W., Schneider, J.J., 2006. Multi-agent-based order book model of financial markets. Europhysics Letters 75 (3), 510.

Sandas, P., 2001. Adverse selection and competitive market making: empirical evidence from a limit order market. The Review of Financial Studies 14 (3), 705–734.

Shiller, R.J., 1981. Do stock prices move too much to be justified by subsequent changes in dividends? The American Economic Review 71, 421–436.

Shleifer, A., Summers, L.H., 1990. The noise trader approach to finance. The Journal of Economic Perspectives 4 (2), 19–33.

Smith, E., Farmer, J.D., Gillemot, L., Krishnamurthy, S., 2003. Quantitative Finance 3, 481.

Smith, V.L., Suchanek, G.L., Williams, A.W., 1988. Bubbles, crashes, and endogenous expectations in experimental spot asset markets. Econometrica, 1119–1151.

Summers, L.H., 1986. Does the stock market rationally reflect fundamental values? The Journal of Finance, 591–601.

Taranto, D.E., Bormetti, G., Bouchaud, J.-P., Lillo, F., Tóth, B., 2016. Linear models for the impact of order flow on prices I. Propagators: transient vs. history dependent impact. Quantitative Finance. In press.

Torre, N., Ferrari, M., 1997. Market Impact Model Handbook. BARRA Inc., Berkeley. Available at http://www.barra.com/newsletter/nl166/miminl166.asp.

Tóth, B., Lempérière, Y., Deremble, C., De Lataillade, J., Kockelkoren, J., Bouchaud, J.-P., 2011. Anomalous price impact and the critical nature of liquidity in financial markets. Physical Review X 1 (2), 021006.

Tóth, B., Palit, I., Lillo, F., Farmer, J.D., 2015. Why is equity order flow so persistent? Journal of Economic Dynamics and Control 51, 218–239.

Tóth, B., Eisler, Z., Bouchaud, J.-P., 2016. The square-root impact law also holds for option markets. Wilmott Magazine 2016 (85), 70–73.

Tóth, B., Eisler, Z., Bouchaud, J.-P., 2017. The short-term impact of trades is universal. Market Microstructure and Liquidity. In press.

Weber, P., Rosenow, B., 2005. Order book approach to price impact. Quantitative Finance 5 (4), 357–364.

Wyart, M., Bouchaud, J.-P., Kockelkoren, J., Potters, M., Vettorazzo, M., 2008. Relation between bid–ask spread, impact and volatility in order-driven markets. Quantitative Finance 8 (1), 41–57.

Zarinelli, E., Treccani, M., Farmer, J.D., Lillo, F., 2015. Beyond the square root: evidence for logarithmic dependence of market impact on size and participation rate. Market Microstructure and Liquidity 1 (02), 1550004.

Empirical Validation of Agent-Based Models[*]

Thomas Lux[*,1], Remco C.J. Zwinkels[†]

Christian Albrechts Universität zu Kiel, Germany
†Vrije Universiteit Amsterdam and Tinbergen Institute, The Netherlands
1Corresponding author: e-mail address: lux@economics.uni-kiel.de

CONTENTS

[*]We gratefully acknowledge the very detailed and careful comments by three anonymous reviewers. Very useful feedback and comments have also been provided by Robert Axtell, Herbert Dawid, Cees Diks, and Blake LeBaron.

1 INTRODUCTION

The primary field of development of agent-based models in economics has been the theory of price formation in financial markets. It is also in this area that we find the vast majority of attempts in recent literature to develop methods for estimation of such models. This is not an accidental development. It is rather motivated by the particular set of 'stylized facts' observed in financial markets. These are overall statistical regularities characterizing asset returns and volatility, and they seem to be best understood as emergent properties of a system composed of dispersed activity with conflicting centrifugal and centripetal tendencies. Indeed, 'mainstream' finance has never even attempted an explanation of these stylized facts, but often has labeled them 'anomalies'. In stark contrast, agent-based models seem to be generically able to relatively easily replicate and explain these stylized facts as the outcome of market interactions of heterogeneous agents.

The salient characteristics of the dynamics of asset prices are different from those of dynamic processes observed outside economics and finance, but are surprisingly uniform across markets. There are highly powerful tools available to quantify these dynamics, such as GARCH models to describe time-varying volatility (see Engle and Bollerslev, 1986) and Extreme Value Theory to quantify the heaviness of the tails of the distribution of asset returns (see e.g. Embrechts et al., 1997). For a long time very little has been known about the economic mechanisms causing these dynamics. The traditional paradigm building on agent rationality and consequently also agent homogeneity has not been able to provide a satisfying explanation for these complex dynamics. This lack of empirical support coupled with the unrealistic assumptions of the neoclassical approach has contributed to the introduction and rise of agent-based models (ABMs) in economics and finance; see e.g. Arthur (2006) in the previous edition of this handbook.

Whereas the strength of ABMs is certainly their ability to generate all sorts of complex dynamics, their relatively (computationally) demanding nature is a drawback. This was, among others, a reason why Heterogeneous Agent Models (HAMs) were developed as a specific type of agent based models. Most HAMs only consider two very simple types of agents. Specifically, most models contain a group of fundamentalists expecting mean reversion and chartists expecting trend continuation. The main source of dynamics, however, is a switching function allowing agents to switch between the two groups conditional on past performance. Interestingly, even such simplified and stylized versions of ABMs are capable of replicating the complex price dynamics of financial markets to a certain degree; see e.g. Hommes (2006) for an overview. Recent research has also collected catalogs of stylized facts of macroeconomic data, and agent-based approaches have been developed to explain those (e.g. Dosi et al., 2013, 2015).

Due to the aforementioned background of ABMs, the early literature has typically been relying on simulations to study the properties of models with interacting agents. By doing so, authors were able to illustrate the ability of ABMs to generate complex dynamic processes resembling those observed in financial markets. There are, however, several good reasons why especially ABMs should be confronted with empirical data. First of all, ABMs are built on the notion of bounded rationality. This generates a large number of degrees of freedom for the theorist as deviations from rationality can take many forms. Empirical verification of the choices made in building the models can therefore enforce discipline in model design. Second, by confronting ABMs with empirical data, one should get a better understanding of the actual law of motion generating market prices. Whereas simulation exercises with various configurations might generate similar dynamics, a confrontation with empirical data might allow inference on relative goodness-of-fit in comparison to alternative explanations. This is especially appealing because the introduction of ABMs was empirically motivated in the first place. Finally, empirical studies might allow agent based models to become more closely connected to the 'mainstream' economics and finance literature. Interestingly, certain elements underlying ABMs have been used in more conventional settings; see for example Cutler et al. (1991) or Barberis and Shleifer (2003), who also introduce models with boundedly rational and interacting agents. Connections between these streams of literature, however, are virtually non-existent. By moving on to empirical validation, which could also serve as a stepping stone towards more concrete applications and (policy) recommendations, the ABM literature should become of interest and relevance to a broader readership.

While ABMs are based on the behavior of and interaction between individual agents, they typically aspire to explain macroscopic outcomes and therefore most empirical studies are also focusing on the market level. The agent based approach, however, by definition has at its root the behavior of individual agents and, by doing so, any ABM necessarily makes a number of assumptions about individual behavior. Stepping away from the rational representative agent approach implies that alternative behavioral assumptions have to be formulated. Whereas rational behavior is uniquely defined, boundedly rational behavior can take many forms. Think, for example, of the infinite number of subsets that can be extracted from the full information set relevant for investing, let alone the sentiment that agents might incorporate in their expectations. To address these two issues, Hong and Stein (1999) define three criteria the new paradigm should adhere to, which serve as a devise to restrict the modeler's imagination. The candidate theory should (i) rest on assumptions about investor behavior that are either a-priori plausible or consistent with casual observation; (ii) explain the existing evidence in a parsimonious and unified way; and (iii) make a number of further predictions that can be subject to out-of-sample testing. Whereas empirical evidence at the macro-level mainly focuses on criteria (ii) and (iii), micro-level evidence is necessary to fulfill criterion (i) and thereby find support for the assumptions made in building the agent based models. This is especially pressing for the reduced form models discussed in Section 3, as a number of assumptions are made for example regarding the exact functional form of the heterogeneous groups.

Taking ABMs to the data is not straightforward due to an often large number of unknown parameters, nonlinearity of the models leading to a possibly non-monotonic likelihood surface, and sometimes limited data availability. As such, one needs to make choices in order to be able to draw empirical inferences. In this review, we distinguish between two approaches. The first approach covers (further) simplifications of ABMs and HAMs to reduced form models making them suitable for estimation using relatively standard econometric techniques. These reduced form models are often sufficiently close to existing econometric models, with the additional benefit of a behavioral economic underpinning. The second approach is less stringent in the additional assumptions made on agent behavior, but requires more advanced estimation methods. Typically, these methods belong to the class of simulation-based estimators providing the additional benefit that the model is not fitted on the mean of the data, as typically is the case when using standard estimation techniques, but on the (higher) moments. This creates a tighter link between the original purpose of ABMs of explaining market dynamics and the empirical approach.

All in all, the empirical literature on agent based models has been mounting over the past decade. There have been interesting advances in terms of methods, models, aggregation approaches, as well as markets, which we will review in this chapter. The empirical results generally appear to be supportive of the agent-based approach, with an emphasis on the importance of dynamics in the composition of market participants. The estimation methods and exact functional forms of groups of agents vary considerably across studies, making it hard to draw general conclusions and to compare results across studies. The common denominator, however, is that virtually all studies find evidence in support of the relevance of the heterogeneity of agents. Allowing agents to switch between groups generally has a positive effect on model fit. These results typically hold both in-sample and out-of-sample. In view of the dominance of financial market applications of agent-based models, most of this survey will be dealing with attempts at estimating ABMs designed to explain asset price dynamics. We note, however, that the boundaries between agent-based models and more traditional approaches are becoming more and more fuzzy. For example, recent dynamic game-theoretic and microeconomic models (Blevins, 2016; Gallant et al., 2016) also entail a framework of a possibly heterogeneous pool of agents interacting in a dynamic setting. Similarly, heterogeneity has been allowed for in standard macroeconomic models in various ways (e.g., Achdou et al., 2015). However, all these approaches are based on inductive solutions of the agents' optimization problem while models that come along with the acronym ABM would typically assume some form of bounded rationality. We stick to this convention and mainly confine attention to ABMs with some kind of boundedly rational behavior. Notwithstanding this confinement, models with a multiplicity of rational agents might give rise to similar problems and solutions when it comes to their empirical validation.

Being boundedly rational agents ourselves, this chapter no doubt suffers from the heuristics we have applied in building a structure and selecting papers. As such, this review should not be seen as an exhaustive overview of the existing literature, but rather as our idiosyncratic view of it. The remainder of the chapter is organized as follows. In Section 2 we discuss which insights economists can gain from other fields when it comes to estimation of ABMs. Whereas Section 3 discusses reduced form models, Section 4 reviews the empirical methods employed in estimation of more general variants of agent-based models. It also proposes a new avenue for estimation by means of state-space methods, which have not been applied in agent-based models in economics and finance so far. Section 5 discusses the empirical evidence for ABMs along different types of data at both the individual and the aggregate level that can be used to validate agent-based models. Section 6, finally, concludes and offers our view on the future of the field.

2 ESTIMATION OF AGENT-BASED MODELS IN OTHER FIELDS

The social sciences seem to be the field predestined for the analysis of individual actors and the collective behavior of groups of them. However, agent-based modeling is not strictly confined to subjects dealing with humans, as one could, for example, also conceive of the animals or plants of one species as agents, or of different species within an ecological system. Indeed, biology is one field in which a number of potentially relevant contributions for the subject of this review can be found. Before we move on to such material, we first provide an overview over agent-based models and attempts at their validation in social sciences other than economics.

2.1 SOCIOLOGY

Sociology by its very nature concerns itself with the effects of interactions of humans. In contrast to economics, there has never been a tradition like that of the 'representative agent' in this field. Hence, interaction among agents is key to most theories of social processes. The adaptation of agent-based models on a relatively large scale coincided with a more computational approach that has appeared over the last decades. Many of the contributions published in the *Journal of Mathematical Sociology* (founded in 1971) can be characterized as agent-based models of social interactions, and the same applies to the contributions to *Social Networks* (founded in 1979). The legacy of seminal contributions partly overlaps with those considered milestones of agent-based research in economic circles as well, e.g. Schelling's model of the involuntary dynamics of segregation processes among ethnic groups (Schelling, 1971), and Axelrod's analysis of the evolution of cooperation in repeated plays of prisoners" dilemmas (Axelrod, 1984). Macy and Willer (2002) provide a comprehensive overview over the use of agent-based models and their insights in sociological research. More recently, Bruch and Atwell (2015) and Thiele et al. (2014) discuss strategies for validation of agent-based models.

These reviews not only cover contributions in sociology alone, but also provide details on estimation algorithms applied in ecological models as well as systematic designs for confrontation of complex simulation models with data (of which agent-based models are a subset). A systematic approach to estimation of an interesting class of agent-based models has been developed in network theory. The pertinent class of models has been labeled 'Stochastic Actor-Oriented Models' (SAOM). It formalizes individuals' decisions to form and dissolve links to other agents within a network setting. This framework bears close similarity to models of discrete choice with social interactions in economics (Brock and Durlauf, 2001a, 2001b). The decision to form, keep or give up a link is necessarily of discrete nature. Similar to discrete choice models, the probabilities for agents to change from one state to another are formalized by multinomial logit expressions. This also allows the interpretation that the agents' objective functions contain a random idiosyncratic term following an extreme value distribution. The objective function naturally is a function evaluating the actor's satisfaction with her current position in the network. This 'evaluation function' is, in principle, completely flexible and allows for a variety of factors of influence on individuals' evaluation of network ties: actor-specific properties whose relevance can be evaluated by including actor covariates in the empirical analysis (e.g., male/female), dyadic characteristics of pairs of potentially connected agents (e.g., similarity with respect to some covariate), overall network characteristics (e.g., local clustering), as well as time-dependent effects like hysteresis or persistence of existing links or 'habit formation' (e.g., it might be harder to cut a link, the longer it has existed).

Snijders (1996) provides an overview over the SAOM framework. For estimation, various approaches have been developed: Most empirical applications use the method of moments estimator (Snijders, 2001), but recently also a Generalized Method of Moments (GMM) approach has been developed (Amati et al., 2015). Maximum likelihood estimation (Snijders et al., 2010) and Bayesian estimation (Koskinen and Snijders, 2007) are feasible as well. The set-up of the SAOM approach differs from that of discrete choice models in economics in that agents operate in a non-equilibrium setting, while the discrete choice literature usually estimates its models under rational expectations, i.e. assuming agents are operating within an equilibrium configuration correctly taking into account the influence of each agent on all other agents' utility functions. While the SAOM framework does not assume consistency of expectations, one can estimate its parameters under the assumption that the data are obtained from the stationary distribution of the underlying stochastic process. If the model explicitly includes expectations (which is typically not the case in applications in sociology) these should then have become consistent. Recent generalizations include an extension of the decision process by allowing for additional behavioral variables besides the network formation activities of agents (Snijders et al., 2007) and modeling of bipartite networks, i.e. structures consisting of two different types of agents (Koskinen and Edling, 2012). The tailor-made R package SIENA (Snijders, 2017) covers all these possibilities, and has become the work tool for a good part of sociological network research. Economic applications include the analysis of managers' job mobility on the creation of interfirm ties (Checkley and Steglich, 2007), and the analyses of link formation in the interbank money market (Zappa and Zagaglia, 2012; Finger and Lux, 2017). A very similar approach to the estimation of network models of human interactions within the context of development policy can be found in Banerjee et al. (2013).

2.2 BIOLOGY

Agent-based simulation models have found pervasive use in biology, in particular for modeling of population dynamics and ecological processes. The range of methods to be found in these areas tends to be wider than in the social sciences. In particular, various simulation-based methods of inference are widely used that have apparently hardly ever been adopted for validation of ABMs in the social sciences or in economics. Relatively recent reviews can be found in Hartig et al. (2011) and Thiele et al. (2014), who both cover ecological applications along with sociological ones. Methods used for estimation of the parameters of ecological models include Markov Chain Monte Carlo (MCMC), Sequential Monte Carlo (SMC), and particle filters, which are all closely related to each other. In most applications, the underlying model is viewed as a state-space model with one or more unobservable state(s) governed by the agent-based model and a noisy observation that allows indirect inference on the underlying states together with the estimation of the parameters of the pertinent model. In a linear, Gaussian framework for both the dynamics of the hidden state and the observation, such an inference problem can be solved most efficiently with the Kalman filter. In the presence of nonlinearities and non-Gaussianity, alternative, mostly simulation-based methods need to be used. An agent-based model governing the hidden states by its very nature typically is a highly nonlinear and non-Gaussian process, and often can only be implemented by simulating its defining microscopic laws of motion. The simulation-based methods mentioned above would then allow to numerically approximate the likelihood function (or if not available, any other objective function) via some population-based evolutionary process for the parameters and states, in which the simulation of the ABM itself is embedded.

Markov Chain Monte Carlo samples the distribution of the model's parameters within an iterative algorithm in which the next step depends on the likelihood of the previous one. In each iteration, a proposal for the parameters is computed via a Markov Chain, and the proposal is accepted with a probability that depends on its relative likelihood vis-à-vis the previous draws and their relative probabilities to be drawn in the Markov chain. After a certain transient this chain should converge to the stationary distribution of the parameters allowing to infer their expectations and standard errors. In *Sequential Monte Carlo*, it is not one realization of parameters, but a set of sampled realizations that are propagated through a number of intermediate steps to the final approximation of the stationary distribution of the parameters (cf. Hartig et al., 2011). In an agent-based (or population-based) framework, the simulation of the unobservable part (the agent-based part) is often embedded via a so-called *particle filter* in the MCMC or SMC framework. Proposed first by Gorden et al. (1993) and Kitagawa (1996), the particle filter approximates the likelihood of a state-space model by a swarm of 'particles' (possible realizations of the state) that are propagated through the state and observation parts of the system. Approximating the likelihood by the discrete probability function summarizing the likelihood of the particles, one can perform either classical inference or use the approximations of the likelihood as input in a Bayesian MCMC or SMC approach.

Advanced particle methods use particles simultaneously for the state and the parameters (Kitagawa, 1998). With the augmented state vector, filtering and estimation would be executed at the same time, and the surviving particles of the parameters at the end of one run of this so-called 'auxiliary' particle filter would be interpreted as parameter estimates. Instructive examples from a relatively large pertinent literature in ecology include Golightly and Wilkinson (2011), who estimate the parameters of partly observed predator-prey systems via Markov Chain Monte Carlo together with a particle filter of the state dynamics, or Ionides et al. (2006), who apply frequentist maximum likelihood based on a particle filter to epidemiological data. MCMC methods have also been applied for rigorous estimation of the parameters of traffic network models, cf. Molina et al. (2005). An interesting recent development is Approximate Bayesian Computation (ABC) that allows inference based on MCMC and SMC algorithms using objective functions other than the likelihood (Sisson et al., 2005; Toni et al., 2008). Since it is likely that for ABMs of a certain complexity, it will not be straightforward to evaluate the likelihood function, these methods should provide a welcome addition to the available toolbox.

2.3 OTHER FIELDS

Agent-based models can be viewed as a subset of 'computer models', i.e., models with an ensemble of mathematical regularities that can only be implemented numerically. Such models might not have units that can be represented as agents, but might take the form of large systems of complex (partial) differential equations. Examples are various models of industrial processes (cf. Bayarri et al., 2007), or the fluid dynamical systems used in climate change models (Stephenson et al., 2012). In biology, one might, in fact, sometimes have the choice to use an agent-based representation of a certain model, or rather a macroscopic approximation using, for example, a low-dimensional system of differential equations (cf. Golightly et al., 2015, for such an approach in an ecological model). Similar approximation of agent-based models in economics can be found in Lux (2009a, 2009b, 2012). The same choice might be available for other agent-based models in economics or finance (see below Section 4.3). In macroeconomics, dynamic stochastic general equilibrium (DSGE) models are medium-sized systems of non-linear difference equations that have also been estimated in recent literature via Markov Chain Monte Carlo and related methods (e.g., Amisano and Tristani, 2010).

In climate modeling, epidemics (Epstein, 2009), and industrial applications (Bayarri et al., 2007), models have become so complex that an estimation of the complete model often becomes unfeasible. The same applies to computational models in anthropology such as the well-known model of Anasazi settlement dynamics in northeastern Arizona (Axtell et al., 2002). The complexity of such models also implies that only a limited number of scenarios can be simulated and that different models can at best be compared indirectly. The epistemological consequences of this scenario are intensively discussed in climate change research as well as in the social sciences (cf. Carley and Louie, 2008). In the context of very complex models and/or sparse data, empirical validation is often interpreted in a broader sense than estimation proper. Aiming to replicate key regularities of certain data is known in ecology as pattern-oriented modeling (cf. Grimm et al., 2005). This is equivalent to what one would call 'matching the stylized facts' in economics. As far as patterns can be summarized as functions of the data and a simulated agent-based model could be replicated without too much computational effort, a more rigorous version of pattern-oriented modeling would consist in a method-of-moments approach based upon the relevant patterns. However, even if only a small number of simulations of a complex simulation model can be run, estimation of parameters through rigorous exploitation of the (scarce) available information is possible. Within the framework of industrial applications and epidemiological dynamics, Bayarri et al. (2007), Higdon et al. (2008), and Wang et al. (2009) provide a systematic framework for a Bayesian estimation approach that corrects the biases and assesses the uncertainties inherent in large simulation models that can neither be replicated often nor selectively modified. In the analysis of complex models of which only a few replications are available often so-called emulation methods are adopted to construct a complete response of model output on parameters. Typically, emulator functions make use of Gaussian processes and principal component analysis (e.g., Hooten and Wikle, 2010; Heard, 2014; Rasouli and Timmermans, 2013). One might envisage that such a framework could also be useful for macroeconomics once agent-based models of various economic spheres are combined into larger models.

3 REDUCED FORM MODELS

The literature on agent-based models was initially purely theoretical in nature. As such, the benchmark models did not take the restrictions into account that empirical applications require. A number of issues in the theoretical models need to be addressed before the models can be confronted with empirical data, especially when focusing on market level studies. One direction is to use advanced econometric techniques, which we will discuss in Section 4. Another direction is to rewrite the model in a reduced form. Bringing HAMs to the data introduces a trade-off between the degree of micro-foundation of the (empirical) model and the appropriateness of the model for estimation. A first choice is the form of the dependent (endogenous) variable. Several models, such as, for example, Day and Huang (1990) and Brock and Hommes (1997), are written in terms of price levels. This poses no problems in an analytical or simulation setting, but could become problematic when turning to calibration or estimation. Most standard econometric techniques assume that the input data is stationary. This assumption, however, is typically violated when using financial prices or macroeconomic time series.

The second issue is the identification of coefficients. The theoretical models contain coefficients that might not all be identified econometrically, which means that one could not obtain an estimate of all the behavioral parameters of a model but that, for instance, only composite expressions of the primitive parameters can be estimated. A third issue relates to the switching mechanism that is typically applied in HAMs. Allowing agents to switch between strategies is, perhaps, the identifying characteristic of HAMs and an important source of dynamics in simulation settings. At the same time it poses a challenge for empirical work, as the switching function is by definition non-linear which could create a non-monotonic likelihood surface.

A final issue we want to discuss here, is the choice of the fundamental value in asset-pricing applications. The notion of a fundamental value is intuitively appealing and central to the behavior of 'fundamentalists' in HAMs. Empirically, though, the 'true' fundamental value is principally unobservable. As there is no objective choice for the fundamental value, any estimation of a model including a fundamental value will therefore inevitably suffer from the 'joint hypothesis problem', cf. Fama (1991). We will discuss these four issues in more detail in the following subsections.

3.1 CHOICE OF DEPENDENT VARIABLE

Whereas several HAMs are principally written in terms of price levels, empirical studies using market data are hardly ever based on price levels due to the non-stationarity issue. Possible solutions to this issue include working with alternative econometric methods, such as, e.g., cointegration techniques (Amilon, 2008; Frijns and Zwinkels, 2016a, 2016b) or simulation techniques (Franke, 2009; Franke and Westerhoff, 2011), but the more typical solution is to reformulate the original model such that the left hand side variable is stationary.

Two main approaches consist of empirical models in terms of returns, $\Delta P_t = P_t - P_{t-1}$ with P_t the asset price at time t, and empirical models in terms of price deviation from the fundamental, $P_t - P_t^*$. The choice between the two is driven by the underlying HAM, or more specifically its micro-foundation and market clearing mechanism.[1] Micro-founded equilibrium models based on a Walrasian auctioneer, such as Brock and Hommes (1997, 1998), assume the existence of an all-knowing auctioneer who collects all supply and demand schedules and calculates the market clearing price. These models are typically written in terms of price levels. It is not possible to convert these into price changes because prices are modeled as a non-linear function of lagged prices. Disequilibrium models based on the notion of a market maker, see Beja and Goldman (1980), Day and Huang (1990), or Chiarella (1992) for early examples, assume that net demand (supply) causes prices to increase (decrease) proportionally, without assuming market clearing. These models are typically written in terms of price changes or are easily reformulated as such.[2]

---

[1] See Hommes (2006) for a more in-depth discussion about different forms of market clearing in HAMs.
[2] Note that time series of price changes are not necessarily stationary because price levels can have different orders of magnitude if the sample period is long enough. As such, an empirical model based on returns or

The most widely applied configuration is the model with a market maker in terms of price changes or returns (see e.g. Frankel and Froot, 1990; Reitz and Westerhoff, 2003; Reitz et al., 2006; Manzan and Westerhoff, 2007; De Jong et al., 2009, 2010; Kouwenberg and Zwinkels, 2014, 2015). The empirical models are typically of the form:

$$\Delta P_t = c + w_t^f \alpha (P_{t-1} - P_{t-1}^*) + w_t^c \beta \Delta P_{t-1} + \varepsilon_t \tag{1}$$

in which w_t^f and w_t^c are the fundamentalist and chartist weights, respectively, ε_t is the noise factor and c, α, and β are the coefficients to be estimated. Given that both the left hand and right hand side variables are denoted in differences, the stationarity issue is largely extenuated. At the same time, there is no (explicit) micro-foundation in the sense of a utility or profit maximizing framework that motivates the behavior of the two groups of agents in this model.

In a series of papers, Alfarano et al. (2005, 2006, 2007) set up a HAM with trading among speculators and a market maker that results in a dynamic process for log returns. They derive a closed-form solution for the distribution of returns that is conditional on the structural parameters of the model and estimate these parameters via an approximate maximum likelihood approach. In a follow-up study, Alfarano et al. (2008) derive closed form solutions to the higher moments of the distribution.

The second approach is to write the model in terms of price deviations from the fundamental value, $x_t = P_t - P_t^*$, or a variant thereof. The implicit assumption that is made, is that the price and fundamental price are cointegrated with cointegrating vector $(1, -1)$, such that the simple difference between the two is stationary.[3] One example of this approach is Boswijk et al. (2007), who initially base their study on the Brock and Hommes (1998) model in terms of price levels:

$$P_t = \frac{1}{1+r} \sum_{h=1}^{H} n_{h,t} E_{h,t}(P_{t+1} + y_{t+1}), \tag{2}$$

with $E_{h,t}(\cdot)$ denoting the expectation of agents of group h, $n_{h,t}$ their number at time t, y_t the dividend and r the risk-free interest rate. Dividing the left and right-hand side of Eq. (1) by dividend y_t and assuming that $y_{t+1} = (1+g)y_t$, Eq. (2) can be written in terms of price-to-cash flow

$$\delta_t = \frac{1}{R^*}\{1 + \sum_{h=1}^{H} n_{h,t} E_{h,t}(\delta_{t+1})\} \tag{3}$$

in which $\delta = P_t/y_t$ and $R^* = (1+g)/(1+r)$. Assuming a fundamental value based on the Gordon growth model, the fundamental is given by $P_t^* = \frac{1+g}{r-g} y_t$, such that

---

log price changes would technically speaking be the preferred solution. It remains challenging, however, to have a micro-founded model that lends to a formalization in terms of log-prices.

[3] This is not a very restrictive assumption, as this is a characteristic one would expect from a properly chosen fundamental value estimate.

the fundamental price-to-cash-flow ratio is given by $\delta_t^* = \frac{1+g}{r-g}$. Finally, Boswijk et al. (2007) use $x_t = \delta_t - \delta_t^*$ as the input to their empirical model. This approach has been applied, among others, by Chiarella et al. (2014).

Clearly, the choice of model has consequences on the results but also on the interpretation of the results. The deviation type models assume that x_t is the variable that investors form expectations about, whereas the return type models assume that ΔP_t is the variable that investors form expectations about. Theoretically these should be equivalent, but we know from social psychology that people respond differently to such different representations of the same information. For example, Glaser et al. (2007) find in an experimental study that price forecasts tend to have a stronger mean reversion pattern than return forecasts. Furthermore, in the deviation type models the two groups of agents rely on the same type of information, namely x_{t-1} or last period's price deviation. Fundamentalism and chartism are subsequently distinguished by the coefficients in the expectations function, in which a coefficient > 1 (< 1) implies chartism (fundamentalism). This interpretation, however, is not exactly the same as with the original models of fundamentalists and chartists because chartists do not expect a price *trend* to continue but rather expect the price deviation from fundamental to increase. Furthermore, this setup is rather restrictive in that it does not allow for the inclusion of additional trader types. In the return based models, on the other hand, agents use different information sets as indicated in Eq. (1). This allows for more flexibility as any trader type can be added to the system. De Jong et al. (2009), for example, include a third group of agents to their model, internationalists, next to fundamentalists and chartists.

There is also an important econometric difference between the deviation and return type models. In the deviation type models, the two groups are not identified under the null of no switching because both rely exclusively on x_{t-1} as information; the switching parameter is a nuisance parameter; see Teräsvirta (1994). As a result, the statistical added value of switching is to be determined using a bootstrap procedure. In the return-based models, however, this issue does not hold as both groups remain identified under the null of no switching, and the added value of switching is therefore determined by means of standard goodness-of-fit comparisons.[4]

3.2 IDENTIFICATION

The original HAMs have a relatively large number of parameters, which might not all be identified in an estimation setting. As a result, the econometrician will have to make one or more simplifying assumptions such that all parameters are identified. As in the previous subsection, here we can also make the distinction between models based on a Walrasian auctioneer and models based on a market maker.

---

[4]The exact goodness-of-fit test is conditional on the estimation method.

Brock and Hommes (1997) build their model using mean-variance utility functions, resulting in a demand function of group h of the form

$$z_{ht} = \frac{E_{ht}(P_{t+1} + y_{t+1} - RP_t)}{a_h \sigma^2} \tag{4}$$

in which $R = 1 + r$, a is the coefficient of risk aversion, and σ market volatility. Now assume a very simple structure of the expectation formation rule:

$$E_{ht}(P_{t+1} + y_{t+1} - RP_t) = \alpha_h(P_{t-1} + y_{t-1} - RP_{t-2}) \tag{5}$$

such that

$$z_{ht} = \frac{\alpha_h(P_{t-1} + y_{t-1} - RP_{t-2})}{a_h \sigma^2}. \tag{6}$$

The empirical issue with such a demand function, is that the coefficients a_h and α_h cannot be distinguished from each other. One solution is to take $\alpha_h' = \alpha_h / a_h \sigma^2$, assuming volatility is constant such that α_h' is also a constant that can be estimated. This assumption, however, is at odds with the initial motivation of HAMs to provide an economic explanation for time-varying volatility. Therefore, the following steps are typically taken. Summing up the demand functions over groups and equating to supply yields the market clearing condition:

$$\Sigma_h n_{ht} \frac{E_{ht}(P_{t+1} + y_{t+1} - RP_t)}{a_h \sigma^2} = z_{st} \tag{7}$$

in which n_{ht} is the proportion of agents in group h in period t, and z_{st} is the supply of the asset. Brock and Hommes (1997) subsequently assume a zero outside supply of stocks, $z_{st} = 0$, such that

$$RP_t = \Sigma_h n_{ht} E_{ht}(P_{t+1} + y_{t+1}). \tag{8}$$

In other words, by assuming zero outside supply, the risk aversion coefficients a_n drop out of the equation and agents effectively become risk neutral provided all groups h are characterized by the same degree of risk aversion (so that groups only differ in their prediction of future price movements). This step eliminates the identification issue, but also reduces the impact of agent's preferences on their behavior. As an alternative avenue, Hommes et al. (2005a, 2005b) introduce a market maker who adjusts the price in the presence of excess demand or excess supply.

In a setting with a market maker, authors typically start by specifying demand functions of the form

$$\begin{aligned} D_t^f &= \alpha^f(P_t - P_t^*), \\ D_t^c &= \alpha^c(P_t - P_{t-1}) \end{aligned} \tag{9}$$

with superscripts f and c denoting the pertinent reaction coefficients of fundamentalists and chartists, respectively. Note that these are already simplified in the sense that risk preference is not taken into account. This either implies that agents are risk neutral, or that α^f and α^c can be interpreted broader as coefficients capturing both the expectation part and a risk adjustment part, $\alpha^f = \alpha^{f'}/a\sigma$. This works again under the assumption that volatility σ is constant.

Aggregating demand of the two groups yields market demand:

$$D_t^m = n_t^f D_t^f + n_t^c D_t^c \tag{10}$$

such that the price equation is given by

$$P_t = P_{t-1} + \lambda D_t^m + \varepsilon_t \tag{11}$$

in which λ is the market maker reaction coefficient, and ε_t is a stochastic disturbance.

In this setting, the market maker reaction coefficient λ is empirically not identifiable independently of α^f and α^c. Two solutions to this issue have been proposed. Either one assumes that $\lambda = 1$ such that the estimated coefficient equals α^h, or one interprets the estimated coefficient as a market impact factor, equal to $\alpha^h \lambda$. Both solutions entail that both groups have the same price elasticity of demand.

Both solutions described here result in extremely simple models of price formation. They do, however, capture the main behavioral elements of HAMs: boundedly rational expectation formation by heterogeneous agents, consistent with empirical evidence, combined with the ability to switch between groups. In addition, simulation exercises also illustrate that certain variants of these models are still able to generate some of the main stylized facts of financial markets, such as their excess volatility and the emergence and breakdown of speculative bubbles (Day and Huang, 1990; Chiarella, 1992). The ABM character underlying these empirical models essentially represents an economic underpinning of time-varying coefficients in an otherwise quite standard econometric model capturing conditional trends and mean-reversion.

3.3 SWITCHING MECHANISM

One of the main issues in estimating ABMs follows from the non-linear nature of the model that (mainly) arises from the existence of the mechanism that governs the switching between beliefs. As a result, the likelihood surface tends to be rugged making it challenging to find a global optimum. This issue has been explored either directly or indirectly by a number of papers. Several approaches have been used.

As an early example, Shiller (1984) introduces a model with rational smart money traders and ordinary investors and shows that the proportion of smart money traders varies considerably during the 1900–1983 period by assuming the aggregate effect of ordinary investors to be zero. Frankel and Froot (1986, 1990) have a very similar approach. Specifically, Frankel and Froot (1986) assume that market-wide expected returns are equal to the weighted average of fundamentalist and chartist expectations:

$$\Delta s_{t+1}^m = \omega_t \Delta s_{t+1}^f + (1 - \omega_t) \Delta s_{t+1}^c \tag{12}$$

with Δs_{t+1}^m, Δs_{t+1}^f and Δs_{t+1}^c denoting the expected exchange rate changes of the overall 'market', of the fundamentalist group and of the chartist group, respectively, and w_t being the weight assigned by 'the market' to the fundamentalist forecast.[5]

By assuming that chartists expect a zero return, we get

$$\omega_t = \frac{\Delta s_{t+1}^m}{\Delta s_{t+1}^f}. \tag{13}$$

Frankel and Froot (1990) subsequently proxy Δs_{t+1}^m by the forward discount, and Δs_{t+1}^f by survey expectations. In this way, they implicitly back out the time-varying fundamentalist weight ω_t from the data. Apart from making some strong assumptions about agent behavior, this method identifies the time-varying impact of agent groups, but does not identify the drivers of this time-variation.

Reitz and Westerhoff (2003) and Reitz et al. (2006) estimate a model of chartists and fundamentalists for exchange rates by assuming the weight of technical traders to be constant, and the weight of fundamental traders to depend on the normalized misalignment between the market and fundamental price. As such, there is no formal switching between forecasting rules, but the impact of fundamentalists is time-varying. Manzan and Westerhoff (2007) introduce time-variation in the chartist extrapolation coefficient by making it conditional on the current mispricing. Hence, the authors are capturing a driver of dynamic behavior, but do not estimate a full-fledged switching mechanism with switching between groups.

Another approach uses stochastic switching functions to capture dynamic behavior, such as regime-switching models (Vigfusson, 1997; Ahrens and Reitz, 2005; Chiarella et al., 2012) and state-space models (Baak, 1999; Chavas, 2000). The advantage of this approach relative to the deterministic switching mechanism that is typically applied in HAMs is that it puts less structure on the switching mechanism and thereby on the data. Furthermore, there is ample econometric literature studying the characteristics of such models. The drawback is that the estimated model weights have no economic interpretation as is the case for the deterministic switching functions. In other words, the stochastic switching models are able to infer from the data that agents switch between groups, but do not allow to draw inference about the motivation behind switching.[6]

Boswijk et al. (2007) is the first study that estimates a HAM with a deterministic switching mechanism that captures switching between groups as well as the motivation behind switching (in this case, the profit difference between groups). While

---

[5]The superscript m for 'the market' here is different from the one in Eq. (11) denoting a market maker. In Frankel and Froot's approach this rather refers to the portfolio managers or foreign exchange dealers responsible for international investments to whom the fundamentalist and chartist forecasts provide consultancy services. Upon past experience of their performance, the investors decide about the weights they attach to both types of forecasts.

[6]Other econometric techniques that have not yet been applied but which could be interesting include generalized autoregressive score (GAS) models, see Creal et al. (2008).

Boswijk et al. (2007) use U.S. stock market data, De Jong et al. (2009) apply a similar methodology to the British Pound during the EMS crisis and the Asian crisis, respectively. Alfarano et al. (2005) set up an empirical model based on Kirman (1993). In this model, switching is based on social interaction and herding rather than profitability considerations. Alfarano et al. (2005) show that in this model the tail behavior of the distributions of returns is a function of the herding tendency of agents.

Boswijk et al. (2007) rewrite the model of Brock and Hommes (1997) such that it simplifies to a standard smooth transition auto-regressive (STAR) model, in which the endogenous variable is the deviation of the price-earnings ratio from its long-run average and the switching function is a logit function of the form

$$w_t^f = \frac{\exp(\beta \pi_{t-1}^f)}{\exp(\beta \pi_{t-1}^f) + \exp(\beta \pi_{t-1}^c)} \tag{14}$$

in which π^f and π^c are measures of fundamentalists' and chartists' performance, respectively.

In this setup, the coefficient β captures the switching behavior of agents, or their sensitivity to performance differences, and is typically denoted the intensity of choice parameter. With $\beta = 0$, agents are not sensitive to differences in performance between groups and remain within their group with probability 1. With $\beta > 0$, agents are sensitive to performance differences. In the limit, as β tends to infinity, agents switch to the most profitable group with probability 1 such that $w_t^f \in \{0, 1\}$.

The significance of β in this configuration cannot be judged based on standard t-tests as it enters the expression non-linearly. Specifically, for β sufficiently large or sufficiently small, additional changes in β will not result in changes in w_t^f. As such, the standard errors of the estimated β will be inflated. To judge the significance of switching, one therefore needs to examine the model fit.

A second issue with this functional form is that the magnitude of β cannot be compared across markets or time periods. This is caused by the fact that its order of magnitude depends on the exact definition and the distributional characteristics of π_t^f. One way to address this issue, is to introduce normalized (unit-free) performance measures in a logit switching function, as first done in Ter Ellen and Zwinkels (2010):

$$w_t^f = \frac{1}{1 + \exp\left(\beta \left(\frac{\pi_{t-1}^c - \pi_{t-1}^f}{\pi_{t-1}^c + \pi_{t-1}^f}\right)\right)}. \tag{15}$$

The additional benefit of this form is that the distribution of profit differences is less heavy-tailed, causing the estimation to be more precise and less sensitive to periods of high volatility.

Baur and Glover (2014) estimate a model for the gold market with chartists and fundamentalist who switch strategies according to their past performance. They find a significant improvement of fit against a benchmark model without such switching of strategies, but very different estimated parameters in different subsamples of the data. They also compare this analysis with switching depending on selected market statistics and find similar results for the parameters characterizing chartists' and fundamentalists' expectation formation under both scenarios.

3.4 FUNDAMENTAL VALUE ESTIMATE

Whereas the fundamentalist–chartist distinction in HAMs is intuitively appealing and consistent with empirical observation,[7] the exact functional form of the two groups is less straightforward. Chartism is typically modeled using some form of expectation of auto-correlation in returns, which is consistent with the empirical results of Cutler et al. (1991), who find autocorrelation in the returns of a broad set of assets, and it is also consistent with the tendency of people to erroneously identify trends in random data.[8] Fundamentalism is typically modeled as expected mean reversion towards the fundamental value. The main question is, though, what this fundamental value should be.

There are several theoretical properties any fundamental value should have. Therefore, in analytical or simulation settings it is possible to formulate a reasonable process for the fundamental value. Empirically though, one has to choose a specific model. Note, however, that the fundamental value used in an empirical HAM is not necessarily the actual fundamental value of the asset. HAMs are based on the notion of bounded rationality, and it is therefore internally consistent to also assume this for the ability of fundamentalists to calculate a fundamental value. As such, the choice of fundamental value should be based on the question whether a boundedly rational market participant could reasonably make the same choice. In other words, the fundamental value should also be a heuristic.

A number of studies using equity data, starting with Boswijk et al. (2007), use a simple fundamental value estimate based on the Gordon-growth model or dividend-discount model; see Gordon and Shapiro (1956). The model is given by

$$P_t^* = \frac{1+g}{r-g} y_t \qquad (16)$$

in which y_t is dividend, g is the constant growth rate of dividends, and r is the required return or discount factor.

The advantage of this approach is certainly its simplicity. The drawback is that it does not take time-variation of the discount factor into account, as is common in mainstream asset pricing studies, cf. Cochrane (2001). This causes the fundamental value estimate P_t^* to be rather smooth because the discount factor is assumed constant. As such, models using this fundamental value estimate might attribute

---

[7] See for example Bloomfield and Hales (2002).
[8] See again Bloomfield and Hales (2002).

an excessive amount of price volatility to non-fundamental factors. Hommes and in 't Veld (2017) are the first to address this issue and introduce a stochastic discount factor in HAMs. Specifically, next to the typical Gordon growth model they create a fundamental value estimate based on the Campbell and Cochrane (1999) consumption-habit model. The latter constitutes a typical consumption-based asset pricing model and therefore belongs to a different class of asset pricing models than the endowment based HAMs. The authors find evidence of behavioral heterogeneity, regardless of the underlying fundamental value estimate. Whereas Hommes and in 't Veld (2017) do not fully integrate the two approaches, their paper constitutes an interesting first step towards integrating the two lines of research, which might also help in getting the heterogeneity approach more widely accepted in the mainstream finance and economics literature.[9]

Studies focusing on foreign exchange markets typically use the Purchasing Power Parity (PPP) model as fundamental value estimate; see e.g. Manzan and Westerhoff (2007); Reitz et al. (2006); Goldbaum and Zwinkels (2014). Kouwenberg et al. (2017) illustrate the added value of switching using different fundamental value estimates in a forecasting exercise for foreign exchange rates.

Alternatively, a number of studies circumvent the issue of choosing a particular model to proxy for the fundamental value. In each case, this approach yields a parsimonious proxy for a fundamental value, but also alters the exact interpretation of fundamentalist behavior. Furthermore, the approach is typically quite specific to a certain (institutional) framework and thereby less general. For example, De Jong et al. (2010) make use of the institutional framework of the European Monetary System (EMS), and use the central parity in the target zone regime as the fundamental. Whereas this provides a very clear and visible target, the group of fundamentalists no longer expect mean reversion towards the economic fundamental but expect the current institutional framework to be maintained without adjustments to the central parity.

Ter Ellen and Zwinkels (2010) use a moving average of the price level as fundamental value estimate. Whereas this is again a very parsimonious approach, the nature of fundamentalists in such a setup moves towards chartism as all expectations are based on market information. More recently, Frijns and Zwinkels (2016a, 2016b) have taken advantage of the fact that assets trade on multiple markets in formulating a fundamental value. Specifically, they use cross-listed stocks and the spot and derivatives markets, respectively. This changes the exact interpretation of fundamentalists towards arbitrageurs, but retains the stabilizing character of this particular group of market participants relative to the destabilizing chartists.

As we will see in the next section, the necessity of specifying the time development of the underlying fundamental value only applies to reduced-form models. When using a more general approach, it often suffices to assume a general law of

---

[9]In fact, the HAM literature in general has paid relatively little attention to the form of the utility function. All dynamics are generated from the beliefs side. There is certainly scope for further research here.

motion of the fundamental value (e.g., Brownian motion). Estimation would, then, allow to identify, for instance, the variance of the innovations of the fundamental value along with the parameters of the agent-based part of the overall model. If the pertinent methodology allows filtering to retrieve unobserved variables, this would also provide an estimated trajectory of the fundamental value as the residual obtained by filtering the empirical data (raw prices or returns) by the behavioral component implied by the ABM. Note that such an approach is very different from the a priori specification of a plausible fundamental dynamic process in the models reviewed above.

4 ESTIMATION METHODS
4.1 MAXIMUM LIKELIHOOD
4.1.1 General Considerations

By the very nature of agent-based models, maximum likelihood (ML) estimation without any numerical approximation will rarely be possible. Such a completely standard approach will indeed only be possible if the ABM can be represented by a reduced-form equation or a system of equations (e.g., a VAR structure) for which a standard ML estimation approach is available. Examples of such models have been covered in the previous section. Any such statistically convenient framework will be based upon relatively strong assumptions on the behavior of the underlying pool of agents. For instance, in order to end up with a reduced form that is equivalent to a (linear) regime-switching model (e.g. Reitz and Westerhoff, 2003), one has to assume that (i) two different groups of agents with two different linear demand functions exist, (ii) all the agents of one group are characterized by the same elasticities, (iii) markets are always dominated by one of the groups, and (iv) there is a unique (Gaussian) noise factor in each of these regimes. Condition (i) might be relaxed by having a less stringent microstructure based on a market-maker; condition (iii) might be relaxed by allowing for smooth transition models in the statistical implementation of the switching of strategies of agents along some discrete choice formalization.

Still, to be able to derive some simple macroscopic structural form of the agents' aggregate behavior, the stochastic factors have to be conceived a-priori as an additive noise superimposed on the agents' interaction. If, in principle, the agents' behavior is conceived to be of a stochastic nature (reflecting the inability of any model to completely cover all their motivations and idiosyncratic determinants of their behavior), this amounts to evoking the law of large numbers and resorting to the deterministic limiting process for an infinite number of agents in the population.

Maintaining the randomness of individual decisions as via a discrete choice formalization with a finite population would render the noise component of the model much more complicated: The noise would now consist of the set of all the stochastic factors entering the decision of all the agents in the model, i.e. with N agents the model would contain N stochastic processes rather than a single one as in typical structural equations. It is worthwhile to note that for typical candidates of the stochastic utility term in discrete choice models, like the Gumbel distribution, theoretical aggregation results are not available. Aggregation of individual decisions might also be hampered by correlation of their choices if social interactions are an important factor in the agents' decision process.

4.1.2 Maximum Likelihood Based on Numerical Integration

Full maximum likelihood for models with dispersed activity of an ensemble of agents would, in principle, require availability of closed-form solutions for the transient density of the process. Due to the complexity of most ABMs, such information will hardly ever be available. However, certain systems allow at least numerical approximations of the transient density that can be used for evaluation of the likelihood function. Lux (2009a) applies such a numerical approach to estimate a simple model of opinion formation for survey data of a business climate index. The underlying model assumes that agents switch between a pessimistic and optimistic expectation for the prospects of their economy under the influence of the opinion of their peers as well as exogenous factors (information about macroeconomic variables). For this model of social interaction, the transient density of the average opinion can be approximated via the so-called Fokker–Planck or forward Kolmogorov equation. The latter cannot be solved in closed form. However, as it is a partial differential equation, many well-known methods exist to integrate it numerically. It thus becomes possible to use a numerical ML estimator. Application to a business climate index for the German economy shows strong evidence of social interaction (herding), a significant momentum effect besides the baseline interaction and very limited explanatory power of exogenous economic variables.

This framework can, in principle, be generalized to more complex models with more than one dynamic process. Lux (2012) applies this approach to bivariate and trivariate processes. Here the underlying data consists of two sentiment surveys for the German stock market, short-run and medium-run sentiment, and the price of the DAX. The model allows for two interlinked opinion formation processes plus the dynamics of the stock index that might be driven by sentiment along with fundamental factors. Combining pairs of these three processes or all three simultaneously, the transient dynamics can again be approximately described by a (bivariate or trivariate) Fokker–Planck equation. These partial differential equations can again be solved numerically, albeit with much higher computational demands than in the univariate case. As it turns out, social interaction is much more pronounced in short-run than medium-run sentiment. It also turns out that both sentiment measures have little interaction (although they are obtained from the same ensemble of participants). The price dynamics show a significant influence of short-run sentiment which, however, could not be exploited profitably for prediction of stock prices in an out-of-sample forecasting exercise.

4.1.3 Approximate Maximum Likelihood[10]

When full maximum likelihood is not possible, various approximate likelihood approaches might still be feasible. For example, Alfarano et al. (2005) apply maximum likelihood based upon the stationary distribution of a financial market model with social interaction. Results would be close to the exact likelihood case only if the process converges quickly to its stationary distribution. In a similar framework, Kukacka and Barunik (2017) use the non-parametric simulated maximum likelihood estimator of Kristensen and Shin (2012) which uses simulated conditional densities rather than the analytical expressions and is, in principle, universally applicable. They show via Monte Carlo simulations that this approach can reliably estimate the parameters of a strategy-switching model à la Brock and Hommes (1997). They find significant parameters of the expected sign for the fundamentalist and chartist trading strategies for various stock markets, but the 'intensity of choice' parameter turns out to be insignificant which is also found by a number of related studies on similar models.

4.2 MOMENT-BASED ESTIMATORS

4.2.1 General Considerations

A most straightforward way to estimate complex models is the Generalized Method of Moments (GMM) and the Simulated Method of Moments (SMM) approach. The former estimates parameters by matching a weighted average of analytical moments, the later uses simulated moments in cases in which analytical moments are not available. Both GMM and SMM have a long legacy of applications in economics and finance (cf. Mátyás, 1999) and should be flexible enough to also be applicable to agent-based models. However, even this very general approach might have to cope with specific problems when applied to typical agent-based models. One of these is the lack of continuity of many moments when varying certain parameters. To see this, consider an ensemble of agents subject to a discrete choice problem of deciding about the most promising trading strategy at any time, where, for the sake of concreteness, we denote the alternatives again as 'chartism' and 'fundamentalism'. There will be two probabilities $p_{cf}(\cdot)$ and $p_{fc}(\cdot)$ for switching from one alternative to the other, both depending on statistics of the current and past market development. A simple way to simulate such a framework consists of drawing uniform numbers ε_i for each agent i and making this agent switch if $\varepsilon_i < p_{cf}(\cdot)$ or $p_{fc}(\cdot)$ depending on which is applicable.

The important point here is that this type of stochasticity at the level of the individual agent is distinctly different from a standard additive noise at the system level. Even when fixing the sequence of random numbers, any statistics derived from this process will not be smooth under variation of the parameters of the model. Namely,

---

[10]The contributions reviewed in this section use approximations to the likelihood of a model if the latter cannot be expressed in closed form. This is somewhat different from what is usually denoted 'quasi-maximum likelihood'. The latter estimates the parameters of a model by a different, misspecified model to avoid estimating some cumbersome nuisance parameter(s).

if we vary any parameter that enters as a determinant of $p_{cf}(\cdot)$ or $p_{fc}(\cdot)$ and keep the set of random draws constant, there will be a discontinuous move at some point making the agent switch her behavior. The same, of course, applies to all other agents, so that in contrast to a deterministic process with linear noise, a stochastic process with noise at the level of the agent will exhibit in general non-smooth statistics even with "frozen" random draws.

Luckily, this does not necessarily make all standard estimation methods unfeasible. While standard regularity conditions will typically require smoothness of the objective functions, more general sets of conditions can be established that allow for non-smooth and non-differentiable objective functions, cf. Andrews (1993). The more practical problem is that the rugged surface resulting from such a microfounded process would render standard derivative-based optimization routines useless.

Many recent papers on estimation of ABMs in economics have used various methods to match a selection of empirical moments. This should not be too surprising as, particularly in financial economics, the most prominent aim of the development of ABMs has been the explanation of the so-called stylized facts of asset returns. A list of such stylized facts includes (i) absence of autocorrelations in the raw returns at high frequencies or martingale-like behavior, (ii) leptokurtosis of the unconditional distribution of returns, or *fat tails*, (iii) volatility clustering or long-term temporal dependence in squared or absolute returns (or other measures of volatility), (iv) positive correlation between trading volume and volatility, and (v) long-term temporal dependence in volume and related measures of trading activity.

All of these features can be readily characterized by statistical moments of the underlying data, and quantitative measures of 'stylized facts' (i) to (iii) are typically used as the moments one attempts to match in order to estimate the models' parameter. Both in GMM and SMM, parameter estimates are obtained as the arguments of an objective function that consists of weighted deviations between the empirical and model-generated moments. According to our knowledge, stylized facts (iv) and (v) have been used to compare the output of agent-based models to empirical data (e.g., LeBaron, 2001) but have not been exploited so far in full-fetched estimation as all available studies concentrate on univariate series of returns and neglect other market statistics such as volume. Indeed, it even appears unclear whether well-known models that are able to match (i) to (iii) are also capable to explain the long-lasting autocorrelation of volume and its cross-correlation with volatility.

Almost all of the available literature also uses a simulated method of moments approach as the underlying models appear too complex to derive analytical moment conditions. An exception is Ghonghadze and Lux (2016).

4.2.2 Moment-Based Estimation of Structural Models

Within structural equation models Franke (2009) and Franke and Westerhoff (2011, 2012, 2016) have applied SMM estimation to a variety of models and have also conducted goodness-of-fit comparisons across different specifications. All the models considered are formulated in discrete time.

Franke (2009) estimates a model proposed by Manzan and Westerhoff (2007), which combines a market maker dynamics for price adjustments with a standard demand function of fundamentalists and a second group of traders, denoted speculators, who react to stochastic news. The author uses a sample of moments of raw and absolute returns, i.e. their means, autocovariances over various lags, and log absolute returns exceeding a certain threshold as a measure related to the tail index. Since it was found that the correlations between the moment conditions were too noisy, only the diagonal entries of the inverse of the variance–covariance matrix of the moment conditions has been used as weight matrix. Although the usual goodness-of-fit test, the so-called J-test for equality of empirical and model-generated moments, could always reject the model as the true data generating process for a sample of stock indices and exchange rates, the fit of the selected moments was nevertheless considered satisfactory.

Shi and Zheng (2016) consider an interesting variation of the discrete choice framework for switching between a chartist and fundamentalist strategy in which fundamentalists receive heterogeneous news about the change of the fundamental value. A certain fraction of agents then chooses one or the other strategy comparing their pertinent expected profits. In the infinite population limit, analytical expressions can be obtained for the two fractions. The resulting price process is estimated via analytical moments (GMM) from which the usual parameters of the demand functions of both groups and the dispersion of fundamental news relative to the agents' prior can be obtained.

Franke and Westerhoff (2011) estimate what they call a 'structural stochastic volatility model'. This is a model of chartist/fundamentalist dynamics in which both demand functions consist of a systematic deterministic part and a noise factor with different variances for both groups. With an additional switching mechanism between groups this leads to volatility clustering in returns because of the different levels of demand fluctuations brought about by dominance of one or the other group. In their SMM estimation the authors use a weighting matrix obtained from bootstrapping the variability of the empirical moments. Results were again somewhat mixed: While the model could well reproduce the selected moments, the authors found that for two out of six parameters it could not be rejected that they were equal to zero in the application of the model to the US dollar–Deutsche Mark exchange rate series. Note that this implies that certain parts of the model seem to be superfluous (in this case the entire chartist component) and that a more parsimonious specification would probably have to be preferred. In the application to the S&P 500 returns, all parameters were significant. The same applies under a slightly different estimation procedure (Franke and Westerhoff, 2016). In the later paper, the authors also assess the goodness-of-fit of the model via a Monte Carlo analysis (rather than the standard J-test based on asymptotic theory) and found that under this approach, the model could not be rejected.

Franke and Westerhoff (2012), finally, use the SMM approach to conduct a model contest between two alternative formalizations of the chartist/fundamentalist approach: one with switching between strategies based on transition probabilities (the approach of their related papers of 2011 and 2016), and one using a discrete choice framework for the choice of strategy in any period. Further variations are obtained by considering different determinants in these switching or choice probabilities: the development of agents' wealth, herding and the effect of misalignment of asset prices. As it turns out, the discrete choice model with herding component in the fitness function performs best in matching the selected moments of S&P 500 returns.

Somewhat similar in spirit are the recent papers by Grazzini and Richiardi (2015), Lamperti (2015), and Barde (2016). Grazzini and Richiardi use a simulated minimum distance estimator for an agent-based model of price discovery in double auctions. Lamberti (2015) proposes an information-theoretical distance measure. Barde (2016) adopts a similar measure to compare different types of agent-based models. He abstains, however, from direct estimation, but compares the models for a large set of parameter values using the concept of model confidence set (Hansen et al., 2011) to select those models (with pre-specified parameters) that cannot be outperformed by other alternatives at a certain confidence level. As it turns out, the above mentioned model of Franke and Westerhoff (2016) is the one most often represented in the confidence set followed by the model of Alfarano et al. (2008).

4.2.3 Moment-Based Estimation of Models with Explicit Agents

The later is a model that in its original format is not in reduced form but has an ensemble of agents that update their behavior in continuous time. While the agents' aggregate behavior is represented by a Langevin equation in Barde (2016) – and hence the model is transformed into a structural one – Jang (2015) studies simulated method of moments estimation for the same framework on the base of proper micro-simulations. He shows that the objective function is non-smooth (cf. the considerations laid out in Section 4.2.1) and also exhibits very flat areas along various dimensions which makes identification of a global minimum difficult. Jang explores the behavior of the SMM estimator in various ways fixing some parameters, and estimating the remaining ones. He finds certain intervals for some of the parameters in which Hansen's J-test does not reject the model as the 'true' data generating process.

When using a model based upon a proper micro-ensemble of agents, a particular conundrum is the decision about the number of agents. Replicating the market dynamics using the 'true' number of market participants appears out of the question. Since this number is probably in the millions for typical stock and foreign exchange markets of advanced economies, this would impose too high a computational burden on most models. In addition, exact numbers are often not known and might show some variation over time. What is more, practically all models available in the literature would become "uninteresting" with this large number of agents. The reason is that despite being subject to all types of social interaction agents are mostly autonomous in their decisions and with a given intensity of interaction the system will eventually tend to a limiting behavior under a law of large numbers when one increases the number of market participants. Typically the limiting behavior would lead to Gaussian market statistics lacking all the stylized facts of financial returns.

Since the stylized facts appear largely independent of the varying size of different markets, it appears appropriate to design behavioral agent-based models that show robust stylized facts independent of system size. Various avenues to arrive at models that maintain strong coherence of behavior also in large populations are laid out in Aoki (2002), Alfarano et al. (2008), Alfarano and Milakovic (2009), and Irle et al. (2011). Lux (2009a) estimates the system size (number of agents) for macroeconomic survey data of which the number of participants is known, and finds a much smaller (as he calls it) 'effective' system size that he attributes to agents moving in tandem with each other in certain groups. This resonates with the important observation emphasized by Chen (2002) that, in principle, the noise-over-signal ratio of some observable should provide an indication on how many independent contributing factors one should expect in a model explaining its behavior. Indeed, Jang (2015) considers different numbers of agents and finds a monotonic improvement of the goodness-of-fit when increasing the number of agents from 10 to 1000 in his estimation of the Alfarano et al. (2008) model for five foreign exchange rates. In his application, he also finds relatively uniform parameter estimates across markets (assuming $N = 100$), and a contribution of about fifty percent of the agent-based speculative dynamics to the overall volatility of exchange rates.

Ghonghadze and Lux (2016) and Chen and Lux (2016) both continue the line of research initiated by Jang (2015). Ghonghadze and Lux (2016) expand analytical results of Alfarano et al. (2008) to derive a generalized methods of moments estimator, while Chen and Lux use a similar set of moments in an SMM approach. Chen and Lux (2016) come to the conclusion that due to the lack of smoothness of the objective function, a one-time optimization from a given set of initial conditions could lead to almost arbitrary results. Hence, a more systematic exploration of the parameter space is needed. They recommend an extensive grid search followed by an application of a derivative-free optimization method for a range of the best grid values found in the first step. With GMM, more standard optimization routines can be applied, but nevertheless the parameters of the Alfarano et al. (2008) model appear difficult to estimate as there are strong correlations between certain parameters. The system appears near to collinearity and with not too large sample size (say some thousand observations as is typical in financial data) certain sets of parameter values could generate apparently very similar dynamics. Again, a grid search prior to the application of an optimization routine appears useful.

It is also found that very large samples are needed (about 10^5 observations) for SMM to approach the efficiency of GMM. While with sufficiently larger sample sizes, both GMM and SMM estimate the parameters more precisely and show a tendency towards $T^{1/2}$ consistency, in both cases the J-test of goodness-of-fit based on the overidentification restrictions shows severe size distortion. In particular, while the asymptotic χ^2 distribution fits the experimental distribution of the J-test well for a minimal set of moments, it tends to over-accept its null when additional moments are added in the estimation. This behavior stems very likely from the limited added informational content of further moment conditions. This might signal a general problem for GMM/SMM estimation of ABMs in the context of univariate financial data: there are not too many moments one can use in such exercises. Basically, all available studies use some measure of fat-tailedness and clustering of volatility. Adding more moments, one can just add alternative measures (like, e.g., autocovariances over different lags) that are highly correlated with each other.

In the empirical part of their papers, both Chen and Lux (2016) and Ghonghadze and Lux (2016) apply their estimation algorithm to a selection of stock and foreign exchange data as well as the price of gold. Although the estimated parameters are not always very close, overall the results confirm received wisdom: Speculative forces appear stronger in stock markets and the market for gold than in foreign exchange markets. Ghonghadze and Lux (2016) also conduct a forecasting competition between their ABM and a standard GARCH model. While the GARCH has throughout somewhat smaller errors of its volatility forecasts, it turns out that the ABM can add value when combined forecasts from both models are constructed. It is also shown that for medium and long-run horizons (10 to 50 days forecasts) the GARCH model does not 'encompass' the ABM, i.e. the forecasts of the later uses information that is not already covered by the GARCH model (which motivates combining their forecasts).

4.3 AGENT-BASED MODELS AS LATENT VARIABLE MODELS AND RELATED ESTIMATORS

4.3.1 Basic Framework

It has been mentioned in Section 2 that agent-based models of ecological processes have often been framed as state-space or hidden Markov models, and have been estimated by a variety of methods developed for this class of models. Indeed, it appears to us that most models that have been reviewed above can be easily categorized as examples of state-space models or slightly more general latent variable models, so that estimation of ABMs could profit substantially from the rich toolbox developed for such models. As far as we can see, economic ABMs have never been related to the framework of state-space models, with the exception of a recent paper by Grazzini et al. (2017) who, however focus only on Bayesian estimation within such a context and do not emphasize the general proximity of ABMs to state-space models.

In other areas of economics, state-space modeling is more common: For instance, dynamic stochastic general equilibrium (DSGE) models have been estimated with both frequentist and Bayesian methods based upon a state-space representation, cf. Fernández-Villaverde and Rubio-Ramírez (2007), and Amisano and Tristani (2010) for both frequentist and Bayesian methods, as well as the monograph by Herbst and Schorfheide (2016) that focuses completely on Bayesian estimation which has become particularly popular in this area. In financial econometrics, similarly popular areas of applications are stochastic volatility models (e.g. Kim et al., 1998; Carvalho and Lopes, 2007) and Markov-switching models (e.g. Billio and Casarin, 2010). A survey of a range of popular approaches can be found in Lopes and Tsay (2011).

Since state-space modeling seems an important concept in which agent-based models could be nested as a particular subset of cases, we provide here a short introduction together with an illustrative application of important methods for parameter estimation to a prominent ABM. A general state-space model is defined by the stochastic evolution in time of a vector of states, say x_t, and a vector of measurements, say y_t. If x_t follows a general Markov process, the unobserved process for the state vector can be written as

$$x_t = f(x_{t-1}, \varepsilon_t) \tag{17}$$

where ε_t is a summary notation for all stochastic factors that enter into the dynamics of x_t. The vector of observations can be written in a similar general form as

$$y_t = g(x_t, \eta_t) \tag{18}$$

where η_t summarizes all stochastic factors that make the vector of measurements a noisy signal of the states x_t. If Eqs. (17) and (18) are linear systems of equations with Gaussian noises, the optimal approach to parameter estimation and filtering for recovery of the unobserved state vector is the well-known Kalman filter. For nonlinear systems with Gaussian noises, various extensions and approximations to the linear Kalman filter have been developed (see e.g. Grewal and Andrews, 2008). For nonlinear, non-Gaussian state-space models, Markov chain Monte Carlo and particle filter methods have become the state of the art (cf. Doucet et al., 2001).

Many agent-based models can be cast into the framework of Eqs. (17) and (18). Others can be embedded into slightly more general classes of models with latent variables. This basically applies to practically all the ABMs for interaction of heterogeneous investors that we have reviewed in the preceding sections. What distinguishes agent-based models from other state-space models is that Eq. (17) captures some sort of summary statistics of relevant features of the agents averaged over the entire ensemble of actors that is of relevance for the dynamics of the observables y_t, most often asset prices or returns. If the behavior of individual agents is formalized in a stochastic way (taking into account idiosyncratic factors unknown to the modeler), Eq. (17) would not only contain one noise factor for each element of the state vector, but would also be driven by the joint dynamics of agents' changes of behavior and their respective stochastic elements. While we could imagine a state-space formalism in which not a summary measure, but the *exact* features of *each* agent define the vector of states, such a model would presumably be hard or impossible to estimate just because a small number of observed variables would almost surely not contain enough information to track a much larger number of states.

4.3.2 Illustration: A Nonlinear Model of Speculative Dynamics with Two Groups of Agents

We take as an example a simple heterogeneous agent model with two types of traders that has been proposed by Gaunersdorfer and Hommes (2007). In this model, the two types are chartists and fundamentalists, and their demand functions, $z_{c,t}$ and $z_{f,t}$ are particular cases of Eq. (4) of the following form:

$$z_{c,t} = \frac{P_{t-1} + g(P_{t-1} - P_{t-2}) + y - RP_t}{a\sigma^2}$$

$$z_{f,t} = \frac{P_f + v(P_{t-1} - P_f) + y - RP_t}{a\sigma^2} \tag{19}$$

where y is the expected dividend (here assumed to be constant). Risk aversion a and expected variance of price changes, σ^2, are assumed to be the same for both groups, and $R = 1 + r$. Agents' choice of strategy is determined by a discrete-choice approach based upon accumulated profits:

$$U_{h,t} = (P_t + y - RP_{t-1})z_{h,t-1} + \eta U_{h,t-1} \tag{20}$$

for $h = c, t$, with $\eta \in [0, 1]$ a memory parameter for the influence of past profits. Gaunersdorfer and Hommes (2007) assume an infinite population so that the fractions $n_{c,t}$ and $n_{f,t}$ of the two groups within the overall population would be identical to their expectations:

$$n_{h,t} = \frac{\exp(\beta U_{h,t-1})}{\sum_{m=c,f} \exp(\beta U_{m,t-1})} \tag{21}$$

with β the parameter for the *intensity of choice*.

In addition, the authors assume that the fraction of chartists also decreases when the price deviates strongly from its fundamental value so that effectively, the two fractions are given by $\tilde{n}_{c,t}$ and $\tilde{n}_{f,t}$ defined as follows:

$$\tilde{n}_{c,t} = n_{c,t} \exp\left(-\frac{(P_{t-1} - P_f)^2}{\alpha}\right),$$

$$\tilde{n}_{f,t} = 1 - \tilde{n}_{c,t}, \tag{22}$$

with $\alpha > 0$, a constant parameter for the strength of the stabilizing force of the fundamental value. In the stochastic version of the model, a random Gaussian term $u_t \sim N(0, \sigma_u^2)$ is added to the system so that the asset price in a market equilibrium with zero exogenous supply is given by

$$RP_t = \tilde{n}_{c,t} E_{c,t}[P_{t+1} + y] + \tilde{n}_{f,t} E_{f,t}[P_{t+1} + y] + u_t \tag{23}$$

with the expectations given by the first two terms in the numerators of the right-hand sides of Eqs. (19), i.e.

$$E_{c,t}[P_{t+1} + y] = P_{t-1} + g(P_{t-1} - P_{t-2}) + y,$$

$$E_{f,t}[P_{t+1} + y] = P_f + v(P_{t-1} - P_f) + y. \tag{24}$$

Obviously, Eq. (23) is a well-defined equation for the observed variable – the asset price – of this dynamic system. Eqs. (19) through (22) constitute the state dynamics with $\tilde{n}_{c,t}$, and $\tilde{n}_{f,t}$ being unobserved state variables, while P_t is the observable part of the system. In the original model with its assumption of an infinite population this would be a completely deterministic system and, thus, would be a somewhat degenerate case of a state-space system. A case that is more representative of the ABM literature is easily obtained by rather assuming that the population of investors is finite and applying Eqs. (21) and (22) not as deterministic expressions, but to draw binomial random numbers with the pertinent probabilities to independently determine for each agent her choice of strategy at time t. This can simply be achieved by binomial draws with probabilities:

$$Pr(c) = \frac{\exp(\beta U_{c,t-1})}{\exp(\beta U_{c,t-1}) + \exp(\beta U_{f,t-1})} \exp\left(-\frac{(P_{t-1} - P_f)^2}{\alpha}\right)$$

and $\quad Pr(f) = 1 - Pr(c)$ \hfill (25)

with the obvious notation indicating the probability to select the chartist or fundamentalist strategy by $Pr(c)$ and $Pr(f)$, respectively. The stochastic fractions of chartists and fundamentalists generated in this way replace the laws of Eqs. (22) and (23). Eqs. (20) and (25) would then constitute our implementation of the state dynamics which apparently is both highly nonlinear and non-Gaussian. Indeed, in this example the stochastic factors that are symbolized in Eq. (17) by the summary notation ε_t consist of as many stochastic draws as there are agents in the system. However, the state of the system can still be conveniently summarized by the (now stochastic) fractions of chartists and fundamentalists which enter again in the price dynamics as formalized in Eq. (23).

Note that our overall system is of a more general format than the state space formalism introduced in Eqs. (17) and (18). Namely, the unobserved state (here $\tilde{n}_{c,t}$) does not follow an autonomous Markov process but also depends on lagged values of the observation, P_t. In the absence of stochastic factors in the state dynamics, such a process is often characterized as an 'observation-driven process' (cf. Douc et al., 2013). The more general case encountered here would fall under the label of a 'dynamic system with latent variables'. An interesting example from empirical finance with a similar format is a stochastic volatility model with a leverage effect (leading to dependency of the latent volatility process on past realizations of returns, cf. Yu, 2005; Pitt et al., 2014).

The dynamics of the present system is well understood: In particular, for certain parameter values its deterministic 'skeleton' (with $u_t = 0$) is characterized by a locally stable fixed point (with the price equal to the fundamental value) and a limit cycle that also possesses its own domain of attraction. Adding noise of sufficient amplitude, the stochastic system switches repeatedly between these two attractors and the noisy cyclical episodes lead to returns that to some extent show leptokurtosis and volatility clustering (cf. also Lux and Alfarano, 2016). The lower left-hand panel of Fig. 1 exhibits a typical example of the state dynamics (fraction of chartists $n_{c,t}$): Mostly the market is dominated by fundamentalists (namely, when the process is

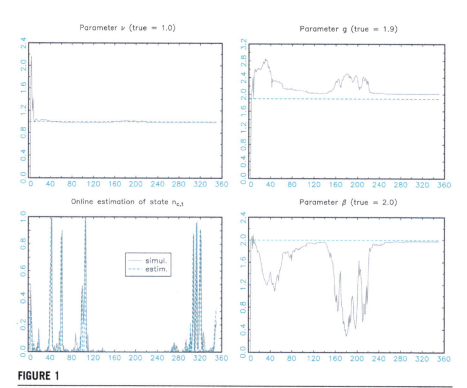

FIGURE 1

Example of on-line estimation via self-organizing state space model. The figure shows the development of the mean of the particle swarm during on-line selection of both the state and the auxiliary particles for a synthetic time series of 1000 observations of asset prices simulated by the model of Gaunersdorfer and Hommes (2007).

close to the fixed point equilibrium), but rapid eruptions of periods with adaption of a chartist strategy by many market participants occur repeatedly (when the stochastic factor drives the dynamics into the domain of the limit cycle).

When bringing such a model to data, one typically would pursue two objectives: (i) estimating the parameters, and (ii) tracking the unobserved state on the base of the observable variables. Moment-based methods (cf. Section 4.2) could be applied for parameter estimation, but they would not provide an avenue for filtering information on unobserved states. Indeed, despite the prominent role of summary variables for agents' states (strategies, expectations, opinions), hardly any attempts have been made in the ABM literature to retrieve information on such unobserved variables.

4.3.3 Estimation of the Model of Gaunersdorfer and Hommes Based on Particle Filter Algorithms

We will now shortly explain how to estimate the parameters and how to track the states of such a highly nonlinear system with dispersed activity via state-space methods. Like many agent-based models, the present framework also has probably too many free parameters, that could not all be estimated at the same time with the limited information available from the price dynamics. We will, therefore, concentrate on four crucial parameters: the reaction parameters of chartists and fundamentalists, g and v, the intensity of choice, β, and the variance σ_u^2 of the noise component of the 'measurement equation' (23). Overall, we adopt the parameters of the simulations conducted by Gaunersdorfer and Hommes (2007): $v = 1.0$, $g = 1.9$, $\beta = 2.0$, $\sigma_u = 10$, $r = 0.001$, $\alpha = 1800$, $a\sigma^2 = 1$, $\eta = 0.99$, $P_f = 1000$, and $y = 1$.

We illustrate the design and performance of Monte Carlo methods developed for state-space models with three basic approaches: (i) frequentist maximum likelihood based on a particle filter, (ii) an evolutionary algorithm known as self-organizing state-space modeling, and (iii) Bayesian sequential Markov chain Monte Carlo. We dispense with many technical details which can be found in the vast statistical literature on this subject and its applications to DSGE models, ecological models as well as in financial econometrics.

Frequentist ML Estimation via a Particle Filter

Denote by $\theta = \{v, g, \beta, \sigma_u\}$ the vector of parameters. The likelihood function with a sample of observations of asset prices P_t, $t = 1, \ldots, T$ is

$$L(P_1, \ldots, P_T | t) = p(P_1 | \theta) \prod_{t=2}^{T} p(P_t | P_{t-1}, \theta) \tag{26}$$

in which in the absence of a closed-form solution for the unconditional density, the first term, $p(P_1 | \theta)$ can be obtained from the simulated stationary distribution on the base of a sufficiently long Monte Carlo simulation of the model. The conditional densities $p(P_t | P_{t-1}, \theta)$ summarize the temporal evolution of the state-space model and can be decomposed as follows:

$$p(P_t | P_{t-1}, \theta) = \int p(P_t | n_{c,t}) P(n_{c,t} | n_{c,t-1}) \, dn_{c,t-1} \tag{27}$$

where we have summarized the state of the latent variables by $n_{c,t}$.

While the first conditional density in the integral can be evaluated analytically in our case (but this need not be so), the second one can only be approximated via simulations.[11] This motivates what has become known as the *particle filter*, i.e. discrete approximation of the terms $p(P_t | P_{t-1}, \theta)$ via a set of 'particles'. The most common approach to particle filtering works as follows[12]:

---

[11] Note that the conditional density of the state process depends not only on $n_{c,t-1}$ but also on $P_{t-1}, P_{t-2}, P_{t-3}$ via Eqs. (19) and (20) which we have skipped for notational convenience. The Markov structure can be easily established by defining: $\hat{P}_t = P_{t-2}$, $\tilde{P}_t = P_{t-1}$.

[12] The application of particle filters goes beyond the realm of state-space and latent variable models. They have, for example, also been successfully applied to large chaotic systems, cf. Lingala et al. (2012).

(i) Initiate a 'swarm' of B particles $n_{c,1}^{(j)}$, $j = 1, \ldots, B$ using random draws from the unconditional distribution $p(n_c, \theta)$. If this is not known, one might simulate the complete state-space system to obtain an approximation of its unconditional density,[13]

(ii) the densities $p(P_1 | n_{c,1}^{(j)}, \theta)$ are computed and the particles are *resampled* using weights $\dfrac{p(P_1 | n_{c,1}^{(j)})}{\sum_m p(P_1 | n_{c,1}^{(m)})}$,

(iii) the resampled swarm is propagated through the state dynamics and the updated states $n_{c,2}^{(j)}$ are obtained,

(iv) steps (ii) and (iii) are repeated for $t = 2, \ldots, T$.

In this way, we obtain an approximation of the likelihood function

$$L(P_1, \ldots, P_T | \theta) \approx \prod_{t=1}^{T} \frac{1}{N} \sum_{j=1}^{B} p(P_t | n_{c,t}^{(j)}, \theta). \tag{28}$$

Under mild regularity conditions, the particle filter is a consistent estimator of the 'true' likelihood (e.g. Künsch, 2005) for baseline state space models. Ionides et al. (2011) show that for general systems with latent variables, an iterated filtering procedure on the base of a particle filter converges to the maximum likelihood estimate when the number of particles goes to infinity. Indeed, our example falls into this general class of models since there is a feedback from the observable variable P_t to the unobservable state $n_{c,t}$ which is absent in the elementary state-space formalism of Eqs. (17) and (18). One important problem is that the resulting approximation of the likelihood function is not a smooth function of the parameters. This is so because the multinomial draws in the resampling step would lead to discrete changes under continuous variation of the parameters of the model. This happens even if the random numbers are kept constant for subsequent iterations in the optimization routine (which one should nevertheless do in order not to introduce *additional* sources of discontinuities in the likelihood function).[14]

Malik and Pitt (2011) have developed a method to make the approximation smooth via a simple transformation but very likely their approach will not provide a full remedy for this problem in an agent-based framework like ours since multinomial draws do not occur only in the resampling step of the particle filter (which Malik and Pitt's method smoothes out) but in the state dynamics as well. We will, therefore, generically have to use optimization algorithms that do not need derivatives as an input. Fernández-Villaverde and Rubio-Ramirez (2007) use simulated annealing to

---

[13] Given the typical size of financial time series, results would also typically not be much different with an ad-hoc initialization that just uses uniform random draws.

[14] We have mentioned already in Section 4.2 that switches of strategy in agent-based models could lead to a lack of smoothness of simulated moments. This also pertains to simulations of the likelihood function via the particle filter algorithm. However, in the later case, the binomial draws implemented with the particle filter constitute an additional second source of discontinuity of the objective function.

find the maximum of the likelihood function. Here, we resort to the versatile Nelder–Mead or simplex algorithm. Table 1 shows the results of a small Monte Carlo study using this particle filter approximation to the likelihood with simulated time series of length $T = 1000$ and $T = 2000$ (used as pseudo-empirical series) and also $B = 1000$ and $B = 2000$ particles.

As we can observe, in this example we get extremely accurate estimates of the parameter v, reasonable estimates of σ_u, and not very precise estimates of the remaining parameters g and β. We also see an improvement of the precision of our estimates when increasing the length of the underlying time series from $T = 1000$ to $T = 2000$. The improvement is, however, smaller than expected under $\sqrt{T}$ consistency. The reason is that we have used the same number of particles B. Since the overall approximation error increases with the length of a series, the approximation of the likelihood function requires an increase of the number of particles to off-set this tendency. Theoretical results on how B shall vary with T for convenient asymptotic behavior can be found in the statistical literature.[15] As we can also observe in Table 1, increasing the number of particles for a constant length of the time series leaves the results basically unchanged. While this result can certainly not be generalized, it indicates that for the present sample sizes, more particles do not lead to a further gain in accuracy of the approximation. Estimated parameters could be used to filter out information on the unobservable state, and the outcome typically appears quite accurate in our application along the lines of the example displayed in the lower left-hand panel of Fig. 1.

Estimation via Self-Organizing State Space Algorithm

A relatively simple alternative avenue to parameter estimation has been proposed by Kitagawa (1998) under this heading. The idea of this approach is to *augment the state space* by *auxiliary particles*. These auxiliary particles cover the unknown parameters. Hence, each particle in our setting would become a vector $\{n_{c,t}^{(j)}, v_t^{(j)}, g_t^{(j)}, \beta_t^{(j)}, \sigma_{u,t}^{(j)}\}$. The state dynamics would be augmented by trivial components:

$$v_{t+1}^{(j)} = v_t^{(j)}, \quad g_{t+1}^{(j)} = g_t^{(j)}, \quad \beta_{t+1}^{(j)} = \beta_t^{(j)}, \quad \sigma_{u,t+1}^{(j)} = \sigma_{u,t}^{(j)}$$

for $j = 1, \ldots, B$ the augmented particles.

---

[15] For instance, Olsson and Rydén (2008) consider parameter estimation using an evenly spaced grid over the parameters for evaluation of the likelihood function and interpolation between the grid points. In the case of piecewise constant functions between the grid points, they show that for asymptotic normality, the grid size M has to decrease faster than $1/T$ and the number of particles has to increase faster than $M^{2/r}T^2$ with r some integer $r \geq 1$. For spline interpolation, the first condition becomes that M has to decrease faster than $1/\sqrt{T}$ while the second condition remains the same. Note that here we adopt the Nelder–Mead algorithm to find the best set of parameters over the rugged surface of the simulated likelihood function so that the results by Olsson and Rydén are not directly applicable. More results on the asymptotics of the maximum likelihood estimator can be found in Kantas et al. (2015).

Table 1 Monte Carlo experiment for estimation of Gaunersdorfer/Hommes model via Maximum Likelihood based on the particle filter

Parameter	ν	g	β	σ_u
True	**1.0**	**1.9**	**2.0**	**10.0**
$T = 1000, B = 1000$				
Mean	0.999	1.585	2.235	10.048
FSSE	0.002	0.642	0.877	0.265
RMSE	0.003	0.712	0.904	0.268
$B = 2000$				
Mean	0.999	1.617	2.186	10.058
FSSE	0.002	0.525	0.846	0.278
RMSE	0.003	0.594	0.862	0.282
$T = 2000, B = 1000$				
Mean	0.999	1.629	2.271	10.085
FSSE	0.001	0.452	0.666	0.202
RMSE	0.001	0.525	0.715	0.218
$B = 2000$				
Mean	0.999	1.619	2.240	10.085
FSSE	0.001	0.493	0.714	0.214
RMSE	0.001	0.565	0.749	0.229

Notes: The table shows the means, finite sample standard errors (FSSE) and root-mean squared errors (RMSE) of 100 replications of each scenario.

The evaluation of the conditional densities in the likelihood function would, then, also exert evolutionary pressure on the auxiliary particles and lead to a selection of those that provide the highest conditional probabilities. By its construction, this approach is executed in one single sweep through the data. An example is shown in Fig. 1. The temporal evolution of the parameters is shown in terms of the mean over all particles for three of the parameters. While the overall length of the time series is $T = 1000$ only the first 350 periods are displayed because the auxiliary parameters have completely converged at this stage, i.e. the shown mean is, in fact, the only value that has survived to this point and can, thus, count as the final estimate.

In this example, the estimation works satisfactorily: the final parameter estimates are close to their 'true' values. Particularly parameter ν is almost exactly identified after just a dozen of observations. Table 2 exhibits the statistics of a set of 100 Monte Carlo replications of the online estimation approach of which Fig. 1 has illustrated one single run. As the table shows overall results with $T = 1000$ and $B = 1000$ are somewhat worse in terms of root-mean squared errors (RMSEs) than with the ML approach. The advantage of this approach is an enormous saving in computation time: We only do one sweep through the data (i.e., estimate *on-line*) while the Nelder–Mead approach usually needed several hundreds of evaluations of the likelihood function over the whole length of the time series. We can, thus, easily increase the number of the particles. Table 2 also shows that the improvement when moving from $B = 1000$

Table 2 Monte Carlo experiment for estimation of Gaunersdorfer/Hommes model via the Self-Organizing State Space Approach

Parameter	v	g	β	σ_u
True	**1.0**	**1.9**	**2.0**	**10.0**
$T = 1000,\ B = 1000$				
Mean	0.988	1.884	1.987	11.866
FSSE	0.044	0.820	1.094	2.470
RMSE	0.045	0.816	1.089	3.086
$T = 1000,\ B = 10{,}000$				
Mean	0.994	1.716	2.071	10.944
FSSE	0.018	0.709	1.108	1.592
RMSE	0.018	0.729	1.105	1.844

Notes: The table shows the means, finite sample standard errors (FSSE) and root-mean squared errors (RMSE) of 100 replications of each scenario.

to $B = 10{,}000$ is, however, not too high and still inferior to the ML results. But one could certainly still increase B at reasonable costs.

One feature of this approach is that a larger time series of observations would not necessarily be of any benefit. With $B = 1000$ particles, the distribution of the auxiliary particles has in almost all cases long become degenerate at the end of a time series of 1000 observations. Hence, no different estimates would be obtained with any longer series. With higher B, the swarm would likely remain heterogeneous for longer time, so that more efficient estimates would require an increase of both T and B at the same time. Despite these limitations, it is also worthwhile to emphasize the good performance of the filter for the state $n_{c,t}$. Note that the tracking of the state in this case is obtained *on-line*, i.e. with moving parameters as shown in the three remaining panels (plus the moving σ_u that is not displayed here). Online estimation or *particle learning* is an active area of research, cf. Carvalho et al. (2010) and Ionides et al. (2011) for examples of more advanced approaches.

Bayesian Estimation

We finally turn to Bayesian estimation, which is strongly connected with state-space approaches in the DSGE community. Andrieu et al. (2010) propose an approach that combines a particle filter with a Metropolis–Hastings sample of the posterior density of the parameters. This and closely related methods have been used by Fernández-Villaverde and Rubio-Ramirez (2007) for DSGE models and Golightly and Wilkinson (2011) for ecological agent-based models. The time-honored Metropolis–Hastings algorithm provides an approach to construct a Markov chain that converges to a stationary distribution equal to the posterior distribution of the parameter one wants to estimate. In order to generate this Markov chain, one needs a *proposal density* for new draws, say $g(\theta_\zeta | \theta_{\zeta-1})$ where ζ is the sequential order of

Table 3 Bayesian estimation of Gaunersdorfer/Hommes model via Particle Filter Markov Chain Monte Carlo

Parameter	$T = 1000$ True	$B = 100$ Mean	S.E.	$B = 1000$ Mean	S.E.
ν	1.0	0.999	0.008	0.999	0.006
g	1.9	1.938	0.124	1.968	0.116
β	2.0	3.139	1.340	2.610	1.362
σ_u	10.0	10.396	0.715	10.184	0.349
LogL		−3754.714	126.023	−3735.381	110.455
Accept. rate		0.352		0.375	

Notes: The table shows the Monte Carlo means and standard errors of the posterior distribution of the parameters from simulations with $B = 100$ and $B = 1000$ particles. The underlying time series has a length of $T = 1000$ while the PMCMC algorithm used 20,000 iterations after discarding a transient of 2000 draws. Fig. 2 contains the transient indicating that convergence to the stationary posterior distribution is very fast.

the chain. Draws from $g(\theta_\zeta | \theta_{\zeta-1})$, say θ^*, are accepted with probability

$$\alpha(\theta^* | \theta_{\zeta-1}) = \frac{p_{\theta^*}(y) p(\theta^*) g(\theta_{\zeta-1} | \theta^*)}{p_{\theta_{\zeta-1}}(y) p(\theta_{\zeta-1}) g(\theta^* | \theta_{\zeta-1})}$$

where $p_\theta(y)$ is the marginal likelihood of the observed data under θ, $p(\theta)$ is the prior of the parameters, and the acceptance rate is restricted to the interval $[0, 1]$ by appropriate constraints. In case the new draw θ^* is not accepted, the chain will continue with the previous values, i.e. $\theta_\zeta = \theta_{\zeta-1}$. Under mild conditions on the likelihood of the process and the proposal density, the chain generated in this way will converge to the posterior distribution of the parameters. Andrieu et al. (2010) show that this convergence property holds also if the marginal likelihood is estimated via the particle filter introduced above. The pertinent method is called Particle Filter Markov Chain Monte Carlo (PMCMC). An important difference to the frequentist estimation presented earlier in this section is, however, that one would *not* initiate the particle filter with the same random seed in each iteration in order to generate random draws of the relative likelihoods.

We illustrate the Bayesian approach in Fig. 2 and Table 3. Since we might not have any clue to what the values of the parameters be prior to estimation, we used uniform priors with support in the interval $[0, 5]$ for ν, g and β and a uniform distribution on $[0, 50]$ for σ_u. For the proposal densities, we used random walks with standard deviations equal to 0.25 for the first three variables and 2.5 for the fourth. The underlying time series had a length of $T = 1000$ and we ran the algorithm with $B = 100$ and $B = 1000$ particles. The posterior distribution was sampled for a Markov chain of a length of 20,000 iterations after discarding the first 2000 iterations as transients.

Fig. 2 shows the complete record or 22,000 iterations including the transients for $B = 100$. As we can see, we can hardly recognize any transient part at all: the Markov chain seems to converge to its stationary distribution very quickly. While this repre-

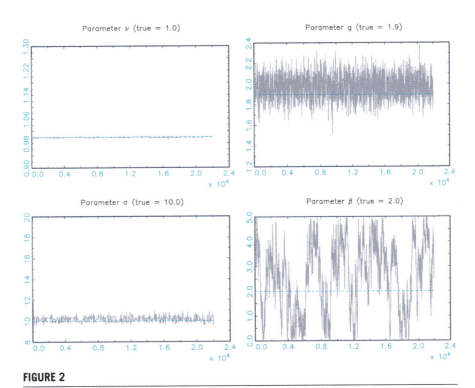

FIGURE 2

Example of an application of PMCMC for the model of Gaunersdorfer and Hommes (2007). The figure shows the development of the posterior distributions of the four parameters v, g, β and σ_u during 22,000 iterations of the PMCMC algorithm with $B = 100$ particles. The statistics of this realization of the algorithm are given in the left panel of Table 3.

sents an estimation for only one replication of our ABM and the standard errors of the posterior distribution are not directly comparable to the finite sample standard errors across 100 simulations with the frequentist approach, results are pretty much in line with our previous findings. We see that the parameter v seems to be almost perfectly identified even with as few as 100 particles followed by σ_u and g with somewhat smaller signal-to-noise ratios. At least in our present example, the mean of the posterior distribution of g is remarkably close to the 'true' value and the signal-to-noise ratio of this parameter is relatively high so as to allow also meaningful inference on this parameter.

This is, however, not the case with β, which eventually wanders across its entire admissible range (that we have fixed to the interval $[0, 5]$ via the choice of its prior). The mean and standard errors of β are so close to those of random draws from such a uniform distribution (2.5 and 1.445) that they appear meaningless, i.e. the data does not provide any information on β beyond that imposed by the distribution of the prior. Still, $\beta > 0$ would be required for the scenario of long periods of fundamentalist dominance with recurrent bursts of chartist activity to be possible at all. The apparent inability to obtain sensible estimates of β resonates with empirical studies (using other methods) that always found it hard to obtain significant estimates of this parameter (see Boswijk et al., 2007; Kukacka and Barunik, 2017).

We note that for the Metropolis–Hastings algorithm the details of implementation are of secondary importance, as the theoretical convergence result holds under very general conditions. One major practical concern is the mixing of the Markov chain. A standard recommendation is an acceptance rate of 0.4, which both of our settings with $B = 100$ and $B = 1000$ get close to. With less mixing, a longer transient would be expected and the chain would have to be simulated over more iterations to obtain a satisfactory representation of the posterior density. The effect of a higher number of particles is a better approximation of the marginal likelihood which should also increase the precision of the estimation of the posterior distribution. This is indeed found to different degrees for the parameter ν, g and σ_u, but not for β underlining the principal problem in estimating this parameter.

Summarizing our findings in this subsection, we believe that the preceding experiments have demonstrated the great potential of sequential Monte Carlo methods for estimation of agent-based models. Adopting the rich toolbox available in this area would bring agent-based models to the same level of statistical rigor and precision as modern macroeconomics. What is more, in contrast to the hitherto popular moment-based estimators, SMC methods do not only allow inference on model parameters, but also filtering of information on unobserved state variables that characterize the agents' beliefs, opinions or attitudes. In the above example, we have also found that different parameters are estimated with very different degrees of precision. In particular, we found that the intensity of choice is almost impossible to estimate which also is in conformity with results obtained by other authors with other methods of inference. How general this phenomenon is and how much it impedes successful validation of agent-based models remains to be seen.

We also note that the Monte Carlo exercises above have been conducted on the base of a model formulated for prices as state variables, not returns. The lack of realism of some of the underlying assumptions such as the assumed dividend process would make an empirical implementation cumbersome. In Lux (2017), the same set of methods is applied to alternative asset pricing models with interacting agents that do not require any assumption on the dividend process. Monte Carlo exercises show very similar tendencies as in the present case, and the models under study are estimated for a selection of financial time series including a comparison of goodness-of-fit.

5 APPLICATIONS OF AGENT-BASED MODELS

Whereas the chapter has so far mainly focused on methods, we will now briefly turn to a description of the applications and results. As indicated before, the comparability of results across studies is rather limited due to the wide variation in both models and methods. It is therefore hard to make general statements about the behavior of agents across markets, or about which model is 'best'. We will, however, provide an overview of what has been found so far using which type of data. We will divide the evidence in three levels: micro (individuals), market, and macro. The micro-level evidence focuses on the questions whether individuals form expectations as typically modeled in ABMs. It therefore serves as a check on the assumptions behind the models. The market level studies focus on one asset each, whereas the macro-level part focuses on general equilibrium models.

5.1 MICRO-LEVEL APPLICATIONS

Because ABM and HAMs step away from the notion of rationality, they introduce a large number of degrees of freedom as there are many ways in which agents can behave boundedly rationally. As such, empirical research into the assumptions on expectation formation in ABMs is crucial. One challenge with micro-level studies is data availability. Whereas market outcomes (i.e., prices, volumes, etc.) are readily observable, market inputs at the individual level are mostly not observable. Therefore, one needs to turn to other sources of data than the standard macroeconomic and finance data bases. Several types of data for individual agents have been used, such as experimental data, survey data, and investment fund data, each with their own advantages and disadvantages. Whereas one can deduct revealed beliefs from experimental data, it is not clear to what extent experimental environments as well as their participants are representative for the real-life setting. Arifovic and Duffy (2018) give an overview of experimental work on ABMs. Survey data, on the other hand, is typically gathered among actual market participants based on actual markets. Unfortunately, it is unknown to the researcher, however, whether or not survey participants state their actual beliefs. This issue is partly mitigated when using publicly available survey data because the survey participant's reputation is at stake. Fund data, finally, consists of actual positions and capital flows, as certain types of funds are by law obliged to provide this information. The question that arises, though, is whether or not the observed actions are driven by beliefs, preferences, or institutional reasons. In what follows, we will give a sample of the empirical evidence from each of these data sources.

Both quantitative and qualitative surveys have been used for research in this area. Taylor and Allen (1992) show, based on a questionnaire survey, that 90% of the foreign exchange dealers based in London use some form of technical analysis in forming expectations about future exchange rates, particularly for short-term horizons. Menkhoff (2010) gathered similar data from fund managers in five different countries, and finds that 87% of the fund managers they survey are using technical analysis. Frankel and Froot (1986, 1990) were among the first to show, based on quantitative survey data, that expectations of market participants are non-rational and heterogeneous. They also find evidence for the chartist–fundamentalist approach employed in many of the heterogeneous agent models. Dick and Menkhoff (2013) use forecasters' self-assessment to classify themselves as chartists, fundamentalists, or a mix. They find that forecasters who characterize their forecasting tools as chartist use trend-following strategies and those that are categorized as fundamentalist have a stronger tendency toward purchasing power parity. For a more extensive overview, see Jongen et al. (2008).

Ter Ellen et al. (2013) are among the first to estimate a dynamic heterogeneous agent model on foreign exchange survey data. They find evidence for three forecasting rules (PPP, momentum, and interest parity) and that investors switch between forecasting rules depending on the past performance of these rules. Goldbaum and Zwinkels (2014) find that a model with fundamentalists and chartists can explain the survey data well. As in Ter Ellen et al. (2013), they find that fundamentalists are mean reverting and that this model is increasingly used for longer horizons. Chartists have contrarian expectations at the 1-month horizon. A model with time-varying weights obtained through an endogenous classification algorithm provides a substantially better fit than a static version of this model. Jongen et al. (2012) also allow the weights on different strategies to vary depending on market circumstances. However, instead of directly explaining the survey expectations, they analyze the dispersion between forecasts. They find that the dispersion is caused by investors using heterogeneous forecasting rules and having private information. This is in line with the earlier findings of Menkhoff et al. (2009) for a dataset on German financial market professionals.

The final data source we discuss here, is fund data. Given that both fund holdings and returns on the one hand and fund flows on the other hand are available, fund data allows us to study the behavior of both mutual fund investors as well as mutual fund managers. Goldbaum and Mizrach (2008) study the behavior of mutual fund investors and are able to estimate an intensity of choice parameter that governs to what extent investors switch between different types of mutual funds. They find that investors switch their allocation of capital between funds of similar styles but with different performance. A few more papers looks into the switching behavior of fund managers. Specifically, the question is to what extent fund managers switch between different styles presumably to maximize the performance of the fund. Using fund return data, the studies test whether the exposure to different styles is time-varying, and whether this time-variation is driven by relative past returns of the styles; see Verschoor and Zwinkels (2013) for foreign exchange funds, Schauten et al. (2015) for hedge funds, and Frijns et al. (2013) and Frijns and Zwinkels (2016a, 2016b) for mutual funds. Interestingly, the latter study finds that although fund managers massively switch capital towards styles that performed well in the recent past, this does not improve the overall performance of the fund nor does it attract more capital inflow. This is an indication that heterogeneity is indeed a behavioral characteristic.

5.2 MARKET-LEVEL APPLICATIONS

Due to the self-referential character of asset markets in ABMs, the behavioral heterogeneity of agents at the micro-level should be reflected in realized prices and returns. If a market is dominated by a particular type of agent, market dynamics should be more similar to the specific expectation formation model of that particular agent. As such, empirical evidence supporting the ABM approach can be identified from market data. A broad range of asset classes has by now been studied. Most papers so far have focused on equity markets. Boswijk et al. (2007) are among the first to estimate a HAM on market data. Specifically, they use historical data of the S&P 500 index and find significant evidence for behavioral heterogeneity at the annual frequency. Lof (2015) is based on the same dataset. Chiarella et al. (2012, 2014) and Amilon (2008) follow suit, on the monthly, weekly, and daily frequency, respectively. De Jong et al. (2009) study the Thai and Hong Kong stock markets simultaneously and find evidence for three types of agents, fundamentalists, chartists, and internationalists. Alfarano et al. (2007) use Japanese stock market data and find evidence for domination of noise traders. All these papers find evidence supportive of the heterogeneity approach in their respective models. Another common finding is that the intensity of choice or switching parameter is not significant based on common measures (i.e., a t-statistic). This finding could imply two things: Either there is no significant switching, or the intensity of choice is rather large such that the standard errors are inflated. Goodness of fit tests tend to suggest that adding switching increases the fit of the models, especially when the heterogeneous groups are well identified (i.e., when the fundamentalist and chartist coefficients are highly significant).

Rather than focusing on the return process of equity markets, a number of authors has employed an ABM to explain the volatility process of equity markets. Franke and Westerhoff (2012, 2016) develop and estimate a stochastic volatility model based on the premise that the stochastic noise terms of fundamentalist and chartist demand are different. By having time-varying weights on the different groups, this creates volatility clustering. Frijns et al. (2013) develop a model in which agents have different beliefs about the volatility process, which converges to a GARCH model with time-varying coefficients in which the ARCH-term and GARCH-term have conditional impacts. Ghonghadze and Lux (2016) apply GMM to the model of Alfarano et al. (2008) and show that the volatility forecasts of the HAM adds value to GARCH forecasts as it is not encompassed by the latter for certain assets and forecasting horizons. A typical finding in the volatility literature is that it is relatively straightforward to outperform a standard GARCH model *in-sample*, but much harder to do so out-of-sample. The volatility forecasting results based on ABMs are therefore encouraging.

Explaining foreign exchange market dynamics has long been an important motivation for the early HAM literature, which is also reflected in the amount of empirical work on this asset class; see Vigfusson (1997), Gilli and Winker (2003), Reitz and Westerhoff (2003), Ahrens and Reitz (2005), Reitz et al. (2006), Manzan and Westerhoff (2007), De Jong et al. (2010), Kouwenberg et al. (2017). The issue with such extremely liquid financial markets, though, is to find expectation formation rules that hold empirically as it is hard to find empirical patterns in such near-efficient markets. Finding behavioral heterogeneity in returns on free-floating exchange rates is therefore challenging. Other financial assets that have been studied using HAMs include credit default swaps (Chiarella et al., 2014; Frijns and Zwinkels, 2016b), and equity index options (Frijns et al., 2013). The largest financial markets in terms of outstanding capital, bond markets, have to our best knowledge not been studied yet. Given that prices of non-financial assets are also a function of the expectation of market participants, ABMs have been estimated on a broad range of markets. Baak

(1999) uses data on cattle prices, Chavas (2000) studies the beef market, Ter Ellen and Zwinkels (2010) the oil market, Baur and Glover (2014) look at gold prices. Lux (2012) can also be mentioned in this respect, as the paper looks into heterogeneity and propagation of sentiment among investors.

Since the unraveling of the global financial crisis, studying the dynamics in the real estate market has become a central theme. Kouwenberg and Zwinkels (2014, 2015) fit a HAM on the Case–Shiller index, representing the US residential housing market. They find very strong evidence in favor of the heterogeneity approach, both in-sample and out-of-sample. Interestingly, their model with the estimated set of co-efficients converges to a limit cycle.[16] In other words, endogenous dynamics play an important role in the US housing market. Eichholtz et al. (2015) follow suit and estimate a HAM on over 400 years of real estate data from Amsterdam. They find that chartist domination is related to periods of upswing in the business cycle. Bolt et al. (2014) estimate a HAM on real estate data from a set of eight countries and also find strong evidence for heterogeneity driven bubbles and crashes.

One of the next steps we expect for this line of research, is a more granular approach. This can go along two lines. First, rather than focusing on stock indices, as most papers currently do, one could estimate ABMs on stock level data. Subsequently, it would be interesting to study the cross-sectional differences in agent behavior between stocks. Results could be linked to the more general asset pricing literature, which has identified numerous cross-sectional anomalies which might be driven by the (time-varying) behavior of boundedly rational agents. Second, with the increasing availability of individual level data, it becomes feasible to estimate (reduced-form) ABMs on groups of traders or individuals. This would allow to draw inference on the personal characteristics of trader types. For example, one can imagine that retail investors display a different type of behavior than professional investors, although both can be boundedly rational in nature. In addition, an interesting extension of the literature would be to compare behavioral heterogeneity across markets, as well as the interaction between markets. Current papers tend to focus on a single asset market. Due to the differences in models and empirical approaches, the results cannot be compared across studies. As such, a direct comparison of behavior across markets is warranted. Furthermore, in the theoretical HAM literature there is an increase in studies looking at multiple asset markets. The empirical follow-up is yet to come.

5.3 APPLICATIONS IN MACROECONOMICS

While agent-based modeling in economics goes beyond financial market applications, estimation of such models has by and large been confined to financial applications. This is not too surprising, as many such models with heterogeneous agents

---

[16]Other papers studying the stability properties of the model using the empirically obtained coefficients find fixed points equilibria; see e.g. Chiarella et al. (2014).

could be cast into traditional structural formats like those of regime-switching models. Even when considering a true ensemble of interacting agents with some stochastic behavioral variation, the overall dynamics still appears convenient enough at least for the rigorous application of moment-based estimation.

Little explicit estimation and goodness-of-fit is found in the macro-sphere. Existing examples are restricted to selected phenomena like the estimation of a model of opinion formation to business survey data in Lux (2009a) or the estimation of a network formation model for banks' activity in the interbank money market by Finger and Lux (2017). Bargigli et al. (2016) go one step further. They combine a network model for the formation of credit links between banks and non-financial firms with the balance sheet dynamics of firms and estimate their model with a rich data set of bank loans to Japanese firms. An interesting methodological aspect is that they use a 'meta-model' to both derive qualitative predictions from their complex model and to use it as an intermediate step for parameter estimation. Hence, in the spirit of 'indirect inference', parameter estimation involves a simple auxiliary stochastic model whose parameters are then matched with the agent-based model. This approach has been inspired by a similar framework adopted from an ABM of an ecological problem (Dancik et al., 2010), and Salle and Yildizoğlu (2014) apply the same concept of meta-modeling to the Nelson and Winter model (Nelson and Winter, 1982) of industrial dynamics as well as to an oligopoly model with heterogeneous firms.

More complex macroeconomic models have mostly been *calibrated* rather than estimated. Axtell et al. (1996) have already discussed how to 'align' complex simulation models that might have been designed to describe similar phenomena in very different languages. Such an alignment aims at finding out in how far there are similarities of observable characteristics between models. In complex macroeconomic data, the pertinent observables have typically been distributions such as those of firm sizes, growth rates, and the relation between size itself and the variance of its growth rate (cf. Bianchi et al., 2007, 2008). A particularly rich set of empirical stylized facts is met by the 'Schumpeter meets Keynes' framework of Dosi et al. (2010, 2013, 2015) that covers both time series properties of output fluctuations and growth as well as cross-sectional distributional characteristics of firms. A recent paper by Guerini and Moneta (2016) proposes to use the fraction of qualitative agreements in causal relationship between a model and data as a criterion for validation of a model that is too complex for rigorous estimation. To this end, they estimate a structural vector autoregressive model for the variables used by Dosi et al. Comparison with simulated model output provides an agreement of 65 to 90 percent of all causal relationships which is viewed as encouraging by the authors.

If heterogeneity is more limited, expanding a standard neo-Keynesian model by a modest degree of interaction of agents could still lead to a framework that can be estimated explicitly. Anufriev et al. (2015) consider heterogeneous inflation expectations with switching between belief formation heuristics according to their past performance. They show that the stabilizing potential of monetary policy depends on the interplay between the central bank's reaction function and the agents' expectation formation. De Grauwe (2011) allows for both boundedly rational, heterogeneous expectations on output and inflation. Jang and Sacht (2016) also follow this approach and replace rational expectations on output and inflation by the outcome of a process of opinion formation of heterogeneous agents. They find that this model provides a satisfactory match to Euro area data when estimated via simulated method of moments. Cornea et al. (2017) estimate a New Keynesian Phillips curve with time-varying heterogeneous expectations. They find significant switching between forward-looking expectations based on fundamentals and naive backward looking expectations. In contrast to other studies, their nonlinear least squares estimation also indicates that the intensity of choice parameter is significantly different from zero.

The so far only attempt at validation of a large-scale macroeconomic model has been made by Barde and van der Hoog (2017). They apply the so-called EURACE model (Dawid et al., 2017) to thirty OECD countries and the Eurozone. Since this is definitely a model that is too complex to subject it to repeated simulation within some parameter estimation loop, they adopt concepts of emulation or meta-modeling (called surrogate modeling in their paper) that have been mentioned in Section 2. Barde and van der Hoog conduct a total of 513 simulations and build model confidence sets of those versions that are not inferior to others following the methodology of Hansen et al. (2011). Adding to the trials those of local minima of the emulation function they attempt to find out whether the search through the later provides significantly better fitting parameters (in terms of an information criterion as objective function). This is mostly not the case. The overall size of the model confidence sets appears reasonably small in most cases which is mainly driven by the matching of the unemployment series while the other macroeconomic series of output and inflation rates add little discriminatory power. One particularly encouraging result appears to be that at least one out of the two particularly successful models (parameter sets) appears in all 31 model confidence sets.

6 CONCLUSION

Estimation of agent-based models has become a burgeoning research area over the last ten years or so. While there has been an older tradition of framing simple models with two groups of agents as regime-switching models, the more recent literature has moved on to develop estimation methods for more general designs of models with heterogeneous, interacting agents. Such models could both summarize the consequences of heterogeneity by some summary measures (like an opinion index) or they could truly consider a finite set of agents with their microeconomic interactions. Research in this vein has been emerging in economics more or less simultaneously with related efforts in other fields (particularly in ecology), unfortunately without too much interaction between these related streams of literature so far.

Estimating agent based models poses certain challenges to the econometrician. For example, the simulated objective functions that one may use to identify the parameters, will often not be a continuous function of the parameters. Because of the simulation of moments or likelihood functions, these functions will be a wiggly image of their unknown theoretical counterparts. At least in those types of models that have been explored so far, this problem seems to be generic. For practical applications, this means that we cannot use the set of convenient gradient-based optimizers that econometricians use for other problems. Otherwise one would almost with certainty end up in some local optimum rather than identifying sensible parameter values. Finding an appropriate optimization routine for non-standard problems (such as Nelder–Mead, simulated annealing, genetic algorithms, and others) can become a research topic in itself, and the best choice might be problem-specific.

While the research on econometric estimation of agent-based models has been growing impressively recently, most of it has so far remained on the level of proof of concept, demonstrating how a particular approach to estimation works with a selected model. Even in finance, the field in which almost all this research resides, it is hard to draw general material conclusions as to which particular model structures perform better than others. However, research on model comparison has recently begun (Franke and Westerhoff, 2012; Barde, 2016) and more along these lines is expected to come. The trend towards estimation might also have a beneficial effect in that it will impose empirical discipline on ABM modeling. It appears to us that there is often a danger of over-parametrization of such models, and even a Monte Carlo exercise could easily reveal that a model has redundant parameters that could never be identified with the data one targets.

As for the reduced-form models, we have seen applications in effectively all possible asset classes. The road ahead therefore no longer lies in analyzing more asset classes, but rather in comparisons between asset classes and more granular studies of individual assets. The former is directly related to the model comparison issues described above. A first step in this direction can be found in Ter Ellen et al. (2017), who provide a comparison of behavioral heterogeneity across asset classes. The granular approach includes, for example, analysis of individual stocks. Individual stock level analysis is especially challenging when it comes to finding the global optimum of the optimization procedure due to the high (idiosyncratic) volatility. A thorough test on the robustness of results to starting values is therefore warranted. A successful asset-level estimation exercise, however, would also help bring the HAM literature closer to the more mainstream asset pricing literature as it becomes possible to connect company characteristics to behavioral heterogeneity. Another step in this direction would be to introduce more sophisticated proxies for the fundamental value. The current proxies are probably too sensitive to the critique that both volatility and risk attitudes are static.

As has been pointed out in Section 2, in epidemiology, climate research, and industrial process dynamics, smaller simulation models have been integrated over time into more comprehensive large models. The smaller models had been validated rigorously in the respective fields and their known dynamic behavior and estimated parameters count as established knowledge. The large models are usually too complex and need too much computation time to be subjected to the same degree of scrutiny. However, methods have been developed to assess biases and to correct the uncertainties of large simulation models. We could imagine that economics could pursue a similar avenue in the medium run: Once a body of knowledge has been collected on ABMs for particular markets (the stock market, labor market, etc.) these could be integrated into a larger macroeconomic simulation framework with validated agent-based microfoundations.

REFERENCES

Achdou, Y., Han, J., Lasry, J.-M., Lions, P.-L., Moll, B., 2015. Heterogeneous Agent Models in Continuous Time. Université de Paris-Diderot.

Ahrens, R., Reitz, S., 2005. Heterogeneous expectations in the foreign exchange market: evidence from daily DM/US Dollar exchange rates. Journal of Evolutionary Economics 15 (1), 65–82.

Alfarano, S., Lux, T., Wagner, F., 2005. Estimation of agent-based models: the case of an asymmetric herding model. Computational Economics 26, 19–49.

Alfarano, S., Lux, T., Wagner, F., 2006. Estimation of a simple agent-based model of financial markets: an application to Australian stock and foreign exchange data. Physica A 370, 38–42.

Alfarano, S., Lux, T., Wagner, F., 2007. Empirical validation of stochastic models of interacting agents: a Maximally Skewed Noise Trader Model. European Journal of Physics B 55, 183–187.

Alfarano, S., Lux, T., Wagner, F., 2008. Time-variation of higher moments in financial markets with heterogeneous agents: an analytical approach. Journal of Economic Dynamics & Control 32, 101–136.

Alfarano, S., Milakovic, M., 2009. Network structure and N-dependence in agent-based herding models. Journal of Economic Dynamics and Control 33 (1), 78–92.

Amati, V., Schönberger, F., Snijders, T., 2015. Estimation of stochastic actor-oriented models for the evolution of networks by generalized method of moments. Journal de la Societé Francaise de Statistique 156, 140–165.

Amilon, H., 2008. Estimation of an adaptive stock market model with heterogeneous agents. Journal of Empirical Finance 15, 342–362.

Amisano, G., Tristani, O., 2010. Euro area inflation persistence in an estimated nonlinear DSGE model. Journal of Economic Dynamics & Control 34, 1837–1858.

Andrews, D., 1993. Empirical process methods in econometrics. In: Engle, R., McFadden, D. (Eds.), Handbook of Econometrics, vol. IV. North-Holland (Chapter 37).

Andrieu, C., Doucet, A., Holenstein, R., 2010. Particle Markov chain Monte Carlo methods. Journal of the Royal Statistical Society, Series B 72 (3), 269–342.

Anufriev, M., Assenza, T., Hommes, C., Massaro, D., 2015. Interest rate rules with heterogeneous expectations. Macroeconomic Dynamics 17, 1574–1604.

Aoki, M., 2002. Open models of share markets with two dominant types of participants. Journal of Economic Behavior & Organization 49 (2), 199–216.

Arifovic, J., Duffy, J., 2018. Heterogeneous agent modeling: experimental evidence. In: LeBaron, B., Hommes, C. (Eds.), Handbook of Computational Economics, vol. 4. Elsevier, Amsterdam, pp. 491–540 (this Handbook).

Arthur, B., 2006. Agent-based modeling and out-of-equilibrium economics. In: Judd, K., Tesfatsion, L. (Eds.), Handbook of Computational Economics, vol. 2. Elsevier/North-Holland.

Axelrod, R., 1984. The Evolution of Cooperation. Basic Books, New York.

Axtell, R., Axelrod, R., Epstein, J.M., Cohen, M.D., 1996. Aligning simulation models: a case study and results. Computational and Mathematical Organization Theory 1 (2), 123–141.

Axtell, R.L., Epstein, J.M., Dean, J.S., Gumerman, G.J., Swedlund, A.C., Harburger, J., Chakravarty, S., Hammond, R., Parker, J., Parker, M.T., 2002. Population growth and collapse in a multiagent model of the Kayenta Anasazi in Long House Valley. Proceedings of the National Academy of Sciences of the United States of America 99 (Suppl. 3), 7275–7279.

Baak, S.J., 1999. Tests for bounded rationality with a linear dynamic model distorted by heterogeneous expectations. Journal of Economic Dynamics and Control 23, 1517–1543.

Banerjee, A., Chandrasekhar, A.G., Duflo, E., Jackson, M.O., 2013. The diffusion of microfinance. Science 341 (6144).

Barberis, N., Shleifer, A., 2003. Style investing. Journal of Financial Economics 68, 161–199.

Barde, S., 2016. Direct comparison of agent-based models of herding in financial markets. Journal of Economic Dynamics and Control 73, 329–353.

Barde, S., van der Hoog, S., 2017. An empirical validation protocol for large-scale agent-based models. Manuscript. University of Bielefeld.

Bargagli, L., Riccetti, L., Russo, A., Gallegati, M., 2016. Network calibration and metamodelling of a financial accelerator agent-based model. Manuscript. Unversità di Firenze.

Baur, D., Glover, K., 2014. Heterogeneous expectations in the gold market: specification and estimation. Journal of Economic Dynamics and Control 40, 116–133.

Bayarri, M., Berger, J., Paulo, R., Sacks, J., Cafeo, J.A., Cavendish, J., Lin, C.-H., Tu, J., 2007. A framework for validation of computer models. Technometrics 49, 138–154.

Beja, A., Goldman, B., 1980. On the dynamic behavior of prices in disequilibrium. The Journal of Finance 35, 235–248.

Bianchi, C., Cirillo, P., Gallegati, M., Vagliasindi, P.A., 2007. Validating and calibrating agent-based models: a case study. Computational Economics 30 (3), 245–264.

Bianchi, C., Cirillo, P., Gallegati, M., Vagliasindi, P.A., 2008. Validation in agent-based models: an investigation on the CATS model. Journal of Economic Behavior & Organization 67 (3), 947–964.

Billio, M., Casarin, R., 2010. Identifying business cycle turning points with sequential Monte Carlo methods: an online and real-time application to the Euro area. Journal of Forecasting 29 (1–2), 145–167.

Blevins, J.R., 2016. Sequential Monte Carlo methods for estimating dynamic microeconomic models. Journal of Applied Econometrics 31, 773–804.

Bloomfield, R., Hales, J., 2002. Predicting the next step of a random walk: experimental evidence of regime-shifting beliefs. Journal of Financial Economics 65 (3), 397–414.

Bolt, W., Demertzis, M., Diks, C., Hommes, C., van der Leij, M., 2014. Identifying Booms and Busts in House Prices Under Heterogeneous Expectations. DNB Working Paper 450.

Boswijk, H.P., Hommes, C.H., Manzan, S., 2007. Behavioral heterogeneity in stock prices. Journal of Economic Dynamics & Control 31, 1938–1970.

Brock, W., Durlauf, S., 2001a. Discrete choice with social interactions. The Review of Economic Studies 68, 235–260.

Brock, W., Durlauf, S., 2001b. Interactions-based models. In: Heckman, J., Learner, E. (Eds.), Handbook of Econometrics, vol. 5. North-Holland, Amsterdam (Chapter 54).

Brock, W., Hommes, C.H., 1997. A rational route to randomness. Econometrica 65 (5), 1059–1095.

Brock, W., Hommes, C.H., 1998. Heterogeneous beliefs and routes to chaos in a simple asset pricing model. Journal of Economic Dynamics and Control 22, 1235–1274.

Bruch, E., Atwell, J., 2015. Agent-based models in empirical social research. Sociological Methods & Research 44, 186–221.

Campbell, John Y., Cochrane, John, 1999. Force of habit: a consumption-based explanation of aggregate stock market behavior. Journal of Political Economy 107 (2), 205–251.

Carley, K.M., Louie, M.A., 2008. Balancing the criticisms: validating multi-agent models of social systems. Simulation Modelling Practice and Theory 16 (2), 242–256.

Carvalho, C., Johannes, M.S., Lopes, H.F., Polson, N., 2010. Particle learning and smoothing. Statistical Science 25 (1), 88–106.

Carvalho, C.M., Lopes, H.F., 2007. Simulation-based sequential analysis of Markov switching stochastic volatility models. Computational Statistics & Data Analysis 51 (9), 4526–4542.

Chavas, J.P., 2000. On information and market dynamics: the case of the U.S. beef market. Journal of Economic Dynamics and Control 24, 833–853.

Checkley, M., Steglich, M., 2007. Partners in power: job mobility and dynamic deal-making. European Management Review 4, 161–171.

Chen, P., 2002. Microfoundations of macroeconomic fluctuations and the laws of probability theory: the principle of large numbers versus rational expectations arbitrage. Journal of Economic Behavior & Organization 49 (3), 327–344.

Chen, Z., Lux, T., 2016. Estimation of sentiment effects in financial markets: a simulated method of moments approach. Computational Economics. In press.

Chiarella, C., 1992. The dynamics of speculative behavior. Annals of Operations Research 37, 101–123.

Chiarella, C., He, X., Huang, W., Zheng, H., 2012. Estimating behavioural heterogeneity under regime switching. Journal of Economic Behavior & Organization 83 (3), 446–460.

Chiarella, C., He, X., Zwinkels, R., 2014. Heterogeneous expectations in asset pricing: empirical evidence from the S&P500. Journal of Economic Behavior & Organization 105, 1–16.

Cochrane, J.H., 2001. Asset Pricing. Princeton University Press.

Cornea, A., Hommes, C.H., Massaro, D., 2017. Behavioural heterogeneity in U.S. inflation dynamics. Journal of Business & Economic Statistics. Forthcoming.

Creal, Drew D., Koopman, Siem Jan, Lucas, Andre, 2008. A general framework for observation driven time-varying parameter models. Journal of Applied Econometrics 28 (5), 777–795.

Cutler, D.M., Poterba, J.M., Summers, L.M., 1991. Speculative dynamics. The Review of Economic Studies 58 (3), 529–546.

Dancik, G.M., Jones, D.E., Dorman, K.S., 2010. Parameter estimation and sensitivity analysis in an agent-based model of *Leishmania major* infection. Journal of Theoretical Biology 262 (3), 398–412.

Dawid, H., Gemkow, S., Harting, P., van der Hoog, S., Neugart, M., 2017. Agent-based macroeconomic modelling and policy analysis: the EURACE@UNIBI model. In: Chen, S.-M., Kaboudan, M. (Eds.), Handbook of Computational Economics and Finance. University Press, Oxford. In press.

Day, R.H., Huang, W., 1990. Bulls, bears and market sheep. Journal of Economic Behavior & Organization 14, 299–329.

De Grauwe, P., 2011. Animal spirits and monetary policy. Economic Theory 47, 423–457.

De Jong, E., Verschoor, W., Zwinkels, W., 2009. Behavioural heterogeneity and shift-contagion: evidence from the Asian Crisis. Journal of Economic Dynamics and Control 33 (11), 1929–1944.

De Jong, E., Verschoor, W., Zwinkels, R., 2010. Heterogeneity of agents and exchange rate dynamics: evidence from the EMS. Journal of International Money and Finance 29 (8), 1652–1669.

Dick, C.D., Menkhoff, L., 2013. Exchange rate expectations of chartists and fundamentalists. Journal of Economic Dynamics and Control 37 (7), 1362–1383.

Dosi, G., Fagiolo, G., Napoletano, M., Roventini, A., 2013. Income distribution, credit and fiscal policies in an agent-based Keynesian model. Journal of Economic Dynamics and Control 37 (8), 1598–1625.

Dosi, G., Fagiolo, G., Napoletano, M., Roventini, A., Treibich, T., 2015. Fiscal and monetary policies in complex evolving economies. Journal of Economic Dynamics and Control 52, 166–189.

Dosi, G., Fagiolo, G., Roventini, A., 2010. Schumpeter meeting Keynes: a policy-friendly model of endogenous growth and business cycles. Journal of Economic Dynamics and Control 34 (9), 1748–1767.

Douc, R., Doukhan, P., Moulines, E., 2013. Ergodicity of observation-driven time series models and consistency of the maximum likelihood estimator. Stochastic Processes and Their Applications 123 (7), 2620–2647.

Doucet, A., De Freitas, N., Gordon, N. (Eds.), 2001. Sequential Monte Carlo Methods in Practice. Springer, Berlin.

Eichholtz, P., Huisman, R., Zwinkels, R.C.J., 2015. Fundamentals or trend? A long-term perspective on house prices. Applied Economics 47 (10), 1050–1059.

Embrechts, P., Klüppelberg, C., Mikosch, T., 1997. Modelling Extremal Events for Insurance and Finance. Springer, Berlin.

Engle, R.F., Bollerslev, T., 1986. Modelling the persistence of conditional variances. Econometric Reviews 5, 1–50.

Epstein, J., 2009. Modelling to contain pandemics. Nature 460 (687).

Fama, E.F., 1991. Efficient capital markets: II. The Journal of Finance 46 (5), 1575–1617.

Fernandez-Villaverde, J., Rubio-Ramírez, J.F., 2007. Estimating macroeconomic models: a likelihood approach. The Review of Economic Studies 74 (4), 1059–1087.

Finger, K., Lux, T., 2017. Network formation in the interbank money market: an application of the actor-oriented model. Social Networks 48, 237–249.

Franke, R., 2009. Applying the method of simulated moments to estimate a small agent-based asset pricing model. Journal of Empirical Finance 16, 804–815.

Franke, R., Westerhoff, F., 2011. Estimation of a structural stochastic volatility model of asset pricing. Computational Economics 38, 53–83.

Franke, R., Westerhoff, F., 2012. Structural stochastic volatility in asset pricing dynamics: estimation and model contest. Journal of Economic Dynamics and Control 36 (8), 1193–1211.

Franke, R., Westerhoff, F., 2016. Why a simple herding model may generate the stylized facts of daily returns: explanation and estimation. Journal of Economic Interaction and Coordination 11 (1), 1–34.

Frankel, J.A., Froot, K.A., 1986. Understanding the US Dollar in the Eighties: the expectations of chartists and fundamentalists. Economic Record, Special Issue, 24–40.

Frankel, J.A., Froot, K.A., 1990. Chartists, fundamentalists and trading in the foreign exchange market. The American Economic Review 80 (2), 181–185.

Frijns, B., Gilbert, A., Zwinkels, R., 2013. Market timing ability and mutual funds: a heterogeneous agent approach. Quantitative Finance 13 (10), 1613–1620.

Frijns, B., Zwinkels, R., 2016a. Time-Varying Arbitrage and Dynamic Price Discovery. Working paper.

Frijns, B., Zwinkels, R., 2016b. Speculation in European Sovereign Debt Markets. Working paper.

Gallant, A.R., Hong, H., Khwaja, A., 2016. A Bayesian approach to estimation of dynamic models with small and large number of heterogeneous players and latent serially correlated states. Manuscript. Penn State University.

Gaunersdorfer, A., Hommes, C., 2007. A nonlinear structural model for volatility clustering. In: Teyssîrè, G., Kirman, A.P. (Eds.), Long Memory in Economics. Springer, Berlin.

Ghonghadze, J., Lux, T., 2016. Bringing an elementary agent-based model to the data: estimation via GMM and an application to forecasting of asset price volatility. Journal of Empirical Finance 37, 1–19.

Gilli, M., Winker, P., 2003. A global optimization heuristic for estimating agent based models. Computational Statistics and Data Analysis 42, 299–312.

Glaser, M., Langer, T., Reynders, J., Weber, M., 2007. Framing effects in stock market forecasts: the difference between asking for prices and asking for returns. Review of Finance 11 (2), 325–357.

Goldbaum, D., Mizrach, B., 2008. Estimating the intensity of choice in a dynamic mutual fund allocation decision with Bruce Mizrach. Journal of Economic Dynamics and Control 32 (12), 3866–3876.

Goldbaum, D., Zwinkels, R., 2014. An empirical investigation of heterogeneity and switching in the foreign exchange market. Journal of Economic Behavior & Organization 107B, 667–684.

Golightly, A., Henderson, D., Sherlock, C., 2015. Delayed acceptance particle MCMC for exact inference in stochastic kinetic models. Statistics and Computing 25, 1039–1055.

Golightly, A., Wilkinson, D., 2011. Bayesian parameter inference for stochastic biochemical network models using particle Markov chain Monte Carlo. Inference Focus 1, 807–820.

Gordon, N., Salmond, D., Smith, A., 1993. Novel approach to nonlinear/non-Gaussian Bayesian state estimation. IEE Proceedings F 140, 107–113.

Gordon, M.J., Shapiro, E., 1956. Capital equipment analysis: the required rate of profit. Management Science 3 (1), 102–110.

Grazzini, J., Richiardi, M., 2015. Estimation of ergodic agent-based models by simulated minimum distance. Journal of Economic Dynamics and Control 51, 148–165.

Grazzini, J., Richiardi, M., Tsionas, M., 2017. Bayesian estimation of agent-based models. Journal of Economic Dynamics and Control 77, 20–47.

Grewal, M., Andrews, A., 2008. Kalman Filtering: Theory and Practice with MATLAB, 3rd ed. John Wiley, Hoboken, NJ.

Grimm, V., Revilla, E., Berger, U., Jeltsch, F., Mooij, W.M., Reilsback, S.F., Thulke, H.-H., Weiner, J., Wiegand, T., DeAngelis, D.L., 2005. Pattern-oriented modeling of agent-based complex systems: lessons from ecology. Science 310, 987–991.

Guerini, M., Moneta, A., 2016. A method for agent-based validation. Manuscript. Scuola Superiore Sant'Anna, Pisa.

Hansen, P.R., Lunde, A., Nason, J.M., 2011. The model confidence set. Econometrica 79 (2), 453–497.

Hartig, F., Calabrese, J., Reineking, B., Wiegand, T., Huth, A., 2011. Statistical inference for stochastic simulation models – theory and application. Ecology Letters 14, 816–827.

Heard, D., 2014. Statistical Inference Utilizing Agent-Based Models. Ph.D. thesis. Duke University.

Herbst, E.P., Schorfheide, F., 2016. Bayesian Estimation of DSGE Models. Princeton University Press.

Higdon, D.M., Gattiker, J., Williams, B., Rightley, M., 2008. Computer model calibration using high-dimensional output. Journal of the American Statistical Association 103, 570–583.

Hommes, C., 2006. Heterogeneous agent models in economics and finance. In: Tesfatsion, L., Judd, K. (Eds.), Handbook of Computational Economics, vol. 2: Agent-Based Computational Economics. Elsevier, Amsterdam, pp. 1109–1186.

Hommes, C., Huang, H., Wang, D., 2005a. A robust rational route to randomness in a simple asset pricing model. Journal of Economic Dynamics and Control 29 (6), 1043–1072.

Hommes, C., in 't Veld, D., 2017. Booms, busts and behavioral heterogeneity in stock prices. Journal of Economic Dynamics and Control 80, 101–124.

Hommes, C.H., Sonnemans, J.H., Tuinstra, J., van de Velden, H., 2005b. Coordination of expectations in asset pricing experiments. The Review of Financial Studies 18 (3), 955–980.

Hong, H., Stein, J., 1999. A unified theory of underreaction, momentum trading, and overreaction in asset markets. The Journal of Finance 54 (6), 2143–2184.

Hooten, M.B., Wikle, C.K., 2010. Statistical agent-based models for discrete spatio-temporal systems. Journal of the American Statistical Association 105, 236–248.

Ionides, E.L., Bhadra, A., Atchadé, Y., King, A., 2011. Iterated filtering. The Annals of Statistics 39 (3), 1776–1802.

Ionides, E., Breto, A., King, A., 2006. Inference for nonlinear dynamical systems. Proceedings of the National Academy of Sciences of the United States of America 103, 18438–18443.

Irle, A., Kauschke, J., Lux, T., Milakovic, M., 2011. Switching rates and the asymptotic behavior of herding models. Advances in Complex Systems 14 (3), 359–376.

Jang, T., 2015. Identification of social interaction effects in financial data. Computational Economics 45 (2), 207–238.

Jang, T., Sacht, S., 2016. Animal spirits and the business cycle: empirical evidence from moment matching. Metroeconomica 67 (1), 76–113.

Jongen, R., Verschoor, W.F.C., Wolff, C.C.P., 2008. Foreign exchange rate expectations: survey and synthesis. Journal of Economic Surveys 22 (1), 140–165.

Jongen, R., Verschoor, W.F.C., Wolff, C.C.P., Zwinkels, R.C.J., 2012. Explaining dispersion in foreign exchange expectations: a heterogeneous agent approach. Journal of Economic Dynamics and Control 36 (5), 719–735.

Kantas, N., Doucet, A., Singh, S., Maciejowski, J., Chopin, N., 2015. On particle methods for parameter estimation in state-space models. Statistical Science 30, 328–351.

Kim, S., Shephard, N., Chib, S., 1998. Stochastic volatility: likelihood inference and comparison with ARCH models. The Review of Economic Studies 65 (3), 361–393.

Kirman, A., 1993. Ants, rationality, and recruitment. The Quarterly Journal of Economics 108, 137–156.

Kitagawa, G., 1996. Monte Carlo filter and smoother for non-Gaussian nonlinear state space models. Journal of Computational and Graphical Statistics 5, 1–25.

Kitagawa, G., 1998. A self-organizing state-space model. Journal of the American Statistical Association 93, 1203–1215.

Koskinen, J., Edling, C., 2012. Modelling the evolution of a bipartite network—peer referral in interlocking directorates. Social Networks 34, 309–322.

Koskinen, J., Snijders, T., 2007. Bayesian inference for dynamic social network data. Journal of Statistical Planning and Inference 137, 3930–3938.

Kouwenberg, R., Markiewicz, A., Verhoeks, R., Zwinkels, R.C., 2017. Model uncertainty and exchange rate forecasting. Journal of Financial and Quantitative Analysis 52 (1), 341–363.

Kouwenberg, R., Zwinkels, R., 2014. Forecasting the US housing market. International Journal of Forecasting 30 (3), 415–425.

Kouwenberg, R., Zwinkels, R., 2015. Endogenous price bubbles in a multi-agent system of the housing market. PLoS ONE 10 (6), e129070.

Kristensen, D., Shin, Y., 2012. Estimation of dynamic models with nonparametric simulated maximum likelihood. Journal of Econometrics 167 (1), 76–94.

Kukacka, J., Barunik, J., 2017. Estimation of financial agent-based models with simulated maximum likelihood. Journal of Economic Dynamics and Control 85, 21–45.

Künsch, H.R., 2005. Recursive Monte Carlo filters: algorithms and theoretical analysis. The Annals of Statistics 33, 1983–2021.

Lamperti, F., 2015. An Information Theoretic Criterion for Empirical Validation of Time Series Models. LEM Working Paper 2015/02. Sant'Anna School of Advanced Studies, Pisa.

LeBaron, B., 2001. Empirical regularities from interacting long- and short-memory investors in an agent-based stock market. IEEE Transactions on Evolutionary Computation 5, 442–455.

Lingala, N., Namachchivaya, N.S., Perkowski, N., Yeong, H.C., 2012. Particle filtering in high-dimensional chaotic systems. Chaos 22 (4), 047509.

Lof, M., 2015. Rational speculators, contrarians, and excess volatility. Management Science 61, 1889–1901.

Lopes, H.F., Tsay, R.S., 2011. Particle filters and Bayesian inference in financial econometrics. Journal of Forecasting 30 (1), 168–209.

Lux, T., 2009a. Rational forecasts or social opinion dynamics? Identification of interaction effects in a business climate survey. Journal of Economic Behavior & Organization 72 (2), 638–655.

Lux, T., 2009b. Stochastic behavioural asset-pricing models and the stylized facts. In: Hens, T., Schenk-Hoppé, K. (Eds.), Handbook of Financial Markets: Dynamics and Evolution. North-Holland, Amsterdam (Chapter 3).

Lux, T., 2012. Estimation of an agent-based model of investor sentiment formation in financial markets. Journal of Economic Dynamics and Control 36 (8), 1284–1302.

Lux, T., 2017. Estimation of agent-based models using sequential Monte Carlo methods. Journal of Economic Dynamics and Control. In press.

Lux, T., Alfarano, S., 2016. Financial power laws: empirical evidence, models, and mechanisms. Chaos, Solitons and Fractals 88, 3–18.

Macy, M., Willer, R., 2002. From factors to actors: computational sociology and agent-based modeling. Annual Review of Sociology 28, 143–166.

Malik, S., Pitt, M.K., 2011. Particle filters for continuous likelihood evaluation and maximisation. Journal of Econometrics 165 (2), 190–209.

Manzan, S., Westerhoff, F., 2007. Heterogeneous expectations, exchange rate dynamics and predictability. Journal of Economic Behavior & Organization 64, 111–128.

Mátyás, L., 1999. Generalized Method of Moments Estimation. University Press, Cambridge.

Menkhoff, L., 2010. The use of technical analysis by fund managers: international evidence. Journal of Banking & Finance 34 (11), 2573–2586.

Menkhoff, L., Rebitzky, R.R., Schröder, M., 2009. Heterogeneity in exchange rate expectations: evidence on the chartist–fundamentalist approach. Journal of Economic Behavior & Organization 70, 241–252.

Molina, G., Bayarri, M., Berger, J., 2005. Statistical inverse analysis for a network microsimulator. Technometrics 47, 388–398.

Nelson, R., Winter, F., 1982. An Evolutionary Theory of Economic Change. Belknap Press, Cambridge.

Olsson, J., Rydén, T., 2008. Asymptotic properties of particle filter-based maximum likelihood estimators for state space models. Stochastic Processes and Their Applications 118, 649–680.

Pitt, M., Malik, S., Doucet, A., 2014. Simulated likelihood inference for stochastic volatility models using continuous particle filtering. Annals of the Institute of Statistical Mathematics 66 (3), 527–552.

Rasouli, S., Timmermans, H., 2013. Using emulators to approximate predicted performance indicators of complex microsimulation and multiagent models of travel demand. Transportation Letters 5, 96–103.

Reitz, S., Westerhoff, F.H., 2003. Nonlinearities and cyclical behavior: the role of chartists and fundamentalists. Studies in Nonlinear Dynamics and Econometrics 7 (4), 3.

Reitz, S., Westerhoff, F., Wieland, C., 2006. Target zone interventions and coordination of expectations. Journal of Optimization Theory and Applications 128, 453–467.

Salle, I., Yildizoğlu, M., 2014. Efficient sampling and meta-modeling for computational economic models. Computational Economics 44 (4), 507–536.

Schauten, M., Willemstein, R., Zwinkels, R., 2015. A tale of feedback trading by hedge funds. Journal of Empirical Finance 34, 239–259.

Schelling, T., 1971. Dynamic models of segregation. Journal of Mathematical Sociology 1, 143–186.

Shi, Z., Zheng, M., 2016. Structural estimation of information-driven heterogeneity. Manuscript. Chinese University of Hong Kong.

Shiller, J., 1984. Stock prices and social dynamics. Brookings Papers on Economic Activity 2, 457–508.

Sisson, S., Fan, Y., Tanaka, M., 2005. Sequential Monte Carlo without likelihoods. Proceedings of the National Academy of Sciences of the United States of America 104, 1760–1765.

Snijders, T., 1996. Stochastic actor-oriented models for network change. The Journal of Mathematical Sociology 21, 149–172.

Snijders, T., 2001. The statistical evaluation of social network dynamics. Sociological Methodology 31, 361–395.

Snijders, T., 2017. Siena algorithms. Manuscript.

Snijders, T., Koskinen, J., Schweinberger, M., 2010. Maximum likelihood estimation for social network dynamics. Annals of Applied Statistics 4, 567–588.

Snijders, T., Steglich, C., Schweinberger, M., 2007. Modeling the co-evolution of networks and behavior. In: van Montfort, K., Oud, H., Satorra, A. (Eds.), Longitudinal Models in the Behavioral and Related Sciences. Lawrence Erlbaum.

Stephenson, D., Collins, D., Rougier, J., Chandler, R., 2012. Statistical problems in the probabilistic prediction of climate change. EnvironMetrics 23, 364–372.

Taylor, M.P., Allen, H., 1992. The use of technical analysis in the foreign exchange market. Journal of International Money and Finance 11, 304–314.

Ter Ellen, S., Hommes, C., Zwinkels, R., 2017. Comparing Behavioral Heterogeneity Across Asset Classes. Working paper.

Ter Ellen, S., Verschoor, W.F.C., Zwinkels, R.C.J., 2013. Dynamic expectation formation in the foreign exchange market. Journal of International Money and Finance 37, 75–97.

Ter Ellen, S., Zwinkels, R., 2010. Oil price dynamics: a behavioral finance approach with heterogeneous agents. Energy Economics 32 (6), 1427–1434.

Teräsvirta, T., 1994. Specification, estimation and evaluation of smooth transition autoregressive models. Journal of the American Statistical Association 89, 208–218.

Thiele, J., Kurth, W., Grimm, V., 2014. Facilitating parameter estimation and sensitivity analysis of agent-based models: a cookbook using NetLogo and 'R'. Journal of Artificial Societies and Social Simulation 17, 11.

Toni, T., Welch, D., Strelkowa, N., Ipsen, A., Stumpf, M., 2008. Approximate Bayesian computation scheme for parameter inference and model selection in dynamical systems. Journal of the Royal Society Interface 6, 187–202.

Verschoor, W., Zwinkels, R., 2013. Do foreign exchange fund managers behave like heterogeneous agents? Quantitative Finance 13, 1125–1134.

Vigfusson, 1997. Switching between chartists and fundamentalists, a Markov regime-switching approach. International Journal of Financial Economics, 291–305.

Wang, S., Chen, W., Tsui, K.L., 2009. Bayesian validation of computer models. Technometrics 51, 439–451.

Yu, J., 2005. On leverage in a stochastic volatility model. Journal of Econometrics 127 (2), 165–178.

Zappa, P., Zagaglia, P., 2012. Network Formation in the Euro Interbank Market: A Longitudinal Analysis of the Turmoil. Working paper. University of Italian Switzerland.

EXPERIMENTS

Heterogeneous Agent Modeling: Experimental Evidence[*]

Jasmina Arifovic[*,1]**, John Duffy**[†]

[*]*Simon Fraser University, Burnaby, BC, Canada*
[†]*University of California, Irvine, CA, United States*
[1]*Corresponding author: e-mail address: arifovic@sfu.edu*

CONTENTS

1 INTRODUCTION

The world consists of heterogeneous agents who differ from one another in numerous respects. Modeling such heterogeneity presents the economics profession with a

[*]We thank two referees for their thoughtful comments and suggestions on an earlier draft.

number of challenges. For instance, which dimensions of heterogeneity are the most empirically relevant? What range of heterogeneity should be allowed? Do agents simply differ in their preferences or do they also depart in various predictable degrees from the rational choice framework? In this chapter we show how experimental evidence on agent-type heterogeneity can be used to answer these questions and how experimental evidence has been used to construct parsimonious yet rich heterogeneous agent models. We further demonstrate how such experimentally validated heterogeneous agent models can explain a number of important economic phenomena that would be difficult to explain using the standard homogeneous, rational actor approach.

As a motivating example, consider the pricing of assets subject to uncertain dividend realizations. Experimental tests, beginning with Smith et al. (1988), have consistently found that inexperienced subjects over-price such assets relative to the asset's rational expectations fundamental value (see Palan, 2013 for a survey). On the other hand, once a group of subjects has experienced a price "bubble," they are less prone to exhibit mis-pricing in repeated interactions. Thus, inexperience and experience provide one dimension of heterogeneity that can matter for the incidence of price bubbles, as documented by Dufwenberg et al. (2005). An alternative dimension on which agents can display heterogeniety is in their cognitive abilities or the degree of bounded rationality. Bosch-Rosa et al. (2018) and Hanaki et al. (2017) report that the mixture of cognitive abilities in a population of agents, as measured by simple tests, matters for the incidence of asset price bubbles. In particular, they find that bubbles are less likely among more cognitively sophisticated subjects and more likely among groups with mixed cognitive abilities.

The development of heterogeneous agent models came about as the result of the failure of homogeneous, representative agent models to adequately capture micro-level properties of macroeconomic and financial time series data. A further reason is the development of advanced computing power that enabled the use of computational algorithms to solve the more complicated heterogeneous agent models beginning in the second half of the 1990s, e.g., with Campbell (1998), Den Haan (1996), and Krusell and Smith (1998). These researchers and others in the large literature on heterogeneous agent models that has blossomed since (see surveys, e.g., by Heathcoate et al., 2009, Krueger et al., 2016, and Ragot, 2018) have sought to match *distributional* field data on wealth, employment, wage earnings, and educational status, among other factors, using models where agents are allowed to differ in these dimensions and others and where markets are incomplete. At the same time, data on certain features of these heterogeneous-agent models, for instance data on individual's cognitive abilities, or their expectations about future variables, are not generally available, and so modelers have often used the short-cut assumption that agents are unboundedly rational and possess rational expectations. Nevertheless, as already noted, agents *can* differ in the boundedness of their rationality and in their forecast specifications and these differences are often important, micro-level building blocks for heterogeneous-agent representations, e.g., in the literature on learning in macroeconomics (Sargent, 1993; Brock and Hommes, 1997, 1998; Grandmont,

1998; Evans and Honkaphoja, 2001). Perhaps as a consequence, some researchers have begun to conduct controlled experiments addressing expectation formation and the extent of bounded rationality in the laboratory. A further use of laboratory experiments has been to address questions of equilibrium selection in settings, e.g., bank runs, where there can be multiple rational expectations equilibria, and where theory is silent about the conditions under which a particular equilibrium is selected.

The use of controlled laboratory experimental evidence to validate as well as to provide evidence for heterogeneous agent models is a relatively recent methodology, but it has also spawned the development of the literature in agent-based modeling (see Duffy, 2006 for a survey). Once a laboratory experiment has been programmed, it is a simple matter to automate the responses of the human subjects with robot players. Some laboratory experiments involve interactions between human subjects and robot players in an effort to reduce noise, e.g., Hommes et al. (2005), discussed below. Gode and Sunder (1993) took the logical step of completely replacing the human subjects with robot players in their exploration of behavior in continuous double oral auctions, and this work was influential in the blossoming of the agent-based approach to social science research. Many agent-based modelers use experimental data to calibrate or validate their heterogeneous agents, but most do not, as they find the constraints of laboratory environments too confining. In this chapter we discuss the development of heterogeneous agent models that *were* conditioned on experimental data, or that were used to validate experimental findings. In some instances (e.g., Arifovic et al., 2017 discussed in Section 4.2.2) heterogeneous agent models are used to help design experiments.

The experimental evidence we discuss comes primarily from studies involving the "convenience sample" of university student subjects. This population has been dismissed by some with the dubious claim that students "are not real people" (List, 2011, p. 4). Field data studies involving "real actors" might seem to be more empirically valid, but these studies often involve a considerable loss of control relative to laboratory studies that can make causal inference more difficult, if not impossible (Falk and Heckman, 2009). In defense of the use of undergraduate subjects, we note that economic models are often so general and parsimonious that there do not exist any real-world "professionals" who might be expected to outperform the student subjects. Indeed, Frechette (2015) reports that among 13 experimental studies that have compared the performance of student subjects with professionals, the professionals do no better than the student subjects in 9 of these studies. Among the other 4 studies, professionals are closer to theoretical predictions than students in just 1 study, while students are closer than professionals in the other 3 studies! Thus, it seems that not much is lost, and greater control is gained by examining data from laboratory experiments with student subjects. Indeed, in several instances there are striking parallels between the heterogeneity observed in the laboratory and that found in studies using non-experimental field data.

This survey adds to, builds upon and extends several prior reviews of the experimental evidence for heterogeneity and the use of such data as a rationale for heterogeneous agent modeling. Duffy (2006) provides a survey detailing the complementarities between human subject experiments and agent-based models, which necessarily involve heterogeneous, interacting agents possessing various degrees of rationality. Many heterogeneous agent models are derived in the context of macroeconomic or financial market settings, which we also focus on here.[1] Prior surveys of experiments related to macroeconomics and finance can be found in Assenza et al. (2014), Duffy (2006, 2010, 2016), and Hommes (2011, 2013). In addition to providing an update to these surveys, we emphasize the role of heterogeneity in agent or subject types for better understanding aggregate phenomena.

The rest of this chapter is organized as follows. Section 2 discusses heterogeneity and bounded rationality in both optimization and forecasting tasks. In that section we make a distinction between "learning to optimize" and "learning to forecast" experiments. Section 3 discusses the consequences of heterogeneous agent types for monetary policy. Finally, Section 4 discusses evidence for heterogeneity in equilibrium selection among models of interest to macro economists, including bank run models and network economy models admitting multiple types of payments.

2 HETEROGENEITY AND BOUNDED RATIONALITY IN DECISION MAKING

In this section we discuss evidence that experimental subjects' choices depart in several different ways from the homogeneous rational actor model. Specifically we focus on the dynamics of group decision making, individual intertemporal optimization and expectation formation. We wish to emphasize at the outset that we view the homogeneous rational actor model as an important benchmark for economic analysis. Indeed, without this benchmark, we would not be able to characterize the many ways in which agents exhibit heterogeneous behavior.

2.1 GROUP DECISIONS ON PROVISION OF A PUBLIC GOOD

One of the simplest group decision-making experiments that reliably reveals heterogeneity in decision-making among members of a group is the linear public goods game, as first studied by Isaac and Walker (1988). This is an N-player game and while it is typically played in the laboratory with small numbers of subjects, in principle, it can be played with any population of size N, and so we include it here in our discussion of macroeconomic experiments.[2] In this game, the N players repeat-

---

[1]For heterogeneous agent models derived from games or microeconomic settings, see Mauersberger and Nagel (2018) appearing in this volume.

[2]Indeed, Issac et al. (1994) report experiments with large group sizes of $N = 40$ and $N = 100$. More generally, we regard games with $N \leq 2$ to be the domain of game theory or decision theory (and the subject of the chapter by Mauersberger and Nagel, 2018), while games with $N > 3$ present aggregation issues and games with large N tend to approximate the competitive market conditions that are often assumed to hold in macroeconomic and finance settings.

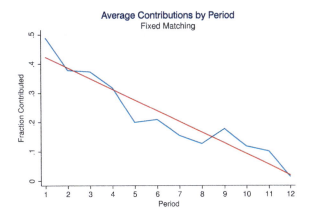

FIGURE 1

Fraction of endowment contributed to the public good in 4-player public good games with $M = 0.4$ under fixed matchings. Averages from eight 4-player groups. Source: Duffy and Lafky (2016).

edly decide whether or not to contribute some portion of their (typically common) endowment, w, to a public account with the remainder going to their private account. Contributions to the public account yield a public good benefit to all N players. Denote the amount that agent i contributes to the public account by c_i. In the public good game, player i's payoff is given by:

$$\pi_i = w - c_i + M \sum_{j=1}^{N} c_j \qquad (1)$$

The key assumption made in this game is that $1/N < M < 1$. While it *would* be efficient for all to set $c_i = w$, in which case $\pi_i = MNw > w$ by the assumption that $M > 1/N$, since the marginal per capita return (MPCR) to contributing to the public good, $M < 1$, it is in fact a dominant strategy for each *individual* agent to contribute nothing to the public good, i.e., to set $c_i = 0$. Thus, this public good game is essentially an N-player prisoner's dilemma game.

By contrast with the rational choice prediction of no contribution, subjects in experimental public good games generally *do* contribute positive amounts to the public good, though these amounts decline with repetition of the game. Fig. 1 shows a typical pattern of giving to the public account (public good) over 12 periods when $N = 4$ and $M = 0.4$. Subjects were incentivized to maximize the payoff function π_i in every period of the experiment. As the figure shows, on average subjects contribute about 1/2 of their endowment to the public good in the first period, but this contribution declines to nearly zero by the 12th and final period.

The pattern of over-contribution and gradual decay in contributions to public goods can be accounted for by *heterogeneity* in the choices of subject participants. Evidence for such heterogeneity has been produced by Fischbacher et al. (2001) us-

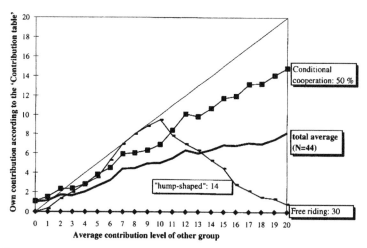

FIGURE 2

Type heterogeneity in a one-shot public good game. Source: Fischbacher et al. (2001).

ing a simple "strategy-method" design.[3] In this design, subjects are presented with the payoff function of the public good game with $N = 4$, $w = 20$, and $M = 0.4$ and were asked to make two types of decisions. The first decision was to indicate how much they would contribute. The second decision involved completion of a contribution schedule showing how much each subject would contribute conditional on the average contribution of the other 3 subjects in their group. Specifically, for each (integer) average contribution amount the other 3 subjects, $0, 1, 2, \ldots 20$ of their 20 token endowment, each subject supplied 21 conditional responses indicating how much they would conditionally contribute. Finally, subjects were matched in groups of four. One, randomly chosen subject's decision was made according to his contribution table while the other three subjects' choices were made according to their unconditional contribution decision; since the determination of which decision was chosen was random, subjects were incentivized to seriously consider both decisions. Then subjects were paid according to the outcome of their group's total contribution. The results of this experiment are nicely summarized in Fig. 2 which reports on the average contribution schedule amounts of selected classes of subjects. The contribution schedules of 22 of the 44 subjects (50%) are consistent with reciprocity or "conditional cooperation" as indicated by the close alignment of the conditional cooperation amounts with the 45 degree line. Thirteen subjects (about 30%) submitted a contribution schedule with 0 for all 21 entries. These subjects are labeled "free riding" types since they are playing according to the raitonal best response. Six subjects (about 14%) are hybrids of the conditional cooperator and free-riding types; they

---

[3]In a strategy method experiment, one elicits each subject's complete contingent strategy as opposed to simply asking subjects to make a choice. The strategy is then typically played on the subjects' behalf, thus incentivizing subjects to truthfully reveal their strategy.

are conditionally cooperative up to point (around $1/2$ of ω) and then become more like free-riders giving rise to the label of "hump-shaped" in Fig. 2 The remaining 6 percent of subjects are not easily classifiable.

Importantly, this heterogeneity in contribution decisions can be used to account for the pattern of initial over-contribution to the public good and the subsequent decay in such contributions over time. For instance, Ambrus and Pathak (2011) show that the presence of two player types, selfish (free-riders) and reciprocal (conditional cooperators) alone suffices to generate this pattern. The initial positive contribution levels are all due to the reciprocal types who start out contributing positive amounts. By contrast, the selfish types contribute nothing. At the end of each round, individual payoffs, π_i, are realized and the group payoff component, $M \sum_{i=1}^{N} c_i$ can be inferred (or more typically, it is simply revealed). The reciprocal types learn that the group average is less than would obtain if all others were contributing levels similar to their own contribution levels and so these types conditionally adjust their giving downward in the next round, given this new information. This downward adjustment explains the decline in contributions over time. Note that this pattern of behavior requires some measure of both of these two distinct, heterogeneous player types, a theme that we will see again and again in this chapter.

In addition to the over-contribution and decay pattern in public good experiments, there are other features of this environment pointing to heterogeneity in subject behavior. For instance, while average contributions in public goods games begin at around 50% of the total endowment, typically more than half of subjects begin by equally splitting their endowment between the private and public accounts. There is also considerable variation in individual contributions as a percentage of endowment. Individual contributions show no consistent monotonic pattern over time. Some increase, some decrease, and some follow a "zig-zag" pattern. Thus, subject behavior in this environment is best described as being 'persistently' heterogeneous. Further, increases in the MPCR lead to an increase in the average rate of contributions, especially in small group sizes. Additionally, increases in the size of the group also lead to an increase in the average rate of contributions. This is particularly true in later repetitions and for small values of the MPCR. Finally, there is experimental evidence for a "restart effect"; that is, if after 10 periods there is a surprise announcement that the public good game is restarting anew, subjects' contributions in period 11 increase relative to those in period 10.

Standard theory provides little help in understanding this degree of heterogeneity in choices and behavior over time. But this behavior can be accounted for by an individual evolutionary learning model (IEL) proposed by Arifovic and Ledyard (2012). The IEL model is based on an evolutionary process which is individual and not social. In the IEL, each agent is assumed to carry a collection of possible strategies in their memory. These remembered strategies are continually evaluated and the better ones are used with higher probability. IEL is particularly well-suited to repeated games with large strategy spaces such as subsets of the real line (as in the public good game) We discuss the details of the IEL implementation and other applications where it is used for validation of experimental data in Section 5. Here, we focus on the results related to public good games.

Arifovic and Ledyard (2012) extend the payoff function (Eq. (1)) used in the public goods experiments to include other regarding preferances, specifically altruism and envy considerations and they assume that the extent of these other-regarding preferences varies across agents. In other words, some agents can be completely selfish, some more or less altruistic as well as more or less envious. This corresponds to the interpretation that human subjects walk into the lab with given type of other regarding preference.

In order to incorporate other regarding preferences into IEL learning, Arifovic and Ledyard used the following utility (payoff function):

$$u^i(c) = \pi^i(c) + \beta^i \bar{\pi}(c) - \gamma^i \max\{0, \bar{\pi}(c) - \pi^i(c)\} \tag{2}$$

where $\pi^i(c)$ is the standard public good payoff as given in Eq. (1), $\bar{\pi}(c)$ is the average payoff of all N players (revealed at the end of each round), $\beta^i \geq 0$ indicates how altruistic player i is,[4] and $\gamma^i \geq 0$ defines how 'spiteful' or 'envious' agent i is. That is, i loses utility when i's payoff is below the average payoff in this group. Arifovic and Ledyard model the heterogeneity by assuming that each subject i comes to the lab endowed with a value of (β^i, γ^i) which is distributed, independently and identically, in the population according to a distribution $F(\beta, \gamma)$.

With linear other-regarding preferences (ORP), for given (N, M) and heterogeneity across (β, γ), Arifovic and Ledyard show that three types of Nash Equilibrium strategies: free riding or selfishness $(c^i = 0)$, full contribution or altruism $(c^i = w)$, and contributing an amount equal to the average or fair-minded behavior $(c^i = \bar{c} = (\sum_i c^i)/N)$. Thus, the introduction of ORP adds the possibility of different equilibrium levels of contributions. However, that theory is still static, i.e., it predicts constant levels of contribution, and thus, cannot account for the observed patterns of public good contributions over time.

Arifovic and Ledyard further assume a specific distribution of types, $F(\cdot)$. Some agents, P% of the population, are purely "selfish"; that is, they have the type $(0, 0)$. The rest, $(1 - P)\%$ of the population, have other-regarding preferences where the (β^i, γ^i) are distributed identically, independently, and uniformly on $[0, B] \times [0, G]$.

Arifovic and Ledyard use the experimental data of Isaac and Walker (IW) to find 'good' values for (P, B, G).[5] For each IW treatment, (M, N), and for each parameter triple, (P, B, G), they conducted 40 trials. Each trial involves a draw of a new type from $F(\cdot)$ for each agent. Those types were selected randomly as follows. Each agent became selfish with probability P. If an agent's type turned out to be selfish, then her utility was based only on her own payoff. That is, $\beta^i = \gamma^i = 0$. If the agent

---

[4] Here altruism refers to a preference for higher values of the average payoff to all agents.
[5] In their approach to learning in general, Arfiovic and Ledyard's methodology is to find parameters that provide a 'loose' fit for one set of data, and then use these parameters to generate simulation data for other experiments.

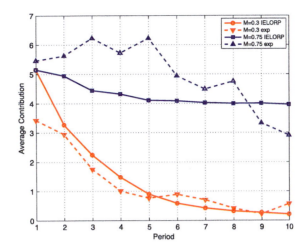

FIGURE 3

IEL and experimental data for $N = 4$.

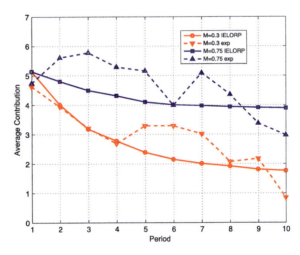

FIGURE 4

IEL and experimental data for $N = 10$.

did not become selfish, then a set of values of β^i and γ^i was drawn uniformly and independently from the ranges $[0, B]$, and $[0, G]$ respectively. Arifovic and Ledyard conducted a grid search over the values for P, B, and G to minimize the NMSE between the simulation and experimental data. The data they used was average contribution over all ten periods and average contributions over the last three periods.

Fig. 3 shows IEL simulation and experimental data for treatments where $N = 4$ and M takes on either a low value of 0.3 or a high of 0.75. Fig. 4 shows the same comparison but for $N = 10$.

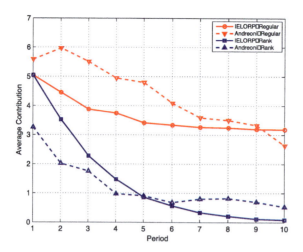

FIGURE 5

IEL and Andreoni's *Regular* and *Rank* treatment.

Further, Arifovic and Ledyard examine how their model performs out of sample using parameter values estimated from IW's data, but in comparions with other experimental datasets. Here, we illustrate the out of sample prediciton exercise using data reported by Andreoni (1995) for two public good treatments. Andreoni used $(N, M) = (5, 0.5)$ for both treatments, *Regular* and *Rank*.[6] In Fig. 5, we present the pattern of average contributions for Andreoni's data and for the IEL simulations.

Finally, Arifovic and Ledyard were also able to 'generate' the aforementioned *restart* effect, which has been a huge puzzle for both theory and simulation models. Andreoni (1988) was the first to present evidence of the *restart* effect (later replicated by Croson, 1996). The key experimental finding is that average public good contributions by fixed groups of N subjects increase after a surprise restart of the public good game but then began to decline again. IEL simulations also capture this pattern for public good contributions as can be seen in (Fig. 6).

Arifovic and Ledyard demonstrate the robustness of the IEL (with ORP) to a wide range of changes in its parameter values.[7]

2.2 INTERTEMPORAL OPTIMIZATION

A workhorse framework for intertemporal optimization is the lifecycle model of consumption and savings due to Modigliani and Brumberg (1954) and Ando and

---

[6]In the *Regular* treatment, subjects' payoffs were the same as in IW. In the *Rank* treatment, subjects were paid according to their payoff ranking in order to encourage greater free-riding behavior.

[7]Most behavioral models are parameterized to fit a specific experimental dataset. Such models are not typically robust to slight parameter changes. However, IEL is generally robust to changes in its parameter values across different applications.

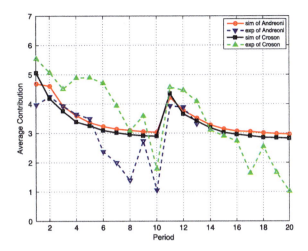

FIGURE 6

Restart effect: A surprise restart of the public good game following period 10. IEL simulations compared to the experimental data of Andreoni (1988) and Croson (1996).

Modigliani (1963). An early experimental evaluation of this model was conducted by Johnson et al. (2001), who asked subjects to suppose that they had just turned age 35 and would live for 40 more years (periods) before dying at age 75. Subjects were instructed that their annual salary would be $25,000 until retirement at age 65, after which they would get 0. They could borrow or save at a known, constant 4 percent interest rate and it was also known that there was no inflation, discounting, taxes or other expenses to be paid nor any uncertainty. Consumption choices were made once per year (period) and what was not consumed was automatically saved. In one treatment using this environment, subjects were asked to make 40 choices as to how much they would consume in every period (year), and they could condition these choices on information about their accumulated asset position (from savings). Subjects were paid a flat fee for their answers since there was no objective right or wrong answer to these decisions. However, in a later treatment, the same subjects were asked to reconsider the same lifecycle problem and rank their *preferences* over five different financially feasible lifetime consumption profiles, each of which exhausted their resources in the final 75th period of life. The five consumption profile choices were:

1. $21,841 per year, every year, i.e., constant consumption.
2. $16,008 at age 35, growing by 2% per year thereafter.
3. $11,240 at age 35, growing by 4% per year thereafter.
4. $28,592 at age 35, falling by 2% per year thereafter.
5. $23,420 from age 35 until age 65, then $10,921 from 65 to 75.

The distribution of subjects' consumption profile choices is shown in Table 1.

First, as is evident from Table 1, subjects clearly exhibit *heterogeneous* preferences with regard to lifecycle consumption profiles, with a majority of subjects

Table 1 Frequency of subjects choosing alternative profiles

Profile number	1 (0%)	2 (2%)	3 (4%)	4 (−2%)	5 (Step)
First choice	0.23	0.31	0.25	0.13	0.08
Second choice	0.23	0.44	0.15	0.11	0.07

favoring positive growth in their consumption profile over time (choices 2 and 3). Second, Johnson et al. examined the relationship between subjects' consumption choices over 40 periods (from age 35–75) in the first treatment to their expressed first choice consumption profile in the later treatment. Specifically, they calculate the average annual absolute percentage deviation between each subject's most preferred consumption profile and his/her actual consumption choices. For those whose preferred profile was the constant consumption profile (choice 1), the mean deviation is 15 percent; for those preferring the 2 percent, 4 percent, −2 percent, or the step function profile (choices 2–5, respectively), the mean deviations were 21, 25, 37, and 46 percent, respectively. Thus, not only are subjects heterogeneous in their preferences, they are also heterogeneous in the bounded rationality of their decision-making.

A criticism of the Johnson et al. experiment is that the payoffs subjects faced were *hypothetical* and their true preferences were unknown. Subsequent experiments testing intertemporal consumption–savings policies have sought to remedy this problem by inducing subjects to hold specific (concave) preferences over consumption so that the subjects can be rewarded with money payments on the basis of how close their lifecycle consumption profile is to the theoretically optimal consumption path.[8] See, for example, Carbone and Hey (2004), Carbone (2006), Ballinger et al. (2003, 2011), Carbone and Duffy (2014), and Meissner (2016). As in Johnson et al., there is no uncertainty about how long agents will live and the lifecycle income process is known, and possibly stochastic. These studies also report that in certain environments, subject's consumption choices deviate substantially from the unconditional optimal path or even the conditionally optimal path that conditions on a subject's current asset position (wealth). Carbone and Hey (2004) identify four player types, (i) those who understand the basic nature of the problem and behave in a near optimal-manner, (ii) those who are pre-occupied with present consumption and discount the future heavily, (iii) those who seem to like to accumulate wealth and build up large asset positions, and (iv) those who engage in consumption bingeing, building up stocks of wealth over cycles of around 4 or 5 periods and then consuming all of that wealth. Ballinger et al. (2011) report that cognitive abilities, as measured by performance in two non-verbal, visually oriented tests (the Beta III test and a working-memory span test) are correlated with performance in lifecycle consumption planning. Those with high cognitive abilities, perform better (closer to the optimal path) than those with lower cognitive abilities, controlling for demographic and other non-cognitive characteristics.

---

[8] In these experiments, the utility function over consumption in period t, $u(c_t)$ converts a subject's consumption choice into money earnings using the induced mapping u, which is typically a concave function.

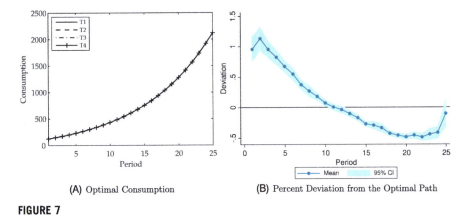

(A) Optimal Consumption

(B) Percent Deviation from the Optimal Path

FIGURE 7

Optimal consumption path and percent deviation from the optimal path in the experiment of Duffy and Li (2017).

Even within the same incentivized lifecycle consumption–savings problem, subjects exhibit heterogeneity with respect to their departures from the optimal or conditionally optimal consumption path. For instance, Duffy and Li (2017) study a lifecycle consumption/savings problem with no uncertainty or discounting, where subjects have induced logarithmic preferences over consumption and face a known lifecycle income profile and a known fixed interest rate on savings. The optimal consumption path in this environment is increasing over the lifecycle (due to the positive interest rate and lack of any discounting), as shown in panel A of Fig. 7, but the behavior of subjects is at odds with this prediction; the mean percentage by which subjects deviate from the optimal consumption path (together with a 95% confidence interval) is shown in panel B of Fig. 7.

As Fig. 7B clearly reveals, subjects consume, on average, more than the optimal amount in the first 10 periods (equivalent to 23 years in model time) and as a consequence, they have less savings later on in life so that in those later periods they under-consume relative to the optimal path. Duffy and Li report that this aggregate pattern of over-consumption followed by under-consumption can be explained by heterogeneity in subject's lifecycle consumption and savings decisions. They report that nearly 50 percent of subjects can be regarded as hand-to-mouth consumers, consuming all (or nearly all of their income) in each period while the remaining subjects can be characterized as conditionally optimal consumers, who make calculation mistakes, but can be viewed as re-optimizing their consumption/savings plan at each new period of the lifecycle, conditional on their current asset holdings. The presence of these two types explains both the over- and under-consumption phenomenon and its magnitude. In the early periods of life, when income is greater than the optimal consumption path, the presence of hand-to mouth consumers means that average consumption is greater than optimal. When income is less than the conditionally optimal amount in the later (retirement) periods of life, the presence of the hand-to-mouth consumers means that average consumption is below the optimal level. Interestingly, Campbell and Mankiw (1989) used a similar, two-type model with 50 percent hand-to-mouth consumers and 50 percent rational consumers to explain volatility in aggregate U.S. quarterly consumption data.

2.3 EXPECTATION FORMATION

Heterogeneity in expectation formation is also well documented using laboratory experiments. In many models in macroeconomics and finance, expectations matter for optimizing choices, and the results of those choices in turn determine the realizations of the variables that agents were forecasting. This belief–outcome interaction can be complicated for subjects (not to mention theorists), and so typically experimentalists have asked subjects to choose actions with expectations implicit, or to form expectations only and to be paid on the basis of the accuracy of those expectations, see, e.g., Schmalensee (1976), Dwyer et al. (1983), Smith et al. (1988), and Kelley and Friedman (2002).

For instance, in one early experiment, Hey (1994) asked subjects to forecast a random time series variable, X_t. The law of motion for X_t was autoregressive, i.e., $X_t = \mu + \rho X_{t-1} + \epsilon_t$, where μ, and ρ are fixed parameters and ϵ_t is a mean zero noise term with variance σ^2, but subjects were *not* aware of this data generating process. They could choose a prior history of $k \leq 50$ past values for X_t and after observing this history, they were asked to form forecasts. They were incentivized to form accurate forecasts in each of 20 periods, t, as the payoff function for each subject, i, in each period t, was a quadratic scoring rule of the form $\pi_i = \max[a - b(X_{i,t}^e - X_t)^2, 0]$, where $X_{i,t}^e$ denotes subject i's time t expectation of X_t; the actual value of X_t was revealed ex-post and then earnings were determined. Hey reports that few subjects, just 2 out of 48 (4%), formed the rational expectation, $EX = \frac{\mu}{1-\rho}$, while 2/3 (66%) of subjects could be characterized as adaptive learners. The remaining 30% were not characterizable using either rational or adaptive expectations!

2.3.1 Asset Pricing Experiments

Hey's experiment has an exogenous data generating process. To capture endogenous belief–outcome interaction, it is necessary for expectations to matter for the variables that subjects are forecasting. A simple framework in which this is the case is an asset pricing model studied experimentally by Hommes et al. (2005). In this model there is a 1 period, risk free bond paying a known, fixed return of r per period and long-lived risky asset (e.g., a stock) paying stochastic, i.i.d. dividends each period with a mean value of $\bar{d}$. The co-existence of these two types of assets requires, via arbitrage, that the price of the risky asset is given by:

$$p_t = \frac{1}{1+r}(p_{t+1}^e + \bar{d}) \tag{3}$$

where p_{t+1}^e is the expectation of the risky asset at time $t+1$. Under rational expectations, $p_{t+1}^e = p_t = p^f \equiv \frac{\bar{d}}{r}$, so that the rational expectation equilibrium (REE) price path should be $p_t = p^f$. Hommes et al. (2005) study whether subjects can price the risky asset consistent with this rational expectations prediction in a laboratory experiment. However, they study a slightly altered version of this pricing equation wherein the price of the risky asset is generated by:

$$p_t = \frac{1}{1+r} \left((1 - \eta_t) p_{t+1}^e + \eta_t p^f + \bar{d} + \epsilon_t \right)$$

where ϵ_t is a mean zero noise term and $\eta_t \in (0, 1)$ is a time-varying weight assigned to fundamental traders' price forecasts, i.e., those who correctly price the asset according to its fundamental value, p^f. The remaining weight, $(1 - \eta_t)$, is given to non-fundamental, adaptive learning agents. In the Hommes et al. (2005) experiment, the fundamental traders are robot players, and the weight assigned to their rational expectations price forecast, η_t, diminishes as the system converges. The human subjects, six per group, comprise the non-fundamental forecasters. In each period t, each human subject i forms a forecast of the price in period $t + 1$, $p_{i,t}^e$, and each is paid according to the ex-post accuracy of their own forecast using the same quadratic scoring rule as in Hey' study. Differently from Hey, the experiment is a group-decision making task since p_{t+1}^e in the equation used to determine p_t is taken to be the average of the six human subjects' forecasts, i.e., $p_{t+1}^e = \frac{1}{6} \sum_{i=1}^6 p_{i,t+1}^e$. Notice further that expectations now matter for actual price realizations so that there is belief–outcome interaction. Subjects in the experiment were asked to forecast a price for the asset in the interval [0, 100] and were not told any details of the equation determining the realization of p_t, though they know r and $\bar{d}$ and, in principle, could compute $p^f = \frac{\bar{d}}{r}$. In contrast to Hey (1994), subjects in the Hommes et al. design have the incentive to coordinate their expectations over time, so heterogeneity should now only be transitory, and may disappear with experience; the presence of the robot fundamental traders helps in this regard. A further difference is that subjects in the Hommes et al. experiment make forecasts of the price in period $t + 1$ in period t, but the price they forecast in period t is not revealed until period $t + 2$, so, in effect, they are forecasting two periods ahead.

Fig. 8 shows the time series of price forecasts over 50 periods from ten different groups of six forecasters. Several observations are evident. First, only a few groups (2, 5) have converged to the REE price, equal to 60 in this experiment by the end of 50 periods. These groups were found to be comprised of individuals whose forecast rules were of an AR(1) nature, including naive best response, $p_{t+1}^e = p_{t-1}$ or past averaging $p_{t+1}^e = \frac{1}{t-1} \sum_{j=1}^{t-1} p_{t-j}$. Second, there is tremendous coordination on price forecasts *within* each group, a kind of group specific expectation norm. Third, many groups' expectations result in an oscillatory path for prices that sometimes appears to be convergent (groups 4, 7, 10) and sometimes not (groups 1, 6, 8, 9). Both sets of groups are found to be employing an AR(2) expectation formation process of the form: $p_{t+1}^e = \alpha + \beta p_{t-1} + \gamma (p_{t-1} - p_{t-2})$. The estimated value of γ is found to be positive, indicating that if subjects see a positive (negative) trend in the past two prices, they expect prices to continue to increase (decrease). This trend-extrapolation

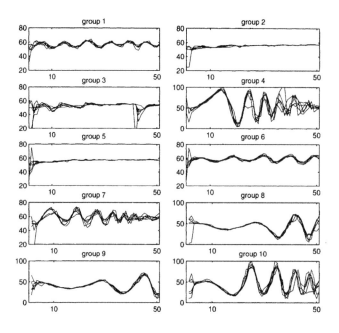

FIGURE 8

Individual price forecasts (p_{t+1}^e) over time, from Hommes et al. (2005).

behavior explains the oscillatory pattern for prices in these groups. Finally, some groups' expectation rule, e.g. group 3, are simply not well understood. Hommes et al. conclude that 75 percent of their subjects can be classified using linear adaptive rules that depart from the rational expectations equilibrium prediction.

Hommes et al. (2008) studied a slightly different version of this same experiment where $p^f = 60$ as before but where the robot players and the noise term were eliminated and the price forecast interval was enlarged by a factor of 10 to [0, 1000]. Their aim was to explore the possibility of rational bubbles, which can be derived as follows. Using the law of iterated expectations, we can expand the price equation as: $p_t = \sum_{i=1}^{n}(1+r)^{-i}\bar{d} + (1+r)^{-n}E_t(p_{t+n})$. Taking the limit as n goes to infinity, $p_t = \sum_{i=1}^{\infty}(1+r)^{-i}\bar{d} + \lim_{n\to\infty}(1+r)^{-n}E_t(p_{t+n})$. Assuming a limit exists, denote the last term by b_t, so that the rational expectations solution consists of a fundamental and a bubble term $p_t = p^f + b_t$. To be a rational bubble, the bubble term must grow at rate r. Hommes et al. did not find evidence for rational bubbles in this strict sense, but they did report that in 5 of their six experiments, prices periodically hit the upper bound of 1000 – more than 15 times fundamentals – before trending down again. They show that this pattern in again driven by positive feedback, trend-following expectation formation rules. Hüsler et al. (2013), using Hommes' data, showed that for the groups in which bubbles arose, the bubble growth rate was "super-exponential". In particular, the rate of change of prices is well approximated by an equation of the form $\log\left(\frac{p_t}{p_{t-1}}\right) = r + \gamma p_{t-1}$, where $\gamma > 0$ is the anchoring weight placed on the more recent price; the positive weight on the latter means that the prices grows at a rate greater than r (super-exponential). Hüsler et al. further show that alternative functional forms for the growth rate of prices (exponential growth or anchoring on lagged returns as opposed to lagged prices) do not perform as well in explaining the path of price bubbles.

The heterogeneity of expectation formation rules means that a single model of adaptive behavior will not suffice to explain the experimental data from these asset pricing experiments. Anufriev and Hommes (2012) therefore propose the use of a heuristic switching model, based on Brock and Hommes (1997) to explain the experimental data of Hommes et al. (2005, 2008). In this simulation model, the price forecasts of several heuristic models, $p^e_{h,t+1}$, indexed by h get aggregated up with weights $n_{h,t}$ to generate the mean price expectation that enters the data generating equation of the model:

$$\bar{p}^e_{t+1} = \sum_{h=1}^{H} n_{h,t} p^e_{h,t+1}$$

The fitness of rule h is updated every period based on past performance,

$$U_{h,t-1} = \mu U_{h,t-2} - (p_{t-1} - p^e_{t-1})^2$$

where $\mu \in (0, 1)$ denotes a memory term. Finally the fitness of each heuristic is used to determine the weight given to it in the expectation equation for $\bar{p}^e_{t+1}$:

$$n_{h,t} = \lambda n_{h,t-1} + (1 - \lambda) \frac{e^{\beta U_{h,t-1}}}{\sum_{h=1}^{H} e^{\beta U_{h,t-1}}}.$$

The four heuristic rules for expectation formation were:

1. Adaptive Expectations (ADA): $p^e_{t+1} = 0.65 p_{t-1} + 0.35 p^e_t$.
2. Weak Trend Following (WTR): $p^e_{t+1} = p_{t-1} + 0.4(p_{t-1} - p_{t-2})$.
3. Strong Trend Following (STR): $p^e_{t+1} = p_{t-1} + 1.3(p_{t-1} - p_{t-2})$.
4. Anchoring and Adjustment (LAA): $p^e_{t+1} = 0.5((t - 1)^{-1} \sum_{j=0}^{t-1} p_j + p_{t-1}) + (p_{t-1} - p_{t-2})$.

These rules were motivated by the estimation results of subjects' individual forecasts, where similar learning rules with only a few significant lags were quite common.

The first rule is a standard adaptive expectations rule while the second and third rules are "trend" following rules, that seek to exploit trends in the most two recent price realizations (between dates $t - 1$ and $t - 2$). The final rule is a flexible anchoring and adjustment rule which puts weight on the hypothesized fundamental price, approximated by the sample average, $(t - 1)^{-1} \sum_{j=0}^{t-1} p_j$, and also gives some weight to price trends.

The model is initialized with equal weights on all four heuristics and a specific choice of parameter values, $\beta = 0.4$, $\eta = 0.7$, and $\delta = 0.9$. In- and out-of-sample

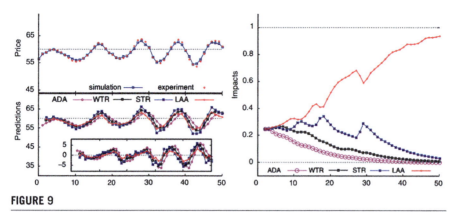

FIGURE 9

Experimental data versus one-step ahead prediction from Anufriev and Hommes's HSM for Group 6 of Hommes et al. (2005).

simulations provide a good fit to the experimental data. An example is shown in Fig. 9, which reports simulation results for group 6 in the asset pricing experiment, which followed an oscillatory path around the REE. As the figure reveals, all four rules in the heuristic switching model initially have some weight, but ultimately the more flexible anchoring and adjustment rule (LAA) becomes dominant in explaining the persistent fluctuations in prices; the adaptive (ADA) and the two trend following rules (WTR and STR) miss the turning points in prices and are thus given less weight over time. In other groups, especially those that converge to the REE, all rules have similar forecasting success and thus all four continue to have weight in the heuristic switching model over time.

2.3.2 Cobweb Model Experiments

A second experimental environment in which there is belief–outcome interaction and evidence for heterogeneous expectations is the Cobweb model of Ezekiel (1938) which is the framework first used by Muth (1961) to formulate the rational expectations hypothesis. This model consists of equations for the demand and supply of a single, perishable good. Demand is a decreasing function of the period t, market price, $D(p_t)$, while supply, which must be chosen one period in advance, is an increasing function of the price expected to prevail at time t, $S(p_t^e)$, based on information available through period $t - 1$. Hommes et al. (2007) elicit price forecasts from $i = 1, 2, \ldots, 6$ subjects, and given these forecasts they optimally solve for the supply that each forecaster i would bring to the market. Thus aggregate supply is given by $\sum_{i=1}^{6} S(p_{i,t}^e)$ and, since the demand side is exogenously given, market clearing implies that the equilibrium price is given by:

$$p_t = D^{-1}\left(\sum_{i=1}^{6} S(p_{i,t}^e)\right) + \epsilon_t \qquad (4)$$

where ϵ_t is an added i.i.d. mean 0 noise term reflecting fundamental uncertainty. Subjects were incentivized to chose $p^e_{i,t}$ as close to p_t as possible as their payoff function was again determined by a quadratic-loss scoring rule. The main treatment variable was a supply function parameter that varied the amount of nonlinearity in supply, and so affected whether the steady state price, p^*, was stable, unstable or strongly unstable under Ezekiel's benchmark choice of naive expectations, $p^e_t = p_{t-1}$, though for more general adaptive learning specifications, the steady state could be stable and the limit of the learning process. The main issue they examined was the validity of the RE prediction that $p^e_t = p^*_t + \epsilon$. They found that the REH found some support in the case where the steady state was stable under naive expectations, but that it did not predict well in the unstable or strongly unstable environments. More precisely, while the mean realized price over the sample of 50 periods was always close to p^* the sample variance was larger and more persistent the greater was the instability of the system under the naive expectations benchmark. Off-the-shelf adaptive learning processes such as past averaging of prices or error-correction approaches were also not as useful in explaining experimental data from the Cobweb model as these models led to too regular fluctuations and predictable autocorrelation patterns not found in the data.

Indeed, an explanation of these findings also requires an explicitly heterogeneous-agent model. Arifovic (1994) was the first to use a *genetic algorithm* to explain experimental findings for the cobweb model similar to those reported by Hommes et al. (2007). Genetic algorithms are computer programs that mimic naturally occurring evolutionary processes: selection based on relative fitness, reproduction and mutation on a population of candidate solutions to an optimization problem. These algorithms, first developed by Holland (1975) (see also Goldberg, 1989), have been shown to be ideal function optimizers for "rugged landscapes" as the population basis of the search and the evolution of new strategies over time avoids the possibility that the algorithm gets stuck at (prematurely converges to) local optima. In a typical Genetic Algorithm, there exists a population of candidate solutions or "chromosomes" coded in some manner, typically a binary encoding. There is also a fitness criterion, e.g., a profit, utility or payoff function that is the objective of the optimization problem and that is used to evaluate the chromosomes. Initial populations of solutions (chromosomes) are typically randomly generated, over some reasonable domain for the solution space. Then solutions are evaluated for their fitness. The most fit solutions are probabilistically more likely to survive into the next "generation" of candidate strategies in a reproduction step to the algorithm. This reproduction step is followed by a crossover step, where pairs of solution strings are randomly matched, a cut-point is randomly determined and the genetic material (binary encodings to one side of the cut point) are swapped in a process mimicking genetic recombination. Finally, encodings are subject to some mutation as well, with some small probability, e.g., a bit is flipped from a 0 to a 1 or vice versa. This process then repeats over multiple generations until some convergence criterion is met or a maximum number of generations has passed. Along this path, genetic algorithms thus consist of very heterogeneous populations of candidates solutions or strategies. In Arifovic's (1994) application to the Cobweb model, the population of chromosomes represented a population of different firms' decision rules as to how much quantity to bring to the market in a given period (demand was automated). Aggregate quantity together with exogenous market demand determined the market price, which was used to evaluate each firm's profits, the fitness criterion. Arifovic found that genetic algorithm simulations, like the experiments of Hommes et al. converged to the rational expectations solution in the stable case and to a neighborhood of the REE in the unstable case, and that the volatility of the heterogeneous agent genetic algorithm was a good approximation to the heterogeneity observed in experimental data. While Arifovic's simulations considered the optimal quantity decision of firms, Hommes and Lux (2013) used a genetic algorithm model on populations of price forecasts in order to address the price volatility in the Hommes et al. (2007) Cobweb model experiments as the system was made more unstable. Like Arifovic (1994), they found that simulations of the genetic algorithm for price forecasts yielded a good match to the experimental data. This match to the experimental data relies upon the genetic algorithm's use of past fitness, its heterogeneity of different solutions, and the genetic operators, which allow for the development of new strategies.

More recently, Arifovic and co-authors have begun working with multiple population genetic algorithms, one population for each decision-maker. These algorithms, which Arifovic refers to as "individual evolutionary learning" (IEL) algorithms are close cousins to genetic algorithms. In addition to having different populations of strategies (different GAs) for each decision-maker, IEL avoids the use of the crossover operation of the genetic algorithm (mutation alone often suffices for experimentation) and it allows for more dynamic specifications of the strategy space, permitting the evolution of conditional strategies. The IEL algorithm was described earlier in connection with the public good game (see Section 2.1) and will also be discussed later in connection with experimental studies of equilibrium selection (bank runs (3.1) and adoption of new payment systems (3.3)).

2.3.3 Positive Versus Negative Feedback

The asset market experiment and the cobweb model experiments differ in two important dimensions. First, in the Cobweb model (Eq. (4)), $p_t = f(p_t^e)$, requiring one step-ahead-forecasts for prices. By contrast in the asset market experiment (Eq. (3)) $p_t = f(p_{t+1}^e)$, requiring two step-ahead forecasts for prices. Second, and more importantly, in the asset market experiment, there is *positive* feedback between price expectations and price realizations, i.e., $\partial f/\partial p_{t+1}^e > 0$ while in the Cobweb model there is negative feedback, i.e., $\partial f/\partial p_t^e < 0$. Positive feedback mechanisms, as in the asset pricing model are associated with strategic complementarities; an increase on one agent's price forecast causes others to choose higher price forecasts as well. By contrast, negative feedback systems are associated with strategic substitutability; a higher price forecast (higher expected demand) by one oligopolist provides incentives for the another oligopolist to lower his or her price forecast.[9] It turns out that

---

[9] See, e.g., Haltiwanger and Waldman (1985).

this difference matters for the speed of convergence to the rational expectations equilibrium, as shown in experimental research by Fehr and Tyran (2001, 2008), Potters and Suetens (2009), Sutan and Willinger (2009), Heemeijer et al. (2009), and Cooper et al. (2017). Here we focus on the work of Fehr and Tyran, Heemeijer et al., and Cooper et al.

In Fehr and Tyran (2001), human subjects play a 4-player "price-setting" game. In each of $2T$ periods, subject i chooses a price P_i and earns a real payoff that is a function of the time t average price chosen by other players, $\bar{P}_{-i,t}$ and the time t nominal money supply M_t:

$$\pi_{i,t} = f\left(P_i, \bar{P}_{-i,t}, M_t\right)$$

The function f yields a unique, dominance-solvable equilibrium for every value of M, is homogeneous of degree 0 in all arguments, and $f_{P_{-i,t}} \geq 0$, so there is a weak, strategic complementarity in price-setting. They conduct a treatment where subjects' earnings are paid according to the above, real payoff function. In addition, there is also a *nominal* payoff treatment where subjects' earnings are reported to them in nominal terms, $P_{-i,t}\pi_i$. In both of these treatments, there is a nominal shock: the nominal money supply is known to be a constant level M for the first T periods and then to decline to a permanently lower level λM, $\lambda < 1$ for the last T periods. The question is then whether subjects will adjust their prices downward at date T from P to λP.

Their results show that, in the *real* payoff treatment, the adjustment to a new, equilibrium nominal price, λP occurred almost instantaneously. However, the adjustment in the second, *nominal* payoff treatment was very sluggish, with nominal prices adjusting slowly to the new equilibrium. Fehr and Tyran characterize this as *money illusion* that depends on whether subjects are paid in real, price adjusted or in nominal terms. This adjustment is more difficult in the normal payoff function treatment where subjects have to correctly deflate their nominal payoff function. In addition, arising from the strategic complementarity in price settings, the failure of some subjects to adjust to the nominal shocks may make it a best response for others who are not subject to money illusion to only partially adjust to the shock.

In order to isolate the latter possibility, Fehr and Tyran (2001) also conduct individual-decision making experiments under both the real and nominal payoff functions where the other $n - 1$ players are known to the human subjects to be robot players that are not subject to money illusion and that adjust prices downward proportional to the shock, at the time of the shock. Their results show that, in this treatment, the extent of price sluggishness is greatly reduced.

Fehr and Tyran (2008) consider not only the prior case where there is a strategic complementarity in price setting, but also the case where there is a strategic substitutability in price setting, i.e. $f_{P_{-i,t}} \leq 0$. Their results show that money illusion and the resulting nominal inertia in response to a fully anticipated monetary shock is greatly reduced in the case of strategic *substitutes* relative to the case of strategic *complements*. This leads to much faster adjustment toward the post-shock equilibrium.

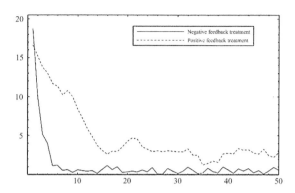

FIGURE 10

Absolute deviation of median market price from the REE price over 50 rounds, positive versus negative feedback treatments, pooled data. Source: Heemeijer et al. (2009).

Heemeijer et al. (2009) studied two simple linear models for price determination:

$$p_t = \frac{20}{21}(123 - p_t^e) + \epsilon_t \quad \text{(negative feedback)}$$

$$p_t = \frac{20}{21}(3 + p_t^e) + \epsilon_t \quad \text{(positive feedback)}$$

where p_t^e was taken to be the average of 6 subject forecasts for p_t. Both models have the same rational expectations equilibrium prediction, namely that $p_t = 60 + \epsilon_t$. Nevertheless, that path by which groups of 6 subjects learned this equilibrium was very different depending on whether they were in the positive or negative feedback treatment. Under negative feedback, convergence obtained rather quickly, within 5 periods, on average. However, under positive feedback, there was only a very slow oscillatory movement toward the equilibrium price of 60. Indeed, average prices and volatility under positive feedback were significantly greater at the 5% significance level as compared with the negative feedback case. Fig. 10 illustrates the absolute difference between the median market price and the equilibrium price over all groups and the 50 rounds of Heemeijer et al.'s experiment.

The explanation for this difference again lies in the value of different forecasting rules in the two environments. When there is positive feedback, if enough agents use trend-following rules, other forecasters find that trend following is profitable and prices often deviate substantially from fundamentals. By contrast, in markets with negative feedback, as the number of individuals adopting trend following rules becomes sufficiently great, the incentives for contrarian, fundamental-based strategies become greater and so trend-following strategies do not survive very long in such negative feedback systems. Bao et al. (2012) consider the same two models, but examine how subjects react to unanticipated shocks to the fundamental value of the price. They report that under the negative feedback system, there is a rapid adjustment to the new, post-shock equilibrium, but under the positive feedback system, the adjustment to the shock is slow; initially the price under-reacts to the change, but over time there is over-reaction. Bao et al. use a heuristic switching model to explain this under- and over-reaction pattern.

Within a given type of feedback (positive or negative), players can also be heterogeneous with regard to their depths of reasoning, i.e., their beliefs about others – see the chapter by Mauersberger and Nagel (2018) for further details in the context of the Beauty Contest Game (Nagel, 1995). They can also be heterogeneous in terms of their knowledge of the data generating process or the history of play by others. For instance, Cooper et al. (2017) induce heterogeneity about the history of play by periodically replacing players in an N-player beauty contest game with new players, coincident with changing the (interior) equilibrium period of the game. They find that the periodic addition of a single, inexperienced player (and removal of an experienced player) in a population of size 4, can have large effects on the speed of convergence to the new equilibrium when the environment is characterized by strategic complementarities (positive feedback) but not when it is characterized by strategic substitutability (positive feedback). This pattern follows from the manner in which the experienced subjects react to the play of the inexperienced subjects; in the substitutes case, too high (or too low) a choice by the inexperienced subject can be counteracted by lower (higher) choices by the experienced subjects but in the complements (positive feedback) environment, the experienced subjects find it more difficult to counteract the errant behavior of the inexperienced subject and thus convergence to the new equilibrium occurs more slowly. These findings show how even a small amount of heterogeneity can nevertheless have large, differential impacts on outcomes.

2.4 LEARNING TO FORECAST VS. LEARNING TO OPTIMIZE EXPERIMENTAL DESIGNS

The expectation formation experiments discussed in the previous section decouple the expectation formation problem from optimization decisions. This is a common practice in the macroeconomic learning literature as well (see, e.g., Evans and Honkapohja, 2001).[10] The maintained assumption is that while agents may be boundedly rational in expectation formation, they have no trouble optimizing given their incorrect forecasts. The experiments that have followed this approach are known as "learning to forecast" experiments, since subjects' only aim to get the expectation of future variables correct; indeed, subjects usually have little knowledge of the system they are operating in (a topic we shall return to shortly). The trading decisions necessary to assure arbitrage between the two assets in the asset market or profit maximization in the cobweb model commodity market are simply automated for subjects. Indeed, in the experiments of Hommes et al. (2005, 2008), subjects are simply instructed that they are forecast "advisors" to some firm.

---

[10] See the chapter by Branch and McGough (2018) for modeling bounded rationality in forecasting as well as bounded rationality in decision-making in macroeconomic models.

The use of such learning to forecast experiments dates back to the work of Marimon and Sunder (1993, 1994) who studied savings behavior in two period overlapping generations models. They found that in old age (period 2) subjects were often failing to spend all of their savings, so they chose to automate the problem so that subjects, in the first, young period of their lives only had to forecast the price level that would prevail in the second and final period of their lives when they were old. Given this price forecast, the optimal saving and consumption decisions was automatically computed for subjects.

However as we have seen in the public good and intertemporal consumption/savings experiments, some subjects are not very good at solving optimization problems (or applying backward induction). In those "learning to optimize" experiments, subjects' forecasts are not explicitly elicited but are rather implicit in subjects' optimizing decisions. Nevertheless, it is instructive to understand the extent to which subjects can both form expectations *and* optimize conditional on those expectations. Such an exercise was considered by Bao et al. (2013) who compared the performance of subjects in learning to forecast and learning to optimize treatments of the cobweb model experiment (described above) as well as additional treatments where subjects did both tasks (forecast and optimize) or in the case where subjects are simply forecasting prices, their payoffs were determined according to a quadratic loss scoring rule between their forecasted price and the actual price resulting from the average forecasts of a group of 6 subjects. In the learning to optimize treatment, the six subjects were in the role of supplier choosing a quantity of the good in period t, $q_{i,t}$, to bring to the market. The payoff to each of the 6 subjects was given by the net profit resulting from this quantity choice, i.e., $\pi_{i,t} = p_t q_{i,t} - c(q_{i,t})$, where p_t is the actual market price determined via the market clearing condition and c was an induced (and known) cost function. In a third treatment subjects were asked to form both forecasts and choose quantities while in a fourth treatment, subjects were matched in teams, where the forecasting task was performed by one team member and the optimizing task by another, and they shared the equal weighted payoff from both activities.

Bao et al. (2013) report that the speed of convergence to the RE price is fastest when subjects only have to forecast prices, that is, in the learning-to-forecast experiment. In second place (in terms of speed of convergence) is the treatment where one subject is specialized in forecasting and the other is specialized in optimizing. In third place was the treatment where subjects were asked to make optimal quantity decisions only (learning to optimize), followed by the treatment where subjects were asked to both forecast and optimize, which had the slowest time to convergence. Heterogeneity in price forecasts and quantity decisions was also significantly greatest in this last treatment where subjects had to perform both forecasting and optimizing roles. The elicitation of the two different decisions reveals that a majority of subjects 59.5% were not making quantity decisions that were optimal given their price forecasts. By contrast, in the team setting, quantity decisions were optimal given price forecasts for a majority of subject pairs (69.4%), suggesting that heterogeneity in price forecast/quantity outcomes may be reduced in teams relative to individuals. Bao et al. further report that subjects' forecast rules in this negative feedback environment were a mix of adaptive and contrarian rules, with more than 50 percent of subjects being classified as adaptive learners.[11]

2.5 ADAPTIVE VERSUS EDUCTIVE LEARNING

The studies of expectation formation discussed in the prior sections presume that agents have limited or no knowledge of the data generating process for the variables they are seeking to forecast. It is natural to think that agents in such settings would adapt their expectations of the variables they are forecasting over time in an inductive manner based on past outcomes, to develop new forecasts that better approximate the data generating process. A second approach to modeling learning asks not whether an equilibrium is eventually reached under adaptive learning, but whether the equilibrium is eductively stable, in the sense of Guesnerie (1992, 2002). Eductive learning departs from adaptive learning in that all agents perfectly know the data generating process. Assuming common knowledge of the rationality of other actors, the question is whether agents can *deduce* that the equilibrium path associated with the data generating process is associated with a particular REE, thereby facilitating coordination on that REE. Eductive stability can be illustrated with respect to the same Cobweb model used to study adaptive learning. In a linear demand and supply model, the market clearing price in a Cobweb economy is given by:

$$p_t = \mu + \alpha \bar{p}_t^e + \epsilon_t$$

where $\bar{p}_{t+1}^e$ denotes the average of all supplier's forecasts and ϵ_t is again an i.i.d. mean 0 noise term. Assume now that μ and α are constants known to all forecasters; under the adaptive expectations view, these parameters are unknown and have to be learned. The equation for p_t yields a unique rational expectations equilibrium in which:

$$p_t^* = \bar{p}_t^{e,*} + \epsilon_t, \quad \text{where } \bar{p}_t^{e,*} = \frac{\mu}{1-\alpha}$$

The REE can be shown to be eductively stable provided that $|\alpha| < 1$. Intuitively, if this condition is satisfied, then starting from any initial price, an iterative reasoning process, performed in notional or mental time, leads agents to the REE. By contrast, as Evans (2001) has pointed out, the REE is stable under adaptive learning so long as $\alpha < 1$, which is a less restrictive condition. Bao and Duffy (2016) exploit this difference to assess the extent to which subjects can be characterized as either adaptive or eductive learners. To conduct this test, they had to put the two theories on an informationally equivalent footing; since the eductive approach assumes complete knowledge of the data generating process while adaptive learning does not, they chose to inform subjects of the equation for prices including the values they chose

---

[11]Bao et al. (2017) study learning-to-forecast versus learning-to-optimize in a positive feedback system. They find that asset price bubbles are a robust feature and even larger in magnitude in learning-to-optimize treatments.

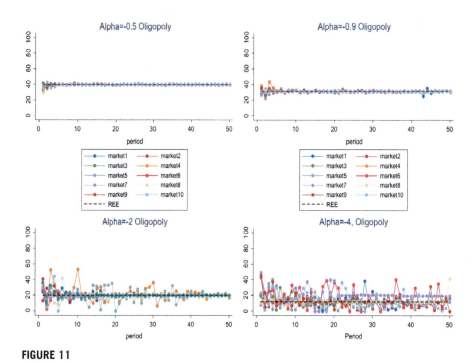

FIGURE 11

Average expectations of prices over time in the Oligopoly treatment of Bao and Duffy, four different values for α: 0.5, 0.9, -2.0, and -4.0.

for $\mu = 60$ and $\alpha \in \{-0.5, -0.9, -2, -4\}$. In one treatment, subjects were matched in groups of three and the average forecast of the three players was used to determine $\bar{p}_t^e$ in each of 50 periods; subjects were again paid according to a proper scoring rule. Fig. 11 shows the evolution of these average forecasts over time for 10 different cohorts in each of the four treatments where $\alpha = 0.5$, 0.9, -2, and -4, respectively.

When $|\alpha| < 1$, consistent with both the adaptive and eductive learning hypotheses, expectations converged to REE. However, in the two treatments where $\alpha < -1$, convergence was slower or did not occur within the time frame of the experiment. Bao and Duffy show that these differing results are due to the presence of roughly equal numbers of adaptive and eductive type players (as well as a sizable fraction of subjects who are not classifiable). The presence of the two types and the relative influence of each matters for whether the system converges or does not converge to the REE, evidence once again that type heterogeneity matters.

3 HETEROGENEITY AND MONETARY POLICY

We next turn to a more complicated setting, the New Keynesian model of monetary policy, where coordination problems can arise if the equilibrium of the model is not determinate or locally unique (i.e., it is indeterminate). Generally speaking, central banks wish to avoid such settings, in favor of those where the equilibrium is unique, and there is a large theoretical and experimental literature addressing the extent to which policy can play such a coordinating role.

3.1 NEW KEYNESIAN EXPERIMENTS

A number of recent papers has focused on studying the effects of monetary policy in *forward-looking* versions of the sticky price, New Keynesian model (as developed in Woodford, 2003):

$$x_t = E_t x_{t+1} - \sigma^{-1} \left(i_t - E_t \pi_{t+1} - r_t^n \right) \tag{5}$$

$$\pi_t = \beta E_t \pi_{t+1} + \kappa x_t \tag{6}$$

$$i_t = f(E_t \pi_{t+1}, E_t x_{t+1}) \tag{7}$$

$$r_t^n = \rho r_{t-1}^n + \epsilon_t \tag{8}$$

The first equation, for the output gap, x_t, is an expectational IS curve, with σ representing the intertemporal elasticity of substitution. The second equation, for inflation, π_t, is the New Keynesian Phillips curve, with β equal to the period discount factor, and κ a parameter that captures the stickiness of prices. The third equation represents the specification of the central bank's policy rule for the nominal interest rate, i_t. Finally, the natural rate of interest, r_t^n, evolves according to an autoregressive process with a mean zero error term, ϵ_t.

Expectations of future inflation, $E_t \pi_{t+1}$ and of the output gap, $E_t x_{t+1}$, play a crucial role in the dynamics of this system. The central bank manages these expectations through the interest rate (policy) rule.

A number of recent papers have studied the behavior of the above system in the context of learning-to-forecast experiments. In these experiments, subjects are asked to forecast next period's inflation rate and output gap and then, subjects' mean or median expectations for inflation and the output gap are substituted into Eqs. (5) and (6) in place of rational expectations. The experimental studies investigate issues related to the stability of economies under different interest rate policy rules, the role of the expectational channel in the reduction of the variance of output and inflation, and the role of different monetary policies in the management of the economies at the zero-lower bound. In all of these settings, the main finding is that there is heterogeneity in subjects' expectations and this heterogeneity plays a crucial role in the dynamics and stability of these economies over time.

For example, Pfajfar and Zakelj (2014) simplify the model by using x_{t-1} as the naive expectation for $E_t x_{t+1}$, and studying only expectations for inflation, $E_t \pi_{t+1}$, in a laboratory environment. Thus, in these experiments subjects are asked to forecast just inflation, knowing only qualitative features of the underlying model and seeing historical time series on inflation, the output gap and interest rates. In addition, they add AR(1) shocks to (5) and (6), respectively. The average of 9 subjects' inflation forecasts is used for $E_t \pi_{t+1}$ and then the model generates data for x_t, π_t, and i_t.

They study two kinds of policy rules of the form:

$$i_t = \gamma(\bar{\pi} - \bar{\pi}_t) + \bar{\pi} \tag{9}$$

were $\bar{\pi}$ is the central bank's target inflation rate and $\bar{\pi}_t$ is either actual inflation at time t or the time t expectation of the inflation rate at $t + 1$. Thus, the first case is a contemporaneous policy rule that requires the central bank to respond to current deviations from the inflation target and the second one is a forward looking rule where the central bank reacts to deviations of expected inflation from the target. The other treatment variable is γ, which takes on 3 different values, 1.35, 1.5, and 4. The Taylor principle is satisfied for all three of these values which implies that, under rational expectations, the equilibrium is determinate (locally) and stable, again locally, under a certain specification of adaptive learning. When the policy rule conditions on expectations of $(t+1)$ inflation, policies with higher γ are much more effective in reducing the standard deviations of inflation expectations. Overall, the policy that conditions on current π_t rather than on future $E_t \pi_{t+1}$ delivers the best performance in terms of stabilization of the experimental economies both in terms of inflation variability and output fluctuations. Essentially, the π_t rule reduces the weight that subjects' expectations play.

In addition, the paper analyzes heterogeneity in subjects' expectations by considering different expectational models. Besides rational expectations, the authors also consider 12 alternative expectation formation models studied in the literature. To characterize subjects' expectation formation process, a new test for rationality based on the difference between agents' perceived law of motion and the actual law of motion is also introduced in a heterogeneous expectations environment. Overall, only 30% to 45% of subjects conform to rational expectations while other subjects' behavior can be explained by trend extrapolation, adaptive learning or sticky information. More importantly, switching between different models fits the experimental data far better than a single model.

Assenza et al. (2014) discuss how monetary policy can manage the self-organization of heterogeneous expectations in a laboratory experiment. Their experimental design uses a contemporaneous inflation targeting policy rule (without weight on the output gap) and small i.i.d. shocks instead of autocorrelated shocks that have been implemented in other experiments. The 3 main treatments of their experiment feature different Taylor rule reaction coefficients and inflation targets. In treatment (a), monetary policy is weakly responsive (the reaction coefficient equals 1) and the inflation target is 2%. Treatment (b) involves aggressive monetary policy (the reaction coefficient equals 1.5) and the same 2% benchmark inflation target. Treatment (c) increases the inflation target to 3.5% while preserving the aggressive monetary policy condition.

Two types of aggregate patterns are observed in treatment (a): convergence to a non-fundamental steady state and exploding inflation and output (see Fig. 12). By

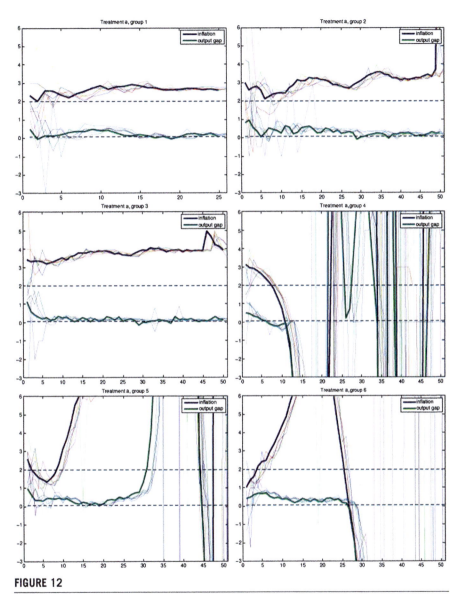

FIGURE 12

Experimental results in Assenza et al. (2014): weakly responsive monetary policy. Blue thick line: realized inflation; green thick line: realized output gap; thin lines: individual forecasts for inflation and the output gap.

contrast, all the sessions in treatment (b) exhibit nice convergence to the fundamental steady state (see Fig. 13). Both convergence to the fundamental steady state and persistent oscillations emerge in treatment (c) (see Fig. 14). The stabilizing effects of

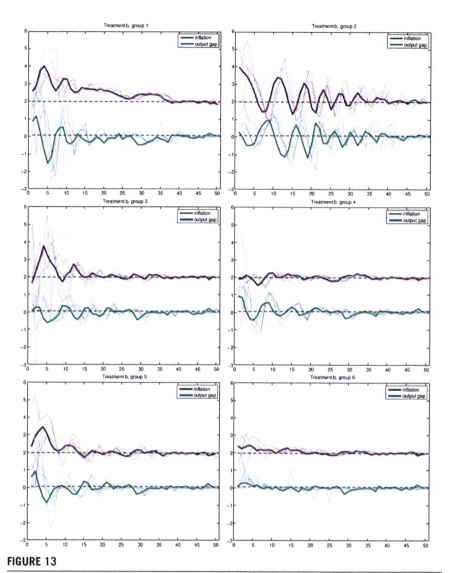

FIGURE 13

Experimental results in Assenza et al. (2014): aggressive monetary policy. Blue thick line: realized inflation; green thick line: realized output gap; thin lines: individual forecasts for inflation and the output gap.

monetary policy appear to come from the aggressiveness of the policy rule, and not the inflation target.

The authors can explain these paths for inflation and the output gap using the heuristic switching model developed by Anufriev and Hommes (2012) in which agents switch between 4 different forecasting rules by evaluating their relative past

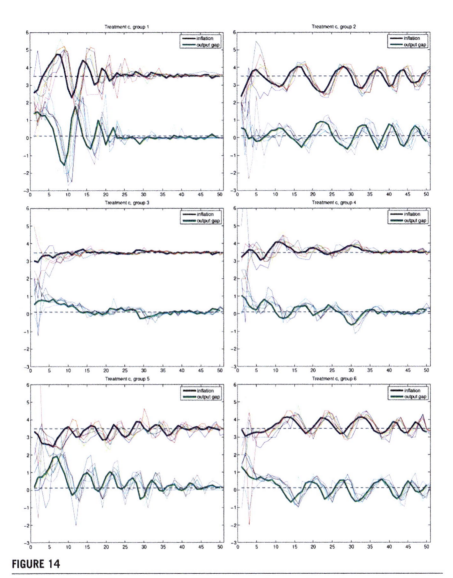

FIGURE 14

Experimental results in Assenza et al. (2014): aggressive monetary policy and high inflation target. Blue thick line: realized inflation; green thick line: realized output gap; thin lines: individual forecasts for inflation and the output gap.

performance (described earlier in the chapter). Simulation results demonstrate that all types of aggregate patterns observed in the experiment can be replicated by the heuristic switching model. Hommes et al. (2017) replicate the experimental results from the Assenza et al. learning-to-forecast experiment using a genetic algorithm to determine price forecasts. The genetic algorithm simulations match the experimental data in terms of the response to different policy rules.

Mauersberger (2018) introduces a new, learning-to-forecast experimental design within a micro-founded New Keynesian model framework, where subjects forecast individual, rather than aggregate, outcomes in an economy based on the linearized heterogeneous expectations New Keynesian model (Woodford, 2013). Unlike Woodford (2013) which features an exogenous preference shock and a mark-up shock, there are no exogenous shocks in the Mauersberger's setup.

Subjects are randomly assigned to be either household advisors or firm advisors. Households, firms and the central bank are computerized. Household advisors are asked to forecast the deviation of household's real expenditure from its long run, steady state level (called 'usual level' in the experiment). Firm advisors need to submit forecasts of the deviation of a firm's optimal price in the next period from the current general price level. Aggregate outcomes are computed using medians of subjects' expectations and choices made by computerized households and firms that are based on these expectations.

Like other experiments, Mauersberger studies the effects of monetary policies that differ in the degree of aggressiveness. He uses a contemporaneous, inflation targeting rule with a zero lower bound, i.e.:

$$i_t = \max(0, \bar{i} + \phi_\pi (\pi_t - \bar{\pi})) \qquad (10)$$

where $\bar{i}$ is a steady state level of the nominal interest rate.

However, his results differ from the previous experimental literature as he finds that a much more aggressive Taylor rule is required for stability and convergence of the experimental economies within 50 periods, i.e., the convergence to the rational expectations steady state can only be obtained when the Taylor rule reaction coefficient is equal to 3. At the group level, heterogeneity is rather pronounced for lower Taylor rule coefficients (0.5 or 1.5), but it vanishes under a more aggressive monetary policy.[12]

Mauersberger uses Thompson sampling algorithm (Thompson, 1933) to explain expectation formation in his experiment. This is an algorithm where agents update their beliefs in a Bayesian manner. However, agents do not choose the optimal action implied by their posterior. Instead, they make a random draw from the posterior each time that an action must be taken and best respond to this random draw. Using the method of *simulated paths* where two initial experimental observations are used to update the algorithm, and, afterward, the dynamic paths of the economies are solely determined by the algorithms' choices and outcomes, Mauersberger shows that Thompson sampling performs well in capturing the features of the experimental data. It generates quite a bit of heterogeneity and volatility for ϕ_π equal to 0.5 and 1.5. However, these are substantially reduced in case of $\phi_\pi = 3$.

---

[12]Note that, for example, Assenza et al. (2014) experimental results indicate convergence for the Taylor rule inflation coefficient of 1.5.

He then compares the performance of Thompson sampling to a number of learning/adaptive models that have been standardly used to investigate expectations in macroeconomic environments: two forms of adaptive learning, least-square learning and constant gain learning (Evans and Honkapohja, 2001), and the heuristic-switching model (Anufriev and Hommes, 2012) which was discussed earlier in the chapter. In addition to the mean-squared error calculated over 50 periods, he uses other statistical measures to better assess the behavior of the models, such as the first and second moments, the mean squared distance from the REE and an index of intra-period dispersion. The heuristic-switching model results in a relatively fast convergence to the rational expectations steady state even when the Taylor rule coefficient is 1.5, which is at odds with Mauersberger's experimental data. Comparing Thompson sampling and the three other benchmark models, Thompson sampling provides a good fit to the data along a number of dimensions (convergence, volatility patterns, individual dispersion etc.).

3.2 NEW KEYNESIAN EXPERIMENTS AT THE ZERO LOWER BOUND

Further evidence for the need for heterogeneous agent models comes from experiments that study the effects of monetary and fiscal policy on subjects' expectations in the New Keynesian model when interest rates are near the zero lower bound, as they were in much of the developed world for a period of time following the 2007–2008 global financial crisis. These experiments reveal a variety of reactions to policy efforts to stimulate the economy when interest rates cannot be driven lower. Arifovic and Petersen (2017) study the effects of monetary and fiscal policy on subjects' expectations in a learning-to-forecast experiment using the linearized New Keynesian framework described earlier by equations (5), (6), and (8).

Compared with the earlier experiments that we discussed, Arifovic and Petersen introduce a binding constraint on nominal interest rates.[13] The nominal interest rate is $i^* = 75$ basis points in the steady state, and cannot be reduced below zero in the event of sufficiently low inflation or output gap. Thus, the Taylor rule in their experimental economy is given by:

$$i_t = \begin{cases} i^* + \phi_\pi (\pi_t - \pi_t^*) + \phi_x x_t, & \text{if } i_t \geq 0 \\ 0, & \text{otherwise} \end{cases} \tag{11}$$

They selected their shock sequences using a social evolutionary learning algorithm in Arifovic et al. (2012) and the same set of shock sequences is used in all treatments. In order to push the laboratory economies toward the zero lower bound, large exogenous demand shocks are introduced in the middle of the shock sequences.

---

[13]Note that Mauersberger (2018) also implements the same constraint. However, the focus of his study is not on the policies related to zero lower bound.

Arifovic and Petersen conduct four different treatments. In their baseline treatment, the central bank implements a standard Taylor rule and a constant inflation target (*Constant*). The state-dependent target treatment and the directional state-dependent treatment are designed to test the effectiveness of quantitative and qualitative forward guidance through explicitly announcing either the state-dependent inflation target (quantitative forward guidance, *SD*), or the direction in which the target is moving (qualitative forward guidance, *Dir. SD*). Finally, by adding an expansionary Ricardian fiscal policy to the baseline treatment, the fiscal policy treatment (*FP*) allows the authors to evaluate the effects of both monetary and fiscal policy near the zero lower bound.

They find that the state-dependent inflation target (*SD* and *Dir. SD*) treatments do not bring significantly greater stability than the standard Taylor rule (*Constant*) treatment. This is more pronounced when fundamentals improve slowly. Arifovic and Petersen argue that the poorer performance of the state-dependent inflation target policies is due to a loss of confidence in the central bank's ability to stabilize the economy. If the confidence in inflation targeting is lost during the *crisis*, expectations diverge further and further away from the target inflation values. In these experimental economies, the central bank is fully committed to its state-dependent policy to keep interest rates low even after the economy starts recovering. Unlike the rational expectations framework, where credibility and commitment are equated, in the experimental economies, subjects do not necessarily perceive the central bank's announcements as credible. As Arifovic and Petersen put it, "subjects need to *see it to believe it*".

On the other hand, an anticipated fiscal policy intervention (the *FP* treatment) results in significantly faster and more stable recoveries. The explanation for this behavior is most likely related to the fact that state-dependent inflation targeting monetary policies provide a promise of future recovery when the future is uncertain while anticipated expansionary fiscal policy stimulates demand with certainty.

Hommes et al. (2016) also design a learning-to-forecast experiment to evaluate the effects of monetary and fiscal policy at the zero lower bound. By adopting a nonlinear New Keynesian framework with multiple equilibria (a low inflation steady state and a targeted high inflation steady state), the authors can test the implications of adaptive learning models near the zero lower bound. More specifically, with aggressive monetary policy and a fixed amount of government spending, only the targeted steady state is locally stable under learning. The local instability of the low inflation steady state makes deflationary spirals possible under large pessimistic shocks. Another theoretical prediction is that the targeted steady state is globally stable under learning if both aggressive monetary policy and a fiscal switching rule that further increases government spending at the zero lower bound are implemented.

The four treatments are constructed based on variations along two dimensions. The first dimension is a type of policy regime: the policy regime M is a combination of aggressive monetary policy and constant government spending while the policy regime F replaces constant government spending with the fiscal switching rule.

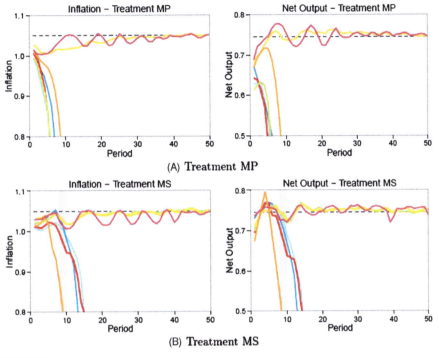

FIGURE 15

Hommes et al. (2016): aggressive monetary policy only, for pessimistic expectations (top panels) and "bad news" shocks (bottom panels). Overview of experimental results of the 4 treatments, 7 groups each. Left panels: realized inflation. Right panels: realized net output. Dashed lines depict targeted equilibrium levels. Shaded areas indicate expectational news shocks.

The second dimension is related to two types of expectational shocks: In scenario P, pessimistic expectations are induced by making "historical" information about inflation and net output accessible to subjects at the beginning of the experiment; in scenario S, late expectational shocks are realized in the form of "bad" news reports.

In treatment MP, 5 out of 7 groups succumb to deflationary spirals because monetary policy cannot eliminate the adverse effects of initial pessimism. In treatment MS, monetary policy seems to be effective as 3 out of 7 groups converge to the targeted steady state despite the onset of late expectational shocks (see Fig. 15). In the two treatments with the fiscal switching rule, neither form of expectational shocks is destructive enough to generate deflationary spirals as all groups converge to the targeted steady state eventually (see Fig. 16). The slow convergence by some groups is due to the fact that the fiscal switching rule can only anchor subjects' inflation expectations when net output recovers.

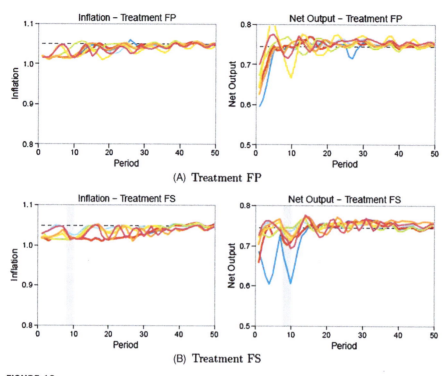

FIGURE 16

Hommes et al. (2016): aggressive monetary policy and fiscal switching rule, for pessimistic expectations (top panels) and "bad news" shocks (bottom panels). Overview of experimental results of the 4 treatments, 7 groups each. Left panels: realized inflation. Right panels: realized net output. Dashed lines depict targeted equilibrium levels. Shaded areas indicate expectational news shocks.

4 HETEROGENEITY IN EQUILIBRIUM SELECTION

Models that admit a multiplicity of equilibria are commonplace in economics, but they pose a real challenge as they invalidate the use of standard comparative statics analysis; if one does not know which equilibrium to focus on, it is not possible to determine how changes in the exogenous variables or parameters of the model affect the endogenous variables of the model. A potential solution to this problem is to use experimental evidence to validate a focus on a particular equilibrium. In certain cases, this approach works well, but in other cases, as we shall see, there is also heterogeneity in the equilibrium that groups of subjects coordinate upon, and heterogeneous agent models help to understand this phenomenon.

We first consider the case of bank run models, where there generally exist two equilibria, one where all depositors keep their money in the bank and another where all run on the bank to withdraw their deposits Second, we consider coordination problems and equilibrium selection in the adoption of new payment methods. In these two applications, we show how heterogeneity in agent types and behaviors is a main driver of the equilibrium selection process.

4.1 BANK RUNS

The experimental literature on bank runs demonstrates how heterogeneity in subjects' expectations influences outcomes and equilibrium selection using the canonical bank run model of Diamond and Dybvig (1983). This intertemporal model involves just three periods. In period 0, all depositors deposit their endowments of money into a bank, which has exclusive access to a long-term investment opportunity. The depositors are willing to deposit their funds with the bank because the contract the bank offers the depositors provides the depositors with insurance against uncertain liquidity shocks. In period 1, some fraction of depositors learn that they have immediate liquidity needs (are *impatient*) and must withdraw their deposits early. The remaining fraction learn they are patient and can wait to withdraw their deposit in the final period 2. The bank uses its knowledge of these fractions in optimally deriving the deposit contract, which stipulates that depositors may withdraw the whole of their unit endowment at date 1 while those who wait until period 2 to withdraw can earn $R > 1$. While there exists a separating, Pareto efficient equilibrium where impatient types withdraw early in period 1 and patient types wait until the final period 2, there also exists an inefficient pooling equilibrium where uncertainty about the behavior of other patient types causes all patient types to withdraw their deposits in period 1 which results in a *bank run*. In that case, the bank has to liquidate its long-term investment in period 1 and depending on the liquidation value of this investment, it may have insufficient funds to honor its deposit contract in period 1.

The possibility of this bank-run equilibrium is the focus of a number of experimental studies including Madiés (2006), Garratt and Keister (2009), Schotter and Yorulmazer (2009), Arifovic et al. (2013), Arifovic and Jiang (2017), Kiss et al. (2012, 2014), and Brown et al. (2017). Here we will focus on the papers by Arifovic et al. (2013) and Arifovic and Jiang (2017) as the experimental results are followed by modeling of their dynamics using evolutionary algorithms, but we briefly summarize other experimental studies of bank runs.

These studies typically dispense with the non-strategic impatient types (or model them using robot players) and consider n-player coordination games were all players are patient, or strategic, i.e., the players can choose to withdraw in period 1 or 2. Madiés was the first to demonstrate that for certain parameterizations of the model, an inefficient run equilibrium can be selected by laboratory subjects, though less than full (partial runs) are more common. Further he showed that a suspension of convertibility or full (but not partial) deposit insurance can work to prevent such runs. Similarly, Garratt and Keister (2009) showed that inefficient run equilibrium were not selected unless some subjects faced stochastic liquidity demand shocks causing them to withdraw early. Schotter and Yorulmazer (2009) consider the case where the bank run is already in progress and consider how insider information about the solvency of the bank matters for the speed and severity of the panic. Kiss et al. (2012)

examine whether observability of prior depositors withdrawal decisions in a sequential move game or lack of such observability in a simultaneous move game together with varying rates of and deposit insurance affects the incidence of bank runs. They find that without observability, both full and partial deposit insurance are effective in decreasing the incidence of bank runs, while with observability, neither level of deposit insurance coverage makes much difference. Kiss et al. (2014) focus further on observability, examining the precise social network structure of which depositors decisions are observed by subsequent depositors. They report that the social information network structure matters for the incidence of bank runs. Brown et al. (2017) report experimental evidence that a run by depositors at one bank can trigger a run at another bank, especially if the run at the first bank may signal something about the fundamentals of the second bank. Similarly, Chakravarty et al. (2014), Duffy et al. (2017), and Choi et al. (2017) have reported experiments examining how deposit withdrawals at one bank can have contagious effects on withdrawal decisions at other, explicitly connected banks (2, 4, and 6–15 banks respectively), using a variety of different interbank network structures; the main takeaway from this research is that the details of the network structure matter for the incidence of such contagions.

Arifovic et al. (2013) use a 2-period version of the Diamond–Dybvig model with $N = 10$ *patient* subjects who play the role of depositors. These players start out with one unit of money already deposited with the bank and choose to withdraw early in period 1 or wait to withdraw later in period 2. Subjects who choose to withdraw early in period 1, are promised a payment of r, and subjects who choose to withdraw later, in period 2, receive a maximum payoff of R. Arifovic et al. vary the rate of return, r, to withdrawing early ($r < R$). This rate determines the value of a coordination parameter, η, that measures the minimum fraction of depositors required to wait (until period 2) so that waiting entails a higher payoff than withdrawing early (in period 1). In other words, if the fraction of subjects who choose to wait is greater than η, those who choose to wait receive a higher payoff than those who choose to withdraw. Otherwise, if the fraction of those who choose to wait falls below the value of η, then these *patient* subjects receive a lower payoff. Thus, the payoff to the depositor who chooses to withdraw is

$$\pi_1 = \min\left\{r, \frac{N}{e}\right\} \tag{12}$$

and the payoff for those who choose to wait is

$$\pi_2 = \max\left\{0, \frac{N - er}{N - e}R\right\} \tag{13}$$

Note that if $e > \hat{e} \equiv N/r$, the bank will not have enough money to pay all early withdrawers the promised rate r, and those who choose to wait until period 2 will receive a zero payoff.

Arifovic et al. ran experimental sessions with 7 or 9 phases where each phase corresponded to one value for η, and lasted for 10 experimental periods. The values of η changed in either an ascending, descending or randomized order to control for

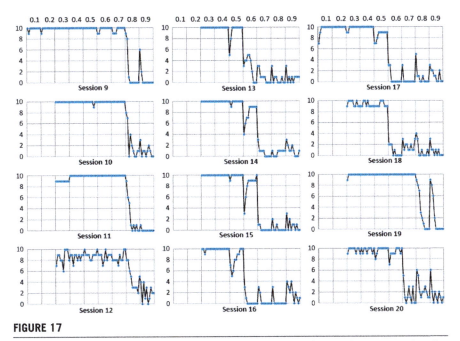

FIGURE 17

Arifovic et al.'s (2013) results for different values of η, values of η are given on top of each panel, and number of subjects who chose to 'wait' on the y-axis.

"order effects". They find that whether coordination-based bank runs occur or not depends on the value of the coordination parameter, η. In particular, the value of the coordination parameter can be divided into three regions: "run", "no-run" and "indeterminacy", characterized, respectively, by high (with $\eta > 0.8$), low (with $\eta < 0.5$), and intermediate (with η between 0.6 and 0.7) values of the parameter. When the coordination parameter lies in the run (no-run) region, strategic uncertainty is low: subjects are almost unanimous in their choices, and all experimental economies stay close or converge to the run (no-run) equilibrium. In setting with the coordination parameter located in the indeterminacy region, subjects are much less certain as to what the 'right' choice is; as a result, the outcomes of the experimental economies vary widely and become difficult to predict.

Fig. 17 shows their results for values of η between 0.1 and 0.9, for sessions 9–20. The values of η are given at the top of each panel, and the number of subjects (out of 10) who were not withdrawing, on the left side of each panel.

In order to capture the learning behavior in the experimental data, Arifovic et al. combine the evolutionary algorithm (Temzelides, 1997) with logit regression models to estimate the rate of experimentation from the experimental data.[14] The evolution-

---

[14]Temzelides (1997) proves a limiting case that as the probability of experimentation approaches zero the economy stays at the no-run equilibrium with probability 1 when $\eta < 0.5$.

ary algorithm consists of two elements. The first is myopic best response, which, in the context of the DD model, is "withdraw" if the number of depositors choosing to wait in the previous period, z_{t-1} (i.e. $N - e_t$), is $\leq z^*$, the number of depositors who choose to wait that equated the payoffs associated with 'wait' or 'withdraw'. Otherwise, the best response is to wait. In the context of this model, experimentation means to flip one's strategy from "withdraw" to "wait" or vice versa.

In the experiments, subjects have information about r (and subjects can deduce η from the payoff tables throughout the experiment). Subjects are not directly informed about z_{t-1}, but most of the time, subjects can refer to the payoff table to deduce z_{t-1} from their own payoffs in the past period. For the evolutionary algorithm, Arifovic et al. assume that if a subject cannot deduce whether $z_{t-1} > z^*$, she skips the first part of the algorithm and does not update her strategy; otherwise, she updates her strategy to the best response. For experimentation, they assume that if a subject can deduce the exact value of z_{t-1}, her experimentation rate depends on z_{t-1} and η; otherwise, her experimentation rate depends only on η. The value of the rate of experimentation is to be estimated from the experimental data with logit models. They sort all the observations on the subjects' individual behavior depending on whether or not they were able to observe or deduce z_{t-1} and best respond to it. Then, they estimate rates of experimentation for different groups using logit regressions. Using the estimated rates of experimentation, they evaluate the performance of the algorithm in two ways. The first one is to use the algorithm's simulated paths and compare the outcomes with the experimental economies. The second is to use one set of data, the Chinese data, to estimate the rate of experimentation, and apply the algorithm to predict the action choice in each of the Canadian observations.[15] The algorithm performed well in terms of predictive power along both dimensions.

Given the above described results, in a follow-up paper, Arifovic and Jiang (2017) introduce an extrinsic "sunspot" variable to the above model and investigate how it affects the coordination outcome. Their hypothesis was that the power of the sunspot as a coordination device increases with the extent of strategic uncertainty. To test this hypothesis, they chose three experimental treatments with three values of the coordination parameter – 0.2, 0.9, and 0.7. Under their hypothesis, the power of the extrinsic signal is likely to be very weak when $\eta = 0.2$, weak when $\eta = 0.9$, and strong when $\eta = 0.7$.[16] Their results show that the randomly generated 'sunspot' announcements did no affect the outcomes of the sessions that were conducted for either $\eta = 0.2$ that all converged to the 'no-run' equilibrium or for $\eta = 0.9$ where they all converged to the run equilibrium. Where the announcement 'evolved' into serving as a coordination device was in the sessions conducted with $\eta = 0.7$. The results observed in these sessions are shown in Fig. 18. The circles on the upper edges of

---

[15] They ran experiments at one location in China, and two locations in Canada.

[16] The announcements that all subjects receive had the following wording: 'The forecast is that e^* or more people will choose to withdraw,' or 'The forecast is that e^* or fewer people will choose to withdraw.' A specific integer number that equalizes the payoffs of 'withdraw' and 'wait' for a given η was substituted for e^* in the experimental instructions.

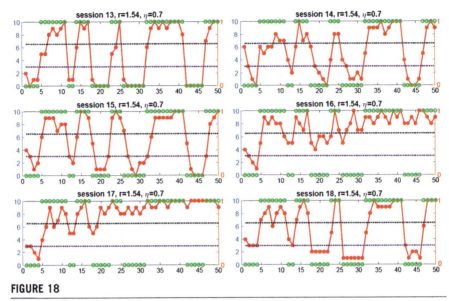

FIGURE 18

Arifovic and Jiang's (2017) results for the value of the coordination parameter $\eta = 0.7$, $N = 10$.

the panels represent periods when 'optimistic' announcements were broadcasted, and the circles on the lower edges represent periods when 'pessimistic' announcements were broadcasted. (These data were not presented to the subjects on their graphical interface.) The solid lines present the number of subjects who decided to wait in each period (out of 10). The figure illustrates that in 4 out of 6 sessions the subjects coordinated on following the extrinsic variable.

4.2 ADOPTION OF A NEW PAYMENT SYSTEM

To conclude our chapter on the role of heterogeneity of expectations we describe the work of Arifovic et al. (2017), ADJ, on the adoption of a new payment system. This is another important coordination problem, where heterogeneity in agent behavior plays an important role in equilibrium selection.

ADJ develop a model of the introduction of a new payment instrument, "e-money," that competes with the existing payment method, "cash". The new payment method is more efficient for both buyers and sellers in terms of per transaction costs and exclusive use of the new payment system is the socially efficient equilibrium. Such cost-saving motives lie behind the various attempts to introduce such new payment methods.

In their theoretical environment, there are a large number of buyers (consumers) and sellers (firms) in the market, each of unit measure. Each seller $i \in [0, 1]$ is endowed with 1 unit of good i. The seller derives zero utility from consuming her own good and instead tries to sell his good to buyers. The price of the good is fixed at

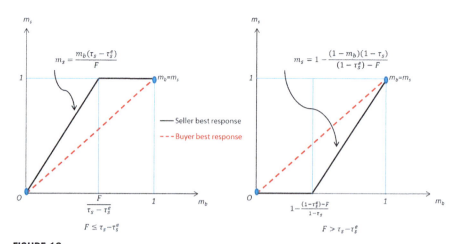

FIGURE 19

Symmetric equilibria.

one. Each buyer $j \in [0, 1]$ is endowed with 1 unit of money. In each period, the buyer visits all sellers in a random order. The buyer would like to consume one and only one unit of good from each seller, and the utility from consuming each good is $u > 1$.

There are two payment methods: cash and e-money. Each cash transaction incurs a cost, τ_b, to buyers, and a cost, τ_s, to sellers. The per transaction costs for e-money are τ_b^e and τ_s^e for buyers and sellers, respectively. Sellers have to pay an up-front cost, $F > 0$, that enables them to accept e-money payments.[17]

In the beginning of each trading period, sellers decide whether to accept e-money at the one-time fixed cost of F or not. Cash, being the traditional (and legally recognized) payment method, is universally accepted by all sellers. Simultaneous with the sellers' decision, buyers make a portfolio choice as to how to divide their money holdings between cash and e-money. After sellers have made acceptance decisions and buyers have made portfolio decisions, the buyers then go shopping, visiting all of the stores in a random order. When a buyer enters store i, she buys one unit of good i if the means of payment are compatible. Otherwise, there is no trade.

Under the certain assumptions about the cost structure of the model, such that e-money saves on per transaction costs for both buyers and sellers; that buyers prefer cash trading to no trading; the net benefit to the society of carrying all transactions in e-money is positive; and that $F \leq 1 - \tau_s^e$, there are at least two symmetric, pure strategy equilibria. See Fig. 19.

In one of these equilibria, $m_b = m_s = 1$: all sellers accept e-money, and all buyers allocate all of their endowment to e-money – call this the all-e-money equilibrium (this equilibrium always exists provided that $F \leq 1 - \tau_s^e$). There is a second sym-

---

[17] For example, to rent or purchase a terminal to process e-money transactions.

metric pure strategy equilibrium where $m_b = m_s = 0$ and e-money is not accepted by any seller or held by any buyer – call this the all-cash equilibrium. In both equilibria, there is no payment mismatch, and the number of transactions is maximized at 1. In the case where $F = \tau_s - \tau_s^e$, there exists a continuum of possible equilibria in which $m_s \in (0, 1)$ and $m_b = m_s$.

The e-money equilibrium is socially optimal as it minimizes total transactions cost. Note that buyers are always better off in the all-e-money equilibrium relative to the all cash equilibrium. The seller's relative payoff in the two equilibria, however, depends on the fixed cost, F, and on the savings on per transaction costs from the use of payment 2. If $F = \tau_s - \tau_s^e$, then the seller's payoff is the same in the cash and e-money equilibria; if $F < \tau_s - \tau_s^e$, then the seller's payoff is higher in the e-money equilibrium than in the cash equilibrium; finally, if $F > \tau_s - \tau_s^e$, then the seller's payoff is lower in the e-money equilibrium than in the cash equilibrium.

4.2.1 Experimental Design and Results

The experimental set-up was designed to match the model as closely as possible, but without the continuum of buyers and sellers of unit mass. They conduct experiment with 14 subjects in each session, who are randomly and equally divided into roles of sellers (7) and buyers (7). The roles remained fixed during a session. The subjects played a repeated, market game, that consisted of 20 markets per session.

Each market consists of two stages. The first stage is a payment choice stage. Each buyer was endowed with seven experimental money (EM) units and had to decide how to allocate his/her seven EM between the two payment methods. At the same time, sellers decide whether or not to accept the new payment method; they always accept the old payment method, cash in the experiment.

During the second stage, each buyer visits each seller in a randomly determined order. Depending on whether or not a seller accepts payment 2 and what a buyer has in their portfolio the transition may or may not take place.[18]

In addition to making payment choices in the first stage, subjects were also asked to forecast other participants' payment choices for that market.

The main treatment variable is the fixed cost to accept the new payment method, T, which a seller has to pay at the beginning of each period if she accepts payment two. They use three different values, $T = 1.6$, 2.8, and 3.5, and conduct 4 sessions for each treatment. In all treatments $\tau_s^e = \tau_b^e = 0.1$, and $\tau_s = \tau_b = 0.5$

Their results show that the new payment method will take off if the fixed cost is low so that both sides benefit by switching to the new payment method. If the fixed cost is high such that the seller endures a loss in the equilibrium where the new payment method is used relative to the equilibrium where it is not accepted, some sellers nevertheless respond by accepting the new payment method initially, fearing to lose business, but they mostly eventually learn over time to resist the new payment method and pull the economy back to the old payment method. If neither

---

[18] If seller accepts both payments, then the transaction will always take place.

side displays much will-power to move behavior toward one equilibrium or the other, then the economy may linger in the middle ground between the two equilibria.

4.2.2 Learning and Prediction

The theoretical model described above is static and thus, cannot account for diverse patterns of behavior observed in experimental economies. It also has multiple equilibria, and the theory does not provide guidance as to which equilibrium will be selected. On the other hand, the adoption of a new payment method is inherently a dynamic process. ADJ's experiment suggests that this dynamic process involves some learning over the repeated markets of our design. The heterogeneity of subjects' expectations and subsequent action, their adaptation and interaction results in selection the of different outcomes.

In order to model the dynamic environment inhabited by agents with heterogeneous expectations, ADJ use the IEL model (discussed earlier) to explain their experimental data. The IEL model mimics the experimental setting closely. Thus, each of the seven artificial buyers and sellers in has as a set of J rules, with each rule consisting of a single number. For buyer i, $i \in \{1, 2, \ldots, 7\}$, a rule $m^i_{b,j}(t) \in \{0, 1, \ldots, 7\}$, where $j \in \{1, 2, \ldots, J\}$, represents the number of EM units the buyer places in e-money in market t. For seller $i \in \{1, 2, \ldots, 7\}$, a rule $m^i_{s,j}(t) \in [0, 1]$, where $j \in \{1, 2, \ldots, J\}$ and J is the total number of rules, represents the probability that the seller accepts e-money.

The updating of the algorithm is done in the usual way, and involves *experimentation, computation of hypothetical payoffs, replication*, and the selection of the action that is actually used in a given market. The way the hypothetical payoffs are computed is key to the algorithms good performance in capturing the dynamics observed in the experimental sessions.[19]

They first simulated the model for the values of T that were used in the experiments. The simulations provide a very good fit to the experimental data. Given the IEL model's good performance, ADJ then used that model to investigate the value of T that would be necessary to make the IEL converge to the payment 1 (cash only) equilibrium. They found reliable convergence to the payment 1 equlibirum when T was equal to 4 or higher. They then tested this prediction in a new experimental treatment with $T = 4.5$. The experimental sessions for this new treatment converge very close to the all-payment-1 equilibrium.

Fig. 20 presents data from ADJ's experiments (top panels) and IEL simulations (bottom panels) for the four values of T used in their experiment: 1.6, 2.8, 3.5, and 4.5. In these figures, the average frequency with which sellers accept the new payment method is indicated by the dashed line, while the average fraction of buyers' income held in the form of the new payment method is indicated by the solid line. The first row of panels reports these averages from 4 experimental sessions for each value of

---

[19]Space limitations do not allow us to describe the algorithm in full detail, but interested readers can look at ADJ (2017).

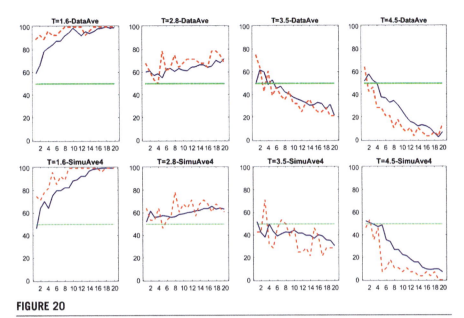

FIGURE 20

Experimental data and simulated data for the four treatments of Arifovic et al. (2017).

T, while the second row of the panels are averages from 4 IEL simulations for each value of T. As Fig. 20 makes clear, there is an impressive fit between the experimental data and the IEL simulations.

5 CONCLUSION

Heterogeneity in agents' expectations and decision-making is well documented in the experimental literature. The evidence we have surveyed in this chapter makes a solid case for the use of heterogeneous agent models to better comprehend such questions as lifecycle consumption and savings, contributions to public goods and expectation formation. Heterogeneous agent models are also important for understanding how agents approach coordination problems and predicting which equilibrium they may choose to coordinate upon. Two computational models of heterogeneous agent behavior, the individual evolutionary model and the heuristic switching models are shown to do well in terms of their fitting to experimental data.

Nevertheless, these heterogeneous-agent models have their limitations. The heterogeneity they capture is all within an individual. For instance, the heuristic switching model is essentially a homogeneous agent model where different heuristics are applied probabilistically. The IEL model imposes heterogeneity exogenously according to the genetic operators. Future work on the modeling of heterogeneous agents could explore how heterogeneity takes place both *between* and within individuals and how such heterogeneity might arise endogenously rather than being exogenously imposed.

The evidence we provide on heterogeneity also stands in contrast to much agent-based modeling and macroeconomic researchers solving heterogeneous agent models using computational methods. The latter seek to replicate heterogeneity observed in data at the *aggregate level*, e.g., wealth distributions, or the distributions of city sizes. In this effort, the empirical validity comes from the aggregate distributional or emergent outcomes that their models are able to generate and *not* from the empirical validity of individual-level heterogeneous agent characteristics. In our view, the more micro-level validation of individual behavior that we focused on in this survey is an important check on the internal validity of heterogeneous agent models and should be viewed as complementary to the more aggregate-level validation.

We conclude by emphasizing that heterogeneous agent behavior is commonplace and not something that needs to be fixed. Sometimes heterogeneity is a persistent phenomenon, as in differences in cognitive abilities or types, but at other times heterogeneity may be a more transient phenomenon, as in the process by which agents come to learn a strongly stable rational expectations equilibrium. If one's concern is with long run behavior in stationary environments that are not subject to shocks, then heterogeneous agent models might not hold much appeal. But in a world that is frequently buffeted by shocks, the short-to-medium-run reactions of agents might be more the phenomena to study, and such data can be collected in the laboratory and used to construct and validate heterogeneous agent models.

Even in the stationary environments that are not subject to shocks, in cases where there is a strong positive feedback (near unit root), heterogeneity of expectations matters, and coordination on boom and bust cycles may arise and may be explained by heterogeneous agent models.

REFERENCES

Ambrus, A., Pathak, P., 2011. Cooperation over finite horizons: a theory and experiments. Journal of Public Economics 95 (1–2), 500–512.

Ando, A., Modigliani, F., 1963. The "Life Cycle" hypothesis of saving: aggregate implications and tests. The American Economic Review 53, 55–84.

Andreoni, J., 1988. Why free ride? Strategies and learning in public goods experiments. Journal of Public Economics 37, 291–304.

Andreoni, J., 1995. Cooperation in public-goods experiments: kindness or confusion? The American Economic Review 85, 891–904.

Anufriev, M., Hommes, C., 2012. Evolutionary selection of individual expectations and aggregate outcomes in asset pricing experiments. American Economic Journal: Microeconomics 4, 35–64.

Arifovic, J., 1994. Genetic algorithm and the Cobweb model. Journal of Economic Dynamics and Control 18, 3–28.

Arifovic, J., Bullard, J., Kostyshyna, O., 2012. Social learning and monetary policy rules. The Economic Journal 123, 38–76.

Arifovic, J., Duffy, J., Jiang, J.H., 2017. Adoption of a new payment method: theory and experimental evidence. Manuscript.

Arifovic, J., Jiang, J.H., 2017. Do sunspots matter? Evidence from an experimental study of bank runs. Manuscript.

Arifovic, J., Jiang, J.H., Xu, Y., 2013. Experimental evidence on bank runs as pure coordination failures. Journal of Economic Dynamics and Control 37, 2446–2465.

Arifovic, J., Ledyard, J., 2012. Individual evolutionary learning, other regarding preferences, and the voluntary contribution mechanism. Journal of Public Economics 96, 808–823.

Arifovic, J., Petersen, L., 2017. Stabilizing expectations at the zero lower bound: experimental evidence. Journal of Economic Dynamics and Control 82, 21–43.

Assenza, T., Heemeijer, P., Hommes, C.H., Massaro, D., 2014. Managing Self-Organization of Expectations Through Monetary Policy: A Macro Experiment. CeNDEF Working Paper. University of Amsterdam.

Ballinger, T.P., Palumbo, M.G., Wilcox, N.T., 2003. Precautionary saving and social learning across generations: an experiment. Economic Journal 113, 920–947.

Ballinger, T.P., Hudson, E., Karkoviata, L., Wilcox, N.T., 2011. Saving behavior and cognitive abilities. Experimental Economics 14, 349–374.

Bao, T., Duffy, J., 2016. Adaptive versus eductive learning: theory and evidence. European Economic Review 83, 64–89.

Bao, T., Duffy, J., Hommes, C., 2013. Learning, forecasting and optimizing: an experimental study. European Economic Review 61, 186–204.

Bao, T., Hommes, C.H., Makarewicz, T., 2017. Bubble formation and (in) efficient markets in learning-to-forecast-and-optimise experiments. The Economic Journal 127, F581–F609.

Bao, T., Hommes, C., Sonnemans, J., Tuinstra, J., 2012. Individual expectations, limited rationality and aggregate outcomes. Journal of Economic Dynamics and Control 36 (8), 1101–1120.

Bosch-Rosa, C., Meissner, T., Bosh-Domènch, A., 2018. Cognitive bubbles. Experimental Economics 21, 132–153.

Branch, W.A., McGough, B., 2018. Heterogeneous expectations and micro-foundations in macroeconomics. In: Handbook of Computational Economics, vol. 4. Elsevier, pp. 3–62 (this Handbook).

Brock, W., Hommes, C.H., 1997. A rational route to randomness. Econometrica 65, 1059–1095.

Brock, W., Hommes, C.H., 1998. Heterogeneous beliefs and routes to chaos in a simple asset pricing model. Journal of Economic Dynamics and Control 22, 1235–1274.

Brown, M., Trautmann, S.T., Vlahu, R., 2017. Understanding bank-run contagion. Management Science 63, 2272–2282.

Campbell, J.Y., 1998. Asset Prices, Consumption, and the Business Cycle. NBER Working Paper 6485. National Bureau of Economic Research, Inc.

Campbell, J.Y., Mankiw, N.G., 1989. Consumption, income, and interest rates: reinterpreting the time series evidence. In: Blanchard, O.J., Fischer, S. (Eds.), NBER Macroeconomics Annual 1989.

Carbone, E., 2006. Understanding intertemporal choices. Applied Economics 38, 889–898.

Carbone, E., Duffy, J., 2014. Lifecycle consumption plans, social learning and external habits: experimental evidence. Journal of Economic Behavior & Organization 106, 413–427.

Carbone, E., Hey, J.D., 2004. The effect of unemployment on consumption: an experimental analysis. The Economic Journal 114, 660–683.

Chakravarty, S., Fonesca, M.A., Kaplan, T.R., 2014. An experiment on the causes of bank run contagions. European Economic Review 72, 39–51.

Choi, S., Gallo, E., Wallace, B., 2017. Financial Contagion in Networks: A Market Experiment. Working Paper.

Cooper, K., Schneider, H.S., Waldman, M., 2017. Limited rationality and convergence to equilibrium play. Games and Economic Behavior 106, 188–208.

Croson, R., 1996. Partners and strangers revisited. Economics Letters 53, 25–32.

Den Haan, W.J., 1996. Heterogeneity, aggregate uncertainty and the short term interest rate. Journal of Business and Economic Statistics 14, 399–411.

Diamond, D.W., Dybvig, P.H., 1983. Bank runs, deposit insurance, and liquidity. Journal of Political Economy 91, 401–419.

Duffy, J., 2006. Agent-based models and human subject experiments. In: Tesfatsion, L., Judd, K.L. (Eds.), Handbook of Computational Economics, vol. 2. North-Holland, Amsterdam, pp. 949–1011.

Duffy, J., 2010. Experimental macroeconomics. In: Durlauf, S., Blume, L. (Eds.), Behavioral and Experimental Economics. In: The New Palgrave Economics Collection. Palgrave Macmillan, New York, pp. 113–119.

Duffy, J., 2016. Macroeconomics: a survey of laboratory research. In: Kagel, J.H., Roth, A.E. (Eds.), Handbook of Experimental Economics, vol. 2. Princeton University Press, Princeton, pp. 1–90.

Duffy, J., Karadimitropoulou, A., Parravano, M., 2017. Financial Contagion in the Laboratory: Does Network Structure Matter? Working Paper.

Duffy, J., Lafky, J., 2016. Birth, death and public good provision. Experimental Economics 19, 317–341.

Duffy, J., Li, Y., 2017. Lifecycle consumption under different income profiles: evidence and theory. Manuscript.

Dufwenberg, M., Lindqvist, T., Moore, E., 2005. Bubbles and experience: an experiment. The American Economic Review 95 (5), 1731–1737.

Dwyer Jr., G.P., Williams, A.W., Battalio, R.C., Mason, T.I., 1983. Tests of rational expectations in a stark setting. The Economic Journal 103, 586–601.

Evans, G.W., 2001. Expectations in macroeconomics: adaptive versus eductive learning. Revue Économique 52, 573–582.

Evans, G.W., Honkapohja, S., 2001. Learning and Expectations in Macroeconomics. Princeton University Press, Princeton.

Ezekiel, M., 1938. The Cobweb theorem. The Quarterly Journal of Economics 52, 255–280.

Falk, A., Heckman, J.J., 2009. Lab experiments are a major source of knowledge in the social sciences. Science 326, 535–538.

Fehr, E., Tyran, J.-F., 2001. Does money illusion matter? The American Economic Review 91, 1239–1262.

Fehr, E., Tyran, J.-F., 2008. Limited rationality and strategic interaction: the impact of the strategic environment on nominal inertia. Econometrica 76, 353–394.

Fischbacher, U., Gächter, S., Fehr, E., 2001. Are people conditionally cooperative? Evidence from a public goods experiment. Economics Letters 71, 397–404.

Fréchette, G.R., 2015. Laboratory experiments: professionals versus students. In: Fréchette, G.R., Schotter, A. (Eds.), Handbook of Experimental Economic Methodology. Oxford University Press, Oxford, pp. 360–390.

Garratt, R., Keister, T., 2009. Bank runs as coordination failures: an experimental study. Journal of Economic Behavior & Organization 71, 300–317.

Gode, D.K., Sunder, S., 1993. Allocative efficiency of markets with zero-intelligence traders: market as a partial substitute for individual rationality. Journal of Political Economy 101, 119–137.

Goldberg, D.E., 1989. Genetic Algorithms in Search, Optimization, and Machine Learning. Addison-Wesley, Reading, MA.

Grandmont, J.-M., 1998. Expectation formation and stability in large socio-economic systems. Econometrica 66, 741–781.

Guesnerie, R., 1992. An exploration of the eductive justifications of the rational-expectations hypothesis. American Economic Association 82, 1254–1278.

Guesnerie, R., 2002. Anchoring economic predictions in common knowledge. Econometrica.

Haltiwanger, J., Waldman, M., 1985. Rational expectations and the limits of rationality: an analysis of heterogeneity. American Economic Review 75, 326–340.

Hanaki, N., Akiyama, E., Funaki, Y., Ishikawa, R., 2017. Diversity in Cognitive Ability Enlarges Mispricing in Experimental Asset Markets. GREDEG Working Paper No. 2017-08.

Heathcote, J., Storesletten, K., Violante, G., 2009. Quantitative macroeconomics with heterogeneous households. Annual Review of Economics 1, 319–354.

Heemeijer, P., Hommes, C., Sonnemans, J., Tuinstra, J., 2009. Price stability and volatility in markets with positive and negative feedback. Journal of Economic Dynamics and Control 33, 1052–1072.

Hey, J., 1994. Expectations formation: rational or adaptive or . . . ? Journal of Economic Behavior & Organization 25, 329–349.

Holland, J.H., 1975. Adaptation in Natural and Artificial Systems. University of Michigan Press, Ann Arbor.

Hommes, C.H., 2011. The heterogeneous expectations hypothesis: some evidence from the lab. Journal of Economic Dynamics and Control 35, 1–24.

Hommes, C.H., 2013. Behavioral Rationality and Heterogeneous Expectations in Complex Economic Systems. Cambridge University Press, Cambridge.

Hommes, C.H., Lux, T., 2013. Individual expectations and aggregate behavior in learning-to-forecast experiments. Macroeconomic Dynamics 17, 373–401.

Hommes, C.H., Makarewicz, T., Massaro, D., Smits, T., 2017. Genetic algorithm learning in a New Keynesian macroeconomic setup. Journal of Evolutionary Economics 27, 1133–1155.

Hommes, C.H., Massaro, D., Salle, I., 2016. Monetary and Fiscal Policy Design at the Zero Lower Bound: Evidence from the Lab. CenDEF Working Paper. University of Amsterdam.

Hommes, C.H., Sonnemans, J., Tuinstra, J., van de Velden, H., 2005. Coordination of expectations in asset pricing experiments. The Review of Financial Studies 18, 955–980.

Hommes, C.H., Sonnemans, J., Tuinstra, J., van de Velden, H., 2007. Learning in cobweb experiments. Macroeconomic Dynamics 11 (Suppl. 1), 8–33.

Hommes, C.H., Sonnemans, J., Tuinstra, J., van de Velden, H., 2008. Expectations and bubbles in asset pricing experiments. Journal of Economic Behavior & Organization 67, 116–133.

Hüsler, A., Sornette, D., Hommes, C.H., 2013. Super-exponential bubbles in lab experiments: evidence for anchoring over-optimistic expectations on price. Journal of Economic Behavior & Organization 92, 304–316.

Isaac, R.M., Walker, J.M., 1988. Group size effects in public goods provision: the voluntary contribution mechanism. The Quarterly Journal of Economics 103, 179–199.

Issac, R.M., Walker, J.M., Williams, A.W., 1994. Group size and the voluntary provision of public goods. Journal of Public Economics 54, 1–36.

Johnson, S., Kotlikoff, L.J., Samuelson, W., 2001. Can people compute? An experimental test of the life-cycle consumption model. In: Kotlikoff, L.J. (Ed.), Essays on Saving, Bequests, Altruism, and Life-Cycle Planning. MIT Press, Cambridge, MA, pp. 335–385.

Kelley, H., Friedman, D., 2002. Learning to forecast price. Economic Inquiry 40, 556–573.

Kiss, H.J., Rodriguez-Lara, I., Rosa-Garcia, A., 2012. On the effects of deposit insurance and observability on bank runs: an experimental study. Journal of Money, Credit, and Banking 44, 1651–1665.

Kiss, H.J., Rodriguez-Lara, I., Rosa-Garcia, A., 2014. Do social networks prevent or promote bank runs? Journal of Economic Behavior & Organization 101, 87–99.

Krueger, D., Mitman, K., Perri, F., 2016. Macroeconomics and household heterogeneity. In: Taylor, J., Uhlig, H. (Eds.), Handbook of Macroeconomics, vol. 2B. North-Holland, Amsterdam, pp. 843–922.

Krusell, P., Smith Jr., A.A., 1998. Income and wealth heterogeneity in the macroeconomy. Journal of Political Economy 106, 867–896.

List, John A., 2011. Why economists should conduct field experiments and 14 tips for pulling one off. The Journal of Economic Perspectives 25, 3–16.

Madiés, P., 2006. An experimental exploration of self-fulfilling banking panics: their occurrence, persistence, and prevention. Journal of Business 79, 1831–1866.

Marimon, R., Sunder, S., 1993. Indeterminacy of equilibria in a hyperinflationary world: experimental evidence. Econometrica 61, 1073–1107.

Marimon, R., Sunder, S., 1994. Expectations and learning under alternative monetary regimes: an experimental approach. Economic Theory 4, 131–162.

Mauersberger, F., 2018. Monetary policy rules in a non-rational world: a macroeconomic experiment. Manuscript.

Mauersberger, F., Nagel, R., 2018. Levels of reasoning in Keynesian Beauty Contests: a generative framework. In: Hommes, C., LeBaron, B. (Eds.), Handbook of Computational Economics, vol. 4. Elsevier, pp. 541–634 (this Handbook).

Meissner, 2016. Intertemporal consumption and debt aversion: an experimental study. Experimental Economics 19, 281–298.

Modigliani, F., Brumberg, R.H., 1954. Utility analysis and the consumption function: an interpretation of cross-section data? In: Kurihara, Kenneth K. (Ed.), Post-Keynesian Economics. Rutgers University Press, New Brunswick, NJ, pp. 388–436.

Muth, J.F., 1961. Rational expectations and the theory of price movements. Econometrica 29, 315–335.

Nagel, R., 1995. Unraveling in guessing games: an experimental study. The American Economic Review 85, 1313–1326.

Palan, S., 2013. A review of bubbles and crashes in experimental asset markets. Journal of Economic Surveys 27 (3), 570–588.

Pfajfar, D., Zakelj, B., 2014. Experimental evidence on inflation expectation formation. Journal of Economic Dynamics and Control 44, 147–168.

Potters, J.J.M., Suetens, S., 2009. Cooperation in experimental games of strategic complements and substitutes. The Review of Economic Studies 76, 1125–1147.

Ragot, X., 2018. Heterogeneous agents in the macroeconomy: reduced-heterogeneity representations. In: Hommes, C., LeBaron, B. (Eds.), Handbook of Computational Economics, vol. 4. Elsevier, pp. 215–253 (this Handbook).

Sargent, T.J., 1993. Bounded Rationality in Macroeconomics. Oxford University Press, Oxford.

Schmalensee, R., 1976. An experimental study of expectation formation. Econometrica 44, 17–41.

Schotter, A., Yorulmazer, T., 2009. On the dynamics and severity of bank runs: an experimental study. Journal of Financial Intermediation 18, 217–241.

Smith, V.L., Suchanek, G.L., Williams, A.W., 1988. Bubbles, crashes, and endogenous expectations in experimental spot asset markets. Econometrica 56 (5), 1119–1151.

Sutan, A., Willinger, M., 2009. Guessing with negative feedback: an experiment. Journal of Economic Dynamics and Control 33, 1123–1133.

Temzelides, T., 1997. Evolution, coordination, and banking panics. Journal of Monetary Economics 40, 163–183.

Thompson, W.R., 1933. On the likelihood that one unknown probability exceeds another in view of the evidence of two samples. Biometrika 25 (3/4), 285–294.

Woodford, M., 2003. Interest and Prices: Foundations of a Theory of Monetary Policy. Princeton University Press.

Woodford, M., 2013. Macroeconomic analysis without the rational expectations hypothesis. Annual Review of Economics 5 (1), 303–346.

Levels of Reasoning in Keynesian Beauty Contests: A Generative Framework*

10

Felix Mauersberger*, Rosemarie Nagel[†,1]

*Department of Economics and Business, Universitat Pompeu Fabra, Barcelona GSE, Barcelona, Spain

[†]Department of Economics and Business, Universitat Pompeu Fabra, Barcelona GSE, ICREA, Barcelona, Spain

[1]Corresponding author: e-mail address: rosemarie.nagel@upf.edu

CONTENTS

*We thank Larbi Alaoui, Jess Benhabib, Antoni Bosch, Pablo Brañas-Garza, Christoph Bühren, Antonio Cabrales, Gabriele Camera, John Duffy, Björn Frank, Willemien Kets, Anita Kopanyi-Peuker, Kiminori Matsuyama, Shabnam Mousavi, Mechthild Nagel, Antonio Penta, Michael Reiter, Ricardo Serrano-Padial, Edouard Schaal, Shyam Sunder, Michael Woodford, three anonymous referees, and the editor Cars Hommes for valuable comments. For financial support we both thank the Barcelona GSE; Felix Mauersberger acknowledges the FPI grant from the Spanish Ministry of Science and Innovation and Rosemarie Nagel the grant MINECO-ECO2014-56154-R from the Spanish Ministry of Education.

Handbook of Computational Economics, Volume 4, ISSN 1574-0021, https://doi.org/10.1016/bs.hescom.2018.05.002

"Because of the success of science, there is a kind of a pseudo-science. Social science is an example of a science which is not a science. They follow the forms. You gather data, you do so and so and so forth, but they don't get any laws, they haven't found out anything. They haven't got anywhere – yet. Maybe someday they will, but it's not very well developed."

(Richard Feynman, radio interview, 1981)

"[This] is the principal problem of classical economics: how is the absolutely selfish 'homo economicus' going to act under given external circumstances?"

(John von Neumann, 1932)

1 INTRODUCTION

Aiming to improve the design of cockpits, US Air Force researchers in 1950 obtained body measures from 4063 pilots, containing 140 dimensions from size to thumb length. For every dimension, the "approximate average" was defined as 0.3 times the standard deviation above or below the sample mean. For the ten most vital dimensions, between 990 (waist circumference) and 1713 (neck circumference) pilots belonged to the average defined this way. However, not a single pilot was "approximately average" with respect to all ten dimensions. Not only did the *average pilot* simply not exist, Daniels (1952) concluded that "the 'average man' is a misleading and illusory concept." As prominently argued by Kirman (1992), the "reduction of the behavior of a group of heterogeneous agents even if they are all themselves utility maximizers, is not simply an analytical convenience as often explained, but is both unjustified and leads to conclusions which are usually misleading and often wrong."

This chapter shows that laboratory experiments can be used as an effective tool to uncover the usually rich heterogeneity of behavioral responses. For our context, we define *heterogeneity* as the existence of several distinct types which have to be described using various specifications with different parameters or even different functional forms. *Homogeneity*, in contrast, means that all agents can be defined by the same specification. It is important to distinguish between heterogeneity and *randomness*: heterogeneity points to systematic differences in a specification, so that at least one structural parameter differs across the population. A situation where the population can be described by the same specification and differences only come from random draws from a well-defined distribution may more accurately be described by randomness.

We distinguish two dimensions of heterogeneity: firstly related to situations; and secondly related to behavior across games and within a game. While there is a myriad of different games and models in economics upon which experiments are often built, the benchmark solutions are typically based on an equilibrium concept, i.e. a well-defined fixed point based on maximization. Laboratory experiments, however, reveal how empirical behavior can be quite different across games: in some situations, equilibrium provides a good approximation of subjects' behavior (on average or individually) and in some it fails to do so. Within games there can be much heterogeneity among a group of agents, which is what Kirman (1992) conjectures and which is very frequently observed in the laboratory. The benchmark solution, on the other hand, might specify a homogeneous outcome for all.

In this chapter, we first review the different and disconnected areas of experimental economics within interactive decision making, each with one representative or *archetypal*, meaning "primitive" or "original" (Oxford English Dictionary, 2018) game or market and a few variations experimented on in the laboratory. We also discuss typical (heterogeneous) behavioral responses. We then offer a novel perspective by showing that the reduced forms (best response functions) of these seemingly unrelated games can be considered as special cases of a canonical game (see definition below), a generalization of the so-called Beauty Contest (BC) game. The basic BC game is characterized by a best response or optimal action as a function of others' (aggregated) actions. The word *canonical* refers to a "general rule or standard formula" (Oxford English Dictionary, 2018). Analogously, a musical canon repeats the melody in different voices. Here a canonical formulation brings together different *archetypal* games into one. In other words, all these games draw from a generative base (inspired Chomsky, 1957) that is universal.[1] The Keynesian metaphor will serve as this base, the seed, out of which emerges a multitude of models which we transform and theoretically and experimentally analyze. Examples include reduced forms (e.g. best response functions) of micro and macroeconomics, including public good games, ultimatum games, Bertrand, Cournot, some auctions, asset markets, New-Keynesian models, and general equilibrium models with sentiments/animal spirits.

The main part of this canonical form consists of the basic Beauty Contest game, which has a long history in (experimental) economics. In the original Beauty Contest game as it was first adopted by the experimental economics literature, all players "choose a number between 0 and 100 and the target or winning choice is the one closest to 2/3 times the average of all chosen numbers", where "2/3" is the main parameter of the game that can be varied. Therefore the best response function corresponds to the choice of a player equal to the target (Ledoux, 1981; Moulin, 1986); see Nagel, 1995 for the first experimental laboratory implementation).[2] The name "Beauty Contest game" was adopted by Duffy and Nagel (1997) from the Keynesian (1936) metaphor describing a contest or coordination game where newspaper readers have to pick faces which they believed to be chosen by most other readers, thus the average, the modes, or the median:

> *"[P]rofessional investment may be likened to those newspaper competitions in which the competitors have to pick out the six prettiest faces from a hundred photographs, the prize being awarded to the competitor whose choice most nearly*

---

[1]Chompsy (1957) first used the word "generative" for a grammar as the rules guiding understandable language, which has later also been used in music theory (see e.g. Baroni et al., 1983).

[2]Nagel et al. (2017) provide a historical account of this game, showing the convergence of the macro and micro version and their applications.

corresponds to the average preferences of the competitors as a whole; [...] It is not a case of choosing those [faces] which, to the best of one's judgment, are really the prettiest, nor even those which average opinion genuinely thinks the prettiest. We have reached the third degree where we devote our intelligences to anticipating what average opinion expects the average opinion to be. And there are some, I believe, who practice the fourth, fifth and higher degrees."

(Keynes, 1936, Chapter 12.V).

Keynes speaks of several reasoning procedures, identifying unreasonable types (own taste, average opinion), and then higher order belief types of third, fourth degree and even higher. Yet, in this contest higher order beliefs collapse all in a choice corresponding to the first order belief. This is easy to see since best response to a face believed to be chosen by the average is equal to this face. Furthermore, each face can be chosen in equilibrium by all participants.

In fact, the aforementioned 2/3-of-average Beauty Contest experiment brings about behavioral belief patterns that can be described according to Keynes' idea of different levels of reasoning. In such a game, the equilibrium, where all players choose zero, is unique and can be obtained through iterated elimination of dominated strategies. All choices above $66.66 = 100 \cdot \frac{2}{3}$ are weakly dominated by 66.66. If one player chooses 66.66 and believes that others do the same, then all choices above 44.44 are eliminated, and so on, until zero will be the only choice that remains.

In contrast to this iterative process, the actual behavior observed in the experimental data can be better described by the level-k model (Nagel, 1995). This model postulates heterogeneous types and consists of one (or several) reference point(s) and (finite) iterated best replies. A reference point in interactive decision-making is typically the choice of a naive or non-strategic player, a focal point, or an intuitive choice or simple heuristics – characterized by level 0 of reasoning. In the original Beauty Contest game, the reference point is assumed to be 50, i.e. the mean of uniform random choices (that would result from insufficient reasoning). The best response to 50 is $33.33 = 50 \cdot \frac{2}{3}$, which can be referred to as level 1. A more sophisticated level-2 player may anticipate this behavior and decide to give a best response to level 1 reasoning, which would be $22.22 = 33.33 \cdot \frac{2}{3}$. A level-3 player may anticipate that behavior and best respond to that, and so on. This path can be pursued to arbitrary levels of reasoning with infinite depth in the limit, corresponding to playing the Nash equilibrium of zero.

Subjects who are not familiar with the game and the underlying theory typically select choices near or at level 0 to level 3. Therefore, also more sophisticated subjects need to respond with rather low levels of reasoning in such untrained subject pools. Thus, we provide a method attending to von Neumann's concern, how "homo economicus" should behave in external circumstances. If the Beauty Contest game is played a repeated number of rounds and subjects can observe the winning number in previous rounds, the results will be a slow convergence to equilibrium due to self-fulfilling beliefs of low levels of reasoning by other players with the reference point being the average of the preceding period. Not always is it possible to understand the reasoning process behind a choice. We therefore also discuss elicitation methods (e.g. strategy method, written comments and brain imaging studies), cognitive and population measures, to better understand heterogeneity in human reasoning in general, and in economic experiments in particular.

The level-k model and related models (Stahl and Wilson, 1994, 1995; Camerer et al., 2004; Crawford et al., 2013) have been applied to describe behavior in many different games in the laboratory and field. It has been extended and applied in behavioral microeconomics (see, e.g., Alaoui and Penta, 2017; survey by Crawford et al., 2013; Crawford, 2013), in epistemic game theory (Kets, 2012), and recently also in behavioral macroeconomics (see e.g., García-Schmidt and Woodford, 2015; Farhi and Werning, 2017).

The canonical form for these archetypal games together with a behavioral model as a framework for economic heterogeneity provides a generative structure or laws Feynman believed is missing in the social sciences. Furthermore, this framework has several advantages: first, an encompassing structure of many situations highlights why similar behavioral patterns can be identified in so many experiments on seemingly different situations across economics. In particular, if the parsimonious behavioral model does not explain behavior, one can check whether this "failure" relies on the underlying game structure or on other features, e.g., related to the subject pool. Second, this encompassing structure of situations can in turn explain why, as compared to individual decision-making, only few parsimonious behavioral game theory models have been constructed for interactive experiments.[3] Third, based on tractable relationships between identified situations and a limited number of parsimonious models, one can use observed behavior in one laboratory experiment to forecast or get an idea of subjects' behaviors in a completely different experimental setting. Fifth, the identification of a general structure may put an end to the existing repetition of experiments that conduct the same game only in slightly different contexts, and thus leaves room for the emergence of new directions in experimental economics outside this general structure, for example experiments on more complicated games.

This chapter proceeds as follows: in Section 2 we give an overview of the different areas and the newest developments in experimental economics, exemplifying heterogeneous behavior in one archetypal game within each area, and we present boundedly rational models; Section 3 provides a framework for seemingly unrelated archetypal models through a generalization of the Beauty Contest game; Section 4 discusses experimental results structured by the level-k or similar models within a systematic series of Beauty Contest and related games; Section 5 presents how different elicitation methods reveal reasoning procedures of human subjects; Section 6 concludes.

---

[3] We will not discuss individual decision making in this chapter. Dhami (2016) offers an excellent overview of behavioral economics, including behavioral game theory and the large area of individual decision-making. Also see Camerer (1995) for a comprehensive account on individual decision-making.

2 AN OVERVIEW OF EXPERIMENTAL ECONOMICS

This section gives a broader overview of experimental economics of interactive decision making to readers that are unfamiliar with this field. Experiments have been used as a tool in a wide range of fields in economics. While experiments with underlying research questions from different fields seem quite disconnected from each other at the first sight, we demonstrate in Section 3 that those games can be connected through a generalization of the Beauty Contest game. The reader that is familiar with experimental economics may skip this section.

In Section 2.1, we present the different areas within experimental economics in the same order as presented in the first Handbook of Experimental Economics (Kagel and Roth, 1995, vol. I). The hypotheses that are tested in the laboratory are initially motivated by economic questions specified through (game) theoretic models and equilibrium solutions based on maximization principles. Based on these hypotheses, experimenters constructed series of experiments mainly consisting of systematic changes of parameters within a few archetypal games or market structures. In some studies, the theoretical benchmarks were corroborated, while in others they were rejected. Both cases incited new work in experimental economics: when theoretical results were initially corroborated, follow-up studies were initiated testing the robustness of those results; when theoretical results were rejected, mechanisms were studied that might eventually bring about the equilibrium outcome. We present the most important games with a few variations to illustrate heterogeneity of human behavior contrasted by the (often homogeneous) theoretical solutions. In Section 2.2, we exemplify the newest developments since the late 1990s, guided by the second Handbook of Experimental Economics (Kagel and Roth, 2016, vol. II). While the first handbook covers the links between economic theory and actual behavior through laboratory experiments, in the last 20 years, experimenters have also attempted to answer questions of external validity, e.g. whether laboratory findings can be replicated in economic decision making in the real world, i.e. the field. In Section 2.3. we discuss different descriptive behavioral models of interactive decision-making that have been motivated by robust laboratory findings (see also surveys by Camerer, 2003; Crawford et al., 2013, and Dhami, 2016).

2.1 EXPERIMENTAL ECONOMICS AREAS WITH ARCHETYPAL GAMES AND MARKETS

Table 1 presents the different topics until the early 1990s. Column 1 (Table 1) states initiating questions, typically inspired by economic theory that led to the different areas of experimental economics (column 2): public goods provision, bargaining, coordination problems, auctions, financial markets, industrial organization, and individual decision making. The data collection led to the development of parsimonious behavioral models discussed in Section 2.3 (column 3).

Since subjects are typically unfamiliar with the tasks or games presented to them, most experiments include repetitions of the same game either with the same or

Table 1 Overview of experimental economics until beginning 2000s

Initiating questions	First wave: definitions of areas, series of experiments, collections of data	Second wave: development of parsimonious models, stylized facts
Inspiring theory	Theoretically driven experiments	Resulting behavioral models or other developments
Free riding vs. giving, public goods provision, punishment	Public good games	Cultural influences
Multiplicity of equilibria	Coordination games Keynesian beauty-contest games	Focal points; global game theory (noise)
Dominance solvable games	p-Beauty Contest games	Level k, learning
Fairness vs. strategic behavior Bargaining in psychology	Bargaining games (e.g. ultimatum game)	Focal points, social preferences, culture, learning models, quantal response equilibrium
Industrial organization Walrasian equilibrium	Industrial organization (Bertrand games, posted offers, etc.) Markets of buyer and seller competition	Zero intelligence
Bubbles vs. fundamental value Rational expectations	Asset markets (double auction design, call market)	Bubbles disappear with repetition of same subjects in same situation Heuristic-switching model
Revenue equivalence	Auctions	Risk aversion as explanation
Expected utility, psychology	Individual decision making	Non-expected utility models (rank-dependent U, hyperbolic discounting etc.), prospect theory, biases

changing subjects over time. This way the experimenter is able to study patterns of first-period behavior and also learning from play over time, which has been studied by a complementary theory literature (e.g. Fudenberg and Levine, 1998). Furthermore, an experimental study typically contains various treatments (experimental setups), which include different variations of some baseline treatment, also referred to as control group. This way the experimenter is able to make some causal inferences of a parameter change under ceteris paribus condition. For example, in the next section we will show the effect of punishment on behavior in public goods experiments, although the theoretical outcome is the same in a punishment and non-punishment treatment.

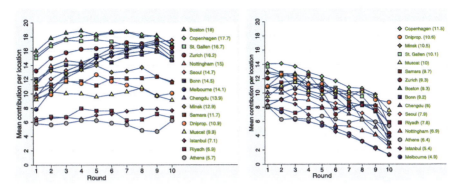

FIGURE 1

Mean contributions in a public goods game over 10 periods in two different environments. Each line corresponds to the average contribution of a particular subject pool. Numbers in parentheses indicate mean contributions (out of 20). Left: no punishment opportunity; Right: punishment opportunity (subjects can decide to punish individual subjects at the end of every round). Modified from Herrmann et al. (2008).

2.1.1 Public Good Provision

Public good games (Ledyard, 1995; Vesterlund, 2016) study situations related to the problem of free-riding. The basic game consists of N subjects within a group, who are asked to contribute all or part of their endowments. The total contribution is multiplied by a factor M ($\frac{M}{N} < 1$), redistributed equally among the members of the group and added to every individual's amount not contributed. Social optimality is attained if all players contribute their endowment to the common good. By contrast, there is an inefficient "free-riding" equilibrium with a dominant strategy, i.e. to give nothing. The main focus of the experimental results is under which conditions people contribute, especially conditionally on what others give. The initial experiments studied investigate hypotheses related to e.g., effects of group size, the multiplication parameters of the contributed amounts and information about others' contributions. A clear result is that in repeated PG games within the same group, in first rounds average giving is around 50% of the endowment but slowly decays over time.

Since the equilibrium is inefficient, experimenters and theorists need to find ways and mechanisms to deter equilibrium behavior. One effective way is punishment of free riders or low contributors. Indeed, contributions then typically do not decay but rather increase over time, despite the fact that the original equilibrium is maintained, due to costly punishment also for the punisher. This is a great example that theoretical outcomes may or may not occur in very similar setups (Fehr and Gachter, 2000).

In the last decade especially cultural heterogeneity in different societies, e.g. Russia, Switzerland, African countries etc., using students as subjects, comparing contributions, punishment, and anti-punishment (how the punished person strikes back to the cooperator) were provided. Fig. 1 shows that average contributions over time across many different countries decay without a punishment rule (left panel), while being stable or increasing over time in the presence of punishment (right panel). (Mean) contributions are very heterogeneous both across groups and within groups due to different conditional cooperation levels by individuals.[4] The authors (Herrmann et al., 2008) attribute distinct levels of contribution and effectiveness of punishment to different degrees of norm compliance in various countries. Guererk et al. (2006) construct an understudied design letting subjects decide which institution to implement: one with punishment or without. In the beginning, most groups opt for the no-punishment option, but quickly converge to the punishment rule leading to higher cooperation.

2.1.2 Bargaining

In the area of *bargaining* (Kagel and Roth, 1995; Camerer, 2003), there was a big debate on how to interpret the discrepancy between data and theoretical solutions. The *ultimatum game* (UG; Güth et al., 1982) is the archetypal game, in which a proposer has to divide a pie (amount of money provided by the experimenter), and a responder can only accept or reject the proposal. A rejection leads to both players receiving nothing and an acceptance to the distribution offered by the proposer. Any offer can be an equilibrium choice that needs to be accepted, with the lowest positive acceptable offer being the subgame-perfect equilibrium. The modal outcome in such experiments is the equal split. Small offers (below 30%) are typically rejected. In order to understand the driving forces in bargaining, many factors in the classical setup have been varied in experiments, including the number of possible offers and counteroffers over time a la Rubinstein (1982), the outside options, the number of bargainers on each side, the information about the pie size etc. The simplest version of a bargaining game in this context is the "dictator game" (without responder behavior).

Camerer and Fehr (2006) attribute the heterogeneity in behavior to a dichotomy of types in the population that is inspired by theoretical biology (Gintis, 2003): self-regarding individuals, who act without applying a particular notion of fairness, and strong reciprocators, who are characterized by giving others altruistic rewards for cooperation and norm-conformity, and applying altruistic punishment in case of norm-violations.

Fig. 2 shows average results in ultimatum games with subjects from different cultures and small scale societies by Henrich et al. (2001). The authors argue that different market and trading rules among the members can identify the different patterns of behavior. For instance, the Lamelara, being predominantly a whale-hunter culture, rely on cooperation for daily fishing, which might explain higher offers in ultimatum games. On the other hand, small scale societies who experience less coordination among group members like Machigueng offer much less when being proposers. In Section 2.3 we discuss the fairness models that rationalize such behavior with social preferences.

---

[4]See Arifovic and Duffy (2018) for further details.

Group	Country	Mean offer[a]	Modes[b]	Rejection rate[c]	Low-offer rejection rate[d]
Machiguenga	Peru	0.26	0.15/0.25 (72)	0.048 (1/21)	0.10 (1/10)
Hadza (big camp)	Tanzania	0.40	0.50 (28)	0.19 (5/26)	0.80 (4/5)
Hadza (small camp)	Tanzania	0.27 (38)	0.20 (8/29)	0.28 (5/16)	0.31
Tsimané	Bolivia	0.37	0.5/0.3/0.25 (65)	0.00 (0/70)	0.00 (0/5)
Quichua	Ecuador	0.27	0.25 (47)	0.15 (2/13)	0.50 (1/2)
Torguud	Mongolia	0.35	0.25 (30)	0.05 (1/20)	0.00 (0/1)
Khazax	Mongolia	0.36	0.25		
Mapuche	Chile	0.34	0.50/0.33 (46)	0.067 (2/30)	0.2 (2/10)
Au	PNG	0.43	0.3 (33)	0.27 (8/30)	1.00 (1/1)
Gnau	PNG	0.38	0.4 (32)	0.4 (10/25)	0.50 (3/6)
Sangu farmers	Tanzania	0.41	0.50 (35)	0.25 (5/20)	1.00 (1/1)
Sangu herders	Tanzania	0.42	0.50 (40)	0.05 (1/20)	1.00 (1/1)
Unresettled villagers	Zimbabwe	0.41	0.50 (56)	0.1 (3/31)	0.33 (2/5)
Resettled villagers	Zimbabwe	0.45	0.50 (70)	0.07 (12/86)	0.57 (4/7)
Achuar	Ecuador	0.42	0.50 (36)	0.00 (0/16)	0.00 (0/1)
Orma	Kenya	0.44	0.50 (54)	0.04 (2/56)	0.00 (0/0)
Aché	Paraguay	0.51	0.50/0.40 (75)	0.00 (0/51)	0.00 (0/8)
Lamelara[e]	Indonesia	0.58	0.50 (63)	0.00 (3/8)	0.00 (4/20)

Note: PNG = Papua New Guinea.
  [a] This column shows the mean offer (as a proportion) in the ultimatum game for each society.
  [b] This column shows the modal offer(s), with the percentage of subjects who make modal offers (in parentheses).
  [c] The rejection rate (as a proportion), with the actual numbers given in parentheses.
  [d] The rejection rate for offers of 20 percent or less, with the actual numbers given in parentheses.
  [e] Includes experimenter-generated low offers.

FIGURE 2

Ultimatum game in small scale societies. Source: Henrich et al. (2001).

In Section 4 we will show disaggregated behavior in UGs both in the first period and after learning has occurred; and in Section 5, we show results for incomplete information UGs.

2.1.3 Coordination Games

Coordination games (see also Ochs, 1995; Camerer, 2003) will be the main focus of attention in this chapter in the following sections with the Keynesian Beauty contest as its corner stone. Behavior in such games is particularly prone to bringing about heterogeneity due to the multiplicity of equilibria, often being Pareto-ranked (some equilibria give all members higher payoffs than other equilibria which, however, might provide secure payoffs or are risk-dominant). Thus, even rational players cannot coordinate a priori to a single prediction by introspection. Therefore, experimentation can be useful and necessary to periodically study equilibrium selection. A simple example is whether we meet at the Empire State Building or at Grand Central Station in New York. Two strangers might resolve the coordination problem differently than two New Yorkers. The focus of the literature on coordination games has offered potential solutions. In general groups of 2–3, maybe also 4 individuals coordinate rather well, while groups larger than 4 typically converge to inefficient equilibria or fail to coordinate altogether. Experimental researchers introduce different methods that subjects also in large groups achieve coordination, e.g. by means of communication. The theoretical literature, e.g., shows that payoff perturbations can lead to a unique equilibrium (initiated by Carlson and Van Damme, 1993 on global games), which we will discuss in Sections 3 and 4.

2.1.4 Industrial Organization

Industrial organization was one of the early areas in experimental economics, starting with Sauermann and Selten (1959) on complicated oligopoly games with demand inertia that led to the theoretical paper of subgame perfection Selten (1965).[5] Experimental industrial organization is surveyed e.g. by Brandts and Potters (2017), Holt (1995), and Davis and Holt (1993). The main topic of this area studies the question of price formation and production in monopolies, oligopolies, and Walrasian markets through different market institutions. Plott and Smith (1978) study the emergence of prices and gains from trade in a private goods market. In the experiments, discrete supply functions are constructed by inducing privately known costs to sellers, who all possess one unit of a good, and demand functions by giving privately known reservation values to buyers who all want to buy one unit of the good. Thus, there is exogenous heterogeneity of types (seller vs. buyer) and sellers or buyers, respectively, can have different values. In the complete information efficient equilibrium the price is such that supply equals demand.

One possible trading mechanism is the double auction, introduced by Smith (1962), in which buyers' bids and sellers' asks together with the resulting contract prices are displayed publicly on a blackboard or on participants' screens. Once an announced bid is higher than an announced ask, trade occurs. The resulting prices converge fast to equilibrium which might be the best example of theory coinciding with observed behavior. The equilibrium in this context is the Pareto-optimal Walrasian equilibrium equating demand and supply and high trading efficiency.

---

[5] See also a discussion by Abbink and Brandts (2010), Nagel et al. (2016).

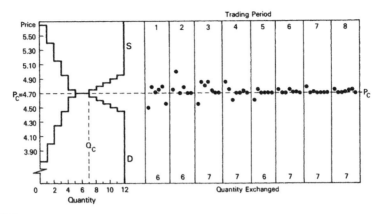

FIGURE 3

Contract prices (dots) in a double auction and the Walrasian equilibrium (datched lines) over time, with supply and demand schedules (left side); from Ketcham et al. (1984).

Fig. 3 shows demand and supply functions of a market (left side of graph) and the resulting contract prices within different time intervals. Only in the first trading periods most contract prices are off equilibrium. However, from period 4 onwards, within a period only initial contract prices are below (above) the equilibrium, and then players coordinate on the equilibrium price. Notably, not all theoretical requirements need to be fulfilled: e.g. a handful of agents on each side suffices instead of an infinite number of agents; demand and supply functions do not need to be commonly known among acting agents, but instead each agent only knows her own cost or willingness to pay.

Gode and Sunder (1993) provide a simple zero intelligence model in which computer programs randomly choose bids and asks (thus, producing high heterogeneity of behavior), constrained by own cost, reservation values and the trading rules. They find that markets populated by automaton traders following such simple rules will converge quickly to the equilibrium. However, the distribution of the surplus depends on the intelligence of traders, giving more to those who are more sophisticated. Thus, humans can easily exploit such mechanical traders. These results are fairly robust to parameter changes. Neither shifting supply or demand curves, reducing the number of sellers to the monopoly case, providing insider information, or incomplete information about the true state of the world offsets the Walrasian equilibrium behavior in most repetitions.

2.1.5 Asset Markets

Sunder (1995) discusses *asset markets* as stylized situations of financial markets, studying information asymmetries between traders. Sunder (2007) highlights that a key development in experimental finance nowadays are experiments to understand the causes and sources of financial bubbles, while before the 2000s, experimental finance dealt with the acquisition and aggregation of information in financial markets.

In the simplest case (Smith et al., 1988) all subjects are identical, endowed with the same number of shares, money that pays no interest, and information about fundamental values (FV), dividend payments of shares per period, and a finite horizon after which the shares are worthless. Trading is done via the double auction, explained in the previous section, or a call market. In the later orders are cleared by a single price, equating demand and supply constructed through the bid-quantity and ask-quantity tuples of participants. Everyone can choose to be a buyer or seller of shares. In reality, it is difficult to separate the fundamental value of an asset apart from the bubble component of realized prices.

Fig. 4 shows a typical outcome of such an asset market played over 15 periods with an occurring bubble. The known fundamental value decreases over time, being zero after 15 periods (see horizontal lines, rational expectation prices). Only the asset pays a dividend while money holdings do not. The solid increasing and decreasing lines represent the realized contract prices in each period and the other dots are subjects' asks and bids, which are quite dispersed although all subjects are ex-ante identical.

Haruvy et al. (2014) conduct bubble experiment and classify players into 3 types based on De Long et al. (1990): fundamental (who are guided by fundamental values), speculative (who exploit momentum traders), and momentum traders (who follow the trend of the contract prices) to explain the presence of bubbles.

If the same group of subjects plays again in the same setup (a multiple period market as described above), once or twice, maintaining the same parameters, the bubble disappears and behavior becomes rather homogeneous with respect to bids and asks. Systematically changing fundamental values (decreasing, increasing, or constant over time), introducing interest rates for money holding results in bubbles. Yet, increasing or constant FVs result in prices closer to the FV than decreasing FV, suggesting that the later produces more confusion in subjects than the former (Breaban and Noussair, 2015). In this paper the authors also test and analyze the influence of individual characteristics (such as risk aversion, loss aversion, cognitive measures) on pricing behavior.

Based on the large amount of experiments with such financial markets, it is easy to predict whether or not a bubble occurs – e.g. the degree of strategic complementarities in the underlying system and the characteristics of subjects are decisive factors. However, as in the real world, one cannot predict the magnitude or time period of the bursting of the bubble. Yet, as mentioned above, one can predict under which conditions bubbles should be smaller or bigger (on average). (See also the discussion on asset markets by Arifovic and Duffy, 2018.[6])

2.1.6 Auctions

Auction experiments (Kagel, 1995) represent the best interaction between theory, laboratory, and reality. Think of a restaurant owner, who buys her fish, seeing the fish

---

[6]In 2010 researchers working in this area created the *Society of Experimental Finance*.

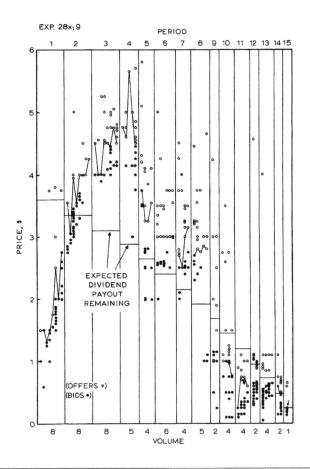

FIGURE 4

Chart of an asset market with all bids and offers and the resulting contract prices (joined by line segments) in sequence for experiment session 28x showing the price dynamics both within and across trading periods in one market. The horizontal lines present the fundamental values for each period. Source: Smith et al. (1988).

coming into the auction hall, and competing with the daily returning other buyers. She clearly knows the auction rules and her willingness-to-pay. As stated already above, understanding or testing behavior related to mathematical models with lab experiments has some advantages over naturally occurring data in the field. Here, certain parameters can be induced by the experimenter as drawing the privately known willingness to pay of each participant from a known, given distribution, in order to calculate a private-value equilibrium. This allows to precisely know deviations of behavior from rational solutions. The first main focus of laboratory experiments in this area consisted of comparing realized revenues and behavior between different auction rules in private and common value single good auctions. Theoretically, average revenues are the same in certain classes of auctions. Kagel and Levin (2002) review

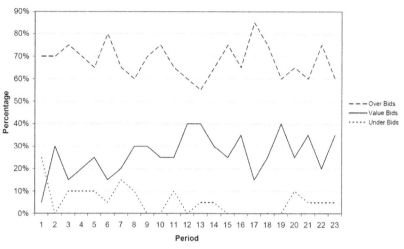

FIGURE 5

Kagel and Levin (1993): Second price auction data as reanalyzed by Garrat and Wooders (2010); bid $< \pm\$0.05$ of value $=$ value; $\frac{2}{3}$ of bids are above private value, although this is strictly dominated.

the influence of the requirements in the newly arising multi-unit auctions starting with the Federal Communications Commission (FCC) auction in the US since 1994. The FCC realized that spectrum auctions more effectively assign licenses than either comparative hearings or lotteries. Here, theorists and experimenters greatly interacted to solve challenging questions such as which auction types to implement or how to deal with bundling of objects.

Let us exemplify heterogeneous behavior in a second-price private value auction with a dominant strategy equilibrium (bidding own private value). All players receive a private value, i.i.d. drawn from a known distribution. The highest bidder will receive the object, paying the second highest bid. The same theoretical results hold for the English auction in which a player quits when an ascending clock reaches her private value, and the last remaining player receives the object for a price determined by the value at which the second last bidder dropped out.

Fig. 5 presents behavior over time for a second price auction categorized by three types: overbidding, i.e. bidding above one's private value (approximately 70%); value bidding (20% in the beginning and then 30%); and underbidding, i.e. bidding below one's value (10% in the beginning and then 0%). Players do not converge to the simple dominant strategy equilibrium over time. This is in contrast to behavior in English auctions, where subjects drop out once their value is reached by the ascending clock. The reasoning procedure for finding the equilibrium bid is much harder for the second price than for the English auction. In the later potential losses are salient, when staying in, once the clock surpasses the private value. However, in the second price auction, a player seems to hope to receive a lower price than her own value and at the same time to augment the chance of winning by an increase of the bid. Since typically subjects do not incur losses, they cannot learn to avoid such wrong reasoning. Similarly, common value auctions produce overbidding and the winner typically pays a much higher price than her private value (called winner's curse). This is due to the difficulty in understanding the theoretical implications of correlated private signals of the common value. Furthermore, players do not learn to avoid such errors neither in the field nor in the laboratory. In the laboratory, each period a new common value together with correlated private values is drawn. An environment like this one being subject to unremitting changes does not allow to draw clearcut implications about the optimal bidding behavior.

2.2 NEW QUESTIONS AND AREAS SINCE THE LATE 90s

Many critiques about experimental economics have repeatedly been expressed, typically from outside this field. The three main concerns were the choice of subject pools (mainly undergraduate students at universities), the question of external validity of laboratory results, and low payoffs. For this purpose, the robustness of laboratory experiments with undergraduates has been tested using different subject pools such as chief executive officers, traders from the stock market, etc. (See example of the ultimatum game above.) Recently, Kagel and Roth (2016) issued the second volume of the Handbook of Experimental Economics containing the newest developments with these and other kinds of questions which we briefly summarize in the remainder of this section.

Field Experiments

All chapters of Kagel and Roth (2016) discuss field experiments, probably the most prevalent experimental methodology besides laboratory experiments (see also survey by Harrison and List, 2004; Banerjee and Duflo, 2018). A field experiment contains a targeted intervention by a researcher in the real world for the purpose of collecting appropriate data to answer a research question. In a field experiment, the researcher does not typically create an artificial setting that she controls but exerts control over some environment or some aspect of subjects' real life. This is usually done by randomly dividing the subject pool into a "treatment" group, being subjected to an intervention or policy, and a "control group", being a comparable group not undergoing that intervention.[7] The challenges of field experiments are usually categorized into "internal validity" considerations, referring to concerns how to consistently estimate the treatment effect, and "external validity" considerations, referring to questions to what extent one can generalize the results of the field study (see Banerjee and Duflo, 2009 and Duflo, 2006 for more detailed discussions). The Internet has become experimenters' playground to set up such natural experiments. For example, Hossain and Morgan (2006) introduce different shipping and handling charges to examine

---

[7]Consider in contrast to that a natural experiment, where the researcher uses some event that happens to randomly divided group of interest into "treatment" and "control."

Table 2 New questions and new areas of experimental economics

New questions after the collection of data	Third wave: leaving the economic laboratory and other new areas
External validity Policy implications Incentives (high, low) Subject pools: experts vs. students Influences of socio-economic variables	Field experiments (RCT) e.g. auctions in the fields, FCC Auctions (multi-unit auctions and bundles of auctions) Incentives field vs. lab Development experiments $\Rightarrow$ policy implications Experiments with different populations (children, small scale societies, professionals e.g. football players etc.) Cross-cultural experiments
Risk in interactive decision making	Price Lists (a series of ordered binary lottery choices) combined with behavior in games
Unraveling in markets	Market design Matching in the field
Male vs. female; happiness, ethics	Gender experiments, personal characteristics, ethics (lying experiments) and happiness surveys, cognitive IQ, strategic IQ
Expectation formation, forecasting, discounting, policy implications, central bank communication	Macroeconomics, finance, political economics experiments $\Rightarrow$ policy implications
How can biological data inform decision making?	Neuroeconomics (especially individual decision making) lesion patients, animals vs. humans; new technologies from the natural sciences: e.g., fMRI, eye-trackers, skin conductance

shopping behavior. Entirely different field experiments introduce (network) structures using Facebook and other social media or online experiments via Mechanical Turk. (For methodological questions about such experiments, see Chen and Konstan, 2018.) Yet, doing the abstract games we discussed above with subject pools different from students also constitute field experiments. As a summary, in the laboratory, many features are controllable by the experimenters, i.e., the induced values of an abstract object in an auction, which in the field is typically known to the subject himself for the real object.

Table 2, column 1, states the main new questions and challenges: *macroeconomic experiments* (Duffy, 2016; see also the chapter by Arifovic and Duffy, 2018); *political economy experiments* with a focus on committee bargaining and voting issues (Palfrey, 2016); Roth (2016) discusses *market design* related, e.g. to school choices, labor markets, kidney exchange, etc. While unraveling in public good games can be offset through punishment, markets such as labor markets or school choices also suffer from inefficiencies, if the institutions are not well designed. Roth compares different matching mechanisms. The most prominent one is the Gale–Shapley (1962) algorithm, with which, for example, unraveling of early matching within a market is largely offset. Frechette (2016), summarizing studies with different subject pools, such as experts, children[8] and even animals, concludes that results are mostly similar across different kinds of subjects. Kagel and Levin (2016) discuss newest developments in *auction* designs and data, especially raised through questions of Federal Communications Commission (FCC) auction designs introduced in the mid-90s, involving multi-unit auctions. Erev and Haruvy (2016) discuss *learning* in simple decision tasks.

The new field of *neuroeconomics* (Camerer et al., 2016) is a first start to bridge the gap between experimental economics and the natural science, linking biological data like brain activity or eye-movements to the behavioral data within existing or new economic experiments. We will discuss this field with a few examples at the end of Section 5.

Gender Experiments

Gender issues have constituted a large topic in empirical economic research, stressing in particular differences in outcomes as wages between men and women based on discrimination. Niederle (2016) discusses heterogeneity of behavior driven by gender and race, taking a different approach. The main result of this experimental topic seems to be that women dislike competition, first documented in Gneezy et al. (2003). They show that this dislike is a main difference between men's and women's entry rates in tournament games (only the winners receive a payment). The reason is related to women's underconfidence of own performance, which contrasts with men's overconfidence. The tasks in such experiments are, for example, about solving mazes or simple calculations in which men and women roughly earn the same with performance-based payments. Fig. 6 shows the percentage of entry rates into standard tournaments (ST) based on the probability of winning the tournament. In general men's entries are much higher than women's. Affirmative action (AA, reserving one of the two winner positions for the highest performing women) considerably helps improve entry by women and decrease men's entry rates.

2.3 BOUNDEDLY RATIONAL MODELS

In the beginning of the 90s, behavioral economics emerged with several new modeling tools of structuring actual behavior in a consistent way (see Table 1, column 3) in order to understand the relationship between actual behavior and theory across the different areas mentioned in the previous section. The special issue in *Games and Economic Behavior* (1995) documents the shortcomings of fully rational concepts

---

[8]See also Harbaugh and Krause (2000) who started to conduct research on experimental games with children, showing, e.g., when theory of mind develops in children in sharing tasks.

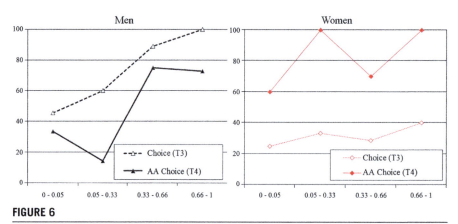

FIGURE 6

Percentage of participants entering the tournaments as a function of probability of winning the specific tournament (T3 is the standard tournament (ST) and AA T4 is the tournament with affirmative action). Modified from Niederle et al. (2013).

such as Nash equilibrium (Nash, 1951) in describing behavior observed in experiments and presents the first important alternatives:

Learning Models

Given a large body of data in the area of bargaining models and market or auction, Roth and Erev (1995) develop reinforcement learning, a learning mechanism originating from psychology, into economic games.[9] This model requires low rationality, without the need to know the precise environment of the game. Subjects update their propensity to play a given strategy through the payoff feedback of their actual past actions. This theory is quite different from the Bayesian learning literature dominating the field of theoretical learning in the game-theoretic and econometric literature. However, both reinforcement learning and Bayesian learning (including fictitious play, which has a Bayesian foundation) have been combined in a more general model, the experience-weighted attraction (EWA) model, by Camerer and Ho (1999). Subjects not only update propensities of chosen but also they keep track of hypothetical payoffs from actions that are not played, which requires more knowledge of the environment than the basic reinforcement model. Camerer (2003) and Erev and Haruvy (2016) provide an overview of such models (see also chapter by Arifovic and Duffy, 2018).

According to the basic forms of reinforcement learning and EWA, players follow the same learning rule regarding the way they make decisions. Stochasticity in those

---

[9]Reinforcement learning models are also found in the machine learning literature. Other examples of algorithms found in the machine learning literature that have been used in economics are hill climbing (Nagel and Vriend, 1999) and Thompson sampling (Mauersberger, 2018).

models is a primitive form of accounting for variation in decision-making over time or in the cross-section.

Quantal Response Equilibrium Model (QRE)

At the same time the so-called quantal response equilibrium model was developed by McKelvey and Palfrey (1995), orthogonally to the learning literature. Agents make mistakes (as their hands may tremble; Selten, 1975) in choosing a best response. By doing so, they form equilibrium beliefs about their opponents that are true in expectation (see survey by Goeree et al., 2014).

Like in reinforcement learning and EWA, players are homogeneous in the basic form of QRE in the way they make decisions. However, quantal response equilibrium model is a stochastic model, allowing decisions to differ over several dimensions such as over repetitions of the game, and the cross-section. Heterogeneity in observed behavior can emerge through random draws. For example, if players start in the same way, stochasticity can push them into different directions and thus also create different payoffs. Rogers et al. (2009) and Breitmoser (2012) expand quantal response equilibrium to include heterogeneity by introducing individual-specific λ-parameters into a logistic equilibrium.

Level-k

The level-k model is an alternative boundedly rational reasoning model (see survey by Crawford et al., 2013), which contains heterogeneity at its core based on the idea that subjects have different degrees of sophistication as mentioned before.[10] This model was developed by Nagel (1995) within the beauty contest experiment and is discussed together with related models in more detail in Section 4.1.2. A requirement or assumption of this model is that the decision-maker knows the strategic environment of the game. This means that it is not obvious that level-k prevails if the decision-maker is not given exact knowledge about the game's parameters. In fact, a large literature (see e.g. Gigerenzer et al., 1999; Hommes, 2013) documents that individuals use heuristics in the absence of precise information about their environments. Heterogeneity can still be observed, because individuals may adopt quite different heuristics. While level-k can be considered a particular heuristic itself, one specific heuristic element contained in level-k thinking is level 0, often corresponding to focal points or reference points. (See e.g. Nagel, 1995; Fehr et al., 2017.)

Social Preference Models

Social preference models cover a fair amount of behavioral models to explain deviations from rational choice models (see surveys by Camerer, 2003 and Cooper and

---

[10]An earlier approach based on stepwise reasoning was eductive learning (Guesnerie, 1992), which investigates whether agents learn an equilibrium by a process of introspection. In contrast to that, level-k postulates that agents use finite iterated steps of reasoning.

Kagel, 2016). The main feature is the expansion of the utility function by specifically considering the preferences or intentions of other individuals. The difference to boundedly rational models is that they require no mistakes or "trembles" such as in the QRE model or in the reinforcement model and are based on the assumption of consistent beliefs as QRE. Therefore, social preference models cannot explain non-maximizing rejection rates as they should not happen in equilibrium. Examples for social preferences include reciprocity, describing the intrinsic desire of an individual to treat other individuals according to how they treat this individual (Rabin, 1993; Falk and Fischbacher, 2006; Dufwenberg and Kirchsteiger, 2004); inequity aversion, describing the aversion against inequalities both in favor or against a particular individual (Fehr and Schmidt, 1999; Bolton and Ockenfels, 2000); and quasi maximin, describing the notion that a decision-maker may care about society's average payoff and the minimum payoff apart from her own payoff (Charness and Rabin, 2002). The literature shows that individuals are heterogeneous regarding their development of such social preferences. Heterogeneity comes about through different parameter constellations in the same or across populations, e.g. the intensity how much you care about your own payoff versus the payoff of the other player(s).

Crawford et al. (2013) discuss the boundedly rational models level-k and quantal response equilibria and others. Crawford (2013) distinguishes between two types of models deviating from full rationality: the first category is "boundedly rational" models, including frameworks that relax the assumption of individual optimization; the second one is "optimization-based" models, which presume some notion of optimality but relax any other assumptions than optimization. While the first category includes models like reinforcement learning, the second category includes models of reference-dependent preferences (Kahneman and Tversky, 1979; Tversky and Kahneman, 1991; Koszegi and Rabin, 2006), models of limited information about the causal structure of the environment to allow for heuristics and biases (Tversky and Kahneman, 1974; Rabin, 2002), and behavioral game theory models of learning such as adaptive models (Woodford, 1990; Milgrom and Roberts, 1990, 1991; Selten, 1991; Crawford, 1995; Fudenberg and Levine, 1998; Camerer and Ho, 1999; Camerer et al., 2002), level-k (Crawford et al., 2013), and "cognitive hierarchy" models (Camerer et al., 2004). Crawford argues that models of the second category (relaxing other assumptions than optimization) are superior to purely boundedly rational models in explaining common phenomena in microeconomics such as systematic overbidding in auctions, bubbles and crashes and finance, the winner's curse and informational naiveté, the latter usually referring to situations where not all available information is used.

3 THE KEYNESIAN BEAUTY CONTEST: A GENERATIVE FRAMEWORK FOR ARCHETYPAL GAMES IN ECONOMICS

In this section we develop a new concept encompassing seemingly different models into one framework. While this section is far from being complete, we hope to inspire a fruitful discussion of structuring models with the aim to make better behavioral predictions in the laboratory and in the field supported by empirical and theoretical validations.

One strength of experimental economics is the systematic control over the parameters of a game or a class of games to test compliance with theoretical predictions, causality issues, and to study behavioral regularities or behavior over time. We choose an approach that helps explain the emergence of heterogeneity by the game structure, i.e. aspects of the environment that are under the control of the experimentalist. Many of the features of the games we bring together in this section have been discussed as overarching themes of common structures by other researchers (as e.g. strategic substitutes and complements and discrete vs. continuous strategies). However, the new idea here is to show that seemingly unrelated situations, some studied in Section 2, can largely be encompassed as special cases of a general function, which is also generative (Chomsky, 1957).

We combine the original *Beauty Contest game*, which is a best response function of aggregated opponent choices, with two additive terms: 1) a constant (representing e.g. a fundamental value of a share or a pre-announced choice of a player) and 2) an idiosyncratic random term (see also Benhabib et al., 2015).[11] This linear function becomes a canonical form for including many seemingly different archetypal models or their abstract simplifications as special cases: e.g. the general equilibrium model with sentiments/animal spirits, New-Keynesian model, asset markets, Cobweb, Cournot reaction functions, ultimatum games, some auctions, and also discrete choice games as stag hunt games, market entry games.

We hope such a common functional form across different models together with level-k will encourage new theoretical, behavioral, and experimental research, to make better predictions that are useful for designing better institutions in the real world. Once we understand the more general structure of those strategic interactions we can more easily understand the driving forces of human behavior and the heterogeneity that may emerge even if the theoretical solutions suggest homogeneous outcomes.

We will show in Section 4 how parameter changes that do not affect the equilibrium outcome may change actual out-of-equilibrium behavior as observed in the laboratory. Conversely, equilibrium differences might not induce behavioral changes due to subjects' cognitive limitations.

3.1 THE BEAUTY CONTEST AS A CANONICAL FORMULATION

Definition 1. Suppose there are N individuals and, at any time $t = 1, ..., T$, every individual i chooses (simultaneously to the N-1 other individuals) an action $y_t^i \in \mathbb{Y}^m$, where $\mathbb{Y}^m$ is an m-dimensional space. We refer to a game as a *Beauty Contest game*

---

[11]Our endeavor resembles Bergemann and Morris (2013). However, while they start with a similar general equation as ours, they are interested in different information structures within their formulation and resulting equilibria.

Table 3 Classification of archetypal games

Optimal choice (best response) for player i:

$$y_t^i = \hat{E}^i \{ c_t + b \cdot f(y_t^1, ..., y_t^N) + d \cdot f(y_{t+1}^1, ..., y_{t+1}^N) + \epsilon_t^i \}$$

	Anti-coordination games **Strategic substitutes** **Negative feedback** *f* decreasing function	Coordination games **Strategic complements** **Positive feedback** *f* increasing function
1. Continuous choice variable: from interval (e.g. [0,100]); or any number	**either substitutes or complements:** *Basic case:* Beauty Contest game ($b<0$ or $b>0$)[a] *General case:* General equilibrium model with sentiments/animal spirits ($b<0$ or $b>0$)	
	strategic heterogeneity: for some players $b<0$ and for some $b>0$	
	Cournot game	Bertrand game Minimum/median effort game some auctions BC with (un)known fundamental Asset market (learning to forecast)
	Ultimatum game Cobweb model	New-Keynesian model (learning to forecast)[b]
	neither substitutes nor complements: public goods, two-person BC with tournament payoff, harmony game (dominant strategy)	
2. Discrete choice variable: from interval (e.g. [1,2,3....7]; or [A,B])	Lowest unique bid auction (LUPI) Entry (chicken) game	Keynesian Beauty Contest Stag hunt game Battle of Sexes
	Global games (congestion) Negative assortative matching	Global games (Attack or not) Positive assortative matching
	strategic heterogeneity: matching pennies (hide and seek), fashion cycles	
	neither substitutes nor complements: prisoner's dilemma, harmony game (dominant strategy)	

y_t^i: choice of individual i in period t; $\hat{E}^i$: subjective (possibly non-rational) belief of individual i in period t; $f(.)$: aggregation function (linear for the continuous case; we allow step functions for the discrete strategy space).

[a] To avoid confusion with other variables such as price, we call this parameter b in our chapter, instead of p as in the experimental literature.
[b] Degree of positive feedback depends on interest rate rule.

if individual i's best response/optimal action is:

$$y_t^i = \hat{E}_t^i\{c_t + b \cdot f(y_t^1, ..., y_t^N) + d \cdot f(y_{t+1}^1, ..., y_{t+1}^N) + \epsilon_t^i\} \tag{1}$$

where $b, d \in \mathbb{R}^{m \times m}$. $c_t \in \mathbb{R}^m$ is a common, deterministic, possibly time-varying process, $\hat{E}_t^i$ denotes the subjective belief of individual i held at time t and $\epsilon_t^i \in \mathbb{R}^m$ is an idiosyncratic exogenous, stochastic process.

$f^{(i)}(.) : \times_{j=1}^N \mathbb{Y}^m \to \mathbb{Y}^m$ produces a vector $y^{agg,i} \in \mathbb{Y}^m$ whose q-th element $(q = 1, ..., m)$ contains either the average, minimum, maximum, median, mode, action least chosen, an action chosen by at least $h \le N$ agents or the sum (provided they exist) of the q-th elements of all individuals' $(j = 1, ..., N)$ present action vectors y_t^j or future action vectors y_{t+1}^j.[12] If $f(.)$ uses the mode, the action least chosen or an action chosen by at least $h \le N$ agents and that statistic is not unique, the one that gives individual i the higher payoff is chosen for $y^{agg,i}$.

In many cases, $c = c_t, \forall t$ reduces to a constant. We limit ourselves to the average, minimum, maximum, median, mode, action least chosen or the sum as aggregation rules, since they are of great importance for economic games and markets.[13] While optimality conditions like Eq. (1) are normally solved by concepts like rational expectations or Nash equilibrium, other less standard solutions concepts are possible of which we discuss one in detail later in Section 4: level k. From Section 2, we will reformulate the public good game, the ultimatum game, several coordination games, an asset pricing market, an auction, and several other games not discussed in detail before.

We present examples from the economic theory literature and the corresponding experimental literature. Note that (1) can describe the optimal action (or best response) for games and setups that differ in several dimensions. Table 3 only contains four of the most important dimensions:

1. **Continuous vs discrete choices:** When strategies are chosen from a finite, discrete set, the typical examples are normal form games with 2 or more strategies; when there are 2 players the experimental literature has essentially defined only five important symmetric games: the prisoners dilemma, chicken game, stag-hunt game, matching pennies, and the harmony game.[14] Contrary to that, strategies can be chosen from a continuous set, i.e. from real numbers, which would be the case in an ultimatum game, an investment or consumption game where you decide the amount to invest or to consume, and in the standard p-Beauty Contest

---

[12] The sign after c need not be positive, as a negative sign can be introduced by b or d.

[13] This kind of aggregation excludes, for example, some asymmetric three player games, in which a player cannot be represented by a constant or the two opponents with a simple aggregation rule. Furthermore, we confine ourself to a linear function as all the games we discuss have this form. Arifovic and Duffy (2018) discuss the non-linear case by Fehr and Tyran (2001, 2007, 2008).

[14] These five symmetric games essentially entail the important characteristics of conflict and cooperation as dominant strategy, multiplicity of equilibria, (in)efficiency of equilibria. There is a long tradition to categorize the important 2x2 games in psychology and economics (see e.g. Rapoport et al., 1976).

game. A Bertrand or public good game is just the continuous version of a PD game. We also will show the effects on behavior when choices can be from the entire real numbers or contrary when the choice set is bounded.

2. **Strategic complements (coordination) vs strategic substitutes (anticoordination):** Loosely speaking, a game of strategic complements is one where an individual has to match others' actions and can thus also be called coordination game. Conversely, a game of *strategic substitutes* is one where an individual i has to act in an opposite way towards others so that the game can alternatively be called anticoordination game (see e.g. Vives, 2010). In the context of the Beauty Contest game, choices are complements (substitutes) if $f(.)$ is an increasing (decreasing) function of another individual's choice y^{-i}. Speaking of "increasing" and "decreasing" highlights an important assumption of an ordered strategy space that is often imposed in case of strategic substitutes and complements. The case of increasing (decreasing) functions is often referred to as positive (negative) feedback, as stressed in Heemeijer et al. (2009).

This terminology can serve as a means of classification for economic environments in both microeconomics and macroeconomics. Bertrand games are commonly characterized by strategic complementarities, because if firms decrease prices, other firms have an incentive to curb prices as well. The Cournot model is, on the other hand, a good example of strategic substitutability, as the higher the quantity a particular firm produces, the lower the quantity another firm produces. In macroeconomics, strategic complementarities play a role in the presence of search frictions (Diamond, 1982), information frictions (Bryant, 1983) and increasing returns (Weitzman, 1982). See Cooper (1999) for an early book for the role of strategic complementarity in macroeconomics. In New-Keynesian DSGE models, there is also an interplay between strategic complements and strategic substitutes (see e.g. Woodford, 2003). On the one hand, prices should be high if other firms charge high prices and consumption should be high if other households consume due to the link between consumption and income. On the other hand, through following e.g. a Taylor-type interest rate rule, the central bank introduces strategic substitutability into the model, as an aggressive interest-rate response to undesired inflation raises the real interest rate, thus curbs consumption through the "dynamic IS" equation and hence reduces inflation through the "Phillips curve."[15]

However, even if $f(.)$ is not differentiable, which is usually the case at least over some domain in games with a discrete strategy spaces, one can categorize games into strategic substitutes and complements. (See e.g. Amir, 2005 for a survey.) A game has strategic complementarities if it is "supermodular", implying that agents are incentivized to match other's actions similarly to the continuous space. (See Topkis, 1979, Vives, 1990, and Milgrom and Roberts, 1990 for the theory of supermodular games.) Conversely, a game has strategic substitutes if it

---

[15] See Assenza et al. (2014) for a more detailed discussion.

is "submodular", implying that agents are incentivized to choose opposite actions to others. Furthermore, according to the axiom of choice in mathematics, an order can be defined over every set (Zermelo, 1904).

3. **Dynamic versus static:** The game can be a one-shot game or a dynamic game. In a dynamic game, the payoff in one round can depend on the decisions in previous rounds. The best-response function in Table 3 introduces a dynamic element by allowing the optimal choice of an individual in a certain period to depend on her belief about future actions and outcomes of other players. The static setup would be a special case with $d = 0$. In microeconomic experiments, the repeated interaction of the same static game is the usual research agenda. We will also discuss dynamic games in which state variables are introduced, for example in forecasting in Beauty Contest games where the constant c becomes time-varying.

4. **Simultaneous versus sequential moves:** Games can be played in extensive form (players decide sequentially) or in normal form (players decide simultaneously).

At the end of Section 3, we will discuss other features.

3.2 CONTINUOUS STRATEGY SPACE

Basic Beauty Contest Game

The most basic example for a Beauty Contest game (*guessing game*) has originally been created by Ledoux (1981) and Moulin (1986)[16] and was experimentally tested by Nagel (1995).

The task is that one's choice has to be closest to b times the average:

$$y^i = b\hat{E}^i \frac{1}{N} \sum_{j=1}^{N} y^j \tag{2}$$

of all chosen numbers by the participants, where $y^i \in [0, 100]$ has been restricted to an interval between 0 and 100, imposing integers or real numbers, typically with two decimals. This is a Beauty Contest game with $c = 0$ and $f(.) = b \cdot$ average, $d = 0$ and $\epsilon_t^i = 0$.

If $0 \le b < 1$ the game has a unique Nash equilibrium $y^{eq} = 0$. If $b = 1$, any number can constitute a Nash equilibrium, all choosing the same number. With a closed interval choice set and $n > 2^{17}$ the (stable) equilibrium zero, starting at the upper bound can be reached through an iterated elimination of dominated strategies (see also example in the introduction). In open intervals, typically iterated best reply structures lead to the (stable) equilibrium. Finally, if $b > 1$ and a closed interval, there are two Nash equilibria, $y^{eq1} = 0$ and $y^{eq2} = $ *upper bound of the interval*. However, only one of these two equilibria is stable: $y^{eq2} = 100$.

---

[16]See Nagel et al. (2016, 2017) for a historical account of Beauty Contests.

[17]The theoretical case of $n = 2$ we discuss in Section 4 together with experimental implementations.

If $b > 0$, the game has strategic complements, as players have an incentive to increase actions when others do so, while if $b < 0$, the game has strategic substitutes, as players need to do the opposite of others. When $b < 0$ and $c = 0$, choices need to include negative numbers. We will alter the number of players, payoff functions, add constants, different information structure about parameters, etc., when discussing experiments related to this game to show how sensitive changes are in terms of equilibrium outcomes, off the equilibrium path structures, and consequentially on behavior. The following games and markets provide part of such changes.

The General Beauty Contest Game

Angeletos and La'O (2010) and Benhabib et al. (2015) show that in a general-equilibrium macroeconomic framework with sentiments (or animal spirits), the equilibrium conditions can be reduced to

$$y_{it} = b\hat{E}_t^i Y_t + \epsilon_t^i \tag{3}$$

where Y_t is the aggregate market outcome, which can, in a simplified fashion, for example be proxied by the average $Y_t = \frac{1}{N}\sum_{j=1}^{N} y_t^j$. $\epsilon_t^i \sim N(c, \sigma^2)$ is an idiosyncratic, private sentiment shock drawn from a distribution which is common knowledge, representing the exogenously given firm specific consumer sentiments.[18] If $b < 0$, the game exhibits strategic substitutes, while for $b > 0$ the game exhibits strategic complements. (d is equal to 0.)

This game is isomorphic to the most general Beauty Contest game discussed in this chapter, $y_t^i = c + b\hat{E}_t^i Y_t + \epsilon_t^i$ with $\epsilon_t^i \sim N(0, \sigma^2)$, being experimentally investigated by Benhabib et al. (2018a, 2018b). If $c = 0$, the Nash equilibrium is playing the private signal $y^{eq} = \epsilon_t^i$, since when all play their signal, the average will be zero and thus the choice for an individual i equals the private signal. If $c > 0$, then the equilibrium becomes $y_t^i = \frac{c}{1-b} + \epsilon_t^i$ and is reached again through an iterated procedure of best reply in an open interval of choices.

Benhabib et al. (2015, 2018a, 2018b) also discuss the case when signals are not precise. Instead, revealed signals are convex combinations of the idiosyncratic signal and a common signal part. In this case players face a signal extraction problem. Since every time a private and a common part is drawn, there can be persistent fluctuations in equilibrium due to this common part. We will discuss an experimental implementation of this theory.

3.2.1 Games of Strategic Substitutes

The Cournot Market

Firm i in the Cournot market (with $N > 2$ firms) chooses the quantity it produces y^i as to maximize its individual profit $\pi^i = py^i - \gamma y^i$ where p is the market price

---

[18] Sunspots and sentiments are conceptually related to correlated equilibria. Imperfectly correlated signals can create multiplicity of equilibria, as shown by Aumann (1974, 1987) for discrete strategy spaces and by Maskin and Tirole (1987) for continuous strategy spaces.

and $\gamma > 0$ is the marginal cost of producing one unit of the good. Let the (inverse) market demand be $p = a - \psi \sum_{j=1}^{N} y^j$. The first-order condition (and thus the target) is therefore

$$y^i = \psi^{-1}(\gamma + a) - \sum_{j=1}^{N} \hat{E}^i y^j \qquad (4)$$

The Cournot game can thus be interpreted as a Beauty Contest game of strategic substitutes with $c = \psi^{-1}(\gamma + a)$, $b = 1$, $d = 0$ and $f(.) = -\sum_{j=1}^{N} \hat{E}^i y^j$ and $\epsilon_t^i = 0$, as this is a standard textbook Cournot market without any exogenous shocks.[19]

Cobweb Market

In Cobweb models (see e.g. Kaldor, 1934; Nerlove, 1958), producers have to produce their commodities first before selling them to buyers. This time lag raises a role for expectations, which can be particularly well illustrated in agricultural markets. Hence, the market can be considered as a price forecasting game so that a producer maximizes profits if her forecast corresponds to the actual price realization: $p_t^{e,i} = p_t$.

Suppose a farmer expects a high price for potatoes. In this case, she would plant more potatoes to harvest at the end of the period. However, if other agents think the same way, the higher supply of potatoes would in fact reduce the price. This is the reason for negative feedback in the Cobweb model so that the reduced form equation is: $p_t = \max\{0, c - b\bar{p}_t^e\}$ where $c, b > 0$ are positive constants, the max operator ensures that prices are non-negative and $\bar{p}_t^e = \frac{1}{N} \sum_{j=1}^{N} p_t^{e,j}$ is the average price expectation in the market for the end of period t.[20] It is easy to see that this is a Beauty Contest game with $d = \epsilon = 0$. For further details see Arifovic and Duffy (2018).

3.2.2 Games of Strategic Complements

Bertrand Market

Let all firms' marginal cost for a product be γ. Firms are submitting prices simultaneously. Assume that the firm with the lowest price obtains the entire market for the product consisting of Q units, so that the individual firm i needs to set the product price p^i as $p^i = \hat{E}^i \min\{\gamma, p^1, \ldots, p^j, \ldots, p^N\} - \eta$ where $\eta > 0$ is small (in order to ensure that player i is below every other player's price). Hence, the Bertrand game can be thought of as a Beauty Contest game with $c = -\eta$, $b = 1$, $d = 0$, and $f(.) = \min\{\gamma, p^1, \ldots, p^j, \ldots, p^N\}$. Note that firms earn higher profits, if they are

---

[19] Solving for y^i yields $y^i = \frac{1}{2}\psi^{-1}(\gamma + a) - \frac{1}{2}\sum_{j=1, j\neq i}^{N} \hat{E}^i y^j$. Hence, an alternative way of viewing the Cournot game is as a Beauty Contest game with $c = \frac{1}{2}\psi^{-1}(\gamma + a)$, $b = \frac{1}{2}$, and $f(.) = -\frac{1}{2}\sum_{j=1, j\neq i}^{N} \hat{E}^i y_j$, i.e. where players need to decide based on the sum of output of all other players excluding themselves.

[20] Hommes et al. (2007) run a Cobweb experiment with a non-linear aggregation function due to non-linear aggregate supply given by a tanh-function.

able to set higher prices p^i, as firms' profit is given by $\pi^i = p^i q^i - \gamma q^i$. The unique (inefficient) Nash equilibrium is, however, $p^i = p^1 = \cdots = p^N = p^{eq} = \gamma$.

Auctions

In a first-price sealed bid auction, all participants simultaneously submit their bids in a way that no agent knows the bid of other participants. In a buyer auction, the individual with the highest bid wins.[21] Hence, every participant chooses a bid y^i so that $y^i = \hat{E}^i \max\{\gamma_i, y^1, \ldots, y^j, \ldots, y^N\}$, where $\gamma_i \geq 0$ may be the seller's (privately known) redemption value. It is easy to see that this is a Beauty Contest game with $c = 0$, $b = 1$, $d = \epsilon = 0$. The γ_i can be thought of as being given by a constructed player called "nature". In Bayesian Nash equilibrium each player chooses $(n-1)/n^* \gamma_i$.

Asset Markets

Campbell et al. (1997) and Brock and Hommes (1998) outline a standard mean-variance asset pricing model with heterogeneous expectations and two assets: a riskless asset with perfectly elastic supply and a risky asset with fixed, perfectly inelastic supply. One very simple design to introduce asset markets as a laboratory setup is a "learning to forecast" design in which subjects are only paid for forecasting and based on subjects' forecast the computer optimizes for them. A particular subject j is then paid according to a distance function such as $U_t^j = A - B(\hat{E}_t^j p_{t+1} - p_{t+1})^2$, i.e. how close her forecast for period $t + 1$, $\hat{E}_t^j p_{t+1}$, is to the realized price in $t + 1$, p_{t+1}.

Campbell et al. (1997) and Brock and Hommes (1998) both use a market clearing asset pricing model (i.e. with a Walrasian auctioneer setting the equilibrium price). In terms of learning-to-forecast experiments, this leads to a two-period ahead forecasting game (as in Hommes et al., 2005). For the positive feedback asset market Heemeijer et al. (2009) implement a learning-to-forecast asset market, using a market maker price adjustment rule. The reason for this is that they want to compare positive versus negative feedback markets. An asset market with a market maker reduces to a one-period ahead forecasting game with the same timing as in the classical cobweb model with negative feedback.

Under market clearing, the price, being the target in learning-to-forecast experiments, can be expressed by $p_t = \frac{1}{1+r}(\bar{p}_{t+1}^e + \bar{y} + u_t)$ where $\bar{p}_{t+1}^e = \frac{1}{N}\sum_{j=1}^N \hat{E}_t^j p_{t+1}$ is the average belief in the market at period t about the price in period $t + 1$, r is the interest rate, $\bar{y}$ is the mean dividend and u_t captures supply and demand shocks in the market.

This is a Beauty Contest game of strategic complements with $c = \frac{\bar{y}}{1+r}$, $b = 0$, $d = \frac{1}{1+r}$, $f(.)$ being the average and the shock being the same for all individuals:

$\epsilon_t^i = \epsilon_t = \frac{u_t}{1+r}$. The current price p_t is given as a temporary equilibrium, being a function of the average belief of the price in the next period, $t+1$.

Another model of price formation is a market maker, like a Walrasian auctioneer, calling out prices and aggregating the asset demand for a given price (Beja and Goldman, 2015). Under this mechanism, the price is determined by a linear function $p_t = c + b\bar{p}_t^e + u_t$, where $\bar{p}_t^e = \frac{1}{N}\sum_{j=1}^{N}\hat{E}_t^j p_t$ is the average forecast in the market at period t about the current price in t. (See e.g. Heemeijer et al., 2009.) It is easy to see that this is also a Beauty Contest game. For further details see Arifovic and Duffy (2018).

New-Keynesian Models

A heterogeneous expectations version of the New-Keynesian model as encountered in Woodford (2003), Galí (2008), or Walsh (2010) can, under some restrictions of the expectations operator (see Branch and McGough, 2009), be written as

$$y_t = \bar{y}_{t+1}^e - \sigma(i_t - \bar{\pi}_{t+1}^e - \rho) + g_t \tag{5}$$
$$\pi_t = \kappa y_t + \beta\bar{\pi}_{t+1}^e + u_t \tag{6}$$
$$i_t = \rho + \phi_\pi(\pi_t - \pi) \tag{7}$$

where y_t denotes the output gap, π_t inflation, t the time-subscript, and $\bar{\pi}_{t+1}^e$ and $\bar{y}_{t+1}^e$ the mean expected future values of output gap and inflation, being the average forecast of all subjects. The model is closed under an inflation targeting rule for the nominal interest rate i_t with a constant inflation target π.

Similarly to the asset market case, we consider a learning-to-forecast game, in which subjects are incentivized to forecast inflation and output gap, being generated as temporary equilibrium where inflation and output gap of period t depend on $\bar{\pi}_{t+1}^e$ and $\bar{y}_{t+1}^e$, respectively, which are the average of all subjects' forecasts for period $t+1$. An individual subject j is then paid according to a distance function such as $U_{t+1}^j = A - B(\hat{E}_t^j \pi_{t+1} - \pi_{t+1})^2$, i.e. how close her forecast for period $t+1$ (given in period t), $\hat{E}_t^j \pi_{t+1}$, is to the realized inflation in $t+1$, π_{t+1}, and similarly for the output gap. It is easy to see that this model is a special case contained in the Beauty Contest definition, since we allowed the variable of interest to be a vector. For the sake of simplicity, however, we describe the New-Keynesian model as a univariate forecasting game of inflation at time t, π_t.

To reduce the dimensionality of this forecasting game to a single dimension, we use the ad-hoc assumption that expectations of the output gap are equal to its long-run steady state value,[22] obtained by using Eq. (6):

$$\bar{y}_{t+1}^e = \kappa^{-1}(1-\beta)\pi \tag{8}$$

---

[22]To keep the task for subjects simple, laboratory experiments have used different ad-hoc assumptions. Pfajfar and Zakelj (2014) use naive expectations about the output gap. Assenza et al. (2014), Arifovic and Petersen (2017), and Mauersberger (2016) use forecasts generated by subjects for both inflation and output gap.

Substituting (8) into (5), the system becomes

$$y_t = \kappa^{-1}(1-\beta)\pi + \sigma\phi_\pi\pi - \sigma\phi_\pi\pi_t - \sigma\bar{\pi}^e_{t+1} + \kappa g_t \tag{9}$$

$$\pi_t = \kappa y_t + \beta\bar{\pi}^e_{t+1} + u_t \tag{10}$$

By inserting (9) into (10) and rearranging one obtains the target that subjects need to forecast at time $t-1$:

$$\pi_t = c + d\bar{\pi}^e_{t+1} + v_t \tag{11}$$

with $c \equiv \frac{(1-\beta)+\kappa\sigma\phi_\pi}{1+\kappa\sigma\phi_\pi}\pi$ and $d \equiv \frac{\beta-\kappa\sigma}{1+\kappa\sigma\phi_\pi}$ and v_t being a composite shock at time t. It is easy to see that the New-Keynesian model can be considered to be a Beauty Contest game with $c > 0$, $d > 0$, $b = 0$, $f(.) = \bar{\pi}^e_{t+1}$, and a common random term $\epsilon^i_t = v_t$ being the same for every individual i. For further details see Arifovic and Duffy (2018).

3.2.3 Public and Private Information
Unknown Constant Fundamental

Morris and Shin (2002) consider the following Beauty Contest game:

$$y^i = (1-r)\hat{E}^i \frac{1}{N}\sum_{j=1}^{N} y^j + r\hat{E}^i c \tag{12}$$

where $0 \leq r \leq 1$. Agents do not have full knowledge of c. However, agents observe a public signal of c, denoted as $z = c + \eta$ where $\eta \sim N(0,\sigma^2_\eta)$ is a Gaussian random shock, and also a private signal of c, being denoted as $x^i = c + \xi^i$, where $\xi^i \sim N(0,\sigma^2_\xi)$ is a Gaussian random shock. Hence, agents face a *signal-extraction problem*. In equilibrium, agents play a convex combination of these two signals, denoted as $y^i = \theta x^i + (1-\theta)z$, where $\theta = \frac{(1-r)\sigma^2_\eta}{(1-r)\sigma^2_\eta+\sigma^2_\xi}$. While Morris and Shin (2002) consider the case of strategic complements, one could also consider a game of this type with strategic substitutes, which would be obtained if $r > 1$ or more generally as $y^i = b\hat{E}^i \frac{1}{N}\sum_{j=1}^{N} y^j + \lambda\hat{E}^i c$.

3.2.4 Other Games
Public Goods Games

The public good game we mentioned in Section 2 is neither attributed to strategic complements nor substitutes since other player's decisions do not enter an individual i's best response. There is a dominant strategy both in public good games with a boundary solution and public good games with an interior solution. Yet other player's decisions are also payoff-relevant. Consider N individuals that are asked to contribute an amount y^i_t to a joint project (that is non-excludable and non-rivalrous in consumption) at time t from their endowment e^i_t. A boundary solution is obtained, if, by contributing y^i_t, individual i obtains the payoff $u^i_t = e^i_t - y^i_t + m\sum_{j=1}^{N} y^j_t$.

It is easy to see that individual i's dominant strategy is $y_t^i = 0$. An interior solution is obtained, if, individual i receives a payoff function of for example $u_t^i = e_t^i + n \cdot y_t^i - y_t^{i,2} + m \sum_{j=1}^N y_t^j$ (similar to Keser, 1996) with a dominant strategy $y_t^i = \frac{m+n}{2}$ for all players i. However, despite the absence of strategic substitutes or complements, this can be seen as a Beauty Contest game with $c = 0$ for the boundary-solution case and $c = \frac{m+n}{2}$ for the interior-solution case with $b = d = \epsilon = 0$.

3.3 DISCRETE STRATEGY SPACE AND MULTIPLICITY

As mentioned before, classifying games into games of strategic substitutes and complements requires an ordered strategy space. An order obviously exists in games with continuous strategy spaces, because numbers can be ranked from "lowest" to "highest." One can also categorize games with discrete strategy space into games of strategic substitutes and complements. (See e.g. Amir, 2005.) A game has strategic complementarities if it is "supermodular", implying that agents are incentivized to match other's actions similarly to the continuous space. It is easy to see that a prisoner's dilemma (PD) game can be considered as a public good game with two strategies, say 0 and 100, and two players, reduced from a continuous [0, 100]-interval. Similarly, a stag-hunt game corresponds to a minimum effort game with a reduced strategy space.

A contrary case to the PD is the harmony game. In the harmony game, the dominant action for all players is also Pareto-efficient, while this is not the case in the PD.

3.3.1 Strategic Complements
The Original Keynesian Beauty Metaphor

Keynes (1936) outlined the following game: Each individual i has to make a choice y^i out of a finite, discrete set (A, B) so that in a contest with N individuals:

$$y^i = \hat{E}^i \text{ Mode}\{y^1, y^2, \ldots, y^i, \ldots, y^j, \ldots, y^N\} \tag{13}$$

where $\hat{E}^i$ denotes the subjective belief of individual i, accounting for the information friction that individual i may not know the choices of the other individuals $j = 1, \ldots, N$. An equilibrium strategy combination is given by any choice, provided that all players make this choice. This is a Beauty Contest game with $f(.)$ being the model. One can also formulate this game for the continuous case, in which case it is easy to see that it would be a Beauty Contest game with $b = 1$, $c = 0$, $d = 0$. However, this game does not induce higher order beliefs despite the fact that Keynes inserts higher order reasoning mentioned in the introduction into this game. If a player believes that face A is chosen by most others, then she herself has also to choose face A. Thus, there is no higher order belief involved. This property holds for all games discussed in this subsection unless otherwise stated.

Table 4 Stag-hunt game

	Stag	Hare
Stag	2, 2	0, 1
Hare	1, 0	1, 1

Table 5 Van Huyck et al. (1991): Median effort game

		Median value of X chosen						
		7	**6**	**5**	**4**	**3**	**2**	**1**
Your choice of X	7	1.30	1.15	0.90	0.55	0.10	−0.45	−1.10
	6	1.25	1.20	1.05	0.80	0.45	0.00	−0.55
	5	1.10	1.15	1.10	0.95	0.70	0.35	−0.10
	4	0.85	1.00	1.05	1.00	0.85	0.60	0.25
	3	0.50	0.75	0.90	0.95	0.90	0.75	0.50
	2	0.05	0.40	0.65	0.80	0.85	0.80	0.65
	1	−0.50	−0.05	0.30	0.55	0.70	0.75	0.70

Stag-Hunt Game

Consider for example a 2×2 *stag-hunt game*, whose payoff matrix is depicted in Table 4. In this game payoffs are high, if both players either play stag or hare, but lose out if one player plays stag and the other hare. Hence, players are well-off, if they choose the same actions, i.e. the mode of $\{y^1, y^2\}$ being unique, while they lose out if they choose different actions, i.e. $\{y^1, y^2\}$ having two modes. This is a Beauty Contest game in the discrete strategy space with $f(.)$ being the mode.

Minimum/Median Effort Game

Similarly to the stag-hunt game whose two equilibria can be Pareto-ranked, Van Huyck et al. (1990,1991) introduce a game into the laboratory where players choose a number between 1 and 7 with the interpretation that a higher number represents higher effort. Each number is associated with a fixed payoff depending on a player's own choice and the minimum or median choice of all other players. An example of such a payoff structure is given in Table 5. In an equilibrium all have to choose the same number, with all choosing 7 being the Pareto optimal equilibrium and all choosing 1 being the risk dominant equilibrium.

Global Games

A latent assumption in the Keynesian Beauty Contest game is common knowledge about the economic fundamentals. Morris and Shin (2001) purport that this symmetry in knowledge is the source of indeterminacy in equilibrium. Consequently, they show that the presence of some uncertainty about the fundamentals can eliminate the multiplicity in equilibria. Carlsson and van Damme (1993), who introduced the term "global games", have shown that small perturbations in the payoff matrices or in the

Table 6 Global games (entries represent players' payoffs)

	Status quo (if $M < f(\theta)$)	Alternative (if $M \geq f(\theta)$)
Attack	$-\lambda$	ψ
Not attack	0	0

information in generalized 2×2 games with multiple equilibria can generate a unique rationalizable equilibrium.

Angeletos et al. (2007) interpret global games as scenarios of regime switch. There are two possible regimes: "status quo" and "alternative" (Table 6). Like in the original Beauty Contest game, there is a discrete set of actions $K = (0, 1)$. Each player can choose one action being preferred in the status quo regime, "not attack" ($k^i = 0$), and one action being preferable in the alternative regime, "attack" ($k^i = 1$). The payoff from not attacking can be normalized to zero and the payoff from attacking can be $\psi > 0$ if the status quo is given up and $-\lambda < 0$ if retained. This implies that individuals should optimally attack, if they expect the status quo to be abandoned. Whether the status quo is abandoned or not depends on whether the aggregate mass of attackers M exceeds a certain critical mass $f(\theta)$, which is a monotonically decreasing function of θ. If less than $f(\theta)$ agents choose attack, all choosing attack earn $-\lambda$, if more than $f(\theta)$ agents attack, all those who attack earn ψ. If θ is common knowledge, there are two equilibrium outcomes: everyone attacking and nobody attacking. A unique equilibrium is only attained, if there is heterogeneous information in the form of a noisy signal about the fundamental. If a private signal of the form $x^i = \theta + \sigma_\epsilon \epsilon^i$ is drawn where ϵ follows a standard normal distribution, Morris and Shin (1998, 2001) show that the size of the attack K is monotonically decreasing in θ and the regime switch occurs if and only if $\theta < \theta^*$, where $\theta^* = 1 - \frac{\psi}{\lambda}$. If there is in addition a public signal of the form $z = \theta + \sigma_\xi \xi$ with ξ following a standard normal distribution, Morris and Shin (2002) show that a unique equilibrium requires $\sigma_\xi \epsilon \leq (2\pi)^{1/2} \sigma^2 \xi$. The survey by Angeletos and Lian (2016) mentions numerous applications for global games: currency crises (Obstfeld, 1996), bank runs (Goldstein and Pauzner, 2004; Rochet and Vives, 2004; Corsetti et al., 2006), debt runs (He and Xiong, 2012), the role of credit rating agencies (Holden et al., 2014), business cycles (Schaal and Taschereau-Dumouchel, 2015), and the particular role of prices as public signals (Angeletos and Werning, 2006). [23]

Schelling (1960)

Schelling (1960) purports that a game of coordination is at the same time a game of conflict, e.g. arranging a time for a meeting involves coordination on a time and avoiding possible scheduling conflicts. These games can be considered to be equivalent to the Keynesian Beauty Contest game. If coordination is supposed to be

---

[23] Global games have also been formulated for strategic substitutes. See e.g. Karp et al. (2007).

tacit, according to Schelling, whether individuals converge to an outcome depends on whether expectations coordinate on a focal point.

He also understood segregation as an outcome of coordination: supposing individuals want to have a certain number of neighbors of the same ethnicity, then, for instance, one black household moving away may induce other black households to move away. More formally, an individual has to make a choice y^i of a location $x \in X$, with the best response

$$y^i = x^* \text{ s.t. at least } h > 0 \text{ individuals choose } x^* \tag{14}$$

Schelling conducted an early experiment about this by playing with different types of pennies on the chessboard that needed to be surrounded by other pennies (Dixit, 2006). This is a Beauty Contest game with $c = 0$, $b = 1$, $d = 0$ and $f(.)$ being the choice made by at least h individuals.

11–20 Game

Arad and Rubinstein (2012a) propose a two-player game in which each player chooses an integer in a fixed interval, say 11 to 20. The player receives her choice as a payoff and a large bonus (e.g. a payoff of 20 in addition) if she is exactly one below her opponent's choice. In Arad and Rubinstein's original game, there is no Nash equilibrium in pure strategies but only a mixed strategy equilibrium corresponding to playing 15, 16, 17, 18, 19 and 20 with probabilities 25%, 25%, 20%, 15%, 10%, 5% respectively.

Alaoui and Penta (2016a, 2016b) have thus slightly modified the game, also giving the bonus in the case of a tie, which renders the equilibrium unique at 11. The game is therefore also dominance solvable as the BC-game. Fragiadakis et al. (2017) have modified the game by giving individuals the bonus if they are $r = 3$ (in some games $r = 4$) below the opponent's choice and an additional smaller bonus in case of ties, which allows a more distinctive analysis for belief elicitation in cognitive hierarchy models. This game has multiple equilibria, e.g., both choosing either 11, 12, or 13, if $r = 3$, as undercutting is not possible for these numbers.

3.3.2 Strategic Substitutes

Hawk–Dove Game

An example of strategic substitutes would be a game with the individual best response being:

$$y^i = \text{Choice least made in } \ldots \{y^1, y^2, \ldots, y^i, \ldots, y^j, \ldots, y^N\} \tag{15}$$

where y^i may again be a choice out of a finite, discrete set $\{A, B, \ldots\}$.

Eq. (15) can be considered to be an accurate description of payoffs the hawk–dove game, in which whose payoff-matrix is depicted in Table 7.

If player 1 (2) plays dove so that $y^1 = D$ and player 2 (1) plays hawk $y^2 = H$, then both choices satisfy $y^i = \text{Choice least made in } \ldots \{y^1, y^2\}$, which are equilibria. This is not the case if both play either hawk or dove.

Table 7 Hawk–dove game

	Hawk (H)	**Dove (D)**
Hawk (H)	−1, −1	1, 0
Dove (D)	0, 1	1/2, 1/2

Ultimatum Game

$N = 2$ players need to split a pie of size $c > 0$. Both announce y^1, y^2 (possibly at different point in times) how much of the pie they claim. A requirement is that $y^1 + y^2 \leq c$, as the allocation is otherwise not feasible, in which case every player receives a low default payoff. Each player i's best-response given by $y^i = c - y^{-i}$. Hence, if players move simultaneously, the ultimatum game can be considered a Beauty Contest game with strategic substitutes where $c > 0$, $b = -1$, $d = 0$, $f(.) = y^{-i}$ trivially being the choice of the other player and no random element ($\epsilon = 0$). All combinations of offers and demands with the requirement $y^i + y^{-i} = c$ are equilibria. If played sequentially,[24] with one player making the offer and one accepting or rejecting it, the lowest positive offer accepted is the subgame perfect equilibrium. However, if there is competition between proposers (responders), the game is of strategic complements, as the competitors have to increase their offers (decrease their demands) if the others also do it. Then the equilibrium with the highest possible offer (lowest demand) is unique and subgame perfect.

3.3.3 Matching

The fact that in the Keynesian Beauty Contest game one must *match* the action of the average reveals the link to a widely used concept in economics: matching. The Keynesian Beauty Contest game is an example of *one-to-many matching*. Other forms of matching are *many-to-one matching*, for example one university admitting many students or just *one-to-one matching*, meaning that two agents pair up. Examples would be employee-employer hirings, school choice, marriage markets, kidney exchange etc.

One distinguishes between *positive assortative matching* on the one hand, which resembles strategic complementarities and means that agents match with similar agents. The opposite would be *negative assortative matching*, which resembles strategic substitutability and means that agents match with agents of dissimilar or opposite characteristics. Heterogeneity is the root of matching problems, including the Keynesian Beauty Contest game, as in the presence of homogeneity any matching problem would become trivial. See Roth et al. (1990) for a more detailed treatment of two-sided matching markets.

---

[24] In dynamic coordination games, there are good reasons to believe that the players move asynchronously. For example, either players alternate in moves or because opportunities to switch actions may arrive randomly to different players. The question whether such an asynchronous nature of moves would help or hinder coordination has been investigated by a large theoretical literature, including for instance Lagunoff and Matsui (1997), Gale (1995), Morris (2014), Matsuyama (1991), and Matsui and Matsuyama (1995).

Table 8 Matching pennies (Hide and Seek)

	Head (H)	Tail (T)
Head (H)	1, −1	−1, 1
Tail (T)	−1, 1	1, −1

3.3.4 Strategic Heterogeneity

Another possibility is a game in which some agents face strategic complements, i.e. need to match other agent's actions, while others face strategic substitutes, i.e. need to do the opposite of others' actions. This has been labeled as strategic heterogeneity (Monaco and Sabarwal, 2016).

Matching Pennies

A well-known textbook example is matching pennies (or hide and seek). This is a game with two players (A and B). Every player has a coin and secretly has to turn it on the head or tail side. They then simultaneously reveal their choices. If the coins match (both showing either head or tail), player A gains the coin of B. If the coins do not match, B gains the coin of A. This can easily be illustrated by a payoff matrix shown in Table 8.

It is easy to see that this game has a unique mixed strategy Nash equilibrium in which both players play each action with probability 50%.

While this seems a stylized example, several real world applications have been found. For example, some sport games are isomorphic to matching penny games (or "generalized matching penny games" (Goeree et al., 2003) with perturbed payoff structures). In soccer penalty kicks, both the kicker and the goalkeeper have two actions – left and right – and one of them has to match the other's action, while the other one has to do the opposite of the opponent.

Fashion Cycles

A somewhat similar case to matching pennies is the evolution of fashion. Matsuyama (1992) studies fashion cycles in a simple model with two actions – red and blue – and two types: conformists who like dressing like others and non-conformists who like dressing differently from others. A vital difference to matching pennies is the path dependence in the dynamic version of the game, since agents switch between red and blue over time depending on both their type and on what the majority chooses. Matsuyama shows that, depending on the share of the types and the matching patterns, this can lead to a stable limit cycle in which Nonconformists become fashion trend-setters switching their actions periodically, while Conformists follow with some inertia.

The Colonel Blotto Game

The Colonel Blotto game can be framed as every player being the commander of an army, having a fixed number of troops. At the beginning of each round, every player has to distribute her number of troops across a fixed number N of battlefields without observing the opponents' choices. Once every player has decided upon her allocation of troops, the battle begins according to the following rules: on every battlefield, the player who has deployed the most troops will win. The player(s) having won the most battlefields is (are) the winner(s) of that round. The Colonel Blotto game as a static game shares some similarity with the fashion cycles model, since there are both motives to match the decisions of the majority, i.e. put many (few) troops on battlefields if opponents put many (few) troops there, but also do the opposite to the majority, i.e. avoid investing troops in a field in which many players put many troops.

3.4 OTHER DIMENSIONS

There are certainly many other dimensions, which may contain further sources of heterogeneity. We distinguish between dimensions that are induced by the game structure on the one hand and dimensions that are related to the experimental implementation.

3.4.1 Game Structure

- **Number of human players:** Players can play against other human players or against machines or nature. There can be one player, which would constitute a game against nature, typically different from playing against humans, as it does not involve e.g. forming higher order beliefs. We will show examples with various numbers of players. The two-player case, which is standard in many textbook games, is often very different both in theory and in the observed outcomes from the case with more than two players (Sutan and Willinger, 2009). It crucially depends on the context whether the number of players empirically makes a difference: Bao et al. (2016) use experimental groups of more than 20 subjects for a learning-to-forecast experiment in an asset market setup, finding that behavior is similar to the experiments with small groups. In contrast to that, Arifovic et al. (2018) investigate whether sunspot announcements have different effects on small groups (of 10 persons) as opposed to large groups (of 80–90 persons) in a bank-run setting, where people decide whether or not to withdraw their money from the bank. They find that none of their large groups coordinate on a random sunspot signal, while small groups sometimes do. (See chapter by Arifovic and Duffy, 2018.)
- **Role of information:** There is often a distinction between imperfect and incomplete information. What is meant by these terms may vary slightly depending on the context. In game theory, imperfect information means that agents are not informed about the actions chosen by other players. Yet, they know the "type" of other players, their possible strategies/actions and their preferences or payoffs. Incomplete information, on the other hand, means that players do not know the "type" of the other players, so that they may lack information about their strategy profile or their payoff. Angeletos and Lian (2016) define imperfect information as agents being uncertain about a fundamental value, e.g. merely receive a signal about the fundamental value, while incomplete information is

defined as agents not being informed about the whole distribution of information across the population, e.g. they do not know which signals other agents receive.

Another debate is whether subjects should be given the functional form of the best response function or the data-generating process. (See Hommes, 2011 for a detailed survey.) While the functional forms of the best responses are often given to the subjects in experimental games, it is often argued (see e.g. Hommes, 2011) that the laws of markets are unknown by market participants so that in experimental finance or macroeconomics, subjects are usually only provided with qualitative information (e.g. Hommes et al., 2005) or no information at all (e.g. Adam, 2007).

- **Calibration:** By characterizing games as complements or substitutes, we made distinctions only according to whether $f(.)$ is increasing or decreasing in the actions of others. However, another important consideration is how much $f(.)$ increases or decreases in the actions of others, which may depend on exogenous parameters that need to be calibrated. For example, we will exemplify below that it makes a difference whether in a simple best response function of $y_t^i = b \cdot \frac{1}{N} \sum_{j=1}^{N} y_t^j$ the coefficient b is chosen to be 0.67 or 0.95.

- **Payoff function:** Players may be rewarded according to a tournament payoff so that one or several winners of the game are paid a fixed prize. As opposed to that, all players can alternatively be rewarded according to a (quadratic) distance function between own choice and the target choice, the outcome of the games. Typically, tournament payoffs produce more outliers, as incentives are too weak or non-existing for most of the players. Deviations are therefore more likely (Sonnemans and Tuinstra, 2010). Theoretical properties can also be very different between these two different payoff schemes which we will discuss in more detail in Section 4.

  A particularly important feature is flatness of the payoff function (around the equilibrium). With a too flat payoff function, suboptimal behavior may not be punished sufficiently, because subjects may face too weak incentives to think about making better decisions.

- **Payoff heterogeneity:** Players can be subdivided into different groups that interact with each other but that are assigned different tasks or that have different payoff functions. For example, if a general equilibrium model is implemented into the laboratory, some players may play firms and others households.

- **Order statistics:** As implied by the function $f(.)$ in Table 3, there are different ways how the action of other players can be aggregated. Hence, the payoff can depend on the sum, mean or median of the (other) participants' actions. The median obviously excludes single outliers in the interaction. However, more intricate dependencies such as network structures can be possible where only some neighbors determine a player's payoff.

- **Type of interaction between several players:** The experimenter has some degree of freedom on how persons interact in an experiment. People can interact with each other directly or anonymously. Furthermore, the experimenter may choose to divide the subjects into subgroups that may play against each other, e.g. in a network with different neighborhoods. In particular, in repeated games the matching mechanism may matter, as players can be randomly matched in each round (repeated one-shot games) or keep playing against the same person (supergames).

3.4.2 Experimental Implementation

- **Sociological dimensions:** Sometimes the researcher's focus is on sociological dimensions such as gender, ethnic group or age. We have already discussed in Section 2 how results depend on culture and gender.
- **Methodology:** The researcher may want to address whether the methodology used makes a difference. For example, he may wonder whether it makes a difference that the data is collected in the laboratory or from the field.
- **Cognitive dimensions:** The experimenter may want to address whether cognitive dimensions, such as risk preferences, IQ, emotions etc., matter for the outcome. This often requires some test, for instance an IQ test, before the game or some form of priming, e.g. inducing a certain type of emotion.
- **Framing:** Game-theoretic experiments and Beauty Contest games (see e.g. Nagel, 1995; Duffy and Nagel, 1997; Ho et al., 1998) usually have an abstract framing without describing any concrete situation. Other games have an economic framing, explicitly communicating to participants that they are for example forecasters in a virtual macroeconomy, investors in a financial market or firms choosing production in an oligopoly market. A concrete framing is often chosen in more sophisticated games, as an abstract framing often further increases the level of complication. Game theoretically, the language or the contexts that are presented should not induce differences in optimal behavior. However, humans might react very differently to small changes in the presentation of the same mathematical models.
- **Structural knowledge:** In microeconomic experiments, most aspects of the game structure, such as parameters of the game, as e.g. the b-parameter, number of players, are typically communicated to the subjects in advance. There might be a historical reason behind this informational setup. At the outset of the experimental economics literature, the main hypotheses tested in the laboratory were whether subjects play the equilibrium. Initial tests were conducted in their strongest form, i.e. by confronting players with the same or similar information as a theorist would need to analyze the game. However, the rationality requirements or more so common knowledge of rationality are outside the control of the experimenter. Furthermore, assuming the level of knowledge about the structure of the model is not always realistic and in fact there are strands of the economic literature, such as the macroeconomic learning literature (Marcet and Sargent, 1989; Sargent, 1993; Evans and Honkapohja, 2001), where the underlying environment is unknown to the decision-maker in the model. For an experimental implementation, this can mean that the parameters are unknown, or that the relationship between variables is only given in a qualitative way, e.g. whether one variable increases when another variable increases. This is a possible motivation to also analyze be-

havior under less information than a theorist in the abstract might have and to test whether agents are able to learn the rational expectations equilibrium over time. In this chapter subjects will always know the structure of the model, like the theorist. Arifovic and Duffy (2018) discuss experiments with less knowledge. This also gives rise to experiments which are much more complicated than in the microeconomic world (see e.g. Adam, 2007) or only described qualitatively (see e.g. Nagel and Vriend, 1999; Lei and Noussair, 2002; Hommes et al., 2005, 2008; Heemeijer et al., 2009; Bao et al., 2012; Pfajfar and Zakelj, 2014; Mauersberger, 2016; Sonnemans and Tuinstra, 2010). Such experiments can be considered to test the theoretical predictions of a large adaptive learning literature and bounded rationality literature in finance and macroeconomics (see e.g. Sargent, 1993; Evans and Honkapohja, 2001), which hypothesizes that agents do not know the coefficients of the underlying model equations, but they need to learn them from past data acting like econometricians, or their perceived law of motion is misspecified.

4 BEHAVIORAL REGULARITIES IN BC-EXPERIMENTS AND LEVEL-K

In Section 3 we show that the generalization of the Beauty Contest game provides a framework for many seemingly different models. In this section we introduce a behavioral model that is useful for encompassing or structuring behavior in many different (BC)-experiments, with the idea to suggest a framework for boundedly rational behavior. The main focus in the BC experimental literature is about the study of cognitive ability by subjects to understand the rules of the game, and the ability to outguess or predict the behavior of others, called strategic intelligence. Based on the behavioral patterns in the first BC-experiment implemented in the lab, Nagel (1993, 1995) introduced a level of reasoning model, later called level k, to describe these behavioral regularities. She provides empirical evidence and visualization for the simplest formulation of level k by using an appropriate, simple experimental game.

Over the past 25 years it could be shown that this behavioral model forms a framework for classifying and structuring heterogeneous behavior in the lab and in the field across many different situations. First of all it describes how bounded rational players interact. Also, in the spirit of von Neumann's question posed at the beginning of this chapter, the model suggests how homo economicus should interact with nonrational or boundedly rational players, or react to other external circumstances. More generally, what kind of heuristics do subjects formulate? Do structural changes of the game that may or may not shift the equilibrium also alter behavior? This section is by no means a complete survey of BC games, nor does it cover all experimental or theoretical papers discussing level-k applications. However, we hope to discuss the important issues about a framework of behavioral patterns which will raise new interesting questions.

Guided by the game or market models discussed in Section 3, we organize the variations of the Beauty Contest game that differ along several dimensions: the magnitudes, and the signs of the game's parameters, i.e. whether the game is characterized by strategic substitutes or by strategic complements; the information structure given to the subjects; the payoff function determining subjects' rewards; unique versus multiple equilibria, and the presence of exogenous stochastic, payoff-(ir)relevant elements.

Yet, we also take into account factors independent of the mathematical formulations, as for example the characteristics of the subject pool. Do people react differently when they are informed about the level of sophistication of other subjects? Since behavioral heterogeneity in experiments is often due to cognitive differences between subjects, typically equilibrium play is initially not observed in the laboratory, even if the equilibrium is unique and payoff-maximizing for all players, and thus socially optimal. We show different layers of heterogeneity. In the first period and over time on the one hand and across subjects on the other hand. The quest is also how to design the game to obtain efficiency-enhancing or optimal choices instantaneously. We discuss the simple structures of the BC games. The experimental literature on more sophisticated BC games and markets such as asset markets, Cobweb, and New-Keynesian models, mentioned in Section 3, are discussed by Arifovic and Duffy (2018).

4.1 THE BASIC BC EXPERIMENT

The main features of most of the games we discuss is the aggregation of behavior as an average or another order statistic such as the median, with $n \geq 2$ or $n = 2$ players. Nagel (1995) introduces the basic BC game ($y^i = b \hat{E}^i \frac{1}{N} \sum_{j=1}^{N} y^j$ and tournament payoffs) to the experimental literature. A large number of players, between 15 and 18, interacts for 4 periods within the same group. In this experiment, there are two salient results: first-period behavior is far away from the equilibrium, all choosing zero, but behavior slowly converges over time towards zero. To find regularities, the pen-and-paper experiment consists of BC games with the parameters $b = 1/2, 2/3$, and $4/3$. Each group is exposed only to one parameter value and every subject was only allowed to participate only in one group.

4.1.1 First Period Choices

Fig. 7 shows first period behavior of different subject pools with $b = 2/3$, including Nagel's laboratory data in the first row, first graph. Choices are highly dispersed but with clear patterns, spikes near and at 22, 33, and 50. There are also choices near 67, because some subjects may calculate $100 \cdot (2/3)$. Out of all subjects only few choose zero. We discuss the entire figure in Section 4.1.4.

4.1.2 The Level-k Model and Related Models

The Basic Level-k Model

Nagel (1995) conceptualized the basic level-k model (then called "steps of reasoning model") based on her own experience as a subject in a two-period 2/3-BC-classroom experiment (see Nagel et al., 2017). She participated in this classroom experiment

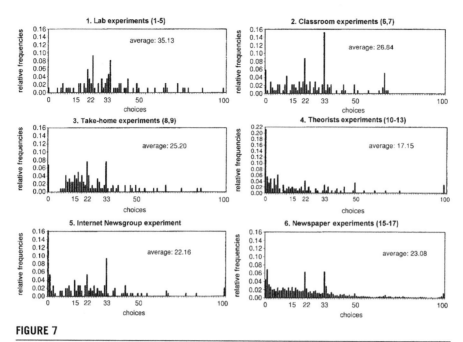

FIGURE 7

Bosch et al. (2002): Relative frequency of choices and pooled averages within the six different subject pools ($b = 2/3$). Group sizes range from 15 to 18 in the lab, 80–100 in the classroom, 20–30 for theorists, 40 in the newsgroup, and 2000–3000 in the newspaper experiments. (The number in parentheses indicate the different session numbers within each subject pool.) For the complete dataset, see Nagel et al. (2018).

as a graduate student at the London School of Economics in 1991 in a game theory lecture by Roger Guesnerie. Support for level-k has been found in the aforementioned experimental datasets and also in the written comments requested from the subjects.[25]

The model consists of a reference point, called level 0 and (finite) iterated best replies. Within the behavioral interactive realm this rule might also have a flavor of a generative principle, which should be studied in the future. It is assumed that all (naive) players in a Beauty Contest game choose randomly, with an average of 50 in the interval [0, 100], for insufficient reasoning. A level-1 (L1) player anticipates this and chooses the best response, $50 \cdot 2/3 = 33.33$, if $b = 2/3$. A level-2 (L2) player anticipates a level-1 player's choice and chooses $22.22 = 50 \cdot (2/3)^2$. Using the same logic, a level-k (Lk) player reacts to level $k - 1$ (Lk-1) player with $50 \cdot (2/3)^k$. That way, a player who believes that all players will come to the same conclusion and iterates infinitely, will reach the equilibrium zero. Given that equilib-

---

[25] This idea of players with different degrees of sophistication has, for example, theoretically been explored independently by Stahl (1993), calling the levels of sophistication "smart$_n$". See Banerjee et al. (1996) for a survey on evolutionary game theory from a purely theoretical perspective.

rium play typically does not win, a player who chooses it, is likely to suffer from a curse of knowledge of the mathematical solution, being ignorant of a winning strategy against boundedly rational subjects (see Camerer et al., 1989 who discuss this curse in the context of information asymmetries). Of course, one cannot expect that subjects make such degenerate choices. For instance, they might just make an approximation to $50 \cdot 2/3$ such as 30. Thus, Nagel allowed for noise by constructing intervals around such theoretical numbers and interim intervals, using the geometric mean to capture the geometric decrease of the level ks. Nagel (1995) rejects the hypothesis that choices are explained by applying a finite number of steps of the iterated elimination of weakly dominated choices starting at 100.

The model suggests heterogeneity due to subjects' different anticipation or beliefs of what others will do. Level-0 reasoning might be understood as system I behavior, i.e. intuitive response without considering the strategic environment. Higher level ks could be related to deliberate reasoning (system II; Kahnemann, 2011), considering the consequences of others' choices. The simplification in this model is that higher level-k players assume that all others are just one level lower than oneself. Most importantly, the level-k model fills a modeling gap for behavior placed between non-strategic, irrational or random behavior and an equilibrium strategy. It is based on a cognitive reasoning procedure that does not require consistency of beliefs,[26] therefore it is a non-equilibrium model. Yet, in the limit, typically an equilibrium is reached. Most other boundedly rational models we discussed in Section 2.3 do not specifically model heterogeneity, according to our definition spelled out in the introduction, as they assume the same parameterization for all subjects which are distinguished by different random draws from a generated probability distribution.

Georganas et al. (2015) show that level-k distributions across players are stable over many games, but one cannot predict this stability for single subjects across different types of games. However, when presenting variations within a class of games, then the researcher can classify many subjects through one level-k choice, e.g. games are distinguished only through parameter changes such as the b-parameter. (See e.g. Coricelli and Nagel, 2009, doing a brain imaging study with subjects playing standard Beauty Contest games; or Costa-Gomes et al., 2001, where the same subject plays many different 3×3 normal form games with rationalizable equilibria.) Additional players can be classified according to the L-k-rule that most closely corresponds to their choices.

Variations and Extensions of the Basic Level-k Models

Stahl and Wilson (1994, 1995) specify players who best respond to a probability distribution of lower level players in addition to Nagel's level-k types. Camerer et al. (2004) suggest a one-parameter cognitive hierarchy model with types at each level following a Poisson distribution of lower levels, with an estimated parameter of 1.5

---

[26]Consistent beliefs about strategies means that a player's subjective probability distribution about opponents' play corresponds to the objective probability distribution (see Kneeland, 2015).

being reasonable for a wide class of experiments. See also the surveys by Camerer (2003) and Crawford et al. (2013). Chong et al. (2016) augment the level-k model by stereotype biases, allowing intermediate cases between players with correct beliefs about others' distribution of reasoning levels and a maximum bias with all opponents adopting the most frequently occurring lower level of reasoning.

The following models make important contributions to aspects not covered by the simple level-k versions. Goeree et al. (2016) note that there is a formal connection between level-k and what they call subjective heterogeneous quantal response equilibrium (SQRE). SQRE means that players have non-rational, possibly heterogeneous beliefs about the choices of other players that are inconsistent with their actual choices. A level-k type believes that opponents' choices are concentrated on type $k-1$. While earlier papers like Stahl and Wilson (1995) take the parameter that governs rationality (λ) to be common to all players, SQRE represents the version with heterogeneous skill parameters, so that a higher level of reasoning (k) is associated with a higher skill parameter (λ). Goeree and Holt (2004) introduce the "noisy introspection (NI)" relying on the assumption that choices made under higher orders of the "I think that you think" process are increasingly more difficult to predict. Level-k thus corresponds to the special case in which the rationality parameters for a level-k player take the form $\lambda_0 = \cdots = \lambda_{k-1}$ and $\lambda_k = \cdots = \lambda_\infty = 0$.

A few recent papers have responded to the fact that level-k vary across settings, for instance when beliefs about opponents' sophistications are varied (see, e.g., Agranov et al., 2012; Alaoui and Penta, 2016a; Georganas et al., 2015). The distinction between a player's cognitive bound and his beliefs has been introduced, for instance, in the models of Strzalecki (2014), Georganas et al. (2015), and Alaoui and Penta (2016a). The basic idea in these models is that players with a higher ability of reasoning will react differently in a subject pool with equal minded subjects than with those of lower reasoning types. Players with lower L-ks will not adjust their levels upwards in more sophisticated subject pools. The question of identifying whether given observed behavior is due to "rationality" or "cognitive" bounds is studied by Friedenberg et al. (2015) and by Alaoui and Penta (2017). The meanings of the two bounds are slightly different in the two papers. Friedenberg et al. (2015) distinguish between "bounded reasoning about rationality" and "bounded reasoning about cognition." A subject can be classified as cognitive if she uses some "method" or "theory" as to how to play the game. Being cognitive does not imply rationality, as the subject may use some boundedly rational heuristic. On the other hand, a rational subject is obviously cognitive, as rationality is one possible "method". Friedenberg et al. exploit Kneeland's (2015) ring games to disentangle the two bounds. Alaoui and Penta (2017) instead develop so-called "tutorial" and "replacement" methods, which can be applied to general games, with no special restriction on the payoff structure. Their methods serve to disentangle a subject's cognitive bound, meaning his or her understanding of a situation, from his beliefs over the opponent's own understanding.

The model of Endogenous Depth of Reasoning (EDR) in Alaoui and Penta (2016a) also takes into account that players' cognitive bound may vary systematically with the payoff structure: increasing the stakes of the game induces players to perform more rounds of reasoning. Alaoui and Penta (2016a) provide an experimental test of the EDR model. The EDR model is based on the axiomatic approach developed in Alaoui and Penta (2016b), which provides foundations to endogenizing players' depth of reasoning through a cost–benefit analysis. Cognitive costs also play a role in the rational inattention literature (Sims, 2003), in which agents pay a cost of precisely observing certain variables. In the vein of that literature, one can say a level-k player is (ir)rationally inattentive to higher level players.

A Critical Comment on Level 0

One main criticism against the level-k model concerns the apparent arbitrary or free level-0 specification, e.g. a focal point, naïve behavior or anchor, depending on the situation.[27] Constructing such a variable might be comparable to the identification of reference points in prospect theory (Kahnemann and Tversky, 1979) or the question of how focal points are found (Schelling, 1960) with a need of empirical validation. Another similar concept is salience which has recently attained a lot of interest in the individual decision making literature (Bordalo et al., 2012). "Salience refers to the phenomenon that when one's attention is differentially directed to one portion of the environment rather than to others, the information contained in that portion will receive disproportionate weighting in subsequent judgments" (Taylor and Thompson, 1982). Also learning models need to specify initial conditions of first-period behavior, which are typically exogenous (see, e.g., Roth and Erev, 1995). This question of the starting point of the reasoning process can thus be seen as a bridge to individual decision-making. Do subjects in a game focus first on the situation or the rules as if each one of them was playing in isolation or against nature? Decision theory has produced a tool case of heuristics which is still, to some extent, unexploited by experimenters on interactive decision making. Most applications of the level-k model specify level 0 as an aggregation of uniformly random players' behavior. However, we will also show that other specifications are used in the experiments, discussed below. For some situations, researchers have also suggested multiple reference points to explain the data.

Level-k as a Descriptive and Predictive Model

The level-k model is, first of all, a descriptive model of behavior which provides a classification of different reasoning types and its distribution, given the experimental data. Ex ante one might very well know which are the modal choices, when level 0 can be clearly specified. The most important contribution of this model comes from the large number of empirical observations that most subjects engage in no more than

---

[27]Brandenburger et al. (2017) write: "A central feature of their identification strategy is that they (authors on level-k) impose auxiliary assumptions about beliefs. This comes in the form of assumptions about the behavior of Level-0 types, which pins down the beliefs of Level-1 types. With this, their notion of iterative reasoning can be conceptually distinct (in subtle ways) from rationality and mth-order belief of rationality (i.e., even in simultaneous move games)."

3 levels. Frequency distributions over these choices are not predicted by the model. Therefore, it should not be possible to predict the average choice, for example. There are, however, ways to have some better indication of future behavior: Obviously, replications of the same underlying experiment should produce similar results regarding the level-k distributions. Thus, knowing the sophistication of the subject pool gives some hints about how behavior may emerge. Most importantly, the goodness of equilibrium as a predictor depends on how many levels are needed to reach equilibrium: in case few levels of reasoning are needed, average behavior can be expected to be close to equilibrium; conversely, if a high number of levels are needed, behavior (above all in early rounds) can be expected to be far from equilibrium. Together with learning rules and the strategic environment (as strategic substitutes or strategic complements), one can indicate whether behavior converges to the equilibrium in the short, medium or long run.

Level-k as a Prescriptive Model

"The problem of prescriptive analysis can be stated as follows: How should a decision analyst advise a client, friend, or himself/herself on how to make a decision?" (Eppel et al., 1992, p. 281). In an interactive decision making problem, one has to consider whether one just consults one player, like "my client" or an entire group. We restrict ourselves here to the one-advisee case. Probably a decent rule-of-thumb advice that can be given to agents is telling them to choose according to level 1 to 2, identifying of course the reference point first. "Don't think too deeply what others are thinking" might be a good advice for real life that has already been formulated by Seneca: "Nothing is more hateful to wisdom than too much cleverness (cunning)." The advisor needs to know the opponents' sophistication or whether players have already interacted for a longer time.[28]

Level-k Modeling in Micro- and Macroeconomic Theory

The stability of limited reasoning (level-k being between 0 and 3), empirically validated through many different experiments, has motivated further work in the micro- and recently also in the macroeconomic theory literature. In applied microeconomics, Crawford et al. (2009), for example, introduce level-k reasoning to the design of optimal auctions. Crawford (2013) use level-k to propose efficient bargaining mechanisms. Kets and Sandroni (2017) extend the level-k model to provide a good model description about how a player's identity affects her reasoning, and use this to study the optimal composition of teams.

In the macroeconomic literature, García-Schmidt and Woodford (2015) introduce a continuous level-k model (which could represent an average of several discrete level-k types) into a standard New-Keynesian model in which households optimize over an infinite horizon. With the introduction of bounded rationality they can justify

---

[28] Another mention of those thoughts can also be found in E.A. Poe's (1958) "The purloined letter", which distinguishes the mathematician from the poet, and the combination of both, which is ultimately the best reasoner as based on logical reasoning and enough intuition for human behavior.

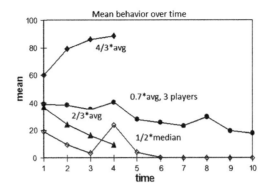

FIGURE 8

Beauty Contest game: Mean behavior over time. Data source: Nagel (1995), Duffy and Nagel (1997) with median; Ho et al. (1998) with 3 players.

the missing increase in inflation after the financial crisis, 2007. A subsequent application of level-k in macroeconomics by Farhi and Werning (2017) introduces level-k into an overlapping generation model with occasionally binding liquidity constraints. Their results differ from García-Schmidt and Woodford (2015), because an overlapping generation model represents a finite horizon. They show that if monetary policy commits to future interest-rate policy, it has particularly weak effects when level-k is combined with incomplete markets. Conversely, under rational expectations, monetary policy would have a rather strong effect. Such papers are now inspiring level-k applications in different macroeconomic contexts. Angeletos and Lian (2016) discuss the relationship between rational expectations equilibrium and "solution concepts that mimic Tâtonnement or Cobweb dynamics, Level-k Thinking, Reflective Equilibrium, and certain kinds of cognitive discounting." They also discuss relaxations of higher-order uncertainty.

4.1.3 Behavior over Time in the Basic BC Game

Nagel (1995) also studies behavior over time, repeating the same game for four periods with the same subjects. After each period, information about all choices, the average and the target number, $2/3 \cdot$ average, and the winning number, are written on the blackboard. Behavior under $b = 1/2$ and $b = 2/3$ converges, albeit at different rates, to zero but stays considerably above zero. If $b > 1$ and $y^i \in [0, 100]$, there are two equilibria: one stable one (100) and one unstable one (0). Nagel shows that if $b = 4/3$, behavior converges to 100, the stable equilibrium. Fig. 8 shows mean behavior over time, slowly decreasing, for different parameter values, group size, and order statistics, i.e. mean or median (Duffy and Nagel, 1997). When the influence of a single player is high ($n = 3$), the mean decreases more slowly than when it is low, as it is the case in the median game.

The level-k model together with a simple adjustment model (called directional learning; Selten and Stoecker, 1986) explain this slow convergence. The idea is that a player in period t, who iterated too many (few) levels from a reference point (say $\frac{2}{3} \times$ average in $t - 1$), as compared to the target t, will iterate less (more) in the next period, $t + 1$. As a result, even if every subject understands that the target should be zero, there is self-fulfilling slow convergence. Using Nagel's (1995) data, Stahl (1996) combines her level-k model with a "law of effect" learning model: Agents start with a propensity to use a certain level of reasoning, and over time the players learn how the available rules perform and switch to better performing rules. He rejects Bayesian-rule learning in favor of this level-k model.

Fig. 9 shows individual behavior from period t to period $t + 1$ for the parameters $b = 1/2$ and $2/3$. Each dot presents a players choice in two consecutive periods. Behavior over time is "flocking" (Raafat et al., 2009), i.e. the variance across players shrinks over time. Flocking occurs faster for $b = 1/2$ than for $b = 2/3$.

4.1.4 Heterogeneity of Subject Pools in Lab- and Field-BC Games

Bosch-Domènech et al. (2002) report on one period BC-games with different populations, including newspaper experiments, in which newspaper readers of the *Financial Times*, *Expansion*, and *Spektrum der Wissenschaft* were invited to participate in a Beauty Contest game similar to Nagel (1995) with $b = 2/3$. Fig. 7 shows the first-period laboratory data (Nagel, 1995), classroom and take home experiments of economics undergraduate in their second year, economists in various conferences, in an online newsgroup experiment and the newspaper contests in Bosch-Domènech et al. (2002).

Behavior is heterogeneous both across different subject pools and within every population. However, there are clear regularities. While undergraduate students hardly ever choose the equilibrium zero, more than 20% of game theorists choose it. On the other hand, outliers selecting 100 or numbers close to 67 are quite similar across populations. According to written comments in many of the BC studies of those subjects who choose 100, they express their frustration of not knowing what a well informed choice could be. This way, they also attempt to increase the average so that low rationality players can win. A choice of 67 can be rationalized since it comes from the game-theoretic property of deleting all (weakly) dominant strategies greater than $100 \cdot (2/3)$. In all datasets, there are clear spikes around 50, 33, and 22, albeit with different frequencies according to the level-k model. Since newspaper readers can reflect upon the game for several weeks, some participants involve parties or newsgroups to participate in the game, to finally submit more informed choices. Indeed those participants had a much higher than average chance to select the winning number. The newsgroup data (last row on the left in Fig. 7) represent a small study, executed by a participant of a newspaper experiment. His choice was less than one integer away from the winning number of our experiment, as he chooses the winning number of his data set.

Bosch et al. (2010) apply a mixture model, which means that the model contains several distributions, to explain behavior in Bosch et al. (2002). They find that four distributions, a uniform distribution, accounting for random behavior, beta distributions for level 1, 2, and infinity (choice zero) explain the actual data best. While

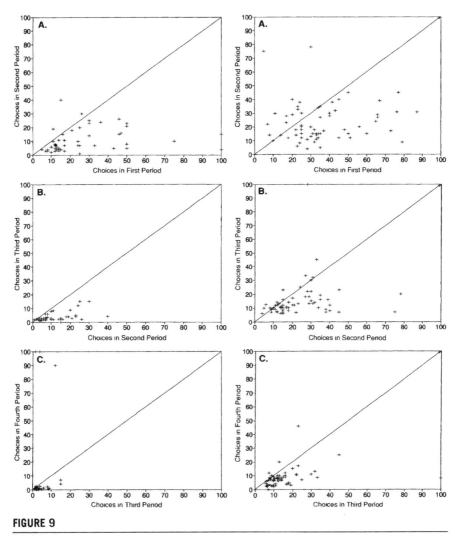

FIGURE 9

Observations over time from periods 1–4, transition between two subsequent periods; left panel: $b = \frac{1}{2}$; right panel: $b = \frac{2}{3}$. Source: Nagel (1995).

all mixtures across different populations have the same means, the frequencies and variances are clearly distinguished across populations. The beta distribution suggests that players do not only have degenerate beliefs and resulting choices, but also tremble. This can be in their beliefs, e.g. they miscalculate or make a shortcut of, e.g., $50 \cdot 2/3$, being 30, or they can tremble in their action, e.g. reaching 22.22 as their second order outcome but choose 25. There is direct evidence for such behavioral results in subjects' comments which the authors requested and subsequently analyzed (see Section 5.5 for more details about this methodology).

4.1.5 Two Person Games

Two Person BC-Games vs $n > 2$-Person BC Game

A natural question is whether players, choosing positive non-dominated choices, are rational and think that opponents are (non)rational or whether players do not understand the logic of the game. Grosskopf and Nagel (2008), Chou et al. (2009), and Nagel et al. (2017) implement several two-person guessing games, in which the target is again $\frac{2}{3} \times$ average. With a tournament payoff, zero becomes a weakly dominant equilibrium strategy, since the lower number of the tuple always wins. However, perhaps surprisingly, Grosskopf and Nagel find that most subjects do not choose zero. Even game theorists playing the game among themselves do not always choose the equilibrium. Chou et al. (2009) repeat the two-person guessing game changing the instructions in simple ways. They demonstrate that behavior is closer to the game theoretical prediction, of zero, if the game is presented in a less abstract way or if hints are given to the subjects, as using the isomorphic game "the lower number always wins". Thus, they conclude that deviations from the game-theoretic solution represent a lack of understanding of the game-form and thus speak of *game-form recognition*. Finding the dominant strategy in this game is cognitively too demanding.

Nagel et al. (2017) resolve the thinking puzzle in such a simple game. With tournament payoffs subjects do not understand that it is sufficient to be closer to the target than the opponent, rather than being as close as possible to the target. The reason is that the best reply to the midpoint (average) of two numbers multiplied with 2/3 is always pointing to the lower choice. In the "hitting the target" game two players must be paid according to the distance of their choice to the target. As a result, theoretically the iterated elimination of *strictly* dominated strategies leads to the equilibrium, albeit with different elimination steps than if $n > 2$, given the large influence of a single player (that is 100, 50, 25... etc. when $b = 2/3$ and $n = 2$, instead of 100, 66.66, 44.44...). Therefore, zero is not a dominant choice. Nagel et al. (2017) show that the distributions of two persons, $n > 2$ persons, fixed payoff, or distant payoffs all show the same behavioral patterns as observed in the Bosch et al. (2002) study. In addition to that, the professionals also choose in all versions the $n > 2$ patterns, the level-k reasoning with 50 as a focal point, albeit with more choices closer or at zero. The first two boxplots in Fig. 11 show the distributions of choices for $n = 2$ for fixed payoffs and quadratic payoffs with no significant difference. Economics professors (prof) also choose positive numbers (third boxplot).

A rather new method is to let each subject play against oneself in the hope to induce equilibrium choices or less random behavior. In Bosch-Rosa et al. (2016) on the "one-person Beauty Contest", each subject has to choose two numbers between 0 and 100 and the subject is paid for every chosen number according to the distance to 2/3 of the average of the two chosen numbers (cf. our two-person distance treatment). An unusually high share of subjects (more than 50% of about 350 subjects) find the Nash equilibrium (i.e. the payoff-maximizing answer). Fragiadakis et al. (2017) play two-person Beauty Contest games as in Costa-Gomes and Crawford (2006): Subjects need to be as close as possible to the target, $b \cdot$ *choice of the other player*, where the interval and b can be different for the two players. In some treatments, subjects need to recall (after some other tasks) their choices or play against their own previous play trials from memory. They find that the payoff-maximizing actions are more likely chosen by those who use level-k driven strategies, compared to those who behave according to non-identifiable patterns. The authors interpret this finding in the following way: level-k reasoning is easier to remember and thus best reply more likely.

11–20 Game

In the original BC-game, the target is quite complicated to understand. Instead, consider the so-called 11–20 ("11 to 20") game, which can be argued to be closer to a real life situation. For example, a tourist may wonder at what time she should leave the beach at the end of the weekend, if she just needs to be on the road a bit earlier than the other drivers, yet wanting to stay as long as possible. Alaoui and Penta (2016a, 2016b) modify the 11–20 game by Arad and Rubinstein (2012a). Two players have to choose a number between 11 and 20, each being paid a dollar amount equal to her choice. Additionally, a player receives a bonus of 20 if her choice is by one lower than the other player's decision. Ties are solved by a random draw. The equilibrium choice 11 is reached by iterated elimination of strictly dominated strategies (20, 19, 8 . . . 11). Level-k behavior is observed with most choices corresponding between L0 and L3 (17–20). The modal choices are either 18 (L2) or 19 (L1). Arad and Rubinstein (2012a, 2012b) observe this kind of behavior, although the equilibrium is in mixed strategies with 15 being the highest probability to be chosen and 20 the lowest. Thus, level-k is a better descriptive model than the theoretical mixing model or the equilibrium 11. An increase of the bonus produces indeed an increase of reasoning, as predicted by Alaoui and Penta who incorporate payoff concerns into the simple level-k model. Because of the ease of understanding this game and at the same time showing important features of level-k, it should be used as a (better) alternative to the basic BC game, especially in populations with known lower cognitive abilities. In such subject pools behavior in BC games are typically concentrated between 35 and 50.

Goeree et al. (2014) consider a variant of the one-shot play of Arad and Rubinstein's (2012a) 11–20 game, where the numbers are arranged on a line with 20 always being the rightmost number (thus being the choice of the level-0 player) and people win if they pick the number to the left of their opponent's choice. They introduce several treatments with different ordering of numbers. For example, if the numbers are ordered in a declining pattern: 19, 18, 17, . . . , 11, 20 then a level-1 player would pick 11. However, the modal choice in this example is 19. The three authors show that the NI-k model helps resolve this puzzle and fits the data better than the level-k model. It turns out that 20 and 19, wherever the later is positioned are the model choices. This can also just mean that they do not understand the rules of the game, but instead those who play 19 order the strategy space according to the natural ascending order.

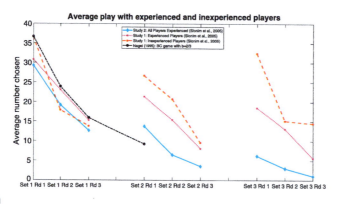

FIGURE 10

Numbers chosen in "guess $\frac{2}{3}$· average" Beauty Contest game. From Slonim (2005): study 1: new, inexperienced players enter in the course of the game (dashed lines) and experienced players (dotted lines); study 2: all players experienced (solid lines); we added the four periods from Nagel (1995) (dotted–dashed lines). Modified from Slonim (2005).

4.1.6 Mixing Experienced with Inexperienced Subjects

Making informed choices is typically evoked through experience. Slonim (2005) demonstrates that limited cognitive reasoning survives and is optimal when experienced players know that inexperienced ones regularly enter a game. He runs a nine period Beauty Contest game in which only one player stays until the end, while after three consecutive rounds all other subjects are replaced by new ones. Fig. 10 shows that the behavior of newly entering players (the first observation of all line-segments dashed lines) are obviously very similar while informed players (first observations of dotted lines) learn to play a best response to first-period behavior of the new entrants. Such kind of best reply choices are most likely observed in any experiment, in which experienced and inexperienced subjects interact. That is why experimenters typically exclude graduate students and colleagues from their experiments and try to track whether subjects participated in similar games before. In real (non-laboratory) markets, such interactions of informed or experienced vs. uninformed or unexperienced agents are certainly typical which might prevent equilibration. All this can be very well controlled in laboratory experiments. In Section 5, other approaches to improve decision-making such as team reasoning are discussed.

Alaoui and Penta (2016a, 2016b) mix students from more quantitative faculties with humanity students in one of their heterogeneous subject treatments on 11 to 20 game, discussed above. They find that the former group decreases their level of reasoning in the 11 to 20 games against humanity students, while humanity students do not react to such a more sophisticated subject pool. The general finding is that more sophisticated players adjust their level-k downwards when predicting less sophisticated players, and thus heterogeneity emerges within the same subject differentiating between various opponent pools. Less sophisticated players do not respond to more sophisticated players. This indicates that the cognitive bounds of a player seem to be binding as modeled in Alaoui and Penta (2017).

4.1.7 Strategic Substitutes vs. Strategic Complements

Camerer and Fehr (2006), Fehr and Tyran (2008), and Hommes (2013) note that if choices are substitutes, rational agents need to behave in the opposite way to other agents, while if choices are complements, rational agents have an incentive to imitate their opponents. Thus, one can expect that under strategic substitutability outcomes are closer to the rational solution, as less rational behavior is mitigated by rational players, while outcomes are further away from the rational benchmark under strategic complementarities, as less rational behavior is reinforced by rational players.

Sutan and Willinger (2009) study the effects in two different one-shot BC-games with the same interior solutions (discussed also in more detail below), one with strategic substitutes and the other with strategic complements. They find that subjects in the game with strategic substitutes choose the equilibrium much more frequently than subjects in the game with strategic complements. Heemeijer et al. (2009) and Bao et al. (2012) add small or large shocks exogenous shocks to Beauty Contest games and indeed find striking differences in aggregate market behavior under strategic complements, where prices oscillate persistently around fundamentals, and strategic substitutes, where markets quickly settle down to the rational equilibrium. Along the chapter we will give other examples (see also Arifovic and Duffy, 2018).

Group Size

Hanak et al. (2016) investigate how this "strategic environment effect" interacts with group size, conducting each of the two Beauty Contest games with $n = 2, 3, 4, 5, 6$ subjects, larger groups with $n = 8, 16$, and also a situation in which subjects do not know n. They find that as long as groups consist of 5 individuals or more, equilibrium play is more frequent under strategic substitutes than complementaries, corresponding to the earlier result of Sutan and Willinger (2009). Since the "strategic environment effect" is not predicted by the standard level-k, a more sophisticated cognitive hierarchy model is needed to explain the different patterns across games. Alternatively, a level-k (or cognitive hierarchy model) with trembles drawn from a logit distribution can explain the observed results. Arifovic and Duffy (2018) discuss other effects of group size.

4.2 DE-FRAMING THE RULES TO (DE-)ANCHOR BELIEFS

In most studies we cited above, subjects' payoffs only depend on the behavior of all players (typically including oneself), abstracting from many additional features that can influence the behavior and payoffs in more realistic settings. Our above discussion shows that it is very difficult to predict opponents' actions in the first period. Furthermore, the intuitive midpoint together with few reasoning steps produce result in numbers far from equilibrium. However, the equilibrium has ideal properties such

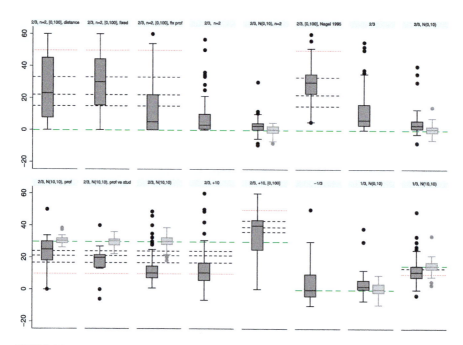

FIGURE 11

Boxplots of different BC-games varying b, $c = 10$, and $N(.,.)$ of ϵ^i, the interval $[0, 100]$ (if not indicated, it is the real line); subject population (professionals = prof. vs. students = stud.); fix = fixed payoff; dist = distance payoff; long-dashed lines represent the (average) equilibrium, and the gray boxplots the equilibrium with noise; dotted lines = L0, short-dashed lines = L1–L3. Data from Benhabib et al. (2018a, 2018b) and Nagel et al. (2017).

as uniqueness and Pareto optimality (in case of a distance function) and equitable payoffs. Thus, the plausible interpretation of deviations from equilibrium is cognitive limitations.

In the remainder of this section, we discuss variations of parameters mentioned in Section 3, to shift behavior in systematic ways.

Fig. 11 provides an overview of some parameter changes we introduce in the following subsections, together with the resulting behavior in boxplots, the equilibrium, and, when adequate, also level-k reasoning. The treatments are shown with parameters $b = -2/3$, $2/3$, and $1/3$; added constants and/or idiosyncratic shocks. The theoretical equilibrium brings about dispersion only with an inclusion of an idiosyncratic noise term, indicated with $N(.,.)$ in the graph. We show that dispersion exists even for subjects that ought to be highly sophisticated, such as economics professors' choices, who were typically invited to participate before a seminar on the topic (prof. = either playing among themselves, or against an existing student distribution, unknown to them (see prof. vs. stud.)).

4.2.1 Interior Equilibrium

Corner solutions have the special property that out of equilibrium behavior can only be in one direction. For example, in a standard public good game there can only be over- but no undercontribution compared to the equilibrium outcome of contributing nothing. In the Beauty Contest games it can also be interesting to move the rational solution into the interior of the strategy space, which we discuss in the following.

An Open Choice Set – Deframing the Rules to De-Anchor Beliefs

Until recently, in most Beauty Contest games the choice sets always constituted a bounded interval, only including positive numbers. Thus, the equilibrium can be attained through an iterated elimination of dominated strategies. Benhabib et al. (2018a, 2018b) allow choices from all real numbers. Those kinds of open sets can be found in reality, e.g. when a person can be a seller or a buyer at the same time and thus prices can be negative or positive. Allowing any number in the choice set of the Beauty Contest game introduces much lower guesses than in sets bounded between 0 and 100 (see Fig. 11, 2/3, no boundaries vs 2/3, [0, 100]; boxplots 6 and 7, first row). The reason is that in the bounded set, the midpoint serves as a natural anchor and is far away from a corner solution. Without those boundaries, zero becomes a natural focal point, although almost all subjects choose positive numbers when $b > 0$. The median choice decreases from about 33 (Nagel, 1995) to 15 in the open set. However, the focal point and thus level 0 of level-k reasoning becomes zero. This alteration eliminates higher-order beliefs different from zero. Yet, in the experiments not only choices of zero are observed. The newspaper comments of those subjects who find the equilibrium indicate that 80% of the observed choices are between 0 and 10, because they do not believe that others will choose zero. This can explain the choices also in this new setup which is basically "focal or reference point reasoning" with noise. Yet, the noise is only towards higher positive numbers and not negative choices.

Benhabib et al. (2018a, 2018b) introduce b-values that are negative. This provides a change from games with the property of positive feedback to negative feedback, without manipulating other properties of the game. Fig. 11 shows that negative b-values ($-1/3$; boxplot 5, second row of Fig. 11) result in aggregate (average or median) behavior that is much closer to zero than when $b > 0$. Level-k reasoning can easily explain this effect: if I think others choose negative numbers, then my best response will be positive, but if all subjects act in the same way, I should choose a negative number etc. However, choices resulting from higher-order reasoning cannot so easily be distinguished from choices resulting from lower reasoning, as a negative choice can result from L2 or L0. Since more than half of the subjects choose negative numbers, we interpret this as a large share of naive choice, being close to, say, $-2/3$ average, suggesting a negative outcome. Other measures as reaction time or even brain scans can provide more conclusions about the matter, which we discuss in the section on elicitation methods.

Calibration of Coefficients

While the above section discusses the sign of the coefficients, their magnitude matters as well. An important finding that has repeatedly been documented in the experimental literature is that if the b-coefficient is sufficiently close to 1 but still exhibits a unique equilibrium, behavior does not dynamically converge to the rational solution even after many repetitions. Several explanations can be provided for that: first, strategic complements are relatively strong for a high b-coefficient, e.g. $b = 0.95$, so that the effect described in detail by Camerer and Fehr (2006), Fehr and Tyran (2008), and Hommes (2013), mentioned in the above paragraph, that rational players have an incentive to mimic irrational players is particularly distinct. Second, for $b \approx 1$ beliefs tend to become (almost) self-fulfilling. Hence, players are not strongly punished for having non-equilibrium beliefs and those beliefs can be sustained more easily. (See Hommes, 2013 for a more detailed discussion about self-fulfilling beliefs.) Third, even small mistakes or misperceptions of b may suffice to introduce a unit root into the process, under which outcomes would not converge. (See Mauersberger, 2016 for a more detailed discussion.)

Sonnemans and Tuinstra (2010) conduct simple Beauty Contest game experiments, setting $b = 0.67$ in one treatment and $b = 0.95$ in another treatment. Independently of whether they provide information about the b-parameters to their subjects or not, they find fast coordination among the cross-section of subjects for $b = 0.95$, but no or only slow convergence to the rational solution in those groups. Conversely, groups with $b = 0.67$ converge fast to the rational solution, while there is much heterogeneity in the initial periods. Non-convergence in most groups for $b = 0.95$ has also been found by Heemeijer et al. (2009). Bao and Hommes (2017), conducting a learning-to-forecast experiment with a framing related to housing markets, have three treatments with b-values of 0.95, 0.86 and 0.71. For $b = 0.95$, they find explosive behavior, for $b = 0.86$ persistent fluctuations and for $b = 0.71$ fast convergence to the rational solution.

4.2.2 Public and Private Information – Anchoring Beliefs

Beauty Contest Games with a Known Constant

A simple way to move the efficient equilibrium in a Beauty Contest game into the interior, was first introduced by Güth et al. (2002). Subjects are told to be close to $y^i = c + b\hat{E}^i \frac{1}{N} \sum_{j=1}^N y^j$ with a bounded interval 0 to 100. They find that the commonly known constant $c = 50$ is chosen by many participants in the first round, but also report some subjects choosing close to $c \times 2/3$ or $c \times 2/3 + c$. The equilibrium in this game is 60. Choices therefore converge fast to 60 in repeated rounds. However, choosing c as the midpoint, does not change the focal point of the basic BC game.

Therefore, Benhabib et al. (2018b) provide two new treatments with $c = 10$: firstly, only allowing subjects to choose numbers within the closed interval 0 to 100, and secondly, allowing another set of subjects to choose from all real numbers (see also Fig. 11, boxplot second row, 2/3, +10; and 2/3, +10 [0, 100]; and the horizontal short-dashed lines which represent levels 0 to 3; equilibrium 30). Within a closed boundary, 50 remains the focal point and most numbers are between to 30 (about $50 \cdot (2/3)$) and 43 ($50 \cdot (2/3) + 10$), consistent with Güth et al. (2002) findings of the reference point being 50. However, without a boundary, most subjects seem to choose 10 as their level-0 belief; or level 1 (two possibilities: near $16 = 10 \cdot (2/3) + 10$; or alternatively, $6.66 = 10 \cdot (2/3)$; or L2 (near 21), instead 30, the equilibrium). The resulting average behavior is around $c = 10$ and thus most choices being between level 0 and 1. We want to stress here, how sensitive behavior reacts to the specifications of the rules: changing the choice set, from boundary to non-boundary, shifts average behavior from about 35 to 10. Furthermore, the anchor c does not provide instantaneous equilibrium behavior, as it is not near or equal to the equilibrium choice.

Common but Unknown Constant

Shapiro et al. (2014) as well as Baeriswyl and Cornand (2014) test the Morris and Shin (2002) Beauty Contest model with a common unknown additive constant c to the BC game. They find that level-k is a good descriptive model in standard settings when information is symmetrically distributed among players, giving only private information. However, subjects' behavior in the asymmetric case is mainly driven by focal points such as choosing halfway between the public and the private signal, or choosing one of these two signals. Thus, whether the equilibrium is instantaneously learnable depends very much upon whether naive players receive an equilibrium strategy as a reference point or not. Behavior over time remains heterogeneous since off-equilibrium payoffs are rather flat and similar to equilibrium payoffs, which impedes learning towards the equilibrium.

Idiosyncratic Precise Shocks with Zero Mean – Equilibrium Anchors

Benhabib et al. (2018a, 2018b) add to the b-average component an idiosyncratic payoff relevant shock ϵ^i drawn from a normal distribution with zero mean, implementing the abstract model of a general equilibrium with sentiments (Benhabib et al., 2015). In each of the eight periods, subjects know the parameter b, differing in each period, and each receives a privately known idiosyncratic shock. There is no feedback between periods, in order to study behavior without learning through realized payoffs. Since drawn signals could result to be negative or outside a boundary, the experiment implements an unbounded choice set, the real number line. Subjects' payoff is given by a quadratic distance function between their choice, y^i, and the target as given in Eq. (3). The experimental results demonstrate that the signal ϵ^i becomes an individual anchor, being indeed the modal choice with the average choice being close to zero, for all, positive or negative, b-parameters. Thus, level-k reasoning finally breaks down: in equilibrium everybody has to choose her signal, and subjects at least on average do so, such that sunspots can be considered a subtle reference point system. This is because these signals coordinate the behavior of strategic and naive subjects: both make the same kind of choice and earn high payoffs. This signal structure can be called "strategic nudging". Fig. 11 shows some typical patterns for $b = 2/3$ and $b = 1/3$ and an added ϵ^i (see row 1, boxplots 5 and 8, and rows 2, 7, and 8), with a mean close to zero.

Idiosyncratic Noisy Shocks

In the same experiment of the previous paragraph, in a slightly modified setup (also based on Benhabib et al., 2018a) players receive correlated noisy signals about the idiosyncratic payoff-relevant shocks ϵ^i. The private noisy signal (called hint) given to each subject is a convex combination of the private, payoff relevant shock ϵ^i and a common shock z, with both shocks drawn from two normal distributions with zero mean. Neither the realization of the private shocks nor the common shocks are known independently. The parameters are constructed such that in equilibrium a player chooses $1.5 \cdot hint$. Here, on average, subjects choose about $0.5 \cdot hint$, which is closer to its equilibrium than average choices in the original Beauty Contest game with an open choice set. Yet, this new game represents an analytically more sophisticated problem. The reason for higher payoff outcomes is that the majority chooses from three kinds of simple heuristics: the modal group of subjects ignores the hint altogether and chooses zero; some choose (near) the noisy signal, thus treating the signal as if it were precise; or others compute a choice resulting from a hint, expecting that the common component shock z is zero. Since the noisy signals become focal points for subjects but are at the same time known from the perspective of the analyst, they are a suitable feature for predictive behavior. The analytical solutions of games with signals are, however, more sophisticated, especially with noisy signals, than in the original Beauty Contest game.

Order Effects from Different Idiosyncratic Shock Treatments Within the Same Subjects

Benhabib et al. (2018a) have subjects play several b-Beauty Contest games with precise or imprecise signals without information between rounds, and then the b-Beauty Contest games without signals. The resulting means in those b-Beauty Contest games without signals are then close to zero, as if subjects played a game with a public announcement "$\epsilon^i = 0$" for all players.

Therefore, the implementation of signals in Benhabib et al. (2018a, 2018b) can be considered to solve Keynes' level-k "problem" by proposing Keynesian sentiments denoted by ϵ^i, to alleviate the need of subjects to do complicated calculations. They just can use their anchor. The analytical treatment of this game is, however, more sophisticated, especially with noisy signals, than in the original Beauty Contest game. In the next paragraph we show, however, that when these added shocks are not equilibrium choices, then behavior is again distorted from the efficient equilibrium as it has already been the case in the treatments with the commonly known constant c.

Idiosyncratic Shocks with Nonzero Means

Benhabib et al. (2018b) add a treatment in which idiosyncratic signals, ϵ^i, are drawn i.i.d. from $N(c, \sigma^2)$, $c > 0$. The resulting equilibrium is $(b \cdot c/(1 - 2/3)) + \epsilon^i$ (see Benhabib et al., 2018a, 2018b). This means, if e.g. $c = 10$, then one should choose $20 + \epsilon^i$. However, the authors show that subjects choose their signals as an anchor, ignoring the effect of the mean signals on the average; some also just choose $2/3 \cdot \epsilon^i$ or $2/3 \cdot \epsilon^i + c$ which both can be considered as level-1 reasoning as in the case of the treatment $2/3 \cdot avg + 10$. If subjects are Economics professors, average play is higher, but still different from the equilibrium mean. When each professor plays against the student populations they choose lower numbers (and thus lower level ks), and typically one step higher than the student population, as if they played "best reply" against this student population, anticipating that students play around c. Fig. 11 shows these treatments in the second row, $\frac{2}{3}$, $N(10, 10)$, which is isomorphic to the game $\frac{2}{3} + 10$ with $N(0, 10)$, and also the behavior is the same.

Bayona et al. (2016) conduct a laboratory three-person supply schedule experiment with privately known (un)correlated costs. In the Bayesian equilibrium, predictions for positively correlated costs result in steeper supply functions, and thus more collusive behavior and greater market power than do uncorrelated costs. Subjects receive private signals about the (un)correlated costs. They find that most subjects bid as predicted by the equilibrium in the simple, uncorrelated cost treatment, where the constant term of the linear supply schedule chosen by the subjects is around the own signal cost. However, in the more sophisticated, correlated cost environment their bids display large heterogeneity and considerable deviations from equilibrium with the average behavior being close to the uncorrelated case. The reason for these similarities are easy to understand: in the uncorrelated case subjects are asked to reason in a simple strategic environment. In the correlated case, subjects largely ignore the feature of correlation or are unable to incorporate it in their reasoning. As a consequence, best response behavior results in behavior close to the uncorrelated case. Since naive subjects still make some profits, learning is impeded and it is optimal for sophisticated players (who understand the correlation implication) to mimic unsophisticated behavior.

4.2.3 Stochastic Common Shocks
Common Time Varying Shock
Another version of the BC game that has been implemented in the lab is $y_t^i = b\hat{E}^i \frac{1}{N} \sum_{j=1}^{N} y_t^j + \epsilon_t$. In this version ϵ_t is a commonly known realization for all participants. Over time, ϵ_t could for example be determined by a random walk: $\epsilon_t = \epsilon_{t-1} + \xi_t$. In this case, the experimental literature documents that the convergence in a BC game with a common and known constant found by Güth et al. (2002) is severely mitigated.

Lambsdorff et al. (2013) implement a price setting game with the target price of $4/5 \cdot (\text{average} + 5) + \epsilon_t/10$ with 5 being explained to the subjects as the "cost of a raw material" and ϵ_t as a "business indicator" being a randomly selected integer from the interval $[-15, 15]$.[29] Subjects choose the business indicator as a simple heuristic ϵ_t instead of the equilibrium $(20 + \epsilon_t/2)$. This shows again that reference points can wrongly anchor subjects' behavior.

In another Beauty Contest experiment, Giamattei and Lambsdorff (2015) phrase the game as a macroeconomic model of the Keynesian multiplier with a time-varying

---

[29] In their paper, this variable is called c. We refer to it as ϵ to stress that this variable is stochastic.

component ϵ_t being an exogenous, non-stationary sequence of investments driven by random shocks. Participants have to decide upon their individually optimal consumption in a way that they have to be close to $4/5 \cdot$ income, where $4/5$ is the marginal propensity to consume. Income is calculated as the average consumption over all subjects + the investment ϵ_t. Again, subjects choose the investment component as an anchor. The authors implement two treatments: Firstly, in the so-called Keynes-treatment, subjects are punished both for upward and downward deviations, while, secondly, in the White-treatment they are only punished for upward deviations of consumption, meaning too low savings. This setup reflects the debate of Keynes and White whether only deficits on the current account should be punished as argued by the latter. Keynes instead advocated punishing both surpluses and deficits.

Giamattei and Lambsdorff (2015) find that due to boundedly rational reasoning, asymmetric punishment of deficits leads to permanent under-consumption. To the best of our knowledge Keynes himself did not apply his own Beauty Contest reasoning process to the model of consumption behavior in games with the so-called Keynesian multiplier. Instead, he pondered that consumers can reason their way to equilibrium instantaneously (thus infinity reasoning), given a simple maximization argument. "Net income is what we suppose the ordinary man to reckon his available income to be when he is deciding how much to spend on current consumption" (Keynes, 1936, p. 56). Yet, in his lecture notes Keynes (1973, p. 181) deplored his approach: "I now feel that if I were writing the book again I should (…) have a subsequent chapter showing the difference it makes when short-period expectations are disappointed."

Giamattei (2017) uses the BC framework with a common time varying shock to test the role of limited reasoning on inflation inertia and disinflation. In his game four price setters have to set inflation rates which are strategic complements with $b = 2/3$. The added random process ϵ_t reflects the part of the inflation rate which can be set by the central bank. The task of the central bank as a fifth player is to reduce inflation. Giamattei (2017) shows that Cold Turkey, a sudden change in ϵ_t, does not help to quickly reduce inflation as proposed by theory. Instead subjects show a large degree of inertia which could be better accounted for by a more gradual approach of lowering ϵ_t.

Guessing a Time Varying Shock

Another (extreme) situation which is independent of other players can be represented by a Beauty Contest equation of the form $y^i = \epsilon^i$ where $c = f(.) = 0$ and ϵ^i being a random element chosen by the computer. In that case, the task becomes an *individual decision-making problem*. In the next paragraph we give one out of possibly many examples.

Khaw et al. (2017) conduct an individual decision-making experiment in which subjects need to estimate the probability of drawing a green ring with replacement out of a box with green and red rings. Subjects see each period a draw and submit their draw-by-draw estimate. This probability can be considered to be a continuous random shock, since it is computer-generated and varies stochastically. They find that participants systematically depart from the optimal Bayesian prediction and can be explained by a model of inattentive adjustment. On average behavior is close to Bayesian reasoning with a high variance.

4.3 MULTIPLE EQUILIBRIA (BC GAME WITH $b = 1$)

Beauty Contest games with $b = 1$ represent the original Keynesian Beauty Contest game. The target is typically to choose what most others select. In this setup, there is no higher order reasoning necessary. If a player believes that others, on average, choose a number x, then her best response is also x. However, as stated in the level-k model, the question is what most players pick, as e.g., the focal point (level 0), or what a naive person would play.

4.3.1 Minimum Effort Game

In Van Huyck et al. (1991), players' payoffs depend on their own choice (1, 2, ..., or 7, which enters as a cost) and the minimum choice of all players (which enters as a benefit). Any choice can form an equilibrium, chosen by all. This can be labeled as a minimum effort game, as the payoff is the greatest if all players choose 7, while it is the least if at least one player chooses one. Heterogeneity in behavior thus induces efficiency losses in this game. For groups of size 14 to 16, there is heterogeneity in the first period as there are many different arguments about optimal play, given the belief of a possible minimum play. After the third round, in all sessions the minimum was 1 with a simple reasoning: best response to a minimum 1 in the previous period is to play 1. This is very different when playing repeatedly in groups of two persons which fostered coordination to the efficient equilibrium a great deal, since 12 out of the 14 groups achieved this equilibrium. If one sees that the other player played a high number, one is inclined to play a high choice as well, with little mismatch within a pair.

Fig. 12 depicts the choices in period 1 for all treatments in Van Huyck et al. (1991) median effort game. In the baseline treatment that combines Gamma and Gammadm, there is one payoff-dominant $(7, \ldots, 7)$ and one secure equilibrium in the set of strict equilibria $(3, \ldots, 3)$. In the first period, 70% of the subjects choose neither of the two but instead an action between the payoff-dominant and the secure equilibrium. Over time, behavior converges to the inefficient equilibrium selected by the "historical accident" of the initial median choice. In the second treatment, Omega, in the set of strict equilibria there is only a payoff-dominant equilibrium $(7, \ldots, 7)$ and no secure equilibrium, which is chosen by 52% of the subjects in the first period. In the third treatment Phi, in the set of strict equilibria there is only a secure equilibrium $(4, \ldots, 4)$, which is the modal choice played by 41% of all players in period 1. Over time, the equilibrium is selected by the "historical accident" of the initial choice.

Experimenters have investigated which institutional designs can increase efficiency in these basic coordination games. We will present just a few such attempts. Van Huyck et al. (1991) vary the payoff structure so that they can investigate two salient equilibrium selection principles: payoff-dominance, being the equilibrium

TABLE II
DISTRIBUTION OF CHOICES IN PERIOD 1

| | Treatment | | | | | | | | |
| | Gamma | | Gammadm | | Combined (baseline) | | Omega | | Phi | |
Action	Nm.	(Pr.)	Nm.	(Pr.)	Nm.	(Pr.)	Nm.	(Pr.)	Nm.	(Pr.)
7	5	(18)	3	(11)	8	(15)	14	(52)	2	(7.5)
6	3	(11)	1	(4)	4	(7)	1	(4)	3	(11)
5	8	(30)	7	(26)	15	(28)	9	(33)	9	(33)
4	8	(30)	11	(41)	19	(35)	3	(11)	11	(41)
3	3	(11)	5	(18)	8	(15)	0	(0)	2	(7.5)
2	0	(0)	0	(0)	0	(0)	0	(0)	0	(0)
1	0	(0)	0	(0)	0	(0)	0	(0)	0	(0)
Total	27	(100)	27	(100)	54	(100)	27	(100)	27	(100)

Notes. Nm. = number of subjects. Pr. = percent of subjects.

FIGURE 12

Table II in Van Huyck et al. (1991).

that would give the largest payoff, and security, meaning that choosing an action whose smallest payoff is at least as large as the smallest payoff for any other action. Weber et al. (2001) investigate whether coordination could be achieved by randomly appointing a group leader who encourages the group to select large numbers. This limited one-way communication does not improve efficiency, since large (8–10 subjects) groups are not able to coordinate towards the efficient outcome, and small (two subjects) groups attain efficiency independently of whether they had the leader's announcement or not. Camerer (2003) surveys those kinds of coordination games.

4.3.2 Public and Private Signals

Fehr et al. (2017) investigate multiplicity of equilibria in an experiment, where two agents in a repeated interaction of 80 periods need to simultaneously choose an integer from 0 to 100, being rewarded according to a quadratic loss function, penalizing their distance from the other player's number. The extrinsic information was displayed as a randomly-drawn integer in the interval from 0 to 100. Each player in turn receives a signal of this number, being the same as this number with a fixed probability p. The treatments differ according to whether the signal is public or private or both and according to the preciseness of the signal: the baseline (N) is without signals; in treatment P75 (P95) subjects receive a private signal with a precision probability of 75% (prob = 95%); in treatment AC subjects receive a precise private signal but the signal is only revealed to each subject with probability 90%; in treatment C subjects receive a public signal with precision probability of 75%; in treatment CP subjects receive a public and a private signal, both with a precision probability 75%; in treatment CC subjects receive two public signals.

The results, being depicted in Fig. 13, show that public signals are not strictly necessary for sunspot-induced behavior or coordination. Even in the absence of extrinsic

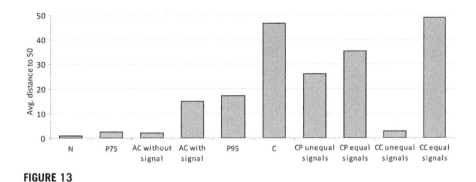

FIGURE 13

Fehr et al. (2017, Fig. 3): Average distance of choices from the secure action (avg. distance from 50).

information (treatment N and the observations of treatment AC without signal), subjects tend to coordinate on choosing 50, the middle of the interval. If the signal is imprecise (P75) or if two signals are difficult to aggregate because they are not highly correlated (CC unequal signals), the focal point of 50 dominates in determining subjects' choice. On the other hand, if the signal is precise (P95), there is one signal (C) or the signals are highly correlated (CC equal signals), there is a clear tendency to follow the action indicated by the signal. If a public signal is combined with a private one (CP), the ability to coordinate behavior on any number is impeded and payoffs are lower on average.

The coordination result resembles one particular finding in the experimental macroeconomics literature (discussed in more detail by Arifovic and Duffy, 2018). In the learning-to-forecast experiment in a New-Keynesian framework by Assenza et al. (2014), one treatment is run with an inflation targeting interest rate rule with coefficient 1, which induces a continuum of RE steady state equilibria. They find coordination on one of these arbitrary equilibria or coordination on unstable inflationary or deflationary spirals.

4.3.3 Global Games

As explained in Section 3, payoff disturbances in coordination games with multiple equilibria can theoretically lead to a unique equilibrium. Heinemann and Noussair (2015) provide a more extensive survey of this literature. Cabrales et al. (2007) test the global game theory based on Carlsson and Van Damme (1993) in a two-person game with two actions for each player and random matching between players each period. In the complete information control treatment, many pairs converge quickly to the Pareto optimal equilibrium while the minority converges to the risk dominant one. In the incomplete information case, each player receives an idiosyncratic noisy discrete signal about the actual payoff of the safe action. Payoffs for the alternative and risky action, is either zero when the other player chooses the safe action or 15 if both players choose the alternative, which is the Pareto-optimal equilibrium. After some periods of miscoordination, almost all pairs coordinate on the global game solution, the risk dominant equilibrium.

For groups of 15 subjects, Heinemann et al. (2004) test the main prediction by global games departing from the speculative currency attack model by Obstfeld (1996) and Morris and Shin (1998). At the beginning of each period, a payoff-relevant random variable Y is drawn from a uniform distribution with known support. Y can be interpreted as the fundamentals of the setup so that higher (lower) values of Y represent worse (better) fundamentals.

There are two treatments: complete information (CI) where Y is known to all 15 subjects and private information (PI), where Y is imperfectly revealed to each of the 15 subjects by idiosyncratic noisy signals. These signals are drawn randomly from a uniform interval $X_i \sim [Y - \epsilon, Y + \epsilon]$ with ϵ being small. Agents then have to choose between two actions, A and B: A, which can be interpreted as "not attacking", is a safe choice yielding a fixed payoff F. The other action, B, which can be interpreted as "attacking", yields a payoff which depends on the total number of subjects choosing B. The critical threshold is given by a monotonically decreasing function $a(Y)$: should less than $a(Y)$ players choose B, all who choose B earn 0, while if more or equal to $a(Y)$ players choose B, the attackers earn a payoff equal to the fundamental Y.

Testing the theory requires that the distribution of Y values is chosen so that there exist values of $Y \leq F$, for which the dominant strategy is choosing A and similarly there exist values of $Y \geq a^{-1}(1)$ so that an individual subject is incentivized to attack by selecting B. Under complete information, there are multiple equilibria, either all players choosing A or all players choosing B, for Y lying in the interval $(F, a^{-1}(1))$. Once information is incomplete, there exists a unique threshold value of the noisy signal above which all subjects should choose B, i.e. to attack, and below which they should not attack and thus choose A.

The main aim of Heinemann et al. is twofold: first, comparing the stability of the complete information game with its multiplicity of equilibria to that of the private information game; second, whether subjects use threshold strategies that are predicted by the global game threshold. The results show that subjects play the threshold strategies in both the private and complete information treatments and estimated thresholds in general lie below the global game predictions X^* or Y^* but are higher than the payoff-dominant strategy of choosing B if $Y > F$. In contrast to Cabrales et al., Heinemann et al. find much coordination over time on a common threshold and therefore little heterogeneity in the complete information treatment, where Y is publicly known and there are in theory multiple equilibria. Conversely, in the incomplete information treatment there is less coordination because of variation of signals between players and therefore more persistent heterogeneity in behavior.

Another paper that tests global game theory is Cornand (2006), who adds two treatments, one where subjects receive a private and a public signal and a second in which subjects receive two noisy public signals. She finds that subjects tend to overreact to the public signal even when they also receive a private signal. However, subjects' behavior tends to be more random if they receive two noisy public signals.

This result implies that if institutions make public announcements, they would be well-advised to coordinate on one single message.

Heinemann et al. (2009) use the full information original (2004) design but additionally, collect data on subjects' degree of risk aversion and their subjective beliefs about the decisions of other subjects. This additional information is required to compare two possible channels of strategic uncertainty in the context of the global games refinement: uncertainty about monetary payoff versus uncertainty about risk attitudes. Their findings are as follows: firstly, adding to a behavioral model either noise to the payoffs or heterogeneity about risk attitudes, performs well in terms of in-sample and out-of-sample performance; secondly, more risk-averse agents are less likely to play the risky choice B; thirdly, players under- (over-) estimate the success probability of coordination when a low (high) number of players choosing B is required to exceed the threshold. In such kind of games of strategic complements players just have to best respond to their subjective beliefs of B-choices of others, which is therefore just level-1 reasoning.

Duffy and Ochs (2012) extend Heinemann et al.'s (2004) design by introducing a dynamic setting so that players repeatedly play the game deciding whether to attack or not, given the history of previous decisions of other players. The result is that even if there is a cost for waiting to attack, they do not find much difference between the thresholds in the dynamic game and in the static game. This is good news in terms of that the simultaneous attack game is a good approximation of the dynamic game.

Szkup and Trevino (2011) also embark on the Heinemann et al. (2004) design to investigate how costly information acquisition impacts on behavior in global games. Here subjects can choose the precision of the private signal received, where more precise signals are costlier. Their results display large heterogeneity, showing that only 30% subjects choose the equilibrium middle level of precision and as opposed to their theory, there is a positive correlation between choosing more precise signals and the frequency of choosing to attack.

4.3.4 Ultimatum Games (Played in Extensive Form)

We described in Section 3 an ultimatum game with simultaneous moves, which is a Beauty Contest game with proposer's demand for himself equals $b = -1$ times the choice of the opponent plus a constant that presents the size of the pie. Typically, this game is played in extensive form, i.e. the proposer sends an offer to the responder, who then reacts only to this stated offer. Experiments like Roth et al. (1991), conducted in several countries, show in two-person games between 50% and 70% of proposers' offers (pie size minus demand) lie between 40% to 50% of a given pie, which is (near) the focal point, an intuitive answer (thus level-0 interpretation), or can also be seen as a best response to the (equal split) norm, expected as the responder's acceptance level (thus level-1). Offers below 30% are typically rejected by the responder. Over time, behavior remains rather stable tilted towards equal splits. However, there are cultural differences across different countries. For example, Japanese

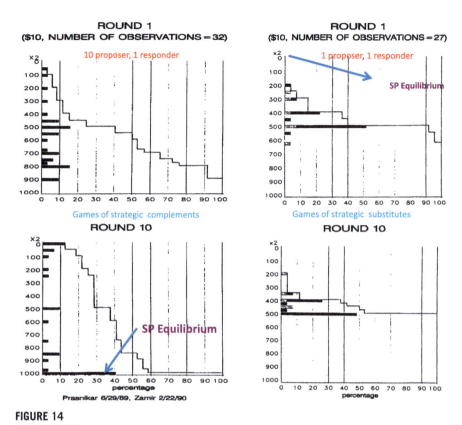

FIGURE 14

Roth et al. (1991): Distribution of accepted (black part of columns) and rejected (crosshatched part of columns) market offers in the United States. The left figure presents 10-proposer markets and the right figure markets with one single proposer.

students choose lower offers which are also accepted, given that the norm is some-what different as already discussed in Section 2 (bargaining).

Roth et al. (1991) also increase the number of proposers in an ultimatum game and thus turn the game into a Bertrand game with strategic complements with no cultural differences. Behavior converges to the unique subgame perfect equilibrium (40% of offers result in SPE-play), giving almost all of the share to the responder. Analo-gously, competing responders (Grosskopf, 2003) induce small proposer offers, which are accepted as responders would find themselves unable to punish self-regarding proposers unilaterally. Fig. 14 presents the first and the 10th period distributions of accepted and rejected offers for the 10 proposers (left figures) and one single pro-poser (right figures). Over time, there is more heterogeneity in the 10 player games than in the one player game, since in the former resulting equilibrium payoffs are rather small, and thus deviations are not punished.

4.4 AUCTION IN THE LABORATORY AND THE FIELD

Here we give some examples of auctions experiments and the interpretation of the data through the level-k model (for an extended discussion see Crawford et al., 2013 and Crawford, 2013).

LUPI

An experimental game conducted in the field that shares the features of the lowest unique bid auction is the LUPI (lowest unique positive integer) game. LUPI is a Swedish lottery game, asking individuals to choose an integer from 1 to K. The winner is the person choosing the lowest integer that nobody else picks. The equilibrium varies depending on the number of players. Östling et al. (2011) calculate the Poisson–Nash equilibrium, a mixed equilibrium, assuming the number of players playing the game every day, is Poisson-distributed. They find that observed play in both laboratory and field data is fairly close to equilibrium play over time. To explain the heterogeneity in player choices, they use a cognitive hierarchy model by Camerer et al. (2004) which assumes a poison distribution by a level-k play over all lower levels.

Auctions with Private Signals

Georganas and Nagel (2011) use a two-player English clock common value auction of a take-over game in the laboratory to test whether agents with a toehold advantage (one owning more shares of the firm than the other) bid more aggressively. The intuition for this theory is the following: imagine bidders want to acquire a company in an auction, in which the value corresponds to the sum of the two private values of the two bidders. One player owns already a larger share (toehold) of the firm than the other. If the player with the larger share wins the bidding, he does not have to pay the full price; if he loses, he receives a lucrative compensation from the winning party. In equilibrium the low toeholder bids close to his signal and the large toeholder has an exploding bid, involving a high level of reasoning to reach the equilibrium bid. Actual larger toeholds increase the winning probability and the payoff of their owners. While these results are in line with theory, they are not nearly as strong as predicted by theory. Bids of higher toeholders are only significantly higher than of lower toeholders, if they own more than 20% of the shares. Behavior can be explained by the level-k model: both bidders bid according to level 1 types, where level 0 is bidding equal to signal value (truthful bidding). This kind of level 0 is equivalent to assuming that the level 0 bidder chooses uniform randomly over the known signal interval. There is also no learning over time. The authors explain this finding by the fact that the payoff function does not penalize deviations from the equilibrium harshly enough.

Crawford and Iriberri (2007) explain behavior in first price private value and first and second price common value with the winner's curse (winning the object, but loosing money), using a level-k reasoning model. They conclude that level-k has much of the same implications as equilibrium auction theory. Furthermore, a level-k model based on types up to L2 can explain the winner's curse in common-value auctions and overbidding in private-value auctions. The intuitive explanation for this is that level-0 types randomly choose a bid or are truthtelling, which can provide an anchor above the equilibrium. Level-1 types anticipate this and give a best response, also being above equilibrium. Crawford and Iriberri also show empirically that a mixture level-k model up to level 2 outperforms the "cursed equilibrium model" by Eyster and Rabin (2005) using three experimental datasets: Kagel and Levin (1986), Avery and Kagel (1997), and Goeree et al. (2002).

4.5 OTHER GAMES WITH DISCRETE STRATEGY SPACES

4.5.1 A Ring Game – Spatial Reasoning

Kneeland (2015) implements a new experiment based on a ring structure which does not require the experimenter to specify level-0 players. In her ring structure with four players, each player chooses from three possible actions. Player 1's payoff may depend on player 2's action, while player 2's payoff may depend on player 3's action; and player 3's payoff depends on player 4's action and player 4's payoff depends on player 1's action. A player with first-order rationality only considers her belief about her neighbor's action, while a player with second-order rationality considers the neighbor's belief about her neighbor's action etc. Since optimal actions differ according to the depth of reasoning, this allows inferring the depth of reasoning of different players: Kneeland (2015) finds that 93% of subjects are at least first-order rational, 71% are at least second-order rational, 44% are at least third-order rational and 22% are at least fourth-order rational. Note, that the author formulates the belief reasoning along the spacial component due to the network structure.[30]

Friedenberg et al. (2015), using the data of Kneeland (2015), find that a large share of subjects that apply reasoning about cognition does not necessarily apply reasoning about rationality. More specifically, approximately 50% of the subjects that are first-order or second-order rational can be considered as applying higher levels of cognition.

Decomposing the (average) behavior into several types made it possible to understand further deviations or (non)-convergence to plausible, efficient or other mathematical solutions. This in turn gave the researchers ideas to construct new designs obtaining different (favorable) outcomes. This will be discussed in the next sections.

4.5.2 Schelling Matching

Benito et al. (2011) let subjects play Schelling's spatial proximity model. There are two types (that ought to represent for example white and black), to each of which N subjects are assigned. The neighborhood of each subject consists of the right-hand

---

[30]Analogously, a question of interest is reasoning in a time space, i.e. how far players look ahead. While a rational player should infinitely ahead (in an infinitely repeated game or a game with stochastic ending), Orland and Roos (2013) find that agents look ahead not more than four periods in an individual-decision making problem of price-setting. Woodford (2018) analyzes the effects of monetary policy with agents that only look ahead a finite number of periods and a value function learned from past experience to assess their situation after that finite number of periods.

and the left-hand neighbor. Subjects' payoff is such that they are most happy if they have at least one neighbor of the same type. In the first treatment, subjects move sequentially and without cost, i.e. one subject starts deciding upon her position in the circle, then the next one follows etc. Even after the circle is complete, a subject can move between two other subjects. In the second treatment, subjects are required to move simultaneously so that they make decisions about moving at the same time. The results of both treatments are identical to Schelling's prediction, as they both end up in the segregated equilibrium. In a later paper, Benito et al. (2015) extend Schelling's model by incorporating moving costs. Both the theoretical and the experimental results show that there is not full segregation in equilibrium. They also note that the degree to which players act strategically increases considerably with the moving costs.

4.5.3 Mixed Equilibrium Games in Lab and Field

Crawford and Iriberri (2007) explain the experimental results of the "hide and seek"-game by Rubinstein and Tversky (1993; "RT") and Rubinstein et al. (1996; "RTH"). Their experiment works as follows: Subjects were divided into hiders and seekers. The hider puts a prize in one of four boxes arranged in a row. Those boxes are marked by A, B, A, A. The seeker's task is to find the prize, only being allowed to open one box. This is similar to a matching pennies game, since one player wins by matching the opponent's choice while the opponent wins by mismatching. The A–B labeling is important to account for a "naturally occurring landscape" as in a hide-and-seek game but represents a tractable setting. It is argued that "B" is salient in the spirit of Thomas Schelling (1960). It is also argued that the two "end A" locations are salient in the sense of Christenfeld (1995). Rubinstein and Tversky (1993) argue that due to these two saliences render the remaining location, "central A", "the least salient place." Rubinstein et al. (1996) verify this choice as the modal behavior for both hiders and seekers, and was even more prevalent for seekers than hiders. Crawford and Iriberri (2007) propose a level-k explanation for this choice behavior. Level 0 is constrained to salient choices; level-1 hiders then best responds to that by using the non-salient location, "central A". While level-1 seekers match the anticipated behavior of level-0 hiders, level-2 seekers choose "central A" with probability 1 etc. Thus, the equal mixing in Nash-equilibrium is not observed. These games have not been played over long time horizon.

Field Experiments

Chiappori et al. (2002) note that evidence on players mixing strategies is based almost exclusively on laboratory experiments and express several criticisms on that methodology: first, laboratory experiments are "simplistic, artificial setting[s]"; second, stakes in the form of payoffs are low in laboratory experiments; third, subjects have other preferences than maximizing their payoffs such as "attempting to avoid looking foolish". It has also been argued that laboratory experiments contain too few rounds for subjects to gain significant experience (Palacios-Huerta, 2003). These criticisms have been responded by new directions.

Thus, papers like Walker and Wooders (2001), Chiappori et al. (2002), Palacios-Huerta (2003), Apesteguia and Palacios-Huerta (2010) propose the use of sports data that represent "generalized" matching penny games, i.e. where the Nash equilibrium is not necessarily (0.5, 0.5). Walker and Wooders analyze data on serves to start rallies in Grand Slam tennis tournaments, Chiappori et al. (2002) use the full sample of penalty kicks in the French and Italian elite soccer leagues over a period of three years, and Palacios-Huerta analyzes data on major professional soccer games in Spain, Italy, England and other countries. All three studies find the data to be consistent with Nash equilibrium. Apesteguia and Palacios-Huerta (2010) use data on penalty kicks in professional soccer tournaments as a natural experiment to test the hypothesis that agents make use of the first-mover advantage, since the team starting with penalty kicks is determined by a coin toss of the referee. The authors return a positive answer, showing that subjects are aware of the advantage of going first and rationally respond to it by systematically choosing to kick first when given the chance to choose the order. In contrast, in multi-period laboratory experiments with a mixed-strategy equilibrium, reinforcement models explain behavior over time better than the Nash equilibrium (see e.g. Erev and Roth, 1998).

Multi-Dimensional Iterative Reasoning: Colonel Blotto Game

This mixed equilibrium game by Arad and Rubinstein (2012b) is the most complicated situation we present here. Two players have to divide a given number of points (troops) into a specified number, e.g. 6, of battlefields. The person who has filled a field with more points than the opponent wins a fixed prize; a payoff of zero is awarded in cases of ties. The experiment is either run in the laboratory with students or conducted online with many participants as a tournament version of the Colonel Blotto Game. Three different dimensions of decision-making are involved in the multi-dimensional iterative reasoning extracted from the actual decisions: 1. In how many fields to concentrate, i.e. to invest most of the troops; 2. Whether to fill "disregarded" fields with one or two troops. 3. Into which fields to assign a large number troops (first, middle or last location). Separately, in each dimension, L0 chooses the intuitive category (e.g. an equal amount of troops); L1 chooses a category that properly responds to L0 within the dimension, etc. Despite the 250 million possible strategies, nine strategies were chosen by about 30% of the subjects. Another astonishing result is that the winners of both subject pools chose a distribution of (2, 31, 31, 31, 23, 2) across the six fields. The experimental results thus clearly document that patterns occur.

5 ELICITATION METHODS

In the previous section we presented a range of structural changes to the original Beauty Contest game to explain resulting behavioral heterogeneity and discrepancy with the theoretical benchmarks of mostly homogeneous solutions. Here we present other methods to create variation in behavior, which are not related to structural changes. This can be, for example, through inducing time pressure, i.e. giving subject limited time, instead of unlimited decision time.

Another important aspect in understanding the general patterns of behavior is to know the reasoning processes behind a choice. When classifying outcomes into certain categories, the same outcome can be created through various channels of cognitive procedures or emotional reactions. Consider two examples of choice: The first one is an equal split in an ultimatum game. Is the person acting according to some fairness principles or does he act strategically as he anticipates that the opponent expects a fair outcome? Secondly, how can one distinguish whether a subject plays a random choice, seemingly unrelated to the rules of the game, and a deliberate choice? For example, a subject in the 2/3 average Beauty Contest game chooses 22, classified as a level 2 choice. However, her written explanation states "this is my age". By coincidence, this gives a high chance of winning when playing with undergraduate students. In the following, we present some elicitation methods which help reveal underlying thought processes and other ideas to induce behavioral changes.

5.1 STRATEGY (VECTOR) METHOD

One of the earliest and most used methods to systematically reveal reasoning processes behind choices in experimental economics has been the so-called strategy method. Selten (1967) introduces it for experiments with a two-step procedure. In the first step, subjects acquire knowledge about the game by playing it in the standard or direct response form reacting to actions of others. In a second step, subjects have to construct strategies with actions for each possible situation (information sets) they could possibly reach. The experimenter then calculates the payoffs according to a tournament structure. Each player's strategy is matched with all other strategies, e.g. in a two-person Cournot game there are thus $n(n-1)$ interactions for each player who is not matched with herself. Then the average payoff for all interactions are calculated.

There are only few experimental papers that utilize this two-step method, as originally introduced, e.g., Selten et al. (1997), and Keser (1996) in oligopoly games with cost asymmetries and demand inertia. Selten et al. (1997) find that subjects do not maximize profits based on expectation formation or backward induction in a 100-period Cournot game. Instead, in the initial periods of a programmed strategy, a common pattern among subjects is a formulation of a goal, an ideal point, which is a production outcome pair based on some fairness considerations. The ideal point can be interpreted as a reference point. Over time, the program describes a "measure for measure", that is, a move by the opponent towards one's own ideal point is responded by one's own move towards the ideal point, while a move away from the ideal point is followed by also moving away.

Mitzkewitz and Nagel (1993; MN) implement the strategy method without the direct response mode, for an experiment on ultimatum games with incomplete formation of the pie on the side of the responders. They pondered that these games are simple enough to understand without the first step. We describe this game in more

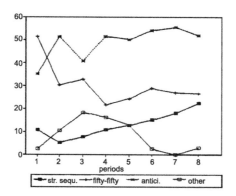

FIGURE 15

Types of (strategic) offer behavior in ultimatum offer games; *y*-axis denotes relative frequency of each type. str. sequ. = sequential equilibrium strategy of accepting all or all positive offers; fifty-fifty: proposal to split pie 50–50 and near 50–50; antici = anticipation strategy based on forming beliefs about an anticipated level of acceptance of the opponent. Source: Mitzkewitz and Nagel (1993).

detail as the rules allow for constructions of several reference points of the level-k model. The pie size is determined by rolling of a six-sided die. Proposers know the amount and specify an offer in offer games (demands, in demand games) for each possible amount. Responders respond to all possible offers (demands), not knowing the specific pie. Choices are from [0, 0.5, 1..., pie size]. With this method (see e.g. survey by Brandts and Charness, 2011), the researchers obtain information even at nodes typically not reached, for example low offers.

MN offer a three-step descriptive theory, resembling level-k. Let us exemplify this for the offer game. In a first step, a naive proposer, ignoring the information structure, offers half of the pie, assuming that the responder will accept half of the pie. A more sophisticated player assumes as a reference point half of the expected pie (3.5/2) in the offer games, and thus ponders to best respond with a rounded offer of 1.5 or 2 (second step). In a third step, offers are rounded downwards, when the offer is greater than half of the actual pie. This is one of the so-called anticipation strategies.

MN classify behavior according to equal split, anticipation strategies and sequential equilibrium strategies, allowing also for small deviations from these strategies. Equal split is the modal choice observed in the first period but this decays over time, as proposers gain a better understanding of the informational advantage for themselves. This decrease is not observed in complete information games, implying that the informational structure plays an additional role to determine fairness norms. Thus, as in level-k, beliefs do not need to be consistent, but instead learning mechanisms might converge to equilibrium strategies. Fig. 15 reflects the proportion of different reasoning patterns over time in an offer game.

Fischbacher et al. (2001) use the strategy method to understand conditional giving in public good games (see also Arifovic and Duffy, 2018). This also allows to understand the (slow) decrease of average giving in those games over time.

Stahl and Wilson (1994, 1995) construct several 3 × 3 normal-form games with dominance-solvable solutions. Each subject has to state an action and belief distribution of other players' actions for all games, without any feedback between the games. Given this strategy vector method, they classify subjects according to a level-k model which includes that a level-k player gives a best response to a distribution of lower levels (0 to k − 1), using also maximum likelihood estimations.

Risk Elicitation Method

Holt and Laury (2002) also use a kind of strategy vector method, a so-called list elicitation, to measure risk attitudes of subjects. In an individual decision-making task, subjects are confronted with a list of two lottery alternatives in each row (or one sure payoff increasing from row to row compared to a fixed lottery; see Heinemann et al., 2009). The rows are ordered in such a way that subjects should reveal their risk attitudes by choosing lotteries from one column for several rows and then switch once to the column of the other lotteries. At the switching point, the subject reveals the equivalence between the two lotteries (the certainty equivalence, in case of sure payoffs). This method produces a heterogeneity measure of risk attitudes. Typically there are few risk-loving subjects, while most show risk-averse attitudes. Since the beginning of this century, this kind of risk elicitation has been linked to behavior in games to analyze the relationship between strategic uncertainty and risk attitudes of a single subject (see, e.g., the literature cited in Heinemann et al., 2009).

5.2 RESPONSE TIME (RT)

Measuring response time is probably one of the least inflicting methods to understand features of the reasoning procedures, since subjects cannot notice that the analyst collects these data. It has been widely used in psychology to understand the difference between deliberation in thought processes and random, spontaneous, or intuitive choices. Using computers to solicit behavior either in the computer laboratory or with online platforms like Qualtrics®, the researcher can obtain reaction times for each choice accurately up to 50 milliseconds. Rubinstein (2007) analyzes reaction time (RT) in several experiments, among others the Beauty Contest games, ultimatum games, etc. For the Beauty Contest game data he finds that the RT of those who choose 22 (4%) was 157 seconds while the RT among the 8 who choose 20, 21, 23, 24, 25 was only 80 seconds. He concludes that "[t]his must mean that there is little in common between the choice of 22 and the rest of the category which Nagel called 'Step 2'." However, a choice of 20 can be made faster, as the subject, e.g., might jump from 50 to 30 to 20 without any precise mental calculations while a choice of 22.22 requires higher calculation time. Yet, both 22.22 and 20 might involve level-k thinking, one with precise and the other one with rough calculations. These discrepancies of data interpretations call for a collaboration between researchers, using different methods to arrive at a more conclusive understanding of actual behavior. For a survey on experiments with RT see Brañas-Garza et al. (2017).

5.3 MOUSELAB, EYE-TRACKING

An increasing literature uncovers the reasoning processes through various (new) choice elicitation techniques. Costa-Gomes et al. (2001) use mouselab tracking techniques by hiding the information of payoffs in normal form games behind boxes on the computer screens which subjects need to click to receive the information. The authors specify possible look-up-ex-ante rules. For instance, for level 1 reasoning the player only needs to look up her own choices, while level 2 reasoning requires look-ups of payoffs from the other player. Roos and Luhan (2013) study whether subjects use all available information in a more complicated setup, where information is only revealed if subjects "buy" it. They find that 75% of the expectations formed in their setup did not use all information available. Brocas et al. (2014) find evidence for level-k thinking in betting games when using this technique. The eye-tracking results of Müller and Schwieren (2011) suggest that subjects in Beauty Contest experiments actually think (or look) more steps ahead than their chosen numbers reveal. Chen and Krajbich (2017) implement eye-trackers while subjects play two-person Beauty Contest games with tournament payoffs. They are in particular interested when subjects realize that 0 is an optimal strategy. The measure of pupil dilation and eye movements are clearly distinguishable between those who switch to the winning strategy (epiphany learners) as compared with subjects who do not learn the winning strategy.

5.4 CONTINUOUS TIME DECISION-MAKING

Whether a choice is determined randomly or with deliberation can be elicited by letting the subjects continuously choose within a given time interval. Agranov et al. (2015) introduce this method in a basic Beauty Contest game and pay subjects according to their choices in a particular time period, chosen at the end, unknown to the subjects ex ante. They find a clear distinction between those who do not understand the rules of the game, identified by random walk behavior, and those who discover either level 1 or level 2 choices after some learning has occurred.

5.5 WRITTEN COMMENTS, CHATS, AND OTHER COMMUNICATION TOOLS, TEAM DECISIONS

Nagel (1993), Bosch et al. (2002), and many others nowadays ask subjects to explain their choices in a written form during or after the experiments. These comments reveal especially random choices or very clear-cut reasoning procedures like choosing $50 \cdot p^k$ in Beauty Contest games. Bosch et al. classify over one thousand comments sent to the experimenters in collaboration with three different newspapers. One interesting finding is that those who comment on the equilibrium (80% of those equilibrium commentators) typically choose numbers between 0 and 10, thus remaining far from the winning choice in these newspaper experiments around 14 to 17.

Burchardi and Penczynski (2014) allow written communication within two-person teams, playing the basic Beauty Contest game and analyze the reasoning procedure related to level k. Sbriglia (2008) provides subjects with comments written by the winners of previous rounds, giving advice on how to choose in Beauty Contest games. This increases the speed of convergence to equilibrium.

The most commonly used communication tool is through the direct application of the so-called cheap talk where one or all subjects send messages related to the action space, e.g. I will choose "action" A (see e.g. Charness, 2000 for stag-hunt games and PD games). In the former, one-sided messages achieve coordination but in PD games messages are not truthful and thus behavior does typically not achieve efficiency.

5.6 ASKING FOR GUESSES

Haruvy (2002) proposes direct elicitation of beliefs to support level-k behavior, additionally to analyzing the actions of the same players. He discovered that explicit beliefs exhibit level-k patterns. Arjona et al. (2017) ask one set of subjects for their choices and another set about their guesses about opponents' distribution of choices in Arad and Rubinstein (2012a) modified two-person 11–20 games, in which a bonus payment is given to the player whose choice is by $R = 3$ steps (AR use $R = 1$) lower than his opponent (e.g. one chooses 20 and the other chooses 17 and therefore receives a bonus addition to the payment of 17). They distinguish more clearly between level-k choices and noisy choices than when $R = 1$ as in AR. About 74% of the guesses and the actual choices can be classified as level 0 (choice 20), level 1 (choice 17), level 2 (choice 14), or level 3 (choice 11).

5.7 PERSONAL CHARACTERISTICS AND TRAINING

A question of interest is to what extent intrinsic characteristics play a role. The subject pool can be quite heterogeneous and thus might create heterogeneous experimental outcomes. Subjects can be inexperienced or experts, students or professionals. Some studies concentrate on children as subjects. Grueneisen et al. (2015) test whether six-year olds can form higher-order beliefs in strategic interaction with peers and return a positive answer, in contrast to previous literature.

Clearly, decision-making very much depends on the context of the environment but also on personal characteristics of a subject. These can be objective measures such as age, gender, training with math, but also cognitive abilities which need to be elicited through various (psychological) tests, such as IQ tests. These characteristics might also influence the reaction towards others induced by expectations about other agents' characteristics.

The careful study on gender has entered experimental economics in the last 15 years (see a survey by Niederle, 2016). Whether there are gender differences related to level-k in BC games depends very much on the details of the experimental design. Cubel and Sanchez-Pages (2017) find that females display less depth of reasoning than males without financial incentives, but no differences prevail in payment treatments. Yet, making mixed gender composition salient induces lower choices for females as compared to males. The reason is that in general women believe that they are better in reasoning in such types of games than men, and correspondingly males believes this as well, which leads them to use less depth of reasoning. The authors relate their finding to stereotype threat (Steele, 1997), which states that members of negatively stereotyped groups indeed choose worse in fear of confirming the stereotype.

Training in certain cognitive realms like chess players (Bühren and Frank, 2012) shows no difference in behavior in BC-experiments, while economists obviously play closer to equilibrium (Bosch-Domènech et al., 2002). Dickinson and McElroy (2010) show that sleep deprivation when playing the BC results in diverting even further from equilibrium play. The authors call up the subjects at several times of the day, also at night. Gill and Prowse (2016) find that subjects with a higher cognitive ability, measured by the Raven test, choose numbers closer to the equilibrium in Beauty Contest games over time, but not in the initial periods. They also investigate the connections between level-k behavior and non-cognitive abilities. Furthermore, cognitive ability improves reasoning in the BC games (Burnham et al., 2009; Brañas-Garza et al., 2012). Additionally, cognitively more able individuals who believe that others are more clever than themselves revise their choices in BC games downwards. This is not the case for those who have lower scores in cognitive ability (Fehr and Huck, 2016).

Bosch-Rosa et al. (2016, see also above) devised the one person BC game, together with other cognitive measures (Raven test) and the results in the original Beauty Contest game to construct an index to discriminate between "high sophistication" and "low sophistication" subjects. High types among themselves (without knowing this grouping) create no bubbles in subsequent asset markets, unlike when only low types interact with each other (see also Arifovic and Duffy, 2018). Levine et al. (2017) also combine several IQ tests, BC-games, and "bubble" experiments, randomly distributing the subjects to different groups. They show that subjects with high strategic IQ (measured by Beauty Contest games) and cognitive intelligence (measured by cognitive reflection test (CRT) and other tests) result in higher earnings in subsequent asset markets as compared to players of the type "low" within these measures.

5.8 NEUROECONOMICS

Since the early 2000s, biological data were gathered as a new source of explaining heterogeneity in behavior through collaborations with neuroscientists (see survey by Camerer et al., 2016). This leads to new design challenges when implementing technical instruments like fMRI (frequency magnetic resonance imaging) scanners measuring brain activity (via blood oxygen levels, known as BOLD signals, which are considered a proxy for cellular activity) and eye-tracking (following eye movements and pupil dilation etc.).

In experimental economics typically "between"-subject comparison is implemented, i.e., a design where one group of subjects participates only in one particular setup and their behavior is compared with the one of subjects in another setup. The economic researcher is typically interested in seeing the isolated consequences due to a single exogenous change in the design. The situations, interactions or decisions are mostly repeated, to understand the difference in perception of new situations and learning over time.

In contrast to economics, in neuroscience, multiple observations from various parameter changes or setups (e.g. playing against computer or playing against humans) are required from the same subject. The reason for these differences in design is that brain activity produces high variance also within a single subject and not only between subjects, and imaging requires contrasting brain activities through different tasks for the statistical analysis. Furthermore, the usage of individualized technological instruments like eye-trackers, skin conductances typically cannot be used for more than a few, or is restricted to even only to one subject, especially when using fMRI. There have been many more brain image studies about individual decision-making (e.g. risk attitudes, intertemporal choices, human well-being etc.) than interactive games (social preferences and strategic behavior we discussed in Sections 2 and 4).

In this section, we describe two studies, which on the one hand provide a biological foundation of level-k reasoning, and on the other hand show differences in brain activity when dividing subjects into high and low earners according to their realized payoffs. Coricelli and Nagel (2009) study behavior in Beauty Contest games using fMRI brain imaging. All subjects are invited one by one to participate in various games with different b-parameters, playing every other period either against nine computer programs, who just choose randomly between 0 and 100, or against nine human subjects who are recorded the same way. There is no feedback between rounds. They also solve calculation tasks related to the level-k calculations as $50 \cdot (2/3)$ or $50 \cdot (2/3)^2$. This is all known to the participants. All subjects behave as level 1 when playing against the randomized computer programs. However, with human opponents most choices are still related to level-1 reasoning, while about 1/3 of the subjects reveal level-2 or higher levels. Brain activity of these two different reasoning types are well distinguishable with higher activity in the medial prefrontal cortex (mPFC) for level-2 players, a theory of mind area (i.e. thinking what others are thinking) and rostral anterior cingulate cortex (rACC) for level-1 players which is related to self referential thinking (see Fig. 16). Yet, there are also brain regions which produce similar activities for high and low reasoning types, as in the superior temporal sulcus (STS), posterior cingulate cortex, and bilateral temporo-parietal junction (TPJ), which are areas responsible for general planning. When playing against the computer, no differential activity in these areas was noted, but only in the calculation area as angular gyrus. This is similar as in the simple calculation tasks we added at the end within the scanner.

Concluding this study, even though the level-k model is specified as a mental model of calculation $50 \cdot (2/3)^k$, the interpretation of putting oneself into the shoe of others can be now supported with brain activity. Furthermore, newspaper participants, who write comments like "I think that the average will be 50 therefore I will choose 33, but others will think alike and therefore I choose 25", reveal a reasoning process beyond mental calculations with theory of mind ideas involved, which is visualized in the mPFC.

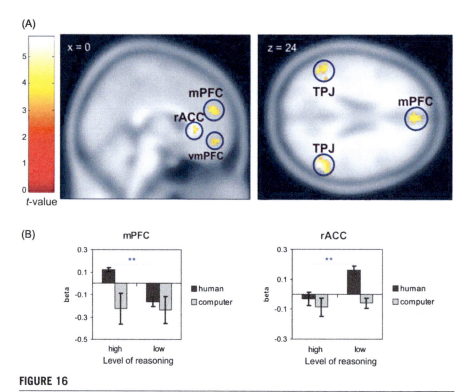

FIGURE 16

Coricelli and Nagel (2009): Patterns of behavior and brain activity for low and high levels of reasoning. The bar charts show the differences of BOLD signals for low vs high reasoning types playing either against humans or computer programs.

The second study is by Smith et al. (2014), who implement a bubble experiment as in Smith et al. (1988, also mentioned in Section 2) with a risky asset and risk-free cash, interacting for 50 periods. Two or three subjects are placed in an fMRI machine and 9–21 subjects as usual in front of the computer. The authors classify players into low, medium and high earners showing differences in trading behavior and brain activity between the three different earning types. Fig. 17 exemplifies heterogeneity in terms of trading behavior and brain activity: average right anterior insula activity of low earners oscillates around 0, while high earners on average show an activity peak that coincides with the beginning of selling units 5–10 periods before the peak of the bubble. The authors interpret this result with high earners producing some physical discomfort and therefore exit the asset market before the crash occurs.

6 DISCUSSION

In the 1950s, the Air force quickly acknowledged the heterogeneity of its pilots and demanded that cockpits should fit pilots falling within the 5 to 95 percent range on

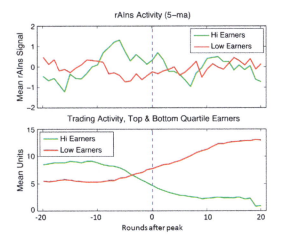

FIGURE 17

Smith et al. (2014): Average right anterior insula activity in high earners and low earners shows that low earner activity fluctuates around 0, whereas high earner activity shows a peak that coincides with the beginning of the sell-off of units shown in (A) (5–10 periods before the price peak).

each dimension (Rose, 2016, p. 9). Adjustable seats were introduced, being an innovation at the time. How to fit economic theory to heterogeneity is less obvious, but we hope to have shown that experimental economics contributes to the understanding of subjects' behavior in the relevant 5 to 95 percent ranges.

To understand metaphorically the rich amount of regularity we have explored as a contrast to the mostly homogeneous rationality benchmark, we introduce the tuning fork (see Nagel et al., 2016, p. 79; Nagel, 2018). It has most of the vibrational energy at the fundamental frequency. In contrast humans with all their shortcomings and rich set of emotions would then represent the instruments, each with different overtones, which however, also have their regularities, as expressed with the level-k model. This helps establish a more positive view of human interaction, as in an orchestra with its diversity, and the tuning fork as an important coordination device. But no instrument would like to be only a tuning fork, pure and poor.

In this chapter, the models, representing economic situations, draw on a universal basic structure, the Beauty Contest game, as a canonical structure to create several archetypal games in (experimental) economics that at first seem disconnected. Identifying a particular game or function within a general structure can give the analyst a hunch about how individual subjects in the laboratory would empirically behave. An encompassing function containing a best response to others' behavior and further exogenous parameters seems a natural candidate: a reasonable or thoughtful subject forms possibly sophisticated beliefs in her mind about the play of a single opponent, or group of opponents and other external features. In such a mind – an aggregation of choices might be represented by an average or reference point. A second step is thereafter to best reply towards to this belief and so on, to maybe reach equilibrium.

Herbert Simon (1996, p. 34ff) has pondered about such a Cournot (1838) equilibrium tatonnement process "each firm, with limited cleverness, formed an expectation of its competitor's reaction to its actions, but that each carried the analysis only one move deep. But what if one of the firms, or both, tries to take into account the reactions to the reactions? They may be led into an infinite regress of outguessing" (Simon, 1996, p. 37). Von Neumann started from the other end, the equilibrium, asking "how is the absolutely selfish 'homo economicus' going to act under given external circumstances?" The key answer, more parsimonious than maybe first thought, has been given by the Keynesian Beauty Contest metaphor with several degrees of reasoning. While the game had been widely used in the macroeconomic literature (see, e.g., discussion by Nagel et al., 2017), the reasoning process has been ignored for almost 60 years. With our chapter we hope to contribute to a behavioral (micro-)foundation of macroeconomics, for which Keynes has made some initial suggestions.

The level-k model, an empirically validated model in the spirit of Keynes, has been a successful descriptive (boundedly) rational model to account for these kinds of observations and questions, proposing limited reasoning. The so-called black box has been opened but restrained at the same time, bridging the gap between fully rational reasoning and beliefs, and random behavior. Yet, in describing heterogeneity of subjects' all types of reasoning can be found seated side by side. Knowing the presence of different types might identify the mistakes of (aggregate) behavior or failures of coordination to provide tools for improving either the institutional environment or the play of a single agent.

While we consider Beauty Contest games only with linear aggregation rules, we hope this can be seen as a starting point and potential future research efforts can be directed towards how the definition of Beauty Contest game can be extended, restricted or refined. Still, one will also need to understand how interactive situations not in this class can be identified and potentially generalized or systematized.

In a similar spirit, level-k has at least two limitations: first, it represents a (descriptive) model being silent about how the distribution of types emerges. Yet, if the researcher knows the subject pool, the result can be more easily predicted, as there is an astonishing robustness of results depending on the population. Second, subjects do not always have enough information or knowledge about the best response function to engage in reasoning about other players' reasoning depth. In those cases, focal or reference points, random behavior, moral laws, heuristics or intuition are guiding principles without the need of higher-order reasoning. Notably, reference points as the key elements of the level-k model are in need of empirical validation. Here a link to the rich studies and heuristics from individual decision making might become of help.

Over time adaptive processes with more or less information feedbacks provide additional patterns, which are covert in more detail in the chapter by Arifovic and Duffy. The authors discuss behavior, for example, in NK-models that fall into our classification of BC-games but are more complicated. Finally, the knowledge of the environment is often either not known or too complicated to allow reasoning about other subjects' reasoning.

There is yet, another criticism about the content presented in this chapter and maybe about the current state of some parts of experimental economics. Returning to our initial example of the air force, the pilots owed the invention of the adjustable seat to a visionary scientist who detected the extent of heterogeneity. This was possible because he measured painstakingly many dimensions of pilots' bodies. Here, we presented different situations with focus on single variable decisions. As a contrast, Reinhard Selten asked for experimental studies of complicated situations with many different decision variable and actors. He stated many examples from the very beginning of his career in economics in the 1950s such as oligopolies (see Abbink and Brandts, 2010; Nagel et al., 2016). Another example of a more complicated structure is also Arad and Rubinstein (2012b) which we presented above. Such studies will reveal further interesting heuristics (e.g. how a single subject copes with many decision variables; see Selten et al., 2012), analogously to the adjustable seat situation. We hope that further inquiries in this vein result in fruitful collaborations among experimental economists, akin to computer scientists who provide new tools for exploring and understanding heterogeneity in big data science.

REFERENCES

Abbink, K., Brandts, J., 2010. Drei Oligopolexperimente. In: The Selten School of Behavioral Economics. Springer, Berlin, Heidelberg, pp. 53–72.

Adam, K., 2007. Experimental evidence on the persistence of output and inflation. The Economic Journal 117 (520), 603–636.

Agranov, M., Caplin, A., Tergiman, C., 2015. Naive play and the process of choice in guessing games. Journal of the Economic Science Association 1 (2), 146–157.

Agranov, Marina, Potamites, Elizabeth, Schotter, Andrew, Tergiman, Chloe, 2012. Beliefs and endogenous cognitive levels: an experimental study. Games and Economic Behavior 75 (2), 449–463.

Alaoui, L., Penta, A., 2016a. Endogenous depth of reasoning. The Review of Economic Studies 83 (4), 1297–1333.

Alaoui, L., Penta, A., 2016b. Cost–benefit analysis in reasoning. Mimeo.

Alaoui, L., Penta, A., 2017. Reasoning About Others' Reasoning. Barcelona GSE Working Paper 1003.

Amir, R., 2005. Supermodularity and complementarity in economics: an elementary survey. Southern Economic Journal 71 (3), 636–660.

Angeletos, G.-M., Hellwig, C., Pavan, A., 2007. Dynamic global games of regime change: learning, multiplicity, and the timing of attacks. Econometrica 75, 711–756.

Angeletos, G.-M., La'O, J., 2010. Noisy business cycles. In: NBER Macroeconomics Annual 2009, vol. 24. University of Chicago Press, pp. 319–378.

Angeletos, G.-M., Lian, C., 2016. Incomplete information in macroeconomics. In: Handbook of Macroeconomics, vol. 2.

Angeletos, G.-M., Werning, I., 2006. Crises and prices: information aggregation, multiplicity, and volatility. The American Economic Review 96 (5), 1720–1736.

Apesteguia, J., Palacios-Huerta, I., 2010. Psychological pressure in competitive environments: evidence from a randomized natural experiment. The American Economic Review 100 (5), 2548–2564.

Arad, A., Rubinstein, A., 2012a. The 11–20 money request game: a level-k reasoning study. The American Economic Review 102 (7), 3561–3573.

Arad, Ayala, Rubinstein, Ariel, 2012b. Multi-dimensional iterative reasoning in action: the case of the Colonel Blotto game. Journal of Economic Behavior & Organization 84 (2), 571–585.

Arifovic, J., Duffy, J., 2018. Heterogeneous agent modelling: experimental evidence. In: Handbook of Computational Economics, vol. 4. Elsevier, pp. 491–540 (this Handbook).

Arifovic, J., Hommes, C., Kopanyi-Peuker, A., Salle, I., 2018. Are sunspots effective in a big crowd? Evidence from a large-scale bank run experiment. Mimeo.

Arifovic, J., Petersen, L., 2017. Stabilizing expectations at the zero lower bound: experimental evidence. Journal of Economic Dynamics and Control 82, 21–43.

Arjona, D.R., Fragiadakis, D.E., Kovaliukaite, A., 2017. The predictive success of theories of strategic thinking: a non-parametric evaluation.

Assenza, T., Heemeijer, P., Hommes, C., Massaro, D., 2014. Managing Self-Organization of Expectations Through Monetary Policy: A Macro Experiment. CeN-DEF Working Paper 14-07.

Aumann, R.J., 1974. Subjectivity and correlation in randomized strategies. Journal of Mathematical Economics 1, 67–96.

Aumann, R.J., 1987. Correlated equilibrium as an expression of Bayesian rationality. Econometrica 55, 1–18.

Avery, C., Kagel, J.H., 1997. Second-price auctions with asymmetric payoffs: an experimental investigation. Journal of Economics & Management Strategy 6 (3), 573–603.

Baeriswyl, R., Cornand, C., 2014. Reducing overreaction to central banks' disclosures: theory and experiment. Journal of the European Economic Association 12 (4), 1087–1126.

Banerjee, A.V., Duflo, E., 2009. The experimental approach to development economics. Annual Review of Economics 1 (1), 151–178.

Banerjee, A.V., Duflo, E. (Eds.), 2018. Handbook of Economic Field Experiments, vol. 2, pp. 3–654.

Banerjee, A., Weibull, J.W., Binmore, K., 1996. Evolution and rationality: some recent game-theoretic results. In: Economics in a Changing World. Palgrave Macmillan, London, pp. 90–117.

Bao, T., Hennequin, M., Hommes, C., Massaro, D., 2016. Coordination on Bubbles in Large-Group Asset Pricing Experiments. Working paper. University of Amsterdam.

Bao, T., Hommes, C., 2017. When Speculators Meet Constructors: Positive and Negative Feedback in Experimental Housing Markets. CeNDEF Working Paper. University of Amsterdam.

Bao, T., Hommes, C., Sonnemans, J., Tuinstra, J., 2012. Individual expectations, limited rationality and aggregate outcomes. Journal of Economic Dynamics and Control 36, 1101–1120.

Baroni, M., Maguire, S., Drabkin, W., 1983. The Concept of Musical Grammar. Music Analysis 2, 175–208.

Bayona, A., Brandts, J., Vives, X., 2016. Supply Function Competition, Private Information, and Market Power: A Laboratory Study. CEPR Discussion Paper 11378. Center for Economic and Policy Research (CEPR), London.

Beja, A., Goldman, M.B., 2015. On the dynamic behavior of prices in disequilibrium. The Journal of Finance 35, 235–248.

Benhabib, J., Bühren, C., Duffy, J., Nagel, R., 2018a. Strategic nudging. Mimeo.

Benhabib, J., Duffy, J., Nagel, R., 2018b. De-framing the rules to (de)-anchor beliefs in beauty contest games. Mimeo.

Benhabib, J., Wang, P., Wen, Y., 2015. Sentiments and aggregate demand fluctuations. Econometrica 83, 549–585.

Benito, J., Branas, P., Hernandez, P., Sanchis, J., 2011. Sequential vs. simultaneous Schelling models. The Journal of Conflict Resolution 55 (1), 33–59.

Benito, J., Branas, P., Hernandez, P., Sanchis, J., 2015. Strategic behavior in Schelling dynamics: a new result and experimental evidence. Journal of Behavioral and Experimental Economics 57, 134–147.

Bergemann, D., Morris, S., 2013. Robust predictions in games with incomplete information. Econometrica 81 (4), 1251–1308.

Bolton, G., Ockenfels, A., 2000. ERC: a theory of equity, reciprocity, and competition. The American Economic Review 90, 166–193.

Bordalo, Pedro, Gennaioli, Nicola, Shleifer, Andrei, 2012. Salience theory of choice under risk. The Quarterly Journal of Economics 127 (3), 1243–1285.

Bosch-Domènech, A., Montalvo, J.G., Nagel, R., Satorra, A., 2002. One, two, (three), infinity, ...: newspaper and lab beauty-contest experiments. The American Economic Review 92 (5), 1687–1701.

Bosch-Domènech, A., Montalvo, J.G., Nagel, R., Satorra, A., 2010. A finite mixture analysis of beauty-contest data using generalized beta distributions. Experimental Economics 13 (4), 461–475.

Bosch-Rosa, C., Meissner, T., Bosch-Domènech, A., 2016. Cognitive bubbles. Experimental Economics. Forthcoming.

Brañas-Garza, P., Garcia-Muñoz, T., González, R.H., 2012. Cognitive effort in the beauty contest game. Journal of Economic Behavior & Organization 83 (2), 254–260.

Brañas-Garza, P., Meloso, D., Miller, L., 2017. Strategic risk and response time across games. International Journal of Game Theory 46 (2), 511–523.

Branch, W., McGough, B., 2009. A new Keynesian model with heterogeneous expectations. Journal of Economic Dynamics & Control 33, 1036–1051.

Brandenburger, A., Danieli, A., Friedenberg, A., 2017. How many orders do player's reason? An observational challenge and solution. Mimeo.

Brandts, J., Charness, 2011. The strategy versus the direct-response method: a first survey of experimental comparisons. Experimental Economics 14, 375–398.

Brandts, J., Potters, J., 2017. Experimental industrial organization. In: Handbook of Game Theory and Industrial Organization. Edward Elgar Publishing. Forthcoming.

Breaban, A., Noussair, C.N., 2015. Trader characteristics and fundamental value trajectories in an asset market experiment. Journal of Behavioral and Experimental Finance 8, 1–17.

Breitmoser, Y., 2012. Strategic reasoning in p-beauty contests. Games and Economic Behavior 75, 555–569.

Brocas, I., Carrillo, J.D., Wang, S.W., Camerer, C.F., 2014. Imperfect choice or imperfect attention? Understanding strategic thinking in private information games. Review of Economic Studies 81 (3), 944–970.

Brock, W.A., Hommes, C., 1998. Heterogeneous beliefs and routes to chaos in a simple asset pricing model. Journal of Economic Dynamics & Control 22 (8–9), 1235–1274.

Bühren, C., Frank, B., 2012. Chess players' performance beyond 64 squares: a case study on the limitations of cognitive abilities transfer. Talent Development and Excellence 4 (2), 157–169.

Burchardi, K.B., Penczynski, S.P., 2014. Out of your mind: eliciting individual reasoning in one shot games. Games and Economic Behavior 84, 39–57.

Burnham, T.C., Cesarini, D., Johannesson, M., Lichtenstein, P., Wallace, B., 2009. Higher cognitive ability is associated with lower entries in a p-beauty contest. Journal of Economic Behavior & Organization 72 (1), 171–175.

Bryant, J., 1983. A simple rational expectations Keynes-type model.. The Quarterly Journal of Economics 98, 525–528.

Cabrales, A., Nagel, R., Armenter, R., 2007. Equilibrium selection through incomplete information in coordination games: an experimental study. Experimental Economics 10, 221–234.

Camerer, C., 1995. Individual Decision Making. Princeton University Press, Princeton, NJ.

Camerer, C.F., 2003. Behavior Game Theory: Experiments in Strategic Interaction. Princeton University Press, Princeton, NJ.

Camerer, C., Cohen, J., Fehr, E., Glimcher, P., Laibson, D., 2016. Neuroeconomics. In: Handbook of Experimental Economics, vol. 2.

Camerer, C., Fehr, E., 2006. When does "economic man" dominate social behavior? Science 311, 47.

Camerer, C., Ho, T.H., 1999. Experience-weighted attraction learning in normal-form games. Econometrica 67, 827–874.

Camerer, C., Ho, T.H., Chong, J.-K., 2002. Sophisticated experience-weighted attraction learning and strategic teaching in repeated games. Journal of Economic Theory 104, 137–188.

Camerer, C.F., Ho, T.H., Chong, J.K., 2004. A cognitive hierarchy model of games. The Quarterly Journal of Economics 119 (3), 861–898.

Camerer, Colin F., Loewenstein, George, Weber, Martin, 1989. The curse of knowledge in economic settings. Journal of Political Economy 97 (5), 1232–1254.

Campbell, J.Y., Lo, A.W.C., MacKinlay, A.C., 1997. The Econometrics of Financial Markets. Princeton University Press, Princeton, NJ.

Carlsson, H., Van Damme, E., 1993. Global games and equilibrium selection. Econometrica 61 (5), 989–1018.

Charness, G., 2000. Self-serving cheap talk: a test of Aumann's conjecture. Games and Economic Behavior 33 (2), 177–194.

Charness, G., Rabin, M., 2002. Understanding social preferences with simple tests. The Quarterly Journal of Economics 117, 817–869.

Chen, W.J., Krajbich, I., 2017. Computational modeling of epiphany learning. Proceedings of the National Academy of Sciences 114 (18), 4637–4642.

Chen, Y., Konstan, J., 2018. Online field experiments: a selective survey of methods. Mimeo.

Chiappori, P.A., Levitt, S., Groseclose, T., 2002. Testing mixed-strategy equilibria when players are heterogeneous: the case of penalty kicks in soccer. The American Economic Review 92 (4), 1138–1151.

Chompsy, Noam, 1957. Syntactic Structures. Mouton, The Hague.

Chong, J.K., Ho, T.H., Camerer, C., 2016. A generalized cognitive hierarchy model of games. Games and Economic Behavior 99, 257–274.

Chou, E., McConnell, M., Nagel, R., Plott, C., 2009. The control of game form recognition in experiments: understanding dominant strategy failures in a simple two person "guessing" game. Experimental Economics 12, 159–179.

Christenfeld, N., 1995. Choices from identical options. Psychological Science 6 (1), 50–55.

Cooper, R., 1999. Coordination Games. Complementarities and Macroeconomics. Cambridge University Press, Cambridge, UK.

Cooper, D., Kagel, J., 2016. Other-regarding preferences: a selective survey of experimental results. In: Kagel, J., Roth, A. (Eds.), Handbook of Experimental Economics, vol. 2.

Coricelli, G., Nagel, R., 2009. Neural correlates of depth of strategic reasoning in medial prefrontal cortex. Proceedings of the National Academy of Sciences 106 (23), 9163–9168.

Cornand, C., 2006. Speculative attacks and informational structure: an experimental study. Review of International Economics 14, 797–817.

Corsetti, G., Guimaraes, B., Roubini, N., 2006. International lending of last resort and moral hazard: a model of IMF's catalytic finance. Journal of Monetary Economics 53, 441–471.

Costa-Gomes, M.A., Crawford, V.P., 2006. Cognition and behavior in two-person guessing games: an experimental study. The American Economic Review 96 (5), 1737–1768.

Costa-Gomes, M.A., Crawford, V.P., Broseta, B., 2001. Cognition and behavior in normal-form games: an experimental study. Econometrica 69 (5), 1193–1235.

Cournot, A.A., 1838. Recherches sur les principes mathématiques de la théorie des richesses par Augustin Cournot. L. Hachette.

Crawford, V., 1995. Adaptive dynamics in coordination games. Econometrica 65, 103–143.

Crawford, V., 2013. Boundedly rational versus optimization-based models of strategic thinking and learning in games. Journal of Economic Literature 51, 512–527.

Crawford, V.P., Costa-Gomes, M.A., Iriberri, N., 2013. Structural models of nonequilibrium strategic thinking: theory, evidence, and applications. Journal of Economic Literature 51 (1), 5–62.

Crawford, V.P., Iriberri, N., 2007. Level-k auctions: can a nonequilibrium model of strategic thinking explain the Winner's curse and overbidding in private-value auctions? Econometrica 75 (6), 1721–1770.

Crawford, V.P., Kugler, T., Neeman, Z., Pauzner, A., 2009. Behaviorally optimal auction design: examples and observations. Journal of the European Economic Association 7 (2–3), 377–387.

Cubel, M., Sanchez-Pages, S., 2017. Gender differences and stereotypes in strategic reasoning. The Economic Journal 601, 728–756.

Daniels, G.S., 1952. The Average Man? No. TN-WCRD-53-7. Air Force Aerospace Medical Research Lab, Wright-Patterson AFB, OH.

Davis, D.D., Holt, C.A., 1993. Experimental Economics. Princeton University Press.

De Long, J.B., Shleifer, A., Summers, L., Waldmann, R., 1990. Noise trader risk in financial markets. Journal of Political Economics 98 (4), 703–738.

Dhami, S., 2016. Foundations of Behavioral Economic Analysis. Oxford University Press.

Diamond, P.A., 1982. Aggregate demand management in search equilibrium. Journal of Political Economy 90, 881–894.

Dickinson, D.L., McElroy, T., 2010. Rationality around the clock: sleep and time-of-day effects on guessing game responses. Economics Letters 108 (2), 245–248.

Dixit, A., 2006. Thomas Schelling's contributions to game theory. Scandinavian Journal of Economics 108, 213–229.

Duffy, J., 2016. Macroeconomics: a survey of laboratory research. In: Kagel, J.H., Roth, A.E. (Eds.), Handbook of Experimental Economics, vol. 2. Princeton University Press.

Duffy, J., Nagel, R., 1997. On the robustness of behaviour in experimental 'beauty contest' games. The Economic Journal 107 (445), 1684–1700.

Duffy, J., Ochs, J., 2012. Equilibrium selection in entry games: an experimental study. Games and Economic Behavior 76, 97–116.

Duflo, E., 2006. Field Experiments in Development Economics. Econometric Society Monographs, vol. 42, p. 322.

Dufwenberg, M., Kirchsteiger, G., 2004. A theory of sequential reciprocity. Games and Economic Behavior 47, 268–296.

Eppel, T., Matheson, D., Miyamoto, J., Wu, G., Eriksen, S., 1992. Old and new roles for expected and generalized utility theories. In: Edwards, Ward (Ed.), Utility Theories: Measurements and Applications. Kluwer Academic Press, Boston, pp. 271–294.

Erev, I., Haruvy, E., 2016. Learning and the economics of small decisions. In: Kagel, J.H., Roth, A.E. (Eds.), The Handbook of Experimental Economics, vol. 2. Princeton University Press, pp. 638–716.

Erev, I., Roth, A., 1998. Predicting how people play in games: reinforcement learning in experimental games with unique, mixed strategy equilibria. The American Economic Review 88, 848–881.

Evans, G.W., Honkapohja, S., 2001. Learning and Expectations in Macroeconomics. Princeton University Press.

Eyster, E., Rabin, M., 2005. Cursed equilibrium. Econometrica 73 (5), 1623–1672.

Falk, A., Fischbacher, U., 2006. A theory of reciprocity. Games and Economic Behavior 54, 293–314.

Farhi, E., Werning, I., 2017. Monetary Policy, Bounded Rationality, and Incomplete Markets. No. w23281. National Bureau of Economic Research.

Fehr, E., Gachter, S., 2000. Cooperation and punishment in public goods experiments. The American Economic Review 90, 980–994.

Fehr, D., Heinemann, F., Llorente-Saguer, A., 2017. The Power of Sunspots: An Experimental Analysis. Working paper.

Fehr, Dietmar, Huck, Steffen, 2016. Who knows it is a game? On strategic awareness and cognitive ability. Experimental Economics 19, 713–726.

Fehr, E., Schmidt, K., 1999. A theory of fairness, competition and cooperation. The Quarterly Journal of Economics 114, 817–868.

Fehr, E., Tyran, J-F., 2001. Does money illusion matter? The American Economic Review 91, 1239–1262.

Fehr, E., Tyran, J.-F., 2007. Money illusion and coordination failure. Games and Economic Behavior 58, 246–268.

Fehr, E., Tyran, J.-R., 2008. Limited rationality and strategic interaction: the impact of the strategic environment on nominal inertia. Econometrica 76, 353–394.

Fischbacher, U., Gächter, S., Fehr, E., 2001. Are people conditionally cooperative? Evidence from a public goods experiment. Economics Letters 71 (3), 397–404.

Fragiadiakis, D., Kovaliukaite, A., Arjona, D.R., 2017. Testing Cognitive Hierarchy Assumptions. Working paper.

Fréchette, Guillaume R., 2016. Experimental economics across subject populations. In: Kagel, John H., Roth, Alvin E. (Eds.), The Handbook of Experimental Economics, vol. 2. Princeton University Press, pp. 435–480.

Friedenberg, A., Kets, W., Kneeland, T., 2015. Bounded reasoning: rationality or cognition. Mimeo.

Fudenberg, D., Levine, D., 1998. The Theory of Learning in Games. MIT Press, Cambridge and London.

Gale, D., 1995. Dynamic coordination games. Economic Theory 5 (1), 1–18.

Gale, D., Shapley, L.S., 1962. College admissions and the stability of marriage. The American Mathematical Monthly 69, 9–14.

Galí, J., 2008. Monetary Policy and the Business Cycle. Princeton University Press, Princeton, NJ.

García-Schmidt, M., Woodford, M., 2015. Are Low Interest Rates Deflationary? A Paradox of Perfect-Foresight Analysis. No. w21614. National Bureau of Economic Research.

Garratt, R., Wooders, J., 2010. Efficiency in second-price auctions: a new look at old data. Review of Industrial Organization 37, 42–50.

Georganas, S.C., Healyb, P.J., Weber, R.A., 2015. On the persistence of strategic sophistication. Journal of Economic Theory 159 (Part A), 369–400.

Georganas, S., Nagel, R., 2011. Auctions with toeholds: an experimental study of company takeovers. International Journal of Industrial Organization 29 (1), 34–45.

Giamattei, Marcus, 2017. Cold Turkey vs. Gradualism: Evidence on Disinflation Strategies from a Laboratory Experiment. Passauer Diskussionspapiere. Volkswirtschaftliche Reihe, No. V-67-15.

Giamattei, M., Lambsdorff, J. Graf, 2015. Balancing the current account – experimental evidence on underconsumption. Experimental Economics 18 (4), 679–696.

Gigerenzer, G., Todd, P.M., ABC Research Group, 1999. Simple Heuristics That Make Us Smart. Oxford University Press.

Gill, David, Prowse, Victoria, 2016. Cognitive ability and learning to play equilibrium: a level-k analysis. Journal of Political Economy 126 (4), 1619–1676.

Gintis, H., 2003. Strong reciprocity and human sociality. Journal of Theoretical Biology 206, 169.

Gneezy, U., Niederle, M., Rustichini, A., 2003. Performance in competitive environments: gender differences. The Quarterly Journal of Economics 118 (3), 1049–1074.

Gode, D., Sunder, S., 1993. Allocative efficiency of markets with zero-intelligence traders: market as a partial substitute for individual rationality. Journal of Political Economy 101, 119–137.

Goeree, J.K., Holt, C.A., 2004. A model of noisy introspection. Games and Economic Behavior 46 (2), 365–382.

Goeree, J.K., Holt, C.A., Palfrey, T.R., 2002. Quantal response equilibrium and overbidding in private-value auctions. Journal of Economic Theory 104 (1), 247–272.

Goeree, J.K., Holt, C.A., Palfrey, T.R., 2003. Risk averse behavior in generalized matching pennies games. Games and Economic Behavior 45 (1), 97–113.

Goeree, J.K., Holt, C.A., Palfrey, T.R., 2016. Response Equilibrium: A Statistical Theory of Games. Princeton University Press, Princeton.

Goeree, J.K., Louis, P., Zhang, J., 2014. Noisy introspection in the 11–20 game. The Economic Journal.

Goldstein, I., Pauzner, A., 2004. Contagion of self-fulfilling financial crises due to diversification of investment portfolios. Journal of Economic Theory 119, 151–183.

Grosskopf, B., 2003. Reinforcement and directional learning in the ultimatum game with responder competition. Experimental Economics 6, 141.

Grosskopf, B., Nagel, R., 2008. The two-person beauty contest. Games and Economic Behavior 62, 93–99.

Grueneisen, S., Wyman, E., Tomasello, M., 2015. "I know you don't know I know ..." children use second-order false belief reasoning for peer coordination. Child Development 86 (1), 287–293.

Guererk, O., Irlenbusch, B., Rockenbach, B., 2006. The competitive advantage of sanctioning institutions. Science 312, 108–111.

Guesnerie, R., 1992. An exploration of the eductive justifications of the rational-expectations hypothesis. The American Economic Review, 1254–1278.

Güth, W., Kocher, M., Sutter, M., 2002. Experimental 'beauty contests' with homogeneous and heterogeneous players and with interior and boundary equilibria. Economics Letters 74, 219–228.

Güth, W., Schmittberger, R., Schwarz, B., 1982. An experimental analysis of ultimatum bargaining. Journal of Economic Behavior & Organization 3, 367–388.

Hanak, N., Sutan, A., Willinger, M., 2016. The Strategic Environment Effect in Beauty Contest Games. GREDEG Working Papers 2016-05. Groupe de REcherche en Droit, Economie, Gestion (GREDEG CNRS), University of Nice Sophia Antipolis.

Harbaugh, W.T., Krause, K., 2000. Children's altruism in public good and dictator experiments. Economic Inquiry 38 (1), 95–109.

Harrison, G.W., List, J.A., 2004. Field experiments. Journal of Economic Literature 42 (4), 1009–1055.

Haruvy, E., 2002. Identification and testing of modes in beliefs. Journal of Mathematical Psychology 46 (1), 88–109.

Haruvy, E., Noussair, C.N., Powell, O., 2014. The impact of asset repurchases and issues in an experimental market. Review of Finance 18 (2), 681–713.

He, Z., Xiong, W., 2012. Dynamic debt runs. The Review of Financial Studies 25, 1799–1843.

Heemeijer, P., Hommes, C., Sonnemans, J., Tuinstra, J., 2009. Price stability and volatility in markets with positive and negative expectations feedback: an experimental investigation. Journal of Economic Dynamics and Control 33.

Heinemann, F., Nagel, R., Ockenfels, P., 2004. The theory of global games on test: experimental analysis of coordination games with public and private information. Econometrica 72, 1583–1599.

Heinemann, F., Nagel, R., Ockenfels, P., 2009. Measuring strategic uncertainty in coordination games. The Review of Economic Studies 76, 181–221.

Heinemann, F., Noussair, C., 2015. Macroeconomic experiments. Journal of Economic Studies 42 (6), 930–942.

Henrich, J., Boyd, R., Bowles, S., Camerer, C., Fehr, E., Gintis, H., McElreath, R., 2001. In search of homo economicus: behavioral experiments in 15 small-scale societies. The American Economic Review 91, 73.

Herrmann, B., Thöni, C., Gächter, S., 2008. Antisocial punishment across societies. Science 319 (5868), 1362–1367.

Ho, T.H., Camerer, C., Weigelt, K., 1998. Iterated dominance and iterated best response in experimental "p-beauty contests". The American Economic Review 88 (4), 947–969.

Holden, S., Natvik, G., Vigier, A., 2014. An equilibrium theory of credit rating. Mimeo. University of Oslo.

Holt, C.A., 1995. Industrial organization: a survey of laboratory research. In: Handbook of Experimental Economics, vol. 349, pp. 402–403.

Holt, C.A., Laury, S.K., 2002. Risk aversion and incentive effects. The American Economic Review 92 (5), 1644–1655.

Hommes, C., 2011. The heterogeneous expectations hypothesis: some evidence from the lab. Journal of Economic Dynamics and Control 35 (1), 1–24.

Hommes, C., 2013. Behavioral Rationality and Heterogeneous Expectations in Complex Economic Systems. Cambridge University Press, Cambridge.

Hommes, C., Sonnemans, J., Tuinstra, J., Van de Velden, H., 2005. Coordination of expectations in asset pricing experiments. The Review of Financial Studies 18 (3), 955–980.

Hommes, C., Sonnemans, J., Tuinstra, J., Van De Velden, H., 2007. Learning in cobweb experiments. Macroeconomic Dynamics 11 (S1), 8–33.

Hommes, C., Sonnemans, J., Tuinstra, J., Van de Velden, H., 2008. Expectations and bubbles in asset pricing experiments. Journal of Economic Behavior & Organization 67 (1), 116–133.

Hossain, T., Morgan, J., 2006. Plus shipping and handling: revenue (non) equivalence in field experiments on eBay. Advances in Economic Analysis & Policy 6 (2), 1429.

Kagel, J., 1995. Auctions: a survey of experimental research. In: Kagel, John H., Roth, Alvin E. (Eds.), Handbook of Experimental Economics.

Kagel, J.H., Levin, D., 1986. The winner's curse and public information in common value auctions. The American Economic Review, 894–920.

Kagel, J., Levin, D., 1993. Independent private value auctions: Bidder behaviour in first-, second-and third-price auctions with varying numbers of bidders. The Economic Journal 103, 868–879.

Kagel, J., Levin, D., 2002. Common Value Auctions and the Winner's Curse. Princeton University Press, Princeton, NJ.

Kagel, J., Levin, D., 2016. Auctions: a survey of experimental research. In: Kagel, J., Roth, A. (Eds.), Handbook of Experimental Economics, vol. 2.

Kagel, J., Roth, A. (Eds.), 1995. The Handbook of Experimental Economics. Princeton University Press, Princeton, NJ.

Kagel, J., Roth, A. (Eds.), 2016. The Handbook of Experimental Economics, vol. 2. Princeton University Press, Princeton, NJ.

Kahneman, D., 2011. Thinking, Fast and Slow. Macmillan.

Kahneman, D., Tversky, A., 1979. Prospect theory: an analysis of decision under risk. Econometrica 47, 263–292.

Kaldor, N., 1934. The equilibrium of the firm. The Economic Journal 47, 60–76.

Karp, N., Lee, I.H., Mason, R., 2007. A global game with strategic substitutes and complements. Games and Economic Behavior 60, 155–175.

Keser, C., 1996. Voluntary contributions to a public good when partial contribution is a dominant strategy. Economics Letters 50 (3), 359–366.

Ketcham, J., Smith, V.L., Williams, A.W., 1984. A comparison of posted-offer and double-auction pricing institutions. The Review of Economic Studies 51, 595–614.

Kets, W., 2012. Learning with fixed rules: the minority game. Journal of Economic Surveys 26 (5), 865–878.

Kets, W., Sandroni, A., 2017. A Theory of Strategic Uncertainty and Cultural Diversity. Working paper.

Keynes, J.M., 1936. The General Theory of Interest, Employment and Money. Macmillan, London.

Keynes, J.M., 1973. In: Moggeridge, D. (Ed.), The Collected Writings of J.M. Keynes. XIV. Macmillan for the Royal Economic Society, London, pp. 492–493.

Khaw, M.W., Stevens, L., Woodford, M., 2017. Discrete adjustment to a changing environment: experimental evidence. Journal of Monetary Economics 91, 88–103.

Kirman, A., 1992. Whom or what does the representative individual represent? The Journal of Economic Perspectives 6, 117–136.

Kneeland, T., 2015. Identifying higher-order rationality. Econometrica 83 (5), 2065–2079.

Koszegi, B., Rabin, M., 2006. A model of reference-dependent preferences. The Quarterly Journal of Economics 121, 1133–1165.

Lagunoff, R., Matsui, A., 1997. Asynchronous choice in repeated coordination games. Econometrica 65 (6), 1467–1477.

Lambsdorff, J.G., Schubert, M., Giamattei, M., 2013. On the role of heuristics—experimental evidence on inflation dynamics. Journal of Economic Dynamics and Control 37 (6), 1213–1229.

Ledoux, A., 1981. Concours résultats complets. Les victimes se sont plua jouer. Jeux et Stratégie, 10–11.

Ledyard, J.O., 1995. Public goods: a survey of experimental research. In: Kagel, J., Roth, A. (Eds.), Handbook of Experimental Economics, pp. 111–194.

Lei, V., Noussair, C.N., 2002. An experimental test of an optimal growth model. The American Economic Review 92 (3), 549–570.

Levine, S.S., Bernard, M., Nagel, R., 2017. Strategic intelligence: the cognitive capability to anticipate competitor behavior. Strategic Management Journal 38 (12), 2390–2423.

Marcet, A., Sargent, T.J., 1989. Convergence of least squares learning mechanisms in self-referential linear stochastic models. Journal of Economic Theory 48 (2), 337–368.

Maskin, E., Tirole, J., 1987. Correlated equilibria and sunspots. Journal of Economic Theory 43, 364–373.

Matsui, A., Matsuyama, K., 1995. An approach to equilibrium selection. Journal of Economic Theory 65 (2), 415–434.

Matsuyama, K., 1991. Increasing returns, industrialization, and indeterminacy of equilibrium. The Quarterly Journal of Economics 106 (2), 617–650.

Matsuyama, K., 1992. Custom Versus Fashion: Path-Dependence and Limit Cycles in a Random Matching Game. Discussion Paper 1030. Department of Economics, Northwestern University.

Mauersberger, F., 2016. Monetary Policy Rules in a Non-Rational World: A Macroeconomic Experiment. Columbia Working Paper Series.

Mauersberger, F., 2018. Thompson Sampling: Endogenously Random Behavior in Games and Markets. SSRN Working Paper.

McKelvey, R.D., Palfrey, T.R., 1995. Quantal response equilibria for normal form games. Games and Economic Behavior 10 (1), 6–38.

Milgrom, P., Roberts, J., 1990. Rationalizability, learning and equilibrium in games with strategic complementarities. Econometrica 58, 1255–1277.

Milgrom, P., Roberts, J., 1991. Adaptive and sophisticated learning in normal form games. Games and Economic Behavior 3, 82–100.

Mitzkewitz, M., Nagel, R., 1993. Experimental results on ultimatum games with incomplete information. International Journal of Game Theory 22, 171–198.

Monaco, A.J., Sabarwal, T., 2016. Games with strategic complements and substitutes. Economic Theory 62 (1–2), 65–91.

Morris, S., 2014. Coordination, timing and common knowledge. Research in Economics 68 (4), 306–314.

Morris, S., Shin, H.S., 1998. Unique equilibrium in a model of self-fulfilling currency attacks. The American Economic Review 88 (3), 587–597.

Morris, S., Shin, H.S., 2001. Rethinking multiple equilibria in macroeconomic modeling. In: NBER Macroeconomics Annual 2000, vol. 15. MIT Press, pp. 139–182.

Morris, S., Shin, H.S., 2002. Social value of public information. The American Economic Review 92 (5), 1521–1534.

Moulin, H., 1986. Game Theory for the Social Sciences. NYU Press.

Müller, J., Schwieren, C., 2011. More than meets the eye: an eye-tracking experiment on the beauty contest game. Mimeo.

Nagel, R., 1993. Experimental Results on Interactive Competitive Guessing. Discussion Paper No. B-236. University of Bonn.

Nagel, R., 1995. Unraveling in guessing games: an experimental study. The American Economic Review 85, 1313–1326.

Nagel, R., 2018. The rational man as a tuning fork. https://www.upf.edu/documents/8394861/161895668/a+change+-+the+rational+man+as+a+tuning+fork.pdf/81440ce1-967e-82f6-3acd-5ba1bd287ef7.

Nagel, R., Bayona, A., Kheirandish, R., Mousavi, S., 2016. Reinhard Selten, the dualist. In: Frantz, R., Chen, S.H., Dopfer, K., Heukelom, F., Mousavi, S. (Eds.), Routledge Handbook of Behavioral Economics.

Nagel, R., Bosch-Domenech, A., Charness, G., Garcia-Montalvo, J., Hurkens, S., Lopez Nicholas, A., Matthies, N., Rockenbach, B., Satorra, A., Selten, R., Thaler, R.H., 2018. Dataset One, Two, (Three), Infinity, …: Newspaper and Lab Beauty-Contest Experiments. https://x-econ.org/xecon/#!Detail/10.23663/x2544.

Nagel, R., Bühren, C., Frank, B., 2017. Inspired and inspiring: Hervé Moulin and the discovery of the beauty-contest game. Mathematical Social Sciences 90, 191–207.

Nagel, R., Vriend, N., 1999. An experimental study of adaptive behavior in an oligopolistic market game. Journal of Evolutionary Economics 9, 27–65.

Nash, J., 1951. Non-cooperative games. Annals of Mathematics, 286–295.

Nerlove, M., 1958. Adaptive expectations and cobweb phenomena. The Quarterly Journal of Economics 72, 227–240.

Niederle, M., 2016. Gender. In: Kagel, J., Roth, A. (Eds.), Handbook of Experimental Economics, vol. 2.

Niederle, M., Segal, C., Vesterlund, L., 2013. How costly is diversity? Affirmative action in light of gender differences in competitiveness. Management Science 59, 1–16.

Obstfeld, M., 1996. Models of currency with self-fulfilling features. European Economic Review 40, 1037–1047.

Ochs, J., 1995. Coordination problems. In: Kagel, John H., Roth, Alvin E. (Eds.), Handbook of Experimental Economics, pp. 195–251.

Orland, A., Roos, M.W., 2013. The New Keynesian Phillips curve with myopic agents. Journal of Economic Dynamics and Control 37 (11), 2270–2286.

Östling, R., Wang, J.T., Chou, E.Y., Camerer, C.F., 2011. Testing game theory in the field: Swedish LUPI lottery games. American Economic Journal: Microeconomics 3, 1–33.

Oxford English Dictionary Online, 2018. Oxford University Press. http://www.oed.com. (Accessed 23 March 2018).

Palacios-Huerta, I., 2003. Professionals play minimax. The Review of Economic Studies 70 (2), 395–415.

Palfrey, T.R., 2016. Experiments in political economy. In: Kagel, J., Roth, A. (Eds.), Handbook of Experimental Economics, vol. 2, pp. 347–434.

Pfajfar, D., Zakelj, B., 2014. Experimental evidence on expectation formation. Journal of Economic Dynamics and Control 44, 147–168.

Plott, C.R., Smith, V.L., 1978. An experimental examination of two exchange institutions. The Review of Economic Studies 45 (1), 133–153.

Poe, E.A., 1958. The purloined letter. In: The Complete Tales and Poems of Edgar Allen Poe. Random House, NY, pp. 215–216.

Raafat, R.M., Chater, N., Frith, C., 2009. Herding in humans. Trends in Cognitive Sciences 13, 420–428.

Rabin, M., 1993. Incorporating fairness into game theory and economics. The American Economic Review 83, 1281–1302.

Rabin, M., 2002. Inference by believers in the law of small numbers. The Quarterly Journal of Economics 117, 775–816.

Rapoport, A., Guyer, M., Gordon, D., 1976. The 2x2 Game. The University of Michigan Press, Ann Arbor.

Rochet, J.-C., Vives, X., 2004. Coordination failures and the lender of last resort: was Bagehot right after all? Journal of the European Economic Association 2, 1116–1147.

Rogers, B.W., Palfrey, T.R., Camerer, C.F., 2009. Heterogeneous quantal response equilibrium and cognitive hierarchies. Journal of Economic Theory 144 (4), 1440–1467.

Roos, M.W., Luhan, W.J., 2013. Information, learning and expectations in an experimental model economy. Economica 80 (319), 513–531.

Rose, T., 2016. The End of Average: How to Succeed in a World That Values Sameness. Penguin, UK.

Roth, A., 2016. Experiments in market design. In: Kagel, J., Roth, A. (Eds.), Handbook of Experimental Economics, vol. 2, pp. 290–346.

Roth, A., Erev, I., 1995. Learning in extensive-form games: experimental data and simple dynamic models in the intermediate term. Games and Economic Behavior 8, 164–212.

Roth, A., Marilda, A., Sotomayor, O., 1990. Two-Sided Matching. A Study in Game-Theoretic Modeling and Analysis. Cambridge University Press.

Roth, A., Prasnikar, V., Okuno-Fujiwara, M., Zamir, S., 1991. Bargaining and market behavior in Jerusalem, Ljubljana, Pittsburgh, and Tokyo: an experimental study. The American Economic Review 81, 1068.

Rubinstein, A., 1982. Perfect equilibrium in a bargaining model. Econometrica, 97–109.

Rubinstein, A., 2007. Instinctive and cognitive reasoning: a study of response times. The Economic Journal 117 (523), 1243–1259.

Rubinstein, A., Tversky, A., 1993. Naive Strategies in Zero-Sum Games. Working Paper 17-93. The Sackler Institute of Economic Studies.

Rubinstein, A., Tversky, A., Heller, D., 1996. Naïve strategies in competitive games. In: Albers, W., Güth, W., Hammerstein, P., Moldovanu, B., van Damme, E. (Eds.), Understanding Strategic Interaction – Essays in Honor of Reinhard Selten. Springer-Verlag, Berlin, pp. 394–402.

Sargent, T.J., 1993. Bounded Rationality in Macroeconomics. Clarendon Press, Oxford.

Sauermann, H., Selten, R., 1959. Ein Oligopolexperiment. Zeitschrift für die Gesamte Staatswissenschaft (Journal of Institutional and Theoretical Economics) 3, 427–471.

Sbriglia, P., 2008. Revealing the depth of reasoning in p-beauty contest games. Experimental Economics 11 (2), 107–121.

Schaal, E., Taschereau-Dumouchel, M., 2015. Coordinating business cycles. Mimeo. NYU.

Schelling, Thomas, 1960. The Strategy of Conflict. Harvard University Press, Cambridge, MA.

Selten, R., 1965. Spieltheoretische Behandlung eines Oligopolmodells mit Nachfrageträgheit: Bestimmung des dynamischen Preisgleichgewichts. Zeitschrift für die Gesamte Staatswissenschaft (Journal of Institutional and Theoretical Economics) 121, 301–324.

Selten, R., 1967. Die Strategiemethode zur Erforschung des eingeschränkt rationalen Verhaltens im Rahmen eines Oligopolexperiments. In: Sauermann, H. (Ed.), Beiträge zur experimentellen Wirtschaftsforschung. Mohr, Tübingen, pp. 136–168.

Selten, R., 1975. Reexamination of the perfectness concept for equilibrium points in extensive games. International Journal of Game Theory 4 (1), 25–55.

Selten, R., 1991. Anticipatory learning in two-person games. In: Selten, Reinhard (Ed.), Game Equilibrium Models I: Evolution and Game Dynamics. Springer, New York, Berlin, London, Tokyo, pp. 98–154.

Selten, R., Mitzkewitz, M., Uhlich, G.R., 1997. Duopoly strategies programmed by experienced players. Econometrica, 517–555.

Selten, R., Pittnauer, S., Hoehnisch, M., 2012. Dealing with dynamic decision problems when knowledge of the environment is limited: an approach based on goal systems. Journal of Behavioral Decision Making 25, 443–457.

Selten, R., Stoecker, R., 1986. End behavior in sequences of finite Prisoner's Dilemma supergames: a learning theory approach. Journal of Economic Behavior & Organization 7 (1), 47–70.

Shapiro, D., Shi, X., Zillante, A., 2014. Level-k reasoning in a generalized beauty contest. Games and Economic Behavior 86, 308–329.

Simon, H.A., 1996. The Sciences of the Artificial. MIT Press.

Sims, C.A., 2003. Implications of rational inattention. Journal of Monetary Economics 50 (3), 665–690.

Slonim, R.L., 2005. Competing against experienced and inexperienced players. Experimental Economics, 55–75.

Smith, A., Lohrenz, T., King, J., Montague, P.R., Camerer, C.F., 2014. Irrational exuberance and neural crash warning signals during endogenous experimental market bubbles. Proceedings of the National Academy of Sciences 111 (29), 10503–10508.

Smith, V.L., 1962. An experimental study of competitive market behavior. Journal of Political Economy 70 (2), 111–137.

Smith, V.L., Suchanek, G.L., Williams, A.W., 1988. Bubbles, crashes, and endogenous expectations in experimental spot asset markets. Econometrica 56, 1119–1151.

Sonnemans, J., Tuinstra, J., 2010. Positive expectations feedback experiments and number guessing games as models of financial markets. Journal of Economic Psychology 31, 964–984.

Stahl, D.O., 1993. Evolution of smart$_n$ players. Games and Economic Behavior 5 (4), 604–617.

Stahl, D.O., 1996. Boundedly rational rule learning in a guessing game. Games and Economic Behavior 16 (2), 303–330.

Stahl, D.O., Wilson, P.W., 1994. Experimental evidence on players' models of other players. Journal of Economic Behavior & Organization 25 (3), 309–327.

Stahl, D.O., Wilson, P.W., 1995. On players' models of other players: theory and experimental evidence. Games and Economic Behavior 10, 218–254.

Steele, C.M., 1997. A threat in the air: how stereotypes shape intellectual identity and performance. The American Psychologist 52 (6), 613–629.

Strzalecki, Tomasz, 2014. Depth of reasoning and higher-order beliefs. Journal of Economic Behavior & Organization, 108–122.

Sunder, S., 1995. Experimental asset markets: a survey. In: Kagel, John H., Roth, Alvin E. (Eds.), Handbook of Experimental Economics.

Sunder, S., 2007. What have we learned from experimental finance? In: Developments on Experimental Economics. Springer, Berlin, Heidelberg, pp. 91–100.

Sutan, A., Willinger, M., 2009. Guessing with negative feedback: an experiment. Journal of Economic Dynamics and Control 33 (5), 1123–1133.

Szkup, M., Trevino, I., 2011. Costly Information Acquisition in a Speculative Attack: Theory and Experiments. Working paper.

Taylor, S.E., Thompson, S.C., 1982. Stalking the elusive vividness effect. Psychological Review 89 (2), 155–181.

Topkis, D., 1979. Equilibrium points in non-zero sum n-person submodular games. SIAM Journal on Control and Optimization 17 (6), 773–787.

Tverksy, A., Kahneman, D., 1991. Loss aversion in riskless choice: a reference-dependent model. The Quarterly Journal of Economics 106, 1039–1061.

Tversky, A., Kahneman, D., 1974. Judgment under uncertainty: heuristics and biases. Science 185, 1124–1131.

Van Huyck, J., Battalio, R., Beil, R., 1990. Tacit coordination games, strategic uncertainty, and coordination failure. The American Economic Review 80, 234.

Van Huyck, J., Battalio, R., Beil, R., 1991. Strategic uncertainty, equilibrium selection, and coordination failure in average opinion games. The Quarterly Journal of Economics 106, 885–910.

Vesterlund, L., 2016. Using experimental methods to understand why and how we give to charity. In: Kagel, J., Roth, A. (Eds.), Handbook of Experimental Economics, vol. 2.

Vives, X., 1990. Nash equilibrium with strategic complementarities. Journal of Mathematical Economics 19, 305–321.

Vives, X., 2010. Information and Learning in Markets: The Impact of Market Microstructure. Princeton University Press, Princeton and Oxford.

Walker, M., Wooders, J., 2001. Minimax play at Wimbledon. The American Economic Review 91 (5), 1521–1538.

Walsh, C.E., 2010. Monetary Theory and Policy, 3rd edition. MIT Press, Cambridge.

Weber, R., Camerer, C.F., Rottenstreich, Y., Knez, M., 2001. The illusion of leadership in weak-link coordination games. Organizational Science 12, 582–598.

Weitzman, M.L., 1982. Increasing returns and the foundations of unemployment theory. The Economic Journal 92, 787–804.

Woodford, M., 1990. Learning to believe in sunspots. Econometrica 58, 277–307.

Woodford, M., 2003. Interest and Prices: Foundations of a Theory of Monetary Policy. Princeton University Press.

Woodford, M., 2018. Monetary Policy Analysis when Planning Horizons Are Finite. Working paper prepared for the NBER Macroeconomics Annual Conference.

Zermelo, E., 1904. Beweis, dass jede Menge wohlgeordnet werden kann (reprint). Mathematische Annalen 59, 514–516.

NETWORKS

Empirical Analyses of Networks in Finance

11

Giulia Iori[*,1], Rosario N. Mantegna[†,‡,§]

*Department of Economics, City, University of London, London, United Kingdom
†Department of Physics and Chemistry, University of Palermo, Palermo, Italy
‡Department of Computer Science, University College London, London, United Kingdom
§Complexity Science Hub Vienna, Vienna, Austria
1Corresponding author: e-mail address: g.iori@city.ac.uk

CONTENTS

Handbook of Computational Economics, Volume 4, ISSN 1574-0021, https://doi.org/10.1016/bs.hescom.2018.02.005

1 INTRODUCTION

At the end of the 90s of the last century a new multidisciplinary research area took off. This research area is today called "network science". Network science is a multidisciplinary research area analyzing and modeling complex networks from the perspective of several disciplines. The major ones are computer science, economics, mathematics, sociology and psychology, and statistical physics.

The onset of the financial crisis of 2007 triggered an enormous interest in applying networks concepts and tools, originating from several different disciplines, to study the role of interlinkages in financial systems on financial stability. The vast literature covers today both theoretical and empirical aspects. It is out of the scope of the present review to cover all the research lines today present in the analysis and modeling of economic and financial systems with network concept and with tools designed specifically for this concept. We will focus instead on a selection of studies that perform empirical analyses of some crucial areas of the financial system.

Our review complements others that have been published in the last few years. Allen and Babus (2008) review theoretical work on networks with application to systemic risk, investment decisions, corporate finance, and microfinance. Bougheas and Kirman (2015) review theoretical and empirical studies on systemic risk that implement networks and complex analysis techniques. Iori and Porter (2016) review agent based models of asset markets, including heterogeneous agents and networks. Grilli et al. (2017) focus on recent theoretical work related to credit networks, discussing in particular agent based computational approaches. Benoit et al. (2017) review studies that identify sources of systemic risk both using regulatory data and market data to produce measures of systemic risk. Aymanns et al. (2018) in this volume review computational approaches to financial stability considering multiple channels of contagion such counterparty risk, funding risk, and common assets holding. While there is some overlap between these papers and the present review, our review has a more empirical focus, exploring a broad range of methodologies that have been applied to the study of financial networks, such as the investigation and modeling of the interbank market, network reconstruction techniques, multilayer characterization of interbank exposures, indirect channels of contagion, proximity based networks, association networks, and statistically validated networks.

Specifically, the empirical studies of the interbank market will be discussed in detail because this market is of major interest for studies of systemic risk of national financial systems and of the global financial system. Recent studies of the systemic risk of the banking system of different countries and of the global financial system have also shown the importance of indirect links present between financial actors. The intensity of these indirect links are for example associated with the degree of similarity of the portfolio of assets owned by the financial institutions. An action of a distressed bank acting on a specific asset and triggering a fire sale of the asset can in fact impact other financial actors even in the absence of direct financial contracts between financial entities. Moreover, the understanding of the dynamic of contagion of distress has promoted the study of networks of influence between financial actors. For the above reasons in finance we have empirical studies covering four distinct types of networks. They are (i) the customary event or relationship networks as, for example, networks of market transactions or networks of the interbank loans exchanged between pairs of banks, (ii) proximity based network, i.e. networks obtained starting from a proximity measure often filtered with a network filtering methodology able to highlight the most significant pairwise similarity or dissimilarity present in the system, (iii) association network, i.e. networks where a link between two financial actors is set if a statistical test against a null hypothesis is rejected for a pair of financial actors (one example of association network is a network summarizing the Granger-causality relationships between all pairs of financial actors of a given financial system), and (iv) statistically validated networks, i.e. event or relationship networks where a subset of links is selected according to a statistical validation of each link performed by considering the rejection of a random null hypothesis assuming the same heterogeneity as observed in financial complex systems.

The review is organized as follows. Section 2 provides a historical perspective of the development of the new interdisciplinary research area of network science. Section 3 discusses the network approaches to the study of the stability of financial systems with a special focus on the interbank market. The section discusses the structure of national interbank markets, typical approaches in the setting and analysis of stress test scenarios, the detection of systemically important financial institutions, and the modeling of lending relationships. The methodological aspects that are considered are related to the problem of network reconstruction and to the multilayer nature of financial networks. Section 3 discusses the classes of financial networks that are different from relationship or event networks. Specifically, it discusses proximity based networks, association networks, and statistically validated networks. Contributions originating from network science, econophysics, and econometrics are illustrated and discussed. Section 4 discusses the indirect channels of contagion with an emphasis on portfolios overlap and firm–bank credit relationships. In Section 5 we conclude with a discussion on the state of the art and perspectives of empirical investigations performed in economic and financial systems.

The review also contains two appendices written to make the chapter self-contained so that readers not directly working in the field of network science could find a guide about tools and concepts that are usually defined and used in different disciplines. Appendix A briefly describes concepts and definitions used in the study of complex networks and provide a basic vocabulary needed to understand the following sections. In Appendix B we recall some econometrics systemic risk measures that have been also used and discussed in the systemic risk studies performed using network concepts.

2 A BRIEF HISTORICAL PERSPECTIVE ABOUT THE USE OF NETWORK SCIENCE IN ECONOMICS AND FINANCE

The main driver of the development of the new research area of network science was originally the invention of the World Wide Web and the rapid development and use of it that quickly involved hundreds of millions of people. Another strong input came in 2003–2004 with the creation of the first social network Myspace and the extraordinary success of Facebook. Studies about so-called complex networks benefited from the knowledge previously accumulated in several distinct disciplines. In mathematics Erdös and Rényi (1960) discovered in the 60s of the last century that a simple random graph presents an emergent phenomenon as a function of the average degree, i.e. the average number of connections each node has in the network. The emergent phenomenon concerns the setting of an infinite spanning component comprising the majority of nodes. In an infinite network this spanning component sets up exactly when the average degree is equal to one and it is absent for values lower than one. In sociology and psychology networks were used to understand social balance (Heider, 1946), social attitude towards the setting of relationships in social networks (Wasserman and Faust, 1994), and some puzzles about social networks as the so-called small world effect (Travers and Milgram, 1967). In statistical physics a pioneering paper was the one on the small world effect (Watts and Strogatz, 1998). Another seminal paper in statistical physics was the paper of Barabási and Albert that introduced the concept of scale free network and presented the preferential attachment model (Barabási and Albert, 1999). In computer science the growing importance of the physical Internet motivated the empirical analysis of it. This analysis was showing that the degree distribution of the network has a power-law behavior (Faloutsos et al., 1999). During the same years a small group of computer scientists focused on the properties of information networks with the aim of finding new solutions for the development of efficient search engines of the World Wide Web. Prominent examples of these efforts are the papers of Marchiori (1997) and Kleinberg (1998) that paved the way to the famous PageRank algorithm (Brin and Page, 1998). An early use of statistical physics concepts in the development of models for social networks can be encountered in the development of the so-called exponential random graphs (Holland and Leinhardt, 1981; Strauss, 1986).

The use of network concept in economics and finance was sporadic and ancillary during the last century. A prominent exception to this status was the model about the process of reaching a consensus in a social network introduced by the statistician Morris H. DeGroot (DeGroot, 1974). Another classic area where the role of a social network was considered instrumental to correctly interpret empirical observations was the area of the modeling of the labor market. In fact the type of a social network that it is present among job searchers and their acquaintances turned out affecting the probability of getting a job of the different social actors (Granovetter, 1973; Boorman, 1975; Calvo-Armengol and Jackson, 2004). Another pioneering empirical study used the concept of network to describe the social structure of a stock options market. The study concluded that distinct social structural patterns of traders affected the direction and magnitude of option price volatility (Baker, 1984).

The interest about the use of network concepts in the modeling of economic and financial systems started to growth at the beginning of this century and become widespread with the onset of the 2007 financial crisis. A pioneering study was published about the stability of the financial systems (Allen and Gale, 2000). During the first years of this century the studies of economic and financial systems performed by economists with network concepts can be classified in two broad areas (Allen and Babus, 2008). The first area concerns studies primarily devoted to the theoretical and empirical investigation of network formation resulting from the rational decisions of economic actors and from their convergence to an equilibrium presenting a Paretian optimum (Goyal and Vega-Redondo, 2005; Vega-Redondo, 2007; Jackson, 2008; Goyal, 2012). Another line of research initiated by the pioneering work of DeGroot (1974) was considering the problem of learning in a distributed system. In parallel to these attempts scholars economists and financial experts in collaboration with colleagues having a statistical physics background performed a series of studies focused on the topological structure of some important financial networks. The most investigated network was the network of interbank credit relationships (Boss et al., 2004; Iori et al., 2006; Soramäki et al., 2007). Another research area focused on the development of methods able to provide proximity based networks starting from empirical financial time series (Mantegna, 1999; Onnela et al., 2004; Tumminello et al., 2005) or generated by financial models (Bonanno et al., 2003).

3 NETWORK APPROACHES TO FINANCIAL STABILITY: THE INTERBANK MARKET

Financial systems have grown increasingly complex and interlinked. A number of academics and policy-makers have pointed out the strong potential of network representation[1] and analysis to capture the intricate structure of connectedness between financial institutions and sectors of the economy. Understanding of the growth, structure, dynamics, and functioning of these networks and their mutual interrelationships is essential in order to monitor and control the build-up of systemic risk, and prevent and mitigate the impact of financial crises.

The recent global financial crisis has illustrated how financial networks can amplify shocks as they spill over through the financial system, by creating feedback loops that can turn relatively minor events into major crises. This feedback between the micro and macro states is typical of complex adaptive dynamical systems. The regulatory efforts to maintain financial stability and mitigate the impact of finan-

---

[1] In financial networks nodes usually represent financial agents such as banks, non-bank intermediaries, firms, investors, and central banks. The edges may represent credit relationships, exposures between banks, liquidity flows, etc.

cial crises has led to a shift from micro-prudential to macro-prudential regulatory approaches. Traditional micro-prudential approaches have relied on ensuring the stability of individual financial institutions and limiting idiosyncratic risk. However, while financial market's participants have clear incentives to manage their own risk and prevent their own collapse, they have limited understanding of the potential effects of their actions on other institutions. The recent emphasis on the adoption of a macro-prudential framework for financial regulation stems from the recognition that systemic risk depends on the collective behavior of market participants acting as a negative externality that needs to be controlled by monitoring the system as a whole. The new regulatory agenda has also brought to the fore the concept that institutions may be "too interconnected to fail", in addition of being "too big to fail", and the need for methods and tools that can help to better identify and manage systemically important financial institutions.

Network analysis in finance has been used to address two fundamental questions: (i) what is the effect of the network structure on the propagation of shocks?, and (ii) what is the rational for financial institutions to form links?, with the ultimate goal of identifying the incentives, in the form of regulatory policies, that would induce the reorganization of financial system into network structures that are more resilient to systemic risk. The first question is the one that has been more extensively studied in the literature. Several authors have analyzed how the financial network structure affect the way contagion propagates through the banking system and how the fragility of the system depends on the location of distressed institutions in the network. Other authors have directed their efforts to develop algorithms for the reconstruction of bilateral exposures form aggregate balance sheet information. A number of papers have focused on detecting long lasting relationships among banks in an effort to understand the determinants of links formation. Others have looked at possible network location advantages. A smaller but growing number of papers have focused on how policy and regulations can influence the shape of the network in order to minimize the costs of systemic risk. Theoretical papers are briefly reviewed in Section 3.1. While these papers provide important insights, the connectivity structure of real financial networks departs significantly from the stylized structures assumed, or endogenously derived, by the seminal paper of Allen and Gale (2000) and subsequent work. Given the empirical emphasis of this review, the characterization of real, or reconstructed, networks of interbank exposure and empirical approaches to estimate the danger of contagion owing to exposures in the interbank bank is the main focus of Sections 3.2 to 3.6. Section 3.7 summarizes complementary approaches developed to quantify systemic risk based on econometric methods while potential benefit arising from location advantages are discussed in Section 3.8.

3.1 INTERBANK NETWORKS CONNECTIVITY AND CONTAGION: THEORETICAL CONTRIBUTIONS

Theoretical work has produced important insights to better understand the role of markets interconnectivity on financial stability. Allen and Gale (2000) were the first to show that interbank relations may create fragility in response to unanticipated shocks. In their seminal paper Allen and Gale suggested that a more equal distribution of interbank claims enhances the resilience of the system to the insolvency of any individual bank. Their argument was that in a more densely interconnected financial network, the losses of a distressed bank are divided among more creditors, reducing the impact of negative shocks to individual institutions on the rest of the system. In contrast to this view, however, others have suggested, via computational models, that dense interconnections may function as a destabilizing force (Iori et al., 2006; Nier et al., 2007; Gai and Kapadia, 2010; Battiston et al., 2012; Anand et al., 2012; Lenzu and Tedeschi, 2012; Georg, 2013; Roukny et al., 2013). Haldane (2013) has reconciled these findings by observing that highly interconnected financial networks are "robust-yet-fragile" in the sense that connections serve as shock-absorbers within a certain range but beyond it interconnections facilitate financial distress to spread through the banking system and fragility prevails.

More recent theoretical papers have confirmed these earlier computational results. Glasserman and Young (2015) show that spillover effects are most significant when node sizes are heterogeneous and the originating node is highly leveraged and has high financial connectivity. The authors also show the importance of mechanisms that magnify shocks beyond simple spillover effects. These mechanisms include bankruptcy costs, and mark-to-market losses resulting from credit quality deterioration or a loss of confidence.

Acemoglu et al. (2015) focus on the likelihood of systemic failures due to contagion of counterparty risk. The paper shows that the extent of financial contagion exhibits a phase transition: when the magnitude of negative shocks is below a certain threshold, a more diversified pattern of interbank liabilities leads to a less fragile financial system. However, as the magnitude or the number of negative shocks crosses certain thresholds dense interconnections serve as a mechanism for the propagation of shocks, leading to a more fragile financial system. While Acemoglu et al. (2015) characterize the best and worst networks, from a social planner's perspective, for moderate and very large shocks. Elliott et al. (2014) show how the probability of cascades and their extent depend, for intermediate shocks and for a variety of networks, on integration (how much banks rely on other banks) and diversification (number of banks on which a given bank's liabilities are spread over). Their results highlight that intermediate levels of diversification and integration can be the most problematic. Cabrales et al. (2017) investigate the socially optimal design of financial networks in diverse scenarios and their relationship with individual incentives. In their paper they generalize the Acemoglu et al. (2015) results by considering a richer set of possible shocks distributions and show how the optimal financial structure varies in response to the characteristics of these distributions. The overall picture that emerges from this literature is that the density of linkages has a non-monotonic impact on systemic stability and its effect varies with the nature of the shock, the heterogeneity of the players, and the state of the economy.

A large number of theoretical papers based on Agent Based simulations have investigated how the topological structure of the matrix of direct and indirect exposures between banks affects systemic risk. For a recent review of this literature we refer the interested readers to Grilli et al. (2017).

A different branch of the theoretical literature focuses on network formation mechanisms that reproduce features of trading decisions observed empirically. Of particular relevance to interbank lending markets, are theories on the formation of core–periphery networks.[2]

Anufriev et al. (2016) build a model of endogenous lending/borrowing decisions, which induce a network. By extending the notion of pairwise stability of Jackson and Wolinsky (1996) they allow the banks to make binary decision to form a link, which represents a loan, jointly with the direction of the loan, its amount, and its interest rate. In equilibrium, a bipartite network is found in which borrowers and lenders form generically a unique component, which well represents interbank markets when aggregating transactions at the daily scale. van der Leij et al. (2016) provide an explanation for the emergence of core–periphery structure by using network formation theory and find that while a core–periphery network cannot be unilaterally stable when banks are homogeneous such structure can form endogenously, if allowing for heterogeneity among banks in size. Heterogeneity is indeed a common characteristics of models that generate stable core–periphery structures. In Farboodi (2015) banks are heterogeneous in their investment opportunities, and they compete for intermediation benefits. A core–periphery network is formed with investment banks taking place at the core, as they are able to offer better intermediation rates. In Bedayo et al. (2016) intermediaries bargain sequentially and bilaterally on a path between two traders. Agents are heterogeneous in their time discounting. A core–periphery network is formed with impatient agents in the core. In Castiglionesi and Navarro (2016) heterogeneity in investments arises endogenously with some banks investing in safe projects, and others in risky projects. The interbank network allows banks to coinsure future idiosyncratic liquidity needs, however, establishing a link with banks that invest in the risky project, reduces the ex-ante probability of serving its own depositors. If counterparty risk is sufficiently high, the trade off leads to a core–periphery like structure. The core includes all the banks that invest in the safe project and form a complete network structure among themselves while the periphery includes all the gambling banks. In Chang and Zhang (2016) banks are heterogeneous in the volatility of their liquidity needs. More volatile banks trade with more stable banks, creating a multi-tier financial system with the most stable banks in the core. However, banks do not have incentives to link with other banks in the same tier, and hence, their network structure is more like a multipartite network than a core–periphery network.

---

[2]A network core–periphery structure indicates that some nodes are part of a densely connected core, and others are part of a sparsely connected periphery. Core nodes are well-connected to peripheral nodes and peripheral nodes are not directly connected among them.

3.2 THE STRUCTURE OF NATIONAL INTERBANK NETWORKS

The mapping of interbank networks has been done for several countries, notably by Sheldon and Maurer (1998) for Switzerland; Inaoka et al. (2004) for Japan (BoJ-NET); Furfine (2003), Soramäki et al. (2007), and Bech and Atalay (2010) for the US Federal funds market (Fedwire); Boss et al. (2004), Elsinger et al. (2006), and Puhr et al. (2012) for Austria; Degryse and Nguyen (2007) for Belgium; van Lelyveld and Liedorp (2006) and Propper et al. (2013) for the Netherlands; Upper and Worms (2004) and Craig and von Peter (2014) for Germany; De Masi et al. (2006), Iori et al. (2008), and Finger et al. (2013) for the Italian based e-MID; Cont and Wagalath (2013), Tabak et al. (2010a) for Brazil; Wells (2004) and Langfield et al. (2014) for the United Kingdom; Martinez-Jaramillo et al. (2014) for Mexico; León (2015) for Colombia. In Fig. 1 we show an example of the typical shape of the interbank network. Specifically, we show the Austrian interbank market investigated in Boss et al. (2004). These studies of the interbank market have revealed a number of stylized facts and regularities. Interbank networks are sparse and display fat tailed degree distributions, with most banks attracting a few connections, and few banks concentrating most of the connections. While some papers identify a scale-free degree distribution (Boss et al., 2004; Inaoka et al., 2004; Soramäki et al., 2007; Propper et al., 2013; Bech and Atalay, 2010; Bargigli, 2014; León, 2015), others have reported heterogeneity but observe a departure from a strict power-law distribution of links (Martinez-Jaramillo et al., 2014; Craig and von Peter, 2014; Fricke and Lux, 2014; in't Veld and van Lelyveld, 2014) and propose to model the interbank market in terms of a core periphery network.

It might be worth noting that the fact that it is difficult to discriminate between a power-law scale free distribution and a core periphery network is not an accident of the empirical investigations performed in the interbank market. There are two important reasons explaining why it might be so difficult to discriminate between the two different models in empirical data. The first reason is that in empirical data a finite cut-off of a scale free distribution is unavoidable in finite systems and therefore empirically detected scale free distribution are typically observed only for a limited number of decades of the degree. The second reason is a theoretical reason that it is related to a mathematical property associated with a scale free system. In fact it has been proved by Chung and Lu (2002) that power-law random graphs with degree distribution proportional to $k^{-\beta}$ with exponent β in the interval [2, 3] (including therefore scale free networks) almost surely contain a dense subgraph (i.e. a core) that has short distance to almost all other nodes. Therefore, also random scale free networks are almost surely characterized by the presence of a core in it. This fact makes the empirical discrimination between a scale free and a core periphery model difficult to asses because, due to the presence of a "core" also in the scale free network, core periphery or scale free can be quantified closely by a fitness indicator (see, for example, the comparison provided in Craig and von Peter, 2014 by using data of the German interbank market and simulations).

Interbank networks show disassortative mixing with respect to the bank size, so small banks tend to trade with large banks and vice versa; clustering coefficients are

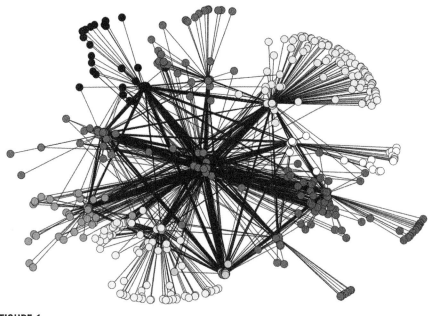

FIGURE 1

The interbank market network of Austria. Data are from September 2002. Nodes are labeled with a gray scale grouping banks according to regional and sectorial organization. Reproduced from Boss et al. (2004).

usually small and interbank networks satisfy the small-world property.[3] Tabak et al. (2010a), Craig and von Peter (2014), Fricke and Lux (2014), and in't Veld and van Lelyveld (2014) point to a correlation between the size of financial institutions and their position in the interbank funds hierarchy in the respective Brazilian, German, Italian, and Dutch interbank markets. In these markets large banks tend to be in the core, whereas small banks are found in the periphery. The cores of the networks, composed of the most connected banks, processed a very high proportion of the total value of credit.

The dynamical evolution of interbank networks, as the subprime crisis unfolded, has been closely monitored in an attempt to identify early-warning signals of the building up of systemic risk. Fricke and Lux (2015) and Squartini et al. (2013) have analyzed respectively the e-MID market and the Dutch market. In both markets the networks only display an abrupt topological change in 2008, providing a clear, but unpredictable, signature of the crisis. Nonetheless, when controlling for banks' degree heterogeneity, Squartini et al. (2013) show that higher-order network properties, such as dyadic and triadic motifs, revealed a gradual transition into the crisis, starting

---

[3] A network is a small world network if the mean geodesic distance between pairs of nodes grows no faster than logarithmically as the number of nodes while the average clustering coefficient is not negligible.

already in 2005. Although these results provide some evidence of early warning precursors based on network properties, at least for the Dutch interbank market, a clear economic interpretation for the observed patterns is missing.

3.3 **MULTILAYER NETWORKS**

When institutions are interconnected trough different types of financial contracts, such as loans of different maturities, derivatives, foreign exchange and other securities, it is critical to go beyond single-layer networks to properly address systemic risk. Multilayer networks explicitly incorporate multiple channels of connectivity and constitute the natural environment to describe systems interconnected through different types of exposures.

Taking into account the multilayer nature of networks can modify the conclusions on stability reached by considering individual network layers (see Boccaletti et al., 2014 and Kivela et al., 2014 for recent reviews). Contrary to what one would expect, the literature shows that the coupling of scale free networks may yield a less robust network (Buldyrev et al., 2010). In the case of single-layer networks, scale free networks are known to be much more robust to random failures than networks with a finite second moment e.g. of Poisson networks. Indeed, scale free networks continue to have a giant component even if most of the nodes are initially damaged. A finite percolation threshold in these networks is a finite size effect, i.e. the percolation threshold disappears in the limit when the network size becomes large. The robustness of multilayer networks can be evaluated by calculating the size of their mutually connected giant component (MCGC). The MCGC of a multilayer network is the largest component that remains after the random damage propagates back and forth thought the different layers. The percolation threshold for the mutually connected component is finite also for multiplex networks formed by layers of SF networks as in the case of a multiplex in which the layers are formed by Poisson networks. Exceptions to this finding would occur when the number of links (i.e. the degree) of interdependent participants coincides across the layers. That is, scale free networks robustness is likely to be preserved if positively correlated layers exist, such that a high-degree vertex in one layer likely is high-degree in the other layers as well (Kenett et al., 2014).

A number of financial markets have been characterized as multilayer networks. Montagna and Kok (2016) model interbank contagion in the Eurozone with a triple-layer multiplex network consisting of long-term direct bilateral exposures, short-term bilateral exposures, and common exposures to financial assets. Bargigli et al. (2015) examine a unique database of supervisory reports of Italian banks to the Banca d'Italia that includes all interbank bilateral exposures broken down by maturity and by the secured and unsecured nature of the contract. The authors found that layers have different topological properties and persistence over time.

Cont et al. (2013) use a set of different kinds of interbank exposures (i.e. fixed-income instruments, derivatives, borrowing, and lending) and study the potential contagion in the Brazilian market. Poledna et al. (2015) identify four layers of exposure among Mexican banks (unsecured interbank credit, securities, foreign exchange and derivative markets). Aldasoro and Alves (2015) analyze the multiplex networks of exposure among 53 large European banks. Langfield et al. (2014) analyze of different layers of the UK interbank system.

León (2015) studies the interactions of financial institutions on different financial markets in Colombia (sovereign securities market, foreign exchange market, equity, derivative, interbank funds). The approximate scale free connective structure of the Colombia interbank market is preserved across the layers in the multilayer mapping with financial institutions that are "too connected to fail" that are present across many of the network layers. This positive correlated multiplexity, coupled with the ultra-small world nature of the networks analyzed, suggest that the role of too connected financial institutions is critical for the stability of the market, not only at the single layer level, but for the market overall.

While a multilayer representation provides a more accurate characterizing the financial system, studies so far have mostly performed a comparison between the different layers. Future steps would require investigating the interconnections and interdependencies between these different layers and the implications of these interdependencies for financial stability.

3.4 FINANCIAL REGULATIONS AND NETWORK CONTROL

Of critical importance in macro-prudential policy is the identification of key players in the financial network. In September 2009, the G20 leaders requested the Financial Stability Board (FSB)[4] to designate "Global Systemically Important Financial Institutions" (G-SIFIs). As a result, the FSB, IMF, and BIS cooperatively adopted the three valuation points – size, interconnectedness, and substitutability – as the evaluation criterion for G-SIFIs (IMF-BIS-FSB, 2009).

As we have discussed, financial networks are often characterized by skewed degree distributions, with most financial firms displaying few connections, and few financial firms concentrating many connections. In these networks the failure of a participant will have significantly different outcomes depending on which participant is selected. Those participants who are "close" (according to some measure of distance) to all other participants in the network can potentially generate widespread cascading failures if they default. A rising amount of financial literature has encouraged the usage of network metrics of centrality for identifying the institutions that are systemically important (Haldane and May, 2011; León and Murcia, 2013; Markose et al., 2012). In a broad sense, centrality refers to the importance of a node in the network. The centrality indicators typically used are constructed from measures of distance of a bank from the other banks in the network, where distance is expressed in terms of: (1) paths of length one, i.e. the number of incoming or outgoing links, for degree

---

[4]The Financial Stability Board is an international body representing central bankers and international financial bodies such as the Basel Committee on Banking Supervision (BCBS), and its mission is to promote financial stability.

centrality; (2) geodesics (shortest) paths (no vertex is visited more than once), for betweenness; (3) walks (vertices and edges can be visited/traversed multiple times) for eigenvector centrality, Pagerank, Sinkrank, and Katz (see Appendix A for the mathematical definition of commonly used centrality measures). Another popular iterative centrality measure is hub and authority centrality. Acemoglu et al. (2015) introduced the notion of harmonic distance over the financial network to captures the propensity of a bank to be in distress when another bank is in distress. Markose et al. (2012) proposes a measure adapted from epidemiological studies (defined as the maximum eigenvalue for the network of liabilities expressed as a ratio of Tier 1 capital) to identify the most systemic financial institutions and determine the stability of the global OTC derivatives markets. Drehmann and Tarashev (2013) explore two different approaches to measuring systemic importance: one related to banks' participation in systemic events (PA) and another related to their contribution to systemic risk (GCA). The contribution approach is rooted in the Shapley value methodology, first proposed by Shapley (1953) for the allocation of the value created in cooperative games across individual players. Shapley values are portions of system-wide risk that are attributed to individual institutions. Because Shapley values are additive, the sum of these portions across the banks in the system equals exactly the level of system-wide risk. PA assigns a higher (lower) degree of systemic importance to an interbank lender (borrower) than GCA. The reason for this is that PA attributes the risk associated with an interbank transaction entirely to the lending counterparty, i.e. the counterparty that bears this risk and can eventually transfer it onto its creditors in a systemic event. By contrast, GCA splits this risk equally between the two counterparties. GCA is computed by focusing on each subsystem or subgroup of banks that belong to the entire system, and calculating the difference between the risk of this subsystem with and without a particular bank. Averaging such marginal risk contributions across all possible subsystems delivers the systemic importance of the bank.

A novel measure of systemic importance, based on the concept of feedback centrality, is the DebtRank (DR), introduced by Battiston et al. (2012) which measures the fraction of the total economic value that is potentially lost in the case of the distress (and not necessarily default) of a particular node. This method complements traditional approaches by providing a measure of the systemic importance of a bank even when default cascades models predict no impact at all. Applications of DR based stress test analysis (see Thiago et al., 2016 for the Brazilian interbank market, and Battiston et al., 2015 for the Italian interbank market) show that systemically important FIs do not need to be large and that traditional indicators of systemic risk underestimate contagion risk.

The identification of SIFIs is crucial to direct regulatory efforts and, for example, to assess the opportunity to limit institutions' exposures, set up some form of regulatory fees or capital surcharges, or to introduce an insurance fund financed through institution-specific insurance premia (Chan-Lau, 2010). Such an approach has recently also been taken in the IMF's Interim Report for the G20 (IMF, 2010), which outlines that an ideal levy on financial institutions should be based on a network model that would take into account all possible channels of contagion. The new

Basel III rules (Basel Committee on Banking Supervision, 2013) in addition to higher capital requirements with a countercyclical component, and a framework for liquidity regulation, include limiting contagion risk as a new objective, in particular for SIFIs.

Several proposals have emerged with the purpose of creating the right incentives for institutions to control the risk they pose to the financial system. In the existing literature on prudential capital controls (Korinek, 2011), optimal policy measures are derived as tax wedges that could be implemented in a variety of equivalent ways. The opportunity cost of not receiving interest can be viewed as a Pigouvian tax. Along these lines, proposals have emerged to base capital requirements not on the risk of banks assets, but on banks' systemic importance, reflecting the impact their failure would have on the wider banking system and the likelihood of contagious losses occurring. Tarashev et al. (2010) set up a constrained optimization problem in which a policymaker equalizes banks' Shapley values subject to achieving a target level for the expected shortfall of assets to liabilities at the level of the system. Similarly Webber and Willison (2011) solve the constrained optimization problem for a policymaker who seeks to minimize the total level of capital in the UK banking system, subject to meeting its chosen systemic risk target. They show that optimal systemic capital requirements are increasing in balance sheet size (relative to other banks in the system), interconnectedness, and contagious bankruptcy costs. The paper illustrates, however, that risk-based systemic capital requirements derived in this way are procyclical and point to the need of approaches that would be explicitly countercyclical.

Gauthier et al. (2012) use different holdings-based systemic risk measures (e.g., marginal expected shortfall, ΔCoVaR, Shapley value) to reallocate capital in the banking system and to determine macroprudential capital requirements in the Canadian market using credit register data for a system of six banks. Alter et al. (2015) perform a similar exercise and compare the benchmark case, in which capital is allocated based on the risks in individual banks portfolios, and a system-based case, where capital is allocated based on some interbank network centrality metrics. Using the detailed German credit register for estimation, they find that capital rules based on eigenvectors dominate any other centrality measure, saving about 15 percent in expected bankruptcy costs.

Taxes imposed on banks in the form of contributions to a rescue fund have also been suggested. Markose et al. (2012) advocate a stabilization super-spreader fund, derived from her eigen-pair centrality measure. Like a 'bail in' escrow fund, the funds are deployed at the time of potential failure of a financial institution to mitigate tax payer bailouts of the failing bank. Similarly Zlatić et al. (2015) apply DebtRank to model cascade risk in the e-Mid market and determine a Pigouvian taxation to finance a rescue fund, which is used in the case of default of single financial players.

Poledna and Thurner (2016) and Leduc and Thurner (2017) have proposed to use a transaction-specific tax that discriminates among the possible transactions between different lending and borrowing banks. A regulator can use the systemic risk tax (SRT) to select an optimal equilibrium set of transactions that effectively 'rewire' the interbank network so as to make it more resilient to insolvency cascades. The SRT was introduced and its effect simulated using an agent-based model in Poledna and Thurner (2016), while Leduc and Thurner (2017) prove analytically that an SRT can be applied without reducing the total credit volume and thus without making the system less efficient. Using an equilibrium concept inspired by the matching markets literature the paper shows that the SRT induces a unique equilibrium matching of lenders and borrowers that is systemic-risk efficient, while without this SRT multiple equilibrium matchings exist, which are generally inefficient.

3.5 STRESS-TEST SCENARIO ANALYSIS

A number of papers have used counterfactual simulations to test the stability of financial systems and assess the danger of contagion due to credit exposures in national interbank markets. The approach consists in simulating the breakdown of a single, or possibly more, banks and subsequently assess the scope of contagion. The baseline stress-test model runs as follows: a first bank defaults due to an exogenous shock; the credit event causes losses to other banks via direct exposures in the interbank market and one or more additional banks may default as a result; if this happens, a new round of losses is triggered. The simulation ends when no further bank defaults. Simulations are then repeated by assuming the unanticipated failure of a different bank, possibly spanning across the all system or focusing on the most important institutions.

Overall, the evidence of systemic risk from these tests is mixed. Risk of contagion has been reported, as a percentage of banking system's total assets lost, by Degryse and Nguyen (2007) for Belgium (20%), Mistrulli (2011) for Italy (16%), Upper and Worms (2004) for Germany (15%), and Wells (2004) for the UK (15%). By contrast, little possibility for contagion was found by Blavarg and Nimander (2002) for Sweden, Lubloy (2005) for Hungary, and Sheldon and Maurer (1998) for Switzerland. Furfine (2003) and Amundsen and Arnt (2005) also report only a limited possibility for contagion. Cont et al. (2013) show that in the Brazilian banking system the probability of contagion is small, however the loss resulting from contagion can be very large in some cases.

Recent studies have shown that not taking into account possible loss amplification due to indirect contagion associated with fire sales and bank exposures to the real sector can significantly underestimate the degree of fragility of financial system. We will discuss these effects in Sections 4.1 and 4.2.

3.6 NETWORK RECONSTRUCTION

A major limitation of the stress-test analysis is that often the full network of interbank liabilities is not available to regulators. For most countries bilateral linkages are unobserved and aggregate balance sheet information are used for estimating counterparty exposures. Formally the problem is that the row and column sums of a matrix describing a financial network are known but the matrix itself is not known. To estimate bank-to-bank exposures, different network reconstruction methods have been proposed. The most popular approach for deriving individual interbank liabilities from aggregates has been to minimize the Kullback–Leibler divergence between the liabilities matrix and a previously specified input matrix (see Upper, 2011 for a review). This network reconstruction approach is essentially a constrained entropy maximization problem, where the constraints represent the available information and the maximization of the entropy ensures that the reconstructed network is maximally random, given the enforced constraints.

One drawback of the Maximum Entropy (ME) method is that the resulting interbank liabilities usually form a complete network. However, as we have seen, empirical research shows that interbank networks are sparse. The maximum entropy method might thus bias the results, in the light of the theoretical findings that better connected networks may be more resilient to the propagation of shocks. This is confirmed by Mistrulli (2011), who analyzes how contagion propagates within the Italian interbank market using actual bilateral exposures and reconstructed ME exposures. ME is found to generally underestimate the extent of contagion. Similarly Solórzano-Margain et al. (2013) showed that financial contagion arising from the failure of a financial institution in the Mexican financial system would be more widespread than from simulations based on reconstructed network based on ME algorithm.

Mastromatteo et al. (2012) have proposed an extension to the ME approach using a message-passing algorithm for estimating interbank exposures. Their aim is to fix a global level of sparsity for the network and, once this is given, allow the weights on the existing links to be distributed similarly to the ME method. Anand et al. (2014) have proposed the minimum density (MD) method which consists in minimizing the total number of edges that is consistent with the aggregated interbank assets and liabilities. They argue that the MD method tends to overestimate contagion, because minimize the number of links, and therefore can together with the ME method be used to provide upper and lower bounds for stress test results. However, increasing the number of links has a non-monotonous effect on the stability of a network, thus attempts to derive bounds on systemic risk by optimizing over the degree of completeness are unlikely to be successful. Montagna and Lux (2013) construct a Monte Carlo framework for an interbank market characterized by a power law degree distribution and disassortative link formation features via a fitness algorithm (De Masi et al., 2006).

The ME approach is deterministic in the sense that the method produces a point estimate for the financial network that is treated as the true network when performing stress tests. Probabilistic approaches to stress-testing have been attempted by Lu and Zhoua (2011), Halaj and Kok (2013), Squartini et al. (2017), Bargigli (2014), Montagna and Lux (2013), and Gandy and Veraart (2017). Such approaches consist in building an ensemble of random networks, of which the empirical network can be considered a typical sample. This allows to analyze not only the vulnerability of one particular network realization retrieved from the real data, but of many plausible alternative realizations, compatible with a set of constrains. However, to generate a realistic random sample it is crucial to impose the relevant constrains on the simulated networks, reproducing not just the observed exposures but also basic network properties. Cimini et al. (2015) introduce an analytical maximum-entropy technique to reconstruct unbiased ensembles of weighted networks from the knowledge of empirical node strengths and link density. The method directly provides the expected value of the desired reconstructed properties, in such a way that no explicit sampling of reconstructed graphs is required. Gandy and Veraart (2017) have proposed a reconstruction model, which, following a Bayesian approach, allows to condition on the observed total liabilities and assets and, if available, on observed individual liabilities. Their approach allow to construct a Gibbs sampler to generate samples from this conditional distribution that can be used in stress testing, giving probabilities for the outcomes of interest. De Masi et al. (2006) propose a fitness model, where the fitness of each bank is given by their daily trading volume. Fixing the level of heterogeneity the model reproduces remarkably well topological properties of the e-Mid interbank market such as degree distribution, clustering, and assortativity. Finally Iori et al. (2015) introduce a simple model of trading with memory that correctly reproduces features of preferential trading patterns observed in the e-Mid market.

An international study lead by several central banks has been conducted to test the goodness of network reconstruction algorithms (Anand et al., 2017). Initial results suggest that the performance of the tested methods depends strongly on the similarity measure used and the sparsity of the underlying network. This highlights that in order to avoid model risk arising from calibration algorithms, structural bilateral balance sheet, and off balance sheet, data are crucial to study systemic risk from financial interconnections.

Another common critique to stress test studies of contagion is the lack of dynamics in terms of banks' behavioral adjustments. Critics stress the importance to include indirect financial linkages, in terms of common exposures and business models, as well as fire sales or liquidity hoarding contagion driven by fear and uncertainty. To address these concerns, a few papers have explored the role of funding and liquidity risk via simulation experiments. The idea of liquidity risk as banks start fire-selling their assets, depressing overall prices in the market, was initially explored by Cifuentes et al. (2005) and has been further investigated in a simulation framework by Nier et al. (2007), Gai and Kapadia (2010), Haldane and May (2011), Tasca and Battiston (2016), Corsi et al. (2016), Cont and Wagalath (2013), Caccioli et al. (2014), and Poledna et al. (2014). The role of funding risk induced by liquidity hoarding is explored in Haldane and May (2011), Chan-Lau (2010), Espinosa-Vega and Solé (2011), Fourel et al. (2013), Roukny et al. (2013), and Gabrieli et al. (2014). Finally, simultaneous impact of market and funding liquidity risk is explored by Aikman et al. (2010) and Manna and Schiavone (2012).

While this body of work has considerably improved our understanding of the effects of the networks structure on the spreading of systemic risk unfortunately data on a range of relevant activities (securities lending, bilateral repos, and derivatives trading) remain inadequate. Moreover, the activities of non-bank market participants, such as asset managers, insurance and shadow banks, and their interconnections remain opaque. A proper assessment of systemic risk relies on a better understanding of the business models of these players and their interactions and on enhanced availability of individual transactions data.

3.7 ECONOMETRICS SYSTEMIC RISK MEASURES

Due to limited availability of supervisory data to capture systemic risk stemming from contagion via bilateral exposures, approaches have been suggested to derive systemic risk from available market data. A number of econometric measures, beyond Pearson correlation, have been proposed to measure the degree of correlation and concentration of risks among financial institutions, and their sensitivity to changes in market prices and economic conditions. Popular ones include Value-at-Risk (CoVaR) by Adrian and Brunnermeier (2016), CoRisk by Chan-Lau (2010), marginal and systemic expected shortfall by Acharya et al. (2012), distressed insurance premium by Huang et al. (2012), SRISK by Brownlees and Engle (2016), distance to distress by Castren and Kavonius (2009), and POD (probability that at least one bank becomes distressed) by Goodhart and Segoviano Basurto (2009). While these approaches are not network based, they are briefly mentioned here (see Appendix B for technical definitions) for completeness as they provide complementary methodologies to assess systemic risk and financial fragility. The underlying assumption behind these "market based" systemic risk measures is that the strength of relationships between different financial institutions, based on correlations between their asset values, is related to the materialization of systemic risk. The rationale is that common movements in underlying firms' asset values are typically driven by the business cycle, interbank linkages or shift in market sentiment that affects the valuation of bank assets simultaneously. By assuming that these are likely causes of contagion and common defaults, systemic risk should be captured by the correlations of observable equity returns.[5] However the importance of short-term changes to market data might be overestimated, and the mechanisms that lead to the realization of systemic defaults are not well understood. In particular, when markets function poorly, market data are a poor indicator of financial environments. Correlations between distinct sectors of the financial system became higher during and after the crisis, not before, thus during non-crisis periods, correlation play little role in indicating a build-up of systemic risk using such measures. Moreover, measures based on probabilities invariably depend on market volatility, and during periods of prosperity and growth, volatility is typically lower than in periods of distress. This implies lower estimates of systemic risk until after a volatility spike occurs, which reduces the usefulness of such a measure as an early warning indicator. Overall these measures may be misleading in the build up to a crisis as they underprice risk during market booms.

3.8 LOCATION ADVANTAGES IN INTERBANK NETWORKS

In addition to having implications for financial stability, holding a central position in the interbank networks, or establishing preferential relationships, may lead to funding benefit. The exploration of potential location advantages has been the focus of recent

---

[5]Equity return correlation are normally used because the equity market is the most liquid financial market and thus new information on an institution's default risk can be incorporated in a timely way.

papers. Bech and Atalay (2010) analyze the topology of the Federal Funds market by looking at O/N transactions from 1997 to 2006. They show that reciprocity and centrality measures are useful predictors of interest rates, with banks gaining from their centrality. Akram and Christophersen (2013) study the Norwegian interbank market over the period 2006–2009. They observe large variations in interest rates across banks, with systemically more important banks, in terms of size and connectedness, receiving more favorable terms. Temizsoy et al. (2017) show that network measures are significant determinants of funding rates in the e-MID O/N market. Higher local measures of centrality are associated with increasing borrowing costs for borrowers and decreasing premia for lenders. However, global measures of network centrality (betweenness, Katz, PageRank, and SinkRank) benefit borrowers who receive a significant discount if they increase their intermediation activity, while lenders pay in general a premium (i.e. receive lower rates) for centrality. This effect is interpreted by the authors, as driven by the market perception that more central banks will be bailed out if in distress, because "too connected to fail". The expectation of implicit subsidies could create moral hazard and provide incentives for banks to become systemically important, exacerbating system fragility. Thus Temizsoy et al. (2017) suggest that monitoring how funding cost advantages evolve over time can act as an effective early warning indicator of systemic risk and provide a way to measure the effectiveness of regulatory policy to reduce the market perception that systemically important institutions will not be allowed to default.

During the crisis, increased uncertainty about counterpart credit risk led banks to hoard liquidity rather than making it available in the interbank market. Money markets in most developed countries almost came to a freeze and banks were forced to borrow from Central Banks. Nonetheless there is growing empirical evidence that banks that had established long term interbank relationships had better access to liquidity both before and during the crisis (Furfine, 2001; Cocco et al., 2009; Liedorp et al., 2010; Affinito, 2012; Brauning and Fecht, 2012; Temizsoy et al., 2015).

Early papers on interbank markets focus on the existence of lending relationships in the US Federal Funds markets (Furfine, 1999, 2001). Furfine (1999) shows that larger institutions tend to have a high number of counterparties while Furfine (2001) finds that banking relationships have important effects on borrowing costs and longer relationship decreases the interest rate in the funds market. Affinito (2012) uses data from Italy to analyze interbank customer relationships. His findings are that stable relationships exist and remain strong during the financial crisis. Liedorp et al. (2010) examine bank to bank relationships in the Dutch interbank market to test whether market participants affect each other riskiness through such connections. They show that larger dependence on interbank market increases risk, but banks can reduce their risk by borrowing from stable neighbors. Brauning and Fecht (2012) show that German lenders anticipated the financial crisis by charging higher interest rates in the run-up to the crisis. By contrast, when the sub-prime crisis kicked in, lenders gave a discount to their close borrowers, thus pointing to a peer monitoring role of relationship lending. Temizsoy et al. (2015) analyze the structure of the links between financial institutions participating in the e-MID interbank market. They show that, particularly after the Lehman's collapse, when liquidity became scarce, established relationships with the same bank became an important determinant of interbank spreads. Both borrowers and lenders benefited from establishing relationship throughout the crisis by receiving better rates from and trading larger volume with their preferred counterparties.

Cocco et al. (2009) suggest that size may be the main factor behind the Portuguese interbank funds connective and hierarchical architecture. Small banks acting as borrowers are more likely to rely on lending relationship than larger banks. Thus they suggest that financial institutions do not connect to each other randomly, but rather interact based on a size-related preferential attachment process, possibly driven by too-big-to-fail implicit subsidies or market power.

Hatzopoulos et al. (2015) have investigated the matching mechanism between lenders and borrowers in the e-MID market and its evolution over time. They show that, when controlling for bank heterogeneity, the matching mechanism is fairly random. Specifically, when taking a lender who makes l transactions over a given period of time and a borrower who makes b transaction over the same period, and such that they have m trades in common over that period, Hatzopoulos et al. (2015) show that m is consistent with a random matching hypothesis for more than 90% of all lender/borrower pairs. Even though matches that occur more often than those consistent with a random null model (which they call over expressed links) exist and increase in number during the crisis, neither lenders nor borrowers systematically present several over expressed links at the same time. The picture that emerges from their study is that banks are more likely to be chosen as trading partners because they are larger and trade more often and not because they are more attractive in some dimension (such as their financial healthiness).

Overall the empirical evidence suggests that, particularly at a time of deteriorating trust towards credit rating agencies, private information acquired through repeated transactions plays an important role in mitigating asymmetric information about a borrower's creditworthiness and can ease liquidity redistribution among banks. These results show that interbank exposures are used as a peer-monitoring device. Private information acquired through frequent transactions, supported liquidity reallocation in the e-MID market during the crisis by improving the ability of banks to assess the creditworthiness of their counterparties. Relationship lending thus play a positive role for financial stability and can help policymakers to assess market discipline. Furthermore, the analysis of patterns of preferential relationships may help identifying systemically important financial institutions. If a bank, who is the preferential lender to several borrowers defaults, or stop lending, this may pose a serious funding risk for its borrowers who may find it difficult to satisfy their liquidity needs from other lenders and may be forced to accept deals at higher rates. This may eventually put them under distress and increase systemic risk in the system. Similarly if preferential borrowers exit the interbank market, such lenders may find it difficult to reallocate their liquidity surplus if they fail to find trusted counterparties. The resulting inefficient reallocation of liquidity, may in turn increase funding costs of other borrowers and again contribute to the spread of systemic risk. In this sense relationship lending provides a measure of the financial substitutability of a bank in the interbank market. Thus when establishing if a bank is too connected to fail, regulators should not only look at how connected a bank is, but also at how preferentially connected it is to other players. Finally, reliance on relationship lending is an indicator of trust evaporation in the banking system and monitoring the effect of stable relations on spreads and traded volume may help regulators to identify early warning indicator of a financial turmoil.

4 NETWORKS AND INFORMATION FILTERING

So far we have primarily considered what we have called relationship or event networks. Event or relationship networks are the most common types of networks that are investigated in finance. In these networks a link between two nodes is set when a relationship or an event is occurring between them in a given period of time. For example two banks are linked when a credit relationship is present between them. In addition to this type of networks other classes of networks have been investigated in finance. We call these types of networks (i) proximity based networks, (ii) association networks, and (iii) statistically validated networks.

4.1 PROXIMITY BASED NETWORKS

In proximity based networks a similarity or a dissimilarity measure (i.e. technically speaking a proximity measure, see a reference text of Data Mining for a formal definition as, for example, Han et al., 2011) computed between all pairs of elements of a system is used to determine a network. The network obtained highlights the most relevant proximities observed in the system. Let us make an example to clarify the concept. Let us consider two banks having no credit relationship in the interbank market connecting them in a given time period. Is this meaning that the two banks are isolated the one to the other unless a chain of bankruptcy of banks occurs? The general answer is no. We can see this by considering the fact that the two banks have both a portfolio of assets and that the two portfolios can present a given degree of similarity. Two banks characterized by a high degree of similarity of their portfolios will be impacted by market dynamics and by exogenous news in a similar way in spite of the fact that they do not present direct credit relationship. For example, the fire sale of a distressed bank of a given asset will impact all those banks having large weights of that asset in their portfolios. The interlinkages associated with different degree of similarity of the set of elements of a given system can therefore be summarized and visualized in a network. In the literature these networks are sometime called with different names. For example, in neuroscience they are called functional networks because they are obtained starting from the functional activity detected by functional magnetic resonance signals detected in different regions of the brain. The proximity can be estimated by considering features of the considered elements that can be numeric, binary or even categorical.

4.1.1 The Minimum Spanning Tree

The first example of proximity based network was introduced in Mantegna (1999). This study proposed to obtain a network starting from a dissimilarity measure estimated between pairs of stocks traded in a financial market. A dissimilarity measure between two financial stocks can be obtained by first estimating the Pearson correlation coefficient ρ between the two time series of return of stocks and then obtaining a dissimilarity d (more precisely a distance) through the relation $d = \sqrt{2(1 - \rho)}$. By following this approach, one can always associate a similarity or dissimilarity matrix to any multivariate time series and use this matrix to define a weighted complete network. The weight of each link being the value of the proximity measure.

For this type of weighted complete networks all information which is present in the proximity matrix is retained and it has associated the same degree of statistical reliability. However, in real cases this ideal condition is hardly verified. In fact, not all the information present in a proximity matrix has the same statistical reliability. The specific level of reliability depends on the way the proximity measure is obtained and limitations are always present when the estimation of the proximity measure is done with a finite number of experimental records or features. The unavoidable presence of this type of limitation is quantified by random matrix theory (Metha, 1991) in a very elegant way. For example, the eigenvalue spectrum of the correlation matrix for a random Gaussian multivariate set is given by the Marčenko–Pastur distribution (Marčenko and Pastur, 1967). Several studies have shown that the Marčenko–Pastur distribution computed for a correlation matrix of n stocks with a finite number of records widely overlaps with the ones empirically observed in financial markets although also clear deviations from this null hypothesis are observed (Laloux et al., 1999; Plerou et al., 1999).

In empirical analyses, it is therefore important and informative to perform a meaningful filtering of any proximity matrix obtained from a multivariate system described by a finite number of records or features. One of the most effective filtering procedures of a proximity matrix is the extraction from it of its minimum (for dissimilarity) or maximum (for similarity) spanning tree (Mantegna, 1999). The minimum spanning tree is a concept of graph theory and it is the minimum (or maximum) tree connecting all the nodes of a system through a path of minimal (maximal) length. The minimum spanning tree can be determined by using Prim's or Kruskal's algorithms. The information it selects from the original proximity measure is related to the hierarchical tree that can be obtained from the same proximity matrix by using the hierarchical clustering procedures known as single linkage. For more details about the extraction of minimum spanning trees from a proximity matrix one can consult (Tumminello et al., 2010).

In Fig. 2 we show an example of minimum spanning tree obtained for a set of 100 highly capitalized stocks traded in the US equity markets during the time period January 1995–December 1998. In the MST several stocks, such as, for example, BAC (Bank of America Corp.), INTC (Intel Corp.), or AEP (America Express), are linked with several stocks belonging to the same economic sector (financial, technology, and utility sector respectively) whereas others (the most notable case is General

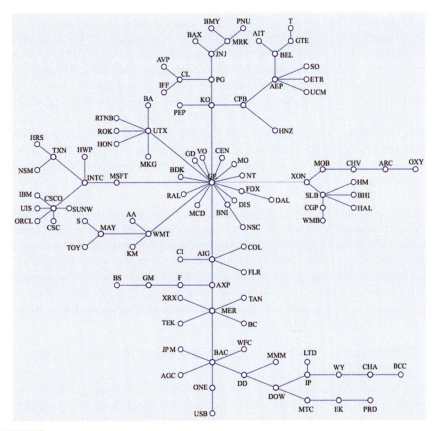

FIGURE 2

Minimum spanning tree of a set of 100 highly capitalized stocks traded in the US equity markets during the time period January 1995–December 1998. The similarity measure used to obtain the tree was the Pearson linear correlation measured between each pair of 1 day stock returns. Each circle represents a stock labeled by its tick symbol. The clustering of stocks according to their economic sector and subsector is evident. Reproduced from Bonanno et al. (2001).

Electric Company (GE)) are linked to stocks of different sectors. In general the clustering in terms of economic sectors of the considered companies is rather evident. Since the original proposal of Mantegna (1999), minimum spanning trees have been investigated in a large number of empirical studies involving different financial markets operating worldwide or in diverse geographical areas. The classes of assets and geographically located markets investigated through the proximity based network methodology comprises[6]: stocks traded in equity markets geographically located in

---

[6]The following references are not exhaustive. For an attempt to cover a wider number of reference see Bonanno et al. (2004), Tumminello et al. (2010), Marti et al. (2017).

US (Mantegna, 1999; Bonanno et al., 2001; Onnela et al., 2002; Miccichè et al., 2003; Bonanno et al., 2003; Onnela et al., 2003; Precup and Iori, 2007; Eom et al., 2007; Tumminello et al., 2007; Brida and Risso, 2008; Zhang et al., 2011), in Europe (Coronnello et al., 2005), in Asia (Jung et al., 2006; Eom et al., 2007; Zhuang et al., 2008), market indices of major stock exchanges (Bonanno et al., 2000; Coelho et al., 2007; Gilmore et al., 2008; Song et al., 2011), bonds and interest rates (Di Matteo and Aste, 2002; Dias, 2012, 2013), currencies (McDonald et al., 2005; Mizuno et al., 2006; Górski et al., 2008; Jang et al., 2011; Wang et al., 2012, 2013), commodities (Sieczka and Holyst, 2009; Barigozzi et al., 2010; Tabak et al., 2010b; Kristoufek et al., 2012; Zheng et al., 2013; Kazemilari et al., 2017), interbank market (Iori et al., 2008), housing market (Wang and Xie, 2015), credit default swaps market (León et al., 2014).

As for other data mining approaches, there are multiple approaches to perform information filtering. The choice of specific approach depends on the posed scientific question and on the ability of the filtering process to highlight the information of interest. This is similar to the case of hierarchical clustering where there is no a priori recipe to select the most appropriate algorithm performing the clustering. In addition to the approach of the minimum spanning tree several other approaches have been proposed in the literature to perform information filtering on networks. We will discuss some examples in the following subsection.

4.1.2 Other Types of Proximity Based Networks and the Planar Maximally Filtered Graph

One of the first alternative approaches to the minimum spanning tree was the one proposed in Onnela et al. (2004) where a network is built starting from a correlation matrix by inserting links between two nodes when their correlation coefficient is above a given threshold. This approach is retaining a large amount of information but suffers by the arbitrariness in choosing the threshold. Moreover, the network can cover only part of the system when the correlation threshold is relatively high. When the threshold is selected by considering an appropriate null model as, for example, an uncorrelated multivariate time series characterized by the same return distributions as in real data, most of the estimated correlation coefficient are rejecting the null hypothesis of uncorrelated returns ending up with an almost complete correlation based graph.

To highlight information present in the system by selecting links in a proximity based network richer than the minimum spanning tree without inserting an arbitrarily selected threshold the use of a network topological constraint was proposed in Tumminello et al. (2005). Specifically, Tumminello et al. (2005) introduce a method to obtain a planar graph starting from a similarity or a dissimilarity matrix. The method of the network construction requires that the network remains always planar, i.e. can be embedded in a surface of genus 0, until all the nodes of the system are included in the network. The resulting network has the property of including the minimum (or maximum in case of similarity) spanning tree and of presenting also loops and cliques of 3 and 4 nodes. The planar maximally filtered graph is therefore extracting an amount of information larger than the minimum spanning tree but still linear in the number of nodes of the system. In fact the minimum spanning tree selects $n - 1$ links among the possible $n(n - 1)/2$ links and the planar maximally filtered graph selects $3(n - 2)$ links. The approach of filtering the network under topological constraints can be generalized (Aste et al., 2005) by considering the embedding of the network into surfaces with genus larger than 0. The genus is a topological property of a surface. Roughly it is given by the integer number of handles observed in the connected, orientable surface. Unfortunately, this general approach which is very well defined from a mathematical point of view, is pretty difficult to implement computationally already for values of the genus equal to 1.

The study of proximity based networks is strongly interlinked with methodological approaches devoted to detect hierarchical structure and clustering of the considered nodes. Examples of this type of interlinkages are the clustering procedure achieved by considering Potts super-paramagnetic transitions (Kullmann et al., 2000). Within this approach, in the presence of anti-correlation, the methodology associates anti-correlation to a physical repulsion between the stocks which is reflected in the obtained clustering structure. Another approach to hierarchical clustering is using maximum likelihood procedure (Giada and Marsili, 2001, 2002), where authors define the likelihood by using a one-factor model, then varied to detect a clustering with high likelihood. In Tumminello et al. (2007) authors introduce the so-called average linkage minimum spanning tree, i.e. a tree associated with the hierarchical clustering procedure of the average linkage. An unsupervised and deterministic clustering procedure, labeled as directed bubble hierarchical tree, often finding high quality partitions based on the planar maximally filtered graph, is proposed in Song et al. (2012). Other clustering approaches have relied more on concepts originating from network science as it is the case for the approaches (i) using the concept of modularity maximization for cluster detection obtained from a correlation matrix (MacMahon and Garlaschelli, 2013), and (ii) using the concept of p-median to construct every cluster as a star network at a given level (Kocheturov et al., 2014).

4.2 ASSOCIATION NETWORKS

Another class of networks is the class we name association networks. In this type of networks two nodes of a complex system are connected in a network by computing a quantity that is putting in relation node i with node j of a given system. The quantity computed can be a complex indicator as, for example, the partial correlation between the time evolution of node i with node j or an indicator of the rejection of a statistical test against a given null hypothesis.

A prominent example of association network is the partial correlation network investigated in Kenett et al. (2010). Partial correlation is a measure of how the correlation between two variables, e.g., stock returns, is affected by a third variable. Kenett et al. (2010) define a proxy of stock influence, which is then used to construct a partial correlation network. The empirical study performed on stocks traded at the US equity markets concluded that stocks of the financial sector and, specifically, of investment services sub-sector, are taking a special position in the association network based on partial correlation. Partial correlation networks have also been investigated by Anufriev and Panchenko (2015) for publicly traded Australian banks and for their connections to domestic economic sectors and international markets.

In their paper, Billio et al. (2012) propose a method to construct a directed network starting from a statistical test performed between each pair of time series of a multivariate system. Specifically they investigate Granger-causality between monthly return time series, and starting from the time series they infer a network of dependencies of hedge funds, publicly traded banks, broker/dealers, and insurance companies. In other words an association network of Granger-causal relations among these institutions is identified via the pairwise Granger-causality test. Granger causality is a statistical notion of causality based on the forecast power of two time series. Time series j is said to "Granger-cause" time series i if past values of j contain information that helps predict i above and beyond the information contained in past values of i alone. In their investigation authors conclude that their results show a pronounced asymmetry in the degree of connectedness among hedge funds, publicly traded banks, broker/dealers, and insurance companies sectors, with banks playing a much more important role in transmitting shocks than other financial institutions.

Another example of association networks concerns the networks obtained when performing pairwise co-integration tests. First attempts to produce association networks based on pairwise co-integration test are reported in Yang et al. (2014) and Tu (2014).

The need of many statistical tests to be used for the construction of an association network raises some problems directly originating form the pairwise nature of the performed tests. For example, in the case of Granger-causality test, as pointed out by Basu et al. (2017), direct pairwise estimation does not take into account indirect effects on the pair under consideration. For example in a system with 3 nodes and 2 "true" Granger causal dependencies: $B \to C, C \to A$, a Granger causal test would detect an additional (spurious) pairwise Granger causal effect $B \to A$, due to indirect effect through C. In fact a similar concern arises with the use of CoVaR, since these models estimate the covariance of an institution with the rest of the system without conditioning it on all other participants. Such inconsistency may impose large economic costs; for example, a number of institutions that are not highly interconnected may end up being wrongly classified as inter-connected under such approaches.

To address this problem Basu et al. (2017) develop and estimate a measure of network connectivity that explicitly recognizes the possibility of connectivity of all the firms in the network, in contrast with extant measures of systemic risk that, either explicitly or implicitly, estimate such connections using pair-wise relationships between institutions. The system-wide approach, is based on the Lasso penalized Vector Auto-Regression (LVAR) model that only focuses on estimating the strongest interconnections, while forcing weaker relationships to zero. Basu et al. (2017) also consider explicitly the problem of the control of the family-wise error rate. In fact when a large number of statistical tests are performed to obtain an association network the absence of the control of the family-wise error rate can produce a large number of false positive. This problem was first recognized in Tumminello et al.

(2011) where the concept of the so-called statistically validated network was introduced (see next section). In Tumminello et al. (2011) it was shown that the so-called Bonferroni correction is highly precise but often characterized by low power and therefore associated with a relatively low accuracy. For this reason, as it is common in statistical approaches needing a control of the family-wise error rate the approach based on the control of the false discovery rate (Hochberg and Tamhane, 1987) was proposed.

A similar system-wide approach was developed in Diebold and Yimaz (2014). However the Diebold and Yimaz (2014) approach requires fitting full vector autoregressive models, simultaneously for all firms, and use variance decomposition of the forecast error of the fitted model to define the network topology and extract connectivity measures. Since the number of parameters to be estimated, even for the simplest lag-1 VAR model in this approach is quadratic in the number of institutions under consideration, the model can only be estimated for a limited number of firms (15 in Diebold and Yimaz, 2014). The advantage of the LVAR model lays on the fact that it needs significantly lower number of time points to estimate as long as the underlying network is approximately sparse, and can be applied to more realistic setting involving all important banks of the economy.

Barfuss et al. (2016) have recently introduced an information filtering methodology (LoGo) to produce parsimonious models associated with a meaningful structure of dependency between variables of interest. The strength of this methodology is that the global sparse inverse covariance matrix is produced from a simple sum of local inversions. This makes the method computationally very efficient and statistically robust. Applied to financial data the method results computationally more efficient than state-of-the-art methodologies such as Glasso producing, in a fraction of the computation time, models that can have equivalent or better performances but with a sparser inference structure.

4.3 STATISTICALLY VALIDATED NETWORKS

In the previous section we have seen that a statistical test is performed to asses the existence of an undirected or directed link between each pair of nodes of the system in the study of association networks. Moreover, a statistical validation procedure can also be performed in ordinary networks to detect those links that are presenting marked differences from a given null hypothesis. According to Tumminello et al. (2011), when statistical tests are performed to highlight specific links (or the absence of links) between pairs of nodes of the investigated systems, we say we are in the presence of statistically validated networks detected against a given null hypothesis. The value of this statistical approach primarily relies on the fact that most systems of interest are highly heterogeneous with respect to economic or financial actions taken in a given period of time (e.g. number of loans, number of syndicated loans, amount of loans provided to firms, etc.) and therefore detecting over-expression or under-expression of interaction with respect to a null hypothesis taking into account for the heterogeneity of the action of each node can highlight important properties of the analyzed system.

The first example of statistical validation in weighted network is the work of Serrano et al. (2009). In this paper the statistical validation is performed on the outgoing weight of each node of the network statistically compared with a null hypothesis of uniform distribution of the total node strength in the outgoing arcs. In their paper authors statistically validate each link by deciding, which of the links carry disproportionate fraction of the weights of a given node. Specifically they compare the empirical value of each link of a node with a null model that considers all links of each node as equally probable. By performing the statistical validation node-by-node they select only those links that reject the null hypothesis therefore obtaining what they call the "multiscale backbone" of the system. It is worth noting that the method is not affected by the heterogeneity of the strength of nodes allowing for a selection of nodes working at all scales of the weight of links. Their approach was then generalized to the case of non-uniform distribution of weights by Radicchi et al. (2011).

Heterogeneity is a typical fingerprint of almost all complex systems. Economic and financial systems do not deviate from this general property and in fact economics was one of the first disciplines where power law distributions were documented and modeled. Vilfredo Pareto discovered a power law distribution in the wealth distribution of individuals in many countries and historical time periods as early as in 1897 (Pareto, 1897). An indication about the essential heterogeneity of economic and financial systems can be seen in the observation that the majority of economic and financial networks are presenting a degree distribution with a pronounced level of leptokurtosis. This observation has motivated network scientists to investigate complex network by estimating the deviation observed from the basic heterogeneity observed in the system.

The first approach designed to perform statistical tests of the over-expression of a given node action (e.g. participating to a credit relationship, performing a market transaction, etc.) against a null hypothesis taking into account the heterogeneity of the nodes was first presented for undirected interaction in Tumminello et al. (2011) and then extended to directed interaction and to the investigation of under-expression of interactions in Hatzopoulos et al. (2015). The method is designed for complex systems where two sets of agents repeats an action involving two actors a number of times in a given time interval. For example the two sets of agents can be (i) calling mobile phone subscribers and (ii) receiving mobile phone subscribers. Another example is the one where the two sets of agents are (i) lending banks and (ii) borrowing banks in the interbank market. Usually these complex systems are highly heterogeneous systems and therefore detecting links that are rejecting a null hypothesis taking into account the heterogeneity of the activity of each node in a statistical test can highlight informative interlinkages of the investigated system. In Fig. 3 we show the statistically validated network of the Italian segment of the e-MID market obtained in Hatzopoulos et al. (2015) from data of the maintenance period from 10 September 2008 to 9 December 2008.

It should be noted that the methodology used to obtain a statistically validated network needs performing a large number of statistical tests, that are usually done on all links of a large network. These means that this statistical procedure needs the

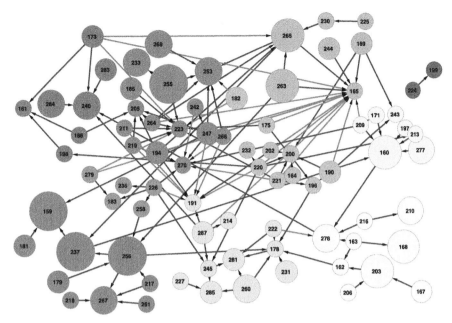

FIGURE 3

Statistically validated network (with the Bonferroni multiple hypothesis test correction) of the Italian segment of the e-MID market during the maintenance period from 10 September 2008 to 9 December 2008. Arrows originate from the lender aggressor. The different gray levels indicate the node membership obtained by applying a community detection algorithm. Light gray links are under-expressed links, while black links are over-expressed ones. Reproduced from Hatzopoulos et al. (2015).

so-called control of family-wise error rate. Tumminello et al. (2011) were the first pointing out the need of multiple hypothesis test correction when statistical tests are used to select or construct networks. Family-wise errors arise from the fact that when a large number of statistical tests are simultaneously performed a certain number of false positive are unavoidably observed due to the parallel repetition of the statistical test many times.

There are different types of procedures to correct multiple hypothesis testing procedures to avoid the presence of false positive. The most restrictive multiple hypothesis test correction is the so-called Bonferroni correction (Hochberg and Tamhane, 1987) that is performed by setting the statistical threshold as $\alpha_B = \alpha/N_t = 0.01/N_t$, where α is the chosen univariate statistical threshold and N_t is the number of tests to be performed. The Bonferroni correction controls the number of false positive therefore ensuring a high degree of statistical precision to the multiple hypothesis test performed. Unfortunately, in some cases it does not guarantee sufficient statistical accuracy because it may provide a large number of false negative. The procedure controlling the false discovery rate introduced in Benjamini and Hochberg (1995) reduces the number of false negative by controlling the expected proportion of rejected null hypothesis without significantly expanding the number of false positive. For this reason the multiple hypothesis test correction controlling the false discovery rate is today widely used also when investigating statistically validated or association networks.

Statistically validated networks originating from bipartite networks have been investigated in a variety of systems. The methodology was first illustrated by investigating the bipartite relationship between genomes and proteins in simple organisms, the price dynamics of financial stocks described in terms of categorical variables and the Internet Movie Database (Tumminello et al., 2011). It has also been used to detect and classify investment strategies of single investors (Tumminello et al., 2012). The methodology is rather flexible and easily adapted to directional relationships such as the ones of any form of communication from a caller to a receiver, any form of loan provided from a lender to a borrower or any form of market transaction from a seller to a buyer, etc. With this generalization of the methodology statistically validated networks have been detected and analyzed in mobile phone communication networks (Li et al., 2014a, 2014b) and in the empirical investigation of the e-MID interbank market (Hatzopoulos et al., 2015).

5 INDIRECT CHANNELS OF CONTAGION

The evaluation of the fragility and resilience of the financial system is a research area where different types of networks need to be taken into account. In fact, finance is probably one of the research areas where both relationships networks and proximity networks play a role in the correct assessment of systemic risk of the system. In the following subsections we will discuss the role of two major indirect channels of contagion that can be detected by using information about similarity of banks' characteristics. The first subsection discusses the role of overlapping portfolios of assets owned by banks and the second concerns the bank–firm credit relations and the indirect channel of contagion that can originate from them.

5.1 OVERLAPPING PORTFOLIOS AND FEEDBACK EFFECTS

Systemic risk is the research area where the use of event or relationship networks and proximity based networks is jointly required for a realistic model of the financial system. In fact, both direct and market mediated indirect channels of contagion need to be taken into account for the estimation of systemic risk of the financial system. One indirect channel can be highlighted by estimating the amount of overlapping of portfolios of different institutions. Market impact of portfolio deleveraging in stress scenarios can in fact induces contagion paths that are indirect (Cont and Wagalath, 2013; Huang et al., 2013; Caccioli et al., 2014). The magnitude of these additional market mediated contagion paths depends on the portfolios overlap of economic actors acting in the financial system (Cifuentes et al., 2005; Braverman and Minca, 2014; Cont and Schaanning, 2017). The most prominent aspect of this approach concerns fire sales occurring during market downturns. It is documented that financial institutions in the presence of financial distress can be forced to fire sales of assets (Kyle and Xiong, 2001; Manconi et al., 2012; Cont and Wagalath, 2013). Due to market impact fire sales can generate a positive feedback loop that will increase endogenous risk (Shin, 2010) creating a channel of contagion for those financial institutions with high similarity in the holding of given assets.

Recent papers have proposed possible methods to include fire sales induced contagion channels into macro-stress tests (Duarte and Eisenbach, 2015; Greenwood et al., 2015; Cont and Schaanning, 2017). In Duarte and Eisenbach (2015) authors construct a systemic risk measure quantifying vulnerability to fire-sale spillovers using detailed regulatory balance sheet data for US commercial banks and repo market data for broker-dealers. They find that fire sale externalities can be substantial, even for moderate shocks in normal times. For example, they estimated that for commercial banks a 1 percent exogenous shock to assets in 2013 in the first quarter can produce fire sale externalities of the order of 21 percent of system capital. Greenwood et al. (2015) introduced a model where fire sales propagate shocks across bank balance sheets. Authors showed how this contagion spreads across the banking sector, and how it can be estimated empirically using balance sheet data. In particular, authors computed bank exposures to system-wide deleveraging, as well as the spillovers induced by individual banks. The study presents an application to European banks. Cont and Schaanning (2017) suggest an operational framework able to quantify the impact of deleveraging in stress scenarios when the financial institutions are subjected to portfolio constraints. The authors show that this price mediated loss contagion may be quantified through a liquidity-weighted overlaps across portfolios. The paper also performs a case study using data on European banks. By performing the case study authors show that indirect contagion effects affect the outcome of bank stress tests and lead to heterogeneous losses of banks which cannot be replicated in a stress test without deleveraging effects. The study highlights the difference between insolvency and illiquidity clarifying that the presence of different levels of illiquidity and insolvency can lead to substantially different loss estimates compared to standard models just based on leverage targeting.

Risk metrics based on the mechanism of portfolio rebalancing through fire sales require the full knowledge of the portfolio holdings of each institution in the economy. However, such detailed information may not be available, especially at frequency higher than a quarter. Di Gangi et al. (2015) propose to apply the maximum entropy approach to the inference of the network of portfolio weights in order to estimate metrics of systemic risk due to fire sales spillovers, starting form a reduced information set. The authors show that this approach, while underestimating systemic risk in interbank networks (Mistrulli, 2011), works well when applied to reconstruct the exposures of US commercial banks available via FFIEC Call Reports. Gualdi et al. (2016) propose a method to assess the statistical significance of the overlap between heterogeneously diversified portfolios, in order to investigate patterns of portfolio overlap. When applied to a historical database of SEC 13-F filings, the authors find that the proposed proxy of fire sale risk, after reaching a peak in 2008 had subsequently decreased. However fire sale risk has been increasing again from 2009 to the end 2013 and the number of securities that can be involved in a potential fire sale has been steadily growing in time, with an even stronger proliferation of contagion channels.

5.2 FINANCIAL SECTOR AND THE REAL ECONOMY

Another important channel of indirect contagion of banks due to external shocks is the indirect channel due to common exposure to firms. When a large firm get distressed it will present difficulties in paying back the loans obtained from a number of banks. In other words the links existing from the real economy to the financial sector can act as channels of contagion from a firm or a set of firms to the banking system especially in a period of economic crisis when a state of financial distress may impact simultaneously many firms or firms of an entire economic sub-sector. The impact of the bank–firm network on systemic risk and its role as channel of contagion is investigated theoretically in Lux (2016). In this study, the author proposes a stochastic model of a bipartite credit network observed between banks and the non-bank corporate sector. The model is based on stylized facts observed empirically in large data sets of bank–firm loans for some countries. The model is investigated computationally and it shows a pronounced non-linear behavior under shocks. In fact, the default of a single unit will typically have no immediate avalanche effect, but might lead to a wide collapse of the entire system in a certain number of cases. The model and its numerical investigations suggest that when one distinguishes between contagion due to interbank credit and due to joint exposures to counterparty risk via loans to firms, the later channel appears more important for contagious spread of defaults. Other recent papers that assess how the interbank network structure affects lending to the wider economy via macro-finance ABM simulations are Gabbi et al. (2015) and Gurgone et al. (2017). In the first paper, firms behavior is exogenous and stochastic, and lending to firms short term. In the second firm dynamics are endogenized, lending to firms is long term, and banks implement precautionary liquidity hoarding strategies. Both papers show that constrains to interbank lending affect rates and volumes on the bank–firm credit markets. Instability arising from this channel dominates direct knock-on effects. However, the connectivity of the interbank market has a non-monotonous effect on macro-financial stability.

Starting from 2010 a series of empirical studies have considered the structure of the bank–firm network observed by considering the credit network provided by the banking system of to the firms operating in a given country. The first studies were conducted by analyzing the credit relations of Japanese banks with large Japanese firms (De Masi et al., 2011), and a subset of the Italian banking and corporate system (De Masi and Gallegati, 2012). More recently, the bank interlinkages originating from joint exposure to firms have been investigated also in Brazil (Miranda and Tabak, 2013) and China (Wang and Yang, 2017). The bank–firm network has been investigated by focusing on the topology of the projected network of banks (De Masi et al., 2011), by considering the time evolution of the credit relationships arising from the clustering of the bank–firm relationships investigated with tools of community detection directly applied to a bipartite network (Marotta et al., 2015), and by highlighting the backbone of the credit relationships (Marotta et al., 2016).

The analysis of the Japanese credit market of 2004 performed in De Masi et al. (2011) pointed out that big Japanese banks privileged in that period of time long-term contracts. An analysis performed by using the minimum spanning tree disclosed a highly hierarchical backbone, where the central positions of MSTs were occupied by the largest banks. A strong geographical characterization of the various branches of the trees was also observed, while the clusters of firms did not show apparently specific common properties. Moreover, authors observed that while larger firms presented multiple lending in large, the demand for credit of firms with similar sizes was very heterogeneous.

In the analysis performed directly on the bank–firm bipartite network (Marotta et al., 2015), the analysis was repeated for each calendar year of the 32-year-long time period ranging from 1980 to 2011. In this study, authors investigated the time evolution of the networked structure of the credit market by tracking the time evolution of detected groups of banks and firms. The different groups were then characterized by analyzing the composition of the groups with respect to the over-expression of attributes of firms and banks. Specifically, authors considered as attributes the economic sector and the geographical location of firms and the type of banks. With their analysis authors were able to detect a long term persistence of the over-expression of attributes of communities of banks and firms together with a slow dynamic of changes from some specific attributes to new ones. In Marotta et al. (2016) authors detected the backbone of the weighted bipartite network of the Japanese credit market relationships. The backbone was detected by adapting the method introduced in Serrano et al. (2009). The analysis was done with a yearly resolution and covered the time period from 1980 to 2011. The study showed the time evolution of the backbone by detecting changes occurring in network size, fraction of credit explained, and attributes characterizing the banks and the firms present in the backbone.

6 CONCLUDING REMARKS

Starting from the end of the last century networks have been used to analyze and model financial systems. In the present review we primarily focused on empirical analyses of financial networks. In particular we have extensively discussed (i) analyses and modeling of the interbank market and (ii) different types of networks that have been empirically investigated in finance. In fact, finance is one of the disciplines where in addition to the customary study of event or relationship networks there is also a large number of investigations of association networks and statistically validated networks.

Empirical analysis needs access to accurate and cured data. Finance is one of the research areas with an extremely high rate of production of business data. Most of economic and market activities are today performed or assisted with tools of information technology and therefore market activities are producing a gargantuan amount of data. Some of these data are transparent and easily accessible other are distributed, confidential, and extremely hard to obtain also for monitoring authorities. For this reason many methods have been proposed to reconstruct interlinkages which are present between financial actors starting from aggregate information publicly released by them. In this review we discuss some of the attempts performed in this direction during the last years.

Our review has shown that many efforts have been done and are continuously done to properly detect and model the interlinkages that are of relevance for the evaluation of the fragility and resilience of the financial system. Several approaches have considered interbank credits in the presence or absence of collaterals and by considering different maturities of the loans. Some of these networks have been investigated to detect systemic important financial institutions defined with a variety of criteria ranging from their size to their interconnectedness with respect to a specific market or to groups of markets. In addition to the direct channels of contagion, a series of recent studies have also considered indirect channels of contagion that can originate from similarity of the banking activities. The wide variety of the methods and approaches proposed shows the importance that interlinkages certainly play in systemic risk assessment and it indicates that currently there is no widespread consensus on the way the fragility of the financial system can be detected and monitored efficiently. The research community is therefore considering multiple approaches partly overlapping that are covering different channels of contagion and different feedback mechanisms. The scientific falsification of the different approaches proposed will provide information that will allow the research community to gradually converge towards a successful consensus methodology. Some recent work in this direction has started. For example Anand et al. (2017) perform a systematic comparison of network reconstruction methodologies from 24 financial networks. These authors show that while some approaches work better than others, performance depends on the network characteristics, such as, for example, its sparsity. Thus, for the moment, we believe that the methods proposed and presented throughout this review need to be considered in parallel until a consensus methodology will eventually emerge.

The network approach to the analysis and modeling of complex financial systems is a truly interdisciplinary activity involving scholar with background in disciplines as different as economics, finance, mathematics, statistics, computer science, physics, econometrics, and social sciences. Typically the cultural background of the researcher connotes the specific approach to the study and some of the different disciplines seem not to communicate among them. In this review we have made efforts to cite empirical investigations of financial systems performed in finance, financial mathematics, econophysics, and econometrics. These different research communities present overlaps of themes, results, and fruitful interactions but also cases of isolation within each specific community of research are frequent. We hope that our review might provide a wider perspective and might promote the diffusion of knowledge obtained by the different research communities bridging the efforts done and cross fertilizing future results.

ACKNOWLEDGMENTS

We would like to thank the many colleagues with whom we have shared the excitement to work in this interdisciplinary area of research, exchanging and creating knowledge and ideas. In particular we are grateful to our co-authors: H. Aoyama, T. Aste, G. Bonanno, G. Caldarelli, C. Coronnello, G. De Masi, T. Di Matteo, Y. Fujiwara, G. Gabbi, M. Gallegati, G. Gur-Gershgoren, G.A. Gurgone, V. Hatzopoulos, H. Iyetomi, S. Jafarey, Z.Q. Jiang, K. Kaski, D.Y. Kenett, J. Kértesz, L. Kullmann, M.X. Li, F. Lillo, A. Madi, L. Marotta, S. Miccichè, G. Monte-Rojas, V. Palchykov, J. Piilo, J. Porter, D.M. Song, G. Tedeschi, A. Temizsoy, M. Tumminello, N. Vandewalle, W.J. Xie, and W.X. Zhou for fruitful discussions. For valuable comments on an early version of this chapter we thank seminar participants at the Workshop Handbook of Computational Economics, Amsterdam (June 2017). Finally we thank two anonymous referees for their valuable comments and the two Editors, Cars Hommes and Blake le Baron, for providing us the opportunity to contribute this chapter to the Handbook and for their constructive feedback.

APPENDIX A **BASIC CONCEPTS IN NETWORK SCIENCE**

Among its definitions, the Oxford Dictionary states that a network is "A group or system of interconnected people or things". More generally, a network is a collection of elements connected by a number of links or interlinkages. This is a rather generic definition. The lack of a more precise definition is probably related to the fact that network science is a truly multidisciplinary research area. In fact network studies have been performed within the research communities of social sciences, mathematicians, statistical physicists, computer scientists, biologists, chemists, medical scientists, and economists. Therefore in network science is not unusual to encounter approaches, methodologies, and technical languages that are reflecting the characteristic of the research community that has originated the studies and the results. One prominent example is graph theory. Graph theory is a well defined research are of mathematics where the object of interest are graphs (i.e. networks) primarily described in terms of a collection of points joined together in pairs by lines. In this last case the definition of a network (here a graph) is much more precise but appropriate just for the purposes of graph theory and not always usable for wider use of the concept of networks. For these reasons we will consider ourselves satisfied with a generic definition saying that a network is a collection of elements connected by a number of links or interlinkages.

Studies about networks have been performed by many scholars in different disciplines since the solution of the so-called Königsberg bridge problem from Euler in 1735. However a large scale interest towards this type of problems triggered at the beginning of the nineties of the last century when the fast development of the World Wide Web manifested the huge importance information networks have in all human activities. Starting from that period several communities of researcher started to work on network problems. Basic concepts about networks can today be easily found in several authoritative books (Newman, 2010; Barabási, 2016) and reviews (Boccaletti et al., 2006). Hereafter we briefly recall a few basic concepts just to set up the terminology we are using in the present review in a way that the reader will find the basic information discussed in this review self-contained.

In a mathematical representation networks are described in terms of graphs. A graph $G = (V, E)$ is a mathematical object consisting of a set V of vertices (also called nodes) and a set E of edges (also called links). Edges are defined in terms of pairs $\{i, j\}$ of distinct vertices i, j belonging to the set V. In undirected networks the order of vertices is not informative. The number of vertices N_v is called the order of the graph. The number of edges N_E is called the size of the graph. A graph $G_S = (V_{G_S}, E_{G_S})$ is a subgraph of $G = (V_G, E_G)$ if $V_{G_S} \subseteq V_G$ and $E_{G_S} \subseteq E_G$. A graph $G_I = (V_{G_I}, E_{G_I})$ is an induced subgraph of $G = (V_G, E_G)$ if $V_{G_I} \subseteq V_G$ is a pre-specified set of vertices and $E_{G_I} \subseteq E_I$ are the edges observed among them. In some cases vertices have self-links (i.e. both edges connected to the same vertex, sometimes also called self-loops). A graph with either self-links and/or multi-edges between two vertices is called a multi-graph or a multiplex. A graph without self-links and without multi-edges is addressed as a simple graph. A graph where the relationship between vertex i and vertex j is directional is called a directed graph. Directed graphs have directed edges also called arcs. In a directed graph the direct edge $\{i, j\}$ is different from $\{i, j\}$. Conventionally, the formalism $\{i, j\}$ states that the directionality is from the tail i to the head j. Note that in a simple directed graph we might have up to 2 directed edges between two vertices. When both are present one says that the two arcs are mutual.

Two vertices $i, j \in V$ are adjacent if joined by an edge belonging to set E. Two edges $e_i, e_j \in E$ are adjacent if connected by a vertex belonging to set V. The degree of a vertex is the number of incident edges on it. A degree sequence is obtained by arranging the degree of vertices in non-decreasing order and associating to each vertex its degree. A degree distribution is the probability distribution of the degree observed in a specific network. In a directed graph one can consider both in-degree and out-degree sequence and/or distribution. A walk on a graph G from an initial vertex i to a final vertex j is the path associated with a sequence of vertices and edges connecting the two vertices in the graph. A walk with n edges (where n is counting edges each time they are encountered including multiple counts) has length n. A walk without repeated vertices and repeated edges is called a path. A walk, of length at least three, beginning and ending at the same vertex but with all vertices distinct from each other is called a cycle.

A vertex i is reachable from a vertex j if there exists at least a walk connecting i to j. A graph G is said to be connected if every vertex is reachable for every other one. A component of a graph is a maximally connected subgraph. The component with the largest number of vertices is called the largest connected component. In the case of directed graphs the concept of connectedness is specialized in two cases. A directed graph is weakly connected if the underlying undirected graph is connected. A directed graph is strongly connected if every vertex i is reachable by every other vertex j through a directed walk. A widely used notion of distance between two vertices of a graph is defined as the length of the shortest path(s) between the two vertices. Another indicator is the diameter of a network defined as the maximum length of shortest paths observed in the network. When an edge of a graph has associated a numerical weight the graph is called a weighted graph. The notion of degree is generalized to take into account the weights of the edges. The generalization is called the strength of the vertex and it is the sum of the weights of all incident edges. When edges are weighted the length of a walk (or of a path) is defined as the sum of the values of the edges composing the walk (path).

Some basic network structures have gained special attention due to their specificity. We are briefly recalling some of these specific network structures hereafter. A complete graph is a graph where every vertex is linked to every other vertex. A complete subgraph is called a clique. A d-regular graph is a graph where all vertices have degree d. A connected graph with no cycles is called a tree. The disjoint union of trees is called a forest. A directed graph whose underlying graph is a tree is called a directed tree. Directed tree may show a root, i.e. a unique vertex from which there is a directed path to any other vertex of the graph. When a root is present in a directed tree the tree is called a rooted tree. A bipartite graph is a graph where the set of vertices can be classified in two disjoint sets and edges are present only between a pair of vertices of different type (for example, actors and movies, authors and papers, students and courses, etc.). From bipartite networks it is quite common to extract one or two projected, i.e. networks containing only vertices of the same type. A graph is planar if its edges can be embedded on a surface like a plane or a sphere, without crossings of the edges.

The information about the edges present in a network are summarized in the adjacency matrix or in the edge list. The adjacency matrix is a square matrix $n \times n$ of elements A_{ij} different from zero when an edge is present between node i and node j. In the presence of an edge, the value of the element is 1 for unweighted networks and equal to the weight of the link w_{ij} for weighted ones.

Networks are investigated under several respects. For example they are investigated both by considering properties of single vertices and edges and by considering a series of ensemble properties of vertices or of groups (also called communities or partitions) of them. Other investigations concerns the relative abundance of structures of a few vertices called triads in social sciences and motifs in natural sciences. Among the measures of single vertex there is the degree (with the corresponding indicator of the strength) and other centrality measures as, for example, the betweenness. The betweenness is a centrality measure obtained by considering which fraction of all shortest paths connecting all pairs of vertices are passing through a specific vertex or edge. Other measures as the clustering coefficient are measuring the degree of local compactness of a network. The local clustering coefficient of vertex i is defined as the ratio between the number of edges observed among the first neighbors of node i and the total number of edges possible among them. The global clustering coefficient computes the fraction of paths of length 2 that are closed.

The most investigated ensemble property of vertices is the degree (and/or strength) distribution. The degree distribution can present a characteristic scale or can be a broad distribution. The characteristics of the degree distribution have been often put in relation with widespread models of networks. A generic model characterized by the same degree distribution of the one of the system of interest and with no additional information is addressed as a configuration model of the considered network. In real networks configuration models are often used as statistical null models to detected structures and regularities that cannot be associated with the type of heterogeneity of the considered system.

The most widespread models of networks are the Erdös–Rényi model (Erdös and Rényi, 1960), the small world model (Watts and Strogatz, 1998), the preferential attachment model (Barabási and Albert, 1999), and the core–periphery model (Borgatti and Everett, 2000). The classic Erdös–Rényi model (Erdös and Rényi, 1960) is a model of random connection between all pair of vertices belonging to a network. The surprising result obtained by Erdös and Rényi was to conclude that in an infinite system the presence of a spanning cluster, i.e. a connected cluster covering large part of the vertices, occurs abruptly ad a function of the average degree in a way that is reminiscent of a percolation phenomenon. The small world model was proposed to solve the apparent puzzle of the observation of many networks that present a high degree of clustering simultaneously with the presence of a short average path length. By studying a transition from a d-regular network to a random network, Watts and Strogatz were able to show that the presence of a very limited number of links connecting remote regions of the network are able to decrease significantly the average path length without equally affecting the degree of local clustering thus providing a rational for the frequent observation of "small world" phenomena. The Barabási–Albert scale free network is a type of network presenting a high heterogeneity of the degree of vertices. One way to generate this wide class of network is by hypothesizing a network growth process based on preferential attachment. The core–periphery model originated in the field of social sciences was originally motivated by a series of studies on national elites, interlocking directorates, and scientific citation networks. These previous studies triggered the developing of a formal model proposed by Borgatti and Everett (2000) where vertices belong to a "core" or to a "periphery". The vertices that belongs to the core are strongly interconnected between them and have also links with vertices of the periphery. The vertices of the periphery have links with vertices of the core but do not have links between them.

The investigation of triads, i.e. subnetworks involving three actors and their links, and their interpretations was originally introduced in studies of social networks performed during the seventies of the last century (Wasserman and Faust, 1994). The same structures have also been investigated in other types of networks such as biological networks (Milo et al., 2002) where they have been labeled as 3-motifs and generalized as k-motifs. Real networks present local structures where vertices have a degree of interconnectedness towards internal vertices much more pronounced that the one observed towards external vertices. When this type of structures are detected in a network it is said that the network is presenting a community (i.e. a cluster) structure. Several methods and algorithms have been proposed to properly detect this type of structures. Comprehensive reviews about the problem of community detection can be found in Fortunato (2010) and Fortunato and Hric (2016).

APPENDIX B ECONOMETRICS SYSTEMIC RISK MEASURE

The first step in market based approaches to quantify systemic risk is to compute the system-wide loss distribution and define a set of systemic events, which are states of the world that occur with a small probability but in which aggregate losses exceed a critical threshold. The systemic importance of a particular bank is then set equal to the expected losses it generates, conditional on systemic events. In other words, systemic importance is measured as the expected participation of individual institutions in systemic events. CoVaR measures the value-at-risk (VaR) of financial institutions conditional on other institutions experiencing financial distress. It provides a boundary on a large loss for some institution(s), given that a particular institution is stressed to a certain degree. While the $q\%$ VaR gives the minimum large loss that is not exceeded $(1 - q\%)$ of the time, $CoVaR_q^{j|i}$ gives the q-percent VaR value for institution j when institution i is at its q-percent VaR value. If one of the institution is replaced by the overall financial system, then CoVaR estimates the size of the losses to the system caused by financial distress of one institution. CoVaR examine the spillover effect from one bank's failure to the whole system, but underplays the importance of institutional size by design. Another disadvantage of CoVaR is that it can be used only to identify systemically important institutions but cannot appropriately aggregate the systemic risk contributions of individual institutions.

The expected shortfall (ES) is the expected loss conditional on the loss being greater than a given limit (usually the 95% VaR). The marginal expected shortfall (MES) of a financial firm is the short-run expected equity loss conditional on the banking sector stock index decreases to its lower fifth percentile (note that the MES can be expressed as a function of the COVAR). Systemic Expected Shortfall is defined as the amount of a bank's equity drop below its target level (which is a fraction of its assets) in case of a systemic crisis when the aggregate banking capital is less than a fraction of aggregate assets. Acharya et al. (2012) show that the SES is related to the MES measured during bad markets outcomes, scaled up by a factor to account for the worse performance in a true crisis. Benoit et al. (2017) show that systemic risk rankings of financial institutions based on their MES tend to mirror rankings obtained by sorting firms on market betas capturing systematic risk rather then systemic risk.

The DIP indicator of systemic risk, is defined as the insurance premium that protects against the distressed losses of banks portfolio. Technically, it is the risk neutral price of a hypothetical insurance contract calculated issued to protect against loses that equal or exceed a fixed level (for example, 10% of the gross liability of all the sampled financial institutions). DIP is similar to the MES measure in that both focus on each bank's potential loss conditional on the system being in distress exceeding a threshold level, and both are coherent risk measures. The threshold definition however is different. The extreme condition is defined by the percentile distribution in the MES setting but by a given threshold loss of the underlying portfolio in the case of DIP. The risk premium comprises two components: the default risk premium, which reflects uncertainty about a financial institution's creditworthiness; and the liquidity risk premium, which reflects market liquidity. The DIP is designed to capture the risk emanating from both deteriorating creditworthiness among financial institutions but also increased risk aversion or price volatility. Unlike the CoVaR and the MES, the DIP uses the incidence of default instead of the plunge of stock prices. The variable utilized by this measure is the default probability of the financial institutions based on their CDS spreads.

Goodhart and Segoviano Basurto (2009) estimate individual banks default probabilities from structural approaches or securities prices and aggregate them at the system level using copulas. From the obtained multivariate distribution of defaults, they derive several banking distress measures.

REFERENCES

Acemoglu, D., Ozdaglar, A., Tahbaz-Salehi, A., 2015. Systemic risk and stability in financial networks. The American Economic Review 105 (2), 564–608.

Acharya, V., Engle, R., Richardson, M., 2012. Capital shortfall: a new approach to ranking and regulating systemic risks. The American Economic Review 102 (3), 59–64.

Adrian, T., Brunnermeier, M., 2016. CoVaR. The American Economic Review 106 (7), 1705–1741.

Affinito, M., 2012. Do interbank customer relationships exist? And how did they function in the crisis? Learning from Italy. Journal of Banking & Finance 36 (12), 3163–3184.

Aikman, D., Alessandri, P., Eklund, B., Gai, P., Kapadia, S., Martin, E., Mora, N., Sterne, G., Willison, M., 2010. Funding liquidity risk in a quantitative model of systemic stability. In: Rodrigo Alfaro, A., Rodrigo Cifuentes, S. (Eds.), Financial Stability, Monetary Policy and Central Banking, pp. 371–410.

Akram, Q., Christophersen, C., 2013. Norwegian overnight interbank interest rates. Computational Economics 41 (1), 11–29.

Aldasoro, I., Alves, I., 2015. Multiplex Interbank Networks and Systemic Importance – An Application to European Data. BIS Working Paper No. 603.

Allen, F., Babus, A., 2008. Networks in Finance. Wharton Financial Institutions Center Working Paper No. 08-07. Available at SSRN: https://ssrn.com/abstract=1094883.

Allen, F., Gale, D., 2000. Financial contagion. Journal of Political Economy 108 (1), 1–33.

Alter, A., Craig, B., Raupach, P., 2015. Centrality-based capital allocations. International Journal of Central Banking 11 (3), 329–377.

Amundsen, E., Arnt, H., 2005. Contagion Risk in the Danish Interbank Market. Danmarks Nationalbank Working Paper No. 2005-25.

Anand, K., Gai, P., Marsili, M., 2012. Rollover risk, network structure and systemic financial crises. Journal of Economic Dynamics and Control 36 (8), 1088–1100.

Anand, K., Craig, B., von Peter, G., 2014. Filling in the Blanks: Network Structure and Interbank Contagion. Bank of Canada Working Paper No. 2014-26.

Anand, K., van Lelyveld, I., Banai, A., Soeren, F., Garratt, R., Halaj, G., Fique, J., Hansen, I., Jaramillo, S.M., Lee, H., Molina-Borboa, J.L., Nobili, S., Rajan, S., Salakhova, D., Silva, T.C., Silvestri, L., de Souza, S.R.S., 2017. The missing links: a global study on uncovering financial network structures from partial data. Journal of Financial Stability. https://doi.org/10.1016/j.jfs.2017.05.012. In press.

Anufriev, M., Panchenko, V., 2015. Connecting the dots: econometric methods for uncovering networks with an application to the Australian financial institutions. Journal of Banking & Finance 61, S241–S255.

Anufriev, M., Deghi, A., Panchenko, V., Pin, P., 2016. A Model of Network Formation for the Overnight Interbank Market. CIFR Paper No. 103/2016. Available at SSRN: https://ssrn.com/abstract=2763964.

Aste, T., Di Matteo, T., Hyde, S.T., 2005. Complex networks on hyperbolic surfaces. Physica A: Statistical Mechanics and Its Applications 346 (1), 20–26.

Aymanns, C., Farmer, J.D., Kleinnijenhuis, A.M., Wetzer, T., 2018. Models of financial stability and their application in stress tests. In: Hommes, C., LeBaron, B. (Eds.), Handbook of Computational Economics, vol. 4. Elsevier, pp. 329–391 (this Handbook).

Baker, W.E., 1984. The social structure of a national securities market. American Journal of Sociology 89 (4), 775–811.

Barabási, A.L., 2016. Network Science. Cambridge University Press, Cambridge, UK.

Barabási, A.L., Albert, R., 1999. Emergence of scaling in random networks. Science 286 (5439), 509–512.

Barfuss, W., Massara, G.P., Di Matteo, T., Aste, T., 2016. Parsimonious modeling with information filtering networks. Physical Review E 94 (6), 062306.

Bargigli, L., 2014. Statistical ensembles for economic networks. Journal of Statistical Physics 155 (4), 810–825.

Bargigli, L., di Iasio, G., Infante, L., Lillo, F., Pierobon, F., 2015. The multiplex structure of interbank networks. Quantitative Finance 15 (4), 673–691.

Barigozzi, M., Fagiolo, G., Garlaschelli, D., 2010. Multinetwork of international trade: a commodity-specific analysis. Physical Review E 81 (4), 1–23.

Basel Committee on Banking Supervision, 2013. Global Systemically Important Banks: Updated Assessment Methodology and the Higher Loss Absorbency Requirement. Bank for International Settlements Report.

Basu, S., Das, S., Michailidis, G., Purnanandam, S., 2017. A System-Wide Approach to Measure Connectivity in the Financial Sector. Available at SSRN: https://ssrn.com/abstract=2816137.

Battiston, S., Puliga, M., Kaushik, R., Tasca, P., Caldarelli, G., 2012. Debtrank: too central to fail? Financial networks, the FED and systemic risk. Scientific Reports 2, 541.

Battiston, S., di Iasio, G., Infante, L., Pierobon, F., 2015. Capital and contagion in financial network. In: Bank for International Settlements (Ed.), Indicators to Support Monetary and Financial Stability Analysis: Data Sources and Statistical Methodologies, vol. 39. Bank for International Settlements.

Bech, M.L., Atalay, E., 2010. The topology of the federal funds market. Physica A: Statistical Mechanics and Its Applications 389 (22), 5223–5246.

Bedayo, M., Mauleon, A., Vannetelbosch, V., 2016. Bargaining in endogenous trading networks. Mathematical Social Sciences 80 (C), 70–82.

Benjamini, Y., Hochberg, Y., 1995. Controlling the false discovery rate: a practical and powerful approach to multiple testing. Journal of the Royal Statistical Society, Series B, Methodological 57 (1), 289–300.

Benoit, S., Colliard, J.E., Hurlin, C., Pérignon, C., 2017. Where the risks lie: a survey on systemic risk. Review of Finance 21 (1), 109–152.

Billio, M., Getmansky, M., Lo, A.W., Pelizzon, L., 2012. Econometric measures of connectedness and systemic risk in the finance and insurance sectors. Journal of Financial Economics 104 (3), 535–559.

Blavarg, M., Nimander, P., 2002. Inter-bank exposures and systemic risk. Sveriges Riksbank Economic Review 2002 (2), 19–45.

Boccaletti, S., Latora, V., Moreno, Y., Chavez, M., Hwang, D.U., 2006. Complex networks: structure and dynamics. Physics Reports 424 (4), 175–308.

Boccaletti, S., Bianconi, G., Criado, R., del Genio, C., Gomez-Gardenes, J., Romance, M., Sendina-Nadal, I., Wang, Z., Zanin, M., 2014. Structure and dynamics of multilayer networks. Physics Reports 544 (1), 1–122.

Bonanno, G., Vandewalle, N., Mantegna, R.N., 2000. Taxonomy of stock market indices. Physical Review E 62 (6), R7615.

Bonanno, G., Lillo, F., Mantegna, R.N., 2001. High-frequency cross-correlation in a set of stocks. Quantitative Finance 1, 96–104.

Bonanno, G., Caldarelli, G., Lillo, F., Mantegna, R.N., 2003. Topology of correlation-based minimal spanning trees in real and model markets. Physical Review E 68 (4), 046130.

Bonanno, G., Caldarelli, G., Lillo, F., Miccichè, S., Vandewalle, N., Mantegna, R.N., 2004. Networks of equities in financial markets. The European Physical Journal B, Condensed Matter and Complex Systems 38 (2), 363–371.

Boorman, S.A., 1975. A combinatorial optimization model for transmission of job information through contact networks. Bell Journal of Economics 6 (1), 216–249.

Borgatti, S.P., Everett, M.G., 2000. Models of core/periphery structures. Social Networks 21 (4), 375–395.

Boss, M., Elsinger, H., Summer, M., Thurner, S., 2004. Network topology of the interbank market. Quantitative Finance 4 (6), 677–684.

Bougheas, S., Kirman, A., 2015. Complex financial networks and systemic risk: a review. In: Commendatore, P., Kayam, S., Kubin, I. (Eds.), Complexity and Geographical Economics. In: Dynamic Modeling and Econometrics in Economics and Finance, vol. 19. Springer, Cham.

Brauning, F., Fecht, F., 2012. Relationship Lending and Peer Monitoring: Evidence from Interbank Payment Data. Available at SSRN: https://ssrn.com/abstract=2020171.

Braverman, A., Minca, A., 2014. Networks of Common Asset Holdings: Aggregation and Measures of Vulnerability. Available at SSRN: https://ssrn.com/abstract=2379669.

Brida, J.G., Risso, W.A., 2008. Multidimensional minimal spanning tree: the Dow Jones case. Physica A: Statistical Mechanics and Its Applications 387 (21), 5205–5210.

Brin, S., Page, L., 1998. The anatomy of a large scale hypertextual Web search engine. Computer Networks and ISDN Systems 30, 107–117.

Brownlees, C., Engle, R., 2016. SRISK: a conditional capital shortfall index for systemic risk assessment. The Review of Financial Studies 30 (1), 48–79.

Buldyrev, S.V., Roni, P., Geralk, P., Stanley, H.E., Havlin, S., 2010. Catastrophic cascade of failures in interdependent networks. Nature 464, 1025–1028.

Cabrales, A., Gottardi, P., Vega-Redondo, F., 2017. Risk-sharing and contagion in networks. The Review of Financial Studies 30 (9), 3086–3127.

Caccioli, F., Shrestha, M., Moore, C., Farmer, J.D., 2014. Stability analysis of financial contagion due to overlapping portfolios. Journal of Banking & Finance 46, 233–245.

Calvo-Armengol, A., Jackson, M.O., 2004. The effects of social networks on employment and inequality. The American Economic Review 94 (3), 426–454.

Castren, O., Kavonius, I.K., 2009. Balance Sheet Interlinkages and Macro-Financial Risk Analysis in the Euro Area. ECB Working Paper No. 1124.

Castiglionesi, F., Navarro, N., 2016. (In)Efficient Interbank Networks. Cahiers du GREThA 2016-13. Groupe de Recherche en Economie Théorique et Appliquée.

Chan-Lau, J.A., 2010. Regulatory Capital Charges for Too-Connected-to-Fail Institutions: A Practical Proposal. IMF Working Paper No. 10/98.

Chang, B., Zhang, S., 2016. Endogenous Market Making and Network Formation. Systemic Risk Centre Discussion Paper No. 50. Available at SSRN: https://ssrn.com/abstract=2600242.

Chung, F., Lu, L., 2002. The average distances in random graphs with given expected degrees. Proceedings of the National Academy of Sciences of the United States of America 99 (25), 15879–15882.

Cifuentes, R., Shin, H.S., Ferrucci, G., 2005. Liquidity risk and contagion. Journal of the European Economic Association 3 (2–3), 556–566.

Cimini, G., Squartini, T., Gabrielli, A., Garlaschelli, D., 2015. Estimating topological properties of weighted networks from limited information. Physical Review E 92 (4), 040802.

Cocco, J., Gomes, F., Martins, N., 2009. Lending relationships in the interbank market. Journal of Financial Intermediation 18 (1), 24–48.

Coelho, R., Gilmore, C.G., Lucey, B., Richmond, P., Hutzler, S., 2007. The evolution of interdependence in world equity markets? Evidence from minimum spanning trees. Physica A: Statistical Mechanics and Its Applications 376, 455–466.

Cont, R., Schaanning, E.F., 2017. Fire Sales, Indirect Contagion and Systemic Stress Testing. Norges Bank Working Paper No. 2/2017. Available at SSRN: https://ssrn.com/abstract=2541114.

Cont, R., Wagalath, L., 2013. Running for the exit: distressed selling and endogenous correlation in financial markets. Mathematical Finance 23 (4), 718–741.

Cont, R., Moussa, A., Santos, E.B., 2013. Network structure and systemic risk in banking systems. In: Fouque, J.-P., Langsam, J.A. (Eds.), Handbook of Systemic Risk. Cambridge University Press.

Coronnello, C., Tumminello, M., Lillo, F., Micciche, S., Mantegna, R.M., 2005. Sector identification in a set of stock return time series traded at the London Stock Exchange. Acta Physica Polonica, Series B 35 (9), 2653–2679.

Corsi, F., Lillo, F., Marmi, S., 2016. When micro prudence increases macro risk: the destabilizing effects of financial innovation, leverage, and diversification. Operations Research 64 (5), 1073–1088.

Craig, B., von Peter, G., 2014. Interbank tiering and money center banks. Journal of Financial Intermediation 23 (3), 322–347.

De Masi, G., Gallegati, M., 2012. Bank–firms topology in Italy. Empirical Economics 43 (2), 851–866.

De Masi, G., Iori, G., Caldarelli, G., 2006. A fitness model for the Italian interbank money market. Physical Review E 74 (6), 066112.

De Masi, G., Fujiwara, Y., Gallegati, M., Greenwald, B., Stiglitz, J.E., 2011. An analysis of the Japanese credit network. Evolutionary and Institutional Economics Review 7 (2), 209–232.

DeGroot, M.H., 1974. Reaching a consensus. Journal of the American Statistical Association 69 (345), 118–121.

Degryse, H., Nguyen, G., 2007. Interbank exposures: an empirical examination of systemic risk in the Belgian banking system. International Journal of Central Banking 3 (2), 123–171.

Di Gangi, D., Lillo, F., Pirino, D., 2015. Assessing systemic risk due to fire sales spillover through maximum entropy network reconstruction. SSRN Electronic Journal. Available at SSRN: https://ssrn.com/abstract=2639178.

Di Matteo, T., Aste, T., 2002. How does the Eurodollar interest rate behave? International Journal of Theoretical and Applied Finance 5 (1), 107–122.

Dias, J., 2012. Sovereign debt crisis in the European Union: a minimum spanning tree approach. Physica A: Statistical Mechanics and Its Applications 391 (5), 2046–2055.

Dias, J., 2013. Spanning trees and the Eurozone crisis. Physica A: Statistical Mechanics and Its Applications 392 (23), 5974–5984.

Diebold, F.X., Yimaz, K., 2014. On the network topology of variance decompositions: measuring the connectedness of financial firms. Journal of Econometrics 182 (1), 119–234.

Drehmann, M., Tarashev, N., 2013. Measuring the systemic importance of interconnected banks. Journal of Financial Intermediation 22 (4), 586–607.

Duarte, F., Eisenbach, T.M., 2015. Fire-Sale Spillovers and Systemic Risk. FRB of New York Staff Report No. 645. Available at SSRN: https://ssrn.com/abstract=2340669.

Elliott, M., Golub, B., Jackson, M.O., 2014. Financial networks and contagion. The American Economic Review 104 (10), 3115–3153.

Elsinger, H., Lehar, A., Summer, M., 2006. Risk assessments for banking systems. Management Science 52, 1301–1314.

Eom, C., Oh, G., Kim, S., 2007. Topological properties of a minimal spanning tree in the Korean and the American stock markets. Journal of the Korean Physical Society 51 (4), 1432–1436.

Erdös, P., Rényi, A., 1960. On the evolution of random graphs. Publication of the Mathematical Institute of the Hungarian Academy of Sciences 5 (1), 17–60.

Espinosa-Vega, M.A., Solé, J., 2011. Cross-border financial surveillance: a network perspective. Journal of Financial Economic Policy 3 (3), 182–205.

Faloutsos, M., Faloutsos, P., Faloutsos, C., 1999. On power-law relationships of the internet topology. Computer Communication Review 29 (4), 251–262.

Farboodi, M., 2015. Intermediation and voluntary exposure to counterparty risk. Mimeo. Princeton University.

Finger, K., Fricke, D., Lux, T., 2013. Network analysis of the e-MID overnight money market: the informational value of different aggregation levels for intrinsic dynamic processes. Computational Management Science 10 (2), 187–211.

Fortunato, S., 2010. Community detection in graphs. Physics Reports 486 (3), 75–174.

Fortunato, S., Hric, D., 2016. Community detection in networks: a user guide. Physics Reports 659, 1–44.

Fourel, V., Heam, J.-C., Salakhova, D., Tavolaro, S., 2013. Domino Effects when Banks Hoard Liquidity: The French Network. Banque de France Working Paper No. 432.

Fricke, D., Lux, T., 2014. Core–periphery structure in the overnight money market: evidence from the e-MID trading platform. Computational Economics 45 (3), 359–395.

Fricke, D., Lux, T., 2015. On the distribution of links in the interbank network: evidence from the e-MID overnight money market. Empirical Economics 49 (4), 1463–1495.

Furfine, C., 1999. Microstructure of the federal funds market. Financial Markets, Institutions & Instruments 8 (5), 24–44.

Furfine, C., 2001. Banks as monitors of other banks: evidence from the overnight federal funds market. Journal of Business 74 (1), 33–58.

Furfine, C.H., 2003. Interbank exposures: quantifying the risk of contagion. Journal of Money, Credit, and Banking 35 (1), 111–128.

Gabbi, G., Iori, G., Jafarey, S., Porter, J., 2015. Financial regulations and bank credit to the real economy. Journal of Economic Dynamics and Control 50, 117–143.

Gabrieli, S., Salakhova, D., Vuillemey, G., 2014. Cross-Border Interbank Contagion in the European Banking Sector. Banque de France Working Paper No. 545.

Gai, P., Kapadia, S., 2010. Liquidity hoarding, network externalities, and interbank market collapse. Proceedings of the Royal Society A 466, 2401–2423.

Gandy, A., Veraart, L.A.M., 2017. A Bayesian methodology for systemic risk assessment in financial networks. Management Science 63 (12), 4428–4446.

Gauthier, C., Lehar, A., Souissi, M., 2012. Macroprudential capital requirements and systemic risk. Journal of Financial Intermediation 21 (4), 594–618.

Georg, C.P., 2013. The effect of the interbank network structure on contagion and common shocks. Journal of Banking & Finance 37 (7), 2216–2228.

Giada, L., Marsili, M., 2001. Data clustering and noise undressing of correlation matrices. Physical Review E 63 (6), 061101.

Giada, L., Marsili, M., 2002. Algorithms of maximum likelihood data clustering with applications. Physica A: Statistical Mechanics and Its Applications 315 (3), 650–664.

Gilmore, C.G., Lucey, B.M., Boscia, M., 2008. An ever-closer union? Examining the evolution of linkages of European equity markets via minimum spanning trees. Physica A: Statistical Mechanics and Its Applications 387 (25), 6319–6329.

Glasserman, P., Young, H.P., 2015. How likely is contagion in financial networks? Journal of Banking & Finance 50 (C), 383–399.

Goodhart, C.A.E., Segoviano Basurto, M.A., 2009. Banking Stability Measures. IMF Working Paper No. 9(4).

Górski, A., Kwapień, J., Oświęcimka, P., Drożdż, S., 2008. Minimal spanning tree graphs and power like scaling in FOREX networks. Acta Physica Polonica A 114 (3), 531–538.

Goyal, S., 2012. Connections: An Introduction to the Economics of Networks. Princeton University Press, NJ.

Goyal, S., Vega-Redondo, F., 2005. Network formation and social coordination. Games and Economic Behavior 50 (2), 178–207.

Granovetter, M.S., 1973. The strength of weak ties. American Journal of Sociology 78 (6), 1360–1380.

Greenwood, R., Landier, A., Thesmar, D., 2015. Vulnerable banks. Journal of Financial Economics 115 (3), 471–485.

Grilli, R., Iori, G., Stamboglis, N., Tedeschi, G., 2017. A networked economy: a survey on the effects of interaction in credit markets. In: Gallegati, M., Palestrini, A., Russo, A. (Eds.), Introduction to Agent-Based Economics. Academic Press.

Gualdi, S., Cimini, G., Primicerio, K., Di Clemente, R., Challet, D., 2016. Statistically validated network of portfolio overlaps and systemic risk. Scientific Reports 6, 39467.

Gurgone, A., Iori, G., Jafarey, S., 2017. Liquidity Hoarding in a Macroeconomic Agent-Based Model with an Interbank Market. Available at SSRN: https://ssrn.com/abstract=3045820.

Halaj, G., Kok, C., 2013. Assessing interbank contagion using simulated networks. Computational Management Science 10 (2), 157–186.

Haldane, A., 2013. Rethinking the financial network. In: Jansen, S.A. (Ed.), Fragile Stabilität. Springer Fachmedien Wiesbaden, Wiesbaden.

Haldane, A.G., May, R.M., 2011. Systemic risk in banking ecosystems. Nature 469 (7330), 351–355.

Han, J., Pei, J., Kamber, M., 2011. Data Mining: Concepts and Techniques. Elsevier Science.

Hatzopoulos, V., Iori, G., Mantegna, R.N., Micciché, S., Tumminello, M., 2015. Quantifying preferential trading in the e-MID interbank market. Quantitative Finance 15 (4), 693–710.

Heider, F., 1946. Attitudes and cognitive organization. The Journal of Psychology 21 (1), 107–112.

Hochberg, Y., Tamhane, A.C., 1987. Multiple Comparison Procedures. Wiley, NJ.

Holland, P.W., Leinhardt, S., 1981. An exponential family of probability distributions for directed graphs. Journal of the American Statistical Association 76 (373), 33–50.

Huang, X., Zhou, H., Zhu, H., 2012. Systemic risk contributions. Journal of Financial Services Research 42, 53–83.

Huang, X., Vodenska, I., Havlin, S., Stanley, H.E., 2013. Cascading failures in bi-partite graphs: model for systemic risk propagation. Scientific Reports 3, 1219.

IMF, 2010. A Fair and Substantial Contribution by the Financial Sector. IMF Interim Report for the G-20.

IMF-BIS-FSB, 2009. Guidance to Assess the Systemic Importance of Financial Institutions, Markets and Institutions: Initial Considerations, Background Paper. Report of the International Monetary Fund, the Bank for International Settlements, and the Financial Stability Report to the G20 Financial Ministers and Central Bank Governors.

Inaoka, H., Ninomiya, T., Taniguchi, K., Shimizu, T., Takayasu, H., 2004. Fractal Network Derived from Banking Transactions: An Analysis of Network Structures Formed by Financial Institutions. Bank of Japan Working Paper No. 04-E-04.

in't Veld, D., van Lelyveld, I., 2014. Finding the core: network structure in interbank markets. Journal of Banking & Finance 49, 27–40.

Iori, G., Porter, J., 2016. Agent based modelling for financial markets. In: Chen, S.-H., Kaboudan, M. (Eds.), The Oxford Handbook on Computational Economics and Finance. Oxford University Press.

Iori, G., Jafarey, S., Padilla, F.G., 2006. Systemic risk on the interbank market. Journal of Economic Behavior & Organization 61 (4), 525–542.

Iori, G., de Masi, G., Precup, O., Gabbi, G., Caldarelli, G., 2008. A network analysis of the Italian overnight money market. Journal of Economic Dynamics and Control 32 (1), 259–278.

Iori, G., Mantegna, R.N., Marotta, L., Micciche, S., Porter, J., Tumminello, M., 2015. Networked relationships in the e-MID interbank market: a trading model with memory. Journal of Economic Dynamics and Control 50, 98–116.

Jackson, M.O., 2008. Social and Economic Networks. Princeton University Press.

Jackson, M.O., Wolinsky, A., 1996. A strategic model of social and economic networks. Journal of Economic Theory 71, 44–74.

Jang, W., Lee, J., Chang, W., 2011. Currency crises and the evolution of foreign exchange market: evidence from minimum spanning tree. Physica A: Statistical Mechanics and Its Applications 390 (4), 707–718.

Jung, W.S., Chae, S., Yang, J.S., Moon, H.T., 2006. Characteristics of the Korean stock market correlations. Physica A: Statistical Mechanics and Its Applications 361 (1), 263–271.

Kazemilari, M., Mardani, A., Streimikiene, D., Zavadskas, E.K., 2017. An overview of renewable energy companies in stock exchange: evidence from minimal spanning tree approach. Renewable Energy 102, 107–117.

Kenett, D.Y., Tumminello, M., Madi, A., Gur-Gershgoren, G., Mantegna, R.N., Ben-Jacob, E., 2010. Dominating clasp of the financial sector revealed by partial correlation analysis of the stock market. PLoS ONE 5 (12), e15032.

Kenett, D.Y., Gao, J., Huang, X., Shao, S., Vodenska, I., Buldyrev, S.V., Paul, G., Stanley, H.E., Havlin, S., 2014. Network of interdependent networks: overview of theory and applications. In: D'Agostino, G., Scala, A. (Eds.), Networks of Networks: The Last Frontier of Complexity. Understanding Complex Systems. Springer, Cham.

Kivela, M., Arenas, A., Barthelemy, M., Gleeson, J.P., Moreno, Y., Porter, M.A., 2014. Multilayer networks. Journal of Complex Networks 2 (3), 203–271.

Kleinberg, J.M., 1998. Authoritative sources in a hyperlinked environment. Journal of the ACM 46 (5), 604–632.

Kocheturov, A., Batsyn, M., Pardalos, P.M., 2014. Dynamics of cluster structures in a financial market network. Physica A: Statistical Mechanics and Its Applications 413, 523–533.

Korinek, A., 2011. The new economics of capital controls imposed for prudential reasons. IMF Economic Review 59 (3), 523–561.

Kristoufek, L., Janda, K., Zilberman, D., 2012. Correlations between biofuels and related commodities before and during the food crisis: a taxonomy perspective. Energy Economics 34 (5), 1380–1391.

Kullmann, L., Kertesz, J., Mantegna, R.N., 2000. Identification of clusters of companies in stock indices via Potts super-paramagnetic transitions. Physica A: Statistical Mechanics and Its Applications 287 (3), 412–419.

Kyle, A.S., Xiong, W., 2001. Contagion as a wealth effect. The Journal of Finance 56 (4), 1401–1440.

Laloux, L., Cizeau, P., Bouchaud, J.P., Potters, M., 1999. Noise dressing of financial correlation matrices. Physical Review Letters 83 (7), 1467–1470.

Langfield, S., Liu, Z., Ota, T., 2014. Mapping the UK interbank system. Journal of Banking & Finance 45, 288–303.

Leduc, M.V., Thurner, S., 2017. Incentivizing resilience in financial networks. Journal of Economic Dynamics & Control 82, 44–66.

Lenzu, S., Tedeschi, G., 2012. Systemic risk on different interbank network topologies. Physica A: Statistical Mechanics and Its Applications 391 (18), 4331–4341.

León, C., 2015. Financial Stability from a Network Perspective. CentER Dissertation Series. CentER, Tilburg University.

León, C., Murcia, A., 2013. Systemic Importance Index for Financial Institutions: A Principal Component Analysis Approach. ODEON No. 7. Available at SSRN: https://ssrn.com/abstract=2408093.

León, C., Leiton, K., Pérez, J., 2014. Extracting the sovereigns CDS market hierarchy: a correlation-filtering approach. Physica A: Statistical Mechanics and Its Applications 415, 407–420.

Li, M.X., Palchykov, V., Jiang, Z.Q., Kaski, K., Kertész, J., Micciché, S., Tumminello, M., Zhou, W.X., Mantegna, R.N., 2014a. Statistically validated mobile communication networks: the evolution of motifs in European and Chinese data. New Journal of Physics 16 (8), 083038.

Li, M.X., Jiang, Z.Q., Xie, W.J., Micciché, S., Tumminello, M., Zhou, W.X., Mantegna, R.N., 2014b. A comparative analysis of the statistical properties of large mobile phone calling networks. Scientific Reports 4, 5132.

Liedorp, F.R., Medema, L., Koetter, M., Koning, R.H., van Lelyveld, I., 2010. Peer Monitoring or Contagion? Interbank Market Exposure and Bank Risk. De Nederlandsche Bank Working Paper No. 248.

Lu, L., Zhoua, T., 2011. Link prediction in complex networks: a survey. Physica A: Statistical Mechanics and Its Applications 390 (6), 1150–1170.

Lubloy, A., 2005. The domino effect on the Hungarian interbank market. Kozgazdasagi Szemle (Economic Review) 42 (4), 377–401.

Lux, T., 2016. A model of the topology of the bank? Firm credit network and its role as channel of contagion. Journal of Economic Dynamics and Control 66, 36–53.

MacMahon, M., Garlaschelli, D., 2013. Community detection for correlation matrices. Physical Review X 5 (2), 021006.

Manconi, A., Massa, M., Yasuda, A., 2012. The role of institutional investors in propagating the crisis of 2007–2008. Journal of Financial Economics 104 (3), 491–518.

Manna, M., Schiavone, A., 2012. Externalities in Interbank Network: Results from a Dynamic Simulation Model. Bank of Italy Temi di Discussione (Economic Working Papers) No. 893.

Mantegna, R.N., 1999. Hierarchical structure in financial markets. The European Physical Journal B, Condensed Matter and Complex Systems 11 (1), 193–197.

Marčenko, V.A., Pastur, L.A., 1967. Distribution of eigenvalues for some sets of random matrices. Mathematics of the USSR, Sbornik 1 (4), 457–483.

Marchiori, M., 1997. The quest for correct information on the web: hyper search engines. Computer Networks and ISDN Systems 29 (8), 1225–1235.

Markose, S., Ginsante, S., Shaghaghi, A.R., 2012. 'Too interconnected to fail' financial network of US CDS market: topological fragility and systemic risk. Journal of Economic Behavior & Organization 83 (3), 627–646.

Marotta, L., Micciché, S., Fujiwara, Y., Iyetomi, H., Aoyama, H., Gallegati, M., Mantegna, R.N., 2015. Bank–firm credit network in Japan: an analysis of a bipartite network. PLoS ONE 10 (5), e0123079.

Marotta, L., Micciché, S., Fujiwara, Y., Iyetomi, H., Aoyama, H., Gallegati, M., Mantegna, R.N., 2016. Backbone of credit relationships in the Japanese credit market. EPJ Data Science 5 (1), 1–14.

Marti, G., Nielsen, F., Bińkowski, M., Donnat, P., 2017. A review of two decades of correlations, hierarchies, networks and clustering in financial markets. arXiv preprint arXiv:1703.00485.

Martinez-Jaramillo, S., Alexandrova-Kabadjova, B., Bravo-Benitez, B., Solorzano-Margain, J.P., 2014. An empirical study of the Mexican banking system's network and its implications for systemic risk. Journal of Economic Dynamics and Control 40, 242–265.

Mastromatteo, I., Zarinelli, E., Marsili, M., 2012. Reconstruction of financial networks for robust estimation of systemic risk. Journal of Statistical Mechanics: Theory and Experiment 2012 (03), P03011.

McDonald, M., Suleman, O., Williams, S., Howison, S., Johnson, N.F., 2005. Detecting a currency's dominance or dependence using foreign exchange network trees. Physical Review E 72 (4), 046106.

Metha, M.L., 1991. Random Matrices. Academic Press.

Micciché, S., Bonanno, G., Lillo, F., Mantegna, R.N., 2003. Degree stability of a minimum spanning tree of price return and volatility. Physica A: Statistical Mechanics and Its Applications 324 (1), 66–73.

Milo, R., Shen-Orr, S., Itzkovitz, S., Kashtan, N., Chklovskii, D., Alon, U., 2002. Network motifs: simple building blocks of complex networks. Science 298 (5594), 824–827.

Miranda, R., Tabak, B., 2013. Contagion Risk Within Firm–Bank Bivariate Networks. Central Bank of Brazil, Research Department No. 322.

Mistrulli, P.E., 2011. Assessing financial contagion in the interbank market: maximum entropy versus observed interbank lending patterns. Journal of Banking & Finance 35 (5), 1114–1127.

Mizuno, T., Takayasu, H., Takayasu, M., 2006. Correlation networks among currencies. Physica A: Statistical Mechanics and Its Applications 364, 336–342.

Montagna, M., Kok, C., 2016. Multi-Layered Interbank Model for Assessing Systemic Risk. ECB Working Paper No. 1944.

Montagna, M., Lux, T., 2013. Hubs and Resilience: Towards More Realistic Models of the Interbank Markets. Kiel Working Paper No. 1826.

Newman, M., 2010. Networks: An Introduction. Oxford University Press, Oxford, UK.

Nier, E., Yang, J., Yorulmazer, T., Alentorn, A., 2007. Network models and financial stability. Journal of Economic Dynamics and Control 31 (6), 2033–2060.

Onnela, J.P., Chakraborti, A., Kaski, K., Kertész, J., 2002. Dynamic asset trees and portfolio analysis. The European Physical Journal B, Condensed Matter and Complex Systems 30 (3), 285–288.

Onnela, J.P., Chakraborti, A., Kaski, K., Kertész, J., Kanto, A., 2003. Dynamics of market correlations: taxonomy and portfolio analysis. Physical Review E 68 (5), 056110.

Onnela, J.P., Kaski, K., Kertész, J., 2004. Clustering and information in correlation based financial networks. The European Physical Journal B, Condensed Matter and Complex Systems 38 (2), 353–362.

Pareto, V., 1897. Cours d'Economie Politique. https://www.institutcoppet.org/wp-content/uploads/2012/05/Cours-déconomie-politique-Tome-I-Vilfredo-Pareto.pdf. https://www.institutcoppet.org/wp-content/uploads/2012/05/Cours-déconomie-politique-Tome-II-Vilfredo-Pareto.pdf.

Plerou, V., Gopikrishnan, P., Rosenow, B., Amaral, L.A.N., Stanley, H.E., 1999. Universal and nonuniversal properties of cross correlations in financial time series. Physical Review Letters 83 (7), 1471.

Poledna, S., Thurner, S., 2016. Elimination of systemic risk in financial networks by means of a systemic risk transaction tax. Quantitative Finance 16 (10), 1599–1613.

Poledna, S., Thurner, S., Farmer, J.D., Geanakoplos, J., 2014. Leverage-induced systemic risk under Basel II and other credit risk policies. Journal of Banking & Finance 42, 199–212.

Poledna, S., Molina-Borboa, J.L., Martínez-Jaramillo, S., van der Leij, M., Thurner, S., 2015. The multilayer network nature of systemic risk and its implications for the costs of financial crises. Journal of Financial Stability 20, 70–81.

Precup, O.V., Iori, G., 2007. Cross-correlation measures in the high-frequency domain. European Journal of Finance 13 (4), 319–331.

Propper, M., van Lelyveld, I., Heijmans, R., 2013. Network dynamics of TOP payments. Journal of Financial Market Infrastructures 1 (3), 3–29.

Puhr, C., Seliger, R., Sigmund, M., 2012. Contagiousness and Vulnerability in the Austrian Interbank Market. Oesterreichische Nationalbank (Austrian Central Bank) Financial Stability Report 24, pp. 62–78.

Radicchi, F., Ramasco, J.J., Fortunato, S., 2011. Information filtering in complex weighted networks. Physical Review E 83 (4), 046101.

Roukny, T., Bersini, H., Pirotte, H., Caldarelli, G., Battiston, S., 2013. Default cascades in complex networks: topology and systemic risk. Scientific Reports 3, 2759.

Serrano, M.Á., Boguná, M., Vespignani, A., 2009. Extracting the multiscale backbone of complex weighted networks. Proceedings of the National Academy of Sciences of the United States of America 106 (16), 6483–6488.

Shapley, L.S., 1953. A value for n-person games. In: Kuhn, H., Tucker, A. (Eds.), Contribution to the Theory of Games, vol. II. Princeton.

Sheldon, G., Maurer, M., 1998. Interbank lending and systemic risk: an empirical analysis for Switzerland. The Swiss Journal of Economics and Statistics 134 (4), 685–704.

Shin, H.S., 2010. Risk and Liquidity. Oxford University Press.

Sieczka, P., Holyst, J.A., 2009. Correlations in commodity markets. Physica A: Statistical Mechanics and Its Applications 388 (8), 1621–1630.

Solórzano-Margain, J., Martínez-Jaramillo, S., Lopez-Gallo, F., 2013. Financial contagion: extending the exposures network of the Mexican financial system. Computational Management Science 10 (2), 125–155.

Song, D.M., Tumminello, M., Zhou, W.X., Mantegna, R.N., 2011. Evolution of worldwide stock markets, correlation structure, and correlation-based graphs. Physical Review E 84 (2), 026108.

Song, W.M., Di Matteo, T., Aste, T., 2012. Hierarchical information clustering by means of topologically embedded graphs. PLoS ONE 7 (3), e31929.

Soramäki, K., Bech, M.L., Arnold, J., Glass, R.J., Beyeler, W.E., 2007. The topology of interbank payment flows. Physica A: Statistical Mechanics and Its Applications 379, 317–333.

Squartini, T., van Lelyveld, I., Garlaschelli, D., 2013. Early-warning signals of topological collapse in interbank networks. Scientific Reports 3, 3357.

Squartini, T., Cimini, G., Gabrielli, A., Garlaschelli, D., 2017. Network reconstruction via density sampling. Applied Network Science 2 (1), 1–13.

Strauss, D., 1986. On a general class of models for interaction. SIAM Review 28 (4), 513–527.

Tabak, B.M., Serra, T.R., Cajueiro, D.O., 2010a. Topological properties of stock market networks: the case of Brazil. Physica A: Statistical Mechanics and Its Applications 389 (16), 3240–3249.

Tabak, B.M., Serra, T.R., Cajueiro, D.O., 2010b. Topological properties of commodities networks. The European Physical Journal B, Condensed Matter and Complex Systems 74 (2), 243–249.

Tarashev, N., Borio, C., Tsatsaronis, K., 2010. Attributing Systemic Risk to Individual Institutions. BIS Working Paper No. 308.

Tasca, P., Battiston, S., 2016. Market procyclicality and systemic risk. Quantitative Finance 16 (8), 1219–1235.

Temizsoy, A., Iori, G., Montes-Rojas, G., 2015. The role of bank relationships in the interbank market. Journal of Economic Dynamics and Control 59, 118–141.

Temizsoy, A., Iori, G., Montes-Rojas, G., 2017. Network centrality and funding rates in the e-MID interbank market. Journal of Financial Stability 33, 346–365. https://doi.org/10.1016/j.jfs.2016.11.003.

Thiago, C.S., de Souza, S.R.S., Tabak, B.M., 2016. Network structure analysis of the Brazilian interbank market. Emerging Markets Review 26, 130–152.

Travers, J., Milgram, S., 1967. The small world problem. Phychology Today 1, 61–67.

Tu, C., 2014. Cointegration-based financial networks study in Chinese stock market. Physica A: Statistical Mechanics and Its Applications 402, 245–254.

Tumminello, M., Aste, T., Di Matteo, T., Mantegna, R.N., 2005. A tool for filtering information in complex systems. Proceedings of the National Academy of Sciences of the United States of America 102 (30), 10421–10426.

Tumminello, M., Coronnello, C., Lillo, F., Micciché, S., Mantegna, R.N., 2007. Spanning trees and bootstrap reliability estimation in correlation-based networks. International Journal of Bifurcation and Chaos 17 (07), 2319–2329.

Tumminello, M., Lillo, F., Mantegna, R.N., 2010. Correlation, hierarchies, and networks in financial markets. Journal of Economic Behavior & Organization 75 (1), 40–58.

Tumminello, M., Micciché, S., Lillo, F., Piilo, J., Mantegna, R.N., 2011. Statistically validated networks in bipartite complex systems. PLoS ONE 6 (3), e17994.

Tumminello, M., Lillo, F., Piilo, J., Mantegna, R.N., 2012. Identification of clusters of investors from their real trading activity in a financial market. New Journal of Physics 14 (1), 013041.

Upper, C., 2011. Simulation methods to assess the danger of contagion in interbank markets. Journal of Financial Stability 7 (3), 111–125.

Upper, C., Worms, A., 2004. Estimating bilateral exposures in the German interbank market: is there a danger of contagion? European Economic Review 45 (4), 827–849.

van der Leij, M., in't Veld, D., Hommes, C., 2016. The Formation of a Core Periphery Structure in Financial Networks. Tinbergen Institute Discussion Paper TI 2014-098/II.

van Lelyveld, I., Liedorp, F., 2006. Interbank contagion in the Dutch banking sector: a sensitivity analysis. International Journal of Central Banking 2 (2), 99–133.

Vega-Redondo, F., 2007. Complex Social Networks. Cambridge University Press.

Wang, G.J., Xie, C., 2015. Correlation structure and dynamics of international real estate securities markets: a network perspective. Physica A: Statistical Mechanics and Its Applications 424, 176–193.

Wang, G.J., Xie, C., Han, F., Sun, B., 2012. Similarity measure and topology evolution of foreign exchange markets using dynamic time warping method: evidence from minimal spanning tree. Physica A: Statistical Mechanics and Its Applications 391 (16), 4136–4146.

Wang, G.J., Xie, C., Chen, Y.J., Chen, S., 2013. Statistical properties of the foreign exchange network at different time scales: evidence from detrended cross-correlation coefficient and minimum spanning tree. Entropy 15 (5), 1643–1662.

Wang, Y., Yang, X.G., 2017. Banks–firms credit network in China. In: 2017 36th Chinese Control Conference (CCC), pp. 11308–11313.

Wasserman, S., Faust, K., 1994. Social Network Analysis: Methods and Applications. Cambridge University Press, Cambridge, UK.

Watts, D.J., Strogatz, S.H., 1998. Collective dynamics of small-world networks. Nature 393 (6684), 440–442.

Webber, L., Willison, M., 2011. Systemic capital requirements. Macroprudential Regulation and Policy 60, 44–50.

Wells, S., 2004. Financial interlinkages in the United Kingdom's interbank market and the risk of contagion. Bank of England Quarterly Bulletin 44 (3), 331.

Yang, C., Chen, Y., Niu, L., Li, Q., 2014. Cointegration analysis and influence rank? A network approach to global stock markets. Physica A: Statistical Mechanics and Its Applications 400, 168–185.

Zhang, Y., Lee, G.H.T., Wong, J.C., Kok, J.L., Prusty, M., Cheong, S.A., 2011. Will the US economy recover in 2010? A minimal spanning tree study. Physica A: Statistical Mechanics and Its Applications 390 (11), 2020–2050.

Zheng, Z., Yamasaki, K., Tenenbaum, J.N., Stanley, H.E., 2013. Carbon-dioxide emissions trading and hierarchical structure in worldwide finance and commodities markets. Physical Review E 87 (1), 012814.

Zhuang, R., Hu, B., Ye, Z., 2008. Minimal spanning tree for Shanghai–Shenzhen 300 stock index. In: Evolutionary Computation CEC 2008 (IEEE World Congress on Computational Intelligence), pp. 1417–1424.

Zlatić, V., Gabbi, G., Abraham, H., 2015. Reduction of systemic risk by means of Pigouvian taxation. PLoS ONE 10 (7), e0114928.

Heterogeneity and Networks[*]

12

Sanjeev Goyal

Faculty of Economics and Christ's College, University of Cambridge, Cambridge,
United Kingdom
e-mail address: sg472@cam.ac.uk

CONTENTS

1 INTRODUCTION AND OVERVIEW

Social, economic and infrastructure networks are an important feature of an economy. Empirical research has highlighted the presence of great heterogeneity in these networks. We see this heterogeneity in Twitter (the number of followers ranges from less than ten to well over a million), in production networks (where real estate and finance form hubs), and in transport networks (airlines typically operate hub-spoke routes). This heterogeneity in connections raises two questions: one, how does network structure shape behavior at an individual and at the system level and two, what are the processes that give rise to such unequal networks? In this chapter I will argue one, that networks can have large and differentiated effects on behavior and two, that social and economic pressures facilitate the formation of heterogeneous networks.

---

[*]I thank Gustavo Paez for expert research assistance and am grateful to Joerg Kalbfuss, Alan Walsh, and two referees for helpful comments. I thank Cars Hommes for editorial guidance and for suggestions on an earlier draft.

Handbook of Computational Economics, Volume 4, ISSN 1574-0021, https://doi.org/10.1016/bs.hescom.2018.03.003

Thus networks can play an important role in understanding the diversity in economic outcomes that is observed empirically. I will draw heavily on two recent survey papers, Goyal (2016, 2017). Bramoulle et al. (2016) provide a panoramic overview of recent research on the economics of networks. Easley and Kleinberg (2010) offer a broad inter-disciplinary introduction to the study of networks.

The key methodological innovation of the early research on the economics of networks in the 1990s was the introduction of graph theory alongside purposeful agents. Two ideas were central: the study of how the network architecture shapes human behavior and the study of how purposeful individuals form links and thereby create networks. Over the past two decades, economists have developed a sophisticated understanding of the scope of these ideas and they are increasingly being used to address a wide range of applied questions.

To develop the main arguments in a straightforward way, I will concentrate on covering four research papers in some detail: a model of local strategic substitutes on a network Bramoulle and Kranton (2007), a model of trading in networks Choi et al. (2017), a model of simultaneous network formation and behavioral choice with local strategic substitutes Galeotti and Goyal (2010), and finally, a model of network formation where payoffs are determined by trade and intermediation benefits Goyal and Vega-Redondo (2007). In the first two papers the network is exogenous, and the latter two papers should be seen as a generalization in which the network is treated as endogenous.

The rest of the paper is organized as follows. Section 2 presents basic notation and terminology on networks. Section 3 discusses the theory of network formation, while Section 4 examines the effects of networks on behavior by presenting a framework that combines individual choice, networks and markets. Section 5 presents a discussion of models in which individuals choose actions as well as choose links, while Section 6 concludes.

2 NETWORKS: TERMINOLOGY

I begin by introducing some notation and a few basic concepts about networks. For a general overview of graph theory, see Bollobas (1998); for an introduction of network concepts to economics, see Goyal (2007), Jackson (2008) and Vega-Redondo (2007).

A network g comprises a collection of nodes $N = \{1, 2, \ldots, n\}$ with $n \geq 2$, and the links (g_{ij}), $i, j \in N$, between them. A node may be an individual, a firm, a project, a city or a country, or even a collection of such entities. A link between them signifies a relation. In some instances it is natural to think of the link as bidirectional: examples include friendship, research collaboration and defense alliance. In other instances, a link is unidirectional: examples include investment in a project, citation, a web link, listening to a speech or following a tweet. In this section I will focus on undirected graphs; the concepts and terminology extend naturally to directed networks.

In case $g_{ij} = 0$ in g, $g + g_{ij}$ adds the link $g_{ij} = 1$, while if $g_{ij} = 1$ in g then $g + g_{ij} = g$. Similarly, if $g_{ij} = 1$ in g, $g - g_{ij}$ deletes the link g_{ij}, while if $g_{ij} = 0$

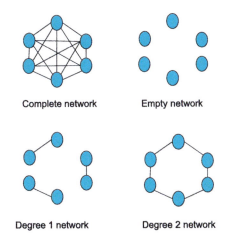

Complete network   Empty network

Degree 1 network   Degree 2 network

FIGURE 1

Regular networks.

in g, then $g - g_{ij} = g$. Let $N_i(g) = \{j \,|\, g_{ij} = 1\}$ denote the nodes with whom node i has a link; this set will be referred to as the *neighbors* of i. Let $\eta_i(g) = |N_i(g)|$ denote the number of connections/neighbors of node i in network g. Moreover, for any integer $d \geq 1$, let $\mathcal{N}_i^d(g)$ be the *d-neighborhood* of i in g: this is defined inductively, $\mathcal{N}_i^1(g) = N_i(g)$ and $\mathcal{N}^k(g) = \mathcal{N}_i^{k-1}(g) \cup (\cup_{j \in \mathcal{N}_i^{k-1}} N_j(g))$. So the 2-neighborhood of i includes the neighbors of i and the neighbors of the neighbors of i.

There is a path from i to j in g either if $g_{ij} = 1$ or there exist distinct nodes $j_1, \ldots, j_m$ different from i and j such that $g_{i,j_1} = g_{j_1,j_2} = \cdots = g_{j_m,j} = 1$. A component is a maximal collection of nodes such that there is a path between every pair of nodes. A network g is said to be connected if there exists only one component, i.e., there is a path from any node i to every other node j.

Let $\mathbf{N}_{k_1}(g), \mathbf{N}_{k_2}(g), \ldots, \mathbf{N}_{k_m}(g)$ be a partition of nodes: two nodes belong to the same group if and only if they have the same degree. A network is said to be *regular* if every node has the same number of links i.e., $\eta_i(g) = \eta \; \forall i \in N$ (and so all nodes belong to one group in the partition). The *complete* network, g^c, is a regular network in which $\eta = n - 1$, while the *empty* network, g^e, is a regular network in which $\eta = 0$. Fig. 1 presents regular networks.

Once we step outside the class of regular networks, a wide variety of networks arise. A *core-periphery* network contains two groups: the periphery, $\mathbf{N}_1(g)$, and the core, $\mathbf{N}_2(g)$. Nodes in the periphery have a link only with nodes in the core; nodes in the core are fully linked with each other and have links with a subset of nodes in the periphery. The star (or hub-spoke) network is a special case in which the core contains a single node. The nested split graph is a partition of nodes $\{\mathbf{N}_1, \ldots, \mathbf{N}_m\}$ into two or more sets such that for $j \in \mathbf{N}_{m-s}$, $s = \{0, 1, \ldots, m - 1\}$, $g_{j,k} = 1$ if and only if $k \in \mathbf{N}_l$, where $l > s$. Fig. 2 presents a range of such networks.

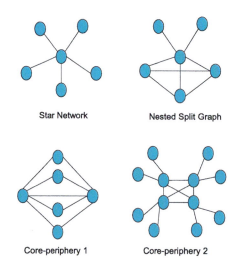

Star Network

Nested Split Graph

Core-periphery 1

Core-periphery 2

FIGURE 2

Irregular networks.

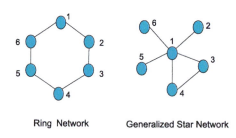

Ring Network

Generalized Star Network

FIGURE 3

Differences in networks.

It is important to note that networks allow for a very rich range of possibility, that go beyond degrees. To bring out this point in a simple way, consider a degree-2 regular network and a (generalized) star network with the same number of links. This is presented in Fig. 3.

Now observe that as the number of nodes increases, 'distance' between the nodes is unbounded in the ring but it is bounded above by 2 in the star network. In the regular network, all nodes are essentially symmetric, while in the core-periphery network the hub nodes clearly have many more connections and are more 'central' than the other nodes.

3 THE THEORY OF NETWORK FORMATION

The finding that the social structure has large effects on individual behavior and payoffs suggests that individuals have an incentive to create networks that are advantageous to themselves. This observation has inspired the theory of network formation. In this section I briefly sketch the building blocks of the theory. The exposition borrows heavily from Goyal (2016, 2017).

The beginnings of the theory of network formation can be traced back to the work of Boorman (1975), Aumann and Myerson (1988) and Myerson (1991). The general framework and a systematic theory of network formation was first presented in Bala and Goyal (2000) and in Jackson and Wolinsky (1996). The two papers present complementary approaches to the process of network formation.[1]

I first take up the approach of *unilateral link formation*. This approach was introduced in Goyal (1993) and systematically studied in Bala and Goyal (2000). Consider a collection of individuals, each of whom can form a link with any subset of the remaining players. Link formation is unilateral: an individual can decide to form a link with another individual by paying for the link. It takes time and effort to sustain a link. A link with another individual allows access, in part and in due course, to the benefits available to the latter via his own links. Thus individual links generate externalities whose value depends on the level of decay/delay associated with indirect links. As links are created on an individual basis, the network formation process can be analyzed as a noncooperative game. The paper allows for general payoffs: utility increases in the number of people accessed and it decreases in the number of maintained links

There are interesting practical examples of this type of link formation – hyperlinks across web-pages, citations, 'following' relations on Twitter, and gifts. But the principal appeal of this model is its simplicity. This simplicity allows for a systematic study of a number of central questions concerning social and economic networks.

Bala and Goyal (2000) provide a characterization of the architecture of equilibrium networks. The equilibrium networks have simple architectures: star (hub-spoke) networks and the cycle are salient. This prediction of great heterogeneity in connections and the presence of highly connected 'hub' nodes is an important theoretical contribution. In the star network, the central hub node will generally earn much larger payoffs as compared to the peripheral nodes. Thus, the theory provides a foundation for the idea that social structures may sustain great inequality.[2]

---

[1] In these models, nodes themselves create links; for an early analysis of firms creating networks see the work on airline routing networks and pricing by Hendricks et al. (1995, 1999).

[2] The processes leading to unequal connections have also been studied by statistical physicists and other scientists. In particular, physicists have been developed a model to derive a scale-free or power law degree distribution. (A power law degree distribution takes the form $f(k) = \alpha k^{-\beta}$, with $\alpha > 0$ and $\beta > 0$). Barabasi and Albert (1999) formulate a dynamic model of network formation in which, at every point in time, a new node arrives and forms new links with existing nodes. The probability that the new node connects to an existing node is proportional to the number of links the existing node has. This is referred to

I turn next to *two-sided or bilateral link formation*. This approach was introduced and developed in Jackson and Wolinsky (1996). A link between two players requires the approval of both the players involved. This is the natural way to think about link formation in a number of social and economic contexts such as the formation of friendship ties, co-authorship, collaborations between firms, trading links between buyers and sellers, and free trade agreements between nations.

The simplest way to think of two sided link formation is to imagine an announcement game along the lines of the game sketched by Myerson (1991). Each player announces a set of *intended* links. A link between two individuals A and B is formed if both A and B announce an intention to create a link. In a context where links are two sided there are elements of "cooperation" involved in the formation of a link, and so solving such games calls for new concepts.

It is useful to begin the discussion with the familiar notion of Nash equilibrium as this will illustrate some of the conceptual issues that arise in the study of network formation with two-sided links. If every player announces that she wants to form no links then a best response is to announce no links. In other words, the empty network is a Nash equilibrium for any network formation game. To overcome this type of coordination failure, Jackson and Wolinsky (1996) propose the concept of *pairwise stable networks*.

A network is said to be pairwise stable if no individual wishes to delete a link and if no two unlinked individuals wish to form a link: Pairwise stability looks at the attractiveness of links in a network g, *one at a time*. Formally, every link present in a stable network must be profitable for the players involved in the link. For every link not present in the network it must be the case that if one player strictly gains from the link then the other player must be strictly worse off.

The second important contribution of the Jackson and Wolinsky (1996) paper was the finding that there is typically a tension between the requirement of strategic stability and of social efficiency. This highlights the presence of externalities in linking activity and remains a recurring theme in the subsequent research in this area.

The great attraction of pairwise stability is its simplicity. For any network it is relatively easy to check whether the two conditions are satisfied. The theoretical properties of this solution concept have been developed systematically and the solution concept has been widely applied. For a survey of this work, see Bloch and Dutta (2012) and Jackson (2008).

The theory of network formation has been and remains a very active field of research; for book length overviews, see Goyal (2007) and Jackson (2008). For a recent overview on network formation models and their applications, see Bramoulle et al. (2016).

---

as *preferential attachment*. This model yields power law degree distributions under suitable assumptions. Strategic models of network formation, like Bala and Goyal (2000) and Jackson and Wolinsky (1996), show that unequal networks arise when rational agents form links based on calculations of costs and benefits of links. In addition, the explicit consideration of costs and benefits permits an analysis of social welfare and the role of policy interventions.

4 NETWORKS AND INDIVIDUAL BEHAVIOR

This section introduces a framework for the study of behavior in networks. It will develop the argument that behavior in networks is shaped both by the nature of strategic interaction and by the structure of the network. These two forces can lead to significant heterogeneity in behavior and in payoffs for individuals, who are otherwise identical. I will draw heavily on Goyal (2007); for related surveys of this field, see Jackson and Zenou (2014) and Bramoulle and Kranton (2016).[3]

Games on networks consist of the set of players, the actions each of the players can choose, a description of the network of relationships between the players and a specification of how the actions and the network together define the payoffs accruing to each player.

The formulation of the strategies of players located in a network raises a number of considerations. Perhaps the first issue that needs to be discussed is whether players are obliged to choose the same action for all links or whether they have the freedom to choose link specific actions. It is reasonable to model individuals as choosing a single action in some contexts – such as consumer search about product prices or other characteristics. However, in some other contexts – an example would be effort in research projects – it is clear that individuals have the choice of putting different amounts of resources in different projects and frequently do exercise this option. However, the single action for all links model has the great merit of being very simple to work with and indeed most applications to date have worked with this formulation.

Suppose each player i takes an action s_i in S, where S is a compact subset of $\mathbb{R}_+$. The payoff (utility or reward) to player i under the profile of actions $s = \{s_1, \ldots, s_n\}$ is given by $\Pi_i : S^n \times \mathcal{G} \to \mathbb{R}_+$. In what follows, $s_{-i} = \{s_1, s_2, \ldots, s_{i-1}, s_{i+1}, \ldots, s_n\}$ refers to the profile of strategies of all players, other than player i.

We now turn to the role of networks in mediating effects of actions across players. A network has a number of different attributes – such as neighborhood size, distance, degree distribution – and it is clear that these attributes will play more or less important roles depending on the particular context under study. So there are many different ways in which network structure can be brought into the payoff function.

4.1 LOCAL INTERACTIONS

Individuals are more affected by the actions of those who are "close by" – such as neighbors, friends, partners, and colleagues. The simplest case arises when only actions of neighbors matter and the actions of non-neighbors have no effects on an

---

[3] In this chapter I will restrict attention to static models. Network structure can have profound effects on learning and contagion dynamics. For an early paper on learning dynamics, see Bala and Goyal (1998), and for a survey of how networks affect macroeconomic volatility, see Carvalho (2014).

individual's payoffs. This is the case of pure *local* effects.[4] This subsection studies a game with local effects. The next section takes up more general network effects.

A game with pure local effects exhibits *positive externality* if the payoffs are increasing in actions of neighbors, and it exhibits *negative externality* if they are decreasing in actions of neighbors. Turning next to strategic relations, a game with pure local effects is said to exhibit *strategic complements* or *strategic substitutes* depending on whether the marginal returns to own action for player i are increasing or decreasing in the efforts of her neighbors.

I now present a simple game on networks with local effects. Suppose each player chooses an action $s_i \in S$, where S is a compact interval in $\mathbb{R}_+$. Following Bramoulle and Kranton (2007), suppose that the payoffs to a player i, in a network g, faced with a profile of efforts $s = \{s_1, s_2, \ldots, s_n\}$, are given by:

$$\Pi_i(s|g) = f\left(s_i + \sum_{j \in N_i(g)} s_j\right) - c s_i \tag{1}$$

where $c > 0$ is the marginal cost of effort. Assume that $f(0) = 0$, $f'(\cdot) > 0$ and $f''(\cdot) < 0$. Define $\hat{s}$ to be such that $f'(\hat{s}) = c$. Moreover, the payoffs are an increasing function of others actions and the marginal payoffs are a decreasing function of others actions. Therefore, this is a game of positive externalities and strategic substitutes. 'Local public goods' is perhaps the natural interpretation of actions in this model.

The action set is compact, the payoffs are continuous in the actions of all players, and strictly concave in own action, and so it follows from standard considerations that a Nash equilibrium in pure strategies exists. We now examine how an equilibrium is sensitive to the structure of the network.

Define the sum of efforts of neighbors to be:

$$\bar{s}_i = \sum_{j \in N_i(g)} s_j.$$

From the strict concavity of $f(\cdot)$, it follows that if $\bar{s}_i \geq \hat{s}$ then marginal returns to effort are lower than the marginal cost and so optimal effort is 0, while if $\bar{s}_i < \hat{s}$, then marginal returns from effort to player are strictly larger than marginal costs c and so optimal effort is positive, and given by $\hat{s} - \bar{s}_i$.

Proposition 1. *A profile of actions* $s^* = \{s_1^*, s_2^*, \ldots, s_n^*\}$ *is a Nash equilibrium if and only if for every player i either*

1. $\bar{s}_i^* \geq \hat{s}$ *and* $s_i^* = 0$ *or*
2. $\bar{s}_i^* \leq \hat{s}$ *and* $s_i^* = \hat{s} - \bar{s}_i^*$.

---

[4]While the actions of direct neighbors have an effect on my payoff, the actions of the neighbors of my neighbors will also typically matter: as they change actions, their neighbors will react and this will affect my payoffs. So, there is a chain of indirect affects working through the different paths of connections.

So in equilibrium there are potentially two types of players: one, those who receive aggregate effort from their neighbors in excess of $\hat{s}$ and exert no effort on their own, and two, players who receive less than $\hat{s}$ aggregate effort from their neighbors and contribute exactly the difference between what they receive and $\hat{s}$. An implication is that an individual will choose $\hat{s}$ if and only if each of her neighbors choose 0. So we start by examining specialized equilibria, i.e., outcomes in which every player chooses either $\hat{s}$ or 0.

We will use the concept of *independent sets*. An *independent set* of a network g is a set of players $I \subseteq N$ such that for any $i, j \in I$, $g_{ij} \neq 1$, i.e., no two players in I are directly linked. A *maximal independent set* is an independent set that is not contained in any other independent set.

Every network contains a maximal independent set: number the players $1, 2, \ldots, n$. Now start by placing player 1 in I, and look for players $j \notin N_1(g)$. If player $2 \notin N_1(g)$, then include her in the independent set, I, if not then include her in the complement set I^c. Suppose, to fix ideas, that $1, 2 \in I$. Next consider player 3: if player $3 \notin N_1(g) \cup N_2(g)$, then include her in I, while if she is then include her in I^c. Move next to player 4 and proceed likewise until you reach player n. At each stage, a player is included in the set if she is not a neighbor of any player who is already included in the set. This process is well defined, and will lead to a maximal set of players I such that for any pair of players $i, j \in I$, $g_{ij} \neq 1$.

Observe that in the empty network there exists a unique maximal independent set and this is the set of all players N. In the complete network, on the other hand, there are n distinct maximal sets, each of which contains a single player. In the star network, there are two maximal independent sets: a set that contains only the central player and a set that contains all the peripheral players.

Maximal independent sets have an intimate connection with specialized Nash equilibria: assign the action $\hat{s}$ to every member of a maximal independent set and assign action 0 to every player who is not a member of this maximal independent set. This configuration constitutes an equilibrium in view of the characterization provided in Proposition 1.

Moreover, it is immediate that in any non-empty network, a maximal independent set must be a *strict* subset of the set of players N. Thus every such network is characterized by extreme heterogeneity in effort levels – with some players being experts and contributing $\hat{s}$ while others contribute 0 – across otherwise identical individuals.

Proposition 2. *There exists a specialized equilibrium in every network. In the empty network the unique equilibrium is specialized and every player chooses $\hat{s}$, so there is no free riding. In any non-empty network there exists a specialized equilibrium with experts and free riders.*

This result gives us a first impression of how networks matter: when we move from the empty network to any non-empty network this gives rise to the possibility of significant free riding, with a subset of players exerting maximal effort while others exert no effort at all. For instance, in the star network there are two specialized equilibria: one, where the central player chooses $\hat{s}$ and all the peripheral players

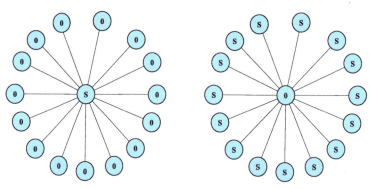

FIGURE 4

Heterogeneity in a star network.

choose 0; two, every peripheral player chooses $\hat{s}$, and the central player chooses 0. Fig. 4 illustrates these equilibria.

We now turn to the possibility of outcomes in which everyone contributes positively. Define an equilibrium strategy profile in which all players choose positive effort as a *distributed equilibrium*. It is easy to see that there does not always exist such an equilibrium. Take the star network. In a distributed equilibrium it must be the case that for every player i, $s_i > 0$ and $s_i + \bar{s}_i = \hat{s}$. Let s_c denote the central player's effort. For any peripheral player l, Proposition 1 says that $s_l + s_c = \hat{s}$, while for the central player, $s_c + \sum_{j \neq c} s_j = \hat{s}$. These equalities cannot be simultaneously satisfied since $s_l > 0$ for every peripheral player in a distributed equilibrium.

Distributed equilibria, however, arise naturally in regular networks: there exists a symmetric distributed equilibrium s^* such that $f'(s^* + ks^*) = c$. Every player chooses $s_i^* = \hat{s}/(k + 1)$.

Turning next to the distribution of payoffs: in a specialized equilibrium the active players will earn $f(\hat{s}) - c\hat{s}$, while the free riders will earn at least $f(\hat{s})$. If c is large then networks can give rise to large heterogeneity in payoffs.

This subsection focused on games of pure local effects: we showed how networks can generate large behavioral heterogeneity and correspondingly large payoff inequality. The study of games with local effects remains an active field of research, see e.g., Gagnon and Goyal (2017). We now turn to an example of general network effects.

4.2 TRADING IN NETWORKS

Supply, service and trading chains are a defining feature of the modern economy. They are prominent in agriculture, in transport and communication networks, in international trade, and in finance. The routing of economic activity, the allocation of surplus and the efficiency of the system depend on the prices set by these different in-

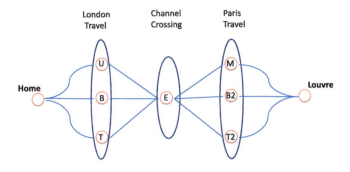

FIGURE 5

Transport network: London to Paris.

termediaries. The goal here is to propose a simple model of price setting in a network of intermediaries.

By way of motivation, consider a tourist who wishes to travel by train from London to see the Louvre in Paris. The first leg of the journey is from home to St. Pancras Station. There are a number of different taxi companies, bus services and the Underground. Once at St. Pancras Station, the only service provider to Paris Nord Station is Eurostar. Upon arriving at Paris Nord, there are a number of alternatives (bus, Metro and taxi) to get to the Louvre. The network consists of alternative paths each constituted of local transport alternatives in London and in Paris and the Eurostar Company. Each of the service providers sets a price. The traveler picks the cheapest 'path'. Fig. 5 represents this example.

Building on this example, Choi et al. (2017) propose the following model: there is a source node, S, and a destination node, D. A path between the two is a sequence of interconnected nodes, each occupied by an intermediary. The source node and the destination node and all the paths between them together define a network. The passage from source to destination generates a surplus. First let us consider the simple case where this surplus is known and set it equal to 1. Intermediaries (who have zero cost) simultaneously *post a price*. The prices determine a total cost for every path between S and D. The tourist moves along a least cost path: so an intermediary earns payoffs only if she is located on it. This completes the description of a game on a network.

To build some intuition for how networks matter, let us consider two simple networks. The first network has two paths between S and D, each with a distinct intermediate node. The two intermediaries compete in price: this is a simple game of strategic complements. Standard arguments – a la Bertrand – tell us that both firms will set a price equal to 0. The second network contains a single line with two nodes between S and D. The two intermediaries are now engaged in bilateral Nash Bargaining and the strategies are strategic substitutes (assuming that the sum of demands must equal the value of surplus). As in the Nash bargaining model, there are a number of possible outcomes.

Turning to the general model, every intermediary i simultaneously posts a price $p_i \geq 0$. Let $p = \{p_1, p_2, \ldots, p_n\}$ denote the price profile. The network g and the price profile p define a cost for every path q between S and D:

$$c(q, p) = \sum_{i \in q} p_i. \tag{2}$$

Let Q be the set of all paths between S and D. Payoffs arise out of active intermediation: an intermediary i obtains p_i only if he lies on a feasible least cost path. A *least cost path* q' is one such that $c(q', p) = \min_{q \in Q} c(q, p)$. Define $c(p) = \min_{q \in Q} c(q, p)$. A path q is feasible if $c(q, p) \leq v$, where v is the value of economic 'good' generated by the path. All paths generate the same value v. If there are multiple least cost paths, one of them is chosen randomly to be the active path. Given g, p and v, denote by $Q^v = \{q \in Q : c(q, p) = c(p), c(p) \leq v\}$ the set of feasible least cost paths, and intermediary i's payoff is given by:

$$\pi_i(p, v) = \begin{cases} 0 & \text{if } i \notin q, \; \forall; q \in Q^v \\ \frac{\eta_i^v}{|Q^v|} p_i & \text{if } i \in q, \; q \in Q^v, \end{cases} \tag{3}$$

where η_i^v is the number of paths in Q^v that contain intermediary i.

A node is said to be *critical* if it lies on all paths between S and D. Choi et al. (2017) develop the following characterization of equilibrium pricing.

Theorem 1. *In every network, there exists an equilibrium. In any equilibrium p^*, $c(p^*) \notin (0, v)$. Thus there is either complete or zero surplus extraction by intermediaries.*

Observe that if there is trade and there exist critical traders then intermediaries must extract all surplus: if not then a critical trader can raise its price and increase profits strictly. However, critical traders are not necessary for surplus extraction. This is because of possible coordination failures along chains of traders that enhance the market power of non-critical traders. These coordination problems give rise to multiple equilibria.[5]

This multiplicity and the possibility of very different allocations of surplus motivates an experimental study of pricing. Choi et al. (2017) choose networks that allow us to examine the roles of coordination, competition and market power. These networks are depicted in Fig. 6.

The ring networks with four, six and ten traders allow us to focus on coordination and competition. For every choice of S and D, there are always two competing paths of intermediaries. In Ring 4, for any non-adjacent pair, there are two paths with a single intermediary each. Ring 6 and Ring 10 allow for situations with a higher (and possibly unequal) number of intermediaries on either path.

---

[5] To see this, note that in a cycle a path may price itself out of the market (by traders setting very high prices) and then the other path can extract full surplus.

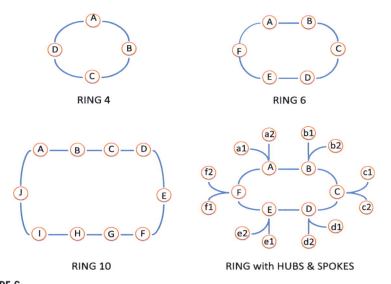

FIGURE 6

Networks in the laboratory.

The Ring with Hubs and Spokes network allows for a study of the impact of market power: for instance, if $\mathcal{S}$ is located at a_1 and $\mathcal{D}$ is located at a_2, intermediary A is a pure monopolist, while if $\mathcal{D}$ is b_1 instead, then the intermediaries A and B play a symmetric Nash demand game. This network also creates the space for both market power and competition to come into play. For instance, if $\mathcal{S}$ is located at a_1 and $\mathcal{D}$ is located at e_1, then there are two competing paths: a shorter path (through A, F, and E) and a longer path (through A, B, C, D, and E). Traders A and E are the only critical intermediaries.

Fig. 7 presents intermediation costs in different treatments. To put these experimental variations into perspective, observe that in Ring 4, there is a unique equilibrium that corresponds to the Bertrand outcome. In every other network, whenever there are at least two intermediaries on every path, there exist both efficient and inefficient equilibria.[6]

In Ring 4, intermediation costs are around five percent of the surplus. In the other rings, intermediation costs vary between ten and twenty percent of the surplus. The overall conclusion is that intermediation costs in all ring networks are modest and, between the two efficient equilibria, are much closer to the one with zero intermediation cost, especially in the smaller rings.

In the Ring with Hubs and Spokes, when $\mathcal{S}$ and $\mathcal{D}$ are served by a sole critical intermediary, the authors find a surplus extraction of 99 percent! Finally, when there

---

[6]Observe that an equilibrium is inefficient if no trade takes place, and this happens if the cost of using any path exceeds the value v.

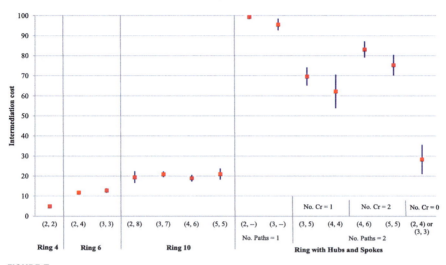

FIGURE 7

Costs of intermediation.

are two competing paths and critical traders, the intermediation cost ranges between 62 percent and 83 percent. In the case without critical intermediaries, this cost falls sharply to around 28 percent, which is comparable to the low-cost outcome found in Rings. These observations are summarized as follows:

Finding 1. *The presence of critical traders is both necessary and sufficient for large surplus extraction by intermediaries. In Rings with four, six, and ten traders, intermediation costs are small (ranging from 5 percent to 20 percent). In the Ring with Hubs and Spokes, with critical traders, intermediation costs are large (ranging from 60 percent to over 95 percent).*

I turn now to the issue of how surplus is divided between critical and non-critical intermediaries. Table 1 presents the average fraction of intermediation costs charged by critical traders, conditional on exchange. The number within parentheses is the number of group observations. Looking at the last 20 rounds, we observe that 67 percent to 80 percent of intermediation costs go to the critical trader(s). In all the cases, regardless of whether an exchange takes place along the shorter or longer path, the number of non-critical traders is at least as large as the number of critical traders. This is consistent with the pricing behavior of different intermediaries, as reported in Fig. 8.[7] This leads to:

---

[7]The numbers along the *x*-axis indicate the length of the two shortest paths between S and D in the different treatments.

Table 1 Surplus division among intermediaries

Network	(#Cr,#Paths, $d(q), d(q')$)	Rounds		
		1 ~ 20	**21 ~ 41**	**41 ~ 60**
Ring with hubs and spokes	(1, 2, 3, 5)	0.56 (20)	0.68 (26)	0.72 (25)
	(1, 2, 4, 4)	0.48 (16)	0.56 (13)	0.67 (10)
	(2, 2, 4, 6)	0.73 (16)	0.77 (19)	0.80 (24)
	(2, 2, 5, 5)	0.65 (8)	0.67 (8)	0.74 (11)

Notes. The number in a cell is the average fraction of costs charged by critical traders. The number of observations is reported in parentheses. #Cr denotes the number of critical intermediaries, #Paths denotes the number of paths connecting buyer and seller, $d(q)$ denotes the length of path q between buyer and seller.

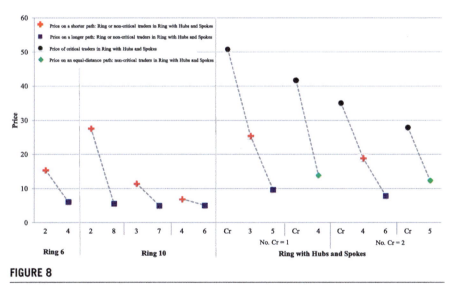

FIGURE 8

Price behavior across intermediary types.

Finding 2. *In the Ring with Hubs and Spokes, critical intermediaries set higher prices and earn a much higher share of surplus than non-critical intermediaries.*

The experiments establish that subjects avoid coordination problems. As a result, trade always takes place, critical traders make large profits while non-critical traders make very little profits.

The results are sharp but it is possible to argue that criticality is too demanding: a node that lies on most (but not all) paths has the same status as compared to a node that lies on only one path. Moreover, all critical paths have equal status in the model. It may be argued that the location in the path – upstream or downstream – should matter. Related work with alternative pricing protocols develops these points. For auctions, see Kotowski and Leister (2014) and Gottardi and Goyal (2012); for bargaining, see Condorelli et al. (2016), Gofman (2011), and Manea (2017); for bid-and-ask prices, see Acemoglu and Ozdaglar (2007), Blume et al. (2007) and Gale and Kariv (2009).[8]

In this section I have considered games with local and global effects. For a general discussion on the nature of strategic interaction in networks, see Goyal (2007). An early paper that consider games on a network with a combination of local and global (market) effects is Goyal and Moraga-Gonzalez (2001). For more recent surveys on the subject, see Jackson and Zenou (2014) and Bramoulle and Kranton (2016). An important message from this literature is that, by varying the strategic structure of payoffs, we can bring different elements of networks into play. The two examples discussed in this section illustrate this general point. In the public goods game, maximal independent sets are important for understanding behavior, while in the pricing game it is criticality (and related notions of betweenness centrality) that are relevant. Moreover, the discussion also shows how heterogeneity in network properties can have powerful effects on choice, on payoffs, and on welfare.

5 COMBINING ACTIONS AND LINK FORMATION

This section will present models that combine choices on actions and linking. I will draw upon original papers by Galeotti and Goyal (2010) and Goyal and Vega-Redondo (2007), and a recent survey paper by Vega-Redondo (2016).

We invest time in acquiring information ourselves, but we also link with others and learn from them. I start with some general observations on patterns of communication. The classical early work of Lazarsfeld et al. (1948) and Katz and Lazersfeld (1955) found that personal contacts play a dominant role in disseminating information which in turn shapes individuals decisions. In particular, they identified 20 percent of their sample of 4,000 individuals as the primary source of information for the rest. The Law of the Few subsumes these empirical findings: in social groups, a majority of individuals get most of their information from a very small subset of the group, viz., *the influencers*. Moreover, research suggests that there are minor differences between the observable economic and demographic characteristics of the influencers and the others. This suggests that individual interactions may play an important role in sustaining such high levels of heterogeneity.

---

[8]For an extended discussion on trading outcomes under different pricing protocols, see Choi et al. (2017).

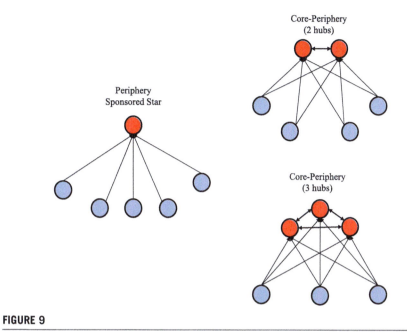

FIGURE 9

Core-periphery networks.

5.1 THE LAW OF THE FEW

Motivated by these observations, and building on Bala and Goyal (2000) and Bramoulle and Kranton (2007), Galeotti and Goyal (2010) propose the following model of activity and interactions. Suppose individuals choose to personally acquire information and to form connections with others to access the information these contacts acquire. Their main finding is that every (strict) equilibrium of the game exhibits the 'Law of the Few'. The network has a core-periphery architecture; the players in the core acquire information personally, while the peripheral players acquire no information personally but form links and get all their information from the core players. The core group is small relative to the number of individuals.[9] Fig. 9 presents a collection of core-periphery networks.

As usual, let $N = \{1, 2, \ldots, n\}$ with $n \geq 3$ be the set of players and let i and j be typical members of this set. Each player i chooses a level of personal information acquisition $x_i \in X$ and a set of links with others to access their information, which is represented as a (row) vector $\mathbf{g}_i = (g_{i1}, \ldots, g_{ii-1}, g_{ii+1}, \ldots, g_{in})$, where $g_{ij} \in \{0, 1\}$, for each $j \in N \setminus \{i\}$. We will suppose that $X = [0, +\infty)$ and that $\mathbf{g}_i \in G_i = \{0, 1\}^{n-1}$. We say that player i has a link with player j if $g_{ij} = 1$. A link between player i and j

---

[9]A number of subsequent papers have explored models that combine behavior and formation of structure; see e.g., Baetz (2014) and Hiller (2012).

allows both players to access the information personally acquired by the other player. The set of strategies of player i is denoted by $S_i = X \times G_i$. Define $S = S_1 \times \cdots \times S_n$ as the set of strategies of all players. A strategy profile $\mathbf{s} = (\mathbf{x}, \mathbf{g}) \in S$ specifies the personal information acquired by each player, $\mathbf{x} = (x_1, x_2, \ldots, x_n)$, and the network of relations $\mathbf{g} = (\mathbf{g}_1, \mathbf{g}_2, \ldots, \mathbf{g}_n)$.

The network of relations $\mathbf{g}$ is a directed graph; let G be the set of all possible directed graphs on n vertices. Define $N_i(\mathbf{g}) = \{j \in N : g_{ij} = 1\}$ as the set of players with whom i has formed a link. Let $\eta_i(\mathbf{g}) = |N_i(\mathbf{g})|$. The closure of $\mathbf{g}$ is an undirected network denoted by $\bar{\mathbf{g}} = cl(\mathbf{g})$, where $\bar{g}_{ij} = \max\{g_{ij}, g_{ji}\}$ for each i and j in N. In words, the closure of a directed network involves replacing every directed edge of $\mathbf{g}$ by an undirected one. Define $N_i(\bar{\mathbf{g}}) = \{j \in N : \bar{g}_{ij} = 1\}$ as the set of players directly connected to i. The undirected link between two players reflects bilateral information exchange between them.

The payoffs to player i under strategy profile $\mathbf{s} = (\mathbf{x}, \mathbf{g})$ are:

$$\Pi_i(\mathbf{s}) = f\left(x_i + \sum_{j \in N_i(\bar{\mathbf{g}})} x_j\right) - cx_i - \eta_i(\mathbf{g})k, \tag{4}$$

where $c > 0$ reflects the cost of information and $k > 0$ is the cost of linking with one other person. As in Section 3, assume that $f(y)$ is twice continuously differentiable, increasing, and strictly concave in y. Also assume that there is a $\hat{y} > 0$ such that $f'(\hat{y}) = c$.

It is easy to see, using arguments from Section 3, that every player must access at least $\hat{y}$ information. Moreover, the perfect substitutability of own and neighbors' information and the linearity in the costs of acquiring information imply that if a player personally acquires information then the sum of the information he acquires and the information acquired by his neighbors must equal $\hat{y}$. We next observe that if some player acquires $\hat{y}$, and if $k < c\hat{y}$, then it is optimal for all other players to acquire no information personally and to form a link with this player. For a strategy profile $\mathbf{s} = (\mathbf{x}, \mathbf{g})$, let us define $I(\mathbf{s}) = \{i \in N | x_i > 0\}$ as the set of players who acquire information personally, and let $y_i(\bar{\mathbf{g}}) = \sum_{j \in N_i(\bar{\mathbf{g}})} x_j$ be the information that i accesses from his neighbors. So we know how much information everyone must access. Now we turn to the distribution of personal information acquisition, the aggregate information acquired in a social group and the structure of social communication. Galeotti and Goyal (2010) establish:

Proposition 3. *Suppose payoffs are given by (4) and $k < c\hat{y}$. In every strict equilibrium $\mathbf{s}^* = (\mathbf{x}^*, \mathbf{g}^*)$: (1) $\sum_{i \in N} x_i^* = \hat{y}$, (2) the network has a core-periphery architecture, hubs acquire information personally and spokes acquire no information personally, and (3) for given c and k, the ratio $|I(\mathbf{s}^*)|/n \to 0$ as $n \to \infty$.*

Galeotti and Goyal (2010) provide the following intuitive explanation for this result. In this model, returns from information are increasing and concave while the costs of personally acquiring information are linear. This implies that on his own an individual would acquire a certain amount of information, which for the purposes of this discussion is normalized so that $\hat{y} = 1$. The second element in this model is the substitutability of information acquired by different individuals. This implies that if A acquires information on his own and receives information from player B then in the aggregate he must have access to 1 unit of information (else he could strictly increase his payoff by modifying personal information acquisition). The third and key element is that links are costly and rationally chosen by individuals. The implication of this is that if A finds it optimal to maintain a link with B then so must every other player. Hence, the group of individuals who acquire information must be completely linked and the aggregate information acquired in the society must equal exactly 1. Moreover, since linking is costly, A will only link with B if B acquires a certain minimum amount of information. Since total information acquired is 1, it follows that there is an upper bound to the number of people who will acquire information: this upper bound is independent of the number of players n. And so the proportion of information acquirers will be negligible in a large group. Finally, we observe that since the aggregate information acquired in the group is 1, everyone who does not personally acquire information must be linked to all those who acquire information, yielding the core-periphery network.

The result mentioned above is derived in a setting where individuals are ex-ante identical. A recurring theme in the empirical work is that influencers have demographic characteristics which are similar to those of others. But this work also finds that they have distinctive attitudes which include higher attention to general market information and enjoyment in acquiring information, see e.g., Feick and Price (1987). This motivates a study of the consequences of small heterogeneity in individual characteristics. Our main finding is that if an individual has a slight cost advantage in acquiring information (or a greater preference for information) then in equilibrium this person is always the unique hub. Small heterogeneities thus help select individuals who play dramatically different roles in social organization.

A natural way to model this difference is to suppose that some players have slightly lower costs of acquiring information. Galeotti and Goyal (2010) consider a situation where $c_i = c$ for all $i \neq 1$, while $c_1 = c - \epsilon > 0$, where $\epsilon > 0$ is a small number. Let $\hat{y}_1 = \arg\max_y f(y) - c_1 y$. Clearly, as long as $\epsilon > 0$, $\hat{y}_1 > \hat{y}$, and $\hat{y}_1 \rightarrow \hat{y}$ as $\epsilon \rightarrow 0$. They establish the following result on strict Nash equilibria:

Proposition 4. *Suppose payoffs are given by (4), $c_i = c$ for all $i \neq 1$ and $c_1 = c - \epsilon$, where $\epsilon > 0$. If $k < f(\hat{y}_1) - f(\hat{y}) + c\hat{y}$ then in a strict equilibrium $\mathbf{s}^* = (\mathbf{x}^*, \mathbf{g}^*)$: (1) $\sum_{i \in N} x_i^* = \hat{y}_1$. (2) the network is a periphery-sponsored star and player 1 is the hub, and (3) either $x_1^* = \hat{y}_1$ and spokes choose $x^* = 0$, OR, $x_1^* = [(n-1)\hat{y} - \hat{y}_1]/[n-2]$ and $x^* = [\hat{y}_1 - \hat{y}]/[n-2]$.*

This result shows that a very small difference in the cost of acquiring information is sufficient to separate the player who will acquire information and act as a hub from those who will acquire little or no information personally and will only form connections.

Following on Galeotti and Goyal (2010) the intuition for this result may be explained as follows: First, observe that for the low cost player the optimal information level is greater than the optimal information level for other players, i.e., $\hat{y}_1 > \hat{y}$. From the arguments developed in Proposition 2 we know that aggregate information acquired by all players other than player 1 will be at most $\hat{y}$. This implies that in equilibrium, player 1 must acquire information personally, $x_1 > 0$. If $x_1 = \hat{y}_1$, the best reply of every other player is to acquire no information and to form a link with player 1. In case $x_1 < \hat{y}_1$ we know, from arguments in Proposition 1, that $x_1 + y_1 = \hat{y}_1$ and so there is a player $i \neq 1$ with $x_i > 0$ and $x_i + y_i(\bar{\mathbf{g}}) = \hat{y}$. If some player wants to link with i then so must everyone else. But then player i accesses all information $\hat{y}_1$; since $\hat{y}_1 > \hat{y}$, this contradicts Proposition 1. Thus *no* player must have a link with player $i \neq 1$ in equilibrium. Hence, i must form a link with player 1, and, from the optimality of linking, so must every other player. Finally, since every player is choosing positive effort, the equilibrium values of x_1 and x_i can be derived from the two equations $x_1 + (n-1)x_i = \hat{y}_1$ and $x_1 + x_i = \hat{y}$.

We briefly note that payoffs may be very unequal in the core-periphery networks: so in the case of a single hub for instance the central player earns $f(\hat{y}) - c\hat{y}$, while the spokes each earn $f(\hat{y}) - k$. In the event that $c\hat{y}$ is much larger than k, the payoff of the hub players is much smaller than the spokes. On the other hand in the case of multiple hubs, it is possible the hubs earn a great deal more than the spokes. So information investment activity and linking can lead to very specialized patterns of behavior and very heterogeneous networks.

5.2 INTERMEDIATION RENTS AND NETWORK FORMATION

In the trading game, we showed that intermediaries earn large payoffs if and only if they are 'critical'. In this section, we consider a network formation game in which traders seek to link with each other to carry out exchange and also to extract intermediation rents by becoming critical. We wish to understand whether criticality is sustainable in such an environment and how the payoffs are distributed.

The discussion here is based on Goyal and Vega-Redondo (2007). Suppose traders can exchange goods and that this creates a surplus of 1. Networks are relevant because this exchange can be undertaken only if these traders know each other personally or there is a sequence of personal connections which indirectly link the two traders. In the case where traders know each other they each get one-half of the surplus. If they are linked indirectly then the allocation of the surplus depends on the competition between the intermediary agents. Following the discussion in Section 3, suppose that competition between paths between any two players j and k leads to full dissipation of market power: in other words intermediaries only make money if they are critical. We have thus combined the model of trading in networks above with a model of network formation.

We will consider a game of network formation in which players propose links. So a strategy for player i is $s_i = \{s_{i,1}, \ldots, s_{i,n}\}$, where $s_{i,j} \in \{0, 1\}$. A link is formed between players i and j if both propose a link to each other, i.e., $s_{ij} = s_{ji} = 1$. Denote by $\mathcal{C}(j, k; g)$ the set of players who are critical to connect j and k in network g and let $c(j, k; g) = |\mathcal{C}(j, k; g)|$. Then, for any strategy profile $s = (s_1, s_2, \ldots, s_n)$, the (net) payoffs to player i are given by:

$$\Pi_i(s_i, s_{-i}) = \sum_{j \in C_i(g)} \frac{1}{c(i, j; g) + 2} + \sum_{j,k \in N} \frac{I_{\{i \in C(j,k)\}}}{c(j, k; g) + 2} - \eta_i^d(g)c, \qquad (5)$$

where $I_{\{i \in C(j,k)\}} \in \{0, 1\}$ stands for the indicator function specifying whether i is critical for j and k, $\eta_i^d(g) = |\{j \in N : j \neq i, g_{ij} = 1\}|$ refers to the number of players with whom player i has a link, and $c > 0$ is the cost per link. $C_i(g)$ refers to the component of individual i in network g.

I now discuss the incentives to form and delete links and the nature of pairwise stable networks. It is easily seen that the star, the cycle containing all players and hybrid cycle-stars (in which there is a cycle and all players outside the cycle have a single link to a single node in the cycle) are all pairwise stable. In the star the center earns a payoff of $(n - 1)[1/2 + ((n - 2)/6) - c]$, and has no incentive to a delete a single link so long as $c < 1/2 + (n - 2)/3$. Two spokes have no incentive to form a link between them if $c > 1/6$, while no spoke has an incentive to delete a link if $c < 1/2 + (n - 2)/3$. Thus a star is pairwise stable so long as $1/6 < c < 1/2 + (n-2)/3$.

In a cycle every player gets a payoff of $(n - 1)/2 - 2c$. An additional link is clearly not attractive since it does not create any extra surplus while it increases costs. Deleting one link is not attractive for an individual player as it makes a neighboring player critical for all transactions, which lowers individual payoffs by at least $(n - 2)/6$. This clearly exceeds the cost c, for large enough n. Similar arguments can be used to show that hybrid cycle-star networks are pairwise stable (for some range of costs).

I now turn to deviations that involve greater coordination. Consider the case of two players choosing to add a link between themselves and delete a subset of links with others. To see how this may have large effects, consider the cycle network containing all players. Consider two players that are far apart in the cycle and establish a direct link. By simultaneously breaking one link each, they can produce a line and become central in it. In a line, they must pay intermediation costs to a number of others, but at the same time they both occupy prominent centrality positions in the line network. This deviation is illustrated in Fig. 10.

Under some circumstances such deviations may be profitable and they have the effect of sharply restricting the set of 'equilibrium' networks. This possibility leads to a consideration of strict bilateral equilibrium networks. Goyal and Vega-Redondo (2007) propose the following definition.[10]

Definition 1. A network g^* can be supported in a *strict bilateral equilibrium (SBE)* if the following conditions hold:

---

[10]For a more detailed discussion of solution concepts in network formation games, see Goyal (2007). Here the strictness refers to the requirement that for every player the proposed strategy profile is strictly better than any network the player can attain on his own, given the strategy profile of all other players. This is the second condition in the definition.

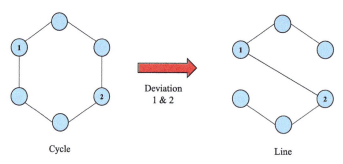

FIGURE 10

Bilateral deviations from cycle.

- There exists a strategy profile s^* which supports g^* as a bilateral equilibrium.
- For any $i \in N$, and every $s_i \in S_i$ such that:

$$g(s_i, s^*_{-i}) \neq g(s^*),$$
$$\Pi_i(g(s^*)) > \Pi_i(g(s_i, s^*_{-i}));$$

- For any pair of players, $i, j \in N$ and every strategy pair (s_i, s_j) with $g(s_i, s_j, \mathbf{s}^*_{-i-j}) \neq g(s^*)$,

$$\Pi_i(g(s_i, s_j, s^*_{-i-j})) \geq \Pi_i(g(s^*_i, s^*_j, s^*_{-i-j}))$$
$$\Rightarrow \quad \Pi_j(g(s_i, s_j, s^*_{-i-j})) < \Pi_j(g(s^*_i, s^*_j, s^*_{-i-j})). \quad (6)$$

Goyal and Vega-Redondo (2007) provide the following (partial) characterization of strict bilateral equilibrium networks.

Proposition 5. *Suppose payoffs satisfy (5) and that n is large. If $1/6 < c < 1/2$ then the unique strict bilateral equilibrium network is the star, while if $1/2 < c < 1/2 + (n-2)/6$ then the star and the empty network are the only strict bilateral equilibrium networks. If $c > 1/2 + (n-2)/6$ then the empty network is the unique strict bilateral equilibrium network.*

There are four arguments in the proof. The *first* argument exploits access and intermediation advantages to show that an equilibrium network is either connected or empty. The *second* argument demonstrates agglomeration pressures: a minimal network with long paths cannot be sustained. This is because players located at the 'end' of the network benefit from connecting to a *central player* in order to save on intermediation costs (cutting path lengths) while a central player is ready to incur the cost of an additional link because this enhances her intermediation payoffs because she shares the intermediation rents with fewer other players. This deviation is illustrated in Fig. 11.

The *third* argument builds on the above example of bilateral deviations to show that a cycle or a hybrid cycle-star network is not sustainable. The *fourth* argument

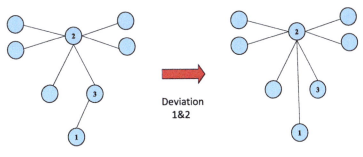

FIGURE 11

Incentives in minimal networks.

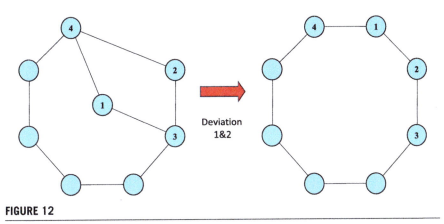

FIGURE 12

Instability in networks with two cycles.

rules out networks with two or more cycles. It is here that the requirement of strictness is invoked. Fig. 12 illustrates how players 1 and 2 are indifferent between the network with two cycles and a network in which there is only one cycle.

Proposition 5 covers large societies and assumes that $c > 1/6$. Goyal and Vega-Redondo (2007) show that in small societies too strategic pressures will create the potential for a 'structural hole' and there will be players who earn large intermediation payoffs by spanning them. In case $c < 1/6$, the star is not an equilibrium, since peripheral players have a strict incentive to link up. For large societies, the above arguments show that no other network is a strict bilateral equilibrium. Thus if $c < 1/6$ then there exist no strict bilateral equilibria.

I conclude this discussion with a comment on payoff inequality. In the star network the central player earns $(n - 1)[1/2 + ((n - 2)/6) - c]$ while each of the peripheral players makes $[1/2 + ((n - 2)/3) - c]$. The payoff difference between the central player and the peripheral player is large, and in particular, the ratio of the two payoffs is unbounded, as n gets large.

The discussion above shows that strategic linking pushes toward an extreme form of market power with a single critical node. One ingredient of the model that plays an important role in the analysis is that only a critical node can earn intermediation rents. In a recent paper, van der Leij et al. (2016) extend this model to allow for smoother competition between paths: here multiple paths may earn intermediation rents depending on a competition parameter δ, that allows in the one extreme for full collusion and in the other extreme for Bertrand competition (as in the model above). They also show that small initial differences in size of banks can feedback to create a core-periphery network with large banks in the core. In particular, their model can reproduce the observed core-periphery structure in the Dutch interbank market for reasonable parameter values.

5.3 RELATED WORK

For a more extensive survey of games with actions and linking, see Vega-Redondo (2016). Here I would like to briefly mention the closely related line of work on link formation in a setting where actions are strategic complements, Koenig et al. (2014). The basic game has linear quadratic payoffs, as in the paper by Ballester et al. (2006). I briefly discuss this paper now.

Koenig et al. (2014) show that if individuals form links to maximize centrality, then the linking process leads to *nested split graphs*: these are networks with a clear hierarchical structure (for an illustration, see Fig. 2). There is a top group of high effort players, who are linked to all players choosing efforts below them. The second level effort players are in turn linked to all players choosing effort below them, and so forth. For an early derivation of nested graphs in a model of network formation, see Goyal and Joshi (2003). A similar structure is also identified in related papers by Hiller (2012) and Baetz (2014), who study a setting like Galeotti and Goyal (2010), except that actions are strategic complements (and not substitutes).

An important general message from this literature is that, in a rich variety of settings, purposeful linking activity leads to sharply structured networks with significant heterogeneity in degree, in behavior across nodes, and in individual payoffs.

6 CONCLUDING REMARKS

We started with the observation that heterogeneity is a defining feature of real world social, economic and infrastructure networks. I have tried to argue, with the help of simple models, how heterogeneous networks give rise to very widely varying forms of behavior and potentially significant inequality. Furthermore, I have presented models that combine activity in networks with linking behavior to show how heterogeneous network structures are a natural outcome in a wide range of circumstances. Thus networks are important for understanding the diversity in economic outcomes that has been empirically noted.

REFERENCES

Acemoglu, D., Ozdaglar, A., 2007. Competition and efficiency in congested markets. Mathematics of Operations Research 32 (1), 1–31.

Aumann, R., Myerson, R., 1988. Endogenous formation of links between players and coalitions: an application to the Shapley Value. In: Roth, A. (Ed.), The Shapley Value. Cambridge University Press, Cambridge, pp. 175–191.

Baetz, O., 2014. Social activity and network formation. Theoretical Economics 10 (2), 315–340.

Bala, V., Goyal, S., 1998. Learning from neighbours. Review of Economic Studies 65, 595–621.

Bala, V., Goyal, S., 2000. A non-cooperative model of network formation. Econometrica 68 (5), 1181–1231.

Ballester, C., Calvo-Armengol, A., Zenou, Y., 2006. Who's who in networks. Wanted: the key player. Econometrica 74, 1403–1417.

Barabasi, A.-L., Albert, R., 1999. Emergence of scaling in random networks. Science 286, 509–512.

Bloch, F., Dutta, B., 2012. Formation of networks and coalitions. In: Bisin, A., Benhabib, J., Jackson, M. (Eds.), Social Economics. North-Holland, Amsterdam.

Blume, L., Easley, D., Kleinberg, J., Tardos, E., 2007. Trading networks with price-setting agents. In: Proceedings of the 8th ACM Conference on Electronic Commerce EC 2007. New York, NY, USA.

Bollobas, B., 1998. Modern Graph Theory. Springer-Verlag, Berlin.

Boorman, S., 1975. A combinatorial optimization model for transmission of job information through contact networks. Bell Journal of Economics 6 (1), 216–249.

Bramoulle, Y., Galeotti, A., Rogers, B., 2016. The Oxford Handbook of the Economics of Networks. Oxford University Press.

Bramoulle, Y., Kranton, R., 2007. Public goods in networks. Journal of Economic Theory 135, 478–494.

Bramoulle, Y., Kranton, R., 2016. Games played on networks. In: Bramoulle, Y., Galeotti, A., Rogers, B. (Eds.), Oxford Handbook on Economics of Networks. Oxford University Press.

Carvalho, V., 2014. From micro to macro via production networks. Journal of Economic Perspectives 28 (4), 23–48.

Choi, S., Galeotti, A., Goyal, S., 2017. Trading in networks: theory and experiments. Journal of the European Economic Association 15 (4), 784–817.

Condorelli, D., Galeotti, A., Renou, L., 2016. Bilateral trading in networks. Review of Economic Studies 01, 1–40.

Easley, D., Kleinberg, J., 2010. Crowds, Networks and Markets: Reasoning About a Highly Connected World. Cambridge University Press.

Feick, L.F., Price, L.L., 1987. The market maven: a diffuser of marketplace information. Journal of Marketing 51 (1), 83–97.

Gagnon, J., Goyal, S., 2017. Networks, markets and inequality. American Economic Review 107 (1), 1–30.

Gale, D., Kariv, S., 2009. Trading in networks: a normal form game experiment. American Economic Journal: Microeconomics 1 (2), 114–132.

Galeotti, A., Goyal, S., 2010. The law of the few. American Economic Review 100, 1468–1492.

Gofman, M., 2011. A Network-Based Analysis of Over-the-Counter Markets. Mimeo. Wisconsin–Madison.

Gottardi, P., Goyal, S., 2012. Intermediation in Networks. Mimeo. EUI and Cambridge.

Goyal, S., 1993. Sustainable Communication Networks. Tinbergen Institute Discussion Paper, TI 93-250.

Goyal, S., 2007. Connections: An Introduction to the Economics of Networks. Princeton University Press, Princeton.

Goyal, S., 2016. Networks in economics: a perspective on the literature. In: Bramoulle, Y., Galeotti, A., Rogers, B. (Eds.), The Oxford Handbook of the Economics of Networks. OUP.

Goyal, S., 2017. Networks and markets. In: Honore, B., Pakes, A., Piazzesi, M., Samuelson, L. (Eds.), Advances in Economics: Eleventh World Congress of the Econometric Society. CUP.

Goyal, S., Joshi, S., 2003. Networks of collaboration in oligopoly. Games and Economic Behavior 43 (1), 57–85.

Goyal, S., Moraga-Gonzalez, J.L., 2001. R&D networks. Rand Journal of Economics 32 (4), 686–707.

Goyal, S., Vega-Redondo, F., 2007. Structural holes in social networks. Journal of Economic Theory 137, 460–492.

Hendricks, K., Piccione, M., Tan, G., 1995. The economics of hubs: the case of monopoly. The Review of Economic Studies 62 (1), 83–99.

Hendricks, K., Piccione, M., Tan, G., 1999. Equilibrium in networks. Econometrica 67 (6), 1407–1434.

Hiller, T., 2012. Peer Effects in Endogenous Networks. Bristol Economics Working Papers no. 12/633. University of Bristol.

Jackson, M.O., 2008. Social and Economic Networks. Princeton University Press, Princeton.

Jackson, M.O., Wolinsky, A., 1996. A strategic model of economic and social networks. Journal of Economic Theory 71 (1), 44–74.

Jackson, M.O., Zenou, Y., 2014. Games on networks. In: Young, Peyton, Zamir, Shmuel (Eds.), Handbook of Game Theory, vol. 4.

Katz, E., Lazarsfeld, P.F., 1955. Personal Influence: The Part Played by People in the Flow of Mass Communications. The Free Press, New York.

Koenig, M., Tessone, C.J., Zenou, Y., 2014. Nestedness in networks: a theoretical model and some applications. Theoretical Economics 9, 695–752.

Kotowski, M., Leister, M., 2014. Trading Networks and Equilibrium Intermediation. Mimeo. University of California, Berkeley.

Lazarsfeld, P.F., Berelson, B., Gaudet, H., 1948. The People's Choice: How the Voter Makes Up His Mind in a Presidential Campaign. Columbia University Press, New York.

van der Leij, M., in 't Veld, D., Hommes, C., 2016. The Formation of a Core-Periphery Structure in Heterogeneous Financial Networks. Mimeo. University of Amsterdam.

Manea, M., 2017. Intermediation and resale in networks. Journal of Political Economy. Forthcoming.

Myerson, R., 1991. Game Theory: Analysis of Conflict. Harvard University Press, Cambridge MA.

Vega-Redondo, F., 2007. Complex Social Networks. Cambridge University Press, Cambridge, England.

Vega-Redondo, F., 2016. Links and actions in interplay. In: Bramoulle, Y., Galeotti, A., Rogers, B. (Eds.), The Oxford Handbook of the Economics of Networks. Oxford University Press.

OTHER APPLICATIONS

Electric Power Markets in Transition: Agent-Based Modeling Tools for Transactive Energy Support

13

Leigh Tesfatsion

Economics Department, Iowa State University, Ames, IA, United States
e-mail address: tesfatsi@iastate.edu

CONTENTS

Handbook of Computational Economics, Volume 4, ISSN 1574-0021, https://doi.org/10.1016/bs.hescom.2018.02.004

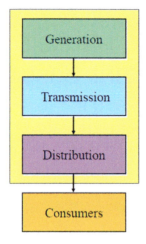

FIGURE 1

Traditional vertically-integrated electric utility company.

1 INTRODUCTION

1.1 BACKGROUND MOTIVATION

Traditionally, U.S. electric power systems were organized as collections of regulated vertically-integrated utility companies.[1] Each utility company controlled all generation, transmission, and distribution of electric power in a designated geographical area for the purpose of servicing power consumers in this area; see Fig. 1. In return, the utility company was guaranteed a rate of return ensuring a suitable profit margin.

Starting in the mid-1990s, prodded by successive rule-making from the U.S. Federal Energy Regulatory Commission (FERC), wholesale power systems in many parts of the U.S. have been substantially restructured into partially decentralized systems based more fully on market valuation and allocation mechanisms. These restructuring efforts were driven by a desire to ensure efficient power production and utilization, reliable power supplies, and affordable power prices for consumers.

As depicted in Fig. 2, the basic design ultimately proposed by FERC (2003) for U.S. wholesale power systems envisions private *Generation Companies (GenCos)* who sell bulk power to private companies called *Load-Serving Entities (LSEs)*, who in turn resell this power to retail consumers. These transactions between GenCos and LSEs take place within a wholesale power market consisting of a *Day-Ahead Mar-*

---

[1]For a detailed discussion of the U.S. electric power industry, including its historical development and current physical and institutional arrangements, see NAS (2016). Although this chapter takes a U.S. perspective, the electric power industries in many regions of the world are undergoing similarly rapid transformations; see, for example, Newbery et al. (2016) and Oseni and Pollit (2016). The agent-based modeling tools and transactive energy system approaches discussed in this chapter are applicable for all of these regions.

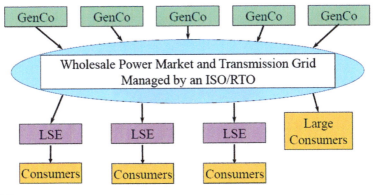

FIGURE 2

Basic design of a restructured wholesale power system as envisioned by FERC (2003).

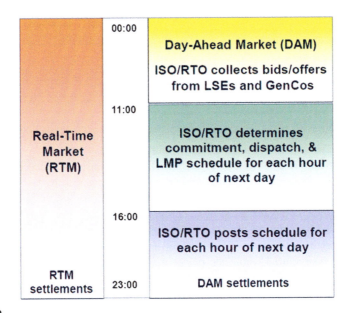

FIGURE 3

Daily parallel operation of day-ahead and real-time markets in an ISO/RTO-managed wholesale power system as envisioned by FERC (2003).

ket (DAM) and a *Real-Time Market (RTM)*, operating in parallel, which are centrally managed by an *Independent System Operator (ISO)* or *Regional Transmission Organization (RTO)*; see Fig. 3. Any discrepancies that arise between the day-ahead generation schedules determined in the DAM based on estimated next-day loads and

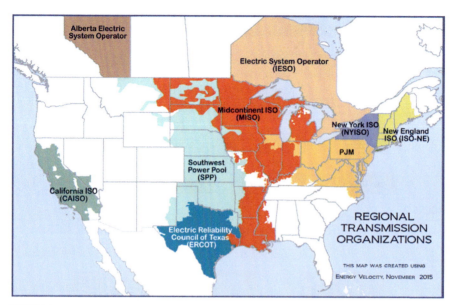

FIGURE 4

The nine North American energy regions with ISO/RTO-managed wholesale power markets. Public domain source: EIA (2016).

the actual needs for generation based on real-time loads are handled in the RTM, which thus functions as a real-time balancing mechanism.[2]

The physical power flows underlying these transactions take place by means of a high-voltage transmission grid that remains centrally managed by the ISO/RTO in order to ensure open access at reasonable access rates. Transmission grid congestion is managed in the DAM and RTM by *Locational Marginal Pricing (LMP)*.[3]

The basic FERC design depicted in Figs. 2 and 3 has to date been adopted by seven U.S. regions encompassing over 60% of U.S. generating capacity; see Fig. 4. Six of these restructured wholesale power markets entail interstate commerce and hence are under FERC's jurisdiction. The seventh, the Electric Reliability Council

---

[2]A GenCo is an entity that produces (supplies) power for an electric power grid. A *load* is an entity that consumes (absorbs) power from an electric power grid. An LSE is an entity that secures power, transmission, and related services to satisfy the power demands of its end-use customers. An LSE aggregates these power demands into "load blocks" for bulk buying at the wholesale level. An ISO/RTO is an organization charged with the primary responsibility of maintaining the security of an electric power system and often with system operation responsibilities as well. The ISO/RTO is required to be independent, meaning it cannot have a conflict of interest in carrying out these responsibilities, such as an ownership stake in generation or transmission facilities within the power system. See FERC (1999) and NERC (2016) for formal definitions.

[3]LMP is the pricing of electric power according to the time and location of its withdrawal from, or injection into, an electric power grid.

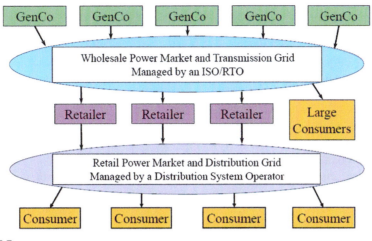

FIGURE 5

Original basic design envisioned for an electric power system with fully restructured retail and wholesale power markets.

of Texas (ERCOT), was deliberately restructured to avoid interstate commerce and hence Federal jurisdiction. Since retail transactions in all seven regions typically involve only local commerce over lower-voltage distribution grids, these transactions are regulated by state and local agencies. In consequence, by and large, retail prices paid by U.S. retail electric power users are regulated flat rates charged on a monthly basis that are not directly responsive to changes in wholesale power prices.

Nevertheless, attempts have repeatedly been made in the U.S. to restructure retail power system operations. The basic idea has been to replace LSEs by a competitive retail market enabling a large number of retailers to sell electric power to price-taking businesses and households at market-clearing prices. The design envisioned circa 2010 for a power system restructured at both the wholesale and retail levels is depicted in Fig. 5. A key aspect to note in Fig. 5 is that all power-flow arrows still point down, just as they do in Figs. 1 and 2, reflecting the traditional idea that businesses and households are passive loads that consume power taking prices/rates as given.

As it happens, however, the design in Fig. 5 has not come to pass; it has been overtaken by two related trends. First, "variable energy resources" are increasingly being substituted for thermal generators (e.g., coal-fired power plants) in response to growing concerns regarding environmental pollution from thermal generation (Ela et al., 2016). Second, technological developments such as advanced metering and intelligent devices are permitting businesses and households to become more active participants in power system transactions (Kabalci, 2016).

Variable energy resources (VERs) are renewable energy resources, such as wind turbines and solar (photovoltaic) panels, whose power generation cannot be closely controlled to match changes in demand or to meet other system requirements. For example, generation from wind turbines and solar panels can abruptly change due to sudden changes in wind speed and cloud cover. The growing penetration of VERs thus tends to increase the volatility of net power demands (i.e., customer power demands minus non-controllable generation) as well as the frequency of strong ramp events (i.e., rapid increases or declines in net power demands).

Volatility and strong ramp events make it difficult for system operators to maintain a continual real-time balance between power supply (i.e., generation net of transmission losses) and net power demands, an essential physical requirement for the reliable operation of power grids.[4] Since large thermal generators (especially nuclear and coal-fired) tend to have slow ramping capabilities, they are not an effective means for countering real-time fluctuations in net power demands. Although large-scale energy storage devices could in principle be deployed to offset these real-time fluctuations, to date this deployment has not been cost effective. Consequently, power system researchers are turning their attention to the possible use of more nimble types of resources for balancing purposes.

In particular, power system researchers are investigating the possibility of introducing various forms of aggregators able to harness ancillary services[5] from collections of *distributed energy resources (DERs)* owned by businesses and households connected to distribution grids. Examples of DERs include *distributed generation* (e.g., rooftop solar panels), plug-in electric vehicles, battery storage systems, and household appliances with energy storage capabilities and flexible power needs that permit collections of these appliances to function as *prosumers*, i.e., as entities that can produce or consume power depending on local conditions.

Harnessing of services from DERs for real-time operations requires voluntary participation by DER owners, hence it requires the creation of value streams that can be used to compensate DER owners appropriately for provided DER services. In addition, it requires technological developments such as advanced metering and intelligent devices that enable DERs to respond in a timely and accurate manner to real-time electronic signals.

Fig. 6 envisions a future *transmission and distribution (T/D)* system. An ISO/RTO-managed wholesale power market operating over a high-voltage (HV) transmission grid is tightly linked through DER/load aggregators to a distribution system operating over a lower-voltage (LV) distribution grid. The participants in the distribution system include DERs (distributed generation, storage, prosumers), locally managed by intelligent price-responsive software agents, as well as conventional (non-price-responsive) loads. An important characteristic of such a system is that data, signals, and power can flow up as well as down between the transmission and distribution levels.

---

[4]Imbalance between power supply and net power demand on a grid that exceeds tight tolerance limits will quickly induce a chain of events resulting in a power blackout.

[5]*Ancillary services* are services necessary to maintain reliable operation of an electric power system. Examples include various types of generation capacity held in reserve for possible later real-time use to balance deviations between scheduled power supply and actual net power demands.

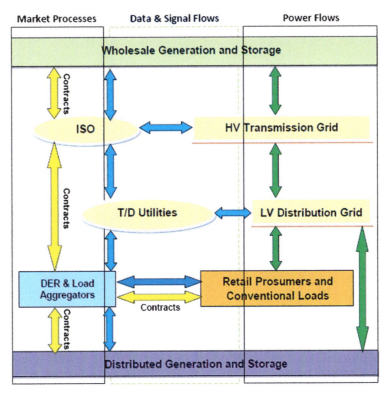

FIGURE 6

A tightly linked T/D system with distributed energy resources (DERs), prosumers, DER/load aggregators, and contract-based transactions.

Another important characteristic of such a system is a prevalence of contract-based transactions that permit transactor responsibilities to be expressed in clear legally-enforceable terms. Indeed, Fig. 6 is only a partial depiction of the many contractual relationships already engaged in by modern power system participants. Missing are directly negotiated bilateral contracts between wholesale power buyers and sellers, self-scheduled in the wholesale power market in order to secure transmission access, as well as various types of financial contracts (e.g., financial transmission rights) secured by system participants in order to hedge against price and quantity risks.

1.2 CHAPTER SCOPE

In view of the developments outlined in Section 1.1, a critical concern is how to design appropriate economic and control mechanisms to handle demand and supply transactions among the increasingly heterogeneous and dispersed collection of participants in modern electric power systems. Responding to this concern, the GridWise

Architecture Council (2015) has formulated a new *Transactive Energy System (TES)* framework for power systems. This TES framework is defined (p. 11) to be "a set of economic and control mechanisms that allows the dynamic balance of supply and demand across an entire electrical infrastructure using value as a key operational parameter."

Given the complexity of TES designs, their validation prior to real-world implementation requires many different levels of investigation ranging from conceptual analysis to field studies (Widergren et al., 2016). Moreover, to avoid adverse unintended consequences, this validation needs to include a careful consideration of behavioral incentives; TES participants should not perceive opportunities to game system rules for own advantage at the expense of system reliability and efficiency (Gallo, 2016).

Fortunately, agent-based modeling is well suited for these purposes. As detailed in IEEE (2016), Ringler et al. (2016), and Tesfatsion (2017a), TES researchers are increasingly turning to agent-based modeling tools in an attempt to bridge the gap between conceptual TES design proposals and validated real-world TES implementations.

This handbook chapter discusses current and potential uses of *Agent-Based Modeling (ABM)* as a support tool for TES research, with a stress on general methodological and practical concerns. Section 2 provides a broad overview of *Agent-based Computational Economics (ACE)*, a specialization of ABM to the study of systems involving economic processes. Although the precise meaning of ABM continues to be debated in the literature, specific modeling principles have been developed for ACE that carefully distinguish it from other types of modeling and that highlight its particular relevance for TES research.

Seven specific modeling principles underlying ACE model design are presented and explained in Section 2.1. Taken together, they express the fundamental goal of many agent-based modelers: namely, to be able to study real-world systems as historical processes unfolding through time.

Section 2.2 divides the various objectives being pursued by ACE researchers into basic categories: empirical understanding; normative design; qualitative insight and theory generation; and method/tool advancement. Section 2.3 identifies distinct aspects of empirical validation that researchers tend to weight differently, depending upon their objectives: namely, input validation; process validation; in-sample prediction; and out-of-sample forecasting. Although differential weighting by objective is commonly done, it is argued that ACE modeling permits researchers to strive for a more comprehensive approach to empirical validation that simultaneously considers all four aspects.

Section 2.4 considers the increasingly important role that ACE models are playing as computational laboratories for the development and testing of policy initiatives in advance of implementation. A taxonomy of *policy readiness levels (PRLs)* is proposed for policy initiatives ranging from conceptual modeling (PRL 1) to real-world policy deployment (PRL 9). It is noted that ACE modeling is helping to bridge the difficult gap between the conceptual research (PRLs 1–3) typically undertaken at universities and the field studies and deployments (PRLs 7–9) typically undertaken by industry. Section 2.5 argues that this PRL taxonomy could facilitate the development of standardized presentation protocols for ACE policy models that appropriately take into account model purpose and level of model development.

Section 3 briefly reviews early ACE research on electric power systems, with an emphasis on seminal contributions. Section 4 provides a general overview of TES research undertaken to date. The next two sections focus on ACE computational laboratories as a support tool for the design of TES architectures. Section 5 discusses current and potential ACE support for TES research on demand-response initiatives designed to encourage more active demand-side participation in T/D system operations. Section 6 discusses current and potential ACE support for TES research on contract design, with a stress on the need for contracts that facilitate flexible service provision in a manner that is both incentive compatible and robust against strategic manipulation. Concluding remarks are given in Section 7.

2 AGENT-BASED COMPUTATIONAL ECONOMICS: OVERVIEW
2.1 ACE MODELING PRINCIPLES

Agent-based Computational Economics (ACE) is the computational modeling of economic processes (including whole economies) as open-ended dynamic systems of interacting agents.[6] The following seven modeling principles collectively characterize the ACE modeling approach:

(MP1) *Agent Definition:* An *agent* is a software entity within a computationally constructed world capable of acting over time on the basis of its own *state*, i.e., its own internal data, attributes, and methods.

(MP2) *Agent Scope:* Agents can represent individuals, social groupings, institutions, biological entities, and/or physical entities.

(MP3) *Agent Local Constructivity:* The action of an agent at any given time is determined as a function of the agent's own state at that time.

(MP4) *Agent Autonomy:* Coordination of agent interactions cannot be externally imposed by means of free-floating restrictions, i.e., restrictions not embodied within agent states.

(MP5) *System Constructivity:* The state of the modeled system at any given time is determined by the ensemble of agent states at that time.

(MP6) *System Historicity:* Given initial agent states, all subsequent events in the modeled system are determined solely by agent interactions.

---

[6]Some of the materials in this section are adapted from Tesfatsion (2017b). Annotated pointers to ACE tutorials, publications, demos, software, research groups, and research area sites are posted at the ACE website (Tesfatsion, 2017c). For broad ACE/ABM overviews, see Arthur (2015), Chen (2016), Kirman (2011), and Tesfatsion (2006).

(MP7) *Modeler as Culture-Dish Experimenter:* The role of the modeler is limited to the setting of initial agent states and to the non-perturbational observation, analysis, and reporting of model outcomes.

Considered as a collective whole, modeling principles (MP1)–(MP7) embody the idea that an ACE model is a computational laboratory permitting users to explore how changes in initial conditions affect outcomes in a modeled dynamic system over time. This exploration process is analogous to biological experimentation with cultures in Petri dishes. A user sets initial conditions for a modeled dynamic system in accordance with some purpose at hand. The user then steps back, and the modeled dynamic system thereafter runs forward through time as a virtual world whose dynamics are driven by the interactions of its constituent agents.

The explicit statement of these modeling principles permits ACE to be distinguished more clearly and carefully from other modeling approaches, such as standard game theory and general equilibrium modeling within economics, and standard usages of state-space modeling by economists, engineers, and physicists. It also permits more precise comparisons between ACE and important historical antecedents, such as system dynamics (Rahmandad and Sterman, 2008) and microsimulation (Richiardi, 2013).

Modeling principle (MP1) provides a concise definition of an ACE agent as a software entity capable of taking actions based on its own local state. Here, "state" refers to three possibly-empty categories characterizing an agent at any given time: data (recorded physical sensations, empirical observations, statistical summaries, ...); attributes (physical conditions, financial conditions, beliefs, preferences, ...); and methods (data acquisition, physical laws, data interpretation, logical deduction, optimization routines, learning algorithms, decision rules, ...). There is no presumption here that the data acquired by an agent are accurate or complete, or that the methods used by an agent to process data are without error.

An agent's state represents the *potential* of this agent to express various types of behaviors through its actions. The agent's *actual* expressed behaviors within its virtual world, while conditioned on the agent's successive states, are also constrained and channeled by interactions with other agents.

An important corollary of (MP1) is that agents in ACE models are *encapsulated* software entities, i.e., software entities that package together data, attributes, and methods. This encapsulation permits an agent's internal aspects to be partially or completely hidden from other agents. A person familiar with *object-oriented programming (OOP)* might wonder why "agent" is used in (MP1) instead of "object," or "object template" (class), since both agents and objects refer to encapsulated software entities. "Agent" is used in ACE, and in ABM more generally, to stress the intended application to problem domains that include entities capable of various degrees of self-governance, self-directed social interactions, and deliberate masking of intentions. In contrast, OOP has traditionally interpreted objects as passive tools developed by a user to aid the accomplishment of a user-specified task.

The "state" conceptualization in (MP1) differs in two important ways from state depictions in standard state-space modeling:

(i) *Diversity of State Content:* The expression of an agent's state in terms of data, attribute, and method categories is broader than the standard depiction of states as vectors of real-valued variables.

(ii) *Variability of State Dimension:* An agent's state is not restricted to lie within a fixed finite-dimensional domain.

Regarding (ii), an agent's state can evolve over time in open-ended ways. For example, an agent can continue to augment its data $\mathbb{D}(t)$ over successive times t without need to rely on fixed-dimensional sufficient statistics, and its attributes $\alpha(t)$ can also vary over time. Moreover, the agent's methods $\mathbb{M}(t)$ might include a domain $\mathbb{R}(t)$ of possible decision rules plus a genetic algorithm g that involves mutation and recombination operations. When g operates on $\mathbb{R}(t)$, given $\mathbb{D}(t)$ and $\alpha(t)$, the result $g(\mathbb{R}(t); \mathbb{D}(t), \alpha(t))$ could be a modified decision-rule domain $\mathbb{R}(t + \Delta t)$ that has different elements than $\mathbb{R}(t)$ and possibly also a different dimension than $\mathbb{R}(t)$.

Modeling principle (MP2) expresses the intended broad scope of the agent definition provided in (MP1). In particular, in contrast to many agent definitions proposed in the general ABM literature, (MP2) makes clear that ACE agents are not restricted to human representations. Such a restriction would require modelers to make unnecessary distinctions between human actions and the actions of all other kinds of entities. Instead, (MP1) is in accordance with the standard dictionary meaning of agent as any entity, whether person or thing, able to take actions that affect subsequent events.

Another way of viewing (MP2) is that it calls for a broad *agent taxonomy*, i.e., a broad classification of agents into ordered groups or categories. As illustrated in Fig. 7, agents in ACE models can span all the way from passive entities with no cognitive function (e.g., grid transformers) to active entities with sophisticated decision-making capabilities (e.g., DER/load aggregators). Moreover, agents (e.g., distribution systems) can have other agents (e.g., households) as constituent members, thus permitting the modeling and study of hierarchical organizations.

The remaining five ACE modeling principles (MP3)–(MP7) imply that ACE models are state-space models in initial value form (Tesfatsion, 2017d). Specifically, an ACE model specifies how an ensemble of agent states varies over time, starting from a given ensemble of agent states at an initial time. Modern economic theory also relies heavily on state-space modeling. However, modeling principles (MP3)–(MP7) sharply differentiate ACE models from standard economic state-space models.

Specifically, (MP3)–(MP7) require agent autonomy conditional on initial agent states. In contrast, standard economic state-space models incorporate modeler-imposed rationality, optimality, and equilibrium conditions that could not (or would not) be met by agents acting solely on the basis of their own local states at each successive point in time. For example, rational expectations assumptions require ex ante agent expectations to be consistent with ex post model outcomes. Consequently, the derivation of rational expectations solutions is a global fixed-point problem requiring the simultaneous consideration of all time periods.

The seven modeling principles (MP1)–(MP7) together require an ACE model to be *fully* agent based. That is, all entities capable of acting within an ACE

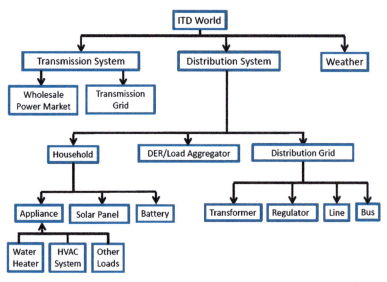

FIGURE 7

Partial agent taxonomy for an ACE modeling of an integrated transmission and distribution (ITD) system. Down-pointing arrows denote "has-a" relationships and up-pointing arrows denote "is-a" relationships.

computationally-constructed world must be modeled as some form of agent. This requirement has two key advantages. First, it enhances conceptual transparency; all factors affecting world events must be clearly identified as an agent or agent component. Second, it facilitates plug-and-play model scalability. The number of previously-typed agents can easily be increased, since this does not require changes to the interfaces between agent types. Also, *high-level architectures (HLAs)*[7] can be designed for ACE models that facilitate enlargement of their scope through inclusion of new agent types.

For ACE researchers, as for economists in general, the modeling of decision methods for decision-making agents is a primary concern. Here it is important to correct a major misconception still being expressed by some commentators uninformed about the powerful capabilities of modern software: namely, the misconception that ACE decision-making agents cannot be as rational (or irrational) as real people.

To the contrary, the constraints on agent decision making implied by modeling principles (MP1)–(MP7) are constraints inherent in every real-world economic system. As seen in the ACE learning research linked at Tesfatsion (2017e), the decision methods used by ACE agents can range from simple behavioral rules to sophisticated

---

[7] An HLA is a general purpose framework that manages the interactions among a "federation" (collection) of "federates" (simulation entities) (IEEE, 2010). The goal is to promote the interoperability and reuse of simulation systems.

anticipatory learning algorithms for the approximate achievement of intertemporal objectives. A concrete demonstration of this assertion within a macroeconomic context is provided by Sinitskaya and Tesfatsion (2015).

A second common misconception is the incorrect belief that (MP1)–(MP7) rule out any consideration of stochasticity. To the contrary, stochastic aspects can easily be represented within ACE models. Agent data can include recorded realizations for random events, agent attributes can include beliefs based on probabilistic assessments, and agent methods can include *pseudo-random number generators (PRNGs)*. A PRNG is an algorithm, initialized by a seed value, that is able to generate a number sequence whose properties mimic the properties of a random number sequence.

PRNGs can be included among the methods of decision-making agents, thus permitting these agents to "randomize" their behaviors. For example, a decision-making agent can use PRNGs to choose among equally preferred actions or action delays, to construct mixed strategies in game situations to avoid exploitable predictability, and/or to induce perturbations in action routines in order to explore new action possibilities.

PRNGs can also be included among the methods of other types of agents, such as physical or biological agents, in order to model stochastic processes external to decision-making agents. For example, the Weather agent in Fig. 7 might use a PRNG to generate a weather pattern for each simulated year that affects the operations of Appliance agents and Solar Panel agents. These operational effects could in turn induce changes in the decisions of the DER/Load Aggregator agent and Household agents.

An important constraint affecting the ACE modeling of stochasticity is that the modeling principles (MP1)–(MP7) require an ACE model to be dynamically complete. Thus, ACE modelers must identify the *sources* of any stochastic shocks affecting events within their modeled worlds, not simply their impact points, because all such shocks must come from agents actually residing within these worlds. This requirement encourages ACE modelers to think carefully about the intended empirical referents for any included stochastic shock terms. It also facilitates successive model development. For example, a Weather agent represented as a highly simplified stochastic process in a current modeling effort can easily be modified to have a more empirically compelling representation in a subsequent modeling effort.

Another key issue is whether modeling principles (MP1)–(MP7) imply ACE models are necessarily pre-statable. As stressed by Longo et al. (2012) and Koppl et al. (2015), the real world "bubbles forth" with an ever-evolving state space, driven in part by random (acausal) events. This renders infeasible the pre-statement of accurate equations of motion for real-world state processes.

ACE modeling addresses this issue in two ways. First, there is no requirement in ACE modeled worlds that the agents residing within these worlds be able to accurately depict laws of motion for their states in equation form, or in any other form. Second, data can be streamed into ACE models in a manner that prevents even the modeler from being able to accurately pre-state future model outcomes.

More precisely, suppose an ACE model has no run-time interaction with any external system during times $t \in [t^o, T]$ for some finite horizon T. Then, in principle, the modeler at time t^o could pre-state all model outcomes over the time interval $[t^o, T]$, conditional on a given specification of agent states at time t^o, in the same manner that he could in principle pre-state all possible plays of a chess game with a given closure rule.

Nevertheless, (MP1)–(MP7) do not imply that ACE agents have complete state information. Consequently, ACE agents can experience events over time that they have no way of knowing in advance. For example, suppose an ACE model consists of a Weather agent interacting over times $t \in [t^o, T]$ with a variety of other agents, as depicted in Fig. 7. At the initial time t^o the modeler might know the weather pattern that the Weather agent will generate over $[t^o, T]$, or be able to pre-state this weather pattern based on the modeler's time-t^o knowledge (or control) of the Weather agent's data, attributes, and methods. However, if other agents have no access to the Weather agent's internal aspects, they will experience weather over $[t^o, T]$ as a stochastic process.

Alternatively, an ACE model can have run-time interactions with an external system. For example, as discussed by LeBaron and Tesfatsion (2008, Section III) and Borrill and Tesfatsion (2011, Section 2.1), an ACE model can be *data driven*; that is, it can include conduit agents permitting external data to be streamed into the model during run-time that are unknown (or unknowable) by the modeler at the initial time t^o. In this case the modeler at time t^o will not be able to pre-state future model outcomes, even in principle.

A particularly intriguing case to consider is when the data streamed into an ACE modeled world include sequences of outcomes extracted from real-world processes. For example, real-world weather data could be streamed into the Weather agent in Fig. 7 that this agent then uses to generate weather patterns for its computational world. These weather data could include thermal or atmospheric noise data accessible to decision-making agents, such as Household agents, enabling them to use "truly random" numbers in place of PRNGs to randomize their decision-making processes.

2.2 ACE OBJECTIVES AND SCOPE

Current ACE research divides roughly into four strands differentiated by objective. One primary objective is *empirical understanding*: What explains the appearance and persistence of empirical regularities? ACE researchers seek possible causal mechanisms grounded in the successive interactions of agents operating within computationally-rendered virtual worlds. A virtual world capable of generating an empirical regularity of interest provides a candidate explanation for this regularity.

A second primary objective is *normative design*: How can ACE models be used as computational laboratories to facilitate the design of structures, institutions, and regulations resulting in desirable system performance over time? The ACE approach to normative design is akin to filling a bucket with water to determine if it leaks. A researcher constructs a virtual world that captures salient aspects of a system operating under a proposed design. The researcher identifies a range of initial agent state specifications of interest, including seed values for agent PRNG methods. For each such specification the researcher permits the virtual world to develop over time driven solely by agent interactions. Recorded outcomes are then used to evaluate design performance.

One key issue for ACE normative design is the extent to which resulting outcomes are efficient, fair, and orderly, despite possible attempts by strategic decision-making agents to game the design for personal advantage. A second key issue is a cautionary concern for adverse unintended consequences. *Optimal* design might not always be a realistic goal, especially for large complex systems; but ACE models can facilitate *robust* design for increased system resiliency, a goal that is both feasible and highly desirable.

A third primary objective of ACE researchers is *qualitative insight and theory generation*: How can ACE models be used to study the *potential* behaviors of dynamic systems over time? Ideally, what is needed is a dynamic system's *phase portrait*, i.e., a representation of its potential state trajectories starting from all feasible initial states. Phase portraits reveal not only the possible existence of equilibria but also the basins of attraction for any such equilibria. Phase portraits thus help to clarify which regions of a system's state space are credibly reachable, hence of empirical interest, and which are not. An ACE modeling of a dynamic system can be used to conduct batched runs starting from multiple initial agent states, thus providing a rough approximation of the system's phase portrait.

A fourth primary objective of ACE researchers is *method/tool advancement*: How best to provide ACE researchers with the methods and tools they need to undertake theoretical studies of dynamic systems through systematic sensitivity studies, and to examine the compatibility of sensitivity-generated theories with real-world data? ACE researchers are exploring a variety of ways to address this objective ranging from careful consideration of methodological principles to the practical development of programming, visualization, and empirical validation tools.

2.3 ENABLING COMPREHENSIVE EMPIRICAL VALIDATION

Modelers focused on the scientific understanding of real-world systems want their models to have empirical validity ("consistency with real world data"). Below are four distinct aspects of empirical validation which, ideally, a model intended for scientific understanding should simultaneously achieve:

EV1. Input Validation: Are the exogenous inputs for the model (e.g., functional forms, random shock realizations, data-based parameter estimates, and/or parameter values imported from other studies) empirically meaningful and appropriate for the purpose at hand?

EV2. Process Validation: How well do the physical, biological, institutional, and social processes represented within the model reflect real-world aspects important for the purpose at hand? Are all process specifications consistent with essential scaffolding constraints, such as physical laws, stock-flow relationships, and accounting identities?

EV3. Descriptive Output Validation: How well are model-generated outputs able to capture the salient features of the sample data used for model identification? *(in-sample fitting)*

EV4. Predictive Output Validation: How well are model-generated outputs able to forecast distributions, or distribution moments, for sample data withheld from model identification or for data acquired at a later time? *(out-of-sample forecasting)*

In practice, economists relying solely on standard analytical modeling tools do not place equal weight on these four aspects of empirical validation. Particularly for larger-scale economic systems, such as macroeconomies, analytical tractability issues and a desire to adhere to preconceived rationality, optimality, and equilibrium ideals have forced severe compromises.

In contrast, an ACE model is an open-ended dynamic system. Starting from an initial state, outcomes are determined forward through time, one state leading to the next, in a constructive manner. This process does not depend on the determination, or even the existence, of equilibrium states. ACE thus provides researchers with tremendous flexibility to tailor their agents to their specific purposes.

In particular, ACE researchers can match modeled biological, physical, institutional, and social agents to their empirical counterparts in the real world. This ability to match modeled agents to empirical counterparts, important for scientific understanding, is also critical for normative design purposes. Robustness of proposed designs against strategic manipulation can only be assured in advance of implementation if the modeled decision-making agents used to test the performance of these designs have the same degree of freedom to engage in strategic behaviors as their empirical counterparts.

ACE modeling thus permits researchers to strive for the simultaneous achievement of all four empirical validation aspects EV1 through EV4. This pursuit of comprehensive empirical validation will of course be tempered in practice by data limitations. Even in an era of Big Data advances, data availability and quality remain important concerns. Computational limitations, such as round-off error, truncation error, and error propagation, are also a concern. Advances in computer technology and numerical approximation procedures are rapidly relaxing these limitations. In the interim, however, as expressed by Judd (2006, p. 887), numerical error must be traded off against specification error:

> *"The key fact is that economists face a trade-off between the numerical errors in computational work and the specification errors of analytically tractable models. Computationally intensive approaches offer opportunities to examine realistic models, a valuable option even with the numerical errors. As Tukey (1962) puts it, 'Far better an approximate answer to the right question ... than an exact answer to the wrong question ...'."*

Empirical validation of ACE models in the sense of EV1 through EV4 is a highly active area of research. Extensive annotated pointers to this research can be found at Tesfatsion (2017f).

Table 1 Policy Readiness Level (PRL) classifications for normative design research

Development level	PRL	Description
Conceptual idea	PRL 1	Conceptual formulation of a policy with desired attributes
Analytic formulation	PRL 2	Analytic characterization of a policy with desired attributes
Modeling with low empirical fidelity	PRL 3	Analysis of policy performance using a highly simplified model
Small-scale modeling with moderate empirical fidelity	PRL 4	Policy performance tests using a small-scale model embodying several salient real-world aspects
Small-scale modeling with high empirical fidelity	PRL 5	Policy performance tests using a small-scale model embodying many salient real-world aspects
Prototype small-scale modeling	PRL 6	Policy performance tests using a small-scale model reflecting expected field conditions apart from scale
Prototype large-scale modeling	PRL 7	Policy performance tests using a large-scale model reflecting expected field conditions
Field study	PRL 8	Performance tests of policy in expected final form under expected field conditions
Real-world deployment	PRL 9	Deployment of policy in final form under a full range of operating conditions

2.4 AVOIDING PREMATURE JUMPS TO POLICY IMPLEMENTATION

Ideally, changes in a society's current institutional and regulatory policies should be guided by research that is strongly supported by empirical evidence. Reaching a point where a proposed new policy is ready for real-world implementation will typically require a series of modeling efforts at different scales and with different degrees of empirical verisimilitude. Moving too soon to policy implementation on the basis of over-simplified models entails major risk of adverse unintended consequences.

Consider, for example, the *Policy Readiness Levels (PRLs)*[8] proposed in Table 1 for research directed towards the normative design of institutional and/or regulatory policies. Due to relatively limited data and computational capabilities, policy researchers at universities tend to work at PRLs 1–3. In contrast, policy researchers within industry, government, and regulatory agencies tend to work at PRLs 7–9.

The interim PRLs 4–6 thus constitute a "valley of death" that hinders the careful step-by-step development and testing of policy proposals from conceptual formula-

---

[8] These PRLs mimic, in rough form, the *Technology Readiness Levels (TRLs)* devised by the U.S. Department of Energy (DOE, 2011a, p. 22) to rank the readiness of proposed new technologies for commercial application.

tion all the way to real-world implementation. Fortunately, ACE modeling is well suited for bridging this valley because it facilitates the construction of computational platforms[9] permitting policy model development and testing at PRLs 4–6. This will be illustrated in Section 5, which focuses on the use of ACE platforms for the design and evaluation of transactive energy system architectures.

All nine levels in the PRL taxonomy are essential for ensuring conceptual policy ideas are brought to real-world fruition. Explicit recognition and acceptance of this tiered model valuation could encourage policy researchers to become more supportive of each other's varied contributions.

Another important point is that the PRL taxonomy does not necessarily have to represent a one-way road map from initial concept to completed application. Rather, PRLs 1–9 could constitute a single concept-to-application iteration in an ongoing *Iterative Participatory Modeling (IPM)* process. Extensive annotated pointers to IPM studies can be found at Tesfatsion (2017f).

2.5 TOWARDS STANDARDIZED PRESENTATION PROTOCOLS FOR ACE POLICY MODELS

The classification of policy models in accordance with policy readiness levels (PRLs), as proposed in Section 2.4, could also help resolve another key issue facing ACE policy researchers. Specifically, how can ACE models and model findings undertaken for policy purposes be presented to stakeholders, regulators, and other interested parties in a clear and compelling manner (Wallace et al., 2015, Sections 3–4, 6)?

Most ACE models are not simply the computational implementation of a model previously developed in equation form. Rather, ACE modeling often proceeds from agent taxonomy and flow diagrams, to pseudo-code, and finally to software programs that can be compiled and run. In this case the software programs *are* the models. On the other hand, it follows from the modeling principles presented in Section 2.1 that ACE models are initial-value state space models. Consequently, in principle, the software program for any ACE model can equivalently be represented in abstract form as a system of discrete-time or discrete-event difference equations, starting from user-specified initial conditions. These analytical representations become increasingly complex as the number of agents increases.

The practical challenge facing ACE policy researchers then becomes how best to present approximations of their models to interested parties who are unable or unwilling to understand these models in coded or analytical form. Most ACE policy researchers resort to verbal descriptions, simple graphical depictions for model components and interactions, Unified Modeling Language (UML) diagrams,[10] and/or

---

[9]In the current study the term *computational platform* is used to refer to a software framework together with a library of software components that permit the plug-and-play development and study of a family of computational models.

[10]The *Unified Modeling Language (UML)* is a general-purpose modeling language intended to provide a standard way to design and visualize conceptual and software models. UML diagrams enable partial graph-

pseudo-code expressing the logical flow of agent interactions over time. Anyone wishing to replicate reported results is referred to the original source code.

The lack of presentation protocols for ACE policy models (and for ACE models more generally) has been severely criticized by economists who directly specify their models in analytical or statistical terms using commonly accepted approaches. At the very least, it complicates efforts to communicate model features and findings with clarity, thus hindering the accumulation of knowledge across successive modeling efforts.

Fortunately, the development of presentation protocols for agent-based models is now an active area of research (Tesfatsion, 2017d,g). For example, the ODD (*O*verview, *D*esign concepts, and *D*etails) protocol developed by Grimm et al. (2006, 2010a) has been widely adopted by ecologists who use agent-based models. To date, however, proposed protocols such as ODD have attempted to provide "one size fits all" requirements for the presentation of models, regardless of purpose and development level.

For policy research, a better way to proceed would seem to be the adoption of multiple standardized presentation protocols tailored to the PRL of a modeling effort. For example, a protocol for PRL 1–3 models could require a complete model presentation within the confines of a typical journal article. In contrast, a protocol for PRL 4–7 models could consist of two sets of presentation requirements: one set for a summary model presentation to be reported within the confines of a typical journal article; and a second set for a complete model presentation (source code, documentation, and test-case simulation data) to be reported at a supplementary website repository.

3 EARLY ACE RESEARCH ON ELECTRIC POWER SYSTEMS

This section briefly surveys pioneering ACE research on electric power systems. Much of this early work was motivated by a desire to understand the substantial restructuring of U.S. electric power systems starting in the mid-1990s; see Section 1.1.

Sheblé (1999) was among the earliest works stressing the potential usefulness of agent-based computational tools for the simulation and analysis of restructured electric power markets. The book covers a wide range of market and operational aspects pertinent for these restructuring efforts, referencing a series of earlier publications by the author and his collaborators. In particular, unusual for a power engineering text at the time, careful attention is paid in this book to auction market design and to

---

ical representations of a model's structural (static) and behavioral (dynamic) aspects. UML has become increasingly complex in successive version releases and is not specifically tailored for dynamic systems driven by agent interactions. Perhaps for these reasons, UML as a general modeling tool has not been widely adopted by ACE/ABM researchers to date; see Collins et al. (2015) for further discussion of these points.

the potentially strategic bid/offer behaviors of auction traders. As noted in the preface, this work was strongly motivated by earlier seminal work by Schweppe et al. (1988) proposing a competitive spot pricing mechanism for real-time electric power transactions.

In parallel with this agent-based modeling work, a series of studies appeared that proposed *multi-agent system (MAS)* approaches for the decentralized control of electric power systems by means of intelligent software agents; see, e.g., Ygge (1998). The distinction between MAS studies and agent-based studies of electric power systems is interesting and important. Roughly stated, in the MAS studies the ultimate goal is to construct software agents whose decentralized *deployment* within a real-world electric power system would permit a more efficient achievement of *centralized* system objectives. In contrast, in the agent-based studies the ultimate goal is to develop high-fidelity *models (representations)* of real-world electric power systems using collections of interacting software agents. This distinction will be concretely demonstrated in later sections of this chapter.[11]

In another series of pioneering studies, Derek Bunn and his collaborators developed various agent-based models permitting them to explore the impacts of alternative trading arrangements for real-world electric power markets undergoing restructuring; see Bower and Bunn (2000, 2001), Day and Bunn (2001), Bunn and Oliveira (2001, 2003), and Bunn (2004). For example, the authors were able to study with care a number of actual market rules and settlement arrangements implemented for the England and Wales wholesale power market.

Nicolaisen et al. (2001) developed an agent-based model of an electric power market organized as a double auction with discriminatory pricing. They used this platform to study market power and efficiency as a function of the relative concentration and capacity of market buyers and sellers. The buyers and sellers have learning capabilities, implemented as a *modified* version of a reinforcement learning algorithm due to Roth and Erev (1995). The modifications were introduced to overcome several perceived issues with the original algorithm, such as zero updating in response to zero profit outcomes.

In a pioneering study of retail electricity markets, Roop and Fathelrahman (2003) developed an agent-based model in which consumers with learning capabilities choose among retail contracts offering three different pricing options: standard fixed rate; time-of-day rates; and real-time pricing. Retail customers make contract choices over time based on the modified Roth–Erev reinforcement learning algorithm developed by Nicolaisen et al. (2001).

During this time, various research groups were also beginning to develop agent-based computational platforms permitting systematic performance testing for electric power market designs. Examples include: *AMES (Agent-based Modeling of*

---

[11]Specifically, the IRW Test Bed covered in Section 5.2.1 is an agent-based modeling of an electric power system, whereas the PowerMatcher covered in Section 5.3 is a decentralized control mechanism for electric power systems whose deployment is based on the bid/offer interactions of distributed intelligent software agents.

Electricity Systems) (Tesfatsion, 2017i) developed at Iowa State University by Koesrindartoto et al. (2005) and Sun and Tesfatsion (2007); *EMCAS* (*E*lectricity *M*arket *C*omplex *A*daptive *S*ystem) developed at Argonne National Laboratory by Conzelmann et al. (2005); *Marketecture* developed at Los Alamos National Laboratory by Atkins et al. (2004); *MASCEM* (*M*ulti-*A*gent *S*ystem for *C*ompetitive *E*lectricity *M*arkets) developed at the Polytechnic Institute of Porto, Portugal, by Praça et al. (2003); *N-ABLE*^{TM} developed at Sandia National Laboratories by Ehlen and Scholand (2005); *NEMSIM* (*N*ational *E*lectricity *M*arket *SIM*ulator) developed at CSIRO by Batten and Grozev (2006); *PowerACE* developed at the University of Karlsruhe by Weidlich and Veit (2008b); and the *Smart Grid in a Room Simulator* developed at Carnegie Mellon University by Wagner et al. (2015).

The pioneering electricity market experiments conducted by Vernon L. Smith and his collaborators also deserve recognition; e.g., Rassenti et al. (2003). Human-subject experiments provide important benchmark data for the design of software agents in agent-based electricity market models. For example, Oh and Mount (2011) demonstrate that suitably designed software agents are able to replicate the behavior of human subjects in three different market contexts relevant for electric power systems.

For detailed historical accounts of early ACE research on electric power systems, see Marks (2006, Section 4), Weidlich (2008, Section 3.3), and Weidlich and Veit (2008a). For a survey covering more recent ACE research on electric power systems, see Ringler et al. (2016). Annotated pointers to a sampling of this research can be found at Tesfatsion (2017a).

4 TRANSACTIVE ENERGY SYSTEMS RESEARCH: OVERVIEW

As discussed in Section 1.1, the growing participation of variable energy resources in modern electric power systems at both the transmission and distribution (T/D) levels has increased the need for flexible power and ancillary service provision in support of T/D operations. *Transactive Energy System (TES)* researchers are attempting to address this need.[12]

A TES is a set of economic and control mechanisms that permits supply and demand for power to be balanced over time across an entire electrical infrastructure, where these mechanisms are designed to enhance value for the transacting parties consistent with overall system reliability. An *electrical infrastructure* consists of electrical devices connected to a physical grid. The electrical devices are capable of power supply (generation) and/or power absorption (consuming/storing power), and the grid permits the delivery of power from supplier devices to absorption devices. The grid

---

[12]For broad introductions to TES research, see GridWise Architecture Council (2015), IEEE (2016), and Widergren et al. (2016). For useful broad overviews of smart grid research, see Kabalci (2016) and Tuballa and Abundo (2016). For surveys specifically focused on agent-based electric power system research, see Gallo (2016), Guerci et al. (2010), Ringler et al. (2016), and Weidlich and Veit (2008a).

can range from a small-scale microgrid, such as an industrial park grid, to a large-scale T/D grid spanning a wide geographical region.

A key characteristic of TES architectures is a stress on decentralization. Information technology is viewed as the nervous system that will permit management of an electrical infrastructure to be shared by a society of distributed resource owners, customers, and other stakeholders. The necessity of using a common physical grid to implement power and ancillary service transactions provides a natural source of alignment among stakeholder objectives. The challenge is to exploit this natural alignment to build a market-based transaction network that results in sustainable business operations for all stakeholders while still preserving the incentive and opportunity to innovate. The ultimate TES objective is to achieve "a loosely coupled set of controls with just enough information exchange to allow for stability and global optimization through local action" (GridWise Architecture Council, 2015, p. 10).

TES researchers are currently investigating a variety of innovative ideas for T/D system design (IEEE, 2016; Widergren et al., 2016). One such idea is the possibility of instituting various forms of *distributed energy resource (DER)* aggregators able to manage collections of business and household DERs as demand-side resources able to adjust their power usage in accordance with real-time T/D operational requirements. To be manageable, the DERs must be intelligent devices able to send, receive, interpret, and respond to real-time signals. TES researchers are also studying new contractual forms that permit flexible market-based bids/offers for power and ancillary services in support of T/D operations.

As indicated in Fig. 8, the implementation of these and other forms of TES initiatives for T/D systems implies tighter feedback connections between operations at the T/D system levels. Consequently, TES research focusing on T/D systems has been guided by three major premises.

First, to ensure the efficient reliable operation of future T/D systems, researchers need to consider with care the *integrated* operation of these systems *over time*. Second, researchers need to develop *scalable* TES approaches that permit the efficient flexible procurement of power and ancillary services from distributed T/D resources as the number and diversity of these resources continues to increase. Third, to evaluate the technical and financial feasibility of these approaches in advance of implementation, researchers need to develop *computational platforms* that permit integrated T/D systems to be modeled and studied as coherent dynamic systems with grid sizes ranging from small to realistically large, and with an appropriate degree of empirical verisimilitude.

As seen in Section 2, ACE modeling permits the modular and extensible representation of complex open-ended dynamic systems. Thus, ACE models can function as computational platforms within which researchers can develop and evaluate TES initiatives for T/D systems in accordance with the above three premises. Edgier yet, as demonstrated by Borrill and Tesfatsion (2011, Section 6.3) for a general enterprise information storage system and by Kok (2013, Part III) for a TES architecture, ACE modeling principles can be directly used to design system architectures that dramatically simplify storage and management of information.

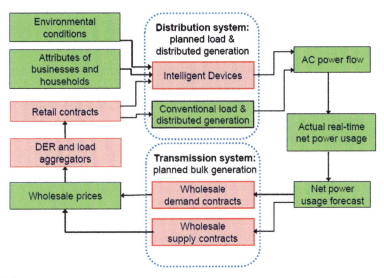

FIGURE 8

Schematic depiction of an integrated T/D system with intelligent devices, DER and load aggregators, and contracts facilitating flexible power and ancillary service provision. *Net power usage* refers to load minus non-controllable generation.

For concreteness, the next two sections focus on the current and potential use of ACE modeling as a support tool for TES research in two areas critical for the successful implementation of TES architectures in T/D systems: namely, demand response and contract design.

5 ACE SUPPORT FOR TES RESEARCH ON DEMAND RESPONSE
5.1 OVERVIEW

In traditional U.S. electric power systems based on vertically integrated utilities (Fig. 1), the power usage of residential, commercial, and industrial customers was generally assumed to be highly unresponsive to price changes. Utilities typically charged their customers a flat hourly rate for power usage, plus additional fixed charges, on an extended (e.g., monthly) basis. A critical utility operator function, referred to as "load following," was then to ensure that real-time customer power usage was continually balanced by real-time power generation, whatever form this power usage took.

Thus, customers became accustomed to extracting power from the grid without any consideration of its actual production cost or environmental impact. Paraphrasing Bunn (2004, p. 5), customers were essentially the holders of power call options that were unconstrained in volume up to fuse box limits and that could freely be exercised at customer convenience.

This traditional conception of customer power usage as externally determined load in need of balancing has been carried forward into U.S. restructured wholesale power markets (Fig. 2). Although, in principle, LSEs participating in day-ahead markets are permitted to submit hourly demand bids for the next-day power needs of their customers in two parts – a price-responsive demand schedule and a fixed power amount – most LSE hourly demand bids currently take a fixed form.

As far back as 2002, power economists have forcefully argued the need for participants on both sides of a power market, buyers and sellers, to be able to express their reservation values[13] for power in order to achieve an efficient pricing of power; see, e.g., Stoft (2002, Chapter 1-1), Kirschen (2003), Rassenti et al. (2003), and Tesfatsion (2009). However, given the relatively primitive state of metering technology, it was not feasible for power customers to adjust their power usage in real time in response either to system operator commands or to automated signals. Consequently, power customers continued to play a largely passive role in power system operations.

Fortunately, recent breakthroughs in metering technology, referred to as *Advanced Metering Infrastructure (AMI)*, have radically improved the potential for more active customer participation (Kabalci, 2016). AMI broadly refers to an integrated system of meters, communication links (wired or wireless), and data management processes that permits rapid two-way communication between power customers and the agencies (e.g., utilities) that manage their power supplies.

In particular, AMI enables the implementation of *demand-response* initiatives designed to encourage fuller demand-side participation in power system operations. Power system researchers are currently exploring three basic types of demand-response initiatives[14]:

(i) Incentive-Based Load Control: Down/up adjustments in the power usage of business and household devices are made either in response to direct requests from designated parties[15] or via device switches under the remote control of designated parties, with compensation at administratively set rates.

---

[13]Roughly, a *buyer's reservation value* for a good or service at a particular point in time is defined to be the buyer's maximum willingness to pay for the purchase of an additional unit of this good or service at that time. A *seller's reservation value* for a good or service at a particular point in time is defined to be the minimum payment that the seller is willing to receive for the sale of an additional unit of this good or service at that time. See Tesfatsion (2009).

[14]For broad surveys of type (i)–(iii) demand-response research, see IEEE (2016), Rahimi and Ipakchi (2010), Ringler et al. (2016), and Siano (2014). For demand-response deployment in the U.S., see FERC (2008) and FERC (2015).

[15]These designated parties can be ISOs/RTOs or utilities. They can also be intermediaries who manage collections of customer-owned demand-response resources in accordance with the operational requirements of ISOs/RTOs or utilities.

(ii) Price-Responsive Demand: Down/up power usage adjustments are undertaken by businesses and/or households in response to changes in power prices communicated to them by designated parties.
(iii) Transactive Energy: Demands and supplies for power and ancillary services by businesses and households are determined by decentralized bid/offer-based transactions within a power system organized as a TES.

The implementation of these demand-response initiatives can result in curtailments (or increases) in total power withdrawal from the grid, or in shifts in the timing of power withdrawals from the grid with no significant change in total power withdrawal. In some cases, demand response resources might be willing and able to offset curtailments (or increases) in their power withdrawals from the grid by resorting to local "behind the meter" generation and storage facilities, such as an onsite wind turbine or a small-scale battery system with no grid connection.

A key goal of type-(i) initiatives is to permit ancillary services to be extracted from demand-side resources in support of system *reliability*. A key goal of type-(ii) initiatives is to enhance system *efficiency* by permitting business and household customers to express their reservation values for power at different times and locations. A key goal of type-(iii) initiatives is to enhance the reliability *and* efficiency of system operations by enabling a balancing of demands and supplies for power and ancillary services across an entire electrical infrastructure on the basis of business and household reservation values.

Researchers focusing on type-(i) and type-(ii) demand response initiatives have primarily stressed metering, control, and planning aspects for system operators and power customers. For example, Bitar et al. (2014, Chapters 2–3) and Parvania et al. (2013) investigate the ability of type-(i) demand response programs to provide reserve services for system operators. Yoon et al. (2014) study various forms of control strategies for type-(i) initiatives designed to maximize the net benefits of building residents subject to constraints. Thomas et al. (2012) propose a type-(ii) intelligent air-conditioning system controller able to determine optimal next-day power usage for a household based on the household's comfort/cost trade-off preferences, conditional on price signals for next day retail power usage and a forecast for next-day environmental conditions. Wang and He (2016) propose a two-stage co-optimization framework for a customer whose stage-1 decision is to install a battery energy storage system and whose stage-2 decision is to join one of several offered type-(i) and type-(ii) demand response programs.

However, some work has explored the effects of type-(ii) demand response initiatives on power system operations over time. For example, Thomas and Tesfatsion (2016, 2017) use an ACE computational platform to investigate the effects of price-responsive household demands for power on integrated T/D system operations over time by means of systematic computational experiments.[16] Zhou et al. (2011) de-

---

[16]Interestingly, regularities observed in these simulation findings permitted Thomas and Tesfatsion (2017) to develop a detailed mathematical analysis of cobweb dynamics.

velop an agent-based computational platform to study the effects of price-responsive power demand by commercial buildings, modeled as autonomous agents with reinforcement learning capabilities, that compete to offer demand response services into a wholesale power market operating over a transmission grid. Making use of the Policy Readiness Levels (PRLs) proposed in Section 2.4, this agent-based work can roughly be classified as PRL 4.

TES researchers focusing on type-(iii) demand response initiatives are interested in understanding the potential effects of these initiatives on the end-to-end operations of entire T/D systems. The work of these TES researchers can roughly be divided into three categories:

[PRLs 1–3] Conceptual discussion supported by graphical depictions and/or by relatively simple analytic modeling: e.g., Bitar et al. (2014, Chapter 4), Rahimi et al. (2016).

[PRLs 4–6] Performance studies making use of agent-based computational platforms: e.g., Broeer et al. (2014), Kahrobaee et al. (2014) Karfopoulos et al. (2015, Sections 1–4), Kok (2013, Section III), Pinto et al. (2011), Santos et al. (2015).

[PRLs 7–8] Relatively large-scale performance tests in laboratory or field settings: e.g., AEP (2014), Karfopoulos et al. (2015, Sections 5–6), Kok (2013, Section IV), Kok and Widergren (2016), PNNL (2015).

As stressed by Ringler et al. (2016, Section 5), the application of agent-based modeling to the study of integrated T/D system operations with smart grid capabilities, such as TES architectures, is still relatively new. Moreover, the source code developed for most of these studies is not publicly available.

A key exception is work based on GridLAB-D (2017), an open-source agent-based computational platform developed by researchers with the U.S. Department of Energy at Pacific Northwest National Laboratory. As explained by Chassin et al. (2014), GridLAB-D permits the customized simulation of a distribution system populated with residential, commercial, and industrial customers that own a wide range of electrical devices.

The first illustration discussed below is a type-(ii) price-responsive demand study by Thomas and Tesfatsion (2016, 2017). This study is conducted in part by means of an ACE computational platform referred to as the *Integrated Retail and Wholesale (IRW) Test Bed* (Tesfatsion, 2017h). The IRW Test Bed simulates the successive daily operations of an electric power system consisting of retail and wholesale power sectors subject to distribution and transmission grid constraints. GridLAB-D is used to model non-price-responsive electrical devices owned by distribution system households.

The second illustration discussed below is a type-(iii) transactive energy study focusing on PowerMatcher (2016), a TES architecture based on agent-based modeling principles that has been tested in multiple field settings. An exceptionally clear, detailed, and thought-provoking report on PowerMatcher is provided by Kok (2013), the original developer.

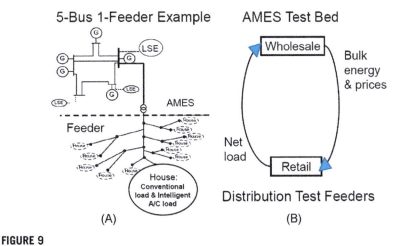

FIGURE 9

(A) Illustration of the IRW Test Bed; and (B) the basic IRW feedback loop.

5.2 ACE DEMAND RESPONSE STUDY UNDERTAKEN WITH THE IRW TEST BED

5.2.1 The IRW Test Bed

As illustrated in Fig. 9, the IRW Test Bed models the integrated grid-constrained operations of retail and wholesale power sectors over time. The IRW Test Bed has four key components:

- *C1:* Wholesale power sector, implemented by means of the AMES Wholesale Power Market Test Bed (AMES, 2017).
- *C2:* Retail power sector, implemented in part by GridLAB-D (2017).
- *C3:* C++ modeling of price-responsive loads.
- *C4:* MySQL database server to facilitate data storage and transfer among C1–C3.

AMES (*A*gent-based *M*odeling of *E*lectricity *S*ystems)[17] is an open-source ACE computational platform that permits the simulation over successive 24-hour days of a wholesale power market adhering to standard practices in U.S. ISO/RTO-managed wholesale power markets. Fig. 10 depicts the principal types of agents comprising AMES (V4.0). These agents include a physical entity (transmission grid), institutional entities (day-ahead and real-time markets), and decision-making entities (ISO and market participants). Each AMES agent is characterized at any given time by its internal state (data, attributes, methods). For visual clarity, Fig. 10 only lists some of

---

[17]Pointers to downloadable AMES software, manuals, and publications can be accessed at the AMES homepage (AMES, 2017). The capabilities of the latest AMES release (V4.0) are discussed and demonstrated by Krishnamurthy et al. (2016), who use AMES (V4.0) to develop an 8-zone test system based on data and structural aspects of the ISO-managed New England power system (ISO-NE).

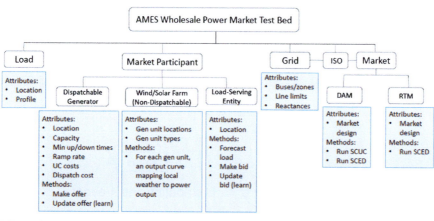

FIGURE 10

Partial agent taxonomy for AMES (V4.0).

the more important attributes and methods for each agent, not the agent's complete state.

More precisely, the decision-making agents in AMES include an *Independent System Operator (ISO)*, *Load-Serving Entities (LSEs)*, and *Generation Companies (GenCos)*. The methods of the AMES decision-making agents can include, in particular, learning methods for updating current methods on the basis of past events.[18] This permits AMES users to investigate the degree to which changes in power market rules or other exogenously specified power system aspects would open up market power opportunities that AMES decision-making agents could exploit for their own personal advantage at the expense of overall system performance.[19]

The LSEs and GenCos participate in an ISO-operated two settlement system consisting of a *Day-Ahead Market (DAM)* and a *Real-Time Market (RTM)* operating over a high-voltage transmission grid. Transmission grid congestion in each market is managed by *Locational Marginal Prices (LMPs)*. The daily DAM and RTM operate in parallel with each other and are separately settled; cf. Fig. 3.

During the morning of each day D the GenCos and LSEs submit into the DAM a collection of supply offers and demand bids, respectively, for all 24 hours H of day

---

[18] AMES includes a *Java Reinforcement Learning Module (JReLM)* that permits decision-making agents to be assigned a wide variety of reinforcement learning methods.

[19] For example, Li and Tesfatsion (2011, 2012) use AMES to explore the extent to which GenCos can learn to withhold generation capacity in ISO-managed wholesale power markets in order to increase their net earnings. GenCo learning methods and the price-sensitivity of LSE demand bids are systematically varied across computational experiments as two key treatment factors.

D + 1. For each hour H, these offers and bids take the following general form[20]:

$$\text{GenCo Price-Responsive Supply: } \pi = a + 2bp \tag{1}$$

$$\text{LSE Price-Responsive Demand: } \pi = c - 2dp \tag{2}$$

$$\text{LSE Fixed Demand: } p = \text{FD(H)} \tag{3}$$

where π ($/MWh) denotes price, p (MW) denotes power, FD(H) (MW) denotes a fixed (non-price-responsive) demand for power, and a ($ /MWh), b ($/(MW)^{2}h), c ($/MWh), and d ($/(MW)^{2}h) are positive constants. The power levels in (1) through (3) represent constant power levels to be maintained during the entire hour H, either as injections into the grid (power supplies) or as withdrawals from the grid (power demands).

Given these offers and bids, the ISO solves *Security-Constrained Unit Commitment (SCUC)* and *Security-Constrained Economic Dispatch (SCED)* optimization problems subject to standard system constraints[21] in order to determine: (i) generation unit commitments; (ii) scheduled generation dispatch levels; and (iii) a price $\text{LMP}^{DA}(\text{B}, \text{H}, \text{D} + 1)$ ($ /MWh) at each transmission grid bus B for each hour H of day D + 1. A generator located at bus B is paid $\text{LMP}^{DA}(\text{B}, \text{H}, \text{D} + 1)$ for each MW it is scheduled to inject at B during hour H of day D + 1, and an LSE located at a bus B must pay $\text{LMP}^{DA}(\text{B}, \text{H}, \text{D} + 1)$ for each MW its household customers are scheduled to withdraw at bus B during hour H of day D + 1.

The RTM runs each hour of each day.[22] At the start of the RTM for hour H on day D + 1, the ISO is assumed to know the actual household power usage for hour H of day D + 1. The ISO then solves a SCED optimization problem to resolve any discrepancies between the generation *scheduled* in the day-D DAM for dispatch during hour H of day D + 1, which was based on day-D LSE demand bids, and the generation needed during hour H of day D + 1 to balance *actual* household power usage. Any needed adjustments in the DAM-scheduled power supplies and demands at a bus B for hour H of day D + 1 are settled at the RTM LMP at bus B for hour H of day D + 1.

GridLAB-D (2017) is an open-source agent-based computational platform for the study of distribution systems that provides detailed physically-based models for a wide variety of appliances and devices owned by residential, commercial, and industrial customers. The distribution system for the IRW Test Bed currently consists of residential households with both conventional (non-price-responsive) and price-responsive loads. The conventional loads are generated by means of GridLAB-D.

---

[20]In current ISO/RTO-managed wholesale power markets, LSEs are permitted to submit hourly demand bids consisting of two parts: a price-responsive demand function; and a fixed (non-price-responsive) quantity demand.

[21]These system constraints include: power balance constraints; line and generation capacity limits; down/up ramping constraints; and minimum down/up-time constraints.

[22]In actual U.S. ISO/RTO-managed wholesale power markets the RTM is conducted at least once every five minutes.

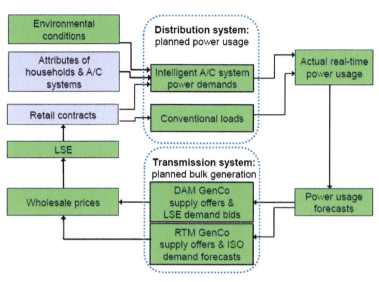

FIGURE 11

Feedback loop for the IRW Test Bed.

As detailed in Thomas et al. (2012), the price-responsive loads in the IRW Test Bed are currently generated as price-responsive demands for *air-conditioning (A/C)* power usage. The price-responsive A/C demand for each household is determined by an intelligent A/C controller operating in accordance with physical and economic principles. Each day the controller determines the household's optimal next-day A/C power usage based on the household's comfort/cost trade-off preferences, next-day power prices announced today by the LSEs, and a forecast for next-day environmental conditions.

Fig. 11 depicts the feedback loop process by which real-time power usage is determined over time in the IRW Test Bed.

5.2.2 A Demand-Response Study Using the IRW Test Bed

Thomas and Tesfatsion (2016, 2017) study the effects of price-responsive A/C load on the integrated operation of wholesale and retail power sectors using a simplified version of the IRW Test Bed. Hereafter this study is referred to as the *IRW Test Case*. This section reports some of the findings for this IRW Test Case in order to illustrate more concretely the capabilities of the IRW Test Bed for demand-response research.

The transmission grid lines for the IRW Test Case are specified with sufficiently large capacity that congestion does not arise. Hence, the grid effectively consists of a single bus B. There is only one GenCo and one LSE, each located at bus B. The GenCo is automatically committed in the DAM each day without need for unit-commitment optimizations.

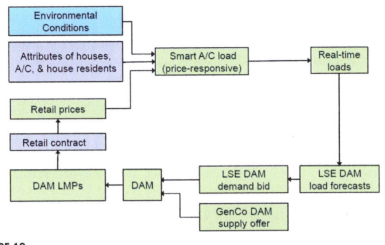

FIGURE 12

Feedback loop for the IRW Test Case. Since retail prices and real-time loads are not affected by RTM imbalance adjustments, these adjustments are not depicted.

The LSE serves as a wholesale power purchasing agent for 500 households populating the distribution system. The power usage of each household arises solely from air conditioning (A/C). The A/C load of each household is managed by a smart controller (Thomas et al., 2012), responsive to both price and environmental conditions, that reflects the specific comfort/cost trade-off preferences of the household. The GenCo has sufficient capacity to meet the power needs of the 500 households. Line capacities for the distribution grid are large enough to avoid grid congestion.

The feedback loop determining retail prices and real-time loads over time for the IRW Test Case is depicted in Fig. 12. A more detailed description of this loop will now be provided.

The supply offer submitted by the GenCo to the day-D DAM for any specific hour H of day D + 1 takes the price-elastic form (1). This supply offer gives the GenCo's reservation value (marginal production cost) for each successive megawatt (MW) of power it might be required to generate during hour H of day D + 1; that is, it represents the GenCo's *marginal cost function.*

The demand bid submitted by the LSE to the day-D DAM for any specific hour H of day D + 1 takes the fixed-demand form (3).[23] This fixed-demand bid is a forecast of household load for hour H of day D + 1. The LSE sets this forecast equal to the actual household load observed for hour H on day D − 1.

The RTM runs 24 hours of each day. The ISO is correctly able to forecast actual household power usage for hour H of day D + 1 at the start of the RTM for hour H

---

[23] As previously noted in Section 5.1, the vast majority of LSE demand bids in current U.S. ISO/RTO-managed wholesale power markets are not price responsive.

of day $D + 1$. The ISO uses the RTM for hour H of day $D + 1$ to resolve any discrepancies between the generation scheduled in the day-D DAM for dispatch during hour H of day $D + 1$ and the actual amount of generation needed during hour H of day $D + 1$ to balance actual household power usage for hour H of day $D + 1$. These discrepancies are settled at the RTM LMP for hour H of day $D + 1$.

The retail contracts offered by the LSE to the 500 households take one of two possible forms: (i) a *flat-rate* retail contract with a flat rate R ($/MWh) set to ensure the LSE breaks even over time; or (ii) a *dynamic-price* retail contract with one-way communication (LSE to households) in which DAM LMPs, marked up by a non-negative percentage m, are passed through to households as next-day retail prices. More precisely, under dynamic-price retail contracts, the *retail price* charged by the LSE to each household for power usage during hour H of day $D + 1$ is given by

$$r(H, D + 1) = [1 + m]\text{LMP}^{DA}(B, H, D + 1) \tag{4}$$

where $\text{LMP}^{DA}(B, H, D + 1)$ ($/MWh) is the LMP determined in the day-D DAM at bus B for hour H of day $D + 1$.[24]

As detailed in Thomas et al. (2012), the *net benefit (benefit minus cost)* attained by household h from the purchase and use of electric power during any hour H of any day D is given by

$$\text{NB}^h(H, D) = \text{Comfort}^h(H, D) - \alpha^h \text{EnergyCost}^h(H, D) \tag{5}$$

In (5), the comfort (Utils) attained by household h depends on the interior thermal conditions experienced by h during hour H of day D. Also, the energy cost ($) charged to h depends on two factors: (i) h's power usage during hour H of day D; and (ii) the form of h's retail contract, either flat-rate or dynamic-price.

The key parameter α^h (Utils/$) in (5) is a trade-off parameter measuring the manner in which household h trades off comfort against cost. The higher the value of α^h, the greater the weight that h places on energy cost savings relative to thermal comfort.[25]

A simplified version of the IRW Test Case with a postulated download-sloping aggregate demand curve for households is first used to derive, analytically, a set of necessary and sufficient conditions for market efficiency and system stability under

---

[24]Retail prices are typically reported in cents/kWh, not in $/MWh, which would require a conversion factor be given on the right-hand side of (4). This price conversion is ignored here for ease of exposition.

[25]More precisely, α^h measures the benefit to h of an additional dollar of income. It permits costs measured in dollars to be expressed in benefit units (Utils), so that comfort/cost trade-offs can be calculated. The precise sense in which α^h quantifies the trade-off between comfort satisfaction and energy cost for h is explained in some detail in Thomas et al. (2012, Appendix). Roughly, it is shown that α^h can be derived as the shadow price for h's budget constraint in a more fully articulated constrained benefit maximization problem: namely, the maximization of h's benefit from consumption of multiple goods/services (including thermal comfort) subject to a budget constraint. Thus, α^h measures h's *marginal benefit of income* at the optimization point, i.e., the drop in the maximized value of h's benefit that would result if h had one less dollar of income to spend.

	m	Alpha = Zero		Alpha = Low		Alpha = Medium		Alpha = High	
		Flat	Dynamic	Flat	Dynamic	Flat	Dynamic	Flat	Dynamic
Avg. LSE Net Earnings ($)	0.00	0.00	0.00	0.04	0.00	0.08	0.00	0.04	0.00
	0.20		9.11		7.67		6.17		4.79
	0.40		18.21		14.84		11.40		8.35
	0.60		27.32		21.51		15.69		10.95
Avg. Gen Net Earnings ($)	0.00	12.59	12.59	10.96	10.99	9.24	9.30	7.59	7.64
	0.20		12.59		10.66		8.62		6.73
	0.40		12.59		10.32		7.98		5.89
	0.60		12.59		9.97		7.33		5.16
Avg. Utility (Utils)	0.00	10446.29	10446.29	8581.52	8587.73	6707.30	6733.29	4879.86	4913.59
	0.20		10446.29		8216.86		5996.66		3870.66
	0.40		10446.29		7845.11		5275.68		2882.13
	0.60		10446.29		7473.19		4563.41		1965.76
Avg. Energy Cost ($)	0.00	1.82	1.82	1.58	1.58	1.33	1.33	1.09	1.09
	0.20		2.19		1.84		1.48		1.15
	0.40		2.55		2.08		1.60		1.17
	0.60		2.92		2.29		1.67		1.17

FIGURE 13

LSE, GenCo, and household welfare outcomes for a range of IRW Test Case treatments exhibiting point-convergent cobweb dynamics.

both dynamic-price and flat-rate retail contracting. A complete analysis of short-run welfare outcomes under each form of contracting is also provided. A key finding is that the use of dynamic-price retail contracts induces braided cobweb dynamics consisting of two interweaved cobweb cycles for power and price outcomes. These braided cobweb cycles can exhibit either point convergence, limit cycle convergence, or divergence depending on a small set of structural parameters characterizing power supply and demand conditions.

Simulation studies are then conducted for the full IRW Test Case to examine the form of the aggregate demand curve for the 500 households with price-responsive A/C controllers under varying price conditions, all else equal. It is shown that this aggregate demand curve is well-approximated by a linear downward-sloping curve in the power-price plane. A systematic sensitivity study is then conducted for the full IRW Test Case with the following three aspects taken as treatment factors: (i) the form of retail contracts, either flat-rate or dynamic-price; (ii) the mark-up m in (4) that determines the percentage by which retail prices are marked up over wholesale prices in the case of dynamic-price retail contracts; and (iii) the household comfort-cost trade-off parameter α^h in (5). Four values are tested for m: $[0.0, 0.2, 0.4, 0.6]$. Also, four values are tested for α^h: $[0, \text{Low}, \text{Medium}, \text{High}]$.

Fig. 13 compares welfare outcomes realized for the LSE, the GenCo, and the households for a range of treatments exhibiting point-convergent cobweb dynamics. For simplicity, only treatments with α and m values commonly set across all households are shown. A key finding indicated by the outcomes reported in Fig. 13 is that dynamic-price retail contracts with a positive mark-up m result in *worse* welfare outcomes for the GenCo and for household residents with $\alpha > 0$ than flat-rate retail contracts.

5.2.3 Implications of Demand-Response Study Findings

Retail customers participating in dynamic pricing programs are price-takers who determine their power usage in response to prices set by LSEs or other intermediaries on the basis of wholesale power market outcomes. The findings reported in Section 5.2.2 demonstrate that dynamic pricing can result in real-time system reliability issues that system operators would need to handle by direct load or generation controls.

These findings suggest that permitting retail customers to submit price-responsive bids/offers into a retail market process in advance of retail price determination might result in better system performance than dynamic pricing. Under the bid/offer option, retail customers play a pro-active role in the determination of retail prices. Moreover, system operators can include appropriate constraints in the retail market process to shape resulting retail power usage as required for system reliability with minimal disruption to system efficiency.

Economists have of course known for decades that possibly divergent cycles can arise for prices and quantities in "cobweb" market models for which a lag exists between the decision to produce a nonstorable good and its actual production. Economic research on this topic remains active; see, e.g., Ezekiel (1938), Hommes (1994), Arango and Moxnes (2012), and Lundberg et al. (2015). Power engineers have raised similar concerns for real-time power markets; see, e.g., Contreras et al. (2002), Roozbehani et al. (2012), and Masiello et al. (2013).

For example, Roozbehani et al. (2012) analyze the global properties of a system of nonlinear differential equations derived for an ISO-managed real-time power market. The authors make various simplifying assumptions (e.g., non-binding capacity constraints for generation and transmission grid lines) that reduce the ISO's optimization problem in each successive period to a straightforward economic dispatch problem in which expected load (power consumption) is balanced by scheduled generation (planned power supply). Power supplies and demands are specified as parameterized functional forms interpreted as the optimal solutions for myopic price-taking utility-maximizing producers and consumers. The discrepancy between scheduled generation and subsequent actual power consumption (hence actual power supply) then results in a form of cobweb cycling for market prices. Given a sufficiently large "Maximal Relative Price Elasticity," roughly defined to be demand price elasticity in ratio to supply price elasticity, the authors prove that prices can become increasingly volatile over time.

All of these cobweb studies highlight a common cautionary concern for demand-response researchers: namely, initiatives designed to encourage the more active participation of retail customers in power system operations must be designed with care in order to avoid adverse unintended consequences for power system operations. In what way, then, does the IRW Test Bed provide additional capabilities for demand-response researchers in general, and for TES researchers in particular, to address this concern?

The IRW Test Bed is an ACE computational platform. Its modular extensible architecture permits systematic studies of alternative demand-response initiatives in a plug-and-play mode. In scope, it covers the entire range of T/D operations, and it permits these operations to play out over time as an open-ended dynamic process. Since analytical tractability is not an issue, the user's initial specifications for physical conditions, institutional arrangements, and the decision-making processes of human participants (including learning processes) can be as strongly grounded in empirical reality as warranted by the user's purpose. Last but not least, the IRW Test Bed is open source software, thus permitting later researchers to build directly and systematically upon previous findings.

Referring back to the policy readiness levels (PRLs) proposed in Section 2.4, previous studies of cobweb cycle effects within electric power systems have largely been conceptual studies at PRLs 1–3. In contrast, the IRW Test Bed studies by Thomas and Tesfatsion (2016, 2017) are PRL-4 studies that incorporate several salient aspects of real-world T/D systems. By exploiting the capabilities of the IRW Test Bed to model increasingly larger systems with increasingly greater degrees of empirical verisimilitude, demand-response researchers could bridge the gap from PRL 3 to PRL 7.

5.3 POWERMATCHER: A TES ARCHITECTURE FOR DISTRIBUTION SYSTEMS

TES researchers stress the desirability of two-way communication between retail customers and distribution system operators (or their intermediaries). In particular, they assert that distribution system operations should be based more fully on demand bids and supply offers from retail customers, not simply on the responsiveness of price-taking retail customers to signaled prices. The negative results reported for dynamic pricing in Section 5.2.2 suggest that bid/offer-based designs for retail customer transactions should indeed be carefully considered.

This section reports on PowerMatcher (2016), a TES architecture for distribution systems developed by Koen Kok in collaboration with industry partners (Kok, 2013). PowerMatcher is fully based on agent-based modeling principles; it implements a decentralized bid/offer-based mechanism for the real-time management of collections of customer-owned *distributed energy resource (DER)* devices by means of intelligent software agents.

Specifically, PowerMatcher organizes a collection of DER devices into a network of "transaction nodes." Communication is restricted to two-way exchanges of information between adjacent transaction nodes, where this information must be required for the support of transactions between these adjacent nodes. Thus, local information specific to individual DER devices that is not needed to support nodal transactions is not included in these nodal communications.

This communication protocol permits a dramatic simplification in overall information and storage requirements. In addition, it facilitates other desirable TES design attributes, such as: privacy protection for DER owners; an ability to accommodate a wide variety of DER devices; and an ability to incorporate an increasing number of DER devices over time.

As detailed in Kok (2013), the transaction nodes envisioned by PowerMatcher for a particular collection of DER devices consist of four distinct types of software agents participating in real-time transactions: *Objective Agent*; *Local Device Agent (LDA)*; *Concentrator*; and *Auctioneer*. An Objective Agent is a software agent that carries out external control actions for specific types of business applications. An LDA is a software agent that communicates bids for power to an adjacent Concentrator or to the Auctioneer (if adjacent) on behalf of a DER device, where each bid indicates the amount of power the device stands ready to consume (absorb) or produce (supply) as a function of the power price.[26]

A Concentrator aggregates bids for power from adjacent Concentrators and/or from adjacent LDAs and communicates these aggregated bids either to an adjacent Concentrator or to the Auctioneer (if adjacent). The Auctioneer is a single software agent that functions as the top-level aggregator for the entire collection of DER devices. The Auctioneer aggregates bids for power from adjacent Concentrators and immediately communicates a price signal back to these adjacent Concentrators. Each of these Concentrators then immediately communicates a price signal back to the adjacent Concentrators or adjacent LDAs from which it received bids. Each LDA uses its received price signal, together with its bid, to determine the amount of power it is required to consume (absorb) or produce (supply).

The price signal communicated by the Auctioneer to its adjacent Concentrators, conditional on the bids it has just received from them, can be designed to achieve particular objectives. For example, the collection of DER devices could constitute a microgrid in island mode,[27] and the price signals that the Auctioneers sends to its adjacent Concentrators, conditional on received bids, could be power prices selected to ensure a continual balance between power supply and power demand on this microgrid.

As reported by Kok (2013, Table 1.1, p. 8) and Widergren et al. (2016), Power-Matcher has performed well in both agent-based simulation and field studies. These studies have included a wide variety of DERs, such as: industrial freezing houses; large industrial Combined Heat and Power (CHP) systems; residential micro-CHP systems; heat pumps; electrical vehicles; and battery storage devices. In these studies, PowerMatcher has demonstrated the following abilities: maintain end-user privacy; ensure incentive compatibility for participating DER owners; reduce peak-load demand, important for system reliability; perform congestion management in distribution networks; integrate renewable energy sources (e.g., wind power); and scale to systems involving more than a million DER device owners.

To facilitate understanding of PowerMatcher's decentralized layered market architecture, it is useful to consider a concrete example. Specifications and outcomes will briefly be reported for a PowerMatcher test case conducted at Iowa State University (Tesfatsion et al., 2017).

---

[26] Kok (2013) uses "bid" to refer either to a demand bid or a supply offer.

[27] "A microgrid is a group of interconnected loads and distributed energy resources within clearly defined electrical boundaries that acts as a single controllable entity with respect to the grid. A microgrid can connect and disconnect from the grid to enable it to operate in either grid-connected or island mode." DOE (2011b, p. vii).

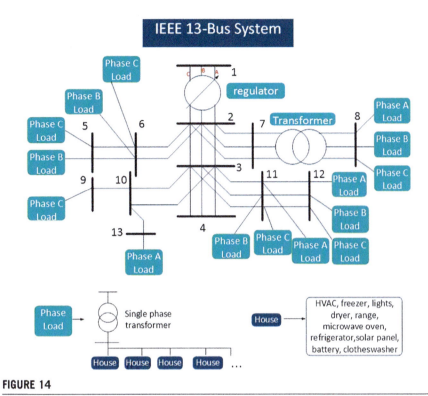

FIGURE 14

Distribution grid for the ISU PowerMatcher Test Case, implemented using GridLAB-D (IEEE13.glm).

The distribution grid for this test case, depicted in Fig. 14, is a 13-bus grid populated with 180 households by instantiating 12 households at each of 15 phase loads. Each of these 180 households has two types of load: (i) conventional (non-price-responsive) load; and (ii) price-responsive load arising from an electric air-conditioning (A/C) system locally managed by an A/C controller with bang-bang (ON/OFF) control settings. To ensure household diversity, households are initialized with randomly distributed structural attributes (e.g., different floor sizes) and with randomly distributed inside air temperatures.

The current state of each household is measured by its current inside air temperature, T_a, determined by current weather conditions, past A/C control settings, and structural household attributes. The goal of each household is to ensure that T_a is maintained between a lower temperature level T_1 and an upper temperature level T_2.

The distribution system is managed by a *Distribution System Operator (DSO)* tasked with ensuring the reliability of system operations. The goal of the DSO is to ensure that aggregate household A/C power usage for each day D closely tracks a target 24-hour load profile for A/C power usage during day D. In pursuit of this goal, the DSO uses a PowerMatcher design based on two-way communication to manage aggregate household A/C power usage.

More precisely, the DSO and households engage in the following iterative seven-step process:

- **Step 1:** The A/C controller for each household collects data on the state of the household at a specified *data check rate*.
- **Step 2:** The A/C controller for each household sends a state-conditioned demand bid to the DSO for A/C power usage at a specified *bid refresh rate*. This demand bid expresses the household's demand for power (kWh) as a function of the power price ($/kWh).
- **Step 3:** The DSO aggregates all household demand bids into an aggregate demand bid at a specified *aggregate bid refresh rate*. This aggregate demand bid expresses aggregate household demand for A/C power (kWh) as a function of the power price ($/kWh).
- **Step 4:** The DSO uses this aggregate demand bid to determine a price signal whose corresponding aggregate demand for A/C power is closest to the DSO's target aggregate A/C power usage.
- **Step 5:** The DSO communicates this price signal to the A/C controller for each household at a specified *price signal rate*.
- **Step 6:** The A/C controller for each household uses this price signal, together with the household's latest updated state-conditioned demand bid, to determine a desired ON/OFF power response.
- **Step 7:** The A/C controller for each household sends ON/OFF power signals to the household's A/C system at a specified *power control rate*.

The demand bid for A/C power usage reported to the DSO by each household at each bid refresh point takes one of three possible forms, depending on the household's current inside air temperature state T_a[28]:

- **ON ($T_a \geq T_2$):** The house is too hot. The A/C system must stay (or be switched) on, regardless of price; hence, the A/C system has no power usage flexibility.
- **OFF ($T_a \leq T_1$):** The house is too cold. The A/C system must stay (or be switched) off, regardless of price; hence, the A/C system has no power usage flexibility.
- **May Run ($T_1 < T_a < T_2$):** The A/C system stays (or is switched) on if and only if the power price Π does not exceed the maximum price $\Pi^*(T_a)$ that the household is willing to pay for its ON power usage level P^*, where $\Pi^*(T_a)$ is an increasing function of T_a; see Fig. 15.

The procedure used by the DSO to aggregate household A/C power demand bids at any given time is illustrated in Fig. 16. For simplicity, only two households are depicted, each in a May Run state ($T_1 < T_a < T_2$). The maximum acceptable ON-power

---

[28] This demand bid formulation for A/C power usage is similar to the demand bid formulation presented by Kok (2013, Section 8.1.2) for the power usage of a freezer.

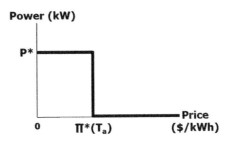

FIGURE 15

The general form of a household's state-conditioned A/C power demand bid for the "May Run" case in which the household's inside air-temperature state, T_a, is within the household's desired temperature range (T_1, T_2).

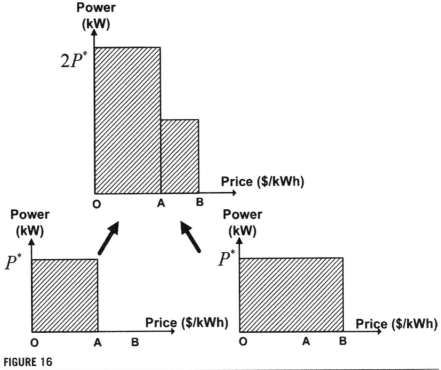

FIGURE 16

Illustration of the procedure used by the DSO in the ISU PowerMatcher Test Case to aggregate household A/C power demand bids. For simplicity, only two bids are depicted, each taking a "May Run" form.

price function for each household takes the simple form

$$\Pi^*(T_a) = \theta \cdot \left[\frac{T_a - T_1}{T_2 - T_1}\right] \text{ for } T_1 < T_a < T_2, \tag{6}$$

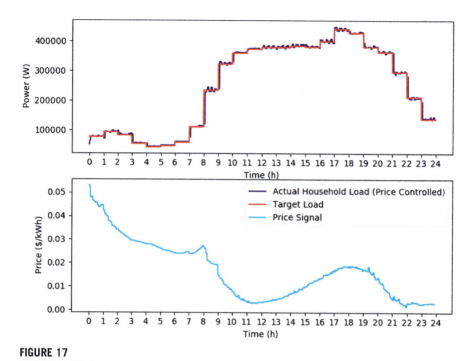

FIGURE 17

Illustrative findings for the ISU PowerMatcher Test Case. Given suitable time-step specifications, the DSO is able to use price signals to ensure that aggregate household A/C load closely tracks the DSO's target 24-hour A/C load profile.

where $\theta > 0$. Household one has a lower inside air temperature T_a than household two. Hence, the value of (6) for household one (labeled A) is smaller than the value of (6) for household two (labeled B).

Fig. 17 reports illustrative outcomes for the ISU PowerMatcher Test Case. As indicated, given suitable time-step specifications for the data check rate, bid refresh rate, aggregate bid refresh rate, price signal rate, and power control rate, the DSO is able to use price signals to ensure that the aggregate A/C load arising from the A/C power usage demands of the 180 households populating the distribution grid closely tracks the DSO's target 24-hour A/C load profile.

This simple test case raises a number of additional issues in need of careful study. For example, if current U.S. distribution systems were to implement a PowerMatcher design managed by a DSO, would this improve the efficiency and reliability of their operations? What precise form would the DSO's objective(s) and constraints have to take to ensure this improvement? And could this be done in a way that ensures revenue sufficiency for the DSO, i.e., coverage of all incurred costs by incoming revenues?

More generally, a DSO with PowerMatcher Auctioneer capabilities could function as an intermediary between a collection of business and/or household device owners on a lower-voltage distribution grid and a wholesale power market operating over a high-voltage transmission grid. In this case broader DSO objectives could be considered, such as the appropriately compensated harnessing of ancillary services from the devices for the support of integrated T/D operations.

For this broader case, another key issue arises: namely, how might the participation of the DSO in the wholesale power market be facilitated by an appropriate form of contract? This issue is addressed below in Section 6.2.

6 ACE SUPPORT FOR TES RESEARCH ON CONTRACT DESIGN
6.1 OVERVIEW

A *contract* is an agreement between two or more parties. *Contract design* is the study of contract formulation in relation to intended contract purpose. Interestingly, the 2016 Nobel Prize in Economics[29] was awarded to two economists, Oliver Hart and Bengt Holmström, for their work on contract design (Royal Swedish Academy of Sciences, 2016).

Markets organized as persistent institutions often rely on explicit legally-binding contracts to provide a careful statement of participant responsibilities as well as the penalties that would apply should participants fail to carry out these responsibilities. Market institutions can take many forms, including: bilateral exchanges permitting individually negotiated bilateral trades; over-the-counter markets managed by a geographically dispersed collection of dealers; and auction markets for which submitted bids/offers are centrally cleared by an auctioneer.

Modern power systems encompass a wide variety of market institutions ranging from bilateral exchanges for financial risk-hedging instruments to ISO/RTO-managed auction markets for the purchase and sale of electric power and ancillary services (NAS, 2016, Chapter 2). These various market forms are based explicitly or implicitly on contractual arrangements. For example, the business practice manuals published by U.S. ISOs/RTOs are legal documents that set out, in excruciating detail, the roles, responsibilities, information access rights, and compensation rules governing the various participants in ISO/RTO-managed markets and supporting processes.

To date, most studies focusing on contract design for electric power systems have focused on the operations of a single wholesale or retail market.[30] However, by definition, a *Transactive Energy System (TES)* is a set of economic and control mechanisms

---

[29]The official title of this prize is the Sveriges Riksbank Prize in Economic Sciences in Memory of Alfred Nobel.

[30]A general overview of economic and power system research pertinent for the study of physical contracting in modern electric power systems is provided by Bosćan (2016, Chapter 1), Bosćan and Poudineh (2016), and Oliveira et al. (2013, Section 2). A *physical contract* is a contract for which the delivery and receipt of a good or service is expected. See, also, Deng and Oren (2006) and Yu et al. (2012, Section I) for a summary review of research focusing on the use of financial contracting to hedge price and quantity risks arising from electric power system transactions.

to ensure the balancing of demands and supplies for power across an entire electrical infrastructure. Consequently, TES contract design research requires a broader scope.

TES researchers are well aware of the need to put TES transactions on a secure contractual footing. Consider, for example, the following assertions by the GridWise Architecture Council (2015, p. 12):

> *"A TE system must clearly define transactions within the context of that system. The following questions (and possibly others not anticipated here) must be able to be answered: Who are the transacting parties, what information is exchanged between them to create a transaction, and what is exchanged between them to execute a transaction? What are the rules governing transactions? What is the mechanism(s) for reaching agreement?"*

TES researchers are also well aware of the need to ensure incentive compatibility for their proposed TES architectures, in the sense that these architectures should ensure sustainable business models for all TES participants.

Nevertheless, most TES researchers to date have not explicitly focused on contract design as an important component of TES architectural design. In particular, insufficient attention has been paid to the need to ensure that TES contractual relationships are robust against strategic behavior, i.e., robust against the possibility that transactors with learning capabilities might discover ways to manipulate these contractual relationships for personal advantage at the expense of overall system performance.

The next section uses an illustrative example to indicate how ACE modeling tools could facilitate the development of TES contract designs for flexible power and ancillary service provision that are both compatible with transactor incentives and robust against transactor strategic manipulation.

6.2 ACE SUPPORT FOR TES CONTRACT DESIGN: ILLUSTRATIVE EXAMPLE

As discussed in Section 1.1, the participation of non-controllable generation (e.g., wind, solar) in U.S. electric power systems is rapidly growing. As discussed in Section 5, the implementation of various forms of demand response in these systems is encouraging more active demand-side participation. The combined effect of these two developments has been a substantial increase in the uncertainty and volatility of *net load*, i.e., load minus non-controllable generation.

Consequently, system operators tasked with the real-time balancing of net load by means of controllable generation are now seeking ways to ensure greater flexibility in the provision of this controllable generation. However, three issues have impeded these efforts.

First, rigidity in product definitions is hindering appropriate compensation for valuable forms of flexibility in controllable generation, such as flexibility in ramp-rate and duration. Second, eligibility restrictions are preventing the achievement of an even playing field for potential providers of controllable generation. Third, the required payment of market-cleared controllable generation in advance of actual real-time generation,[31] plus variously required out-of-market make-whole payments for controllable generation (e.g., uplift payments for unit commitment costs), are providing opportunities for strategic manipulation.

Several recent studies (Tesfatsion et al., 2013; Heo and Tesfatsion, 2015; Li and Tesfatsion, 2018) have explored the possibility that all three of these issues could be ameliorated through the use of standardized contracts for power and ancillary services permitting swing (flexibility) in their contractual terms. This swing contract design is intended for use by any dispatchable resource participating in a centrally-managed wholesale power market. These participants could include, for example, entities managing large collections of *Distributed Energy Resource (DER)* devices as dispatchable virtual power plants (generators) or as dispatchable virtual batteries (prosumers).

The swing contract proposed in these studies permits a resource to offer the availability of power paths with variously specified attributes, such as start-location, start-time, power level, ramp rate, and duration. Moreover, each of these attributes can be offered as a range of values rather than as a point value, thus permitting greater flexibility in real-time implementation.

For illustration, consider the following swing contract that permits a dispatchable resource to offer power paths with swing (flexibility) in both their power level and their ramp rate:

$$SC = [b, t_s, t_e, \mathcal{P}, \mathcal{R}, \phi] \tag{7}$$

b = location where service delivery is to occur;

t_s = power delivery start time;

t_e = power delivery end time;

$\mathcal{P} = [P^{min}, \ P^{max}]$ = range of power levels p;

$\mathcal{R} = [-R^D, \ R^U]$ = range of down/up ramp rates r;

ϕ = performance payment method for real-time services.

In (7), t_s and t_e denote specific calendar times expressed at the granularity of time periods of length Δt (e.g., 1 h, 1 min), with $t_s < t_e$. The power interval bounds $P^{min} \leq P^{max}$ can represent pure power injections (if $0 \leq P^{min}$), pure power withdrawals or absorptions (if $P^{max} \leq 0$), or bi-directional power capabilities (if $P^{min} \leq 0 \leq P^{max}$). The down/up limits $-R^D$ and R^U for the ramp rates r (MW/Δt) are assumed to satisfy $-R^D \leq 0 \leq R^U$. The location b, the start time t_s, and the end time t_e are all specified as single values in (7). However, the power levels p and the down/up ramp rates r are specified in swing form with associated ranges $\mathcal{P}$ and $\mathcal{R}$.

As discussed at greater length in Heo and Tesfatsion (2015), the performance payment method ϕ in (7) that designates the mode of ex post compensation for actual

---

[31] The DAM/RTM two-settlement system requires day-ahead payments to be made to DAM-cleared resources for their next-day scheduled services in advance of any actual service performance.

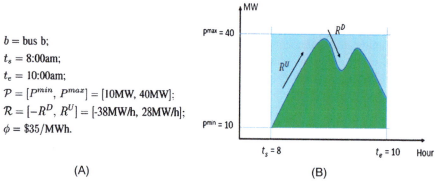

b = bus b;

t_s = 8:00am;

t_e = 10:00am;

$\mathcal{P} = [P^{min}, P^{max}] = [10MW, 40MW]$;

$\mathcal{R} = [-R^D, R^U] = [-38MW/h, 28MW/h]$;

ϕ = \$35/MWh.

(A)   (B)

FIGURE 18

(A) Illustrative swing contract with power and ramp rate swing offered by a DER aggregator into an ISO-managed day-ahead wholesale power market. (B) Possible power path the ISO could signal the DER aggregator to follow in real-time operations.

real-time service performance can take a wide variety of forms, such as a specified flat rate for energy and/or a power-mileage compensation for ramping. Moreover, ϕ can include penalties or incentive payments to encourage accurate following of real-time dispatch instructions.

To understand the obligations of the seller and buyer of this swing contract, should it be cleared, a more concrete example might be helpful. Consider a DER aggregator that manages a large collection of DER devices owned by retail customers. Assume the number and diversity of these devices permits the DER aggregator to function as a dispatchable virtual power plant with controllable down/up power within predictable ramp rate limits.

Suppose the DER aggregator offers a swing contract into an ISO-managed day-ahead market (DAM) at an availability price $\alpha = \$100$, with $\Delta t = 1$ h. Under this contract the DER aggregator offers to inject power into the transmission grid at bus b from 8:00 am to 10:00 am on the following day. The offered power levels range from 10 MW to 40 MW, but the required down/up ramp rates r to achieve these power levels must satisfy -38 MW/h $\leq r \leq 28$ MW/h.

Suppose, also, that the performance payment method ϕ appearing among the terms of this swing contract requires the DER aggregator to be paid the price $\phi = \$35/MWh$ for each MWh of energy it delivers. This payment is a pay-for-performance obligation. That is, the payment is not due until after the actual delivery of energy has been made. However, if the swing contract is cleared by the ISO, the DER aggregator is immediately entitled to receive its availability price $\alpha = \$100$.

Fig. 18A summarizes the contractual terms of this swing contract, and Fig. 18B depicts one possible power path that the ISO could dispatch in real-time operations in accordance with these contractual terms. The darkened (green) area under this power path is the corresponding energy (MWh) delivery, to be compensated ex post at the rate of \$35/MWh.

		Current DAM	Proposed SC DAM
Similarities		• Conducted day-ahead to plan for next-day operations • ISO-managed • Participants can include all dispatchable resources • Subject to same physical constraints: e.g. transmission, generation, ramping, & power-balance constraints	
Differences	• Optimization formulation	SCUC & SCED	Contract clearing
	• Settlement	Locational marginal pricing	Contract-determined prices
	• Payment	Payment for next-day service before actual performance	Payment for availability now & performance ex post
	• Out-of-market payments	Make-whole payments (e.g., for unit commitment)	No out-of-market payments
	• Info released to participants	UC, DAM LMPs, & next-day dispatch schedule	Which contracts have been cleared

FIGURE 19

Comparison of swing contract DAM with current DAM designs for U.S. ISO/RTO-managed wholesale power markets.

Li and Tesfatsion (2018) develop an analytic model of an ISO/RTO-managed DAM for which any market participant with dispatchable resources is able to offer services from these resources using a swing contract. They demonstrate that the ISO/RTO can determine the optimal market clearing of these swing contracts by means of a *mixed integer linear programming (MILP)* formulation, solvable using standard MILP solution software.

In particular, as depicted in Fig. 19, this optimal market clearing of swing contracts accomplishes both *Security Constrained Unit Commitment (SCUC)* and *Security-Constrained Economic Dispatch (SCED)* subject to the usual types of physical constraints. Moreover, it does so without requiring any performance payments to be made in advance of actual performance, or any out-of-market uplift payments to be made for unit commitment costs.

Tesfatsion et al. (2013) and Heo and Tesfatsion (2015) discuss in detail a long list of potential advantages that could result from the use of swing contracts in a linked sequence of ISO/RTO-managed power markets with planning horizons ranging from years to minutes. These assertions are supported by simple analytical swing-contract examples. Hence, in terms of the *Policy Readiness Levels (PRLs)* defined in Section 2.4, these studies would be classified as PRL 2.

In contrast, Li and Tesfatsion (2018) provide a specific analytic optimization formulation for achieving the optimal market clearing of DAMs permitting swing contracting for all dispatchable resources, and they demonstrate the effectiveness of this formulation by means of a numerical application. Thus, this work is at PRL 3. However, any real-world implementation (PRL 9) of these swing-contract ideas will require substantial preliminary work to be carried out at each of the intervening PRL levels 4–8. In particular, it will require a crossing of the "valley of death" (PRLs 4–6).

Researchers at Iowa State University are currently developing an ACE computational platform at PRL 5 for the express purpose of studying the performance of swing contracts for DER aggregators within *integrated transmission and distribution (ITD)* systems. This platform, referred to as the *ITD Test System*, is an extended version of the IRW Test Bed discussed in Section 5.2.1; see Fig. 8 for a depiction of its intended final form. The ITD Test System will retain a key ability of the IRW Test Bed: namely, the ability to model decision-making agents as strategic agents with learning capabilities and local objectives.

An ACE computational platform, such as the ITD Test System, would permit many critical issues to be explored for swing contract market designs at successively greater scales and with successively greater empirical fidelity. A number of these issues are highlighted by Gallo (2016, Sections 2–3).

For example, would the two-part pricing permitted by swing contracting, in particular the ex-ante payment for service availability versus the ex-post payment for actual service performance, result in more appropriate compensation for the *full* range of services provided by thermal generation, including ancillary service performance? If so, this would alleviate the well-known "merit order effects" that have arisen in ISO/RTO-managed wholesale power markets due to the increased penetration of renewable energy resources with subsidized or naturally low marginal production costs.[32]

Also, would this two-part pricing help to resolve the "missing money" problem, i.e., the inability of some resource owners participating in current electric power markets to recover their full costs without various types of out-of-market payments? Would it eliminate the need for capacity markets in which payments are made for capacity availability without any direct tie-in to real-time performance? Would the elimination of payments in advance of performance, and out-of-market payments, reduce opportunities for participants to exercise market power at the expense of overall system reliability and efficiency?

Of course, subsequent to these PRL 4–6 studies, prototype large-scale studies and field work at PRLs 7–8 would have to be undertaken to test the performance of swing contract market designs in expected field conditions. Presumably such studies would be undertaken in collaboration with industry and/or national laboratory partners.

---

[32] This "merit order effect" is roughly described as follows. The penetration of low-cost renewable energy resources pushes more expensive thermal generation further down the generation dispatch queue and thus possibly out of the market, raising their risk of insolvency. Yet, thermal generation is currently needed to firm up renewable energy (e.g., wind, solar, hydro) in adverse weather conditions (e.g., low wind, cloud cover, drought).

7 CONCLUSION

Electric power systems are extraordinarily complicated heterogeneous-participant systems in rapid transition toward transactive energy designs. The overall goal of this chapter is to introduce readers to a computational modeling approach, *Agent-based Computational Economics (ACE)*, that is well suited for the study of these complex evolving systems.

The chapter begins with a broad historical overview of the U.S. electric power industry. Seven principles characterizing the ACE modeling approach are next presented and explained, and two potential ACE advantages are stressed: namely, the facilitation of more comprehensive approaches to empirical validation; and the ability to bridge the gap between conceptual design modeling and real-world design implementation. On the downside, it is noted that the absence of standardized presentation protocols currently hinders the readability and acceptance of ACE research efforts.

The use of ACE modeling tools for electric power systems research is then addressed, with a particular focus on the ability of ACE computational platforms to facilitate the design and study of *Transactive Energy System (TES)* frameworks. A TES framework is a set of economic and control mechanisms that permits the supply and demand for power to be efficiently balanced across an entire electric power system on the basis of transactor reservation values in a manner consistent with system reliability.

Two types of TES initiatives are discussed at some length for illustration: namely, demand response programs intended to encourage more active demand-side participation in electric power systems; and new contractual designs meant to facilitate the flexible market-based provision of power and ancillary services in electric power systems. These illustrations suggest that ACE computational platforms could play a critical role in the TES development process, permitting researchers to ensure that good TES designs move from conceptual formulation to real-world implementation.

ACKNOWLEDGMENTS

This work has been supported by funding from the Department of Energy (DOE/OE), the Pacific Northwest National Laboratory (PNNL), and the ISU Electric Power Research Center (EPRC). The author is grateful to the handbook editors and an anonymous referee for useful comments received on a preliminary chapter draft, and to Swathi Battula, Yanda Jiang, Koen Kok, Dheepak Krishnamurthy, Wanning Li, Shanshan Ma, Hieu Trung Nguyen, Abhishek Somani, Auswin George Thomas, Zhaoyu Wang, and Steve Widergren for useful discussions on related topics.

REFERENCES

AEP, 2014. Ohio gridSMART© Demonstration Project Final Technical Report. https://www.smartgrid.gov/project/aep_ohio_gridsmartsm_demonstration_project.

AMES, 2017. The AMES Wholesale Power Market Test Bed: homepage. http://www2.econ.iastate.edu/tesfatsi/AMESMarketHome.htm.

Arango, S., Moxnes, E., 2012. Commodity cycles, a function of market complexity? Extending the cobweb experiment. Journal of Economic Behavior & Organization 84, 321–334.

Arthur, W.B., 2015. Complexity and the Economy. Oxford University Press, Oxford, UK.

Atkins, K., Barrett, C.L., Homan, C.M., Marathe, A., Marathe, M.V., Thite, S., 2004. Agent-based economic analysis of deregulated electricity markets. In: Proceedings of the Sixth IAEE European Conference on Modelling in Energy Economics and Policy. Zürich, Switzerland.

Batten, D., Grozev, G., 2006. NEMSIM: finding ways to reduce greenhouse gas emissions using multi-agent electricity modelling. In: Perez, P., Batten, D. (Eds.), Complex Science for a Complex World: Exploring Human Ecosystems with Agents. Australian National University, Canberra, Australia, pp. 227–252.

Bitar, E., Poola, K., Varaiya, P., 2014. Coordinated Aggregation of Distributed Demand-Side Resources. Final Project Report: PSERC Publication 14-12.

Borrill, P.L., Tesfatsion, L., 2011. Agent-based modeling: the right mathematics for the social sciences? In: Davis, J.B., Hands, D.W. (Eds.), Elgar Companion to Recent Economic Methodology. Edward Elgar, Northampton, MA, pp. 228–258. http://www2.econ.iastate.edu/tesfatsi/ABMRightMath.PBLTWP.pdf.

Boscán, L.R., 2016. Essays on the Design of Contracts and Markets for Power System Flexibility. Thesis. Doctoral School of Economics and Management, Copenhagen Business School.

Boscán, L.R., Poudineh, R., 2016. Flexibility-Enabling Contracts in Electricity Markets. Oxford Institute for Energy Studies, University of Oxford.

Bower, J., Bunn, D.W., 2000. Model-based comparison of pool and bilateral markets for electricity. Energy Journal 21 (3), 1–29.

Bower, J., Bunn, D.W., 2001. Experimental analysis of the efficiency of uniform-price versus discriminatory auctions in the England and Wales electricity market. Journal of Economic Dynamics and Control 25 (3–4), 56–11592.

Broeer, T., Fuller, J., Tuffner, F., Chassin, D., Djilali, N., 2014. Modeling framework and validation of a smart grid and demand response system for wind power integration. Applied Energy 113, 199–207.

Bunn, D.W., 2004. Structural and behavioural foundations of competitive electricity prices. In: Bunn, D.W. (Ed.), Modelling Prices in Competitive Electricity Markets. John Wiley & Sons, pp. 1–17.

Bunn, D.W., Oliveira, F.S., 2001. Agent-based simulation: an application to the new electricity trading arrangements of England and Wales. IEEE Transactions on Evolutionary Computation 5 (5), 493–503.

Bunn, D.W., Oliveira, F., 2003. Evaluating individual market power in electricity markets via agent-based simulation. Annals of Operations Research 121 (1–4), 57–77.

Chassin, D.P., Fuller, J.C., Djilali, N., 2014. GridLAB-D: an agent-based simulation framework for smart grids. Journal of Applied Mathematics 2014. https://doi.org/10.1155/2014/49230.

Chen, S.-H., 2016. Agent-Based Computational Economics. Routledge Publishers, New York, NY.

Collins, A., Petty, M., Vernon-Bido, D., Sherfey, S., 2015. A call to arms: standards for agent-based modeling and simulation. Journal of Artificial Societies and Social Simulation 18 (3), 12. http://jasss.soc.surrey.ac.uk/18/3/12.html.

Contreras, J., Candiles, O., de la Fuente, J.I., Gómez, T., 2002. A cobweb bidding model for competitive electricity markets. IEEE Transactions on Power Systems 17 (1), 148–153.

Conzelmann, G., Boyd, G., Koritarov, V., Veselka, T., 2005. Multi-agent power market simulation using EMCAS. In: Proceedings of the IEEE Power Engineering Society General Meeting, vol. 3, pp. 2829–2834.

Day, C.J., Bunn, D.W., 2001. Divestiture of generation assets in the England and Wales electricity market: a computational approach to analysing market power. Journal of Regulatory Economics 19 (2), 123–141.

Deng, S.J., Oren, S.S., 2006. Electricity derivatives and risk management. Energy 31, 940–953.

DOE, 2011a. DOE Technology Readiness Assessment Guide. DOE G 413.3-4A. Office of Management, Department of Energy.

DOE, 2011b. DOE Microgrid Workshop Report. Office of Electricity Delivery and Energy Reliability, Department of Energy.

Ehlen, M.A., Scholand, A., 2005. Modeling interdependencies between power and economic sectors using the N-ABLE agent-based model. In: Proceedings of the IEEE Power Engineering Society General Meeting, vol. 3, pp. 2842–2846.

EIA, 2016. U.S. Energy Information Administration (EIA). http://www.eia.gov/.

Ela, E., Milligan, M., Bloom, A., Botterud, A., Townsend, A., Levin, T., Frew, B.A., 2016. Wholesale electricity market design with increasing levels of renewable generation: incentivizing flexibility in system operations. The Electricity Journal 29, 51–60.

Ezekiel, M., 1938. The cobweb theorem. The Quarterly Journal of Economics 52 (2), 255–280.

FERC, 1999. Regional Transmission Organizations. FERC Order No. 2000, Final Rule.

FERC, 2003. Notice of White Paper. U.S. Federal Energy Regulatory Commission.

FERC, 2008. Wholesale Competition in Regions with Organized Electric Markets. Final Rule: Order 719. U.S. Federal Energy Regulatory Commission. http://www.ferc.gov/whats-new/comm-meet/2008/101608/E-1.pdf.

FERC, 2015. Assessment of Demand Response and Advanced Metering. Federal Energy Regulatory Commission Staff Report.

Gallo, G., 2016. Electricity market games: how agent-based modeling can help under high penetrations of variable generation. The Electricity Journal 29, 39–46.

GridLAB-D, 2017. GridLAB-D: the next generation simulation software. http://www.gridlabd.org/.

GridWise Architecture Council, 2015. GridWise Transactive Energy Framework Version 1.0. PNNL-22946 Ver1.0.

Grimm, V., Berger, U., Bastiansen, F., Eliassen, S., Ginot, V., Giske, J., Goss-Custard, J., Grand, T., Heinz, S., Huse, G., Huth, A., Jepsen, J.U., Jørgensen, C., Mooij, W.M., Müller, B., Pe'er, G., Piou, C., Railsback, S.F., Robbins, A.M., Robbins, M.M., Rossmanith, E., Rüger, N., Strand, E., Souissi, S., Stillman, R.A., Vabo, R., Visser, U., DeAngelis, D.L., 2006. A standard protocol for describing individual-based and agent-based models. Ecological Modelling 198, 115–126.

Grimm, V., Berger, U., DeAngelis, D.L., Polhill, J.G., Giske, J., Railsback, S.F., 2010a. The ODD protocol: a review and first update. Ecological Modelling 221, 2760–2768.

Guerci, E., Rastegar, M.A., Cincotti, S., 2010. Agent-based modeling and simulation of competitive wholesale electricity markets. In: Rebennack, S., Pardalos, P.M., Pereira, N.S., Iliadis, N.A. (Eds.), Handbook of Power Systems II: Energy Systems. Springer, Berlin, pp. 241–286.

Heo, D.Y., Tesfatsion, L., 2015. Facilitating appropriate compensation of electric energy and reserve through standardized contracts with swing. Journal of Energy Markets 8 (4), 93–121.

Hommes, C.H., 1994. Dynamics of the cobweb model with adaptive expectations and nonlinear supply and demand. Journal of Economic Behavior & Organization 24 (3), 315–335.

IEEE, 2010. IEEE Standard for Modeling and Simulation (M&S) High Level Architecture (HLA): framework and rules. https://standards.ieee.org/findstds/standard/1516-2010.html.

IEEE, 2016. Transactive energy: everyone gets into the act. IEEE Power & Energy Magazine 14 (3). Special issue.

Judd, K., 2006. Computationally intensive analyses in economics. In: Tesfatsion, L., Judd, K. (Eds.), Handbook of Computational Economics, vol. 2: Agent-Based Computational Economics. Elsevier, Amsterdam, pp. 881–893 (Chapter 17).

Kabalci, Y., 2016. A survey on smart metering and smart communication. Renewable & Sustainable Energy Reviews 57, 302–318.

Kahrobaee, S., Rajabzadeh, R.A., Soh, L., Asgarpoor, S., 2014. Multiagent study of smart grid customers with neighborhood electricity trading. Electric Power Systems Research 111, 123–132.

Karfopoulos, E., Tena, L., Torres, A., Salas, P., Jorda, J.G., Dimeas, A., 2015. A multi-agent system providing demand response services from residential consumers. Electric Power Systems Research 120, 163–176.

Kirman, A., 2011. Complex Economics: Individual and Collective Rationality. Routledge, New York.

Kirschen, D.S., 2003. Demand-side view of electricity markets. IEEE Transactions on Power Systems 18 (2), 520–527.

Koesrindartoto, D., Sun, J., Tesfatsion, L., 2005. An agent-based computational laboratory for testing the economic reliability of wholesale power market designs. In: Proceedings of the IEEE Power Engineering Society General Meeting, vol. 3, pp. 2818–2823.

Kok, K., 2013. The PowerMatcher: Smart Coordination for the Smart Electricity Grid. SIKS Dissertation Series No. 2013-17. Dutch Research School for Information and Knowledge Systems, TNO, The Netherlands. http://dare.ubvu.vu.nl/handle/1871/43567.

Kok, K., Widergren, S., 2016. A society of devices: integrating intelligent distributed resources with transactive energy. IEEE Power & Energy Magazine 14 (3), 34–45.

Koppl, R., Kauffman, S., Felin, T., Longo, G., 2015. Economics for a creative world. Journal of Institutional Economics 11 (1), 1–31.

Krishnamurthy, D., Li, W., Tesfatsion, L., 2016. An 8-zone test system based on ISO New England data: development and application. IEEE Transactions on Power Systems 31 (1), 234–246.

LeBaron, B., Tesfatsion, L., 2008. Modeling macroeconomies as open-ended dynamic systems of interacting agents. The American Economic Review: Papers and Proceedings 98 (2), 246–250.

Li, H., Tesfatsion, L., 2011. ISO net surplus collection and allocation in wholesale power markets under locational marginal pricing. IEEE Transactions on Power Systems 26 (2), 627–641.

Li, H., Tesfatsion, L., 2012. Co-learning patterns as emergent market phenomena: an electricity market illustration. Journal of Economic Behavior & Organization 82 (2–3), 395–419.

Li, W., Tesfatsion, L., 2018. A swing-contract market design for flexible service provision in electric power systems. In: Meyn, S., Samad, T., Glavaski, S., Hiskens, I., Stoustrup, J. (Eds.), Energy Markets and Responsive Grids: Modelling, Control, and Optimization. In: The IMA Volumes in Mathematics and Its Applications. Springer. In press. http://lib.dr.iastate.edu/econ_workingpapers/21.

Longo, G., Montévil, M., Kauffman, S., 2012. No entailing laws, but enablement in the evolution of the biosphere. In: GECCO Proceedings. arXiv:1201.2069v1 [q-bio.OT].

Lundberg, L., Jonson, E., Lindgren, K., Bryngelsson, D., 2015. A cobweb model of land-use competition between food and bioenergy crops. Journal of Economic Dynamics and Control 53, 1–14.

Marks, R., 2006. Marked design using agent-based models. In: Tesfatsion, L., Judd, K.L. (Eds.), Handbook of Computational Economics, vol. 2: Agent-Based Computational Economics. Elsevier, Amsterdam, pp. 1339–1380.

Masiello, M., Harrison, J., Mukerji, R., 2013. Market dynamics of integrating demand response into wholesale energy markets. The Electricity Journal 26 (6), 8–19.

NAS, 2016. Analytic Research Foundations for the Next-Generation Electric Grid. National Academies of Science, The National Academies Press, Washington, DC. https://www.nap.edu/download/21919.

NERC, 2016. Glossary of Terms Used in NERC Reliability Standards. North American Electric Reliability Corporation.

Newbery, D., Strbac, G., Viehoff, I., 2016. The benefits of integrating European electricity markets. Energy Policy 94, 253–263.

Nicolaisen, J., Petrov, V., Tesfatsion, L., 2001. Market power and efficiency in a computational electricity market with discriminatory double-auction pricing. IEEE Transactions on Evolutionary Computation 5 (5), 504–523.

Oh, H., Mount, T.D., 2011. Using software agents to supplement tests conducted by human subjects. In: Dawid, H., Semmler, W. (Eds.), Computational Methods in Economic Dynamics. Springer, New York, pp. 29–56.

Oliveira, F., Ruiz, C., Conejo, A.J., 2013. Contract design and supply chain coordination in the electricity industry. European Journal of Operational Research 227, 527–537.

Oseni, M.O., Pollit, M.G., 2016. The promotion of regional integration of electricity markets: lessons for developing countries. Energy Policy 88, 628–638.

Parvania, M., Fotuhi-Firuzabad, M., Shahidehpour, M., 2013. Optimal demand response aggregation in wholesale electricity markets. IEEE Transactions on Smart Grid 4 (4), 1957–1965.

Pinto, T., Morais, H., Oliveira, P., Vale, Z., Praça, I., Ramos, C., 2011. A new approach for formation and management in the scope of electricity markets. Energy 36 (8), 5004–5015.

PNNL, 2015. Pacific Northwest Smart Grid Demonstration Project Technology Performance Report. https://www.smartgrid.gov/document/Pacific_Northwest_Smart_Grid_Technology_Performance.html.

PowerMatcher, 2016. PowerMatcher homepage. http://www.PowerMatcher.net.

Praça, I., Ramos, C., Vale, Z., Cordeiro, M., 2003. MASCEM: a multi-agent system that simulates competitive electricity markets. IEEE Intelligent Systems 18 (6), 54–60.

Rahimi, F., Ipakchi, A., 2010. Demand response as a market resource under the smart grid paradigm. IEEE Transactions on Smart Grid 1 (1).

Rahimi, F., Ipakchi, A., Fletcher, F., 2016. The changing electrical landscape. IEEE Power & Energy Magazine 14 (3), 52–62.

Rahmandad, H., Sterman, J., 2008. Heterogeneity and network structure in the dynamics of diffusion: comparing agent-based and differential equation models. Management Science 54 (5), 998–1014.

Rassenti, S., Smith, V.L., Wilson, B., 2003. Controlling market power and price spikes in electricity networks: demand-side bidding. Proceedings of the National Academy of Sciences of the United States of America 100 (5), 2998–3003.

Richiardi, M., 2013. The missing link: agent-based models and dynamic microsimulation. In: Leitner, S., Wall, F. (Eds.), Artificial Economics and Self Organization: Agent-Based Approaches to Economics and Social Systems. In: Lecture Notes in Economics and Mathematical Systems, vol. 669. Springer, Berlin, pp. 3–15 (Chapter 1).

Ringler, P., Keles, D., Fichtner, W., 2016. Agent-based modelling and simulation of smart electricity grids and markets – a literature review. Renewable & Sustainable Energy Reviews 57, 205–215.

Roop, J.M., Fathelrahman, E., 2003. Modeling Electricity Contract Choice: An Agent-Based Approach. Pacific Northwest National Laboratory Report PNNL-SA-38282.

Roozbehani, M., Dahleh, M.A., Mitter, S.K., 2012. Volatility of power grids under real-time pricing. IEEE Transactions on Power Systems 27 (4), 1926–1940.

Roth, A.E., Erev, I., 1995. Learning in extensive form games: experimental data and simple dynamic models in the intermediate term. Games and Economic Behavior 8, 848–881.

Royal Swedish Academy of Sciences, 2016. Oliver Hart and Bengt Holmström: Contract Theory, Scientific Background on the Sveriges Riksbank Prize in Economic Sciences in Memory of Alfred Nobel. https://www.nobelprize.org/nobel_prizes/economic-sciences/.

Santos, G., Pinto, T., Morais, H., Sousa, T.M., Pereira, I.F., Fernandes, R., Praca, I., Vale, Z., 2015. Multi-agent simulation of competitive electricity markets: autonomous systems cooperation for European modeling. Energy Conversion and Management 99, 387–399.

Schweppe, F.C., Caramanis, M.C., Tabors, R.D., Bohn, R.E., 1988. Spot Pricing of Electricity. Kluwer, Boston, MA.

Sheblé, G.B., 1999. Computational Auction Mechanisms for Restructured Power Industry Operation. Kluwer, Boston, MA.

Siano, P., 2014. Demand response and smart grids – a survey. Renewable & Sustainable Energy Reviews 30, 461–478.

Sinitskaya, E., Tesfatsion, L., 2015. Macroeconomies as constructively rational games. Journal of Economic Dynamics & Control 61, 152–182.

Stoft, S., 2002. Power System Economics: Designing Markets for Electricity. IEEE Press & Wiley–Interscience, John Wiley & Sons, Inc., New York.

Sun, J., Tesfatsion, L., 2007. Dynamic testing of wholesale power market designs: an open-source agent-based framework. Computational Economics 30 (3), 291–327.

Tesfatsion, L., 2006. Agent-based computational economics: a constructive approach to economic theory. In: Tesfatsion, L., Judd, K.L. (Eds.), Handbook of Computational Economics, vol. 2: Agent-Based Computational Economics. Elsevier, Amsterdam, pp. 831–880.

Tesfatsion, L., 2009. Auction basics for wholesale power markets: objectives and pricing rules. In: Proceedings of the IEEE Power and Energy Society General Meeting. Calgary, Alberta, CA, July. http://www2.econ.iastate.edu/tesfatsi/AuctionBasics.IEEEPES2009.LT.pdf (electronic).

Tesfatsion, L., 2017a. Agent-based electricity market research. http://www2.econ.iastate.edu/tesfatsi/aelect.htm.

Tesfatsion, L., 2017b. Modeling economic systems as locally-constructive sequential games. Journal of Economic Methodology 24 (4), 384–409. http://lib.dr.iastate.edu/econ_workingpapers/23.

Tesfatsion, L., 2017c. Agent-based computational economics: growing economies from the bottom up. http://www2.econ.iastate.edu/tesfatsi/ace.htm.

Tesfatsion, L., 2017d. Elements of dynamic economic modeling: presentation and analysis. Eastern Economic Journal 43 (2), 192–216. https://doi.org/10.1057/eej.2016.2.

Tesfatsion, L., 2017e. ACE research area: learning and the embodied mind. http://www2.econ.iastate.edu/tesfatsi/aemind.htm.

Tesfatsion, L., 2017f. Empirical validation and verification of agent-based models. http://www2.econ.iastate.edu/tesfatsi/empvalid.htm.

Tesfatsion, L., 2017g. Presentation and evaluation guidelines for agent-based models. http://www2.econ.iastate.edu/tesfatsi/amodguide.htm.

Tesfatsion, L., 2017h. Integrated transmission and distribution system project. http://www2.econ.iastate.edu/tesfatsi/ITDProjectHome.htm.

Tesfatsion, L., 2017i. AMES Wholesale Power Market Test Bed: homepage. http://www2.econ.iastate.edu/tesfatsi/AMESMarketHome.htm.

Tesfatsion, L.S., Silva-Monroy, C.A., Loose, V.W., Ellison, J.F., Elliott, R.T., Byrne, R.H., Guttromson, R.T., 2013. New Wholesale Power Market Design Using Linked Forward Markets. Sandia National Laboratories Report SAND2013-2789.

Tesfatsion, L., Wang, Z., Nguyen, H.T., Battula, S., Takkala, R.R., 2017. Development of an Integrated Transmission and Distribution Test System to Evaluate Transactive Energy Systems. Quarterly Report for PNNL Contract 339051. Iowa State University.

Thomas, A.G., Jahangiri, P., Wu, D., Cai, C., Zhao, H., Aliprantis, D., Tesfatsion, L., 2012. Intelligent residential air-conditioning system with smart-grid functionality. IEEE Transactions on Smart Grid 3 (4), 2240–2251.

Thomas, A.G., Tesfatsion, L., 2016. Using test systems to explore integrated T&D system operations with smart grid functionality: a demand response illustration. In: IEEE Power and Energy Society General Meeting. Boston, MA, July.

Thomas, A.G., Tesfatsion, L., 2017. Braided Cobwebs: Cautionary Tales for Dynamic Retail Pricing in End-to-End Power Systems. Economics Working Paper No. 17028. Department of Economics, Iowa State University, Ames, IA. http://lib.dr.iastate.edu/econ_workingpapers/30/.

Tuballa, M.L., Abundo, M.L., 2016. A review of the development of smart grid technologies. Renewable & Sustainable Energy Reviews 59, 710–723.

Tukey, J.W., 1962. The future of data analysis. The Annals of Mathematical Statistics 33 (1), 1–67.

Wagner, M.R., Bachovchin, K., Ilic, M., 2015. Computer architecture and multi time-scale implementations for smart grid in a room simulator. IFAC-PapersOnLine 47 (30), 233–238.

Wallace, R., Geller, A., Ogawa, V.A. (Eds.), 2015. Assessing the Use of Agent-Based Models for Tobacco Regulation. Institute of Medicine of the National Academies, National Academies Press, Washington, DC.

Wang, Z., He, Y., 2016. Two-stage optimal demand response with battery energy storage systems. IET Generation, Transmission & Distribution 10 (5), 1286–1293.

Weidlich, A., 2008. Engineering Interrelated Electricity Markets: An Agent-Based Computational Approach. Physica-Verlag, Springer, Berlin.

Weidlich, A., Veit, D., 2008a. A critical survey of agent-based wholesale electricity market models. Energy Economics 30 (4), 1728–1759.

Weidlich, A., Veit, D., 2008b. PowerACE: ein agentenbasiertes Tool zur Simulation von Stromund Emissionsmärkten. In: Proceedings of the Multikonferenz Wirtschaftsinformatik. Garching.

Widergren, S., Kok, K., Tesfatsion, L., 2016. Transactive energy webinar. IEEE Smartgrid, March 10. http://smartgrid.ieee.org/resources/webinars/past-webinars.

Ygge, F., 1998. Market-Oriented Programming and Its Application to Power Load Management. Ph.D. thesis. Department of Computer Science, Lund University. Available at: http://www.enersearch.se/ygge.

Yoon, J.H., Baldick, R., Novoselac, A., 2014. Dynamic demand response controller based on real-time retail price for residential buildings. IEEE Transactions on Smart Grid 4 (1), 121–129.

Yu, N., Tesfatsion, L., Liu, C.-C., 2012. Financial bilateral contract negotiation in wholesale power markets using Nash bargaining theory. IEEE Transactions on Power Systems 27 (1), 251–267.

Zhou, Z., Zhao, F., Wang, J., 2011. Agent-based electricity market simulation with demand response from commercial buildings. IEEE Transactions on Smart Grid 2 (4), 580–588.

PERSPECTIVES ON HETEROGENEITY

Modeling a Heterogeneous World

14

Richard Bookstaber*, **Alan Kirman**[†,1]

*Office of the Chief Investment Officer, University of California, Oakland, CA, United States
†School for Advanced Studies in the Social Sciences (EHESS), Paris, France
[1]Corresponding author: e-mail address: alan.kirman@ehess.fr

CONTENTS

As physicians, we are ambivalent about heterogeneity in medicine. We actively suppress it – ignore it, tune it out – because doing so is crucial for establishing the efficacy of tests, drugs, and procedures. But heterogeneity is ubiquitous in complex systems, including all of biology and human society.... we recognize that suppressing it exacts a heavy price and struggle to take it into account.

Davidoff (2009) (p. 2580)

Heterogeneity is the reality of our world. We have an economic system that is composed of individuals who differ in their characteristics and in their choices, and who change themselves and their environment through their interactions. The simple fact that agents differ from one another is the basic driving force behind all economic activity. To put it simply, if agents were identical there would be little interest in their interacting with each other. When agents are too similar in their beliefs or characteristics we are rapidly led to "no trade" theorems which are so much at odds with the amount of trade that actually prevails that it is clear that one must take full account of the interaction between agents.

Handbook of Computational Economics, Volume 4, ISSN 1574-0021, https://doi.org/10.1016/bs.hescom.2018.03.004

Heterogeneity almost inevitably leads the economy to be a complex adaptive system.[1] The economic system is composed of many parts and the interaction between these parts leads to aggregate behavior which is intrinsically different from that of its components, a characteristic called emergence. In its most apparent form, emergence can lead to congestion or stampedes, even though on an individual basis no one is taking action intended toward that end. In terms of the economy, it can be locally stable but globally unstable.

This complexity leads to computational irreducibility, where analytical methods fail the task. The economy is not susceptible to being modeled as a system in which individuals behave according to some axioms where their behavior generates an equilibrium which can be shown to exist and whose characteristics can be solved. Furthermore, having many heterogeneous agents can lead the system to be over-identified, so even if the tools of standard methods could be applied, the result will not be a closed system. There is not a unique solution.[2] As a result, heterogeneous agent models move from deductive to simulation.

Integrating heterogeneity into the economist's worldview not only changes the approach to analyzing models, it also changes the objective of the models. If heterogeneity matters, a different set of heterogeneous agents will lead to a different result. And this in turn means that rather than seeking a theoretical result, we are in the world of pragmatism, of engineering, of case studies. And, it means we must delve into the real world.[3]

We will illustrate the nature of heterogeneity with three examples. One is drawn from a model of a microeconomic market, one from the setting of a potential shock to a financial market, and one that looks at the heterogeneity of the financial system. Agent-based models have been put to task for each of these cases. We have chosen these three examples to illustrate our basic point. The first example is based on a market for a perishable good, fish, for which we have detailed information on every transaction and where the participants have heterogeneous characteristics. We

---

[1] Although it is worth observing that it is not necessary for a system to be heterogeneous in order to be complex. A collection of particles or individuals who are, at the outset, identical, may change their states as they interact with other particles and the result will be configurations of particles in different states which will be difficult or even impossible to predict from an analysis of the particles in isolation. A classical example is Conway's "Game of Life" in which simple systems of interacting particles generate complex evolving patterns which may never converge to any particular stationary pattern. This sort of view has entered into economics quite recently (see e.g. Miller and Page, 2007 and Kirman, 2010 and Hommes, 2013).

[2] Romer's (2018) critique of macroeconomics focuses on the problems of over-identification within the real economic system.

[3] We are arguing here for a radical position, but there have been a number of contributions which have suggested something of a compromise in which one builds models based on "stylized facts" and which in simple forms are tractable. Hommes (2006) in the Handbook of Computational Economics, Volume 2 summarized this, quite extensive, literature. Eschewing theory as a goal is far from universally accepted at the present time and two chapters in the current Handbook of Computational Economics, Volume 4, treat partly tractable heterogeneous agent models in macroeconomics (Branch and McGough, 2018) and in finance (Dieci and He, 2018).

observed that aggregation over heterogeneous agents led to the emergence of what could be considered as the "Law of Demand" but which was not satisfied for the individuals. We then looked at another stylized fact, that of the emergence of loyalty between buyers and sellers. Here, we could obtain analytic results but only in the very simplest version of the model. From this we had to simulate to see whether our results carried over to more general but still simple versions of the model. Finally to look at several stylized facts simultaneously we built a simple agent based model in which agents learned to use behavioral rules. No a priori rationality was attributed to the participants.

In our second example, we look at the complex interaction between the components of a market when there is a change in volatility and the transmission of the reactions to that change from one type of agent to another. Here we do not specify the rationality of the agents on the basis of theory but rather use the behavioral rules which each of the various types of agents that we describe not only use but claim to use. We substitute an empirically based specification for a theoretically based one, and in so doing distance ourselves from models with behavioral axioms. Our last example examines the feedbacks from one part of a large financial institution to another. Again, the different functions of the various agents are associated with different rules and the sort of cascading events that, for example, characterized the Bear Sterns collapse can be clearly seen in this sort of framework. Notice that, as we make more realistic assumptions about the actors in the market or institution, the model becomes more specific and cannot be simply applied to any financial institution. We move from theory to pragmatism. In our presentation here we will not delve into the details of the models themselves, leaving that to other sources.[4] If we are to understand heterogeneous agent models, we need to understand the richness of heterogeneity in various settings just as much as we need to understand the models within those settings, and we will focus on the former. Simply knowing that there is heterogeneity is sufficient to understand important characteristics, such as complexity, computational irreducibility, emergence, and a lack of ergodicity, that can lead standard economics to fail.

1 HETEROGENEITY AND STANDARD ECONOMICS

Many economists, particularly those who have been trained in general equilibrium theory, will react negatively to the idea that the heterogeneity of economic agents has been ignored. After all, if agents are identical why would there be any trade? Yet what we typically analyze is the equilibrium that, we argue, results from such trades. Heterogeneity is therefore clearly taken into account. Nevertheless, there are two objections to this argument.

---

[4]The model for the market example is in Kirman and Vriend (2001), the agent-based model for the financial system and for shocks to that system is in Bookstaber et al. (2017).

First, we do allow heterogeneity of preferences and of endowments in our basic versions of the general equilibrium models. Yet the heterogeneity of endowments or income is often reduced to assuming that, while there is a distribution of income that distribution is fixed. And whilst we allow for preferences to differ, we confine them to a very small set of all possible preferences, to the ones that satisfy certain axioms which economists have argued correspond to rationality. But this limitation is due to the introspection of economists and not to how we observe people behaving in real life.

Second, and worse, even with this highly restrictive approach, although we argue that voluntary trades lead to an equilibrium, we have been unable to prove that an economy out of equilibrium would through such trades, whether they take place between individuals or through an organized market, ever reach an equilibrium. To avoid the inconvenience of this sort of difficulty, which results from the problem of aggregating over individuals with different characteristics, macroeconomists have turned to the fiction of the "representative agent", the person whose behavior corresponds to the behavior of the economy as a whole. This approach purports to retain the rigor of the analytic approach, but only does so by removing the essential contribution of heterogeneity and the implications that arise from it.

Although it would be unfair to argue that macroeconomists have totally ignored these problems. There has been increasing interest in different types of heterogeneity, whether it concern the fundamental characteristics of agents such as their preferences or their attitude to risk, or even the extent of their rationality. Bounded rationality as proposed by Herb Simon, has received increasing attention but, in general, has been regarded as being more within the context of "behavioral economics" rather than in the domain of standard economic analysis.

A number of important economists such as Akerlof (2007) have argued that macroeconomic dynamics are heavily dependent on the heterogeneity of the individuals in the economy, yet their contributions have not had a major impact on the way in which macroeconomics has developed in the last few decades. The way in which the dynamic interaction between stock markets and the macro economy has been understood by the economics profession has evolved significantly over the last thirty years. Shiller (2003) argued, while the rational representative agent framework and the related Efficient Market Hypothesis represented the dominant theoretical modeling paradigm in financial economics during the 1970s, the behavioral finance approach has gained increasing ground within the economics community over the last two decades.

The main reason for this significant paradigm shift is well known: Following Shiller (1981) and LeRoy and Porter (1981), a large number of studies have documented various empirical regularities of financial markets – such as the excess volatility of stock prices – which are clearly inconsistent with the Efficient Market

Hypothesis.[5] During the 1990s several researchers[6] have developed models of financial markets with heterogeneous agents which follow on from the seminal work by Beja and Goldman (1980). In such models agents switch between forecasting rules and tend to use the rule which is currently the most successful. Thus the heterogeneity of agents in terms of their forecasts is the result of their learning from experience. Ever since, financial market models with heterogeneous agents using rule-of-thumb strategies have become central in the behavioral finance literature.[7]

Yet, many have argued that in the sort of perfectly competitive economy where individuals have negligible influence on aggregate outcomes, there is no need for any consideration of heterogeneity in society. As Wolgast (1994, 224) asserts: "From the atomistic standpoint, the individuals who make up a society are interchangeable like molecules in a bucket of water-society a mere aggregate of individuals". But it is difficult to reconcile this with a longstanding philosophical point of view. For example consider Locke's view when he says: "We are all a sort of chameleons, that still take a tincture from things near us: nor is it to be wondered at in children, who better understand what they see, than what they hear" (Locke, 1693, 67).

Indeed, once we allow for the sort of externalities suggested in this phrase, particularly in tastes or preferences, one runs into logical problems and the idea that a social norm, or social contract will emerge becomes questionable. Even the most minimal social contract allowing some liberty of choice to individuals is impossible as Sen (1970) has shown.

Furthermore, precisely how the social contract is established is left unstated though a number of authors associate with Hobbes, the view that a social contract emerges as a norm, (see e.g. Ullmann-Margalit, 1977) a view relatively recently formalized and developed by economists such as Young (2015). But what distinguishes Adam Smith (1776) from that view is that in the earlier literature what was supposed to emerge was a social contract which delimited the freedom of choice. Smith it is claimed, with his "invisible hand", developed the idea that somehow what will emerge from a group of very different individuals, acting in their own interest, is spontaneous order rather than a contract delimiting the bounds of the freedom of choice. But no mechanism was proposed to explain how the order emerged. Later economists such as Walras argued that markets will achieve this and even today many distinguished economist refer to the First Fundamental Theorem of Welfare Economics as the "Invisible Hand Theorem". But this is inappropriate because that theorem is about the properties of an equilibrium state and not about how it is attained. Reading Walras and his modern followers leads one to suspect that they never

---

[5] See e.g. Frankel and Froot (1988, 1990), Shiller (1990), Allen and Taylor (1990), and Brock et al. (1992), among many others.
[6] See e.g. Day and Huang (1990), Chiarella (1992), Kirman (1993), Lux and Marchesi (1999), and Brock and Hommes (1998).
[7] See e.g. Chiarella and He (2001, 2003), De Grauwe and Grimaldi (2006), and Dieci and Westerhoff (2010).

actually visited markets. Had they done so our "market" models would have looked very different.

In fact, markets give us excellent examples of complex systems. Different individuals come together to trade and the relations that build up between the participants create a network whose structure has an influence on the final aggregate outcomes. The network itself evolves over time as a result of the experience that individuals have with their activity. Rules evolve over time to constrain the behavior of those in the market. There is self-organization as individuals change their trading partners in the light of their experience. The way in which the rules and norms evolve governs the evolution of the aggregate activity.

In the next section we look at an example of a specific market, the Marseille fish market, which although a very small is already too complex to reduce to a standard economic model.

2 HETEROGENEITY IN MICROECONOMICS: FISH MARKETS

If one is interested in how specific markets function, fish markets are quite a good place to start. The goods that are being sold are perishable and there is, as a result, no need to consider inventories. Furthermore, there is a substantial literature analyzing such markets from Roman times.

We will take as our empirical example the Marseille wholesale fish market. At the time that the data was collected, the wholesale fish market for Marseille, situated at Saumaty on the coast at the Northern edge of Marseille, was open every day of the year from 2 a.m. to 6 a.m. Over 500 buyers and 45 sellers came together, although they were not all present every day and more than 130 types of fish were sold. Prices were not posted. All transactions were pairwise. There was little negotiation and prices can reasonably be regarded as take it or leave it prices given by the seller. The data set consists of the details of every individual transaction made over a period of three years. The data was systematically collected and recorded by the Chambre de Commerce de Marseille which managed the market at that time. The following information is provided for each transaction:

1. The name of the buyer
2. The name of the seller
3. The type of fish
4. The weight of the lot
5. The price per kilo at which it was sold
6. The order of the transaction in the daily sales of the seller.

The data runs from January, 1988 through June, 1991. The total number of transactions for which we have data is 237,162.

Thus we have a very complete picture of the behavior of all the participants over three years and one approach would have been to analyze the individuals and to try to establish some specific behavioral features which were common to all of them.

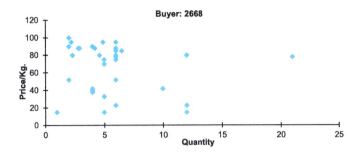

FIGURE 1

Transactions of one buyer for one species of fish. Source: Härdle and Kirman (1995).

As will quickly become apparent this would not have been appropriate and would not have led to an understanding of the evolution of the aggregate behavior of the market.

Why would the individualistic approach not have worked here? There are a number of reasons. There are many different agents with different functions who participate but are not all present all of the time. Some are buying for large supermarkets or supermarket chains, others are small retailers, yet others are buying for their restaurants or for the organizations for whom they cater. Thus, we are dealing with a collection of heterogeneous agents who interact regularly and from this interaction emerges certain aggregate behavior.

Yet, trying to model the behavior of the individuals in isolation will give one a very poor picture of the overall evolution of the market. For example, in Härdle and Kirman (1995) we showed that if one plots the quantities purchased by an individual against the price at which they were transacted, the result seems almost random. This is illustrated in Fig. 1 where the purchases of one individual of one species of fish are shown.

Thus there is little to suggest that there is a monotone declining relation between the price paid and the quantity purchased. This is, of course, but one illustration of the many thousands of such relationships that we analyzed but there was no consistent evidence of the sort of behavior that theory might lead us to expect.

However, if we now examine the aggregate data for a single fish we see something like the monotonic relation, just mentioned, emerging. This, even though we used a non-parametric estimation which is much more exacting than fitting a pre-determined functional form. This can be seen in Fig. 2.

Now if we go one step further and aggregate over all types of fish the result is even more striking. This can be seen in Fig. 3.

What we see clearly is that the aggregate relationship is not the sum of many similar individual relationships but has characteristics resulting from the aggregation

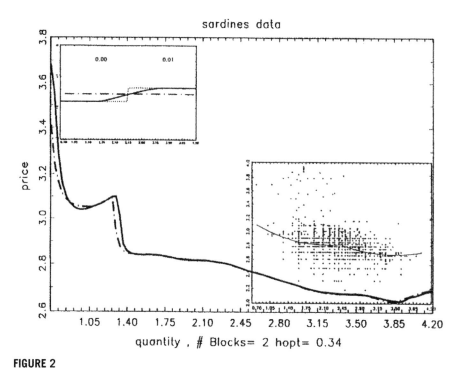

FIGURE 2

Aggregate price quantity relation for one fish species. Source: Härdle and Kirman (1995).

itself. But this is an empirical observation and no theoretical argument is presented to explain how this sort of phenomenon emerges.[8]

Consider now, a second question. How do the relationships between buyers and sellers emerge on such a market? In order to answer this question we started in Weisbuch et al. (2000) by reducing the problem to the simplest possible case and obtained a theoretical solution. However, the question that immediately arises is whether this result holds in more general cases. But first let us spell out the model of a simplified version of the Marseille fish market that we built to try to answer this question. We started from the assumption that links between buyers and sellers are created and reinforced as a result of the experience that the participants have with those links.

---

[8]This remark deserves a fuller explanation. What was done here was to make a non-parametric fit over the points corresponding to the averages of all the observations in a "bin". This means that one is looking at all the transactions within a certain quantity interval and then averaging over the observations in that interval. There is, in fact, a distribution of prices in each interval and whether the average reflects that distribution depends very much on the nature of the distribution. Using a non-parametric fit penalizes the smoothness of the fit but at a high level of aggregation the monotonic character of the function is very clear. It should also be remembered that buyers are not always present and that some, such as expensive restaurants, have highly inelastic demand so one is not simply aggregating over random draws from a given distribution.

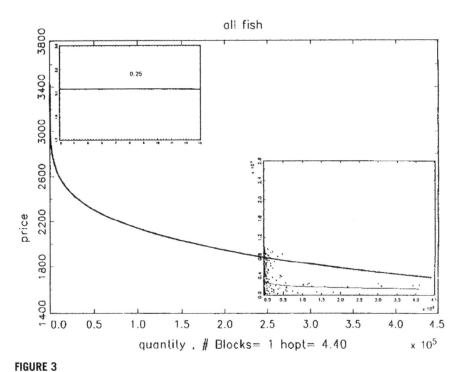

all fish

FIGURE 3

Price quantity relation aggregated over all fish species. Source: Härdle and Kirman (1995).

Thus, we consider a situation in which buyers do not anticipate the value of choosing sellers but rather develop relationships with sellers on the basis of their previous experience.

To be more precise, think of a *buyer i* who trades with different sellers and records the profit he made in the past from each of them. So at any point in time he knows what the profit is that he has from these visits and he updates his probability of visiting any seller on that basis. So, denote by $J_{ij}(t)$ the cumulated profit, up to period t, that buyer i has obtained from trading with seller j.

Then the probability $p_{ij}(t)$ that i will visit j in that period is given by,

$$p_{ij}(t) = \frac{e^{\beta J_{ij}(t)}}{\sum_k e^{\beta J_{ik}(t)}} \tag{1}$$

where β is a reinforcement parameter which describes how sensitive the individual is to past profits. This non-linear updating rule will be familiar from many different disciplines and is also widely used in statistical physics. It is known as the "logit" rule or, in game theory as the "quantal response" rule. The rule is based on two simple principles. Agents make probabilistic choices between actions. Actions that have generated better outcomes in the past are more likely to be used in the future. Such a process

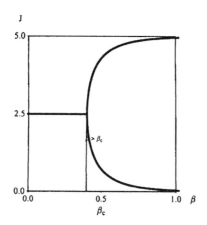

FIGURE 4

The transition from symmetric to asymmetric solutions to the probability of visiting each of two sellers. Source: Weisbuch et al. (2000).

has long been adopted and modeled by psychologists (see e.g., Bush and Mosteller, 1955). It is a special form of reinforcement learning. It has also been widely used in evolutionary and experimental game theory (see Roth and Erev, 1995) and a more elaborate model has been constructed by Camerer and Ho (1999). This approach has the great advantage that it requires no specific attribution of rationality to the agents other than that they are more likely to do what has proved to be successful in the past.

Using the learning rule that we have given we know the probability for agent i to visit seller j and can therefore calculate the expected gain from that visit.

However, to be able to solve this model we need to simplify even further and look at the case where there are just two sellers and furthermore each time a buyer visits one of the sellers he receives a fixed profit of Π. The reader will, by now, have understood that we are purifying our model so much that it is in danger of becoming totally unrealistic. As a Chinese philosopher said, "water that is too pure has no fish in it"! What turns out to be important in this very simple model is that for each buyer there is a critical value of β, call it β_c.

In this case, when $\beta \leq \beta_c$ the importance attached to previous experience is below the critical value β_c there is a single solution and the cumulated profits from both sellers and hence the probabilities of visiting them are the same.

However, when $\beta > \beta_c$ there is a rapid transition at $\beta = \beta_c$. By which we mean that as soon as β passes above the critical value the probabilities of visiting each seller become rapidly very different. All of this is illustrated in Fig. 4.

This very simple example suggests that as beta passes a critical value buyers are most likely to attach themselves to one seller. This critical value depends on the amounts that agents buy and the frequency with which they purchase. Thus empirically one would expect buyers who visit the market frequently and who buy large quantities to be loyal to one seller whereas the other buyers would shop around amongst sellers. This is precisely what we observe on the actual market with a heavy concentration of large and regular buyers who buy from a single seller, whereas the smaller and less frequent participants bought from several sellers. Yet it is difficult to argue that this evidence can be seen as a justification for our extremely simplistic model. We need to move to a more general case.

But, even dealing with three sellers and several buyers proves difficult to handle analytically. To see whether our results in the simplistic theoretical model carried over to this case we ran simulations with agents probability of choosing a seller depending monotonically on their previous success with the seller in question. Again we used the logit rule to translate previous profits into probabilities. In the simulation with three sellers and 30 buyers the results from the theoretical model were confirmed. Buyers who had beta values below their critical threshold shopped around while those whose values were above their critical threshold became loyal to one seller. Those who became loyal were again those who came to the market frequently and bought large quantities. This was clearly reflected in the data as explained by Weisbuch et al. (2000). One might have thought that the presence of the shoppers would interfere with the evolution of loyalty since the shoppers might prevent the loyal buyers from obtaining what they needed. It turns out that this was not the case and the buyers were divided into two distinct classes exactly as they were on the actual Marseille fish market.

Notice how we proceeded here, we started from an extraordinarily simple model in order to examine this feature of buyers' behavior. To see if this result was at all robust we had to resort to simulations. Yet there are many other questions about the behavior of the buyers on this market which remain unanswered and in order to consider these we had to change strategies and abandon our simplistic theoretical model and develop a different approach.

This brings us back to the essential point of this chapter. As soon as one wants to build a rather general model of even a simple market such as that of a wholesale fish market, with trading over time between heterogeneous agents solving an analytical model becomes intractable, and thus we are pushed toward an agent-based model.

In one sense the previous model is a special case of an agent-based model where the rule that the agents use can be thought of as determining the choice of seller in a particular way depending on the success of transactions with that seller in the past. However, as we have said, once the rules are extended to cover a variety of choices the behavior of the model quickly becomes too complicated to model formally. Suppose, however, that our aim is to analyze several features of the market at the same time. The way to proceed is to abandon the passage by a theoretical model and construct an agent-based model from the outset. In doing so we hope to find some of the salient aspects of the real empirical markets that interest us as emergent features.

Indeed, in Kirman and Vriend (2001) we used the agent-based approach to develop a simple model which reproduces three of the features of the Marseille fish market. These are first, the division between loyalty and shopping behavior on the part of buyers that we have already mentioned. Second, price dispersion even for the same species. And third, the way sellers decide which customers to give priority.

In our simple agent-based model agents interact with each other and learn in so doing. This evolution is the natural one if one starts with the data for a particular market and wishes to construct a model which captures the basic characteristics of the aggregate behavior of that market. Note that in this relatively simple situation we would like to see if the market participants learn which decision rules to use and how these compare with the rules that the buyers use in reality. For, as Lucas (1986) said,

> *In general terms, we view or model an individual as a collection of decision rules (rules that dictate the action to be taken in given situations) and a set of preferences used to evaluate the outcomes arising from particular situation–action combinations. These decision rules are continuously under review and revision; new decision rules are tried and tested against experience, and rules that produce desirable outcomes supplant those that do not. I use the term "adaptive" to refer to this trial-and-error process through which our modes of behavior are determined.*

Analyzing how agents learn in this market is particularly valuable, because we cannot detect their rules from the data. For this we would need to know how much each seller brought to the market and how many potential buyers he saw. However, later, when we examine a financial market we can use rules which the agents acknowledge that they use. Here, we will assume that the buyers were identical to start with and see whether they learn to behave heterogeneously.

In the simple simulated model we developed in Kirman and Vriend (2001), ten initially identical sellers and one hundred initially identical buyers met in the market hall for five thousand days for a morning and an afternoon session. They traded single individual units of a perishable commodity. Here we make two simplifications. The morning and afternoon sessions correspond to the idea that there are several opportunities to trade during the day. Taking two periods allows us to take account of the idea that the possibility of trading later in the day has an influence on the prices that buyers will accept and sellers will propose early in the day. It would, of course, be more realistic to consider more trading opportunities in the day. The single unit assumption is frequently used but can be criticized on the grounds that when buyers require different amounts this may influence what they pay.

On each day the sequence of events is the following:

In the morning before the market opens the sellers purchase their supply outside the market for a given price that was identical for all sellers and constant through time. Thus, we assume that the participants on the Marseille have no influence on what happens in the outside world. The market opens and the buyers enter the market hall. Each buyer requires one unit of fish per day. All buyers simultaneously choose the queue of a seller. The sellers then handle these queues during the morning session. Once the sellers have supplied all the buyers who are willing to purchase from them the morning session ends. All those buyers who are still unsatisfied choose the queue of a seller in the afternoon. Of course, the only sellers present in the afternoon are those who did not sell all their stock in the morning. Sellers now sell to those buyers who are willing to purchase from them and the end of the afternoon session is then reached. All unsold stocks perish. Those buyers who did purchase fish, resell that

condition	action	strength
if	then	....
.. ..	....	....
.. ..	....	....

FIGURE 5

A simple classifier system.

fish outside the market, at a given price that is identical for all buyers, and constant through time. Each buyer can visit at most one seller in the morning and one seller in the afternoon.

What are the decisions with which the actors are faced? Buyers have to choose a seller for the morning session. They then have to decide which prices to accept or reject during the morning session. If necessary, they also have to decide on a seller for the afternoon. Lastly, they must decide which prices to accept or reject during the afternoon session. Sellers have also four decisions to make. They must decide what quantity to supply. They must decide how to handle the queues with which they are faced. They must decide which prices to set during the morning session and which prices to set during the afternoon session.

In the model developed by Kirman and Vriend (2001), each individual agent uses a Classifier System (see Holland, 1992) for each decision and this means that each agent updates four such systems every time he takes an action. Fig. 5 represents such a system.

Each classifier system consists of a set of rules. Each rule has a condition "if......." and an action "then......" and in addition each rule is assigned a certain strength. The classifier system decides which of the rules will be the active rule at a given point in time. It does this by checking the conditional part of the rule and then chooses amongst all of those rules for whom the condition is satisfied. The choice is made as if the system ran an auction. Each rule makes a "bid" to be the current rule and this bid = current strength + ε, where ε is white noise, a normal random variable with mean 0 and fixed variance. The rule with the highest "bid" in this auction becomes the active rule. The white noise means that there was always some experimenting going on and there was always some probability that a rule, however bad, will be chosen.

What the agents in this model are doing is learning by an even simpler version of reinforcement learning than that encountered previously. Details of the particular rules in the simulation model of the Marseille fish market can be found in Kirman and Vriend (2001).

Although such an approach seems to be innocent of theoretical pre-suppositions it should be noted that the very choice of the rules amongst which the agent chooses has an impact on the outcomes. Ideally, one would like to start with agents who are totally ignorant. However, this would imply that they would somehow generate a set of rules with which they would experiment. This pushes the analysis back many stages to a very fundamental level. What is done here is in line with standard practice, which is to provide the agents with a set of rules and simply note that this, to some extent, conditions the outcomes of the process. As an example, consider the fact that we would like agents to learn how to handle the queues with which they are faced. In an ideal world we would like the agents to realize that their handling of the queues is important and then we would like them to work out for themselves how to handle them. As it is, by giving different rules explaining how to handle queues the modeler is already biasing the behavior of the seller by suggesting to him what it is that is important in generating his profit. However, what is not biased is the choice amongst the rules presented. Thus, the rule chosen will be the best available for handling queues amongst those presented, given the agent's experience, but he might well himself have focused on some other aspect of the market. In the previous model we simply established the pattern of loyalty but did not suggest any macroeconomic consequences of that feature.

In our case we used a specific measure of loyalty and then let sellers learn how to use this measure to determine how they handle queues.

What probability will be chosen depends on whether the seller learns to favor loyal customers or not. Which price is charged depends on how successful that choice turns out to be.

With these reservations it is still worth examining the results of the simulations and to see to what extent they reflect reality.

What happens is that 90% of the buyers actually get a higher payoff by being loyal. What this means is that when basically loyal customers shop around, as they do stochastically from time to time, the profit realized is lower on average than when they buy from their regular supplier. Thus, there is no incentive to deviate from their practice of buying from their normal seller. Furthermore, nine out of ten of the sellers get a higher profit when dealing with loyal buyers. In other words, the profit on average from a loyal customer is higher than from a random shopper.

How is it possible that both buyers and sellers do better from their transactions with their regular partners? The answer is simple, profit is made only when a transaction takes place, so shoppers may sometimes get better prices but they also risk not finding the fish they want. This will depend on how sellers learn to handle their customers in function of their loyalty. The question then becomes how, in the agent-based model, do loyal buyers tend to be handled by sellers? In all but one of the cases, sellers learned to give priority in service to loyal buyers but to charge them higher prices than random shoppers. Buyers learn that when they become loyal their profit is higher since they are more likely to be served even though they pay higher prices. Thus, loyalty is profitable both to buyers and sellers.

What about the one seller who did not find loyal customers more profitable than shoppers? This seller learned to charge low prices to loyal customers but to give them low priority in the queue. One might ask why he did not learn to adopt the more profitable strategy learned by the other sellers. The answer here is that, with the sort of local learning that is going on, a move towards better service and higher prices for loyal customers can never develop. To make such a move would imply increasing prices and improving service. However, buyers will immediately observe the higher prices and will not necessarily immediately observe that their priority in the queue has improved. This will lead them to reduce their probability of visiting this seller. But as soon as this seller observes that his customers are drifting away, he will go back to his former behavior and will therefore never learn his way to the more profitable strategy. But it is interesting to note that in the model this seller still makes positive profits so that he does not disappear. Thus, there is at least one explanation for the heterogeneity in terms the dispersion of profits that one observes on the market. We were not able to obtain data for the profitability of the different buyers but there is a consensus on the market that some sellers make considerably more profit than others and the argument of our model would be that they have simply reinforced on more profitable rules. One of the arguments for uniformity of behavior, that is for the elimination of heterogeneity, is that less profitable behavior will be driven out as a result of competition. However, within the context of the simplified model of this market this will not necessarily happen.

This very simple rudimentary artificial fish market model managed then to reproduce some of the features of the real market. For example, it is interesting to note that, on average, in the Marseille fish market loyal buyers pay higher prices than shoppers. Those buyers who buy more than 50% of their fish per year from one seller pay, on average, 5% more than the other buyers even though almost all the large buyers are loyal. Thus, here we observe the emergence of a clear organizational feature which has had a very specific consequence for the market price distribution. Such a model has the advantage that it can always be extended to examine other aspects of the real market, whereas to attempt to construct a theoretical model which incorporates all of these is a more than ambitious task.

Up to this point we have considered, in the context of a specific example, how the results from an extremely simplistic theoretical model of a particular market can carry over to a more general simulation. Then we examined to what extent in an agent-based model of the same market agents could learn which rules to adopt. As we observed this depends to a certain extent on which rules we allow them to choose from. However, we did not impose any criterion of what is "economically reasonable" and showed how in such a setting realistic rules could emerge and reflect the empirical data for agents' choices on the real market.

This changes with the next two examples, which put us face-to-face with the complexity of financial markets. In these examples we are not only faced with different types of agents who interact continuously, but each type of agent has a particular role to fulfill within the financial system along with particular rules that are characteristic of that role. The choice is then, between making assumptions as to the nature of the rules that are followed by the participants in each role or basing the rules in the model on the observed and advertised behavior of the actors. This means that we are then restricting our model to the particular situation, in our case, the market that we study, and in doing so, moving toward realism and away from the general approach in economics that s rooted in abstract, theoretical models. As Bookstaber (2017) argues, for large complex systems the idea of finding an adequate theoretical model is illusory.

3   HETEROGENEITY IN FINANCIAL MARKETS: THE IMPLICATIONS OF A VOLATILITY SHOCK

Over the course of 2017, U.S. equity market volatility as measured by the VIX, a widely-trade equity volatility index, dropped to one of its lowest points in history, perhaps not coincidentally during a time of growing concentration in strategies that were selling (or shorting) volatility. It is in the periods of low volatility such as this that risk can be increasing under the covers, as the perception of lower risk leads leverage and concentration to expand, what is called the volatility paradox.[9] Thus the immediate question during this period is the implication of a sudden surge in volatility from such a low level. What is the dynamic through which a volatility shock might propagate across the financial system?

A conventional stress test will assess positions that have explicit volatility exposure, such as positions in options, in the VIX and other volatility-based instruments, and in other instruments that have their payoffs determined as a function of volatility. But such a stress test will underestimate the effect, because there are dynamics triggered by other strategies that do not have explicit volatility exposure but that have a link to the volatility of assets and to the assets themselves. A rise in volatility will trigger actions for these strategies, leading to selling of the underlying assets, and this in turn will lead volatility to rise even more, creating a positive feedback between the volatility of the market and the assets in the market.

To understand these effects we need to identify the various agents in the market that have a direct or indirect link into volatility. It is the heterogeneity of the types of agents that will determine the nature of the dynamics.

The agents that are the source for cascading losses across equity markets and possible contagion into other assets classes are primarily driven by forced selling across funds using a strategy called volatility targeting, risk parity, and other strategies that will be forced to quickly rebalance their portfolios when volatility rises.

Volatility-linked agents. The positions of these agents include volatility products like the VIX, as well as products like options and derivatives that have a functional relationship to volatility.

---

[9]See, for example, Brunnermeier and Sannikov (2014), and http://rick.bookstaber.com/2011/12/volatility-paradox.html.

Volatility targeting agents. Volatility targeting is a strategy used by portfolio managers. It targets a level of volatility for the portfolio that is typically set based on the manager's mandate. For example, the manager might follow a strategy that will seek to keep the portfolio's volatility near 12%. If the volatility of the market is 12%, the fund can be fully invested. However, if the volatility of the market rises to 24%, the fund will sell half of its holdings in order to stay in line with its 12% target.

Risk parity agents. This strategy allocates portfolio weights to have the same total dollar volatility in each asset class. Risk-parity is used in a portfolio with holdings in a range of asset classes, such as equities, bonds, currencies, and commodities. The asset classes vary in their typical level of volatility. Equities tend, for example, to be more volatile that bonds. Risk-parity strategies use leverage to adjust holdings of underlying assets, buying more of the lower volatility assets relative to the higher volatility ones. If the volatility of one of the asset classes rises, the fund will need to sell some of that asset class in order to maintain equal dollar volatility across the asset classes it is holding.

The heterogeneity of the agents is important for the implications of a volatility shock in at least two ways. First, these agents differ significantly in their time horizon. The volatility-linked agents will see losses with the surge in volatility, and will need to reduce their positions immediately. The target volatility agents will only reduce positions as the rise in volatility is seen as having a non-transient component, and their adjustments will be in a weekly to monthly time scale. And the risk parity agents will have an even longer time horizon, because they generally make asset adjustment with a monthly or even quarterly time frame.

Another way heterogeneity will have an effect is the contagion that occurs based on the actions of the various agents. The volatility-linked agents will largely reside only in the volatility space, though they will also have an effect on the underlying market if they are engaged in dynamic hedging.[10] For the volatility targeting agents, as volatility rises they will be making adjustment in to their overall portfolio. Thus any action from a rise in volatility in one of the markets they hold will be across the broader set of markets in their portfolio. The investment strategy of risk parity agents is to hold a multi-asset class portfolio, so any adjustment in one asset class will naturally pass through to changes in other asset classes.

And, finally, there is heterogeneity in terms of the institutions executing these strategies; these agents can include bank/dealers, asset managers, hedge funds, pension funds and insurance companies. They will act based on differing decision times and objectives.

---

[10]Dynamic hedging typically involves replicating an option-like return by continuously adjusting exposure with changes in the market price. This can lead to positive feedback, as occurred with dynamic hedging during the stock market crash on October 19, 1987. In that event, the widespread use of a hedging strategy known as portfolio insurance led to the algorithmic selling of stock market indexes as the equity markets dropped. The intent of the selling was to reduce exposures and stem further losses, but it exacerbated the decline by creating positive feedback – the further prices declined, the more selling there was from the portfolio insurance hedging, with that selling driving prices down even further.

3.1 THE INTERACTION OF HETEROGENEOUS AGENTS: MARKET VOLATILITY SHOCKS

The first phase of a potential market unwind could be sparked by a sudden rise in expected volatility, which might, for example, come as the result of a drop in the equity market. This effect is likely to be magnified because many types of agents in the VIX market are short volatility. Even a one day change in the VIX will trigger actions by the volatility agents because they rebalance daily based on their returns, and some will be forced to get out of their positions if in the face of a large negative return. A potential flashpoint can arise from those who are short volatility – and thus who will face a negative return if volatility rises. Many of these investors are in what are called the inverse exchange-traded indexes of the VIX.[11]

Because they are short, these volatility agents will have to buy volatility, and a flood of buying will lead volatility to rise further. The higher volatility could in turn lead to a sell-off in equities, sparked by forced selling across funds using volatility targeting and risk parity agents that are rebalancing their portfolios when volatility rises.[12]

The following diagram (Fig. 6) shows the flow through key agent strategy types and the timing of effects on high-level asset classes.

The heterogeneity of the agents in the positive feedback loop obviously adds complexity to the dynamic. The cascade can occur over a number of different time frames, with agents that have different trigger points for having to liquidate their positions, and that have exposure to various other markets. It may well be that instability of the market to a sudden rise in volatility could be demonstrated with a less complicated model, one with fewer types of agents and with less heterogeneity, and in that respect the description of the model here is unnecessarily complicated.

However, the objective of the agent-based approach is not to demonstrate in a parsimonious way that in theory instability can occur, but rather to trace out how it might occur within the real-world financial system, and that requires faithfulness to the realities of the market structure and participants. By specifying these agents with their different strategies, time frames, and institutional characteristics in an agent-based model, the problem of assessing the impact of a rise in volatility can be framed within its market setting where we can draw on our knowledge of the agents who participate in markets in order to populate our artificial markets with agents who resemble their real-life counterparts.

---

[11] The two notable inverse exchange-traded indexes are the XIV and the SVXY. The XIV is an exchange-traded note (ETN) that holds short positions in the VIX. Its prospectus indicates that it will unwind if the net asset value falls more than 80% intraday, with investors receiving the end of day value. Given this is a known threshold, anything close to a 80% rise in VIX futures would likely trigger buying by the ETN provider and/or market participants in anticipation of an unwind. The SVXY is an exchange-traded fund (ETF), and it also holds short positions in the VIX. Unlike the XIV, it does not have a set threshold to unwind according to its prospectus. That said VIX futures currently have a margin requirement, and any decline in value of the inverse volatility indexes to the margin level could trigger a rapid forced unwind.

[12] For description of the current risk from low volatility and the implications of a rise in volatility, see IMF (2017), page 28.

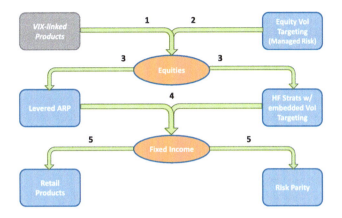

FIGURE 6

Positive feedback and cascades from a volatility shock. (1) A spike in volatility forces selling by leveraged agents that are short the VIX and increased hedging by those that a range of volatility-linked products, creating downward pressure on equity markets. (2) Agents that are sensitive to realized volatility, like those with managed-risk styles, reduce exposure in order to maintain a constant volatility, which applies further pressure to equities. This in turn increases volatility. (3) Volatility targeting and alternative risk premium hedge funds reduce exposure as equities drop and realized volatility rises. (4) Pressure on these strategies causes contagion from the equity markets into fixed income. (5) Risk-parity products, which rebalance less frequently, are drawn in, readjusting away from equities in order to maintain equal volatility across their asset classes. As risk targeting agents, they also reduce exposure across all asset classes as equity volatility spreads to other asset classes.

4 HETEROGENEITY IN THE MACRO-FINANCIAL SYSTEM

Economic models depict the macroeconomic world in the abstract: "assume there are N banks, K asset managers, and M markets." Where, it goes without saying, the banks and asset managers are non-descript, and they and the markets are all homogeneous. But financial vulnerabilities and risks do not occur in an abstract world. We have a concrete financial system. We know the N banks. They include Citi, Morgan Stanley, and Deutsche Bank. We know the K asset managers and hedge funds. They include Bridgewater, PIMCO, and Citadel.

The banks are heterogeneous. Each has its own focus and business franchise; some have major prime brokerage operations, some are aggressive in fixed income derivatives and swaps, others are major market makers for high yield bonds. Similarly, the asset managers and hedge funds each have their own approaches to risk and liquidity management, market focus, holding periods and leverage. A fund such as Renaissance Capital which focuses on liquid markets and has holding periods measured in days is going to have a different effect on the system than one like Cerberus which focuses on illiquid distressed debt.

Furthermore, the many functions of banks – prime brokerage, funding, market making, and derivatives – belie the conventional economic representation of them as monolithic entities. Their financing desks and prime brokerage create credit transformations as they allow less credit-worthy investors to receive funding from lenders who demand very high credit quality in their loans. Their trading operations create liquidity transformations where less liquid assets such as structured products which package less liquid instruments into larger-scale and more liquid structures, and where they make markets for the less liquid securities such as corporate bonds. They create risk transformations through derivatives that alter the return characteristics of various securities. Overall, the financial system is more akin to a production processing plant, where each agent takes in a flow and outputs a flow that is altered in some manner than it is to a simple network with one-dimensional nodes.[13]

Fig. 7 illustrates the vast heterogeneity of the agents operating in the financial system. It is a schematic of the relationships of the various agents, and, in the case of the bank, the subagents that operate within it. Each box is a type of agent, operating on its own sorts of heuristics. The links between the agents represent contractual relationships, such as loans and swaps, and the exchange and brokering of assets. (Note that this schematic is a close-up of only one part of the system. It shows only one bank, whereas of course in the overall financial system there are many banks, and similarly for the other types of agents.)

Fig. 7 is highlighted by colored outlines to point out the segments of the market involved in three major activities: the trading of assets, the supply of funding to facilitate holding those assets, and the maintenance of collateral to secure that funding.

Asset-related agents. The agents that are involved in the flow of assets and cash between investors are highlighted by green. The agents holding the assets include mutual funds, hedge funds, the trading and investment arms of insurance companies and pension funds, and retail investors. Intermediating in this process are trading desks, exchanges, and others types of market makers.

Funding-related agents. Funding moves from cash providers to those who are using the funding to finance their investment activities, most notably hedge funds. At the center of funding activities are the banks that access short-term funding, such as through repurchase agreements, and lend it through their prime brokerage operations or their financing desk, both for clients and for their own market making activities.[14] The agents involved in the funding process are highlighted in Fig. 7 by the purple outline.

Collateral-related agents. Secured funding flows are matched by flows of collateral to agents that supply that funding.[15] The agents that are key to collateral flows are

---

[13] Bookstaber et al. (2015) describes the financial system in a production plant context, and applies a standard tool for analyzing a complex production process, signed directed graphs, to understand the complexity of the system.

[14] A description of the flow of funding and the agents involved in that process, as well as the vulnerabilities that can arise in the funding activities, is presented in Aguiar et al. (2014).

[15] A description of the flows of collateral and the agents involved in that process is presented in Aguiar et al. (2016).

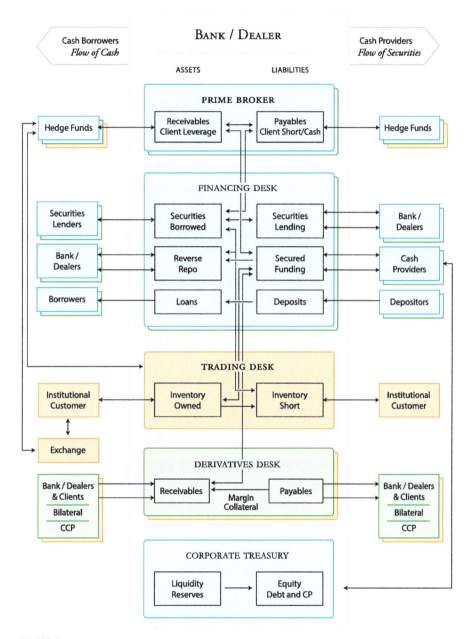

FIGURE 7

Agents in the financial system. Fig. 7 illustrates the heterogeneity of agents in the financial system, centered on the bank/dealer and the various subagents contained within it. The agents can be described by agents dealing with assets (in yellow), funding (in blue), and collateral (in green). Many functions have agents of multiple types.

highlighted in Fig. 7 by the boxes outlined in green. Stresses in the asset market will transfer down through the funding agents to those involved with collateral, possibly leading to a withdrawal of funding or an increase in margin requirements. This in turn can work back up through funding to cause forced selling by leveraged investors.

Agent heuristics. Each type of agent employs a different type of heuristic. For example, a cash provider lends to the finance desk of the banks based on a collateral haircut that is determined by the quality of collateral and the volatility of the market, and will cap the amount it will lend based on the permanence of its capital and the credit quality of its counterparties. Hedge funds will adjust their asset holdings based on their current leverage versus the maximum leverage allowed from their funding counterparties and also based on redemption pressure form their investors. The trading desk of the bank will make markets based on its capacity for holding inventory, which in turn is determined by risk limits and available funding, and by its current inventory. And, of course, the various agents within each type will differ as well.

Often the heuristics are coarse and rule-of-thumb, and the lack of precision and fine tuning to all the available information may not be the result of computational limitations, but of operating in a world that is fraught with the radical uncertainty marked by anticipatable events and unchartered states of nature.[16] But if we want to know an agent's heuristics, we can always ask. Paradoxically, it is in times of crisis that the heuristics of many of the agents are the clearest, perhaps because that is when the specter of radical uncertainty is at its height. The actions in times of crisis are often predetermined based on governance principles, risk management guidelines, and contractual bounds such as margin requirements. The subtle judgments of investment decisions become dominated by coarse efforts to hoard capital by pulling back on lines of credit, and to reduce exposure by liquidating broadly, perhaps subject to keeping positions on assets that are providing collateral for funding.

4.1 THE INTERACTION OF HETEROGENEOUS AGENTS: A CASE STUDY OF BEAR STEARNS

To see how the wide range of heterogeneous agents become employed in an agent-based modeling scenario, consider the case of the failure of two large hedge funds in Bear Stearns' asset management business, and the subsequent failure of Bear Stearns itself.[17]

This case involves agents in all three areas of the financial system. In terms of assets, the two hedge funds at the center of failure focused on the less liquid credit and mortgage instruments, holding $18 billion of assets by the end of 2006. In terms of funding, Bear Stearns had nearly $40\times$ leverage, supported through commercial

---

[16]Coarse heuristics as a response to radical uncertainty, and the superiority of these heuristics to standard optimization in the face of radical uncertainty, is discussed in Bookstaber and Langsam (1985), Gigerenzer (2008), Gigerenzer and Brighton (2009), Gigerenzer and Gaissmaier (2011).

[17]This example is taken from Bookstaber and Kenett (2016).

paper and repurchase (repo) agreements. Its hedge funds supported their $18 billion of assets by 10× leverage. In terms of collateral, the two Bear Stearns hedge funds posted collateral with other banks to support $16 billion of loans, and the parent reused collateral posted by hedge fund clients through its prime broker as collateral for loans in the repo market.

Shortly after Bear Stearns Enhanced Leveraged Fund began operation in 2006, the benchmark index for its portfolio began to fall (point 1 in Fig. 8). The fund experienced redemptions that led to forced selling, and cash providers demanded more collateral (point 2) while banks refused to roll over their repo funding (point 3). One of the repo lenders, Merrill Lynch, seized $850 million of collateral that Bear Stearns had posted against their loans, and began to liquidate the collateral, which further weakened the subprime market (point 4). The drop in price then led to similar actions by other collateral holders, leading to further drops in funding, and more sales both from the hedge funds due to margin calls and from the holders of the collateral. Ultimately, Bear Stearns, the parent company for the hedge funds, stepped in to provide nearly $2 billion to the lenders to take over the collateral (point 6). This weakened Bear Stearns balance sheet, leading to stricter terms of funding, with cash providers – through the repo market and money market funds – demanding more collateral and raising funding rates (point 7). Meanwhile, hedge fund clients of Bear Stearns prime broker pulled out, reducing cash and collateral that could be reused for its own funding purposes (point 8). Derivative and swap counterparties also demanded more collateral (point 9).

The failure of Bear Stearns was the end result of a spiral passing through agents in the asset markets, funding, and counterparty space. A model that does not differentiate these types of agents – or even that does not consider the heuristics of the individual agents – cannot deal with the realities of these market events.[18]

5 CONCLUSION

Taking heterogeneity as the starting point in our economic inquiry may lead to a paradigm shift that has been long awaited by some economists yet dreaded by many others. Certainly, it is difficult to understand how an economic model can be effective if it ignores the central information about the agents, how they interact, and how their interactions can alter the environment. The key feature of agent-based models is that they do not require the generalized representation that is required to compress a model into a computationally reducible form. In the agent-based approach, the agents

---

[18]In the case of Bear Stearns and other dynamics during the 2008 crisis, the heuristics of specific firms played a critical role. The aggressive nature of Merrill Lynch which was manifest in its demand for collateral, and the predatory of another firm, Goldman Sachs, which marked AIG's collateral at crippling level, are two examples. The implications of Goldman Sachs's aggressive actions in precipitating the 2008 crisis are discussed in Chapter 13 of Bookstaber (2017).

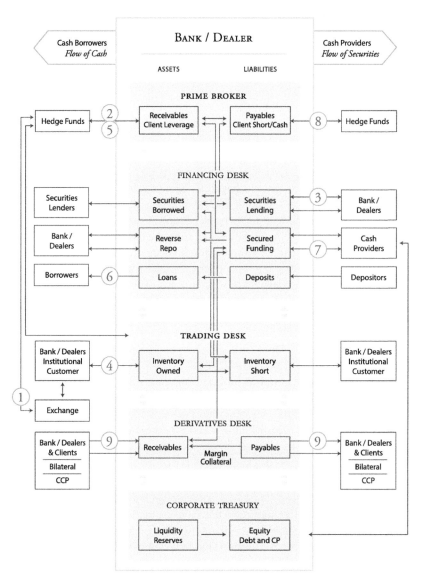

FIGURE 8

Bear Stearns case study. Fig. 8 shows the various agents embroiled in the cascade progressing from the failure of the Bear Stearns hedge funds to the failure of Bear Stearns itself. (1) The prices of benchmarks for the hedge funds' positions drops. (2) The hedge funds' begin to receive margin calls. (3) Funding from the repo markets begins to weaken. (4) Banks start to sell collateral to recover their secured loans. (5) The selling drops prices further, increasing margin calls. (6) As other banks withdraw, Bear Stearns becomes the sole source of funding. (7) Cash providers begin to limit funding to Bear Stearns itself. (8) Hedge funds pull positions from Bear Stearns' prime broker, further reducing its sources of funding. (9) Derivatives dealers demand collateral from Bear Stearns.

can be specified with realism and in detail. Indeed, even in terms of agent-based models themselves, those that employ "let there be B banks" generalizations are missing the essential power that these models can bring to bear.

With heterogeneity comes complexity that is immune from assault by the standard economic arsenal, and that creates emergent phenomena where the aggregate results are more than a simple aggregating up of the actions of the individuals. As a result, in place of the rigorous mathematical tools buttressed by regularity conditions that lead to an assured solution, we have simulations. And in the end those simulations with many heterogeneous agents and an over identified system might not yield a unique solution at all. But such is our world.

In standard macro-economic models there is little place for heterogeneity, for as Sargent says, "All agents inside the model, the econometrician, and God share the same model."[19]

Hand in hand with heterogeneity comes behavior couched in heuristics. If all agents have a "god-like" view of the world, with all available information, and operate in an optimal way given the information, they will have similar decision rules. But, as we increase heterogeneity we move along a path away from the standard full-information optimization that has been chosen to respect the axioms of rationality – as least as economists define the term – and toward the more varied world of heuristics. This move might be justified because we are fallible; or because we do not have the computational or cognitive wherewithal to do this massive optimization; or because, we face a future with unanticipatable states, one marked by future with radical uncertainty, where optimization for the current world is not optimal.[20]

And in the end, with heterogeneity comes pragmatism rather than theory, because if heterogeneity really matters, each problem can only be addressed by understanding the nature of the specific, and this in terms requires an inquiry into the nature of the real world where the model is operating. Agent-based models are one means of expressing this more pragmatic approach, and these rely on simulations rather than the analytic approach favored by most economic theorists. However expressed, we cannot be successful if we cast away the reality of the world, if we assume away the heterogeneity that paints our markets and our economic system.

REFERENCES

Aguiar, Andrea, Bookstaber, Richard, Kenett, Dror, Wipf, Tom, 2016. A Map of Collateral Uses and Flows. OFR Working Paper no. 16 (06).

Aguiar, Andrea, Bookstaber, Richard, Wipf, Thomas, 2014. A Map of Funding Durability and Risk. OFR Working Paper no. 14 (03).

---

[19] Thomas Sargent, quoted in Evans and Honkapohja (2005), page 566.

[20] See Soros (2013) on fallibility, Lucas (1986) on constrained optimization, Gigerenzer (2008) on computational limitations, and Bookstaber and Langsam (1985) on the optimality of using coarse heuristics in the face of radical uncertainty.

Akerlof, George A., 2007. The missing motivation in macroeconomics. American Economic Review 97 (1), 5–36.

Allen, H., Taylor, M., 1990. Charts, noise and fundamentals in the London foreign exchange market. Economic Journal 100 (400), 49–59.

Beja, A., Goldman, M., 1980. On the dynamic behavior of prices in disequilibrium. Journal of Finance 35 (2), 235–248.

Bookstaber, Richard, 2017. The End of Theory. Princeton University Press, Princeton, NJ.

Bookstaber, Richard, Glasserman, Paul, Iyengar, Garud, Luo, Yu, Venkatasubramanian, Venkat, Zhang, Zhizun, 2015. Process systems engineering as a modeling paradigm for analyzing systemic risk in financial networks. Journal of Investing 24 (2), 147–162.

Bookstaber, Richard, Kenett, Dror, 2016. Looking Deeper, Seeing More: A Multilayer Map of the Financial System. OFR Brief no. 16 (06).

Bookstaber, Richard, Langsam, Joseph, 1985. On the optimality of coarse behavior rules. Journal of Theoretical Biology 116 (2), 161–193. https://doi.org/10.1016/S0022-5193(85)80262-9.

Bookstaber, Richard, Paddrik, Mark, Tivnan, Brian, 2017. An agent-based model for financial vulnerability. Journal of Economic Interaction and Coordination. https://doi.org/10.1007/S11403-017-0188-1.

Branch, W.A., McGough, B., 2018. Heterogeneous expectations and micro-foundations in macroeconomics. In: Handbook of Computational Economics, vol. 4. Elsevier, pp. 3–62 (this Handbook).

Brock, William A., Hommes, Cars H., 1998. Heterogeneous beliefs and routes to chaos in a simple asset pricing model. Journal of Economic Dynamics and Control 22 (8–9), 1235–1274.

Brock, W., Lakonishok, J., LeBaron, B., 1992. Simple technical trading rules and the stochastic properties of stock returns. Journal of Finance 47 (5), 1731–1764.

Brunnermeier, Markus, Sannikov, Yuliy, 2014. A macroeconomic model with a financial sector. American Economic Review 104 (2), 379–421.

Bush, Robert R., Mosteller, Frederick, 1955. Stochastic Models for Learning. Wiley, Hoboken, NJ.

Camerer, Colin, Ho, Teck Hua, 1999. Experience-weighted attraction learning in normal form games. Econometrica 67 (4), 827–874. https://doi.org/10.1111/1468-0262.00054.

Chiarella, C., 1992. The dynamics of speculative behaviour. Annals of Operations Research 37, 101–123.

Chiarella, Carl, He, Xue-Zhong, 2001. Asset price and wealth dynamics under heterogeneous expectations. Quantitative Finance 1 (5), 509–526. https://doi.org/10.1088/1469-7688/1/5/303.

Chiarella, Carl, He, Xue-Zhong, 2003. Dynamics of beliefs and learning under a_L-processes – the heterogeneous case. Journal of Economic Dynamics and Control 27 (3), 503–531. https://doi.org/10.1016/S0165-1889(01)00059-8.

Davidoff, Frank, 2009. Heterogeneity is not always noise: lessons from improvement. Journal of the American Medical Association 302 (23), 2580–2586. https://doi.org/10.1001/jama.2009.1845.

Day, R.H., Huang, W., 1990. Bulls, bears and market sheep. Journal of Economic Behavior & Organization 14, 299–329.

De Grauwe, Paul, Grimaldi, Marianna, 2006. The Exchange Rate in a Behavioral Finance Framework. Princeton University Press, Princeton, NJ.

Dieci, R., He, X.Z., 2018. Heterogeneous agent models in finance. In: Handbook of Computational Economics, vol. 4. Elsevier, pp. 257–328 (this Handbook).

Dieci, Roberto, Westerhoff, Frank, 2010. Heterogeneous speculators, endogenous fluctuations and interacting markets: a model of stock prices and exchange rates. Journal of Economic Dynamics and Control 34 (4), 743–764.

Evans, George W., Honkapohja, Seppo, 2005. An interview with Thomas J. Sargent. Macroeconomic Dynamics 9 (4), 561–583. https://doi.org/10.1017/S1365100505050042.

Frankel, Jeffrey A., Froot, Kenneth, 1988. Chartists, fundamentalists and the demand for dollars. Greek Economic Review 10, 49–102.

Frankel, Jeffrey A., Froot, Kenneth, 1990. Exchange Rate Forecasting Techniques, Survey Data, and Implication for the Foreign Exchange Market. IMF Working Paper no. 90 (43).

Gigerenzer, Gerd, 2008. Rationality for Mortals: How People Cope with Uncertainty, Evolution and Cognition. Oxford University Press, Oxford.

Gigerenzer, Gerd, Brighton, Henry, 2009. Homo heuristics: why biased minds make better inferences. Topics in Cognitive Science 1 (1), 107–143. https://doi.org/10.1111/j.1756-8765.2008.01006.x.

Gigerenzer, Gerd, Gaissmaier, Wolfgang, 2011. Heuristic decision making. Annual Review of Psychology 62 (1), 451–482. https://doi.org/10.1146/annurev-psych-120709-145346.

Härdle, Wolfgang, Kirman, Alan, 1995. Nonclassical demand: a model-free examination of price quantity relations in the Marseille fish market. Journal of Econometrics 67 (1), 227–257. https://doi.org/10.1016/0304-4076(94)01634-C.

Holland, John H., 1992. Adaptation in Natural and Artificial Systems: An Introductory Analysis with Applications to Biology, Control and Artificial Intelligence, 2nd ed. MIT Press, Cambridge, MA.

Hommes, Cars H., 2006. Heterogeneous agent models in economics and finance. In: Tesfatsion, Leigh, Judd, Kenneth L. (Eds.), Handbook of Computational Economics: Agent-Based Computational Economics. Elsevier, Amsterdam, pp. 1109–1186.

Hommes, Cars H., 2013. Behavioral Rationality and Heterogeneous Expectations in Complex Economic Systems. Cambridge University Press, Cambridge.

International Monetary Fund, 2017. Global Financial Stability Report: Is Growth at Risk? Washington, DC.

Kirman, Alan, 1993. Ants, rationality and recruitment. Quarterly Journal of Economics 108 (1), 137–156. https://doi.org/10.2307/2118498.

Kirman, Alan, 2010. Complex Economics: Individual and Collective Rationality. Routledge, New York, NY.

Kirman, Alan, Vriend, Nick, 2001. Evolving market structure: a model of price dispersion and loyalty. Journal of Economic Dynamics and Control 25 (3–4), 459–502.

LeRoy, S., Porter, R.D., 1981. The present-value relation: tests based on implied variance bounds. Econometrica 49 (3), 555–574.

Locke, John, 1693. Some Thoughts Concerning Education, Defining Gender, 1450–1910. A. and J. Churchill, London.

Lucas, Robert E., 1986. Adaptive behavior and economic theory. Journal of Business 59 (4), S401–S426.

Lux, Thomas, Marchesi, Michele, 1999. Scaling and criticality in a stochastic multi-agent model of a financial market. Nature 397 (6719), 498–500. https://doi.org/10.1038/17290.

Miller, John H., Page, Scott E., 2007. Complex Adaptive Systems: An Introduction to Computational Models of Social Life. Princeton Studies in Complexity. Princeton University Press, Princeton, NJ.

Romer, Paul, 2018. The trouble with macroeconomics. American Economist. Forthcoming.

Roth, Alvin E., Erev, Ido, 1995. Learning from extensive-form games: experimental data and simple dynamic models in the intermediate term. Games and Economic Behavior 8 (1), 164–212. https://doi.org/10.1016/S0899-8256(05)80020-X.

Sen, Amartya, 1970. The impossibility of a Paretian liberal. The Journal of Political Economy 78 (1), 152–157.

Shiller, Robert, 1981. Do stock prices move too much to be justified by subsequent changes in dividends? American Economic Review 71 (3), 421–436.

Shiller, Robert J., 1990. Market volatility and investor behavior. American Economic Review 80 (2), 58–62.

Shiller, Robert J., 2003. From efficient markets theory to behavioral finance. Journal of Economic Perspectives 17 (1), 83–104.

Smith, Adam, 1776. An Inquiry into the Nature and Causes of the Wealth of Nations. W. Strahan and T. Cadell, London.

Soros, George, 2013. Fallibility, reflexivity, and the human uncertainty principle. Journal of Economic Methodology 20 (4), 309–329. https://doi.org/10.1080/1350178X.2013.859415.

Ullmann-Margalit, Edna, 1977. The Emergence of Norms. Clarendon Press, Oxford.

Weisbuch, Gerard, Kirman, Alan, Herreiner, Dorothea, 2000. Market organisation and trading relationships. Economic Journal 110 (463), 411–436. https://doi.org/10.1111/1468-0297.00531.

Wolgast, Elizabeth, 1994. A World of Social Atoms. Prentice-Hall, Englewood Cliffs, NJ.

Young, H.P., 2015. The evolution of social norms. Annual Review of Economics 7, 359–387.

Index